QB
209
.E52
1994

Encyclopedia of
time.

$95.00

DATE			

BAKER & TAYLOR

ENCYCLOPEDIA
of
TIME

Garland Reference Library of Social Science
(Vol. 810)

ENCYCLOPEDIA
of
TIME

Edited by

SAMUEL L. MACEY

Garland Publishing, Inc.
New York & London
1994

Library of Congress Cataloging–in–Publication Data

Encyclopedia of time / edited by Samuel L. Macey.
    p.   cm. — (Garland reference library of social science ;
vol. 810)
    Based on the author's Time: a bibliographical guide published
by Garland in 1991.
    Includes index.
    ISBN 0–8153–0615–6 (alk. paper)
    1. Time—Encyclopedias.   I. Macey, Samuel L.   II. Macey,
Samuel L.   Time.
QB209.E52   1994
529'.03—dc20   93-43355
                                         CIP

Printed on acid-free, 250-year-life paper
Manufactured in the United States of America

*For June, Elizabeth, Caroline,
Matthew, and Elizabeth Christine*

CONTENTS

INTRODUCTION

The great majority of the publications in the large, interdisciplinary, and dynamic discipline of time studies, which serves in the vanguard of so many areas of modern research, have appeared as recently as the past twenty-five years.

The production of this encyclopedia has grown directly out of my *Time: A Bibliographic Guide* published by Garland at the end of 1991. Though that bibliography contains some 6,000 entries divided into twenty-five major disciplines and about 100 subdisciplines, it would have taken about fifty such volumes to document the entire canon of time-related books and articles published by 1990. The details of these approximations appear in the introduction to the bibliography. *Time: A Bibliographic Guide* provided the first "atlas" for recognizing as a whole the size, shape, and ramifications of this new discipline. The *Encyclopedia of Time* has used that atlas to locate the subjects which have been energized by a concern with time, to identify their relationships with other such subjects, and to help in identifying appropriate articles and potential authors.

In many articles—like those on calendars or clocks—the presence of time is strongly implicit, but when that is not so the reader should be aware that time is always implicit in the title of an article in this encyclopedia and that the contributor will concentrate on aspects of the subject concerned with time. Furthermore, since contributors are generally leading scholars in the particular subjects on which they write, they will give the reader some sense of the present knowledge and future possibilities for research in those subjects.

The procedure for bringing this encyclopedia into being has involved consulting with advisers on the selection of subjects and contributors before arranging when and by whom the articles should be written. Because time has permeated virtually all of the disciplines in the modern world, it has been necessary to work with a wider range of advisers and contributors for the *Encyclopedia of Time* than would normally be necessary for its approximately 360 articles. It has also been necessary to ensure that articles have been read by a specialist in the particular field before they have come to me for further editing. My job has been to ensure a uniformity in format and style, but to achieve this without attempting to impose any hint of the rigid editorial censorship that might destroy the rich variety of conjectures, opinions, and hypotheses inherent in so dynamic and diffuse an evolving interdisciplinary discipline. Sometimes—as, for example, with the many references to circadian rhythms and biological clocks both within and across disciplines—some duplication and even disagreement has been unavoidable.

The interdisciplinary nature of the *Encyclopedia of Time* has meant that the format and style must be understandable by the intelligent reader from any discipline. The result has been a conscious attempt to avoid jargon, to explain as many special terms as possible that the specialist author feels unable to avoid, and to eliminate most abbreviations. The attempt to simplify language and avoid jargon provides one form of entry into the subject of time. It was also felt necessary to provide alternative methods of entry to the individual subjects and authors beyond alphabetizing the titles of the articles themselves in the main body of the text. Each title is, therefore, grouped under an alphabetized disciplinary heading at the beginning of the encyclopedia; the index provides page references to where both authors and subjects may be found; and most articles conclude with cross references to related articles and a suitable list of further readings, in addition to the initials of their authors keyed to the list of contributors.

The format of an encyclopedia inhibits the use of notes. The names of scholars mentioned in the text will, however, often be found under the "Further Readings" to the article, which are intended as a guide rather than as a comprehensive bibliography. The format used for the further readings has been widely employed by North American scholars whose work in time studies cuts across the disciplines and comes very close to Basic Style *A* in *The Chicago Manual of Style*, 13th edition, Section 16.5, and to that recommended in *The MLA Style Manual*. I have also followed these publications in other appropriate areas. With respect, however, to the preference for the use of first names or initials, which varies both among scholars and between disciplines, I have made no attempt to impose a consistent form.

No previous encyclopedia has dealt with the multidisciplinary study of time and the present undertaking would hardly have been possible without the prior publication of *Time: A Bibliographic Guide*. The sheer size and dynamic growth of the study of time means that, like the *Bibliographic Guide*, the *Encyclopedia of Time* cannot possibly be a definitive publication. But it is all the more stimulating for that. Here, then, is the first "atlas" mapping out in a prose text rather than in a bibliography the extent and nature of the study of time in a whole variety of disciplines and subdisciplines. And here some 200 of the foremost international scholars in time studies make their individual contributions to our understanding of that large, wide-ranging, and dynamic discipline which has been at the cutting edge of this century's research in virtually all areas of human endeavor and enterprise.

In the course of writing three books on time that dealt respectively with literature and philosophy, religion and the history of ideas, and social and economic history, I became acutely aware of the need for the multidisciplinary bibliography that I eventually produced. But the credit for suggesting to me that there should now be an *Encyclopedia of Time* belongs entirely to Gary Kuris of Garland Publishing. Both he and the officers of that company have given me

invaluable editorial and technical support without which this work would hardly have been possible. There are many other people to whom I am also much indebted. First and foremost come the advisory board and the contributors whose names are listed immediately after this introduction. I am indebted to Lee Edmunds and Charles Sherover for advice concerning articles and contributors, and also to Jean Cleary, John Schofield, and the late Gerhart Friedmann for suggesting corrections. All are colleagues and many are friends who have generously interrupted their own research in order to support this project. And behind them is an equally impressive group of unnamed readers who have contributed by reviewing these articles in the light of their own particular specializations.

I am grateful also to the University of Victoria and to the Canada Council for financial aid over many years related to the study of time; to Corpus Christi College, Cambridge, which by electing me a visiting fellow in 1972 facilitated my early research into temporal matters; to the Institute of Management Services through which as a member and fellow for over thirty years I have been been able to retain an active interest in industrial engineering; and to The International Society for the Study of Time, of which I am currently the immediate past-president. Many colleagues from that society—which has members in thirty-three countries and more than twenty disciplines—have made considerable contributions to this endeavor. My indebtedness both to them and to J. T. Fraser, the society's founder, is very great.

I am also indebted to my colleagues at the University of Victoria, to the staff of the McPherson Library, to the Faculty Microcomputer Demonstration Facility, and to three research assistants—Janelle Jenstad, Chris Venour, and Nick Mount—who have given me considerable help. My obligation to Nick Mount, who has worked through the entire collection of articles, is particularly great. Though the credit very properly belongs to all those who have contributed, any faults that may remain are my own. Finally, and above all, I am grateful to a surprisingly generous wife who has shared with me in the excitement of dealing with such a rich and varied manuscript.

ADVISORY BOARD

CONTRIBUTORS

Dr. Fred D. Abraham [F.D.A.]
Department of Psychology
University of Vermont

Dr. Ralph H. Abraham [R.H.A.]
Department of Mathematics
University of California at Santa Cruz

Dr. Barbara Adam [B.A.]
School of Social and Administrative Studies
University of Wales

Dr. Martin J. Aitken [M.J.A.]
Laboratory for Archaeology
Oxford University

Dr. Paul K. Alkon [P.K.A.]
English Department
University of Southern California

Dr. Geraldine A. Allen [G.A.A.]
Department of Biology
University of Victoria

William J. H. Andrewes [W.J.H.A.]
Collection of Scientific Instruments at Harvard
Harvard University

Dr. Josephine Arendt [J.A.]
School of Biological Sciences
University of Surrey

Dr. Alex Argyros [A.A.]
School of Art and Humanities
The University of Texas at Dallas

Dr. Jacob A. Arlow [J.A.A.]
King's Point, New York

Mark H. Aultman [M.H.A.]
Attorney and Counselor at Law
Worthington, Ohio

Dr. Anthony F. Aveni [A.F.A.]
Department of Physics and Astronomy
Colgate University

Chris H. Bailey [C.H.B.]
Former Managing Director
American Clock and Watch Museum
Bristol, Connecticut

Silvio A. Bedini [S.A.B.]
United States National Museum
Smithsonian Institution

Dr. P.-M. Bélanger [P.-M.B.]
School of Pharmacy
Laval University

Dr. Gene D. Block [G.D.B.]
Department of Biology
University of Virginia

Dr. Richard A. Block [R.A.B.]
Department of Psychology
Montana State University

Dr. Eva T. H. Brann [E.T.H.B.]
Department of Philosophy
St. John's College, Annapolis

Jeffery C. Bridger [J.C.B.]
Department of Rural Sociology
Pennsylvania State University

Dr. Johanna Broda [J.B.]
Instituto Investigaciones Historicas
Mexico City

Dr. Bernard Brugerolle [B.B.]
Département de pharmacologie médicale
Groupe Hospitalier de la Timone
Marseilles

Dr. J.-P. Bureau [J.-P.B.]
Laboratory of Clinical Psychology
University of Montpellier, Nîmes

Dr. John T. Burns [J.T.B.]
Department of Biology
Bethany College

Dr. Bill Bytheway [B.By.]
Swansea, Wales

Dr. Scott S. Campbell [S.S.C.]
Institute of Chronobiology
New York Hospital—Cornell Medical Center

Dr. Ann Cartwright [A.C.]
Institute of Social Studies in Medical Care
Hampstead, London

David Charlton [D.C.]
Editor, *Management Services*
Institute of Management Services
London, England

Dr. C. Chatfield [C.C.]
School of Mathematical Sciences
University of Bath

Dr. Cheng Chung-Ying [C.C.-Y.]
Department of Philosophy
University of Hawaii

Dr. Russell M. Church [R.M.C.]
Department of Psychology
Brown University

Dr. C. J. S. Clarke [C.J.S.C.]
Faculty of Mathematical Studies
University of Southampton

Dr. Eric F. Clarke [E.F.C.]
Faculty of Music
City University of London

Dr. Michael P. Closs [M.P.C.]
Department of Mathematics
University of Ottawa

John Clute [J.C.]
London

Dr. Vincent Colapietro [V.C.]
Department of Philosophy
Fordham University

Dr. Peter G. Coleman [P.C.]
School of Medicine
University of Southampton

Dr. Caroline L. Collins [C.L.C.]
Department of Psychology
University of Victoria

Dr. George W. Collins, II [G.W.C.,II]
Department of Astronomy
Case Western Reserve University

Dr. Germaine Cornélissen [G.C.]
Chronobiology Laboratories
University of Minnesota

Dr. Martin Currie [M.C.]
Department of Economics
University of Manchester

Dr. Kenneth G. Denbigh [K.G.D.]
London

Dr. Charles De Paolo [C.D.]
Department of English
Borough of Manhattan Community College
City University of New York

Dr. Martin Dillon [M.D.]
Department of Philosophy
State University of New York at Binghampton

Dr. Roger A. Dixon [R.A.D.]
Department of Psychology
University of Victoria

Dr. Betsey D. Dyer [B.D.D.]
Department of Biology
Wheaton College

Dr. Charles W. Eddis [C.W.E.]
The Unitarian Church of Montreal

Judie English [J.E.]
Department of Biochemistry
University of Surrey

Magali Ferrero [M.F.]
Laboratoire d'Economie et de Sociologie du Travail
Aix-en-Provence

Robert J. Fleck [R.J.F.]
U.S. Geological Survey
Branch of Isotope Geology
Menlo Park

Dr. Thomas R. Flynn [T.R.F.]
Department of Philosophy
Emory University

Dr. George A. Ford [G.A.F.]
Department of English
University of Rochester

Dr. J. T. Fraser [J.T.F.]
Westport, Connecticut

Dr. William J. Friedman [W.J.F.]
Department of Psychology
Oberlin College

Ingrid C. Friesen [I.C.F.]
Department of Psychology
University of Victoria

Dr. George Gale [G.G.]
Department of Philosophy
University of Missouri

Dr. Richard M. Gale [R.M.G.]
Department of Philosophy
University of Pittsburgh

Dr. Glenn Gass [G.Ga.]
School of Music
Indiana University

Dr. Pierre Gervais [P.G.]
Hôpital Fernand-Widal
Paris

Dr. Alex Gonzalez [A.G.]
Department of Psychology
California State University

Dr. Paul J. Green [P.J.G.]
Harvard-Smithsonian Center for Astrophysics
Harvard University

R. John Griffiths [R.J.G.]
Prescot Museum, Merseyside

Dr. Reuben Gronau [R.G.]
Department of Economics
Hebrew University of Jerusalem

Dr. Jean De Groot [J.D.G.]
School of Philosophy
The Catholic University of America

Dr. Barry R. Gross [B.R.G.]
Department of History and Philosophy
York College
City University of New York

Dr. John G. Gunnell [J.G.G.]
Department of Political Science
State University of New York at Albany

Dr. Franz Halberg [F.H.]
Chronobiology Laboratories
University of Minnesota

Dr. Steve Handel [S.H.]
Department of Psychology
University of Tennessee

Dr. Linda Hantrais [L.H.]
Department of European Studies
Loughborough University

Dr. Paul E. Hardin [P.E.H.]
Department of Biology
Texas A & M University

Dr. Ron Harre [R.H.]
Linacre College
University of Oxford

Dr. Edward R. Harrison [E.R.H.]
Department of Physics
University of Massachusetts

Dr. John Hassard [J.H.]
School of Management and Economics
University of Keele

Dr. J. Woodland Hastings [J.W.H.]
Department of Cellular and Developmental
Biology
Harvard University

John P. Heap [J.P.H.]
Computing Services Unit
Leeds Polytechnic

Dr. Bertrand P. Helm [B.P.H.]
Department of Philosophy
Southwest Missouri State University

Dr. John P. Hittinger [J.P.H.]
Department of Philosophy
College of St. Francis, Joliet

Dr. Louis A. Hobson [L.A.H.]
Department of Biology
University of Victoria

Donald R. Hoke [D.R.H.]
Outagamie Museum
Appleton, Wisconsin

Dr. Barbara M. Hopkins [B.M.H.]
Department of Chemistry
Xavier University

Dr. W. J. M. Hrushesky [W.J.M.H.]
Division of Medical Oncology
Albany Medical College

Dr. Drew A. Hyland [D.A.H.]
Department of Philosophy
Trinity College
Hartford, Connecticut

Dr. Richard Ivry [R.I.]
Department of Psychology
University of California at Berkeley

Dr. Janet L. Jackson [J.L.J.]
Netherlands Institute for the Study of Criminality
and Law Enforcement
Leiden

Dr. Jo Ellen Jacobs [J.E.J.]
Department of Philosophy
Milliken University

Julia S. Johnson [J.S.J.]
Department of Health and Social Welfare
Open University

Dr. Huw R. Jones [H.R.J.]
Department of Geography
University of Dundee

Dr. Martha Sharp Joukowsky [M.S.J.]
Center for Old World Archaeology and Art
Brown University

Dr. Peter Kalkavage [P.K.]
St. John's College, Annapolis

Dr. Leonie Kellahar [L.K.]
Centre for Environmental and Social Studies in
Ageing
University of North London

Dr. Frank M. Kirkland [F.M.K.]
Department of Philosophy
Hunter College
City University of New York

Dr. George L. Kline [G.L.K.]
Department of Philosophy
Bryn Mawr College

Dr. Klaus K. Klostermaier [K.K.K.]
Department of Religion
University of Manitoba

Dr. Jonathan D. Kramer [J.D.K.]
Department of Music
Columbia University

Dr. Edwin C. Krupp [E.C.K.]
Griffith Observatory
Los Angeles

Dr. Gaston Labrecque [G.L.]
Le Centre Hospitalier
Laval University

Dr. John Lachs [J.L.]
Department of Philosophy
Vanderbilt University

Dr. David S. Landes [D.S.L.]
Department of History
Harvard University

Marvin Lanphere [M.L.]
U.S. Geological Survey
Menlo Park

Dr. Peretz Lavie [P.L.]
Diagnostic Sleep Laboratory
Israel Institute of Technology
Haifa

Nicola Le Feuvre [N.Le F.]
Department of Sociology
University of Toulouse

Prof. Dr. Björn Lemmer [B.L.]
Zentrum der Pharmakologie
J. W. Goethe-Universität

Dr. Robert Levine [R.L.]
Department of Psychology
California State University at Fresno

Dr. Donald W. Livingston [D.W.L.]
Department of Philosophy
Emory University

Dr. Judy Lochhead [J.Lo.]
Department of Music
State University of New York at Stony Brook

Dr. George R. Lucas, Jr. [G.R.L.]
Division of Research Programs
National Endowment for the Humanities

Dr. Françoise J. J. Macar [F.J.J.M.]
CNRS Lab. de Neurosciences Fonctionnelles
Neurosciences Cognitives
Marseilles

Andrew McArthur [A.M.]
Department of Biology
University of Victoria

Dr. John J. McDermott [J.J.M.]
Department of Philosophy
Texas A & M University

Dr. Samuel L. Macey [S.L.M.]
Department of English
University of Victoria

Dr. Joseph E. McGrath [J.E.M.]
Department of Psychology
University of Illinois
Champaign

Dr. Peter K. McInerney [P.K.M.]
Department of Philosophy
Oberlin College

Dr. Michael L. McKinney [M.L.M.]
Department of Geology
University of Tennessee

Leslie-Jean MacMillan [L.-J.M.]
Department of Biology
University of Victoria

Dr. David R. Maines [D.R.M.]
Department of Sociology
Wayne State University

Dr. Glenn Martin [G.M.]
Department of Philosophy
Radford University

Dr. Robert E. Meagher [R.E.M.]
Department of Philosophy
Hampshire College, Amherst

Dr. Murray Melbin [M.M.]
Department of Sociology
Boston University

Dr. Jacob Meskin [J.M.]
Religion Department
Williams College

Prof. Dr. John A. Michon [J.A.M.]
CB Haren, The Netherlands

Dr. Susan Milbrath [S.M.]
Department of Interpretation
Florida Museum of Natural History

Dr. Philip Mosley [P.M.]
Department of English
Pennsylvania State University
Worthington Scranton Campus

Dr. David Mott [D.M.]
Department of Music
York University

Nicholas James Mount [N.J.M.]
Victoria, British Columbia

Dr. S. Nakayama [S.N.]
School of Business Administration
Kanagawa University

Dr. Gerald Newsom [G.N.]
Department of Astronomy
Ohio State University

Dr. John D. North [J.D.N.]
HJ Paterswolde
The Netherlands

Dr. Jack Ofield [J.O.]
Department of Telecommunications and Film
San Diego State University

Dr. Keith A. Olive [K.A.O.]
School of Physics and Astronomy
University of Minnesota

Dr. Lance Olsen [L.O.]
Department of English
University of Idaho

Dr. Kristina Ovaska [K.O.]
Victoria, British Columbia

Dr. J. D. Palmer [J.D.P.]
Department of Zoology
University of Massachusetts

Dr. David A. Park [D.A.P.]
Department of Physics
Williams College

Dr. Jann Pasler [J.P.]
Department of Music
University of California at San Diego

Naina Patel [N.P.]
Central Council for Education and Training in
Social Work
Leeds

Dr. Robert Patterson [R.P.]
Department of Psychology
Washington State University

Dr. Dorothy H. Paul [D.H.P.]
Department of Biology
University of Victoria

Dr. Richard Perkins [R.Pe.]
Buffalo, New York

Keith Potter [K.P.]
Department of Music
Goldsmith's College

Dr. Jeff L. Pressing [J.L.P.]
Department of Music
La Trobe University, Australia

Dr. Ira Progoff [I.P.]
Dialogue House, New York

Dr. John Protevi [J.Pr.]
Newtown Square, Pennsylvania

Dr. Ricardo J. Quinones [R.J.Q.]
Center for Humanistic Studies
Claremont-McKenna College

Dr. Albert I. Rabin [A.I.R.]
Department of Psychology
Michigan State University

Dr. Andrew J. Reck [A.J.R.]
Department of Philosophy
Tulane University

Dr. Robert G. B. Reid [R.G.B.R.]
Department of Biology
University of Victoria

Dr. Alain E. Reinberg [A.E.R.]
Chronobiologie et Chronopharmacologie
Fondation A. De Rothschild, Paris

Prof. Dr. Ludger Rensing [L.Re.]
Department of Biology
University of Bremen

Dr. Jürgen P. Rinderspacher [J.P.R.]
Fn. Evangelische Theologie
Universität Münster

Dr. Richard A. Ring [R.A.R.]
Department of Biology
University of Victoria

Dr. Herbert L. Roitblat [H.L.R.]
Department of Psychology
University of Hawaii at Manoa

Dr. Lewis Rowell [L.R.]
School of Music
Indiana University

Dr. C. L. N. Ruggles [C.L.N.R.]
School of Archaeological Studies
University of Leicester

Dr. Merritt Ruhlen [M.R.]
Palo Alto, California

Dr. Henry J. Rutz [H.J.R.]
Department of Sociology
Bogazici University, Istanbul

Dr. Frank B. Salisbury [F.B.S.]
Department of Plant, Soil and Biometeorology
Utah State University

Dr. Alan Sandage [A.S.]
Department of Astronomy
Carnegie Institute of Washington
Passadena

Dr. David S. Saunders [D.S.S.]
Department of Zoology
University of Edinburgh

Dr. Frank Schalow [F.S.]
Department of Philosophy
Loyola University, New Orleans

Dr. Lawrence E. Scheving [L.E.S.]
College of Medicine
University of Little Rock

Dr. Tom Schuller [T.S.]
Continuing Education
University of Edinburgh

Dr. Charlene H. Seigfried [C.H.S.]
Department of Philosophy
Purdue University

Said Shahtahmasebi [S.S.]
Centre for Social Policy Research and
Development
University of Wales

Dr. Gayle L. Smith [G.L.S.]
Department of English
Pennsylvania State University
Worthington Scranton Campus

Dr. Quentin Smith [Q.S.]
Department of Philosophy
Antioch College

Dr. Michael H. Smolensky [M.H.S.]
Health Science Center at Houston
University of Texas

Dr. Steven C. Snyder [S.C.S.]
Cardinal Meunch Seminary
Fargo, North Dakota

Dr. Robert P. Sonkowsky [R.P.S.]
Department of Classical Studies
University of Minnesota

Dr. Marlene P. Soulsby [M.P.S.]
Department of German
Pennsylvania State University
Worthington Scranton Campus

Dr. Joan Stambaugh [J.S.]
Department of Philosophy
Hunter College
City University of New York

Carlene E. Stephens [C.E.S.]
Division of Engineering
National Museum of American History
Smithsonian Institution

Dr. F. Richard Stephenson [F.R.S.]
Department of Physics
University of Durham

Dr. M. S. Stern [M.S.S.]
Department of Religion
University of Manitoba

Dr. Ruth M. Stone [R.M.S.]
Folklore Institute
Indiana University

Dr. John J. Stuhr [J.J.S.]
Department of Philosophy
University of Oregon

Dr. Fred Gillette Sturm [F.G.S.]
Department of Philosophy
University of New Mexico

Dr. Hardja Susilo [H.S.]
Music Department
University of Hawaii at Manoa

Dr. Kenneth R. Thornton [K.R.T.]
School of Health Information Science
University of Victoria

Dr. Anthea Tinker [A.T.]
Age Concern Institute of Gerontology
King's College
University of London

Dr. James W. Truran [J.W.T.]
Enrico Fermi Institute
University of Chicago

Dr. Verena Tunnicliffe [V.T.]
Department of Biology
University of Victoria

Dr. A. J. Turner [A.J.T.]
Le Mesnil-le-Roi, Paris

Horacio Vaggione [H.V.]
University of Paris-VIII

Dr. Richard Velkley [R.V.]
Department of Philosophy
Stonehill College

Dr. Bruce Venable [B.V.]
St. John's College
Santa Fe

Dr. Charles Walcott [C.W.]
Cornell Laboratory of Ornithology
Cornell University

Dr. Lawrence C. H. Wang [L.C.H.W.]
Department of Zoology
University of Alberta

Dr. J. M. Waterhouse [J.M.W.]
Department of Physiological Sciences
University of Manchester

Dr. G. Clare Wenger [G.C.W.]
Centre for Social Policy Research and
Development
University of Wales

Dr. Eric White [E.W.]
English Department
University of California at Santa Barbara

Dr. Kevin White [K.W.]
School of Philosophy
Catholic University
Washington

Dr. Dennis A. Whitmore [D.A.W.]
Dunstable, Bedfordshire

Dr. Dianne Willcocks [D.W.]
City Campus
Sheffield Hallam University

Rev. Allan B. Wolter [A.B.W.]
Monastery of Santa Barbara
Franciscan Friary, Santa Barbara

Dr. Michael O. Woodburne [M.O.W.]
Department of Earth Sciences
University of California at Riverside

Dr. F. Eugene Yates [F.E.Y.]
Department of Medicine
University of California at Los Angeles

Dr. Michael Young [M.Y.]
Institute of Community Studies
Bethnal Green, London

Dr. Dan Zakay [D.Z.]
Department of Psychology
Tel-Aviv University

Dr. Michael Zeilik [M.Z.]
Dept. of Physics and Astronomy
University of New Mexico

Professor Robert Zweig [R.Z.]
Department of English
Borough of Manhattan Community College
City University of New York

ARTICLES LISTED BY MAJOR DISCIPLINE

LIST OF ILLUSTRATIONS

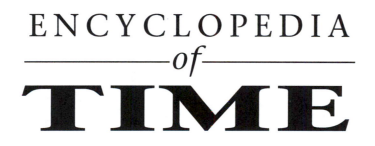

ENCYCLOPEDIA
of
TIME

AGE OF THE OLDEST STARS AND THE MILKY WAY

There was a time in the history of the universe before either stars or galaxies existed. A principal problem in stellar and galactic evolution is to date the formation of the oldest stars in our galaxy. This age dates our galaxy, and by extension other galaxies as well.

The dating of stars became possible beginning with developments in the 1920s when the source of stellar energy was identified by A.S. Eddington, Robert d'Adkinson, F. Houtermans, and others as the conversion of hydrogen to heavier chemical elements in nuclear reactions in the interiors of the stars.

The exact mechanism for the conversion of hydrogen to helium was discovered in 1938 independently by C.F. von Weizsäcker and by H. A. Bethe, both relying on the increased knowledge of nuclear reactions then available. The development opened the way for an eventual understanding of stellar evolution and an understanding of the Hertzsprung–Russell (HR) diagram—of E. Hertzsprung and H.N. Russell—where the stellar surface temperature is plotted versus the radiated luminosity. The HR diagram provides a decisive representation of stellar physics from which the evolutionary state of stars as they age can be read.

Massive stars are observed to radiate the energy they generate at a rate more than a million times higher than the power output of the sun. Such stars consume their available supply of hydrogen in less than 10 million years. Less massive stars radiate at a lower rate, and therefore live longer. The lifetime of a star is determined by how long it takes for it to exhaust all its nuclear fuel in the conversion of its initial hydrogen content into the heavier chemical elements by nuclear reactions in the stellar interior.

The oldest stars in the galaxy can be identified from the faintest luminosity level attained by a particular feature in the HR diagram. As stars burn their hydrogen, changing to helium, they become slightly brighter and slightly larger. This changes their position relative to younger stars in the HR diagram. Eventually, when about 10 percent of the initial hydrogen becomes helium, a major change of radius occurs. In technical terms, the star leaves the main sequence in the diagram. It is at this stage that the precise age of the star can be determined. The fainter the main sequence termination point, the older the star, because it takes a longer time for a low-luminosity star to reach the 10 percent hydrogen exhaustion point than for stars of high luminosity, which burn their fuel at a faster rate.

Stars in the compact globular clusters that exist in our galaxy have the faintest turnoff luminosities (that is, the luminosity at the sequence termination point) known. Beyond doubt these are the oldest stars in the galaxy. Calculating how much time is required to convert 10 percent of the hydrogen into helium at the rate determined by the known faint luminosity level of the main sequence termination point shows that the age of the system of globular clusters in the galaxy is 14 billion years. The error of the determination by this method is estimated to be less than 15 percent.

The compact globular clusters were the first aggregates to form in the galaxy as it collapsed from a larger volume when the protogalaxy that became the Milky Way decoupled from the general expansion of the universe. The time from the beginning of the big bang to the formation of the first globular clusters is well determined from the dynamics of galactic collapse. The collapse time is short, and is of the order of only a billion years. Therefore, the age of the universe dated in this way is 15 billion years, again, known to an accuracy of about 2 billion years. This age, dated here via stellar evolution, is similar to the age of the chemical elements determined from radioactive decay, and to the age of the universe determined from the properties of its expansion (see **Expansion of the Universe**). The agreement of these three independent time scales is the principal evidence for a creation event for the universe to have occurred about 15 billion years ago.

[A.S.]

See also Expansion of the Universe; Star and Galaxy Formation.

FURTHER READINGS

Sandage, A. "The Population Concept, Globular Clusters, Subdwarfs, Ages, and the Collapse of the Galaxy." *Annual Review of Astronomy and Astrophysics* 24 (1986): 421–458.

———. "The Size and Shape of the Universe: The Quest for the Curvature of Space." *Endeavour*. New Series (Pergamon Press) 14.3 (1990): 104–111.

AGING AND TIME

In twentieth-century Western society it is common to think of time as an attribute of aging. That is to say, aging, human or otherwise, cannot and does not take place unless time passes; time is the precondition for any concept of aging. The converse position, that time does not exist unless the maturing, growing old, and ultimate disintegration of animate things is observed, recorded, or measured in terms of time elapsing, is perhaps less commonly held. Nonetheless, time and the maturing of animate and inanimate things are ideas which run in parallel and which are often seen as being conceptually interdependent.

In other cultures, and at other times in Western civilization, different relationships between time and aging to the one being proposed here as currently dominant—that time is the pre-existing concept and context within which aging has its shape—have existed. Aristotelian thinking, for example, held that time was entirely the duration of an event and did not exist independently of events. Thus, human aging as a series of events, with whatever categories or cutoff points a particular society may have constructed to identify phases or stages of life, constituted a unit of time, which might be subdivided into smaller units of time. The idea that time could stand on its own, independent of events—including the events by which a life may be described—is an idea which only appears in Western thinking long after Aristotle.

In early thinking up to Galileo, at the time of the Renaissance in Europe, there was a resistance to—even a horror of—the idea of limitless space and infinite time. Arthur Koestler in his *The Act of Creation* wrote of this pre-Renaissance period that "Aristotelian doctrine held that not even God could create an empty space or infinite time." Time—and space—only came to be invested with new meaning in the Newtonian age, during and after the eighteenth century. Newton, and others like him, saw time and space as absolutes in themselves—existing regardless of the duration of events, whether these were human lifetimes or larger-scale historical episodes. At this point the human life span came to be construed within time. Thus, in the eighteenth century through to the early twentieth century, human and nonhuman aging were not seen as having any influence on or relevance for philosophical conceptions of time. With Einstein's general theory of relativity in the earlier part of the twentieth century, the idea of time was reconstructed and reintegrated in an interactive way within the world which came to be seen as important for the recognition and calibration of time. Again, Koestler says of this later period that "time had lost its awesome cast-iron character."

The idea that time is an absolute entity, independent of others, can then be contrasted with notions of time as an entity either within or relative to other entities. These two sets of constructions can be seen at work in other cultures which lie beyond the Western culture within which Aristotelian, Newtonian, and Einsteinian conceptions of time have emerged. Mircea Eliade, for instance, noted when studying Asian culture that time appeared to be regarded as both linear and circular. In a rough way we may think of these distinct categories as parallel to the Newtonian and the Einsteinian models which suggested that, respectively, time was more or less absolute, or more or less relative to other realities. It is crucial to note, however, that in Western society, these categories have generally been treated as mutually exclusive, whereas in many other cultures, the possibility and capacity of holding both these concepts of time simultaneously is more characteristic. This variation in flexibility otherwise finds its epistemological correspondence in positivist and structuralist thinking. It is further echoed in sociological and anthropological debates about the relationships between structure and function, the fixed and the mutable, the continuous and the discontinuous.

These observations about time, entangled as they are with aging as one manifestation of the passing of time, can be transferred to ideas and theories which are currently held about age and aging; that is to say, age can be conceptualized as being an absolute or relative concept. Similarly, aging processes can take on absolute or relative complexions. From the matrix shown below (see

Figure 1) we can construct a continuum which allows us to place ideas and theories about aging in relation either to the thinking that both time and aging are fixed and absolute concepts or entities, or that time and aging are both entirely flexible, mutable, and fluid ideas.

CHRONOLOGICAL AGE

It is argued that chronology—the length of time which has elapsed in the course of a life—is a fixed variable; time can be measured precisely in terms of years, and this allows the measurement of time between events and between stages in a life. Chronological age is a commonly used measurement that can be applied to individuals and to groups and the "calculations" can be expressed simply. It conveys apparently straight-forward messages about individuals and about the periods they live, or have lived, through. But beyond this, the question has been raised as to whether the chronological age of an individual is a measure of anything of consequence since chronology, to mean something, needs to be set against other factors which take account of differences within individuals and of the differing contexts in which they live out their lives.

PHYSICAL AND BIOLOGICAL AGE

The proposal that living organisms have an inner clock or pacemaker which controls development, maturity, and decline according to a predetermined program is an idea that places aging toward the more fixed end of the absolute-relative time continuum. There is evidence to indicate how each individual's physical development through life is biologically influenced by the normal activity of the hypothalamus and pituitary glands, suggesting that, to a degree, aging can be regarded as an absolute process, determined by biology, which is common to the whole human race. Insofar as it has been demonstrated and is accepted that there are genetic influences on individual "clocks," this idea is reinforced. But at this point it has to be admitted that individuals and groups age differently according to different rates.

AGING AND PSYCHOLOGICAL DEVELOPMENT

If the human aging process can be shown to have fixed physiological elements which, although important at the individual level, do not constitute a way of relating aging to the passage of time in a universal manner, how far can it be argued that human age is an absolute state in terms of psychic development? Is it the case that

people's psychological development is fixed in relation to the passing of time? Theories about human psychic and emotional states frequently rest upon the idea that there are stages to be passed through and that these follow particular sequences, one stage following upon the more or less successful completion of an earlier phase, and psychic maturity being thereby achieved. Developmental theories—for instance those of Freud, Jung, Adler, and of many others—emphasize different pathways toward psychic maturity: some of these have physiological components, others are entirely spiritual, and still others rest upon interactional and relational developments between people.

Both biological and psychological notions of development lead to frameworks for considering aging which have time at their base. These frameworks may fall under headings such as the life cycle, the life-span, and the life course. All suggest a progression through time and each approach places emphasis on more or less fixed features of human constitution or the human condition. Life-cycle approaches—such as the seven ages, or several stages, of man—suggest an inevitable trajectory of development and growth, of diminishment and decline, which is likely to be founded upon physiological and corresponding functional change. Life-span approaches appear to allow for considerable fluctuation of development and change within the span of three-score years and ten or more, and in this respect may be seen as approaches to aging, within time, which consider one set of entities in relation to others. But insofar as life-cycle and life-span frames for age and aging are set by universal chronologies and individual "clock" physiologies, they may be veering toward the fixed pole of the time continuum.

It is argued that life-course approaches, in contrast, do not rest on the idea of life as a cycle in which physiological and functional decline eventually return individuals to their infantile

	TIME	
	Absolute	Relative
AGE — Absolute	1	2
AGE — Relative	3	4

Figure 1. Aging and Time

beginnings. This way of considering aging may be viewed as taking into account the passage of time according to patterns which depend on characteristics particular to the individual rather than to the species, an individually rather than physiologically, or even neurologically, constructed life course.

At the same time, individuals or groups—cohorts in which the group has the same chronological starting point—are also seen as living through time and through society's time or history. This suggests a series of approaches to thinking about time and aging that are at least partly framed within structures created by society. To a greater or lesser extent these structures may use the three principle underpinnings of chronology, physiology, and psychology to which allusion has been made. However, it is arguable that the approaches are structured by society or culture and that individuals or groups of people are assigned to positions in categories determined by society.

Gerontologists—as distinct from geriatricians and psycho-geriatricians, who are predominantly concerned with the physiological and medical aspects of aging—have been increasingly concerned about developing and elaborating theories for understanding human aging that reflect the variability which gerontologists would claim is to be observed in the aging process across cultures. Out of this strand of thinking have emerged a set of ideas which place the aging process firmly within a range of social contexts, in that aging is seen to be constructed and then explained by culturally and temporally specific characteristics.

One way of grouping these approaches to aging, suggested by J. Bond and P. Coleman, is that "all our social behaviour, our attitudes and values, are the result of the organisation and structure of the society in which we live." In other words, aging and time are juxtaposed and interrelated in ways that suggest a relative interdependence rather than an independence resting on the absolute nature of either entity. The analysis by Bond and Coleman makes one further distinction, namely, that aging and time as components of social structure can be seen either as aligned and arising from consensus in society or as arising out of splits and conflicts within society.

SOCIAL AGE
It has been suggested—for instance, by Meyer Fortes when writing about time and social structure—that in many societies—particularly in preliterate and preindustrial societies—chronological age "calculated by reference to a dating system" is not a generally recognized way of thinking or acting about age and aging. Referring to a 1956 cross-cultural study of aging, Fortes notes that it is citizenship—politico-jural rights and duties—rather than family which tended to be associated with status, and so with social age in society. Events, ceremonies, and rites of passage may mark, in public ways, the stages through which an individual passes and by which he or she achieves a changed status and therefore ages in social terms. While the physiological gradient is observed, the symbolic acts that mark the various stages of social aging may refer to realities associated with social ages which are ahead or in the past. The cross-cultural evidence suggests that though biological age provides the "gradient" along which social aging progresses, societies and cultures identify and name the phases associated with the aging process in ways that relate symbolically rather than chronologically to the passing of time.

A further set of theories has been proposed to explain events as they have been observed in Western society since at least the 1940s. The first two of these are defined as consensual in Bond and Coleman's scheme of things, since they can be thought of as supporting the social structure of Western society. They have been termed respectively the disengagement theory of aging and the activity theory of aging.

DISENGAGEMENT THEORY
First proposed by E. Cumming and W. Henry in 1961 in *Growing Old*, the idea was that "Disengagement is an inevitable process in which many of the relationships between a person and the other members of society are severed and those remaining are altered in quality." As more time passes and biological gradients peter out or become steeper and more difficult to negotiate, incapacitating disease and the prospect of death will, as this theory proposes, make it necessary for society—which means the individual and the collectivity—to prepare itself for the individual's final disappearance from the scene. Disengagement theory is posited on the notion that society sets up self-protective norms so that its equilibrium can be maintained even in the face of the disruption which death represents, and that these norms are at their most structured and forceful where aged rather than nonaged people are concerned. This is a theory that has been challenged, not least because it has been thought to condone indifference to older people. It is a sociological theory that ostensibly rests upon

physiological changes which are likely to accompany aging, though an alternative and non-consensual theory—structured dependency—offers a different analysis of withdrawal from public life on the part of older people. But before discussing conflicting theories of aging, consider a theory that sets up a different kind of consensual framework within which to view aging.

ACTIVITY THEORY

In 1963, R.J. Havighurst suggested that—in contradistinction to disengagement theory and an acquiescent withdrawal from life—the ideal was the continuation of a level of activity into old age which was in line with that which had been habitual at younger ages. Where activities and relationships had been lost, it was in the interests of individuals and of society to replace these, so that changes and deficits would not be conspicuous or disruptive to society as a whole.

These contrasting ideas about aging seem to be associated with contrasting notions about time. On the one hand, disengagement theory may be said to weigh very heavily the consequences of the passing of time on individuals and therefore on society. The passage of time and the accompanying associations with physiological incapacity are seen, at least in Western society, as the determinants of norms. To this extent, the relativity of time in relation to aging is reduced but not absent. In activity theory, on the other hand, the denial of the passage of time works to place the individual life span as the absolute entity—aging, or rather, nonaging—within time. This approach generates the criticism that activity theory is simply an ideal developed as a counterpoint to disengagement theory, with little basis in reality.

STRUCTURED DEPENDENCY

Rather than holding to theories of aging which say that everything works to preserve society's status quo, others would argue that the way time, its passing, and what is meant by aging and age-appropriate interactions between people are dealt with, shows splits and conflicts between different parts of society. The theory of structured dependency takes as a starting point the observations made—at least about many post-industrial societies—that older people tend to be less engaged than those at other ages in the mainstream activities of society. This is the same empirical starting point as used for disengagement theory. But structured dependency theory explains this withdrawal not as an agreed or consensual one between the old and the others,

but as a consequence of strictures placed around older people that force them into retirement, both in terms of paid employment and in terms of social activity beyond the world of work and even extending into the heart of family relationships.

In proposing the idea that dependency may be associated with old age and following on from this that society builds structures which give this group of people little room for maneuver and make them dependent on a restricted range of resources, a model is being put forward that suggests a high degree of manipulation on the part of society. However, it needs to be stressed that structured dependency is a concept which applies equally to groups that have not experienced as much passing time as have older groups of people. Manipulation is a mechanism that entails the holding of entities within a fluid system where everything can be relative to everything else. It is conceivable that the theory of structured dependence could flow into that of structured, or unstructured, independence, where time and its passing—age—are in relationships that are not fixed, though they may be defined.

In conclusion, it is clear that in thinking and acting about age and aging, time in itself does not always feature prominently and explicitly. However, time and time passing is frequently implicit in ideas about aging. To varying degrees, time and age are viewed as absolute entities, but more frequently it can be argued that one or the other of these elements is seen as relative and variable—at the individual level or else at the level of society or culture.

[L.K.]

See also **Aging Populations; Ethnicity and Aging; Politics and Aging; Social Gerontology.**

FURTHER READINGS

Bond, J., and P. Coleman, eds. *Aging in Society: An Introduction to Social Gerontology*. London: Sage, 1990.

Eliade, M. *The Myth of the Eternal Return*. Princeton: Princeton UP, 1965.

Fortes, M. *Time and Social Structure and Other Essays*. London School of Economics Monographs on Social Anthropology 40. London: Athlone P, 1970.

Koestler, A. *The Act of Creation*. London: Hutchinson, 1964.

AGING POPULATIONS

The age structure of a population evolves in response to earlier changes in fertility, mortality, and migration. In developed countries, the major cause of changing age structures has been volatility of fertility in the last half century, embracing the low fertility of the 1930s Depression era, the prolonged postwar baby boom, and the subsequent collapse of fertility (the baby bust) in the 1970s and 1980s (see Figure 1).

A major planning problem has been, and will continue for some time to be, the provision of resources to meet the considerable needs of the baby-boom cohort, sandwiched as it is between two much smaller low-birth cohorts. The baby boom had to cope with crowded classrooms and teacher shortages during its earlier years and exerted great pressure on labor and housing markets in the 1970s and 1980s. Toward the end of the century, competition for career advancement in middle age is likely to be intense, but the real crunch will come when the baby boomers reach retirement age. Figure 1 shows that this will not occur until around 2015. However, any complacency is misplaced, because the numbers at the younger and older ends of the elderly range will change very differently in the short term. Those in their sixties will not increase significantly since they will be the survivors of the low-birth cohort of the Depression, but there will be appreciable increases among the super-elderly (eighty plus), who are particularly demanding of state resources for care and support at a time when the family unit seems increasingly ill adapted to shoulder the burden of the aged. The trend shown by United States projections in Figure 1 is typical of developed countries, although the actual proportions of the elderly are somewhat higher in European populations not subject to American levels of net immigration of younger population. Thus, the proportion of population over sixty-five

years in Sweden had reached 18 percent in 1990 and is projected, under medium-variant assumptions, to reach 23 percent in 2025. Moreover, migration on retirement produces particularly high concentrations of the elderly in areas like Florida, the American Southwest, and the south coast of England.

There is much contemporary concern in developed countries about the implications of aging populations for productivity and dependency, but the problems are often overstated. It is not always appreciated that the elderly proportion levels off under conditions of reasonably stable fertility and mortality of the type experienced in developed countries between 1975 and 1990 and expected to continue during the 1990s (Figure 1). It must also be appreciated that the current aging of populations has not increased significantly the total dependency burden (the proportion of the total population aged zero to fourteen and sixty-five plus) since the larger elderly cohorts are compensated by the smaller cohorts of children. One needs, however, to consider the changing internal composition of both the working population and the dependent population. Under conditions of sustained lower fertility, the lower proportion of younger workers in the labor force poses particular problems for those labor-intensive occupations like nursing which depend heavily on large numbers of young recruits. More generally, the benefits stemming from the greater flexibility and mobility of younger workers are an important consideration in human resources planning.

As for the dependent population, there is a greater cost per capita of supporting the elderly than children, mainly because of the rapidly escalating costs of health care for the super-elderly. There is also a major problem concerning the funding of state pension systems. These systems are generally based on an intergenerational transfer of resources from workers to the retired, rather than on workers paying into a fully funded pension scheme from which they will eventually be entitled to draw an annuity. In other words, current benefits to those retiring are financed by taxes on current workers. This has posed problems in the 1980s and early 1990s because of the association of growing numbers of the retired with the eroding tax base of sagging economies. A short-term response in several countries has been to increase taxes and trim benefits.

Medium-term policy adjustments might include immigration coming back to favor, although

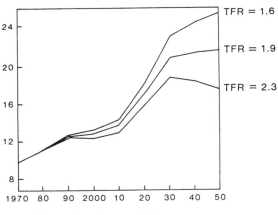

Figure 1. Aging populations.

the social and political costs could outweigh the advantages of a younger labor force and more substantial tax base; more retraining and redeployment of older workers could substitute for the flexibility that a younger labor force usually provides; and the funding problem of pension systems could be eased by reversing the trend toward younger retirement, which would also accord with health improvements at these ages.

In the longer term, some governments might follow the example of France in trying to enhance fertility levels through the provision of financial and other incentives to parents. But governments in most developed countries are reluctant to infringe upon basic human rights in procreation and family-size choice, and are sensitive to the association of pronatalist "social engineering" with prewar Fascism and postwar communism. It seems, therefore, that the major response of governments to aging population structures will be in institutional mechanisms within the broad field of economic and social policies.

[H.R.J.]

See also **Human Fertility Trends.**

FURTHER READINGS

Johnson, P., C. Conrad, and D. Thomson. *Workers Versus Pensioners.* Manchester: Manchester UP, 1989.

Schulz, J., A. Borowski, and W. Crown. *Economics of Population Aging: The Graying of Australia, Japan, and the United States.* New York: Auburn House, 1991.

Tout, K. *Ageing in Developing Countries.* Oxford: Oxford UP, 1989.

ALBERTUS MAGNUS (CA. 1200–1280)

Albert of Lauingen, a scientist, philosopher, and theologian known even in his own day as "the Great," was an Aristotelian in natural philosophy. His defense of the extramental reality of time, not only against St. Augustine's Platonic "psychologizing" of time, but also against Averroes (Ibn-Rushd), the influential Arabian commentator of Aristotle, is perhaps his most significant contribution to this problem.

Albert believed that natural philosophy, rather than metaphysics or psychology, was the primary discipline in which time is properly studied. He held that time's existence as a real attribute of events of the physical universe is self-evident to all observers whose minds are not clouded by false preconceptions. Albert argued that because time is an attribute of the events of the physical universe, time's mode of being is analogous to motion's. Time does not possess enduring being (*esse permanens*), as do rocks, trees, and stars; time has successive being (*esse successivum*) which flows and is always losing what was had and gaining what is to come. Albert believed that the present moment or "now," which is all of time that exists, is a flowing reality that is the end of the past and the beginning of the future. He followed Aristotle's definition of time, arguing that "time is the number of the events of the physical universe according to prior and posterior." Time is an attribute of the changes and interactions of physical beings in the universe. Albert believed that, although all physical events are temporal, time is primarily an attribute of the fundamental motion of the universe, the circular motion of the outer sphere of fixed stars, since it is the most uniform and continuous; secondarily, time numbers all other events. Thus, there is one time of the universe and not as many times as events.

Averroes thought Aristotle held that in order to exist, time requires a mind to number events, since a number requires a numberer. Albert explicitly rejected this interpretation and argued that "the soul never numbers anything unless there exists in the soul a principle of number taken from things themselves" (*Physica* 4.3.16). Albert believed that time exists in nature according to a form of temporal discretion (that is to say, number) inherent in the material events themselves. Thus, he held that, materially and formally, time exists as a flowing, successive being, even if no soul exists.

Albert argued that there is no common or univocal measure between time and eternity, but he held that only by understanding time can we form a notion of God's eternity. For Albert, eternity is "a period (*spatium*) which lacks beginning and end and which has in itself no prior and posterior and no succession, because it measures (*mensurat*) not what is made or is a copy but rather what is immovably permanent" (*Physica* 4.4.1). The terms *spatium* and *mensurat* are not quantitative terms but analogous terms referring to the subsistent actuality of God's absolute being.

Albert's concern is with the being and nature of time, with *chronos*, rather than the measurement of time, chronometrics. His analysis, complementing those of mathematical physics, has enduring philosophic value.

[S.C.S.]

FURTHER READINGS

Albertus Magnus. *Physica* in *Opera Omnia*. Ed. Paul Hossfeld. Münster: Aschendorff, 1987.

Maier, Anneliese. *Metaphysische Hintergründe der spätscholastischen Naturphilosophie*. Rome: Edizioni di storia e letteratura, 1955. 47–137.

Snyder, Steven C. "Albert the Great's Analysis of Time in Its Historical and Doctrinal Setting." Ph.D. dissertation, University of Toronto, 1984.

Weisheipl, James A., ed. *Albertus Magnus and the Sciences*. Toronto: Pontifical Institute of Mediaeval Studies, 1980.

ALEXANDER, SAMUEL (1859–1938)

Time for Samuel Alexander is one of the two aspects of Space-Time, the ultimate reality or irreducible stuff out of which all that exists emerges. To the ancients, as to modern classical science, the underlying reality was matter and motion. Time was a lesser reality.

Alexander considered the most characteristic feature of thought during the first quarter of the twentieth century to be the discovery of time. Philosophy with Bergson, and science with Minkowski, Einstein, Lorentz, and others began to take time seriously. In a comparable manner Alexander, a British philosopher, moving from Einstein's space-time (lower case) and his special theory of relativity, developed a whole philosophical system grounding ultimate reality in Space-Time (capitalized).

In Alexander's usage, Space (capitalized) signifies space as a whole, and Time (capitalized) signifies time as a whole. When he writes of space or time he writes of parts of the whole. Space-Time is itself "the infinite matrix of all finites." It is "the nurse and mother of all becomings." Time has no reality apart from Space, or Space apart from Time. As separate concepts both are abstractions from the four-dimensional reality.

In Alexander's view, human beings in their conscious minds and bodily brains are examples of a pattern of mind and body which is universal and followed not only by all entities in the universe but by Space-Time itself. Mind is a form of Time. Time is the mind of Space. Space is the body of Time. Time animates Space, causing a restlessness of Space-Time which generates matter in the form of discrete entities. A creative thrust builds on material entities to bring into being living creatures, and goes on to the further level of mind and consciousness. Matter, life,

and mind are successive emergent qualities of primordial Space-Time.

Alexander argues that Space is generated in Time, and that Space is the trail of Time. The world is the body of God, an evolving creation of what is at root Space-Time. God's deity, or divine quality, is presently aspiring to a new unimaginable stage of existence beyond the human quality of mind or soul.

Unless change is used by Bergson as a loose expression for motion, Alexander disagrees with Bergson's comment that change is the stuff of things. For Alexander, Space-Time is a system of motions, and could be called Motion, if Motion is understood in a special comprehensive sense in which there is nothing such as matter that moves, and if matter is deemed to be a product of Motion.

Alexander is a process philosopher. For him, time is not something which happens to things that exist in space. There is nothing which is not temporal, and no reality but that of events. The only ultimate reality is the system of events he prefers to call Space-Time.

Alexander comments that we learn much more directly about the nature of Time from the expectation of the future than from the remembrance of the past. The only eternity which can be construed in terms of experience is infinite Time (in its capitalized sense). Space (in its capitalized sense) not only contains present time, but is full of memory and expectation. In 1921, he pointed out that thinkers had only just begun in their speculations to take time seriously, and to realize that in some way or other Time is an essential ingredient in the constitution of things. "To realize the importance of Time as such is the gate of wisdom."

Samuel Alexander, who grew up in Australia, was educated in classics and mathematics at Balliol College, Oxford. He became interested in the mind-body problem and studied psychology and neurology in London and Freiburg. In 1893, he was elected to a chair in philosophy at the University of Manchester, where he stayed until and after retirement.

[C.W.E.]

See also **Bergson, Henri; Gravity, Time, and Space; Physics; Relativity Theory; Whitehead, Alfred North.**

FURTHER READINGS

Alexander, Samuel. *Space, Time, and Deity*. The Gifford Lectures at Glasgow, 1916–1918. 1920; reprint, New York: Dover, 1966.

―――. *Spinoza and Time*. London: Allen and Unwin, 1921. (Also in *Philosophical and Literary Pieces*, ed. John Laird.) See especially section v.

―――. "Theism and Pantheism." *The Hibbert Journal* (January 1927). (Also in *Philosophical and Literary Pieces*, ed. John Laird.)

Stiernotte, Alfred P. *God and Space-Time*. New York: Philosophical Library, 1954.

ALLERGY AND POLLEN

The chronobiological phenomenon is very important in the pathophysiology of human respiratory allergic diseases produced by the interaction of allergens with the immunologic system. Indeed, circadian and circannual rhythms have been detected in allergens from acrids, spores, and molds, as well as in pollinization.

CIRCADIAN RHYTHMS IN POLLINIZATION

The circadian rhythm of anemophilous pollens may vary from one region to another and from one plant to the next. For instance, the release of pollen from grass begins early in the morning of a sunny day and it reaches its highest level by the end of the afternoon. On the other hand, maximal release of pollen from plantains (of genus *Plantago*) occurs in the morning, while the pollen released by trees—such as elm, ash, and oak—is largest by midnight. In the United States, peak pollen values of ragweed are found before 10:00 A.M.

The circadian rhythms of plants are endogenous. Their main characteristics are as follows: (1) rhythms are controlled by an external signal (such as light or darkness), but they may be synchronized to an external rhythm with a slightly different period; (2) rhythms are present in isolation but their amplitude may be gradually reduced; and (3) temperature does not influence the rhythms of plants. Thus, the variations reported in the biological rhythms of different plants are explained by differences in their genetic background.

CIRCANNUAL RHYTHMS

Allergists must also be aware of the circannual rhythms in pollinization because this knowledge will help them to determine the cause of allergic reactions observed in the respiratory, ocular, and even cutaneous systems. In temperate climates, three periods can be defined for the release of pollens, and it must be noted that pollen from wall pellitory are released during all three periods. The first period occurs early in the season. Pollinization begins at the end of winter; the exact time of year depends on the latitude.

Pollen originating from trees with much sap in their roots and trunk are involved in this first period. The second period takes place at the end of the spring or at the beginning of summer. This is the main season for pollinization. The main sources of pollen in the air are grass, perennial plants, and trees in full growth. Weeds, plantains, rumex, and sheep sorrel also begin to release pollen at this time of year. The third period occurs late in the summer and at the beginning of the fall. Pollen coming from herbaceous plants found in fields without too many plants and those taking some time to bloom are involved in this period.

Physicians must realize that the plasma levels of cortisol and catecholamines are lowest during the main season for pollinization. Thus, the defense mechanisms of humans are lowest when pollinization is highest and this fact may explain the importance of the pathological problems caused by pollens in humans at that time of the year.

[P.G. and G.L.]

See also **Biological Rhythms and Medicine; Biological Rhythms in Epidemiology and Pharmacology; Histamine and Allergic Rhinitis.**

FURTHER READINGS

Baillaud, L. "Les rythmes biologiques: point de vue d'un botaniste sur quelques problèmes de biologie générale." *Separatum Experimentia* 27 (1971): 489.

Frankland, A.W. "Allergènes polliniques en Grande-Bretague." *Atlas Européen des pollens allergisants*. Ed. J. Charpin and R. Surinyach. Paris: Sandoz, 1974.

ALLOCATION OF TIME

Economics is the discipline dedicated to the allocation of scarce resources. Time definitely falls within this definition. That time is a prime factor in the production process has been recognized for ages. Households sell firms the time (and effort) of their members in return for wages; households also sell capital services, whose returns (interest, dividends, and rents) depend, in part, on the duration for which they are used by the firms.

The adage "time is money" is not confined to the production sector. It relates to the home sector as well; indeed, time is the fundamental scarcity in the home. Because of a physical limit on the amount of available time (say, twenty-four hours a day), time is not a costless resource: it can be sold on the market for a price (the wage rate), and even when there are limits on how much time a person can sell on the market (such as a maximum working hours restriction), there are many activities that compete for that scarce resource.

The fact that travel time and the value people assign to their time affects their travel decisions has long been recognized in economic literature. In 1963, J. Mincer demonstrated that households' decisions on their labor supply, fertility, and the demand for housemaids are affected by the value assigned to home time. Two years later, G. Becker formalized the modern theory of the allocation of time. Drawing an analogy to production theory, he reformulated consumption theory so that the sources of utility are activities rather than individual goods. The household "produces" these activities ("commodities" in Becker's terminology) by combining time and goods purchased in the market or produced at home. This production is subject to several constraints: existing technology, the amount of time available, and the available money income (to acquire the goods). Time can be converted into money by selling it on the labor market. Along with preferences, technology, time and income constraints, and the rate at which time can be sold on the market determine consumption patterns and the allocation of time (including labor supply). The greater one's income, or the higher the wage rate, the higher the value assigned to one's time, and hence the greater the effort to conserve it: if possible, households will substitute goods for time in the production of each activity, and time-intensive activities (rest or sleep) will be curtailed while goods-intensive activities are expected to expand.

Becker's theory of the allocation of time and household production has been applied to explain several patterns of household behavior. It was employed by Becker himself and by R. Willis, in 1973, to explain fertility patterns: higher wages raise the cost of raising children; hence, women earning high wages tend to have fewer children but invest more in each child (a wife's wage and schooling have been shown to be more important factors explaining fertility patterns than a husband's wage and schooling). Better educated people tend to be more efficient workers in their market jobs and at home. The impact of schooling on home technology and on consumption was explored by R. Michael in 1973, and on the demand for health services by M. Grossman in 1972. A long list of economists have analyzed the role of time in travel-related

decisions, including its effect on the choice of mode of transport, place of residence, and the place of work. People with higher income and wages will try to save time by choosing faster modes of travel to cut down on commuting time. These time savings are often associated with higher money costs. The traveler chooses the faster mode only if the cost of time savings is lower than his or her subjective value of time. Data on the choice of travel mode allowed empirical economists to estimate the value people assign to the saving of travel time. Most studies concur that commuters assign to their time a value which is much lower than their wage rate (only a quarter to a half), either because they cannot increase their earnings by increasing work and reducing travel time, or because travel is more enjoyable than work. These values are routinely incorporated in cost-benefit calculations of investment in transport facilities (freeways, underground trains, location of airports, bridges, and faster modes of travel), where the value of time saving is known to be one of the major benefits.

Becker's theory revived interest in the measurement of time budgets. Data on time budgets were first collected in the Soviet Union in the early 1920s. A few attempts to collect such data were made in the United States in the mid-1930s, but in general the collection of such data was much more advanced in Europe (in particular in the Communist countries) than in North America. In the mid-1960s the United Nations sponsored an international study of time budgets (as reported by A. Szalai in 1972) which included close to a dozen countries. This study triggered large systematic surveys in the United States and elsewhere of time use patterns based on twenty-four-hour time diaries.

These surveys show that in most countries total weekly working hours (combining market work and work at home) ranged between fifty-five and sixty-five hours and were about the same for men and women. There is, however, a sharp gender-based difference between work in the market and at home. The intra-family allocation of time is often affected by relative wages (along with social norms). Men, who in general enjoy higher wages, specialize in market work, while women, who have a lower wage, work more at home. Data from the end of the 1970s and early 1980s show that whereas men spend forty to fifty-five hours in the market and only five to fifteen hours working at home, the home job occupies close to thirty hours of women's time. The variation in men's allocation of time is affected mostly by age (that is, entry into the labor force and retirement), and marriage status. Women's allocation of time, on the other hand, is also (perhaps even more) affected by their schooling level and whether they have young children; the latter are the two prime factors determining *married* women's labor force participation and time use patterns (employed married women spend far more hours on work than married women who are not employed).

No time series (see **Time Series**) exists on time use, but most data sources indicate that total work time has diminished over the last three decades, while leisure time has increased (there seems also to have been a decline in hours of sleep). These trends are common to both men and women, in spite of the sharp increase in married women's labor force participation. For women, the increase in leisure is explained by a sharp decline in work at home, assisted partly by the proliferation of timesaving devices at home.

An activity that has drawn special attention because of its social implications is child care. In the past, bringing up children in the Western world was associated with their mothers' withdrawal from the labor force. This tendency has weakened in many countries during the last two decades. Time use surveys indicate that although schooling has a strong positive correlation with labor-force participation, women with more education do not spend less time on child care (although they may spend more time on educational activities rather than on menial chores). The data, though scarce, also indicate that this activity has not declined over time.

Conventionally, the standard national accounts relate (with few exceptions) only to the production activity taking place in the market. The exclusion of home output (specifically housewives' services) results in a serious underestimate of the measure of economic activity, and may bias intercountry comparisons and changes in national output over time, since economic development shifts economic activities out of the home and into the market. The output in the home sector does not bear a price tag and economists have devised different methods to estimate its value. These estimates indicate that the value of this output, which is produced mostly by women, accounts for more than a third of the Gross Domestic Product.

[R.G.]

See also **Social Time; Use of Time; Work and Time.**

FURTHER READINGS

Becker, Gary S. "A Theory of the Allocation of Time." *Economic Journal* 75 (1965): 493–517.

Gronau, Reuben. "Home Production—A Survey." *Handbook of Labor Economics*. Volume 1. Ed. O. Ashenfelter and R. Layard. Amsterdam: North-Holland, 1986. 273–304.

Juster, F. Thomas, and Frank P. Stafford. "The Allocation of Time: Empirical Findings, Behavioral Models, and Problems of Measurement." *Journal of Economic Literature* 29 (1991): 471–522.

ALTERNATE HISTORY

Alternate histories are essays or narratives exploring the consequences of an imagined divergence from known historical events. In 1857, Charles Renouvier named such works "Uchronias" to suggest their role as utopian versions of past time, although now "uchronia" also refers to the related genre of utopias set in the future. The first book-length alternate history is Louis Geoffroy's *Napoléon et la conquête du monde— 1812 à 1832—Histoire de la monarchie universelle* (1836; Napoleon and the conquest of the world— 1812 to 1832—History of the universal monarchy). Also known as *Napoléon apocryphe* (the apocryphal Napoleon), this is an account of Napoleon's victorious Russian campaign, invasion of England, and establishment of a French monarchy that first governs all Europe and later the entire world. This is only partially a Bonapartist's nostalgic utopia portraying a technologically advanced Francophile (and Francophone) world that might have been had Napoleon avoided defeat in Russia. Geoffroy also provides a devastating critique of that world's shortcomings as a terrifyingly efficient police state. Napoleon becomes a foreshadowing of Orwell's Big Brother in Geoffroy's powerful warning against the dangers of any future superpower created along the lines suggested by the historical Napoleon's ambitions. Thus, from its first fully realized example in Geoffroy's *Napoléon apocryphe*, alternate history displays a Janus-like ability to point attention backwards to what was and might have been, and also forward to future possibilities.

Historians call speculations about alternate history "counterfactuals." A famous example is Robert W. Fogel's *Railroads and Economic Growth: Essays in Econometric History* (1964), which considers how America might have developed had there been no railroads during the nineteenth century. Many historians dispute the utility of such counterfactual speculation as a method of arriving at valid knowledge about the past. As imaginative literature, alternate history has been less controversial but infrequent outside of science fiction. The term sometimes includes narratives more accurately described as parallel history, which is to say accounts of our planet that present a totally different past or present not caused by a divergence from real history at some key moment such as a French victory at Waterloo. Parallel histories simply present a past differing from the one we know without assigning any particular reasons for the differences.

Alternate history is an effective vehicle for commentary on the human condition, as in Simon Leys's witty *La mort de Napoléon* (1986; the death of Napoleon), in which Napoleon secretly returns from St. Helena only to live out his days anonymously as a successful bourgeois happy at last in private life. Alternate histories usually identify a pivotal event as the crucial turning point whose outcome shapes subsequent history. In Philip K. Dick's brilliant novel of an Axis victory in World War II, *The Man in the High Castle* (1962), it is the assassination of Franklin D. Roosevelt that leads to American defeat. In Winston S. Churchill's ingenious essay, "If Lee Had Not Won the Battle of Gettysburg" (1931), Confederate victory is presented as an outcome that would have prevented World War I. Borderline novels like Vladimir Nabokov's *Ada* (1969) share features of the parallel world and alternate history narrative. On publication in 1949 George Orwell's *Nineteen Eighty-Four* was primarily a futuristic uchronia portraying a bleak future as a metaphor describing current totalitarian tendencies, whereas after 1984, Orwell's masterpiece has also achieved the power of an alternate history showing what our world might have been as a warning against what it might still become. Whatever their value for analysis of historical causation, a vexed topic at best, alternate histories invite attention to important questions about past and future possibilities, as well as present choices and their consequences.

[P.K.A.]

See also **Futuristic Fiction; Utopias and Dystopias.**

FURTHER READINGS

Alkon, Paul K. *Origins of Futuristic Fiction*. Athens: U of Georgia P, 1987.

Hacker, Barton C., and Gordon B. Chamberlain. "Pasts That Might Have Been, II: A Revised Bibliography of Alternative History." *Alternative Histories: Eleven Stories of the World as It Might Have Been*. Ed. Charles G. Waugh and Martin H. Greenberg. New York: Garland, 1986. 301–363.

AMERICAN INDIANS: TIME IN OUTLOOK AND LANGUAGE

DIVERSITY OF LANGUAGES AND CULTURES

The term "American Indians" refers to all societies that were indigenous to the North and South American continents and the Caribbean islands at the time of European incursions beginning at the end of the fifteenth century. This represents a widely diverse group of cultures, approximately 2,000 in number, speaking languages that belong to more than 150 different language families, whose homelands range geographically from north of the Arctic Circle to the southern tip of South America, from mountain ranges to vast plains, from deserts to tropical rain forests. Many have been nomadic while others have long histories of living in urban centers and practicing settled agriculture. Historically, at least two civilizations developed—the Mesoamerican and the Andean—in which measurement of temporal changes and calendric systems reached a very sophisticated level. More recently there have been regional efforts to articulate a "Pan-Indian" consciousness, largely among societies which have become cut off from their cultural heritages, including the Native American Church in the United States and Canada. These tend to be characterized by a superficial eclecticism, largely interpreted from the perspective of the dominant non-Indian culture. Given this wide diversity, it is difficult to make generalizations about an American Indian concept of time, or to identify a typical "American Indian" view on any matter, except to state that none of these cultures possesses the current view of "time" and "temporality" which is held within the world of European civilization.

THE LANGUAGE OF TIME AND TEMPORALITY

Exact equivalents for the vocabulary of time in European languages are largely lacking in the languages of Indian-America. It is often difficult to distinguish between temporal terms and spatial terms, or among terrestrial, celestial, and cosmic temporality. In the Mayan languages, for example, the same word, *kin* or *k'ij*, refers to "sun," "day," "age," or "eon." Siouan languages have terms referring to obvious observable environmental changes: day (with reference to night), month (with reference to lunation), the four seasons, and year. Lacking was a term for "week" until contact with European Catholics, when reference had to be made to the "space between ceremonies" (reference is to Sunday mass). Although the phases of the moon might be used for this purpose, there is little evidence that this occurs in any of the languages. Although the two rattlesnakes in the Aztecan "Eagle's Bowl" are divided into twelve segments each, presumably indicating twelve hours in a day, and twelve hours in a night, words for "hour" are difficult to find. In Quechua, the expression "potatoes come to boil" seems to refer to a period of approximately an hour, although the Spanish "hora" and "media-hora" are used by the Mayan speakers indicating no concern for those "periods of time" until contact with the Europeans. The names given to months usually refer to a changing scene: "egg-laying," "egg-hatching," "guanaco pregnancies," and "young guanacos" by the Ona of the Andes; and "loosening of bark" and "finding first bird eggs" by their neighbors the Yahgan. Such naming points to an early effort to discern patterns of rhythmic order in the midst of arbitrary activity, looking both to recurring patterns with the earthly environment and to the orderly movements of celestial bodies and configurations.

COSMOLOGICAL DIMENSIONS: SPACE-TIME COORDINATES

The fundamental concern for such temporal descriptions and measurements is cosmological, an effort to discover and maintain order in the lived-world. The Maya-Guarani myth of origins opens with the words "Our very first father created his own body out of the primeval darkness," and the struggle between creative order and destructive chaos is viewed as a continuing dialectical process. The parallel Apapokuva-Guarani myth of origins refers to a primordial cross which "our great father" directs to the east and sets down as the earth's support. The act of creation begins with the creator's own self-emergence, the establishment of spatiotemporal quadrants within which the earth is formed. The integration of "space" and "time" is characteristic of many Amerindian cultures. The same words are often used to refer both to the spatial coordinates "east" and "west," and to the temporal events "rising of the sun" and "setting of the sun." The solar solstices, which become crucial to the description of temporality, are referred to in the languages of those cultures which engage in astronomical observation as "sun stands still in middle of sky." The Maya observed Venus "stand still," and there seems to be some evi-

dence of observation of lunar "standstills" as well. A stele at the Maya site Chichen Itza proclaims the discovery, after a lengthy process of observation, that five Venus cycles (of 584 days each) is equivalent to eight solar years. Among the Mayan societies only four out of the eighteen deities who bear the months can be deities who bear the years. Each of the four is associated, as well, with one of the cardinal directions, and the new year is entered according to the direction of its deity-bearer. Puebloan dances, which observe the high points of the ceremonial year, are performed in sets of four, honoring the spatial directions and at the same time celebrating the order of temporality. At the dance held in Tewa-speaking societies for the preparation of the ground for planting in February, the spirits who assist are heralded in the chanting that accompanies the dance as "coming from all directions," and this is carried out with repeated reference to the four cardinal directions. The "originating winds" in Tupi-Guarani myths of origins are correlated with the four cardinal directions, as well as with the four seasons—clearly spatiotemporal.

CALENDRICS AND CEREMONY

Although hunting animals and the gathering of wild plants are incorporated in the sequence of ritual, the appearance of calendars coincides with the domestication of plants. The Iroquois calendar, for example, is divided into two sections. The first extends from harvest of cultivated crops rituals in September through the new year ceremony in February ("when the Pleiades shine through the smoke hole of the long house"); the second, or summer half, includes ceremonies for maple sugar gathering (late March), wild berry picking (late May), wild fruit gathering (late July), as well as dances for the growth and harvesting of corn, beans, and squash (June and July), and the green corn dance (late August). The Puebloan ceremonial calendar features animal dances in the winter half, and rituals dealing with rain and fertility during the spring and summer. A special sun priest is responsible for regular observation of the sun's movement with reference either to natural points on the horizon, or to drawn points on a wall from which will be determined the correct time for specific ceremonies to begin. In the Quechua language the name for an horizon point, either natural formation or carved, used in solar observation is *Intihuatana* ("Hitching post of the sun"), although these may be more important as shrines for solar ritual. The most elaborate calendric systems were developed by the Mayans in Mesoamerican civilization, and by the Incans based on earlier astronomico-ceremonial efforts in Andean civilization. They involve two or more calendars which are not in accord and require a process of imbrication resulting in a complex view of "time." The Mayan calendric system is the most elaborate, including the sacred calendar of 260 days, the solar calendar of 365 days, the correlation of these two of fifty-two solar years ("calendar round"), the Venus calendar of 584 days, and the correlation of calendar round and Venus, or 104 solar years, with yet another calendar in which the total sum of temporal coordinates for any given day recurs only once every 374.44 solar years. Such a highly complex understanding of patterns of order is a rejection of both a simple cyclical view of temporal progression and a purely lineal concept.

CONCEPTS OF HISTORY AND DESTINY
In addition to the multiple calendars developed by the Mayan and spread to a limited extent throughout parts of Mesoamerican civilization, with efforts to calculate the correlation of calendars and calendric elements into a virtually indefinite past and indefinite future, Mayan culture also held to a long count. The long count introduced a fixed date, corresponding to 3113 B.C., that becomes a dividing point, calculations proceeding forward or backward from it. Whether referring to a highly significant event that gives profound meaning to history, or in an effort to locate a cosmic center in which all temporal changes are ultimately related and grounded, the long count indicates that "time" is more than processes that can be reduced to mathematical calculations and astronomical observations. The Puebloan notion of emergence from the point of origin and wandering through a series of levels or planes of existence until the "center" is found where the people have settled refers to a sacred history which is teleological, and to the concept of growth in spirituality. There is a similarity between Puebloan "planes of existence" and the Mesoamerican view of four cosmic ages already passed, each having ended cataclysmically, and a final fifth age which possibly faces a violent end unless the human community cooperates in maintaining the cosmic order. Among Tupi-Guarani speaking societies found throughout the eastern half of South America there is a similar anxiety about an impending catastrophe that will bring cosmic order to an end and mark a return to primordial chaos. This has given rise to "messianic" movements led by diviner-shamans (*pajé*) who pre-

dict the end and lead entire societies in a search for the "land without sorrow," which had been established at the point of origin as a place for escaping chaos. Similar is the myth of the return of Quetzalcoatl or Kulkulcan within Mesoamerican cultures, and the 1780 Tupac-Amaru uprising in the vice-royalty of Peru appealed to a cognate notion. The movement, however, is not linear but helical.

[F.G.S.]

See also **Archaeoastronomy; Aztec Calendar; Maya Calendars and Chronology; Meaning of Time in Primitive Societies; Primitive Time-Reckoning.**

FURTHER READINGS
Aveni, A., ed. *Archaeoastronomy in the New World.* Cambridge: Cambridge UP, 1982.

Carlson, J.B., and W.J. Judge, eds. *Astronomy and Ceremony in the Prehistoric Southwest.* Albuquerque: Maxwell Museum, 1987.

Givens, D. *An Analysis of Navajo Temporality.* Washington: University Presses of America, 1977.

Léon-Portilla, M. *Time and Reality in the Thought of the Maya.* Boston: Beacon P, 1973.

Sturm, F.G. "The Concepts of History and Destiny Implicit in the Apapokuva-Guarani Myth of the Creation and Destruction of the Earth." *"Love and War: Hummingbird Lore" and Other Selected Papers from LAILA/ALILA's 1988 Symposium.* Ed. Mary H. Preuss. Culver City: Labyrinthos, 1989. 61–66.

Tedlock, B. *Time and the Highland Maya.* Albuquerque: U of New Mexico P, 1982.

Williamson, R., ed. *Archaeoastronomy in the New World.* Los Altos: Ballena, 1981.

ANALYTIC PHILOSOPHY

The major issue addressed in the writings on time by analytic philosophers is whether time is nothing but a static order of events running from earlier to later or requires in addition that these events also are past, present, or future and shift in respect to such determinations. The latter, called "temporal becoming," is supposed to be the very essence of time, but it occasions perplexities concerning *what* does the shifting and the sort of *shift* involved. It must be some mysterious transcendent entity X that shifts, since temporal relations between events and times are fixed. The nature of the shift is equally perplexing, for it must occur at a particular rate. A rate of change involves a comparison between one kind of change and a change of time. In the case of temporal becoming, however, it is change of time that is compared to change of time, resulting in the tautology that time passes or shifts at the rate of one second per second, surely an absurdity since this is not a rate of change of change at all. In a move that suggests desperation, some have claimed that temporal becoming is a *sui generis* type of change that defies analysis but is accessible to us through ineffable intuition.

To escape such perplexities, many analytic philosophers have attempted a "linguistic reduction" of tensed or temporal indexical propositions reporting an event as past, present, or future into tenseless or non-indexical propositions that describe a temporal relation of precedence or simultaneity between the reported event and another event or time. The former is expressed by the use of a sentence that is not freely repeatable in time, the latter through a sentence that is timelessly true or false. This is supposed to effect an "ontological reduction" of an event's being past, present, or future to its being respectively earlier than, simultaneous with, or later than some other event or time. It is generally conceded that such a linguistic reduction does not work, because an indexical proposition is not identical with any indexical one. This is due to the fact that one can have a propositional attitude to one of them that one does not have to the other; for example, I can believe (or know, and so forth) that event E occurs now but not believe that it occurs (tenselessly) at time t_7. The proponents of temporal becoming have drawn the wrong moral from this failure—that there is a Mr. X out there doing "The Shift." They have overlooked the fact that two sentences can express different propositions and yet report one and the same event or state of affairs in that their respective nominalizations are coreferring; for example, "This is water," and "This is a collection of H_2O molecules," though differing in sense, report the same event or state—this being water is nothing but this being a collection of H_2O molecules. It could be claimed that the same holds for the appropriate uses of indexical and non-indexical sentences. For example, the utterance at t_7 of "Georgie flies at this time (at present)" reports one and the same event as does an utterance at any time of the non-synonymous sentence, "Georgie flies (tenselessly) at t_7," since Georgie's flying at this time is the same event as Georgie's flying at t_7, given that this time is t_7. This effects the same ontological reduction of the becoming of events to their bearing temporal relations to each other as does the linguistic reduction. The "coreporting reduction" also shows the absurdity of the "psychological reduction," according to which an

event's being present and so forth requires a relation to a perceiver whereas an event's having a temporal relation to another event or time does not. Since Georgie's flying at this time is identical with Georgie's flying at t_7, it would violate Leibniz's law, which requires that identicals are indiscernible (have all their properties in common), if the former but not the latter were to have the property of being dependent on a perceiver.

[R.M.G.]

See also **McTaggart, John McTaggart Ellis; Russell, Bertrand Arthur William.**

FURTHER READINGS

Gale, Richard M., ed. *The Philosophy of Time*. New York: Anchor Doubleday, 1967.

———. *The Language of Time*. London: Routledge & Kegan Paul, 1968.

ANASAZI ARCHAEO-ASTRONOMY

The Anasazi people inhabited what is now the greater four corners area of the Southwest United States. Their direct descendants are the Pueblo people of today. The Anasazi were a sedentary agricultural people; their basket maker predecessors cultivated corn perhaps as early as 1000 B.C. During the height of the classic Anasazi culture some thousand years ago, these prehistoric people occupied two major sites: Mesa Verde and Chaco Canyon. A regional center developed in the San Juan basin around Chaco by A.D. 1110; as many as seventy communities dispersed among 50,000 square kilometers may have been integrated into a socioeconomic and ritual network connected by a road system. Favorable weather in the San Juan region during this time supported the development of the Chacoan system.

How did the Anasazi regulate and track time? We can approach a reconstruction of this crucial aspect of the society by examining first the nature of time in the historic Pueblo societies— a posture that enables a culturally appropriate view. The Pueblo people (see **Pueblo Ethnoastronomy**) interweave sacred and secular time, which are governed by astronomical observations of the sun, moon, and stars. Certain high religious officials have the responsibility and authority to set ritual dates. They do so by making anticipatory observations to forecast and announce celebratory dates ahead of time. By using ethnographic analogy, we can generate hypotheses about Anasazi astronomy that can be checked against the archaeological record.

Anasazi archaeoastronomy has achieved mixed results so far—in part because the practitioners are few, in part because astronomical knowledge is not part of the standard tool kit of field archaeologists. But the situation appears to be improving, largely because astronomers and archaeologists are beginning to work actively together. As a result, we are on the brink of some limited insights into the probable practices of Anasazi astronomy.

The most important cycle of time for the Pueblos is the seasonal year, which is typically tracked by horizon calendars observed by the sun priest at sunrise from a point in or near the pueblo. Anticipatory observations are made about two weeks prior to the solstices. Of the Anasazi sites tested so far, about one-third have reasonable horizon calendars: these include Pueblo Bonito in Chaco Canyon, Tsankawi Pueblo on the Pajarito Plateau, and Kuaua Pueblo along the Rio Grande River Valley.

A secondary strategy employed in the historic pueblos used a special opening or window in an east wall to cast sunlight on an opposing wall at or after sunrise. Distinct markers were hung or embedded in the adobe on the viewing wall to track the seasons. The best Anasazi analogues to this type of interior observational technique occur in Hovenweep National Monument at Hovenweep Castle, Unit Type House, and the Cajon Group ruins with small portals. Hovenweep Castle and the Cajon ruins work at sunset; Unit Type House just after sunrise. In all three locations, the horizon profiles lack the relief for tracking horizon calendars. For all, the throw from the shadow-casting edges is large enough so that the linear motion on the receiving wall is typically a few centimeters per day from the sun's angular positional change in the sky. For Unit Type House and Hovenweep Castle, photographs taken just prior to 1900 clearly show that the portals were original parts of the buildings and so not a consequence of modern restoration. The evidence so far hints that interior light and shadow casting played an important role in Anasazi seasonal timekeeping.

Exterior light and shadow casting was not an important timekeeping technique in historic times. It may have been used more extensively by the Anasazi, though perhaps more for ritual than calendric purposes. The three-slab site atop Fajada Butte in Chaco Canyon has been much investigated; so has the Holly site at Hoven-

weep. In both these cases, light and shadow cast by rock edges fall onto panels of rock art at important seasonal times of the year. Other possible sites have been noted, especially among the rock art in the Petrified Forest at a variety of locations. These exterior sites generally suffer from a lack of resolving power for reliable calendric forecasting, especially if we consider the standard achieved by the historic Pueblo sun priests—within a day of the astronomical date of the solstices. Hence, these sites may have served as sun shrines for offerings to the sun with a light and shadow display that served a commemorative rather than a calendric function.

We have no firm evidence so far of prehistoric monthly lunar calendars, though such a count of days would have a unique sequence tied to the phases of the moon. For example, we know that historic Pueblo calendar sticks were used to track the months; no conclusive prehistoric analogue has been found in the archaeological record so far. Neither has any rock art in the Anasazi region been demonstrated to display the measure of a lunar tally.

Occasional claims have been made that the Anasazi noted the 18.6-year standstill cycle of the moon. Among a few other places, the hypothesis that this interval was recognized has been applied for the Fajada three-slab site and for the Chimney Rock Archaeological Area in Colorado. The most convincing case is made for Chimney Rock, where the natural rock pillars (after which the site is named), act as a natural foresight when viewed from the site of Chimney Rock Pueblo, a Chacoan outlier that was occupied from about A.D. 1075–1175. The orientation allows a spectacular anticipation and forecasting of the major lunar standstills. For about two and a half years prior to the standstill, the moon rises between the pillars for one or two days per month. Starting after the summer solstice, the moon appears as a waxing crescent. Finally, near the winter solstice, the full moon stands between the pillars at around sunset. Hence, the priest in charge of the moon watching could forecast the date of the standstill and also the full moon nearest the winter solstice—an important conjunction among the historic Pueblos.

[M.Z.]

See also **Archaeoastronomy; Mesoamerican Archaeoastronomy; Pueblo Ethnoastronomy.**

FURTHER READINGS

Zeilik, M. "Keeping the Sacred and Planting Calendar: Archaeoastronomy in the Pueblo Southwest." *World Archaeoastronomy*. Ed. A.F. Aveni. Cambridge: Cambridge UP, 1989. 143–166.

ANESTHESIA AND PAIN

Analgesic and anesthetic drugs have been shown to exhibit temporal variations of their activity, toxicity, and kinetics according to their time of administration.

PAIN SENSATION IS NOT CONSTANT ALONG THE TWENTY-FOUR HOURS OF THE DAY

Before one can produce an adequate pain relief with drugs, it must be kept in mind that the pain sensation itself varies along the twenty-four-hour scale: the exacerbation of pain over a twenty-four-hour period is observed every day by physicians. It has been demonstrated in human beings that induced or spontaneous dental pain is maximal in the evening. Moreover, a circadian rhythm of pain induced by a radiant heat has been shown by P. Proccacci et al., with the highest pain occurring in the morning (6:30 A.M.). Concerning rheumatologic diseases, many examples may be cited: for instance, in rheumatoid arthritis, joint pain, stiffness, and joint size are well known to vary, with a maximum occurring between 2:00 A.M. and 4:00 A.M. As mentioned elsewhere, the maximal pain may be observed at different moments depending on the pathology. Although each patient has his or her "own" pain and individual variations may occur (as documented by F. Lévi et al.), this rhythmicity must be taken into account when treating with analgesic drugs. Circadian changes in pain can also be detected in animals and are in agreement with human data; they suggest that these variations may depend on temporal variations of endogenous substances (endorphins and enkephalins), or transmitters involved in the pain pathways; for instance, temporal changes have been detected in the concentration of beta-endorphin in different discrete areas of the rat brain.

THE TOXICITY AND THE EFFICIENCY OF ANALGESIC AND ANESTHETIC DRUGS VARY ALONG THE TWENTY-FOUR HOURS: LOCAL ANESTHETICS

Local-anesthetics-induced mortality varies in rodents depending on the hour of injection: the maximal mortality occurs during the dark period (activity period in rodents). These data may indicate that in diurnal animals such as man, increased susceptibility to the acute toxicity of local anesthetics may occur more frequently during the activity phase, that is, during the day. A. Reinberg and M.A. Reinberg demonstrated in both human teeth and skin a significant circadian rhythm of the duration of local anaesthesia induced by lidocaine and betoxycaine: the longest duration of anesthesia was found to be at 3:00 P.M. with a peak-through difference of more than 100 percent of the twenty-four-hour mean. Under conditions of daily dental practice, L. Pollman also demonstrated that the duration of the effect of mepivacaine depended on the time of the day: the longest duration occurred at 3:00 P.M.; both the onset of pain and the disappearance of numbness followed a similar circadian rhythm. These data agree well with previous animal data and they are of great interest in daily dental surgery: they seem to indicate that the maximal duration of the effect of local anesthetics occurs in the late afternoon in man. At present, these findings are well established and are taken into account by many dental practitioners in daily dental practice.

MORPHINE AND RELATED ANALGESICS

Very few investigations have been conducted on the chronopharmacology of narcotic analgesics. In a study on patient control analgesia during gastric surgery, D.A. Graves et al. demonstrated a circadian variation in morphine dosing rate requirements: the maximum demand for morphine occurred at 9:00 A.M., the lowest demand being observed at 3:00 A.M. A similar study of S. E. Auvil-Novak et al. confirmed this temporal variability in demand for drugs.

Different results were obtained by G. Labrecque et al. in patients undergoing thoracic or abdominal surgery: the analgesia induced by a constant infusion of morphine or by subcutaneous injections of this drug every four hours were compared, pain being assessed by the patient with a visual analog scale (and not by the estimation of morphine dosing rate requirements as used in the two first studies). The maximal pain was observed between 6:30 and 7:15 P.M.

THE TEMPORAL CHANGES IN THE TOXICITY AND THE EFFICIENCY OF ANALGESIC AND ANESTHETIC DRUGS

Two kinds of mechanisms may be involved with analgesic and anesthetic drugs, namely, temporal variations of the mode of action of the drug, and/or temporal changes in its pharmacokinetics (chronokinetics). The mechanism of action of local anesthetics involves a block of nerve conduction by decreasing or preventing the large transient increase in the permeability of the membrane to sodium ions that is produced by a slight depolarization of the membrane. Thus, drug-induced changes by local anesthetics in membrane permeability of nerve cells to ions are the main mode of action of these drugs.

Circadian changes in the effects of local anesthetics may result from temporal changes in membrane properties. In order to evaluate temporal changes of penetration of local anesthetics through biological membranes, temporal variations of the passage of bupivacaine, etidocaine, and mepivacaine into red blood cells were investigated in mice: a circadian variation of the passage of the three anesthetic agents was demonstrated with a maximum occurring at 4:00 A.M. for bupivacaine and at 10:00 A.M. for etidocaine and mepivacaine. Concerning the second kind of mechanism involved, chronokinetic changes of the local anesthetics may be evoked; for instance, circadian variations of lidocaine kinetics were documented in rats: when lidocaine was given at 4:00 P.M. its elimination half-life was shorter than when given at 10:00 A.M., 10:00 P.M., or 4:00 A.M. and the peak (Cmax) was higher. Similar chronokinetics of bupivacaine were reported in mice: after a single 20 mg/kg/i.p. (milligram per kilogram of body-weight by intraperitoneal route) injection of this drug at 10:00 A.M., 4:00 P.M., 10:00 P.M., or 4:00 A.M. pharmacokinetic parameters were found to depend greatly on the hour of administration: these data also showed that at the highest plasma levels obtained the highest toxicity (10:00 P.M.) of the drug was also observed.

Because these drugs are very often used, it is particularly important to take into account temporal variations of analgesic and anaesthetic drugs in experimental or clinical practice. Temporal periodicity analyses of therapeutic and toxic ratios may eventually contribute to a better understanding of the lethality and margin of safety of these agents.

[B.B.]

See also **Biological Rhythms in Epidemiology and Pharmacology.**

FURTHER READINGS

Bourdalle-Badie, C., et al. "Biological Rhythms in Pain and Anesthesia." *Annual Review of Chronopharmacology* 6 (1990): 155–182.

Bruguerolle, B., and M. Prat. "Temporal Variations in the Erythrocyte Permeability to Bupivacaine, Eti-docaine, and Mepivacaine in Mice." *Life Sciences* 45 (1989): 2587–2590.

Lemmer, B., and R. Wiemers. "Diurnal Variations in the Local Anaesthetic Effect of Carticaine Plus Epinephrine (Ultracain D-S®) in Patients with Caries—Studies with an Electronic Pulptester." *Annual Review of Chronopharmacology* 5 (1988): 253–256.

Pollman, L. "Circadian Changes in the Duration of Local Anaesthesia." *Journal of Interdisciplinary Cycle Research* 12 (1981): 187–191.

Reinberg, A., and M.A. Reinberg. "Circadian Changes of the Duration of Action of Local Anaesthetic Agents." *Naunyn-Schmiedeberg's Archiv für Pharmacologie* 297 (1977): 149–152.

ANIMAL TIMING AND SCALAR TIMING THEORY

Animals have been found capable of exquisite temporal judgments concerning durations ranging from microseconds in bat echolocation to a year or longer in seasonally migrating species. Much of the laboratory work on animal timing has been in the range of one to a few seconds. For example, in classical or Pavlovian conditioning, there is an optimal interval between the conditional stimulus (CS) and the unconditional stimulus (US). On each trial, the experimenter presents a CS, such as a bell, and after some interval presents a US, such as a bit of food. After a few of these presentations, the conditional stimulus comes to elicit a response (salivation) very similar to that originally elicited by the unconditional stimulus. The optimal delay between conditional stimulus and unconditional stimulus presentations to support maximal conditioning depends on the unconditional stimulus and on the response being measured.

Several hypotheses have been offered to explain why conditioning is better with some intervals than others. These include the hypothesis that the animal's brain needs some amount of time to process the conditional stimulus before it can pair the processed conditional stimulus with the presented unconditional stimulus and thereby associate them. This hypothesis is important because it attributes the animal's temporal performance to a nontemporal mechanism: The animal is presumed to respond to some event that takes place over time, rather than to respond to time itself. This hypothesis is inadequate, however, because the duration of the optimal interval between the conditional and unconditional stimuli depends on the unconditional stimulus and the response being measured, not on the conditional stimulus. For example, rabbits can be trained with a buzzer as the conditional stimulus and a weak electric shock as the unconditional stimulus. When the response being measured is the rabbit's nictitating membrane response (the rabbit closes a membrane over its eye in response to the stimulus), the optimal interval between the conditional and unconditional stimuli is 0.5 seconds. When the response being measured is a change in the rabbit's heart rate, the optimal interval between the conditional and unconditional stimuli is 6.75 seconds. The nictitating membrane response shows that the buzzer is fully effective within 0.5 seconds; therefore, delays in reaching an effective level cannot be the cause of the optimal interval for the heart rate response. It appears instead that the optimal interval between the conditional and unconditional stimuli is adapted to the behavioral system involved and timed to deal effectively with the predicted unconditional stimulus event.

Many techniques have been used to study animal timing. One of these involves a variation on the matching-to-sample procedure. Each trial begins with an event, such as illumination of a light, whose duration is the critical feature. This event is followed after a delay by the presentation of two response alternatives, such as two levers. If the duration is less than some criterion (for example, one second) the correct response might be to push the left lever. If the duration is longer than the criterion (for example, four seconds) then the correct response is to push the right lever. The animal's choice of the left or the right lever is an indication of the animal's judgment concerning the duration of the timing signal. The temporal bisection point, or the duration at which they are equally likely to respond short as long, is the geometric mean of the two durations used in training, located halfway between the two durations when plotted on a log scale.

Another method used to study timing in animals is called the peak procedure. Two kinds of trials are intermixed. Each trial begins with the presentation of a timing signal. On "fixed-interval" (FI) trials the animal is rewarded for making a particular response (for example, pressing a lever) at the end of a predetermined interval. On "empty" trials the reward is not presented at the usual time. On the FI trials, the animal typically increases its response rate over the course of the interval, responding at the highest rate just before the reward is to be delivered. Until the reward is delivered, the animal has no

way to know whether a given trial is an FI trial or an empty trial, and its response on empty trials mimics that on FI trials until the time at which food would be delivered if it were an FI trial. The rate of responding then diminishes in a nearly symmetric pattern for the rest of the trial.

The peak rate—the maximum observed rate of responding—is changed by changing the proportion of FI and empty trials. The peak time—the time of the peak response rate—is not affected by the proportion of reinforced trials, but is affected by prefeeding the animal with lecithin or protein snacks, which move the peak time earlier, or prefeeding with carbohydrates, which moves the peak time later. Neither of these affects the peak rate. These and other findings suggest that dopamine plays a role in determining the speed of the animal's internal clock. Increases in dopamine increase clock speed and decreases in dopamine decrease clock speed.

John Gibbon, Russell Church, and their associates have developed a theory of animal timing called scalar timing theory. It attributes the animal's timing performance to the use of an internal clock that can time a wide variety of events. The clock consists of a pacemaker, which produces pulses at more or less regular intervals; a switch, which gates the pulses and either passes them or blocks them from the rest of the system; and an accumulator, which counts the pulses. The clock is analogous to an electronic stop watch. The accumulator displays the elapsed time, and the switch can start and stop the timing of an event.

The assumption that the pacemaker produces pulses at regular intervals suggests that the animal's clock, like a stopwatch, measures time along a scale that is linear with real time. Superficially, linear time appears difficult to reconcile with some of the findings of animal timing, such as the location of the temporal bisection point at the geometric mean of the two training intervals, or the finding that judged differences between intervals depends on the size of the difference relative to their total duration. Judging a small difference between short durations is easier than an equal difference between two long durations. The ratio of the just differentiable difference in duration to the length of the duration is a constant. This relation is called Weber's law. These findings support the hypothesis that subjective time is measured along a logarithmic scale; nevertheless, a number of other findings are inconsistent with logarithmic timing.

The starting point is crucial on a logarithmic scale. The difference in logarithms between two and five seconds is large compared with the difference between twenty-two and twenty-five seconds (as can be readily checked on a calculator). As a result, an animal using a logarithmic time scale should prefer an ongoing interval to a fresh interval of the same duration. For example, if a rat is given a choice between one lever that has been available for twenty-two seconds and another lever that has been available for only two seconds, both of which will deliver food for a response after another three seconds, it should prefer the twenty-two-second lever if it is using logarithmic time and be indifferent if it is using linear time. In fact, rats are indifferent between the two alternatives in this comparison.

Scalar timing theory reconciles this discrepancy between apparent logarithmic and apparent linear timing by proposing that animals use ratios to compare durations rather than their difference, and by proposing that the standard deviation of a judged duration increases proportionally with the magnitude of the duration. Scalar timing theory is consistent with the known facts of animal timing, without becoming involved in the future discounting inherent in logarithmic scales.

[H.L.R.]

See also **Internal-Clock Models.**

FURTHER READINGS

Gibbon, J. "Origins of Scalar Timing." *Learning and Motivation* 22 (1991): 3–38.

Killeen, P., and J.G. Fetterman. "A Behavioral Theory of Timing." *Psychological Review* 95 (1984): 274–295.

Roitblat, H.L., and K.N.J. Young. "Time and Order: A Comparative Perspective." *Cognitive Models of Psychological Time*. Ed. R.A. Block. Hillsdale: Erlbaum, 1990. 119–152.

ANTHROPIC PRINCIPLE

In astronomy, the anthropic principle states that as we look out on the universe we must expect to find all the conditions necessary for our existence. It was stated in this form by the astrophysicist Brandon Carter in 1974 and implies, for example, that any astronomer, anywhere in the universe, must find that the universe is (roughly) between 10 and 20 billion years old. This is because if it were much younger there would not have been enough time for the formation of a planetary system and the interval of biological evolution necessary to produce an astronomer, while if it were much older there would be few if any habitable planets left.

The principle has also been stated in more radical forms. These statements arise from a study of the values of some of the numerical constants that determine the structure of matter and the formation of stable planetary systems. We do not know at present why these constants have the values they do, but it appears that if the values of quantities such as the gravitational constant, the electric charge of the proton, and the number giving the strength of nuclear forces were much different from what they are, life as we know it, perhaps any life at all, would be impossible. Some have concluded that these are only lucky coincidences or else the result of our incomplete understanding, but others have been led to suggest stronger anthropic principles: that the universe was planned to be such that life could evolve in it (Fred Hoyle) or even that its structure and development were conditioned by the lives and consciousnesses that it would later contain (John Wheeler). Clearly, such statements can neither be proved nor disproved, and so they lie outside the bounds of ordinary scientific discourse.

[D.A.P.]

FURTHER READINGS

Barrow, John D., and Frank J. Tipler. *The Anthropic Cosmological Principle*. New York: Oxford UP, 1986.

Davies, Paul C.W. *The Accidental Universe*. Cambridge: Cambridge UP, 1982.

APOCALYPSE

The word "apocalypse," derived from the Greek term for "revelation," is represented in the Bible primarily by the Book of Daniel and the Book of Revelation. "Apocalyptic" writing is concerned in large part with the future and depicts a cosmic struggle between the forces of good and evil. This kind of literature features God's chosen people, whether the Jews or Christians, as a suffering minority, victimized by earthly tyrants and by empires embodying satanic forces. Although apocalyptic writing responds to specific historical circumstances, it transcends history as well, for it is concerned with the consummation of time. This concern with "the last things," or with "eschatology," focuses not only on the phases of individual existence (death, resurrection, judgment), but also on the last events of the "present" age in which evil will be defeated by good. The most common historical scheme found in apocalyptic literature is a twofold one: the present age will be annihilated and replaced by a new age over which God will reign.

Apocalyptic and prophetic literature differ from one another in purpose. Prophets such as Amos delivered messages primarily to reform their people. One instance of this is Amos's stern reproof of Israelite oppression, idolatry, and incorrigibility (Amos 4:1–13), which is followed, in short order, by an exhortation to repentance, at the pain of exile (5:21–27). As God's prophetic spokesman, Amos warns Israel of the terrible historical consequences of apostasy. The author of Daniel, on the other hand, was less concerned with reforming his community than he was with revealing, through symbolic language, that present trials and tribulations were occurring in accordance with God's plan; his emphasis is therefore on the future. Thus, although the prophet was God's spokesman, he was concerned primarily with mundane events and with the preservation of religious and cultural traditions. The apocalypticist, on the other hand, transcended the limits of history, circumstance, and empire, and was convinced that God would intervene decisively into the temporal world. This is illustrated by Daniel's vision of Michael delivering Israel from bondage in the name of God (Daniel 12:1), a vision including the resurrection, judgment, and spiritual transfiguration of the dead. Daniel's vision exceeds the limitations of time: "And many of them that sleep in the dust of the earth shall awake, some to everlasting life, and some to shame and everlasting contempt. And they that be wise shall shine as the brightness of the firmament; and they that turn many to righteousness as the stars for ever and ever" (Daniel 12:2–3).

Apocalyptic writing was usually composed in atmospheres of religious oppression. The Book of Daniel, for example, was composed during the reign of Antiochus IV Epiphanes, who persecuted the Jews. This book endowed Antiochus with cosmic stature; he is symbolized by a beast's horn which "made war with the saints, and prevailed against them; Until the Ancient of days came, and judgment was given to the saints of the most High; and the time came that the saints possessed the kingdom" (Daniel 7:21–2). Elevated above his historical context, Antiochus becomes a figure whom God alone can defeat. This conflict of good and evil, subsuming earthly history, is an important feature of apocalyptic writing. The Book of Revelation, like its apocalyptic precursor, the Book of Daniel, was also written during a time of persecution, specifically that of emperor Domitian in A.D. 93. In Revelation, Daniel's mythic figures become firmly established in St. John's apocalyptic drama, and St. John's apocalypse, in turn, would shape prophetic writings throughout the Middle Ages. The imagery of Revelation—of the opening of seals and of the bestial antichrist who would contend with Christ—conveys a full-scale theodicy, justifying the ways of God to man and explaining the meaning and purpose of evil. With the undoing of each seal on the scroll, a new historical and spiritual phase is revealed, a process culminating in a thousand-year reign of Christ on earth, a final struggle with Satan, followed by the Last Judgment: "But the rest of the dead lived not again until the thousand years were finished. This is the first resurrection. Blessed and holy is he that hath part in the first resurrection: on such the second death hath no power, but they shall be priests of God and of Christ, and shall reign with him a thousand years" (Revelation 20:5–6). In Revelation, Daniel's fourth beast becomes a great, seven-headed dragon with ten horns, representing Satan and the persecution of the faithful. Forming an anti-trinity composed of a sea beast, a land beast, and the dragon, this image symbolized, for St. John, the Roman Empire under Domitian. But deliverance is also envisioned. Christ, symbolized as a divine warrior and as a lamb with seven horns and seven eyes (the seven spirits sent into all the earth [Revelation 5:6]), will conquer universal evil.

The apocalyptic tradition extends well into the nineteenth and twentieth centuries, especially among Protestants who have speculated on the Book of Revelation, ascribing apocalyptic significance to contemporary events. Examples from the seventeenth and eighteenth centuries include the "fifth monarchy men," who, during the English Civil War (1642–60), derived their name and purpose from Daniel 2, "the fifth monarchy" referring to the final kingdom of God. Similarly, the French Revolution was endowed with apocalyptic importance by many English and German enthusiasts, many of whom recanted their beliefs once they realized that these events were not fulfilling the biblical design.

For apocalyptic thinkers, whether Jewish or Christian, time is the context of divine activity, the medium in and through which God's plan will be realized. In their view, history is important only insofar as it serves God's purposes, which ultimately transcend the temporal world and time itself.

[C.D.]

See also **Eschatology; Millenarianism; Prophecy.**

FURTHER READINGS

Bloom, Harold, ed. *The Revelation of St. John the Divine.* Modern Critical Interpretations. New York: Chelsea House, 1988.

Cohn, Norman. *The Pursuit of the Millennium: Revolutionary Millenarians and Mystical Anarchists of the Middle Ages.* New York: Oxford UP, 1977.

Farrer, Austin. *A Rebirth of Images: The Making of St. John's Apocalypse.* Albany: State U of New York P, 1966.

Friedrich, Otto. *The End of the World: A History.* New York: Coward, McCann & Geoghegan, 1982.

Stuhlmueller, C. "Apocalyptic." *New Catholic Encyclopedia.* Ed. Rev. William J. McDonald et al. 18 vols. New York: McGraw-Hill, 1967. 1:663a-664a.

AQUINAS, ST. THOMAS (1224/25–1274)

The foundation of Aquinas's understanding of time is Aristotle's treatment of the subject in *Physics* IV.10–14, a text which he read in a Latin translation with the help of commentaries by Averroes and Albertus Magnus and on which he composed a commentary himself. The most important theme in Aquinas's writings involving the notion of time is the divine eternity or "timelessness"; he interpreted the biblical opposition between time and eternity in terms of its elaboration by neo-Platonic authors, notably Boethius and Augustine, and to a lesser extent pseudo-Dionysius and the author of the *Book of Causes.* Despite small variations in vocabulary and emphasis, his understanding of time remained constant throughout his career. The procedure here will be to summarize the principal clarifications made in Aquinas's above-mentioned commentary, which is his most important treatment of time, and to draw on his other works as occasion warrants. The main references and quotations used are based on the Bekker edition of Aristotle's *Physics*, and the Leonine edition of Aquinas's commentary on *Physics* IV.

THE DEFINITION OF TIME

Aquinas always cites Aristotle's definition of time in *Physics*—"the number of motion according to the before and after"—as canonical. He defends the definition from the charge of circularity by answering in his commentary on *Phys-*

ics IV that the "before and after" mentioned are those (or, according to some manuscripts, "is that") caused in motion by magnitude, not those (or "that") measured by time itself.

TIME AND THE SOUL

Aristotle asks in *Physics* whether there would be time if there were not soul, answering that if soul, which alone is capable of numbering, could not exist, then no numerable, hence no number, and hence no time would exist, although without soul, if there were motion, there would also be time as a "whenever" (*utcumque*) being. Aquinas comments that since number depends on a numberer in the way that things numbered do, and since the being of things numbered does not depend on the intellect of a soul—although it might depend on a causative divine intellect—neither does number of things depend on the intellect of a soul. He then explains that the conditional "if it is impossible for there to be a numberer, it is impossible for there to be anything numerable" is in a sense true, although it does not follow that "if there is no numberer, there is no numerable." Finally, he clarifies the being of time by comparing it to that of its substratum, motion: if motion had fixed being in things, one could say absolutely that, even if soul did not exist, there would be number of motion, or time, in the same way that there would be numbers of things; but motion does not have fixed being, or anything actual except its indivisible and dividing part, although the totality of motion is grasped by the soul's comparison of a mobile thing's prior and posterior disposition; so, too, time has no being outside the soul except in its indivisible part, the now, although the totality of time is grasped by the soul's ordering activity of numbering before and after in motion. This is why Aristotle says that without soul, time is "*utcumque*," to wit, "imperfectly" a being: neither it nor motion has "perfect" being outside the soul.

TIME, ETERNITY, AND EVITERNITY

Aquinas states that Aristotle's explanation of how the now, like a moving body, is both ever the same and ever different leads easily to an understanding of eternity: insofar as it corresponds to an ever-different mobile thing, the now distinguishes before and after in time, and by its flow causes time as a point does a line; if the ever-different disposition is subtracted from the mobile thing, there remains a substance always in the same state, in which one understands an ever-standing, non-flowing now which has no before and after. Just as the now of time is understood as the number of a mobile thing, so, as Aquinas argues, the now of eternity is understood as the number, or rather the oneness, of a thing always in the same state.

Elsewhere, Aquinas presents a more elaborate route from Aristotle's discussion of time to an understanding of eternity, one subordinated to the principle that the human intellect must approach knowledge of the simple through what is better known to it, the composite, and consisting in the removal of two aspects mentioned by Aristotle, namely the successive motion of which time is the number and the beginning and end of the things which time measures. This leaves eternity as "whole simultaneous" and "interminable" respectively, or, in its complete and authoritative definition by Boethius, "the whole, simultaneous and perfect possession of interminable life." God, being supremely immutable, is eternal, is His own eternity, and is alone properly called eternal. Time and eternity are each a "duration," which is a feature following upon anything's being actual. Nothing except God is its own duration. Eternity is the measure of permanent being. Created things recede from permanence of being, and so from eternity, in one of two ways: some have a being which is a subject of transmutation, as is the being of corruptible things, or consists in transmutation, as does the being of motion, and these are measured by time; others, which recede less from eternity, have a being which neither consists in nor is a subject of transmutation, but do have some actual or potential transmutation "joined to" them. These latter include the heavenly bodies, to which is joined transmutability with respect to place, and the angels, to whom is joined transmutability with respect to choice, acts of understanding, affections, and, in a way, place; the being of heavenly bodies and that of angels are measured by eviternity (aevum), a third kind of duration intermediate between time and eternity, as argued by Aquinas in Summa Theologiae I.

THE UNITY OF TIME
Aquinas, in his commentary on Physics IV, mentions a difficulty arising from Aristotle's argument that time is something pertaining to motion because we perceive time and motion together: if the motion meant is outside the soul, we would not perceive time in perceiving motion within the soul; if it is the motion of the soul itself, time will not be a thing of nature, but a mere "intention" of the soul; and if it is any

motion whatsoever, there will be as many times as there are motions. Aquinas responds by stating that there is one first motion, that of the first moveable thing (the outermost heavenly body of the geocentric cosmos), which is the cause of all other motions and of the transmutable being of other moveable things. Whoever perceives any motion perceives transmutable being and consequently the first motion upon which time follows; hence, whoever perceives any motion perceives time, although time follows upon the one first motion by which all others are caused and measured, so that there is only one time.

Aquinas returns to this theme in discussing Aristotle's remark that a regular circular locomotion is the measure of time. Aquinas notes that the most uniform and regular circular motion is the first motion, which circles the entire firmament daily and which—as the first, simplest, and most regular motion—is measure of all others; motion which is measure and number of other motions must be regular, because a measure must be most certain and therefore uniform. From this we may gather that if the first cycle measures every motion, and motion is measured by time inasmuch as it is measured by a motion, then it is necessary to say that time is the number of the first cycle according to which time itself is measured and by which all other motions are measured through the measuring of time. Grasp of the real, numerical unity of time requires reference to the unity of the first motion, for otherwise time's unity might be thought to be merely specific, like that of several threesomes. Time takes its unity from the first motion because it is not merely its measure (as it is of other motions), but also its accident.

Analogously, as Aquinas argues in Summa Theologiae I, there is only one eviternity, the being of all eviternal things being measured by the first and simplest among them.

THE BEGINNING OF TIME
The one point in Aristotle's discussion of time from which Aquinas distances himself is Aristotle's suggestion that motion and therefore time are without beginning or end. "According to his opinion," Aquinas says, movement never began and will never fail. Aristotle says that every now of time is both a beginning and an end on the supposition that motion is perpetual; but if it were said that motion began and will end, it would follow that one now would be a beginning but not an end of time and another would be an end but not a beginning. What Aquinas suggests hypothetically here he asserts categor-

ically in more theological contexts, namely that time has both a beginning and an end.

Aristotle's arguments for a perpetual material universe, being in open conflict with the scriptural assertion in the first verse of Genesis that God created the world "in the beginning," were central to the theological mistrust of his works in thirteenth-century Paris. St. Bonaventure argued that the notion of a perpetual world is philosophically untenable both because beginninglessness is incompatible with creatureliness and because an infinite time is untransversable. Aquinas offers a middle way, arguing on the one hand that Aristotle's arguments on this point neither are nor are intended to be demonstrative, and on the other hand (notably in the polemic *On the Eternity of the World*) that although the Catholic faith teaches that the world had a beginning of its duration, there would be nothing contradictory—and there is a comparable argument in *Summa Theologiae* I—in its being both created (dependent on God for its being) and "eternal."

THE END OF TIME

The remark introducing Aristotle's discussion of the things that are in time, that time measures both motion and being moved, occasions an important distinction in Aquinas's commentary: whereas motion is measured by time both according to its essence and according to its being or duration, other things are measured by time according to their transmutable being or duration, but *not* according to their essence. As Aquinas indicates elsewhere, however, there is a difference in such things between perfection "according to nature" ("full-grown man") and perfection "according to time" ("right size for his age"), for they need time to reach fullness of perfection. This is most importantly true of the human being, who, like the angel, is perfected by the beatific vision, but who, unlike the angel, begins not yet capable of this perfection and so is given a "longer way" in order to acquire it. The human being is essentially an intelligence which depends on the human senses and body, and so on time, for its perfection, and hence is rational, discursive, temporal, and historical. The acts by which human beings merit beatitude and the virtues which perfect these acts are formed in time. All of the theological virtues, but notably faith and hope, are not merely temporal in formation and exercise, but also futural in orientation. Among the "parts" of the fundamental cardinal virtue of prudence are included the three time-bound ones mentioned by Cicero:

memory of the past, understanding of the present, and the most important aspect of prudence, providence for the future.

The purpose of the motion of the heavenly bodies and hence of all motion is the production and perfection of human beings, in particular the number of the elect. Accordingly, the most significant temporal events are the creation of human beings, the Fall, the history recorded in the Old Testament, the incarnation and life of Christ, the history of the church, the general resurrection, and the Last Judgment. After this last event, motion, having achieved its end, will cease, so that its number, time, as Aquinas says quoting *Apocalypse* 10.6, "will be no more."

[K.W.]

See also **Albertus Magnus; Aristotle; Augustine.**

FURTHER READINGS

Bianchi, Luca. *L'errore di Aristotele: La polemica contro l'eternità del mondo nel XIII secolo.* Florence: La Nuova Italia Editrice, 1984.

Mansion, Augustin. "La théorie aristotélicienne du temps chez les peripatéticiens médiévaux." *Revue néoscholastique de philosophie* 36 (1934): 275–307.

Pegis, Anton C. "The Notion of Man in the Context of Renewal." *Theology of Renewal.* Ed. L.K. Shook. New York: Herder and Herder, 1968. 1:250–264.

Quinn, John M. "The Doctrine of Time in St. Thomas: Some Aspects and Applications." Catholic University of America Dissertation, 1960.

Redpath, Peter A. "The Ontological Status of Time in the *Commentary on the Sentences*, the *Commentary on the Physics*, and the *Summa Theologiae* of Thomas Aquinas." State University of New York Dissertation, 1974.

ARCHAEOASTRONOMICAL FIELD TECHNIQUES

A large part of archaeoastronomical research has consisted of measuring the orientation of alignments formed by architectural features at well-preserved archaeological sites, such as rows of standing stones in prehistoric Britain, or the sides of large ceremonial buildings in pre-Columbian Mesoamerica, to see whether they align on significant astronomical events at the horizon such as the sun rising or setting on significant days of the year, the extreme northerly or southerly rising or setting points of the moon, or the rising or setting points of prominent stars.

In order to determine the astronomical significance, if any, of a point on the horizon as viewed from a particular spot on the ground, the investigator needs to determine the declination ("celestial latitude") of the point on the celestial sphere directly behind the point being observed. This can be simply calculated from the azimuth (orientation) and altitude of the point, together with the observer's latitude. If reasonably high precision (say, to better than one degree) is required, then a theodolite (surveyor's transit) is needed to measure the azimuth and altitude. Since a theodolite can only measure relative, not absolute, azimuths, the direction of due north has to be determined accurately. This can be done by taking timed observations of the sun using an accurate timepiece.

Once one knows the declination of a point, one knows (at least in principle) the astronomical bodies rising and setting there at any given epoch. In practice, a further correction must be made for atmospheric refraction, which can vary according to weather conditions: recent investigations by Bradley Schaefer and others have suggested that in certain situations, variations due to refraction can be far greater than was previously suspected. Another factor that must be taken into account in the case of a star is "extinction," which may cause a star's light to be so dimmed near to the horizon that its rise or set cannot be seen. This is especially important at high latitudes, where stars set nowhere near vertically, and the extinction of a star a short way above the horizon could significantly affect the orientation of a structure built to align upon it. Finally, also of importance for stars is the effect of precession, which alters the declination of a given star significantly over a period of a few centuries. This means that if the date of the architectural feature is not accurately known (as is, for example, the case with almost all British prehistoric data), it is possible to fit a reasonably bright star to almost any alignment by choosing an appropriate date within the available range of possibilities. Thus, it is almost impossible to attest with any confidence that a given alignment was associated with a given star at a given date unless the site can be dated fairly accurately by independent means, or unless it can be determined—again by independent means such as written evidence—that the alignment in question was associated with that particular star.

With points such as the last in mind, Gerald Hawkins set out in 1966 a methodology for gathering and analyzing archaeoastronomical data. This was expanded by Anthony F. Aveni in the Mesoamerican context in 1980.

An essential problem is that although an architectural feature such as a row of stones may be aligned upon an astronomical event, this may not have been intentional. Where, as in prehistoric Britain, there is little or no independent evidence to corroborate a putative astronomical alignment (see **British Archaeoastronomy**), recourse must be made to statistical analysis. This means that great attention must be paid to the fair selection of data. Clive Ruggles, in an archaeological and statistical reappraisal of 300 western Scottish sites undertaken in an attempt to reassess the earlier conclusions of Alexander Thom, has presented detailed and rigorous criteria for selecting data at sites such as the free-standing British megalithic settings. Where there are independent cultural data, different criteria may be important. For example, the alignment from the central entrance of the governor's palace at the classic Maya site of Uxmal to the distant site of Cehtzuc points at an extreme rising point of Venus. This would not seem significant if taken in isolation, but its intentionality is supported by our general knowledge of the importance of Venus to the Mayans, and in particular by the presence of Venus iconography around the entrance in question. The way in which one determines data selection criteria in different situations, where the availability of independent cultural evidence may vary widely, is one of the central methodological issues still facing archaeoastronomy.

[C.L.N.R.]

See also **Archaeoastronomy; British Archaeoastronomy; Mesoamerican Archaeoastronomy.**

FURTHER READINGS

Aveni, A.F. *Skywatchers of Ancient Mexico.* Austin: U of Texas P, 1980.

Hawkins, G.S. *Astro-archaeology.* Cambridge: Smithsonian Institution Astrophysical Observatory (Research in Space Science, Special Report no. 226), 1967.

Ruggles, C.L.N. *Megalithic Astronomy: A New Archaeological and Statistical Study of 300 Western Scottish Sites.* Oxford: British Archaeological Reports (British Series 123), 1984.

———. "The Stone Alignments of Argyll and Mull: A Perspective on the Statistical Approach in Archaeoastronomy." *Records in Stone.* Ed. C.L.N. Ruggles. Cambridge: Cambridge UP, 1988. 232–250.

Schaefer, B.E. "Basic Research in Astronomy and its Applications to Archaeoastronomy." *Archaeoastronomy in the 1990s.* Ed. C.L.N. Ruggles. Loughborough: Group D Publications, 1992.

Šprajc, I. "Venus-Rain-Maize Complex in Mesoamerican World Views." *Journal for the History of Astronomy* 24 (1993): 17–70.

ARCHAEOASTRONOMY

BASIC DEFINITIONS

Archaeoastronomy is the interdisciplinary study of ancient astronomical systems based on both the written and unwritten record. It has become a meeting ground for at least three established inquiries into ancient astronomy:

1. *Astroarchaeology*—The name given to a field methodology for retrieving astronomical information from the study of alignments of heavenly bodies with landscape and ancient architecture. It has attracted a wide following among people from the hard quantitative sciences, including astronomers and engineers. Commonly employed in the 1960s and 1970s, this term is rapidly becoming obsolete and is often replaced by the term "alignment studies."

2. *The History of Astronomy*—A traditional discipline that usually deals only with written texts, and is concerned with the extent of ancient cultures' astronomical knowledge (especially the Old World's knowledge of astronomy).

3. *Ethnoastronomy*—A branch of cultural anthropology that draws its evidence about astronomical practice from the ethnohistorical record and ethnographic studies of contemporary cultures. Ethnoastronomy focuses on the influence of a society's knowledge of astronomy on its cultural behavior. For an amplification of the foundations of the discipline in anthropological theory, see Iwaniszewski in *World Archaeoastronomy*, ed. A.F. Aveni.

PHILOSOPHICAL BACKGROUND FOR ARCHAEOASTRONOMICAL STUDIES

Archaeoastronomy holds that human beings have always been interested in the cosmos and that this interest has influenced humanity's development. Events that took place in the heavens impinged directly upon the minds of ancient people, who attempted to classify the universe and find temporal order in celestial events. Hunter-gatherers and later sedentary societies could hardly overlook the periodic precision of celestial cycles. Also, the tides, menstrual cycles, lunar phases, and cycles of planetary motion were considered periodic phenomena functioning within a harmonious universe. To early observers, there appeared to be an association between events on earth and the cycles of the heavens. Based on observations of such occur-

rences, humans developed calendars. At first calendars were simple: tally marks represented the passage of time and solar positions at the horizons were noted, as exemplified in Figure 1. However, as agricultural, religious, and socioeconomic needs became linked to methods of keeping time in a particular culture, increasingly accurate methods for time's measurement were developed. From archaeological as well as cultural remains, we realize how much astronomical concepts influenced many ancient societies.

EARLY DEVELOPMENT OF THE FIELD

Archaeoastronomy owes its origin in part to the development of astroarchaeology which began at the turn of the century. Then, British astronomer Sir J. Norman Lockyer published *The Dawn of Astronomy* (1894), in which he suggested that Egyptian temples and pyramids were components of an orientation calendar based on astronomical principles. He contended that walls, doorways, and axes of buildings were arranged deliberately to "orient" or align with the rising and setting positions of the sun (especially on the solstices when the sun reaches its northernmost and southernmost positions on the local horizon) and other celestial bodies. These speculations by Lockyer about ancient Egyptian religion and society were condemned by archaeologists, who ignored the crucial early chapters of Lockyer's book in which he explained the rudiments of astroarchaeological methodology much as it is employed today.

THE STONEHENGE CONTROVERSY AND MEGALITHIC ARCHAEOASTRONOMY

Nearly half a century later, Scottish engineer Alexander Thom began survey work in the 1930s at more than 200 megalithic sites, and a trickle of his publications reached some professional journals in the 1950s. Thom's work culminated in three monographs and a series of papers published in the British *Journal for the History of Astronomy* and its supplement, *Archaeoastronomy*. Despite some constructive reactions, Thom's work, like Lockyer's, was passionately criticized by the British archaeological community. Thom's findings implied that neolithic geometry and metrology were sufficiently developed to keep precise lunar and solar time. His basic conclusions were as follows:

1. Astronomical alignments using the sun and moon incorporate not only standing stones, but also notches and peaks on the distant horizon.

2. The study of ring metrology implies that a common unit, the megalithic yard (0.83 meters), was employed in the construction of most megalithic structures. Thom suggested that the basic parameters associated with these stone configurations, derivable from geometry involving Pythagorean right triangles, consisted of integral numbers of megalithic yards.

3. Most of the worked stones in the British Isles are arranged in the forms of flattened circles, "eggs," and ellipses rather than true circles. Thom classifies these forms into a few basic categories.

In 1965, another astronomer, Gerald Hawkins, brought the controversy to public attention with a series of papers and a book proposing that Stonehenge, the most famous of all the megalithic monuments, was intended principally to function as a device for predicting eclipses of the moon. Hawkins argued that this could be done by sighting solar and lunar positions at the horizon through openings in the standing stones, and computing eclipse cycles by counting architectural elements in the structure (see Figure 2). Actually, some of these ideas had already been anticipated by C. A. Newham, though his publication had not been widely circulated.

Hawkins's conclusions, like Thom's, dramatically opposed the contemporary view of the intellectual level of prehistoric man in the British Isles about 3000 B.C. Their pioneering work opened up the question of the level of sophistication of mathematics, astronomy, and timekeeping in ancient societies.

Several investigators have reexamined megalithic alignments in the field and criticized the sort of high precision astronomy advocated by Thom on archaeological, astronomical, and statistical grounds. They conclude that while a real concern for keeping time by the movements of the sun and moon is demonstrated by alignments in the architecture, Thom exaggerated the precision of their data. Critics such as C.L.N. Ruggles argue that one cannot conclude that the megalithic structures were precise astronomical observatories, though there is little doubt they functioned as part of an astronomically timed set of rituals. Similarly, megalithic geometry was not as precise as Thom suggested. People involved with megaliths created a measuring unit and several categories of deliberately distorted circles but these methods of measurement were not as precise as indicated by Thom. Investigators like A. Burl and E.W. Mackie have attempted to integrate megalithic astronomy into our understanding of the prehistoric cultures of Europe ca. 3000 B.C. Studies concluded in the 1980s—such as the work on recumbent stone circles by Burl and Ruggles, and the work of Ruggles and Martlew on stone rows on the island of Mull—demonstrated that archaeoastronomical investigations now have begun to pass into the mainstream of British archaeology. Today, investigations about the astronomical significance of the arrangement of stone structures are routinely incorporated into a series of questions such as those on site placement pertaining to drainage, visible accessibility of landscape features, proximity to water, and soil considerations.

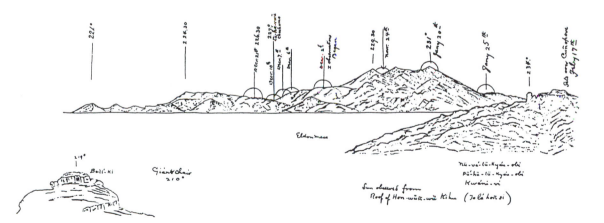

Figure 1. *American Indian reference to horizon calendar. The sun's position is noted on important days of the year. From the journal of A.M. Stephen, an early traveler to the American Southwest (Ref. Parsons 1936).*

One pattern that has begun to emerge from these studies is that—while not in acutely precise ways—both the southerly lunar extreme and prominent landscape features such as mountains were being interlinked by builders of the sites. Thus, one is impelled to think of the megalithic sites less as scientific observatories intended to predict accurately lunar phenomena, such as eclipses, and perhaps more as areas in which rituals took place. For example, people might have arranged these sites so that the moon would be in its proper setting over a mountain and more or less aligned with a set of megaliths for the purpose of conducting worship or celebrating a festival.

THE ASTRONOMICAL BACKGROUND FOR ARCHAEOASTRONOMICAL STUDIES

One problem in studying archaeoastronomy is that most modern people are far less familiar with astronomical phenomena than their ancient ancestors. Furthermore, what we learn in textbooks of astronomy we tend to view through technological aids such as the telescope or computer, and so it is becoming more difficult for us to understand how ancient people viewed the cosmos with the naked eye.

To remedy this problem, Aveni, in his *Skywatchers of Ancient Mexico*, has given considerable attention to the principles of "naked-eye" astronomy that might have been employed by ancient cultures. He also has contrasted elsewhere some of the differences between "naked-eye" celestial phenomena in the tropics and the higher latitudes, suggesting that the environment and ecology of the culture may have played a significant role in the type of astronomy that was developed. To summarize, the principal horizon-based events likely to have concerned early cultures in developing schemes for marking time are:

1. The rising and setting of stars at the local horizon.

2. The rising and setting of the sun, especially its extreme positions on the horizon (attained on the solstices), at the equinox, at the date of zenith passage (in the tropics), or on dates of the year connected with key agricultural or ritual events.

3. The rising and setting of the moon at its extremes, which occurs every 18.61 years.

4. The rising and setting of the planets, especially at their extremes.

5. The heliacal rising and setting of stars and planets, which mark the annual dates of the appearance and disappearance of these objects relative to the sun.

In an article entitled "Archaeoastronomy," in *Advanced Archaeological Method and Theory* (1981), Aveni has produced a checklist of some of the most obvious celestial phenomena not necessarily occurring at the horizon.

A second problem in the development of the field of archaeoastronomy stems from the diverse disciplinary turfs—such as astronomy, anthropology, archaeology, statistics, history of religion, and history of art—with which this interdiscipline is concerned. Should archaeoastronomers simply gather and analyze data, leaving it for the more well-informed cultural anthropologist to interpret, or should they formulate a problem and define its scope before undertaking an investigation? Two salient points, as discussed by R. Williamson, have emanated from this debate: first, there is a need for both organized data gathering on a widespread basis, and the development of a methodology that can be defined and practiced universally; on the other hand, when individuals who are totally uninformed begin to dabble in another discipline and extend their ideas prematurely to the printed page, they can often create falsehoods that propagate through the literature and may be difficult to eliminate. Therefore, while it might be suggested that anthropologists and archaeologists can learn many of the principles of ancient astronomy relatively quickly, it is even more difficult for astronomers and other scientists interested in archaeoastronomical research to understand fully the anthropological ramifications of an ancient people's knowledge. As discussed by Aveni in his edited *World Archaeoastronomy*, the 1980s and early 1990s have brought considerable interdisciplinary progress.

FIELD TECHNIQUES

A large part of archaeoastronomical research has consisted of analyzing standing structures for astronomical alignments (astroarchaeology). The modern methodology for gathering and analyzing such data was first outlined by Hawkins and later expanded by Aveni in *Skywatchers of Ancient Mexico*, while the surveying techniques have been described by C.L.N. Ruggles. Principal equipment includes a surveyor's transit and an accurate timepiece. Computer programs are available for reducing data in the field.

MESOAMERICAN ARCHAEOASTRONOMY

Twentieth-century studies of the art, iconography, architecture, and written documents surviving the Spanish conquest have revealed the sophistication of Mesoamerican cultures. As British megalithic astronomical studies developed in the 1970s, archaeoastronomy in Mesoamerica began to flourish. The field has proven to be quite productive in the past decade because the cultural context for astronomical questions can be viewed in clearer focus than in the Old World. For one thing, the Mesoamerican culture that practiced astronomy existed in the more recent past. For another, knowledge of the culture is readily accessible through Hispanic contact. Abundant evidence can be derived from written records, historical documents, and numerous well-preserved archaeological ruins in addition to the living remains of indigenous cultures that exist from the southwestern United States through Central America.

Field studies, combined with evidence from allied disciplines, reveal that astronomical information is incorporated within the architecture of a large number of Mesoamerican ceremonial buildings. Here we offer only a few specific examples, referring the reader to the summary chapter in Aveni's *Skywatchers of Ancient Mexico*, and *World Archaeoastronomy*, where a number of original references together with those mentioned in this section are listed.

TEOTIHUACAN, ALTA VISTA, AND THE PECKED CROSSES

Calendric and astronomical knowledge was propagated throughout Mesoamerica through use of an orientation device called the pecked cross. About seventy petroglyphs of remarkably similar structure have been found carved in the floors of buildings and on prominent rock outcrops; these consist of cup-like depressions pecked into the rock or stucco matrix with a percussive device. Though they tend to cluster around Teotihuacan, where they probably originated, a few of the pecked circles have also been found in the Maya region, for instance as at the ruins of Uaxactun and Seibal. On most of these devices there are twenty holes on each axis (twenty is the base of the Mesoamerican counting system). Employing the techniques discussed in the previous section, J. Dow in 1967, and later Aveni and Gibbs in 1976, found that the axes of the markers, and lines passing over some distance from one marker to another, matched favorably with astronomical orientations. The Pleiades star group fit the orientation of the Teotihuacan grid, which is skewed $15^{1}/_{2}$ degrees clockwise from the cardinal points (the four chief directions of the compass). The orienta-

tion is marked by a pair of pecked circles three kilometers apart. Interestingly, the Pleiades star group underwent heliacal rise on the day of solar zenith passage of Teotihuacan. Moreover, the Pleiades also transited the zenith of Mesoamerican skies and they were employed in Aztec time to mark the beginning of a fifty-two-year sacred calendar round. Thus, this particular star group was probably chosen as a stellar-solar cross-check device for marking the start of the year.

Also part of a complex set of alignments in Figure 3, a summer solstice orientation is marked by pecked crosses at the ruins of Alta Vista (Chalchihuites). A site lying within twenty kilometers of the tropic of Cancer, it dates, as J.C. Kelley pointed out, from the Tlamimilolpa-Xolalpan phase of the Teotihuacan culture (ca. A.D. 600). Why might solar alignments be anticipated at the tropic? It is there that the sun seems to turn when it reaches its zenith at noon precisely on the first day of summer, the longest day. After reaching its greatest northerly rising and setting positions along the local horizon on the same day, the sun slowly marches back toward the southern sky to complete its cycle. The Alta Vista markers look almost exactly like those at Teotihuacan 650 kilometers away and at Uaxactun, 1700 kilometers distant. It is possible that the elements that make up the design were used as

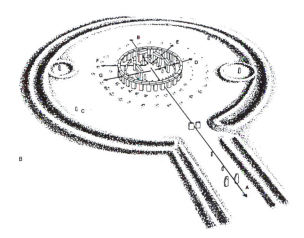

Figure 2. Sketch showing how Stonehenge was aligned to mark key solar and lunar references in the calendar. (A) View at ground level. Each upright that makes up the megalithic horseshoe weighs more than thirty tons. Source: Photo by the author. (B) Plan showing some of the proposed time markers discussed in the text. Copyright © 1982 Hansen Planetarium, Salt Lake City, Utah. Reproduced with permission.

part of a calendrical tally system. As Aveni, Hartung, and Kelley have indicated, the evidence suggests a rather specific and detailed common mode of transmission of knowledge of Mesoamerican space and time over a wide area of Mesoamerica.

C. Coggins has discussed the possible political implications of the use of the pecked cross symbol. Given the developed nature of the Teotihuacan state, it is possible that its rulers sought a methodology for organizing the calendar and disseminating it to all points of the empire. She argues that they did so in their influence on the Maya city of Tikal.

Scholars are not sure which principles of organized timekeeping were passed on to the Aztecs (whose empire involved a larger area of Central Mexico in the fourteenth to fifteenth century) by the Teotihuacans, but the Aztec capital, Tenochtitlan (today Mexico City), possessed at least one astronomically oriented building (the Templo Mayor). Also, Spanish chronicles inform us that ritual offerings to the gods were made at regular intervals at sites on the horizon periphery of the city. Some of these directions may have been fixed through an orientation principle that included astronomical considerations.

MAYA VENUS OBSERVATORIES

One of a class of round structures, the Caracol of Chichén Itza, discussed by Aveni and others in his *Native American Astronomy*, is a Maya-Toltec building located in northern Yucatan. It incorporates in its asymmetric ground plan alignments to particular celestial phenomena observable within the local horizon. Paramount among these phenomena is Venus, for which the extreme setting positions coincide with both a pair of alignments taken through narrow horizontal sighting shafts at the top of the building and the directions perpendicular to the base of the building, as well as the perpendicular to the base of the building. These alignments are corroborated by other evidence, for the circular form of the building is known to symbolize Quetzalcoatl-Kukulcan, the Venus god, in the form of the god of the wind. Moreover, the Venus Table in the Dresden Codex, a Maya written document, also originated in the same time and place as the Caracol. The intervals in which Venus could be observed were tabulated in the Dresden Codex and this data has derived from observations of Venus at the standstill positions.

Venus alignments can also be found at Uxmal in the Palace of the Governor. The principal doorway of this structure aligns with Venus at its southerly rising extreme, the line of view intersecting the largest structure at Cehtzuc, another site 6 kilometers away. This discovery raises the possibility that *intersite* alignments may have been a factor in the planning of Maya ceremonial centers.

The Uxmal-Venus orientation scheme is supported by the occurrence of carvings of the Venus hieroglyphic symbol, the same one appearing in the Venus Table in the Dresden Codex, on the cornice of the palace. Finally, the number eight in Maya dot-bar notation is carved on a pair of large rain-god masks that form part of the north and south cornerstones of the building. Eight days is the mean interval of disappearance of the planet prior to the heliacal rise. Venus's importance to Maya astronomy has become obvious from these discoveries. I. Sprajc gave a recent summary of this in *Archaeoastronomy*.

SUN-WATCHING SCHEMES

One of the special architectural devices the Maya likely employed to mark the solstices and equinoxes is illustrated in Figure 4. An observer would stand on an east-facing pyramid and view the sunrise over a series of three smaller buildings constructed on a common base. When the sun reached the summer and winter standstills, it was positioned over the northern and southernmost buildings, respectively, while at the equinox it was perched over the central building. Several examples of this architectural-solar calendar have also been discovered at sites in the Petén rain forest of Guatemala.

The sun would also be sighted when it passed the zenith, by the passage of its light through vertical tubes built into the architecture; examples occur in Structure P at Monte Albán, and at the ruins of Xochicalco. However, there is no evidence that any of the cultures of Mesoamerica either divided the time of day or marked the solar course by following the shadow cast by a gnomon—practices developed in the early astronomy of the classical world.

From a sizeable data base on building orientations with assignable temporal provenance in the Maya area, Aveni and Hartung, in *Native American Astronomy*, have proposed that the solar orientation calendar evolved from an earlier form based on solstice-fixed horizon points to positions that marked the sunrise and sunset at twenty-day intervals reckoned from the zenith passage. F. Tichy had independently proposed the idea of twenty-day divisions in central Mexico, which he found extant in the alignments of colonial churches.

ARCHAEOASTRONOMY IN NORTH AMERICA

Increased activity in North American archaeoastronomy is evidenced by a survey of recently published papers in the journals which Aveni compiled in *Archaeoastronomy in the 1990s*, edited by C.L.N. Ruggles. This survey demonstrates that about one-third of all the studies on cultures on both new world continents focus on North America, particularly the southwest United States (a subject dealt with in *Astronomy and Ceremony in the Prehistoric Southwest*, edited by Carlson and Judge). For example, medicine

wheels (in an area in the Rocky Mountains) are among those structures which scholars believe are astronomically oriented. These hub-like circular structures average fifteen meters in diameter, and stacks of boulders (cairns) are positioned about them. J.A. Eddy found cairn-to-cairn alignments at the Bighorn medicine wheel in northern Wyoming, which may have functioned as a device to warn of the coming of winter. The alignments point to the rising azimuths of those three bright stars that undergo heliacal rising at intervals of one lunar month. Furthermore, the three months indicated are those of summer, the only time when weather conditions render the mountain habitable. The Moose Mountain medicine wheel, Saskatchewan (a radiocarbon date on the Moose Mountain wheel corresponds to about 2000 B.C.), exhibits a similar pattern of

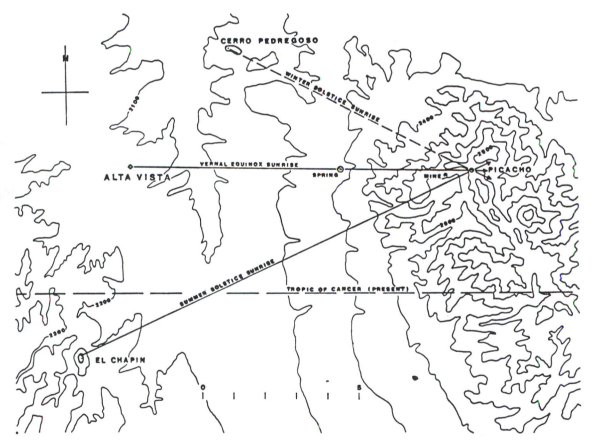

Figure 3. Archaeoastronomy pays particular attention to ways in which ancient cultures expressed the marking of astronomical time by means other than writing, such as in this complex scheme from Alta Vista (Chalchihuites), Mexico, ca. A.D. 600, which involved the alignment of the axis of a pecked circle with June solstice sunrise over a prominent peak. The site is situated at the tropic of Cancer, where this date also marks the passage of the sun across the zenith. Its most prominent building has the corners cardinally aligned; that is, they point to the rising and setting equinox sun.

spokes and cairns. Eddy's studies, supported by archaeological data from T. and A. Kehoe, raise questions about the viability of complex time-keeping among nomadic versus sedentary peoples. They suggest that the people who built these structures had long ago maintained a semi-sedentary life and that they were cognizant of many of the fundamental timekeeping concepts outlined above. Because the cultural record is thin and no historical documents exist, criticisms of this work parallel many of those leveled at Thom and Hawkins. For example, a recent statistical survey of more than 100 medicine wheels by Vogt in *Astronomies and Cultures*, edited by Ruggles and Saunders, offered evidence for a general astronomical orientation but failed to support any theories on specific stellar associations at specific sites. Other studies of calendrical warning devices dependent on solar sightings have been made in the Anasazi region at Fajada Butte, such as those by Sofaer and Williamson.

In a series of essays in *Archaeoastronomy*, M. Zeilik has made some attempt at unifying ideas in the North American field. Following on the early work of such North American ethnologists as Fewkes and Cushing, which suggests that sun-watching at the horizon (especially at solstice) was a widespread and common practice, others have begun to seek stronger ties between archaeoastronomy and anthropology.

ARCHAEOASTRONOMY IN THE ANDEAN WORLD

Compared to studies in Mesoamerica, South American studies are in their infancy. Early alignment work on disparate cultures of the South American continent have yet to be synthesized with the large corpus of ethnographic material, though recent collections of works—such as *Time Calendars in the Inca Empire*, edited by Ziolkowski and Sadowski—seem to indicate that such a process is now underway.

Popular arguments about the astronomical orientation of the famous Nazca lines on the coast of Peru have been largely discredited (see Aveni's *The Lines of Nazca*); however, studies of the astronomical significance of structures in the Inca empire are still pursued because of the numerous references in the Spanish chronicles to the practice of astronomy and the construction of calendars. In Williamson's *Archaeoastronomy in the Americas*, Zuidema and Aveni have interpreted the ceque system of Cuzco, the Inca capital, at least in part as an astronomical sighting and counting scheme which also served

as a mnemonic device that related this knowledge to information about kinship, the descendance of the monarchy, and ritual behavior.

The ceque system is an organization of forty-one radial lines (ceques) emanating from Coricancha, the Temple of the Sun, each delineated by 328 sacred places (huacas) that overlay the entire capital and its surrounding landscape. Several astronomical sightings are made with the ceque system, among them:

1. The December solstice sunrise was marked by a pair of vertical pillars on a ceque line observed from the Temple of the Sun.

2. A line running from an ornately carved rock outcrop north of Cuzco to a pair of pillars on a distant hill denotes the June solstice sunset point.

3. A sight line running from the Ushnu, a small pyramid in the present Plaza de Armas, to four pillars on Cerro Picchu marks the commencement of ground-breaking for annual planting. The date indicated in the chronicles is mid-August, or when the sun sets at a point precisely opposite to the point from which it rose on the day it passed the nadir (the "anti-zenith" sunset). This line is interpreted as an embodiment of the Incaic vertical symbolism often discussed by such Andean ethnologists as B.J. Isbell in *To Defend Ourselves*.

The anonymous chronicler writing in about 1570, cited by V. Maurtua in 1906, mentions that the four pillars that marked the course of the sun also served an agricultural function. They were said to be visible from at least two to three leagues from the city. The chronicler says they were "high on a hill overlooking Cuzco from the west," and when the sun passed the first pillar, the people prepared themselves for planting in the higher altitudes, where ripening takes longer. When the sun entered the space between the two middle pillars, this indicated that it was time to plant in Cuzco. The August date he quotes for the latter event is consistent with the relative situation of the Plaza de Armas and Cerro Picchu. Evidence suggests that the whole device is an agricultural sun-watcher's calendar.

Just how important a role time-marking systems played in the architecture of Cuzco remains a subject of controversy. The conclusion that the structures are astronomically aligned has been challenged by disputes over the straightness of ceques and the precision of other architectural features. Nonetheless, archaeoastronomical study of Cuzco offers arguments that find ethnohistory converging with archaeoastronomy. It accounts not only for the position and function of horizon pillars, but also for the chronicler's description of ceques. Continued excavation of the several predicted huaca sites may disclose whether these structures were accurate instruments of astronomy.

OTHER AREAS OF ACTIVITY

E.C. Baity's bibliography of 1973 in *Current Anthropology* lists practically all the work on archaeoastronomy that had been published up to that time. In addition, one should mention the revival of alignment studies in Egypt by G.S. Hawkins and E.C. Krupp in which some of Lockyer's early work is reassessed, and the newly initiated European studies, which, especially in central Europe, focus on Medieval church orientations—see article in Aveni's *World Archaeoastronomy*—and in the south on pre-Roman ruins in a collection of articles edited by G. Romano. Astronomical alignments in medieval Islamic religious architecture represent a fertile area of work for the future, particularly with regard to the qibla, or determination of the local direction of Mecca, which has been discussed by D. King in Aveni and Urton's *Ethnoastronomy*. Astronomy and architecture also have been linked in Hawaiian architecture by daSilva and Johnson, in Antillean architecture by Robiou-LaMarche, in sub-Saharan African architecture by Lynch and Robbins, Easter Island (Liller), pre-Roman ruins in Menorca and other Mediterranean islands (Hoskin), and in Southeast Asian architec-

ture by Stencel. See other references to tropical ethnoastronomy and archaeoastronomy in Aveni and Urton's *Ethnoastronomy*. It is surprising that so few detailed studies have started on the African and Asian continents, and that the field methods of astroarchaeology remain practically untried in the Greco-Roman world except for the singular, rather fruitful attempt by W.B. Dinsmoor in the *Proceedings of the American Philosophical Society* in 1939.

SUMMARY: THE FUTURE OF ARCHAEOASTRONOMY

Discussions of current attitudes to archaeoastronomy can be found in Williamson's *Archaeoastronomy in the Americas* and in the Oxford III symposium volumes of *Archaeoastronomy in the 1990s*, edited by Ruggles (UP of Colorado, 1993), and *Astronomies and Cultures*, edited by Ruggles and Saunders. Most opinions point to the conclusion that progress in the field can be made only if archaeoastronomers possess knowledge of the culture involved. Also, as Ruggles has argued, statistical techniques are necessary in order to determine whether a purported orientation might be due to pure chance. In addition, an interpretive approach can employ ethnohistorical and inscriptional evidence as well as architectural and topographic data gathered through appropriate instrumentation in the environment of the ruins. This is often preferable to the shotgun techniques of matching alignments with horizon events, and it can lead to very different results. For example, in the Incaic

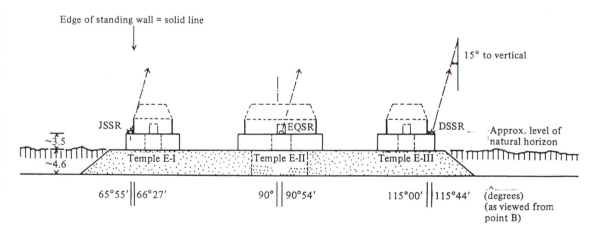

Figure 4. *Uaxactun, Guatemala, Group E, an ancient Maya solar observatory (Ref. Aveni, 1980, Figure 100).*

studies, one is surprised to find astronomical sighting directions that emanate from several different points in the Cuzco area. One of these directions, the zenith sunrise-anti-zenith sunset line, was of primary importance, serving as an embodiment of the up-down dualism that enters so frequently into Andean thought. Without the ethnohistorical data it is unlikely that these conclusions could ever have been reached. It will be interesting to learn whether the zenith principle, also common in Mexico, holds in other equatorial zone astronomies such as those of Polynesia, Java, and central Africa. To answer this question there is a need for field anthropologists, like B. Tedlock and G. Urton in the New World, to relate their studies specifically to cosmological and astronomical questions, which prove to be of great importance to indigenous societies.

In Maya studies, recent breakthroughs in the decipherment of hieroglyphic writing have begun to reveal that the Mayas viewed their own history as one that closely united dynastic ceremonial and astronomical events (this idea is suggested in the works of Schele and Miller, and Schele and Friedel). These studies have begun to lead archaeoastronomers to testable hypotheses. As a consequence, such studies have become more a part of the mainstream disciplines of cultural anthropology, history of religion, ethnohistory, and Maya studies.

While a genuine union of all the relevant academic enterprises, conducted by individuals with contrasting outlooks, motives, and approaches seems quite impossible, the sharing of information among them will advance the study of the astronomies and timekeeping systems of ancient non-Western cultures. Joint research projects by anthropologists and astronomers have become more commonplace, and three journals have been established to promote interaction and to disseminate information on archaeoastronomy: *Archaeoastronomy*, supplement to the *Journal for the History of Astronomy*, Churchill College, Cambridge, England; *Archaeoastronomy Bulletin*, Center for Archaeoastronomy, College Park, Maryland; and *Astronomy and the Human Sciences*, of which the publication in Strasbourg is pending.

As a result of the closer contact among related disciplines, archaeoastronomers have begun to ask a new set of broader questions, all of which are related to the study of time: Why did ancient societies develop astronomy? What role did astronomy play in their scientific and reli-

gious view of the world? What accounts for variations in the development of astronomy? What universal questions can be perceived from cross-cultural comparisons? Does the ability to speculate on the abstract world really depend on the achievement of a certain level of social, economic, cultural, religious, or scientific development in all societies? These questions have more to do with cosmological and ideological rather than scientific astronomical systems. Because they raise the level of discussion and expand it to areas where it can be addressed meaningfully by all scholars of antiquity, these questions also explain the broad interdisciplinary interests associated with the study of archaeoastronomy.

[A.F.A.]

See also **Anasazi Archaeoastronomy; Archaeoastronomical Field Techniques; British Archaeoastronomy; Chinese Astronomy; Maya Astronomy; Mesoamerican Archaeoastronomy; Pueblo Ethnoastronomy.**

FURTHER READINGS

Aveni, A.F., ed. *Archaeoastronomy in Pre-Columbian America.* Austin: U of Texas P, 1975.

——, ed. *Native American Astronomy.* Austin: U of Texas P, 1977.

——. *Skywatchers of Ancient Mexico.* Austin: U of Texas P, 1980.

——, ed. *World Archaeoastronomy.* Cambridge: Cambridge UP, 1989.

——, ed. *The Lines of Nazca.* Philadelphia: American Philosophical Society, 1990.

Aveni, A.F., and G. Urton, eds. *Ethnoastronomy and Archaeoastronomy in the American Tropics, Annals of the New York Academy of Sciences* vol. 385. New York: New York Academy of Sciences, 1982.

Carlson, J.B. and W.J. Judge, eds. *Astronomy and Ceremony in the Prehistoric Southwest.* Albuquerque: Maxwell Museum, 1987.

Hawkins, G.S. *Stonehenge Decoded.* New York: Delta-Dell, 1965.

Heggie, D., ed. *Archaeoastronomy in the Old World.* Cambridge: Cambridge UP, 1982.

Lockyer, J.N. *The Dawn of Astronomy.* 1894; reprint, Cambridge: MIT P, 1964.

MacKie, E.W. *Science and Society in Pre-historic Britain.* London: Paul Elek, 1977.

Romano, G., ed. *Primo Seminario Sulle Ricerche Archaoastronimche in Italia* (Estratto dal *Giornale di Astronomia*), 1985.

Ruggles, C.L.N., ed. *Records in Stone.* Cambridge: Cambridge UP, 1988.

——, ed. *Archaeoastronomy in the 1990s.* Loughborough: Group D Publications, 1992.

Ruggles, C.L.N., and N.J. Saunders, eds. *Astronomies and Cultures*. Niwot: UP of Colorado, 1993.

Schele, L. and M. Miller. *Blood of Kings*. Fort Worth: Kimbell Museum, 1986.

Thom, A. *Megalithic Sites in Britain*. London: Oxford UP, 1967.

———. *Megalithic Lunar Observations*. London: Oxford UP, 1971.

Thom, A., and A.S. Thom. *Megalithic Remains in Britain and Brittany*. London: Oxford UP, 1978.

Williamson, R., ed. *Archaeoastronomy in the Americas*. Santa Barbara: Ballena P, 1981.

Ziolkowski, M., and R. Sadowski, eds. *Time Calendars in the Inca Empire*. Oxford: B.A.R., 1989.

ARCHAEOLOGICAL DATING METHODS

The most direct way by which an archaeological stratum can be dated is by means of an object, usually a clay tablet or a coin, on which the date, or the year of a king's reign, is inscribed; the latter requires the availability of a calendar of reigns that is continuous to the present day, or that can be dated in some other way. The earliest calendar is the Egyptian one; this begins at the start of the first dynasty around 3000 B.C., and is fixed in calendar years through the recorded observation of an astronomical event that is datable by calculation. Dating of events prior to 3000 B.C. is only possible through natural physical "clocks" (*chronometric techniques*), or through the correlation that has been established between past global climate and variations that have occurred in the earth's orbital motion (eccentricity of the orbit, obliquity of the ecliptic, and precession of the equinoxes). These variations result from gravitational perturbations due to the changing configuration of the planets—which are themselves calculable. Such a correlation, first proposed in detail by M. M. Milankovitch around 1941, makes possible rather accurate dating of the successive glacial and interglacial periods that conditioned the life of early man; the fossil flora and fauna of an archaeological site allow attribution to a warm or cool period and other evidence (such as the tool technology) may point to a particular period. However, chronometric methods give more direct and objective dating.

CHRONOMETRIC TECHNIQUES

The process of radioactive decay is immutable and hence provides a clock immune to environmental influences. *Potassium-argon dating*, of crucial importance in the study of early homi-

nids, is based on the accumulation, in volcanic lava and elsewhere, of argon-40 produced from the slow decay of potassium-40; the latter is present in naturally occurring potassium as a trace component. During a volcanic eruption, the previously accumulated argon (a gas) is released and this is the event which is dated. It can be used when there is association of human occupation with volcanic products. *Uranium-series dating* is similarly based on the slow build-up of radioactive products (thorium-230, protactinium-231) following the precipitation of calcium carbonate as calcite, typically in caves; at precipitation, only uranium is present. It is important in giving a time scale for human development from 500,000 years onward.

Radiocarbon dating relies on the minute amount of weakly radioactive carbon-14 that is present in the "carbon exchange reservoir" consisting of the atmosphere, the oceans, and living fauna and flora; on removal from the reservoir, such as by death, there is slow decay of radioactivity—by a factor of two every 5,730 years; the extent to which the radioactivity of the sample has fallen below that of the reservoir enables the time elapsed since removal from the reservoir to be evaluated. The radioactivity of the reservoir is determined by the production rate of carbon-14 in the upper atmosphere by cosmic rays, and the amount of non-radioactive carbon in the reservoir. It is the most widely used of all techniques and covers the period from about 400 to 40,000 years ago. It has high precision, around ± 100 years, but because there have been small variations in the radioactivity of the reservoir in the past, the basic ages obtained have to be quoted in "radiocarbon years." Conversion of these to calendar years is possible back to about 10,000 years ago by measurement of dendrochronologically dated wood (see below) and further back by comparison with uranium-series dates on coral. Dates in radiocarbon years are usually quoted as "so many years B.P.," the letters standing for "Before Present," with "Present" defined as A.D. 1950.

There is another category involving radioactivity in which the dating clock is based on the cumulative effect of nuclear radiation on crystal structure. The setting-to-zero of the effect is the event which is dated and the nuclear radiation is provided by trace amounts of potassium-40, thorium, or uranium that are naturally present in the sample and/or its surroundings. *Fission track* formation is one effect that is used; this is mainly applicable to minerals of volcanic origin and the zeroing occurs through heating during the eruption. Trapping of electrons at crystal defects in minerals such as quartz, feldspar, calcite, coral, and hydroxyapatite is an effect of more general use and measurement can be by means of *luminescence* or by *electron spin resonance* (ESR), according to sample. In addition to heating, for some of these sample types the zeroing may be by exposure to daylight; in the case of biogenic crystals, there are zero trapped electrons at formation. For luminescence dating, the main applications are to pottery, burnt stone, and wind- and water-borne sediment; for ESR, to the tooth enamel of early humans. Luminescence may be observed either by heating the sample (*thermoluminescence*—TL) or by shining light on it (*optically stimulated luminescence*—OSL); the age range is roughly from ten years ago to several hundred thousand years ago. The ESR technique extends back to several million years ago.

Amino acid racemization and *obsidian hydration* are the two principal techniques based on chemical change. At formation, the aspartic acid, for example, of a protein molecule is present in its L form; thereafter, slow conversion to the D form commences and continues until an equilibrium mixture of the two is reached. Epimerization (similar to racemization, but more complex) of isoleucine is another reaction used, particularly in ostrich eggshells. Like the slow formation of hydration rims on freshly cleaved obsidian, the amino acid technique is strongly influenced by environmental conditions, temperature in particular; site-by-site calibration against radiocarbon is usual, and there is then extrapolation beyond the range of the latter technique. Loss of nitrogen from bone and uptake of fluorine and uranium are some other processes from which dating information can be obtained; study of the diffusion profile of ingoing fluorine, obtained by means of a nuclear microprobe, is a recent sophistication.

Archaeomagnetic dating utilizes the changing direction of the earth's magnetic field, a fossilized record of this being provided by the weak but permanent magnetization acquired by clay and stones on cooling down after baking and by sediment during deposition (or consolidation). Region-by-region calibration using kilns, hearths, and silted-up ditches of known age is necessary. On a larger time scale, complete reversals of the earth's field provide a worldwide geomagnetic chronology, calibrated by means of the potassium-argon technique.

Finally, there is the conceptually simple technique of *dendrochronology*—the counting of rings which form annually in some species of trees. Because the pattern of wide and narrow rings is dependent on climate an ancient timber having upwards of fifty rings has a distinctive signature which can be matched to a master chronology for the region concerned. In Europe and the southwestern United States, such chronologies have been established for nearly ten millennia by means of fossil trees whose growth periods overlap.

[M.J.A.]

See also **Archaeology; Geochronometry.**

FURTHER READINGS
Aitken, Martin J. *Science-Based Dating in Archaeology.* London: Longman, 1990.

ARCHAEOLOGY

The word archaeology derives from two Greek words: *archaio*, meaning "ancient," and *logia*, meaning "knowledge," "theory," or "science." The word is used to describe the scientific inquiry, methodology, location, study, interpretation, and curation of past material remains. It has come to denote that branch of learning which scientifically studies the physical remains of prehistoric and historic human activities in relation to their environment. In its broad sense, archaeology's aim is to understand the interrelationships between people and to establish their cultural chronologies so the past may be reconstructed and its processes understood while ensuring its preservation and conservation.

The scope of archaeology is enormous and includes diversity in subject and time ranging from the stone tools made in Africa some 4 million years ago to recent times. Because archaeology can involve excavation and the physical disruption of remains, it represents a nonrenewable resource; each site is irreplaceable, fragile, and should be excavated by a professional scholar. An archaeologist is a trained professional who excavates and analyzes the past and reconstructs its social and cultural processes. Archaeologists must be theoretical scientists who are able to define research problems and who have a thorough knowledge of their area of expertise.

THE SUBJECT AREA
In the twentieth century, archaeology is worldwide in scope; there is archaeology both on land and underwater from Japan to Russia and from

Alaska to South Africa. Lost civilizations unknown prior to archaeological research include the Sumerians of Lower Mesopotamia, the Harappan civilization of India, the Shang civilization of China, and the Olmecs of Central America. The discipline covers a wide range of approaches and specialization from the study of ancient languages and natural sciences to the practical methodology and techniques of field work.

The aim of archaeology is to recreate fully and accurately human cultural development from the Paleolithic (Stone Age—the period before ca. 10,000 B.C.E.) through the Bronze and Iron Ages of Asia, Europe, and Africa (known as "Old World" archaeology) to the civilizations of America (or "New World" archaeology), including the western hemisphere—North America, Mesoamerica, and South America (Peru and Venezuela). The archaeology of Islam, India and Pakistan, China, Japan, Southeast Asia, Oceania, the circumpolar regions, and Australia are also specialist disciplines. Archaeology involves the study of all aspects of society: its temporal and spatial cultural processes and the reconstruction of its cultural history, including settlement patterns, demography, technology, economy, exchange systems, organization of domestic life, mortuary practices, kinship, social stratification, ritual, art, and religion.

Prehistoric archaeology concentrates on the time before the advent of written or pre-written sources and extends, if we accept the East African dates for *Australopithecus afarensis*, from 4 million to some 5,000 years ago; during this time, material remains are of particular importance. Once written sources become available in the Middle East, ca. 3,200 B.C.E., human activity is now considered history, and in this field the archaeologist and the historian work closely. Although written records often provide a fuller understanding of thought processes and behavior, they present their own problems of decipherment and interpretation, while archaeology supplies a broader context for otherwise unavailable information. The Trojan War in Homer's *Iliad* can be assessed only in light of the archaeological remains of the Mycenaean civilization in Greece and the Aegean.

Traditionally, archaeology has been academically oriented. In the United States, prehistoric archaeology is taught in anthropology departments along with cultural anthropology and linguistics, whereas classical archaeology is often found in art history and classics departments. In each of the large branches of archaeology, there are chronological and geographical sub-disciplines. Paleolithic archaeology has its major emphasis on physical anthropology, history, and geology (geoarchaeology). Sub-disciplines of historical archaeology include classical (Greek and Roman), Near Eastern (Biblical, Palestinian, Anatolian, Mesopotamian, and Persian), museology, underwater, and industrial archaeology. Classical, medieval, and industrial archaeology, as well as Egyptology and Assyriology, are based on the written record in addition to art history.

Because of the interwoven nature of past and present, American archaeologists studying Native Americans believe that archaeology is anthropology. Anthropological archaeology can incorporate linguistics, folklorism, ethnology, demographics, and physical anthropology; cultural anthropology places emphasis on learned social, linguistic, technological, and familial behaviors.

Specializations within archaeology also include cognitive archaeology, conservation archaeology, environmental archaeology, cultural resource management (CRM), ethnoarchaeology, experimental archaeology, and paleoethnography. An additional field is contract archaeology, which is research conducted under the aegis of federal or state legislation before highway or urban construction is undertaken. Ecofact study of non-artifactual remains—pollen, shell, seeds, and bones—can help in the reconstruction of vegetation and climate. Bone analysis can determine diet, butchering patterns, sex, ages of animal populations, and seasonality of yields. And DNA and gene analysis is being used to reconstruct heredity. The links between all of these fields are found in archaeological analysis, methodology, and concepts of interpretation.

HISTORY OF ARCHAEOLOGY

In the past twenty years, there has been a marked increase in the number of discoveries, but in its infancy during the eighteenth and nineteenth centuries, archaeology was fostered by antiquarians and dilettantes who were little more than treasure hunters collecting antiquities or filling museum cases with interesting curios. In 1650, English Archbishop Ussher asserted that the world began in 4004 B.C.E. This date was accepted as fact until the nineteenth century when, in 1816, Christian J. Thomsen (1788–1865), curator of the Danish National Museum, arranged the museum galleries by material: stone, bronze, and iron, which became known as the *three age system* for prehistoric technological and chronological periods. Thomsen's student, Jan Worsaae (1821–1885), proved Thomsen correct through excavation, and Sir John Lubbock (1834–1913) coined the terms "Paleolithic" to mean the Old Stone Age and "Neolithic" for the New Stone Age. In 1798, Napoleon took savants to Egypt, and in 1822, Champollion (1790–1832) deciphered the Rosetta stone. Paul Emile Botta (1702–1870) excavated in Iraq at Nineveh and Khorsabad, to be followed by Austin Henry Layard (1817–1894), who excavated Nimrud and Babylon. These were no more than plundering expeditions for museums, with little or no understanding of methodology and technique. Then, for the first time, excavations started to answer questions about the antiquity of man. General Pitt-Rivers (1847–1900) excavated at Dorset, and his excavations and detailed publications marked the beginning of modern archaeology. Instead of excavating for objects, archaeologists began to excavate for information and realized that the geological record indicated that man had a much greater antiquity than 4004 B.C.E.!

Archaeology began some 150 years ago with studies of pre-Roman and Roman remains in France and Great Britain, searches for biblical origins in Palestine, and examinations of the monuments of Egypt, the pre-Viking remains of Scandinavia, the temples of Greece, and the remains of Mesopotamia. The theoretical side of archaeology has often focused on regional specializations and diversities in interpretation. (For example, whether or not colonialist, nationalist, or imperialist ideologies are espoused through the archaeological record.) The evolution of American archaeological thought, from 1950 to 1975, brought about gradual changes within the discipline; the *new archaeology* evolved which emphasized research designs, including the studies of cultural and human ecology. These archaeologists stressed that artifacts should be examined in relation to their cultural contexts with emphasis on cultural processes and regional relationships so that all-inclusive culture systems could be known.

THE ARCHAEOLOGICAL SITE

An archaeological site is any place of past human activity. Each site is distinct for its environmental, spatial, temporal, and artifactual remains. A site can serve a unique specialized function such as a battlefield, a butchering station, a burial (the Sutton Hoo ship burial in England, or Huang Ti's burial in Xi'an, China), or a ceremonial sacred activity (Stonehenge in

England, or Easter Island in Polynesia). Multipurpose sites include towns and cities like Mohenjo-Daro in Pakistan, which served many functions such as habitation, administration, manufacture, and ceremony; in general, these site types span an extended time period. Prehistoric sites can be located in plains or riverside terraces (Olduvai Gorge in Tanzania), or in caves (Chou Kou Tien, near Beijing, China). They can be artificial mounds built up by successive habitation, known in the Near East as *tells* or *tels* (Jericho, Israel), *tepes* (Tepe Yahya, Iran), or *höyüks* (Çatal Höyük or Troy in Turkey). The most famous are monumental cities (Ur in Iraq, or Pompeii in Italy). There are also other specialized sites, such as underwater installations like the Ulu Burun shipwreck off the southwestern Turkish coast. Sites that are a testimony to ancient technical genius because of the enormity and craftsmanship of their remains include the Olmec heads of Mexico, the Inca cities of Peru, and the Sphinx of Egypt.

STRATIGRAPHY

Strata are the various layers of human or geologic origin which comprise archaeological sites. These remains include soils, architecture, burials, pits, and other features. Stratigraphy is the interpretation of how archaeological deposits came to be buried through environmental factors and human intervention. When Thomas Jefferson (1743–1826) excavated a burial mound in Virginia, he recognized the principles of stratigraphy, as did the Englishman Sir Flinders Petrie at Tell-el Hesi in Palestine. It was Petrie who prioritized the importance of stratigraphy for the study of Middle Eastern tells.

Stratigraphy is dependent on three assumptions: *superposition*, *association*, and *correlation*. Superposition reasons that in any undisturbed archaeological site, the strata (levels) on the bottom were deposited first, and are older or earlier than those above them. Those artifacts found in a sealed archaeological context are assumed to be contemporary and culturally associated. Therefore, strata containing similar assemblages are reasoned to be of similar age. Correlation reasons that once associations between archaeological data are determined, artifacts can be cross-culturally matched and are therefore contemporary. Much like coins, diagnostic artifacts such as index fossils or horizon markers, characterize and date an archaeological deposit; thus, sites having similar artifactual evidence share a similar cultural development.

ARTIFACTS

Most important to an artifact is its context—its immediate surroundings—together with its horizontal and vertical provenience, and its association with other artifacts. The analysis of stones (for example, obsidians and marbles) and metals helps to pinpoint origins and trade routes. The study of inorganic and organic ecofacts, including faunal (bones) and floral (pollen) analysis, aids in the reconstruction of agricultural systems, pastoralism, and food collection and production. Such archaeological data bases are constantly expanding because of their cultural relevance.

Artifacts have formal attributes that can be measured, identified, and described. Typical attributes include material, manufacture, shape, and decoration, as well as specifics such as length, width, thickness, color, and weight. (These attributes are assumed to be a nonrandom standard followed by the maker.) Classifications and typologies are composed of artifact types—a defined cluster of attributes. *Seriation* is the ordering of specific artifact types over a time sequence (similar to the ordering of automobiles over time). A group of objects found in association is known as an *assemblage*, and a full assemblage can be described as a *culture*. It is assumed that a regularly occurring assemblage of artifacts represents the shared behavior of a group of people. When an excavated stratum or strata represents through its physical remains a way of life of a particular group, such as the classical Greeks, the data collected have a known and recognizable set of ideas that are assumed to be the cultural products of the society. One of the goals of archaeology is to order culture into time slots and thus to construct a cultural chronology as well as to identify cultural groups and understand their development.

DATING, TECHNOLOGY, AND ANALYSIS

Time is assumed to be a period during which something exists and can be measured; it is a continuum of events that succeed one another from the past to the present. The two types of dating in archaeology are referred to as absolute and relative. In order to establish absolute and relative dating sequences, soil study, climatology, botany, zoology, geology, and chemistry may be used. Relative dating is based on the chronological sequence of objects, as mentioned earlier. Two expressions used for the dating of archaeological deposits are *Terminus ante quem* (a Latin phrase meaning "time before which"), and *Terminus post quem* (meaning "time after which"). *Terminus ante quem* assumes that dateable material found on a floor gives an *ante quem* for the floor, that is to say, it had to have been built before the material collected on it. The dateable material under the floor gives a *terminus post quem* for the floor, since the floor must have been built after that material was deposited.

Absolute dating is a date given in specific years with reference to a specific time scale. Also known as chronometric or calendrical dating, absolute dating relies on time scales such as B.P. (*Before Present* or 1950), B.C. (*Before Christ*), and A.D. (*Anno Domini*, or *After Christ*). For the latter two terms, it is becoming common to substitute B.C.E. (*Before the Common Era*) and C.E. (*Common Era*).

In the last thirty years, archaeology has used scientific analyses and techniques; thus, the physical and biological sciences are usually incorporated into archaeological research. Geochronological dating determines the absolute age of an archaeological deposit by its association with geological processes. Well-known geochronological techniques include radiocarbon (C^{14}), potassium-argon, alpha-recoil tracks, amino acid racemization, fission track, and thermoluminescence. Other methods used for determining absolute dates include archaeomagnetic or paleomagnetic dating, varve analysis, and dendrochronology (tree-ring dating).

PRE-EXCAVATION EXPLORATION

Archaeological inquiry is undertaken to resolve a particular problem or question. A systematic research design includes a blueprint and timetable for pre-excavation research, an excavation strategy, recording and analysis of the data collected, and its interpretation and publication so that it becomes part of the public record. Not only does it involve the specification of the general and specific goals, but it also involves the study, in-depth analyses, and sequence ordering of the material remains, relative and absolute dating methods, and the evaluation and synthesis of the results of the research.

Archaeology involves aboveground reconnaissance as well as excavation. A variety of methods are used for the recording of topographic surface features, artifacts, and natural resources such as water supply or mineral deposits. Pre-excavation exploration also includes extensive library research and the referral to old and new maps, toponyms, legends, and folkways, but its chief involvement is with field walking, surveys, and sampling for an understanding of the site and its context. Preliminary analysis involves a knowledge of who the site's occupants were, how long they lived there, and its probable relationship to other sites. The research goals are important—what problems will be solved by the site's excavation? What staff specialists are needed? With ever-increasing knowledge, there has been increased use of statistics, systems analysis, and computer application for quantification of remains, mapping, and site visualization.

For a detailed image of the ground and subsurface features, aerial and ground photography are essential, including remote sensing, photogrammetry, and photomapping. Outlines of buried structures can be seen with infrared photographs. Plant life is often stunted over buried structures due to reduced soil moisture, so soil and crop marks can be clues to buried remains. Technological advances used to locate subsurface features have been brought about with the use of the electrical resistivity meter which measures the resistant moisture of the soil, the proton magnetometer or gradiometer, which identifies magnetic differences between buried structures, and seismic surveys that employ ground-penetrating radar. There is, however, no substitute for the ground search survey, which is the close reconnaissance of the ground by site walking. Based on the evidence from surface and subsurface features, artifact collections, and documents, the professional archaeologist decides where to excavate.

EXCAVATION

Surveying is essential to the accurate recording of an archaeological site. After a reference datum is established, differences in height or topography are measured using a level (transit, theodolite, or electronic surveying equipment) with a staff or target. The site grid is the surveyed horizontal dimensions of regularly sized, equally spaced squares to enclose and control the site. The excavation grid follows the same lines as the site grid by using trenches of regular squares with balks or earth partitions set between them which serve to control the stratigraphy. From measured reference points, features are plotted to scale both for horizontal maps, known as *plans*, and for *sections*, which are the vertical profiles of the excavation.

Excavation is one of the principal methods of data acquisition in archaeology. It involves practical methods for the systematic removal of soils and remains and their accurate recording,

conservation, and interpretation. Appropriate methods and tools vary with each site. The tools of archaeology include not only the pick, the hoe, the trowel, and the brush, but also the notebook, for any excavation requires extensive and accurate field notes in addition to ongoing library research.

PROFESSIONAL ETHICS IN ARCHAEOLOGY

Archaeology is a field which requires professional morality, responsibility, and competence. The archaeologist must adhere to a code of ethics. Art collectors and dealers have contributed to the exploitation of archaeological sites by illicit excavations, the production of forgeries, and enhancement of the commercial value of archaeological objects. The Archaeological Institute of America's code of ethics is accepted by most archaeologists. Archaeologists should "(1) Seek to ensure that the exploration of archaeological sites be conducted according to the highest standards under the direct supervision of qualified personnel, and that the results of such research be made public; (2) Refuse to participate in illegal trade of antiquities derived from any excavation in any country after 30 December 1970 when the A.I.A. Council endorsed the UNESCO Convention on Cultural Property, and refrain from activities that enhance the commercial value of such objects; [and] (3) Inform appropriate authorities of threats to, or plunder of, archaeological sites, and of the illegal import or export of archaeological material."

Archaeology today is a vast intellectual exchange with powerful new interpretative tools, but remains are endangered by events such as the Gulf War, increased tourism, road and housing developments, and the attrition caused by agricultural products such as chemical fertilizers and herbicides. There has been a popularization of the subject with television programs, books, and educational courses, but some of the interested public concentrates on the lunatic fringes—*Raiders of the Lost Ark*, van Daniken's writings, and Atlantis. There is, therefore, an urgency for communication and representation between archaeologists and federal, state, and local authorities, the private sector, and the general public to further the goals and discipline of archaeology for the preservation of the world's patrimony.

[M.S.J.]

See also **Archaeological Dating Methods; Geochronometry.**

FURTHER READINGS

Ashmore, Wendy, and Robert J. Sharer. *Discovering Our Past: A Brief Introduction to Archaeology*. Mountain View: Mayfield Publishing, 1988.

Binford, Lewis Roberts. *In Pursuit of the Past: Decoding the Archaeological Record*. New York: Thames and Hudson, 1983.

Ceram, C.W. [Kurt W. Marek] *Gods, Graves, and Scholars: The Story of Archaeology*. Trans. E.B. Garside. London: Victor Gollancz, 1952.

Daniel, G. *150 Years of Archaeology*. London: Duckworth, 1975.

Harris, Edward, ed. *Principles of Archaeological Stratigraphy*. 2nd ed. San Diego: Academic P, 1989.

Heizer, Robert Fleming, Thomas R. Hester, and Carol Graves. *Archaeology, a Bibliographical Guide to the Basic Literature*. New York: Garland, 1980.

Knudson, S.J. *Culture in Retrospect: An Introduction to Archaeology*. Prospect Heights: Waveland P, 1985.

Sharer, Robert J. *Archaeology: Discovering Our Past*. Mountain View: Mayfield Publishing, 1987.

Sherratt, Andrew, ed. *The Cambridge Encyclopaedia of Archaeology*. New York: Cambridge UP, 1980. Includes bibliography.

Trigger, Bruce G. *A History of Archaeological Interpretation*. New York: Cambridge UP, 1989.

The World Atlas of Archaeology. London: M. Beazley, 1985. Includes bibliography.

ARISTOTLE (384–322 B.C.)

Aristotle's fundamental treatment of time is found in *Physics* IV.10–14, where he defines time as the number of motions with respect to before and after. For Aristotle, time is an attribute of motion. In *Physics* IV, Aristotle is concerned with defending our ordinary perception of motion from place to place against philosophers like Parmenides, who claimed all change is illusory. One facet of his defense of motion is refuting the idea that motion from place to place is a series of instantaneous leaps from one place of rest to another. Even when it varies in speed, motion is smooth and continuous, and it always takes time.

Both motion and time are continuous, Aristotle believes, because of their dependence on magnitude, that is, distance or the size of body. Body is associated with the notion of place, while magnitude abstracts from body and place and is closer to the geometrical notions of line segment, bounded surface, and solid. Since motion from place to place covers some distance, or magnitude, motion is continuous because magnitude is. Since time measures or numbers motion, time is continuous because motion is. Aristotle first introduces "before" and "after"

in relation to time in the context of establishing the dependence of time on motion and magnitude. Accordingly, he says the before and after (*to proteron kai husteron*) are first in place.

How they are first in place is not spelled out. Things in different places could be before and after because of their relation to a common reference point, as in the terms "in front of" and "behind," possible translations of *proteron* and *husteron* respectively. In this case, "the before" and "the after" are units brought into relation through a third thing. However, the two terms could be viewed as related primarily to one another—"the before and after"—and not to a common reference point. In this case, however, it is difficult to see how, on the basis of Aristotle's analysis of place in *Physics* IV.1–5, the before and after in place would be anything more than mere difference in place. Place must be conceived in relation to motion for difference in place to constitute before and after. Given that the context for the account of time is the correlation of place, motion, and time, it is natural to interpret the before and after in place in relation to motion, and this is the interpretation adopted here. On Aristotle's model of motion, any individual movement tends toward an end—a natural culmination or intended destination—on the attainment of which the motion ceases. Hence, it is the directionality of motion that gives ordering to difference in place, making one point "before" (*proteron*) and another "after" (*husteron*). Thus, even if we take "the before and after" as a unit originally, their relation still depends on the reference point of their common end in motion. Nevertheless, Aristotle believes that, in perception at least, the before and after are presented to us independent of their common end.

We see the independence of before and after from the end of motion in Aristotle's conviction that time is dependent not on any particular motion taken in its entirety, that is, as involving starting point and ending point, but on motion as a substratum for before and after. Aristotle distinguishes the before and after in motion from its substratum by characterizing the substratum as that which, being whatever it may be, *is* before and after. Thus, he makes the before and after an attribute that is always present in motion, the substratum. He makes this distinction between motion and its attribute because he believes that we recognize time has passed when we perceive just the before and after in motion. Thus, even though the before and after are present in motion because motion is ordered to an end, it is not necessary to know or perceive the end to perceive before and after. Indeed, they are themselves the means by which we come to know motion.

"Nows"—indivisible instants—mark before and after, making possible the recognition of a continuous interval between them. The "nows" that mark corresponding points in different simultaneous movements are themselves the same in substratum, because they mark simultaneous times. Thus, different perceptions of time based on different motions which occur simultaneously involve the same before and after. Accordingly, although our primary perception of time is in the movement of the heavenly bodies, we can know time has passed, even without access to this primary timekeeper, by noticing movement within the soul. Hence, the substratum for time is not dependent on the before and after of any particular motion. Aristotle believes the world is eternal and that there has never been a time when there was not *something* in motion.

Because its number is most easily known, the uniform, circular movement of the heavens is the standard by which other motions are measured in time. That standard does not itself insure the uniform flow of time, however. Arguing against the idea that time is the motion itself of the celestial sphere, he says that, in this case, if there were many worlds, there would be many times simultaneously, a notion he regards as absurd. Time is not any particular motion but the number of motion. One reason Aristotle gives for calling time number is that time is not fast or slow, and no number by which we count is fast or slow.

Aristotle says that the before and after are countable by virtue of the "now." He takes the present now to be indivisible and uses the term to designate past or future instants as well as the present instant. He explains the character of the instant, again by reference to the correlation of the continua of place, motion, and time, when he says the moving object is similar to the point, and the now to the moving object. By means of the moving object, we know motion and the before and after. But it is by means of the now that the before and after are countable. In one way, the now is the same, because there is a permanent present instant which, by following the moving object, marks new "befores" and "afters." But in another way, the now is always different, because each stage of motion marked has a different number when counted.

In addition to this treatment of the role of the now in passage, Aristotle also treats the now as the link between past and future. Time is both divided at the now and unified by the now. Past and future meet in the now, and this was true of earlier nows also. However, this does not mean the now serves at the same time as an end point of the past and a first point of the future. This is because the now is different from a point, which remains and thus actually divides a line into segments. By contrast, the now divides only potentially, because it follows the moving object and does not stop. Seen from this vantage point, the role of the now is to mark off periods of time which may be compared in length of duration to other periods.

The way the function of the now implicates periods of time has led some to interpret Aristotle's statement that time is the number of motion as meaning that time is a metric concept and is number in the sense of magnitude or duration. Aristotle says that time is number in the sense of what is numbered rather than what numbers, and magnitude is one possible understanding of what is numbered. However, the role of before and after in the definition of motion suggests that Aristotle means time to be number in the sense of ordinal number, such as first, second, or third. Before and after are attributes of ordered series, and the successiveness of motion, in Aristotle's account, is such an ordered series. The numbering of nows then implicates the metric function of time secondarily through the duration established between before and after.

One problem Aristotle recognizes to be involved in this account of time is whether there would be time without a soul to count it. He responds that as long as there were motion, there would be before and after. And these are time, insofar as they could be counted. They are not truly countable, however, without there being a soul to count them. Another problem Aristotle addresses is one to which his own treatment of the present might be subject. This is the problem of the reality of past and future. Neither what was nor what will be are presently. In particular, the present cannot have duration, since part of any present duration will be in the past and part in the future. The present is only a durationless instant. But in this case, how can time be real, since durationless instants cannot be parts of time, nor together make up a period of time?

As scholars have interpreted Aristotle's account, the reality of past and future is secured through his persisting now. The now cannot exist without continuous time in which to serve as a marker. Furthermore, the fact that the now does not actually divide time implies that past and future are not essentially different. In addition, it is by means of the now that we come to know time as duration. Because it follows the moving object, the reality of time is ensured finally by the reality of persisting objects.

A different way that time figures prominently in Aristotle's philosophy is in the issue of the truth or falsity of propositions about future contingent events. In *On Interpretation* IX, Aristotle says that concerning events in the past or present, a statement either affirming or denying their occurrence must be true. If the affirmative proposition is true, its denial is false, and *vice versa*. This is not the case with statements about events in the future. If it were, then all future events would be predetermined. Thus, Aristotle believes that propositions about future events have different logical properties than propositions about the present or past. The status of future contingent propositions has been the subject of much discussion because of its relation to the issue of whether Aristotle believed all genuine possibilities are actualized at some time or another.

[J.D.G.]

See also **Aquinas, St. Thomas.**

FURTHER READINGS

Hintikka, Jaako. *Time and Necessity in Aristotle.* Oxford: Clarendon P, 1973.

Hussey, Edward. *Aristotle's Physics: Books III and IV.* Translated with notes. Oxford: Clarendon P, 1983. 138–175.

Inwood, Michael. "Aristotle on the Reality of Time." *Aristotle's Physics.* Ed. Lindsay Judson. Oxford: Clarendon P, 1991. 151–178.

Sorabji, Richard. *Time, Creation, and the Continuum: Theories in Antiquity and the Early Middle Ages.* Ithaca: Cornell UP, 1983.

Waterlow, Sarah. "Aristotle's Now." *Philosophical Quarterly* 34.135 (1984): 104–128.

ARROW OF TIME

The world, and everything in it, gets older. Creatures are born, live, and die; a mountain range may be formed in some geological event but is finally worn flat by the processes of nature. One may say that it, too, dies. Our minds learn, think, and forget. Memory and prediction are very different experiences. Natural processes such as these define a direction of time from past toward future that is called the arrow of time. It may seem silly to ask why everything ages in the same direction; that is, why there is nobody who grows younger at the same pace, but in the opposite sense of time, as from that in which we grow older. If one looks at the physical bases of life and change, however, the silly question cannot be avoided.

The question arises because everything is made of atoms. The mathematical laws that govern the behavior of atoms and molecules and the fields of force that control them do not distinguish past from future. Imagine that one could make a motion picture of some of the molecules of a gas in a steady state, bouncing around in a confined space. Now if the film were run backward, we would see the same kind of behavior and there would be no way to find out, by looking at the two versions, which was the correct one. On the other hand, if one is given a segment of an ordinary narrative film, unless it shows something extremely organized such as a dance routine or a figure skater, one can tell at once in which direction the film is supposed to be viewed. There is a paradox here: how is this possible if the things and actors of the film are all composed of atoms and molecules whose behavior at the microscopic level is time-symmetric? Somehow, in the transition between samples of matter composed of a few particles and samples composed of a very large number of them, a new characteristic of the world emerges—the arrow of time.

A few examples will illustrate the distinction. If a kettle of hot water is set on the ground, it cools off; a cool kettle set there does not heat up. Heat always flows from warm to cool and never the other way. Also, the molecules of a gas are never seen spontaneously bunching together. If the density of the gas is initially large in one part of a container, observation a little later shows that the molecules have spread out so that they are evenly distributed throughout the container. Such processes are called irreversible, and very nearly every event observed on the macroscopic scale is of this kind. Irreversibility introduces a directionality in the flow of events that distinguishes past from future. Is the distinction absolute? That is, is it inherent in the very nature of things, or is it in some way an artifact of the large numbers involved?

For more than a century the paradox of time's arrow has occupied physicists, chemists, and mathematicians. Much is now understood, but there is still no simple and clear argument that answers every question. Some of the questions are too technical to discuss here, so this article will focus on one simple example of irreversible behavior in order to show how it can arise in a system governed by the reversible equations of Newtonian mechanics. It involves the density of an idealized gas, which is an observable macroscopic property, and the argument will show how the random and reversible motion of its atoms can lead to the "irreversible" change in density just mentioned; the quotation marks are used because in this case the definition of irreversibility involves a subtlety that conceals the resolution of the paradox. It will soon be apparent that the resolution involves time in a fundamental way.

AN EXAMPLE

Consider a tube one meter long, with gas molecules moving around in it at a speed of 100 meters per second (such speeds are typical of ordinary gases under ordinary conditions). Suppose that initially all the molecules are in the left half of the tube. Experience shows that the density of the gas will soon become even, and suggests that the molecules will *never* again all be found in the left half.

Start with a gas consisting of a single molecule. Of course, in this case, the suggestion is not true. If the molecule is observed fifty times, how often will it—that is, all the gas—be found in the left half of the tube? Common sense says half the time, but we must put in a proviso: the observations must not be made too close together. If we find it in the left half and then make forty-nine more measurements in the next 1/10,000 second, we will continue to find it in almost the same place. The measurements must be taken at least 1/100 second apart for the commonsense expectation to be correct. A motion picture of this molecule would show perfectly reversible behavior.

Now put in two molecules, and observe the tube every 1/100 second. One-fourth of the observations will show them both in the left half of the tube, and in general if there are N molecules one will have to look about 2^N times before finding them all on the left side. This will happen, on the average, at intervals given by:

$$T = (1/100) \times 2^N \text{ seconds.}$$

A real gas contains a huge number of molecules, but the tendency is clear if we consider only a few. The table shows T corresponding to several values of N.

TABLE

N	T
1	1/50 second
10	10 seconds
20	10,500 seconds = 3 hours
50	350,000 years
100	4 x 10^{20} years

The last figure is billions of times the age of the universe. Even though on the longest scale of time the gas molecules wander in a reversible way that makes no distinction between past and future, the scale is so immense that if one threw 100 molecules into the left side of the tube they would, with overwhelming probability, not all be found there again within any reasonable time. A refinement of the argument shows what one would intuitively expect: that over long intervals of time the distribution of molecules is effectively uniform along the tube and that perceptible departures from uniformity are rare and of short duration. The conclusion: One should be careful about using the word "never."

This example shows how, in a very simple situation, irreversibility is an illusion produced by large numbers, but the real world, including our perception of it, is much more complicated. For example, how did the molecules get into the left side of the tube in the first place? Possibly by human intervention. Then, should the body and brain of the experimenter be included in the analysis? The laboratory? The society that produced the laboratory? There is no simple formulation. At what point should one say the process to be analyzed actually started? There is an opinion among scientists (but only an opinion) that one must go all the way back and that the origin of irreversibility is bound up with the origin of the universe.

[D.A.P.]

See also **Passage of Time.**

FURTHER READINGS

Landsberg, Peter. *The Enigma of Time*. Bristol: Adam Hilger, 1982.

Morris, Richard. *Time's Arrows*. New York: Simon & Schuster, 1984.

Park, David. *The Image of Eternity*. Amherst: U of Massachusetts P, 1980.

ASPIRIN®

Despite the introduction of many new drugs, Aspirin® (acetylsalicylic acid, ASA) is widely used to relieve pain, fever, and inflammation. However, the chronopharmacology of ASA has not been completely evaluated. The data available to date indicate that 500 milligrams of ASA was 40 percent more effective against dental pain when ingested between 9:00 A.M. and noon than between 8:00 P.M. and 2:00 A.M. Similarly, chronokinetic studies showed that absorption of salicylate was faster and more complete in the morning and the renal excretion was 30 percent faster at night.

The daily use of ASA is now recommended for the prevention of recurrent myocardial infarction (MI) or for patients with unstable angina. Recent data obtained in a study of 22,071 physicians indicated that ASA was associated with a 60 percent reduction in the incidence of morning myocardial infarction, compared to a 34 percent reduction for the remaining hours of the day. These data, as well as those indicating that ASA produced twice as many irritations of the gastric mucosa when ingested at 10:00 A.M. than at 10:00 P.M., suggest that patients with recurrent myocardial infarction or unstable angina should be instructed to take their prophylactic dose of ASA at 9:00 P.M. Further research is needed on the clinical chronopharmacology of ASA.

[G.L.]

See also **Anesthesia and Pain; Biological Rhythms and Medicine.**

FURTHER READINGS

Ridker, P.M., et al. "Circadian Variation of Transient Myocardial Infarction and the Effect of Low–Dose Aspirin in a Randomized Trial of Physicians." *Circulation* 82 (1990): 897–902.

ASSOCIATION FOR THE SOCIAL STUDIES OF TIME (ASSET)

ASSET, the Association for the Social Studies of Time, was founded in 1984 and holds its annual meetings in the United Kingdom. Its international membership receives an annually updated bibliography and bulletin. The secretary of ASSET is Tom Schuller, I.C.S., 18 Victoria Park Square, Bethnal Green, London E2 9PF.

[B.A.]

ASTHMA

Asthma is a chronic disease typically characterized by inflammation and hyperreactivity of the lung tissue and spasms of the smooth muscles of the airways. Often these conditions exist in concert with excessive mucus production by specialized cells of the airways. As a result, breathing is difficult and labored with heightened risk of death from respiratory failure. Epidemiologic studies prove that for most patients, asthma is a nighttime disease. Approximately 90 percent of those affected with asthma experience severe enough symptoms overnight to awaken them from sleep at least once monthly. One survey found that sleep was disrupted by asthma nightly in nearly 40 percent of the patients and three times a week in about 60 percent. In children, loss of sleep due to asthma may be detrimental to schooling. In adults, it can affect job performance. In addition, a feared consequence of asthma is death due to a severe episode of the disease. Asthma mortality is most common overnight; one investigation found that ninety-three of 219 deaths from asthma occurred between midnight and 8:00 A.M.

There are numerous hypotheses as to why asthma occurs at night. Initially, it was thought that some aspect of sleep itself was the cause of nighttime asthma. However, studies have shown that asthma can occur in patients nocturnally even when they are purposely kept awake. Some investigators have hypothesized that the disease manifests itself nocturnally because of the exposure of patients and bedding in the bedroom to allergens to which the airways are hyperreactive. For the majority of asthma sufferers, however, this is an insufficient reason for asthma attacks to occur at night. Finally, some have proposed that when the patient assumes a supine sleeping position at night, asthma results from the reflux of acid from the stomach causing a reflex spasm of the airways. While this phenomenon explains why asthma occurs in a small number of patients, it does not explain the nocturnal preference of asthma in the majority of sufferers.

Asthma, in part, occurs at night due to the influence of specific circadian rhythms of the body which modulate airway function and status during the twenty-four hours of the day. First, the resistance of the passageways of the lung to the air flow varies greatly during the twenty-four hours in asthmatics. The resistance of the airways is considerably greater overnight than during the daytime. In fact, the day-night variation in airway resistance may amount to 40 to 50 percent of the mean level during the twenty four hours. This is due to day-night patterns in the secretion of such hormones as epinephrine, which influences the muscle tone of the airways, and cortisol, which modulates airway inflammation. Airway inflammation intensifies nocturnally. This results in markedly increased airway hyperreactivity to both non-specific environmental irritants such as air contaminants, and specific allergens such as house dust. Finally, the day-night differential in the risk of asthma represents the twenty-four-hour temporal patterns of those chemical mediators occurring secondary to immune reactions which underlie asthma crises.

In addition to circadian rhythms, asthma is known to exhibit other temporal patterns, although these have been less well studied. In premenopausal women who suffer from asthma, it is not uncommon for the disease to worsen during the premenstrual and menstrual phases of the fertility cycle. This pattern results from menstrual cycle-related variations in hormone concentrations which affect airway function. In both men and women, asthma commonly displays seasonal patterns. These are believed to represent variation in the type and quantity of environmental allergens to which one is exposed during the year in addition to seasonal rhythms in biological function.

[M.H.S.]

See also **Beta-Agonist Medications; Biological Rhythms in Epidemiology and Pharmacology; Theophylline.**

ATOMICITY OF TIME

Greek philosophers in the sixth and fifth centuries B.C. identified dual aspects of time—*being* (the Parmenidean continuity aspect) and *becoming* (the Heraclitean transience aspect)—that to this day remain unreconciled. Time extends continuously from the past to the future (the being aspect), and things change in time (the becoming aspect). Augustine's paradox of time is that things in time change in time. Do things actually change in time, or do they appear to change because we move in time? If we move in time, then we change in time. Evidently, temporal location does not exhaust the properties of time.

In theoretical physics, time is fully spatialized and time and space have no distinction in four-dimensional space-time. Events of the phys-

ical world are displayed in space-time; they are fixed and never change, and space-time decomposes into the different spaces and times of observers in relative motion. The becoming or transience aspect of time (the part that cannot be spatialized), which consists of an awareness of change in the sensible world, is banished from the physical world as a psychological or metaphysical characteristic of the observer. The problem for the physicist and the philosopher, in Whitrow's words, is "How do we get the illusion of time's transience without presupposing transient time as its origin?"

ZENO'S PARADOX AND THE BIRTH OF ATOMIC TIME

Zeno the Eleatic, by devising paradoxes of motion, tried to prove that all apparent change in the sensible world is illusory. In one of Zeno's paradoxes, Achilles and a tortoise hold a race in which the tortoise starts with a lead of 100 units of distance. While Achilles runs the 100 units of distance the tortoise travels one unit, and while Achilles runs this further unit the tortoise travels 1/100 of a unit, and so on, without limit. Hence, said Zeno, because of the infinity of subdivisions of distance, Achilles never overtakes the tortoise, thus demonstrating the illusory nature of change in the sensible world. Although readers armed with infinitesimal calculus might find this argument unconvincing, philosophers still debate the significance of Zeno's paradoxes; at issue is the assumed mathematical continuity of time.

Xenocrates, a student of Plato and his successor as head of the academy in Athens, developed the concept of atomic time, which has since occasionally figured in solutions of Zeno's paradox. If time consists of indivisible moments, often referred to as chronons, motion consists of imperceptible jerks that can, it is said, explain how Achilles overtakes the tortoise. Also, transition from time atom to time atom might explain our awareness of transience.

THE KALAM UNIVERSE

Perhaps Zeno's paradoxes and Xenocrates's atomicity of time influenced a school of Indian philosophers (a Buddhist sect) in the first century B.C. that developed a theory of momentary time, and probably inspired Bakillani, a medieval Arab scholar.

In the tenth and eleventh centuries A.D. the ilm al-kalam, a religious school of Arab philosophers, rejected the Aristotelian philosophy of more orthodox Muslim theology. Using the atomic theory of the Epicureans of the Greco-Roman world, the scholars of the kalam, the mutakallimun, sought to demonstrate the total dependence of the material world on the will of the supreme being—the sole agent. Atoms, they said, are isolated by voids and their configurations are governed not by natural agents but by the will of the sole agent.

Bakillani of Basra, who lived in Baghdad where he died in 1013, proposed that time also is atomic. In each atom of time the sole agent dissolves the world and recreates it in slightly different form. The world is created not once but repeatedly. The twelfth-century *The Guide for the Perplexed* by Moses Maimonides, a Jewish scholar, serves as a primary source of information on the kalam theory of atomic time. Maimonides wrote, "An hour is divided into sixty minutes, the minute into sixty seconds, the second into sixty parts, and so on; at last, after ten or more successive divisions by sixty, time-elements are obtained, which are not subjected to division, and in fact are indivisible."

But continual recreation poses a problem. The countless creations are isolated in atoms of time and have no connection with one another. How then can human beings arrange them in an orderly sequence? The kalam solution anticipated the theory of occasionalism (see below). In each atom of time, the sole agent creates not only a material world, but also a corresponding mental world of remembered events linking together the time atoms.

The mutakallimun sought to demonstrate the total dependence of the world on the will of the sole agent and unintentionally stumbled on a remarkable theory that unifies the dual aspects of time. In each "now," or atom of time, the material world stretches away in space and memories of the past and expectations for the future stretch away in time; everything exists in a frozen state of being. Then everything dissolves and in a new atom a new state of being exists. Transient acts of becoming transform whole states of being. Shorn of its extreme theism, the kalam theory accounts moderately well for our complex experience of time. A. N. Whitehead wrote, "In every act of becoming there is the becoming of something with temporal extension, but. . .the act itself is not extensive." In other words, temporal acts of becoming cannot be spatialized in the same way as temporal states of being. The atomic theory of time harmonizes the extensive and nonextensive aspects of time.

MONADS

René Descartes in the first half of the seventeenth century found by introspection that he possessed an immaterial mind: "I think, therefore I am." Yet his body was no more than a machine in a world of matter in motion. How could an immaterial mind interact with a material body? In *A Discourse on Method,* he argued that the supreme being repeatedly recreates both the material world and its coincident mental world (a theory known as occasionalism). Probably Descartes knew of the medieval kalam theory from the well-known work of Maimonides.

The kalam time atoms were also forerunners of the monads invented in the second half of the seventeenth century by Gottfried Leibniz. According to Leibniz, monads are the fundamental components of the world; they exist in isolation and their inner worlds are coordinated by pre-established harmony (a theory known as parallelism). Leibniz had a copy of *The Guide for the Perplexed,* and its marginal notes in his handwriting indicate that he was aware of the kalam atomic theory.

Whether physics will ever adopt the characteristics of atomic time, thus making the observer and transient time an integral part of the physical world, is a matter for speculation.

[E.R.H.]

See also **Descartes, René; Leibniz, Gottfried Wilhelm; Pre-Socratics; Whitehead, Alfred North.**

FURTHER READINGS

Burnet, J. *Early Greek Philosophy.* London: Black, 1920. 130–196.

Harrison, E.R. *Cosmology: The Science of the Universe.* New York: Cambridge UP, 1981.

———. *Masks of the Universe.* New York: Macmillan, 1985.

MacDonald, D.B. "Continuous Recreation and Atomic Time in Muslim Scholastic Theology." *Isis* 9 (1927): 326–344.

Maimonides, M. *The Guide for the Perplexed.* New York: Dover, 1927. Part I, Chapters 72–76.

Whitehead, A.N. *Process and Reality: An Essay in Cosmology.* Ed. D.R. Griffin and D.W. Sherburne. New York: Macmillan, 1978.

Whitrow, G.J. *The Natural Philosophy of Time.* 2nd ed. Oxford: Clarendon Press, 1980.

Wolfson, H.A. *The Philosophy of the Kalam.* Cambridge: Harvard UP, 1976.

AUGUSTINE (354–430)

Augustine's interest in the question of time extends across the entire corpus of his works and embraces a diversity of concerns from music and poetry to philosophy and theology. Augustine finds in time the *vestigium,* or footprint of eternity, a path to be followed from the finite to the infinite. In his view, nowhere is the course of time more transparent to the unalterable design of eternity than in the experience of life-time, human life-time, the unquestionable matrix of Augustine's theory of time.

Augustine's most focused and succinct inquiry into the nature of human temporality is to be found in Book XI of his *Confessions.* The reflections on experienced time presented there help not only to explain the curious structure of the *Confessions,* but also to disclose the core of Augustine's understanding of the human soul.

Earlier, in the *Soliloquies,* Augustine states that he desires to know God and the soul, nothing more. That same twofold desire impels and directs Augustine in the *Confessions,* wherein he addresses first the activity of the soul and then the activity of God. Thus, while the first nine books of the *Confessions* are autobiographical, telling the temporal story of his soul, the last three books are theological, commenting on the eternal story of God. In between, in Book X, Augustine explores the labyrinth of memory and meditates on the memory of God. Then, in Book XI, Augustine conducts a sustained philosophical investigation of time, wherein he reveals the unique relationship between the soul and God, between autobiography and the Bible, between time and eternity.

The first nine books of the *Confessions* comprise Augustine's response to the question, "Who are you?" (Book X), a question that he addresses to himself. These books tell a story, spread across time as the "fallen" self is spread across time. Time is indeed the medium both of the self and of its story. In the midst of Book XI, however, Augustine wonders skeptically about the very existence of time. The past, he suggests, does not exist, for it is no longer. Similarly, the future does not exist, for it is not yet. Nor does the present exist, for any true present, indivisible into past and future, is without extension. And if time does not exist, neither does the self. Augustine and his life story are thus called radically into question. The self, dispersed in time, shares in the nothingness of time. Led by his own doubt to a personal and temporal void,

Augustine becomes a desperate question to himself, a question inseparable from that of time.

Augustine's startling response to this question of time and self, a response etched in his *Confessions* and developed fully in his treatise *On the Trinity,* is that time, or more specifically the soul's own life-time, does not exist unless the soul creates it. The soul's time is for the soul to create through its own activities of memory, expectation, and attention. For the soul there is really only one time, the imaginatively extended present, constituting the presence of the past through memory and the presence of the future through expectation. It is in such a moment that Augustine himself composes his autobiography, virtually creating his life-time with his own words.

The autobiographical moment and act, in which Augustine summons his life-time in speech, reflect the biblical moment and act in which God reveals in words the creation of time and of all reality. It is not surprising that the story of the soul should reflect the story of God, for the soul, according to Augustine, is the image of God in what it is and in what it does. The soul speaks and its speech is creative, just as God speaks and his speech is creative. The soul creates its own life-time, its own personal reality, just as God creates all time and reality itself. Before the soul and God utter their respective words, there is nothing.

Neither Augustine's autobiography nor the Bible, however, are the heart of the matter. Both are mere accounts, respectively, of human and divine creativity. Both are once removed from what they relate. Their outspoken words recall earlier unsounded words, those inner expressions of will that virtually constitute reality. God's creative word constitutes all time and all reality. The soul's creative word constitutes its own life-time and its own personal reality. God creates in eternity, to which all time is present, whereas the soul creates in that extended present to which its own imagined past and future are present through memory and expectation. The soul acts in the image of God. It cannot do otherwise. Time is the *imitatio* of eternity.

Augustine's bold assertion of the soul's temporality, its immersion in time, personal and historical, together with his understanding of human will and imagination as virtually constitutive of experienced reality have not been lost on later thinkers such as Hobbes, Kant, Hegel, Marx, and Heidegger. Few ideas have left a deeper stamp on the course of Western theory and practice. What has been all but lost within the Western philosophical tradition, however, is the integrity of Augustine's vision—embodied in the very structure of the *Confessions*—in which temporality is but the image of eternity, and humanity but the image of God.

In the *Confessions,* and with relentless regularity elsewhere, Augustine makes clear that human creativity must yield to divine creativity. Stated most simply, Augustine confessed that the soul, however profoundly it may experience its own creative imagination and will to be, "must come to realize that it is a creature" (*de moribus Ecclesiae* I.21). Sin, as Augustine understands it, is not a matter of doing what God would never do, but rather of doing what only God properly does. Sin, in short, is the imitation of God, the mimicking of properly divine activity, just as time is the imitation of eternity. Sinfulness and temporality together are the medium of human life, "original" to lived human experience.

Thus, Augustine laments in the *Confessions* that he has virtually "come apart" in time, "torn into so many pieces" by time's irrepressible turbulence. The experience of time, confesses Augustine, means the *distentio* or dispersion of the soul (Book X). Fallen into time, the soul's integrity is lost beyond reach, shredded into multiplicity. Only eternity can bring unity to time. Only God, in whom Augustine sees all of his scattered moments and selves "gathered into one," can bring stillness and peace to human life. "He that made us, remade us," writes Augustine in *Epistles*. In the moment of truth, the moment of conversion, in which the soul is remade in time, "every drop of time becomes precious" (*Confessions* XI). It is in precisely this moment, this transient *now* transparent to eternity, that Augustine composes his *Confessions* and, as he sees it, tells the truth about time.

[R.E.M.]

FURTHER READINGS

Jordan, Robert. "Time and Contingency in St. Augustine." *Augustine: A Collection of Critical Essays*. Ed. R.A. Markus. Garden City: Anchor, 1972. Chapter 11.

Meagher, Robert E. "Conversion." *Augustine: An Introduction*. New York: Harper & Row, 1978. Chapter 2.

O'Connell, Robert J. "Eternity and the Fall into Time (Book XI)." *St. Augustine's Confessions: The Odyssey of Soul*. Cambridge: Harvard UP, 1969. Chapter 15.

O'Daly, Gerard. "The Measurement of Time." *Augustine's Philosophy of Mind*. Berkeley: U of California P, 1987. Chapter 6.

Ricoeur, Paul. "The Aporias of the Experience of Time: Book XI of Augustine's *Confessions*." *Time and Narrative*. Trans. K. McLaughlin and D. Pellauer. Chicago: U of Chicago P, 1984. Volume 1, Chapter 1.

AZTEC CALENDAR

As the dominant people of Mexico on the eve of the Spanish conquest, the Aztecs were the heirs of ancient Mesoamerican culture. With respect to their astronomical knowledge, they carried on and further developed calendrical traditions that had their roots some 2,000 years before their own time.

The Aztec calendar was primarily solar and consisted of a year of 365 days combined with a 260-day ritual calendar, and the Venus cycle of 584 days. It was based on a cyclical philosophy of time that was one of the foundations of Prehispanic cosmology. The solar year (called *xíhuitl* in Náhuatl, the language of the Aztecs) consisted of eighteen months of twenty days, with a remainder of five days. The ritual cycle (called *tonalpohualli*, "the counting of the days") was composed of thirteen vigesimal units. The combination of both cycles formed major units of fifty-two years, called *xiuhpohualli* ("the counting of the year"), which was the Aztec "calendar round" or ancient Mexican century in the so-called short count. Every two of these units, or 104 years, coincided also with sixty-five years of the Venus cycle (the common denominators of the Venus cycle of 584 days and the solar year of 365 days were eight solar years that had Venusian symbolic connotations).

As far as is known today, the Aztecs did not clearly distinguish these successive "calendar rounds" from each other. The basic traits of the Aztec calendrical system have been known for a long time and there exists a long tradition of specialized research based on written texts and pictorial documents, as well as on iconographical and archaeological records.

THE 260-DAY CALENDAR: THE TONALPOHUALLI

The 260-day cycle was formed by the combination of a "week" of twenty days represented by signs, mostly of animals, and a "week" of thirteen days designated by numbers. In this count, each day received one of the twenty signs and a number between one and thirteen. The combination of sign and number repeated itself only once every 260 days.

To these days, the Aztecs attributed a favorable, unfavorable, or neutral meaning that had great significance for daily life. Additionally, several series of gods exercised their influence on the days: (1) The thirteen "lords of the days," *Tonalteuctin*, accompanied them in an ever repeating cycle of thirteen. Each of these gods was associated with a bird. (2) The nine "lords of the night," *Yohualteuctin*, formed another cycle, a "week" of nine nights with a rather obscure significance. (3) There existed a series of gods or regents of the twenty-day signs who were at the same time (with one displacement) regents of the twenty weeks of the *tonalpohualli*. The thirteen "lords of the days," the nine "lords of the nights," the "lords of the twenty-day signs," and the "lords of the twenty weeks of thirteen days" were, to a large extent, the same gods. (4) Additionally, the *tonalpohualli* was combined with different colors, with the five world-directions, and with their associated animals.

From these multiple divine influences resulted the augural meaning of individual days. The *tonalpohualli* was a complex astrological system, and its interpretation for divinatory ends was carried out by a specialized branch of priesthood called *tonalpouhque*. By this calendar the following matters of everyday life were regulated: the name days of children, dates for marriages, interpretation of dreams, medical treatments, and prognoses for all kinds of undertakings. However, these dates were also crucial for political history: they determined the days of the succession of kings, the initiation of battles, and other important dates in Aztec historical record keeping.

Originally, the 260-day calendar may have been derived from solar observation; however, the Venus cycle has also been suggested, and scholars have not reached an agreement on this point. The preponderant divinatory use of the *tonalpohualli*, unfortunately, has obscured the issue of the astronomical importance of the Aztec calendrical system.

THE SOLAR YEAR: THE XIUHPOHUALLI

The other cycle of time used by the Aztecs was the *xíhuitl*, the solar year of 365 days that was divided into eighteen chronological units of twenty days, and a remainder of five days.

The sequence of Aztec months is documented in the sources; however, there existed variants for their names, and the year-beginning still constitutes an unresolved problem. According to the Spanish chronicler, Fray Bernardino de Sahagún, the year began with the Indian month of *Atlcahualo*, corresponding to Febru-

ary. During each of these months a major religious festival took place that involved an ample social participation from all sectors of Aztec society. These festivals were in tune with seasonal rhythms, agricultural activities, and events of political and military importance. Their elaborate ceremonialism can be reconstructed in detail; however, their astronomical implications are still too little known.

THE FIFTY-TWO-YEAR CYCLE: THE XIUHMOLPILLI

From the combination of the 365-day calendar with the *tonalpohualli* resulted the designation of Aztec days and years. Thus, the *tonalpohualli* constituted the base of the elaborate calendar system. A date was fixed in three ways: (1) by the day name; (2) by the day's position within the twenty-day period; and (3) by the name of the year, for example *one Malinalli* (day name) *five Toxcatl* (day of the month) *one Tochtli* (name of the year). The solar year could only begin with one of four day-signs, the so-called year-bearers (the signs *House, Rabbit, Reed,* and *Flint*) which increased their number each year by one and were numerically distinguishable as *one Rabbit, two Reed, three House, four Flint, five Rabbit,* and so on until the fifty-second year-bearer *thirteen Flint*. Only after 13 x 4 = 52 years did a complete date repeat itself. In this count seventy-three *tonalpohualli* were covered (52 x 365 = 73 x 260 = 18,980 days). After fifty-two years, the combinations of the 365-day and the 260-day cycles were exhausted, and a new big cycle with exactly the same dates began. This event was celebrated by a solemn rite, the "new fire ceremony," which denoted that the world would continue to exist for another fifty-two years. This ceremony was tied to the observation of the Pleiades' meridian passage at midnight.

An important issue that is not sufficiently understood yet is how the Aztecs corrected their calendar periodically in order to keep it in tune with the seasons. Presumably they did so, maybe every four or every fifty-two years, but the precise method still remains open to debate.

Astronomical observation was the condition for the development of the calendar, since only by such observation, maintained patiently throughout many generations and centuries, could such an exact system arise. However, the calendar was also a social construct, and the effort of its elaboration consisted in seeking common denominators to be applied to the observation of nature as well as to society. This cyclical philosophy of time was important for everyday life. The Aztec calendar was closely linked to seasonal rhythms and agricultural cycles; it imposed a socially defined measure of time by which it regulated economic, political, and religious activities of Aztec state society.

[J.B.]

See also **Maya Calendars and Chronology.**

FURTHER READINGS

Aveni, Anthony F. *Skywatchers of Ancient Mexico.* Austin: U of Texas P, 1980.

Broda, Johanna. *The Mexican Calendar as Compared to Other Mesoamerican Systems.* Acta Ethnologica et Linguistica no. 15. Vienna: Institut für Völkerkunde der Universität Wien, 1969.

Caso, Alfonso. *Los Calendarios Prehispanicos.* Mexico City: Instituto Nacional de Antropología e Historia, 1967.

Edmonson, Munro S. *The Book of the Year: Middle American Calendrical Systems.* Salt Lake City: U of Utah P, 1988.

Tichy, Franz. *Die geordnete Welt indianischer Völker (Ein Beispiel von Raumordnung und Zeitordnung im Vorkolumbischen Mexiko).* Stuttgart: Franz Steiner Verlag, 1991.

BAUDELAIRE, CHARLES (1821–1867)

As Samuel Macey has argued, for the romantic poets—though not for the bourgeoisie whose lives tended to proceed with clockwork regularity—the Watchmaker God of the eighteenth century would become the clockwork devil. For none of the romantics was this reaction against bourgeois values more true than for Charles Baudelaire and for Edgar Allan Poe, by whom Baudelaire was so strongly influenced. Indeed, Baudelaire's translations of Poe date from 1856 to 1865. After a voyage to India and the dissipating of the patrimony that he inherited, Baudelaire spent much of the rest of his life living in miserable poverty in the literary and artistic quarters in Paris, haunted by exotic visions and memories. Though in 1861 he published the drug-related work *Les Paradis artificiels, opium et haschisch*, which reflects one of the interests with which many romantics have been associated, the slightly earlier *Les Fleurs du mal* (1857) epitomizes his poetry of macabre romanticism involving an uncompromising hatred for the increasing domination of the clock.

By night or by day, Baudelaire's hatred for the clock remains unequivocal. In "L'Examen de minuit," the clock as it strikes midnight makes us question the manner in which we have used the day that has passed, but in "Rêve parisien," the clock is just as terrifying at midday, "La pendule aux accents funèbres / Sonnait brutalement midi." In "Madrigal triste," human beings shudder at the thought that the hour will inevitably strike and they will be "convulsant quand l'heure tinte." William Paley's twenty editions of his *Natural Theology* during the first twenty years of the nineteenth century might still use the analogy with a clock to convince the clergy and the bourgeoisie that God must be a watchmaker, but some poets at least were now warning men and women about a clockwork devil.

In Baudelaire's "L'Horloge," the warning becomes even more explicit: "Horloge! dieu sinistre, effrayant, impassible, / Dont le doigt nous menace et nous dit: 'Souviens-toi!'" As he points out in "Le Voyage," it matters little to time whether we travel or stay at home. In either event, the final dark journey to Hades is inevitable, Time "mettra le pied sur nôtre échine," and thereafter "nous embarquerons sur la mer des Ténèbres." Just as in Shakespeare's *King Lear*, the message concerning death is that "The ripeness is all." In "L'Imprévu," where the clock again warns of damnation, "L'Horloge, à son tour, dit à voix basse: 'Il est mûr. . . .'" But Baudelaire goes beyond Shakespeare's lack of a Christian optimism through which to mellow the ripeness. Time is now endowed by the romantics with a quality of clockwork diabolism very different from those Renaissance years when he had still been honored by Catholic and Protestant alike as the father of truth.

[S.L.M.]

See also **Clock Metaphor; Father Time; Poe, Edgar Allan.**

FURTHER READINGS

Baudelaire, Charles. *Les Fleurs du mal*. Ed. Antoine Adam. Paris: Éditions Garnier Frères, 1959.

Macey, Samuel L. *Clocks and the Cosmos: Time in Western Life and Thought*. Hamden: Archon Books, 1980.

BERDYAEV, NICOLAS (NIKOLAI ALEKSANDROVICH BERDYAEV) (1874–1948)

In his first book (1901), Berdyaev defended a "Kantian-Marxist" ethical theory, epistemology, and philosophy of history. But within a few years he had turned away from Marxism toward a theistic and subjectivistic philosophy of existence. Berdyaev was banished from Russia by Lenin's government in 1922 and spent the rest of his life in Western exile. In a late text, he identified the "conquest of the deadly flux of time" as a continuing and central philosophical concern. There may be some exaggeration in this claim, but it is clear that he regarded the problem of time of decisive importance for his own existential philosophy.

Berdyaev appears to have been the first critic to understand (in the early 1920s) that the distorted view of historical time common to Marx himself and the Russian Marxists involves a morally unacceptable reduction of the historical (pre-Communist) *present* to the status of mere means for the realization of the remote historical (Communist) *future* as end. Marxists not only devalue and instrumentalize living persons; they also perversely claim that present strife, hatred, and violence will necessarily lead to future harmony, brotherhood, and freedom. The corollary of the Marxist "deification of future generations of happy human beings" is the mythologizing "reification" of the historical future as, in effect, a kind of "vampire" which relentlessly devours both the historical present and the historical past. Berdyaev unequivocally rejects the Marxist position, on both Kantian and Christian grounds, as a violation of the intrinsic, non-instrumentalizable value of the human person.

In his own speculative ontology of time, Berdyaev draws a sharp distinction between cosmic, historical, and existential time, symbolized respectively (if less than perspicuously) by the geometrical circle, straight line, and point. Both cosmic and historical time are forms of unwelcome objectification, although there is deeper human meaning in the latter than in the former. But existential time is uniquely characterized by unobjectified spirituality, creativity, and subjectivity. It is a delusion, Berdyaev insists, to seek the "fullness and perfection" of human life in either a remembered historical past or an anticipated historical future. Such fullness and perfection are to be found only in the existential *present*, but this is not a "part" or "aspect" of time. Rather, it is an "emergence" out of time—an emergence, in some sense, into eternity. Berdyaev insists that whatever in the order of history is of genuine significance results from an irruption of the order of existential, "metahistorical" time into the historical process. The latter is marked by inescapable tragedy, and the "end of history," for Berdyaev, represents a welcome overcoming of historical time by existential time, which, in turn, involves an overcoming of every system of fixed and universal objectifications by the individual subjectivity and creativity of free "divine-human" persons.

[G.L.K.]

See also **Existentialism; Kant, Immanuel; Marx, Karl; Russian Thinkers on the Historical Present and Future.**

FURTHER READINGS

Berdyaev, N. *Smysl istorii: Opyt filosofii chelovecheskoi sud'by.* 1923 (Berlin); reprint, Moscow: Mysl', 1990. (Translated by George Reavey as *The Meaning of History.* 1936; reprint, Cleveland: Meridian, 1962.)

———. *Novoe srednevekov'e: Razmyshlenie o sud'be Rossii i Evropy.* Berlin: Obelisk, 1924. (Translated by Donald Attwater as *The End of Our Time.* London: Sheed & Ward, 1933.)

BERGSON, HENRI (1859–1941)

Bergson's radical critique of the notion of time reflects this French philosopher's leading role in the late nineteenth- and early twentieth-century reaction against scientific and mechanistic thought. Bergson also rejected Kantian idealism, in which time is assimilable to space, and knowledge is the product of formal mental construction. In proposing a theory of the self as an organic whole, he anticipated some of the tenets of the phenomenologists and existentialists, though they did not always share his fundamental optimism. He also encouraged a widespread religious revival, and his spiritual ideas developed from the critique of time he elaborated in his earliest work, *Essai sur les données immédiates de la conscience* (1889, translated as *Time and Free Will*).

Bergson was elected to the Académie Française in 1914 and was awarded the Nobel Prize for Literature in 1927. His other main works are *Le Rire* (1900, translated as *Laughter*), *Introduction à la métaphysique* (1903, translated as *Introduction to Metaphysics*), *L'Evolution créatrice* (1906, translated as *Creative Evolution*), and *Les Deux sources de la morale et de la religion* (1923, translated as *The Two Sources of Morality and Religion*). Though long since considered unfashionable, Bergson's philosophy had a considerable impact on modernist art, while his theories of time and memory appear to have been influential on literary figures as diverse as Proust, Péguy, Pirandello, Shaw, and Woolf.

CHRONOLOGICAL TIME VERSUS DURATION

Bergson believes that chronological time is merely a symbol of space and is therefore distinct from the immeasurable flow of duration (*durée*), which is no less than the essence of life itself. As an arbitrary system of fixed points measurable by mathematics, chronological time perceives reality as conforming to natural law, an intellectual conception underlying all physical science. By subdividing time into a series of consecutive moments, the intellect attempts to fix an unstable and ceaseless flow. Bergson argues that since things do not depend on chronological time for their existence, all standards of measurable time are relative. Chronological time is, therefore, a mere convenience that enables us to organize and rationalize our everyday lives.

Duration, by contrast, is a continuous progression of time in which past, present, and future dissolve into an unbroken flux. Duration implies succession as a mutual penetration of temporal units without mutual externality. Conversely, space implies mutual externality of temporal units without succession. Founded on change, duration leads to perpetual recreation of the self in its immediacy. It is a dynamic process of sustained becoming that cannot be halted or isolated at a particular point of being; thus, the becoming *is* our being. We live, move, and have our being in time. Its subdivision into a series of static moments is, therefore, false: according to Bergson, "It is quite possible to divide an object, but not an act." Bergson perceives a link between time and space via a process of "endosmosis," whereby time "is space in so far as it is homogeneity, and duration in so far as it is succession." However, endosmosis is at best a concession to science, and there may well be an element of parody in Bergson's use of the term.

Bergson believes that we apprehend duration through intuition, though he can only explain intuition by analogy with certain pure mathematical principles. Intuition also reveals the instinctive and anti-material life force (*élan vital*), whose creative power can lead us away from intellectual inhibition toward spiritual truth and positive action. Hence, freedom and necessity combine in Bergson's formulation: "Spirit borrows from matter the perceptions on which it feeds, and restores them to matter in the form of movements which it has stamped with its own freedom." Bergson believes that the function of art is to express this dynamic fusion of thought and action.

MEMORY

In his second major work, *Matière et mémoire* (1896, translated as *Matter and Memory*), Bergson argues that mind and matter intersect in memory. If duration stresses the persistence of the past into the present, then the faculty of memory permits an unlimited preservation of accumulated time. Memory stores the past but never separates it wholly from present perception. Since the act of memory takes place only in the present, each perception is also an opportunity for recollection. However, recollection is more than merely a weakened perception, since Bergson, like Freud, maintains that the failure of memory does not depend on the ability to forget but on the inability to remember.

Bergson insists on a clear distinction between habitual and independent memory. Representing the survival of the past through motor mechanisms, habitual recollection is a fully conscious act of volition, whose function Bergson likens to the focusing of the lens of a camera. Associating but also isolating ideas, this is the form of memory generally studied by psychologists. Occurring wholly by chance, independent recollection is both spontaneous and capricious. For Bergson, this aleatory element may be dangerous in that it detracts from our ability to control our actions and to direct them toward a particular goal. Moreover, the sophisticated nature of independent recollection may cause the subject to be unable to distinguish between the memory itself and present perception. Yet Bergson still maintains that the moments which are suggested to us by the workings of independent recollection have more intrinsic value than those we extract deliberately from duration.

It is important to understand that Bergson links the faculty of memory to action. Memory conditions us for certain patterns of behavior. Bergson thus opposes any emphasis on the past purely for its own sake, for such an outlook carries with it no practical advantage. This aspect of Bergson's thought distances him from Schopenhauer and brings him closer to the pragmatism of Peirce, Dewey, and James.

[P.M.]

See also **Dewey, John; James, William (as Philosopher); Peirce, Charles Sanders.**

FURTHER READINGS

Deleuze, Gilles. *Bergsonism*. New York: Zone Books, 1988.

Lacey, A.R. *Bergson*. London: Routledge, 1989.

Papanicolaou, Andrew C., and Pete A.Y. Gunter, eds. *Bergson and Modern Thought, Towards a Unified Science*. New York: Harwood, 1987.

Pilkington, A.E. *Bergson and His Influence: A Reassessment*. Oxford: Oxford UP, 1976.

BETA-AGONIST MEDICATIONS

Beta-agonist medications are commonly used for the medical management of asthma. This class of medication acts as a bronchodilator, mainly by inducing a relaxation of the smooth muscles which control the cross-sectional diameter of the smaller airways of the lung, thereby easing the effort and difficulty of breathing due to asthma. Even when used as prescribed, these drugs can produce undesirable effects like tremor, restlessness, and increased heart rate. Beta-agonist medication is available in many forms such as elixirs, aerosols, tablets, and parenteral solutions.

Beta-agonist aerosol medications have been prescribed for many decades as a maintenance therapy for asthma. The traditional beta-agonist aerosol medications exert their effect immediately, although they are short acting, having a duration of effect of four to five hours only. Thus they are often prescribed for use several times daily at equal intervals. However, recent studies indicate the use of such aerosol bronchodilator medications three to five times a day can actually result in a decrement of airway function and worsening of the asthmatic condition. For this reason, it is currently recommended that conventional short-acting aerosol bronchodilator medications be used only for the relief of asthma symptoms when they occur. Currently, there is great interest in newer forms of beta-agonist bronchodilator medications which have a longer (twelve-hour) duration of effect. These aerosol medications, which are dosed twice daily, seem to exert excellent therapeutic effect with minimal side effects.

The effectiveness of conventional, short-acting aerosol medications varies according to the time, with reference to circadian (twenty-four-hour) rhythms of airway function, when they are dosed. Their beneficial effect on the airways is greatest when used in the morning on arising from sleep, and in the evening before bedtime. In stable asthma patients, the effect of beta-agonist aerosol medication is negligible when used around midday.

Tablet beta-agonist medications are also used in the medical management of asthma. Presently, sustained-release tablet formulations are used according to a twelve–hour, equal-interval, equal-dosing regimen. Yet many patients continue to experience asthma breakthrough nocturnally. In Europe, some physicians have found it possible to optimize the effectiveness of such tablet medications by dividing the daily dose so that one-third is ingested in the morning and the remaining two-thirds in the evening. This dosing schedule represents a *chrono-optimization* of sustained-release beta-agonist tablets for patients who suffer from nocturnal asthma. Recently, one European pharmaceutical company has developed a beta-agonist tablet chronotherapy. When ingested before bedtime, elevated levels of the drug are achieved in the lungs overnight, resulting in a decreased risk of asthma nocturnally, when symptoms most commonly occur, and without significant incidence of side effects. The chronotherapy of the newer, long-acting beta-agonist aerosol medications (for example, unequal dosing at different times during the twenty-four hours) still awaits exploration.

[M.H.S.]

See also **Asthma; Chronotherapy; Theophylline.**

BIG BANG THEORY

Our earthbound viewpoint dictates how we see the hierarchy of the universe: from the Solar System, past other stars near the sun, our ken extends out into the Milky Way galaxy, and then beyond to other galaxies. The Milky Way, composed of about 10 billion stars like the sun, is like millions of other galaxies scattered throughout the universe. The most naive question we can ask about our universe is perhaps the most profound: "What holds it all up?"

According to currently accepted physics, there are only four known forces in the universe. Two are nuclear forces that act only over distances comparable to the size of an atomic nucleus. A third, the electromagnetic force, can attract or repel over long distances, but is not a force important in cosmology because macroscopic objects like baseballs, people, stars, and galaxies carry no appreciable electric charge. The last remaining force, gravity, although intrinsically the weakest, is the only one of the four forces that is cumulative on cosmic scales. If the universe needs to be "held up," it is to counter the constant tug of gravity that pulls the galaxies toward one another.

It has often been supposed that the universe is essentially uniform and static, but a static cosmology is in direct conflict with our concept of gravity: with no opposing force to prevent it, galaxies must soon begin to fall in toward one another. Einstein recognized this conflict when he developed his general theory of relativity in 1916, and introduced into the equations a fudge factor, the cosmological constant, to keep the universe static against the gravitational attraction. But only a decade or so after his theory was published, astronomers discovered that in the light from galaxies, characteristic atomic emission lines appeared to be Doppler-shifted to lower frequencies, toward the red end of the spectrum. Just as the lowered pitch of a train whistle means it is moving away, the redshifted light from galaxies means they are moving away from each other at velocities comparable to the speed of light. The universe is neither static nor collapsing under gravity: the galaxies are rushing away from one another at enormous speeds as if they were shrapnel from a grenade. No bigger explosion is conceivable than that of the universe itself. We are like the expanding debris of a big bang.

The single observation considered by astronomers to be the most conclusive evidence for the big bang theory is that the sky is filled with a uniform and isotropic background radiation. When the effects of local galactic motions are subtracted, the spectrum of this cosmic microwave background perfectly resembles the radiation of a "blackbody" at 3 degrees K (Kelvin). A blackbody, defined as any object that emits and absorbs radiation equally, has a characteristic and predictable spectral emission for a particular temperature. The universe itself must at all times constitute a blackbody since radiation cannot escape it—the universe is by definition everything, so there is nowhere else for radiation to go. The blackbody radiation that pervades all space is most easily explained as the remnant of the cosmic flash that accompanied the big bang. For the first million years or so after the big bang, space was filled with a hot ionized plasma of electrons and protons much like that in the core of the sun. When the universe cooled down to about 3,000 degrees, the opaque plasma could combine to form hydrogen atoms. Suddenly the universe became transparent, and a blast of radiation characteristic of a 3,000K blackbody streamed unimpeded throughout space. Since the universe before recombination was opaque, this moment is as far into the past as we can ever hope to see. The radiation has been red shifted by a factor of 1,000 by the expansion of the universe, so instead of seeing a 3,000K blackbody, the remnant we see today is that of a 3K blackbody. The tiny deviations from perfect uniformity that were detected in 1992 by the orbiting COBE satellite provide striking additional evidence consistent with standard theories of rapid inflation of the very early universe. Inflation theories predict such background deviations as the primordial perturbations in the young cosmos that eventually turned into today's galaxies.

Nuclear physics testifies further to the huge densities and temperatures associated with the big bang. The relative abundances of helium and hydrogen observed throughout the universe today (about 10 percent helium by number) are only consistent with a universe that was once extremely hot, hot enough to fuse hydrogen to helium in the observed ratio.

To find how long ago the big bang was, in order to derive the age of the universe, seems at first an easy task. Simply measure how fast other galaxies are moving away, observe their distance, and divide distance by velocity to get time. Unfortunately, intergalactic distances are so difficult to estimate that the age (and size) of the universe are still uncertain to within a factor of about two. A further complication is that ever since the big bang occurred, gravity has been decelerating the universal expansion: the velocity of expansion has been changing with time. To know the exact deceleration, we need to know the density of matter in the universe. However, studies of the motion in the grandest associations of celestial objects (galaxies and clusters of galaxies) reveal that nearly 90 percent of the mass in the universe may be invisible.

From several independent forms of evidence, astronomers believe the age of universe to be about 15 to 20 billion years. The fate of the universe is more difficult to predict, since a prediction requires both an estimate of the universe's density and its expansion velocity. At least we know what the possibilities are, and there are only three: (1) expansion continues forever, (2) it slows, stops, and reverses its motion toward infall, or (3) it slows asymptotically and simply stops. The last possibility, as an unstable equilibrium, is as unlikely as a flipped coin balancing on its edge. If the universe expands forever, eventually space becomes highly rarefied and distant galaxies invisible, a possible but rather boring fate. If the big bang eventually stops and reverses direction toward what some have called the big crunch, the universe may be recyclable, its current manifestation only one link in a chain stretching infinitely forward and back in time.

[P.J.G.]

See also **Cosmology; Expansion of the Universe; Gravity, Time, and Space; Relativity Theory; X-Ray Universe.**

FURTHER READINGS
Guth, Alan H. "Starting the Universe: The Big Bang and Cosmic Inflation." *Bubbles, Voids and Bumps in*

Time: The New Cosmology. Ed. James Cornell. Cambridge: Cambridge UP, 1989. 105-146.

Silk, Joseph. *The Big Bang: Creation and Evolution of the Universe.* New York: W.H. Freeman, 1980.

Weinberg, S. *The First Three Minutes: A Modern View of the Origin of the Universe.* New York: Basic Books, 1977.

BIOLOGICAL CORRUPTION

Biological corruption, also known as decomposition of the human body, refers to those chemical reactions occurring after death that result in the breaking apart of complex body structures. The process generally begins one to three hours after the death of an individual. Both the time of its onset and the rate at which it occurs are influenced by many conditions. Intrinsic factors are age, sex, corpulence, cause and manner of death, bacteria present in the body, state of dehydration of the tissues, fever, and drugs. Extrinsic factors include temperature of the environment, moisture, degree of exposure to air, bacteria in the environment, and pressure due to clothing or earth.

Decomposition is favored by moisture and the presence of bacteria, and increases with temperature. Stillborn infants decompose slowly owing to the absence of bacteria in their intestinal tract. The dryness of tissues associated with old age may tend to retard decomposition. Contact with air accelerates the process. An interesting expression that compares the relative rate of decomposition in different environmental media is Casper's law. This law states that a body exposed to the air decomposes twice as rapidly as a body immersed in water, and about eight times as fast as a body buried in the ground. This trend occurs because the air can carry decay-promoting organisms, which need oxygen, to the body.

The order of decomposition of various body parts is determined by the relative abundance of biological catalysts called proteolytic enzymes. Those organs containing the largest number of enzymes decompose first and those with the fewest do so last. Thus, the lining of the larynx and trachea, the stomach, and the intestines are the first to break down, while the blood vessels and the nonpregnant uterus are last.

Some signs of decomposition are color changes, nauseating odors, gas accumulation in the internal organs, and the separation of the epidermis from the dermis (desquamation) due to decomposition of proteins in the binding tissues between the two layers. These signs may appear a few hours after death, depending on the degree of influence of each of the factors that promote decomposition.

Since proteins comprise the major structural constituent of the human body, their decomposition provides the most visible and aromatic evidence of biological corruption. Proteins are composed of long chains of building blocks called amino acids. They first break down into shorter chains called proteoses and peptones, then into intermediate products called ptomaines, and finally into amino acids. The word *ptomaine* comes from the Greek *ptoma*, meaning "corpse." Two commonly occurring ptomaines are putrescine and cadaverine, whose colorful names should give a hint of their scents. Carbohydrates and lipids (fats) present in the body also undergo enzyme-controlled decomposition reactions. Unlike the proteins, putrid odors are not characteristic of the majority of their products.

The process of biological corruption can be retarded by the introduction into the body of chemicals such as formaldehyde, phenol, and certain alcohols. The efficiency of these chemicals is directly related to the amount of time that has elapsed between death and the embalming of a body. Ideally, embalming should occur as soon as possible. It should be remembered that decomposition is only retarded by embalming, and not permanently stopped. Although certain environmental conditions are favorable to maximizing the effects of embalming, no claims are made by modern embalmers that the process will keep a body intact for all time.

[B.M.H.]

See also **Thanatochemistry.**

FURTHER READINGS

Frederick, L.G., and C.J. Strub. *The Principles and Practice of Embalming.* 5th ed. Dallas: Professional Training Schools, Inc. and Robertine Frederick, 1989.

Mayer, Robert G. *Embalming History, Theory, and Practice.* Englewood Cliffs: Appleton and Lange, 1990.

BIOLOGICAL REVOLUTIONS

All evolutionists agree that, regardless of the mechanism and speed of the process, certain manifestations of evolution can be regarded as revolutionary. They are sometimes referred to as "macroevolutionary," having potentiated massive consequences of diversification and exploitation of new environments. Among these revolutions are, in approximate chronological order:

1. The emergence, from nonliving matter, of living organisms that are capable of genetically based, self-regulated reproduction.

2. Sexual reproduction, which produced genetic mixing and variation impossible with asexual reproduction.

3. The photosynthetic oxygenation of the biosphere, which radically altered the conditions of life and triggered major physiological and biochemical revolutions in plants and animals.

4. Endosymbiosis, which resulted in the eukaryotic condition (that is, cells with nuclei and specialized organelles).

5. Multicellularity, which resulted in tissue and organ specialization and diversity of form, including other revolutionary acquisitions such as the digestive, nervous, and endocrine systems.

6. Segmentation, which reinforced the consequences of endosymbiosis, and potentiated further diversity of form.

7. Acquisition of an endoskeleton (vertebral column and associated appendicular skeleton), a versatile anatomical feature that, with modifications, serves alike in the aquatic, terrestrial, and aerial environments. The appearance of the arthropod, and in particular the insect, exoskeleton had almost as great evolutionary consequences.

8. The emergence of multicellular plants and animals on to the land, establishing an independent terrestrial food pyramid.

9. Thermoregulatory and neuromuscular integrations. These permitted first the dinosaurs and then the mammals to become dominant animal forms of the terrestrial environment. They also allowed the ultimate development of consciousness and memory.

10. Logicolinguistic functions, which are most likely the foundation of the biological revolution of human evolution.

There is considerable debate over the mechanism of these revolutions. The orthodox opinion is that they were most likely cumulative adaptations that reached "critical mass," with explosive consequences. The alternative is that these revolutions can largely be considered saltations.

[R.G.B.R.]

See also **Chemical Evolution and the Origin of Life; Endosymbiosis; Evolution of Language; Evolution of the Nervous System; Evolution-** ary **Progress; Gaia Theory; Origin of Sex; Saltatory Evolution.**

BIOLOGICAL RHYTHMS AND MEDICINE

This article is concerned with the definitions, properties, synchronization, and applications of biological rhythms in medicine. When the activity of an organism is investigated as a function of time, nonrandom changes are found in most variables examined. These changes in biological phenomena are periodic and predictable over a given span of time and it is possible to talk about rhythms in biology. The ubiquity of rhythms in biological functions led to the development of a new field called chronobiology which can be defined as the study of the temporal organization of living beings, its control mechanisms, and its alterations. Aging from fetal states to death is another time dimension which is taken into account as well in chronobiological investigations.

DEFINITIONS AND PROPERTIES OF BIOLOGICAL RHYTHMS

Biological rhythms can be characterized and quantified by four parameters: the period, the acrophase, the amplitude, and the rhythm-adjusted mean. The period (t) refers to the average time interval after which an arbitrarily defined state (for example, maximum value) recurs. For instance, a biological rhythm with a t of about twenty-four hours is called circadian (< Latin *circa*, about; *dies*, one day) while a circannual rhythm is an oscillation with a t equal to one year. The acrophase (ø) is the location of peak time of the rhythmic function and is expressed in hours and minutes when the t is equal to twenty-four hours, with midnight as time reference ø. The amplitude (A) is half of the total predictable peak-to-trough difference in a rhythm, and the rhythm-adjusted mean (M) represents the midpoint between the highest and the lowest values of the function.

The properties of biological rhythms are always similar, whether found in unicellular eukaryotes (algus, fongus), plants, or all animal species, including man. These properties can be summarized as follows:

1. *Ubiquity.* Biological rhythms can be detected at the cellular level in tissue culture as well as in multicellular organisms.

2. *Inherited Origin.* The genetic origin of biological rhythms has been demonstrated directly

in drosophila, neurospora, aplisia, and elsewhere, but only indirect evidences have been provided in human cases through studies performed with mono- and dizygotic twins, with phenotypes, and with gender-related differences for some variables.

3. *Persistence Under Constant Environmental Conditions.* Biological rhythms can still be detected in conditions of constant light or darkness and they are said to be free-running which means that their t's differ from twenty-four hours exactly (for example, 24.8 hours in humans) with interindividual differences.

4. *Circadian Oscillators.* Biological rhythms are driven by circadian oscillators (circadian pacemakers or biological clocks). In mammals and certain species of birds, the suprachiasmatic nucleus (SCN) appears to have all properties for an anatomically identified biological clock. The fact that SCN does not control all biological clocks, and also that free-running circadian rhythms may exhibit different periodicities in the same individual, led many investigators to consider that circadian rhythms are controlled in humans by a multioscillatory system rather than by a single clock.

5. *Synchronizers or Zeitgebers.* Organisms use periodic changes (with t = twenty-four hours) of environmental factors (called synchronizers or zeitgebers under these conditions) as signals and cues to reset their biological clocks. In normal setting, the synchronizers are able to calibrate a biological rhythm on a t of twenty-four hours and to reset all acrophases at their respective physiological clock hours. The light-dark cycle (with dawn and dusk or the light-on and light-off cycle) is a strong zeitgeber for many plants and animals, while alternation of (relative) heat and cold, noise and silence, and the absence or presence of certain odors can also be used as zeitgebers. In humans, the alternation of rest and activity related to the constraints and habits of social life is the main synchronizer. However, it is now known that bright light (greater than 2500 lux) may contribute to synchronizing human circadian clocks. It must be noted that synchronizers or zeitgebers do not create rhythms but rather they are able to phaseshift the ø's of a rhythmic function and to calibrate their t.

APPLICATIONS IN MEDICINE

Many investigations in humans have shown that the ø's (acrophases) of biological rhythms are not randomly distributed over twenty-four hours (circadian) or a year (circannual). On the contrary, a temporal organization (anatomy in time) can be found in all functions. The circadian temporal organization of about 1,000 variables has been described in endocrinology, cardiology, hematology, immunology, neurology, and biochemistry (including the liver, kidney, and brain enzymes). This organization in time is characteristic for a given system and the related information has led to the development of chronophysiology, chronopathology, and chronotherapy.

1. *Chronophysiology.* Biological rhythms were detected in human physiology and a temporal organization can be described for each system of a diurnally-active healthy human. For instance, plasma cortisol level is very low and even nil between midnight and 4:00 A.M. but it begins to increase by 4:00 A.M. to reach a peak at awakening time. A circadian rhythm was also detected in the levels of ACTH, a pituitary hormone controlling the secretion of cortisol. As expected, peak ACTH level precedes in phase the ø of cortisol secretion. In the cardiovascular system, studies indicated that blood pressure and heart rate are lowest during the night but start to increase during sleep in the morning hours to reach peak values late in the afternoon or early in the evening. Neither are blood coagulation factors constant throughout the day; coagulation is lowest and highest at 4:00 A.M. and 8:00 A.M., respectively. These data and many others suggest that it is no longer possible to refer to normality without knowing the synchronization of subjects and the time of sampling over the twenty-four-hour scale. Time-reference values need to be considered in human physiology because most biological functions vary with a circadian and/or circannual rhythmicity.

2. *Chronopathology.* Pathological rhythmicities, as well as alteration of biological rhythms, have also been described in diseases. For example, diseases may exhibit a circadian rhythmicity in their symptoms as is the case for nocturnal asthma, rheumatoid arthritis, and myocardial infarction. In addition, diseases can be associated with alterations of the temporal structure. This is the case of the cancerous cell which has usually lost both its anatomy in space (for example, conventional microscopic pathology), and its anatomy in time. The chronopathological approach to diseases leads to a better understanding of

the disease process as in, for example, nocturnal asthma, where the rhythmic changes in the pulmonary physiopathology explain the nocturnal occurrence of the disease.

3. *Chronotherapy.* Description of biological rhythms in physiology, laboratory medicine, pathology, and pharmacology has led to the development of chronotherapy which corresponds to the determination of the optimal time for drug administration. Indeed, investigators have indicated that the administration of medications according to time-reference values can improve both the desired effects (chronoeffectiveness), or reduce the toxicity (chronotolerance) of many medications. It can also reestablish the temporal structure of body functions which were altered by diseases.

In summary, biological rhythms are present in our life, whether we wish to acknowledge them or not. Considerable evidence is now accumulating to indicate that these rhythms must be taken into account to reach a better understanding of human nature both in health and in illness.

[A.E.R.]

See also **Anesthesia and Pain; Biological Rhythms in Epidemiology and Pharmacology; Chronobiology; Circadian Pacemakers; Circannual Rhythms.**

FURTHER READINGS

Reinberg, A. *Les rythmes biologiques.* Paris: Les Presses Universitaires de France, collection Que sais-je?, no. 734, 1989.

Reinberg, A., G. Labrecque, and M.H. Smolensky. *Chronobiologie et chronothérapeutique: Heure optimale d'administration des médicaments.* Paris: Flammarion Médecine-Science, 1991.

Touitou, Y., and E. Haus. *Biologic Rhythms in Clinical and Laboratory Medicine.* Berlin: Springer, 1992.

BIOLOGICAL RHYTHMS AND PSYCHOLOGICAL TIME

In response to the natural alternation in light and darkness, virtually all species have developed endogenous rhythms with frequencies close to twenty-four hours. As F. Halberg has indicated, the pervasive nature of such rhythms suggests that this circadian (< Latin *circa*, about; *dies*, one day) temporal organization is vital to the overall well-being of the organism. Numerous systems and functions are mediated by the circadian timing system, including hormonal output, body core temperature, rest and activity,

sleep and wakefulness, and motor and cognitive performance. In all, literally hundreds of circadian rhythms in mammalian species have been identified, and J. Aschoff noted in 1965 that "there is apparently no organ and no function in the body which does not exhibit a similar daily rhythmicity."

The proof that such rhythms are governed by factors inherent to the organism, rather than by the environmental cues with which they are typically synchronized, can be derived only from studies of organisms living in the absence of external factors that may provide cues to time of day or, more generally, to the passage of time. As reported by J. Aschoff and R. Wever in 1962, and again by Aschoff in 1965, the first such experiments conducted to examine human circadian rhythms established that people exhibit endogenous rhythms averaging slightly longer than twenty-five hours. That is, under time-free conditions, the subjective day continues for about an hour longer than the natural day, although in some people the subjective day can last much longer (up to fifty hours). Thus, a subject who emerges from such an environment after one month may believe that only three weeks have elapsed.

Although there is remarkable interindividual precision in circadian rhythmicity (Wever has reported ± 0.5 hours for the twenty-five-hour period averaged from a sample of 147 subjects), there is considerable variability *within* individuals from one cycle to the next. Indeed, as S.S. Campbell indicated in 1984, only when the circadian timing system is structured by the presence of social and occupational pressures, or by experimental instructions, does it take on the precise character of daily experience. In the absence of the structuring influence of behavioral controls, the circadian sleep-wake system becomes unrecognizable as such, with sleep and waking episodes of varying durations occurring throughout the circadian cycle. Thus, for a given individual, the internal clock governing the circadian timing system is characterized by two distinct features: it is slow relative to sidereal time, and it is quite labile.

PSYCHOLOGICAL TIME

Using data collected under such time-free conditions, Aschoff showed in 1985 that long-term time estimation was strongly related to the free-running circadian period of rest and activity—the longer the subjective day, the longer the subjective perception of an hour. He concluded from these findings that the estimation of one-hour intervals was closely linked to the circadian system in general, and specifically to the sleep-wake cycle. In contrast, it was concluded that the estimation of shorter intervals (on the order of seconds and minutes) was not related to sleep-wakefulness, or to any other aspect of the circadian timing system.

If it is indeed the case that perception of the passage of relatively long intervals is coupled to the circadian timing system, it follows that time estimation should be characterized by the same features that characterize the circadian system. In view of the considerable lability in the temporal organization of human behavior, and the apparent dependence on behavioral structuring for the maintenance of circadian integrity, several questions regarding the adequacy of this system as the basis for an internal chronometer become apparent. Is psychological time also slow and labile? Does the availability of behavioral controls in one's environment influence the accuracy with which psychological time is measured? The answer appears to be in the affirmative on both counts.

Results of virtually all studies of long-term time estimation suggest that human timekeeping capacity is at least as labile as the endogenous circadian system by which it is presumably mediated. Aschoff identified large intra-individual variability as one of the most prominent features in the judgment of one-hour intervals by subjects living for extended periods in isolation. Standard deviations of subjects' estimates in that study ranged from 25 percent to 49 percent of the one-hour interval. The "sloppiness" of psychological time is also apparent in the low frequency with which subjects are accurate in their judgments of the passage of time. In studies—by Campbell in 1986 and P. Lavie and W.B. Webb in 1975—of estimates of interval durations, ranging in length from one to twenty-five hours, subjects were found to be "accurate" (that is, within ± 10 percent of the actual interval) in only about one-fourth of total estimates made.

Despite the sloppiness that characterizes individual estimates of the passage of time, a rather consistent *group* trend emerges in the way in which psychological time is perceived: the "subjective hour" routinely continues for longer than an actual hour. That is, psychological time slows down. All studies of long-term time estimation have demonstrated this tendency for the underestimation of elapsed time, and the range in the duration of the average "subjective hour"

across studies, as reported by Campbell in 1990, is quite small (1.08 to 1.47 hours).

CONCLUSIONS

Thus, as is the case for the circadian system on which it is putatively based, psychological time is characterized by two distinct features: it is slow relative to sidereal time, and it is quite labile. Moreover, as with the circadian timing system, the degree of precision in psychological time depends largely on behavioral structuring. When the human time-keeping system functions in the presence of social and behavioral cues that temporally structure one's environment, it serves as a reasonably accurate mechanism for tracking the passage of time. For example, most of us are reasonably proficient at tracking the passage of a normal day without reference to celestial cues or human-made chronometers. Yet, if required to function without the benefit of cues derived from an environment well-grounded in prior experience, the human "clock" becomes unrecognizable as such. Under these conditions, psychological time is characterized by two properties not typically associated with clocks—sloppiness and sluggishness.

[S.S.C.]

See also **Circadian Pacemakers; Psychology of Time; Sleep-Awake Cycles.**

FURTHER READINGS

Aschoff, J. "Circadian Rhythms in Man." *Science* 148 (1965): 1427–1432.

———. "On the Perception of Time During Prolonged Temporal Isolation." *Human Neurobiology* 4 (1985): 41–52.

Aschoff, J., and R. Wever. "Sontanperiodik des Menschen bei Ausschluss aller Zeitgeber." *Naturwissenschaften* 49 (1962): 337–342.

Campbell, S.S. "Duration and Placement of Sleep in a 'Disentrained' Environment." *Psychophysiology* 21.1 (1984): 106–113.

———. "Estimation of Empty Time." *Human Neurobiology* 5 (1986): 205–207.

———. "Circadian Rhythms and Human Temporal Experience." *Cognitive Models of Psychological Time.* Ed. R.A. Block. Hillsdale: Erlbaum, 1990. 101–118.

Halberg, F. "Physiologic 24-Hour Periodicity: General and Procedural Considerations with Reference to the Adrenal Cycle." *Zeitschrift für Vitamin-, Mormon- und Fermentforschung* 10 (1959): 225–296.

Lavie, P., and W.B. Webb. "Time Estimates in a Long-Term Time-Free Environment." *American Journal of Psychology* 88.2 (1975): 177–186.

Wever, R.A. *The Circadian System of Man: Results of Experiments Under Temporal Isolation*. New York: Springer, 1979.

BIOLOGICAL RHYTHMS IN CLINICAL PRACTICE

Under normal circumstances, and when we are healthy, the body clocks, the many biological rhythms they cause, and the rhythms in our environment are all synchronized to each other with a mean period of twenty-four hours. As a result, we fit efficiently into our rhythmic surroundings. This is changed if we fly to a new time zone, when the new external time cues no longer match the time given by our body clock. The problems of feeling "below par," of having difficulties with sleep and concentration, and of losing our appetite—the symptoms of "jet lag"—all show how important to our well-being is the normal synchrony that exists between our body clocks and the environment.

ABNORMAL BODY CLOCKS

While some problems arise because of "abnormalities" in our lifestyle, there are other people who suffer similar symptoms in spite of attempting to live a normal lifestyle. They generally notice that they are having difficulties with sleep at night and, consequently, are suffering from daytime fatigue and an inability to concentrate. This is quite frequent in blind subjects, though the symptoms can also be found in sighted individuals. The biological rhythms appear not to be adjusted to a solar day but rather to drift continually in and out of phase with it. The problems are most marked when the biological rhythm is phased twelve hours away from the expected position. Lack of adjustment of the body clocks to the twenty-four-hour day is probably due to the absence of light and dark information about external time (in the case of blind patients) or poorly structured patterns of sleep and activity as well as social patterns (in both blind and sighted individuals).

In Delayed Sleep Phase Syndrome, rhythms are adjusted to a twenty-four-hour day but they are phased much later than average. On a freely chosen schedule, therefore, individuals can get enough sleep (say from 3:00 A.M. to 11:00 A.M.), but while trying to live and work normally, this is not possible. A decreased sensitivity of the body clocks to normal external time cues or clocks that tend to run abnormally slowly are two possible explanations of this disorder. Finally, in some cases associated with clinical depression, biological rhythms are adjusted to a twen-ty-four-hour day, but their timing relative to each other, and particularly to sleep, is abnormal.

RHYTHMS IN THE HOSPITAL

As a result of our normal biological time structure many phenomena are not distributed evenly throughout the twenty-four hours. In hospitals, examples can be found by considering nonelective events such as: (1) childbirth and death, (2) the severity of symptoms of illness, and (3) the diagnosis and treatment of the illness.

1. CHILDBIRTH AND DEATH

Childbirth and mortality from cardiovascular disorders are not distributed evenly throughout the twenty-four hours. The frequency of births between 3:00 A.M. and 9:00 A.M. is above the twenty-four-hour average and this follows because the spontaneous onset of labor is most common toward midnight. This in turn might reflect the rhythmic world in which the fetus has lived. Thus, it has been influenced by the normal rhythms of hormones from the mother and placenta and the effects of these have been in evidence for the last trimester of pregnancy, with the fetus normally being most active in the evening.

Deaths from cardiovascular disorders—hemorrhages, cardiac death, and infarcts—all are most frequent between about 6:00 A.M. and noon. During this time, a combination of factors disadvantages the cardiovascular system. Thus, there is an increasing demand on the heart (due to waking up and becoming active), but also a tendency to coronary vasoconstriction (due to increased sympathetic tone), a steep rise in blood pressure (due to both factors), and an increased tendency for thrombus formation (since the fibrinolytic system is less active and the ability of platelets to aggregate is highest then).

2. SYMPTOMS

The existence of biological rhythms means that the severity of symptoms in some diseases are also rhythmic. It has been known for many years that fevers are worst late in the day—an observation that is known now to reflect the increased heat loss through the skin as the hypothalamus lowers the body's core temperature in the evening.

Arthritis and asthma are two diseases which show marked daily changes in the severity of their symptoms. Pain, swelling, and the stiffness of joints in rheumatoid arthritis are all most marked in the hours about waking, in part because the anti-inflammatory effect of the hormone, cortisol, which suppresses the symptoms, is least then. For 70 percent of asthmatics (those suffering from nocturnal asthma), breathlessness and wheeziness, like other allergic responses, are worst in the evening and at night. Again this is caused in part by the low levels of plasma cortisol during the night, but rhythms of histamine release, vagal tone, and plasma adrenaline are also involved. The net result is that there is a tendency for airway resistance to be highest at night in all of us, but for asthmatics, the increase in sensitivity of the bronchioles tends to cause excessive constriction nocturnally.

3. DIAGNOSIS AND TREATMENT

In the cases considered above, the best time to assess the severity of the illness will obviously be when the symptoms are worst. In addition, the diagnosis of a disorder often entails establishing if the value of a variable lies outside limits that are accepted as "healthy." Since many hormones show a rhythm with a high amplitude, a normal value at one time of the day might be quite abnormal at another. For this reason, possible deficits of growth hormone or cortisol secretion should be tested for early in sleep, or just after waking, respectively (because these are the times when the concentrations should be high), and excess secretions are best assessed when values in health are low.

If the symptoms of a disease or its causes are rhythmic, then knowledge of this can be important when treatment is considered. For example, an anti-hypertensive drug should show at least some effect in the hours between 4:00 A.M. and 10:00 A.M. when the greatest rise in blood pressure occurs. In practice, therefore, taking medication first thing in the morning might not be the best time (though it is a convenient one), as the effectiveness of the drug will be declining at the time when it is most needed. Similarly, an asthmatic must have access to a bronchodilator, particularly at night. Drug formulations for asthma and arthritis are now available that, by virtue of their rate of release or the time(s) at which they are taken, ensure adequate concentrations of the drug when it is most needed.

Hormone-replacement therapy also benefits from a knowledge of biological rhythms. Continuous infusions are rather ineffective, since the target tissue becomes refractory to them. By contrast, giving most, if not all, of the hormone at a time when the rhythm naturally peaks is more effective and requires less hormone. Such methods have been used to treat dwarfism and delayed puberty caused by inadequate pituitary secretions.

Both the desired (effectiveness) and undesired (toxicity) effects of a drug can show a daily rhythm. Many drugs when taken orally show a more rapid uptake and metabolism after morning than evening ingestion. Rhythms in blood flow to the gut, liver metabolism, and renal clearance all contribute to this result. In addition, the sensitivity of the body to a given plasma concentration of a drug can show rhythmicity. One example is non-fractionated heparin, often administered to reduce the chance of thrombosis. Bearing in mind that platelets aggregate most readily in the morning and less readily as the day progresses, and that the activity of the fibrinolytic system increases during waking hours, a continuous infusion of heparin at a constant rate might be insufficient immediately after sleep and yet render the chance of hemorrhage unacceptably high about midnight.

Finally, drugs can have toxic side effects that show rhythmicity in their severity. As an example, a dose of aspirin® given at 10:00 A.M. results in double the number of observed bleeding lesions of the stomach when compared with the same dose given at 10:00 P.M. This can also be important in cancer chemotherapy where it is drug toxicity that limits treatment. One example is the antimitotic drug, cisplatin, side effects of which are potential kidney and bone marrow damage. It has been found that administering this drug in the late afternoon rather than in the morning increases dramatically the patient's tolerance of the treatment. Studies indicate that such a protocol is also associated with a more favorable prognosis for patients with some types of ovarian or bladder cancer.

[J.M.W.]

See also **Chronobiology; Biological Rhythms in Epidemiology and Pharmacology.**

FURTHER READINGS

Arendt, J., D.S. Minors, and J.M. Waterhouse, eds. *Biological Rhythms in Clinical Practice.* London: Wright, 1989.

Czeisler, C.A., et al. "Chronotherapy: Resetting the Circadian Clocks of Patients with Delayed Sleep Phase Insomnia." *Sleep* 4 (1981): 1–21.

Minors, D.S. "Chronobiology: Its Importance in Clinical Medicine." *Clinical Science* 69 (1985): 369–376.

Moore-Ede, M.C. "Circadian Rhythms of Drug Effectiveness and Toxicity." *Clinical Pharmacology and Therapeutics* 14 (1973): 925–935.

Reinberg, A., M. Smolensky, and F. Lévi. "Therapeutic Implications of Time Dependences." *Topics in Pharmaceutical Sciences*. Ed. D.D. Breimer and P. Speiser. Amsterdam: Elsevier, 1985. 191–205.

BIOLOGICAL RHYTHMS IN EPIDEMIOLOGY AND PHARMACOLOGY

During their university training, most health professionals are taught the traditional point of view of constancy (homeostasis) in biology. According to this hypothesis, the *milieu interieur* is kept relatively constant and it is assumed that the response of the body to stimuli is comparable no matter the hour of day, the month of the year, and so on. Chronobiologists have a different perspective about the significance of time in biology because they are concerned with predictable variability in biological functions over time. If the symptoms and markers of illness vary in a predictable manner over twenty-four hours or a year, the time when certain epidemiologic surveys are made may result in very different findings. Similarly, if predictable time-dependent variations are found in enzymatic processes or in physiological reactions, the effects of drugs may be quite different depending on the moment of their administration. The purpose of this article is to illustrate that biological rhythms can be detected in human diseases and to present the main concepts of chronopharmacology.

BIOLOGICAL RHYTHMS IN HUMAN DISEASE

Biological rhythms have been detected in the occurrence and symptoms of human diseases. This is exemplified by data obtained from cardiovascular diseases. A twenty-four-hour pattern was reported in the occurrence of myocardial infarction which exhibits two peaks, a major one between 8:00 A.M. and 10:00 A.M. and a secondary one twelve hours later. Conversely, cerebral infarction was most frequent during the night, especially around 3:00 A.M. On the other hand, cerebral hemorrhage occurred more frequently early in the evening, around 7:30 P.M.,

whereas Prinzmetal variant angina was observed mainly between 4:00 A.M. and 8:00 A.M.

Asthma is one disease for which chronobiologic factors have been rather well researched. The dyspnea observed in patients active during the day with allergic asthma was shown to be primarily a nocturnal event and data indicated that the risk of having asthma attacks between 3:00 A.M. and 5:00 A.M. is fifty-fold more likely than in the afternoon. Circadian changes in the physiology of the lungs of asthmatic patients resulted in a nocturnal susceptibility/diurnal resistance rhythm to dyspnea. This difference between night and day was so important that investigators were even able to show in patients with nocturnal asthma that inhalation of normal saline can produce bronchoconstriction at night, but not during the day.

Most clinicians are well aware that the signs and symptoms of arthritis vary within a day and between days. The morning stiffness observed in patients with rheumatoid arthritis (RA) is so characteristic that it has become one of the diagnostic criteria of the disease. In patients with arthritis, pain is not constant throughout the day, but the twenty-four-hour pattern of pain is slightly different in patients suffering from one arthritic disease to another. For instance, patients with evolutive osteoarthritis of the hip or knee report peak pain at 9:00 P.M. while rheumatoid arthritis patients indicate consistently that pain intensity is higher after waking in the morning than in the afternoon or the evening. Due to large interindividual differences in pain patterns, the circadian rhythm of pain intensity must be used as a marker rhythm to optimize the effectiveness of arthritic medications.

CHRONOPHARMACOLOGY

Chronopharmacology involves the study of the effects of drugs as a function of biological timing and on the characteristics of rhythms (that is, period, acrophase, amplitude, and rhythm-adjusted mean). Regular, and thus predictable, changes were detected in the response of organisms to a large variety of drugs. These studies led to the development of new concepts such as chronopharmacokinetics and chronesthesy, and to their applications in everyday practice.

Chronokinetics refers to rhythmic changes in the biovailability, absorption, distribution, metabolism, and excretion of drugs. When a single daily dose of a medication is given at different hours of the day over a period of a few days, circadian rhythms can be demonstrated in the pharmacokinetic parameters (for example, peak height, half-life, time to peak, area-under-the-curve) of this agent. Chronokinetic phenomena have been demonstrated for most classes of drugs including analgesics and anti-arthritics (aspirin®, ketoprofen), antiepileptics (valproic acid, diphenylhydantoin), antibiotics (ampicillin, erythromycin), and for medications used in the treatment of cancer (cispatin), asthma (theophylline, albuterol), and cardiovascular diseases (propranolol, lidocaine). The temporal changes in pharmacokinetics depend on certain physicochemical properties of drugs, on time-dependent variations in blood flow to organs, and in rhythmic changes in metabolic pathways of the liver and kidneys.

The term chronesthesy was proposed to designate rhythmic changes in the susceptibility of a target biosystem to an agent. Chronesthesy can be quantified in humans by measuring the response of an organ to a fixed dose of medication which is reaching the target organ directly without being distributed by the blood. Circadian changes in acetylcholine-induced bronchoconstriction, in cutaneous reactions to histamine or allergens, and in the duration of action of a local anesthetic are examples of this concept. It must also be pointed out that chronesthesy can be found at the molecular level as circadian rhythms were detected in the binding to receptor sites (for example, ovarian estradiol, ß-adrenergic, or benzodiazepine receptors).

Finally, studies carried out in patients taking medications for different diseases have indicated that the toxicity (chronotolerance) and effectiveness (chronoeffectiveness) of drugs also varied as a function of time of day. For instance, studies in healthy volunteers or in arthritic patients showed that the gastro-intestinal side effects produced by anti-inflammatory agents such as aspirin, indomethacin, or ketoprofen are two- to four-fold less frequent when these drugs were ingested in the evening than in the morning. A study in patients with thromboembolism receiving heparin for forty-eight hours with a constant infusion pump indicated that the anti-coagulant effect of this drug is 40 percent greater at 4:00 A.M. than at 8:00 A.M. The importance of hour of drug administration was also observed during chronic administration of medications, as a five–year study in children with acute leukemia indicated that the probability of complete remission was 4.6 times better when the daily dose of 6–mercaptopurine was ingested in the

evening than in the morning. Thus, the data available so far suggest strongly that the chronopharmacological approach for drug administration does improve the effectiveness or reduce the side effects of medications.

[G.L., A.E.R., and M.H.S.]

See also **Anesthesia and Pain; Aspirin®; Asthma; Biological Rhythms and Medicine; Biological Rhythms: Inflammation and Chronopharmacology; Cardiovascular Chronopharmacology.**

FURTHER READINGS

Lemmer, B. *Chronopharmacology: Cellular and Biochemical Interactions.* New York: Dekker, 1989.

Reinberg, A., G. Labrecque, and M.H. Smolensky. *Chronobiologie et chronothérapeutique: Heure optimale d'administration des médicaments.* Paris: Flammarion Médecine-Science, 1991.

BIOLOGICAL RHYTHMS: INFLAMMATION AND CHRONOPHARMACOLOGY

The chronobiology of inflammation and the chronopharmacology of anti-inflammatory drugs deserve special consideration in a discussion on biological rhythms in biology and medicine. Indeed, temporal patterns can be detected in studies carried out in laboratory animals and in the signs and symptoms of arthritic diseases. Furthermore, the effectiveness and toxicity of nonsteroidal antiarthritic drugs (NSAIDs) vary significantly according to the hour of administration. This article will summarize the most pertinent data in these areas.

BIOLOGICAL RHYTHMS IN EXPERIMENTAL INFLAMMATION AND ARTHRITIS

Circadian and circannual variations have been reported in rats synchronized under a twelve-hour light-dark cycle. Indeed, the development of edema produced by carrageenan (Carr) was twice as fast when this agent was injected during the activity (8:00 P.M.) rather than during the rest periods (8:00 A.M.) of rats. A circannual variation was observed also as maximal edema was greater in spring than in winter. Adrenalectomy abolished the circadian variation in edema, but the chronesthesy of the rat paw to different mediators (histamine, bradykinin, and prostaglandins), and the temporal changes in Carr-induced migration of leukocytes into the inflammatory site could not explain the data.

Circadian rhythms have been described in the signs and symptoms of arthritis. In patients with rheumatoid arthritis (RA), intensity of pain was consistently higher after waking in the morning than in the afternoon or evening. The circadian patterns of joint stiffness and joint size were in phase with the circadian rhythm of pain with acrophases occurring in the morning. Grip strength was shown to be highest when the subjective ratings of stiffness, pain, and joint size were least. In contrast, peak pain occurred at 9:00 P.M. in patients with evolutive osteoarthritis of the knee or the hip, and large interindividual variations can be found in the circadian pattern of pain in these patients. The data suggest that the circadian changes in the pathophysiology of arthritis could be used to optimize and individualize the treatment of arthritic patients with NSAIDs.

BIOLOGICAL RHYTHMS IN THE EFFECTS OF ANTI-INFLAMMATORY DRUGS

The chronopharmacology of NSAIDs was studied on edema produced by acute injection of Carr in the hindpaw of rats. The effectiveness of indomethacin (Indo) and phenylbutazone (PHZ) was largest when the drugs were administered at the beginning of the resting period (for example, 8:00 A.M.). A circannual variation was found as PHZ reduced paw edema by 42.6 percent in June, by 12 percent and 24 percent in September and February, and not at all in March and April. In rats with chronic arthritis, oral administration of Indo at the beginning of the activity period (6:00 P.M.) had the largest effect on paw inflammation whereas maximal effect on grip strength occurred at the beginning (9:00 A.M.) or in the middle (3:00 P.M.) of the "rest period." These data suggest that the optimal hour for NSAIDs administration may not be the same for all symptoms of arthritis.

In arthritic patients with coaxarthrosis and gonarthrosis, the best time for NSAIDs administration was studied in 497 patients taking 75 milligrams of sustained-release formulation Indo (Indo SR) at 8:00 A.M. for a week, at noon for another week, and at 8:00 P.M. for the last week. The data indicated that the hour of Indo SR administration producing the optimal analgesic effect differed among patients because of important interindividual variations in the circadian patterns of self-rated pain. Morning or noon doses were most effective when pain occurred predominantly in the afternoon or evening, while the evening doses were preferred by subjects with nocturnal or early morning pain. When the medication was taken at the time preferred by each of the subjects, the analgesic

effect of Indo SR was further increased by 60 percent. It must also be noted that 32 percent of the gastrointestinal (GI) side effects were related to the morning ingestion of Indo, while only 7 percent were obtained after the evening dose of the drug. Similar data were obtained for the gastrointestinal side effects of ketoprofen and aspirin®.

The animal and human data suggest that NSAID administration in accordance with biological rhythms in the symptoms of arthritis leads to an optimization and individualization of drug use by arthritic patients. Furthermore, when the NSAID treatment produces too many side effects, a change in the time of administration is likely to reduce these undesired results. Research is still needed to determine the optimal hour of administration of NSAID in patients with different arthritic diseases, but the data available to date suggest that biological rhythms can be used to enhance the effectiveness of these drugs and to reduce their undesired effects.

[G.L, J.-P.B., and P.-M.B]

See also **Anesthesia and Pain; Biological Rhythms and Medicine; Biological Rhythms in Epidemiology and Pharmacology.**

FURTHER READINGS

Labrecque, G., and A.E. Reinberg. "Chronopharmacology of Non-Steroid Anti-Inflammatory Drugs." *Chronopharmacology: Cellular and Biochemical Interactions.* Ed. B. Lemmer. New York: Dekker, 1989. 545–579.

BODIN, FÉLIX (1795–1837)

Félix Bodin's *Le Roman de l'avenir* (1834; The Novel of the Future), contains an incomplete futuristic novel along with the first criticism devoted to fiction set in future time, for which Bodin invented the term *littérature futuriste*. He complains that the few previous efforts resulted mainly in utopias and apocalypses that do not stir our imagination because in them, action and characterization are subordinated to statement of a thesis. Bodin further objects to apocalypses such as Grainville's *Last Man* (1805), because they encourage despair. His critique of previous futuristic fiction thus links the aesthetic issue of imaginative appeal with the moral question of how readers may best be roused from indifference to their own futures. Bodin eloquently argues that *littérature futuriste* should employ novelistic methods to combine interesting plots with realistic visions of future social and technological possibilities such as aerial warfare and undersea voyages. He predicts that such works will become the epics of the future by providing new sources of the marvelous that are altogether credible, unlike the gods and other supernatural marvels in classical epics. Futuristic fiction alone, Bodin suggests, can appeal to our hunger for the marvelous while also remaining within the bounds of verisimilitude in a scientific age, thereby providing an aesthetically satisfying vehicle for rational speculation. Bodin's manifesto proposing a poetics for futuristic fiction before that genre had been fully developed, or even much practiced, thus remarkably anticipated the techniques perfected by Jules Verne, H.G. Wells, and their successors.

[P.K.A.]

See also Apocalypse; Futuristic Fiction; Grainville, Jean-Baptiste Cousin de; Utopias and Dystopias.

FURTHER READINGS

Alkon, Paul K. *Origins of Futuristic Fiction.* Athens: U of Georgia P, 1987.

BRITISH ARCHAEOASTRONOMY

Archaeoastronomy has its roots in investigations of alignments at prehistoric sites in the British Isles. The most famous of these is the Hele or Heel Stone alignment at Stonehenge: this stone, it is popularly believed, aligns exactly with the rising position of the sun at midsummer solstice. In the north and west of Britain, there are many hundreds of free-standing megalithic sites dating to the third and early second millennium B.C., involving stones sometimes as tall as five meters or more; these are set in the form of rings, short rows of up to five stones, pairs, and single standing stones, as well as more complex formations, and are often apparently associated with other structures such as burial cairns.

These megaliths fascinated the antiquarians of the seventeenth and eighteenth centuries, many of whom noted specific alignments on horizon astronomical events. The first investigator to undertake systematic measurements was the astronomer-editor of *Nature*, Sir Norman Lockyer, who concluded in the early part of the twentieth century that there were many significant alignments upon the sun, moon, and stars at a variety of British megalithic sites. His book, *Stonehenge and Other British Stone Monuments*

Astronomically Considered, sold widely, but was largely ignored by archaeologists.

The main development of "megalithic astronomy," as this field of investigation became known in the 1960s and 1970s, was due to the extensive fieldwork and analysis of Alexander Thom, an amateur astronomer who rose to become emeritus professor of engineering at Oxford University. His investigations of many hundreds of megalithic sites between the 1930s and 1970s led first to the idea of a "megalithic calendar" whereby the year was divided into eight, and possibly sixteen, equal months, demarcated by the horizon positions of the rising or setting sun, and subsequently to the idea of "megalithic lunar observatories," sites where alignments on distant notches in the horizon were used to pinpoint the motions of the moon in its 18.6-year cycle to very high precision.

To numerate scientists, mainly astronomers and engineers, Thom's highly technical approach was very attractive, but archaeologists, who noted with dismay his lack of attention to archaeological knowledge about the megalith builders, suspected that modern astronomers were simply projecting their own cultural context, interests, and goals on the ancient world (a tendency encapsulated in the use of the word "observatory"). Thus Thom's work opened up a gulf between the astronomers and the archaeologists, a gulf which only began to be narrowed in the late 1970s, when constructive critiques began to appear from both sides of the fence.

The essential problem is that although an architectural feature such as a row of stones may be aligned on an astronomical event, this may not have been intentional. In the absence of corroborating evidence, there is an onus on the surveyor to demonstrate that there are significantly more astronomical alignments than one would expect by chance. This inevitably involves recourse to statistical analysis, and makes the objective selection of data an essential priority in the field (see **Archaeoastronomical Field Techniques**). The subjective selection of data was a very important factor in the eventual rebuff of the more extravagant claims of "megalithic astronomy" by authors such as Aubrey Burl and Clive Ruggles in the early 1980s.

The huge passage grave at Newgrange, built and used around the late fourth and early third millennium B.C., illustrates current views about the probable role of astronomy in the prehistoric British Isles. The tomb incorporates a simple, yet elegant and spectacular, alignment on the sun, which, for a few minutes after it rises on days around the winter solstice, enters the passage through a "roof-box" above the entrance and shines down its entire length (almost twenty meters) into the central chamber where the bones of the dead were laid. The tomb was not designed as an observatory where living people would go to observe the sunrise; indeed, the design was such that the sun would continue to shine in after the entrance was blocked. Instead, the interplay with the rising midwinter sun was a deliberate feature of the architecture of the tomb, presumably motivated by a system of beliefs associated with death and ritual.

Others in archaeoastronomy are luckier. While British archaeoastronomy was finding its methodological feet in the 1980s, archaeoastronomy was growing into a thriving discipline in its own right, studying a variety of cases worldwide where our knowledge of the cultural context, through sources other than alignments, is far richer. This has recently led to reassessments of the role of statistics, which must still be used in order to prevent the biased selection and presentation of alignment data, but must not be allowed to blind us to the interpretation of human variation.

A recent project by archaeoastronomer Clive Ruggles and archaeologist Roger Martlew on the Isle of Mull in western Scotland epitomizes the new, integrated approach. Earlier survey and statistical analysis had demonstrated that the short stone rows on the north of the island appeared to be aligned systematically upon the moon at its extreme rising and setting positions in the south. The project attempted to examine this result in its fuller archaeological context through an integrated program of excavation, locational analysis, horizon survey, and statistical investigation. The results of recent work, taken as a whole, suggest that the moon was of special symbolic significance in Britain between about 4000 and 1500 B.C., especially at sites such as the short stone rows of western Scotland and the "recumbent stone circles" of eastern Scotland in places and times where society never became especially complex. In many simple societies, it is the cycles of the moon, rather than those of the sun, that are used to mark time and to delimit seasonal events, and the lunar symbolism apparently incorporated in these sites may well indicate that this was also the case in prehistoric Britain. The archaeological evidence also suggests that symbolic architectural orientations were related not only to horizon astron-omy but often to prominent horizon features such as mountain peaks. In areas such as Wessex, however, where developments in social organization led to the construction of complex sites such as Avebury and Stonehenge, it is possible to discern a definite shift from a predominant concern with the moon to a predominant concern with the sun. According to Burl, this is linked to changing developments in the "cult of the dead"; it may well also indicate calendrical developments by which the cycles of the sun became the predominant mechanism for marking time.

What, then, are the ultimate aims of our observations of astronomy in prehistoric contexts? New, cross-disciplinary approaches to British archaeoastronomy, and its role within world archaeoastronomy as a whole, have shifted the emphasis away from merely how prehistoric people reckoned time by observing the sun or moon toward wider questions. Astronomical observations must be seen not as ends in themselves, or as merely the means of setting up a calendar in terms that seem to us practical, but as part of complex, integrated ideological systems linking the celestial bodies and their cycles to objects, events, and cycles of activity both in the perceived terrestrial world and the divine world. In prehistoric contexts very few direct indicators of these systems may be accessible to us. Astronomical symbolism, however, appears sometimes to be an exception. Identifying changing trends and practices in astronomical symbolism can, in the prehistoric context, provide some very valuable clues about ideological change in particular and social change in general.

[C.L.N.R.]

See also **Archaeoastronomy; Archaeoastronomical Field Techniques.**

FURTHER READINGS

Burl, H.A.W. "Science or Symbolism: Problems of Archaeoastronomy." *Antiquity* 54 (1980): 191–200.

———. *The Stonehenge People.* London: Dent, 1987.

Heggie, D.C., ed. *Archaeoastronomy in the Old World.* Cambridge: Cambridge UP, 1982.

Lockyer, J.N. *Stonehenge and Other British Stone Monuments Astronomically Considered.* 2nd ed. London: Macmillan, 1909.

Ruggles, C.L.N. *Megalithic Astronomy: A New Archaeological and Statistical Study of 300 Western Scottish Sites.* Oxford: British Archaeological Reports (British Series 123), 1984.

———. "Megalithic Astronomy: The Last Five Years." *Vistas in Astronomy* 27 (1984): 231–289.

———, ed. *Records in Stone*. Cambridge: Cambridge UP, 1988.

———. "Recent Developments in Megalithic Astronomy." *World Archaeoastronomy*. Ed. Anthony F. Aveni. Cambridge: Cambridge UP, 1989. 13–26.

Ruggles, C.L.N., and R.D. Martlew. "The North Mull Project." *Archaeoastronomy* (supplement to *Journal for the History of Astronomy*) 14 (1989): S137–149; 16 (1991): S51–75; 17 (1992):

Ruggles, C.L.N., and A.W.R. Whittle, eds. *Astronomy and Society in Britain during the Period 4000–1500 BC*. Oxford: British Archaeological Reports (British Series 88), 1981.

Thom, A. *Megalithic Sites in Britain*. Oxford: Oxford UP, 1967.

———. *Megalithic Lunar Observatories*. Oxford: Oxford UP, 1971.

BUDDHISM

Buddhist tradition holds that the first exposure to the experience of the transience of youth, health, and life at age twenty-nine prompted Prince Gautama to abandon everything and to devote his life to the search for liberation from transience. When he had found enlightenment, the Buddha proclaimed "the four noble truths" to the world, beginning with *sarvam duḥkham*, the insight into the transience of everything, and ending with the teaching of the eightfold path to *nirvāṇa*, the transcendence of everything. He approached his former fellow seekers with the announcement: "Freedom from death has been found." Overcoming the condition of transience—its pains as well as its pleasures—and entering into deathlessness, freedom from desire and delusion, became the central concern of all Buddhists. They designed meditations to convince their practitioners intellectually and emotionally of the undesirability of bodily existence and the "ill of impermanence" (*anicca/anitya*) attaching to all beings.

The transience of everything that has come into existence became the key doctrine in the various Buddhist philosophical schools. Its verbal articulation, often in the context of polemics with other Buddhist and non-Buddhist schools of thought, leads to a variety of philosophies of time. The *Sarvāstivādins* assert the existence of things in past, present, and future. The *Sautrāntikas* criticize this theory and maintain that only the present exists. The *Yogācāras* and the *Madhyāmakas* hold that time is a fiction of the mind and that only *kṣaṇas* (moments, time-atoms) exist, with phenomena coming into existence and going out of existence every moment (*kṣaṇabhaṅga*). The seventh-century compendium *Tattvasangraha* devotes a large section to the proof of momentariness of everything and another section to the examination of the notion of the three modes of time. Śāntarakṣita holds that the theory of momentariness of things is the central doctrine of Buddhism, and by holding and proving it, he believes to have demolished all theories which maintain the existence of a (permanent) material substratum of the world, the existence of a (creator) god, and the existence of an (eternal) soul. His commentator Kamalaśila adds that "The whole purpose of our philosophy reaches its culminating point in this, i.e. the momentariness of everything. What is superficially called 'time' is a mind-construct based on the succession of discrete and intrinsically unrelated moments. While time (*kāla*) is seen only as a conventional designation (without any substance to it), the moment (*kṣaṇa*) is accepted to be a reality (*vāstu*). Things do not owe their transience to a (separate) cause/destruction, but they originate and disappear every moment (because of their intrinsically transient nature)." In the section on *traikalya* (the three modes of time), Śāntarakṣita and Kamalaśila critique in detail those Buddhist schools which assume the (real) existence of past, present, and future. They maintain that "The Buddhist Doctrine is, that there is nothing that has continued existence." They state as the genuine Buddhist position that "The yogis cognize *that* form of the 'present' thing which, directly or indirectly, has become either an effect, or a cause. Subsequently they follow it up with conceptual cognitions, which are common in character, and which are really objectless . . . . As for the Tathāgatā Himself (i.e. the Buddha), His teachings proceed without circumlocution: because the series of His cognitions are entirely devoid of the web of conceptual content."

The second-century Madhyāmaka philosopher Nāgārjuna went even further in his critique of those who attribute any reality to the three modes of time. In his chapter on *kāla* in the *Madhyāmakasūtra* he demonstrates the absurdity of imputing reality status to time by demonstrating the non-existence of past, future, and present.

[K.K.K.]

See also **Hinduism; Indian Traditions and Time; Jainism.**

FURTHER READINGS

Balslev, A.N. *A Study of Time in Indian Philosophy.* Wiesbaden: Harrassowitz, 1983.

Goddard, Dwight, ed. *A Buddhist Bible.* Boston: Beacon P, 1970.

Gupta, Rita. "The Buddhist Doctrine of Momentariness and Its Presuppositions." *Journal of Indian Philosophy* 8 (1980): 47–68.

Izutsu, Toshiko. "The Field Structure of Time in Zen Buddhism." *Eranos Yearbook* 47 (1978).

Jha, Ganganatha, trans. *The Tattvasangraha of Śāntarakṣita with the Commentary of Kamalaśila.* 2 vols. Baroda: Oriental Institute, 1939.

Loy, David. "The Mahāyāna Deconstruction of Time." *Philosophy East and West* 36.1 (January 1986): 13–23.

Mandal, Kumar Kishore. *A Comparative Study of the Concepts of Space and Time in Indian Thought.* Varanasi: Chokhambha, 1968.

Nishitani, Kaiji. "Śūnyatā and Time." *Religion and Nothingness.* Berkeley: U of California P, 1982. Chapter 5.

Schayer, Stanislaw. *Contributions to the Problem of Time in Indian Philosophy.* Warsaw: Polish Academy of Science, 1938.

Sprung, Mervin, trans. *Lucid Exposition of the Middle Way.* The essential chapters from the *Prasannapada* of Candrakirti. Boulder: Prajna Press, 1979.

Steinkellner, Ernst. "Die Entwicklung des Ksanikatvanumāna bei Dharmakirti." *Wiener Zeitschrift für die Künde Südasians* 12–13 (1968–1969).

CALENDAR: CHINESE AND JAPANESE

From early times until their replacement by the modern Gregorian calendar, the Chinese and Japanese used typical lunisolar calendars. The Japanese, who had adopted the Chinese calendrical system during the seventh century, started to compile their own calendars only in the seventeenth century, although the framework of both systems remained basically the same. Hence, unless particularly noted as being Japanese, we treat their characteristics in the same terms.

Successive attempts to produce an improved system for reconciling two fundamentally incommensurable periods—the tropical year and the synodic month—were made throughout the history of Chinese and Japanese calendars. The length of a synodic month varies between 29.0 and 30.1 days. The lunisolar calendar provided for "short" months of twenty-nine days and "long" months of thirty days. Calendar makers attempted to arrange short and long months so that the moon's conjunction would take place on the first day of every month. The day notation of the lunar month represented the phase of the moon; for instance, the fifteenth day of the month had always been a full moon.

In addition, the Chinese had an independent system of solar intervals for indicating seasonal changes, the most important phenomena in the regulation of agriculture. The tropical year was divided into twelve equal intervals of time, the element of a purely solar calendar. The middle point of each interval was called its *interval-center*. The synodic month was always slightly shorter than an equal interval, and thus an interval-center did not occur in certain months. Such months were designated as intercalary months, and in this way the sequence of synodic months was reconciled with the seasons of the tropical year. The year that included an intercalary month had thirteen synodic months. This occurred roughly once every three years.

FREQUENCY OF CALENDAR REFORM

In 2,000 years there were more than fifty revisions of the Chinese calendar, and ten of the Japanese calendar, whereas in the West, there was only one major reform—the Gregorian. For this difference there were two major reasons, the one political and the other technical.

1. *Political*. The idea prevailed among the ancient Chinese that a ruler received his man-

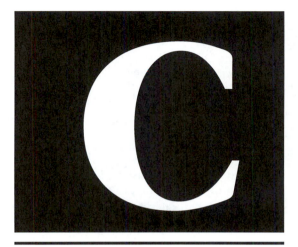

date from heaven. Therefore, after important changes of reign, and always after changes of dynasty in the early period, the new emperor was prompted to reform every institution—especially the official calendar—in order to confirm the establishment of the new order and the new disposition of celestial influences that a new mandate implied. Those people who adopted the new calendar were considered to be subject to the new regime; otherwise, their existence would be jeopardized.

The importance of the calendar to the political order endowed calendrical study with such prestige that the history of Chinese astronomy is, for the most part, the history of calendar calculation.

Gradually, however, the political importance of calendar reform dwindled. Although some rulers initiated reform to proclaim a new order and thus gain popular support, the classic identification of calendar revision with change of dynasty was largely lost by the fifth century.

The traditional Chinese practice of changing the official calendar whenever a dynasty changed was not necessary in Japan because the reigning dynasty was never overturned. Thus the political climate did not encourage calendrical research.

2. *Technical*. By the seventh century, the motive for calendar reform had become simply to correct disagreements of the calendar with observed celestial phenomena. Hence, reforms were carried out whenever a small error was discovered.

EXACT SCIENCE

In ancient China, a mean synodic month of approximately 29.5306 days was used for the purpose of calendrical calculation. In the sixth century, however, it was suggested that the anomalistic months of the sun and moon (or their Keplerian elliptic motions, in modern terms) be taken into consideration in calendar making, and the true synodic month was applied in order to attain better agreement with the actual phases of the moon and for convenience in eclipse prediction. The latter provided the supreme test of accuracy of a calendrical system.

Thus, the art of calendar calculation in traditional East Asia was the most genuine contribution to exact science. Mathematics in ancient and medieval China was largely subordinated to calendrical science. Its foremost problem was the calculation of a preceding grand conjunction, which requires the solution of indeterminate equations.

PURPOSE

The difference of purpose between calendar making in the West and in East Asia is clear. While the Western calendar aimed at schematic convenience for civil and religious purposes, the East-Asian one was intended to tally with astronomical observation. Since the goal of the calendar makers was to represent faithfully the movements of the heavenly bodies, the Chinese calendar was always closely linked with celestial phenomena. Whereas the Western solar calendar could be calculated even by a child, the East-Asian lunisolar calendar requires a professional astronomer's expertise. As a result, people had to depend blindly on the public authority to issue an official calendar.

Daily life was never affected by small errors in the calendar such as those due to the anomalistic actions of the sun and moon. The astronomical attainments of the Chinese calendar were far beyond the concerns of the common people. The failure of eclipse predictions and a small disagreement in dating the full-moon feast were only of ceremonial concern to the ruling authority.

Thus, the astronomical precision of a calendar was closely linked with the official authority and disregarded any civil convenience.

USE OF THE CALENDAR FOR FORTUNE-TELLING

The equivalent of the Hellenistic tradition of horoscopic astrology can be found in the manipulation of calendrical indexes in both China and Japan. Although the basic idea of foretelling the individual's fate was the same, the method employed in each case was distinctly different. The Chinese art, from its outset, was not directly concerned with celestial motions as was Ptolemaic astrology. Chinese fortune-tellers relied heavily on calendrical indications rather than directly upon astronomical computations or observations. Counting cycles based on planetary periodicities in the Western horoscopic arts could be replaced with much simpler abstract cycles attached to the year, month, day, and time of one's birth.

The "stem-branch" system (ten "stems" and twelve "branches" in combination make a sexagenary cyclic indication) of calendrical dating was in this sense purely mathematical. Interpretation depended upon a combination of the five forces (with their auxiliary correlates, such as geographical directions and seasons), and the sexagenary calendrical indexes of the year, month, day, and even hour of the event to be foretold. Thus, Chinese fate calculation is not astrology in any literal sense, but an application of calendrical, or time-numbering, elements to mundane personal affairs.

Closely related to developments in calendrical science was the notion of lucky and unlucky days. Hemerology (< Greek *hemera*, day) was practiced to determine the propitious moment for undertaking any act of daily life. Illustrations and notes in the margins of the official calendar, printed and distributed to the public after the tenth century, were widely used as guides for scheduling personal conduct. The life of Japanese court nobilities in medieval times was heavily influenced by the calendrical indexes, even in such a minor matter as cutting nails, and despite the fact that they were quite ignorant of calendrical science.

MODERNIZATION AND WESTERNIZATION

As calendar making was quite an important part of the social system, westernization in modern times was first infiltrated through calendrical revision at the time of the Jesuits' influence on China. When faced with a superior Western astronomy in the seventeenth century, the Chinese reformers adopted Western astronomical data under the slogan, "Let us melt Western materials and cast them into the mold of the traditional calendar." They accepted the achievements of Western astronomy only as long as it could contribute toward improving the traditional art of calendar making.

In the early eighteenth century, the Japanese discovered that within the traditional framework of the Chinese model of calendrical science substantial elements had already been replaced by Western materials. Since then, the scientific quality of the traditional lunisolar calendar had been improved and reached close to perfection, but still the traditional mold was maintained throughout the Tokugawa period (1603–1867).

Despite the earlier recognition of Western superiority in science, a radical change of political institutions in Japan had to precede the official adoption of the Western Gregorian calendar in 1873. The decisive factor in the adoption of the Gregorian calendar was the high value the government placed on westernization. A Japanese astronomer proposed a more reasonable solar calendar at the time of the reform, but the government preferred the Gregorian, despite its obvious shortcomings, because of diplomatic relations with the West.

On the establishment of the Republic of China in 1912, the Chinese lunisolar calendar was officially abolished.

[S.N.]

See also **Calendar: Western; Chinese Astronomy; European Timekeepers in China and Japan.**

CALENDAR: WESTERN

By keeping a count of the most obvious cycles of nature—days, lunations, and years—calendars help coordinate and reckon the cyclically and linearly varying needs of societies and individuals.

Although such needs arise from a psychobiological matrix shared by all people, their timing is under social and environmental control and hence it differs from place to place and epoch to epoch. At the turn of the millennium there are still scores of calendars in use around the world. This article sketches the history of the Western calendars responsible for the temporal organization of the emerging, global reckoning of time.

All calendrical time reckoning is built on two assumptions which, though essential, are seldom made explicit. One is that there is a partial, but not a complete synchrony between, on the one hand, the cyclically changing intensities of hunger, sleep, and desire for mate, and on the other hand, the apparently eternal cycles of the sun, the moon, the seasons, and the stars.

The other assumption is that these astronomical cycles are stable, whereas human cycles are not and hence solar, lunar, and stellar cycles may be used to help order human rhythms, but not vice versa. We measure the time of our rising in the morning by the position of the sun in the sky, but do not measure the time of the rising of the sun by whenever we happen to wake in the morning.

A necessary background to the use of counted astronomical cycles is the linear progression of days and years. But astronomical rhythms suggest eternal return. They do not manifest linear changes noticeable within individual, tribal, or even national memory. It is likely, therefore, that the linear counting of years has not arisen from anything in the geological or astronomical world, but from the projection of human and animal birth, life, and death on the universe. In this encyclopedia, the linear counting of years is dealt with under **Chronology**.

Notations on bones found in France and estimated to be 28,000–30,000 years old have been interpreted as records of the waxing and waning of the moon for more than two lunations. A bone plaque dating from about 9000 B.C. is believed to show lunations extending to three and a half years, engraved in a format that may be interpreted as indicating the equinoxes and solstices.

How did the carvers of these bones make the observations which they are believed to have recorded? We do not know. But the simplest instrument that can be used to reckon the progress of days and seasons is a sun stick, which is a vertical stick casting a shadow. The changing directions and lengths of the shadow during the day measures the hours of the day. The seasonal variations of the length of the shadow indicate the part of the year. Sundials are refined versions of sun sticks. The part of the sundial whose shadow shows the hours and seasons is called the gnomon, from the Greek, meaning translator, interpreter, or one who knows. Indeed, the gnomon mediates between heaven and earth. It translates the regularities of solar motion into the regularities of a temporal framework that is useful for organizing human actions. The motion of the shadow represents the heavenly domain; the lines engraved on the sundial, the earthly, social world. The two processes are connected by the belief of the dialer that the regularities of the solar motion are permanent.

The stone circles of Scotland, Ireland, and England dating from the late Neolithic and early

Bronze Age are also calendars, but instead of providing a shadow moving on a grid, they are observatories. Their best known example is Stonehenge on the Salisbury Plain, erected some time between 1800 and 1400 B.C. It is believed to have been used for the making of astronomical observations such as the counting of days in lunar months, for determining the days of summer and winter solstices, and possibly for the predicting of eclipses. For what purpose such calendrical data were employed by the people who erected Stonehenge and the other more than 600 stone circles is not known.

The oldest calendrical system whose details and uses are known is that of pre-dynastic Egypt. It was a calendar of 365 days, divided into twelve months of thirty days and five extra days. The beginning of the year was celebrated at the heliacal rising of the brightest star—our Sirius, their Sothis—an event that coincided more or less with the yearly flooding of the Nile and thus signaled the beginning of the fertile season. But since the tropical year is about 365 $1/4$ days long, the civil year of 365 days began to retrogress with respect to the Sothic year. The two new years would coincide every 1,460 years, a period known as the Sothic cycle. Calculations backward from a known coincidence in A.D. 139 suggest that the Egyptian calendar might have been in use as early as 4242 B.C.

The Mesopotamian calendar of Sumer, Babylon, and Assyria admitted both lunar and solar years. The lengths of the months were determined by actual lunations, each beginning with the observation of the first appearance of the lunar crescent. The year began with the new moon that rose closest following the vernal equinox. The division of the ecliptic into equal parts, known today in its later form as the Zodiac with its twelve signs, was also a Mesopotamian invention.

The Egyptians divided the time from sunrise to sunset, and from sunset to sunrise into twelve equal hours, making the length of the hours dependent on the time of the year and on geographical latitudes. Seasonal hours, as they are called, disappeared only with the invention of mechanical clocks. The Sumerians, having realized the impracticality of unequal hours for astronomical purposes, divided the whole day into twelve equal hours. We have inherited the twenty-four-hour division from the Egyptians, and the equal hours from the Sumerians.

Greek calendrical reckoning was chaotic, even though from the sixth century B.C. onward,

Greek astronomers began to derive ways for reconciling the incommensurable lengths of days, lunations, and years. A lunisolar calendrical system that survives to our own age, having been incorporated in the Julian and later in the Gregorian calendar, was proposed in 432 B.C. by the Athenian astronomers Meton and Euctemon. Taking the length of the synodic month to be 29 $1/2$ days and the solar year as 365 $5/19$ days, they discovered that nineteen tropical years were very nearly equal to 235 lunations (6,940 days). This lunisolar unit, known as the Metonic cycle, was combined with the many other calendrical cycles used by the Greeks in agriculture and in keeping order in the tenures of Athenian magistrates.

The ancient Hebrew calendar was fashioned after the Babylonian one, a mute historical witness to the exile of the Jewish people in Babylon during the sixth century B.C. Their pre-Babylonian time-reckoning is virtually unknown. The Hebrew calendar in use today is a partial replacement of the inherited Babylonian system, adopted probably in the fourth century A.D. It consists of twelve lunar months alternating between twenty-nine and thirty days, with two of the months varying in length. The lunar years so constructed have 353, 354, or 355 days. They are kept in phase with the solar year by intercalating a thirty-day month seven times in the nineteen-year Metonic cycle, yielding six kinds of years differing in lengths. Depending on the way the major holidays are situated within each year, there is a total of fourteen different types of years. This complement of years, together with the free-running line of seven-day weeks—also inherited from Babylon—is made more complicated by the requirement that certain religious events must not occur on certain days of the week. The year begins with the celebration of Rosh Hashana, in September or early October.

The earliest Roman calendar—traditionally attributed to Romulus, legendary cofounder of Rome—consisted of six months of thirty days, four of thirty-one days, and an uncounted winter period. Numa Pompilius (traditionally 715–672 B.C.), the legendary second king of Rome, is credited with adding two months for the winter period, thereby lengthening the calendar year to 354 days. The year began in March and ended with the seventh, eighth, ninth, and tenth months. Their names (based on Latin numerals) remain enshrined in the terms *September*, *October*, *November*, and *December*.

The Roman republican calendar is believed to have been promulgated at the turn of the fifth century B.C. It was comprised of twelve months of twenty-eight, twenty-nine, and thirty-one days, adding up to 355 days. The year began in January, a custom that was later adopted by the Julian and the Gregorian calendars. As a result of unreliable intercalations, by the middle of the first century B.C. the spring equinox of the calendar lagged behind the astronomical equinox by eight weeks.

It was during his sojourn to Egypt in 48 B.C. that Julius Caesar began to think of reforming the republican calendar. He secured the cooperation of Sosigenes, an Alexandrian astronomer and philosopher who advised him to abandon the lunar calendar altogether. He also recommended that the new calendar follow the old Egyptian one, but with the year lengthened to 365 $1/4$ days and the months arranged with respect to the solar year. Their lengths alternated between thirty-one and thirty days except for February, which had twenty-eight days. The Julian year thus became 365 days long, with an intercalary day inserted in February every four years. July, named after Julius Caesar, had thirty-one days, whereas August, named after Augustus Caesar, had only thirty days. Possibly because he regarded this as a slight, Augustus ordered his month increased to thirty-one days. To avoid three thirty-one-day months in a row, the lengths of the rest of the months were rearranged leaving us with "Thirty days hath September. . . ."

But the length of the tropical year (as measured with today's instruments) is not 365.25 but 365.24219879 mean solar days, with corrections to be added for the century. Consequently, the difference between the Julian and the tropical year began to accumulate until by the mid-sixteenth century, the calendrical vernal equinox came ten days after the astronomical one. Had the calendar remained uncorrected, Easter, whose date was tied to the calendrical equinox, would have been celebrated later and later in the year, carrying all the movable feasts with it. To assure synchrony between the ecclesiastical and astronomical calendars, the Council of Trent (1545) authorized the pope to arrange for whatever corrections were necessary.

The reasons why an agreement between heavenly and earthly cycles was judged important are complex; it is impossible to present them briefly and under a single perspective. But they may be implied by remembering that the ecclesiastical year is a celebration of the story of the birth, life, death, and resurrection of Christ and, through that story, a representation of the destiny of man on earth. The steadfastness of this yearly cycle with respect to the eternally stable rhythms of nature assured the faithful that the power of the church and of its moral teachings were themselves eternal and timeless. The scientific accuracy of the calendar assumed significance only in the service of the mission of the church.

Although work on the new calendar began soon after the Council of Trent, it was not until 1572, the first year of the reign of Pope Gregory XIII, that the reform was completed and the calendar promulgated. It was immediately adopted by Catholic but not by Protestant lands and towns. From 1582 until the mid-eighteenth century, Europe remained a kaleidoscope of calendars, with neighboring towns often using different systems. Bulgaria did not adopt the Gregorian calendar until 1916, Turkey until 1927.

For much but not all of Christian Europe after about the fifth century, the year began with the first of March; then, from the ninth century on, it began with the Day of Annunciation or Lady's Day on March 25, erroneously identified in the Julian calendar as the day of the vernal equinox. This placed Christ's birth on December 25, again erroneously identified as the day of the winter solstice. In Anglo-Saxon England, the year began on the 25th of December. From the eleventh century it began with January 1, later with March 25, and it remained that way until the Gregorian calendar with its new year on January 1 was adopted in 1752.

The Gregorian year is 365.2425 mean solar days. To ensure this length, the leap year was manipulated: no centennial year is a leap year unless it is divisible by 400. This adjustment makes the Gregorian system gain on the astronomical year no more than one day in 3,560 years, if second order corrections and unpredictable changes in the rate of the earth's rotation are neglected.

All this is but a coarse tuning between the ecclesiastical or social cycle and the cycles of the sun, moon, and the stars. To this system of synchronization one must add the fine tuning of the earthly year demanded by political and economic considerations. For instance, in the United States, Independence Day is always July 4 regardless of the day of the week, just as Thanksgiving Day is the fourth Thursday in November regardless of the day of the month. Lincoln's birthday used to be celebrated on February 12, and Washington's on February 22, until they were combined into a single Presidents' Day on the Monday between the two, thus making it possible for people to have long weekends.

Let this American calendrical fine tuning be an example of the archetype of its kind: an extensive debate that stretched from the second to the eighth centuries and is known as the Easter controversy. The question was: When to celebrate Easter?

All four Gospels concur on the sequence of events that led up to Christ's Passion: the celebration of the Passover, his betrayal and trial, his crucifixion, and his resurrection. They also agree that he was crucified and died on a Friday, the first day of Passover, and rose on the third day thereafter. This places the Resurrection on the first day of the Jewish (and American) week, which is Sunday.

From the early history of Christianity, the Western churches celebrated Easter on Sunday, the day of Resurrection. Eastern churches did so on the day of Crucifixion, which was on the fourteenth day of the Jewish month Nisan, regardless of the day of the week on which it might fall. But the day of Crucifixion so determined was thereby tied to the Jewish Passover, a connection that many of the early Western churchmen would have preferred to eliminate. There ensued a controversy between Eastern and Western preferences to which, one must stress, several fine-tuning controversies of local nature were added. The Council of Nicaea (A.D. 325) favored the Roman custom and ruled that Easter was to be celebrated on the next Sunday after (but not on) the fourteenth day of the paschal moon (month), reckoned from the day of the new moon, inclusive. In its turn, the paschal moon was defined as the calendar moon whose fourteenth day falls on, or is next following the vernal equinox, taken to be the twenty-first of March. The rule assured that Easter would remain in the spring, close to the astronomical equinox, but not tied to Passover.

Although the controversy subsided after the eighth century, differences remained. Thus, in Eastern Orthodoxy the greatest feast of the year is Good Friday and not Easter Sunday. Also, Easter is often later than in the Western church because the Eastern rites use the Julian calendar for establishing the date of the equinox. This introduces a thirteen-day delay (because of the Julian count), and another delay of four days (because the Julian calendar takes the day of the equinox as March 25). Furthermore, in Eastern tradition, Easter must follow the Jewish Passover but never precede or coincide with it.

Calendrical differences in celebration help maintain and even define group identity through temporal segregation. An example is the practice of the three great monotheistic religions to have different days of rest: Muslims have Fridays, Jews Saturdays, and Christians Sundays. The closely woven scheduling systems of industrialized countries are secular examples of temporal segregation by means of the calendar.

The art and science of calendar making, in its earliest form, is indistinguishable from the history of astronomical observations, theory, and measurement. The first formal body of knowledge that may be uniquely identified with the Western calendar is known by its medieval name as the science of computus. Its concern was the preparation of tracts and tables necessary for keeping track of astronomical and ecclesiastical cycles. Computistic literature formed the first extensive elaboration of medieval scientific theory from its second-century beginning to the turn of the first millennium. It reached its mature form in the works of a Northumbrian monk, known to later ages as the Venerable Bede (672–735). In a series of treatises culminating in *De Temporum Rationae* ("On the Reckoning of Time"), he showed how to use the nineteen-year Metonic cycle to calculate Easter tables. He also discussed problems of time measurement and gave examples of useful arithmetic computations.

The years of each Metonic cycle were numbered consecutively from one to nineteen; the number of a year within the Metonic cycle—a lunisolar parameter—was called its golden number. Next, an ecclesiastical lunar calendar had to be calculated, tabulating the dates of the ecclesiastical new moons (as defined by the Council of Nicaea) against the golden numbers. This was an idealized lunisolar table. As a way of identifying the dates of all Sundays in a year, the first seven letters of the alphabet were then placed against the days of each year, beginning with "A" for January 1. The letter that stood against every Sunday of a year was called the dominical letter of the year; it would retrograde for each year by one place, and would leap over a letter for each fourth year. (Hence, we have our leap years.) Using these tables, a paschal table could then be compiled, giving the dates of Easter in the Julian calendar. This table could then be used for the making of Julian paschal tables.

The Gregorian calendar with its systematic corrections for the precise length of the year demanded a recalculation of the dates of the ecclesiastical new moons. This took the form of replacing the table of golden numbers with the table of epacts (from the Greek, meaning intercalation) that took into account not only the years but also the centuries. Likewise, for a Gregorian paschal table, the table of dominical letters had to be revised.

The science of calendar making demanded increasing accuracy in the determination of solar and lunar periods and, through that demand, it promoted observational and theoretical astronomy and its related craftsmanship. Its mode of thinking encouraged the practice of expressing physical change in terms of mathematical relations which, together with the developing skill in measurements, contributed to the later emergence of experimental science.

With the emergence of Western technology, computistic rules were mapped into kinematic variables such as the relative rates of rotations of gears and cams and the linear motion of cam followers. These mechanical elements made possible the construction of the remarkable calendar clocks of the West. They were models of the universe that displayed the motion of the sun, the motion and phases of the moon, and the motion of the planets in (what today is called) real time. They also showed the calendrical positions of the movable and fixed feasts and, through them, reminded the faithful of the life of Christ.

Calendrical rules in geometrical forms were represented as curves on the mater of the astrolabe (its thickest plate), against which the rotating rete (open-work metal plate) defined the positions of the sun, the moon, and the planets. In our own age, the same mathematical relationships are used in the design of calendrical computer programs, such as the software used by this writer. That program can display all days of the Gregorian calendar from 1582 forward to as many future years as a user's patience permits. The historical path from computus to computers traces the shift from the Christian calendar as a support in individual and collective life guided by moral teachings and cosmic purpose to calendars as tools in the service of secular values.

The Islamic calendar is a seventh-century lunar reckoning, serving the purposes of group identification with a religious authority. It contains twelve months alternately of thirty and twenty-nine days, making for a lunar year of 354 days. It regresses with respect to the tropical year by eleven days per year and is kept in phase with the solar year by adjusting the length of the twelfth month. The calendar equates 360 lunations to 10,631 days, with a cumulative error of a day once in about every 1,500 years.

In eighteenth-century France, there was popular demand for a calendar that would be separate from that of the Church and thus lend support to a secular, national identity. In 1793, four years after the storming of the Bastille, the National Convention promulgated the French revolutionary or republican calendar and made it retroactive to the proclamation of the republic on September 22, 1792. The year was divided into twelve thirty-day months, each named according to the season, resembling the Chinese months. The five intercalary days were feasts of virtue, genius, labor, opinion, and reward, with a sixth day for leap years, called the revolution day. Ten-day weeks were introduced, with each day divided into ten hours, each hour into 100 minutes, and each minute into a hundred seconds. But the revolutionary calendar was unable to dislodge the received version and in 1806, under Napoleon Bonaparte, France reverted to the Gregorian system.

In 1929 the Soviet Union introduced a continuous-shift workweek of four days with the fifth day for rest. The system was designed to increase productivity and abolish the seven-day week with its Sunday. But technical difficulties and the inertia of the old calendrical system forced the Soviet government to abandon its plans.

There is yet another Western calendar, used by astronomers around the world, but not broadly known by non-scientists. It was devised by Josephus Scaliger, a sixteenth-century French literary scholar, who named the days of his calendar Julian days after his father, Julius Caesar Scaliger. This calendrical cycle is long enough to contain what Scaliger judged to be the history of mankind.

Its length of 7,980 years is the least common multiple of three historically recognized cycles. They are the twenty-eight-year solar cycle (for which the days of the year recur on the same days of the week), the nineteen-year Metonic cycle, and the fifteen-year cycle of indiction (originally a Roman accounting cycle, still used for dating in the sixteenth century and even appearing in the American *Farmer's Almanac*). Its reference epoch is 4713 B.C., the year when the beginnings of the three cycles last coincided, as seen in ex post facto calculations. Its units are Julian days, abbreviated as JD.

According to Bulletin A of International Earth Rotation Service of the United States Naval Observatory, using as do all astronomical tabulations the system of Julian days, I am writing these lines on 2,448,804.5 JD. The half a day is added because until 1925 the astronomical days began at noon, Greenwich Mean Time. Thereafter, the beginning of astronomical days were made to coincide with the midnight starts of civil days. To be able to use the Julian day system consistently, it was necessary to add 0.5 to their day count.

There is no statement in this article that is not a gross oversimplification of the issues involved. The apparent simplicity of calendars hanging on walls, resting on desks, and displayed on wrist watches masks their great complexity and intricate history. They are living witnesses to the ancient practice of comparing the lengths of days, lunations, seasons, and years among themselves, molding these lengths into a numerical system, and placing this system of astronomical reckoning in the service of the social organization of time.

[J.T.F.]

See also **Aztec Calendar; Calendar: Chinese and Japanese; Chronology; Clocks: The First Mechanical Clocks; Historiography and Process; Maya Calendars and Chronology; Partitioning the Day; Periodization.**

FURTHER READINGS

Bickerman, E.J. *Chronology of the Ancient World.* Revised ed. London: Thames and Hudson, 1980.

Coyne, G.V., et al., eds. *Gregorian Reform of the Calendar.* Specola Vaticana: Pontifica Academia Scientiarum, 1983.

Kalender im Wandel der Zeiten. Karlsruhe: Badischen Landesbibliothek, 1982.

King, H.C. *Geared to the Stars.* Toronto: U of Toronto P, 1978.

Neugebauer, Otto. *The Exact Sciences in Antiquity.* Princeton: Princeton UP, 1954.

Nilsson, M.P. *Primitive Time Reckoning.* 2nd ed. Lund: Gleerup, 1960.

Parise, Frank, ed. *The Book of Calendars.* New York: Facts on File, 1982.

Stevens, W.M. "Cycles of Time: Calendrical and Astronomical Reckonings in Early Science." *Time and Process: The Study of Time VII.* Ed. J.T. Fraser and L. Rowell. Madison: International Universities P, 1992. 27–50.

United States Naval Observatory. *Explanatory Supplement to the Astronomical Ephemeris and the American Ephemeris and Nautical Almanac.* London: Her Majesty's Stationery Office, 1974.

Zerubavel, Eviatar. *The Seven Day Circle: The History and Meaning of the Week.* New York: The Free Press, 1985.

CANCER AND TIME

Cancer takes time to develop—typically the better part of an average human life span—and usually many years to kill. This simple observation indicates that timely intervention can prevent the process of cancerization. It also indicates that earlier detection of cancer is possible and that there is a substantial span of time during which a wide range of complementary treatments may be used to cure a cancer or to control it if it cannot be cured.

The living unit of the body that gives rise to cancer is the cell. The cell "chooses the cancer path" against heavy odds. Many injuries to the cell's reproductive machinery, its DNA, are required in order to give rise to the family of cells eventually recognized as a cancer. In order for a cell to become cancerous, it must endure all of these injuries without repairing them; it must also neither die nor lose its ability to reproduce. A cell that becomes injured, however, has genetic programs that command it to commit suicide if its genetic material is irreparably damaged; it also has complex genetic programs that command it to fix almost any repairable injury to its DNA. If any of the injuries required for cancer can be prevented or repaired, or if cells with these injuries can be selectively killed or cajoled into committing suicide, the development of that cancer will be thwarted.

A person's life cycle and the usually briefer life cycle of a cancer within that person are unfortunately often linked by a common end. There are other natural cycles that are of major importance to the delicate balance between a person and an incipient or established cancer. These include seasonal cycles, fertility cycles of approximately thirty days, and daily or circadian cycles.

Before listing the practical ways in which each of these time cycles affects the balance between a person and a cancer, it is important to consider why all living organisms do all things cyclically. Seasonal, monthly, and daily cycles arose because as life was evolving on this planet the waxing and waning of light, heat, electromagnetism, and gravitational force caused rhythmic changes in energy availability and even in the physical medium in which the evolutionary process was occurring. Even more than the happenstance of the geophysical location of the evolution of life, basic thermodynamic laws have strongly influenced the choice of nonlinear dynamics (rhythms) as the preferred mode of biologic temporal organization.

This rhythmic biologic time structure has evolved to maximize the stability of living things and to ensure that they do not waste precious energy. Life's absolute need for stability requires continuous readjustment of the system to external and internal dynamic requirements. This may be pictured as a cyclical activation and production, stability assessment, and triangulation, or as a reinitiation cycle. If stability is favored by additional activity, a second cycle will be initiated at the optimum time to favor additional stability. If stability is optimum, a nonproductive or minimally productive cycle will be initiated. This will appear as a relatively refractory period during which systemic responses will be damped, thus creating a period with low or no perceptible output.

Biological economy demands that subcellular, cellular, tissue, organ, organismic, population, and ecosystem tasks be initiated and completed at specific optimal times within important timekeeping cycles and in a certain order relative to one another. The regularly undulating responsive/refractory model of behavior clearly favors stability and economy. The stuttering progression to a new state caused by the cyclical readjustment of networks moves the system gradually, allowing time for accurate sensing of a new state, for retriangulation within the new state, and for responses to the new state. The frugality of having the production of one cycle available to trip a second set of product-dependent cycles so that important metabolic tasks may be compartmentalized in both time and space is essential. The cyclical nature of the coordination in time means that if an essential task is not completed in a timely fashion, the organism has a second chance to do so within a defined span (one cycle length). Escape from this sort of temporal ordering has lethal consequences.

Casual observation of biologic time structure reveals certain fundamental frequencies more or less tightly tied to external and internal environmental regularities. The internal, genetically determined, circadian and menstrual cycles are a fair example of two primary rhythms tightly tied to internal genetic timekeeping mechanisms respectively essential for organismic and species survival. Each cycle is also influenced by environmental cycles, the circadian very strongly and the menstrual cycle somewhat less strongly. Cyclic changes between light and dark can lead and shift endogenous circadian cycles, while circadian cycle shifts can affect menstrual cycle regularity. Yearly cycles, which are made clear by the seasonal changes in both our biology and our environment, are also essential temporal reference frames that interact with all other biologic frequency ranges.

SEASONAL BALANCE BETWEEN A PERSON AND A CANCER

The process of cancerization has generally been considered to be irreversible. There is growing evidence, however, that this somewhat static linear biologic view does not tell either the whole or the most accurate story of cancer development. The balance between cancer progression and health is dynamic.

Breast cancer, a disease that will be diagnosed in one of every nine living American women, furnishes an example of the seasonal balance between a person and cancer. Several large studies, on each side of the equator, have demonstrated that the likelihood of the discovery of breast cancer is highest in spring, lowest in fall, and intermediate in winter and summer. Since the average breast cancer takes many years to develop and since these large confirmatory studies derived from culturally diverse populations living in very different climatic and geographic conditions, these observations tell us that breast cancer size (which reflects both the growth of the tumor cells *and* the woman's defenses against that growth) increases more rapidly in springtime than in other seasons. Other measures of breast cancer biology—including the average size of resected tumors, the assessment of their microscopic aggressiveness, the number of lymph glands into which the cancer has spread, the concentration of hormone receptor molecules within the resected breast cancer cells, and the overall survival of women with breast cancer—are all affected by season.

Breast cancer is not the only cancer with yearly rhythmic (nonlinear) biology. As is known through microscopic examination of scrapings from the surface of the cervix ("pap smears"), all of the premalignant and malignant changes of the surface of the uterine cervix are also nonrandomly distributed throughout the year. All premalignant and malignant changes of the cervical surface cells are more frequent in winter months. Moreover, seasonal cancer biology is not limited to women. The discovery of testicular cancer, the most common cancer in men under thirty-five years of age, is also prominently seasonal. Cancers of the two common cell types of the testicle have almost opposite seasonality; the frequency of one type peaks in December or January and the frequency of cancers of the other cell type in August or September.

The realization that the biology of the balance between a person and an incipient cancer is on average predictably different at different seasons for different types of cancer can improve our understanding of cancer biology. If employed, this knowledge will also increase our ability to prevent, diagnose, and treat a cancer by optimally timing our preventive, investigative, or therapeutic program.

Preventive strategies may be most effective and most important to employ at certain times of the year. Mass screening programs for early cancer detection currently conducted at great cost could, if performed at the optimal season, generate fewer false negative, fewer false positive, and more true positive test results, thereby enhancing the effectiveness of cancer screening and substantially diminishing its costs. Therapeutically, careful seasonal modulation of treatment regimens may be more effective and less toxic. It has been demonstrated, for example, that chemotherapy is most damaging to normal tissue at certain seasons and that hormonal therapy may be more effective in some seasons than in others.

FERTILITY CYCLE MODULATION OF HOST-CANCER BALANCE

While seasonality affects us all, the menstrual cycle directly affects only about 52 percent of the world's inhabitants. Each of the members of just over half of the world's population spends about half of her life participating regularly and continuously (aside from periods of pregnancy) in this powerful biological rhythm. Many diverse disease activities have been demonstrated to be affected by this cycle. Cancer is one of them.

During the next twelve months, breast cancer will be diagnosed in almost 180,000 women in the United States. Of these, 60,000 will be cycling, premenopausal women at the peak of their economically productive years. In 1836, Sir A.P. Cooper, surgeon to the king of England, wrote in his textbook of surgery that "breast cancer growth waxes and wanes during the menstrual cycle." In 1894, another English surgeon demonstrated that when the ovaries are removed from a menstrually cycling woman with advanced breast cancer the cancer can shrink and even disappear. Surgical removal of a breast cancer remains the most common initial treatment, but surgery itself adversely affects the ability of the body's immune system to fight cancer. Recent discoveries indicate that the immune system's capacity to fight cancer oscillates during the fertility cycle. Surgical cure of a breast tumor is more likely if surgery is performed in the middle of a woman's menstrual cycle during the week or so following ovulation or, in other words, between two and three weeks from the first day of the menstrual period immediately prior to the operation. The curative advantage to optimally timed surgery is large, perhaps several fold. There are also early indications that the ability of a woman to withstand the toxicities of chemotherapy may also vary with the timing of the treatment in relation to the fertility cycle. These provocative observations indicate that this biological cycle exerts a powerful influence over the balance between a person and a cancer which must be better understood and applied to help women with cancer. The observations also suggest that when this biological cycle is fully understood, all cancer patients will benefit.

TIMING WITHIN THE DAY: CIRCADIAN CYCLES

Most doctors give little thought to the time of day at which a drug is given. In general, patients receive anti-cancer drugs at times that are convenient to the staff administering them. A growing body of data suggests that the therapeutic effect may be maximized and toxicity minimized if drugs are administered at carefully selected times of the day. This potential for a marked improvement in therapeutic index is especially critical for therapies with narrow ratios of efficacy to toxicity, like most anti-cancer treatments. The toxicities of at least twenty chemotherapeutic agents have been shown to be time-of-day dependent in mice. The anti-cancer efficacy of many of these agents, either given singly or in combinations, has also been shown to be time-of-day dependent in experimental studies. Data are now available which show that the toxicity of many common chemotherapeutic agents can be modified by the timing of delivery to cancer patients. In addition, clinical trials are ongoing to determine also if optimal timing has an impact on the response rate and overall survival for cancer patients. The availability of portable infusion pumps capable of delivering single or multiple drugs, each with their optimal circadian scheduling, has made the clinical application and testing of these principles possible.

The current perspectives of the science and practice of medicine are each built on a foundation which denies that the balance between a person and a cancer changes rhythmically and predictably as a function of time of day, time within the fertility cycle, and season. Such basic assumptions are seriously undermined by the examples given in this brief summary. As this foundation crumbles and is replaced by one that recognizes the essential nonlinearity of human biology, the next revolution in cancer prevention, detection, and cure may be expected to begin in earnest.

[W.J.M.H.]

See also **Biological Rhythms and Medicine; Biological Rhythms in Epidemiology and Pharmacology; Chronobiology; Chronobiology of the Cell Cycle.**

CARDIOVASCULAR CHRONOPHARMACOLOGY

Circadian rhythms in the functions of the cardiovascular system are now well established both in healthy subjects and in patients suffering from cardiovascular diseases. The recent development of automatic twenty-four-hour monitoring devices such as the ambulatory blood pressure monitor (ABPM) and the twenty-four-hour electrocardiogram (Holter-ECG) have greatly contributed to our present knowledge about circadian rhythms in the cardiovascular system. The rhythms in heart rate and blood pressure are the most well known periodic functions in this system. Figure 1 shows the systolic blood pressure obtained by ABPM in healthy subjects, primary (essential) hypertensive patients, and those suffering from congestive heart failure showing peak values in blood pressure during daytime with a fall at night. In about 70 percent of secondary hypertensive patients in whom hypertension is due, for example, to a renal disease, this blood pressure rhythm is either abolished or even reversed. Thus, the twenty-four-hour profile in blood pressure can even be of diagnostic value. Significant rhythms within the cardiovascular system have also been described for such factors as blood flow, stroke volume, peripheral resistance, parameters of ECG recordings, the plasma concentrations of cardiovascular-active hormones such as noradrenaline, renin, angiotensin, aldosterone, atrial natriuretic peptide, and plasma cAMP, as well as

in blood viscosity, aggregability, and fibrinolytic activity. In rodents, significant twenty-four-hour rhythms have been demonstrated down to the cellular and subcellular level of the neurotransmitter receptors and the post-receptor mediated signal transduction, for example the ß-adrenoreceptor–adenylate cyclase–cAMP–phosphodiesterase–system.

The onset and symptoms of certain diseases of the cardiovascular system also do not occur at random within a twenty-four-hour day. Myocardial infarction occurs most frequently between 8:00 and 12:00 P.M. rather than at other times of the day. In patients suffering from angina pectoris of the Prinzmetal type, angina attacks, as well as ST-segment elevations in the ECG, occur more frequently at nightly hours around 4:00 P.M., whereas in cases of an angina pectoris with rather stable symptoms, ST-segment depressions in the ECG and angina attacks are registered more often during daytime hours, indicating differences in etiology.

In light of the chronobiological and chronopathological findings described, it is not surpris-

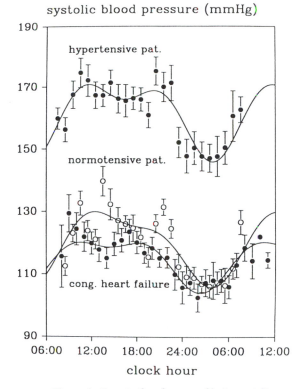

Figure 1. Twenty-four-hour profile in systolic blood pressure in normotensive subjects, patients with primary hypertension, and patients suffering from congestive heart failure.

Chronopharmacodynamics	
Beta-Blockers	**Calcium Channel Blockers**
Acebutolol	Amlodipine
Atenolol	Lacidipine
Bevantolol	Nifedipine
Bopindolol	Nisoldipine
Labetolol	Nitrendipine
Mepindolol	Verapamil
Metoprolol	
Nadolol	**ACE Inhibitors**
Oxprenolol	Captopril
Pindolol	Enalapril
Penbutolol	
Propranolol	**Others**
Sotalol	Clonidin
	Prazosin
	Potassium chloride
Diuretics	
Hydrochloro-	**Nitrates**
thiazide	Glyceryl-trinitrate
Indapamide	Isosorbide-dinitrate
Piretanide	Isosorbide-5-mono-
Xipamide	nitrate

Table 1. Cardiovascular active drugs for which daily variations in their effects were shown in clinical studies.

ing that the pharmacokinetics and the effects of cardiovascular active drugs may also not be constant within the twenty-four hours of a day. This has been convincingly demonstrated in experimental animals as well as clinical studies in man. In Tables 1 and 2, cardiovascular active drugs are listed for which daily variation in their effects or in their pharmacokinetics have been reported in man.

It is a common paradigm in pharmacology that pharmacokinetic parameters—which is to say the behavior of a drug within the body—are considered not to be influenced by the time of day at which a drug is administered. Moreover, concerning drug concentration profiles over a twenty-four-hour span during continuous drug treatment "the flatter the better" is also a common aim in drug targeting. Chronopharmacological studies, however, have now revealed that these paradigms cannot be maintained any longer: Firstly, the functions of organs such as the liver and the kidneys, which are responsible for the metabolism and elimination of drugs, have been shown to be highly circadian phase dependent. Moreover, daily variations in gastric emptying time, gastro-intestinal perfusion, body composition, and fluid distribution have been shown to influence the twenty-four-hour drug concentration profile.

Clinical chronopharmacological studies have revealed that, in general, the pharmacokinetics of lipophilic drugs such as propranolol, nife-

dipine, digoxin, and oral nitrates, showed higher peak drug concentrations and shorter times-to-peak concentrations after morning dosing than after evening dosing. The effects of chronic application of beta-blockers, calcium channel blockers, and angiotensin converting enzyme inhibitors (ACE-inhibitors) on the blood pressure of essential hypertensives were in general more pronounced during daytime than nighttime. Diuretics, on the other hand, seem to lower blood pressure throughout the twenty-four-hour period. However, there is a lack of data concerning results of crossover studies in which morning versus evening dosing has been compared within the same patient. Nevertheless, these data clearly indicate that the dose-response relationship—another important paradigm in pharmacology—can be circadian phase dependent as well. Moreover, there is evidence obtained with organic nitrates and nifedipine demonstrating that a drug's galenic formulation (immediate-release, sustained-release) can be important to whether or not daily variation in its pharmacokinetics or its bioavailability will be present. In conclusion, the chronopharmacological data compiled recently clearly demonstrate that the variable "time-of-day" has to be taken into account in drug treatment of cardiovascular diseases such as hypertension and coronary heart disease.

[B.L.]

See also **Biological Rhythms in Epidemiology and Pharmacology.**

Further Readings

Lemmer, B. *Chronopharmacology: Cellular and Biochemical Aspects.* New York: Dekker, 1989.

———, guest editor. *Recent Advances in the Chronopharmacology of the Cardiovascular System. Part 1. Coronary Heart Disease, Risk Factors, and Congestive Heart Failure. Chronobiology International* 8.5 (1991).

Chronopharmacokinetics	
Beta-Blockers	**Calcium Channel Blockers**
Propranolol	Diltiazem
	Nifedipine
	Verapamil
Nitrates	
Isosorbide-dinitrate	
Isosorbide-5-mononitrate	
Glycosides	**Others**
Digoxin	Dipyridamol
Metildigoxin	Potassium chloride

Table 2. Cardiovascular active drugs for which daily variations in their pharmacokinetics were shown in clinical studies.

————, guest editor. *Recent Advances in the Chrono-pharmacology of the Cardiovascular System. Part 2. Blood Pressure Regulation, Hypertension, and Drug Treatment. Chronobiology International* 8.6 (1991).

CARROLL, LEWIS (CHARLES LUTWIDGE DODGSON) (1832–1898)

Though Lewis Carroll subscribed to the romantic myth regarding the spontaneity of creative art—"I cannot set invention going like a clock"— an examination of *Alice's Adventures in Wonderland* (1865) and its equally worthy sequel, *Through the Looking Glass* (1872), will surely make one suspect that whatever the initial inspiration, the "spontaneous" creation must have been supplemented by some careful "mechanical" revision through which the works were consciously shaped by patterns relating to clocks and time. This should hardly be surprising since Carroll, who wrote a précis of all the letters he wrote or received (the last entry in his system of cross-referencing is numbered 98,721), was one of the most methodical men who ever lived. He was also "a clever mechanist" with music boxes and comparable automata, an academic who held the mathematical lectureship at Christ Church, Oxford, from 1855 to 1881, and an author who published extensively on mathematics throughout his adult life.

There are, of course, many regular patterns in the Alice books, but our concern here is with those related to clocks and time. Each of the works is of almost equal length and divided into twelve parts. On the level of calendar time they exactly divide the twelve months of the year though they last for only twelve hours each. *Alice in Wonderland* takes place on May 4, the birthday of the real Alice Liddell, who was the daughter of the Dean of Christ Church. Exactly six months later, on November 4, *Through the Looking Glass* takes place when the real Alice was precisely seven and a half years old. For obvious reasons, when dealing with an elderly man and a young girl, there is no explicit statement that the two books divide the day and the night just as precisely, but they do so nonetheless. Equally well balanced and appropriate in terms of the calendar, *Alice* is a springtime tale of croquet and the outdoors, while *Looking Glass* is an autumn tale of the indoors and chess.

The twelve parts of *Alice* start with the making of a daisy chain (suggesting the same etymology as Chaucer's "day's eye"), and conclude with Alice's sister engaged in "watching the setting sun." By contrast, when *Looking Glass* starts late in the November day, Dinah (the name of the Liddells' cat) had finished washing the black kitten "earlier in the afternoon." Yet, in the last paragraph of *Looking Glass*, the black kitten—who may be assumed to have spent the night as the wife of the Red King—is scolded by Alice, "As if Dinah hadn't washed you this morning!" Alice herself may exist during the night in the consciousness of the Red King. Tweedledee had told her, "you're only a sort of thing in his dream," but in Chapter XII, which needs to be reread carefully, "He was part of my dream, of course—but then I was part of his dream too!" And she had taken the place of his wife during her noteworthy game of chess. Clearly, the illusions of Lewis Carroll may have followed Alice Liddell right through the looking glass and throughout that highly creative night.

Both the structure and the content of the Alice books are involved with clocks and time. In each case they provide the activating moment at the beginning of the story. For the outdoors Alice of the springtime, the activating moment comes after she found, at first, that there was "nothing so *very* remarkable about the White Rabbit . . . but, when the Rabbit actually *took a watch out of his waistcoat-pocket*, and looked at it, and then hurried on, Alice started to her feet." In *Looking Glass* (again in Chapter I), Alice is kneeling on the mantlepiece at the side of the clock when her fantasy of pretending that "the glass has gone all soft like gauze" turns into reality. Once she is inside "Looking-Glass land," she notices that the "clock on the chimney-piece (you know you can only see the back of it in the Looking-Glass) had got the face of a little old man, and grinned at her."

If the timepieces of the two Chapters I's are a coincidence, the fact that Hatter and Hare, who appear at the peripeteia or turning point of Chapter VII in *Alice* and turn up again thinly disguised as Haigh and Hatta exactly in Chapter VII of *Looking Glass*, can hardly be an unaided coincidence of the creative imagination. Among all of Carroll's characters the Mad Hatter and the March Hare are surely the most clock-dominated. At the tea party, following an important passage concerned with the elasticity of "time," Hatter recalls the occasion when he sang "Twinkle, twinkle, little bat," and the "Queen bawled out 'He's murdering the time! Off with his head!' . . . . ever since that [time] won't do a thing that I ask! It is always six o'clock now." And indeed we learn at some length in the course of the conversation at the tea party that the Mad Hatter's watch is permanently set at the right time for six o'clock tea. Theophilus Carter, who invented an alarm clock bed that tipped its unfortunate occupant on to the floor at a predetermined time, is said to have provided the model for Carroll's Mad Hatter. But the irony is that however gentle his criticism, Lewis Carroll, like many of his Romantic compatriots, was by no means entirely free of the clockwork-like qualities that his art called into question.

[S.L.M.]

See also **Clock Metaphor.**

FURTHER READINGS

Carroll, Lewis. *Alice in Wonderland* and *Through the Looking Glass*. Ed. Donald J. Gray. New York: Norton, 1971.

Macey, Samuel L. *Clocks and the Cosmos: Time in Western Life and Thought*. Hamden: Archon Books, 1980.

CATASTROPHISM

In the study of earth history, the term "catastrophe" embodies the concept that major changes in physical and biological features of the planet have been episodic and not gradual. The idea has had a variable status in the writings of scholars from ancient Greeks to the present due to the scale of catastrophic phenomena: events and side effects of magnitudes outside the human experience occurring at frequencies on the geological time scale. Diluvialism—the shaping of the earth by immense floods—was the predominant form of catastrophe in ancient to Renaissance writings. The biblical record of Noah's flood probably refers to an event in Mesopotamia around 4000 B.C. While local floods can be catastrophic to human communities, we now know that in the 4-billion-year history recorded in earth's rocks, ocean transgression and regression have shaped both geography and organism communities.

As geological studies of the seventeenth and eighteenth centuries developed, every kind of catastrophe—divine and natural—was invoked to explain incongruous observations. Much constraint was placed on the observers by the supposition that the planet was very young and therefore big changes could only occur very rapidly. Nineteenth-century geology responded with a rational framework for scientific explanations in the form of the law of uniformitarianism, an investigative philosophy in which it is assumed that present-day processes also acted in the past. In addition, the antiquity of earth rocks was established by Lord Kelvin's work using radioactive decay rates.

In view of the brief human experience on an ancient planet, it is not surprising that support for catastrophes as major factors in earth evolution was diminished. However, in the second half of the twentieth century, a new role for catastrophes has arisen. The disparate studies of the solar system and of plate tectonics have documented dramatic large-scale phenomena that could well reflect the causes of major episodic catastrophes. But it is the recognition of mass extinctions in the geological record by paleontologists that has demonstrated the effects of such phenomena. At present, an extensive debate exists on the causes of large-scale extinctions documented in the Phanerozoic period (the last 570 million years). The disappearance of many organisms, including the dinosaurs, at the end of the Cretaceous period 65 million years ago is the most celebrated of such catastrophes. Strong evidence supports the periodic impact on the earth of extraterrestrial bodies resulting in major atmospheric and biotic perturbations. The presence at some extinction boundaries of thin layers of iridium, an element found concentrated only in meteorites, was the first clue to the role of bolide impact in evolution. However, other explanations of the evidence such as catastrophic volcanism, sea level changes, and climate changes have also been invoked. The role of such catastrophes in extinction is not unanimously supported; the fossil record of some organisms does not show an abrupt eradication within the very short time demanded by the catastrophic hypotheses.

[V.T.]

See also **Chemical Evolution and the Origin of Life; Dinosaurs; Extinction; Geologic Time Scale.**

FURTHER READINGS

Albritton, C.C. *Catastrophic Episodes in Earth History*. London: Chapman and Hall, 1989.

Brasier, M., ed. *Innovations and Revolutions in the Biosphere*. *Historical Biology* 5.2-4 (1991).

CELESTIAL ORIENTATION AND NAVIGATION

Before the time of satellites and modern radio technology, human as well as animal orientation depended on celestial information. In order to use this information a way to tell time was essential. In finding one's way, it is important to distinguish between two processes: a "compass," which provides a reference direction and enables one to move in a straight line; and a "map," which provides position information and indicates the direction to one's goal.

In human terms, the most primitive compass depends on the sun. During the day its bright disk provides an obvious point of reference in the sky. Yet to use it to determine a reference direction, one must compensate for the sun's apparent movement through the sky. Living organisms possess internal biological clocks, which in the case of humans and many other species of animals, are able to compensate for the sun's movement. Thus, an animal wanting to go south flies with the sun on its left in the morning, toward the sun at noon, and with the sun on its right in the afternoon. A homing pigeon's sun compass is sufficiently accurate that it can head within about 10 degrees of its goal.

For humans, the second process, the "map," also depends upon celestial cues. During the day, human navigators measure the exact position of the sun in the sky to derive their position on the surface of the earth. The basic idea is that the altitude of the sun, that is its distance above the horizon at noon, is a function of one's position along a north-south line. The further south, the higher the sun at noon for any given season. East-west position can be determined by the progress of the sun along its arc. But in order to interpret this information it is essential to know the exact time of day, since a time error of one minute is equivalent to a position error of one nautical mile (about 1.9 kilometers). This need to know the exact time over extended sea voyages was one of the major driving forces behind the invention of more accurate and stable clocks. Thus, for humans, an accurate sense of time is an essential part of celestial navigation.

For animals, the situation is somewhat different. Although many animals are known to use a time-compensated sun compass, to give its full, technical name, I know of no animal that uses time information as part of its navigation. Consider a homing pigeon that has been taken from its home loft and released at a site where it has never been before. When the bird is freed, it circles the release site and then typically sets a roughly direct course for the home loft. If, before release, one confines such a pigeon to a light-tight box and exposes it to an artificial light-dark

cycle six hours out of synchrony with the real day for a period of four to five days, the bird, on being released, no longer heads directly for home. Such a "clockshifted" pigeon flies off at 90 degrees to the correct home direction. The interpretation of such an experiment is straightforward: the bird still knows the direction toward home, but the six-hour clockshift has caused an error in its sun compass. Since the sun appears to move at an average speed of 15 degrees per hour, a six-hour shift would be expected to cause the 90-degree error that is observed.

Pigeons with the same shift, released under overcast skies when the sun is not visible, head directly home. Again, the thinking is that the shift has had no effect on either the compass used under an overcast sky or on the map. All this evidence suggests that whatever cues the pigeons are using, they do not depend on an accurate sense of time.

Many animals are known to use a celestial compass; migratory birds, ants, bees, and butterflies provide just a few examples. Many birds migrating at night use the stars as a compass; some marine, shore-dwelling amphipods apparently are able to use the moon as a compass. This is a very surprising finding because the moon would require a very different sense of time than does the sun; it is hard to imagine one clock that could serve both needs. The reason for this is that the position of the moon is not described by the twenty-four-hour daily rhythm. The moon, as anyone familiar with the ocean tides it causes can attest, has a rhythm of roughly twenty-five hours. This means that in the normal twenty-four-hour day frame of reference the moon's rising and setting occur roughly fifty minutes later every day. For an animal to make use of both the sun and the moon as position references it would need either two separate clocks or some way of compensating for the difference between solar and lunar rhythms. That this is a general problem is made clear by the number of animals that exhibit a tidal rhythm in both their activities and their orientation.

Honey bees also use celestial orientation in both foraging for nectar and in communicating the direction and distance of the food source to other foragers in their hive. A scout bee flies an irregular path searching for flowers with nectar. When she finds a supply, she returns to the hive in a straight "bee line." That this return is based on a compass can be demonstrated by capturing the bee and displacing it. When it is released it flies in a direction parallel to the course that would have taken it home from the flower. This means that the bee does not navigate; that is, it does not correct for its displacement. When the bee reaches its hive, if the nectar supply is sufficiently rich, it performs a dance. This dance, performed on a vertical comb in total darkness, indicates the direction and distance to the food source; the vigor of the dance indicates its richness and the odor clinging to the bee is that of the flowers from which the nectar was gathered. The dancing bee indicates the direction to the food source relative to the position of the sun; vertically up on the comb indicates the direction of the sun. A bee dancing at 90 degrees to the right of vertical is indicating that the food is 90 degrees right of the direction of the sun in the horizontal plane. The honey bee, like other animals, has an internal clock. If a forager is delayed in dancing for an hour or two on its return to the hive, when it does dance, it allows for the movement of the sun. In the example above, a bee delayed for two hours would dance 60 degrees to the right allowing for the 30 degrees of sun movement.

All these examples indicate that while many animals use celestial cues for orientation they must all, in addition, employ an internal biological clock. The use of celestial cues for orientation necessitates a sense of time. But animals use these cues as compasses or directional cues; there is no evidence that any animal uses celestial cues in the sense of position finding or true navigation. Only humans seem to have developed a true celestial navigation system that depends on an accurate sense of time.

[C.W.]

FURTHER READINGS

Able, Kenneth P. "Mechanisms of Orientation, Navigation, and Homing." *Animal Migration, Orientation and Navigation*. Ed. Sidney A. Gauthreaux. New York: Academic P, 1980. 283–373.

Baker, Robin R. *Bird Navigation: The Solution of a Mystery?* New York: Holmes and Meier, 1984.

Frisch, Karl von. *The Dance Language and Orientation of Bees*. Cambridge: Harvard UP, 1967.

Hasler, Arthur D. *Underwater Guideposts*. Amherst: Wisconsin UP, 1966.

CELLULAR RHYTHMS

Endogenous rhythms within cells represent dissipative structures—states of temporal order characteristic of nonlinear dynamic systems far from thermodynamic equilibrium. The period lengths of cellular rhythms range from a few milliseconds for action potentials to annual and longer cycles of reproduction processes. Cellular rhythms are in many cases of decisive significance for the function of a cell or organism: as signals in the transmission of information, as a basis for locomotion of various kinds, and as a "clock" in coordinating processes with respect to a certain time schedule. There also seem to exist rhythms without obvious significance.

For information transmission, the message is often encoded in the frequency of the rhythm rather than in the amplitude. The message is thus encoded in a digitalized form based on amplifying or relaying devices in the mechanism of the rhythm. Electrical and/or concentration waves travel within a cell, along excitable membranes or in the surrounding medium. At the target, the frequency is often translated into analogue signals related to changes in the activity of an enzyme or concentration of second messenger molecules. Action potentials in nerve and muscle cells, as well as potential changes in nonexcitable cells, are well-known examples of this information transfer. Calcium oscillations with period lengths between five and sixty seconds have been detected recently within several cell types. M. J. Berridge and R. F. Irvine have reported that they apparently play an important role in the transmission of signals from the plasma membrane to targets within the cell. They also form traveling waves in space and time, the waves probably exerting local effects by triggering the activity of membrane-bound Calcium-ATPases (ATP = adenosine triphosphate, a high-energy nucleotide which functions as the principal energy-carrying compound in the cells of all living organisms). Calcium and cyclic nucleotides represent rather tightly coupled so-called second messenger systems. It would be surprising, therefore, if corresponding rhythms of cAMP (cyclic form of adenosine monophosphate) were lacking.

Extracellular cAMP-rhythms with period lengths of about two to ten minutes are well known in Dictyostelium. They are often triggered by pacemaker cells and relayed by surrounding cells, which use the travelling cAMP waves to orient themselves before moving toward the aggregation center. During this and later stages in the morphogenesis of this slime mold, oscillations play a fundamental role in the temporal and spatial organization of the developing organism.

The molecular basis of locomotion and movement comprises high-frequency interactions between the proteins actin and myosin or dynein, respectively kinesin and tubulin. These oscillations are asynchronous. The interactions require the hydrolysis of adenosine triphosphate (ATP) and are mainly elicited by elevated calcium concentrations which, in turn, are controlled by nervous inputs or spontaneous rhythms. In smooth muscle cells or ciliated cells, these calcium oscillations or waves cause corresponding contractions or ciliar beats, respectively. A central pacemaker in the human heart, the sino-atrial node, generates rhythms with period lengths of about a second. This excitation rhythm spreads and leads to corresponding contraction rhythms of the atria and ventricles by means of calcium release from intracellular stores.

Temporal coordination of repetitive cellular processes is achieved by endogenous rhythms, which is to say by "clocks." The circadian oscillator is such a clock system, which is present in almost all eukaryotic—and perhaps some prokaryotic—cells. The term "circadian" (<Latin *circa*, about; *dies*, one day) refers to the approximately twenty-four-hour period under constant conditions. Circadian rhythms are endogenous rhythms within individual cells or cell populations which can be entrained by periodic signals, especially by light and temperature changes. The period length under constant conditions adapts rather quickly to different temperatures, a phenomenon known as temperature compensation. As reviewed by L.N. Edmunds, the mechanism of the circadian clock probably contains periodic activity changes of (1) protein, (2) Ca2+ (calmodulin), and (3) membrane-associated processes. Mutation of the period (per) gene originally analyzed in Drosophila, but found also in other organisms, leads to either different period lengths or arhythmicity of the oscillator. The circadian clock controls many cellular processes such as photosynthesis, respiration, bioluminescence, gene activity, protein synthesis, DNA synthesis, and mitosis in a defined sequential or synchronous order. The cell is thus programmed to meet the different requirements during the geophysical day. The circadian rhythms of population of cells or cells within a multicellular organism interact and represent a system of coupled oscillators.

Another coordinative rhythm is the cell cycle clock. Its mechanism consists mainly of two proteins: one (cyclin) increases in its amount from one mitosis to the next, while the other (cdc2 kinase—associated with cyclin) is activated at a defined phase shortly before mitosis and phosphorylates various proteins. As B. Lewin has reported, its activity, furthermore, leads to the degradation of cyclin during mitosis. The cell cycle may be coupled to the circadian clock through common calcium-dependent processes.

Cellular rhythms can thus mutually interact to form a complex temporal and spatial pattern during a day or a proliferation cycle.

[L.Re.]

See also **Chronobiology; Chronobiology of the Cell Cycle; Circadian Pacemakers.**

FURTHER READINGS

Berridge, M.J., and R. F. Irvine. "Inositol Phosphates and Cell Signalling." *Nature* 341 (1989): 197–205.

Edmunds, L.N. *Cellular and Molecular Bases of Biological Clocks*. Berlin: Springer, 1988.

Lewin, B. "Driving the Cell Cycle: Mphase Kinase, Its Partners and Substrates." Meeting review. *Cell* 61 (1990): 743–752.

Rensing, L., ed. *Oscillations and Morphogenesis*. New York: Dekker, 1992.

CHAOS AND DYNAMICAL NAVIGATION OF THE COGNITIVE MAP

First, consider four of the most basic concepts of dynamics as indicated by F.D. Abraham, R.D. Abraham, and C.D. Shaw in 1990: (1) the dynamical system (the vectorfield and the phase portrait are the visual representations of temporal patterns of interacting variables), (2) the dynamical scheme (the dynamical system as a function of control parameters; the response diagram represents this scheme graphically), (3) bifurcations (changes in the attractor patterns with changes in the control parameters), and (4) self-organization (when bifurcations come under the control of the system itself). (For a discussion of dynamics theory see **Dynamics**.)

The following article summarizes a concept of mind as dynamical schemes with interactions involving brain, behavior, cognition, and environment, and considers the holistic combination of these domains in a common state space with shared attractors and bifurcations.

TEMPORAL INTEGRATION AND INSENSITIVITY TO INITIAL CONDITIONS

Consider the following questions: if memories are comprised of chaotic attractors, how much time is required for their expression? How much time does it take the brain to process an attractor? Over how much time must an attractor be integrated to establish its basic properties? If the mind cannot comprehend an instant in time, what kind of time spans are required for comprehension to occur? While there is quite a history on these questions, they are raised only to emphasize the more resolvable queries of the dynamical point of view, and to relate them to the problem of discriminating between attractors representing different processes of mind.

After recognizing that a process of mind requires a sufficient time integration of a chaotic trajectory, we must also recognize that any of the vast number of trajectories that obey that attractor are sufficient to represent it. This is contrary to the popular chaos concept of "sensitivity to initial conditions," and is here called "insensitivity to initial conditions." It should be remembered that many different starting places in the basin of the attractor initiate different trajectories in the attractor, but they all behave similarly, approaching the attractor and then diverging from each other on the attractive surface. But each still obeys the same attractive and divergent forces creating that attractor, and can be used to represent it.

The exact starting time and location of similar memories and other trains of thought or streams of consciousness is unimportant, and their trajectories need not involve an exactly repeatable set of neurons, which makes this "insensitivity" an extension of Karl Lashley's concept of equipotentiality. James Skinner, in 1990, also conjectured that within the brain there may be generalized chaotic processes in memory storage: "If the data compression is the raison d'être for a chaotic dynamical process, and if information storage is by a 'compressed representation' and not a specific 'engram,' will we finally be able to recognize biologically stored information?"

Similarly, Walter Freeman concluded in 1990 (from his research on the olfactory bulb in odor discrimination) that an activated memory is a periodic attractor, and that the stored attractor is chaotic: "I conceive the bulb as carrying a repertoire of learned limit cycle attractors. Each is distinguished by its input basin with respect to receptors and by the spatial amplitude modulation pattern of its output. Random access is facilitated by the chaotic basal state, which keeps the bulb far from equilibrium and ready to move rapidly to any region of optimal convergence."

George Mpitsos, from his work on the marine mollusk, Pleurobranchia californica, also made this insensitivity-equipotentiality point

in 1990: "A set of neural connections may be able to generate many and variable attractors. Some of these may be adaptive for certain environmental demands, while others may have little adaptability. What determines the appropriate responses at any given time, we believe, is not the selection of a particular centrally programmed neural structure or attractor, but rather the process arising from the continual interaction between the animal and the environment. . . .When viewed in this way, the concept of attractor is scale-independent."

Parenthetically, this dynamical view of what might be called William James's "stream of consciousness" may reflect the distinction between concepts of time that are linear, Newtonian, and reversible (such as the Greeks' chronos, J. Henkel's ordinary linear phase, and D. Loye's serial time: the vectorfield or phase portrait), and those that are nonlinear, Bergsonian, and irreversible (including the Greeks' *chairos* [or *kairos*], Henkel's event time, Loye's timeless and spatial time: the response diagram). The temporally linear motion along a trajectory obeys chronos, but the mind, integrating cognitively over periods of time, follows the saltatory, evolutionary, event time of *chairos* (see the related discussions by Henkel in 1989, Loye in 1983, and N. Wiener in 1948). The mind's activity is therefore both dynamic and mnemonic.

SELF-ORGANIZATION AND CHOICE: NAVIGATING THE RESPONSE DIAGRAM

Thus, there can be navigation within the dynamical system with its cognitive equivalent of the phase portrait, as well as self-regulation of behavior within the familiar territory of dynamical schemes via cognitive response diagrams integrated from past experience. But there can also be a consideration of future possibilities, and of potential attractors, including the construction of novel state spaces and attractors. In addition, the mind can also evaluate the present, examine the past, and forecast the future. Choices are conceived both as maneuvering along control parameters, and jumping to new trajectories leading to new attractors.

Consider, for example, the cyclic patterns of the abused wife, her swings between contentment, affection, dependency, pain, and despair, and her spouse's patterns of conciliation, appeasement, and abuse. These patterns could be seen as a response to a quasi-cyclic chaotic attractor that could be modeled by a variant of the famous prey-predator dynamic model.

The forces of the instantaneous vectorfield, the linear time frame of the present, may involve some memory features and choices at saddles leading to alternative outcomes or trajectories toward inevitable events. This would include the coping behavior of an abused wife when confronted by an abusive husband. A saddle in her phase portrait may send her to a friend's home, or just change the time (via a change in trajectory duration) of the abusive episode.

When shifting the time frame to nonlinear considerations of the dynamical scheme, the mind may consider the cognitive metaview of the response diagram solely from a historical, memorial perspective, in which is embedded the current phase portrait. For example, the abused wife may consider historical times prior to the bifurcation to the abusive cycle, identify alternative familial coping strategies, and make a reverse trip on that control parameter and hope for a bifurcation to more desirable behavioral patterns, similar to those from earlier in the relationship. But as we all know, such strategies are difficult to attain.

Thus, one must imagine projections of the response diagram into the future, including information-gathering strategies, new alternatives, new spaces, new dimensions, and new attractors. The abused wife may move along a self-assertion control parameter and perhaps succeed in getting her reluctant spouse to seek family therapy. Or she may perceive a chance to move to a new trajectory, such as leaving her spouse and seeking a shelter or support group or family support of some type, thus creating a new life for herself.

In both the linear saddle choices in the phase portrait and the self-organizational route of choosing bifurcations in the reconstructed response diagram, it is to be remembered that instability occurs at such saddle and bifurcation choice points, and instabilities require a great deal of energy and resolve, compared to following stable phase portraits of current cognitive and life styles, even when these involve pain and discomfort. The same is true when acceptable life attractors abound, seducing one from seeking further growth. At a bifurcation point, demands of chairos are greater; once in the new phase portrait or attractor, the demands of chronos become stronger; there is a waxing and waning of the relative importance of nonlinear and linear time with personal growth.

In summary, we have suggested a simplistic metaphor in which basic concepts of dynamical systems theory are used to provide an initial language for cognitive strategies for choice behavior and projecting the future. These involve dual time frames. One is the linear temporal concept of chronos using the concept of the phase portrait as a cognitive model. The other is the nonlinear temporal concept of chairos using the concept of the response diagram involving self-organization and bifurcations (transformations) as cognitive models and the integration of time into the cognitive map and its navigation.

[F.D.A.]

See also **Bergson, Henri; Chaos Theory; Cognition; Dynamics; Gaia Theory; James, William (as Psychologist); Kairos; Psychology of Time; Saltatory Evolution; Saturn-Cronus.**

FURTHER READINGS

Abraham, F.D., R.H. Abraham, and C.D. Shaw. *A Visual Introduction to Dynamical Systems Theory for Psychology*. Santa Cruz: Aerial, 1990.

Freeman, W. J. "Nonlinear Neural Dynamics in Olfaction as a Model for Cognition." *Chaos in Brain Function*. Ed. E. Basar. Berlin: Springer, 1990. 63–73, 153–161.

Henkel, J. "Toward a Gaia Philosophy: The Dyadic Realities Picture." *The Gaia Review* 1 (1989): 20–30.

Loye, D. *The Sphinx and the Rainbow: Brain, Mind, and Future Vision*. Boulder: Shambhala, 1983.

Mpitsos, G.J. "Chaos in Brain Function and the Problem of Nonstationarity: A Commentary." *Chaos in Brain Function*. Ed. E. Basar. Berlin: Springer, 1989. 162–176.

Skinner, J.E., et al. "Chaotic Attractors in a Model of Neocortex: Dimensionalities of Olfactory Bulb Surface Potentials." *Chaos in Brain Function*. Ed. E. Basar. Berlin: Springer, 1990. 119–134.

Weiner, N. *Cybernetics or Control and Communication in the Animal and the Machine*. New York: Wiley, 1948.

CHAOS THEORY

Chaos theory originated in the study of meteorology during the 1960s, but its appeal today is multidisciplinary. Chaos theory has developed and matured in pure mathematics, astronomy, meteorology, physics, optics, biology, fluid dynamics, paleobiology, thermal convection, laser research, physiology, and other disciplines.

Chaos theory examines the behavior of dynamic systems, whether they are real or theoretical. Dynamic systems are those whose state changes with time. Chaos theory is concerned with nonlinear dynamic systems because they have been found to differ qualitatively from strictly linear systems in their behavior over time.

Chaos theory proposes that complex and apparently random behavior can result from simple, deterministic systems. This challenges the assumptions that complex behavior is due to complex causes, either internal (many components to the system) or external (random or complex influences), and that simple systems behave in simple, predictable ways. For example, the following difference equation models the growth of a population in an environment with limiting resources, where N is a relative measure of population size (ranging from 0 to 1) and r is the intrinsic growth rate of the population:

$$N_{t+1} = rN_t(1-N_t)$$

If this is tried with a hand calculator when $N_t = 0.02$ and $r = 2.7$, it will be found that the population size will rise and then plateau at $N_t = 0.523$. At first glance, this is a simple system behaving simply, but in actuality, the behavior of the system is dependent upon the intrinsic growth rate (r). At low values, the population size does plateau. As the intrinsic growth rate is increased, the population size behaves periodically over time; first a two-year cycle (try r = 3.2), then a four-year cycle (try r = 3.5), then an eight-

year cycle (try r = 3.58). As the intrinsic growth rate is increased further, the behavior of the population becomes chaotic over time (try r = 3.9). Figure 1 illustrates this complexity. The simple, deterministic model exhibits apparent randomness. Overall, this indicates a complex range of behaviors without complex cause.

UNIVERSALITY

Chaos theory also proposes that different dynamic systems share universal aspects of their behavior and that real-world chaotic systems with near infinite complexity can thus be understood using simple models. The difference equation above exhibited the period doubling route to chaos—as the intrinsic growth rate was increased the behavior bifurcated from monotonic to a two-year cycle and then to a four-year cycle and so on until chaotic behavior was observed. The same period doubling route to chaos has been observed in real-world systems. For example, currents in a pot of water will exhibit the period doubling route to chaos as the amount of heat applied is increased—first a general warming, then two currents of rising warm water and falling cool water, then four currents, and so on until boiling (chaos) occurs. A small volume of water has near infinite complexity considering the number of atoms involved, yet the behavior can be understood using very simple deterministic models.

The period doubling route to chaos and the butterfly effect (see below) are universal to all nonlinear dynamic systems. Indeed, the rate at which the bifurcations occur increases at a universal geometric rate in all nonlinear dynamic systems (Feigenbaum's constant).

THE BUTTERFLY EFFECT

If all nature followed simple and universal deterministic rules and if the initial conditions of a system were known with perfect accuracy, the future behavior of this system could be predicted with perfect accuracy using simple deterministic models. If the current conditions of the earth's weather were known with perfect accuracy, the future behavior of the earth's weather could be predicted *ad infinitum*. However, the initial conditions of any real-world system cannot be known with perfect accuracy and the predictions made would rapidly diverge from the actual weather experienced. This is known in chaos theory as sensitive dependence upon initial conditions, or the butterfly effect—the undetected flap of a butterfly's wing in Hong Kong makes long-term weather prediction in

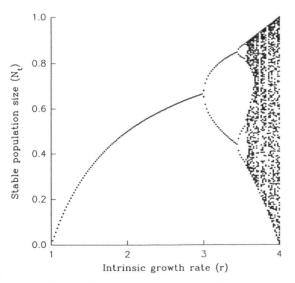

Figure 1. The logistic map based on the population difference equation given. Low values of r have a single stable point while others exhibit periodicity (two or more stable points). Stable chaotic behavior occurs if r exceeds 3.57.

New York impossible. Sensitive dependence upon initial conditions is universal to all nonlinear dynamic systems.

STRANGE ATTRACTORS AND FRACTALS

Though prediction and reality diverge in chaotic systems due to sensitive dependence upon initial conditions, they do not do so infinitely. The behavior of chaotic systems has finite limits, and prediction and reality may temporally be similar at some point in the future. By definition, a chaotic trajectory through time is never repeating and chaotic systems thus have a trajectory through time of infinite length within finite limits. They have fractional dimension (that is, they are fractal). A square plate has finite surface area and zero volume (two dimensions). A cube has finite surface area and finite volume (three dimensions). A chaotic trajectory within a cube has infinite length (surface area) within a finite volume (dimension between two and three). This fractal nature of stable chaotic systems is universal. Additionally, fractal systems are self-similar on all scales. Fluctuations for cotton prices since the late 1800s are identical whether measured per minute, hour, day, month, year, or decade, though individual changes are unpredictable. And all of this is true despite two world wars and a depression.

All dynamic systems have attractors. An attractor is simply the trajectory that the system ends up following over time. The system may start at any point but may be attracted to a two-year cycle (an attractor with period two) or it may fluctuate wildly until it passes some critical point and stops (a point attractor). The latter is an example of unstable chaotic behavior, such as a population crash. As illustrated, chaotic systems can be stable and nonrepeating over time. These systems are attracted to strange attractors—attractors whose trajectory is infinite within finite limits (fractal). Seemingly chaotic fluctuations in population size using the population difference equation given are following a strange attractor. There is hidden order within the chaotic behavior. Chaos theory is concerned with the identification of these strange attractors in natural systems.

PHILOSOPHICAL IMPLICATIONS OF CHAOS THEORY

Chaos theory suggests that the behavior of all systems (stellar, biological, physical, mental, quantum, and so on) could be deterministic in a universal manner. Apparent randomness over time could actually be determined by simple universal laws of behavior. The goal of chaos theory was originally reductionistic, with the hope that knowledge of the simple universal laws of behavior would explain the complex behavior of any natural or theoretical system over time. However, chaos theory now differentiates between the ability to understand the behavior of dynamic systems and the ability to predict the behavior of dynamic systems.

Chaos theory calls into question the Laplacian delusion that complete understanding will bring complete predictability. It has shifted epistemologically from predicting behavior over time (what will the system do?), to understanding the nature of the behavior itself (why does the system do that?). Additionally, chaos theory states that the behavior of dynamic systems is independent of scale and that scale-dependent interpretation or measuring of these systems biases our understanding of them.

[A.M.]

See also **Dynamics; Time Series.**

FURTHER READINGS

Glass, L., and M.C. Mackey. *From Clocks to Chaos: The Rhythms of Life*. Princeton: Princeton UP, 1988.

Gleick, J. *Chaos: Making a New Science*. Harmondsworth: Penguin, 1987.

Laplace, P.S. *Celestial Mechanics*. Trans. N. Bowditch. 4 vols. 1829–39; reprint, New York: Chelsea Publishing, 1966. (Translation of Laplace's *Mécanique céleste* [1799–1825].)

Mandelbrot, B.B. *The Fractal Geometry of Nature*. San Francisco: Freeman, 1983.

Middleton, G.V. *Nonlinear Dynamics, Chaos and Fractals with Applications to Geological Sciences*. St. John's: Geological Association of Canada Publications, 1991.

CHEMICAL EVOLUTION AND THE ORIGIN OF LIFE

Earth was likely formed 4.6 billion years ago from the solar nebula, a mixture of dust and gas surrounding the sun. That dust and gas probably supported the origin of life on earth, which occurred more than 3.5 billion years ago. The estimate of this time is based on the age of ancient sedimentary rocks found in Australia, in which the earliest known fossils of microorganisms were first identified. When examined with an electron microscope, these fossils are quite similar to extant colonies of cyanobacterial cells, relatively advanced life forms, but whether or not they are the ancestors of today's organisms is not known. Thus, chemical evolution, the origin of the genetic code and metabolism, and the origin of the cell must have first occurred during some uncertain period of time prior to 3.5 billion years ago.

The earth's environment presumably became suitable for the accumulation of organic molecules, the building blocks of life forms, after the formation of the moon. The moon was probably derived from an impact between the young earth and an asteroid the size of Mars about 4.4 billion years ago. The heat released by this impact would have sterilized the earth's surface. Some of the subsequent impacts could also have eradicated complex chemicals and life forms at least during the next 0.9 billion years of earth's existence. Thus, the span of time within which the origin of life occurred remains unknown, although most certainly it was less than 0.9 billion years.

The source of simple organic compounds, the raw materials needed to synthesize more complex organic molecules, is uncertain. In the past, we thought that these chemicals were synthesized in the earth's early atmosphere, but recent evidence suggests that this atmosphere did not contain enough hydrogenated chemicals—such as methane, ammonia, and hydrogen sulfide—to support the required syntheses. Rather, organic compounds may have accumulated both as the earth passed through dense clouds of interstellar dust, and as comets and carbonaceous chondrites entered earth's atmosphere. Accumulation of these chemicals is a crucial first step that requires the absence of free molecular oxygen, O_2, a reasonable assumption for the young earth.

The next step in chemical evolution—the polymerization of monomers into simple carbohydrates, peptides, and nucleic acids—is difficult to envisage in the earth's early environment. Clay minerals may have facilitated this process because they have large surface areas per unit volume and are composed of charged crystal lattices to which simple organic monomers can adhere. The probability that chemical bonds could form among these attached monomers is increased and the bonds would be somewhat protected from hydrolysis. Also, these minerals must have been very abundant in the atmosphere and ocean as impacts occurred. However, some scientists consider the formation of polymers on earth to be unlikely and suggest that cells originated on another planet. They further postulate that some of these cells were subsequently transported through space, eventually inoculating the earth. Other scientists believe that polymers were produced in the vicinity of the hot, hydrogen-rich environments provided by rifts separating earth's crust into plates on the deep ocean floor.

The accumulation of polymers in the earth's environment would greatly increase the probability that chemical evolution could continue. We now believe that ribonucleic acid (RNA) was perhaps the most important molecule in the next stages of evolution. In modern cells, RNA has many functions, including transport of genetic messages (messenger RNA), transport of amino acids (transfer RNA), and sites for the assembly of amino acids into proteins (ribosomal RNA). In addition, RNA is autocatalytic, that is, it can accelerate its own reproduction, and this may have allowed formation of a primitive, nonliving genetic code. Present-day RNA viruses, which are now obligate parasites of other organisms, may actually resemble the primitive, self-organizing, independent RNA molecules. Ultimately, development of the simple genetic code found in bacteria would have been impossible without a molecule having greater capacity than RNA to store information. Deoxyribonucleic acid (DNA), the molecule that contains the genetic material of all cells, was an ideal replacement.

In addition to their great importance in RNA and DNA structures, nucleotide phosphates are the primary molecules for energy storage and transfer within extant cells, and therefore must have been in great demand by chemical reactions. Eventually, reductions in the concentrations of free nucleotide phosphates would have limited further syntheses of RNA and DNA. Extant organisms have overcome this difficulty by synthesizing nucleotide phosphates with an electron transport system coupled to a proton gradient across a membrane. Thus, membrane syntheses must have been required early in the evolution of life for these and other purposes, such as concentrating products of chemical reactions by inhibiting their loss through diffusion.

Membranes may have formed in solutions of lipids, polymers of fatty acids and glycerol, and proteins, polymers of amino acids. Indeed, artificial membranes which are remarkably similar to those of extant cells can be made by dissolving lipids and proteins in salty water where they form microspheres. Many scientists believe that these spheres were very abundant in the ocean of the early earth and provided habitats for chemical reactions the products of which were protected against diffusion, thus maintaining steep gradients of chemicals. However, membranes would have limited the access of the contents of microspheres (protocells) to chemical compounds and energy sources in the environment. Hence, if evolution were to proceed beyond some set of organized chemical reactions inside a protocell, transport mechanisms and metabolism were required, eventually giving rise to the origin of a living cell.

[L.A.H., and L.-J.M.]

FURTHER READINGS

Chyba, C., and C. Sagan. "Cometary and Asteroidal Delivery of Prebiotic Organics Versus *In Situ* Production on the Early Earth." *Bulletin of the American Astronomical Society* 22 (1990): 1097.

Dyson, F. *Infinite in All Directions*. New York: Harper & Row, 1988. Chapters 4 and 5.

Greenberg, J.M. "Chemical Evolution in Space." *Origins of Life and Evolution of the Biosphere* 14 (1984): 25–36.

Hartmann, W.K. "Birth of the Moon." *Natural History* 11 (1989): 68–77.

Maher, K.A., and D.J. Stevenson. "Impact Frustration of the Origin of Life." *Nature* 331 (1988): 612.

Oberbeck, V.R., and G. Fogleman. "Estimates of the Maximum Time Required to Originate Life." *Origins of Life and Evolution of the Biosphere* 19 (1989): 549–560.

CHINESE ASTRONOMY

Astronomy in China is part of a cultural tradition that extends back to at least 1300 B.C., the time of the Bronze Age Shang dynasty (1750–1100 B.C.). Shang oracle inscriptions on bones and tortoise shells provide the earliest Chinese texts referring to celestial objects and events, including solar eclipses and lunar eclipses. The date of each divination in the sixty-day calendar cycle is also given. Analysis of these dated inscriptions suggests that the Shang estimated the tropical year's length as 365.25 days and the length of the moon's cycle of phases as 29.53 days. A pictographic character from this era implies early use of the gnomon and shadow measurement by Shang astronomers. Most of the oracular inquiries are thought to have originated in the court of the Shang ruler. Systematic calendrics and astronomical observation appear, then, to have been official business commissioned by the king.

The official character of astronomy was preserved in China for more than three millennia.

Astronomers were government employees chartered by the king to make, record, and report seasonal observations of the sun, moon, and stars. These observations allowed the ruler to formulate, calibrate, and announce a calendar. Through the calendar, the agricultural, economic, and ceremonial activities of imperial China were organized.

China's cosmo-magical state religion was articulated by the actions of the king, who was regarded as the representative on earth of Shang di, the supernatural personification of celestial cosmic order. State-sponsored astronomers also kept track of other heavenly events—including the movements of planets, the appearances of novae and supernovae, and the arrivals and departures of comets. These phenomena were thought to indicate heaven's assessment of the character and authority of the government. It was the ruler's responsibility to respond, through ritual and practical action, to the information provided by the sky, and he ruled with heaven's mandate. Institutionalized astronomy, seasonal ritual, and an official calendar all demonstrated the ruler's ability to harmonize the forces thought to govern nature and the affairs of people.

The primary organizing principle of Chinese astronomy was the daily rotation of the sky. This

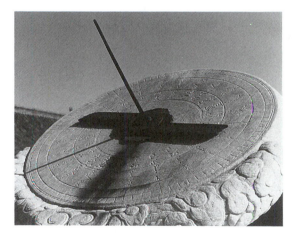

Figure 1. This working Chinese sundial is actually a small gnomon tilted at an angle appropriate for the latitude of Beijing. It measures the passage of time and is, as well, a symbol of the emperor's virtue and ethical government. It stands upon a monumental support in the courtyard of the Hall of Supreme Harmony in Beijing's Imperial Palace. From this hall, the emperor held public audiences and announced the calendar. (Photograph, Robin Rector Krupp)

fundamental movement establishes the meaning and location of the north celestial pole and the celestial equator. The Chinese kept time, followed the seasons, and mapped the stars with a system of celestial references based on the equator and the pole. Circumpolar stars were used to measure the passage of time at night. In addition, the entire sky was split into twenty-eight zones known as *xiu*. Each segment began at the north celestial pole, widened at the celestial equator, and converged again at the south celestial pole. Convenient reference stars marked the boundaries of each *xiu*. These stars and the zones they represented were in turn grouped into four equatorial palaces, seven *xiu* in each. The palaces were associated with the four cardinal directions, named for the four seasons, and symbolized with a talismanic animal and color. The earliest known record of the twenty-eight *xiu* appears on the lid of a ceramic box found in a Zhou dynasty (1100–221 B.C.) tomb with a burial from 433 B.C.

China's earliest star map was painted on the ceiling of a Han dynasty (206 B.C.–A.D. 220) tomb dating from the beginning of the first century B.C. Celestial ceilings continued to appear in high status tombs as late as A.D. 1116. Early star charts and catalogs confirm that the Chinese developed their own system of star names and constellations. The earliest surviving manuscript containing star charts was prepared in A.D. 940 and was found at Dunhuang.

Instruments were developed and refined for timekeeping, calendar keeping, mapping the sky, and measuring the positions of planets and other moving celestial objects. It is likely that a device employing inscribed metal rings for measurement of equatorial coordinates was available by the fourth century B.C. Observations of the planet Jupiter informed Chinese astronomers of its 11.86-year cycle through the stars and inspired the concept of twelve Jupiter stations, each of which corresponded to a creature in the twelve-year cycle of emblematic animals, for which the years were named. Jupiter, known as the "year-star," was honored with its own altar for sacrifices to the "year god" in imperial Beijing.

Although the gnomon was standardized to a height of about eight feet some time after the end of the Zhou dynasty, larger instruments were eventually dedicated to more accurate solstice determination and more precise estimates of the length of the year. A giant gnomon, contrived as a brick tower by the astronomer Guo shou jing, survives from A.D. 1276, the time of the Yuan dynasty (A.D. 1271–1368). With this observatory Guo shou jing confirmed the value of the length of the year quoted in the *Tong tian* calendar of A.D. 1199 and expressed it decimally—rather than fractionally—as 365.2422 days. This is only twenty-six seconds too long, an extraordinary accomplishment (see Figure 1).

The Chinese divided the tropical year into twenty-four intervals. Known as the *qi*, these intervals were nearly—but not exactly—equal in duration. Selected to conform to about fifteen degrees of solar movement along the ecliptic, they were named after seasonal meteorological and astronomical phenomena. A lunar calendar, based upon the moon's phases, was also maintained. It was coordinated with the solar year through the intercalation of seven extra months in a nineteen-year period. Finer tuning later reduced the error of congruence even more, but the intercalation rules remained unchanged. The beginning of the year was determined by the phase of the moon and the position of the sun and usually occurred in what corresponds to early February. At that time, the Ming (A.D. 1368–1644) and Qing (A.D. 1644–1911) dynasty emperors of Beijing would perform sacrifices at the Hall of Prayer for Good Harvests, in the Temple of Heaven complex, on behalf of a successful grain harvest in the coming year. Imperial sacrifices to heaven at winter solstice, to earth at summer solstice, and to the sun and the moon at the equinoxes were offered by the emperor at open-air altars in the four quarters of the capital. Beijing itself was laid out cardinally upon a primary, north-south axis intended to reflect the polar-equatorial ordering principle of the sky. Many monumental tombs—including that of Qin, China's first emperor—also incorporated symbolic cardinal orientation.

Historical records of eclipses, sunspots, comets, novas, supernovas, and other celestial phenomena from China are more complete and continuous than any others in the world. They are valuable today, not only to historians tracing the development of astronomy, but to astrophysicists, who use the ancient data to extend their own base line of observation.

[E.C.K.]

See also **Archaeoastronomy; Calendar: Chinese and Japanese; Eclipses and Time.**

FURTHER READINGS

Aveni, Anthony F. *Empires of Time.* New York: Basic Books, 1989.

Krupp, E.C. *Echoes of the Ancient Skies—The Astronomy of Lost Civilizations*. New York: Harper & Row, 1983.

———. *Beyond the Blue Horizon—Myths and Legends of the Sun, Moon, Stars, and Planets*. New York: Harper Collins, 1991.

Needham, Joseph. "Mathematics and Sciences of the Heavens and the Earth." *Science and Civilisation in China*. Volume 3. Cambridge: Cambridge UP, 1959.

O'Neil, W.M. *Early Astronomy from Babylon to Copernicus*. Sydney: Sydney UP, 1986.

———. *Time and the Calendars*. Sydney: Sydney UP, 1975.

CHRONOBIOLOGY

Chronobiology is the science of objectively quantifying and investigating mechanisms of biologic time structure including rhythmic and age-related manifestations of life.

The term was derived from *chronos* (time), *bios* (life), and *logos* (science), in order to describe the inferential statistical quantification of life's overt and covert makeup in time. Quantitative chronobiologists analyze changes as a function of time by mapping the time structure (chronome) of organisms and by objectively estimating the characteristics of the chronome's constituents, the chrones (see **Chronome**).

IMPORTANCE OF RHYTHMS

Rhythms with different frequencies are found at all levels of biologic integration: ecosystem, population, group, individual, organ-system, organ, tissue, cell, and subcellular structure. Their ubiquity and their critical importance to the survival of both the individual and the species have prompted the development of a new discipline to study these temporal characteristics in the context of the chronome, including trends in development, growth, and aging. (For some of the subdivisions of the science of chronobiology see **Chronohygiene, Chronopathology, Chronophysiology,** and **Chronotherapy**.)

The importance of rhythms, which are the foundation on which the science of chronobiology was built, lies in their ubiquity. Even the most fundamental processes of life, such as DNA and RNA synthesis, exhibit marked circadian rhythms, whereas earlier they were regarded as the most constant features of organisms. The marker rhythms of an in vivo circadian cell cycle time-specify the classical cell cycle and fill in some of its gaps. In growing mouse liver, as in the organ regenerating from partial hepatectomy, daily recurring RNA formation precedes DNA formation, at variance with the former dogma postulating information flow from DNA to RNA to protein without any consideration of rhythmicity and its timing. The critical importance of a circadian cell cycle lies in its eventual use for cancer therapy targeted in time (see **Chronotherapy**).

As prominent circadian rhythmicity was found at different levels of organization, several series of experiments were carried out under rigorous standardized laboratory conditions that investigated the effect of a single physical stimulus such as exposure to noise. Outcomes were as different as no response, convulsion, or even death as a function of the circadian stage at which the organism was exposed to noise. Whether the stimulus was audiogenic or exposure to an endotoxin, or to drugs such as ouabain, or to whole-body irradiation, predictable changes were found as a function of the circadian stage at which the stimulus was applied, albeit with differences in timing. The hours of changing resistance were thus uncovered, and the times of overall largest response by the organism to a fixed stimulus applied at different rhythm stages mapped. The charts that follow serve as a guide for timing the administration of various agents (see Figure 1). The chronotherapy of cancer and high blood pressure are critical applications resulting from this work (see **Chronotherapy**).

"CIRCA" RHYTHMS

Chronobiologic terminology applies the prefix *circa* in five ways: All life involves the recurrence in *about* (the first *circa*) the same sequences of *about* (the second *circa*) the same phenomena with *about* (the third *circa*) the same extent of change at intervals that are *about* (the fourth *circa*) the same, but not necessarily exactly the same. Certain intervals or the periods they represent—such as a day, a week, a month, or a year—correspond to *about* (the fifth *circa*) the length of environmental cycles. These circa-periodicities persist when organisms under ordinary conditions are deprived of the receptor of their major synchronizing environmental cycle, such as the eyes, or are isolated under conditions rendered as constant as possible on earth and show natural periods, described as free-running when they differ with statistical significance from their environmental near *(circa)* match. The foregoing five uses of *circa* thus include the indirect demonstration by free-running periods (see **Free-Running in Chronobiology**) of the genetic basis of rhythms that constitute the mechanisms of life.

These rhythms can be characterized by, among other things, their frequencies, their periods, and the extent and timing of their predictable changes (amplitude and acrophase). Over the past four decades, these rhythm characteristics have been rigorously quantified and documented for different variables at different levels of organization. Today, basic and applied biology, and the health sciences in particular, have opportunities for evolutionary, even revolutionary, progress in prevention, diagnosis, and treatment based on the combination of several new emerging technologies. These include (1) the availability of portable, personal, long-term ambulatory monitors of biologic variables (blood pressure, the ECG and EEG, gastric acidity, and core temperature are cases in point, as these and other variables undergo changes that recur spontaneously and as responses); (2) the availability of data-base systems to acquire and analyze volumes of data obtained from personal monitors; (3) the availability of statistical procedures to analyze and model the biologic dynamics and from them to devise optimal dosage time patterns for specific individuals; (4) the availability of portable, programmed devices to administer therapy, such as physiologic rate-adjusted cardiac pacemakers, defibrillators, or drug pumps; and (5) a chronobiologic understanding of the health effect of rhythms (see Table 1).

CHRONOBIOLOGIC METHODS IN MEDICAL PRACTICE

The employment of chronobiologic methods in routine medical screening, diagnosis, prognosis, treatment, and disease prevention remains a challenge to be met with the realization of the following points regarding chronobiology in human medicine and biology:

1. A visual time-macroscopic inspection of patterns—that is, bioperiodicities—in time plots of physiologic variation;

2. A critical specification in time of any biologic measurement, as well as a systematic and strategic placement of measurements for the appropriate estimation of rhythm characteristics, thus constituting the experimental control or clinical reference standard;

3. An objective, computer-aided, inferential, statistical estimation of the characteristics of trends, rhythms, and noise (the chrones), and of relations among these gauged by cross-spectral coherence;

4. A set of procedures yielding improved old and new dynamic biologic end points—such as amplitude, acrophase, and coherence—for, among other things, human blood pressure, circulating hormones, or the effect of cosmic factors upon the organism;

5. The resolution of rhythms with periods that are only an approximate (*circa* = about) match of environmental cycles, and that under conditions of isolation differ (usually with statistical significance) from their environmental counterparts. Such free-running periods, whether they are discovered after a manipulation of the environment or of the organism, represent a first indirect line of evidence for the heritability of circa-rhythms;

6. The residual sum of squares from the least-squares fit of a model to the data allows testing for statistical significance of any changes in any one or several of the rhythm characteristics. Thus, with P-values (probability that outcome of hypothesis test results from chance alone), the reliability of findings for the given individual can be described;

7. A way to quantify health positively, inside the range of usual variation. Homeostasis equates the range of physiologic variation, often explicitly, with random variation. In so doing, a curtain of ignorance is drawn over the range in which everyday function occurs. Chronobiology lifts this curtain. It introduces a statistical determinism; thereby focus is placed on the rhythm, just as quantum mechanics emphasizes the wave. To carry this analogy further, the resolution of the time course of phenomena becomes possible and statistical predictability replaces random variability up to the point when uncertainty relations prevail; and

8. A generally applicable methodology for the animal laboratory, including the design of special lighting and other environmental conditions, with computer-aided hardware and software for data collection and analysis by methods of chronobiometry.

CONCEPTS AND MECHANISMS OF CHRONOBIOLOGY

Chronobiology provides a better understanding of life's mechanisms in the form of rhythms, their intermodulations, and the reasons for their alterations. Possible applications include the following:

1. A focus on heritability—for example of circadian rhythms—by studies on monozygotic twins reared apart, demonstrating that within-twin-pair differences in rhythm characteristics are smaller than among-twin-pair differences, notwithstanding the different geographic and other environments in which the twins were brought up and continue to live until study time;

2. A focus by genetic engineering on, for example, mutants of fruit flies that macroscopically lack a circadian rhythm and exhibit it again after gene transfer by examining the extent of reconstitution of rhythms in a broader-than-circadian (ultradian-to-infradian) rhythm spectrum and an extension of a molecular biologic approach from a fruit fly to a mold, a hamster, and an herb (mouse-ear cress);

3. An approach resolving some of the individual's interactions with the socio-ecologic environment, such as physiologic synchronization or desynchronization, frequency division and/or multiplication, variance transposition or rhythm scrambling in the face of complex (circadian, circaseptan, or circannual) schedules in shiftwork and transmeridian or transequatorial travel;

4. A set of mechanisms for multiple rhythmic interactions, the so-called feedsidewards (see **Feedsideward**) in biologic networks, that substitute for oversimplified feedbacks along axes. For example, a built-in adrenal cycle exhibits in vitro a spontaneous (α) rhythm; it reacts to the pituitary hormone ACTH in a periodic fashion, as a response (β) rhythm; and it interacts with the pineal as a circadian, unifrequency (γ) or a circadian-circaseptan multifrequency (δ) modulatory rhythm.

5. A view of the *adaptive* Darwinian evolution of species that acquired a chronome, in health or disease, including some rhythmic changes that resonate with geophysical environmental periodicities complemented by a way to look at an internal (integrative) evolution of life on earth as a feature not only of environmental adaptation but also of temporal coordination.

APPLICATIONS IN MEDICINE

Applications in medicine are found not only for treatment optimization, but also for diagnosis, prognosis, and screening for disease risk assessment, and thus for prevention. Such applications include the following:

1. A dimension for chemical and physical treatment of, for example, cancer by timed radiotherapy, high blood pressure with beta-blocking agents or diuretics, asthma with corticosteroids, and a host of other conditions, with timing complementary to dosing (see **Chronotherapy**);

2. A way to reduce if not avoid the toxicity of physical stimuli, such as radiation or a host of drugs. Cases in point are the cardiac drug ouabain, corticosteroids, psychiatric normalizers, anesthetic agents, and cancer chemo-

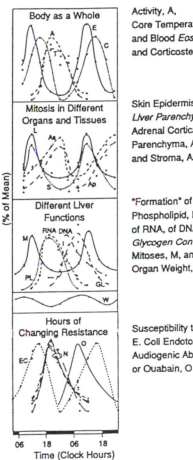

Figure 1. Ubiquity of circadian periodicity found at different levels of organization, characterizing the body as a whole (top), a given phenomenon (mitosis) in different organs and tissues (second), and different functions of a given organ (such as liver, third). In the latter case, a map of the sequence of events is provided, showing a clear lead of RNA over DNA formation. The hours of changing resistance are illustrated in the bottom panel.

therapy with agents such as doxorubicin, cisplatin, arabinosyl cytosine, vincristine, cyclophosphamide, and melphalan, among others. The body's resistance to many other kinds of agents is documented to undergo rhythmic change;

3. A basis for diagnosis of, for example, Addison's disease or Cushing's syndrome by sampling blood for circulating cortisol in the morning or evening, respectively;

4. A chronobiologic approach in particular to the study of time-patterned variation in pathology, such as nocturnal versus diurnal blood pressure elevation, epilepsy, asthma, or filariasis;

5. A basis for prognosis of, for example, hypercortisolism, accelerated blood pressure elevation, or sudden, presumably cardiac, death;

6. A way toward self-help in preventive as well as in medically-guided curative health care;

7. A way to optimize the use of calories, exploiting different effects upon body weight gain as, for example, a function of consuming all daily calories within one hour of awakening or not before twelve hours after awakening;

8. A way to assess the risk of developing diseases such as breast cancer, certain cardio-, cerebro-, reno-, and retinovascular diseases, emotional

Table 1: Tentative period ranges of biologic rhythms*

Domain Region	Range				Illustrative example	Validated from free-running reference period
ultradian	$\tau <$	20		h		
circacentuminutan	$\tau =$	1.7 ±	1	h	EEG-sleep-wakefulness of narcoleptics	
circaoctohoran	$\tau =$	8 ±	1.5	h		
circasemidian	$\tau =$	12 ±	2	h		
circadian	$\tau =$	24 ±	4	h	Human adrenal cortical cycle	Yes
dian	$\tau =$	24 ±	0.2	h	Murine core temperature synchronized by 12 h light alternating with 12 h darkness	Yes
infradian	$\tau >$	28		h		
circadidian	$\tau =$	2 ±	0.5	d		
circasemiseptan	$\tau =$	3.5 ±	1	d	Sudden human death	Yes
circaseptan	$\tau =$	7 ±	1.5	d	Human 17-ketosteroid excretion Egg-laying of *Folsomia candida* Luminescence of *Gonyaulax* Response of *Acetabularia*	Yes
circadecan	$\tau =$	10		d		
circadiseptan	$\tau =$	14 ±	3	d		
circavigintan	$\tau =$	21 ±	3	d		
circatrigintan	$\tau =$	30 ±	5	d	Human gonadal cycle	
circannual	$\tau =$	1 y ±	2	m	Gonadal index of catfish	Yes
circaseptennian	$\tau =$	7 ±	1	y	Gonadal index of marine invertebrates	Yes
circaduodecennian	$\tau =$	12 ±	2	y	Human blood pressure	Yes†

*τ = period; h = hour; d = day; m = month; y = year. Terms coined to approximate validated spectral components, many of them separate physiologic rhythms. By analogy to usage in physics, where frequencies higher than those audible or visible are called ultrasonic and ultraviolet, frequencies higher than one cycle per 20 h are designated as ultradian. By the same token, as frequencies lower than audible or visible are called infrasonic and infrared, rhythms with a frequency lower than one cycle per 28 h are designated as infradian. The suffix -*ennian* instead of -*annual* for periods longer than 1 year serves to avoid the connotation of 'annual' as a suffix after numbers larger than 1 to denote events that repeat themselves within the year, as in *biannual* or *triannual*, meaning twice or thrice a year. The change from *duo-* (used earlier in *circaduodian*) to *di-* is prompted by the desire for consistency (e.g., with *circadiseptan*) and by the need to use an infix that denotes a doubling (rather than the addition of two, as done advisedly in *circaduodecennian*). A term such as *circasemidian* (and, perhaps, others if left unqualified) describes only a spectral component, without any implication as to whether the component represents a rhythm in its own right, rather than merely the waveform of a rhythm with a different (e.g., lower) frequency. Physiologic tests are required to distinguish these possibilities. A single human variable such as blood pressure or heart rate may exhibit spectral components with most if not all of the periods listed.
†Sunspot cycle during same span.

depression, anxiety, alcoholism, and other chemical dependencies;

9. A paradigm of preventive medicine, such as assessment, during pregnancy and in the newborn, of the risk of developing high blood pressure later in life (see **Chronotherapy**); and

10. An approach toward optimizing, by the manipulation of routines or drugs, the eminently multifrequency rhythmic immune system and its earliest changes as it evolves toward diseases such as cancer or acquired immune deficiency syndrome (AIDS). Many individuals who carry an infectious agent (such as a virus) do not exhibit overt pathology. One of the challenges of our day for chronoimmunopharmacology lies in the field of chronobiologic mechanisms underlying (about-daily, -weekly, -monthly, and -yearly) rhythmically recurring deficits in immunity and their prevention by appropriate chronobiologic defense initiatives, complementing the approach by vaccines.

SUMMARY

Applied chronobiology involves a better understanding of underlying mechanisms, a combination of therapeutic applications, and the development of new modalities of preventive interventions. And these illustrate only the medical aspects of dividends offered by chronobiology. To summarize, chronobiology may be seen as a science in its own right with a substantial body of stimulating facts, integrated by unifying mechanisms—such as cephalo-endocrine and cellular feedsidewards and chronomodulation—leading to new principles such as internal as well as adaptive evolution, and offering procedures for various applications throughout human health care, veterinary medicine, animal husbandry, agriculture, and other fields of biology.

Moreover, chronobiology is not only a science in its own right, not only a new broad methodology for study design and analysis, not only a new kind of statistical analysis, and not just an aspect of biology; whether its focus is directed at the integrity of the body or at that of the inseparable socio-ecologic niche and the even broader cosmic environment, chronobiology is a new objective way of invariably approaching any problem in biology broadly. The development of a chronome (chronomo-ontogenesis) in the very premature human infant (see **Chronome**) may reflect chronomo-phylo-

genesis; the multifrequency structure acquired in chronomo-phylogenesis, in turn, may reflect, in part, the solar system at life's origin. If so, chronomo-ontogenesis tells the evolutionary biologist about the basic time structure of earliest life, which in turn may provide solar physicists with a glimpse of the solar system dynamics several billion years ago.

[G.C., F.H., and R.P.S.]

See also **Biological Rhythms in Epidemiology and Chronopharmacology; Chronohygiene; Chronome; Chronopathology; Chronophysiology; Chronotherapy; Circaseptan; Feedsideward; Free-Running in Chronobiology.**

FURTHER READINGS

Cornélissen, G., and F. Halberg. "Toward a 'Chron-Sensus' on Neuroimmunomodulation, with 'Modulation' Operationally and Inferentially Defined." *Ontogenetic and Phylogenetic Mechanisms of Neuroimmunomodulation: From Molecular Biology to Psychosocial Sciences*. Ed. N. Fabris, et al. *New York Academy of Sciences* 650 (1992): 60–67.

Halberg, F. "Chronobiology." *Annual Review of Physiology* 31 (1969): 675–725.

——. "*Quo Vadis* Basic and Clinical Chronobiology: Promise for Health Maintenance." *American Journal of Anatomy* 168 (1983): 543–594.

——. "The Sphygmochron for Chronobiological Blood Pressure and Heart Rate Assessment." *Dialogue in Hypertension* 4.2 (1990): 4–8, and 4.3 (1990): 1–3.

Halberg, F., and A. Ahlgren. "Prologue: Puzzles Regarding Biologic Rhythms and Their Implications for Self-Help in Health Care." *Chronobiology: Principles and Applications to Shifts in Schedules*. Ed. L.E. Scheving and F. Halberg. Alphen aan den Rijn: Sijthoff and Noordhoff, 1980. v–xxiii.

Halberg, F., G. Cornélissen, and F. Carandente. "Chronobiology Meets the Need for Integration in a Reductionist Climate of Biology and Medicine." *Chronobiologia* 18 (1991): 93–103.

Halberg, F., et al. *Glossary of Chronobiology. Chronobiologia* 4, Supplement 1, 1977.

——. "Circaseptan Biologic Time Structure Reviewed in the Light of Contributions by Laurence K. Cutkomp and Ladislav Dérer." *Acta entomologica bohemoslavica* 87 (1990): 1–29.

——. *International Womb-to-Tomb Chronome Initiative Group: Chronobiology in Space*. Minneapolis: University of Minnesota/Medtronic Chronobiology Seminar Series Number 1, December 1991. 21 pages, 70 figures.

——. "Toward Chronobiologic Optimization of Nutrition for Cancer Treatment and Broad Disease Prevention." *The Role of Nutrients in Cancer Treatment, Report of the 9th Ross Conference on Medical*

Research. Ed. A.F. Roche. Columbus: Ross Laboratories, 1991. 2–9.

Reinberg, A., and M.H. Smolensky. *Biological Rhythms and Medicine: Cellular, Metabolic, Physiopathologic, and Pharmacologic Aspects*. New York: Springer, 1983.

Touitou, Y., and E. Haus, eds. *Biological Rhythms in Clinical and Laboratory Medicine*. Berlin: Springer, 1992.

Young, M.W., ed. *Molecular Genetics of Biological Rhythms*. Cellular Clocks Series Number 4. New York: Marcel Dekker, 1992.

CHRONOBIOLOGY OF THE CELL CYCLE

The cell cycle is a series of stages that a cell must go through in sequence if it is to replicate normally. The cell cycle is divided into four phases: (1) the M (mitosis) phase; (2) the G1 or pre-synthetic phase; (3) the S phase or the period of time when DNA synthesis takes place; and (4) the G2 or post-synthetic DNA phase, the time period between the end of the S phase and the beginning of the M phase.

The M or mitotic phase is further subdivided into four components: (1) prophase, which represents the preliminary stage of division; (2) metaphase, the stage during which the chromosomes split and move into a characteristic position; (3) anaphase, the stage during which duplicated chromosomes are moving to opposite poles of the cell; and (4) telophase, the final phase of mitosis during which the major event is that the cell divides into two daughter cells. Some cells undergo proliferation or "run" the cell cycle throughout the life of the organism. Other cells are unable to reproduce themselves after their initial work of organ formation has been completed. Cells incapable of "running" the cycle are said to be "out of cycle" or in a special quiescent phase called *Go* phase. An example of such a cell would be the neuron.

It has been learned recently that the cell cycle is temporally organized, with the time duration of the in vivo mammalian cell taking place with a frequency of about twenty-four hours. Such a frequency is commonly called *circadian* (< Latin *circa*, about; *dies*, a day). During each stage of the cycle characteristic metabolic events take place. The cell-proliferation rhythms are *covert* and therefore must be adequately monitored in order to render them *overt*. If a particular metabolic event can be adequately monitored at frequent intervals along the twenty-four-hour scale, a predictable rhythm in the event can be demonstrated. Unfortunately, in the past, many scientists either underestimated the magnitude of change or they made a priori assumptions that the rhythmic behavior was only a passive consequence either of the light-dark cycle, the sleep-awake cycle, or the timing of meals. A critical mass of data now exists which proves that none of the above are true. The cell-proliferation rhythms are *endogenous*, that is to say generated by the organism. The rhythm seen is only synchronized to the light-dark cycle (either the natural or artificial one), not produced by it.

All mitotically active tissues undergo circadian variation and this has been shown to persist (in, for example, the cornea of rodents) until the day of the organism's death. In the case of the rodent cornea, cell proliferation can be viewed directly after staining the whole tissue. It has been reported that the mitotic (*M*) stage of the cycle will peak about the time the environmental light-dark cycle (natural or artificial) comes on, and the trough occurs about the time the lights go off. It is important to realize that the variation in this tissue may be eight- to ten-fold, with virtually no cells being present in the mitotic phase at trough time.

Other tissues have been evaluated by monitoring the rates of DNA synthesis with radioisotopes. The variation in different parts of the fore- and hind-gut of the rodent may vary four- or five-fold from trough to peak along the twenty-four-hour time scale. The rhythm in the small intestine may vary less, but it is still temporally organized.

In the human skin, the majority of cells in the mitotic stage can be monitored through small biopsies by counting stained chromosomes that are in the process of dividing (metaphase and anaphase). When properly monitored (with sampling at frequent intervals over one or more circadian spans), it was found that the majority of cells in the human skin divide between midnight and 4:00 A.M.

That such circadian variation occurs has only been widely accepted by scientists in recent years. In fact, it had long been dogma that cells divide in a random manner. This idea came about primarily from studies done on the rodent intestinal tract. Such erroneous views brought about many studies, but of these many are today questionable, simply because the rhythm seen in vivo was not recognized. Many of these studies involved measuring the duration of each stage or total generation time of the cell cycle by an inadequate technique that assumed randomness and not rhythmicity.

The rhythm in cell proliferation should not be ignored for many reasons. For example, many anti-cancer agents have as their target primarily those cells that are in the processes of dividing; especially important are those in the intestinal tract and bone marrow. Some agents act on the S phase, some on the M phase, and others at other stages of the cell cycle. The profile of the rhythm can be taken advantage of to effectively reduce toxicity within the organism receiving anticancer drugs. This is done by giving the drug at a time when fewer normal cells are likely to be dividing, thus killing fewer healthy cells and more malignant cells, which, unlike healthy cells, are likely to be dividing at random. This amounts to a *shielding in time* of the healthy tissues while still attacking the tumor. A plethora of data from animal experiments supports this concept. Similar studies are beginning in the clinics and they are very promising. However, more work has to be done before physicians can routinely apply this procedure to the cancer patient.

Consideration of the rhythmic behavior characterizing the in vivo dividing cell may ultimately result in an understanding of the mechanism of cell division in both normal and malignant cells.

[L.E.S.]

See also **Biological Rhythms and Medicine; Biological Rhythms in Epidemiology and Pharmacology; Cancer and Time; Chronbiology; Molecular and Biochemical Rhythms.**

FURTHER READINGS.

Burns, E. Robert, and Lawrence E. Scheving. "Circadian Influence on the Wave Form of the Frequency of Labeled Mitosis in Mouse Corneal Epithelium." *Cell Tissue Kinetics* 8 (1975): 61-66.

Scheving, L.E., et al. "The Potential of Using the Natural Rhythmicity of Cell Proliferation in Improving Cancer Chemotherapy." *Temporal Control of Drug Therapy.* Ed. W.J.M. Hrushesky, R. Langer, and F. Theeuwes. *Annals of the New York Academy of Sciences* 618 (1991): 182–227.

CHRONOHYGIENE

Chronohygiene is concerned with the improvement of health by methods such as the implementation of prophylactic intervention aimed at disease risk-lowering, and by relying on procedures such as the scheduling of food intake, exercise, and other hygienic activities that take

into account the time structure of both the organism and its environment. The latter include relations of people with each other and broad environmental-organismic interactions that can be described as a chronocosmosymbiosis. In the case of health care, chrones are end points for the study of the "health gene configurations." The study of disease genes in the current homeostatic genome initiative may well be complemented by the genome mapping in the light of chrones, such as the circadian rhythm of the human heart rate, which has been shown to be emergenic, that is, a high degree of heritability is found for its circadian amplitude in monozygotic but not in dizygotic twins reared apart.

[G.C., F.H., and R.P.S.]

See also **Chronobiology; Chronome; Chronopathology; Chronophysiology; Chronotherapy.**

FURTHER READINGS

Hanson, B.R., et al. "Rhythmometry Reveals Heritability of Circadian Characteristics of Heart Rate of Human Twins Reared Apart." *Cardiologia* 29 (1984): 267–282.

Lykken, D.T., et al. "Emergenesis: Genetic Traits that May Not Run in Families." *American Psychologist* 47 (1992): 1565–1577.

CHRONOLOGY

Chronology (< Greek "chrono," time; + "logia," science) is the science of dating, of ordering time, and of calculating temporal distances between aligned events. Focusing on classical, on Judeo-Christian (A.M. [*Anno Mundi*] and B.C./A.D.), and on scientific (B.P. [Before Present]) chronologies, this article will survey the development of this science over three millennia of Western history and will suggest that the most significant contributions have occurred in the midst of great intellectual revolutions.

CLASSICAL CHRONOLOGY

In the sixth century B.C., Greek exploration of the Mediterranean stimulated an intellectual revolution that affected the view of the past. At this time, Greek chronologies were based largely on genealogical tables that fused myth and historical fact. Three Greek generational historians—Hecataeus of Miletus, Xanthus of Lydia, and Hellicanus of Lesbos—contributed important works in the generational format. In his *Genealogies*, Hecataeus, who was organizing the new geography, dealt with the problem of chronological order. Fragmentary remains of his speculations indicate that he tried to link the age of humanity with a timeless mythical age. In the fifth century B.C., Xanthus recorded the history of his people up to the downfall of King Croesus and attempted to relate past events to natural occurrences such as earthquakes and droughts. And Hellanicus, in his *Troica*, employed a generational count to calculate the fall of Troy, which he identified as having occurred in 1240 B.C. In his *Attic History*, he advanced beyond the generational count with lists of officeholders kept by cities and temples. Two such lists—that of the priestesses of Hera at Argos and that of the winners of the Carnean games—were particularly useful; with the Argos list, Hellicanus ambitiously tried to arrange a multitude of events from Greek, Sicilian, and Roman history. His use of lists inspired other Greek chronologists to devise ordering sequences: Hippias of Elis used the list of Olympic victors and of magistrates in Sparta (beginning with 755 B.C.) and in Athens (683–682 B.C.).

But the diversity of referents and of theoretical approaches was not conducive to the formulation of a uniform time scale. Even in the case of Herodotus, there is little chronological coherence to the independent histories of the Lydians, Persians, Egyptians, and Greeks. For Herodotus, the sense of regional and of temporal interrelatedness was not a unifying element. His efforts to coordinate Greek and oriental time schemes, such as the Egyptian dynastic lists, did not succeed; hence, throughout his *Histories* (except from the Ionian revolt on), the ethnographic and geographical descriptions lack time frames. Although more systematic and genuinely historical in his dating of the Peloponnesian War, Thucydides's chronological perspective was limited to the linear time of the war between Athens and Sparta.

By the fourth century B.C., the Greeks' exposure to new regions and peoples required the coordination of calendars and the formation of a uniform time frame. Timaeus of Tauromenium (third century B.C.) synchronized comparative lists of Spartan kings, of Athenian magistrates, and of Argive priestesses with the list of Olympic victors. Indebted to earlier chronologists such as Aristotle who had refined this dating practice, Timaeus, in his *Olympionicae*, used the Olympiad scale consistently. In both his chronological study of Olympian victors and fragmentary *History of Rome*, he was concerned with the founding and ascendancy of Rome. Although he mixed

myth and historical fact, Timaeus refrained from ascribing the founding of Rome to gods, heroes, or Trojans; rather, he linked Rome's founding with Carthage. Although inquiring into the factual past, and although moving away from dynastic mythology, Greek historiography generally remained topical and insular. And even though Timaeus had provided the Greeks with a common calendar, which Eratosthenes adapted to his great work, *On Chronology*, the Olympiad scale was intrinsically limited since it could not be extended backwards beyond the first Olympic Games of 776 B.C. Furthermore, the lack of political unity among the city-states precluded its uniform use.

The Romans influenced the development of chronological theory. Abandoning the Greeks' generational model as a means of constructing a basic chronology, the Romans developed a lunar calendar by which they scheduled religious festivals and political gatherings. The inevitable cross-fertilization of Greek and of Roman historiography promoted the reconciliation of their respective chronological systems.

One immediate problem the Romans encountered was that their accounts of ethnographic origin—of Aeneas and of Romulus—inherited from the works of Eratosthenes and Timaeus, contained discrepancies. A chronology reflecting the interdependent histories of Greece and Rome, and of the entire Mediterranean culture, was needed. The most influential attempt at such a synthesis was Castor of Rhodes's *Chronicle*. Based on the works of Apollodorus of Athens (second century B.C.), this work traced events from the Assyrians to 60 B.C. and took the form of chronological tables. A compendium of Mediterranean kingship, the *Chronicle* influenced many great historians, such as Varro, Sextus Julius Africanus, and Eusebius.

JUDEO-CHRISTIAN CHRONOLOGIES: A.M. AND B.C./A.D.

Nearly fifty years before Christianity became the official religion of Rome in A.D. 313, Christian historians were interested in creating a Christian framework for the past, a task that necessarily involved chronology. To understand these early attempts at Christian chronology, it is important first to reflect upon Jewish conceptions of time. Certainly, the Old Testament contained historical records, but these records were not coordinated in a specific time frame. After Alexander the Great (356–323 B.C.), the Jews relied on the Seleucid era for dating years up to the destruction of the temple in A.D. 70, which provided a starting point for a genuinely Jewish era. At an undetermined point, however, the Jews decided to date their origin with the Creation. These years would be designated as A.M. (*anno ab origin mundi*).

Late in the third century, Sextus Julius Africanus, in his *Chronography*, made the first Christian attempt to subsume Near Eastern, Greek, and Roman history under a Judeo-Christian time scheme by calculating that 5,500 years had elapsed between Adam and the birth of Christ. Another significant contribution to patristic chronology came from Constantine's advisor, Eusebius, bishop of Caesarea. In his two major works, the *Chronicle* and the *Ecclesiastical History*, he borrowed from Hellenistic historians, such as Castor of Rhodes, and announced the triumph of Christianity. As for important dates, such as the birth of Christ, Eusebius, like Sextus Julius Africanus, derived his calculations from Scripture, but Eusebius's results were not always uniform; for instance, Eusebius figured Christ's birth to have been 5,198 years from Adam or 2,015 years from Abraham, whereas Africanus designated Christ's birth to have been 5500 A.M. The discrepancy, attributable to different versions of the Old Testament, influenced Eastern historians who would come to rely on Africanus's Latin chronology, upon which they based their liturgical calendar. Those in the West preferred Eusebius's Greek texts, which Jerome would translate into Latin, and which would predominate up until Bede's revision.

Between 400 and 650, Western historians subscribed to the Eusebian chronology in Jerome's Latin translation, whereas only Jordanes, who lived in the East, subscribed to Africanus's system. But the diversity of systems made it difficult to write accurate historiography. In his *History of the Franks*, Gregory of Tours encountered three contradictory liturgical calendars (devised by Eusebius and Jerome, by Paulus Orosius, and by Victorius of Aquitaine). Uncertain about where to situate Frankish history chronologically, he decided to adopt Victorius's calendar that began with Christ's Passion, A.D. 28.

The problem of contradictory liturgical chronologies clearly affected any attempt to write secular historiography. The solution occurred as a natural development of patristic chronological theory. In A.D. 525, Dionysius Exiguus, a Roman scholar, outlined an Easter table based on Christ's birth. Advent was to be celebrated on December 25, a date corresponding to the beginning of the Roman year. Abandoning the Greek chronology entirely, and following the Alexandrian table, which covered a ninety-five year period from 437 to 531, Dionysius calculated Christ's Crucifixion to have occurred in A.D. 34. In 559, when Dionysius's cyclical periods fortuitously coincided with those outlined by Victorius of Aquitaine, the Incarnation became accepted as year 1. Used by the Venerable Bede (672/3–735) in *On Time* and *On the Reckoning of Time*, this linear chronology, beginning with Christ's birth and designated "Anno Domini" or A.D., became the traditional time scheme.

After 1500, at least fifty different dating schemes, or "world eras," existed, claiming to account for the time preceding the Incarnation. In 1573, the great scholar, Joseph Justus Scaliger (1540–1609), in his *Restoration of Chronology*, and later in his *Thesaurus of Dates*, used the new mathematics and astronomy to realign all dates on the basis of what came to be known as the Julian period that began arbitrarily on January 1, 4713 B.C. Dionysius Petavius, S.J. (1583–1652) tried to date events prior to Christ's birth according to the Olympiads, world eras, and the foundation of Rome. His great innovation, the revival of the B.C. scheme, computed history anterior to the Incarnation. By 1650, the B.C. scheme, conducive to both Catholic and Protestant outlooks, received universal application in the West.

CHRONOLOGY AND THE NATURAL SCIENCES: B.P.

The discoveries of early naturalists challenged the adequacy of the B.C./A.D. chronology, a challenge that was subtly strengthened with each new discovery. At the end of the seventeenth century, some naturalists tried to square fossil evidence with the received tradition. The Reverend John Ray (1627–1705), a Cambridge University lecturer, discovered marine fossils inland, but attributed his findings to the great deluge that had supposedly deposited marine life in the mountains. Another seventeenth-century naturalist, Isaac de la Peyrère, courageously published a book arguing that his collection of chipped stones antedated Adam, but his work was burned in 1655. The conventional position found its strongest advocate in Archbishop James Ussher of Armagh, Ireland, who in 1650 determined the year of Creation to have been 4004 B.C.

A preponderance of physical evidence began to prevail in the eighteenth century. When Georges Cuvier (1769–1832), a professor of natural history at the College de France, excavated strata rich with fossils, it became clear that inland seas had deposited these creatures in the distant past. But Cuvier, a devout Huguenot, did not take the step leading to a theory of evolution by suggesting that one species had arisen from another. Rather, he articulated the theory of catastrophism: that vast floods occurred in succession, wiping out old life forms and replacing them with new ones. Charles Lyell (1797–1875), whose theory of uniformitarianism held that geological forces were dynamically reshaping the earth, eventually synthesized disparate theories and scattered evidence to suggest that the earth's chronology exceeded six thousand years. Together with the notion of James Hutton (1726–1797)—in his *Theory of the Earth* (1795)—that the earth was of great antiquity, Lyell's theory suggested that the earth was undergoing dynamic, though imperceptibly gradual, change. To the eighteenth-century mind accustomed to the biblical idea that the earth's chronology extended backward only six millennia, these were astonishing revelations.

Lyell's great work, *Principles of Geology* (1830 and 1833), influenced the young Charles Darwin (1809–1882), who in 1859 published his *On the Origin of Species by Means of Natural Selection,* which suggested that mankind had descended from simian antecedents. Through comparative anatomy, Thomas H. Huxley (1825–1895), a colleague of Darwin's, argued that all animals on earth, and especially the great apes, were related to mankind. Darwin, in *The Descent of Man* (1871), propounded the idea of an unbroken chain of organisms that began with ancient life forms and that evolved to the human species. With the 1868 discovery of Cro-Magnon man in the Dordogne region of France, powerful archeological evidence existed to dispute the biblical scheme. The discoveries of Cro-Magnon, who lived 40,000 years before the present, as well as of Homo Erectus, of Peking Man, and of Australopithecus in the twentieth century, required a revised chronological designation that would incisively convey the relationship between modern man and his primitive ancestors. For modern naturalists, the secular designation B.P. (before present) replaced the B.C./A.D. schemes.

Subject to revision with each new paleontological discovery, modern geological time scales employ the B.P. designation, along with periodization, to convey great temporal magnitudes and significant biological events. Thus, the Precambrian period (the formation of the earth, of the primordial sea, of the first algae and bacteria, and of the first oxygen-breathing animals) extends from 4.5 billion to 570 million B.P.; the Paleozoic (first invertebrates and vertebrates) from 570 to 255 million years B.P.; the Mesozoic (reptiles, mammals, birds, flowering plants) from 225 to 65 million B.P.; and the Cenozoic (first primates, prehominids, humans) from 65 million B.P. to the present. The B.P. perspective allows one to survey eras from the fixed present, and the geological time scale stratifies natural history into eras and periods (for example, the Paleozoic into the Cambrian, Ordovician, Silurian, Devonian, Carboniferous, and Permian).

Facilitating the understanding of one's relationship to temporal periods and events, chronology relates historical facts to each other and at the same time to the chronologist. But even with the most carefully designed scale, one can easily lose a sense of proportion: it is difficult, for instance, to conceptualize the notion of the Precambrian era being 570 million years long. To communicate their findings more effectively, scientific writers have resorted to analogies, figurative models comparing vast magnitudes of geological time with similar but more easily apprehensible time units, such as one hour or one year.

Two examples of analogical prehistoriography will illustrate this innovation. Bernard G. Campbell illustrates the "hour" model: "If the almost six hundred million years of vertebrate evolution is symbolized by one hour of time, then primate evolution has taken seven minutes and man's evolution occurred in the last twelve seconds of that hour." An example of the "year" model is Carl Sagan's "cosmic chronology" in *The Dragons of Eden.* In a "year" model of this type, if the universe, the Milky Way, and the earth in approximate figures are taken as being respectively 15, 10, and 5 billion years old, they would have their respective beginnings on January 1, May 1, and September 1. However, the whole of the modern period since the seventeenth century with which this article has been much concerned would fit comfortably into the last second of that "year," namely between 11:59:59 and midnight. Furthermore, the entire year from which the scientist's B.P. is measured would extend for only the last .002 of that final second. The advantage of an analogical model of this type is that it contextualizes time so that cosmic and natural history exist on a continuum.

Though temporally distant from one another, the four most prominent developments that took place in the history of chronology—the Greek Olympiad (fourth century B.C.), "Anno Domini" (Exiguus, sixth century A.D.), "Before Christ" (Petavius, sixteenth century A.D.), and "Before Present" (twentieth century A.D.)—have arisen in the midst of great intellectual revolutions. The Greek exploration of the greater Mediterranean, and the Greeks' exposure to other cultures, especially to the Romans, freed them from the insularity of heroic legend and myth, thus permitting writers such as Timaeus, Eratosthenes, and Thucydides to develop genuine historiography and a viable though limited chronology: the Olympiad. "Anno Domini," a product of the patristic tradition and of the fortuitous convergence of Victorius's and Dionysius's timetables, became the traditional designation for time posterior to the Incarnation. The adaptation of the B.C. scheme in the seventeenth century is directly attributable to the works of Scaliger and of Petavius whose conclusions, though theologically orientated, applied mathematics and the new science to historical data. Finally, the "B.P." designation, the logical consequence of a scientific and technological revolution in the twentieth century, has separated theology from the natural sciences and has led to a deeper and more comprehensive understanding of the origin of the universe and of life on earth. The possible synthesis of the theological and scientific chronologies remains an evocative problem.

[C.D.]

FURTHER READINGS

Albritton, Claude C., Jr. *The Abyss of Time: Changing Conceptions of the Earth's Antiquity after the Sixteenth Century*. New York: St. Martin's P, 1986.

Breisach, Ernst. *Historiography: Ancient, Medieval, and Modern*. Chicago: U of Chicago P, 1983.

Bronowski, Jacob. *The Ascent of Man*. Boston: Little, Brown, 1973.

Campbell, Bernard G., ed. *Humankind Emerging*. Boston: Little, Brown, 1976.

Eisley, Loren. *Darwin's Century: Evolution and the Men Who Discovered It*. New York: Doubleday Anchor, 1961.

Leakey, Richard E., and Roger Lewin. *Origins: The Emergence and Evolution of Our Species and Its Possible Future*. New York: Dutton, 1977.

Macey, Samuel L. *The Dynamics of Progress: Time, Method, and Measure*. Athens: U of Georgia P, 1989.

Sagan, Carl. *The Dragons of Eden: Speculations on the Evolution of Human Intelligence*. New York: Random House, 1977.

Whitrow, G.J. "Time and Measurement." *Dictionary of the History of Ideas: Studies of Selected Pivotal Ideas*. Ed. Philip P. Wiener. 5 vols. New York: Scribner's, 1973. 4:398b–406a.

Wilcox, Donald J. *The Measure of Times Past: Pre-Newtonian Chronologies and the Rhetoric of Relative Time*. Chicago: U of Chicago P, 1987.

CHRONOME

The term "chronome"—derived from *chronos* (time), *nomos* (rule, law), and *chromosome*—describes features in time, just as cells characterize the spatial organization of life. The chronome complements the genome (derived from *gene* and *chromosome*). The chronome consists of (1) a partly genetic, partly developmental, partly environmental multifrequency spectrum of rhythms that (2) undergo trends with growth, development, maturation, and aging in health and/or trends with an elevation of disease risk, illness, and treatment in disease and of (3) unresolved residuals—stochastic or deterministic chaos. The chronome is genetically coded; it is environmentally synchronized by cycles of the socioecologic habitat niche; and it is influenced by the dynamics of the interplanetary magnetic field.

The chronome constituents, the "chrones," algorithmically formulated end points, are inferentially and statistically validated and resolved by computer.

Chronomes and their chrones: (1) quantify normalcy, allowing an individualized positive health quantification; (2) assess by their alterations the earliest abnormality, including the quantification of an elevated risk of developing one (or several) disease(s), chronorisk, by the alteration of one or several chrones; (3) provide, by the study of underlying mechanisms, a rational basis in the search for measures aimed at the prevention of any deterioration in properly timed, mutually beneficial environmental-organismic interactions.

[G.C., F.H., and R.P.S.]

See also **Chronobiology.**

FURTHER READINGS

Cornélissen, G., and F. Halberg. "Broadly Pertinent Chronobiology Methods Quantify Phosphate Dynamics (Chronome) in Blood and Urine." *Clinical Chemistry* 38 (1992): 329–333.

Halberg, F. "Norberto Montalbetti: 1936–1991." *Bioquimica Clinica* 16 (1991): 43–46.

Halberg, F., and G. Cornélissen. "Consensus Concerning the Chronome and the Addition to Statistical Significance of Scientific Signification." *Biochimica Clinica* 15 (1991): 159–162.

Halberg F., et al. *International Womb-to-Tomb Chronome Initiative Group: Chronobiology in Space*. University of Minnesota/Medtronic Chronobiology Seminar Series, Number 1, December 1991. 21 pages, 70 figures.

CHRONOPATHOLOGY

Chronopathology describes alterations in dynamic parameters in addition to deviations in the overall mean, thus recognizing an elevation in disease risk and covert prepathology before pathology becomes overt and symptomatic. The monitoring of physiologic variables in time, combined with chronobiologic data analysis (chronobiometry), detects unfavorable constellations of certain temporal parameters early, such as in neonates in relation to their familial risk of developing a high blood pressure and/or other cardiovascular diseases later in life or in neonates who have been exposed *in utero* to betamimetic drugs. The amplitude of circannual rhythms has also been related to the risk of developing various civilization diseases, such as blood pressure and circulating aldosterone with respect to cardiovascular disease risk, and circulating prolactin and thyroid-stimulating hormone with respect to cancer of the breast or the prostate.

[G.C., F.H., and R.P.S.]

See also **Chronobiology; Chronohygiene; Chronophysiology; Chronotherapy.**

FURTHER READINGS

Cornélissen, G., et al. "Chronobiologic Approach to Blood Pressure During Pregnancy and Early Extrauterine Life." *Chronobiology: Its Role in Clinical Medicine, General Biology, and Agriculture, Part A*. Ed. D.K. Hayes, J.E. Pauly, and R.J. Reiter. New York: Wiley-Liss, 1990. 585–594.

Halberg, F. "*Quo Vadis* Basic and Clinical Chronobiology: Promise for Health Maintenance." *American Journal of Anatomy* 168 (1983): 543–594.

Halberg, F., G. Cornélissen, and E. Bakken. "Caregiving Merged with Chronobiologic Outcome Assessment, Research and Education in Health Maintenance Organizations (HMOs)." *Chronobiology. . . Part B*. Ed. Hayes, Pauly, and Reiter. (1990): 491–549.

Halberg, F., et al. "International Geographic Studies of Oncological Interest on Chronobiological Variables." *Neoplasms—Comparative Pathology of Growth in Animals, Plants and Man*. Ed. H. Kaiser. Baltimore: Williams and Wilkins, 1981. 553–596.

Syutkina, E.V., et al. "Intrauterine Exposure to Betamimetics Affects Adolescent Circadian Blood Pressure (BP) and Heart Rate (HR) Rhythms." *Biochimica Clinica* 15 (1991): 158–159.

Tarquini, B., et al. "Infradian, Notably Circannual, Cardiovascular Variation Gauging Effect of Intrauterine Exposure to B-Adrenergic Agonists." *Chronobiology. . . Part A*. Ed. Hayes, Pauly, and Reiter. (1990): 595–604.

CHRONOPHYSIOLOGY

Chronophysiology quantifies, in every field of biology, changes within as well as outside the otherwise neglected "normal" ranges of variation. The latter need no longer be regarded or handled as indivisible, as once was the atom. Particularly in the fields of physiology, laboratory medicine, and bioengineering, the normal range gains from being split (like fission) into chrones, that is, rhythms and trends whose characteristics can be objectively quantified along with any other temporal features such as deterministic or stochastic chaos. Yet, more novel physiologic relations within the organism and its socio-ecologic and broader cosmic environments are resolved by the integration (like fusion) of chrones into chronomes and by mapping the relations among chronomes, studied by cross-spectral coherence and coordinated through "feedsidewards" (that is, interactions among multiple rhythmic entities that result in predictable sequences of attenuation, no-effect, and amplification of the effect of one entity—the actor—upon another entity—the reactor—as it is modified by a third entity—the modulator). Heretofore inaccessible dimensions of normalcy (for example, health) and risk elevation are thus quantified, allowing the exploitation of the normal variation in the range in which it occurs, rather than using the abnormal to define the normal.

[G.C., F.H., AND R.P.S.]

See also **Chronobiology; Chronohygiene; Chronome; Chronopathology; Chronotherapy; Feedsideward; Free-Running in Chronobiology.**

FURTHER READINGS

Cornélissen, G., F. Halberg, and B. Tarquini. "Ultradian Rhythms: A Neglected Yet Promising Domain of the Rhythm Spectrum." *XV World Congress of Anatomic and Clinical Pathology, Florence, May 16–20, 1989*. Ed. M. Fanfani and B. Tarquini, 1990. 275–287.

Cornélissen, G., et al. "From Meetings in Florence and Milan: Chronobiology Extends and Integrates the Scope of Anatomic and Clinical Pathology." *Biochimica Clinica* 14 (1990): 203–208.

Halberg, F. "Chronobiologic Engineering." *Infusion Systems in Medicine.* Ed. W.D. Ensminger and J. L. Selam. Mount Kisko: Futura Publishing, 1987. 263–297.

Halberg, F., G. Cornélissen, and B. Tarquini. "Chronobiology and Chronopathology 1990: State of the Art, Parallaxes and Perspectives." *XV World Congress of Anatomic and Clinical Pathology, Florence, May 16–20, 1989.* Ed. M. Fanfani and B. Tarquini, 1990. 245–259.

CHRONOTHERAPY

Chronotherapy is the study of the effects of timed treatment of any modality, which includes, among other subdisciplines, chronopharmacology, the study of timed drug treatment, and chronotoxicology, the study of rhythm-stage-dependent undesired effects of toxic agents, as well as the effect of agents upon temporal parameters. Chronotherapy involves any treatment targeted in time in order (1) to exploit maximal benefit from treatment effects that vary as a function of administration time, specified in relation to the organism's time structure, and/or (2) to correct any detrimental alteration in the organism's time structure itself associated with disease risk elevation, if not pathology. The concepts underlying chronotherapy result directly from the demonstration of the hours of changing resistance, the outcome from exposure to a given (fixed) stimulus differing drastically as a function of when (in relation to the chronome) it is applied. In particular, cancer treatment should be targeted in time, since it further benefits from the mapping of the circadian cell cycle (see **Chronobiology**).

The optimization of the timing of treatment administration is concerned with the improvement of treatment efficacy and with the lowering of treatment toxicity by optimization along the scales of the biologic day and the biologic week and/or other chronome components rather than according to the clock-hours when the physician and the clinical facilities are available, that is, during "regular hours" on workdays, at the convenience of the health care system and the patient. Cancer treatment being usually highly toxic, the drugs used can cause harm to various organs such as the bone marrow, heart, kidney, gut, or nervous system. The cancer may also be hit, but the treatment may not be optimally planned. As a consequence, before killing the cancer, the treatment may kill the patient.

Marker rhythms are helpful for determining when a given agent is less toxic to the host; they make it possible to time treatment to minimize the undesired toxic effects of the treatment. Whereas targeting by tolerance markers lessens the impairment of life quality, it does not necessarily correspond to the optimization of the treatment's efficacy. Large amplitude circadian (and other) rhythms have been mapped for some tumor markers in saliva and urine. Their noninvasive assessability renders them suitable as putative marker rhythms for guiding treatment timing so as to optimize efficacy, whether or not they reflect tumor burden. While target-

CHRONORADIOTHERAPY AT CIRCADIAN PEAK IN HUMAN PERIORAL TUMOR TEMPERATURE DOUBLES THERAPEUTIC GAIN

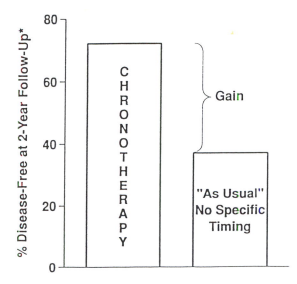

* Excluding 1 or 2 patients/group (total = 8) unavailable at follow-up (Halberg et al., 1977).

Figure 1. In the clinic, a relatively unspecified marker, tumor temperature, served for guiding the radiotherapy of patients with cancer of the oral cavity. The patients were randomly assigned to receive the treatment at one of five different circadian stages, either at the time of their daily peak tumor temperature (left) or four or eight hours before or after that time. Tumor regression rate was largest for those patients receiving the treatment at the time of their peak tumor temperature. Patients treated at that time also had the largest percentage of disease-free survival at a two-year follow-up. The therapeutic gain was double that resulting from treatment "as usual," that is, without consideration of timing (right).

ing treatment in time by tumor markers may increase the chances of killing the cancer, the treatment may still be accompanied by great toxicity. When proliferation markers exhibit ultradians (rhythms with a period shorter than twenty-four hours), there may be more than a single "best time" to treat each day; it can then be attempted as a secondary consideration to choose, among these times of optimal efficacy, those that also optimally shield the host from the treatment's toxicity.

Whether physical, chemical, or other, chronotherapy is concerned with complementing dosing by timing with the use of powerful chronobiologic pilot designs aimed at determining the optimal rhythm stages of treatment administration. Optimization of treatment by timing according to the organism's time structure should precede, as an indispensable "Phase 0," each of the usual Phase I, II, and III trials, in order to guide the incorporation of timing into all phases of clinical trials, concerned, in the case of new drugs, with their toxicity (Phase I), efficacy (Phase II), and a comparison with the best current treatment (Phase III), respectively. Otherwise, we may test drugs on a homeostatic quicksand, losing, to start with preclinically, many valuable, if properly timed, molecules, and/or ignoring the undue toxicity (at certain times) of other drugs that pass through all stages of clinical trials only to be recalled later after they have been marketed for years.

In addition to optimizing the testing of new drugs, as well as the use of established molecules, chronotherapy aims at ways to optimize prosthetic devices. The fully ambulatory, battery-powered, transistorized Bakken pacemaker is the most successful example of engineering to reestablish the most basic rhythm, the heartbeat. The 1 hertz rhythm of the heart, however, is just one component of the heart's chronome. The demonstration that the amplitude of the circadian heart rate rhythm has a heritable dimension is a stimulus for chronobioengineering which aims at the task of optimizing devices by all components of the chronome. Chronobiologic pacemaker-cardioverter-defibrillators and drug pumps are targets for immediate further improvement. Sooner or later, any therapy, whether by electrical or other physical means (chronoradiotherapy has already been tested) or by drugs, will exploit timing as a complement to dosing. The greatest challenge, however, lies in the recognition of the earliest harmful chronome alteration, such as a circadian amplitude-

hypertension and its timely correction. Prosthetic devices for prevention as needed could be the future of chronotherapy *par excellence*.

[G.C., F.H., and R.P.S.]

See also **Cancer and Time; Cardiovascular Chronopharmacology; Chronobiology; Chronopathology; Chronophysiology.**

FURTHER READINGS

Bakken, E., and K. Heruth. "Temporal Control of Drugs: An Engineering Perspective." *Temporal Control of Drug Delivery*. Ed. W.J.M. Hrushesky, R. Langer, and F. Theeuwes. *Annals of the New York Academy of Sciences* 618 (1991): 422–427.

Bakken, E., et al. "Enhancing the Physiologic Effectiveness of Cardiac Stimulators in Heart Rhythms' Management Using Chronobiology." *Chronobiology: Its Role in Clinical Medicine, General Biology, and Agriculture, Part A*. Ed. D.K. Hayes, J.E. Pauly, and R.J. Reiter. New York: Wiley-Liss, 1990. 347–361.

Bourgeois, I.M., et al. "Toward a Chronobiologic Pacemaker." *Chronobiology: Its Role in Clinical Medicine, General Biology, and Agriculture, Part B*. Ed. D.K. Hayes, J.E. Pauly, and R.J. Reiter. New York: Wiley-Liss, 1990. 379–388.

Carandente, A., and F. Halberg. "Drug Industry and Chronobiology: Achievements and Prospects." *Temporal Control of Drug Delivery*. Ed. W.J.M. Hrushesky, R. Langer, and F. Theeuwes. *Annals of the New York Academy of Sciences* 618 (1991): 484–489.

Cornélissen, G., et al. *Toward Phase Zero Preclinical and Clinical Trials: Chronobiologic Designs and Illustrative Applications*. Minneapolis: University of Minnesota Medtronic Chronobiology Seminar Series, Number 6, September 1992. 411 pages.

Halberg, F. "Chronopharmacology and Chronotherapy." *Cellular Pacemakers*. Ed. D.O. Carpenter. New York: Wiley, 1982. 261–297.

Halberg, F., et al. "24-Hour Periodicity and Audiogenic Convulsions in I Mice of Various Ages." *Proceedings of the Society for Experimental Biology* (New York) 88 (1955): 169–173.

———. "Steps Toward a Cancer Chronopolytherapy." *Proceedings of the XIV International Congress of Therapeutics. Montpellier: L'Expansion Scientifique Française*, 1977. 151–196.

Kumagai, Y., et al. "Usefulness of Circadian Amplitude of Blood Pressure in Predicting Hypertensive Cardiac Involvement." *Chronobiologia* 19 (1992): 43–58.

CIRCADIAN PACEMAKERS

Circadian rhythms are ubiquitous. Plants and animals exhibit approximately twenty-four-hour periodicities in many overt behaviors, such as leaf movements in plants and locomotor activity and sleep-wakefulness cycles in animals. In addition, most internal physiological processes, including the levels of many hormones, exhibit circadian fluctuations. Circadian rhythms have also been implicated in a number of sophisticated animal behaviors, including solar orientation, navigation, seasonal reproductive cycles, and time sense in honey bees.

A wealth of experimental data reveals that circadian rhythms are endogenous and are generated by internal timing mechanisms, commonly referred to as *circadian pacemakers*. In some animals these pacemakers have been localized to specific portions of the central nervous and endocrine systems. For example, in mammals, the circadian pacemaker appears to be located in a small region at the base of the hypothalamus called the suprachiasmatic nuclei (SCN). These paired structures, each approximately 7–10 microns (μM, or millionths of a meter) in diameter, contain approximately 10,000 neurons, or nerve cells. The conclusion that this structure contains a circadian pacemaker is based on numerous lines of evidence; the most compelling is that removal or damage to the structure leads to arhythmicity in behavior while transplantation of fetal SCN tissue restores rhythmicity in a previously SCN-lesioned host animal. Furthermore, the natural period of the donor's activity rhythm (which can be modified through mutation) is now reflected in the reestablished locomotor rhythm of the host animal. It has also been possible to record circadian rhythms in electrical activity from isolated tissue slices of the SCN maintained in a specially designed chamber.

While mammals appear to rely on the SCN as circadian pacemakers for controlling behavioral rhythmicity, in birds the pineal appears to play an important role as a circadian pacemaker in the timing of locomotor activity. The pineal of the house sparrow, *Passer domesticus*, exhibits a circadian rhythm in the release of the hormone melatonin when the gland is removed from the bird and placed into culture medium. As with SCN transplants in the hamster, transplantation of the pineal into a pinealecomized bird (one from which the pineal has been removed) restores rhythmicity and, importantly, the phase of the restored rhythm correlates well with the phase of the rhythm of the donor bird just prior to removal of the pineal. The pineal need not be intact for generation of circadian rhythmicity because the isolated gland maintained outside the brain in vitro can be cut into several parts and each part continues to exhibit a circadian

rhythm in melatonin release. Circadian rhythms in melatonin release have also been reported for pineals that have been dispersed enzymatically into individual cells in cell culture. This suggests that individual cells within the avian pineal are capable of generating circadian rhythms.

Circadian pacemakers have also been identified in invertebrates. In the cockroach, the optic lobes of the brain each appear to contain a circadian pacemaker. Removal of the lobes or small lesions to a specific portion of the lobe (the "lobula" region) leads to behavioral arhythmicity. As with vertebrate pacemakers, transplantation of an optic lobe into a surgically rendered lobeless animal restores the circadian rhythm in locomotor activity, and the natural period of the rhythm in constant conditions closely matches the natural period of the rhythm of the donor and not the host animal.

Research on marine mollusks also provides interesting insights into the basis of circadian rhythms. Several opisthobranch mollusks have been studied in some detail. The well-known "sea hare," *Aplysia californica*, exhibits a rhythm in locomotor activity that is controlled by circadian pacemakers located in each eye. The eye can be removed from the animal, placed into a seawater bathing medium, and a precise rhythm in spontaneous impulse frequency can be recorded from the cut end of the optic nerve of the eye. The rhythm is generated by a class of special retinal neurons and in a related mollusk, *Bulla gouldiana*, "the cloudy bubble snail," it has been demonstrated that each of these neurons is capable of generating a circadian rhythm. From these studies, and those involving vertebrates, it is becoming increasingly clear that the cellular and molecular mechanisms generating circadian rhythms occur within the confines of individual neurons and are not the result of neuronal circuitry within the brain.

The study of circadian pacemakers has also revealed another important principle about how circadian rhythms are controlled. In nearly every case that has been studied, it appears that more than one circadian pacemaker is involved in controlling behavioral rhythmicity. For example, in many cases the circadian pacemaker is located in a bilaterally distributed structure, such as the paired suprachiasmatic nuclei. Each nuclei appears capable of controlling locomotor rhythmicity; removal of only one nucleus, however, has very little effect on behavior, suggesting that both normally participate in the control of rhythmic behaviors. Similarly, in the cockroach, a pacemaker is located in each optic lobe and either lobe can control the locomotor rhythm. Interestingly, the two circadian pacemakers appear to be mutually coupled (that is, the two pacemakers run in synchrony) through neuronal connections. Coupling between the two pacemakers, similar to a rubber band joining two swinging pendulums, prevents the two clocks from coming out of synchrony with one another if the animal is exposed to extended periods of darkness. In the mollusks *Aplysia* and *Bulla* there are circadian pacemakers in each eye, and in *Bulla*, similar to the cockroach, the two circadian pacemakers appear to be internally coupled to one another.

Very little is known about the "nuts and bolts" of individual circadian pacemakers. Biochemical and biophysical experiments are just beginning to provide glimpses of the underlying subcellular mechanisms responsible for rhythm generation. It is known, however, that protein synthesis is critical during certain portions of the cycle. Blocking protein synthesis with protein synthesis inhibitors stops the motion of the clock; the clock does not continue to run until the inhibitor is removed. There is also recent evidence from work on the molluskan eye clock that the flow of calcium into the pacemaker cell is critical for synchronization by light cycles. While progress is being made in the study of biological timing, it is becoming clear that a detailed understanding of circadian pacemakers is one of the great challenges to contemporary cell and neural science.

[G.D.B.]

See also **Cellular Rhythms; Chronobiology; Circannual Rhythms; Lunar Monthly and Fortnightly Rhythms; Melatonin.**

FURTHER READINGS

Klein, D., R. Moore, and S. Reppert. *Suprachiasmatic Nucleus: The Mind's Clock*. Oxford: Oxford UP, 1991.

Moore-Ede, M., F. Sulzman, and C. Fuller. *The Clocks that Time Us*. Cambridge: Harvard UP, 1982.

CIRCANNUAL RHYTHMS

"Circannual rhythm" is a term used to describe a repetitive change in any behavioral, morphological, or physiological function of an organism with a "free-running" periodicity of approximately one year. Even though it is typically synchronized with the seasonal changes in nature, the circannual rhythm is initiated endogenously by an internal "clock," and can persist without external *Zeitgebers* (external entraining agents or cues for the endogenous rhythm). Circannual rhythms are most clearly observed in organisms experiencing contrasting seasonal differences in environmental conditions (such as mammalian hibernation and avian migration), although similar rhythms are also expressed in many tropical plants (for example, seed germination) and animals (such as the breeding cycle of tropical birds). The best illustrated free-running circannual rhythmicity in mammals is seasonal hibernation. Hibernation has been observed to occur yearly in golden-mantled ground squirrels kept in the laboratory for four years under constant temperature, constant darkness, constant light, or a constant alternation of light and darkness for twelve-hour periods. The periodicity measured between successive onsets of hibernation is about ten to eleven months; interestingly, the timing for annual immergence into and emergence from hibernation is extremely precise in each individual, often varying only a few days between years.

Ground squirrels not only exhibit a circannual rhythm for hibernation, but also show striking circannual changes in body mass and gonadal activity. Hibernation starts when the body mass reaches its peak in the late summer or early fall, which may be twice the animals' springtime body mass. Gonadal activity, on the other hand, is severely depressed many weeks prior to the initiation of hibernation, but is regained fully at the end of the hibernation season. Thus the circannual rhythms of body mass, gonadal activity, and hibernation seem to be intimately linked. However, experimental manipulations demonstrate that each rhythm can occur in the absence of the others.

The relevant *Zeitgebers* which can synchronize the timing of circannual rhythms with nature include photoperiod, temperature, and food availability. Even though these environmental factors have been found to advance or delay slightly the onset of a particular phase of the circannual rhythm (for example, hibernation), the period of the annual cycle (for example, the onset of hibernation in second year) is not altered by any of these factors.

The neuroanatomical basis and the regulatory mechanisms driving the circannual changes in weight regulation and hibernation remain largely unknown. Lesioning of the suprachiasmatic nuclei, a brain area which is known to play a regulatory role in circadian (twenty-four-hour) rhythms, disrupts the daily organization of activity, but has no disruptive effect on the overall circannual rhythmicity of hibernation and body mass in hibernators. This suggests that circannual rhythms do not arise from simple multiplication of the period of the circadian rhythm. Regardless of the state of our knowledge on how the circannual rhythm is generated and regulated, the functional significance of this biological rhythm is easily perceivable. Circannual rhythms may have evolved to allow the organism to "anticipate" predictable seasonal changes and to begin appropriate physiological adjustments in advance of the ultimate challenges from the environment.

[L.C.H.W.]

See also **Chronobiology; Circadian Rhythms.**

FURTHER READINGS

Gwinner, E. *Circannual Rhythms: Endogenous Annual Clocks in the Organization of Seasonal Processes.* Berlin: Springer, 1986.

Lyman, C.P., J.S. Willis, A. Malan, and L.C.H. Wang. *Hibernation and Torpor in Mammals and Birds.* London: Academic P, 1982.

CIRCASEPTAN

The term "circaseptan" relates to biologic variations of rhythms with a frequency of one cycle in about seven days. In humans, circaseptan rhythms at about 3.5-day, or circasemiseptan variations, are found in various physiologic variables in vivo, in the glutathione content of platelet-rich plasma in vitro, and in the incidence of pathology, such as myocardial infarctions, strokes, and epilepsy. Circaseptan rhythms are also prominent in blood pressure in early extrauterine life, both at term and in prematurity. The endogenicity of circaseptans is supported by their manifestation (or amplification) after a single stimulus that carries no seven-day information, such as organ transplantation, and by their free-run with periods differing slightly but with statistical significance from the exact seven-day societal schedule and other near seven-day changes such as those in geomagnetic disturbances. Circaseptan patterns characterize the effect of repeated shifts (at different intervals) of the daily lighting regimen on oviposition by the springtail, *Folsomia candida*, the linden bug, *Pyrrhocoris apterus*, and the face fly, *Musca autumnalis*, and on the growth of a unicell, *Acetabularia mediterranea*, which upon enucleation shows an about 3.5-day response pattern.

The week is hardly "all culture and no nature." Instead, organisms may "recognize" their nature in the circaseptan (and other) aspects of their chronomes (see **Chronobiology**) awaiting exploitation. For instance, the circaseptan-circadian administration pattern of the immunomodulator lentinan determines whether malignant growth will be inhibited or enhanced in a rat model.

[G.C., F.H., and R.P.S.]

See also **Chronobiology; Chronome; Free-Running in Chronobiology.**

FURTHER READINGS

Halberg, F., et al. "Spectral Resolution of Low-Frequency, Small-Amplitude Rhythms in Excreted 17-Ketosteroid; Probable Androgen-Induced Circaseptan Desynchronization." *Acta endocrinologica. Supplementum* (Copenhagen) 103 (1965): 5–54.

———. "Circaseptan Biologic Time Structure Reviewed in the Light of Contributions by Laurence K. Cutkomp and Ladislav Dérer." *Acta entomologica bohemoslavica* 87 (1990): 1–29.

Hildebrandt, G., and I. Bandt-Reges. "Historische Aspekte der circaseptanen Reaktionsperiodik." *Zeitschrift für Physikalische Medizin* 17 (1988): 383.

CLOCK METAPHOR

During the period of the horological revolution of 1660–1760, between the inventions of Huygens's pendulum escapement and Harrison's marine chronometer, the clock metaphor permeated intellectual thought. That was the century when watchmaking represented the epitome of advanced mechanical engineering. Though also mechanical in nature, the atomic philosophy associated with Democritus, Epicurus, and Longinus lacked an inherent clockwork analogy because this philosophy developed before the advent of mechanical clocks. However, Aquinas, in the early days of mechanically motivated timekeepers, had already compared the functioning of animals to the mechanical action of a clock, and Oresme used the image of a clock to describe the workings of a universe motivated by God, yet moving under its own volition.

But Descartes, in the first half of the seventeenth century, was the first major thinker to incorporate the clock analogy into a philosophical system. The mechanical metaphor seems to have come naturally to a man who had been a military engineer and had toyed with the possibility of constructing human and animal automata. Although Descartes visualized the world as a clock, the concept of the animal as a machine appears repeatedly in the Cartesian canon. It is this concept of the animal as machine that made the greatest impact on both the followers and opponents of Descartes.

From then on, the clock metaphor reigned supreme for about 150 years. This concept was adopted by both the Cartesians and their opponents. The metaphor is found in various forms in the writings of virtually every major philosopher (and a host of minor ones), and it was also popular with theologians and poets. (For more information about theologians' use of the clock analogy in the argument from design, which many people found so persuasive for so long, see also **Watchmaker God**.) The very large number of works referring to the clockwork metaphor demonstrates the importance of the idea.

Although even a representative sampling is beyond the scope of this article, the opening salvo from the battle between Leibniz and Clarke (representing Newton) indicates how fully the clock metaphor of God as watchmaker became integrated into very different schools of thought. Leibniz, who himself uses the clock metaphor for many purposes, writes: "Sir Isaac Newton, and his followers, have also a very odd opinion concerning the work of God. According to their doctrine, God Almighty wants to wind up his watch from time to time . . . and even to mend it, as a clockmaker mends his work."

PHILOSOPHERS AND THE CLOCK METAPHOR

Because Descartes rarely forgot that his fate was in God's hands, his system incorporates a not entirely convincing dualism of body and spirit mediated through the pineal gland. And he teases us elsewhere with such images as "une Ame dans une horloge, qui fait qu'elle monstre les heures." But the mechanical philosophy was potentially atheistic. Those who followed Descartes tended to move toward either the "ideal" and the religious or the material and the atheistic extremes. What is significant is that the clock metaphor was used irrespective of the views of the writer. It was generally employed to explain at least one of the philosopher's most central hypotheses. This can be observed of Malebranche, Clauberg, and Gelineux, the "occasionalists" who tried to find a more satisfactory place for God in the system, and of Mersenne and Henri de Roy, who stayed closer to Descartes.

In England, Bacon did not base his own work on the clock analogy, although he was aware of its potential. Nevertheless, he played a seminal part in the rise of science with which the horological revolution of 1660–1760 was inextricably associated. Bacon and his followers, such as Webster, Petty, and above all Boyle, played a major role in raising the status of the "mechanical arts." In the period with which we are concerned, leading watchmakers like Tompion, Graham, and the Le Roys achieved a position comparable to the nuclear scientists of our own time. In fact, their real income was very much higher.

Furthermore, watchmaking was an occupation with which many leaders of that time were happy to be connected. The king of Poland, the king of Prussia, and the Emperor K'ang Hsi of China initiated and maintained clock factories; like Descartes, Leibniz and Benjamin Franklin took a practical interest in clocks; Louis XVI and Voltaire made large investments in watch factories; George III intervened personally to support Harrison's claim that he had discovered the longitude and had his chronometer tested privately at Kew; and lastly, when Beaumarchais raised a fleet of forty vessels to help the American War of Independence it was not supported by writing The *Marriage of Figaro* or *The Barber of Seville*. In fact, the money came for the most part from his profits as a brilliant watchmaker.

The English philosophers—many of whom were followers of both Bacon and Descartes—were also interested in the clock metaphor. Charlton's *Physiologia* (1654) was the main source through which the atomic theory of Epicurus and Gassendi entered England. He explains the extraordinary smallness of the atom and the exquisite workmanship of the system by an analogy of a ring watch. The clock as an analogy for at least the beast in man was now well enough understood. Hobbes can therefore simultaneously use the extended metaphor of a watch to "explain" the need for the individual man to subordinate himself to the Leviathan or the state. Hobbes's state is a body corporate, which is an "Artificial man." For him, thoughts and actions were determined much like the "Trayne" in a watch; his mechanical action in which man is respectively motivated and restrained through "appetite and fear" is reminiscent of Locke, Hartley, and the later "behaviorists."

The Cartesian analogy for demonstrating mechanical order (watch equals animal) and Hobbes's analogy (watch equals man equals Leviathan) are countered by Cudworth's argument that order is a concept in the mind of the perceiver rather than in the watch. Glanvill, who was associated with the Cambridge Platonists, even uses the clock analogy to underline the potential for progress in experimental philosophy. But he also uses this analogy to indicate the limitations of knowledge. His argument reflects the paradox of an age caught up between material optimism for the future and spiritual orthodoxy from the past. However, Power is so fascinated with the secrets that the microscope can disclose that he generally forgets to control his optimism. Power makes an analogy between looking into the newly evident secrets of life and looking into the wheelwork of a watch.

With Robert Boyle, the watch analogy becomes a maid of all work, but it also "explains" a central element in his philosophy. As a scientist he is conscious of the fact that in the search for a final cause one should not undervalue efficient causes. Knowing that a man has made a watch should not inhibit us from investigating the materials in the spring, wheels, string, chain, or balance. Similarly, in his defense of God, Boyle speaks in the mechanistic idiom. He maintains that God is not, as others would suggest, a mere engine, but is in fact a superior engineer analogous to a man who could make a good watch.

Locke proposes to clear away some of the "rubbish" cluttering up philosophy. By disposing with "innate" ideas in the mind, he can begin with a *tabula rasa*, which among other things facilitates human learning through the mechanical process of "association." Perhaps even more iconoclastic is the contention, supported by a clock metaphor, that we must not assume a relationship between ideas and the physical objects they represent. The clock analogy also plays its part in Locke's demonstration that God has adjusted our senses to our surroundings to make this the best of all possible worlds. Shaftesbury—whom Locke the physician had brought into this world—goes beyond Locke's philosophy when he suggests that there is a "moral sense" inborn in human nature. He makes use of the watch analogy to "explain" what he calls "social or natural Affection."

Leibniz—whose immediate predecessor, Spinoza, made even the mind work along mechanical lines—differed from his mentor by positing a preestablished harmony between mind and matter. He argued that the mind operated with the mechanical nature of a watch; he also held that mind and matter worked in harmony like the clock and the watch in Breguet's *pend-*

ules sympathiques. Leibniz is completely wedded to the clock analogy. But the combination of his piety and contemporary biological discoveries made him insist that, unlike the watch, the machines of nature possess infinite complexity, and "are still machines in their smallest parts." In these thoughts, and when he talks of "organic things . . . evolving by a certain predetermined order," lie the seeds of the plant metaphor. That metaphor—which had earlier been virtually displaced by the clockwork analogy—will prove better suited to the world of evolution and "becoming" that we associate with Darwin.

Though their arguments may have been ingeniously rationalized, Leibniz, Spinoza, and Descartes were all concerned with a dualism between the body and the spirit. In such circumstances, there is always the temptation to move toward one extreme or the other. In the eighteenth century, Bishop George Berkeley took the "ideal" and spiritual extreme, while Julien Offray de La Mettrie (and to a lesser extent David Hartley) took the other. Berkeley, in his early *Principles* (1710), feels obliged to "explain" himself in terms of the clock metaphor. However, he expresses dissatisfaction with this in his *Siris* (1744). For the materialist La Mettrie, the clock analogy fully holds its value, and the atheism of *L'homme machine* achieves a major *succès de scandale* as late as 1748.

After the middle of the eighteenth century—though the concept of man as a machine survives even today—the impact of the watch analogy declines. It is no longer part of the stock-in-trade of virtually every philosopher. Later in the eighteenth century, Hume undermines the clock metaphor, but for different reasons than those urged by Berkeley. By the time of his *Dialogues* (1779), he could safely set up the plant analogy as a worthy opponent.

By then, a developing climate of opinion was reopening the door to biological, and more particularly, botanical analogies. This coincides with a new trend in scientific investigation. The trend leads ultimately to Darwin's *Origin of the Species*, but it can be observed earlier in the inspiration Goethe derived from extensive biological experiments, or Shelley's ability to identify with a "sensitive plant." This new spirit of growth (epitomized by the striving and "becoming" of Goethe's Faust) is more sympathetic to the transcendental and dialectical philosophies than to the mechanical philosophy identified with the clock metaphor.

Poets and the Clock Metaphor

When we look at the relationship between poets and the mechanical philosophy, as epitomized by the metaphor of the clock, two main areas of interest emerge. The first considers how the mechanical philosophy affected poets, and the second regards the way in which poets reacted to the mechanical philosophy.

Hobbes, a leading exponent of the mechanical philosophy in England, employed the watch metaphor to elucidate his central concept in *Leviathan*. In that work, as elsewhere, one frequently finds mechanical determinism underlying his thought. When Hobbes speaks of thoughts themselves, he says, "I will consider them first *Singly*, and afterwards in Trayne, or dependence upon one another." It is therefore natural that in aesthetics he should also give a typically mechanical and deterministic explanation of the creative process. With the help of Dryden he did much to restrict and downgrade the use of fancy and imagination in neoclassical art: "Time and education beget experience; experience begets memory; memory begets judgement and fancy; judgement begets the strength and structure, and fancy begets the ornament of a poem. The ancients therefore fabled not absurdly, in making Memory the mother of the Muses." This mimetic concept of art left little room for creative imagination. Thus, Swift condemns the modern as a spider who "Spins and Spits wholly from himself, and scorns to owe any Obligation or Assistance from without," and Pope suggests that the poet should convey "What oft was *Thought*, but ne'er so well *Expresst*."

Not everybody in the eighteenth century, of course, was satisfied with standards of art requiring close attention to imitation and rules. Cowper complains that Pope "Made poetry a mere mechanic art, / And ev'ry warbler has his tune by heart." Elsewhere, he speaks of the mechanical type of poetry "Beating alternately, in measured time, / The clockwork tintinnabulum of rhyme, / Exact and regular the sounds will be, / But such mere quarter-strokes are not for me." As Donald Greene and others, however, have pointed out, the artists of the Restoration and earlier eighteenth century were not as completely subjugated by rules as some literary historians have led us to believe. Pope himself applauds "Great Wits" who "*snatch a Grace* beyond the Reach of Art," and other influential writers such as Dryden, Temple, and Addison follow the example of Longinus in saying much the same.

Although poets frequently paid lip service to the literary rules and the dramatic unities during the Restoration and eighteenth century, this was a yoke that many artists could not easily accept. For example, in *Peri Bathos*, Pope heavily undercuts the mechanical way of writing poetry. He does so by making his *persona*—the discredited modern projector Martinus Scriblerus—support the division of labor, which had recently been introduced by Tompion, the father of English clockmaking: "To this economy we owe the perfection of our modern watches, and doubtless we also might that of our modern Poetry and Rhetoric, were the several parts branched out in the like manner." Scriblerus then proceeds to indicate how the "principle workman"—which is to say the modern poet—might order various figures of speech from the appropriate sub-trades, and assemble them as though he were performing any mechanical operation. Similarly, another chapter in this work employs an extended metaphor of cookery: a recipe is followed mechanically in order "to make an Epic Poem."

At this time, poets' attitudes toward imitation and mechanical processes of writing were ambivalent. But the mechanical philosophy which compared life to the workings of mechanical devices like clockwork was met almost unanimously with disapprobation by the same group. This negative attitude had already been foreshadowed by the reaction of French poets to Descartes's own animal mechanism, presented in particular through the metaphor of the clockwork dog that lacked a soul. Fontaine and Houdar de La Motte were opposed to making animals "meer [sic] / Machines, or pieces of Clockwork"; Fontenelle noted that watches produce no puppies; and Bougeant pointed out that we cannot caress our watches. Nevertheless, the Cartesian view of animals and even of human bodies as machines has had a profound effect on modern developments in physiology.

Though they are frequently proselytizers of the new science, Dryden and Cowley seem not to have praised animal mechanism. Even Prior, hardly beloved by the Scriblerians, continually undercuts the mechanical philosophy in his long poem *Alma; Or, The Progress of the Mind*. In so doing, he reveals many trends of thought common to his time. Of the atomical theorists, Prior says, "Atoms you cut, and forms you measure, / To gratify your private pleasure"; of "L'homme-machine," "So, if unprejudic'd you scan / The goings of this clock-work, man"; of animal mechanism, "Quoth Mat, to me thou seem'st to mean, / That Alma [the mind] is a mere machine." Significantly, Mat Prior reserves denial of this final heresy for his own namesake.

Indeed, the potential for atheism in mechanical philosophy accounted for the antagonism of most poets. Also, poets tended to be as wary of "system-makers" in philosophy as philosophers were suspicious of poetic imagination. Prior puts it this way, "We system-makers . . . in a point obscure and dark, / We fight as Leibnitz did with Clarke." In *The Battle of the Books*, Swift attacks Descartes the "system-maker" rather than Bacon the experimental philosopher. Pope complains similarly about those who, like Descartes, "Thrust some Mechanic Cause" into God's place. In a footnote to *Dunciad* IV. 470, he says, "whereas they who take this high Priori Road (such as Hobbes, Spinoza, DesCartes, and some better Reasoners) for one that goes right, ten lose themselves in Mists."

Swift puts much of the same argument into more striking language when he speaks of the philosopher who "while his Thoughts and eyes were fixed upon the *Constellation*, found himself seduced by his *lower Parts* into a *Ditch*." That quotation comes from Swift's *A Discourse Concerning the Mechanical Operation of the Spirit*, a work that attacks mechanical philosophy. Laurence Sterne's *Tristram Shandy* makes a similar attack. Not only does it take Locke's association of ideas to ridiculous extremes, but the entire work undercuts the mechanical standards associated with neoclassical rules at their worst. As for the mechanical nature of Walter Shandy, the retired turkey merchant, his antics with the clock, at the beginning, set the pattern for the whole book.

While attacking the mechanical philosophy, poets also tended to take issue with the mechanical habits of the new clock-oriented and frequently bourgeois "moderns." For example, Wycherley's Sir Jasper Fidget must hurry away to business when it is "a quarter and a half quarter of a minute past eleven"; Swift, with tongue in cheek, congratulates Whiston for seeing his comet exactly as predicted "at three Minutes after five, by my own Watch"; and Sterne ironically calls a critic an "admirable grammarian" when he complains that Garrick "suspended his voice in the epilogue a dozen times three seconds and three fifths by a stop-watch, my Lord, each time." In the famous letter about Gulliver's silver fob watch, Swift is able to mock not only travelers' tales and Cartesian animal mechanism, but also the fact that the watch of Gulliv-er—who had "been a sort of projector" or inventor-cum-businessman in his younger days—is "the god that he worships."

Though the poets tended to mock the mechanical approach to life, they were nevertheless part of a new mechanically-oriented age. Just like philosophers who opposed the Cartesian system of philosophy, they were nonetheless obliged to use the clock metaphor of their day. Pope tells us, "Tis with our *Judgements* as our *Watches*, none / Go just *alike*, yet each believes his own"; Chesterfield advises his son, "Wear your learning, like your watch, in a private pocket"; Southey writes, "the hand of the political horologe cannot go back."

And indeed, the hand of the linguistic horologe cannot go back either. Poets—like philosophers and ultimately theologians—have had to look elsewhere for inspiration and idiom. Today, we know that the minds and bodies of even the simplest living organisms are far more complex than even the repeater watch or Vaucanson's mechanical duck that inspired La Mettrie in writing *L'homme machine*. In the period leading up to Darwin and beyond, this knowledge played its part in making the plant metaphor for man and his universe more acceptable than the clock metaphor.

Today, the clock metaphor may well have gone forever. It is a *Zeiterscheinung* closely tied in with the horological revolution that gave it immediacy, status, and meaning. The mechanical view of life, however, is another matter. This concept can be traced back to Democritus. In our own century, it may well be staging a comeback at the expense of the vitalist orientation of biology. The relatively new science of cybernetics provides an example of this development. But there have been other credits on the "mechanical" side of the ledger. If we were asked to "explain" the "mind" of human beings in the present age of electronics, we would surely choose as our metaphor a computer rather than a vegetable.

What can be concluded? The circumstances leading up to and creating the horological revolution led to the clock metaphor becoming part of man's philosophic systems, and indeed, of his very way of thinking. In the tradition of metaphors that live long enough, it eventually faded into the language. Just like ourselves, the clock now has hands and a face. But at least in the London vernacular, only a human being can receive a punch in the clock that may stop his ticker or change the look on his dial. Moreover, our fate frequently depends on which way the pendulum swings, and the manner in which our train of thought makes us tick will often be reflected in whether we work in low gear or high gear. Though the nonmechanical Elizabethan humors are still with us, we are now more likely to unwind or to feel wound up, to have ideas that might be rusty, or to consider that the wheels of our political movement, or the mechanism of our commercial organization might need oiling before the inevitable striking of the eleventh hour when their wheels as well as ours could be in danger of running down.

Scientists, poets, philosophers, and theologians were all obliged to rethink the nature of themselves and their universe in mechanical terms during the period when modern science emerged. Because they wished to envisage those things and concepts that cannot readily be understood in terms of those that can, they felt the need to solidify abstractions through the use of an analogy. For them the watch, rather than today's computer or color television, provided a point of concrete reference with which both authors and readers could empathize. And the watch was widely employed as an analogy for explaining the workings of such disparate objects as human beings, animals, the mind, the state, the world, the universe, and even God— such oversimplifications could not satisfy indefinitely.

The term *revolution* is related to Copernicus's *Revolution of the Heavenly Orbs*, and alerts us to the potential of science for upsetting established order. Yet it is a particular irony of the British horological revolution that while it served in the vanguard of Western technology and science, it also provided the most satisfying symbol of order through which society attempted to regulate the dangers of impending progress. The clockwork universe of the Watchmaker God— like the mechanical philosophy, and the regularity of neoclassical poetry—all reflect the widespread regulating influence of the horological metaphor.

Influenced in part, however, by the developing biological science, there came about a realignment of values after about 1760. The poets reacted against Pope's "clockwork tintinnabulum of rhyme"; philosophers opposed the Christian argument from design; and only the theologians—supported by those followers who were bourgeois—continued to worship a Watchmaker God and the regularity that such a God represented. Though Romantic poets were often as

interested in God as theologians, they came to identify the regularity and order of clockwork with the devil. By the nineteenth century, Tennyson places a clock in hell, E. T. A. Hoffmann invests diabolic qualities in the beautiful automaton Olympia, Baudelaire writes of "Horloge! dieu sinistre," and Edgar Allan Poe illustrates the dangers of the clock in stories like "Devil in the Belfry," "Predicament," and "Pit and the Pendulum." We can still identify with the pejorative qualities ascribed to the human automaton by the Romantics. Furthermore, they recognized in clockwork the original symbol of the diabolism of technological progress, which their pastoralism opposed.

Lewis Mumford has claimed convincingly that "the clock, not the steam engine, is the key machine of the modern industrial age." Virtually every major invention in today's mechanical watch belongs to the horological revolution of 1660–1760, and the child of that revolution is the watch analogy. This metaphor can tell us a great deal about the birth of Western science and technology, and perhaps also something about the paradox of modern men and women being both attracted and repelled by the mechanical aspects of their lives.

[S.L.M.]

See also **Dramatic Unities; Leibniz-Clarke Correspondence; Watchmaker God and Argument from Design.**

Further Readings

Descartes, René. *René Descartes, Selected Philosophical Writings.* Trans. J. Cottingham, R. Stoothoff, and D. Murdoch. New York: Cambridge UP, 1988. See index under "Time" and "Mechanics."

Gregory, Joshua C. "The Animate and Mechanical Models of Reality." *Journal of Philosophical Studies* (1927): 302–14.

Heinrichs, Jürgen. *Das Problem der Zeit in der praktischen Philosophie Kants.* Bonn: Bouvier, 1968.

Kirkinen, Heikki. *Les origines de la conception moderne de l'homme-machine.* Helsinki, 1960.

Laudan, Laurens. "The Clock Metaphor and Probabilism: The Impact of Descartes on English Methodological Thought, 1650-1665." *Annals of Science* 22 (June 1966): 73–104.

Leibniz, G., and S. Clarke. *The Leibniz-Clarke Correspondence: Together with Extracts from Newton's* Principia *and* Optics. Ed. H. G. Alexander. Manchester: Manchester UP, 1956.

Lenoble, Robert. *Mersenne; ou, La naissance du mécanisme.* Paris: J. Vrin, 1943.

Macey, Samuel L. *Clocks and the Cosmos: Time in Western Life and Thought.* Hamden: Archon Books, 1980.

Nicolson, Marjorie. "The Early Stage of Cartesianism in England." *Studies in Philology* 26 (1929): 356–74.

Rosenfield, Leonora Cohen. *From Beast-Machine to Man-Machine.* Enlarged ed. New York: Octagon Books, 1968.

Vartanian, Aram, ed. *La Mettrie's L'Homme Machine* (critical edition with an introductory monograph). Princeton: Princeton UP, 1960.

CLOCKS: AMERICA AND MASS PRODUCTION, 1770–1890

Awareness of time has become automatic in our present daily life, in part because timekeepers have become commonplace. Though mechanical timekeeping devices were developed at least 800 years ago, the availability of clocks in sufficient quantity and at low cost is a relatively modern phenomenon. The mass production of clocks affordable by the general public began in America less than two centuries ago.

Though some clocks were brought from Europe by colonial settlers, the clocks at that time were handmade by craftsmen and consequently so expensive that only the affluent could afford them. By 1700, a few clockmakers began to settle in Boston, Philadelphia, and New York as the population and wealth in the colonies had increased sufficiently to support such craftsmen.

The clock movements these men produced were basically English in style, made of cast brass and forged steel that was laboriously crafted and finished. Considerable skill was needed to create this instrument and engrave a brass dial. This skill was passed on through an apprenticeship system whereby a young lad worked with a master for a period, usually seven years. During this time he received no pay other than clothing, food, and shelter, but assisted the master, eventually learning to construct the clocks himself.

Prior to 1780, virtually all American-made clocks were housed in floor-standing cases, and hence were called "tall clocks." About that time, clockmaker Simon Willard and younger brother Aaron Willard of Grafton, Massachusetts, were the first to depart from the manufacture of the old floor clocks and begin to make smaller clocks that could sit on a shelf or hang on a wall. In 1802, Simon Willard patented an eight-day brass movement wall hanging "improved timepiece," now commonly called the "banjo clock." Though basically handmade, the smaller size of Willard's shelf and wall clocks allowed them to be made and sold cheaper than the tall clocks.

Members of the Willard "school," including several members of the Willard family, their clockmaking associates, and makers who copied the Willard style of products, did a thriving business in the Boston, as well as other areas of eastern Massachusetts, southern New Hampshire, southern Maine, and Rhode Island well into the 1830s making tall and shelf clocks, and into the 1840s making "banjo" timepieces. Few makers of this "school" survived the onslaught of cheap manufactured clocks that arrived from Connecticut by the 1830s. One notable firm operated by Edward Howard at Roxbury, Massachusetts, tooled up in the 1840s to make banjo and high-grade regulators by machine methods. His firm continues to supply high quality, expensive clocks to a limited buying public after more than a century.

In 1798, a United States direct tax was levied nationwide on clocks and watches, among other items. A review of this tax indicates that at that time approximately 8 percent of households in Connecticut owned a clock. Percentages would likely have been considerably lower in other industrialized New England states. Pennsylvania, which had an unusual number of clockmakers in the handcraft period, may have rivaled New England, but it is doubtful if any other southern or mid-Atlantic state had more than a fraction of a single percent of the population owning a clock.

Without question, the man primarily responsible for the mass production of inexpensive clocks affordable by the working family was Eli Terry (1772–1852) of Plymouth, Connecticut. Terry was trained as a brass clockmaker under the old apprenticeship system. Commencing his own business in 1792, Terry began to make clocks with wooden wheels and plates instead of brass and steel, producing a less expensive product to capture a more extensive buying public. Large crude wooden clock movements had been made in rural Connecticut since about 1750, but Terry refined their design and made them more like brass clocks, smaller and better finished. He also increased his production numbers by making them in batches instead of singly. He devised a system of jigs and fixtures to make his wheels and form his levers exactly alike and to drill his plates identically. This system alleviated the need for a single man to be trained in making, finishing, and setting up all the components in a clock movement. Instead, it allowed one trained clockmaker to oversee the making of identical parts by many workmen who each had a modest amount of training in repeatedly making and finishing a specific part or parts.

In 1806, two Waterbury, Connecticut, businessmen, Levi and Abel Porter, hearing of Terry's production advancements, contracted with him to make 4,000 wooden clock movements for tall clocks within a period of three years. In order to accomplish this Terry purchased a sawmill and converted many of his foot powered operations to water power. He successfully completed the contract in 1809. It was not only the first privately funded production of goods in mass quantity, but perhaps the earliest American manufactured product with truly identical and interchangeable parts.

Terry sold his operation in the spring of 1810 to two of his former workmen, Seth Thomas and Silas Hoadley, who continued the business. Terry's clocks and production methods were also copied by more than a dozen other craftsmen in the area. In 1810, Terry began to experiment with the manufacture of a wooden movement shelf clock, and in December of 1812, purchased a mill in which to manufacture it. His new clock, introduced about 1815, sold complete with case for about fifteen dollars in the "pillar & scroll" case, and was an immediate success. In order to protect himself from other makers pirating his new clock, Terry applied for a patent for it that the United States government granted on June 12, 1816. The fear of litigation from infringement of Terry's patent and subsequent revision patents gave Terry control of his shelf clock's manufacture for only a few years. In 1826, he brought a lawsuit against Seth Thomas, claiming a violation of agreements and patent infringement. Though the suit was settled out of court in 1827, it showed that Terry's patents, as written, were unenforceable. With the threat of litigation lifted, many small, undercapitalized operations sprang up within a few years, flooding the market with copies of Terry's wooden movement shelf clocks. The following years saw increased competition that not only drove down prices, but also profits and quality.

Not everyone was impressed by Terry's wooden clock. Even Terry, trained as a brass clockmaker, knew the brass movement clock was superior. But he was shrewd enough to appreciate that at the time the wooden clock had the best profit potential for the available production technology. By 1818, Joseph Ives (1782–1862) of Bristol, Connecticut, had incorporated some of Terry's manufacturing ideas to make cheaper brass and steel movement clocks. Ives used brass produced by a new process that rolled it into sheet form, rather than the old-fashioned and more costly casting method. By the early 1830s, Ives was also using dies to punch out brass wheel blanks from sheet brass stock, preparatory to cutting the teeth. Though less expensive than handmade brass clocks, they were still three to four times the cost of a one-day wood clock.

By 1837, the glut of cheaper clocks had put the industry into an unhealthy financial position. One of the severest depressions in American history occurred that year. Many banks failed, and clockmaker Chauncey Jerome recounted in his autobiography that "in 1837, came the great panic and break-down of business which extended all over the country. Clock makers and almost every one else stopped business. . . .The hard times came down on us and we really thought that clocks would no longer be made. Our firm thought we could make them if any body could, but like the others felt discouraged and disgusted with the whole business as it was then." The troubles were not solved immediately. As a letter of January 26, 1838, written by clockmaker Philip Barnes of Bristol, Connecticut, noted: "Some of the heaviest of banks in this state have failed, and many others are expected daily to follow. . . . Money is ten times as scarce as last year."

In 1838, an important breakthrough came in the production of inexpensive brass clocks with the introduction of a one-day brass weight-driven striking clock by Chauncey Jerome (1793–1868). Jerome had begun his career as a clock casemaker for Eli Terry in 1816, and began making wooden clocks about 1823. Unlike most of its brass movement shelf clock predecessors, which retailed at fifteen to twenty dollars, Jerome's one-day clock had a newly designed movement and sold in a simple ogee (S-curve) molding case retailing profitably at six dollars cash and seven dollars on credit. Jerome's movement was designed by his brother, Noble Jerome (1800–1861), an able mechanic, and patented June 27, 1839. Its success was largely due to its having a minimum number of parts, being inexpensive to make, simple to assemble and repair, and a durable and dependable timekeeper. Sheet brass was used for components, and dies were employed to create both plate and wheel blanks. This movement was the basis of most manufactured clock movements for the century that followed.

Prior to 1840, most American-made clocks were powered by cast iron weights that traveled in channels inside the case. Joseph Ives pioneered the development of American-made spring clocks about 1820 by using a multi-leaf spring similar to a "wagon spring" mounted to the bottom of the clock case. When the clock was wound, this spring was bent upwards at the ends and exerted enough torque, as the spring attempted to return to its original flat position, to power the clock. Though ingenious and workable, such springs could not be produced inexpensively.

About 1835, coiled springs made of brass were introduced at Bristol, Connecticut, in a "beehive" shaped shelf clock made by E.C. Brewster & Company. By 1840, spring clocks began to appear in greater numbers, allowing manufacturers to reduce the size of clocks substantially since tall cases were not needed for weights to travel. Silas B. Terry (1807–1876), son of Eli Terry, developed a process for manufacturing coiled steel springs more cheaply by 1847. Stronger steel springs replaced brass ones, and by 1850, both one-day and eight-day shelf clocks with steel springs were major production items. Between 1840 and 1850, the average clock shrunk in size by at least 30 percent. As materials were expensive and labor cheap, smaller clocks meant greater production savings and hence retail price reductions.

An industrial census taken on October 1, 1845, reported seven Connecticut towns had a total of thirty-one clockmaking operations employing 580 hands and producing 359,500 clocks in the previous twelve months. Five years later only fourteen clock manufacturers were left in Connecticut, eleven of whom were in Bristol (and of the others two had begun in Bristol). In all, fifteen firms employed 703 hands and produced 511,000 clocks in the twelve months prior to June 1, 1850. Within a decade seven of these fifteen firms were gone and five others had undergone bankruptcy or takeovers.

After 1850, the brass movement pendulum shelf clock with steel springs became the standard clock produced, at least until World War II. Though many Connecticut clock businesses did not survive the panic of 1837, seven major manufacturers emerged in the next two decades. Although there were a few smaller operations, these seven firms manufactured all but a small percentage of America's clock products after 1860. Their origins and brief histories are recounted below.

- *The Seth Thomas Clock Company, Thomaston, Connecticut.* This firm was established by Seth Thomas (1785–1859) in 1813 and incorporated in 1853 by Thomas, six years prior to his death. The Seth Thomas Clock Company was highly regarded by other Connecticut manufacturers and produced quality pendulum and marine movement clocks for a century and a half. Between 1883 and 1915, the Seth Thomas firm manufactured better-quality jeweled watches and was the only Connecticut clockmaker to do so. After World War II, the firm suffered a steady decline, culminating in its removal from Connecticut in 1983. The Seth Thomas firm still exists at Norcross, Georgia, though it is now primarily a marketing firm whose clock components are purchased.

- *The New Haven Clock Company, New Haven, Connecticut.* Chauncey Jerome—who began his career as a casemaker for Eli Terry in 1816, and became a major manufacturer of wooden and brass clocks at Bristol, Connecticut—was the first manufacturer to export American clocks, opening up the English market in 1841. Jerome established a clock case factory at New Haven, Connecticut, in 1844, and moved his entire operation there after a fire on April 23, 1845, destroyed his movement factory at Bristol. He built his business into an empire that was incorporated in 1853 as the Jerome Manufacturing Company. It crumbled around him in bankruptcy on February 14, 1856, because of excessive debt and poor management. Jerome's operation was bought by his nephew, Hiram Camp (1811–1893), and merged into the New Haven Clock Company, which Camp had established in 1853 to supply clock movements to the Jerome firm. The New Haven Clock Company was a major producer of a huge line of wood and metal cased clocks and non-jeweled watches. The firm closed and its machinery was sold at auction in 1960.

- *The E.N. Welch Manufacturing Company, Forestville, Connecticut.* Extensive clockmaking operations commenced in 1830 at Forestville, a village in the town of Bristol, Connecticut, by Jonathan C. Brown (1807–1872). During the 1840s, J.C. Brown's operation became the largest in Bristol. However, the business failed in 1856 and his firm and several smaller bankrupt operations were purchased by financial entrepreneur Elisha N. Welch (1809–1887). Welch incorporated his operation in

1864 as the E.N. Welch Manufacturing Company. He formed an auxiliary firm in 1868 with clockmaker Solomon C. Spring called Welch, Spring & Company, which manufactured a better-quality line of shelf clocks and wall regulators until 1884. Welch's operation became the largest and most prosperous in Bristol in the latter part of the nineteenth century, though it approached collapse after Welch's death in 1887. Following more than a decade of financial struggle and interruptions to its manufacturing, the operation was purchased by the Sessions family in 1903. They manufactured clocks as the Sessions Clock Company until 1968, devoting much of their efforts to electric clocks after 1930.

- *The Ansonia Clock Company, New York, New York.* The firm of Terry & Andrews, established in 1841, moved their clockmaking operation to Ansonia, Connecticut, in 1850 at the urging of foundry tycoon Anson G. Phelps. Their factory was destroyed by fire in November of 1854, but Phelps's Ansonia Brass & Copper Company continued the clockmaking operations. The firm was eventually renamed the Ansonia Clock Company in 1873 and the operation was moved to Brooklyn, New York, in 1878. This firm specialized in metal case French-style clocks and china clocks and it made non-jeweled watches. While most firms were doing well in the 1920s, Ansonia's business declined through poor management. In 1929, the operation was purchased by Amtorg, the Russian purchasing agent, and removed to Moscow in the summer of 1930. Some Ansonia workers spent more than a year in Russia setting up Russia's first clock manufacturing operation.

- *The E. Ingraham Company, Bristol, Connecticut.* The firm of Brewster & Ingrahams, formed in 1842, ceased operations in 1852 because of discontent among its partners. After a fire destroyed the factory of the succeeding firm, E. & A. Ingraham, in 1855, and its subsequent bankruptcy, Elias Ingraham formed a new operation in 1857 to manufacture some of his new clock designs. This became known as E. Ingraham & Company in 1860, and manufactured a large line of wooden-cased shelf and wall clocks. In 1913, the firm purchased the bankrupt Bannatyne Watch Company of Waterbury, Connecticut, and became major producers of non-jeweled pocket and wrist watches. Their watchmaking operations at

Bristol ceased in 1963 and their clockmaking in 1978, though Ingraham electric clocks are still manufactured at Laurinburg, North Carolina.

- *The William L. Gilbert Clock Company, Winsted, Connecticut.* Clark, Gilbert & Company bought the old wooden movement clock factory of Riley Whiting in 1841 to manufacture Jerome's inexpensive brass clocks. William L. Gilbert (1806–1890), who began his clockmaking career at Bristol, Connecticut, in 1828, purchased controlling interest in the operation in 1851 and incorporated the Gilbert Manufacturing Company in 1866. A fire destroyed the factory in 1871, but it was rebuilt as the William L. Gilbert Clock Company. In 1932, the firm went into bankruptcy, but emerged in 1934 as the Gilbert Clock Corporation. In 1957, it was taken over by General Computing Machines and ceased operations in 1964.

- *The Waterbury Clock Company, Waterbury, Connecticut* was incorporated March 5, 1857, by the Benedict & Burnham Manufacturing Company to make clocks and use the parent firm's brass. Veteran clockmaker Chauncey Jerome established its casemaking shop and his brother, Noble Jerome, set up its movement manufacturing operation. Though this firm manufactured a large line of clocks, it became well known for its non-jeweled watches after Archibald Bannatyne developed the "Jumbo" watch in 1889. In 1892, Robert and Charles Ingersoll ordered 1,000 of these watches for eighty-five cents each to sell in their mail-order business. Literally millions of "dollar" watches were manufactured by Waterbury for Ingersoll in the next three decades. When Ingersoll went bankrupt in 1922, Waterbury purchased them. By 1917, Waterbury was manufacturing 23,000 clocks and watches a day, but was reduced to a small operation in a largely empty factory after the Great Depression hit in 1929. In 1941, the firm was purchased by two Norwegian businessmen who moved the operation to a new factory at Middlebury, Connecticut, and engineered the "Timex" watch. Now known as Timex Corporation, the firm remains successful to the present time.

The depression years of the 1930s saw serious declines in the mechanical clock industry's profits, workforce, and production. Though synchronous electric clocks brought new promise to the industry after 1929, business prosperity had barely returned when it was interrupted again by World War II. In 1942, clockmaking operations were converted quickly to wartime production, with most firms tooling up to make timing fuses for bombs.

When the war ended and firms reentered clock manufacturing, they faced the need to revitalize antiquated equipment, to reestablish suppliers and markets, and to meet increasing competition from foreign manufacturers. Since their fuse and timing device operations established with government funding during the war were modern and promised to be more lucrative with less investment, the old-fashioned managements resisted spending the money needed to modernize clockmaking operations. As a result, they have virtually abandoned the manufacture of the pendulum clock. Over a period of forty years following the war, most firms gradually ceased clockmaking operations, though a few firms have continued marketing electric clocks or mechanical clocks with components purchased from foreign and domestic suppliers.

[C.H.B.]

See also **Watch Manufacturing in Nineteenth-Century America.**

FURTHER READINGS

Bailey, Chris H. *Two Hundred Years of American Clocks and Watches.* Englewood Cliffs: Prentice-Hall, 1975.

———. "From Rags to Riches to Rags: The Story of Chauncey Jerome." Supplement No. 15 to the *Bulletin* of the National Association of Watch and Clock Collectors. Columbia, 1986.

Battison, Edwin A. *The American Clock 1725–1865.* Greenwich: New York Graphic Society, 1973.

Husher, R.W., and W.W. Welch. *A Study of Simon Willard's Clocks.* Nahant: Husher and Welch, 1980.

Roberts, Kenneth D. *Eli Terry and the Connecticut Shelf Clock.* Bristol: Ken Roberts Publishing, 1973.

———. *The Contributions of Joseph Ives to Connecticut Clock Technology, 1810–1862.* 2nd ed. Fitzwilliam: Ken Roberts Publishing, 1988.

Roberts, Kenneth D., and Snowden Taylor. *Forestville Clockmakers.* Fitzwilliam: Ken Roberts Publishing, 1992.

Shaffer, Douglas H. *Clocks.* New York: Cooper-Hewitt Museum, 1980.

Varkaris, Jane. *The Canada and Hamilton Clock Companies.* Erin, Ontario: Boston Mills P, 1986.

Willard, John Ware. *Simon Willard and His Clocks.* New York: Dover, 1968.

Woodbury, R.S. "The Legend of Eli Whitney and Interchangeable Parts." *Technology and Culture* 1 (Summer 1960): 235–253.

CLOCKS AND WATCHES: THE LEAP TO PRECISION

This article will discuss the development of mechanical clocks and watches as accurate timekeepers from the origins of the pendulum and the balance spring to about 1730, when precision regulators could keep time to within a few seconds a week. This development resulted largely from the demand for an improved method by which both celestial and terrestrial measurements could be made. Owing to the rotation of the earth on its axis, time measurement can provide an alternative to angular measurement for determining the distance between two celestial objects. By measuring angular distance in time, the mechanical clock not only helped astronomers to establish the positions and apparent motions of the sun, the moon, and the stars, but also enabled celestial observations to be used in the determination of terrestrial information. By the second half of the eighteenth century, precision timekeepers had influenced the production of accurate celestial maps and tables, the finding of longitude both on land and at sea, calculations of the finite velocity of light, and the measurement of the size of the solar system.

One of the earliest references to the use of a mechanical clock for scientific purposes is described in a manuscript entitled, "Metrologum de pisce cane et volucre," written by Giovanni da Fontana about 1420. A passage in this work suggests using mechanical clocks for measuring brief intervals, as in timing the rise and fall of rockets. About the same time, the celebrated Paduan physician Michael Savonarola described the use of a mechanical clock in an experiment to compare the temperature of water from the baths of Abano with that of water from the baths of St. Helena. Paulus Almanus, a German monk who made notes on the timekeepers he repaired during his stay in Rome about 1475, described a clock showing the division of the hour into minutes. Nuremberg astronomer Bernhard Walther employed a different method to obtain fractions of an hour: during his observation on January 16, 1484, to determine the difference in time between the rising of Mercury and sunrise, he noted the revolutions of the hour wheel and expressed the fraction of its rotation by counting the number of gear teeth that had passed during his observation. By 1587, Danish astronomer Tycho Brahe was experimenting with clocks that indicated both minutes and seconds, but he found them to be unreliable and preferred to use angular measuring instruments during his observations. Jost Bürgi, who served as clockmaker to Landgrave Wilhelm IV in Kassel and later to Emperor Rudolf II in Prague, produced some of the finest and most ingenious clocks of his time. One of his most important innovations was the remontoire, a device designed to overcome fluctuations in the power transmitted from the driving weight or spring through the wheels of the timekeeper to the escapement. Bürgi also made clocks indicating minutes and seconds, but it was not until 1657, when the pendulum clock introduced the era of precision timekeeping, that the divisions of minutes on the dial became commonplace. With further improvements and the introduction of the long pendulum, the division of the minute into seconds also became practical.

Drawings of mechanical devices with pendulums were made by Leonardo da Vinci in the late fifteenth century and by the Florentine instrument maker, Benvenuto Volpaia, in the early sixteenth century. Between 1637 and 1639, Galileo wrote about his observations on the pendulum and in 1641, during the period when he was afflicted by increasing blindness, he collaborated with his son Vincenzo to design a mechanism to keep a pendulum going. Galileo died in the following year, but Vincenzo did not begin construction of a model of their design until April 1649, when he enlisted the help of a young locksmith, Domenico Balestri, to produce the iron frame and the blanks for the wheel work. The model unfortunately was never completed, for Vincenzo died rather suddenly one month later. Although this model has since disappeared, one of Galileo's pupils, Vincenzo Viviani, made a drawing of the device in its incomplete state. While Viviani's drawing illustrates a new form of escapement to keep a pendulum in motion, it does not include a dial to show the time. Although Viviani asserted in 1659 that the German clockmaker, Johann Philipp Treffler, who was employed by Grand Duke Ferdinand II of Florence, had adapted Galileo's invention to a chamber clock in 1655, no example of this date has survived. Viviani's claim was intended to give credit of the invention to Galileo, because by 1659 a dispute had arisen over priority in the application of the pendulum to clockwork. In that year, Roman clockmaker Giuseppe Campani traveled to Florence to show the Grand Duke Ferdinand II the pendulum clock that he claimed to have invented accidentally in 1656. Campani was greatly surprised to

be shown examples of both Galileo's and Treffler's work as well as a small publication of 1658 entitled *Horologium* that described the pendulum clock invented by the Dutch mathematician and astronomer, Christiaan Huygens.

In a letter to Ismail Boulliau dated December 26, 1657, Huygens records that it was on December 25, 1656, that he made the first model of this type of clock. The oldest surviving pendulum clocks are those made to his design in 1657 in the Netherlands. Huygens employed in his clocks the common verge escapement: this escapement required the pendulum to swing in a wide arc that varied in its amplitude according to the force transmitted through the gearing from the driving weight or spring. To overcome "circular error," the error or variation in the time that it takes a pendulum swinging in a circular path to perform arcs of different amplitude, Huygens proposed two solutions: in *Horologium*, he illustrated a method of minimizing the effects of circular error by reducing the amplitude of the pendulum through gearing between the escapement and the pendulum. In practice, this gearing would have introduced serious problems of friction, and Huygens reverted to improving his former method in which he suspended the pendulum from a thread between two curved pieces of brass known as "cycloidal cheeks." The cycloidal cheeks were designed to act upon the thread and thereby automatically adjust the pendulum's length according to the amplitude of its oscillation. Huygens believed that if in this way he could make the pendulum follow a cycloidal rather than a circular arc, its large or small oscillations would be performed in the same period of time: in theory, therefore, his pendulum clocks would be perfect timekeepers. In his magnum opus, *Horologium Oscillatorium*, that he dedicated to Louis XIV in 1673, Huygens suggested that the pendulum clock could be used to establish a universal and perpetual measure: the length of a seconds-beating pendulum divided into three parts could provide a standard measure that he termed an "hour foot." This appears to be the first attempt to introduce a standard unit of measurement based on a frequency. It was not until the development of the atomic clock that a standard frequency was adopted as the universal standard measure.

Horologium Oscillatorium also describes two ways in which these new accurate clocks could be set to time and regulated: one by the sun, which involved the equation of time; the other by the stars, which involved sidereal time. *The equation of time* is concerned with the fact that through the course of the seasons the observed motion of the sun in the sky is not constant. This is due to the tilt of the earth's axis relative to its path and the earth's elliptical orbit around the sun. Apparent solar time (the time shown by a sundial), and mean solar time (the time shown by a clock), therefore, agree only four times a year (on or about April 15, June 13, September 2, and December 25), and can differ by as much as sixteen minutes. The difference between solar and mean time is known as the equation of time. Pendulum clocks, which required more accurate methods of regulation than earlier timekeepers, demanded a resolution of this discrepancy when a sundial was used to set the clock. Huygens was the first person to use a pendulum clock to calculate the equation of time: his results were first published in 1665 in a rare booklet entitled *Kort Onderwys*. Prior to the invention of the pendulum clock, the equation of time had been calculated since the time of Ptolemy by astronomical observation. After the invention of the pendulum clock, the equation of time was sometimes engraved on sundials, which were commonly used for setting clocks and watches. *Sidereal time* is concerned with the fact that owing to the variations of solar time, greater accuracy could be obtained when pendulum clocks were regulated by the observation of the transit of a star from one night to the next. This system of time measurement, which measured the rotation of the earth on its axis relative to the stars, is known as sidereal time (< Latin *sidereus*, relating to the stars). In the course of one year, the earth, because of its orbit around the sun, will rotate one more time in relation to the stars than it will in relation to the sun. In other words, in 365.2422 days, the time it takes the earth to travel from vernal equinox to vernal equinox, sidereal time will differ from solar time by twenty-four hours. Therefore, a sidereal day is three minutes 56.4 seconds shorter than a mean solar day.

In *Horologium Oscillatorium*, Huygens recommended a simple form of transit instrument in which the observer aligns a window frame or some other regular point of observation with the roof or wall of a neighboring house behind which the observed star can be seen to vanish. A clock can be regulated by the disappearance of the star. This event will be seen to occur three minutes 56.4 seconds earlier each night. John Harrison, the inventor of the first successful marine timekeeper, employed this method for timing his precision clocks. Observatories adopted a telescope mounted on a solid base facing due south to observe the transits by which standard time was established. The first reliable instrument of this type was erected in 1690 by the Danish astronomer, Ole Roemer. Roemer is known to have used pendulum clocks of Huygens's design to time his observations. In 1676, by noticing variations during the year in the times of the eclipses of Jupiter's satellites, Roemer was able to discover the finite velocity of light and estimate its speed.

Salomon Coster and other clockmakers in Holland made pendulum clocks to Huygens's design and, by 1659, these new timekeepers were being manufactured in France by Nicolas Hanet and in England by Ahasuerus Fromanteel. The introduction of the pendulum strongly influenced both the appearance and the design of clocks. Now that time could be measured with some degree of accuracy, the dial with both hour and minute hands became a more prominent feature in the clock's appearance.

Following the application of the pendulum to clocks, the next major advance in precision timekeeping was the invention of the anchor escapement. As discussed earlier, Huygens had tried two methods to overcome the problems of circular error that resulted from using an escapement which required the pendulum to swing in a wide arc. The anchor escapement provided a much simpler solution by reducing the arc of swing of the pendulum and thereby bringing it closer to a cycloidal path. The earliest surviving clock with an anchor escapement was supplied to Wadham College, Oxford, in early 1670 by the famous clockmaker, Joseph Knibb. The invention of this escapement has also been attributed to another well-known clockmaker, William Clement, and to the English experimental philosopher, Robert Hooke, who claimed to have produced an example shortly after the Great Fire of London. The knowledge of this escapement does not appear to have been transmitted to the Continent until 1675, when Huygens included a small drawing of the device in a manuscript dated January 20 of that year. Beside the drawing are the names "Leibnitz" (a celebrated German philosopher and mathematician) and "Roemer," who may have been responsible for supplying the information.

The anchor escapement drawing is not well known and may have been overlooked because it occurs on the same page as a drawing of another of this savant's highly significant contributions to horology, the spiral balance spring. The application of the spiral balance spring for watches ushered in a new era of accuracy for portable timekeepers, similar to that which the pendulum had introduced for clocks. A similar controversy also surrounded this invention. On this occasion, however, Huygens's opponent was Robert Hooke, who claimed to have originated the idea in 1658. Watches with straight balance springs were known to have been made in the 1660s, but it was not until Huygens's spiral design appeared that this device was commonly adopted in watches. The improvements in accuracy made possible by the balance spring rapidly expanded the market for watches in an increasingly time-conscious society.

It was during the last quarter of the seventeenth century that England became preeminent in the production of clocks and watches. There were several reasons for this, but one factor was Louis XIV's revocation, in 1685, of the Edict of Nantes, a law that gave religious liberty to the Hugenots, the French Protestants. In the mass exodus of Protestants that ensued, many of France's best craftsmen fled abroad. England established a supremacy in the production of clocks, watches, and scientific instruments that it retained for more than 100 years, while France struggled to regain the splendor she had known during the earlier period when the French minister Colbert, by encouraging Huygens and other prominent savants to settle in France, had made Paris one of the great cultural and scientific centers of Europe.

The Royal Observatory at Greenwich was founded in 1675 in order to find out "the longitude of places for perfecting Navigation and Astronomy." The Greenwich Observatory became the point on the earth through which the line of Longitude 0 degrees was drawn, the arbitrary line dividing east and west from which universal time is measured. The first "Astronomer Royal" was John Flamsteed, who took great pains to obtain the finest instruments for his observations. His clocks were made by Thomas Tompion, the maker who established England's supremacy in the art of horology. In a letter dated December 11, 1675, to Richard Towneley, Flamsteed illustrated a new form of escapement, similar to the anchor previously mentioned, but designed in such a way that the seconds hand would have a "dead" beat, in other words, no recoil. This is the earliest known illustration of a dead-beat escapement, the escapement that became adopted as one of the standard features of a precision regulator. The device appears to have been suggested by Towneley and first made by Tompion in a clock for Flamsteed's friend and benefactor, Sir Jonas Moore.

Many historians have given credit for the invention of the dead-beat escapement to Tompion's successor, George Graham. It was indeed Graham who, by developing and standardizing the design of precision clocks, popularized this escapement. Graham, who succeeded to Tompion's business in 1713, continued the high standards of craftsmanship, producing scientific instruments in addition to clocks and watches. He employed some of the most prominent clockmakers and instrument makers of the eighteenth century, including John Shelton, John Bird, and Jonathan Sisson, and trained important makers such as Thomas Mudge and William Dutton. It was Graham too who encouraged John Harrison in his early attempts to produce a marine timekeeper (see **Longitude**). Graham established the design of the "precision regulator" (a clock designed specifically for accuracy), and made many significant improvements and innovations in the altitude measuring instruments that, along with his timekeepers, he supplied to most observatories during the first half of the eighteenth century. He was one of the first clockmakers to attempt to design a pendulum that would automatically compensate for variations in temperature. The effects of temperature variation on the accuracy of clocks were not noticeable until there were instruments that could keep a reliable measure of time: in heat a pendulum rod would expand, causing a clock to run slow; in cold, the opposite would occur. These variations had been observed by Flamsteed and other astronomers of his generation. In 1715, Graham attempted to devise a pendulum that would maintain the same period of oscillation regardless of changes in temperature. His first experiments involved the varying coefficients of expansion of different metals, but he abandoned these attempts because the variations were so small. In 1721, he made a pendulum supporting a jar of mercury: as the length of the steel pendulum rod increased in warm weather, the height of the mercury in the jar rose, thereby maintaining the center of gravity of the pendulum. About 1727, without knowledge of Graham's work, John Harrison conducted experiments to determine the difference in the coefficients of expansion of different metals. From the results, Harrison devised his "gridiron" pendulum, a pendulum composed of brass and steel rods assembled in such a way that the expansion or contraction of one metal would be counteracted by the expansion or contraction of the other. "Mr. Graham's quicksilver-pendulum," as it was known at the time, and Harrison's "gridiron" became the two temperature-compensated pendulums most frequently employed in precision clocks for the next 150 years.

The precision clocks in which Harrison used his gridiron pendulums were remarkable in many other ways. By using lignum vitae, a naturally oily wood, for the bearings and anti-friction wheels, and by devising a special form of escapement, this remarkable maker was able to reduce substantially the friction and wear in his timekeepers. Because his "grasshopper" escapement demanded a wide arc of swing, he designed a special form of pendulum suspension with adjustable "cycloidal" cheeks. This was done apparently without prior knowledge of Huygens's work. In his manuscript of 1730, Harrison claimed that his clocks, which were made largely of wood, would keep time to within one second a month and would not need to be cleaned for thirty years.

Clocks that were designed specifically for keeping mean solar or sidereal time were called regulators, because they provided the standard time by which other clocks were regulated. By 1730, the basic design of the regulator was established. A regulator incorporates several special features: a pendulum that automatically compensates for variations in temperature, a special escapement to provide a regular impulse to the pendulum, maintaining power to keep the clock running while it is being wound, and a dial especially designed to indicate clearly minutes and seconds.

[W.J.H.A.]

See also **Definition and Measurement of Time; Longitude; Timekeepers, Domestic: English Influence 1710–1800; Time Measurement and Science.**

FURTHER READINGS

Andrewes, W.J.H. "John Harrison: A Study of His Early Work." *Horological Dialogues*. New York: Journal of the American Section, Antiquarian Horological Society, 1979. 1:11–38.

———. "Time for the Astronomer, 1484–1884." *Vistas in Astronomy*. Ed. Paul Murdin and Peter Beer. Oxford: Pergamon, 1985. 28:69–86.

Bedini, Silvio A. *The Pulse of Time*. Florence: Leo S. Olschki, 1991.

Howse, Derek. "The Tompion Clocks at Greenwich and the Dead-Beat Escapement." *Antiquarian Horology* (December 1970): 18–34, and (March 1971): 114–133.

Huygens, Christiaan. *Horologium Oscillatorium*. Trans. Richard J. Blackwell. Ames: Iowa State UP, 1986.

Landes, David S. *Revolution in Time*. Cambridge: Harvard UP, 1983.

Thorndyke, Lynn. *A History of Magic and Experimental Science*, Vol. 4. New York: Columbia UP, 1934.

CLOCKS: THE FIRST MECHANICAL CLOCKS

The mechanical clock can be defined in various ways, but here it will be taken to have a *mechanical drive* (a falling weight, and later a spring), and a series of gear-wheels leading to an *escapement* (such as the device controlled by the verge and foliot, and much later by the pendulum), which in turn allows the energy stored in the drive to be periodically released in small units, the "ticks" of the clock. Finally, there must be some *indicator* of the passage of time, such as the striking of a bell (the word clock comes from the Late Latin *clocca*, or bell), or possibly one or more hands moving around a dial. In some cases this was an astronomical dial, such as an astrolabe, with or without planetary indications. Many early clocks had no dial whatsoever, but only a bell.

WATER-DRIVEN ALARMS

Anyone who had let go the windlass on a well with a full bucket on the rope knew the principle of the falling-weight drive. Such a drive had been used in antiquity in association with various hydraulic devices—those in particular of Hero (first century A.D.), and Vitruvius (first century B.C.). It had a wide currency in Islam. We may describe the release of the fluid in a hydraulic clock as an "escapement," although the word is now usually reserved for a device in which the energy is released in discrete units.

The oldest detailed Western medieval account of the construction of a water-driven alarm is in an incomplete tenth- or eleventh-century manuscript that was written in the Benedictine monastery of Santa Maria de Ripoll, at the foot of the Pyrenees. The description of the driving mechanism is now missing, but it seems that the weight-operated striking mechanism was very simple, with a rope and weight turning an axle which acted as a flail on small bells hanging from a rod. There was perhaps nothing more by way of dial-work than was needed to reset the alarm, a task no doubt undertaken by the sacristan, as laid down in the rules of the Cistercian, Cluniac, and Benedictine orders.

There must have been an accumulation of valuable experience over the next two or three centuries in the design of mechanical accessories to water-driven alarms. The striking mechanism for the mercury clock described in the books assembled by Alfonso X of Leon and Castile in the late thirteenth century is admittedly a relatively simple affair, but one suspects that much more elaborate versions had by then been developed. It seems more than probable that the first mechanical escapement was inspired by a bell-striking mechanism, and it is surely not without significance that the escapement of Richard of Wallingford's clock functioned in much the same way as the device that he provided to strike its bell.

MONASTIC MECHANICAL CLOCKS FROM THE 1280s

The earliest written record presently available that seems to refer to a mechanical clock is one in the annals of Dunstable Priory, a house of Augustinian Canons in Bedfordshire, England. The date is 1283. The word *horologium* refers ambiguously to any time-telling device, but here it was used for something set up above the rood screen (*pulpitum*), a most inconvenient place for a water clock. More to the point is the fact that this record is one of a cluster of similar records appearing suddenly in English ecclesiastical annals of the last two decades of the thirteenth century. There are records from Exeter (1284), London (Old St. Paul's, 1286), Norwich (1290), Ely (1291), and Christchurch (1292). There follow records for Salisbury (1306), and outside England for San Eustorgio, Milan (1309), Cambrai (1308 or 1318), and one or two more dubious instances. Taken together, these records suggest that some new form of timepiece, *horologium*, had arrived on the scene. The sums of money occasionally mentioned in connection with *horologia* are now relatively large. We are told, for instance, that at St. Paul's (London), one Bartholomew the *orologiarius* drew 281 rations for three quarters and eight days early in 1286, and more later in the same year, after he was joined by William of Pikewell. The first Norwich payment with reference to a *horologium* occurs in 1273–74, and when this "old" clock was mentioned again in 1321, it was in connection with payment for a *chord*.

ASTRONOMICAL MOTIVES

Such records as these lead us to suspect that we are in the presence of a new historical situation from the 1280s. Evidence of a very different sort suggests that the key invention had not been found at least by the year 1271—if Robertus Anglicus is a reliable witness. Every university student of the Middle Ages was expected to know the elements of astronomy, and most acquired their knowledge from the early thirteenth-century book, *On the Sphere*, by Sacrobosco. In 1271, "Robert the Englishman," a scholar teaching in Paris who was lecturing from, and commenting on, the work of Sacrobosco, reached the earlier writer's discussion of equal and unequal hours. Robert added to this his own statement to the effect that makers of clocks (*artifices horologiarum*) were trying to make a wheel that would complete one revolution for every revolution of the celestial sphere, that is, once a day. They had not yet managed to perfect their work, he said. Robert went on to make it clear that a weight-driven clock was at issue, for he mentioned in very general terms a uniformly balanced wheel with a lead weight hung from its axle.

A high proportion of the earliest mechanical clocks of which we have records have some or other astronomical association. At the simplest level, this usually implied a dial in the general pattern of an astrolabe—a representation, that is, of the celestial sphere of fixed stars. The dial might possibly also show the sun, as it moved with the daily motion with respect to the local horizon and meridian line.

TRADITIONS OF PLANETARY REPRESENTATION

Although most early "astronomical" mechanical clocks were doubtless restricted to an astrolabe dial, some were eventually to go far beyond, picking up a separate and also ancient tradition of making geared representations of the various motions of the sun, moon, and planets. The geared mechanism found at the beginning of this century in an ancient wreck on the sea bed off the island of Antikythera gives us an idea of the remarkable technological expertise available even to the Greeks in the first century B.C. This device had a calendarial function, and on it were represented the sun and moon. It reminds us of the planetarium made by Archimedes in the third century B.C. Archimedes's lost work, *On Spheremaking*, is now generally held to have told of the construction of a planetarium somehow enclosed in a star-globe. Cicero saw the planetarium, and described it in enough detail for us to be sure that it was indeed an intricate geared device.

We learn much of the other ancient tradition, that of the anaphoric clock, from the writings of the Roman architect Vitruvius. The word "anaphoric" refers to the fact that the (water-driven) clock showed risings and settings, namely of the heavens over the horizon, by means of an astrolabe dial. On a conventional astrolabe, as known to later centuries, the rete, a fretwork disk, carries the star map, and this rotates above a fixed disk carrying the local coordinate lines (horizon, meridian, and so forth). On the anaphoric clock, the moving star map was on a plate rotating behind a fixed rete of local coordinate lines. This arrangement was adopted by many medieval clockmakers.

There are surprisingly few early medieval references to planetary models as such, but one of the most intriguing of them concerns a gift made in 1232 by the sultan of Damascus to the Holy Roman Emperor, Frederick II. There is a possibility that this is the subject of a short text dating perhaps from the thirteenth century and surviving in at least three manuscript copies from northern Italy.

THE FIRST ESCAPEMENT

It seems that in the 1270s, or thereabouts, a mechanical means of driving astronomical models was found. Where, and by whom, we simply cannot say. Whether by the accident of preservation, or because this was the place of the invention, England seems to have a richer collection of early records than any other country. The records from 1283, 1284, and 1286 are strangely laconic, and give no sign of local pride. Half a century had gone by when Richard of Wallingford wrote what for us is the oldest surviving detailed account of a mechanical clock, so it is not surprising that *he took for granted the design of the escapement*, quoting only the crucial measurements. What is surprising is that his was not what had previously been thought the earliest form of escapement, namely the simple verge and foliot. He used instead a version with two parallel wheels of pins, called "strob" wheels, the pins engaging with a semicircular pallet. Its attendant verge and crossbar are thrown one way by the pins of one wheel, and then stopped and returned by the pins of the other. This arrangement was previously thought to have been invented by Leonardo da Vinci, who

sketched it in the following century. There is no means of knowing whether the simpler verge and foliot, with the familiar crown wheel in place of the "strob" wheels, was an earlier or later alternative. For the time being, at least, we can say no more than that the earliest known mechanical escapement is of the "double wheel and semicircle" type, and that it is known from an English source.

That there was a latent demand for large clocks is suggested by their relatively rapid diffusion. In 1324, Lincoln cathedral was presented with a new clock, and where the gift is recorded there comes a casual statement that clocks are now ubiquitous in cathedral and conventual churches. Richard of Wallingford moved from Oxford to become abbot of St. Albans in 1327, three years after this statement, and he was able to make use of the services of professional clockmakers. They shared the surname Stoke, and were probably members of the same family, although they might simply have been men from the village of that name. Roger and Laurence of Stoke both go under the name of "clockmaker" (*horologiarius*). The existence of this group of clockmakers is of special interest in view of the fact that the name of Roger of Stoke occurs in the rolls of Norwich cathedral in connection with the building of a new and larger clock than that mentioned earlier as dating from 1290. This new work was built from 1321 onward, and the financial accounts show that it had a massive painted and gilded iron dial weighing eighty-seven pounds on which the sun and moon were represented.

RICHARD OF WALLINGFORD

Fragmentary financial records are no substitute for the sort of account left to us by Richard of Wallingford, and we can only regret that we have nothing comparable from the first half-century of the history of the clock. Abbot of St. Albans from 1327 until his death from leprosy in 1336, Richard began to write a treatise on his astronomical clock, but like the clock itself, it seems to have been unfinished at his death.

In the matter of the movement of sun, moon, and stars, not to mention the striking of the bell, this attests to the use of mechanisms of extraordinary and hitherto unsuspected complexity. The "strob" escapement has a surprisingly long beat (nearly eleven seconds). The striking mechanism records the hour with an appropriate number of strokes on the bell—up to twenty-four strokes for the last hour of the day. The striking barrel, with its spiral of pegs to trip the strike, seems to have much in common with the chiming barrels of a later period. It is worth remarking that the clock at the church of San Gottardo in Milan seems to have acquired twenty-four-hour striking in 1335, the year before Richard of Wallingford's death, and once again, we can say nothing of the direction of diffusion of the invention.

From a theoretical point of view, the most remarkable part of the clock is the arrangement that produces a carefully calculated variable velocity for the passage of the sun around the zodiac in the course of the year. This uses an oval contrate wheel, with a pinion lying in a diametral direction. The calculation of the oval was a tour de force indeed, as anyone who tries to repeat it will soon discover. As far as the sun's mean motion is concerned, we cannot expect high absolute accuracy, in view of the essential imperfections of early escapements. We can, however, ask how well the trains of gears were computed, relating the sun's daily and (irregular) annual motion. The fractional error in the mean motion, judged against the best astronomical data available to the Abbot, turns out to be only seven parts in a million. It is important to realize that we are here dealing with a clock in a very different category from those much later specimens that survive from Salisbury and Wells, and which for so long were thought to date from the fourteenth century.

Richard's mechanism for the moon, like so many others in his clock, reminds us of later designs, but far surpasses most of them. The changing phase of the moon throughout the month was shown on his clock in what was to become a standard way—by means of a rotating half-blackened globe—but as for the eclipse mechanism, there are very few parallels from later centuries. When the time is right for an eclipse of the moon, a train of wheels terminating in a rack and pinion draws the moon-globe under the so-called "Head of the Dragon." This is all easier said than done, and one had to be an astronomer of uncommon skill to express in mechanical terms the theoretical conditions for an eclipse to take place. When we add to such devices as this features like the spiral contrate wheel included in the clock to ensure a smooth drive, not to mention the ingenious use of differential gears, we soon realize the hazards of dating extant devices purely in terms of their complexity. Son of a blacksmith as well as England's best astronomer, and in control of the

purse strings of its premier abbey: this was a combination that should not cause us to marvel when we find inferior work done by others centuries later.

GIOVANNI DE' DONDI

Another talented astronomer with resources financial as well as intellectual was Giovanni de' Dondi (1318–1389), whose astronomical clock, or "astrarium," was designed and built in Padua between 1348 and 1364. His masterpiece no longer survives, but there are numerous well-illustrated manuscript copies of the work in which he describes it. It differed conspicuously from the massive iron clocks considered thus far, for it was made of brass, was considerably smaller than the St. Albans clock, and speaking generally, might be said to have fitted more closely into the tradition of astronomical instrument design than into that of machines for public display and the ringing of large bells. Its purpose was to show the positions and motions of the planets, and to do so at a glance, rather than after such lengthy computations as were required of anyone using astronomical tables of the Alfonsine type. To describe it simply as an astronomical clock is to obscure the difference between it and most, if not all, of the astronomical clocks that had gone before it.

Giovanni de' Dondi was the son of another astronomer, Jacopo, who had himself designed and supervised the erection of an important clock for Prince Ubertino of Carrara in 1344. This clock sported a number of astronomical features. Giovanni became famous enough to be befriended by Gian Galeazzo Visconti, duke of Pavia, whose ailing son he attended and in whose palace he lived after 1382. The astrarium was seemingly in de' Dondi's possession until acquired by the duke and installed in the ducal library in or around 1381.

It was built into a seven-faced columnar frame, the upper section of each face bearing a dial, one for the sun, one for the moon, and one for each of the known planets. It was eventually provided with a covering case, the precise form of which is unknown to us. On the lower frame there were also a twenty-four-hour dial, a dial for the fixed feast-days of the church, another for the movable feasts, and one for the lunar nodes, this last being of significance in the calculation of eclipses. Flanking the horary dial there were tabulated times of rising and setting of the sun for Padua. Much ingenuity was shown in the way of providing gears with variable reach, that is, of gearing motions which are effectively of variable eccentricity (as in the case of the complicated Ptolemaic models for Mercury and the moon), by the use of loosely meshing oval gears. These were not at all of the same character—or accuracy—as the oval contrate wheel of Richard of Wallingford's clock, however, and while the Paduan machine was seemingly a more complete mechanical cosmos than that of St. Albans, it was mechanically less satisfying. One suspects that most engineers would agree that its most ingenious feature was its set of three linked chains for providing the discrete motions required for the calendar-work, motions that involve the solar (twenty-eight-year), lunae-solar (nineteen-year) and indiction (fifteen-year) cycles.

The drive of the astrarium used a falling weight in the conventional way, and the escapement was what has generally been supposed the original form of verge and foliot, the only difference being that in place of a crossbar, the verge carried a balance wheel in the form of a crown.

From the time of its completion, de' Dondi's astrarium became one of the marvels of Italy, and it was long to remain so. Leonardo da Vinci and Regiomontanus were among its admirers, and studied it carefully. In about 1529, the Emperor Charles V commissioned Gianello Torriano to repair it. He was unable to do so, but instead made a faithful copy, which ended up in Spain, in the monastery of San Yuste in Estramadura. Like the original, this has completely disappeared from history.

THE RAPID DIFFUSION OF CLOCKWORK

By the middle of the fourteenth century, mechanical clocks were proliferating throughout Europe, and to attract attention, such a clock had to be not only a timekeeper but a showpiece, not only an astronomical world, but a stage on which automata could act out a more familiar scene on the hour, or even more frequently. Saints and the Virgin, emperors and kings, monks and jousting knights, even the skeletal figure personifying time itself, any or all of these might be seen passing across the face of one of the larger clocks at due intervals. Angels turned with the sun, cocks crowed, the tides might be indicated, and the moon showing her appropriate phases—and at St. Albans, at least, be eclipsed when the time was ripe. Jacks were often used to strike the bells. One did not have to be trained in the art of reading the time from an astrolabe to appreciate such things.

The clock erected in the south transept of Strasbourg cathedral in 1354, a few years after

de' Dondi began work on his astrarium, was to become one of the most famous in Europe. Whereas de' Dondi's machine was of the order of a meter in height, the Strasbourg clock reached to eighteen meters or so, and was nearly half as wide as it was high. Surmounting the clock was a gilded cock made of iron, copper, and wood. Flapping its wings and spreading its feathers at noon, the cock opened its beak, put out its tongue and crowed—by means of a bellows and reed. In addition to this and other jack-work, there was the usual astrolabe dial. There was also a painted "zodiac-man," a commonplace in fourteenth-century manuscripts, showing the astrological relationship between the different parts of the body and the signs of the zodiac. Other monumental clocks in German cities were those of Frankenberg (1359), Munich (1371), Cologne (ca. 1372), and Villingen (1401). Like those of Lund (ca. 1380), Prague (1410), Olomouc (1422), and Bologna (1451)—to take four other notable clocks from the following century—the originality these displayed was not in the matter of fundamental mechanical principle, much less in astronomical respects, but in the complexity of their mundane displays. They occasionally included musical automata—as in the case of the cock of Strasbourg and the trumpeters of Lund. In all of them, the result was to create a *dual* pageant, representing microcosm and macrocosm side by side; but there is no doubt that as the years went by, representation of the heavens steadily lost ground to the display of more readily comprehended human activities.

There is not enough evidence to allow us to make generalizations about different regional traditions, but in France, for example, the clock at Bourges (ca. 1423) was relatively free from mundane paraphernalia. Once again, however, we are in a situation where the intellectual ambitions of the scholar responsible for the work were an important determinant of its style—just as was the case with the works of Richard of Wallingford and the de' Dondi family. There are other French clocks that seem to have been suitably frivolous. That at Chartres (ca. 1407), for instance, displayed a procession of singing clerks and priests every hour. This arrangement might well have been a common one, for it seems to have been used on the Norwich clock of 1322–25.

THE CHAMBER CLOCK

The clock in Bourges cathedral was designed by the astronomer Jean Fusoris (ca. 1365–1436), who was most famous as a maker of astronomical instruments. He operated a workshop producing astrolabes, and he built equatoria, including a fine specimen for the bishop of Norwich. (One part of this suffered the indignity of being reused as a clock face in the seventeenth century.) We still have Fusoris's annotated drawings for an astronomical clock that—according to his pupil Henry Arnaut of Zwolle—was built for the duke of Burgundy. Fusoris was a scholar-craftsman, and there were a few others cast in the same mold in most parts of Europe at one time or another.

The 1350s have been suggested as the beginning of the diffusion of the small domestic clock, but firm references are rare before the end of the century. (There are three or four connected with the French court, including an unambiguous one to a payment for an "orloge portative" by Charles V, dated 1377.) If the evidence has been correctly understood, the first small mechanical clock known to history was made in France in 1299 or 1300 by Pierre Pipelard for Philip the Fair (d. 1314). We know of it through the inventory of the personal possessions of Charles V (d. 1380), which speaks of a silver clock, entirely without iron, its silver weights filled with lead. Its scale is unknown, but the silver used for it suggests a small clock.

The fifteenth century saw a rapid growth in the production of chamber clocks, which were personal possessions that could be used as marks of prestige and taste. One of the most conspicuous social consequences of the diffusion of clocks large and small was a widespread awareness of the potentialities of *mechanism*. People became not only conscious of the existence of the finished work, but also caught up in its mystery. From the very first we find the clock as a metaphor in literature. We find it in Dante and Chaucer, for instance. Occasionally the reference may be historically revealing. In the course of an analogy drawn between the clock and love, Froissart tells of the daily rotation of the dial, inscribed with the twenty-four divisions of the day, and the twenty-four pegs that trip the striking mechanism. He tells of the force, the virtue, provided by the lead, and how this must be moderated by the foliot and escape wheel. His actual words rather suggest that he was contemplating the same long-forgotten form of escapement as we find in Richard of Wallingford.

CLOCKS AND THE POPULACE

People were caught up in the excitement of the creation of monumental clocks, not to mention the related economic consequences. Most building accounts are peremptory. Those of Norwich are reasonably full, but for sheer detail there is nothing to compare with the account of the installation of a large bell and clock mechanism in the palace of Peter (Pere) IV of Aragon (1319–1387), at Perpignan, in 1356. Pere had in his employ a number of astronomers, as well as metalworkers engaged in the upkeep of his scientific instruments. He was a patron of astronomy and the cosmographical arts generally, the so-called "Catalan Atlas" of 1375 being perhaps the best known result of his patronage. There is reason to think that he owned at least one clock as early as 1345; later he had several, and he presented others to members of his family, but the great clock of 1356 seems to have been his most ambitious enterprise.

The detailed accounts of the building of this clock give an intimate picture of the event—down to the discount obtained on the 421 eggs used to mix the earth for the lining and the cope of the bell. The accounts cover everything from laundry to the transmission of letters, and they contain the names of more than 600 people who were in some way connected with the enterprise. The social implications of this fact speak for themselves.

Details of the clock mechanism are almost entirely absent from the records. We do learn something of considerable interest: it was unreliable, and to such a degree that by 1387, his heir, King John I, appointed two men to sound the hours in the manner of the cathedral at Barcelona, that is, manually, following a sand-glass.

Pere's clock continued to function badly for decades. Meanwhile other Iberian cities were overtaking Perpignan. By 1378, Valencia cathedral had a clock which struck the quarters. This was built by Juan Aleman, whose name suggests that he was a German clockmaker. There were striking clocks too in Burgos (1384), Palma, Mallorca (1386), Lérida (1390), Barcelona (1393), Seville (1396), and Santiago (1395). In short, most of the principal cathedrals in the peninsula were in possession of striking clocks by the end of the fourteenth century. Although not at the heart of the new European technology, prelates and princes in this region were determined not to let the revolution pass them by. It was a revolution that was transforming the face of Europe, and preparing the way in many different respects for its industrialization.

[J.D.N.]

See also **Clock Metaphor; Dante Alighieri; Instruments of Time Measurement to ca.** A.D. **1275.**

FURTHER READINGS

Bedini, S.A., and F. R. Maddison. "Mechanical Universe: The Astrarium of Giovanni de' Dondi." *Transactions of the American Philosophical Society* n.s., 56.5 (1966): 5–69.

Beeson, C.F.C. *English Church Clocks, 1280 1850.* London: Antiquarian Horological Society, 1971.

———. *Perpignan 1356. The Making of a Clock and Bell for the King's Castle.* London: Antiquarian Horological Society, 1982.

Haber, F.C. "The Cathedral Clock and the Cosmological Clock Metaphor." *The Study of Time II.* Ed. J.T. Fraser and N. Lawrence. New York: Springer, 1975. 399–416.

King, H.C., and J.R. Millburn. *Geared to the Stars: The Evolution of Planetariums, Orreries, and Astronomical Clocks.* Toronto: U of Toronto P, 1978.

Leopold, J.H. *The Almanus Manuscript.* London: Heinemann, 1971.

Lloyd, H.A. *Some Outstanding Clocks over Seven Hundred Years, 1250–1950.* London: Leonard Hill, 1958.

North, J.D. "Monasticism and the First Mechanical Clocks." *The Study of Time II.* Ed. J.T. Fraser and N. Lawrence. New York: Springer, 1975. 381–398.

———. *Richard of Wallingford. An edition of his writings, with introductions, English translations, and commentary.* 3 volumes. Oxford: The University Press, 1976.

Poulle, E. *Equatoires et Horlogerie planétaire du XIIIe au XVIe siècle.* 2 volumes. Geneva: Droz, 1980.

Price, D.J. de S. *Gears from the Greeks: The Antikythera Machine—a Calendar Computer from ca. 80* B.C. New York: Science History Publications, 1975.

Ungerer, A. *Les Horloges astronomiques et monumentales les plus remarquables de l'Antiquité jusqu'à nos jours.* Strasbourg, 1931.

CLUB OF ROME

Growing concern in the 1960s about high rates of population growth and resource depletion led to fears and forecasts of global eco-catastrophe becoming common. The high-water mark of such modern Malthusianism was reached when an informal international association with a restricted, prestigious membership, the Club of Rome, embarked on a breathtakingly ambitious task—a Project on the Predicament of Mankind. It commissioned computer modeling of the global interaction of five basic factors (population, agricultural production, natural resources, industrial production, and pollution). The resultant 1972 book, *The Limits to Growth*, commanded worldwide attention. It forecast catastrophic levels of famine, pollution, and resource depletion leading to the collapse of the global system in the twenty-first century; exponential growth in a finite system could not be accommodated over an indefinite period of time.

The social advocacy of the study and its sponsors was for a self-imposed limitation on growth, embracing birth control programs, capital shifts from manufacturing to agriculture, and the adoption of ecologically harmonious life-styles. The study was well received by biologists well versed in the exponential growth of animal populations up to a critical environmental carrying capacity. But, for many economists, the assumptions about future resource availability did not adequately take into account the way in which the market system provides incentives for substitution, recycling, and new extractive methods.

[H.R.J.]

See also **Malthus, Thomas.**

FURTHER READINGS

Meadows, D.H., D.C. Meadows, J. Randers, and W. Behrens. *The Limits to Growth: A Report for the Club of Rome's Project on the Predicament of Mankind.* New York: Universe Books, 1972.

COEVOLUTION

The evolution of all forms of life on earth has been influenced by both the physical environment and other forms of life. An organism may feed on other organisms, be fed on by them, compete with them for food or space or mates, or interact cooperatively with them. Such interactions have profound ecological implications and evolutionary effects. Competing species may diverge from one another over time, increasing evolutionary success by reducing conflict. Predators and their prey (which in the broad sense include such diverse species as lions and zebras, bison and prairie grasses, or tapeworms and their hosts) engage in an evolutionary "arms race," with each species continuously evolving new adaptations for capture or escape. Many attributes of organisms—such as teeth and claws, armor, poison glands, and visual and auditory senses—reflect coevolutionary selective pressures. Symbiotic species may become increasingly interdependent, until they can scarcely exist separately: flowering plants and their pollinators are a striking example. Coevolution can explain such diverse phenomena as crypsis (camouflage through coloring, shape, or behavior), mimicry (close resemblances among unrelated species), and the occurrence of bright warning colors and patterns such as those of butterflies or tropical fishes.

[G.A.A.]

See also **Evolution of Evolutionism; Speciation.**

FURTHER READINGS

Futuyma, D.J., and M. Slatkin, eds. *Coevolution.* Sunderland: Sinauer Associates, 1983.

COGNITION

Theorizing on the psychology of time has fluctuated between two extremes, the biological and the cognitive. Biological theories propose that psychological time is a product of brain mechanisms, especially those involving one or more internal clocks that a person directly accesses to time behavior and judge duration. Cognitive theories propose that psychological time is a product of information-processing activities—especially those involving attention, memory, and judgment—which a person uses heuristically to time behavior and to use available order and duration information. A complete account may require both kinds of theories. This article emphasizes the cognitive approach, as well as recent cognitive neuroscience research that is beginning to suggest possible syntheses of the two views.

In the late 1800s, several theorists argued that psychological time involves cognitive processes. Jean-Marie Guyau and William James, for example, both proposed that cognitive factors influence the experiencing and remembering of time. During the early to mid-1900s, biological views became influential, and cognitive models became less prominent. The resurgence of cognitive psychology in the second half of the twentieth century brought cognitive models of psychological time to the forefront. Cognitive psychologists use experimental evidence to make inferences about underlying structures that represent temporal information and processes that access and use such representations.

Cognitive processes involve the functioning of several memory, or knowledge, systems. These include the procedural system, which contains information about well-learned movements; the semantic system, which contains information about concepts and linguistic expressions; and the episodic system, which contains information about personal experiences. In addition, a working-memory system contains information about currently activated mental representations. Time is a ubiquitous construct based on the knowledge that these systems represent.

PROCEDURAL KNOWLEDGE

Procedural knowledge, such as the "knowing how" that is expressed in skilled movements, must specify relative intervals between movement components; if this information is imprecise or lacking, movements may not be smoothly coordinated. Motor programs contain information needed to control movements. Timing of activities such as typing and handwriting may be a natural product of output systems tuned to particular task requirements. Timing of activities such as musical production may be directly represented in hierarchical control structures, probably with relative rather than absolute timing between performance components.

SEMANTIC KNOWLEDGE

Semantic knowledge, often regarded as timeless and factual, may be somewhat temporary: Changing circumstances require a person to update attributes of objects and individuals (such as single, married, or divorced). Knowledge concerning temporal concepts and phenomena also changes in the process of development. Children learn facts about temporal experience, such as that time seems lengthened if one is waiting for an event to occur. People also use and appreciate temporal metaphors such as "time is money."

EPISODIC KNOWLEDGE

Psychological time probably relates more intimately to the episodic system than to the other cognitive systems. Episodic knowledge concerns events that a person has experienced in a particular spatiotemporal context. A short-term, or working-memory, system apparently generates contextual information, including relative time-of-event (order) information, and transmits it to the episodic system, which stores it in a more permanent way along with the memory for events per se. Remembering the order and duration of events and episodes (sequences of events) requires this contextual information. Research on judged duration, for example, frequently reveals complex interactions (more technically, "double-dissociations"). These interactions suggest that cognitive processes involved in prospective duration judgment, or experienced duration, differ from those involved in retrospective duration judgment, or remembered duration. Attention to time lengthens experienced duration but has little or no influence on remembered duration. Many models of experienced duration propose that a stimulus information processor and a temporal information processor ("timer") share limited attentional resources. If stimulus processing demands more resources, fewer resources are available for temporal information processing, and experienced duration shortens. Other models, such as the contextual-change model (which follows), can also explain how attentional processes influence experienced duration.

Two classes of cognitive models focus on remembered duration: event-memory and contextual-change models. Event-memory models propose that remembered duration lengthens as a function of the amount of event (stimulus) information subjects encode into memory and retrieve at the time they make a duration judgment. One event-memory model proposes that remembered duration is a cognitive construction based on the number of stored events and their complexity of coding. Although some evidence supports this model, other experiments reveal that remembered duration only indirectly relates to stored and retrievable event information.

Some of these experiments suggest an alternative model, a contextual-change model. It proposes that remembered duration is a cognitive construction based on the availability in memory of contextual changes that occurred during the time period. Various evidence supports this model. If a person performs several different kinds of tasks during a time period, remembered duration is longer than if a person performs only a single kind of task; this is attributable to greater process-context changes. Remembered duration is also longer if there are more changes in environmental or emotional context. Subjects tend to remember the first of two equal durations as being longer, and greater contextual changes that accompany the first of two similar experiences may cause this time-order effect.

Several other cognitive models explain duration judgments made following the performance of specific kinds of tasks. One model emphasizes segmentation of events; it explains the finding that duration judgments lengthen if a time period contains more distinct segments. Another model emphasizes dynamic attending and forming of expectancies; it explains the finding that hierarchical and other structural characteristics of episodes influence duration judgments.

Whether more general models, such as the contextual-change model, can subsume these models or whether these models propose processes unexplainable by more general models is unclear.

BRAIN SYSTEMS AND TEMPORAL COGNITION

Some neuropsychologists and other neuroscientists investigate neural substrates of time-related cognitive processes by studying the effects of brain damage, the psychophysiology of brain systems, and the effects of psychoactive drugs. Cognitive and physiological discoveries are now beginning to clarify and reinforce each other. Improved understanding of brain mechanisms may ultimately lead to a reconciliation of biological and cognitive views on psychological time.

Abnormal functioning of the cerebellum, a result of brain damage or of drugs such as alcohol, disrupts the timing of motor skills. The cerebellar system is clearly dissociable from other brain systems involved in psychological time. For example, amnesics who are not able to acquire new episodic information can still acquire procedural information.

Studies on effects of brain damage and use of physiological recording techniques reveal the brain areas that subserve semantic information processing. These include posterior regions of the frontal lobes, anterior regions of the parietal lobes, and most of the temporal lobes, especially in the left cerebral hemisphere.

Part of the prefrontal cortex of the cerebrum apparently serves as a system for timing short durations and maintaining a working-memory context for present experiences. In doing so, it processes temporal and other contextual information. The prefrontal cortex is directly connected with a memory system located in the medial temporal lobe. This system and its most critical component, the hippocampus, subserves the long-term encoding of episodic memories, which are apparently stored in various areas of the brain that were active during an episode. Damage to the hippocampus causes a syndrome in which a person lives mainly in the present and future, because events that once occupied working memory are not permanently stored.

[R.A.B.]

See also **Guyau, Jean-Marie; James, William (as Psychologist); Memory for Time; Prospective and Retrospective Time; Psychology of Time; Psychophysiology; Time Perception.**

FURTHER READINGS

Block, Richard A., ed. *Cognitive Models of Psychological Time*. Hillsdale: Erlbaum, 1990.

Friedman, William J. *About Time: Inventing the Fourth Dimension*. Cambridge: MIT P, 1990.

Levin, Iris, and Dan Zakay, eds. *Time and Human Cognition: A Life-Span Perspective*. Amsterdam: North-Holland, 1989.

Macar, Françoise, Viviane Pouthas, and William J. Friedman, eds. *Time, Action and Cognition: Towards Bridging the Gap*. Dordrecht: Kluwer, 1992.

Michon, John A., and Janet L. Jackson, eds. *Time, Mind, and Behavior*. Heidelberg: Springer, 1985.

COLLINGWOOD, ROBIN GEORGE (1889–1943)

In his short life, this admirable British philosopher and historian published some fifteen books ranging from philosophy through Roman history, religion, and travel. From 1921 to 1925, he held double posts at Oxford as lecturer in both philosophy and Roman history. In 1935, he was appointed to the Waynflete Chair, from which he resigned in 1937 due to illness. Collingwood writes with a rare grace and wit that makes his works accessible to educated nonspecialists.

In his charming autobiography he describes his admirably eccentric upbringing that might have come off the pages of Evelyn Waugh or Anthony Powell. To the age of thirteen he was educated at home by his father, beginning Latin at four and Greek at six. Obviously gifted at languages, he later read manuscripts for Oxford University Press in French, German, Spanish, and Italian. Collingwood's parents were impoverished intellectual artists able to send him to school at Rugby and Oxford only through the generosity of a family friend. In these places, he tells us, he flourished best when left to his own curiosity to explore intellectual and artistic byways; he bridled under routine assignments.

Collingwood was unusual among philosophers in having practiced, or watched at first hand, the work of other disciplines such as painting, poetry, music, and history, at the last of which he became a master himself. There is in his philosophical writing a realization of the sheer recalcitrance of things despite the graceful claim in his *Essay on Philosophical Method* (1933), that "The prose writer's art is an art that must conceal itself and produce not a jewel that is looked at for its own beauty, but a crystal in whose depths the thought can be seen without distortion or confusion; and the philosophical writer (in especial contrast to the poet) follows the trade not of a jeweller, but of a lens-grinder." So it is ironic that Collingwood came to despise the Oxford realists on the one hand, and G. E. More on the other, both of whom he thought to believe falsely that knowing something was a transparent and direct relation between knower and known. Painting and archeology had taught him there was much more than that to knowing something.

Despite eschewing contemporary analytic rigor, Collingwood anticipated two important trends: the analysis of the history of science contributed by Thomas Kuhn, and the ordinary language analysis of Ludwig Wittgenstein, J. L. Austin, and others. Collingwood held that every inquiry seeks answers to questions, and that those answers presuppose the answer to prior questions. But one cannot reasonably ask forever; ultimately there are presuppositions that are not answers to prior questions. Metaphysics consists in seeking out these absolute presuppositions of an age or a discipline and noting how they change over time. Kuhn actually performed a reasonably similar analysis for which he is justly famous.

In his 1926 essay, "Some Perplexities About Time: With an Attempted Solution," Collingwood advances the theory that many puzzles about time arise from our uncritical talk about it as if time were a one-dimensional space. Spatial parts do exist before and behind us. So if we think in a spatial way about time we shall be tricked into believing that the past and the future somehow exist now, as the space in front and behind us does. And then we are stuck with the impossibility of figuring out how what has ceased to exist and what does not yet exist, both do really exist. There are several similar analyses in the essay. Collingwood holds that time is simply a perpetually changing present. But we must go carefully here, too, for if the present is shrunk too far it becomes a point, which also does not exist. And then there would be no time. To avoid this, he is driven to assign to time another "mode of being besides existence," and to say that both past and future are ideals that are thought of, but not thought of as actually existing. The present, he says, exists as a union of nonexistent pasts and futures that are purely ideal, the past living and the future germinating, into the present.

Admirable as his diagnosis of the perplexity is, it cannot be said that Collingwood offers a solution. Having presciently diagnosed the problem as a misuse of words, he then misuses words to solve it. Had he seen clearly how he spotted the problem, he might well have avoided creating yet another.

[B.R.G.]

See also **Wittgenstein, Ludwig.**

FURTHER READINGS

Collingwood, R.G. *An Autobiography*. Oxford: Clarendon P, 1938.

Donagan, Alan. *The Later Philosophy of R.G. Collingwood*. Oxford: Clarendon P, 1962.

COMPUTER MUSIC

This article will concern itself with the interaction between macro- and microtime in computer music. Music is an art of time not only because it uses time as a carrier of forms. As Jonathan Kramer has pointed out, music deals with time in a very intimate way. Composing music is composing time, that is, shaping it into a variety of temporalities. These temporalities are materials defined at different levels or time scales, which interact in order to create a highly articulated process.

Common music notation deals with pitch and duration organized into a complex, multilevel network. These aspects are manipulated by means of a symbolic representation having as a primitive element the *note* inscribed on music paper. This presupposes a dualistic view of the musical fact: the composer deals pertinently with syntactical time manipulations that operate above the level of the note, leaving undefined the smaller levels (comprised between the beginning and the end of each note) corresponding to the internal structures of sound. In other words, the microtime dimension of sound is not explicitly included in the act of composing, and hence is not connected structurally with the macrotime of figures, phrases, sections, and so on.

This does not means that composers have not tried to integrate features of sound into their compositional microworlds: the use of register as a complementary force in the building of melodic and harmonic materials, as well as the mixtures of instrumental sources in the orchestral works of the nineteenth-century repertoire, often shows a deep concern for controlling sound color as a significant element. However, this concern was manifested—intuitively—within a classic dualistic paradigm, maintaining a separation between syntactical macrotime relations determined through notation and infra-syntactical, nonnotated elements considered simply as sound-carriers of musical discourse.

The evolution of twentieth-century music through the work of Debussy, Stravinsky, Schoenberg, Webern, and Varèse shows a growing awareness of the limitations of this approach and of the necessity to proceed to a structural integration of sound as a composable dimension. Schoenberg stated this clearly in his *Harmonielehre* of 1911: having reaching the point of dissolution of tonal functionality (which constituted the basis of earlier musical logic), the "emancipation of the dissonance" that followed could not aspire to a similar level of rationality without an extension of compositional control to "timbre"—the *klangfarben*, the color of sound—that is, without generalizing compositional syntax to include the shaping of microtime.

As B. Truax and O. Laske have separately argued, the domain of microtime can be said to begin below a threshold of fifty milliseconds. It contains dimensions which are of capital importance for the definition of the qualities of sound: relations of frequency between the partials of a spectrum, and relations of amplitude (envelopes) shaping the temporal behavior of these partials. Compositional manipulation of these dimensions was impossible to realize with the technical means available at the beginning of the century. It was only much later, with the use of the electro-acoustical and digital means developed since 1950, that intervention at this level became possible. The introduction of the digital computer as a compositional tool thus changed the scope of possible temporalities to be composed, providing access to time scales which stand below the level of the note and thereby allowing the composer to control both micro- and macrotime features within a unified field of relationships. Thus, as M. Mathews and J.A. Moorer have respectively shown, the new situation incorporates techniques of (1) sound synthesis, and (2) signal processing as complementary tools to create, manipulate, and describe musical entities. Here the primitive is not the note, but the *sample*, that is, the basic element of what constitutes the numerical definition of sound as a series of discrete steps. It is the availability of this numerical definition that allows the extension of syntactical musical activity to the domain of microtime. This does not mean, however, that the elements manipulated by common music notation are abandoned: they are instead clearly assigned to their specific temporal dimension, which is now articulated within a broader field of musical relations.

In any case, structuring of the microtime of sound is not without immediate consequences for the macrotime. However, the compositional control of the interactions between these different kinds of temporal domains depends on the cognitive paradigm adopted by the composer. A decision has to be made about the status and the nature of these interactions: to consider them as taking place in a continuum which is to be organized in a univocal hierarchical fashion, or to assume a certain kind of noncontinuity, of nonlinearity, in which case micro- and macrotime are taken as disjoint (or relative) dimensions, hence conceiving all possible cross-manipulations as passages between specific localities and globalities.

This question reveals an epistemology of music composition. The possible answers are related to the concepts retained as pertinent, acting as substrata of a given musical thought. The problem, for a composer interested in the extension of a syntax to all possible temporal dimensions, is to find the means to articulate this complexity.

[H.V.]

See also **Mathematics of Musical Time.**

Further Readings

Kramer, J. *The Time of Music.* New York: Schirmer Books, 1988.

Laske, O. "Toward an Epistemology of Composition." *Interface* 20 (1991): 235–269.

Mathews, M. *The Technology of Computer Music.* Cambridge: MIT P, 1969.

Moorer, J.A. "Signal Processing Aspects of Computer Technology." *Foundations of Computer Music.* Ed. J. Strawn and C. Roads. Cambridge: MIT P, 1986.

Truax, B. "The POD System of Interactive Programs." *Foundations of Computer Music.* Ed. J. Strawn and C. Roads. Cambridge: MIT P, 1986.

COMPUTERS AND TIME

The development and use of the electronic digital computer cannot be analyzed without a number of references to time. First, computers are "of our time"—they have been in existence only for about fifty years. Second, they can be used to "create" time—by freeing time that would otherwise be employed in menial and repetitive activity—or to "condense" time—by making possible in a very short time what would otherwise take much longer. Thus computers can be said to remove some of the constraints that time places on human activity.

The development of the computer over time has been dramatic. There have been only a small number of significant basic technological changes, but we have seen amazing changes in the size, speed, and power of computers. Size, speed, and power are all directly related. Since internally the computer involves electrons traveling at something approaching the speed of light, a reduction in the distance traveled can result in significant, relative time savings and hence in the speed of operation of the machine. The power of the computer is directly relative to this speed factor. The faster a particular simple instruction can be carried out, the more instructions can be packed into the same time frame and the more can be carried out. Since all processing is based on processing these simple instructions, power rises as speed increases. The speed and power of computers is measured in a number of ways. One is to use "bench marks" for standard computing tasks and to demonstrate how long a particular machine takes to carry out a range of bench marks. Another is simply to measure the power of the processor in terms of the MIPS (millions of instructions per second) that it is capable of handling.

Modern processors use VLSI (very large scale integration) of components to keep electron travel paths to a minimum. This has the added advantage of presenting a small device to the computer builder, and hence smaller machines to the end user. A small microprocessor can, however, carry out sophisticated tasks. It is this miniaturization which has led to simple "computers" being built into many consumer goods such as washing machines, cars, calculators, and the ubiquitous digital watch.

In a "full-blown" computer, however, the processor is only a small part (in every sense) of the full system. Manufacturers of other components, of peripheral devices, and of software are fighting to keep up with processor development. One of the slowest (all things are relative!) devices in the computer is the device used to store programs and data.

Originally most storage devices were magnetic tapes. The problem with tapes is that they are serial or sequential access devices—it is necessary to wind past the data on the tape that one does not want to access to get to the data that one does. This is a time-consuming process, especially if the sophisticated and relatively expensive processor is sitting idle while the search for data takes place. Most storage devices nowadays are direct or random access devices allowing access to any portion of the data very quickly. The most common is the magnetic disk.

Here again, we have seen shifts in both size and speed of operation, and once more the two are related. Disks are mechanical devices and the shorter distance the read and write head has to move in order to access any track on the disk, the faster the data on that track can be retrieved. A number of "tricks" are employed for further speeding up data access. The most used of these is data caching. When data is accessed from disk, the chances are that subsequent bits of the data that are required will follow directly from the bit of data with which one is currently dealing. To take advantage of this fact, when data is read from the disk, a whole section is transferred to a segment of internal memory (which is much faster than disk). Subsequent retrieval of data can then often take place from this cache of data with another disk access only taking place when the next required piece of data is not in the cache. Another section of disk memory is then read into the cache, and the process continues.

Perhaps the most dramatic time effects of computers have come about from software development. In the early years of computing, all processing was carried out in batch mode. A "job" was submitted to the machine which churned away and eventually produced a batch of output that was returned to the user. The processing would normally take a few hours and the whole turnaround time from the user submitting his job to getting his output would typically be twenty-four hours or more. Nowadays, for the majority of tasks, processing takes place in "real-time" mode—the user interacts directly with the software and results are (to all intents and purposes) immediate. Response times of seconds can now seem frustrating. This makes possible a whole range of applications that were not previously feasible—including such time-critical activities as reservation systems and, more importantly, patient monitoring in life-support systems.

One of the most recent developments in computing is the development of the GUI (graphical user interface). This is a software system that sits between the user and the application software and presents a coherent, standard method of working to the user. Paradoxically, such systems can be slower than other (text-based) interfaces, but the benefits lie in the standardization of the interface across a number of software applications—which reduces the time required to learn a new package and should result in less confusion for the user who makes use of a number of packages on a regular basis.

The future certainly holds further development, and development that will take place at an increasing rate. An infinitude of computer-associated possibilities awaits us—some that we can foresee and many others that we cannot. Only time will tell.

[J.P.H.]

CONTROLLED-RELEASE FORMULATIONS

In the last twenty-five years, long overdue recognition has been given to the fact that living systems are rhythmic, having internal clocks with many periods, ranging in human beings from thousandths of a second to several years. The most prominent clock has a period of about twenty-four hours. It drives the daily cycles of temperature and sleep-wake activity, among many others. This clock is normally entrained by or synchronized with the earthly cycle of light and dark, but even under constant conditions these periodicities assert themselves. The twenty-four-hour clock was first recognized (in plants) by Jean Jacques d'Ortous de Mairan. In 1729, he discovered that a "sensitive" heliotrope plant would open its leaves during the day and fold them at night, even when it was put in a place where sunlight could not reach it.

The existence of internal biological clockworks, and especially the twenty-four-hour "circadian" clock, suggests that there might be important time-of-day variations in the rates or amplitudes of physiological and biochemical processes, and that pharmacologic therapies aimed at any such process might be more efficacious at certain times than at others. Conversely, they might be more toxic or dangerous at certain times. If the time of heightened efficacy does not coincide with the time of highest toxicity, then a new, optimized drug formulation design is suggested, namely to deliver the drug at a nonconstant rate such that it is most active in the body at the time of day of highest beneficial effect and least active at the time of highest potential for toxicity.

To tailor pharmaceutical formulations according to the above timing concept, which might be referred to as optimizing the circadian rhythm phase, requires determination of the rhythms of target processes and reactions and their varying sensitivity to pharmacologic modulation, both beneficial and harmful, at different phases of their daily rhythms. Recently, such data have been forthcoming with respect to processes such as those that regulate blood pressure.

Traditional prescriptions of oral medications (pills, capsules, syrups) have either ignored time or dealt with it casually. Patients are often told to take their medicine "as needed" or "as directed" (which often means little direction was given), or "at mealtimes" (as a reminder). However, many diseases are periodic. For example, asthma attacks tend to occur in the early morning hours more than at other times, and heart attacks and strokes have the highest probability of occurrence between 6:00 A.M. and noon. Liquids, gels, and powders are ordinarily used to "formulate" drugs into dosage forms suitable for patient use. The art of formulation is ancient and was well known to Pharaonic Egyptians, but most formulations, old and new, just give pulses of drugs, without controlling temporal patterns well. More advanced versions assure constancy (no time variation) of levels of drugs in body fluids. These have proved greatly beneficial in many cases, but now the search is for extra benefits to be obtained from working in harmony with biological rhythmic organization.

Pharmaceuticals that deliver drugs in optimal conjunction with circadian rhythms require new drug delivery systems, that is, new formulations. We now have an impressive array of such inventions. Many of these rely on polymer systems. Some impose a membrane barrier between the drug and the biological interface such that the passage of the drug by diffusion from a reservoir to the body is governed by the physical characteristics of that membrane. In a matrix tablet version the dry reservoir acts also as a controlling barrier. Other polymeric systems are arranged so that they act as small pumps (driven by osmotic pressure) that turn on when wet. Still others boost diffusional transports of drugs arising from concentration differences between reservoirs and body fluids by means of very small electric currents. Transdermal systems with delays are available that turn on after they absorb water and so start a chemical reaction preparatory to releasing the drug. Most of these new formulations are based on a combination of chemical engineering, materials science, organic chemistry, physical chemistry, pharmaceutics, pharmacology, biochemistry, physiology, and pathology. These are the relevant sciences, and it can be seen that these new designs are almost spectacularly multidisciplinary in origin.

Controlled-release therapeutic systems can be built with chosen delays so that they begin to function only after a selected number of hours has passed since the system was administered. As an example of the usefulness of delay to achieve a proper rhythm, consider that even in patients with high blood pressure (hypertension), the pressure falls during sleep and rises, sometimes abruptly, when the subject awakens. By then it is too late to take medication to prevent a supernormal surge in blood pressure seen in some of these patients. A new therapeutic system might permit a patient to take the antihypertensive pill at bedtime if the formulation had a built-in delay such that it did not begin to function until approximately 4:00 A.M. (before blood pressure rises). The blood-pressure-lowering drug would then be increasingly active in body fluids at the time of awakening and so optimally prevent establishing hypertension during the following day. Furthermore, by this pattern the therapeutic system could avoid overtreating the patient during sleep, when less medication might be needed.

Even more remarkable than benefits that might accrue from optimal circadian phasing of drug delivery is the design of programmed, pulsatile delivery systems. In at least one instance, a human physiological system has been found to be frequency-modulated rather than amplitude-modulated, as is more common. The frequency-modulated system involves a brain hormone (gonadotropin-releasing hormone, GnRH) that travels from the hypothalamus of the brain to the anterior pituitary gland, where it regulates the release of hormones (luteinizing hormone, follicle-stimulating hormone) that act on the ovary in women and the testis in men to support gametogenesis (ripening of eggs and sperm) and sex hormone production. GnRH has a pulsatile pattern with one pulse about every ninety minutes in human beings. If it is given constantly, even at high levels, it is ineffective. A healthy reproductive system of a young woman depends absolutely on proper pulsing of GnRH according to this ninety-minute clock. In some infertile women the pulsation is lacking, and if it is established by a therapeutic system, fertility returns. Conversely, in many fertile women, a therapeutic system that masks the pulsations with a constant signal produces contraception. Therefore, the clinical effect of the same chemical agent can go one way or the other, depending on the perspective of timing.

The newest generation of formulators for pharmaceuticals explicitly takes time into account in seeking the optimal input function for a drug. New designs stimulate the development of new materials, new geometries and arrangements of existing materials, and new investigations of fundamental biological organization. Just as the science of anatomy (morphology) addresses spatial organization in living systems, the science of physiology addresses functional organization. Functions imply change with time and their organization is temporal. The processes of fertilization, fetal development, birth, growth, maturation, differentiation, adaptation, and senescence all dramatize the salience of time in life. Drugs are molecular agents of a physician's purpose, which is always to produce a salubrious effect on biological processes. Because these processes are usually temporally organized, controlled-release formulations in which, literally, "time is of the essence," acquire new benefits compared to conventional medications.

[F.E.Y.]

See also **Biological Rhythms and Medicine; Biological Rhythms in Epidemiology and Pharmacology; Chronobiology.**

FURTHER READINGS

Heilmann, Klaus. *Therapeutic Systems: Rate-Controlled Drug Delivery—Concept and Development.* 2nd ed. (revised). New York: Georg Thieme Verlag, 1984.

Roseman, Theodore J., ed. *Controlled Release Delivery Systems.* New York: Dekker, 1981.

Stuyker-Boudier, Harry A.J. *Rate-Controlled Drug Administration and Action.* Boca Raton: CRC P, 1986.

COSMOLOGY

Cosmology in the broadest sense is the study of the universes of different societies in different periods of history. In this treatment, cosmology is restricted to studies of the physical universe, with emphasis on developments in the twentieth century.

THE THREE COSMOLOGIES OF THE ANCIENT WORLD

In ancient Greece, pre-Socratic philosopher-scientists—including Thales, Anaximander, and Anaximenes of the sixth century B.C.—originated the idea that the world consists of events controlled by natural rather than supernatural agents, and Pythagoras of Samos advanced the idea of a cosmos harmonized by mathematical relations. From the birth of science emerged the three grand cosmologies of classical antiquity: the infinite atomist universe of evolving stars, planets, and lifeforms popularized by Epicurus and described in the epic poem, *De rerum natura,* by Lucretius; the Aristotelian celestial spheres in endless epicyclic motion elaborated by Ptolemy; and the Stoic cosmos of a finite system of stars surrounded by infinite and empty space proposed by Zeno of Citium and widely accepted in the Greco-Roman world. In the atomist universe, the landscape of history glided by on the river of time; in the Aristotelian universe, the heavens whirled eternally; and in the Stoic cosmos of periodic catastrophic upheavals, history forever repeated itself on the wheel of time.

MEDIEVAL UNIVERSE

In the Middle Ages, the Aristotelian celestial spheres were identified with the neo-Platonic angelic spheres. Beyond the sphere of fixed stars lay the *primum mobile*, introduced by Arab scholars, that was maintained in constant circular motion by divine will. Anselm, archbishop of Canterbury, in the eleventh century introduced the empyrean, the outermost sphere of purest fire where God dwelt. But in the High Middle Ages (thirteenth century), the notion of a finite God, limited in power by Aristotelian logic, was attacked by Etienne Tempier, the bishop of Paris, and his condemnations of 1277 stand as a landmark in the history of cosmology. In the wake of the condemnations, the outer boundary of the medieval universe melted away. Thomas Bradwardine of Oxford, who became archbishop of Canterbury, echoed the ancient philosophy that God is without center or circumference; he extended the empyrean throughout an infinite extramundane void to accommodate an unlimited God. Cardinal Nicholas of Cusa in the fifteenth century used the theological analogy to describe the universe and said, "the universe has its center everywhere and its circumference nowhere." The modern cosmological principle stating that all places are alike in the universe has its roots in theology.

A renascent Stoic universe of a cosmos immersed in infinite mysterious space lasted until the seventeenth century. Following the Copernican revolution in the sixteenth century, Thomas Digges of London dispersed the stars throughout an infinite space (the "court of coelestiall angelles"), and the message of an endless universe of countless inhabited planets was broadcast by the ill-fated Giordano Bruno.

The star-populated heavens became infinite, but biblical scripture still determined the age of the world. From Mosaic chronology (*mosaic* pertains to the biblical Moses), Dante Alighieri, author of *The Divine Comedy*, estimated that Adam and Eve were created in 5198 B.C.; Johannes Kepler, an astronomer, estimated that the world was created in 3877 B.C.; and James Ussher, an Irish bishop, estimated that creation occurred in 4004 B.C.

The Newtonian World System

In the seventeenth century, the Cartesian and then the Newtonian systems of the world outrivaled in scope the cosmologies of antiquity. A mathematized universe, mechanized with Newtonian dynamics and universal gravity, emerged in the eighteenth century. Thomas Wright in 1750 proposed a universe of endless galaxies, and astronomers, notably William Herschel, explored the starry heavens with telescopes of increasing power. Much of cosmology in the eighteenth and nineteenth centuries consisted of religious beliefs in conflict with mounting scientific evidence concerning the age of the earth, sun, and inferentially, the universe. Astronomers often referred to the large distances of the stars and nebulae, and although the finite speed of light had been known since the late seventeenth century, they usually failed to draw attention to the embarrassing conclusion that most starlight had traveled for spans of time vastly greater than that sanctioned by biblical chronology.

Olbers's Paradox

Why is the sky dark at night? In an infinite universe, every line of sight eventually intercepts the surface of a star, and if all stars are similar to the sun, then every part of the sky should blaze as bright as the sun's surface. This startling conflict in cosmology between theory and observation is known as Olbers's paradox. The paradox originated in the sixteenth century and many astronomers, including the astronomer Wilhelm Olbers of Bremen in 1823, have attempted to solve it. The solution, as shown by Lord Kelvin in 1903, depends on realizing that when we look out in space we look back in time. We look back either to the firstborn stars or to the beginning of the universe. Kelvin showed that all visible stars out to the most distant (the firstborn) are insufficient in number to cover the sky. His argument applies also to the modern expanding universe with only slight modification.

Curved and Dynamic Space

According to special relativity theory, the speed of light is the same for all observers, independent of their motion, and four-dimensional space-time decomposes into the different spaces and times of observers in relative motion.

In 1916, Albert Einstein advanced a new theory of gravity; he developed the special theory of relativity into a general theory of curved and dynamic space-time. As Willem de Sitter, a famous Dutch astronomer, said in 1931, this "theory brought the insight that space and time are not merely the stage on which the piece is produced, but are themselves actors playing an essential part in the plot."

Using general relativity theory, Einstein proposed in 1917 the idea of a static universe, of infinite age, that was spatially finite and curved like the surface of a sphere. He separated space-time into a uniformly curved space obeying the cosmological principle and a common (or cosmic) time. Einstein achieved a static universe by invoking a repulsion force, referred to as the cosmological term, that balanced the attraction of large-scale gravity. In the same year, 1917, de Sitter proposed a universe containing no matter, but it was not realized until later that the repulsion of the cosmological term was causing the de Sitter universe to expand.

The Expanding Universe

Edwin Hubble assembled the evidence for an expanding universe in 1929. The theory of an expanding universe, pioneered by Alexander Friedmann in 1922 and Georges Lemaître in 1927, was little known at the time. Various models of an expanding universe were proposed in the 1930s; most models were uniform in space, either infinite or finite in extent, in which all places evolved in synchronism and cosmic time measured the age of the universe. This general pattern forms the basis of modern cosmology.

The expanding space paradigm (receding galaxies are at rest in expanding space) helps us to understand several aspects of modern cosmology. The light received from distant galaxies is red shifted (shifted toward the red end of the spectrum), and the farther away a galaxy, the greater its red shift and its velocity of recession. Light traveling in expanding space between the galaxies has its waves steadily stretched by the expansion of space. At the Hubble distance, the galaxies are receding from us at the velocity of light. The Hubble distance is estimated to be between 10 and 20 billion light-years (a light-year equals the distance light travels in one year, and nearby stars are roughly five light-years away). The expansion of space causes the galaxies beyond the Hubble distance to recede faster than the velocity of light. The expansion of space is governed by general relativity, and the velocity of expansion is not limited by the velocity of light.

The Hubble time of 10 to 20 billion years serves as an approximate measure of the age of the universe. A more precise determination of the age depends on the way in which the expansion occurs. When Hubble first measured the rate of expansion, he obtained a Hubble time that was little more than 1 billion years, considerably less than the age of the earth. Cosmologists in the 1930s and 1940s grappled with the perplexing cosmic age problem. Obviously, nothing in the universe can be older than the universe itself. Why then did the universe appear to be younger than the earth? Various solutions were proposed. Historically, the most interesting was the popular steady-state universe proposed by astronomers Hermann Bondi, Thomas Gold, and Fred Hoyle. In their expanding steady-state universe of infinite age, without beginning or end, matter was continuously created by an unknown mechanism at a rate that compensated for expansion. The created matter formed into new galaxies that occupied the widening gulfs between old galaxies, thus maintaining the same unchanging cosmic scenery.

The revision upward of extragalactic distances in the late 1950s greatly increased the Hubble time, and estimates of the age of the universe matched the age of the oldest stars. Moreover, the case for the steady-state universe collapsed with the discovery of the cosmic background radiation that had been predicted in the late 1940s by George Gamow, a pioneer in big bang cosmology.

THE EARLY UNIVERSE

The discovery of the cosmic background radiation in 1965 by Arno Penzias and Robert Wilson revolutionized cosmology. This thermal radiation, uniformly distributed throughout the universe, has a temperature of 3 degrees Kelvin. It has been cooled by expansion and survives from the time when the universe was 100,000 years old. It provides convincing evidence that the universe in its early stages was extremely hot, as well as dense.

In the beginning, possibly at the Planck epoch of 10^{-43} seconds, the universe may have consisted of a quantum chaos of space-time. Later, at 10^{-35} seconds, the universe may have entered a period of extremely rapid expansion, or inflation, that greatly distended the universe and accounts for various previously unexplained properties of the universe. This inflation, proposed by Alan Guth in 1981, is caused by a state of negative cosmic pressure (or tension) predicted by grand unified theories in particle physics. After the end of inflation, from 10^{-37} to 10^{-6} seconds, a dense sea of structureless hyperweak particles decayed into quarks and electroweak particles, and the electroweak particles then decayed into the weakly interacting leptons and electromagnetically interacting photons. When the temperature dropped to 10^{15} (million billion) degrees Kelvin, at 10^{-6} seconds (one microsecond), the quarks transformed into strongly interacting hadrons. At 10^{-4} seconds, the hadrons and their antiparticles annihilated, leaving relatively few nucleons (protons and neutrons) that survived and constitute the present-day visible universe of stars. The universe then entered a brief lepton-dominated era that terminated with the annihilation of most electrons and positrons.

At cosmic age of one second, the radiation-dominated era began in which nuclear reactions during the first 200 seconds converted a quarter of all nucleons into helium nuclei. Most heavy elements, such as carbon, nitrogen, oxygen, and iron, are synthesized in old and dying stars (as shown by Geoffrey and Margaret Burbidge, William Fowler, and Fred Hoyle), and were not made in the dense and hot early universe, as Gamow hoped. The radiation era ended at age 100,000 years, marking the end of the early universe. In the succeeding dark ages, which are not yet accessible to exploration by astronomers, the galaxies started to form.

The younger the universe, the greater the rapidity of events, and cosmic history seems best told in logarithmic time. The early universe, extending from 10^{-43} to 10^{12} seconds (55 orders), covers ten times more cosmic history than the matter-dominated universe, extending from 10^{12} to $10^{17.5}$ seconds (5.5 orders). Thus, most of cosmic history occurred long before the universe was one second old.

TO THE END OF TIME

The fate of the universe has been a subject of interest throughout history. Within the frame of the modern physical universe we can tentatively explore the far future. The universe will undoubtedly continue to expand and the great clusters of galaxies will continue to move farther and farther apart. In tens of billions of years the galaxies will slowly darken as their stars fade into white dwarfs and other stellar remnants such as neutron stars and black holes.

Perhaps the universe will expand forever and in 10^{24} (a billion billion) years consist mostly of matter engulfed in black holes. According to a theory in particle physics, protons decay on a time scale of 10^{30} or so years, and hence the matter that has survived engulfment in black holes will eventually melt away into radiation. Ultimately, the black holes, ranging from stellar to galactic mass, will disappear, slowly radiating away their mass by Hawking radiation on a time scale of 10^{100} years.

But the fate of the universe is uncertain. According to some cosmological models, expansion will cease at a cosmic age of roughly 50 billion years, and the universe will commence to collapse. As the density and temperature rise, astronomical systems will progressively dissolve: first the great clusters of galaxies, then the galaxies, and finally the stars, and in the eschatological climax, the universe will revert to primordial quantum chaos.

CREATION OF THE UNIVERSE

Modern cosmology has changed the nature of old theological and philosophical concepts. Cosmogenesis, or the creation of the universe, is a prime example. The universe cannot originate at a point in space (for it contains space) and not at a moment in time called the beginning or the big bang (for it contains time). The universe originated in a tenseless sense as a space-time unity. In cosmology, we must distinguish between two kinds of creation. The first kind is cosmogenical, and consists of the creation of a whole universe containing space and time. The second kind is magical, and consists of the creation out of nothing of parts of the universe in preexisting space and time. The oft-quoted statement that cosmology offers a choice between creation all at once, as in the big bang, or little by little, as in the steady-state universe, is wrong because *creation* is used differently in the two cases. If a universe of finite age is cosmogenically created, then so also is a universe of infinite age. Those who seek to evade creation by preferring a universe of infinite age confuse cosmogenical creation with magical creation.

A postulated creator of the universe presumably exists outside space-time and is therefore spaceless and timeless. When we do not like what exists, or seek to influence events beyond our control (such as praying for victory in battle), nothing can be accomplished by supplicating the creator to recreate what is already created. What has been created once cannot be created twice.

If we cannot accept the principle that events displayed in space-time are inalterable, and we dislike the Stoic philosophy that all is predetermined and fate rules the world, we have no alternative but to try and reconstruct our understanding of the nature of time in the physical world. Although there seems little prospect of such a fundamental change in our ideas occurring in the near future, we must not forget how enormous has been the revolution in our understanding of the physical universe in the twentieth century, and we must realize that in cosmology itself the future is always uncertain.

[E.R.H.]

See also **Age of the Oldest Stars and the Milky Way; Big Bang Theory; Cosmology (Philosophy); Expansion of the Universe; Gravity, Time, and Space; Relativity Theory; Space-Time; Star and Galaxy Formation; X-Ray Universe.**

FURTHER READINGS

Bertotti, B., et al., eds. *Modern Cosmology in Retrospect.* Cambridge: Cambridge UP, 1990.

Grant, E. *Much Ado About Nothing: Theories of Space and Vacuum from the Middle Ages.* New York: Cambridge UP, 1981.

Haber, F.C. *The Age of the World: Moses to Darwin.* Baltimore: Johns Hopkins P, 1959.

Harrison, E.R. *Cosmology: The Science of the Universe.* New York: Cambridge UP, 1981.

———. *Masks of the Universe.* New York: Macmillan, 1985.

———. *Darkness at Night: A Riddle of the Universe.* Cambridge: Harvard UP, 1987.

Hubble, E.A. *The Realm of the Nebulae.* New Haven: Yale UP, 1936.

Islam, J.N. *The Ultimate Fate of the Universe.* Cambridge: Cambridge UP, 1983.

North, J.D. *The Measure of the Universe: A History of Recent Cosmology.* Oxford: Clarendon P, 1965.

Silk, J. *The Big Bang.* New York: W.H. Freeman, 1989.

Weinberg, S. *The First Three Minutes.* New York: Basic Books, 1977.

COSMOLOGY (PHILOSOPHY)

Cosmology is the study of the structure and evolution of the universe as a whole. Physical cosmology is that branch of natural science which aims at constructing theoretical models of the universe; these models are based on mathematical equations and imply certain observationally testable consequences. Physical cosmology leaves room for philosophical cosmology since the theoretical models of the universe are open to various interpretations, the soundness of which depends on philosophical principles and arguments. Philosophical cosmology may also offer independent theses of its own, derived from uniquely philosophical methods of reasoning (for example, arguments from a priori truths about time).

A key idea in any cosmological theory is the notion of time. One goal of physical cosmology is to determine if the universe admits of "cosmic time," a universe-wide time. The related aim of philosophical cosmology is to interpret the significance of the cosmic time postulated by physicists and to ask whether there are philosophical grounds to distinguish this cosmic time from a metaphysical time knowable by philosophical reasoning.

A cosmic time is admitted by the main physical cosmological theory advanced today, the big bang theory. According to big bang cosmology, the universe (space as well as its material contents) is now expanding. Several billion years ago (many say about 15 billion years ago) the universe was compressed into a very small volume, smaller than the size of an atom, from which it exploded in a big bang. The big bang theory supposes that the universe on a large scale is *homogeneous* (matter is evenly distributed) and *isotropic* (from each point in the universe, it looks the same in every direction). Since the universe is expanding, this means that on a large scale the expansion of the universe is uniform rather than irregular. This uniformity enables a *privileged reference frame* to be determined from which cosmic time measurements can be constructed. The privileged reference frame is the frame from which the universe appears to be homogeneous and isotropic. The reason the frame is privileged is that the laws of nature formulated from the perspective of this frame take a simpler form than they would if they were formulated from any other reference frame. The estimate some make about the age of the universe, that it began about 15 billion years ago with the big bang, is made from this privileged frame.

The question that may be raised in philosophical cosmology is whether or not this cosmic time constitutes an "absolute time" in the sense that Einstein rejected in his special theory of relativity. "Absolute time" and "relative time" may be defined in terms of the relation of simultaneity. If time is absolute, then this relation is two-termed, and is expressed by sentences of the form "x is simultaneous with y." If time is relative, then the simultaneity relation is three-termed and is expressed by "x is simultaneous with y relative to z," where z is the reference frame relative to which x and y are simultaneous. This suggests that the cosmic time posited by big bang cosmology is not absolute time, since the time measurements are made relative to the privileged reference frame. For example, the assertion that the age of the universe is about 15 billion years old is elliptical for the statement "relative to the privileged reference frame, the universe is 15 billion years old."

A second philosophical question is whether time must begin if physical cosmology posits a beginning of the universe. Standard big bang cosmology regards the universe as beginning to exist about 15 billion years ago with the big bang (although recent theories, such as some quantum cosmological theories, argue the universe is without beginning). If the universe did begin, then cosmic time must begin, since cosmic time is defined in terms of a physical frame of reference from which the universe appears homogeneous and isotropic. There is no such reference frame prior to the existence of the universe and thus no cosmic time.

This raises the deeper philosophical question if cosmic time should properly be identified with *real time* or whether the so-called "cosmic time" is merely an observable succession of changes that take place in physical objects (changes that are not to be identified with real time, but rather changes that take place in real time). There may be philosophical arguments for the existence of a metaphysical time (which would be real time), a time not defined in terms of physical changes or reference frames. Metaphysical time may be defined as both *absolute* (relations of simultaneity are two-termed) and *substantival* (times are moments that exist independently of the physical or mental events that may occupy them). The simplest way to argue for metaphysical time is to claim it is a self-evident a priori truth (which is to say a truth known by intuition or reasoning, not sensory observation) that there is metaphysical time. If there is such a metaphysical time, then there is no reason to think that it began with the big bang. If the universe began with the big bang, there may have been an infinite lapse of empty time before the big bang (or there may be other universes besides our own that occupied this metaphysical time).

Many thinkers, including philosophers, will not be fully satisfied with the claim that it is self-evident a priori truth that there is metaphysical time. On behalf of the claim that there is such an a priori truth, it may be said that people generally assume time to be absolute and not definable in terms of events and reference frames. Defenders of cosmic time as the only real time often say that these beliefs about metaphysical time are due to "scientifically untutored common sense," and that these beliefs should be abandoned or revised in light of current scientific thinking. But the defender of metaphysical time may argue that these beliefs express a genuine philosophical insight into an a priori truth about time.

[Q.S.]

See also **Cosmology; Relativity Theory; Space-Time; X-Ray Universe.**

Further Readings

Craig, William Lane. "God and Real Time." *Religious Studies* 26 (1990): 335–347.

Grünbaum, Adolf. *Philosophical Problems of Space and Time.* 2nd ed. Dordrecht: Reidel, 1973.

Munitz, Milton. *Cosmic Understanding.* Princeton: Princeton UP, 1986.

Sklar, Lawrence. *Space, Time and Space-Time.* Berkeley: U of California P, 1974.

Smith, Quentin. *Language and Time.* New York: Oxford UP, 1993.

CREATIONISM AND EVOLUTION

Creationism is the belief that the world and all of its living inhabitants were created by a supernatural power, or supreme being. It is "fundamentalistic," requiring a literal interpretation of the biblical account of Genesis. The publication of *Origin of Species* in 1859 rocked fundamentalistic assumptions, but the intellectual appeal of evolutionary theory as an explanation of the diversity of life led, in most cases, to a compromise: the Genesis story was taken metaphorically, and, while life itself might be regarded as a special creation (a unique rather than a continuous event), it could thereafter have evolved according to natural laws predetermined by the Creator. While the controversy subsided relatively quickly among orthodox Protestant

groups, the Roman Catholic Church had some difficulty in coming to terms with evolutionism. The English Catholic evolutionist St. George Jackson Mivart was excommunicated in 1900 for refusing to sign an affidavit submitting to the scientific authority of the church. Moreover, publication of *Le Phénomène humain*, which the Jesuit evolutionist, Pierre Teilhard de Chardin, had completed in 1938, was barred by his order and it did not appear until 1955, after his death.

Among the early fundamentalists was Philip Henry Gosse, co-founder of the Plymouth Brethren, and an eminent marine biologist of the mid-nineteenth century. His struggle with evolutionism led to the still-popular creationistic rationale that the world had been created with an appearance of an earlier history, much as Adam must have been created with a navel, and the fossil record was a test of our faith in the Bible. In the United States, creationism took a political and educational turn, with a presidential election and schools and textbooks becoming the arena for antievolutionism. In the 1920s, laws barring the teaching of evolutionary theory were passed in Tennessee, Arkansas, Texas, and Mississippi. In Tennessee, the legislation was challenged in the Scopes "monkey trial," but was not finally repealed until 1967. A more recent phase of "scientific creationism" tries to use scientific data and inferences to counter evolutionism and support creationism. Though it ignores the fact that there can be no logical, naturalistic, scientific proof for the existence of a supernatural being, the debate is illuminating. The major arguments of the scientific creationists include the following, presented here with some of the pros and cons:

- *Evolution has never been observed*: this is true, in a limited sense: thoroughly documented examples of natural speciation have not been observed, although there are some debatable cases. The genetic mechanisms of speciation are, however, understood, and it is possible to engineer genetically new types that meet the definitive requirements of new species. Darwin argued that the span of human consciousness of evolution has been too short, and speciation is too slow to have been witnessed; but in the huge stretch of available geological time, all the manifestations of evolution have been possible.

- *Not enough time has been available for evolution to have occurred*: creationists have often accepted the calculation from biblical history that the special creation occurred in 4004

B.C., and some scientific creationists continue to accept that God literally created the world in six, twenty-four-hour days, and that the only significant geological event subsequent to that was the biblical Flood. The Flood drowned the now-extinct fossil forms, depositing them in the sediments in the order of their demise. If this were the case, and there is no scientific argument to support the contention, there would certainly not have been enough time to produce the diversity of living forms by natural evolution. However, the scientific estimation of the time available for evolution is about 3.5 billion years, and there have been numerous large-scale geological catastrophes that had a major influence on the distribution of plants and animals, thereby explaining some of the discontinuity of the fossil record. The scientific creationists counter that the geological dating methods must be wrong.

- *Evolution is in conflict with the second law of thermodynamics*: a corollary of this law is that entropy, or chaos, tends to increase with time in a closed system. Therefore, the scientific creationists argue that the evolutionary complexification of living forms in the biosphere is physically impossible. By default, only special creation could provide the complex diversity of life. However, order can increase in an open system, such as the biosphere, since it receives the necessary energy in the form of sunlight from outside the system. In like manner, the complexity of an adult human develops from a single cell because energy in the form of food is available from outside the system. And we are all witness to this.

The numerous remaining arguments can be grouped as criticisms of the theory of natural selection: natural selection does not explain evolutionary progress; mutation rates are too slow for evolution to occur; and there appears to have been an early explosive period of diversification that would better fit the special creation model. Also, since evolutionists disagree among themselves about the causes of evolution, they must all be wrong, and by default, creationism must be true.

Paradoxically, a growing number of evolutionists would agree that these criticisms of selection theory are much to the point. There have always been biologists who thought that the major events of evolution were saltatory. And many have concluded that simple point mutations of structural genes, acted upon by natural selection, are per se inadequate to account for evolutionary progress. However, the logical and scientific basis of the theory of the process of evolution is independent of the nature of the mechanism of evolution. The demolition of selection theory would not bring down evolutionism. Therefore, there is no logical weight, nor was there ever any scientific substance, to the argument that the only alternative, if natural selection is not the cause of the diversity of life, is special creation.

[R.G.B.R.]

See also **Catastrophism; Evolution of Evolutionism; Evolutionary Progress; Fossil Record; Saltatory Evolution; Thermodynamics; Time Available for Evolution.**

FURTHER READINGS

Futuyama, D.J. *Science on Trial*. New York: Pantheon, 1982.

Gish, Duane T. *Evolution: The Fossils Say No*. San Diego: Creation-Life Publishers, 1972.

Nelkin, D. *The Creation Controversy: Science or Scripture in the Schools*. New York: Norton, 1982.

CREATION MYTHS

The word "myth" is used here not in the vulgar sense of fantasy, fiction, or untruth, but as it has been widely accepted by historians of religion, which is to say a traditional, pre-scientific narrative about origins, often believed to have been revealed by an ancestor or a deity, and transmitted through many generations by word of mouth. Traditional societies distinguish "true myths," such as creation myths, from "false myths," such as stories explaining the etymology of a certain word or the peculiarities of certain animals. To refer to the Genesis account of Creation as "myth" does not imply disrespect for the biblical tradition, but it qualifies this narrative so that it is not mistakenly set in competition with modern scientific cosmologies. The transition between mythical and philosophical cosmologies is fluid. Myths are important in practical life and are closely connected to theoretical, speculative thought. Thus, the social stratifications of India are justified by a reference to a creation myth, the establishment of the Mosaic law took place on the basis of the biblical creation myth, and out of Greek creation myths there developed Greek philosophies. Modern science, too, received many an inspiration from ancient creation myths.

In creation myths, people expressed their deepest convictions about the nature of the world around them, about the structure of their societies, and about their personal destinies. Beginnings are important to traditional societies, not only because they signal the coming into existence of the world and everything in it, but also because they reveal the real and the ideal structures of human existence in the world. Frequently, creation myths were recited or dramatically performed during new year celebrations, which served to remind the people of their beginnings and their ideal laws. These were often the occasion for renewing the mandate of the ruler as a vice-regent of the deity.

Creation myths often quite matter-of-factly describe the formation of the world and its inhabitants following the thought, desire, and urge of a preexisting divine being. In myths, the consciousness of time emerges together with the awareness of death: the end of life, the transience of created existence brings an asymmetry into the relationship between the creator and his creation. The Bible is fairly alone in suggesting that mortality was the direct result of a transgression of a divine command by the first pair of humans. But many traditions question the inevitability of death and dying and devise methods and practices to attain immortality.

In the classical Western mythical traditions, the "sublunar sphere" was supposed to be the sphere of transience and mortality; the celestial bodies above the moon were believed to consist of incorruptible matter, serving as the abodes of the blessed.

Indian traditions have many different creation myths, not all of which can be harmonized. Like many others, they speak of a demiurge-figure, who (as the supreme's instrument) creates the world. In Manu's account, the creation of "time and the divisions of time, the lunar mansions and the planets" is mentioned immediately after the creation of the sacrifice, which in Manu's philosophy was the source of every good.

The Australian aboriginal people differentiate "dreamtime" from "our time." All the great things happened in "dreamtime," when people had unimaginable creative powers and when the rituals were founded. Our own time can do no better but to remember dream-time and to execute the arrangements laid down by the ancestors.

The search for beginnings is as old as human civilization. Contemporary science has narrowed down the story of the beginning of the universe to "the first three minutes" after the "big bang," which—according to S. Weinberg—is the mythical beginning of *our* time. Recent information obtained through the space probe *Explorer* may lead us back even further, as scientists connected with the experiment believe, to within a few fractions of a second after the big bang, instead of the currently accepted "first three minutes." We are as intrigued as our forebears by the question of "when did time begin?" Obviously, "the first three minutes" were not three minutes in our time. More decisive events took place—cosmically speaking—in these first three minutes than in billions of years afterwards, events which created the conditions for later developments.

Traditionally, *archai* (beginnings) were seen not so much as temporal "firsts" but as exemplary: the "first" was seen as the "best" (as expressed in the Sanskrit *prathama*, the Greek *aristos*, and the Latin *primus*). Going back to the beginnings was an important act in the maintenance and purification of a tradition. And thus one can conclude that cultures with living creation myths are basically world-affirming and possess a positive attitude toward life. They accept the complexity of the present as a meaningful unfolding of their cherished beginnings.

[K.K.K.]

FURTHER READINGS

Abrahamsson, Hans. *The Origin of Death: Studies in African Mythology*. Uppsala: Uppsala UP, 1951.

Brandon, S.G.F. *Creation Legends of the Ancient Near East*. London: Hodder & Stoughton, 1963.

Doria, Charles, and Harris Lenowitz. *Origins*. New York: Anchor P, 1975.

Eliade, Mircea. "Myths of Creation and of Origin." *From Primitives to Zen*. London: Collins, 1967. Chapter 2.

Long, Charles H. *Alpha: The Myths of Creation*. New York: Braziller, 1963.

Maclaglan, David. *Creation Myths*. London: Thames and Hudson, 1977.

Pettazzoni, Raffael. "The Truth of Myth," and "Myths of Beginnings and Creation-Myths." *Essays on the History of Religions*. Leiden: Brill, 1954. Chapters 2 and 3.

Zimmer, Heinrich. *Myths and Symbols in Indian Art and Civilization*. Princeton: Princeton UP, 1972.

CULTURAL DIFFERENCES

As Oswald Spengler maintained in *The Decline of the West*, Volume 1, "It is by the meaning that it intuitively attaches to time that one culture is differentiated from another." Cultures may differ on many aspects of social time—its value, and meaning, as well as how it should be divided, allocated, and measured. The dimensions that are particularly culture-bound include punctuality, temporal perspective, the general pace of life, and the importance of clock time versus event time.

CLOCK TIME VERSUS EVENT TIME

Robert Lauer (1981) argued that the most fundamental difference in the meaning of time is between groups for whom time is measured by social events versus those for whom the clock predominates. In "event time," activities begin and end by mutual consensus—when "the time seems right." Under "clock time," the time on the clock dictates beginnings and endings.

Clock time most often predominates in cultures where "time is money." For example, in the United States—where workers are paid by the hour, lawyers charge by the minute, and advertising is sold by the second—one's time becomes a precious commodity. It is carefully measured, allocated, saved, and spent. Clock time tends to predominate in economically developed cultures.

In event-time societies, modes of time-reckoning tend to express social experience. Sometimes activities occur in finely coordinated sequences, but without observing the clock. For example, anthropologists have described how participants at an Indian wake move from gathering time to prayer time, singing time, intermission, and meal time. They move by consensual feeling—when "the time feels right"—but with no apparent concern for the time on the clock.

Even the language of time may be more or less event-oriented. The Kachin people of North Burma, for example, have no single word equivalent of "time." They use the word *ahkying* to refer to the "time" of the clock, *na* to a long "time," *tawng* to a short "time," *ta* to springtime, and *asak* to the "time" of a person's life. Whereas clock-time cultures treat time as an objective entity—it is a noun in English—the Kachin words for time are treated more like adverbs.

CALENDARS

Many cultures use social activities to define their calendars rather than the other way around. The calendars of the Nuer people from the Upper Nile in the Sudan, for example, are based on the seasonal changes in their environment. They know that the month of *kur* is occurring *because*

they are building their fishing dams and cattle camps. When they break camp and return to their villages, they know it must now be the months of *dwat*.

Most societies have some type of week, but it is not always a week of seven days. The Muysca of Columbia had a three-day week. The Incas of Peru had a ten-day week. Often the length of the week reflects cycles of activities, rather than the other way around. For many, the market is the main activity requiring group coordination. The Khasi people hold their markets every eighth day. Consequently, they have made their week eight days long and named the days of the week after the places where the main markets occur.

PUNCTUALITY

Beginning and ending events according to the time on the clock is a recent phenomenon. Although humankind has been measuring the seasons and weeks for several thousand years, it is only in the last few centuries that timepieces have allowed us to live by the precise hour, let alone the minute and second. Not until the late eighteenth century did the word "punctuality" appear in the English language as it is used today.

Cultural differences in punctuality are often great. When Mexican-Americans make appointments, they often specify whether it is on *"hora ingles"* or *"hora Mexicano."* American Indians and those familiar with them speak of "Indian time." In Trinidad there is a saying that "any time is Trinidad time." Other cultures speak of "rubber time." Each of these express not only an acceptance of lateness, but a more flexible view of the time on the clock for any aspect of scheduling. For example, R. Levine (1990) found that in Brazil, compared to the United States, people needed to arrive earlier for appointments before they were considered early and had to stay later before they were defined as staying late.

Even in event-time cultures, clock time generally plays some role in the scheduling of social activities. Some cultures, however, are not only indifferent to the clock, but downright hostile to it. Anthropologists have described a society of peasants in Algeria, for example, who have no concept of exact times of appointment, have no exact times for eating, despise haste in their social affairs, and label the clock as "the devil's mill."

THE PACE OF LIFE

Punctuality and attention to clock time are reflected in the overall pace of life. The highly industrialized North American, northern European, and Asian countries are often described as prototypically "fast" cultures. A slower pace of life, where promptness and the need to make every minute count are seen as less important, tends to predominate in less developed and more traditional cultures.

Levine (1980) and his colleagues compared walking speed, work speed, and concern with clock time in six countries. They found that Japan had the fastest overall pace of life, followed by the United States, England, Italy, Taiwan, and Indonesia. Other studies have shown a negative relationship between the population size of cities and the speed of their pace of life.

The pace of life may also have characteristic rhythms, including differences in the relationship of "up" time to "down" time. Among the sporadically unemployed, young, black, street corner subculture of the United States, sociologists have observed that people are slow-paced most of the time, but speed up their tempos when they want to do so. Time for the "cool person" is "dead" at such times when money is tight or when he is in jail. But time is "alive" when there is "action."

TEMPORAL PERSPECTIVE AND ORIENTATION

Temporal orientation refers to the relative emphases assigned to the past, present, and future. Temporal perspective refers to images of the past, present, and future. Cultures may differ sharply on either or both dimensions.

Edward Hall (1983) described the temporal orientation and perspective in many American Indian groups. Some, such as the Hopis, have no verb tenses for past, present, and future. The Navajos have difficulty understanding the future in concrete terms. The only real time to them, like the only real space, is the here and now. The Sioux have no single words for "time," "late," or "waiting."

In some cultures, the past, present, and future are neither measured in discrete intervals nor clearly separated. The Trukese, who live on an atoll in the South Pacific, do not distinguish between immediate past and distant past. Time does not "heal all wounds" for the Trukese, so that events which occurred many years ago take on the same immediacy in the present as events which have just taken place.

Cultures also differ in their perceptions of the "size" of the past, present, and future. Although the United States and most northern European industrialized nations tend to be future-oriented, their notions of the future are more limited than those of some other cultures. For example, whereas people in the United States tend to experience difficulty thinking beyond a few years—or, at most, the coming generation—the Chinese may plan for change that might take centuries.

OTHER CULTURAL DIFFERENCES

Cultures differ on many other dimensions of time. For example, to what extent is time conceived as "linear" (progressive and unidirectional) versus "cyclical" (a series of repetitive, alternating events)? Are people "polychronic" (attend to many things at once) or "monochronic" (attend to one thing at a time)? How does a culture distinguish between "private time" and "public time," or "sacred time" and "profane time"? What value is given to behaviors such as patience and waiting, or doing "nothing"?

TIME AND CULTURE SHOCK

Cultural differences are not only large, but often have profound consequences. The "silent language" of time has no written dictionary to help the foreigner along. In an investigation into the roots of culture shock, returning Peace Corps volunteers were asked to rank-order thirty-three items as to how much difficulty they posed for cultural readjustment. The list included issues ranging from "the type of food eaten" to the "personal cleanliness of most people," "the number of people of your own race," and "the general standard of living." But, after "the language spoken," the stressors that posed the greatest adjustment difficulties to the volunteers both related to temporal matters: "the general pace of life" followed by "how punctual most people are."

[R.V.L.]

See also **Psychology of Time; Social Psychology; Time Perception; Time Perspective and Its Measurement.**

FURTHER READINGS

Aveni, A. *Empires of Time: Calendars, Clocks, and Cultures.* New York: Basic Books, 1989.

Hall, E.T. *The Dance of Life: The Other Dimension of Time.* Garden City: Anchor P, 1983.

Lauer, R. *Temporal Man: The Meaning and Uses of Social Time.* New York: Praeger, 1981.

Levine, R. "The Pace of Life." *American Scientist* (September-October, 1990): 450–459.

McGrath, J.E., ed. *The Social Psychology of Time: New Perspectives.* Newbury Park: Sage, 1988.

CURRIE, RUSSELL (1902–1967)

There is little doubt that during the past forty years, nobody has exerted more influence on the study of work systems than did Russell Currie, not only in the United Kingdom but also in Europe and indeed, throughout much of the world. The consensus is that the importance Currie gave to the striving for higher productivity had as its basis his unique concept of human dignity and his confidence in the philosophy and methods that he advocated, resting as they did on the careful, critical examination of time and method study.

Born in Glasgow on July 7, 1902, Currie was educated at Kelvinside Academy, Glasgow, and Fettes College, Edinburgh, followed by a five-year apprenticeship with McKie and Baxter, engineers and shipbuilders of Govan, and evening classes at the Royal Technical College, Glasgow. Currie's first engineering appointment was in India (1924) with the Lukwah Tea Company, Assam. Two years later he joined the British-owned Shanghai Waterworks Company as distribution engineer. In this company, which had the second largest pumping station of its kind in the world, he received steady promotion, moving up through the position of chief mechanical engineer to that of engineer-in-chief in the course of some fifteen years. In the meantime, Currie had achieved his first of a string of engineering qualifications with professional institutions: the Institution of Mechanical Engineers (1935), the Institution of Civil Engineers (1936), and the Institution of Electrical and Production Engineers (1938). He had also been commissioned in the British Territorial Army.

At the outbreak of World War II, Winston Churchill called a conference to organize war production in Canada, Australia, South Africa, India, and the Far East, and Currie was appointed British technical adviser. Still based in Shanghai when Japan attacked Pearl Harbor, he was arrested by the Japanese secret police. Even under arrest, he and his staff contrived to operate the city's water supply under direct instruction from His Majesty's government. Eventually, in 1942, Currie made history by being one of the few prisoners to be exchanged by the Japanese. Home again, he joined Associated Industrial Consultants (AIC) at the request of Admiral Wake-Walker, Third Sea Lord, and spent the rest of the war reorganizing the Scottish shipyards.

Immediately after the first atomic bomb was dropped on Hiroshima in August 1945, the Foreign Office asked Currie to return to Shanghai on diplomatic status. Currie flew into Shanghai—still technically enemy territory—with the Flying Tigers of the United States Air Force, and was the first civilian to land there. The job of securing the pumping stations and keeping the supply going was made more than difficult by the Communist-controlled labor unions. Some six times he was "locked up," though he never came to any physical harm. The water supply secured, he returned to Britain and rejoined AIC in April 1946.

On June 23, 1947, Russell Currie joined Imperial Chemical Industries (ICI) and with this began twenty years of dedication to work study. It is for Currie's pioneering work and contribution to work study that he is best known. At the time the concept of work study was, to say the least, restricted. ICI had 110,000 employees and thirty time study men. In setting up the Central Work Study Department, Currie expanded both the concept and the facilities with the foresight of a pioneer. Twenty years later, there were 2,000 full-time specialists in the work study departments of ICI in Great Britain. Apart from this phenomenal growth, his department had been directly responsible for some 2,500 training and appreciation courses in work study involving more than 40,000 ICI staff of all ranks.

These two vital decades saw the complete development of the science from "time and motion" on the shop floor to "work study"—a change as dramatic as that from alchemy to chemistry or astrology to astronomy. This change was brought about by Currie and the team he built up and inspired. He never claimed to have invented the simple phrase "work study," nor did he claim to have originated any single technique. He was always meticulous in paying tribute to his team. But, without doubt, it was his inspiration that put work study on the map, gave it a worldwide reputation, and raised the subject to a full professional and scientific level.

When several work study organizations merged to become the Work Study Society, Currie was appointed its first president, and it was under his leadership that the society grew into a profession. His recognition as the father figure of work study was by no means restricted to Great Britain. Many countries sought his advice, especially those in the initial stages of establishing and developing work study techniques, many of which had been evolved under his control. He was especially proud of the support Jawaharlal Nehru, prime minister of India, gave to his efforts in establishing the use of work study in that country. When, in 1961, the European Work Study Federation was formed, it was natural that he should be invited to be president of that, too, and two years later he was unanimously reelected for another two-year term of office.

Currie's pioneering efforts in the development of work study techniques in the pre-production field—in research, development, design, and planning; his published works, including the standard British textbook *Work Study*, together with *Financial Incentives Based on Work Measurement*, *Simplified PMTS* (predetermined motion time systems), *The Measurement of Work*, and many other publications; and his work for British industry, the armed services, and the nationalized industries are contributions to productivity which will long be remembered. In 1957, this was recognized in his investiture by Her Majesty as a Commander of the Most Excellent Order of the British Empire (CBE).

Essentially, Russell Currie was a "catalyst" and a super salesman for method study and work measurement techniques. On the one hand, he could recognize and get to the heart of a need for new techniques from his "customer contact" with line managers; on the other hand, he could see the basic value of new techniques developed by his staff and others—or he could provoke them into an effective response to the challenge or need. In all of this could be seen Currie's ability to turn ideas into clearly understood, practical procedures with a new clarity, depth of understanding, and concern for human values and human dignity.

[D.C.]

See also **Industrial Engineering After Taylor; Measurement of Work and Applications; Predetermined Motion Time Systems; Scheduling Through Operational Research; Time Management.**

DANTE ALIGHIERI (1265–1321)

Dante Alighieri, known to history quite simply by his given name, Dante, was the native son of an expanding urban center, Florence, at the time when it had begun to assert its long-lasting cultural hegemony in Europe of the late Middle Ages. Accordingly, in his greatest poem, *The Divine Comedy*, Dante would represent and continue to address the great issues of time and culture that we associate with the renewal of urban life in the cities of western Europe. Dante's poem itself bespeaks his own awareness of a new energy and variety in life, at the same time that it shows the destructive powers of time. Joining the two, Dante can issue his powerful lament (at the beginning of *Paradiso* XVI) for "Our poor nobility of blood" ("O poca nostra nobiltà de sangue"). But this lament, far from being passive, issues in a stirring call to active endeavor:

> Ben se' tu manto che tosto raccorce;
> sì che, so non s'appon di dì in die,
> lo tempo va d'intorno con le force.

("Truly thou art a mantle that quickly shrinks, so that if we do not add to it day by day time goes round it with the shears.")

Already in Dante, time has acquired implements of destruction against which humankind must take strong measures of response. We get some sense of the complexity of Dante's attitudes toward time when we see that in the major work of this poet, who has been called "the chief imagination of Christendom," we find the prototype of future exhortations to make energetic response to the destructive powers of time.

This complexity is seen when we realize that he recoiled against simple exhortations to exploit time that themselves seemed devoid of any higher directions and principles. Thus, he can have his Ulysses, that prototypal Western man, urge his followers to spend the "picciola vigilia d'i nostri sensi ch'è del rimanente" ("brief vigil of our senses that is so left to us") in the pursuit of adventure and exploration. This stirring humanistic creed, however, leads nowhere, and Ulysses is a personage whose life and message help to constitute the mind of hell.

If the *Inferno* is monochromatic, peopled by souls who are driven, obsessed, and single-minded, Dante's *Purgatorio* is the realm of time, where change is possible and where hope revives. But the *Purgatorio* is also penitential, and consequently no place for wasting time. In canto III, Virgil asks for proper directions, "chè perder tempo a chi più sa più spiace" ("for loss of time most grieves him that knows best"); and at the end of canto VI, he urges Dante onward with his sense of the passage of time. In the next canto, Virgil scolds Dante for lingering, and in canto VI, Dante absorbs the lesson, "Segnore, andiamo a maggior fretta" ("My Lord, let us make more haste"). In canto XII, Virgil spurs Dante on by reminding him that "today never dawns again," and in canto XVI, he again prods Dante as he would "the lazy who are slow to use their waking hours." In canto XXIII, Dante, who again appears to be dawdling, is urged by Virgil to go on, "che 'l tempo che n'è imposto / più ultimente compartir si vuole" ("for the time appointed us must be put to better use.")

The exhortations to make proper use of time in the *Purgatorio* are clearly part of penitential purposes and directions, and this might indicate that their origins are in the monastic disciplines and rules. Nevertheless, a new voice is also heard, one that is secular, heroic, and Roman. In Dante's addresses to time, the dominant voice is that of Virgil, and there is another impulse behind Virgil's exhortation, and that is toward an heroic fulfillment.

> "Omai convien che tu così ti spoltre,"
> disse 'l maestro, "ché, seqqendo in piuma,
> in fama non si vien, né sotto coltre.
> Sanza la qual chi sua vita consuma,
> cotal vestigio in terra di sé lascia,
> qual fummo in aere ed in acqua la schiuma."

("Now must thou thus cast off all sloth," said the master, "for sitting on down or under blankets none comes to fame, and without it he that consumes his life leaves such trace of himself on earth as smoke in air or foam on the water.") *Inferno* XXIV. 46–51.

In particular regard to the notion of fame, we see how complex are developments in Dante's poem. Fame is one of the grand human means for rising above the limitations of time. In the Renaissance, fame was to become one of the great motives of action. But as with Ulysses's own exhortations that are urgent yet misdirected, so fame itself can be unreliable and comes under intense spiritual scrutiny. Dante's revered teacher, Brunetto Latini, taught Dante how "man makes himself eternal," and his final words commit to Dante's guardianship the memory of his great work. Throughout the upper Inferno, numerous souls ask that their names be remembered. But in contrast to the deficiencies of their ethical lives, this seems to be too vicarious a method of recovery. Indeed, in the lower Inferno, there are few such requests, and indeed, the final request is for silence. Virgil wishes to persuade the arch-traitor Bocca degli Abati to reveal his identity for the purpose of fame. But Bocca's response reveals the true realities of hell. His only need is for oblivion, as he bitterly responds to Virgil's request, "ché mal sai lusingar per questa lama" ("You flatter badly in this level").

In the *Purgatorio*, fame is no longer an object of address, as penitent souls seek other means by which to transcend their individual lives. Intercession, prayers for the souls of the dead—such remembrance on the part of the living—are the requests that Dante now encounters. But such are Dante's faiths in the powers of the Creation and his own devotion to a revived and purged heroic humanism that great endeavors are not to be permanently denounced in his poem. For instance, in the prologue of the poem (*Inferno* II), when Beatrice comes to the Limbo of the virtuous pagans and persuades Virgil to come to Dante's rescue, her address is fulsome but indicative:

"O anima cortese mantoana di cui la fama ancor nel mondo dura e durerà quanto 'l mondo lontana. . . ."

("O courteous Mantuan soul, whose fame still endures in the world and shall endure as long as the world lasts. . . .")

Even in Paradise (c. IX), Cunizza, a well-known courtesan of the age prior to Dante's, refers to the Provençal poet and later bishop of Marseille, Folco, as one whose fame will endure:

"vedi se far si dee l'omo eccellente, sì ch'altra vita la prima relinqua."

("consider then if man should not make himself excel so that the first life may leave another after it.")

Throughout the most agonizing of spiritual itineraries, the goal of excellence is not abandoned. This is Dante's high motivation, and why he persists in writing his poem, despite the discomfort that it will cause some contemporaries and their families. In the great encounter with his knighted ancestor and crusader, Cacciaguida, from whom Dante credits many of his own attributes, Dante is encouraged to believe that the fame of his work will long outlast his foes.

Dante's poem is another in the many repeated attempts within Western culture to bring the intensely realized world of time and history into some integration and coordination with the unchanging, the mythic, and the eternal. This is why, while he sympathizes with and even shares the mobile energy of Ulysses, and his exhortations to make use of time that would typify energetic Western man, he can only regard these journeyings as footloose and purposeless. To such centrifugalism, he would offer the centripetalism of philosophy, of religion, of a Christocentric world. Rather than the Ulyssean movement outward, Dante favors a circling back. Consequently, one of his most celebrated images, one central for the purposes of time, is the figure of the clock, with which he closes canto X of the *Paradiso*. For Dante, the clock represents the full harmonization of the many energies of life in a common spiritual effort. The medieval philosophers who populate the twelve stations are so integrated and harmonized in their efforts that they are like the mechanical clock.

"Indi, come orologio che ne chiami nell'ora che la sposa di Dio surge a mattinar lo sposo perché l'ami,

che l'una parte l'altra tira e urge,
tin tin sonando con sì dolce nota,
che 'l ben disposto spirto d'amor turge;
così vid' io la gloriosa rota muoversi e
render voce a voce in tempra ed in
dolcezza ch'esser non pò nota
se non colà dove gioir s'insempra."

("Then, like a clock that calls us at the
hour when the bride of God rises to sing
matins to the bridegroom that he may
love her, when one part draws or drives
another, sounding the chime with notes
so sweet that the well-ordered spirit swells
with love, so I saw the glorious wheel
move and render voice to voice with
harmony and sweetness that cannot be
known but there where joy becomes
eternal.")

It should be noted that such is Dante's sense
of the diverse energies of human existence that
it is not the surface of the clock that draws his
attention, but rather the insides, the meshing of
all the parts. Dante is so supreme a witness to
Western understanding about Time because he
was so full a participant in his age, an age when
many crucial changes began to occur.

[R.J.Q.]

See also **Renaissance**.

FURTHER READINGS

Cullman, Oscar. *Christ and Time*. Trans. Floyd V.
Filson. Philadelphia: The Westminster P, 1964.

Ladner, Gerhart B. "Homo viator: Medieval Ideas on
Alienation and Order." *Speculum* 42 (1967): 233–
259.

Masciandaro, Franco. *La problematica del tempo nella
Commedia*. Ravenna: Longo, 1976.

Quinones, Ricardo J. "Dante." *The Renaissance Discovery of Time*. Cambridge: Harvard UP, 1972. 23–105.

DARK MATTER

Astonishing though it may seem, perhaps as
much as 90 percent of the matter in the universe
is completely unidentified. How, then, do we
know it is there? There are several indirect methods
for inferring the existence of this unseen, or
"dark", matter. The visible matter in the universe
is believed to be ordinary matter made up
of protons, neutrons, and electrons. Ordinary
matter becomes visible when stars and galaxies
are formed. Even the gas around galaxies is
"visible" when it is hot and emits X-rays detectable
on earth. By observing the numbers and
brightness of distant galaxies, the amount of
visible matter can be determined.

There is strong evidence, however, that not
all the matter in the universe is visible. Just as
the planets rotate about the sun, the stars and
gas in most galaxies rotate about the center of
the galaxy. By Newton's laws, the mass of a
galaxy within a certain distance from its center
can be determined by measuring how fast the
stars at that distance revolve around the center.
One expects the rotational velocity to drop as
the distance from the center of the galaxy increases.
(The velocity is measured by observing
to what degree the frequency or wavelength of
light emitted by the star is shifted to the blue
[higher frequencies for motion toward the observer]
or red [lower frequencies for motion
away from the observer].) Instead, what is generally
found is that the rotational velocity remains
constant no matter how far it is measured from
the center. The implication of these observations
is that the mass with a given distance from
the center of the galaxy increases as the distance
increases, while the amount of visible matter
stays the same. Thus we can infer the existence
of dark matter.

There are other, more subtle reasons for
invoking the dark matter hypothesis. Though
our understanding of the mechanisms of the
formation of galaxies is far from complete, we
believe that galaxies were formed from tiny
perturbations in an otherwise smooth gas of
matter. Because of gravity, these perturbations
grow and accumulate mass until stars begin to
form. According to Einstein's theory of relativity,
the smaller the perturbation, the more time
it takes to grow. The perturbations also leave a
detectable fingerprint: they distort the light that
makes up the cosmic microwave background
radiation first discovered in 1964 by A. Penzias
and R. Wilson, and recently investigated in
detail by NASA's Cosmic Background Explorer
satellite (COBE). COBE has found these distortions
to be very faint, requiring very small perturbations
and the need for a suitable amount of
time for them to grow. Because of its interaction
with light, perturbations of ordinary matter cannot
grow until relatively late in the history of the
universe. However, dark matter perturbations
can begin to grow earlier. Thus, the existence of
galaxies cannot be reconciled with the faint
signatures of perturbations detected by COBE
unless there is a large amount of dark matter.

Another important indication for the existence of dark matter is based on the early history of the universe, moments after the big bang. Today, the universe appears to be very nearly spatially flat, that is, it appears to be on the borderline between an eventual collapse, and eternal expansion. The typical time-scale to decide the fate of the universe should be the Planck time, which is determined by the physical constants G (Newton's constant), $\hbar$ (Planck's constant), and c (the speed of light) according to the formula:

$$t_P = \sqrt{\frac{\hbar G}{c^5}} = 5.4 x 10^{-44} s.$$

The age of the universe is about 15 billion years, or 10^{61} Planck times. Given the great age of the universe, it is very peculiar that the universe still rests on the borderline of collapse and eternal expansion. A solution to this quandary is called cosmological inflation (a great expansion of the universe just after the big bang). A prediction of inflation is that the universe is actually (to high precision) on the borderline of recollapse. This theory also predicts the amount of matter in the universe necessary to rest on the borderline (more matter and the universe collapses, less and it expands forever).

At a later time in the history of the universe (but still very early by today's standards), about one minute after the big bang, the light element isotopes ^{2}H, ^{3}He, ^{4}He, and ^{7}Li were formed. There is excellent agreement between the theory of their formation, big bang nucleosynthesis, and the observational determination of their abundances. However, this theory also makes a clear prediction: the amount of ordinary matter is necessarily less than the amount of matter necessary to produce a collapse. In fact, big bang nucleosynthesis predicts that no more than 10 percent of the matter in the universe is ordinary matter if the theory of inflation is correct. The remaining 90 percent of the matter in the universe is dark, and must be of some other form than ordinary matter.

What is this dark matter? While some of the dark matter in galaxies might be made of protons and neutrons—perhaps in the form of stars, too small to shine, or maybe locked up in the form of black holes—most of the dark matter cannot be in the form of protons or neutrons. Fortunately, particle physics leaves open several interesting possibilities. Two of the most frequently discussed explanations are neutrinos and the lightest supersymmetric particle, or LSP.

Neutrinos are known particles (there are three different types), but their masses are not measured (indeed, they may not have a mass). If each neutrino has a mass of 1.6×10^{-31} grams (25 billionths of the mass of a proton), there would be enough neutrinos to supply all of the missing mass in the universe. The supersymmetric generalization of the standard model in particle physics also offers dark matter candidates. Supersymmetry associates with all known particles a supersymmetric partner. The partner of the photon, the quantum of light, is called the photino. The lightest of these supersymmetric partners is expected to be stable and can easily supply the missing mass.

The amount of dark matter in the universe also plays a role in determining the age of the universe. Though the age of the universe is most sensitive to the expansion rate of the universe or Hubble parameter, the total amount of matter also plays a key, though technical, role in determining the present age. For example, for an expansion rate of fifty kilometers per megaparsec per second, the age of the universe changes from 13 billion years to 18 billion years as the amount of dark matter is decreased from the amount predicted by inflation to the minimal amount needed from the dynamics of galaxies.

[K.A.O.]

See also **Age of the Oldest Stars and the Milky Way; Big Bang Theory; Cosmology; Expansion of the Universe; Newton, Isaac; Relativity Theory; Solar System; Star and Galaxy Formation; X-Ray Universe.**

FURTHER READINGS

Riordan, Michael, and David N. Schramm. *The Shadows of Creation: Dark Matter and the Structure of the Universe.* New York: W.H. Freeman, 1991.

DEFINITION AND MEASUREMENT OF TIME

In some broad sense, time is defined by the interval between two successive events. However, problems arise when one tries to choose which events to use for establishing a clock that all will agree should serve as a standard. Since all clocks run in response to physical forces, it is a problem in engineering to provide the most accurate and stable clock. Thus, time is usually defined through the method by which it is measured. Time itself is a fundamental aspect of the universe and qualifiers such as "biological time" or "atomic time" simply denote the phenomena whose temporal behavior is described.

However, temporal intervals are not absolute, as believed by Newton, but depend on the relative motion of the observer and clock. Thus, two observers traveling relative to one another will not be able to agree on the interval of time separating two mutually observed events. Fortunately, this effect, which is described by the special theory of relativity, is small for relative motions that are not an appreciable fraction of the speed of light and can generally be corrected for if necessary.

Traditionally, we have expressed time in terms of a sequence of astronomical events such as the successive passing of the sun across a local meridian. While such a definition served early man quite well, close observation showed that the tilt of the earth's axis with respect to its orbit and the elliptical nature of the orbit resulted in a nonuniform motion of the sun across the sky and a variable solar day. Additional observations showed that the rate of rotation of the earth on its axis varied by small amounts during the year. This, coupled with a secular slowing of the spin rate due to tidal interaction with the sun and moon, leads to a variable sidereal day (which is to say, a variable time between successive stellar crossings of the local prime meridian). However, since the affairs of mankind are geared to the rising and setting of the sun, the pressure to tie the civil time to the local solar day is strong.

Because we require that time be uniformly changing, the basic interval of time is unvarying. To accomplish this, the uniform rate of atomic time (see below) is adopted for the interval of time and the actual value is kept within a second of time determined by the motions of the earth. This is done by making adjustments to the local civil time as often as twice a year at the end of June and the end of December. This time is known as *Universal Coordinated Time* (UTC), and is broadcast throughout the world as the civil time standard. However, because of the irregular spin of the earth, it will be only approximately correct for those who wish to locate objects in the heavens. Thus an additional time scale that accounts for the irregular spin of the earth is required. This time scale was historically based on successive passages of stars across the prime meridian at the old Royal Observatory at Greenwich, England. Some corrections were made so that the rate of passage was uniform for reasonable periods of time. This time scale is known as *Greenwich Mean Time* (GMT) because it serves as a basis for what is now known simply as *Universal Time*. Since it accounts for the varia-

tions of the earth's rate of spin, it is continuously adjusted. Despite the similarity of the name, it should not be confused with Universal Coordinated Time. Although the two are kept within one second of each other, their definitions are fundamentally different.

For following the motion of celestial objects in the solar system, one needs a time scale that does not depend on the vagaries of the rotation of the earth. Again, the time scale should be uniform. Since this is the time used to calculate the ephemerides of planets, comets, and the like, an early version of this time scale was known as *Ephemeris Time* (ET), which has now been supplanted by *Terrestrial Dynamic Time* (TDT). The relationship between TDT and UT are given in the *Astronomical Almanac* for each year. While TDT is accurate enough for most problems involving motion in the solar system, the effects of relativity have required the introduction of an additional time scale for the precise dynamics of the solar system.

As indicated above, time is a relative concept depending on the relative motion of the observer and clock. In addition, the rate at which a clock will run depends on the strength of the gravitational field in which the clock is located. Thus, clocks located on the earth will run at fundamentally different rates than those located on spacecraft moving through the solar system. The size of the effect can be determined from the general theory of relativity and is extremely small by most standards. However, the small amounts can be of considerable significance in the navigation of spacecraft and the establishment of fundamental standards of positional reference among the stars. Thus, a time scale known as *Barycentric Dynamical Time* (TDB) has been established. This is simply TDT as it would be measured at the barycenter of the solar system (that is, the center of gravity of the solar system). The typical differences between TDB and TDT are less than 0.002 seconds. For applications where these differences are important, one can find a formula for their calculation in the *Astronomical Almanac*.

ATOMIC TIME: ITS BASIC NATURE AND BASIS AS A STANDARD

To understand how atomic clocks work, it is useful to consider the manner by which atoms radiate light. Isolated atoms—which is to say, those that can be treated as unaffected by the presence of other atoms—radiate light in discrete amounts of energy. The energy corresponds to a discrete frequency and discrete wavelength of radiation. To measure one is to measure the other as they are related by the speed of light. To measure the frequency of a light beam is to measure the interval of time between successive passages of crests of the passing light beam. Thus, the frequency of a beam of light is a specific measure of successive temporal events and hence can be considered to be a clock. The quality of the clock will depend on how accurately one can measure the frequency of the light. The accuracy to which one can in principal measure that frequency is limited only by the Heisenberg uncertainty principle. This argument serves as the basis for the construction of "atomic clocks" that have accuracies ranging from one part in 10^{11} to one in 10^{14}, or about one second in 3,000 to 3 million years. This is by far the most accurate measurement of time presently available with terrestrial clocks. Clocks whose operation is fundamentally governed by these processes are called "atomic clocks," and they form the basis for an international time standard known as *International Atomic Time* or, as abbreviated by the French, TAI. The current definition of the TAI-second is the interval of time corresponding to 9,192,631,770 oscillations of the light wave resulting from a specific atomic transition of the element cesium. While it is true that the great precision of TAI has resulted in its use as a fundamental standard, it does differ from civil time used throughout the world. Between the inception of UTC and 1990, differences of about twenty-five seconds have had to be made to bring agreement between the heavens and the earth. To maintain agreement with historical ephemerides, an additional constant of 32.184 seconds was added to TAI in 1984 to make it agree with TDT. Thus, by 1992, UTC and TAI differed by about a full minute.

Although atomic clocks are based on the behavior of ensembles of atoms, the forces that mediate the atomic events are electromagnetic in nature. Thus, perhaps one should call atomic time *electromagnetic time,* or more correctly *electro-weak time,* to indicate the recent recognition of the relationship between the electromagnetic and weak nuclear forces. These forces mediate the behavior of chemical and mechanical processes. Therefore, one should expect that time measured from atomic events should be identical to time measured from the observation of biological or mechanical events. The accuracy that one gets is determined only by the sophistication of the clock and does not depend on any fundamental aspect of nature.

GRAVITATIONAL TIME: ITS BASIC NATURE AND BASIS AS A STANDARD

When the forces of gravity dictate the sequence of events, they are measured by gravitational time. Thus, the time kept by a pendulum clock is a clear example of gravitational time. Since gravity determines the motion of the planets in their orbits, they too keep gravitational time. So the length of the year is basically a gravitational year. It is the force of gravity that governs the tidal interaction between the earth, sun, and moon. This tidal interaction is a major contributor to changes in the spin rate of the earth. While there are many other factors that are mechanical in nature, it is fair to say that UTC, which forms the basis for the civil time of the earth, is gravitational time.

It is largely an article of faith that after corrections for relativistic effects, gravitational time and atomic time should agree. Indeed, should it eventually be demonstrated that the fundamental forces of nature are all manifestations of the same force seen under differing conditions, one would then be able to justify this assumption. Failing that, only lengthy observations of the small differences between TAI and UT will determine if the differences can be reconciled on the basis of known physical laws. During the first half of this century, some of the best minds of physical science speculated on the possibility that gravitational and electromagnetic time flowed at fundamentally different rates (see Barrow and references therein). Not all of these speculations have been set aside, and only future observation will settle the matter.

THE ZERO-POINT FOR TERRESTRIAL TIME AND TIME ZONES

In addition to the standard interval or rate at which a clock should run, a complete operational definition of time must specify a zero point. That is, we must operationally agree on how to set the clock. To do this we pick some reference point on the earth where the clocks are to be related to the position of the sun. Traditionally, this point has been the meridian of longitude that passes through the old Royal Observatory at Greenwich, England. The transiting of the sun across this meridian could serve as the instant when one should start measuring time. In reality, the definition of the initiation of the "day" is rather more complicated. It was thought more appropriate that the civil day should begin at midnight, even though the astronomer's day begins at noon. Thus, adjustments are made so the local time on the earth allows for the day to begin at local midnight. This requires establishing time zones around the world differing by generally one hour. The existence of twenty-four time zones on a globe with a circumference of about 25,000 miles means that each time zone will have an extent of slightly more than 1,000 miles at the equator. However, the boundaries of time zones are often moved to accommodate social and commercial interests of the population within the zone. Each time zone has acquired a name appropriate for the region that it covers. For example, the continental United States is spanned from east to west by the Eastern, Central, Mountain, and Pacific time zones.

With the systematic shift of one hour between zones, there is a point where the time lags the time by twenty-four hours. Continued westward movement produces a change of twenty-four hours, or one day. This boundary is known as the *International Date Line*, and by convention it is arranged to be twelve hours from Greenwich near the middle of the Pacific Ocean. Crossing this line from east to west yields an advance in the calendar of one full day.

[G.W.C.,II]

See also **Gravity, Time, and Space; Relativity Theory; Standard Time: Time Zones and Daylight Saving Time.**

FURTHER READINGS

The American Almanac. Ed. J.B. Hagen and A. Boksenberg. Washington: U.S.G.P.O., 1992. L1–L3.

Barrow, John D. "The Mysterious Lore of Large Numbers." *Modern Cosmology in Retrospect.* Ed. B. Bertotti, R. Balbinot, S. Bergia, and A. Messina. Cambridge: Cambridge UP, 1990. 67–93.

DEFOE, DANIEL (1660–1731)

Robinson Crusoe, Moll Flanders, Roxana, and *A Journal of the Plague Year* show Defoe's fascination with human time. To create verisimilitude, Robinson Crusoe's adventure is anchored firmly in calendar time. He begins with the phrase "I was born in the year 1632." He notes that he was shipwrecked on September 30, 1659, spent twenty-four years of solitude until the arrival of Friday, and finally departed from his island on December 19, 1686: "after I had been upon it eight and twenty years, two months, and 19 days; being delivered from this second captivity the same day of the month that I first made my escape . . . from among the Moors of Sallee." By such devices as remarking temporal coincidences, Defoe uses chronology for symbolic purposes that go beyond the establishment of

verisimilitude. He invites attention to providential patterns in life that can only be perceived in retrospect but which may show something of how God's will is enacted in human affairs. Thus, specification of time is linked to the novel's religious outlook.

Defoe makes Crusoe's tale of solitary survival into a compelling legend existing for readers in a realm of mythic time detached from the chronology of seventeenth-century history just as the tales of King Arthur dwell outside the arena of historical time despite their medieval setting. *Robinson Crusoe* initiated a genre of tales about heroic endurance in the face of isolation and catastrophe, the Robinsonade, whose vitality is further testimony to the mythic force of Defoe's narrative. It is a tale whose variations are equally recognizable in later settings like that of Johann Rudolf Wyss's *Swiss Family Robinson* or those alien landscapes of the future where an astronaut is stranded alone on Mars in Rex Gordon's *No Man Friday*. We discover in pictures of Neil Armstrong's footprint on the moon echoes of that shattering moment when Crusoe finds the print of a single foot and realizes that solitude has given way to society. *Robinson Crusoe* has become a lens through which we view our time. Defoe's greatest achievement is the creation of a story that transcends the era of its writing, the calendar time of its action, and even the eighteenth-century particularities of its text, so that in various avatars and with complex layers of meaning it has become a central myth of modern civilization.

Within Defoe's narrative, Crusoe's conversion puts him in touch with eternity, a relationship symbolized by the calendar he constructs in the form of a cross and by the day he loses in his reckoning of time during the sickness that heightens his longing for God's mercy. Defoe also dramatizes a decline of religious concerns as Crusoe finally leaves the island with his convert Friday and again enters the realm of historical time where account books are more attractive reading than the Bible to which Crusoe turns in his loneliness. There is, however, no concern with the actual events of history in *Robinson Crusoe*. It deals mainly with interactions between personal time and eternity. It also shows contrasts between primitive eras and later periods, the first symbolized by the empty island with its occasional cannibal visitors, and the latter by the comforts Crusoe establishes with the aid of goods taken from the shipwreck and his own knowledge of how to use them. On returning to civilization, Crusoe never asks about public events during his absence nor, accordingly, does Defoe include in *Robinson Crusoe* any account of such temporal milestones as the restoration of King Charles in 1660 or the fire and plague that devastated London a few years thereafter.

Crusoe remains immersed in private, not public, time. On returning to civilization, he quickly marries and has three children to make up for lost family time. He also reclaims property that has accumulated in value, thanks to the passage of time and the improbable honesty of those who left it in his name during all the years he was stranded on his island. In this, as in many other points, *Robinson Crusoe* departs from the realism apparently signaled by precise chronological specification of its action. Thus, too, Crusoe's marriage does not primarily serve to enhance psychological realism, although hastening to wedlock does seem plausible after almost thirty years of solitude relieved only by the company of a dog, some cats, a parrot, and a pious ex-cannibal. Rather, Crusoe's eventual prosperity, of which marriage and parenthood are a part, provides an ending that recalls that of the Book of Job. So, similarly, young Crusoe's disobedience of his father in running away to sea is described as an "Original Sin," thereby recalling Adam's disobedience of God the Father. Such allusions create for Defoe's narrative a typological dimension in which events of one time replicate those of another.

The overall temporal structure of *Robinson Crusoe*, however, like that of all Defoe's major fiction, with the exception of *A Journal of the Plague Year*, has the deceptive simplicity of a retrospective autobiographical narration proceeding in largely chronological order to provide an account in which the protagonist starts with birth and moves forward to old age. Defoe's choice of this structure shows his concern with portraying the biological cycle of life in time and with portraying too some of the psychological features of crucial moments during that cycle. Defoe's brilliant portraits of childhood in *Moll Flanders* and *Colonel Jack* are unsurpassed in English fiction before Dickens. The biological and psychological passages of female life also receive notable attention in *Moll Flanders* and *Roxana*.

Among English fiction, *Roxana* is remarkable for being set in two times at once: the eighteenth century *and* the late seventeenth century. Various allusions point to *both* periods as the temporal venue of *Roxana*'s action. For us, but not for Defoe, this is paradoxical. Given the conventions established by nineteenth-century fiction, we can more readily accept temporal doublings of the kind found in James Joyce's *Ulysses*, where the action takes place in modern Dublin but alludes symbolically to mythic events of the heroic age narrated in Homer's epic. In *Roxana*, Defoe experimented successfully with a double time scheme that allowed for the immediacy of an eighteenth-century setting and topical interest together with evasion of libel laws by displacement backwards in time of satiric episodes attacking masquerades and other activities contemporary with the novel's 1724 publication.

In *A Journal of the Plague Year*, Defoe entirely focuses on a major historical event. Published in 1722, this account of how London coped with the 1665 plague is the first great historical novel. It invites an imaginative leap from the reader's present to a notable moment of past time. It blends accurate mortality tables showing the plague's actual progress with fictional incidents typifying life during plague time. It is not organized as a journal, that is to say a chronologically presented day-by-day account in diary form. Instead, it is presented as a first-person retrospective narrative in which a survivor only identified as "H.F." sets down his memories of the plague. This form allows departure from chronological order because memories can juxtapose events that were separated at the time of their occurrence. H.F.'s narrative often puts together incidents that occurred separately, and also indulges in considerable repetition and circling around in time. By this and other means in *A Journal of the Plague Year*, Defoe creates a very slow tempo that recreates for readers the dragging pace of what H.F. describes as "the long course of that dismal year." Thus Defoe succeeds as no one previously had in portraying subjective as well as objective features of duration.

[P.K.A.]

See also **Novel.**

FURTHER READINGS

Alkon, Paul K. *Defoe and Fictional Time*. Athens: U of Georgia P, 1979.

Backscheider, Paula R. *Daniel Defoe: His Life*. Baltimore: Johns Hopkins UP, 1989.

Blewett, David. *Defoe's Art of Fiction: Robinson Crusoe, Moll Flanders, Colonel Jack & Roxana*. Toronto: U of Toronto P, 1979.

Novak, Maximillian E. *Realism, Myth, and History in Defoe's Fiction*. Lincoln: U of Nebraska P, 1983.

Richetti, John J. *Defoe's Narratives: Situations and Structures*. Oxford: Clarendon P, 1975.

DÉJÀ VU

The déjà vu experience represents a distortion of the sense of time in which a current set of perceptions is endowed with an inappropriate sense of pastness. There is an insupportable sense of familiarity, of having been through the experience once before. Other mental functions that are distorted in the déjà vu experience are the sense of reality and memory.

Déjà vu is far from an uncommon disorder. It has been associated with many psychopathological states, with anxiety, panic and dissociative experiences, and with various mood and personality disorders. Experiences of déjà vu have also been reported in patients suffering from schizophrenia and organic brain disease, particularly in the temporal lobe. In addition various drugs may induce déjà vu experiences.

What is striking is that déjà vu experiences frequently occur under circumstances that are in no sense unusual. Most studies of the phenomenon concentrate on the nature and configuration of the perceptual elements in the déjà vu experience, trying to demonstrate how certain suggestive similarities in the configuration of the perceptions may mislead the observer into a false sense of familiarity. Even more noteworthy are those cases in which an individual has a sense of déjà vu in a setting with which, in fact, he or she is really quite familiar.

Psychoanalytic investigations of the déjà vu phenomenon take into account the significance, conscious and unconscious, that the experience has for the individual. Clinical studies suggest that the unusual sense of familiarity represents a form of reassurance against emerging anxiety connected with some unconscious danger that has been evoked by the individual's situation. The anxiety is warded off with a familiar mechanism of reassurance. The individual thinks, "I have seen this before, that is to say, I have been through similar experiences of danger and have mastered them. The same (I hope) will happen now." From the perspective of the time experience, one may summarize by saying: In déjà vu, a perception of the present, which portends danger in the future, is reassuringly endowed with a quality of an experience from the past—an experience of the danger that had already been successfully mastered.

[J.A.A.]

FURTHER READINGS

Arlow, Jacob A. "The Structure of the Déjà Vu Experience." *Journal of the American Psychoanalytic Association* 7 (1959): 611–631.

Efron, R. "Temporal Perception, Aphasia and Déjà Vu." *Brain* 86 (1963): 403–424.

Gifford, S. "Sleep, Time and the Early Ego: Comments on the Development of the 24 Hour Sleep-Wakefulness Pattern as a Precursor of Ego Functioning." *Journal of the American Psychoanalytic Association* 8 (1960): 5–42.

Stein, M.H. "Premonition as a Defense." *Psychoanalytic Quarterly* 22 (1953): 69–74.

DERRIDA, JACQUES (1930–)

Born in 1930 near Algiers, Derrida is now a Parisian university philosophy professor. In his *Speech and Phenomena* (1967), a study of Edmund Husserl, Derrida expounds an important philosophy of time and space. Other relevant works include "Ousia and Gramme" (1969), which examines Martin Heidegger's views on the importance of Aristotle's time treatise to the European philosophical tradition, and "Force of Law" (1989), which focuses on the futurity of democracy and justice.

In *Speech and Phenomena*, Derrida discovers a tension between Husserl's demand that knowledge be grounded in intuitive evidence, in a present moment of conscious awareness, and Derrida's own description of how such present moments come about. Human experience is a temporal flux, Husserl writes, in which a present moment of conscious awareness is produced out of an interweaving of past and future, recollection and anticipation. Derrida points out that because of this fundamental contribution by past and future, any moment of conscious awareness is never *simply* present; Husserl's—indeed, all philosophy's—reliance on intuition as the ground of knowledge is thus called into question.

Since the present is now seen as a production out of past and future, Derrida draws the conclusion that the present is made up out of what is different from it. Since by the same token the present never really arrives, but is always delayed due to the role the future plays in its production, Derrida names the interweaving that produces time "différance," which captures both the differing and deferring aspects. Since "space" is what is different from time, Derrida paradoxically defines "différance" as the "becoming-time of space" and the "becoming-space of time." Derrida brings space into the discussion of time because the traditional discussions all center on the present now, which, as we have seen, is always deferred because it is always made up out of what is different from it.

In "Ousia and Gramme," Derrida examines the basic text for European philosophy of time, Aristotle's *Physics*. Derrida locates the interweaving of space and time in Aristotle's use of the Greek term *hama*, which means something like "together at the same time and place." He then shows how Aristotle overlooked some of the more paradoxical consequences of his famous comparison of time as a series of nows to the line as a series of points. Derrida concludes by showing certain commitments to the value of presence in key Heideggerian terms such as "authenticity," and he is careful to point out that his thought on time is only possible on the basis of Heidegger's pioneering work.

In "Force of Law," Derrida shows that "democracy" and "justice" are ideals, and thus must be conceived in terms of a future we are all obligated to work toward realizing. But because the future is always open, is always other than the present which it nonetheless makes up even in delaying its full arrival, "democracy" and "justice" can never be fully realized in a present. They are hence always futural, always "to come." This futurity does not lessen our obligation, however, but increases it, as we can never rest satisfied that our present accomplishments are enough.

[J.Pr.]

See also **Aristotle; Heidegger, Martin; Husserl, Edmund.**

FURTHER READINGS

Derrida, Jacques. *Speech and Phenomena*. Trans. David Allison. Evanston: Northwestern UP, 1973.

———. "Ousia and Gramme." *Margins of Philosophy*. Trans. Alan Bass. Chicago: U of Chicago P, 1982.

———. "Force of Law: The 'Mystical Foundation of Authority.'" *Cardozo Law Review* 11.5–6 (July-August 1990): 919–1045.

DESCARTES, RENÉ (1596–1650)

Time does not seem to have been one of Descartes's major philosophical concerns. One of the central aims of the Cartesian project is to render the material world accessible to mathematical knowing. To accomplish this, Descartes reduces the complex nature of body to the clear and distinct idea of extension. In the *Meditations* (1641), he takes a piece of wax and notes that the only thing that endures throughout change is the wax taken solely as an extended thing capable of infinite variation. He concludes that the true nature of the wax must therefore reside in this extendedness. In spite of time's inclusion in the list of indubitables in *Meditation* I, Cartesian thought in relation to material nature is overwhelmingly a philosophy of space rather than a philosophy of time.

There are, nevertheless, three important ways in which time appears in Descartes: time as history, time in the new physics, and the lived time of the human individual.

Time as history is depicted in the *Discourse on Method* (1637). In this work, Descartes sets out to establish himself as the turning point of human history. He revolutionizes the goal as well as the method of all prior philosophizing by placing the theoretical sciences, notably physics, in the service of man and the improvement of man's temporal condition. In the language of *Discourse* VI, the purpose of physics is "to render us masters and possessors of nature." The crowning science is no longer metaphysics but medicine, which ministers to health, "undoubtedly the chief good and the foundation of all the other goods in this life." Descartes is thus not only the "father of modern philosophy," but also the inventor of a new age, a new time. As Swift depicted with scathing wit in his *Battle of the Books*, it was due primarily to Descartes, to his systematic dismantling of the most cherished assumptions of the past, that we come to speak of "ancients versus moderns."

The second and most obvious locus of time in Descartes is time as it is understood by the new physics. In the *Principles of Philosophy* (1644), Descartes defines substance as "a thing which exists in such a way as to depend on no other thing for its existence." Attributes and modes enter once Descartes considers how substance is humanly conceived. The duration of a thing is "a mode under which we conceive the thing in so far as it continues to exist." Time as the measure of movement is "simply a mode of thought." It differs from duration only in the fact that "in order to measure the duration of all things, we compare their duration with the duration of the greatest and most regular motions which give rise to years and days, and we call this duration time."

Time as the measure of motion is fairly straightforward. It is with the more primitive notion of time as duration that Cartesian time becomes both interesting and problematic. The reason for this lies in the phrase "continues to exist." To put time as duration in its proper context, we must consider Descartes's understanding of motion.

In his *Principles of Philosophy*, Descartes reduces the quality–rich Aristotelian notion of change to the quantitative motion *par excellence*—local motion. The living continuity of change is reduced to "the transfer of one piece of matter, or one body, from the vicinity of the other bodies which are in immediate contact with it, and which are regarded as being at rest, to the vicinity of other bodies." The emphasis here is on motion not as flux or process but rather as a sequence of relative spatial configurations. In this "static" definition of motion, we catch a glimpse of the Cartesian universe as a series of "states of matter" as opposed to a cosmos of developing individual beings.

Descartes's understanding of time as duration is a counterpart to his definition of motion. Time is not the seamless flow encountered in human experience—the time that drove Augustine to distraction—but rather a sum of infinitely many, utterly disconnected parts: "the nature of time is such that its parts are not mutually dependent, and never [like the parts of space] coexist." As he notes in *Le Monde*, it is the time that a mathematical physicist presupposes when he says, for example, that a rock whirled around in a sling tends *at each instant* to go off in a straight line.

In the *Meditations*, Descartes analyzes a human lifespan into "innumerable parts, none of which depends in any way on the others." It is precisely this causal or logical discontinuity of time that Descartes uses to argue for God's existence: "it does not follow from the fact that I existed a little while ago that I must exist now unless there is some cause which as it were creates me afresh at this moment—that is, which conserves me." God emerges as the guarantor of continued existence in time. In Descartes's world there are no individual natures or forms that hold a thing in its being, no "substance" in Aristotle's sense of the term. The continuance of existence in time, as he argues in the *Principles*, is not "given" by the specific natures of individual things, but must be guaranteed by a continual transfinite act of conserving. This is a sort of continual enforcement of the law of inertia, according to which "each and every thing, in so far as it can, always continues in the same state." Continued existence in time, like motion, thus falls under the general principle that God, manifested as nature, always acts in the same way, that is, lawfully. The world's change of state from one moment to the next is only superficially change. In reality it is the perpetual expression of the eternal self-sameness manifested in Descartes's laws of motion, particularly in the

law of inertia. In the *Principles*, Descartes writes: "the very fact that creation is in a continual state of change is thus evidence of the immutability of God." One might also say that it is evidence of the immutability of nature itself rightly understood.

The third locus of time in Descartes is the lived time of the human individual. Time in this sense appears in the last published work, the *Passions of the Soul* (1649). Here, in the Preface, Descartes claims to speak about the passions not as rhetorician or moral philosopher, but solely "as a physicist."

Descartes's project is only in part the mastery of material nature. The other part is man's mastery of himself. Self-mastery is the practical end of the *Passions of the Soul*: "the chief use of wisdom lies in its teaching us to be masters of our passions and to control them with such skill that the evils which they cause are quite bearable, and even become a source of joy." The generally accepted definition of a passion points to the connection between the passions and time: a passion is "everything that occurs or happens *anew*." To be passionate is to be continually at the mercy of the new, to be immersed in time. It is for this reason that wonder is "the first of all the passions." While Descartes grudgingly concedes the utility of wonder, he concludes that "more often we wonder too much rather than too little" and that, having acquired the sciences, "we must attempt to free ourselves from this inclination as much as possible." Armed with an account of the passions offered by a benevolent physicist, man ceases to find himself surprising and thus gains mastery over time as bombardment by the new.

[P.K.]

FURTHER READINGS

Kennington, Richard S. "René Descartes." *History of Political Philosophy*. Ed. Leo Strauss and Joseph Cropsey. Chicago: U of Chicago P, 1987. 421–439.

Simon, Yves. *The Great Dialogue of Nature and Space*. Albany: Magi Books, 1970.

Westfall, Richard S. "Descartes and the Mechanical Philosophy." *Force in Newton's Physics: The Science of Dynamics in the Seventeenth Century*. New York: American Elsevier, 1971. 56–98.

DEVELOPMENTAL PSYCHOLOGY

Developmental psychologists attempt to understand the human experience of time by examining the origins of temporal awareness and the progressive changes in children's grasp of time as they grow older. Developmental research shows that the mature understanding of time is the product of a lengthy process and that many different aspects of time must be mastered.

Perhaps the earliest abilities involve the processing of temporal information in brief auditory and visual stimuli. A number of studies show that even in the first months of life, infants look longer at visual stimuli that flash on and off at particular frequencies. These findings indicate that there is an innate ability to process information about rates of change. Other studies show that very young infants, like adults, can discriminate between stimuli that differ in the durations of their parts or in their overall rhythmic patterns. For example, by one month of age, infants can detect the difference between elementary speech segments, called phonemes, which differ by as little as 0.02 seconds in the times that two of their component sounds begin. This ability may be an important adaptation underlying human speech perception. Research has also shown that even in the first six months of life, infants can discriminate between pairs of auditory patterns that differ by only 0.04 seconds in the time at which part of a rhythmic pattern occurs. Apparently, humans' sensitivity to rhythmic patterns also has an innate basis.

During the first eighteen months of life, infants learn to sequence their own actions and to notice the order in which others' actions take place. Fifteen-month-olds are able to remember the successive movements of an experimenter's hand and to use this information to infer where she must have hidden a toy that was in her hand. This ability is an early form of a general human capacity to build mental representations of temporal order. Recent evidence shows that by two years of age, children possess temporally organized representations of familiar event sequences and can readily learn new sequences. For example, twenty-month-old children can imitate a brief sequence of actions of a toy bear taking a bath.

Gradually, preschool and school-age children build representations of much longer temporal patterns. By four years, most children are aware of the order of the main events in a waking day. Between four and seven years, children learn about the order of the seasons, and in the following years come to represent important features of clock and calendar time. However, some of these representations continue to change into adolescence. For example, school-age children first represent the months of the year as a kind of list, one month following the next, and only later are the months represented as an overall pattern. Adolescents are the first age group who can mentally scan backward through past months or immediately grasp where widely separated months like March and November fall relative to one another.

Another conventional division of time, the past-present-future distinction, is manifest in language. Children correctly use the past and future tenses in their speech before three years of age, and in some languages, tense use begins to appear around two years. It would be incorrect, however, to assume that young children's sense of the past and future resemble that of adults. Three-year-olds often misuse temporal adverbs such as yesterday or tomorrow, indicating a less differentiated sense of the past and future than adults possess. Recent research on children's memory for the time of past events shows that some components of our sense of the past are present by early childhood, whereas others continue to develop well into the school years. One aspect of time memory that is present from early ages is a direct impression of the relative recency of events. For example, four-year-olds can judge which of two school events, one of them seven weeks in the past and the other one week in the past, occurred a longer time ago. However, the ability to locate memories in conventional time is often limited, and young children lack a sense of where different past times fell relative to one another. A mature sense of the past, and the future, depends upon building representations of long-scale time patterns.

Alongside these transitions in the sense of the past and the representation of time patterns is an increase in the sophistication of children's notions of the nature of time itself. Research by Jean Piaget and others has shown the gradual development of the ability to integrate information about the successions and durations of different actions. This work indicates that there are important changes from early to middle childhood in children's grasp of the homogeneity of time. Other studies reveal successive phases in children's understanding of the measurability of time. Six-year-olds choose to count when asked to reproduce a brief duration, and most children of this age realize the importance of counting at a constant rhythm. By nine years, most children also realize that there are arbitrary aspects of time measurement. They recognize that units need not be conventional ones to measure durations accurately and even accept that calendars could be changed without influencing natural durations such as one's age or the length of a day.

From the first months of life through adolescence children show a progressive adaptation to the temporal structure of their environment. The developmental sequence is convincing evidence for the complexity of humans' understanding of time.

[W.J.F.]

See also **Piaget, Jean.**

FURTHER READINGS

Friedman, William J., ed. *The Developmental Psychology of Time*. New York: Academic P, 1982.

Levin, Iris, and Dan Zakay, eds. *Time and Human Cognition: A Life-Span Perspective*. Amsterdam: North–Holland, 1989.

Macar, Françoise, Viviane Pouthas, and William J. Friedman, eds. *Time, Action and Cognition: Towards Bridging the Gap*. Dordrecht: Kluwer, 1992.

DEWEY, JOHN (1859–1952)

John Dewey's pragmatism, filling more than thirty-five volumes of collected works, constitutes nothing less than a revolutionary rejection of traditional philosophies; a wholesale reconstruction of philosophy itself; and a critical articulation of a radically empirical, experientially temporal, and melioristic naturalism—in metaphysics, epistemology, logic, education, ethics, politics, art, and religion.

The centerpiece of this work is Dewey's theory of experience, set forth most fully in his 1925 *Experience and Nature*, the clearest and most comprehensive statement of Dewey's mature view of time. The ultimate goal of this philosophy is not to make theory practical; instead, it is to make practice intelligent. This has large implications for the subject matter and evaluation of philosophy. When philosophy does not begin with actual temporal experience and practical problems, it consigns itself to cultural irrelevance—to the artificial problems of philosophers instead of the real problems of men and women. Similarly, when philosophy does not end in illumination, clarification, and deepening of meaning of the experience and problems that supply its origin, it consigns itself to theoretical abstraction—borne out in dead, antiseptic systems of thought instead of living practice. As a consequence, Dewey's pragmatism is not primarily an attempt to give better or correct answers to old, supposedly timeless philosophical quandaries and puzzles. Instead, it seeks to dissolve old problems and substitute new ones—living problems rooted in, and consonant with, actual changing, temporal conditions of culture. This has implications for philosophy's self-understanding: Philosophy, like all other human activities, is temporal. It is irreducibly tied to time and place, providing no infallible knowledge, no insight into ultimate reality, and no grasp of transcendental values.

Dewey's theory of experience is oriented to, and celebrates, the evolutionary, transient, and open rather than the supposedly permanent, stable, and eternal. For Dewey, recognition of change is necessary for the experience of time—and any notion of time independent of human experience is, for Dewey, nonsensical and literally meaningless. Unwavering attention to this temporality of experience leads Dewey, following William James's radical empiricism, to a new understanding of experience. By "experience," Dewey means the ontologically primary unity of experienc*ing* subject *and* experienc*ed* object. For Dewey, the subject/object dualisms dear to materialists and idealists, realists and antirealists, and empiricists and rationalists are metaphysical fictions. Dewey replaces them with a holistic metaphysics of activity or process that takes experiential time seriously. From this standpoint, the dualisms of traditional philosophies are merely distinctions made by reflection for assorted purposes; they may have functional, but never ontological, status. As Dewey says succinctly, every existent is an event.

Here Dewey makes a central distinction between temporal quality and temporal order. Temporal quality, ontologically more fundamental, is an immediate, ineffable feature of all experience. It is that quality that makes an experience just the particular experience it is. Temporal order, by contrast, is not immediate; it is the result of reflection, a matter of science, a consequence of inquiry into the conditions upon which occurrence of particular temporal qualities depend. Reflection may produce temporal order and this in turn may make possible future control of temporal qualities. But temporal order, as knowledge of the past, does not explain or explain away temporal quality, as experience of the present; temporal quality cannot be reduced to temporal order. Thus, for Dewey, temporal quality is ontologically primary.

This temporal quality involves projection. As Dewey says, again succinctly, we live forward. This is a beginning point for a phenomenology of temporal experience—a phenomenology which Dewey did not develop. It is also an entry into social and political philosophy. Dewey developed these implications throughout his work, but specifically pinpointed their connections with his views on time in essays such as "Time and Individuality." Individuality, Dewey claims, is a temporal matter, a career, and thus something precarious to be achieved rather than something sure and given at birth. The central political and educational issue thus becomes one of how to direct change so as to produce the conditions—especially freedom and intelligence—needed for the development of both individuality and community. Here, Dewey's metaphysics of experiential time has profound social implications, signaling his commitments to progressive education, inquiry, and a democratic way of both government and life.

[J.J.S.]

See also **Phenomenology; Pragmatism.**

FURTHER READINGS

Dewey, John. *Experience and Nature. John Dewey: The Later Works, 1925–1953*, Vol. 1. 1925; reprint, Carbondale: Southern Illinois UP, 1981.

———. "Time and Individuality." *John Dewey: The Later Works, 1925–1953*, Vol. 14. 1940; reprint, Carbondale: Southern Illinois UP, 1988. 98–114.

DICKENS, CHARLES (1812–1870)

Near the end of Dickens's most popular story, *A Christmas Carol*, Scrooge responds to the teachings of the three time spirits by making a vow. "I will live in the past," he affirms, "the Present, and the Future." Scrooge's vow corresponds nicely to the practice of his creator; when Dickens himself presents time in his writings, he allows each of its three phases to have approximately equal weight. Dickens's practice here differs from that of some other novelists in whose writings a single time mode is predominant. Examples would include Proust with his focus on the past, or H.G. Wells on the future, or Henry Green on the present.

Dickens's multiple focus is sometimes misrepresented by his commentators, one of whom said of him: "He never looks back." This is of course an absurd misreading. A large body of Dickens's writings is past-oriented, writings in which he looks back both to historical events in the manner of Scott, and to the pasts of individuals. Illustrative of the historical are the Gordon riots in his novel, *Barnaby Rudge*, or the mass executions in his *Tale of Two Cities* with its memorable opener: "It was the best of times, it was the worst of times."

But more important than Dickens's use of public time-past is his exploration of the private times-past experienced by his individual characters, explorations of crucial episodes remembered from earlier years. In *Great Expectations*, the adult Pip remembers how his whole life was changed because of the "one memorable day" when, as a boy, he had first visited the house of Miss Havisham. And Scrooge's encountering the Spirit of Time Past leads to a marvelous evocation of his lost childhood in a scene that is illustrative of Dickens's mastery of the role of memory in human experience. Such recollective scenes are often heightened by a realization of chances missed. And these accounts of time-past are movingly presented (as Graham Greene says) through Dickens's "secret prose" with its "deliberate and exact poetic cadences, the music of memory, that so influenced Proust."

Of his use of time-present, according to C.P. Caspari's learned study, *Tense Without Time*, Dickens was "the pioneer of historical Present experimentation," a mode in which his narratives shift from traditional past tense into present tense, as, for example, in *David Copperfield*, when four widely separated chapters, each entitled "Retrospect," portray earlier experiences as if they all are happening *now*. Similar experimental methods are illustrated by ten chapters of *Edwin Drood*, including the opium-induced soliloquy of its opening chapter. Such scenes represent private time as experienced by a single individual. But again, as with time past, Dickens shifts to the present in passages featuring public time. A famous example is his long opening paragraph of *Bleak House*, with its cascade of present participles ("Fog creeping into the cabooses of collier-brigs, fog lying out on the yards, and hovering in the rigging of great ships. . . ."), a list that finally culminates in a finite verb in the present tense. In such a passage the social abuses pictured as going on in the 1850s are, in effect, made to seem to be going on *now*, today. Time-present thus provides Dickens the social critic with an effective device for his exposures of corruption and ineptitude.

A different example of time-present is represented by some of Dickens's scenes in which a clock plays an important role. In his early fiction, *Master Humphrey's Clock*, the clock is simply a device for recording time. But in a later novel, *Hard Times*, a clock becomes emblematic of a modern factory economy in which clock time regulates not only the lives of the workers but effects mechanized attitudes upon all levels of society. Mr. Gradgrind, a member of Parliament from Coketown, who is obsessed with hard facts at the expense of human emotions, has in his study "a deadly statistical clock . . . which measured every second with a beat like a rap upon a coffin-lid." The sounds of this awesome mechanism seem to overpower Gradgrind's daughter when she is seeking (without success) her father's advice about marriage; "and the moment shot away into the plumbless depths of the past, to mingle with all the lost opportunities that are drowned there."

Speaking of time-future, John Ruskin exclaimed, after reading Dickens's *Bleak House*: "He [Dickens] is . . . a pure modernist—a leader of the steam-whistle party *par excellence*—and he had no understanding of any power of antiquity except a sort of jackdaw sentiment for cathedral towers." Ruskin is certainly at least half right, for a static society, such as China's, appalled Dickens. Also future-oriented was his contempt for the backwardness (in his view) of the Middle Ages. He was especially contemptuous of medieval instruments of torture, which, like a good Victorian, he could not foresee might be prominently resurrected in the twentieth century.

Nevertheless, although he believed that progress was being made, Dickens was no Utopian, and unlike William Morris, he wrote no Utopias. To reinforce the complexities of his position is his portrait of Mr. Dombey in *Dombey and Son*, who illustrates the terrible mistake of living for the future at the expense of daily life— as evident in the very opening page of this novel. And in other ways he repudiates the "steam-whistle party," not only by showing the drawbacks of industrialism, but by his celebration of the traditional rhythms of country living as in his *Pickwick Papers*, and *The Old Curiosity Shop*. Much of Dickens's life, early and late, was passed in the preindustrial south of England, and he responded recurrently to its traditional sense of time.

In sum, Dickens's own attitudes to time are complex and contradictory, and these complexities lead to the rich diversities of his presentations of times past, present, and future.

[G.H.F.]

See also **Novel.**

FURTHER READINGS

Feltes, N.N. "To Saunter, To Hurry: Dickens, Time, and Industrial Capitalism." *Victorian Studies* 20 (Spring 1977): 247–267.

Ford, George H. "Dickens and the Voices of Time." *Nineteenth-Century Fiction* 24 (March 1970): 428–448.

Franklin, Stephen L. "Dickens and Time: The Clock Without Hands." *Dickens Studies Annual* 4 (1975): 1–35.

Patten, Robert L. "Dickens Time and Again." *Dickens Studies Annual* 2 (1972): 163–196.

Rosenberg, Devia B. "Contrasting Pictorial Representations of Time: The Dual Narratives of *Bleak House*." *Victorian Newsletter* 51 (Spring 1977): 10–16.

Talon, Henri. "Space, Time and Memory in *Great Expectations*." *Dickens Studies Annual* 3 (1973): 122–133.

DINOSAURS

"Dinosaur" is the popular term for two orders of reptiles within the subclass Diapsida: the Saurischia includes the bipedal carnivores and huge quadrupedal herbivores, while the Ornithischia contains only herbivores. Although less than 700 species of dinosaurs are known, they dominated both terrestrial and marine ecosystems for more than 120 million years in the Mesozoic era due to their numbers and ecological impact. Ancestral mammals appeared in the Triassic but could not invade niches occupied by dinosaurs. Most dinosaurs are known only from a few bones, including, for example, the presumed largest animal, "Seismosaurus," estimated (from two bones) to exceed thirty meters in length. Nonetheless, interpretation of bone types and assemblages plus dinosaur tracks indicate behaviors very different from modern reptiles. Many species were social, hunting in packs, browsing in herds, nesting in colonies, and their agility may have rivaled modern mammals. Some may have been warm-blooded. Changing vegetation and climate patterns near the end of the Cretaceous (65 million years ago) caused some extinctions, but many dinosaur groups were still expanding. Their abrupt disappearance may be attributable to the aftereffects of bolide impact on earth. Into the vacated niches stepped the early mammals who then underwent a great diversification. Some researchers argue that the dinosaurs are still with us in the form of their most direct descendants, the birds.

[V.T.]

See also **Catastrophism; Extinction; Fossil Record.**

Further Readings
Norman, D. *The Illustrated Encyclopedia of Dinosaurs.*
New York: Crescent Books, 1985.

DRAMATIC UNITIES

As drama has traditionally been a representational art, much critical discussion has been concerned with its verisimilitude. The three unities of action, place, and time are a convention governing the relation between the "real" world and a believable representation of it. Accordingly, a drama is to represent one main action, take place in a limited setting, and span a time not exceeding one day.

In the *Poetics* (ca. 335 B.C.), Aristotle focuses on tragedy as the imitation of a unified action and makes the observation that most tragedies depict an event as taking place within one revolution of the sun. Later commentators augmented Aristotle's "rule" to include the unities of place and further specified the unity of time. Julius Caesar Scaliger, in the *Poetics* (1561), speaks of the necessity of making dramatic presentation concise and "to have such sequence and arrangement as to approach the truth as much as possible." In *Poetica d'Aristotele* (1570), Lodovico Castelvetro codifies the unities of action, time, and place. Tragedy, in order to be believable, must confine itself to representing an action whose boundaries of time and place are roughly coincident with the audience's "real" experience of time and place. A drama must, therefore, represent a unified action in a limited place which must not exceed twelve hours. The boundaries implied by the three unities guided much Renaissance criticism and continued to be significant through a considerable part of the eighteenth century. Although the unities were never as important in England, they were particularly significant in the French neoclassical theater.

By the eighteenth century, several critics reacted to the three unities by questioning the assumptions on which they rested. Much criticism focused on Shakespeare, whose tragedies did not adhere to the unities of time and place. Samuel Johnson, in his preface to *The Plays of William Shakespeare* (1765), dismissed the unities of time and place as confusing actuality with drama. It is not necessary, Johnson argued, to make a dramatic representation "credible." An audience is fully aware of its detachment from the representation being observed. The audience is always aware of illusory transportations of time and place which are encountered. These

in no way detract from the enjoyment and intellectual benefit that may be gotten from a dramatic performance. As Johnson puts it, "Time is, of all modes of existence, most obsequious to the imagination; a lapse of years is as easily conceived as a passage of hours." The Romantic reaction against "neoclassical" rules, beginning in the latter part of the eighteenth century, signaled the end of the dominant critical attention which the unities had received. Romantic theory, with its emphasis on the imagination, displaced verisimilitude as a unifying structure for the drama, and as competing unifying structures have dominated the attention of critics since the Romantic era, discussion of the unities has become important only as an historical phenomenon.

Insistence on the exact coincidence of "actual chronological" time and "dramatic time" may have given an impetus to "concentration," as T.S. Eliot suggests in "A Dialogue on Dramatic Poetry" (1928), but it does not account for the flexibility of the mind to distinguish between "lived" and "represented" time. Any rules of verisimilitude and its relation to time must necessarily be problematical; for minds themselves may have radically different "experiences" of the same chronological time.

[R.Z.]

Further Readings
Freytag, Gustav. *Die Technik des Dramas.* 10th ed.
Leipzig: S. Hirzel, 1905.
Lapp, John C. "The Unities of Time and Place." *Aspects of Racinian Tragedy.* Toronto: U of Toronto P, 1955. Chapter 2.

DUNNE, J.W. (1875–1949)

In his first career, that of aeronautical engineer, John William Dunne was a figure of some interest as the creator of the first airplane in the United Kingdom designed for military use, around 1907. But he is now mainly remembered for his second career as a writer; and the best-known of his books still remain the nonfiction texts he wrote between the two world wars about the nature of time. In these texts—*An Experiment of Time* (1927; last revised 1934), *The Serial Universe* (1934), *The New Immortality* (1938), *Nothing Dies* (1940), plus the posthumously published *Intrusions?* (1955)—Dunne attempted, in terms of increasing complexity, to explain his initial "discovery"—or, better, intuition—that dreams often had a precognitive aspect.

In the simplest formulation of his beliefs, he argued that precognition demanded that the entire flow of normal time—which he called Time 1—must have in some sense already occurred; and that it could be measured and recorded by an observer in Time 2, or "regressive time," which might also be described as a form of dreamtime. In essence, the observer in Time 2 sees Time 1 as a kind of *geography*: as a road or course whose "flow" can be measured over against Time 2. Dunne claimed that this sense that time was a geography derived from the passage in H.G. Wells's, *The Time Machine* (1895), which describes "duration as a dimension of space." (Wells repudiated Dunne's version of his fictional concept.) However, regardless of the degree of wish-fulfilling fabulation in his concept, and ignoring the impossible complexities of his later formulations, it is clear that Dunne addressed a deep-felt need in his readers.

The period between the two world wars could not, of course, be described as a time of settled peace. It was, rather, a period of aftermath, during which the implications of the Great War jostled distressingly with the implications of developments in physics, biology, psychology, political science, and philosophy. The modernist movements in the arts may be seen as a valiant—and perhaps as the last—attempt by the high culture of the West to comprehend the nature of the world in aesthetic terms. And the attempts, by writers like J.B. Priestley (and many less significant than he) to use the theories of J.W. Dunne to redeem time from the horrors of relativity, can also be seen as a response—perhaps rather less wholesome—to the profound insecurities of the new century.

Dunne's theory of time is more than a geography; it is also a pastoral. What he presents is a vision of a fixed and safe past couched as a vision of the measurability of the future, and as such, it offered a nostalgia-based firmament to writers and dreamers in search of repose. It is with some relief, tinged with melancholy, that one must record a sense that Dunne's recipe decreasingly serves, for those of the late years of this century, to redeem the time.

[J.C.]

See also **Science Fiction; Time Travel: Future; Time Travel: Past; Wells, H.G.**

FURTHER READINGS
Dunne, John W. *An Experiment with Time*. 5th. ed. London: Faber, 1938.

———. *The Serial Universe*. New York: Macmillan, 1938.

DUNS SCOTUS, JOHN (CA. 1266–1308)

Time was not a subject of major interest to this medieval philosopher, but he did discuss it in passing in connection with two other topics of concern as a professional theologian. One was "aeviternity," the other our intellectual memory of worldly events in the afterlife. Scotus was content to accept Aristotle's definition of time as the measure of physical change, being determined primarily by the uniform motion of the outermost heavenly sphere. "Time," he quoted, "is nothing other than the number of motion according to before and after." At the end of the world after the last judgment, time will cease and we will live like the angels in a state of aeviternity.

Aeviternity (or aevum) was the peculiar mode of existence the scholastics attributed to the angels and to Aristotle's pure spirits or intelligences believed to be responsible for the movement of the heavens. Lacking matter, these intellectual beings were incapable of undergoing the generation and corruption characteristic of the material universe and were, according to Aristotle, eternal.

The scholastics, however, believed these beings to possess a kind of "created eternity" or "permanent being," having been given by God "continuous unchanging existence." Some theologians, however, argued that one might distinguish distinct moments of that existence, for while it might be a contradiction for God at the same instant to both create and annihilate an angel, it was not a contradiction to give such a creature existence at one moment but cease to give it existence at any subsequent moment. In this sense all created existence could be considered to consist of successive moments and to be at least "quasi-temporal." By contrast, God as necessary and immutable first cause is altogether atemporal and exists in the "now" of eternity. Others, however, argued that unless some real change took place there was no objective intrinsic ground for distinguishing one moment of an angel's existence from another, an opinion that Scotus seems to have preferred. Though incapable of substantive change, however, an angel was believed to be able to think or will differently from one moment to the next. Scotus tells us that some claimed such changes occurred suddenly, as if in jerks, and hence posited the existence of a "discrete time," an idea that some earlier commentators on Aristotle had referred to as indivisible "time atoms." Scotus, however, rejected this idea as philosophically unjustified.

Because Aristotle had stressed the sense perceptual nature of memory, Scotus believed it important to show that, since we remember our thoughts and our voluntary actions, we must possess intellectual memory as well, something we will retain in the afterlife. "Recollection," he tells us, "is the knowledge of some past act of the person recollecting who now recognizes that action as past." Philosophically analyzed, this implies that our intellect was initially aware of the existence of a personal act on our part, retained an impression of the same, and became once more aware of it after a period of time; second, we perceive the actual flow of time between the present perception and that instant or time when the object of recall existed; and third, we recognize that what is recalled is not present now, or it would not be something recalled. Our knowledge of time is itself a proof that our intellect is capable of intellectual intuition of individual events and not mere abstract knowledge of universals.

[A.B.W.]

See also **Aristotle.**

FURTHER READINGS

Duns Scotus, John. *Opus oxoniense* IV, distinction 43, question 2. Ed. Louis Vivès. Paris, 1891–1895. 20:324–372 (treatise on intellectual memory).

———. *Ordinatio* II, distinction 2. *Opera omnia*. Vatican City: Vatican Polyglot Press, 1950–. 7:161–239 (treatise on aeviternity).

Sorabji, Robert. "Time and Time Atoms." *Infinity and Continuity in Ancient and Medieval Thought*. Ed. Norman Kretzmann. Ithaca: Cornell UP, 1991. 37–85.

DURKHEIM, EMILE (1858–1917)

Emile Durkheim's main contribution to the analysis of time came in the early sections of his *Elementary Forms of Religious Life* (1915), where he argued that the origins of time are "social." Basing his analysis on evidence from studies of primitive societies, he suggests that "The foundation of the category of time is the rhythm of social life." Durkheim was thus the first to focus on the collective social aspect of temporality. Time is not, as Kant argued, a universal category inherent in the mind. Instead, it is essentially a "collective representation," arising from the experience of the collectivity—it is society that provides the framework according to which time is arranged. Durkheim argues that since all members of a society share a common temporal consciousness, time is a social category of thought: collective time is the sum of temporal procedures which interlock to form the cultural rhythm of a given society. Durkheim also suggests that "The rhythm of collective life dominates and encompasses the varied rhythms of all the elementary lives from which it results; consequently, the time that is expressed dominates and encompasses all particular durations."

In modern Western societies, therefore, crucial elements of this framework are work and the clock. In primitive societies, however, temporal frameworks are arranged according to the "periodic recurrence of rites, feasts, and public ceremonies." In such societies, time depends on the rhythms of nature and the repetition of natural events, rather than on the calendar. The Durkheimian approach to the analysis of time suggests, therefore, that time and temporality are primarily derived from social life and become the subject of collective representations. Time is fragmented into a plethora of temporal activities which are reconstituted into an overall temporal rhythm that gives it meaning.

Durkheim's analysis is also reflected in contributions to what have been called the French and American traditions in the sociology of time. In the French tradition, two social anthropologists closely associated with Durkheim—Henri Hubert and Michel Mauss—also emphasize the rhythmical nature of social life through their concept of "qualitative" time. For example, Hubert in 1905 defined time as a symbolic structure representing the organization of society through its temporal rhythms. Like Durkheim, he focuses on time as a collective phenomenon: as a product of collective consciousness. Durkheim's influence on the American tradition is most notable in the work of P. Sorokin and R. Merton, who in 1937 outlined the cyclic-qualitative nature of social time. Following Durkheim, they argue, first, that astronomical time is only one of several concepts of time, and second, that the need for social collaboration is at the root of social systems of time. Also following Durkheim, they suggest that "social time is qualitatively differentiated according to the beliefs and customs common to the group." Above all, they draw attention to the fact that social time is not continuous, but is punctuated by critical and meaningful points of reference. Sorokin and Merton thus argue that calendrical systems arise from and are perpetuated by social requirements—which themselves arise from social differentiation and a widening area of social interaction.

[J.H.]

FURTHER READINGS

Durkheim, E. *The Elementary Forms of Religious Life.* Trans. Joseph W. Swain. Glencoe: Free Press, 1975.

Hubert, H. "Etudes sommaire de la representation du temps dans la religion et la magie." *Annuaire de l'Ecole Pratique des Hautes Etudes* (1905): 1–39.

Sorokin, P., and R. Merton. "Social Time: A Methodological and Functional Analysis." *American Sociological Review* 42 (1937): 615–629.

DYNAMICS

Dynamics (also known as dynamical systems theory) is the branch of mathematics dealing with patterns in space and time. It has coevolved with our concepts of time, providing abstract models and cognitive strategies for calendars, clocks, theories of history, and so on. For example, linear progress is modeled on a geometrical line, and historical cycles on geometrical circles. Since Isaac Newton's *Principia Mathematica* of 1687, the mathematical structures known as differential equations have dominated dynamics. Our current understanding of these models for dynamical processes in nature is based on the revolutionary work of Henri Poincaré a century ago. The chief features of this new understanding are attractors and their bifurcations. There are three types of attractors, namely static, periodic, and chaotic, and we will give examples of these below. The recent developments in this theory, including chaotic and fractal models, are just beginning to have an impact on philosophy and criticism. This article will suggest some applications of dynamics to the theory of time.

HIERARCHIES AND FRACTALS

As a first step, consider the model of time as a hierarchical structure. Time has different strata, or time scales, rather than a single cosmic time or universal clock. Such a model, with eight levels, was proposed by J.T. Fraser in 1975 in Chapter 12 of his *Of Time, Passion, and Knowledge.* In an extreme version of this hierarchical model of time, there might be an infinity of strata, with self-similarity across scales. Such a model was proposed in 1975 by the McKenna brothers in *The Invisible Landscape.* Thus, zoom-

ing into the microstructure of time one gets lost, as each new view is much like the last. This is the structure of the mathematical objects called fractals, which abound in the mathematical theory of dynamics. (For examples, see *The Beauty of Fractals* under *Further Readings.*) The specific fit of a fractal curve to the graph of cultural novelty as a function of time was discussed by Terence McKenna in 1987. Following this trend, we may find among the new ideas of dynamics some models for time with a richer structure than those considered previously: fractal time.

LINES, CYCLES, AND CHAOS

As described above, lines and cycles have long been employed as models for time, on various strata: psychological, social, historical, and so on. For the sake of discussion, let us consider the historical stratum. The linear-progress paradigm for history may be modeled by a geometrical line or curve. We may construct a dynamical model from the concept of a static attractor in dynamical systems theory. Thus, consider the history of a region as represented by a moving point in space, to which each position has a prescribed motion. As history evolves, it must follow these rules of motion, changing from point to point as it moves. This is a dynamical model. Eventually, the path of this history approaches closer and closer to a fixed point, and moves more and more slowly. It essentially stops at the destination, like a train at a station. This model is an example of a static attractor, and it models the idea of linear progress with an apocalypse, an end of history. Of course, this represents a distant view of history: from up close, history is always chaotic.

Next, consider the cyclic paradigm for history. This may be modeled by a geometric circle. We now construct a dynamical model for cyclic history using the periodic attractor of dynamical systems theory. Consider again the history of a region represented as a point moving in a space with a dynamical rule prescribed at each point. Eventually, the moving point gets closer and closer to a loop, then goes around and around this loop, completing each cycle in exactly the same period of time. This model is an example of a periodic attractor, and it models the idea of history repeating itself exactly in periods of a fixed length. These two examples are classic, and have dominated historiography from antiquity. In other strata of time, the static and periodic behavior are also familiar.

But now we have a new model, this time using the chaotic attractor concept of dynamical systems theory. Again, consider the historical stratum for our example, with the history of a region represented by a point moving in a geometrical space of three or more dimensions. The track left by this moving point, a curve which wanders about the space without crossing itself, moves closer and closer to a thick loop which resembles a coil of rope. It then moves around and around the loop, completing each cycle in a different period of time, and never visiting the same point twice. This model is an example of a chaotic attractor, and models a roughly cyclic history, which almost repeats itself, but at unpredictable intervals. As a time series, this behavior appears to be a cyclical model with noise.

Evolution and Bifurcations

Periods of disintegration in the world of ideas, which result in numerous small disciplines scorning each other, are followed by opposing movements of integration, which result in numerous small disciplines in a tightly coupled network. Closely related examples of integrative movements are the study of time, and general evolution theory. The latter, part of the systems theory approach growing since World War II, studies the universal patterns presented by all evolving systems. The recognition of these patterns in human prehistory and history, following the pioneering ideas of Ibn Khaldun and Vico from centuries past, is one of the main projects of general evolution theory. Dynamical systems theory provides models for the space-time patterns observed by general evolution theorists on all levels of the evolutionary hierarchy, and again, we will illustrate these model patterns on the historical level. Consider a dynamical system, characterized by a set of attractors dispersed within a geometrical space of virtual states, which we will call the state "space." This system is generated by a fixed rule of motion attached to each point in the space. After starting at one initial point and following these rules, a model history ends up at one of these attractors, whether a point, a cycle, or a chaotic motion. This fixed system is too rigid to model evolution in the natural world, or in the history of a social system, in which the rules are slowly changing in time. What happens to the dynamical system when the rules of motion shift? The configuration of attractors shifts. And eventually, while wandering about in the state "space," they may be radically altered. Such transformations are called bifurcations, and dynamical systems theory is gradually developing an atlas of them.

The emerging atlas of bifurcations is organized in three categories: subtle, explosive, and catastrophic. These model transformations may be applied to evolutionary studies in any empirical domain to enhance our understanding. For example, imagine a dynamical model with a single attractor, a point. A model history in this context is a curve of linear progress, coming to rest at an apocalyptic state, as described above. But then the rules begin to drift, as environmental factors evolve, for example, and at some time the point attractor becomes a very small cycle, which then grows. In mathematics, this is called a Hopf bifurcation. It is a subtle bifurcation in that at first it is qualitatively invisible. Eventually, one sees that the course of time has changed from a static state to a cyclic oscillation. Similarly, a periodic attractor may subtly change to a chaotic attractor, and one observes that the periods of history gradually become irregular. For the next example, imagine a model with a point attractor as above, where once again the rules gradually begin to drift. And again, the point attractor drifts, and turns into a periodic attractor. But in this case, it suddenly jumps from a point to a cycle of a large girth. This is an explosive bifurcation, and might be applied to a social transformation such as the emergence of civilization, the Renaissance, or the Reformation. Explosive bifurcations of chaotic attractors are characterized by a sudden increase in the magnitude of their chaotic behavior. After one of these, another explosion (in reverse) might suddenly decrease the amount of chaos. This is typical of the transient phase of a social transformation or revolution.

For another example, imagine a model with two point attractors. They represent static conditions for two different apocalyptic states, such as communism and capitalism, or, let us say, A and B. All initial states might be tested, in principle, to see if they evolve to rest at A or B. Those that end up at A fill up a certain area of the state space, called the basin of attractor A. Those that evolve to rest at B fill out the basin of B. Between these two basins there is a thin region of indecision, called the separatrix, which divides the entire state space into the two basins. Now we imagine, in this model, that a history starting up in the A basin has come to rest at A. Then the rules begin to change, and the two point attractors begin to drift about in their basins. The history we are observing tracks A, following its motion closely. The separatrix also moves. Attractor A approaches closer and closer to the separatrix. At the climactic moment, they collide, and vanish! Such an event is called a catastrophic bifurcation. After the event, the rules continue to drift and there is only one attractor, the point B. Our history finds itself near the point where A was when it ceased to be an attractor. This point is now in the basin of B, the only remaining attractor. Our history then rushes off, attracted to B. Here we have a model for a catastrophic social transformation, such as the end of an era. While eras end and are reborn in historical bifurcations, history can only end once.

CONCLUSION

In these examples we have seen just a few of the ways in which dynamical systems theory can extend our view of time. Fractal geometry gives us models for a richer geometry of time, while dynamics provides chaotic models for the behavior of time and an atlas of bifurcations for modeling sudden transformations in evolution. We may combine these into very complex temporal models, in which static periods give way to chaotic motions, and evolution proceeds in epochs alternatively static, periodic, or chaotic, and punctuated by transformations of subtle, explosive, or catastrophic character. Chaotic attractors are themselves fractal objects, and chaos theory empowers us to make more realistic temporal models than those of the past. We may call them models of *kairotic* time.

[R.H.A.]

See also **Hierarchical Theory of Time;** *Kairos*; **Time Series.**

FURTHER READINGS

Abraham, Ralph H., and Christopher D. Shaw. *Dynamics, the Geometry of Behavior.* 2nd ed. Reading: Addison-Wesley, 1992.

Fraser, J.T. *Of Time, Passion, and Knowledge: Reflections on the Strategy of Existence.* New York: Braziller, 1975.

Laszlo, Ervin. *Evolution: The Grand Synthesis.* Boston: Shambhala, 1987.

McKenna, Terence. "Temporal Resonance." *Revision* 10.1 (Summer 1975): 25–30.

Peitgen, Heinz-Otto, and Peter Richter. *The Beauty of Fractals.* Berlin: Springer, 1986.

ECLIPSES AND TIME

Ancient and medieval observations of eclipses have played a major role in the study of time. Applications of these observations include investigation of early calendars, dating of historical events, determination of changes in the length of the day (due to tides and other causes, and estimates of the accuracy of time measurement by the astronomers of antiquity. In calendar studies, eclipses have the attraction that their precise Julian or Gregorian dates can be computed. Hence recorded and calculated dates may be compared. Many recorded times are quoted to the nearest few minutes.

Most early records of eclipses originate from four civilizations: China (later including Korea and Japan), Babylon, Europe, and the Arab dominions. Before the eighth century B.C., only scattered observations—some of dubious reliability—are preserved in history. However, from this time onwards, both Chinese and Babylonian astronomers began to record these phenomena systematically.

CHINA

In ancient China, lunar eclipses were regarded as of little significance. However, it is from this country that the earliest series of solar observations from any part of the world has survived. The *Chunqiu* ("Spring and Autumn Annals")—a chronicle covering the period from 722 to 481 B.C.—notes as many as thirty-six obscurations of the sun. Although no times are reported, the exact dates of most of these events are given in the following form: year of ruler, lunar month, day of month (invariably the first day), and day of the sexagenary cycle, a sixty-day cycle that is independent of any astronomical parameter and has continued to run without interruption down to the present day. When the various dates are converted to the Julian calendar, there is found to be precise accord with the dates of calculated eclipses in thirty-one instances. This represents a remarkable achievement at such an early period. In later Chinese history (especially after 200 B.C.), solar—and eventually lunar—eclipses were consistently reported. The accuracy of dating is uniformly high, but times of day or night are only rarely noted. Similar remarks apply to eclipse observations from Korea and Japan.

BABYLON

According to Ptolemy, Babylonian astronomers began to record eclipses systematically from the

accession of King Nabonassar (747 B.C.). Regular observations probably continued until the first century A.D., after which Babylon ceased to be inhabited. Many eclipses of both sun and moon are recorded on the late Babylonian astronomical texts, but these clay tablets (which are now largely in the British Museum) are so fragmentary that there are many gaps in the extant record. Although the earliest lunar eclipse observation dates from 702 B.C., no references to solar eclipses are preserved before 369 B.C. Dates are expressed in terms of a lunar calendar which has been extensively studied. Before the Seleucid era (311 B.C.), years were counted from the accession of the current ruler. Whenever Babylonian eclipse dates are fully preserved, their Julian equivalents without exception prove to be in exact accord with those of calculated eclipses.

The Babylonian astronomers consistently measured the local times of the various phases of eclipses, mainly to check the accuracy of their own predictions. Times were usually determined relative to sunrise or sunset, whichever was nearest; these are normally well-defined reference moments. After about 200 B.C., lunar eclipse times were frequently measured relative to the culmination of certain marker stars. It is evident that some form of timing device (such as a clepsydra) was used rather than taking altitudes of the sun and moon. However, the precise nature of the instrument is unknown. Although the earliest eclipse timings tend to be rather crude, from about 560 B.C. the Babylonian astronomers systematically estimated time intervals to the nearest *us*. This unit, $1/360$ of the interval for the celestial sphere to make a full revolution, was equivalent to four minutes.

175

Greece and Rome

The use of eclipses in the accurate dating of events recorded in the Greek and Roman classics is well known. To give just one example, the first-century B.C. historian Diodorus notes the occurrence of a total solar eclipse one day after the tyrant Agathocles escaped from Syracuse harbor with a fleet of ships. This event was said to have occurred when Hieromemnon was archon in Athens (and thus during the year 310–309 B.C.). The date of the eclipse has been established by calculation as August 15 in 310 B.C., so this important historical event is accurately fixed in time.

Arab World

Very few eclipse records are preserved from the Occidental world during the Dark Ages. However, from around A.D. 800, both Christian and Muslim annalists began to record the more spectacular eclipses, often providing a rough estimate of the hour of day or night. In most cases, the reported dates (given in terms of the Julian or Islamic calendars) prove to be accurate, although errors in the month are not unusual. There are also several instances of more serious error. For instance, the Muslim chronicler 'Imad al-Din records the occurrence of a total obscuration of the sun when the army of Saladin was crossing the Orontes river. Although 'Imad al-Din, who was with Saladin at the time, stated that the event occurred in Shawwal, the tenth month of 570 A.H. (*anno hegirae*), the calculated date of the eclipse—A.D. 1176 April 11—corresponds to the Ramadan, the ninth month of 571 A.H.

Medieval Muslim astronomers, based largely at Baghdad and Cairo, measured the local times of about thirty lunar and solar eclipses between about A.D. 830 and 1020. Dates were also carefully recorded. The main motive in making these observations was to determine the accuracy of existing eclipse tables. However, in several cases lunar timings were used to estimate the longitude differences between distant cities. Aware of the inaccuracies of conventional clocks, the Muslim astronomers measured time indirectly by determining the altitudes of the sun, moon, or selected bright clock stars at the beginning and end of an eclipse. These results, which were usually expressed to the nearest degree or half-degree, were afterwards reduced to local time using either an astrolabe or conversion tables. Modern reductions of these same measurements give quite reasonable timing errors, averaging four or five minutes.

Length of the Day

Ancient and medieval observations of eclipses, both timed and untimed, yield valuable information on changes in the length of the day in the past. Tidal computations, based on the measured rate of retreat of the moon from the earth (some 3.5 centimeters per year by lunar laser ranging), indicate a steady increase in the length of the day by 2.4 milliseconds per century. It can be seen that over a period of 1000 years (some 365,000 days), the accumulated clock error amounts to about half an hour; in 2000 years the effect will be four times as large, and so on. As a result, the recorded times of historical eclipses, when reduced to Universal Time, tend to be systematically earlier than the times calculated on the assumption of a constant length of day (Ephemeris Time). Ancient observations of eclipses yield a result for this clock error (known as ΔT) of 15,600 seconds at the mean epoch 390 B.C., whereas by medieval times (mean epoch A.D. 950), this had decreased to only about 1,850 seconds. Both results are considerably less than would be expected due to tides alone.

The above figures for ΔT can be readily converted to changes in the length of the day (expressed relative to the standard reference value of 86,400 SI seconds, defined at A.D. 1800). It follows that around 390 B.C. the mean solar day was about 45 milliseconds shorter than at present, while at A.D. 950, the corresponding figure had reduced to 12 milliseconds. Both of these values are considerably less than the expected figures due to tides alone, and indicate marked nontidal variations in the length of day on the millennial time scale. A combination of postglacial uplift, changes in global sea level, and electromagnetic coupling between the core and lower mantle of the earth seems the most likely explanation.

Investigation of individual Babylonian eclipse timings using a smoothed function for ΔT reveals that for observations near sunrise or sunset typical errors amounted to only one or two *us*. However, when measurements were made near midday or midnight—and thus a long way from the reference moments of sunrise and sunset—errors could be as much as forty-five minutes. The difficulties in establishing the instants of midday and midnight using crude clocks are apparent. By comparison, the medieval Arab altitude measurements averaged errors of about 1 degree—or some five minutes of time—throughout the day and night. Although these observations were of similar accuracy to the best of the Babylonian results, their consistency is decidedly superior.

[F.R.S.]

See also **Definition and Measurement of Time.**

ELIAS, NORBERT (1897–1990)

Elias set out to explain the development of time as a social tool. Clocks and calendars, the socially constructed symbols of time, are explicated as tools for social interaction, coordination, orientation, and regulation. To Elias, clock time is a highly sophisticated social construction for the coordination of body, person, society, and nature.

Elias rejects both the Newtonian and the Kantian understanding of time: time is neither about the representation of an objectively existing flow (Newton), nor about a form of intuition prior to experience (Kant). Rather, time is a social institution and clocks are instruments that symbolically represent socially normative processes with regularly recurring patterns of change. This means that clocks are not time. Clocks are tools to compare sequences of events and this always necessitates a third frame of reference with which to standardize the first two. Clocks represent symbolically repeatable patterns of unrepeatable events and as such they may be used as tools for interaction, coordination, and orientation: time as numerical measure is simply symbolic shorthand for known physical processes. In societies without clocks and calendars, location in time must be necessarily event based: questions about when something happened have to be answered in conjunction with a publicly known event. Our contemporary Western understanding of time, in contrast, is a very recent development associated with the symbol of the year and the capacity to synthesize events through symbolic representation. Elias rejects the idea that clock time is an abstraction since there is nothing to abstract time from. The idea of synthesis, in contrast, not only side steps this problem but also points to the central aspect of remembering. Thus, time is to be viewed as a symbol at the highest level of synthesis, bringing together into an orderly and ordered relationship aspects of the universe, the natural and social environment, and personal lives.

Elias's most innovative thoughts on time relate to his elaboration of the dimensionality of time: his fifth dimension. The fact that time assumes the character of a universal dimension,

he argues, is nothing more than a symbolic expression of the experience that everything which exists is part of a continuous flow of events. Time is thus an expression of the endeavor of human beings to define position, duration of intervals, and the speed of changes for purposes of their own orientation. This requires analyses from several perspectives and at several levels. In a four-dimensional universe humans do not yet include themselves as observers and perceivers in their observations and perceptions. Once humanity includes itself as the subject of knowledge in the process of knowing, then the symbolic character of the fourth dimension becomes discernible and we move to a new level of analysis: the fifth dimension of the awareness of awareness. Once human beings not only appreciate that they define and order time but also incorporate that knowledge into their understanding, their analysis has shifted into the fifth dimension.

The key ideas in Elias's theory of time are symbol and synthesis: time as symbol for meaning, interaction, orientation, coordination, and regulation and time as synthesis for universal, physical, biological, and individual levels of processes. To Elias, time is always social time, even as individual experience or as representation of events and processes of nature. It is a social symbol of instrumental value that may take different forms in different societies and historical periods but that remains, nevertheless, a human construction.

[B.A.]

See also **Kant, Immanuel; Newton, Isaac.**

FURTHER READINGS
Elias, Norbert. *Über die Zeit.* Trans. H. Fliessbach and M. Schröter. Frankfurt: Suhrkamp, 1984.
———. *On Time.* Oxford: Blackwell, 1992.

EMERSON, RALPH WALDO (1803–1882)

Emerson's transcendental, correspondential worldview defies common sense notions of time as duration, as a continuum neatly divisible into past, present, and future. For him, time (and space) relations belong to the world of the senses, the Understanding, prudence. The higher powers of Soul, Reason, Intellect, Vision, and Truth transcend the limits of duration and extent. The poet, the philosopher, the wise soul in search of eternal verities must not be constrained by the apparent limitations of time and distance. As Emerson writes in his 1838 journal, "A great man escapes out of the kingdom of time; he puts time under his feet." In moments of self-affirming clarity, the soul absorbs past and future into an eternal now. As Poulet correctly observes, each Emersonian moment is fully representative of the whole.

In the "Discipline" chapter of *Nature*, Emerson acknowledges that time and space teach some concrete, practical lessons, namely that "things are not huddled and lumped, but sundered and individual." He quickly adds, however, "Time and Space relations vanish as laws are known." Similarly, the all-important laws of the soul "are out of time, out of space, and are not subject to circumstance." In "The Over-Soul," he defines the soul in large part by its independence of restrictions we tend to obey unthinkingly; it "circumscribes all things . . . contradicts all experience . . . abolishes time and space." In fact, "The least activity of the intellectual powers redeems us in a degree from the conditions of time."

Although Emerson appears to dismiss the power of time when he says things like, "Time and Space are but physiological colors which the eye makes, but the soul is light," he does appreciate the experience the individual faces. The powers of the eye, and of society, are formidable; most people's senses so dominate the higher faculties of the mind "that the walls of time and space have come to look real and insurmountable; and to speak with levity of these limits is, in the world, the sign of insanity."

So vital was it to Emerson that the individual's spirit and intellect be encouraged to transcend this "wall" that, in a journal entry in 1839, he declared doing so a major purpose of his upcoming lecture series: "I am to invite men drenched in time to recover themselves and come out of time, and taste their native immortal air." Too mindful of time, we venerate the past and anticipate the future, meanwhile failing to live in and fully value the present and our own thoughts. We read history for the wrong reasons, assuming the past is more important than the present and somehow radically different from it. For Emerson, great stretches of time do have a value in our understanding of history, but not because they ennoble the past. Instead, "Time dissipates to shining ether the solid angularity of facts," releasing the true, larger "fable" that underscores the identity of ancient history and our own minds. Intellectual and spiritual self-reliance requires freedom from the authori-

ty of the past. He warns us not to follow slavishly old forms of worship, not to think of revelation as past. The true teacher will "show us that God is, not was; that He speaketh, not spake," he reminds the Harvard Divinity School students.

To help individuals "come out of time," the teacher must help them recognize and value moments of inspiration. He begins "The Over-Soul" with a description of such moments: "There is a difference between one and another hour of life, in their authority and subsequent effect. Our faith comes in moments; our vice is habitual. Yet there is a depth in those brief moments, which constrains us to ascribe more reality to them than to all other experiences." In these moments we experience our oneness with nature, soul, God; past and future are contained in it.

If we look at the effect of time itself on Emerson's views, we find, appropriately enough, little change. In an 1859 journal entry, he writes, "Illusion of time, which is very deep. Who could dispose of it?"

[G.L.S.]

FURTHER READINGS

Emerson, Ralph Waldo. *The Journals and Miscellaneous Notebooks of Ralph Waldo Emerson*. Ed. William H. Gilman, et al. 16 vols. Cambridge: Belknap of Harvard UP, 1960–1982.

———. *The Collected Works of Ralph Waldo Emerson*. Ed. Alfred R. Ferguson, et al. Cambridge: Belknap of Harvard UP, 1971– .

Poulet, Georges. "Emerson." *Studies in Human Time*. Baltimore: The Johns Hopkins P, 1956. Appendix, 323–326.

EMIGRATION

By the seventeenth century, international migrations began to comprise a single global network organized in the interests of the dominant states of northwestern Europe. Two sparsely peopled environments, in particular, attracted migrants who radically changed the population base of those areas over the subsequent centuries.

First, tropical and subtropical coastlands, especially in the Americas, were quickly exploited because of maritime accessibility and the suitability of warm humid climates for production of exotic crops like sugar, cotton, and coffee. Initial labor was provided by European emigrants recruited under an indenture system, whereby an individual would contract to work for an employer abroad for a fixed number of years in exchange for passage and subsistence. But since numbers coming forward under this basically oppressive system were limited, plantation managers quickly turned to slave labor from Africa. About 12 million slaves left Africa before the abolition of slavery in the nineteenth century. British and Dutch colonialists then substituted a semi-slave trade in indentured labor from the huge population and poverty reservoirs of India and China. Two major destinations of such emigrants were new zones of plantation agriculture around the Pacific and Indian Oceans in Malaya, Sumatra, Ceylon, Fiji, Hawaii, Natal, East Africa, and Mauritius. "Coolie" labor was also recruited for tin mining in Malaya and Sumatra and for railway construction in California and East Africa.

The second type of New World environment to attract European investment and settlement was the temperate zone grasslands and woodlands well suited to established European agricultural practices. The huge outpouring from Europe to such environments in the Americas, South Africa, Argentina, Australia, and New Zealand constitutes the most important migratory movement in human history. About 60 million people emigrated between 1820 and 1930. But for three centuries after discovery by Europeans, these lands had received only a trickle of emigrants. Such distant lands were considered fit for military adventurers, deported criminals, paupers, and religious dissidents, but hardly for decent ordinary citizens. What then opened the floodgates in the decades following the Napoleonic Wars? A major factor was the demographic pressure that built up in Europe as mortality rates declined with the onset of modernization. Problems of rural congestion were exacerbated in some areas by transformation of farming structures involving tenant eviction, as in the notorious Highland Clearances in Scotland. The role of emigration as a safety valve to European population growth can be illustrated by the total of 750,000 emigrants from Norway between 1840 and 1914, equivalent to 40 percent of the country's natural increase of population. But the most spectacular, if atypical, case of the bloodletting of a nation was Ireland, where one million people emigrated during the fateful five years following the 1846 potato blight.

Complementing land hunger in Europe was the lure of virgin land in the New World, particularly when accompanied, as in the United States, by liberal government policies of public land distribution at low cost to settlers. Knowledge of the new opportunities overseas grew in the nineteenth century with the development of pamphlets, newspapers, and postal services, while the new railways and steamships brought greater standards of space, speed, and safety to transoceanic and transcontinental travel. The spread of emigration fever was closely related to the progression of fundamental economic, social, and demographic changes across Europe from the northwest to the south and east. Thus, by the late nineteenth century the heaviest emigrations were from Italy, Greece, Austria-Hungary, Russia, and Poland. Emigration from Europe peaked in the decade before World War I. Its levels have fluctuated subsequently in relation to employment conditions overseas (there was little emigration, for example, during the 1930s depression), and the strictness of immigration controls.

Since the mid-twentieth century the major international migrations have all involved emigration from less developed countries. There have been three major streams:

1. From the 1960s, traditional countries of permanent-settlement immigration (United States, Canada, and Australia) have adopted less ethnically discriminatory immigration policies, so that by the 1980s, Asia had replaced Europe as the dominant origin of legal migrants to all three countries.

2. There has been considerable growth in the number of international refugees; this is partly related to the wars and revolutions accompanying the three-fold increase in the number of independent countries between 1950 and 1975. By far the largest resettlement in the West has been by refugees from Vietnam, Laos, and Cambodia in the United States. Between the fall of Saigon in 1975 and 1990, one million refugees from the region settled in the United States. But such movements to the West are exceptional. The great mass of refugees are stranded in poor Third World countries of first refuge.

3. International labor-market systems have emerged in several parts of the world where there is spatial proximity of poor, labor-surplus countries to rich countries with labor shortages in menial occupations. This is the basis of emigration from Mexico and Central America to the United States; from North Africa and Turkey to northern Europe; from Egypt, Jordan, Yemen, India, and Pakistan to Saudi Arabia and the Gulf; from Botswana, Lesotho, and Swaziland to South Africa; and

from Indonesia to Malaysia. While the receiving countries have tried to make such movements strictly temporary, many migrant workers have stayed on to be joined by their families.

The effects of emigration on countries of origin are widely debated. The fact that governments of such countries often initially encouraged, organized, and subsidized emigrants implies that benefits are likely to accrue to the country of origin as well as to the migrants themselves. Pressures on domestic labor markets are eased, and valuable foreign exchange is provided by worker remittances. But there are often problems of demographic imbalance stemming from the selective nature of emigration, with many villages being denuded of young men. At its most acute, emigration can engender a social and economic malaise that George Bernard Shaw recognized in rural Ireland—"a place of futility, failure and endless pointless talk."

[H.R.J.]

See also **Immigration Policies.**

Further Readings

Alonso, W., ed. *Population in an Interacting World.* Cambridge: Harvard UP, 1987.

Guillet, E. *The Great Migration.* Toronto: U of Toronto P, 1963.

ENDOCRINE SYSTEM

The endocrine system is temporally organized, and the concepts of time and rhythm are central to our understanding of how the endocrine system controls the behavior and physiology of vertebrates, including humans. The secretion of hormones and the responses of tissues to the hormones are characterized by important temporal relations that when altered may lead to drastically different consequences. For example, female Syrian hamsters were given injections of insulin at one of four different times of the day for up to nine days. When the hamsters received the insulin at 4:00 P.M. no effects were noticed, but hamsters that received insulin at 10:00 P.M. all died from insulin overdose. Insulin produces a much greater hypoglycemic response at some times of day than at other times. It is apparent that *time* is just as important as *dose* when it comes to the actions of hormones.

Thus, the sensitivity of an organism to a hormone can be expected to vary with the time of the day, that is to say, it is dependent on a circadian rhythm. Circadian rhythms have been found in the effectiveness of thyroxine, a hormone produced by the thyroid gland. For example, tadpoles that resided in water containing thyroxine metamorphosed more rapidly when the thyroxine was present only during the twelve hours of daylight as compared to tadpoles that were in water containing thyroxine only during the twelve hours of nighttime. The time of day with respect to the photoperiod was the crucial factor to understanding thyroxine's ability to induce metamorphosis. Prolactin, a hormone produced by the anterior pituitary gland, has an inhibitory effect on metamorphosis that varies with the time of day. The eventual understanding of many developmental changes in vertebrates will doubtless require a greater understanding of the role of circadian, as well as seasonal and other rhythms.

Already we know that prolactin is an especially important hormone in the temporal organization of vertebrates. The time of the day that prolactin is present in the blood stream in large part determines its function. Prolactin stimulates pigeons to produce cropsac milk, a cheesy mass of sloughed epithelium from the inside of the cropsac which is fed to the young. When prolactin is injected into young pigeons, a cropsac response is obtained at most times of the day, but no response is obtained if the prolactin is injected at dawn! Further study revealed that the rise near dawn in adrenal corticoids in the blood was the determinative factor. The adrenal corticoids were hypothesized to form a *temporal synergism* with prolactin such that the corticoids functioned by setting the phase of the response rhythm to prolactin. Consequently the time lag between corticoid injections and prolactin injections determines the magnitude of the response obtained.

Additional studies on temporal synergism have been performed on a variety of vertebrates, including salamanders such as the spotted newt. Salamanders of this kind are unusual in that they metamorphose twice during their lifetime. The aquatic tadpole metamorphoses into a terrestrial red eft stage. The red eft lives in the woods for a few years and then metamorphoses a second time to become a sexually mature aquatic adult. The migration of the efts back to water before the second metamorphosis, called water drive, was known to be induced by prolactin. However, it was found that a particular time relation of corticosterone and prolactin, the eight-hour relation, was especially effective in causing the water drive.

The most comprehensive application of the concept of temporal synergism has been the research on its regulation of the seasonal cycle of the migratory white-throated sparrow. In this photoperiodic species, the seasonal changes in the length of the photoperiod coupled with seasonal changes in the interpretation of day length (seasonality) cause seasonal changes in fat stores, reproductive development, migratory activity, and orientation of flight. Seasonality is thought to be a consequence of interactions between circadian rhythms. Experiments showed that the seasonal progression of physiological and behavioral changes could be induced by timed injections of corticosterone and prolactin. Thus, the spring conditions of fattening, migratory activity oriented northward, and a developing reproductive system were elicited by daily injections of corticosterone and prolactin separated by a twelve-hour interval. The summer conditions of lean fat stores, no migratory activity, and a regressed reproductive system were induced by daily injections of corticosterone and prolactin separated by an eight-hour interval. Finally, the fall conditions of fattening, migratory activity oriented southward, and a regressed reproductive system were elicited by daily injections of the hormones separated by a four-hour interval. Assays of the circadian rhythms of corticosterone and prolactin in wild sparrows has revealed similar patterns in the timing of natural hormone levels. Thus, the time lag between the circadian releases of hormones in the sparrows is the critical factor to be considered when investigating the regulation of seasonal changes.

In the case of mammals, a similar role for temporal synergism has been discovered. Syrian hamsters, which have a distinct seasonal cycle in fat stores, reproductive development, and hibernation, were demonstrated to change their seasonal state in response to different temporal relations of daily injections of corticosterone and prolactin. The twelve-hour relation of corticosterone and prolactin was found to inhibit reproductive development and the twenty-hour relation of the hormones inhibited fattening. Interestingly, the twenty-hour relation of these same hormones prevented hibernation in the thirteen-lined ground squirrel. Properly timed injections of cortisol and prolactin reduced obesity, hyperinsulinaemia (abnormally high blood insulin levels), and insulin resistance in the Syrian hamster. These effects persisted ten weeks after the termination of the adrenal corticoid and prolactin injections. Also, bromocriptine,

an inhibitor of prolactin, when given at 8:00 A.M. and 2:00 P.M. caused a reduction in fat stores in Syrian hamsters. In humans, timed bromocriptine administration reduced body fat stores in obese subjects and hyperglycemia in Type II diabetics.

It has been discovered that the neurotransmitters serotonin and dopamine, which modify corticosterone and prolactin rhythms, can be pharmacologically manipulated and thereby regulate temporal synergisms of hormones. Again, these studies have involved a wide variety of vertebrates. Potentially, temporal synergisms and the concept of time properly used in the giving of medications may alleviate much human suffering from conditions such as obesity, diabetes, atherosclerosis, and immune disorders. The possible application of the concept of temporal synergisms to human medicine is now in the clinical trial stage.

[J.T.B.]

See also **Chronobiology; Biological Rhythms in Epidemiology and Pharmacology.**

FURTHER READINGS

Burns, J.T., and A.H. Meier. "A Circadian Rhythm in Insulin Overdose in the Golden Hamster (*Mesocricetus auratus*)." *Chronopharmacology and Chronotherapeutics*. Ed. Charles A. Walker, Charles M. Winget, and Karem F.A. Soliman. Tallahassee: Florida A & M University, 1981. 315–318.

——. "The Phase Relation of Corticosterone and Prolactin Injections as a Factor in the Inhibition of Hibernation in the Thirteen-lined Ground Squirrel, *Citellus tridecemlineatus*." *Annual Review of Chronopharmacology* 5 (1988): 57–60.

Burns, John T., Renee Patyna, and Simone Ryland. "A Circadian Rhythm in the Effect of Thyroxine in the Stimulation of Metamorphosis in the African Clawed Frog, *Xenopus laevis*." *Journal of Interdisciplinary Cycle Research* 18 (1987): 293–296.

Joseph, M.M., and Albert H. Meier. "Circadian Component in the Fattening and Reproductive Responses to Prolactin in the Hamster." *Proceedings of the Society for Experimental Biology and Medicine* 146 (1974): 1150–1155.

Meier, Albert H. "Daily Hormone Rhythms in the White-Throated Sparrow." *American Scientist* 61 (1973): 184–187.

Meier, A.H., A.H. Cincotta, and W.C. Lovell. "Timed Bromocriptine Administration Reduces Body Fat Stores in Obese Subjects and Hyperglycemia in Type II Diabetes." *Experientia* 48 (1992): 248–253.

Meier, Albert H., Louis E. Garcia, and M.M. Joseph. "Corticosterone Phases a Circadian Water-Drive Response to Prolactin in the Spotted Newt, *Notopthalmus viridescens*." *Biological Bulletin* 141 (1971): 331–336.

Meier, A.H., et al. "Circadian Variations in Sensitivity of the Pigeon Cropsac to Prolactin." *Journal of Interdisciplinary Cycle Research* 2 (1971): 161–171.

Wilson, John M., and Albert H. Meier. "Resetting the Annual Cycle with Timed Daily Injections of 5–hydroxytryptophan and L-dihydroxyphenylalanine in Syrian Hamsters." *Chronobiology* 6 (1989): 113–121.

ENDOSYMBIOSIS

THE ORIGIN OF COMPLEX CELLS

Complex cells (cells with nuclei and other specialized subcellular compartments) evolved 1 to 2 billion years ago when simple bacteria cells (without compartments) joined together in symbiotic associations. Organisms composed of complex cells (collectively known as the eukaryotes) include animals, plants, fungi, and protocists. Mitochondria, subcellular compartments devoted to the respiratory metabolism of food molecules, are found in nearly all eukaryotes. Mitochondria apparently originated as free-living respiring bacteria that were "acquired" as internal symbionts by other bacteria that are involved in a somewhat less efficient type of metabolism, namely fermentation. Chloroplasts are subcellular compartments, usually filled with the green pigment chlorophyll and in which photosynthesis (the synthesis of food using energy from the sun) occurs. The ancestors of chloroplasts were free-living photosynthetic bacteria, also acquired by a fermenting host cell. Motility structures such as sperm tails and cilia may have originated as free-living motile (spiral-shaped) bacteria which attached to the fermenting host as external symbionts.

TIMING IN COMPLEX CELLS

Cells composed by the symbiotic association of once free-living simple cells have a unique and fascinating problem: How do the independent rhythms and cycles of the simple cells become coordinated to form an efficient and well-organized complex cell? Mitochondria, chloroplasts, and motility structures are in fact extraordinarily well-coordinated subunits of an intricate whole. It is not possible to observe the initial steps in the evolution of this coordination, which occurred 1 to 2 billion years ago, but it is possible to gain an understanding of this coordination by observing symbioses currently in a state of early evolution. One example is the recent (in the past twenty years) establishment of a symbiosis between amoebae and formerly pathogenic bacteria in the laboratory of Kwang

Jeon. At first, pathogenic bacteria invaded Jeon's cultures of amoebae, killing most of them. One of the characteristics of any pathogen is the lack of coordination of its reproductive cycle with that of the host. The resulting overproduction of pathogens drains host energy and resources and may ultimately kill the host.

Any pathogen may be checked by having its rate of reproduction more closely coordinated with that of its host. This seems to be what occurred next in Jeon's amoebae, that is, bacterial replication began to approximate more closely the reproductive cycle of the host cells. Those few amoebae cells not killed in the initial infection apparently had preexisting genes enabling such a coordination to begin. Perhaps this could be defined as "resistance." There is an advantage both to host and to the bacteria. The host experiences less severe pathogenicity. The invading bacteria, if they can keep their host alive and if they succeed in reproducing only when the host reproduces, thus ensuring that they will be passed to the next generation but will not overrun the cell, have acquired a much more stable and dependable environment. This may be the general evolutionary trend for many pathogens—that is, the advantage of coordinating reproductive cycles may outweigh the advantages of quickly reproducing and having to abandon one host for another.

It may be that lethal or near-lethal pathogens are actually recent pathogens and that milder pathogenicity or nonpathogenicity indicates a long evolution with the host. In the case of Jeon's amoebae the relationship between host and bacteria has evolved into a mutually obligate symbiosis. The bacteria, of course, have the advantage of a stable environment, and the amoebae, strangely enough, have evolved a dependency on their bacterial associates. How or why such a dependence could have evolved will be addressed in the next section, which returns to mitochondria and chloroplasts as examples, since more is known about their genetics.

GENETIC INTIMACY AND COORDINATION

Mitochondria and chloroplasts have retained some of the genes of their once autonomous past. These genes have undergone an interesting evolution. Many genes have been lost, such as those coding for characteristics necessary in a free-living bacterium (for example, cell walls), but not in the stable and protective environment of a host cell. Other genes have been lost because they produce similar products to ones being coded for and made by the host and are therefore redundant. Symbionts that accidentally lose unnecessary genes have an advantage in that they can reproduce somewhat more efficiently than if they were weighed down with extra sequences. Most interesting, however, are genes that have been transferred from the symbionts to the host via one of the many mechanisms by which genes are moved across species boundaries. These include "jumping" genes and viruses, both of which can pick up other genes and transfer them, blurring the species boundaries in symbiotic associations.

One result of gene movements is that certain important structures in mitochondria and chloroplasts such as "ATPases," which help cells store energy and which are coded by several genes, are now formed cooperatively by the host and the mitochondria or chloroplasts. That is, some ATPase subunits are coded for by genes held by the nucleus of the host cell and some subunits are coded for by genes retained by the symbionts (chloroplasts and mitochondria). The fact that cooperation is needed to construct an essential structure like the ATPase means that the reproductive cycle of the partners can never be too far out of synchrony. Indeed, mitochondria and chloroplasts are known to divide with remarkable coordination with the reproductive cycle of their hosts. The shared coding not only prevents the cell from being overrun by its symbionts (now unlikely, though in the early evolution a possibility) but also prevents the symbionts from being "left behind" by the host in the event that the host should begin to divide more rapidly, diluting out its partners.

In the case of Jeon's amoebae, less is known about the genetic coordination between the partners, but it is understood that in the brief twenty-year period in which the partners have been evolving, the genes of the host nucleus have undergone changes resulting in an obligate relationship, presumably of advantage to both.

THE ORIGIN OF CIRCADIAN RHYTHMS?

It has been hypothesized that circadian rhythms may have evolved at the same time as complex cells as a mechanism for coordinating the timing of the partners. Circadian rhythms are found only in organisms with complex cells and are cycles of activity of approximately twenty-four hours (< Latin *circa*, about; *dies*, a day) which may be reset by some external input (such as sunrise).

The idea that circadian rhythms originated as mechanisms for coordinating symbionts is an appealing although untested concept. It has been demonstrated that even a slight deviation from a twenty-four-hour cycle will cause a drift in periodicity that might result in a particular cell becoming completely out of synchrony from other cells (with slightly different drifts). Cells that can take cues from each other are more likely to be able to synchronize and the opportunities for chemical communication are certainly there in intimate symbiotic associations. Furthermore, cells that can stay in cycle with some highly regular astronomical event (such as sunrise) are enabled to resist the tendency to drift even as partners drifting together.

[B.D.D.]

See also **Cellular Rhythms; Chronobiology; Circadian Pacemakers; Molecular and Biochemical Rhythms; Molecular Genetics and Biological Rhythms.**

FURTHER READINGS

Dyer, B.D. "Symbiosis and Organismal Boundaries." *American Zoologist* 29 (1989): 1057–1060.

Jeon, K. "Amoeba and X-Bacteria: Symbiont Acquisition and Possible Species Change." *Symbiosis as a Source of Evolutionary Innovation.* Ed. L. Margulis and R. Fester. Cambridge: MIT P, 1991. 118–131.

Kippert, F. "Endosymbiotic Coordination, Intracellular Calcium Signaling, and the Origin of Endogenous Rhythms." *Endocytobiology III.* Ed. J.J. Lee and J.F. Frederick. New York: Annals of the New York Academy of Sciences, 1987. 476–495.

Margulis, L. *Symbiosis in Cell Evolution.* 2nd ed. New York: W.H. Freeman, 1993.

ENVIRONMENT AND ECOLOGY

Time in the natural environment is characterized by rhythmic variation, synchronization, and an all-embracing, complex web of interconnections. Linear sequences take place, but these are part of a wider network of cycles as well as finely tuned and synchronized temporal relations where ultimately everything connects to everything else: the structure of an ecological system is temporal and its parts resonate with the whole, and vice versa. Rhythmicity, therefore, forms nature's silent pulse. All organisms from single cells to ecosystems display interdependent rhythmic behavior. Some of this rhythmicity constitutes the organism's unique identity, some relates to its life cycle, some binds the organism to the rhythms of the universe, and some functions as a physiological clock by which living beings "tell" cosmic time.

The natural environment is thus a temporal realm of orchestrated rhythms of varying speeds and intensities as well as temporally constituted uniqueness. It is a realm of organisms with the capacity for remembering and anticipating, of beings that time their actions, synchronize their interactions, and reckon time. The very essence of life, furthermore, is growth and evolution. In organic processes, therefore, the entropic principle changes its direction from decay, uniformity, and heat-death to growth, variation, and life. This involves the creation and regeneration of time. The use and depletion of time are counterbalanced by its generation and replenishment: decay is compensated by repair through healing and by "superrepair" through the birth-death cycle. Moreover, natural processes vary with context. This means that general principles find unique expression: the rhythmically changing constellations of the stars never repeat themselves in exactly the same way. Springtime, the period when a large proportion of land-based nature comes to life, is incomparably different from wintertime when so much lies dormant. Lastly, a vast range of time spans coexist simultaneously. These extend from the imperceptibly fast to the unimaginatively slow, covering processes that last from nanoseconds to millennia.

Clock time dominates contemporary industrial and industrializing societies. Due to its powerful effects on our social lives and institutions, we are inclined to lose sight of the complexity of times in our environment and to neglect the fact that we too are "clocks": due to its pervasiveness, we tend to ignore that we *are* timepieces beating the multiple pulses of our earth, that we oscillate in synchrony with nature's rhythms. Once we assimilate this knowledge, however, the discrepancy becomes apparent between the artifactual time and its sources. We begin to recognize that our machine-based rhythms beat to a different pulse from the rhythms within which they are embedded. Our own multiple physiological clocks, for example, vary in intensity and rate. Their speed alters with both internal and external conditions, while invariance and uniformity are the characteristics of the artifactual clock time that underpins our contemporary social organization. Rhythmicity and body clocks are part of that which the mechanical clock symbolizes. The human device, however, is out of sync with its multiple sources: idealized invariance, motion without change, and spatialized time are at odds with the temporal, variant, creative, and generative time on which the artifactual time is based.

This discrepancy relates to wider problems. Many of our technical and chemical inventions, for example, are copied from nature. In contrast to the originals, however, the replicas are created in invariant form, as fixed in time and abstracted from the give-and-take of the ecologically interconnected world. Problems arise when the principles of the originals and the copies no longer coincide, when the replicas exclude cybernetic and metabolic principles and the symbiotic relationship of beings with their environments. The human products, created as isolated things rather than interactive, mutually dependent, contextual processes, end up on rubbish dumps instead of contributing to the life-generating activity of our planet. This dilemma extends beyond the artifact copies of nature to the products of human culture generally: cultural products are not temporal, rhythmic, interconnected, and mutually dependent in the same way as is the living environment within which they have been created and upon which they have such a devastating effect. This applies particularly to the products of industrial and industrializing societies. Steam engines, cars, and nuclear power "plants," for example, are rhythmically organized and finely tuned *within* each isolated system, but they are *not* temporally embedded within, and explicitly connected to, the rhythmic structure of their environments. Resource depletion, pollution, and degradation of the environment are some of the inevitable outcomes of the neglect of the temporality of life, of variance, cycles of change and context dependence, of ecological connectedness and generative time. Our present ecological crises, in other words, have a strong temporal dimension.

Beyond the problems associated with the isolation of human products from the interdependencies of nature, present economic strategies tend to be incompatible with environmental concerns. The Western association of time with money, for example, fits uneasily with ecological principles such as durability, sustainability and reusability. Where time is commodified (see **Social Theory**), speed becomes an important economic value—the faster goods move through the economy the better—it increases profit, enhances the Gross Domestic Product, and shows up positively on the corporate and national balance sheet. Moreover, in our present economic system, labor and time tend to be expensive, materials relatively cheap. A very different picture emerges when speed is linked not to profit but to energy use. When time is associated with energy, we become aware that the faster something moves or functions, the higher tends to be its use of resources: it transforms speed from something to be aspired into a liability. Tied to energy, speed does not mean profit. Rather, it constitutes a deficit on the balance sheet. Such a shift in perspective illuminates an otherwise latent tension between economic and ecological concerns and shows how the combination of a high regard for speed and a low value of natural resources facilitates economic systems of planned obsolescence, waste, and pollution.

Closely connected to the association of time with money is the short-term approach to audits. Here too, the picture changes dramatically when, instead, we trace the products' existence from their inception to the rubbish dump, when we take account of the pathways and allow for different intensities to enter our calculations. Once more, clock time plays an important role in our restricted vision and our insensitivity to variance. A time measure that has been standardized and separated from context is by definition not integrated into the rhythms of nature and the varying intensities of processes. A long-term approach to audits and provision for time to become reembodied and recontextualized, in contrast, makes it obvious that most of the irreparable damage to the environment occurs during the early phases of a product, during the extraction of raw materials. Furthermore, the different temporal perspective forces us to recognize and to accept responsibility for the long-term and largely invisible effects of our products. Nuclear power is a case in point. Radiation is a naturally occurring phenomenon, but with the human production of nuclear power we have intensified the concentration and once more produced an ecological hazard, something that cannot be benignly reintegrated into the living environment. Plutonium, for example, has a half-life of 24,000 years. This means that approximately 720 future generations should feature in our contemporary policies, since our generation is responsible for those long-term effects that will determine the present of future generations for thousands of years.

[B.A.]

See also **Social Theory.**

FURTHER READINGS

Adam, Barbara. *Time and Social Theory.* Cambridge: Polity Press, 1990.

Bateson, Gregory. *Mind and Nature: A Necessary Unity.* Glasgow: Fontana, 1980.

Brown, L.R. *The State of the World 1991.* London: Earthscan, 1991.

World Commission on Environment and Development. *Our Common Future.* Oxford: Oxford UP, 1987.

Young, Michael. *The Metronomic Society.* Cambridge: Harvard UP, 1988.

ESCHATOLOGY

"Eschatology," concerned with the "last things" or the purpose and end of history, developed in the Judeo-Christian tradition and has been expressed in many forms. Eschatology not only informs history with cosmic importance, making it the finite matrix within which God justifies his ways to mankind and contends with the spiritual and physical manifestations of evil, but it also transforms time: because it portends the "last things"—God's direct intervention in the world—eschatology describes the culmination of finitude, the cessation of time itself, and its subsumption under God's eternal present. Thus, the climactic stages of eschatological time—apocalypse, millennium, Armageddon, and Last Judgment—are directed, providentially, to the climax of temporality.

JEWISH ESCHATOLOGY

From Israel's profound conviction that Yahweh acted purposefully in history and guided events toward a redemptive goal emerged the idea of a covenant made between them and a god who assured them of material blessings, of victories over their enemies, and of the Promised Land. During the reign of David, Israel's eschatological consciousness took definite form, notably in the Book of Amos, where we hear of the expectation of the day of Yahweh, of God's intervention into temporality (5:18). Though Amos foresees the elimination of Israel's enemies, he still has a dire warning for his apostate people: "Woe unto you that desire the day of the LORD! to what end is it for you? the day of the LORD is darkness, and not light" (Amos 5:18). Along with mixed messages of redemption and chastisement was the promise of a Davidic kingdom that would rule eternally, an eschatological motif that can be found in the Psalms (Psalm 2:1–12).

From the eighth to the sixth century B.C., this sense of a nationalized eschatology was transformed in the prophetic works. The prophets sanctioned the Jewish people for their apostasy, warning that the day of Yahweh would be one of retribution, of sorrow, and of judgment. Prophets such as Amos expected this chastisement to occur, historically, through Assyrian or Babylonian hegemony. Although the prophets did not repudiate a hope for the future, they placed greater emphasis on the need for chastisement and purification, and they lamented the encroachment of paganism on the Jewish liturgy. So, under these conditions, Jewish eschatology became somber and foreboding. In Isaiah, there is the warning that the Jewish people would undergo a purification and that only a remnant would experience this promised future (I Isaiah 21–26). Isaiah's description of the coming of an ideal David became the basis of the messianic tradition, once again projecting a note of hope into their prospectivism: "For unto us a child is born, unto us a son is given: and the government shall be upon his shoulder: and his name shall be called Wonderful, Counsellor, The mighty God, The everlasting Father, The Prince of Peace" (Isaiah 9:6). In Jeremiah, the breaking of the covenant once again threatened castigation; however, there was still hope in the distant future that Yahweh would give Israel a new covenant (31:31–4). Despite the changing tone from eschatological expectation to retributive anticipation, Jewish eschatology retained the central theme that God would redeem His chosen nation.

The yearning for God's intervention became acute with the Exile. Isaiah, in particular, speaks of an imminent time when Yahweh would free His people from bondage and resettle them (13:1–14:23). In Isaiah II, the edict of Cyrus in 538 B.C., which permitted the exiles to return to Jerusalem, was hailed as a new Exodus and a turning point in history; once again, the eschatological promise became popular.

CHRISTIAN ESCHATOLOGY

Eschatology is central to the New Testament and to the teachings of Christ. The New Testament writers affirm that Jesus is the eschatological hope of Israel fulfilled, and that in Christ the power of God had indeed intervened into the world to bring on the future age (Acts 3:12–26). The suffering, death, and Resurrection of Christ constitutes the decisive victory of good over evil, reversing the entire course of history (Revelation 5:12). The early church saw itself as living in the end of time, as an eschatological community, and as the inheritor of a new covenant prophesied by Jeremiah (2 Corinthians 3:4). Gradually, the church began to understand that this eschatology was not imminent, and that the victory of Christ's kingdom was still to come. The eschatological orientation of the

Gospel, however, was never lost, finding its greatest expression in the Book of Revelation, composed by St. John of Patmos in A.D. 93. This, too, is an apocalypse indebted to Jewish apocalyptic literature and uses symbolic language to describe the prospective consummation of historical time.

In the Christian world, apocalyptic eschatology also promised a new and better world under God's direct auspices. At the time of the first millennium, many Christians awaited Christ's imminent return because the thousand-year period spoken of in Revelation was drawing to a close. Relying on the Book of Revelation and on other biblical texts, theological historians such as Joachim of Floris constructed periodical schemes, claiming that his own age was on the eschatological threshold and was the last. Social, political, and economic inequities fueled the eschatological impulse. Before the Reformation, those dissatisfied with the church would indulge in eschatology, whereas, after the Reformation, many Protestant thinkers, most notably Martin Luther, identified the antichrist with the Pope and translated the age-old conflict of good and evil into one between the Roman church and Protestantism. Under the influence of the humanists, however, apocalyptic eschatology was largely discredited, although it flared up with major consequences in revolutionary circles, one of which was led by Thomas Müntzer (1489?–1525). Wherever minorities lived under social and religious oppression, and whenever plagues and wars erupted, eschatological forecasters arose, motivated by zealous piety and the overbearing desire for a better future.

From the mid-eighteenth to early nineteenth century, despite the development and use of analytical research methods and of a secularized approach to history, theological eschatology (as opposed to idealistic, socially progressive, or evolutionary variants) continued to appear. Many sects developed eschatological doctrines. The Adventists, for instance, subscribed to William Miller's computation that Christ would return to earth in 1843–1844 to found the millennium. And the Jehovah's Witness movement was based on Charles T. Russell's assertion in 1835 that Christ had returned to earth secretly in 1874 and would establish the millennium in 1914. Revelation 20, therefore, continued to be the seminal text for eschatological speculation. Idealistic and secular currents in nineteenth-century philosophy, notably among the Germans, influenced English theological historians. In *The Kingdom of Christ* (1842), F.D. Maurice interprets the idea of the imminent kingdom idealistically, envisioning God's reign in the immanent moral perfection of mankind, and hoping for the progress of the kingdom of God in the improvement of the social order.

Twentieth-century proponents of apocalyptic eschatology focus on Christ's life as the central and determining factor of history. For example, Jürgen Moltmann, in the *Evangelische Kommentare* (1968), formulates a theology of hope which focuses on the last things and on the idea that the Resurrection heralds the amelioration of society. And Karl Barth reconsiders the nature and purpose of Christian revelation as an insight into existential truth: that time can be apprehended as eternity, conflating past and future. The contemplation of the *eschaton*, therefore, transforms present consciousness with enlivened hope and freedom.

Engendered by discontent and supported by faith, eschatological speculation informs time with divine purpose and with the possibility of redemption. Paradoxically, this engendering implies the consummation of the finite world.

[C.D.]

See also **Apocalypse; Millenarianism; Prophecy.**

FURTHER READINGS

Bowman, John Wick. "Eschatology of the New Testament." *The Interpreter's Dictionary of the Bible: An Illustrated Encyclopedia.* Ed. George Arthur Buttrick et al. 4 vols. New York: Abingdon P, 1962. 2:135a–140a.

Jenni, Ernst. "Eschatology of the Old Testament." *The Interpreter's Dictionary of the Bible.* 2:126b–133a.

Martin, F. "Eschatology (in the Bible)." *New Catholic Encyclopedia.* Ed. Rev. William J. McDonald. 18 vols. New York, 1967. 5:524b–533b.

Schmithals, Walter. "Eschatology." *Dictionary of the History of Ideas: Studies of Selected Pivotal Ideas.* Ed. Philip P. Wiener. 5 vols. New York: Charles Scribner's Sons, 1973. 2:154b–161b.

Williams, M.E. "Eschatology (Theological Treatment)." *New Catholic Encyclopedia.* 5:533b–538a.

ETHNICITY AND AGING

The future for minority groups among the elderly in Western societies can to a large extent be foreseen by past and current trends pertaining to such processes as international migration, settlement, racial discrimination, changing family structures, and the achievement of old age in a second homeland. The most significant factor for minorities among the elderly is the dual experience of racism and ageism, often referred to as "double" or "triple" jeopardy when combined with the effects of social class or gender discrimination.

The concepts of ethnicity, "race," and culture have undergone various changes in their usage and meaning over time. Currently, the construction of ethnicity focuses on language, cultural patterns, and beliefs and attitudes. Frequently stress is placed on "apparent" attributes such as food and dress. In this sense we all have ethnicity and carry specific ethnic identities which do not remain static over time. With international migration and the emergence of new states, ethnic identities and diversity are expanding across the world. However, ethnicity is frequently associated with minorities and in particular with racial and religious minorities. As A. Sivanandan indicates, discussion of ethnicity often omits the forces of racism and intergroup power relations, implying that multiethnic equality can be achieved with cultural adjustments. For minority elders, problems of racism, poverty, communication, and inaccessible welfare services are intensified by their minority and migrant status. Naina Patel has argued that ethnicity, when viewed in the context of power relations between majority and minority groups, is a significant determinant of how old age is experienced, irrespective of whether the individuals came as migrants, refugees, or dependents.

ETHNIC IDENTIFICATION AND THE MEANING OF OLD AGE

Membership of an ethnic group with its shared culture, customs, language, and meanings provides an important resource and protection against the problems of old age. Different societies place different values, interpretations, and expressions on the past, present, and future. Those minorities which migrated from areas where life expectancy was lower brought with them a concept of old age defined by their past experience. Old age may have meant forty-five years in one society, but can mean seventy or eighty years in another, and may well be higher still in future societies.

PSYCHOLOGICAL EFFECTS

Minority groups among the elderly experience a curtailment of their roles, including a loss of close family and community ties. In the past, they would have been assigned a higher status and revered in a manner that is no longer the case. This is the result of changing family patterns and an increasing emphasis on individualism. For those elders coming to a new country to join their children as "dependents," an absence of roles, the impact of new ways and values (particularly at a time when due to aging, changes may be more difficult to accept), and the frequent inability to communicate in the language of the majority leaves them isolated and disillusioned. There is frequently little possibility of leading an active and independent life. Many such migrants had also aspired to return "home" in their early migration period, and hoped to have earned the wherewithal to make this possible. These hopes are seldom achieved as their families usually settled in low income occupations with little potential to save for old age. As a result the wish to retire "home" will have become a distant reality which has been referred to as the "myth of return."

SOCIAL AND ECONOMIC CONDITIONS
Ethnicity also functions as an active force in determining the social and economic well-being of minority groups among the elderly. Colin Brown's major study of employment and housing conducted in the United Kingdom found that there were wide differentials in pay and an unequal distribution of black and white workers by sector and industry. A disproportionately large number of black people occupied housing in poorer areas. The earlier experience of employment earnings and housing impacts directly on the present income potential and consequent quality of life of minority groups among the elderly. Their poverty is further compounded by a failure to claim benefits (where they exist) because of language difficulties, lack of knowledge of the benefits system, or an inability to deal with officialdom. Similar findings in the United States by Steven P. Wallace suggest that because of the poverty faced by older African Americans, particularly women, a greater reliance is placed on families and informal resources as providers of care. In this respect there has been a growing concern and a developing awareness regarding the need to provide social and health-care services which are culturally appropriate and institutionally indiscriminate to ensure full access by minority groups among older people. Among such people there is now an increasing awareness of their particular status and consequently greater demands for improved rights and entitlements. Should there only be a slow improvement in their circumstances, however, there is a danger that they may develop pessimistic expectations and anticipate that the ultimate fulfillment of their needs will not be satisfied in their own lifetimes.

[N.P.]

See also **Aging and Time; Gender Differences in Aging; Social Gerontology.**

FURTHER READINGS
Brown, Colin. *Black and White: The Third PSI Survey.* Aldershot: Gower, 1984.

Norman, Alison. *Triple Jeopardy: Growing Old in a Second Homeland.* Policy Studies on Ageing, No. 3. London: Centre for Policy on Ageing, 1985.

Patel, Naina. *A "Race" Against Time? Social Services Provision to Black Elders.* London: Runnymede Trust, 1990.

Sivanandan, A. "Black Struggles Against Racism." *Setting the Context for Change.* Ed. Curriculum Development Project Steering Group. Anti-Racist Social Work Education Series, No. 1. London: Central Council for Education and Training in Social Work, 1991. 28–45.

Wallace, Steven P. "The Political Economy of Health Care for Elderly Blacks." *International Journal of Health Services* 20.4 (1990): 665–680.

EUROPEAN TIMEKEEPERS IN CHINA AND JAPAN

From a comparatively early period, time in east Asian countries was measured only by means of the sundial and the water clock. In about the sixth century it was achieved also by means of burning incense known as *hsiang-yin* and *hsiang-chuan* in China and as *kōbandokei* in Japan. Although the Chinese had developed sophisticated timekeepers for astronomical purposes as early as A.D. 1090, natural and political events erased all knowledge of them in succeeding centuries, and by about the time that the mechanical clock emerged in the Western world late in the thirteenth century, the east Asian countries had returned to the use of simple timekeepers. Time and its measurement had become little more than philosophical preoccupations.

The first European mechanical clocks in East Asia were introduced in Japan by Jesuit missionaries desiring to establish missions. Among the gifts presented in 1549 to Yoshitaka Ouchi, governor of Yamaguchi, by a Jesuit mission led by Francis Xavier was a clock provided for the occasion by the Portuguese viceroy to India. A short time later, a second clock was presented to General Toyotomi Hideyoshi, ruler of all Japan, and yet another was brought later in the sixteenth century by a Jesuit missionary to the

Japanese general and statesman, Iyeyashu, founder of the Tokogawa shōgunate.

In due course, native Japanese craftsmen, assisted by missionaries skilled in the practical arts, used their metalworking skills to make clocks based on the foreign models, first producing copies of them and then developing others having a character of their own. Eventually, Japanese clocks were to assume a mechanical form and artistic character recognized as indigenous to Japan.

European clocks were first introduced into China also by Jesuit missionaries who had established the first Christian mission at Macao and later at Chaoching. In 1583, while seeking means to influence ruling authorities and ultimately permission from the emperor for evangelization by the missionaries, the Jesuits learned that the Chinese viceroy Ch'en Jui wished to acquire a "sing-ringing bell," as mechanical clocks were described by the Chinese. The missionaries sought timepieces in Macao without success and then engaged a local Indian blacksmith having knowledge of clockmaking to return with them to Chaoching, where in 1584 he constructed such a clock for the viceroy. Having petitioned for permission to visit the imperial court at Peking to present gifts to Emperor Wan, one of their number, Matteo Ricci, set out from Macao with companions and after many delays and obstacles finally reached the city. Eventually, in January 1601, the foreigners were summoned to the court. Following many postponements, Ricci presented two clocks for the emperor at the court. One was a small spring-driven gilt bronze chamber clock and the other was a large iron tower clock elaborately decorated with figures of dragons and eagles. Pleased with the gifts, the emperor assigned four eunuchs from the college of mathematics to be taught by the missionaries how to maintain the timepieces. Inasmuch as there was no suitable space in the palace for the fall of the weights of the tower clock, Ricci and his companions erected a tower to accommodate it outside the palace walls. Some time later Ricci presented the emperor with a spring-driven table clock encased in gilt metal. The "clocks that struck of themselves," as they were described by the Chinese, had made a tremendous impression on the imperial court and subsequently Ricci personally constructed a brass clock for the emperor which struck the Chinese double-hours twice daily. With support from the Pope in Rome, the Jesuits established a library in 1618 in Peking containing works in all fields of knowledge and featuring science and mechanics in particular. In 1627, a work in the Chinese language was produced entitled, *A Description and Illustration of the Mechanical Marvels of the West*, and describing Western science and technology.

Aware of the imperial proclivity for horological curiosities, missionaries and papal envoys arriving in China thereafter, and diplomatic missions to the Far East, featured among their gifts more and more complicated timepieces, musical clocks, and automata, competing with each other in the splendor of their horological gifts of great complexity. Missionaries of several nationalities who were sent to Peking thereafter were carefully selected for their mechanical skills and their ability to construct clocks and automata. A number of particularly talented French missionaries who were employed at the court were kept fully occupied producing clocks and automata of considerable complexity. Notable among these missionaries were Frère Jacques Brocard, Frère Valentin Chalier, and Frère Charles Slaviczek. Some of their works were masterpieces of horological invention. Chalier spent four months constructing a magnificent timepiece indicating and striking Western hours, minutes, and seconds on one dial and the Chinese mansions of the night on another. So pleased was the emperor with it that he spared no expense in its decoration, and frequently demonstrated it to members of the court, implying that it may have been his own invention. Frère Jean Matthieu de Ventavon designed and constructed an automaton motivated by clockwork in the form of two men carrying a vase between them as they walked. Later, he modified a writing automaton created in Switzerland by Jacques Droz so that it would write messages in the Manchu, Mongolian, and Tibetan languages. A similar writing android was later created by the cooperative efforts of Augustine missionary Pietro Adeodato and the French Lazarist, Frère Charles Paris. Particularly favored at court for their many horological achievements were the Frères coadjuteurs Gilles Thebault and François-Louis Stadlin. The imperial court's preoccupation with horological toys in this period was so considerable that a French missionary complained in his correspondence that he was kept so occupied repairing watches for the Chinese mandarins that he had not been able to find time to study the language.

In 1680, Emperor K'ang Hsi established a series of twenty-seven imperial manufactories within the palace precincts in Peking for the production and practice of a wide range of arts and crafts and other skills, including mapping and planning, cloisonné enamels, glass working, working in tin (paktong?), helmet making, working in jade, gold filigree, gilding, and a manufactory for inkstones, all operating under the board of works. The emperor invited practiced craftsmen from all parts of the empire to staff the studios. Interested in having native craftsmen trained in watch and clockmaking, the emperor established one of the manufactories exclusively for that purpose. There, under Jesuit supervision, Chinese craftsmen learned to repair and maintain the imperial court's numerous timepieces and subsequently to duplicate some of them. They began to produce clocks and watches copied from European examples, and although many of their products were well designed and artfully decorated, they were inferior in technical aspects. A difficulty encountered was the production of sufficiently supple and elastic clock springs; it may have been for this reason that the majority of timepieces produced were weight-driven. By the end of K'ang Hsi's reign the atelier was manned with a large staff, reported to include 100 native workers in 1736. The atelier remained active through subsequent reigns to near the end of the eighteenth century. The clock manufactory underwent substantial expansion under Ch'ien Lung and became professionalized, serving also as a training center for clockmakers who would later be sent out into the provinces. Following Ch'ien Lung's abdication in 1796, the imperial ateliers were terminated and the remaining buildings were destroyed by fire in 1869.

Soon after they had begun to produce timepieces, the Chinese—as had the Japanese—gradually evolved clock forms which were distinctively their own. At first their products demonstrated a strong Western influence on the style of case. Though they used fine Asian woods, they employed altar shapes of Italian, Spanish, and Portuguese prototypes, often decorating the cases with mother-of-pearl or jade inlay. The pagoda form eventually replaced the European case shapes and Chinese-produced clocks assumed subtle East Asian appearances. By the late eighteenth century Chinese clockmakers flourished in several trade centers. The monopoly was conceded, at least for a time, to those Chinese craftsmen who had become Christians and to whom the missionaries had taught the craft. By the beginning of the nineteenth century clockmaking had become a familiar art, and in

1809, the first clockmaking manual in Chinese was published. In Nanking and Canton, as many as 200 craftsmen were engaged in commercial horological production at the same time.

Simultaneous with the development of a native capability to produce timepieces in China, a trade specifically in such items was being developed between China and England and the Continent. By the beginning of the eighteenth century, the East India Company had established a profitable trade by exporting opium from India to China and exporting tea, spices, and silk from China to England. The taste of the Chinese court for elaborately decorated clocks and watches with complicated movements having become known, craftsmen, primarily in England, France, and Switzerland, responded to the new market with a new type of export consisting of jeweled horological toys rendered in gold or silver and decorated with precious gems and containing movements of considerable complexity. Among the most talented of the English artisans who produced outstanding works for this trade was James Cox, and others well-known were William Anthony, Charles Magniac, and William Hughes. In 1783, Cox's son, John Henry Cox, established an outpost in the British compound in Canton for the sale of his father's products.

The horological gifts brought by religious missions to the Chinese imperial court were so well received and their success so well publicized in Europe that forthcoming diplomatic missions to the Far East followed suit with similar gifts. The mission of Lord MacCartney, sent to China on behalf of King George III near the end of the eighteenth century, included two professional clockmakers in the party to maintain the clocks and scientific instruments being brought as gifts to the emperor. The ambassador from the Netherlands stopped at Canton en route to Peking to purchase clocks from the shop of James Cox's successor for presentation at the imperial court. The timepieces were damaged in the course of the journey and when Charles H. Petitpierre was unable to repair them, the task was assigned to Frère Charles Paris, then the official clockmaker at the imperial court.

By the late eighteenth century, however, the import trade met with strong competition and began to diminish. The products of native Chinese craftsmen, although of inferior quality, were sold at lower prices. Furthermore, Emperor Chia Ch'ing and his court began to take a dim view of the craze for these toys of time, inasmuch as they were no longer rarities, and major restrictions were imposed on their importation. Consequently, European merchants who had established outlets at Canton were forced to extend credit and to increase prices. The English lost interest in what had become a less than favorable market and gradually abandoned it to the recently arrived representatives of many of the most prominent Swiss watchmaking firms. The Swiss established manufactories in southern Chinese cities and soon organized outlets for the sale of their mass-produced goods directly in port cities in order to reach a different and lucrative market. The Chinese market consequently expanded beyond the imperial court and many imports were sold to Chinese merchants who in turn sold them at retail to mandarins who presented them as gifts to superiors and officials for gaining favors. It became common practice among the wealthy Chinese to wear two watches simultaneously. This led European watchmakers catering to the China trade to produce watches which were duplicates of each other and sold in sets of two. It was the Opium War, which left China impoverished, that was largely responsible for bringing to an end native Chinese clockmaking activities. At the same time, the war also effectively reduced the importation of Swiss and other European timepieces.

A great number of the fabulous timepieces brought to the Chinese imperial court from European missions have survived. The majority of the watches are for the most part in the National Museum of the Chinese Republic in Taipei, Taiwan, while the imperial clock collection is presently in the Clock Museum, formerly the Palace Museum and the Museum of Antiquities in the old Imperial Palace complex of the Forbidden City in Beijing. There a workshop for their maintenance and repair is also maintained. Although less than 200 clocks are on display, it is reported that more than 1000 others are in storage.

Many more clocks and automata were brought to China than to Japan, not only as gifts but also as objects of trade. This was due not to the greater population of China, but to the fact that although the importation of Western timepieces led to the evolution of a clockmaking tradition in China, neither the intent nor the product served the needs of time measurement, and timepieces remained merely titillating toys for the pleasure of the privileged.

In Japan, on the other hand, the early imported European clocks strongly influenced the evolution of a clockmaking tradition that produced new forms of timepieces that were uniquely Japanese and were both practical and appropriate to the national way of life. In the beginning, Japanese craftsmen copied European clocks without attempting to adapt the mechanism to the Japanese system of time-telling, in which time was reckoned in accordance with periods of variable length. The period of daylight hours was longer and the nighttime hours shorter in the summer months, while the reverse was true in winter. Tradition states that the first clock produced in Japan was a copy of a European timepiece made by a smith named Tsudo Sukezaiema in the late sixteenth century.

Eventually, the Japanese replaced the European dial with one indicating the twelve Chinese signs of the zodiac. Then, by the late seventeenth century, a new mechanism had been devised, incorporating a fixed hand or indicator with adjustable hour plates. In the eighteenth century, the Japanese developed a more sophisticated timepiece having a double escapement, one balance of which served for daylight hours and another for the hours of the night. Although at first Japanese clockmakers continued to use the European verge and foliot escapement, subsequently other escapements were adapted. A work in three volumes published by Hanzo Hosowaka in 1796 describing mechanical toys, automata, and clocks, devoted one volume to a treatise on the construction of timepieces.

Although the major Japanese clockmaking center was Nagasaki, there were also centers in Kyoto, Edo (Tokyo), Osaka, Sendai, and Nagoya. Production remained relatively small as indeed was the demand, for due to the feudal social structure, the chief market was the privileged class. The revolution of 1866 brought an end to civil rule of the Tokugawa shōgunate and the restoration of the mikado. At the same time, Japan was opened to Western influence, and among other drastic changes was the replacement on January 1, 1873, of the former calendar and complex method of timetelling by the European system. All existing clocks and watches became immediately obsolete and relegated to the category of curios.

The clocks first brought as gifts to the countries of the Far East were of immeasurable value in promoting the establishment of the first Christian missions in China and Japan. The mechanical clock and related horological curiosities such as automata also played a significant role in opening up East Asian countries to Western diplomatic and trade missions in the sixteenth and seventeenth centuries. At the same time, the trade in clocks with China and the presentation of such timepieces to Chinese emperors influenced the craft of clockmaking in England, France, and Switzerland in particular, providing stimulation for the development of complicated mechanisms and elaborate workmanship. However, although European trade in timepieces with China for more than a century constituted an important chapter in European world trade, it had little effect on Chinese concepts of the measure of time, temporarily or permanently. The Chinese did not relate mechanical clocks to time and astronomy, but considered them primarily as toys and curiosities. Many Chinese erroneously assumed that when a watch ceased functioning it had died and had to be replaced with another. It was this belief that popularized the purchase of duplicate watches mentioned earlier. Apparently this practice also related to timepieces in public offices. Nineteenth-century photographs of railroad stations or other public buildings occasionally depict as many as six or more clocks in a row on the wall, of which perhaps one was operative.

[S.A.B.]

FURTHER READINGS

Bedini, Silvio A. "Chinese Mechanical Clocks." *Bulletin of the National Association of Watch and Clock Collectors* 7.4 (June 1956): 211–221.

———. "Oriental Concepts of the Measure of Time: The Introduction of the Mechanical Clock Into China and Japan." *The Study of Time II*. Ed. J.T. Fraser and N. Lawrence. New York: Springer, 1975. 451–484.

Bonnant, Georges. "L'introduction de l'horlogerie occidentale en Chine." *La Suisse Horlogere* (August 27, 1959): 767–768.

Chapuis, Alfred. *La Montre Chinois*. Neuchâtel, 1919.

Cipolla, Carlo. *Clocks & Culture 1300–1700*. London: Collins, 1967.

d'Elia, Pasquale. *Fonte Ricciane. Documenti originati concernenti Matteo Ricci e la storia della prima relazioni tra Europa e la Cina 1579–1615*. Rome, 1942–1949. 1:201–212.

Harcourt-Smith, Simon. *A Catalogue of Various Clocks, Watches, Automata, and Other Miscellaneous Objects of European Workmanship Dating from the XVIIIth and the Early XIXth Centuries, in the Palace Museum and the Wu Ying Tien Peiping*. Peking: The Palace Museum, 1933.

Needham, Joseph, Wang Ling, and Derek J. Price. *Heavenly Clockwork: The Great Astronomical Clocks of Medieval China—A Missing Link in Horological History*. Cambridge: Cambridge UP, 1960.

Robertson, Drummond. *The Evolution of Clockwork With a Special Chapter on the Clocks of Japan . . . Together with a Comprehensive Bibliography of Horology*. London: Cassell, 1932.

Weaving, Allen H. "Clocks for the Emperor." *Antiquarian Horology* 19.4 (Summer 1991): 367–387.

EUTHANASIA AND AGING

The debate about euthanasia has recently widened to cover a number of medical decisions about the end of life. This is a welcome development, particularly in relation to older people. A study in the Netherlands by D.J. Van der Maas et al. found that euthanasia—administering lethal drugs at the patient's request—and assisted suicide were more common for patients dying under the age of sixty-five. The study also found that alleviation of pain and symptoms with drugs that might shorten a patient's life occurred with about equal frequency in relation to the number of deaths at all ages, while nontreatment decisions—the withholding or withdrawal of treatment in circumstances where the treatment would probably have prolonged life—were more common among deaths of people aged sixty-five or more.

One reason for these differences with age is that euthanasia is more commonly practiced on deaths from cancer than other causes, and at older ages, cancer accounts for a smaller proportion of deaths. One might wonder whether there are other reasons why euthanasia is less frequently practiced on the old: might their deaths be less predictable, are older people less likely to request euthanasia, or is it because they are less likely to die at home than in hospitals or other institutions? (The Dutch study found that 62 percent of general practitioners, 44 percent of the clinicians, and 12 percent of nursing home physicians said that they had practiced euthanasia.) Many respondents to the Dutch study said that an emotional bond between doctor and patient is necessary for euthanasia and it could be that this happens less for older people. Another possibility is that older people are less likely to be perceived as suffering severe pain. As A. Cartwright, L. Hockey, and J.L. Anderson have reported, while pain is more common among deaths from cancer, confusion and incontinence are more frequent among people dying when they are older.

The following is part of an issue that the London-based Institute of Medical Ethics was urged to consider: "The lives of an increasing number of patients, predominantly but by no means all elderly, are now being prolonged by modern medicine in states of coma, severe incapacity, or pain they consider unrelievable and from which they seek release." The subsequent report of the institute discussed some commonly raised objections to assisting death but thought that these needed to be balanced against strong arguments for the prevention of suffering. The report recognized that many patients now suffer persistent mental and physical distress while awaiting natural death, and suggested that "allowing doctors to assist death could be seen as a way of fulfilling their commitment to prolonging lives of satisfaction and dignity." However, a review in the *British Medical Journal* (1992) of euthanasia around the world does not suggest that current practices are directed at achieving death with dignity for elderly people without a terminal cancer.

[A.C.]

FURTHER READINGS

British Medical Journal. "Euthanasia Around the World." *British Medical Journal* 304 (1992): 7–10.

Cartwright, Ann, Lisbeth Hockey, and John L. Anderson. *Life Before Death*. London: Routledge and Kegan Paul, 1973.

Institute of Medical Ethics Working Party on the Ethics of Prolonging Life and Assisting Death. "Assisted Death." *Lancet* 336 (1990): 610–613.

Van der Maas, D.J., et al. "Euthanasia and Other Medical Decisions Concerning the End of Life." *Lancet* 338 (1991): 669–674.

EVE'S GENETIC LEGACY

Individuals of many species, including humans, do not inherit exactly the same amount of genetic material from each of their two parents. In higher organisms, most of the genetic material carried by an individual is found in the nuclei of the cells. The DNA of the nucleus is inherited equally from an individual's paternal and maternal parents. However, genes are also present in other cellular organelles, such as mitochondria, microbodies, and (in plants) chloroplasts. For example, in humans the DNA occurring in the mitochondria codes for thirty-seven genes. Although this is far fewer than the approximately 10,000 genes of the nuclear DNA, many of these organelle genes are of critical importance, being involved in cellular respiration processes and other essential mitochondrial functions. The DNA present in cell organelles may be inherited from one or from both parents. Mitochondrial DNA in humans is inherited maternally, being passed on to offspring through the egg but not through the sperm. Because mitochondrial DNA (in contrast to nuclear DNA) does not undergo rearrangement and recombination from one generation to the next, but is passed on essentially intact from mother to daughter, it serves as a powerful tool for studying the evolution and migration of human populations. Only the maternal lineage is continuous for genes carried in the mitochondria, since males do not pass on their mitochondrial genes.

Modern techniques of molecular biology, including restriction analysis and gene sequencing, provide a sensitive means of detecting tiny genetic differences between the mitochondrial DNAs of different human lineages. Human populations have been sampled from all parts of the world, and from these samples, mitochondrial DNA differences have been determined. The variability of human mitochondrial DNA is greatest in native African populations, confirming conclusions from existing fossil evidence that humans originated in Africa. Many researchers believe that mutations in human mitochondrial DNA accumulate at a relatively constant rate over evolutionary time; that is, that this DNA behaves like a "molecular clock." If this is true, mitochondrial DNA differences can be used to construct an evolutionary tree from which inferences can be made about the branching pattern, age, and geographic origins of maternal lines. One such inference, based on a number of simplifying assumptions, is that all humans alive today—in other words *modern man*—can be traced back to a common maternal ancestor (belonging to *Homo sapiens*) who lived in Africa about 200,000 years ago. Only the mitochondrial DNA has been passed down in this fashion; the nuclear DNA of present human populations has been inherited from a much larger number of individuals. From this probable point of origin in Africa, *Homo sapiens* has spread outward into Europe, Asia, and Australia, and eventually into the New World.

[G.A.A.]

See also Evolution of Evolutionism.

FURTHER READINGS

Wilson, A.C., and R.L. Cann. "The Recent African Genesis of Humans." *Scientific American* 266 (April 1992): 68–73.

EVOLUTION OF EVOLUTIONISM

Evolutionism, the belief that evolution is a real phenomenon, came of age in 1859 with the publication of Charles Darwin's *On The Origin of Species by Means of Natural Selection, Or The Preservation of Favoured Races in the Struggle For Life.* Evolution is now interpreted in a variety of ways, the loosest definition being "any biological change that has a genetic basis." However, for many people, evolution is of necessity a process with a progressive content, implying the historical development of the diversity of complex organisms of the present time from one or a few very simple cells that emerged as the first life forms about three and a half billion years ago.

Evolutionary theory is about two distinct things: process and mechanism. The Darwinian evidence for the reality of the process of evolution includes the fossil record; biogeography (the study of the geographical distribution of plants and animals); the historical record of changes induced in domesticated plants and animals by human breeders; embryology; and comparative anatomy. Recent molecular biological research confirms what was already concluded from the other points of evidence.

The mechanism that Darwin proposed as the cause of evolution was "natural selection." Some variant characteristics of a species are better "fitted" to the circumstances of existence, thereby enhancing survival and reproduction, and ultimately they come to predominate in the population. Thus, natural selection is a process analogous to the purposeful culling and selection of breeding stock by farmers.

Fifty years before Darwin published *Origin of Species*, the French evolutionist, Jean-Baptiste de Monet, chevalier de Lamarck, had proposed that the most important mechanism of evolution was "the inheritance of acquired characteristics." This implied that any beneficial change that might have happened in an organism during the course of its life might be somehow genetically fixed and so passed on to the next generation. Numerous attempts to demonstrate this have failed to satisfy the rigorous demands of scientific proof.

In all probability, an intuitive perception of natural selection arose in the mists of prehistory. Any hunting people would know that they were able to capture the weakest, slowest, least intelligent prey, and that the fittest survived. There is a strong sense of this in North American aboriginal mythology, for example. It does not follow, however, that knowing about natural selection implies a belief in evolution. The preacher, in Ecclesiastes 9:11 (ca. 500 B.C.), says,

"the race is not to the swift, nor the battle to the strong . . . nor yet favour to men of skill; but time and chance happeneth to them all." This implies a conventional wisdom that the swiftest and strongest and smartest were usually the fittest. But the preacher was no evolutionist. The idea of the inheritance of acquired characteristics was common among the Greeks of Aristotle's period, but was never tied to evolutionism.

Even earlier, the Greeks had discussed the origins of life, particularly human life. Thales and Anaximander (ca. 500 B.C.) wrote about the origin of life in the sea. Xenophanes discussed the significance of fossils found in rock strata in the mountains, and understood that geological and biological changes must have occurred. Empedocles (fifth century B.C.) thought that there had been a progressive series of creations, including the monsters of Greek mythology that succumbed to human superiority.

Among the Greeks, Aristotle is the best candidate as an evolutionist. His system of classification of plants and animals, the *Scala Naturae*, or ladder of nature, places humans at the top of a scale of descending complexity of form and physiology. All this needs to make it an evolutionary escalator is upward movement in time. But Aristotle was convinced that organisms had entelechies, or biological souls, that make them true to type, and despite the general classical Greek familiarity with metamorphoses and metaphysical flux, a true understanding of evolutionary progression seems to have been absent.

In the eighteenth century, French nature philosophers revived the early Greek ideas about the origins of life. George Louis Leclerc, comte de Buffon, might have been the founder of modern evolutionism if he had not equivocated due to religious pressure. He certainly realized that if a species such as the ass could have mutated from the horse then there need be no limit to the process, and all the diversity of life could have arisen from a simple, common ancestor. Buffon had a direct impact on the evolutionism of Charles Darwin's grandfather, Erasmus, whose *Zoonomia* (1794) included a brief but comprehensive Buffonian evolutionism. Likewise, Buffon was the greatest influence on Lamarck.

Lamarck set out his laws of evolution in *Philosophie zoologique* (1809). The most controversial of these laws proposed that organisms respond to a "need" by a movement and by the development of organs appropriate to it. Another law, namely that if organs are used they increase proportionately in time, and if they are not used they regress and atrophy, was intuitively acceptable to most biologists. The perennially thorny issue is the inheritance of acquired characteristics. The influence of Georges Cuvier, who opposed evolutionism on the grounds that all organisms were so well correlated internally that any change would be detrimental, partially eclipsed Lamarckism, but many were persuaded that evolution was real. In Britain the debate was taken up by a number of minor advocates concerned with the mutability of species and natural selection. W.C. Wells, for example, in an 1813 lecture, remarked that "What agriculturalists do by art, seems to be done with equal efficiency, though more slowly, by Nature." Later, the time available for evolution became a major issue when Lord Kelvin calculated a relatively short time on the basis of the rate of cooling of the planet. He was soon proved to be wrong, but the controversy points to the importance of time in relation to evolution.

Robert Chambers's *Vestiges of the Natural History of Creation* (1844) produced a horrified uproar that carried the book through ten printings. The *North British Review* commented that, "Prophetic of infidel times and indicating the unsoundness of our general education, the Vestiges has started into public favor with a fair chance of poisoning the fountains of science and sapping the foundations of religion." Darwin could take a hint; he dropped his unpublished thesis on evolution and gave his attention to the study of barnacles for the next ten years.

Darwin began to think about speciation as a result of his observations on the tortoises and birds of the Galapagos Islands during the voyage of the naval survey ship *H.M.S. Beagle*. But although he had a short essay prepared in 1842, and a full book manuscript for *Origin of Species* by the mid-1850s, he might have procrastinated longer if it had not been for Alfred Russel Wallace, a surveyor and naturalist who, in 1858, sent him a manuscript so close to Darwin's original unpublished essay that Darwin thought he would be accused of plagiarism if he went ahead and published first. But he was given documented priority at a presentation of the "Darwin-Wallace Papers" to the Linnaean Society. The following year *Origin of Species* was published, and an enthusiastic review in the *Times* of London by T.H. Huxley helped it on its way. Church reaction was surprisingly mild: an apocryphal remark attributed to the wife of the bishop of Worcester was, "Descended from an ape? Pray

that it be not so. But if it be so, pray that it not become widely known": faint hope! Churchmen Asa Gray in the United States, Charles Kingsley in England, and Henry Drummond in Scotland all argued eloquently for the conciliation of evolutionism with Christianity. At the 1860 Oxford meeting of the Association for the Advancement of Science, the bishop of Oxford vowed to "smash Darwinism," but he was undone by his own sophistry and Huxley's barbed response, as well as a careful scientific reply by Darwinist J.D. Hooker.

There is no doubt that Darwin borrowed freely from the vocabulary of other authors, with and without acknowledgment. Patrick Matthew contributed "natural selection," E. Blyth "adaptive radiation," Herbert Spencer "survival of the fittest," and the debt to Wallace may never be fully assessed. Progressive evolution is to be found in Buffon, Erasmus Darwin and in book-length detail in Lamarck and Chambers. But a borrowed word or a metaphor or a concept may be meaningless unless perceived and integrated and restated as a convincing synthesis. Darwin provided this, along with the plethora of information and insights for which Victorian biology hungered. Hence we still refer to the "Darwinian Theory," and *Origin of Species* remains the keystone of evolutionism.

Darwinian theory came in for frequent criticism, and Darwin's responses vacillated, leaving him vulnerable to the claims of neo-Lamarckism, which, after Darwin's death in 1882, gained a prominence that it held for forty years. Neo-Lamarckism was an eclectic doctrine containing elements of Lamarck's laws, the influence of the environment, and natural selection. During the neo-Lamarckist ascendancy, the mechanisms of natural selection had barely been demonstrated, and the inheritance of acquired characteristics had barely been refuted, so there was room for endless speculation and polemic.

Darwin's major theoretical problems, the origin of variation and the cellular nature of reproduction, had in part been solved by his contemporary Gregor Mendel. In the 1860s, Mendel elegantly demonstrated that genetic traits are governed by pairs of elements, later called "alleles," that is, the various forms of the "genes." These retained their integrity from one generation to the next. But Mendel's work was ignored during his lifetime and the erroneous Darwinian concept of "blending inheritance," which held that parental characters were homogeneously blended in offspring, remained influential. "Mutation theory" originally proposed that mutations could provide large-scale biological changes that would transcend the effects of blending inheritance.

After the rediscovery of Mendel's work at the beginning of the twentieth century, the nature of mutation and the gene were investigated largely through studies of the fruit fly, *Drosophila*, by T.H. Morgan's research group at Columbia University. They decided that mutations were usually productive of very small changes that were suitable raw material for natural selection, and that the gene was probably a molecular entity, a concept that was not completely confirmed until after J.D. Watson and F.H.C. Crick had proposed the double helix structure of DNA in 1953. Another stream of evolutionary thought led in the direction of theoretical population genetics. By the early 1930s, the leaders in this field, R.A. Fisher and J.B.S. Haldane in Britain, Sewall Wright in the United States, and S.S. Chetverikov in Russia, had provided the mathematical basis for quantification of the effects of natural selection. Fisher argued that in large populations, with unrestricted gene flow, "time and chance" are irrelevant. But Wright thought that in small populations random events such as "genetic drift" could speed up the process. Haldane, wary of over-simplification, observed that "the world is not only queerer than anyone has imagined, but queerer than anyone can imagine. This is a most disturbing thought, and one flees from it by stating the exact opposite." The vast sweep of time available for natural selection to bring about, no matter how gradually, the diversity of the contemporary world was a comfort to incipient skeptics.

The formulae into which selection coefficients and fitness could be factored were the theoretical foundations of neo-Darwinism: an evolutionism that offered natural selection as the all-sufficient cause of evolution, purged of Darwinian vacillations and other historical baggage. It had a romantic appeal for biologists, who had perennially chafed under the criticism that biology was not a true science, since it lacked a mathematical base. For the following four decades, neo-Darwinism, bolstered by its amalgamation with classical genetics and other biological developments as "the modern synthesis," dominated evolutionism. The reduction of heredity to genes, of variation to mutation of genes, and of speciation to the redistribution of gene pools in populations provided an awesome simplicity amidst the mess of

biological forms and functions. Eventually the question had to be asked, "Is it *too* simple?"

In the 1970s the realization began to dawn that even a comprehensive knowledge of genomes (the complete genetic makeup of organisms) could not explain how genes were expressed and how they interacted to produce distinctive whole organisms. It became almost respectable to ask (1) if there had been perhaps too much emphasis on population genetics and not enough on epigenetics (the study of gene expression during development); or (2) too uncritical an acceptance of the perfection of adaptation, and if natural selection might even be more of an obstacle to evolution than its primary cause; and (3) if the course of evolution had ever been the stately gradual phenomenon proposed by orthodoxy. Is there a need for a new synthesis of evolutionary theory? Opinions vary, but there is a consensus that the question is valid and the debate healthy for evolutionism.

[R.G.B.R.]

See also **Biological Revolutions; Evolutionary Progress; Fossil Record; Heterochrony; Metamorphosis; Presocratics; Saltatory Evolution; Time Available for Evolution.**

FURTHER READINGS

Hull, David L. *Darwin and His Critics.* Cambridge: Harvard UP, 1973.

Løvtrup, Søren. *Epigenetics.* New York: Wiley, 1974.

Mayr, Ernst. *The Growth of Biological Thought.* Cambridge: Belknap P of Harvard UP, 1982.

Osborn, Henry F. *From the Greeks to Darwin.* 2nd ed. New York: Scribners, 1929.

Provine, William. *The Origin of Theoretical Population Genetics.* Chicago: U of Chicago P, 1971.

Reid, R.G.B. *Evolutionary Theory: The Unfinished Synthesis.* Ithaca: Cornell UP, 1985.

EVOLUTION OF LANGUAGE

In discussing the evolution of language it is important to distinguish the evolution of the *capacity* for human language from the evolution of particular languages like English, Chinese, or Zulu. That is, one must not confuse the biological basis of language, with which all human beings are born, with the particular cultural manifestations of this capacity in the world's populations.

Just when and how the capacity for language developed is a question that has never been resolved—and perhaps never will be—but it seems reasonable to assume that, since this capacity is so complex and is so intimately connected with human cognition, it must have evolved gradually over a long period of time. Inasmuch as chimpanzees, the closest relative of modern humans, do not possess anything approaching human language, surely the common ancestor of chimps and humans, which lived about 5 million years ago, did not either. Consequently, we must assume that the capacity for language has developed over the past 5 million years. During this interval it seems likely that the various hominids that existed possessed a language faculty that became progressively more complex over time. However, since none of these earlier hominids survived into historical times, we have no direct evidence of what language capacities each may have had. Indeed, there has recently been a heated debate on the linguistic capabilities of the Neanderthal people who inhabited Europe prior to the arrival of modern humans and who mysteriously disappeared around 35,000 years ago. While some scholars have maintained that the Neanderthalers probably had a capacity for language not unlike that of modern humans, others have argued that the particular vocal tract of Neanderthalers, which differs from that of humans, would have made speech as we know it impossible.

There are remarkable parallels between the discovery of the evolutionary explanation for biological and linguistic diversity. In both fields, the evolutionary explanation replaced a biblically inspired static view in which both species and languages were seen as immutable objects, the result of divine creation. The evolutionary explanation in linguistics, however, preceded that in biology by more than seventy years. An English jurist, Sir William Jones, is generally credited with having first recognized, in 1786, that similarities between Latin, classical Greek, and Sanskrit could only be explained by assuming that these three languages (and others as well) had all evolved from a single earlier language, "which perhaps no longer exists," as Jones put it. During the nineteenth century this unattested parent language came to be called Indo-European. Though Lamarck proposed a theory of biological evolution in 1801, it was not until the publication of Darwin's *On the Origin of Species* (1859), and its proposal of natural selection as the chief underlying mechanism, that evolution from a common ancestor became the accepted explanation for biological diversity.

During the nineteenth century it was widely believed that linguistic evolution also entailed *progress* toward more advanced languages. Perhaps not surprisingly the "advanced" languages, identified by their use of inflections on words (for example, the plural marker -*s* in "books" or the past-tense marker -*ed* in "kicked"), were European languages, while Chinese, which generally lacks such inflections, was taken to represent the primitive state from which a more advanced form would emerge. By the end of the century, however, the notion of progress in language was dropped for a number of reasons. First, it was recognized that there was really no evidence that the use of inflections made a language any more efficient than one without inflections. Second, it was clear that the Indo-European languages had for some time been moving away from the complicated system of inflections: modern English, for example, has lost most of the inflections of the original Indo-European language, which existed about 6,000 years ago. But this would mean that English has not progressed, but has rather regressed toward a system that is more similar to Chinese. Third, it was realized that there simply was no correlation between this (or any other) structural property of language and the level of culture of human groups. Today, most linguists maintain that, while languages are constantly changing, they are all roughly equal instruments of communication and there is no evidence of either progression or retrogression in linguistic evolution. In other words, the biological basis of language is uniform and unchanging throughout the entire human species, despite the constant flux that affects its manifestations in all human cultures.

A final issue has to do with the temporal limit of the comparative method in the study of the evolution of language. We have seen that Jones traced most of the languages of Europe back to a single language, Proto-Indo-European, which is generally thought to have been spoken around 4000 B.C. Many modern linguists believe that beyond this date, constant linguistic erosion has destroyed all trace of earlier affinities, so that Indo-European cannot be shown to be related to any other language family. Recently, a number of scholars have demonstrated that this is yet another Eurocentric myth and that the Indo-European family is really one member of an even more ancient family called Eurasiatic, whose languages extend from Europe across Asia and into northern North America (the Eskimo and Aleut). Furthermore, a comparison of all the world's language families with each other indicates that they are all related in a single family, that is, all extant human languages appear to have evolved from a single language. Evidence from human genetics and archaeology suggests that this language may have been the language of a population which apparently migrated out of Africa within the past 100,000 years and eventually populated the entire earth. It is important to stress that this language was not the first language, it was not a primitive language, and it was no doubt not the only language existing at that time. It was merely the language of a population that—for unknown reasons—was highly successful in populating the earth.

[M.R.]

See also **Creationism and Evolution; Eve's Genetic Legacy; Evolutionary Progress.**

Further Readings

Greenberg, Joseph H. "Language and Evolutionary Theory." *Essays in Linguistics*. Chicago: U of Chicago P, 1957. 56–65.

———. "Language and Evolution." *Evolution and Anthropology: A Centennial Appraisal*. Ed. Betty J. Meggers. Washington: Anthropological Society of Washington, 1959. 61–75.

Hawkins, John A., and Murray Gell-Mann, eds. *The Evolution of Human Languages*. Redwood City: Addison-Wesley, 1992.

Ruhlen, Merritt. *A Guide to the World's Languages*. Vol. 1: Classification. Stanford: Stanford UP, 1991.

EVOLUTION OF THE NERVOUS SYSTEM

The evolution of nervous systems spans the history of life, for it started when lipid membranes surrounded simple genetic systems to form the first cells (prokaryotes) roughly 3,500 million years ago. Because lipid (fat) is a good insulating material, biomembranes were from the outset good electrical capacitors. Some 2,000 million years later, eukaryotic (nucleated) cell membranes acquired additional properties which conferred electrical excitability. This came about as specific proteins were inserted in the membranes, some to generate electrochemical gradients across the membranes, thereby charging their capacitance, and others to form low resistance channels through which ions (electrically charged molecules) could pass, making biomembranes electrical conductors.

The structures of ion channel proteins (like all proteins) are encoded in specific DNA sequences (genes). The first, possibly derived from prokaryotes, was probably a gene coding for a potassium (K^+) channel (Figure 1). From it, the process of molecular evolution spawned additional types of K^+-channels, each with slightly different functional properties, and a *new family* of channels for calcium (Ca^{++}), which was to become central to neurochemical signaling. (Molecular evolution occurs, in part, by chance duplications of genes, after which one copy continues serving the original function, while the other may change enough over time for its protein product to take on a new function.) Some 750 million years ago, the Ca^{++}-channel gene spawned a sodium (Na^+) channel gene. With the combined expression of these three genes in nerve cells of the first nervous system, the mechanisms used henceforth for generating nerve impulses were established: influx of Na^+, and sometimes Ca^{++}, followed by efflux of K^+.

Individual ion channels take tenths of milliseconds to open and close in response to mechanical, chemical, or electrical stimuli, and different types differ in their biophysical and biochemical properties. Therefore, the net ion fluxes in and out of cells vary widely, and their interplay gives rise to the varied forms, durations (1–100 milliseconds), and rates of propagation (less than 0.5 to more than 200 meters per second) of nerve impulses. However, the most rapid rates of propagation are achieved only with the assistance of additional insulation (myelin) provided by nonneural cells, a "trick" which has evolved at least three times: that is to say in vertebrates, crustaceans, and earthworms.

Nerve cells are tiny information-processing machines, some with thousands of input and output connections. They have two ways of communicating with each other: chemically and electrically. The mechanisms underlying neurochemical communication evolved in parallel with the mechanisms underlying bioelectricity in early Precambrian eukaryotic cells (Figure 1). Chemical signaling involves the ability to synthesize and secrete "messenger" molecules (neurotransmitters, hormones) and to recognize them as informational signals by means of specific receptor molecules. After diffusing from sender to receiver in a few milliseconds or less, signal molecules bind to their receptors and either (1) cause particular ion channels to open or close, producing changes in transmembrane electrical potential lasting from one to hundreds of milliseconds, and which often trigger nerve impulses, or (2) activate intracellular signal molecules, called second messengers, which take from milliseconds to minutes to instigate biochemical changes inside the receiver cell. These changes may be transient (lasting seconds to hours) or long term (lasting days, weeks, or a lifetime), and underlie the ability of nervous systems to mediate behavioral change, learning, and memory. Second messenger systems are also rooted in Precambrian eukaryotes. Even the sites of electrical coupling between cells, which mediate an almost instantaneous form of intercellular communication, are made of proteins that apparently had antecedents, of uncertain function, in premetazoans. Thus, the human ability to read about the evolution of the nervous system relies on basic bioelectrical and neurochemical mechanisms that existed 750 million years ago, at the time of the first nervous system (Figure 1).

That nervous systems and metazoans made their debuts together is not surprising, for the premier function of nervous systems is to coordinate the activities of a multiplicity of cells. Because nervous systems do not fossilize, their morphological evolution can only be reconstructed by comparing nervous systems in extant animals. That they evolved at all (that is, could change over time while continuing to function) stems from the inherent flexibility of the compartmentalized genetic regulatory systems which arose in Precambrian eukaryotes. Within 50 to 100 million years of the first nervous systems (networks of crisscrossing nerve cells in jellyfish-like animals), the first *central nervous systems* had evolved, probably as condensed parts of the nerve nets. In animals with bilateral symmetry and a fixed axis for locomotion, processing of information from increased numbers of sensory receptors at the "head" end presumably underlay the elaboration of a brain. Two of the three extant types of complex central nervous systems (those in crustaceans and insects, among the arthropods, and squid and octopus, among the molluscs) may be descendants of the first bilaterally symmetric central nervous system, but the third, that is the chordate spinal cord and brain, evolved *de novo*, starting a little more than 500 million years ago (Figure 1).

The progenitor of our spinal cord, a short, dorsal hollow nerve cord, appeared in protochordates, the most primitive of which continue to use a peripheral nerve plexus for coordinating local activities. In more advanced protochordates, the nerve cord lengthened, as it accommodated neural circuits for undulating the body in a new and rapid form of locomotion. It bulged at its anterior end, producing an incipient brain, as neural circuits were added to handle increased sensory input from sense organs on the head. By 500 million years ago, the fore-, mid-, and hindbrain regions of vertebrate brains had become delineated. Their well-defined neural circuits integrated sensory information from a multitude of sources (chemoreceptors, assorted types of mechanoreceptors, image-forming eyes, and a new distance sense, electroreception [useless on land, but retained in lampreys, most fishes, and many aquatic amphibians]). They also coordinated, along with the spinal cord, increasingly rapid, well-directed, and complex movements.

About 395 million years ago, the nervous system of one vertebrate lineage faced new problems associated with life on land, such as the greatly increased importance of gravity and the different transmissivity of sound and electro-

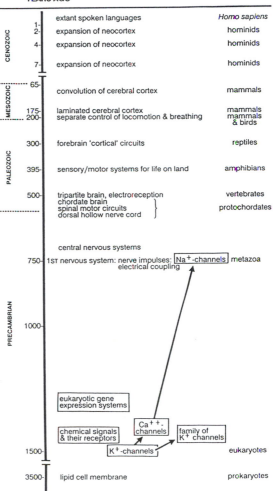

Figure 1. Note the expanded time scale for the Cenozoic era. Molecular features are enclosed in boxes.

magnetic radiation in air. Limbs had to be moved through the less resistive medium—initially just for support and propulsion. Then, some 240 million years later, the coordination necessary for manipulating objects evolved in some mammals and, after another 150 million years, starting about 4 million years ago, for manufacturing and using tools in hominids. Among the many changes in the central nervous system which enabled the new uses of limbs, two were particularly pivotal. First, roughly 300 million years ago, in the forebrains of reptiles, certain neuronal circuits were becoming organized to process and integrate visual, auditory, and olfactory information; some 125 million years later, these well-defined circuits became incorporated into the most distinctive anatomical feature of mammalian brains: the laminated cerebral cortex—to what advantage is the subject of continuing debate. Second, in mammals (and, independently, in birds), the previously interconnected neural control systems for locomotor and ventilatory activities became disengaged. Without independent control of breathing and limb movements, neither the multifarious uses of the forelimbs nor complex vocal communication, including speech, could have evolved.

Between 100 and 65 million years ago, the neocortex in some mammals expanded and became convoluted and folded within the confines of the cranial cavity, as nerve cells and connections were added for increasingly rapid and complex visual and auditory integration and, probably, also for nascent internalized information processing (the forerunner of symbolic thought?). Further increases in brain size of hominids occurred around 7 million years ago (elaborating on neural changes associated with frontally directed eyes and stereoscopic vision and following the evolution of an opposable thumb and upright posture in arboreal primates), 4 million years ago (about the time hominids became bipedal and began using tools), and 2 million years ago (when cranial capacity of hominids surpassed that of the other apes, correlated, presumably, with increased mental dexterity).

The cerebral asymmetry for language and other functions in human brains evolved from complementary specializations (primarily associated with complex social vocalizations) of the right and left cerebral hemispheres in monkeys. Dedicating the two sides of the brain to different functions is not unique to primates, having evolved several times in other mammals and birds, presumably as a space-efficient way to add complex neural programs. Sometime between 1 million and 40,000 years ago, *Homo sapiens*, who had appeared 1.5 million years ago and was using fire 1.4 million years ago, began speaking the language from which extant languages are descended and human intelligence had become a factor influencing the evolution of human brains.

[D.H.P.]

See also **Chemical Evolution and the Origin of Life; Evolution of Evolutionism; Evolution of Language.**

FURTHER READINGS

Anderson, P.A.V., ed. *Evolution of the First Nervous Systems*. New York: Plenum P, 1989.

Fincher, J. *The Brain: Mystery of Matter and Mind*. New York: Torstar Books, 1984.

Hille, B. *Ionic Channels of Excitable Membranes*. 2nd ed. Sunderland: Sinauer, 1992.

EVOLUTIONARY PROGRESS

Evolutionary progress is the production of complex forms from a few simple organisms. Complexity, in this context, implies a high degree of internal integration and self-organization. Darwin was emphatic that we must be very careful in using expressions such as "higher and lower organisms." Likewise, modern neo-Darwinists point out that "lower," or simpler organisms, as they exist at the present time, are the product of as much evolution (as they define it) as "higher" or more complex organisms. Oysters today may look much like the oysters of 300 million years ago, but by the "Red Queen hypothesis" they have been evolving hard to keep up with the passage of time. The logic of all of this depends on the definition of evolution. To define evolution simply as "any genetically based biological change" begs the question, assuming that evolutionary progress is nothing but a complex product of natural selection. By this assumption, there is no necessary correlation between time and progress.

The study of mechanisms for increasing order in organisms can to a degree be subsumed under the title of "biological structuralism," which proposes that evolutionary progress involves internal complexification that is independent of ecological and selective events. Furthermore, there is a school of thought that proposes a universal law of complexification that works at the inanimate level as well as in biological evolution. Such physical principles have recently been sought in nonequilibrium thermodynamics and in chaos theory. However, a physical law that operates to produce ordered organismic complexification runs counter to the concept of emergence.

Emergence doctrine addresses the appearance of biological novelties, whether they be minor phenomena such as new species, or major events such as the emergence of life itself. It has its roots in the philosophy of Hegel and Kant, in relation to the emergence of life, consciousness, mind, and spirit. John Stuart Mill showed that certain qualities of a whole are the sum of the parts, but that some wholes, such as chemical compounds, have a "composition of causes" that are unpredictable and more than simply additive. A complete knowledge of the physico-chemical character of oxygen and hydrogen would not allow a prediction of the qualities of water. G.H. Lewes, a Victorian biologist and philosopher, called the production of such wholes "emergences," in contrast to the additive "resultants." Applying this concept to evolution, the philosopher-evangelist Henry Drummond remarked, "when we pass from the inorganic to the organic we come upon a new set of laws—but the reason why the lower set do not seem to act in the higher sphere is not that they are annihilated but that they are overruled." This is a plain statement of what M. Polanyi later discussed as the "boundary conditions" of the different hierarchical levels of complex wholes. The early twentieth-century emergentists tended to adduce a hidden, transcendent cause for emergence, much in the manner of Henri Bergson's *élan vitale*, which made the doctrine unpopular with materialists.

A. O. Lovejoy, the architect of the "history of ideas," turned emergence theory into an epistemological framework for the materialistic analysis of biological novelty. He categorized emergences in descending order of evolutionary impact as follows: (1) new events, irreducibly different from old ones; (2) new types with new qualities; (3) new qualities in existing organisms; (4) new methods of doing the same old thing; and (5) new population distribution patterns. Neo-Darwinism would only recognize (3), (4), and (5) as the real events of evolution, (1) and (2) being nothing but the cumulative results of the former. But to some biologists, including the structuralists, (1) and (2) are revolutionary and as such require special attention, unbiased by orthodoxy.

[R.G.B.R.]

See also **Biological Revolutions; Chaos Theory; Evolution of Evolutionism; Saltatory Evolution.**

FURTHER READINGS

Reid, R.G.B. *Evolutionary Theory: The Unfinished Synthesis*. Ithaca: Cornell UP, 1985.

Riedl, R. *Order in Living Systems*. London: Methuen, 1978.

EXISTENTIALISM

The concept of time is central to the thought of that family of thinkers known as "existentialists." To the extent that existentialism is a person-centered philosophy, it focuses upon the time-bound character of human existence as finite. The influence of Bergson and especially of Husserl on the treatment of this subject by twentieth-century existentialists is pronounced. Though each philosopher pursues the topic in a distinctive manner, one can distinguish at least seven aspects of time that figure in their discussions.

Existential time is conceived *qualitatively*. The famous temporal "ekstases" of the past as facticity, the future as possibility, and the present as immersion or "presence-to" are not homogeneous concepts, subject to measurement, but differ qualitatively from one another. Similarly, the difference between recent and long past or near and distant future is not merely one of degree. The homogeneous, quantitative time that "contains" physical nature and measures motion is derived from lived, ekstatic temporality.

Although it is experiential and thus psychological, existential time is primarily *ontological* in nature. It denotes a distinct way of being, namely, the human way of being, and is sometimes conceived as coextensive, if not synonymous, with being itself. Existentialists claim to avoid the famous circularity of any attempted definition of "time" by this triad of facticity, possibility, and immersion ("fallenness").

While admitting its dispersive nature, existentialists take time to be *unifying* by virtue of its projective, individuating, and (after Husserl) intentional character. The three temporal ekstases distinguish this existential agent from all others. Each of us "exists" in these three dimensions uniquely. Indeed, living in them is what it means to exist.

Correspondingly, existential temporality has a broadly *moral* character. It can be inauthentic or authentic according as the individual "chooses" the dispersive or the unifying dimension of its time-bound being. Inauthentic temporality lives in nostalgia, dreams unreal possibilities, and dissipates itself in present concerns. Authentic temporality sustains the anguished tension between these "ekstases" in the unity of a temporalizing project.

These philosophers tend to *value* one dimension over the others, usually the future as the locus of possibility, freedom, and responsibility (Kierkegaard, Heidegger), or the present as actualizing the possible and sustaining the past (Sartre). They distinguish the dynamic "moment" from the atemporal "instant," which is the boundary of past and future, the point of existential choice, and the place of insertion of eternity in temporality.

There is a direct link between ecstatic temporality and ontological *freedom*. The freedom which we "are" is a function of the temporal spread or difference which we "exist." Existentialists make ample use of rhetorical tropes to convey this message.

Historicity, or the profoundly historical nature of human existence, is the final feature of temporality that these thinkers share. This implies that time is communal, not just individual. It bears a public and collective dimension that is cumulative and unidirectional. The sedimentation of past actions in the living past of our facticity conditions (but does not determine) our future as destiny.

In addition to philosophy, the existentialist understanding of ekstatic temporality has also been fruitful in psychoanalysis and the social sciences as well as in literature and film.

[T.R.F.]

See also **Bergson, Henri; Heidegger, Martin; Husserl, Edmund; Kierkegaard, Sören Aabye; Sartre, Jean-Paul.**

FURTHER READINGS

Heidegger, Martin. *History of the Concept of Time: Prolegomena.* Trans. Theodore Kisiel. Bloomington: Indiana UP, 1985.

———. *The Concept of Time.* Oxford: Blackwell, 1992.

Kierkegaard, Sören. *The Concept of Anxiety.* Ed. and Trans. Reidar Thomte and Albert B. Anderson. Princeton: Princeton UP, 1980.

Merleau-Ponty, Maurice. *Phenomenology of Perception.* Trans. C. Smith. New York: Humanities P, 1962.

Sartre, Jean-Paul. *Being and Nothingness: An Essay on Phenomenological Ontology.* Trans. Hazel E. Barnes. New York: Philosophical Library, 1956.

EXPANSION OF THE UNIVERSE

Inquiry into the origin, age, formation, and evolution of the universe, defined as everything that is, occupies a branch of philosophy called ontology—the study of existence. The three possible histories of the world, each with many variations on the central theme, are (1) the universe has not always existed but came into being in some event that can be called "creation," evolving into its present state over the finite time of its existence; (2) the universe was created in its present state with little or no fundamental change over time—it has a finite age; or (3) the universe has existed forever but has changed throughout time, being different at different times, cycling through various states.

Until the first third of the twentieth century, the subject was confined to the discipline of metaphysics in schools of philosophy and to the creation stories in all religions, both Eastern and Western, and in all native tribes studied today by anthropologists.

The subject matter became part of rational scientific inquiry with the birth of observational cosmology in the 1920s. This momentous development came about because of the astronomical discoveries on the structure of the universe on its largest scale. The discoveries, begun in the first years of the twentieth century and continuing today, were made possible by the construction of large telescopes of enormous power. The first of these was the 60-inch reflector at the Carnegie Institution of Washington's Wilson Observatory starting in 1909, followed in 1919 by the commissioning of the 100-inch Hooker reflector at the same observatory.

These giant telescopes, following earlier instruments of less power, but which nevertheless pioneered the way, opened up the universe to scientific inquiry. Examples of the forerunner telescopes, showing the astronomical marvels to be discovered, were the great Melbourne reflector in the 1860s, the six-foot castle Burr telescope of Lord Rosse in Ireland in the 1870s, and the one-meter Crossley reflector at the Lick Observatory, reconstructed from a revolutionary telescope by Ainslie Common in England in the 1890s.

The organization of the universe on its largest scale was found to be described by the distribution of galaxies and their clusters and associations. Galaxies are to the large scale structure of the cosmos as atoms are to the microscopic world at the small end of the size distribution of existence.

The nature of galaxies as the prime ingredient of this last hierarchy of the size distribution of cosmic structures was not known at the beginning of the twentieth century. Discoveries by Swedish astronomer Knut Lundmark and United States astronomers H.D. Curtis and E.P. Hubble in the late 1920s established the existence of galaxies as the basic unit to describe the distribution of matter on the largest scale.

The philosophical problem of the "creation" was then reduced to the question of the way this large scale distribution of matter on an astronomical scale came about. "How old are the galaxies?" came close to the ultimate question of how old is the universe, and therefore to the question of its creation.

Is it possible to determine the age of the Milky Way, which is our galaxy? Yes. This is done by identifying the oldest stars in the galaxy and then using the method of reading the Hertzsprung-Russell diagram to identify a particular stage in a star's evolution. From calculations of the stellar structure it is known that this stage occurs when a star has burned about 10 percent of its nuclear fuel, changing its hydrogen to helium (see **Age of the Oldest Stars and the Milky Way**).

Interestingly, this age of the galaxy is about 15 billion years as determined from the principles of nuclear physics applied to stellar evolution, but we can also determine the age of the universe itself in a direct and independent way. The method was found in the late 1920s by employing a discovery concerning the dynamic condition of the galaxies relative to one another on the largest scale. Galaxies are in a state of motion away from each other in all directions, obeying a velocity law such that the velocity of separation from one another is directly proportional to their distance apart.

The discovery of this expansion of the universe is one of the most profound findings in astronomy, if not in all of physical science. The phenomenon is ubiquitous. All galaxies beyond the very local neighborhood of our own galaxy and members of the small group of galaxies around us partake in the expansion. The form of the expansion is linear, meaning that measured velocities increase in direct proportion to distance from any observer.

Take any pair of galaxies anywhere. A linear velocity relation is such that the rate at which the pair is moving apart is directly proportional to their separation. Galaxies twice as distant from each other are separating at twice the velocity as others whose separation is only half as much. Those three times as distant are separating at three times the speed, and so on. This is true no matter where in the velocity field we put an observer. In other words, it is true for observations made from earth, but remains true for all observers no matter where in the universe we make an observation. This is one of the three remarkable properties of a linear velocity field. The other two are (1) a linear field preserves shapes as the expansion continues, only the scale (or the size of the figure) changes, and (2) a linear velocity field is the only form for an expansion field where sometime in the past all particles (matter) in the field can all be at the same place at the same time. This form of field is a sufficient, but not necessary condition, for a "creation" event, starting the expansion from a singularity in time, to have occurred.

But it is incorrect to view the beginning of the expansion as matter expanding into a space that is already there. Matter and radiation (which itself formed the galaxies as it cooled and changed into matter) expand, *creating* the space of the universe as the manifold separates.

The discovery of this most remarkable of all natural phenomena was made in the closing three years of the 1920s. The method of discovery was through spectroscopy. When the light of the galaxies was analyzed by passing it through a prism or a grating, spreading it into a spectrum, it was found that the wavelength of the atomic spectral lines visible in the galaxy spectrum were shifted from their laboratory position toward the red. The fainter and smaller the galaxy (generally meaning greater distance), the greater was the red shift. Red shift increased with distance. Many subsequent experiments showed that the increase was indeed linear—red shift increased directly with distance. If the shift was due to the well-known Doppler effect in stars (and in sound waves such as those generated by an approaching and then receding train or siren on earth), the red shift of the galaxies could be expressed as a velocity.

Red shifts have now been observed for certain types of astronomical objects, called quasars, with equivalent velocities nearly 0.8 times the velocity of light for the most distant of the quasars.

Information on the timing of the creation event, now often called the "big bang," is available from the details of the observed red shift/distance relation. The present rate of expansion, expressed as the velocity per unit distance, and called the Hubble constant, H, contains the direct measure of the time in the past when the expansion began.

Note that the Hubble constant, H, which is velocity per unit distance, has the physical dimension of an inverse time. Hence, one over H—which is to say, the reciprocal rate—is a measure of a cosmologically interesting time. It can be shown that H^{-1} would be the age of the universe from the time the expansion began if there has been no deceleration of the expansion due to the self-gravity of the universe acting on itself.

There would be no deceleration if the mean density of matter in the universe were zero—that is, if there was no matter. On the other hand, the matter density may be just high enough to close space-time upon itself according to the general theory of relativity. Einstein's theory of gravity relates space-time curvature with the presence of matter. The critical density to just "close the universe" is about 10^{-30} grams per cubic centimeter, or about one hydrogen atom in every cubic meter. If the cosmic density is, in fact, this high, the deceleration of the expansion would have been enough to make the determination of the age of the universe, determined from the present value of H, to be too high by a factor of one and a half ($^3/_2$).

In principle, the value of the Hubble constant can be measured by astronomical means. The red shift is routinely measured at the telescope, using a spectrum of a galaxy, by finding the ratio of the observed red shifted wavelengths of atomic spectral lines in the spectrum to the laboratory (rest) wavelengths. This fractional wavelength ratio, times the velocity of light, gives the velocity of recession.

Then, if the distance to the galaxy can be found, the ratio of velocity-to-distance can be determined. ($H = v/r$, where v stands for a galaxy's recessional velocity in kilometers per second, and r for its distance in megaparsecs.) A number of such measurements will determine the mean value of H if the samples of galaxies are distant enough that most of the observed velocities are cosmological (due to the expansion) rather than due to random motions.

The determination of H is one of the most difficult tasks in observational cosmology. It has been measured over the past fifty years, with values ranging from about 600 kilometers per second per megaparsec distance (one parsec is 3.2 light years, which is about 200,000 times the distance from the earth to the sun) determined in the late 1920s, to values between 40 and 80

kilometers per second in current times (ca. 1993). Great advances have been made in measuring galaxy distances since the problem was first approached in the late 1920s, but even by 1993 there still remained uncertainties of a factor of two in the cosmic distance scale, accounting for the factor of two in estimates of the value of H.

If $H = 40$ kilometers per second per million parsecs in distance, the inverse, called the Hubble time, would be 24 billion years. If there is just enough matter to give the critical density so that space-time is flat, the true age of the universe since the big bang is two thirds of this, or 16 billion years. On the other hand, if $H = 80$, the Hubble time would be 12 billion years. If space-time is flat, the age would be two-thirds of this, or 8 billion years.

Despite the uncertainty of a factor of two in these times due to our incomplete knowledge of galaxy distances and therefore of H, either value of the Hubble time is of the same *order* as the age of the oldest stars in our galaxy (see **Age of the Oldest Stars and the Milky Way**) and the age of the chemical elements. The coincidence of the three entirely different time scales to better than a factor of two (which is the present inherent inaccuracy in each of the methods) is taken as proof that a creation event did indeed occur about 15 billion years ago, and that the first of the stated histories of the universe in the introductory paragraph of this article is favored by the evidence.

[A.S.]

See also **Age of the Oldest Stars and the Milky Way; Big Bang Theory; Cosmology; Dark Matter; Gravity, Time, and Space; Origin and Age of the Elements; Relativity Theory; Solar System; Space-Time; Star and Galaxy Formation; X-Ray Universe.**

FURTHER READINGS

Barrow, J.D., and J. Silk. *The Left Hand of Creation*. New York: Basic Books, 1983.

Bernstein, J., and G. Feinberg. *Cosmological Constants*. New York: Columbia UP, 1986.

Eddington, A.S. *Space, Time, and Gravitation*. Cambridge: Cambridge UP, 1921.

Gamow, George. *The Creation of the Universe*. New York: Viking, 1952.

Harrison, E.R. *Cosmology*. Cambridge: Cambridge UP, 1981.

Pauli, W. *Theory of Relativity*. Oxford: Pergamon, 1958.

Sandage, A. "Observational Tests of World Models." *Annual Review of Astronomy and Astrophysics* 26 (1988): 561–630.

EXTINCTION

The disappearance of biological species is a fundamental feature of the evolutionary process. A species becomes extinct in two ways: by leaving no descendants and thus terminating the lineage, or by evolving into another species. In the first instance, the species does not adapt to environmental changes or to superior competitors, while in the second instance, natural selection probably alters the species over time. Examination of the fossil record throughout the Phanerozoic (the last 570 million years) allows calculation of a fairly constant "background" rate of extinction. Meanwhile, the rate of speciation seems to have increased, thus increasing the number of species on the planet.

Extinction occurs because the world is constantly changing and because species have to compete for resources. Paleobiologists document the changing composition of plant and animal communities over time due to speciation and extinction. Three dynamic phenomena are often invoked to explain such changes: continental drift, sea level change, and climate change. In a changing habitat, adaptive fitness of a species may decline and extinction can result as fitter species replace less adaptable ones. Often, related species with similar adaptations became extinct at the same time so that entire genera and families disappeared from the fossil record. Thus, nearly all marsupial mammals disappeared from South America when placental mammals invaded from North America over the Panama land bridge about 5 million years ago coincident with major climate changes over the continent.

Fossil histories record times at which large numbers of species became extinct at the same time; these events are called mass extinctions. Mass extinctions play an important role in evolution: they reduce competition and leave a multitude of vacant niches that allow the radiation of new species which otherwise could not have established themselves. An example is the radiation of mammals after the extinction of dinosaurs. As a consequence, the history of life is not a smooth and gradual evolution but represents periods of slow change punctuated by revolutions.

The largest mass extinctions occurred at the ends of the Ordovician, Permian, Triassic, and Cretaceous periods; over 85 percent of marine species became extinct at the end of the Permian (250 million years ago). There is no consensus on the causes of such extinctions, although catastrophic hypotheses have strong support. Anomalies in the rock record coincident with mass extinctions indicate accumulations of unusual compounds, localized intense heat or vibration, and tsunami inundation. These features support the idea of impact by extraterrestrial bodies (called bolides). Concurrent changes in atmospheric chemistry, radiance, and temperature would affect both plants and animals. Researchers also debate the possibility that there is a regular periodicity of about 26 million years to the occurrence of mass extinctions throughout the Phanerozoic. Some astronomers hypothesize that periodic disruption of the comet cloud associated with the solar system would induce bolide impact. Other theories include periodic volcanic activity associated with deep mantle cycles and rapid climate change. Mass extinction events are relevant to mankind: it is estimated that species loss during the twentieth century rivals that of the end of the Cretaceous. A major difference is the fundamental alteration and occupation of habitats by man that disallows reoccupation by new species.

[V.T.]

See also **Catastrophism; Chemical Evolution and the Origin of Life; Evolutionary Progress; Fossil Record; Geologic Time Scale.**

FURTHER READINGS
Donovan, S.K., ed. *Mass Extinctions: Processes and Evidence*. New York: Columbia UP, 1989.

FAMILY PLANNING POLICIES

The early twentieth-century pioneers of the international family planning movement were individuals like Margaret Sanger in the United States and Marie Stopes in Britain who, in the face of fierce opposition, advocated voluntary motherhood and the right of married women to control their fertility through modern contraceptive devices. They laid the foundations of family planning services now widely provided in Western countries by philanthropic groups and government agencies.

GROWTH OF PROGRAMS IN LESS DEVELOPED COUNTRIES

The first government to provide a family planning program with the aim of reducing national fertility—and thereby controlling the increase of population over time—was India in 1952. But such was the lack of government-perceived urgency throughout the Third World that by 1964, similar national programs had been established only in Pakistan, South Korea, Fiji, and China. By the mid-1960s, however, there was a surge of fertility regulation policies as a response to:

1. The unexpectedly high rates of population growth revealed by the censuses of the 1960s as a result of major disease eradication campaigns in the 1950s.

2. The orthodoxy of the time regarding development which maintained that the critical "takeoff" of a national economy into self-sustained growth required a level of savings and productive investment that high population growth rates seemed to inhibit. This is essentially because a high dependency ratio diverts savings into welfare expenditure. There emerged the economic concept of value of births averted. Accordingly, in 1965, President Lyndon Johnson urged a United Nations audience to "act on the fact that less than five dollars invested in population control is worth $100 invested in economic growth."

3. The development in the early 1960s of oral contraceptives and intrauterine devices encouraged development planners for the first time to believe that Third World fertility rates could be regulated by intervention policies.

Significant impetus was thus given in the mid-1960s to the formation and external funding of national family planning programs in the Third World. In 1962, Sweden was the first developed country to earmark a major part of its foreign aid program to birth control; in 1964 a population office was established within the United States Agency for International Development (AID), and AID missions in Latin America were advised to consider population programs as a priority area; and in 1965, the United Nations began to provide advisory services to family planning programs. By 1976, as many as sixty-three countries in the less developed world, embracing 92 percent of its population, had launched their own programs or endorsed those of private groups like the International Planned Parenthood Federation. In about half of the programs, the explicit aim is to reduce fertility in the interest of national development planning, while in the others, family planning is supported essentially on grounds of health, human rights, and family welfare, regardless of any national demographic impact. It is remarkable how in the space of fifteen years, Third World governments shifted from almost universal indifference or condemnation of family planning to almost universal approval or acceptance.

THE REGIONAL PATTERN

In Asia, under conditions of very large populations and high densities, the great majority of governments are committed to a reduction in population growth rate. With the major exception of Egypt, African nations have generally not developed comparable anti-natalist positions. This is attributable to their high death rates, tribal tensions, and low modernization levels. In the Middle East, the combination of Islamic fundamentalism, labor shortages, and military conflicts has had a similar negative impact.

In Latin America, the majority of its governments have come, somewhat belatedly, to support family planning activities on essentially humanitarian rather than demographic grounds. But the continent has very few governments prepared to back strong anti-natalist policies. One potent contributory factor is the widespread cult of *machismo*. Another is the pattern of settlement, in which vast areas of sparsely peopled "outback" are popularly perceived as offering development potential, even though most of the population lives under conditions of congestion. Also, there has been the suspicion that United States imperialism was imposing birth control as a means of limiting the emerging power of Latin America, with the international family planning movement viewed as a Central Intelligence Agency (CIA) wolf in sheep's clothing. Finally, the Roman Catholic Church exerts a strong influence. At the level of individual behavior, the church's pronouncements on birth control are widely disregarded, but in the political arena, the church's conservative influence on government decision makers is often crucial.

Skepticism, Opposition, and Restructured Programs

Although family planning programs have long been an integral part of the development planning orthodoxy preached by Western advisers, the appropriateness of their role continues to be questioned. The basic assumption of many program planners has come under increasing fire. This assumption is that members of traditional societies desire smaller families but, in the absence of modern contraceptive knowledge and supplies, are unable to realize such desires. There has been a growing appreciation of the distinction between macro- and microconsequences of high fertility. At a national level, high fertility invariably entails high net costs, but at a family level, there may well be net benefits. Therefore, if poor people benefit from large numbers of children, why persuade them to limit their fertility?

There has been particular concern about a few programs which go beyond incentives and disincentives into real coercion of individuals by the state, notably India's vasectomy program in the mid-1970s and China's one-child policy in the early 1980s. In addition, the major donor to the international family planning movement, the United States government, has greatly reduced its support, partly because of its growing ideological objections in the 1980s to government intervention policies and partly as a response to the powerful pro-life, antiabortion lobby.

Many of the early programs were highly centralized, clinic-based and catered largely for an urban *élite*. Such policies were justified on the grounds of cost-effectiveness, but the principal policy challenge now is to reach the rural poor who form the majority in most less developed countries. An effective strategy in this respect in countries like Mauritius and Indonesia has been a labor-intensive motivational program using lower-status, local community workers to gain the confidence of eligible women and to act as the essential link between community and clinic.

A few Third World countries are beginning to restructure their programs even more radically now that demographic goals have been attained. Sub-replacement fertility has been achieved in Hong Kong, Singapore, Taiwan, South Korea, Thailand, Mauritius, Cuba, and a few small Caribbean territories. Emphasis is now being placed there on the social welfare element of their programs, including child spacing, family counselling, reduction of abortion and premature sterilization, and a modification of the contraceptive "method-mix" in the interests of clients' health and convenience.

[H.R.J.]

See also **Human Fertility Trends.**

Further Readings

Donaldson, P., and A. Tsui. "The International Family Planning Movement." *Population Bulletin* 45.3 (1990).

Lapham, R., and G. Simmons, eds. *Organizing for Effective Family Planning Programs*. Washington, D.C.: National Academy P, 1987.

FATHER TIME

The figure of Father Time is derived from Saturn-Cronus, the Greek and Roman child-devouring god of the golden age who probably came to represent time through a mistaken association of Cronus with Chronos. Although the early Christians appropriated the mid-winter festival of Saturnalia, they could not eliminate Saturn-Cronus, whose planet, which is visible in the sky, was a constant reminder of his quondam importance. Saturn-Cronus was eventually reduced to a mere mortal, but he was by no means forgotten, and his attributes were embodied in two new and less-powerful figures: Father Time and Father Christmas. In the past, malevolent and benevolent qualities were attributed to both Father Time and Father Christmas. But Father Time essentially inherited the malevolent aspects of Time the destroyer, and Father Christmas inherited the benevolent aspects associated with the Saturn-Cronus of the golden age.

Father Time fulfilled an important role in Christian eschatology. The single god of Judeo-Christian monotheism is infinite by definition and has always had a problematic relationship with finite time. Satan, although evil, cannot represent infinite time as could the figures of evil in the eastern pantheons because that would imply he enjoyed equal status with God. Father Time, a mortal figure outside the official Christian framework, offered no competition to God. Thus Saturn-Cronus, although attacked by the church fathers, found a useful niche under a new name in the world view of Christianity.

ICONOGRAPHY

The iconography of Saturn-Cronus adapted well to the *memento mori* message of Father Time. Saturn-Cronus's sickle already represented the inevitable harvest of human life after a finite period of time. It now acted also as a reminder to prepare during one's finite lifetime for the eternal life hereafter. Subsequent technological advancement changed the sickle to a scythe in later depictions of Father Time. The sickle was probably the first agricultural implement. It consisted of a curved metal blade with a short handle, and was in use at least 8,000 years ago. The Romans developed the sickle into a scythe by setting the blade at right angles to the handle. As the scythe replaced the sickle throughout the Middle Ages, the iconography of Time as well as that of Saturn and Death changed to reflect the current state of agricultural technology.

Additional iconographic aspects of Father Time were accretions from other allegorical figures. Unlike Saturn-Cronus, who was usually shown with a full head of hair, Father Time had only a single forelock. This feature was taken from Kairos, the personification of opportunity, and signified the opportunity that one ought to seize. Father Time was also given winged feet and shoulders, again attributes imitating the classical figure of Kairos. The wings remind one of the swiftness of Time and graphically express the meaning of *"Tempus fugit."*

The hourglass or sandglass, an invention of the fourteenth century, was first, to our knowledge, added to the iconography of time in the illustrations of Petrarch's *Triumphs* (fifteenth century). Although it was also associated with the figures of death, temperance, and opportunity (or Occasio), the hourglass was particularly suitable for Father Time because the sand running out symbolizes the finite duration of life. As the pendulum clock became popular during the horological revolution of 1660–1760, clocks were sometimes depicted with Father Time. The uninterrupted flow of clock time and the image of the snake biting its own tail—the latter a symbol of Saturn-Cronus which occasionally found its way into the iconography of Father Time, and represented infinity and a cyclic view of time—were not entirely appropriate symbols for the allegory of finite time. Thus the pendulum clock, despite its technological superiority over the hourglass, did not succeed in supplanting it in the iconography of Father Time.

THE CHANGING CHARACTER OF FATHER TIME: MALEVOLENCE TO BENEVOLENCE

As Father Time evolved, the malevolent character he had acquired from Saturn-Cronus gave way to a benevolent and finally even pathetic personality. The figure of Time was initially considered comparable to a figure of Death and viewed as the destroyer of all. For example, in Revelation 14:13–20, Death carries a sickle, with which he reaps the earth, and he wears a golden crown, a relic from Saturn-Cronus. When Christians painted the figure of Death in allegorical works, which they began to do in the eleventh century, he resembled Time. In the Middle Ages and the Renaissance, it was felt that the pagan figure of Time was not respectable enough to appear in Christian allegory and so Death with the sickle often appeared in his stead. The hourglass was added to the iconography of Death and Time at much the same time. In the fifteenth century, some of the illustrators of Petrarch's *Triumphs* made the first iconographic distinctions between Death and Time: Death is given the scythe, and Time is provided with the hourglass and wings in two engravings of circa 1470–75 which may be accredited to Filippo Lippi (Figure 1). The separation of death from Father Time allowed the benevolent aspects of the latter to develop.

In the sixteenth century, Father Time was still mostly seen as a malevolent creature, but he was beginning to be considered the father of Truth, an idea which has its roots in the works of Sophocles and other Greek writers. A woodcut entitled *Truth, the Daughter of Time*, appearing in William Marshall's *Goodly Prymer in Englyshe* of 1535, shows a smiling Time drawing Truth out of a cave. Another woodcut, *Veritas Filia Temporis* of 1536, shows an equally mild Time in a similar scene. Although Christian allegory from the eleventh century onward held that Truth and her sisters—Peace, Justice, and Mercy—were the daughters of God, the implied sacrilege of Time's claim was overlooked by both Mary Tudor and Queen Elizabeth I, who found the Time-Truth allegory politically expedient. The official acceptance of Time's role as the father or revealer of Truth greatly enhanced Time's benevolence.

Sixteenth- and seventeenth-century emblem books reflect the changing perception of Father Time. Both Death and Father Time were being portrayed less severely, but Time continued to be the milder figure of the two. Quarles clearly juxtaposes the characters of Death and Father Time in his *Hieroglyphikes* of 1638: a kindly-looking Time prevents a skeletal and leering Death from snuffing out the candle of life. In the past, the Christian creator of emblems would choose to show the figure of Death, but the more benevolent Time was increasingly being depicted. In *Horati Flacci Emblemata* (1607), Otto Van Veen uses six images of Time and only two images of Death in eleven emblems which treat the subject of impending death.

This more benevolent Father Time gained widespread approval when the horological revolution of 1660–1760, and the subsequent technological explosion had made men perceive the universe as a giant clock. The Father Time of the late seventeenth and early eighteenth centuries had virtually no pejorative connotations in the Newtonian clockwork universe, and was sufficiently popular that he, along with Cupid, was one of very few allegorical figures to survive the scientific attack on allegory as a mode of thought.

Father Time's popularity was brief, however. The scientific revolution that initially made him important promoted worldly attitudes; people now concentrated more on the material quality of their time on earth and rather less on the subsequent step into the hereafter. In particular, erotic love, once at the bottom of the hierarchy in Petrarch's *Triumphs* and perhaps the most worldly of values, conquered Father Time in the eighteenth century. French clocks of this period frequently show Cupid above the dial carrying Time's scythe, and Time below the dial holding the verge-and-foliot mechanism of a clock. The positioning of the two figures has obvious implications, reinforced by the substitution of the foliot for the hourglass. Father Time no longer

reminds one that time must run out for every human being. In *The Lady's Last Stake* (1758–59), Hogarth's exclusion of Father Time indicates the complete victory of love over time in the situation depicted.

Father Time was a pathetic figure during the Augustan age. His *memento mori* message was lost on an age which concerned itself far more with immediate pleasures and social values than spiritual matters. Swift boasted, in *Tale of a Tub* (1704), that "the Writers of and for GRUB-STREET, have . . . nobly triumphed over *Time*; have clipt his Wings, pared his Nails, filed his Teeth, turn'd back his Hour-Glass, blunted his Scythe, and drawn the Hob-Nails out of his Shoes." Pope and Hogarth, disgusted with the secular values of their era, both envisioned the death of Time in their final artistic statements. Pope's *Dunciad IV* (1742–43) describes a reversal of the Genesis creation which extinguishes all things, ending with time itself. Hogarth, in *Tailpiece; or, The Bathos* (1764), painted a naked, dying Father Time surrounded by the pieces of his broken scythe and hourglass.

Victorian sentimentalism, however, revived Father Time, fashioning him into the wise old patriarch we see today at new year. From his malevolent beginnings as the heir of Saturn-Cronus's temporal and destructive qualities, he has become almost as benevolent as his twin, Father Christmas. His relationship with the figure of Death has evolved: at first he was equated with Death, then he gained power over him and was even shown feeling horror at the sight of him. Unlike our medieval and Renaissance ancestors, we no longer view Time's sickle as a *memento mori* message. In an era skeptical of even the existence of a hereafter, Father Time acts as a reminder to make the most of one's life precisely because this earthly life may be the only one we experience.

[S.L.M.]

See also **Indo-Iranian Gods of Time;** *Kairos*; **Saturn-Cronus.**

FURTHER READINGS

Macey, Samuel L. *Patriarchs of Time: Dualism in Saturn-Cronus, Father Time, the Watchmaker God, and Father Christmas.* Athens: U of Georgia P, 1987.

Panofsky, Erwin. *Studies in Iconology.* New York: Harper & Row, 1962.

Petrarch, Francesco. *The Triumphs.* London: John Murray, 1906. Mr. Colvin's Notes upon the Engravings.

Figure 1. The Triumph of Time. *(From* The Triumphs of Francesco Petrarch, *with Mr. Colvin's notes [London: Murray, 1906].) Permission of McPherson Library, University of Victoria.*

Roscher, W.H. "Chronos." In his *Ausführliches Lexikon der griechischen und römischen Mythologie.* Leipzig: Teubner, 1884–90. 1:899.

Saxl, Fritz. "Veritas Filia Temporis." *Philosophy and History: Essays Presented to Ernst Cassirer.* Ed. R. Klibansky and H. J. Paton. New York: Harper & Row, 1963. 197–222.

FEEDSIDEWARD

"Feedsideward" is a term used by chronobiologists to describe the interaction among multiple rhythmic entities that results in predictable sequences of attenuation, no-effect, and amplification of the effect of one entity (the actor) upon another entity (the reactor) as it is modified by a third entity (the modulator).

The endogenous components of the chronome are internally coordinated through feedsidewards (interactions among multiple rhythmic entities) in a network of spontaneous, reactive, and modulatory rhythms.

[G.C., F.H., and R.P.S.]

See also **Chronobiology; Chronome.**

FURTHER READINGS

Halberg, F., S. Sánchez de la Peña, and G. Cornélissen. "Circadian Rhythms and the Central Nervous System." *Circadian Rhythms in the Central Nervous System, Proceedings IX Conference of IUPHAR, Bath, August 4–5, 1984.* Ed. P.H. Redfern et al. London: Macmillan, 1985. 57–79.

Halberg, F., et al. "Cephalo-Adrenal Interactions in the Broader Context of Pragmatic and Theoretical Rhythm Models." *Chronobiologia* 13 (1986): 137–154.

Sánchez de la Peña, S., et al. "Pineal Modulation of ACTH 1–17 Effect Upon Murine Corticosterone Production." *Brain Research Bulletin* 11 (1983): 117–125.

FEMINIST PERSPECTIVES

To be female is to have a paradoxical relationship to time. This assertion characterizes Western feminist writing on time: natural and social times are stripped of their taken-for-granted status and theorized in relation to the times of *work* and *production*, to the *birth-death parameter*, to *history, clock time*, and the decontextualized *commodity*, and to the spheres of *language, religion*, and *politics*. All these dimensions of cultural life, moreover, are considered interdependent and mutually implicating and their times viewed as inseparably tied to each other. Beyond these general agreements on women's uneasy relationship to time and the interdependence of the

dominant approaches to time, feminist analyses of the issues have undergone significant changes. After first demanding equal rights in and to the linear time of history, and after consequently establishing the fundamental difference between patriarchal and matriarchal time, contemporary feminists are striving to come to terms with the complexities and contradictions posed for women by the dominance of clock time and emphases on linearity and finitude. In their quest to transcend the old dualisms, they seek to conceptualize the paradoxes of belonging to a world dominated by the quantitative times of production and death while orienting towards the generative times of reproduction and life.

Women in industrialized and industrializing countries are both integral to the world of standardized, commodified time and clock-based rhythms in education, paid work, and entertainment, and at odds with those times. They are subject to social time structures, deadlines, and schedules. They are tied into an economic life in which labor time is exchanged for money, a life in which employment relations are dependent on time as an abstract exchange value. Yet the times of reproduction and nurturing, of caring, loving, and educating, of household management and maintenance are not so much time measured, paid, spent, allocated, and controlled as time lived and generated. Often this is shared time, enmeshed with significant others, and created in interaction. Such time is not easily quantified. This makes translation into money almost impossible. In a world where money is synonymous with power, any time that cannot be given a money value is by definition associated with a lack of power. Furthermore, emotional work, in contrast to most paid work, is inclined to be subject and task orientated. This means it is not easily governed by externally imposed, fixed timetables, schedules, and deadlines. Rather, it has to be open-ended. Such a time tends to be excluded from the public life of objective time and relegated to the private realm of personal, subjective relations.

Equally out of sync are the decontextualized, standardized clock time of industrial production on the one hand, and the embedded, generative time of reproduction on the other. The clock, it is argued, is a metaphor for the consumptive, thus destructive preoccupation with finitude and death, quantity and measure. Clock time is a finite resource that we consume, a quantity that is running out or, alternatively, a vessel to be filled with a fixed amount: only so much can be achieved in an hour. Time ticks on while the deadlines move ever closer. Efficiency means producing or accomplishing more of something in the same unit of time. It is linked to time pressure, an ever-increasing shortage of time, and the veneration of speed. In contrast to the fixed quantity bounded by individual death and associated with a scarce resource, birth creates time in ongoing cycles of regeneration. It generates a time of creative becoming.

Feminists conceptualize this disjunction between the time of destruction and construction, of consumption and regeneration as one of difference in both transcendence and power. Transcendence, achieved through the externalization of knowledge in fixed form, is associated with power over nature and fellow human beings. Objectifications ranging from art and writing to clocks, steam engines, and airplanes cast the transient world in a permanent mold. In addition, technological products encourage standardization, quantification, measurement, and translation into money. These products of culture allow for contemplation, manipulation, and control. They facilitate power over processes and beings. The extraordinary rise of Western societies to a position of global dominance is generally associated with these temporal processes of externalization, detemporalization, decontextualization, disembedding, and rationalization. As beings whose transcendence is grounded in generative temporality, women find their lives and their histories constituted as the shadow of the world of production. Their time of reproduction and their emphasis on birth and regeneration are rendered invisible by the dominant times of calendars and clocks. Their time-giving becomes subsumed under time consumption and their generative temporality under the construction of permanence in artifacts and symbolic systems, products of science, institutions, and market structures.

The relation between the times of birth and death, however, must not be seen as a duality: those who give and generate time also live *in* time. They are subject to a complexity of times governed by natural and social rhythms, by culturally set rites of passage, by calendars and clocks, religious and social festivals. They are integral to the contemporary world of production and time budgets, of deadlines, time control, and payment for time. Generators of time simultaneously partake in, articulate, and help to maintain the dominant time as a collective construct. Inextricably incorporated into a life of commerce they inevitably collude in the economic relations of time in which speed is venerated and thus find it difficult to defend an open-ended time of care and a reduction in pace. Almost irrespective of appropriateness, faster is considered better in education, transport, sport, and endless other areas of social activity, and deemed more efficient in commerce and production. As the shadows of the world of resource consumption, the time-generating activities are evaluated and judged by criteria based on a finite resource: the abstracted, standardized measure of the clock.

Writing about the paradoxes, the discrepancies, and the mutual implications, feminists are giving shape to the invisible. Their attention to the disattended aspects of Western, commercialized social time may help to recover an essential balance between the consumption and the regeneration of time.

[B.A.]

See also **Social Theory.**

FURTHER READINGS

Adam, Barbara. *Time and Social Theory.* Cambridge: Polity, 1990.

Davies, Karen. *Women and Time: The Weaving of the Strands of Everyday Life.* Aldershot: Avebury, 1990.

Forman, F.J., and Caoran Sowton, eds. *Taking our Time: Feminist Perspectives on Temporality.* New York: Pergamon, 1989.

Irigaray, Luce. *Le temps de la différence, pour une revolution pacifique.* Paris: Lib. Generale Française, 1989.

Kristeva, Julia. "Women's Time," trans. Alice Jardine and Harry Blake. *Signs* 7.1 (1981): 13–35.

FILM

Film (motion pictures, cinema, movies—photographic images that move) is a technological art form that has advanced from its nineteenth-century ancestor, the still photograph, through a series of revolutionary inventions that continue today to alter both the form and the way it can be manipulated to influence our sense of real time. The invention of the camera, especially the movie camera, enables us not only to recapture time, but to analyze and alter it. Events too fast or slow for the human eye to follow—such as hummingbirds' wings beating, plants growing, or raindrops disintegrating—can be filmed and viewed as continuous action. Film, coupled with the invention of sound recording, helps us attempt to reconstruct and sometimes change the past, accelerate the present, and envision the future; but finally, all that we ever witness on film is a mechanical description of the past.

Film is a combined art, being both visual and auditory, existing in both space and time. Narrative film employs dialogue, actors, scenery, furniture, costumes, lighting, and music to tell stories, just the way theatrical plays do. But film also uses space larger than any stage area, makes simultaneous presentation of actions at more than one point in time, and uses far more complex lighting and sound effects. Black and white film, now thought of as "old," has been largely replaced by color film, which heightens even more our sense that film is real.

Film used to be called "living pictures" because it seems to reproduce reality exactly as it exists. In both narrative and documentary film, reality is edited, or arranged, into an expressive whole. Events and people appear to be happening in front of us; indeed, audiences sometimes confuse performers with the roles they are playing and decide that events on the screen are real. This appearance of absolute reality and of time "passing" occurs because film does not stand still on one scene. It moves around, "describing" as it goes; thus, action and description move forward together. Sound synchronized with visual motion further enhances the illusion of real time.

What happens to cause this appearance of motion—of moving forward through time, or backward in time (the "flashback")—is comparable to turning the pages of a picture book slowly, allowing enough time to pass to clear one picture from the mind before looking at the next. When the reader flips the pages, the time between pictures is shortened; one picture is still in the mind when the next one appears. A movie is actually a series of twelve to twenty-four separate pictures or "frames" appearing in such rapid succession that they present one seemingly continuous, lifelike action. This appearance of motion is made possible by two processes that go on in the eyes and mind when a movie is being watched: *persistence of vision (PV)* and the *phi phenomenon*.

Persistence of vision was known to the ancient Egyptians, but was first described scientifically by Peter Mark Roget in 1824. When a picture strikes the eyes, it registers an image on the retina that is carried by the optic nerve to the brain. After the picture is removed the image lingers in the eye (persistence of vision) for one-sixteenth of a second. When the next image replaces it immediately, as on a moving strip of film, the illusion of continuous motion is created. When pictures are shown faster than sixteen frames per second, PV keeps each picture in the eyes while the next few are being shown.

The phi phenomenon was discovered by Gestalt psychologist Max Wertheimer in 1912, and describes our eyes' ability to see, for example, the individual blades of a fan whirling as one circular form, or the illusion of still pictures moving as a single continuous motion at twelve to twenty-four frames per second.

In 1893, Thomas Alva Edison invented the kinetograph, the first true motion picture camera, and the kinetoscope, the first true motion picture projector. Both were culminations of earlier inventions by Edward Muybridge, Etienne-Jules Marey, and Hannibal Goodwin. Edison's inventions both featured three crucial time-conscious mechanisms: (1) a stop-motion device (adapted from the escapement mechanism of a watch) to permit intermittent but regular movement of a roll of film; (2) tiny sprockets that held the perforated film strip steady; and (3) a high-speed shutter that opened to permit light to shine on each frame on the film strip. Camera and projector are synchronized and the projector shows the same twenty-four still pictures of action that the camera photographed. Our eyes do their part with PV and the phi phenomenon and we see the smooth-flowing action just as it took place before the camera.

When all the filming is completed, the director works with an editor to cut and splice together the portions of film that will tell the story. Sound effects, music, and special optical effects are added to clarify meaning, heighten the mood, or emphasize particular ideas. Our sense of empirical time and motion are dramatically affected by techniques used at this stage of film production. *Continuity editing* enables a character to move from one scene in one place through several others in different places while speaking continuous dialogue so that the visual sequence spans a period of time. The *split screen* shows us two events in different places occurring simultaneously. *Parallel cutting* two separate, albeit simultaneously occurring, scenes can build suspense by manipulating real time. For example, a scene of a stalking tiger is spliced to one of a sleeping man and the two scenes are alternated in a single sequence. The tiger is moving in its own time and may take fifteen minutes to reach the man, who sleeps in his own time, but we see them as parallel events with the tiger drawing ever closer in a matter of seconds.

To bridge intervals between events in the present and remembering an event thirty years ago, or envisioning an event in the future, a *lap-dissolve* is used in which the end of one scene is double-printed over the beginning of the next scene so that the transition has a smooth, dream-like quality. A *montage*, which is used to cram many events, even whole eras, into a few seconds, is a series of short scenes cut together to tell part of a story quickly. For example, a speeding train, names of cities, newspaper headlines, theater programs, and applauding audiences may be combined to tell the story of a singer's successful tour. A combination of suitable sounds accompanies the picture montage.

Camera movement manipulates multiple levels of temporality, further affecting our sense of time when watching a film. *Panning* moves the camera horizontally; *tilting* moves it vertically; *zooming* and *dollying* quickly bring us close to something. The technique of *day-for-night* is used to film night scenes during the day by underexposing the film and using filters to increase the contrast or alter the color. *Slow motion*—which causes us to feel that action is suspended in air, much the way astronauts look during moonwalks—results from photographing action at *faster* than twenty-four frames per second, then projecting the film at normal speed.

Film offers a present-tense dream world constructed of vividly lit, larger-than-life images viewed on huge screens in dark theaters. Seeing and hearing stories in this setting has become a riveting, perhaps ecstatic experience for millions of people, who return again and again to renew the sensation of leaving their own reality and entering into the reality of the story. Freed for a few hours from concerns over past and future, the stationary film audience, wrapped in the anonymous dark, focuses on the unending present of the story. Well-constructed films that adhere to the classical elements of order, form, symmetry, narrative economy, psychological complexity, and archetypal themes exert an especially strong appeal for audiences, who repeatedly view them until, over generations, they come to be thought of as "classics." Yet film technology permits a wide range of styles that may or may not adhere to Aristotelian order and may keep the audience off balance, wondering whether the past, present, or future is being shown on the screen. During the course of the twentieth century, tens of thousands of films

have been made in dozens of languages and cultures, forming a visual legacy that powerfully and completely evokes images of vanished time—all possible because of the optical principles of the camera based on the human eye.

[J.O.]

See also **Telecommunications; Television.**

FURTHER READINGS

Brownlow, Kevin. *The Parade's Gone By.* New York: Knopf, 1968.

Cook, David A. *A History of Narrative Film.* 2nd ed. New York: Norton, 1990.

Ellis, Jack C. *A History of Film.* 3rd ed. Englewood Cliffs: Prentice-Hall, 1990.

Fulton, A.R. *Motion Pictures: The Development of an Art from Silent Films to the Age of Television.* Revised ed. Norman: Oklahoma UP, 1980.

Pratt, George C. *Spellbound in Darkness: A History of the Silent Film.* Revised ed. Greenwich: New York Graphic Society, 1973.

FOOD SUPPLY AND POPULATION

Throughout the time that they have inhabited the planet, human beings have been preoccupied by obtaining enough food to live. The only exceptions are modern developed societies where less than 20 percent of disposable income is now spent on food. Traditionally, limitations on food production have restrained population growth by imposing environmental carrying-capacity limits and population ceilings. These restraints operated throughout the long hunting and gathering era, as well as in subsequent agricultural societies of the type described by Malthus in his *Essay on the Principle of Population* (1798). Historical demographers have provided clear evidence of recurrent local subsistence crises in pre-nineteenth-century European peasant communities, with poor harvests leading to mortality surges, emigration, delayed marriage, and lower fertility. The most extreme, and very late, example was the Great Famine in Ireland following the ravages of potato blight in 1846.

Any sustained increase in food availability permitted population growth. This was particularly evident in Europe and European-colonized countries overseas in the nineteenth century. Agricultural productivity had been transformed by a series of advances, collectively termed the Agricultural Revolution, which included enclosure of inefficient open fields, reclamation of fenland and moorland, introduction of new fodder crops like turnips and clover, development of balanced crop rotations, and conservation of soil fertility by marling, liming, and mixed farming. Regional famines were eliminated by the growing economic integration of national territory promoted by new roads, canals, and railways. Later in the century, substantial food imports became available to Europe's expanding population, above all from the newly opened-up wheatlands of the North American interior.

A review of more recent trends in the food/population balance suggests that at a *global* scale the balance has improved significantly in the last half-century. Despite unprecedented population growth, global food production has expanded at an even faster rate, so that the price of most food grains has fallen in real terms. A *second* agricultural revolution in the developed world—based on mechanization, chemical fertilizers, and pesticides—has permitted major increases of production in the West from the 1950s. More recently, similar technological developments in association with the breeding of highly productive cereal strains have brought enhanced yields of the green revolution to appreciable parts of the Third World. However, the food/population ratios that matter for human welfare are not global ones, but those at national, regional, class, and household levels. It is clear that the apparently healthy global position is largely attributable to appreciable production growth in North America, western Europe, and Australia-New Zealand.

The situation in the Third World is much more variable. In Latin America, continuing availability of new cropland in the sparsely peopled interior has been the major factor in modest, but sustained, increases in grain production per capita. Southern and especially eastern Asia has witnessed the biggest success story, disproving dire predictions of chronic food shortages for this densely peopled region. Although there are some lagging countries—notably Bangladesh, where undernutrition remains rife and famine sometimes threatens—most Asian countries have expanded their food output faster than their population—not through any significant increase in cropland in these already crowded countries, but because of yield increases. There were early gains in Japan, Taiwan, and South Korea, countries which benefited in the 1950s from the development of land reform, agricultural research, comprehensive rural infrastructure, and mass education. Many of the more intensive agricultural methods pioneered in these

countries—such as the use of high-yielding varieties of wheat and rice, which became available in the 1960s—were adopted by other parts of Asia, particularly India, Pakistan, and the Philippines. Africa, on the other hand, is a continent in crisis. Food production per head fell there during the 1970s and 1980s. From near self-sufficiency in food in 1970 there has been a decline to a position in which imports provided about 20 percent of the continent's cereal needs in the late 1980s. Contributory factors include widespread political and military strife, severe droughts in ecologically fragile, semiarid zones, and inefficiency, mismanagement, and corruption associated with obsessive state centrism.

The precarious balance between food and population in many parts of the Third World would not be so potentially catastrophic if the huge potential surpluses of North America and western Europe could be made readily available to needy populations. But a complicated mix of commercial and diplomatic considerations among potential donors has thwarted the development of a system of internationally coordinated reserves in the form of a world food bank.

A relatively new appreciation is that demand factors are just as important as supply factors as causes of famine and undernutrition. Access to resources is always mediated through the social structure, and the plain fact is that regardless of global or national food/population ratios, there are always some individuals with inadequate access to food because of their poverty. Consequently, hunger is increasingly regarded as an injustice rather than a misfortune. Indeed, some of the world's worst famines have occurred with no significant aggregate decline in food availability per head—Bengal in 1943, Ethiopia in 1973, and Bangladesh in 1974. Similarly, the relatively healthy overall food situation in Latin America masks the inability of pauperized rural and urban proletariats to purchase adequate food. Food is perhaps the most basic human necessity, but it is far from being thought of as a basic human right.

[H.R.J.]

See also **Club of Rome; Malthus, Thomas.**

FURTHER READINGS

Gittinger, J., J. Leslie, and C. Hoisington, eds. *Food Policy.* Baltimore: Johns Hopkins UP, 1987.

Lee, R., ed. *Population, Food and Rural Development.* Oxford: Clarendon P, 1988.

Sen, A. *Poverty and Famines.* Oxford: Clarendon P, 1981.

FOSSIL RECORD

A fossil (< Latin *fossilis*, dug up) is now understood to represent any aspect of past life, ranging from traces and burrows, to actual ancient cells, to preserved skeletons and other hard body parts. Fossils remain the only tangible evidence of past life on our planet and, in this context, span an interval of time that begins at least about 3.5–3.8 billion years ago. (Throughout this article, GA [< Greek *Giga*, giant] represents one billion years ago, and Ma, one million.)

The geologic time scale is generally divided into two great eons, the Cryptozoic eon (from about 4.5–0.6 GA; during which time life forms are presumed to have evolved, but the actual record of their presence is difficult—though not impossible—to see), and the Phanerozoic eon (from about 0.6 GA to the present; the time of visible life, meaning that fossil evidence is relatively good). In the Cryptozoic eon, the evidence is mostly composed of preserved cells or groups of cells of apparently primitive forms of life, whereas in the Phanerozoic eon most evidence consists of preserved hard parts attributable to more complexly evolved living things. Ichnofossils (traces or burrows made by organisms that may, or may not, be recognized as well on the basis of preserved hard parts) transcend the boundary between these two eons. Also, virus-like, bacteria-like, and other forms of simple organisms typical of the Cryptozoic eon still persist to the present time.

Most fossils consist of hard parts developed as supporting skeletons by invertebrate (shelly) organisms that then lived, and now live, in the sea. Most major kinds (phyla) of invertebrate organisms are known as fossils from the Cambrian period that began about 570 Ma. The marine realm continues to be the most diversely populated by living organisms in the world. Animals commonly preserved as fossils include sponges, corals, clams, oysters, arthropods, and echinoderms. Also preserved are remains of single- or simple-celled marine plants (diatoms, nannofossils, algae), animals (foraminifer), and delicate films of soft-bodied forms such as various kinds of multicellular "worms." Many marine vertebrates are also represented. These include various ancient fish-like forms, as well as ancestors and members of sharks, bony fish, and diverse kinds of reptiles, birds, and mammals.

The continental record of past life is generally less well represented than that of the marine realm. Nevertheless, we have discovered over time a rich array of all major kinds, including fish-like forms that adapted to coastal, brackish, or even freshwater environments, including ancient as well as early and present true fishes, amphibians, reptiles, birds, and mammals.

Thus, the fossil record shows us glimpses of the first life on the planet, the first steps (if not the origin) and diversification of multicellular organisms (metazoans), the early diversification of the major plant and animal phyla, major revolutions in the marine realm, and the invasions and conquests of once living things of the land and air.

SUMMARY OF THE SUCCESSION OF LIFE ON EARTH

It is generally agreed that the earth is about 4.6 GA old, and that identifiable forms of life (visible under the light microscope, at least) first appear in sediments around 3.8–3.5 GA. The earth was most likely without free oxygen before this time, but at least by then free oxygen was present in the ocean (and perhaps in the atmosphere), with both plant-like (photosynthetic) and animal-like (heterotrophic) organisms having evolved. Although the eukaryotic cell (with a nucleus in the cell; the foundation of all multicellular organisms) is not known in rocks older than about 1.7 GA, organisms having attained that level of organization probably were present earlier. In any case, truly multicellular organisms are first preserved in the fossil record at about 600–550 Ma.

This, the youngest interval of Proterozoic strata, and coming just before those at the base of the Phanerozoic eon (and the base of the Cambrian system), is generally termed the Vendian system. These imprints and molds of soft-bodied organisms are found around the world, with only the continents of South America and Antarctica not yet having their representatives. Most of these fossils are recovered from shallow water marine sediments (sandstone, shale, mud) derived from the land. This implies that the environment of deposition usually was oxygenated and that a variety of organisms with hard-to-preserve bodies did not survive predation or microbial decay. The middle Cambrian Burgess Shale fauna (ca. 500 Ma) suggests why this is so (see below). Vendian multicellular animals include representatives of the worms, corals, jellyfish, arthropods, and echinoderms. Multicellular plants (seaweeds) also had evolved by Vendian time.

The base of the Cambrian system approximately heralds the first occurrence of a large variety of organisms with skeletons made of preservable hard parts. The fossils are thus easy to see; hence the beginning of the Phanerozoic (visible life) eon. Based upon the fossils typically found in Cambrian and younger strata, it generally was agreed that virtually all animal phyla with preservable hard parts had evolved at least by Cambrian time, but also that the phyla represented the "settled upon" ways of organizing a body plan to take an effective role in the biosphere. Importantly, most of the fossils in this context were collected from aerobic, shallow water settings in which land-derived sediments predominated or, lacking the input from the land, carbonate (limestone, dolomite) dominated as the major host sediment. Most skeletons were formed of calcium carbonate, aragonite (magnesium carbonate), and siliceous or phosphatic materials.

The Burgess Shale fauna (medial Cambrian age) of British Columbia comprises numerous remains of organisms composed only of carbon films, coated by silicate films. The preserved animals were presumably transported from shallower water into a deep water setting that lacked oxygen and this hindered attack by bacteria and other organisms. In addition to arthropods, which dominate the fauna, there are remains of various kinds of worms, cnidarians, sponges, mollusks, and echinoderms. The use of these familiar names indicates that the fossils could be assigned to groups recognized elsewhere and, in a general sense, were modern in character. Many other Burgess Shale fossils, however, are of uncertain affinities, and this suggests that their morphologies, body plans, and thus "ways of doing business" reflect a number of still experimental stages in this process, which ultimately proved unsuccessful.

GENERAL PATTERNS: INVERTEBRATE FAUNAS

In general terms, the Phanerozoic eon saw not only the Cambrian stabilization of a differentiated marine fauna, but also two other major revolutions in the inhabitants of that realm. The three basic "marine evolutionary faunas" were the Cambrian fauna (ca. 550–500 Ma); the Paleozoic fauna (Ordovician to Permian, ca. 500–250 Ma); and the Modern fauna (Mesozoic and Cenozoic, 250 Ma to the present). The Cambrian fauna was dominated by trilobites, inarticulate brachiopods, monoplacophorans, early sponges, and crinoids. These forms began a decline in the late Cambrian, to be superseded by the Paleozoic fauna. These taxa, dominated by articulate brachiopods, crinoids, corals, cephalopods, and bryozoans (sea lilies), formed a major component of shelly fauna environments until the late Permian, when one of the world's major mass extinctions took place. The elements of the Modern fauna had already been diversifying, however, so the surviving gastropods, bivalves, bony and cartilaginous "fishes," and more evolved bryozoans and echinoids did not originate anew, but expanded as conditions permitted. Nevertheless, the marine fauna experienced three major revolutions before reaching the present day.

GENERAL PATTERNS: PLANT KINGDOM

One of the first major encroachments into the continental realm was made by members of the plant kingdom. Probably following a covering of a green "scum" of bacteria and algae, the continents were first inhabited by seedless vascular plants of relatively simple construction (those reproduced by means of spores, such as modern ferns), but which still had a tubular supporting skeleton that both provided a skeleton and a circulatory system to enable the transport of life-supporting nutrients. The fossil record of these plants begins in the Silurian period (ca. 430 Ma). They and their modern descendants require an aqueous or very humid environment in order to live and reproduce. Other major advances in the plant kingdom include the development of seed-bearing plants (gymnosperms, such as conifers) in the late Paleozoic era (ca. 250 Ma) and the modern flowering plants (angiosperms) in the late Mesozoic era (ca. 130 Ma). For these plants, an aquatic phase is not required for reproduction, and they spread widely over the land surface. In the late Paleozoic era (ca. 250 Ma), tree-sized seedless and gymnosperm plants were major contributors to the vast coal swamps in western Europe and eastern North America. On burial and deformation, these became the fossil-fuel reserves that spawned the industrial revolution millions of year later. It is considered probable that the rise of the flowering plants, hosting numerous niches for various arthropods, provided an impetus for the radiation of primitive insectivorous mammals, now culminating in the world's placental, marsupial, and also the monotreme groups (in decreasing order of modern abundance, but in reverse order of gross—but not necessarily direct—evolutionary development).

EARLY VERTEBRATES, PLANTS, AND INVERTEBRATES

Vertebrate animals underwent a number of experiments beginning in the Cambrian period (with the modern lampreys and hagfish being descendants of the first jawless animals). By the end of the Devonian period (ca. 360 Ma), most experiments had been completed, with the main cartilaginous (sharks) and bony (true fish) groups present by then, as well as before (in the Silurian). They dominate the marine and (mostly bony fish) the freshwater realms today.

It is notable that the first land-dwelling invertebrates (mostly kinds of crustaceans and other arthropods) closely followed the invasion of the truly terrestrial plants in the Silurian period. These invertebrates were the inheritors of the terrestrial environment, as they still are today. Inevitably vertebrate animals capable of land locomotion and life evolved and left the water (in the late Devonian) to exploit the unencumbered food resources not otherwise available to their competitors, the early bony fishes that inhabited the same ponds, lakes, rivers, and swamps. Modern descendants of the fish ancestors of these land vertebrates, the coelacanths, now inhabit near-bathyal depths adjacent to oceanic ridges, but show muscular capabilities of their bodies and fins eerily similar to the kinds of locomotory movements made by their amphibian cousins.

These new land vertebrates were the ultimate ancestors of modern amphibians: frogs, toads, salamanders, and caecelians. In the late Paleozoic, and into the Mesozoic, however, these animals explored a wide variety of ecologic niches, including retreating to a more aquatic existence, without a viable land-living phase. As amphibians, however, all of these animals were virtually tied to an aquatic reproductive phase inherited from their fish ancestors. The amphibians are composed of two major ancient groups: (1) the main line labyrinthodonts (so named because of a complexly folded pattern seen in cross section of their teeth) and (2) the anthracosaurs. The former almost certainly include the ancestors of living amphibians.

REPTILES: THE NEXT MAJOR STEP ON LAND

For vertebrates the next major step on to the land was made by the reptiles, which stemmed ultimately from a group of anthracosaurian amphibians. The first reptiles (in the early Pennsylvanian period, ca. 310 Ma) were relatively small in size, but already showed rearrangements of the skull musculature consistent with a more powerful, grabbing method of prey acquisition than the more rapid, snapping method employed by amphibians, as well as achiev-ing a number of skeletal modifications conducive to a more active mode of locomotion.

AQUATIC REPTILES

Once having arisen, the reptiles diversified into a wide variety of kinds, including ancestors of modern turtles, crocodiles, the tuatara of New Zealand, and lizards and snakes. In addition to turtles, there were a number of reptiles specialized for an aquatic mode of life. The most highly specialized of these were the ichthyosaurs which had a general body plan similar to modern porpoises (mammals). Certainly the ichthyosaurs could not leave the sea to crawl onto the beach to lay their eggs in the sand for hatching (as do living sea turtles). Rather, the ichthyosaurs must have "hatched" their young within the body of the female and given birth to them alive. Indeed, the fossil record shows us skeletons of female ichythyosaurs that apparently died and were preserved in the process of giving birth to their young (also preserved).

GIANTS AND ADAPTATIONS

The gigantic, herbivorous saurischian and, somewhat smaller but still impressive, ornithischian dinosaurs held sway on the land during the Mesozoic era (ca. 265–240 Ma). In addition to their large stature, fossils show that these animals possessed a wide range of adaptations for defense (body spines, mace-like tails, horns), eating (batteries of crushing or grinding teeth), and social activities (cranial crests with resonating chambers). In fact, fossilized nesting grounds of certain dinosaurs indicate that parental care was practiced, a trait not usually associated with reptiles.

MORPHOLOGY AND PRESERVATION

The meat-eating dinosaurs ranged from small, swift, lightly built and long-armed types (coelurosaurs) to larger, more ponderously built animals with formidable arrays of sharp dagger-like teeth in cavernous mouths (*Tyrannosaurus rex* is a typical example of the latter). *Archaeopteryx*, arguably the first bird that appeared in the late Jurassic period (ca. 150 Ma), had a body covered with feathers, but its skeleton was virtually that of a coelurosaurian dinosaur. In fact, had not the limy muds in which it was entombed preserved the delicate body covering of *Archaeopteryx,* it undoubtedly would have been considered to be a small dinosaur.

AN EXTINCTION

The age of reptiles came to a close at the end of the Cretaceous period (65 Ma), with the fossil record showing that many kinds had been diminishing in numbers and diversity for several million years. Whether the ultimate demise of the reptiles (both on land and in the oceans) was triggered by a catastrophic meteoric impact or by the combined effects of climatic deterioration, mountain building, volcanism, and the withdrawal of formerly widespread shallow seas is still under debate. But whether or not the extinctions actually were catastrophic is becoming perhaps clearer. Studies of what appear to be very complete sequences that embrace the Cretaceous/Tertiary (K/T) boundary in Spain, Texas, Tunisia, and the Antarctic suggest that faunal change was gradual, not abrupt. The more traditional view of an abrupt change at the K/T boundary may derive from the study of rock sequences that contain hiatuses or other perturbations and thus give a false impression of a synchronous abrupt change.

SURVIVORS: MAMMALS

One group of reptiles that in one sense did not become extinct at the end of the Cretaceous is the group that gave rise to the mammals. This group, the synapsid or "mammal-like" reptiles, flourished in the late Permian and Triassic of the southern continents (or of Gondwana, the hypothetical land mass which became South Africa, Antarctica, and South America) and may have already evolved some of the more complex physiological attributes of mammals. Many of these reptiles lived in places also partly occupied by glaciers, so that temperatures must have been cool. Whereas some of the large dinosaurs may have had an internally even body temperature due to size alone, the near ancestors of the mammals must have achieved advanced mechanisms for controlling body temperature and the elevated metabolic rates that accompany this. Features that can be interpreted to show the reptile-mammal transition are the development of a secondary palate between the nasal passages and the roof of the mouth; the reduction of tooth replacements from many to two phases; the differentiation of incisors, canines, premolars, and molars in the dentition, and precise occlusion between upper and lower teeth; and the reduction of the number of bones in the lower jaw to one and incorporation of some of the remainder into the inner ear.

MODERN MAMMALS

The reptile-mammal transition was complete by about the end of the Triassic period (ca. 200 Ma) and a number of early experiments were developed, but their dentition was still mostly composed of rather simply constructed teeth with cusps arranged in a linear to somewhat sinuous row on each tooth. Others had more elaborate tooth crowns and were likely herbivorous. Within the Cretaceous period (ca. 110 Ma), however, the record shows the first evidence of modern monotremes, marsupial, and placental mammals. Monotremes (which have hair and give milk, as do mammals, but which lay eggs, as do reptiles) apparently were of Gondwana distribution, rather than limited to Australia and New Guinea, as usually thought. Monotreme fossils are now known from the Cretaceous and younger deposits of Australia, and from those of early Tertiary age in Patagonia. Biogeographic theory suggests that the group must have been present on Antarctica as well, in that Australia was part of that continent until about 55 Ma when it broke away to drift to its present location.

Marsupials (in which the young are born at an early developmental stage and undergo further growth in the female's pouch) and placentals (with a longer pre-birth development within the female) likely evolved, or underwent most of their early (Cretaceous) evolution in the northern hemisphere, with both groups being found in rocks as old as about 110–100 Ma.

MARSUPIAL ADAPTATIONS

Soon thereafter, however, marsupials achieved a major evolutionary presence in South America and, via Antarctica, Australia. Especially in the latter region, marsupials radiated into a wide variety of forms that superficially resembled moles, burrowing rodents, and flying squirrels of other parts of the world, as well as arboreal, somewhat primate-like species and the characteristic kangaroo. The giant, extinct *Diprotodon* was as large as a rhinoceros. Marsupials are found as fossils in many parts of the northern hemisphere, but only in small numbers and limited diversity. The modern American opossum immigrated recently (within the last million years) to North America.

PLACENTAL MAMMALS

Placentals are the dominant mammal group on the land, air, and sea today. No marsupial has ever developed powered (in contrast to gliding) flight as have bats, nor a fully marine adaptation as have whales, porpoises, seals, and walruses.

Overall, mammals of the early Tertiary (65–38 Ma) ranged from shrew to rhinoceros size, and typically possessed teeth with low to tall cusps, the cusps connected to each other by V-shaped arrays of crests that extended toward the outer side of the upper teeth (especially the molars) and toward the inner side of the lower teeth. These "reversed triangles" slid past one another during mastication, cutting the food. The basic dental plan is retained in insectivorous and carnivorous forms; with blunter cusps and a more omnivorous diet there were the primates and rodents, as well as a variety of ancient hoofed (ungulate) herbivores. These included the first horses, tapirs, and rhinos, which already began to show the crests being arranged into definite lophs that traverse the tooth in obliquely parallel fashion. The first horses were small, dog-sized animals with five toes on their feet. Proboscideans and sirenians had evolved by the end of this interval, as well as a variety of unique, extinct, endemic large quadrupeds in South America and Africa.

At about 35–30 Ma, the humid to subtropical environments of the early Tertiary gave way to progressively drier, as well as somewhat cooler, conditions of the medial Tertiary (38–18 Ma). The primitive mammals were replaced with more advanced types (especially herbivores) having taller-crowned teeth with taller crests, apparently in response to eating tougher foodstuffs as plants adapted to the new conditions. A host of deer- and sheep-like forms as well as primitive camels are seen now, as are the first sabre-toothed "cats" (which apparently evolved independently a number of times thereafter). The still lophodont horses now have reduced their toes to three on each foot. Primates began to dwindle, except in Africa, but rodents continued to flourish, and rabbits are newly present, too.

The late Tertiary (18 Ma to the present) saw a general additional increase in aridity, and cooler climates. In general, the landscapes began to be more open and savannah-like, although it is unlikely that grasslands were widespread, contrary to usual interpretations. Still, artiodactyls and perissodactyls with taller-crowned teeth evolved, with the horse family experiencing a great diversity until about 5 Ma. The single-toed modern horse, *Equus*, evolved at about this time and, especially in the northern hemisphere, more truly steppe-like landscapes developed.

Throughout this interval (beginning in the middle Tertiary), the ecology was sufficiently stable (at least in North America) that lineages of families, or even genera, persisted for considerable intervals. Conspicuous novelties generally came into North America from elsewhere, and many of these were carnivorous forms. Proboscideans entered North America from Eurasia at about 14 Ma, having exited Africa for Europe at about 18 Ma.

THE ICE AGES AND EXTINCTION

The Ice Ages began about 2.5 Ma, as the climate deteriorated even more in the northern hemisphere. The ebb and flow of the glaciers forced geographic fluctions of the biomass, and at about 8–9,000 years ago a large component of the world's megafauna (large-sized animals; body mass more than ca. forty kilograms) became extinct. In the Americas, in Europe north of the Sahara, and in Asia north of the Himalayas, animals becoming extinct included giant ground sloths and armadillos, camels, giant bison, a yak, the horse, wooly rhinoceroses, mammoths and mastodons, sabre-toothed "cats," giant wolves, giant beavers, giant peccaries, and bears. In South America, the list includes the last of the endemic notoungulates and litopterns, and many edentates; endemic rodents declined, and many North American immigrants were lost (proboscideans, horses), whereas others were reduced in diversity (camels, cats, cervids). In Australia, the giant *Diprotodon*, giant wombats, kangaroos, giant marsupial "lion," and others also became extinct.

Did man cause these extinctions? Opinions vary, but the timing differs in various places: between 13,000 and 9,000 years ago in North America; ca. 20,000–11,000 years ago in Europe; 12,000–9,500 years ago in sub-Saharan Africa; and 25,000–11,000 years ago in Australia. Also, the extinctions were fewer in sub-Saharan Africa, which apparently experienced a less stressful environmental milieu than did Europe and the Americas.

[M.O.W.]

See also **Biological Revolutions; Catastrophism; Dinosaurs; Evolution of Evolutionism; Evolutionary Progress; Extinction; Geochronometry; Geologic Time Scale; Stratigraphy and Paleontology.**

FURTHER READINGS

Briggs, D.E.G., and P.R. Crowther, eds. *Paleobiology: A Synthesis*. London: Blackwell Scientific Publications, 1990.

Carroll, R. *Vertebrate Paleontology and Evolution*. New York: W.H. Freeman, 1987.

Keller, G. "Extended Period of Extinctions Across the Cretaceous/Tertiary Boundary in Planktonic Foraminifera of Continental-Shelf Sections: Implications for Impact and Volcanism Theories." *Geological Society of America Bulletin* 101 (1989): 1408–1419.

Zinsmeister, J.W., R.M. Feldmann, M.O. Woodburne, and D. H. Elliot. "Latest Cretaceous/Earliest Tertiary Transition on Seymour Island, Antarctica." *Journal of Paleontology* 63 (1989): 731–738.

FOUCAULT, MICHEL (1927–1984)

Foucault's models for understanding historical events and relationships are primarily spatial and comparative rather than temporal and evolutionary. He believed that traditional history of ideas devalued space as dead, fixed, undialectical, and immobile in favor of time conceived as richness, fecundity, life, and dialectic—views he associated with Bergson and Hegel. But his effort to dislodge dialectic, with its totalizing, temporalizing power, restored to time its Dionysian character as disruptive, dispersive, and aleatory. Foucault's early "structuralist" works discounted the diachronic (historical time) in favor of the synchronic (the ahistorical). These "archaeologies" of clinical medicine, mental illness, and the social sciences were comparative studies of accumulated discourse (playing one network of conditions for what qualifies as science-knowledge against another) that seemed to avoid the temporal succession and progressivism of traditional history of ideas. But the epistemic breaks between networks, which he charted in these books, were rigorously periodized, and he placed great store in their event-like character. Time plays an important, if implicit, role in his poststructuralist "genealogies" of sexuality and the penal system, where strategy replaces rule as the key to historical intelligibility. For, as Pierre Bourdieu has noted, the concept of strategy entails the rhythm, orientation, and irreversibility of time.

[T.R.F.]

FURTHER READINGS

Flynn, T.R. "Foucault and the Career of the Historical Event." *At the Nexus of Philosophy and History.* Ed. Bernard P. Dauenhauer. Athens: U of Georgia P, 1987. 178–200.

Foucault, Michel. *Power/Knowledge: Selected Interviews and Other Writings, 1972–1977.* Trans. Colin Gordon et al. Ed. Colin Gordon. New York: Pantheon Books, 1980.

———. *Foucault Live (Interviews, 1966–84).* Trans. John Johnston. Ed. Sylvère Lotringer. New York: Semiotext, 1989.

FRAISSE, PAUL (1911–)

Paul Fraisse is an experimental psychologist who was born in Saint-Etienne, France. He was a student of Albert Michotte and Henri Piéron, and pursued their task in developing psychological research in France. In addition, he has played a prominent role in the vocational training of many scientists.

Fraisse was named professor of experimental psychology at the Sorbonne in 1957 and director of the Institute of Psychology in Paris in 1961. He was the successor to Henri Piéron in 1964 as the head of his laboratory of the *Ecole Pratique des Hautes Etudes*, which he entitled the *Laboratoire de Psychologie Expérimentale et Comparée.* In this laboratory were trained many scientists who themselves founded a number of research teams in France. Topics given special attention at Fraisse's laboratory included the experimental psychology of time; perception and memory; social, industrial, and educational psychology; psycholinguistics, and neuropsychology.

From 1966 to 1969, Fraisse was the president of the International Union of Scientific Psychology. He has been responsible for two scientific collections at the Presses Universitaires de France and for two journals, *L'Année Psychologique* and *French Language Psychology.* He developed the latter in 1980 to promote the diffusion of French psychology and psychoanalysis in English-speaking countries. Fraisse was one of the founders of the *Association de Psychologie scientifique de Langue française,* which organizes regular meetings in Europe. He holds honorary doctorates from several universities around the world and is an associate member of the American Academy of Sciences.

The doctoral theses that Fraisse presented on rhythm and on time perception have been the starting points of numerous works in the field. These theses have been published as two books, *Les Structures rhythmiques* (1956) and *Psychologie du temps* (1957), the latter of which was translated into English in 1963. According to Fraisse, in rhythmic patterns, both the order of events and the intervals between them are perceived. Rhythm perception is the very basis of the experience of duration. Time perception depends on the "density of perceived changes": Duration is judged longer when this density increases. External as well as internal changes related to perception and memory mechanisms are involved. The level of attention devoted to the current configuration of events largely determines the number of changes processed.

Furthermore, attention influences the limits of the "psychological (or perceived) present"—the interval within which all environmental and behavioral changes are perceived as a unity. Within the psychological present, duration is perceived, and only immediate memory is concerned. Beyond it, duration is estimated, with quite different mechanisms being involved.

Fraisse argues that intuitions of time do exist. Even infants are attuned to temporal parameters: They discover duration through the experience of waiting, as when a delay elapses between their feelings of hunger and satiation. This view was thoroughly debated between Fraisse and Jean Piaget, who believed that the mastery of time notions slowly develops during childhood as a result of the relations that are progressively recognized between speed and space.

[F.J.J.M.]

See also **Piaget, Jean; Psychological Present; Rhythm and Meter in Music; Time Perception.**

FURTHER READINGS

Fraisse, P. *The Psychology of Time*. New York: Harper & Row, 1963.

————. *Psychologie du rythme*. Paris: Presses Universitaires de France, 1974.

Fraisse, P., and J. Piaget, eds. *Traité de psychologie expérimentale*. Paris: Presses Universitaires de France, 1963.

FRASER, J.T. (1923–)

Time has traditionally been understood as a measure of change. In other words, time is what a clock measures. Accordingly, the history of the philosophy of time can be seen as a debate concerning which clocks are the fundamental ones.

For example, the theories of special and general relativity, and the emphasis on private time in the early part of the twentieth century, share the basic assumption that whatever time is, it can ultimately be reduced to a single unified concept. In special relativity, time in an inertial frame is assumed to be relative to the observer, and in general relativity, the fundamental fabric of reality is postulated to be a four-dimensional space-time. There is, however, no suggestion in either theory that, over and above its plasticity and relativity, time is anything but a Platonic essence whose basic features have remained constant since creation. Space-time provides essentially the same sort of temporality for a lump of coal as for a mammal. And whereas the work of thinkers such as Henri Bergson and Edmund Husserl, and of novelists like Marcel Proust, emphasized the flows and eddies of internal time consciousness, they did nothing to suggest that there is any other form of temporality besides the dialectic between human subjective time and quantified public time.

J.T. Fraser's strikingly original contribution to the study of time is the idea that we must give up the search for the quintessential clock and instead begin to conceptualize time as a hierarchy of different, but deeply interconnected, temporalities. Whereas time has typically been understood as the agent of change, Fraser contends that it is itself dynamical. Simply, the universe is a clocksmith whose history can be understood as the invention of increasingly intricate clocks.

Specifically, Fraser claims that the correct model for time is that of an evolutionary hierarchy of more and more complex temporalities. A major part of the beauty and persuasiveness of Fraser's theory is that it recasts the fundamental stages of cosmic evolution in temporal terms. Fraser's theory supplements the classificatory system usually employed to describe the evolution of the universe with a temporal description of each stage of the universe's history. Time, therefore, is no longer understood as a background for reality, nor simply as the human experience of flux, but as an evolving palimpsest of emergent temporal levels constitutive of reality.

Fraser's evolutionary model of time does what most genuinely innovative theories do: it does not simply refute older theories, but rather situates them within a larger, more inclusive context. By reformulating the terms with which philosophy can address the issue of time, and by doing so using concepts stemming from the natural sciences, the social sciences, and the arts and humanities, Fraser's theories have done much to place the study of time on a new interdisciplinary footing that promises to solve many heretofore intransigent problems, to open the door to new research, and, with a measure of tragedy that Fraser himself would appreciate, to generate new, higher order problems and paradoxes.

[A.A.]

See also **Hierarchical Theory of Time; Interdisciplinary Studies; International Society for the Study of Time.**

FURTHER READINGS

Fraser, J.T. *Time as Conflict: A Scientific and Humanistic Study*. Boston: Birkhäuser Verlag, 1978.

———, ed. *The Voices of Time.* 2nd ed. Amherst: U of Massachusetts P, 1981.

———. *The Genesis and Evolution of Time: A Critique of Interpretation in Physics.* Amherst: U of Massachusetts P, 1982.

———. *Of Time, Passion, and Knowledge: Reflections on the Strategy of Existence.* 2nd ed. Princeton: Princeton UP, 1990.

———. *Time, the Familiar Stranger.* Amherst: U of Massachusetts P, 1987.

Fraser, J.T., et al., eds. *The Study of Time.* Volumes I-IV, New York: Springer, 1972–1981; Volume V, Amherst: U of Massachusetts P, 1986; Volumes VI-VIII, Madison: International Universities P, 1989–.

FREE-RUNNING IN CHRONOBIOLOGY

Free-running in chronobiology involves the continuance of bioperiodicity with a natural frequency usually at least slightly, yet statistically significantly, different from any known environmental schedule.

The deviation of a circadian rhythm's period from both a precise 24-hour solar and a 24.8-hour lunar day, such as the shortened period observed in the rectal temperature of mice after blinding, led to the definition of free-running. The statistically significant deviations from various other known environmental period lengths of circadian rhythms with similar but not identical periods in different variables of many species constitute an argument for a partly endogenous time structure. The endogenicity of rhythms was first demonstrated and inferentially statistically validated as generalized free-running for the case of circadians in the blinded mouse model. In studies of the effect of the lighting regimen as a synchronizer, the question as to the transducer arose. Do the eyes mediate the effect? To answer this question, two models were studied: the blinded mouse and the mouse born anophthalmic (without vision). In the study on blinded mice, the controls were sham-operated and the mice had on the average consistently high blood eosinophil counts in the middle of the daily light span and low counts during the dark span. By contrast, the blinded mice showed the same result in one study and the opposite effect a few weeks later. It was postulated that the rhythm of the blinded mice may have a circadian period slightly different from that of the twenty-four-hour synchronized control mice. Since it was not practical to bleed a mouse every four hours over a long span, rectal temperature was measured around the clock, in some studies for the lifetime of the groups of mice investigated, and proved to exhibit an appropriate marker rhythm.

This work led to the discovery of free-running rhythms in variables such as eosinophil counts in circulating blood, serum corticosterone, liver glycogen, and liver mitoses. The period of these rhythms differed invariably from twenty-four hours, and also differed among some of the mice. In two groups of mice, one sham-operated and the other blinded, it was found that the daily peaks in the average rectal temperature curves occurred every twenty-four hours in the sham-operated mice, but occurred earlier and earlier each day in the blinded mice. A plot of the circadian acrophases as a function of time postoperation showed a downward drift to earlier and earlier clock-hours for the blinded mice but not for the sham-operated control mice. A

ENDOGENOUS TIME STRUCTURE (CHRONOME) OF INTERNALLY COORDINATED FREE-RUNNING RHYTHMS

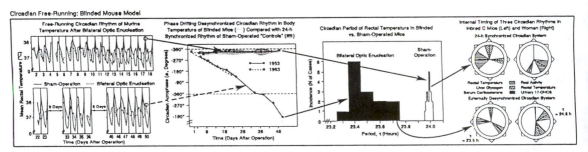

Figure 1. Demonstration of circadian free-running in the blinded mouse model. Whereas the control sham-operated animals had daily peaks in rectal temperature recurring every twenty-four hours, these peaks occurred earlier and earlier each day in the blinded mice (left) corresponding to a downward drift of the circadian acrophase (second left). On the average, the circadian period was shorter than twenty-four hours for the blinded mice (third left); nonetheless, the internal timing of some variables was preserved, as shown for inbred C mice and for a woman isolated from society (right).

histogram of the estimated circadian periods showed that the sham-operated animals had a twenty-four-hour synchronized circadian rhythm (the periods clustering very tightly around twenty-four hours), whereas the mice that had a bilateral optic enucleation had a circadian period shorter than twenty-four hours. Experiments have demonstrated that, a deviant circadian period notwithstanding, the internal timing of three variables was preserved, as shown for inbred C mice (brother to sister mated for more than twenty generations), and for a woman isolated from society, even if the free-running circadian period of the mice was shorter and that of the woman longer than twenty-four hours (see Figure 1). These experiments clearly establish, on an inferential statistical basis, for the individual woman, as well as for a population, the phenomenon of circadian free-running, which led to the demonstration of the endogenicity (that is, of the genetic basis) of the chronome.

Once the fundamental feature of rhythms, found at all levels of organization, is recognized by means of their capability to free-run as a manifestation of their endogenicity, it is important to quantify rigorously their characteristics and their interrelationships as a basis for a definition of health, for their alterations provide harbingers of increased risk, and their mapping can be used to guide the timing of treatment when needed.

[G.C., F.H., and R.P.S.]

See also **Chronobiology; Chronome; Chronophysiology.**

FURTHER READINGS

Halberg, F. "Some Physiological and Clinical Aspects of 24-Hour Periodicity." *Lancet (USA)* 73 (1953): 20–32.

———. "Physiologic 24-Hour Periodicity: General and Procedural Considerations with Reference to the Adrenal Cycle." *Zur Vitamin-, Hormon- und Fermentforschung* 10 (1959): 225–296.

———. "Body Temperature, Circadian Rhythms and the Eye." *La photoregulation de la reproduction chez les oiseaux et les mammifères.* Ed. J. Benoit and I. Assenmacher. Paris, CNRS 172, 1970. 497–528.

———. "*Quo Vadis* Basic and Clinical Chronobiology: Promise for Health Maintenance." *American Journal of Anatomy* 168 (1983): 543–594.

Halberg, F., M.B. Visscher, and J.J. Bittner. "Eosinophil Rhythm in Mice: Range of Occurrence, Effects of Illumination, Feeding and Adrenalectomy." *American Journal of Physiology* 174 (1953): 109–122.

Halberg, F., and M.B. Visscher. "Temperature Rhythms in Blind Mice." *Federation Proceedings* 13 (1954): 65.

Halberg, F., et al. "Physiologic 24-Hour Periodicity in Human Beings and Mice, the Lighting Regimen and Daily Routine." *Photoperiodism and Related Phenomena in Plants and Animals.* Ed. Robert B. Withrow. Washington, D.C.: Publication No. 55, American Association of Advanced Science, 1959. 803–878.

———. *Glossary of Chronobiology. Chronobiologia* 4, Supplement 1, 1977.

FRENCH CLOCKS AND WATCHES, 1660–1830

The invention of the balance spring for watches (1675) and the application of the pendulum to clocks (1658), both of which are innovations associated with Christiaan Huygens, produced fundamental changes in European horology. Their immediate and most obvious effect was an improvement in the accuracy of timekeepers from an error of some twenty to thirty minutes per day to four to five minutes per day. This immense improvement in time-measurement inevitably drew attention to the new timekeepers, attention which was encouraged by publicists such as John Smith and William Derham in England and Henry Sully in France who published explanatory treatises on horology designed for the lay public. Innovation, publicity, and, at last, reliability, all combined to create a greater demand for clocks and watches which quickly became essential tools and status symbols for the rapidly growing commercial, manufacturing, and bourgeois classes of *ancien régime* Europe. Growing demand gave a commercial fillip to European horology and stimulated innovation in both the mechanisms and the decoration of clocks and watches. At the same time, since the proof of a successful technical innovation lay in the improvement that it brought to the performance of a watch or clock, the idea of continuously seeking to improve the precision of the instrument aligned the interests of the more enterprising makers with those of astronomers, physicists, and navigators interested in developing time-measurers of the highest possible precision for their specific purposes. Huygens himself was not a clockmaker but a mathematician, physicist, and astronomer. His intervention in horology brought not only social and intellectual prestige to the subject, but also revealed the intrinsic interest of the subject for savants, and led to a close association between advanced craftsmen and theoreticians. In the course of the eighteenth century, precision clockmaking became, therefore, increasingly assimilated with technical and scientific research, both theoretical and practical. In the *Encyclopédie*, Ferdinand Berthoud, one of the leading, and certainly the most eloquent, of Paris clockmakers wrote that "Up to Huygens horology could be considered as a mechanical art which required only manual work; but the application which it makes of geometry and mechanics for its discoveries, have made this art a science in which manual work is no more than an accessory, and of which the principal part is the theory of the movement of bodies which includes the most sublime parts of Geometry, calculation, Mechanics and Physics."

The association of the practical craft of clockmaking with the theoretical sciences of physics and mathematics combined with the considerable wealth that the most successful clockmakers amassed to raise the social status of horology and thus helped further expansion to take place. While these developments were general to most of Europe, the form that they took in different countries and regions was quite specific, the differences in turn combining to have feedback effects on the individual regions. French horology in the eighteenth century therefore displays the paradox of being both unique in, and characteristic of, horology throughout Europe.

Although the first pendulum clocks to be built to Huygens's design were made in the Hague by Salomon Coster in 1657–59, knowledge of them quickly spread via John Fromanteel to London where they were advertised in late October and early November of 1658, and to Paris in great part via Huygens himself, who made several visits to the city before settling there for nearly twenty years as a *pensionnaire* of the Académie Royale des Sciences in 1666, and the clockmaker Nicolas Hanet, who worked with Coster at The Hague before returning to Paris in the autumn of 1658. Inevitably, the earliest French pendulum clocks closely resembled their Dutch predecessors. They are contained in plain, rectangular cases, usually of oak or walnut veneered with ebony or ebonized pearwood, and have a glazed door in the front behind which is the circular brass chapter ring with Roman hour and Arabic minute numerals, set on a full, velvet-covered plate. The winding hole is normally in or near the center of the dial, and below the chapter ring is a decorated brass swag, sometimes engraved with the maker's name, which covers a stop-start aperture. Early on, a smooth-surfaced arch top was attached, sometimes ornamented with brass finials. Decorative pillars were added to the front of the clock and decorative inlay and veneers appear on the case. The two hands were often finely pierced. The movements of such clocks are normally square; plated, with an external, numbered locking plate; and fitted with a horizontal verge escapement with the pendulum crutch directly attached to the pallet arbor, the pendulum being suspended by a silk thread operating between cycloidal cheeks.

Decorative development of such clocks, which at first were hung on the wall but quickly acquired feet for placing on a piece of furniture or on a wall bracket, was rapid and considerable. An increase in height to give a more elegant, elongated form was reinforced by the appearance of the caddy top, which was also convenient for housing the bells for hour or half-hour striking and for music. Corners tended to be rounded off or treated architecturally, but it is perhaps not until the characteristic rectangular glazed front door was given an arched top, which the top of the case also echoed, that these "religieuse" clocks as they were called can be considered as giving way to the more sinuously rounded and far more luxuriantly decorated clocks typical of the latter part of the reign of Louis XIV and of the Regency. These clocks, placed on elaborate floor-standing pedestals or wall-mounted on smaller plinths, would maintain themselves in a bewildering number of decorative styles throughout the eighteenth century.

Other styles did of course appear. Elaborately inlaid clocks with exaggerated narrow waists known as "Tête de poupée" were popular during the last quarter of the seventeenth century and metal inlay, popularized by Charles Boulle and subsequently known by his name, developed from ca. 1695 onward. Individual white enamel plaques carrying the hour numerals in blue became typical in the last quarter of the seventeenth century. Single piece floor-standing clocks were rare except for regulators, as were metal-cased clocks, but "cartels," clocks contained in elaborately worked gilt wood or gilt bronze cases designed to be applied directly to a wall without a plinth, became popular in the mid-eighteenth century. There was also a vogue for clocks in highly elaborate porcelain surrounds, usually showing shepherds and/or shepherdesses in floral or arboreal settings, from the 1760s onward. Toward the end of the century elaborate figurative gilt bronze cases or supports became popular. Their exuberance, however, produced a reaction during the Empire when a new plainness developed in casemaking, elegance being achieved by line and proportion with decoration heavily restrained. The influence of the rediscovery of Egypt and Hellenistic Greece are both reflected in clockcase design during this period. High precision clocks, which became prestigious during the Revolution and Empire, were particularly susceptible to being placed in austere but exceptionally well-made cases (see Figure 1).

Variation in style following the dictates of fashion is characteristic only of clocks produced for wealthy bourgeois and noble urban customers. For the less wealthy and for use in rural areas and the workaday settings of manufactories or commercial establishments, more robust, less pretentious clocks were produced. Lantern clocks—which were driven by the force of a falling weight rather than by a spring as were the fashionable clocks described earlier—developed in England during the seventeenth century as an (usually) all-brass, smaller version of the larger iron "Gothic" clocks of the fifteenth and sixteenth centuries. Adapted to pendulum control after the mid-century, such clocks began to be imported into France during the last quarter of the seventeenth century, mainly through the ports of Caen and Rouen. Quickly, however, they stimulated local emulation and it was in the same two towns that the first French lantern clocks were marketed. The first treatise in French devoted to clockmaking, the *Horlogéographie pratique ou la manière de faire les horloges à poids. . .*, by Père Beuriot, was also published at Rouen in 1719. It deals specifically with lantern clocks, describing in the minutest detail how to construct them with an alarm or with hour striking.

Although today a book of the greatest rarity, the influence of Beuriot's work was probably considerable, supplying local craftsmen in small towns and villages with basic instruction in how to make a reliable clock for local customers. Often quite rustic in appearance, they normally had iron frames supporting the wheelwork, surmounted by a single bell carried either on a vertical arm or suspended from cross straps, and with a large rectangular or circular dial sometimes surmounted by a decorative fretted headpiece. The movements may or may not have been protected by a case before being hung on the wall or stood on an open bracket, but such clocks were also used inside one-piece floor-standing cases.

Lantern clocks were a regional product. They were made primarily in northwest France in the areas of Normandy, La Manche, Calvados, the Orne, Mayenne, and the Eure. In the northeast, the Ardennes, Alsace, and the Franche Comté, domestic time-telling was assured by large, robust longcase clocks of between two and three meters in height known as "Comtoise" clocks, and as "Morbiers" or "Morez" after two towns in the Franche Comté which were main centers of their production. Like the Normandy lantern clocks, comtoise clocks first seem to have been produced in quantity in the last quarter of the seventeenth century. That this coincides with the moment when clocks acquired a new prestige thanks to their enhanced time-telling capacities after Huygens's innovations is surely not by chance. Since the trains of a comtoise clock are placed side by side and not one behind the other as they are in lantern clocks, the movements are much broader than lantern clocks and can carry a large, usually enameled dial easy to read from a distance. The typical escapement

Figure 1. A seconds-indicating mantel clock with calendar, late eighteenth century, signed Revel.

of the clock until well into the nineteenth century is a horizontal verge often with the escape wheel inverted so that the pallets mesh below rather than above it, but the anchor escapement, and some variants, was also used, displacing the verge almost entirely in the middle of the nineteenth century. Like many public clocks, the comtoise commonly has a double strike for verifying the hour, the striking of which is repeated after an interval of two minutes.

Lantern and comtoise clocks were undeniably the most commonly used clocks in eighteenth-century France, although their popularity may have been rivaled in some areas by a relatively inexpensive but attractive compartmented cylindrical clepsydra (see Figure 2), which could be obtained with either an alarm or with striking work or with both. The clepsydras were manufactured in large numbers by pewterers in the regions of Sens and Chartres to be sold by peddlers in rural regions. Of the development of turret clocks little is yet known in detail, although a fundamental innovation was made by Julien Le Roy. At an unknown date before 1737, when he published descriptions of it, he introduced the earliest form of "flat-bed" turret clock, that is, a clock in which the various trains and their component parts are disposed horizontally in a massive single bar, rectangular frame, instead of being set up vertically in a cubical, "bird-cage" type of frame as had hitherto been prevalent. Le Roy's layout was quickly adopted by other makers, in particular by J.A. Lepaute who made several clocks of this kind. If Julien Le Roy's son, Pierre, perhaps exaggerated when he claimed in 1770 that the horizontal or "flat-bed" form "had led to the abandon of the others," it was certainly used for most royal and noble commissions for clocks for their châteaux by the leading Paris makers. Such a clock was installed at Versailles in 1769 by Pepin and Le Roy, and another at the Hôtel des Monnaies in 1774 by Lepaute. A few years later a new, mixed form was introduced by Robert Robin in which the going train was partially arranged vertically with the other trains horizontally beside it. The clock of this arrangement that he installed in the Jardin des Plantes in 1780 still survives.

The increase in precision consequent upon the introduction of the pendulum had raised for the general public the problem of the equation of time. Because a clock keeps a mean average time, it does not exactly follow true solar time. Since the first pendulum clocks were advertised as "going with the sun," this was a problem, as was the emotional feeling of most people that true time could only be that given by the sun, rather than by a machine. The making of a clock, and even more a watch, which could by ingenious gearing show both times, was a technical challenge to savants and craftsmen in the early eighteenth century. Some of the solutions produced were masterpieces of mechanical ingenuity, and it is notable that Lepaute incorporated an adjustment for the length of the pendulum into his turret clocks, which throughout the year would automatically adjust the length of the pendulum and so the speed of the clock according to the season. By the end of the century, however, clockmakers such as Berthoud and Janvier were campaigning for the adoption of mean time as legal civil time to be observed nationally, and in 1816, this was at last decreed.

By contrast with turret clocks, watches have been well studied. Unlike clockmaking—which was quite sharply demarcated geographically with the luxury trade centered on Paris, and to a lesser degree on regional centers such as Lyon or Marseille, while lantern and comtoise clocks characterized different regions—watchmaking was far more of a national, indeed international, trade. The reason for this is obvious enough. Watches are easily transportable. Labor intensive but requiring little investment for material, tools, and workspace, they are ideally suited to small workshop or domestic production and, because they are of small bulk and weight, can easily be distributed over a wide region. Watchmaking in the sixteenth and seventeenth centuries had been carried out in numerous small centers scattered across France. If the centralizing tendencies of the late seventeenth century meant that by the eighteenth century Paris dictated style and fashion and to a lesser degree dominated the retail trade, the prestige that came to be attached to watches by the great Paris makers such as Julien Le Roy, Lepine, or the Lepaute family combined with the relatively high value of their products and their portability to create ideal conditions for the development of a counterfeit trade. Such counterfeit watches were being made even beyond the French borders and smuggled across the frontiers. While Dutch makers tended to counterfeit English watches, Swiss makers produced well-finished, highly deceptive imitations of the work of the best Paris makers. The signature on an eighteenth-century "French" watch is no guarantee that the object ever had any connection with the maker named. Equally devastating for French manufacture was the competition of the legitimate Swiss production. Toward the middle of the century, Julien Le Roy complained that "the genevans inundate all the southern provinces of the kingdom with their awful watches, apart from the merchants who take them for a considerable value to the fair of Beaucaire, there are many others who every summer carry a great number into the Dauphiné, Provence, the Languedoc and Gascony."

In the course of the eighteenth century there was considerable variation in the style of watches. The preference already evident by 1650 for round watches over oval, hexagonal, cruciform, or other shapes was reinforced by the introduction of Huygens's balance spring in 1675, but its need of space reversed another tendency of the mid-century which was toward the construction of small watches of about twenty to twenty-five millimeters in diameter. Watches with balance springs, an extra wheel to ensure thirty hours duration, and motion work for the action and setting of the minute hand (which the improvement in accuracy had now made worth adding to watches) could not be made so small. First generation balance spring watches were therefore some fifty to sixty millimeters in diameter and something of the shape of an onion or tuber, by which name (oignon) they continue to be known. Fitted with two hands adjusted centrally through the dial, such watches have large balances with the balance spring initially of only two or three coils, later of five or six, protected by a much enlarged, decoratively pierced and chased cock. The maker's name is normally engraved along the edge of the back plate, perhaps to be repeated on the dial; the regulator disk is usually of silver, as less commonly may be the cock and the pillar capitals. Dials were either of chased gilt metal with twelve enameled hour numeral plaques and a minute ring within, or entirely enameled, sometimes with bosses for the hour numerals. Cases are usually of gilt metal, rarely of silver, either plain, engraved, or leather-covered with a pin appliqué decoration. That such watches were destined for wide distribution is underlined by the use of gilt metal rather than gold for the cases.

Accurate, decorative, and relatively robust, the "oignon" was nonetheless cumbersome and inelegant. Reducing the size of watches and streamlining their appearance is a major theme of the development of French horology in the eighteenth century. A second theme is technical. A balance spring, like a pendulum, has its proper period. Of itself it divides time in equal

parts and needs the mechanism of the watch merely as a motive force to give a regular impulse to the balance spring and to count its oscillations. A verge escapement, however, is quite the opposite. The balance has no period of its own and is constantly influenced by the wheel train, an interference that it transmits to the balance spring, upsetting its isochronism. To function properly the balance spring needs to be as free of such interference as possible. Huygens's invention imposed on watchmakers the search for a new escapement.

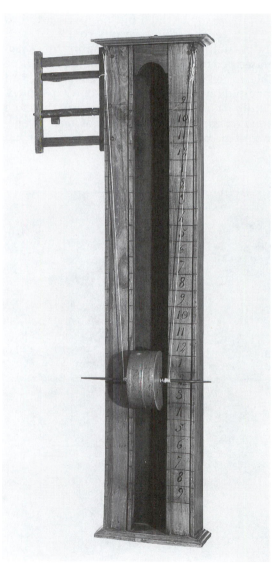

Figure 2. A compartmented falling cylinder clepsydra, early nineteenth century.

Initial attempts were made in England. In ca. 1720–1725, George Graham, developing ideas of Thomas Tompion and others, produced his cylinder escapement. It quickly became known in Paris (perhaps though Henry Sully), where it was adopted by Julien Le Roy ca. 1728, and was eulogistically described by Antoine L'Aîné Thiout in his Traité d'horlogerie (1741). Already widely used by the middle of the eighteenth century, this escapement would retain popularity for standard watches and even small clocks until well into the twentieth century. But the success of the cylinder, unlike that of the verge in earlier centuries, did not prevent further innovation. The assimilation of watchmakers into the progressive research and improvement ethos of eighteenth-century savants combined with the possibilities which balance spring timekeepers seemed to hold out for developing a machine able to keep time accurately enough to find longitude at sea, and led to constant experimentation. The eighteenth century was therefore punctuated by the invention of new escapements and other improvements to watches and clocks. For want of space, and because they are the most historically significant, I mention only the following: the virgule escapement produced by Lepaute in 1767 that greatly reduced the heavy friction of the cylinder of which it is a variant; the duplex, known in a number of forms, of which the commonest is that used by Julien Le Roy ca. 1750; and the lever devised in England by Thomas Mudge in 1754, first used by him in a clock in 1769–70, and applied to watches by Josiah Emery ca. 1782. The full development of these escapements did not, however, necessarily occur during the period with which we are here concerned. The lever escapement, for example, though known to the leading Paris makers through three examples imported into France between 1783 and 1786, was used only by a few of the best makers such as Robin, Breguet, and briefly Louis Berthoud, and was not fully developed and exploited until the second quarter of the nineteenth century. In the same period, the cylinder escapement also enjoyed a vast expansion of production, and in France supplied the mainstay for the cottage industry of an entire region on the plateau of the Maîche in the Jura, around the towns of Maîche and Pontichard.

At the same time as the requirements of the balance spring thus stimulated technical innovation, the desire to produce smaller, thinner, more elegant watches also had consequences for the machine. Already in the early decades of the eighteenth century the oignon was losing favor, and from the end of the first quarter of the century smaller, though still rather thick, double-cased watches were being produced with engraved, repoussé, or enameled cases. In the third quarter of the century the demand for a thin watch led Jean-Antoine Lépine to make radical rearrangements in the layout of the watch. Between 1762 and 1772 he developed his new model. Always using a steel cylinder or the virgule escapement, he suppressed the fusee by using only the central portion of the main spring where variation in the force would be least, and placed this spring in a going barrel. In about 1770, he realized that the back plate of the watch was itself not strictly needed and removed it, supporting the various organs of the watch by bridges or, as for the going barrel, simply leaving them suspended. At the same time, he moved the winding and hand-setting from the front to the back of the watch, thus protecting enamel dials from damage, and incorporated an inner cover.

Figure 3. A two-day marine chronometer by Breguet & fils.

Not only did Lepine's rearrangement of the watch allow it to be far thinner, it also had economic advantages (no costly fusee to manufacture), and removal of the fusee also eliminated an important source of friction. His layout was quickly taken up by other makers, and it was also for Lepine-caliber watches that the first mass-produced ebauches or unfinished movements, those of Japy, were made from 1785 onward. Japy's enterprise, which was quickly imitated by Swiss entrepreneurs, heralds the semi-industrial techniques that would lead to the nineteenth- and twentieth-century domination of world watch markets by Swiss manufacturers. In France, despite the example of Japy, there was only a limited development along these lines. In 1792, in a conscious effort to decentralize watchmaking from Paris and make it more competitive, a new watchmaking community was established at Besançon. But before 1830, this did little more than survive, despite state protection, and a similar, state-supported attempt to set up an automated manufactory at Versailles ca. 1795 failed totally after only a few years.

The strength of Swiss competition meant that whatever chance there might have been for French watchmaking to obtain a substantial share of the world mass market for watches was lost during the period of the revolution and Empire. The inventiveness of the Paris trade and its skill in producing high precision, elegant watches for the luxury and scientific trades, however, remained and affirmed itself. Makers such as Pierre Le Roy, Robert Robin, and Swiss expatriates Ferdinand Berthoud and Abraham-Louis Breguet brought immense prestige to Paris watchmaking. The styles and technical innovations of Breguet were to influence high precision watches for civil use for over half a century after his death in 1823. In the field of precision chronometry for marine use, the work of Pierre Le Roy was brilliant, that of Ferdinand Berthoud impressive by its tenacity, and that of his nephew, Louis Berthoud, exceptional. But the dependence of such makers on state support for their researches and the high prices they demanded meant that they failed to lay the foundations of a viable commercial manufactory of marine chronometers (see Figure 3). Widespread trade in such machines remained the preserve of English makers.

More important commercially was the development in the last quarter of the eighteenth century of various styles of small spring-driven clocks specially designed for traveling. They are characterized by being fully enclosed in strong, relatively plain metal cases, and all are surmounted by a substantial carrying handle. Such clocks are known as "pendules d'officier" (which presumably describes one of their commoner uses), "capucines," or "foncines." The commonest of them are the "capucines," plain, rectangular, brass-cased clocks with corner finials and a centrally-placed bell with carrying handle above. Related to them are various forms of small hanging clocks. In about 1810, such clocks were joined in Breguet's production by very high quality, often complicated clocks with astronomical or calendar indications, of rectangular form, and mounted in gilt bronze cases glazed on all sides. A variant form, in which the movement is enclosed in an unglazed rectangular wooden case usually faced with a rich veneer of rare wood, is clearly related to the plainer variety of rectangular mantel clocks ("borne" clocks) popular during the same period. At the very end of the period covered here, these portable clocks gave rise to the classic "carriage clock" as it was developed by Paul Garnier. This was easily the best quality mass-market clock of the nineteenth century and was long a virtual French monopoly. Although their development falls outside the scope of this survey they are worthy of being noted here as yet another of the eighteenth-century developments that laid the foundations of nineteenth-century horological prosperity in France.

[A.J.T.]

See also Clocks: America and Mass Production, 1770–1890; Clocks and Watches: The Leap to Precision; Longitude; Precision Timekeeping, 1790–1900; Timekeepers, Domestic: English Influence, 1710–1800; Watch Manufacturing in Nineteenth-Century America.

FURTHER READINGS

Allix, Charles. Carriage Clocks: Their History and Development. New York: Apollo, 1974.

Cardinal, Catherine. La montre des origines au XIXe siècle. Fribourg: Office du livre, 1985.

Cardinal, Catherine, and Jean-Claude Sabrier. La Dynastie Le Roy, horlogers du Roi. Tours: Musée des Beaux Arts de Tours, 1987.

Chapiro, A. Jean-Antoine Lépine horloger (1720–1814). Paris: Editions de l'amateur, 1988.

Edey, Winthrop. French Clocks. New York: Walker, 1967.

Landes, David S. Revolution in Time: Clocks and the Making of the Modern World. Cambridge: Belknap P of Harvard UP, 1983.

Maitzner, Francis, and Jean Moreau. *La comtoise, la morbier, la morez, son histoire, sa technique ses particularités, ses complications, sa réparation.* 3rd ed. N.p.: the authors, 1979.

Sabrier, Jean-Claude. *Les horloges lanternes françaises, les trois dernières parties de l'ouvrage du Père Beuriot Horlogéographie pratique rééditée avec une introduction.* London: Rogers Turner Books, 1988.

Tardy. *French Clocks the World Over.* 5th ed. Paris: Tardy, 1981. Parts 1 and 2.

Turner, A.J. *Les montres.* Paris: Fabbri, 1991.

Ungerer, Alfred. *Les horloges d'édifice, leur construction, leur montage, leur entretien, . . .* Paris: the author, [1927].

FREUD, SIGMUND (1856–1939)

Sigmund Freud, one of the outstanding thinkers of the twentieth century and founder of psychoanalysis, was born in the small town of Freiberg in Moravia on May 6, 1856, of Jewish parents. Many of his insights relate to time by demonstrating the extent to which past exterience, often suppressed, affects the present mental condition of the individual.

When he was four years old, Freud's father, a merchant of moderate means, moved his family to Vienna, where Freud received his education, married, practiced medicine, did some basic biological research on the central nervous system of invertebrates, and wrote classic studies on aphasia and cerebral palsy in children. He would have preferred to pursue a career in biological research, but Professor Ernst Wilhelm von Brücke, in whose laboratory Freud served as a research assistant, indicated that the anti-semitism Freud would encounter rendered such a choice inadvisable. Freud was deeply influenced by the evolutionary ideas of Charles Darwin and the materialist theories of the school of Hermann von Helmholtz. Freud had also studied the coca plant and had suggested the use of cocaine as a surface anesthetic but, distracted by personal matters, he delayed performing the crucial experiments which brought fame to his friend and colleague, Carl Koller.

Freud's psychological investigations began after an historic conversation with Josef Breuer in 1883. Breuer, an eminent physician and physiologist whom Freud had met in Brücke's laboratory, described a unique and novel method by which he had relieved the symptoms of a woman suffering from severe hysteria. During hypnosis, the patient would relate what was oppressing her mind and would recollect some highly emotional fantasy or event connected with the onset of her symptoms. Awake, the patient was completely unaware of the "traumatic event" or its connection with her disability. As the patient recollected these painful experiences in increasingly lighter hypnotic trances, and reacted to these recollections with appropriate emotional discharge, the symptoms disappeared. Freud repeated the experiment on several patients during the next twelve years, and became convinced of the validity of Breuer's findings. In 1895, mainly as a result of Freud's initiative and insistence, Breuer and Freud published "Studies in Hysteria." Breuer and Freud reasoned that the symptoms of hysteria are the effects of an undischarged quantity of emotion connected with a painful memory. The task of treatment, therefore, was to transform the repressed memory into a conscious experience and thereby achieve discharge of the pent-up emotions. Breuer did not wish to pursue these problems further, but Freud did. The motives for repressing certain memories, Freud said, are defensive. Repression serves to protect the individual from shame, guilt, fear, humiliation, or other unpleasant effects associated with the memory of certain events.

In an effort to get the patient to recall traumatic events, Freud used hypnosis and suggestion. At first, he felt that all patients suffering from hysteria had been seduced sexually at an early age and that this type of experience was the essential factor in causing hysteria. Later observations convinced him that, in many instances, the reports of experiences of seduction, which he had accepted at face value, had actually been fantasies. It is probable that they were artifacts resulting from Freud's vigorous method of suggestion. Although at first bewildered by this turn in his investigation, Freud came to realize that, in the minds of patients, fantasies may exert an influence as effective as real events and that, contrary to the notions current at the time, children do have sexual wishes and urges. He also changed his method of investigation from hypnosis and suggestion to a technique of free association, urging patients to say, without censorship, whatever thoughts came into their consciousness.

Using this technique, Freud learned that other neurotic symptoms, such as phobias and obsessions, also had meaning. He discovered that his method could reveal hidden meanings in many normal phenomena, such as dreams, slips of the tongue, lapses of memory, jokes, artistic creations, fairy tales, and rituals. All of these had the following characteristic in common: they represented the result of an interplay between opposing or conflicting forces in the mind. This conflict of forces ended in a compromise, and, in the various mental acts that appear in consciousness, the wishes are fulfilled, but only partially and in substitute form. They are disguised, distorted, and rendered unrecognizable. Some of these compromises, like symptoms, may be painful or unacceptable. Others, like dreams, may be quite pleasurable.

Three major works by Freud originated during this period of his investigations (1900–1905). They were *The Interpretation of Dreams*, *Three Essays on Sexuality*, and *Jokes and Their Relationship to the Unconscious*. Sexuality, Freud stated, begins in earliest infancy and not at puberty, as had been thought formerly. Childhood sexuality, furthermore, is capable of the widest developmental variation and it reaches a climax around the ages of three to six in a special set of conflicts over attachment to one's parents. These experiences, known as the Oedipus complex, play a major role in shaping the personality of each individual.

These discoveries alone entitle Freud to a place in history as one of the great liberators of the mentally ill. By insisting that the symptoms and the verbal productions of neurotics, and even psychotics, had a meaning, he served to dispel the deeply rooted prejudice directed against a very considerable segment of humanity. His theories and technical discoveries also made possible a rational system of treating many mental illnesses by psychological methods. Even where his method is not effective in curing the illness, psychoanalysis still enables the doctor to understand the nature of the patient's complaints and difficulty. Knowledge of the early emotional development and its significance in shaping the personality has influenced the theory and practices of educators and has been helpful in devising measures for preventing emotional disorders and delinquency.

But Freud went on to demonstrate how his principles of mental functioning could be applied to the understanding of literature, religion, and group formation. He advanced these theories in several publications, especially *Totem and Taboo* (1913) and *Group Psychology and the Analysis of the Ego* (1921). Freud's insights into the psychological bonds that unite people into groups and organize their activities around common ideals have been applied to the study of many problems of sociology and anthropology. These insights have also made possible forms of psychotherapy in which patients may be treated in groups instead of individually.

Throughout his life, as he confronted new clinical findings, Freud kept revising his theory, as well as his technique. His final exposition of the dynamic forces in human psychology contained the concept of two fundamental drives, Eros, a life-giving force, and Thanatos, a biological force toward quiescence and death. The workings of the mind of the individual he articulated in terms of a structural theory: three organized centers or groups of mental functioning—the ego, the id, and the superego (see **Psychoanalysis**).

At first, a few followers gathered around Freud for weekly meetings at his apartment in Vienna. Ultimately this developed into the International Psychoanalytical Association, which today comprises thousands of members in all parts of the world. In 1909, Freud delivered a series of lectures at Clark University. It was his first and only trip to America, a land that did not impress him. Among other honors, Freud received the esteemed Goethe Prize for Literature.

The final years of his life were marked by an heroic struggle against cancer of the mouth. In spite of intractable pain, Freud carried on his investigations until the very end. In 1938, when the Nazis seized Vienna, Freud's name was prominent on the Nazi proscription list. Only the intervention of the American ambassador to France, William Bullitt, and Princess Marie Bonaparte secured his safe release to England, where he died in September of 1939, after having been made a member of the Royal Society.

[J.A.A.]

See also **Psychoanalysis**.

FURTHER READINGS

Arlow, Jacob A. "Disturbances of the Sense of Time With Special Reference to the Experience of Timelessness." *Psychoanalytic Quarterly* 53 (1984): 13–37.

Freud, Sigmund. *The Standard Edition of the Complete Psychological Works*. 24 vols. London: Hogarth P, 1953–74. See "Time" under Subject Index in Vol. 24.

Gay, Peter. *Freud: A Life for Our Time*. New York: Norton, 1988.

Hartocollis, P. *Time and Timelessness*. New York: International Universities P, 1983.

Jaques, E. *The Form of Time*. New York: Crane Russak, 1982.

Jones, E. *The Life and Work of Sigmund Freud*. New York: Basic Books, 1953.

Kafka, John. "On Reality: An Examination of Object Constancy, Ambiguity, Paradox and Time." *Psychiatry and the Humanities, Volume 2*. New Haven: Yale UP, 1977. 133–158.

FRONTIERS IN TIME AND SPACE

Human wakeful activity after dark slowly increased over thousands of years, and then surged ahead in the past two centuries. People have established continuous processes or nonstop schedules in many spheres of activity that were once intermittent. These include manufacturing, transportation, hospital services, restaurants, retail merchandising, indoor tennis, data processing, broadcasting, and the shipping and delivering of freight.

An analogy between such frontiers in time and the better understood frontiers in space will help us to understand the nature and causes of this expansion. The tests of the idea deal with whether (1) the causes of wakeful endeavors over the twenty-four-hour period are the same as for extending land settlements into uninhabited regions, (2) the pattern of development in colonizing the new region occurs in the same way, and (3) the type of society, its people, and their behavior are the same as on land frontiers. To test this hypothesis, an extensive set of comparisons have been made based on criteria derived from historians' analysis of the American western frontier.

"Frontier" is a concept, not an empirically based descriptor. Even though it had been developed originally in connection with geographic expansion, extending its theoretical compass to include time, and outer space, does not stretch its abstract meaning. And although point-by-point similarities may be demonstrated between a geographic outpost and after-dark activities, the frontier idea is more inclusive than can be shown by looking at only these two forms. Rather than a metaphor, it is conceptually like a "wave," which may have had watery beginnings but now subsumes the undulating motions of light, sound, shock, and water in a single theory.

Expansion of wakeful activity is spurred by the same causes that gave rise to land frontiers. These include desires for relief in the face of density pressures—whether felt as human crowding or overloaded production facilities, and resource scarcity—and the lures for gain in the uncolonized region, whether regarded as pleasing solitude or profit opportunities from new resources.

In documenting the remarkable parallels between the frontiers in time and the American western frontier, a variety of data from chronicles, statistics, and four field experiments confirmed the similarities between colonizing land at the edge of a wilderness and introducing more activity after dark. There was no contradictory evidence for thirteen distinct dimensions:

1. The stages of advance proceed from exploration to production to services and consumption, and occur in waves, with fluctuating advances and even periods of retreat (often in the face of danger, harsh living conditions, or economic decline).

2. There is usually organizational sponsorship; governments and firms promote the ventures, frequently for economic gain by exploiting some resource, such as natural material wealth or idle capacity for productive equipment.

3. The population is sparse and it is more homogeneous, overbalanced by vigorous young adult males who are less enmeshed in social obligations and more willing to face danger.

4. The motives for venturing onto the frontier are mainly relief and opportunity. Some individuals move to escape densities that are unpleasant or harassing to them, seeking more peaceful and solitary regions, but more go to improve their economic lot.

5. Settlements are isolated, have limited contact with one another, and the outposts are rather self-sufficient. Although the connection between the settled center and frontier is important to both, it is far less in people's consciousness than the local affairs of the region itself.

6. The society has less propriety and fewer decorous social norms; more nonconformity, and more immoderate or unconventional customs are tolerated.

7. There are fewer status distinctions and there is less deferential conduct; people are more relaxed and interact in an egalitarian manner.

8. There are novel hardships in the unfamiliar habitats, and distinctive, arduous difficulties in adapting.

9. There is decentralization of power, often the absence of constituted authority, so that obedience to the law is selective, and those present on the frontier make and enforce its particular rules.

10. There is more lawlessness and peril, more outlawry and violence, though some of this is more a matter of reputation than actual experience.

11. People are more helpful and friendly to strangers. Men and women on a frontier are aware of dangers, and the sense of threat itself prompts law-abiding persons to draw together once they conclude that they are not a menace to one another; they welcome the company of others and are more forthcoming to persons seeking assistance (demonstrated experimentally for the nighttime).

12. In a later stage, the dawning realization of a vigorous frontier's development leads the government to introduce policies to manage access to and exploitation of the frontier.

13. Conflicts develop between the frontier and the center of society, usually crystallizing around issues of personal rights or competitive struggles over economic opportunities; the interest groups strive to impose their own priorities and relations between the center and the outlying region is changed by political action.

Recently, the history of the exploration of outer space was tested by Carol J. Auster against this set of attributes. The findings showed substantial agreement. The few points of difference did not contradict but rather supplemented the set. All these studies make up a cumulative effort to establish a model of the general traits of frontiers. The word "frontier" has been linked to geography for so long that it seems to refer to space alone. But the empirical pattern of nighttime wakefulness suggests that the abstract idea of an edge of expansion and development should be enlarged to cover frontiers in time. The idea and the evidence support a case for the general equivalence of space and time.

[M.M.]

See also **Shift Work.**

FURTHER READINGS

Auster, Carol J. "Specification of Melbin's Frontier Hypotheses: An Application to Outer Space Exploration." *Sociological Inquiry* 57 (Winter 1987): 102–112.

Melbin, Murray. "Night as Frontier." *American Sociological Review* 43 (February 1978): 3–22.

———. *Night As Frontier: Colonizing the World after Dark.* New York: Free Press, 1987.

Turner, Frederick Jackson. *The Frontier in American History.* 1893; reprint, New York: Holt, 1920.

FUTURISTIC FICTION

Futuristic fiction is most precisely defined as any narrative explicitly set in future time. It was to such writing that Félix Bodin first applied the term *littérature futuriste* in 1834. In this category are works such as H.G. Wells's *The Time Machine* (1895), whose action starts out in its contemporary readers' present at the Time Traveller's house, but then moves forward to episodes set in distant futures before looping back again to the nineteenth century. In a looser sense, futuristic fiction refers to works that in any way significantly point attention forward to future prospects whether real or imaginary. A classic example of this sort is Jules Verne's *Twenty Thousand Leagues Under The Sea* (1870), whose action takes place during the interval 1866–1868, but revolves around that famous bit of then futuristic technology, Captain Nemo's submarine, the *Nautilus*. Other major works by Verne resort to a similar temporal structure. They are set in a present or immediate past in which is placed some currently impossible vehicle like the spaceship in *From the Earth to the Moon* (1865), or the flying machine in *Robur the Conqueror* (1886). Mary Shelley's *Frankenstein* (written in 1816) is also set in a recent past rather than the future, but centers on the creation of life via scientific means, a feat that belongs to the realm of future possibility. In the looser sense in which works like *Frankenstein* and *Twenty Thousand Leagues Under the Sea* may be termed futuristic fiction, it includes most science fiction and even some varieties of avant-garde literature whose stylistic novelties, if not subject-matter, point toward future prospects.

Futuristic fiction in the strict sense of narratives explicitly set in future time is a relatively new development. There are no examples in classical, medieval, and Renaissance literature. The beginnings were scattered and hesitant. In 1659, there appeared the first book of secular fiction set in future time: Jacques Guttin's incomplete romance *Epigone, histoire du siècle futur* (Epigone: history of the future century). Other obscure experiments followed, but only with publication in 1771 of the first utopia set in future time, *L'An 2440* (The Year 2440) by Louis-Sébastien Mercier, did a work of futuristic fiction attract a wide audience. This best-selling vision of a twenty-fifth-century Paris free alike from repressive government and its symbol, the Bastille, doubtless encouraged those tides of change that rose in 1789.

Following the upheavals of the French Revolution and its aftermath, futuristic fiction gathered momentum. Milestones in this second phase are publication in 1802 of *Les Posthumes* by Restif de la Bretonne; appearance in 1805 of the first of the last men in *Le dernier homme* by Jean-Baptiste Cousin de Grainville; publication in 1826 of Mary Shelley's story of future plague, *The Last Man*; articulation in 1834 of futuristic fiction's first manifesto in Félix Bodin's *Le Roman de l'avenir* (the novel of the future), which stressed the aesthetic advantages of works set in future time as a unique source of realistic marvels; and inauguration of the French dystopian tradition in 1846 with Emile Souvestre's satiric portrait of Tahiti in the year 3000, *Le Monde tel qu'il sera* (The world as it will be). Thereafter, imaginary future settings became increasingly attractive to writers and encountered less resistance from readers. This trend culminated in 1871 with the great success of Sir G.T. Chesney's *The Battle of Dorking* in establishing the future-war tale as a popular vehicle of commentary on the present state of military readiness, and with the even greater success in 1888 of Edward Bellamy's futuristic utopia *Looking Backward 2000–1887*. Echoing Mercier's achievement of the previous century, Bellamy's portrait of Boston in the year 2000 inspired widespread debate about how the future should be shaped. *Looking Backward* also stimulated a raft of counter-utopias, including William Morris's *News From Nowhere* (1890). In 1895, futuristic fiction achieved impressive artistic maturity with *The Time Machine*. Meanwhile, Jules Verne's popularity created a wide audience for his brand of adventure laced with futuristic machinery. Thus, by 1900, futuristic fiction was an established form.

To write its history in the twentieth century would be to outline the development of all those varieties of the printed word and moving picture that have resorted to imaginary futures as a venue for action or argument. Of more importance than such history per se, for which there is scant room here, is the need to recognize what futuristic fiction is and what it is not. It is a form unique to the post-Renaissance era. It transcends many generic as well as media boundaries. It is seldom prediction. Nor is it always science fiction, though without the possibility of future settings, science fiction could hardly have achieved its current scope and power.

If measured by accuracy or even probability in foretelling the future as though it were only prophecy, most of the best futuristic fiction would either score low marks or be impossible to judge for centuries. We cannot defer response to *The Time Machine* while waiting to see whether life on earth will peter out as Wells shows it doing in those haunting scenes of bizarre creatures on a far future beach faintly illuminated by the light of a dying sun. The future setting creates a thought experiment. We are moved by the power of Wells's vision to consider the meaning of our present actions in the light of such a remote possibility of life's bleak finale on our planet. *If* the human story were to end that way—or as Mary Shelley shows it ending in *The Last Man*'s terrible plague—what meaning would it have? How should we *now* live in the face of that prospect? Nor can readers of *The Time Machine* evade its invitation to consider how we *now* treat the poor simply by noting the unlikelihood that exploitation of them will eventually divide the human species biologically into the equivalent of Wells's useless Eloi and savage Morlocks. They are not predictions of future evolution but skillfully dramatized symbols of present class relationships. A future setting allows effective creation of such symbols. So too Orwell's *Nineteen Eighty-Four* (1949) can hardly be dismissed because the world in calendar year 1984 did not exactly resemble that portrayed in his novel. Its purpose, like that of most outstanding futuristic fiction, is to present an imaginary future standing as a metaphor of the actual present, thereby inviting readers both to notice crucial features of that present, and to consider where such features might lead if allowed to flourish. There may be predictive elements, but the best futuristic fiction primarily aims to comment on the present while inviting consideration of how we may shape a better future. Not incidentally, outstanding futuristic fiction also achieves aesthetic effects otherwise unavailable.

The emergence of futuristic fiction is roughly coincidental with the accelerating pace of change induced by the scientific and industrial revolutions of the eighteenth and nineteenth centuries. Whether the rise of modern science and technology caused the invention of futuristic fiction or merely provided its most appropriate subject matter is a moot question. Be that as it may, futuristic fiction, especially in its avatars of science fiction, has become the most characteristic and arguably the most important means of expressing those desires, fears, and possibilities peculiar to our time. Films like Ridley Scott's *Blade Runner* (1982) show how powerfully the genre may be adapted beyond the printed page. Works like *Nineteen Eighty-Four* show how the masters of futuristic fiction may provide our most effective warnings against the nightmares unleashed or abetted by abuse of science.

[P.K.A.]

See also **Alternate History; Bodin, Félix; Grainville, Jean-Baptiste Cousin de; Mercier, Louis-Sébastien; Restif de la Bretonne, Nicolas-Edme.**

FURTHER READINGS

Alkon, Paul K. *Origins of Futuristic Fiction.* Athens: U of Georgia P, 1987.

Cazes, Bernard. *Histoire des futurs: Les figures de l'avenir de saint Augustin au XXIe siècle.* Paris: Éditions Seghers, 1986.

Clarke, I.F. *Tale of the Future From the Beginning to the Present Day: An Annotated Bibliography.* 3rd. ed. London: The Library Association, 1978.

———. *The Pattern of Expectation: 1644–2001.* New York: Basic Books, 1979.

Suvin, Darko. *Metamorphoses of Science Fiction: On the Poetics and History of a Literary Genre.* New Haven: Yale UP, 1979.

GAIA THEORY

The Gaia theory of James Lovelock and Lynn Margulis uses a controversial mechanism to explain the chemistry of the atmosphere, hydrosphere, and lithosphere (soils and surface rock) of earth, which is unique in the sense that earth is the only planet known to have life. The theory suggests that organisms are intricately involved in both producing and regulating the liveability of earth's surface. It is proposed that the mechanism is comprised of networks of feedback loops, any one of which might operate in a manner comparable to a household thermostat. The thermostat both senses the temperature of the room and turns the furnace off or on depending on the temperature. Because there will always be a time lag between a change in temperature and the sensing of that change and the consequent adjustment of the furnace and the resultant increase or decrease of temperature, one would expect that the temperature of a room over a given period of time would cycle regularly up and down through the thermostat set point. Many such feedback loops interacting either directly or indirectly with each other would tend to form a highly complex system challenging to model. The cycles of some feedback loops might tend to damp one another out while some might enhance each other. In the case of the Gaia hypothesis, the thermostats are organisms and their sensitivities to environmental conditions are very basic. That is, in some environments organisms will leave more offspring than in others as a result of natural selection. Furthermore, organisms, by virtue of their ability to take in and release gases, to produce minerals, to change solubilities of compounds, to change albedo (absorption and reflectivity of sunlight), and to do many other significant activities, have the ability to change their environments. Organisms themselves can act as agents of natural selection. Quite simply (perhaps too simply), organisms with a predisposition to producing environments toxic to themselves and presumably to others will at some point be, in effect, selecting against themselves. And thus, organisms with a tolerance for certain conditions and/or an ability to produce environments more conducive to life will tend to leave more offspring.

There are several predictions resulting from this theory of organisms regulating earth conditions.

1. One would expect not only dramatic shifts in organismal populations but also many ex-

tinctions throughout the fossil record. This is indeed the case, indicating perhaps that the evolution of organisms has been the history of many randomly begun experiments, most of which have ultimately failed (at least in a given environment). Failure (extinction) could be the end result of an "error" so mild that the failing organism might be producing only slightly fewer offspring than a "competitor."

2. One would also expect to find earth's chemistry in odd chemical disequilibrium, especially when compared to its two neighbors, the lifeless planets Venus and Mars. Indeed, earth's atmosphere is like a bubbling crucible compared to the stagnant atmospheres of these lifeless neighbors in which most atmospheric reactions were completed long ago. Highly reactive oxygen along with trace (but significant) amounts of methane, hydrogen sulfide, hydrogen, and other gases form the dynamic (even explosive) earth atmosphere, much of it a direct product of organismal activity. Constant input and recycling by organisms are what maintain the only atmosphere we know (outside of science fiction) that is conducive to life.

3. One would expect that in response to perturbation from the outside, the system would (up to some realistic point) be able to "right itself," to get back on course. Perturbations include sudden catastrophes such as the periodic extinctions that have occurred several times in earth history, some of which were apparently precipitated by colliding meteorites or comets. Perturbation may also be steadier as in the case of the sun's luminosity, which since its "birth" has been steadily

increasing. In both of these cases earth has righted itself, regaining diversity again and again after mass extinction. In fact, earth continues to right itself in that (as though run by a competent thermostat) its temperature fluctuates around a mean of about 25 degrees centigrade in spite of the activities of the sun.

The Gaia theory would be best supported if as many of the (hypothetical) feedback loops as possible could be convincingly dissected out of the whole and demonstrated to have some individual thermostat-like activity. One such possible isolated loop is that involving the link between oceanic plankton and climate. It has been observed that marine phytoplankton (photosynthetic organisms) excrete dimethylsulfide, which reacts and forms sulphate and methane sulfonate in aerosol forms. These aerosols are a main source of nuclei for cloud condensation over marine areas. Cloud cover in turn has a profound effect on earth's albedo (absorption and reflectivity), and therefore earth's temperature. And finally, changes in temperature and solar radiation can (to complete the loop) affect the growth of marine phytoplankton (and many other organisms).

The feedback loop is neither altruistic nor goal oriented. The production of dimethyl sulfide is (like any process in an organism) under some direct or indirect genetic control, and varies from species to species, strain to strain. Production seems to be particularly high in tropical species. Regardless of what the immediate benefit might be to an individual organism to secrete a sulfur compound, it is the long-term cumulative effect of the sulfur product that will exert a selection pressure on many populations. In this case, it is expected that cloud cover will both cool the environment and decrease solar radiation and will have a negative influence on algal reproduction, especially tropical species. A decline in tropical species numbers (probably almost immediately replaced by temperate species) means a decline in dimethylsulphide production and ultimately a decrease in cloud cover and the completion of a cycle.

Feedback loops like the one described above may be used to construct computer models of earth chemistry (albeit over-simplified ones). This is, in fact, what has been attempted by J. Lovelock and M. Bremer in their popular computer simulation, "SimEarth." This simulation uses what is known about the effects of the activities of organisms and the presence of organisms on absorption and reflection of heat and light by the earth's surface. The simulation successfully mimics the expected (thermostat-like) fluctuations in temperatures over the course of earth's history, in spite of the increase in solar luminosity.

[B.D.D.]

FURTHER READINGS

Barlow, C. *From Gaia to Selfish Genes*. Cambridge: MIT P, 1991.

Bremer, M. *SimEarth User Manual* (and program disc). Moraga, CA: Maxis, 1991.

Charlson, R.J., J.E. Lovelock, M.O. Andreae, and S.G. Warren. "Oceanic Phytoplankton, Atmospheric Sulfur, Cloud Albedo, and Climate." *Nature* 326 (1987): 655–661.

Lovelock, J. *Gaia: A New Look at Life on Earth*. Oxford: Oxford UP, 1979.

GENDER DIFFERENCES IN AGING

Women and men journey through life by very different routes. In *Pilgrim's Progress*, John Bunyan contrasts Christian's journey, a brief and ageless one, with that of Christiana, whose journey starts when she is a young mother and ends when she is an "aged matron."

LONGEVITY AND AGING

It is almost universal that women, on average, live longer than men. In some countries, this is by as much as eight years (for example, in Finland, France, Peru, and Poland). According to United Nations statistics, only Bangladesh, Bhutan, India, and Iran report a longer life expectancy at birth for males. The consequences of this for the experience of aging are twofold: (1) because of age homogamy in affective relationships, there is a greater likelihood for women to experience loss, particularly in later life; and (2) there will be more women than men over, say, seventy-five years of age (although due to differential mortality rates and patterns of migration, this is not always the case: in Pakistan, for example, there are 30 percent more men aged over seventy-five than women). As a result, when chronological age is used as a regulator in later life, for example, to determine access to welfare services, we are more often talking about women than men.

FAMILY LIFE

Larger numbers of older women who have suffered loss means that more older women live alone. Also, the members of the older generation within the family are more likely to be women. These are women who have served and cared for their families, and who have often regarded themselves as less important than the men and the children. As a result, men can expect to be supported in their final years, largely by the women in the family, whereas the future care of the aging woman is less certain. In many developing countries there are also increasing numbers of older widows as a result of war, famine, urbanization, and migration. For example, K. Tout reports that in Fiji, South Korea, Malaysia, and the Philippines, there are four times as many widowed women as men over age sixty.

LIFELONG INEQUALITIES

Those who have studied the political economy of old age have drawn attention to the processes by which socioeconomic inequalities continue in later life. In Britain, it is older women who, following a life of disadvantage, are most likely to be living in poverty and in substandard housing, and to be in poor health. According to S. Arber and J. Ginn, proportionately twice as many women as men in older age groups are living at or below the poverty line. Conversely, those older people—disproportionately men—who have been able to accumulate or inherit wealth, are able to acquire resources and services to meet their needs. Older people from ethnic minority groups tend to suffer the triple jeopardy of ageism, racism, and a lack of access to services. Gender differences persist, in part because it is often the case with migrant groups that women follow men to become their dependents.

WORK, EMPLOYMENT CAREERS, AND RETIREMENT

In most societies, men and women tend to be engaged in different kinds of work. Certain occupations have become closely identified with one or the other; for example, many jobs in heavy industry have been filled by men in order to draw upon their perceived superior physical strength. This has often resulted in early retirement through disability. In contrast, many of the caring services are largely staffed by women in order to draw upon their supposed caring nature.

Patriarchy ensures that the power secured through employment rests with men. Men are encouraged to aspire to a continuing, well-paid and full working life, whereas women are expected to give priority to domestic responsibilities which may interrupt their employment careers or reduce their employment opportunities. Women are more likely to have lower paid, part-time, temporary, and unpensioned jobs. In many countries the official retirement age for men and women is different. In Britain, for example, women must retire at a younger age. The consequence of all this is that men have a greater chance of approaching retirement in a more economically secure position.

BIOLOGICAL DIFFERENCES AND TIME

With menstruation, pregnancy, childbirth, and the menopause, women much more than men experience biological changes as temporally scheduled phenomena. Feminists have argued that many of these processes and women's relationship to aging are controlled by medicine and, therefore, largely by men. Just as biological differences between the sexes are used to legitimate the disadvantaged position of women in society, so the biological changes that take place with age are used to justify discrimination against older people. Both gerontologists and feminists have argued that discrimination, demeaning images, and loaded language, rather than any natural differences, have all contributed to the powerlessness and low self-esteem of women and older people.

AGEISM THROUGH THE LIFE COURSE

Ageism affects every individual from birth onward. It places constraints on experience, expectations, relationships, and opportunities. Thus, in the words of C. Itzin, the chronology of aging becomes the hierarchy of ageism. Men and women experience both institutional discrimination and internalized prejudices and fears. For women in particular, aging often represents a gradual disqualification from many areas of life. Through cosmetic attempts to mask the signs of aging, they are engaged in "a race against the calendar," according to S. Sontag. At the institutional and societal level old people are often seen as passive and dependent, and as consuming scarce resources. British research has indicated that women in later life are more likely than men to experience chronic ill-health. Institutions for the chronically ill are predominantly occupied by women and predominantly serviced by women. What this means is that older women "living on borrowed time" are blamed for the "burden of care" that an aging population is presumed to impose.

[B.By. and J.S.J.]

See also **Aging and Time; Aging Populations; Social Gerontology.**

FURTHER READINGS

Arber, S., and J. Ginn. *Gender and Later Life*. London: Sage, 1991.

Itzin, C. "Ageism Awareness Training: A Model for Group Work." *Dependency and Interdependency in Old Age*. Ed. C. Phillipson, M. Bernard, and P. Strang. London: Croom Helm, 1986. 114–126.

MacDonald, B., and C. Rich. *Look Me in the Eye*. London: Women's Press, 1985.

Sontag, S. "The Double Standard of Ageing." *An Ageing Population*. Ed. V. Carver and P. Liddiard. Sevenoaks: Hodder and Stoughton, 1978. 72–80.

Tout, K. *Ageing in Developing Countries*. Oxford: Oxford UP, 1989.

United Nations. *Demographic Yearbook 1989*. New York: United Nations, 1989.

Victor, C. *Health and Health Care in Later Life*. Milton Keynes: Open University Press, 1991.

GENERAL PRACTICE ORGANIZATION

General or family practice is the total primary medical care of patients by the physician for patients of both sexes and all ages. It comprises diagnosis, treatment, and follow-up care, and is derived from the "medical model" used by Western countries. In modern general practice, increasing medical knowledge means that the physician requires more time for training and for continuing education. However, the general practitioner, particularly in the new "walk-in" clinics, can increase productivity by such methods as employing modern office technology and seeing patients in succession using several examining rooms.

HISTORY

The Code of Hammurabi in 3000 B.C. prescribed severe penalties for the improper practice of medicine. From early records we know that the Egyptian physician Imhotep practiced in 2900 B.C.; later, the Ebers-Smith papyri listed remedies and surgical treatments. Recorded Greco-Roman medicine began with Asclepius in 1200 B.C., and was centered around healing temples, where Hippocrates taught that each disease had a cause that was often found within the person.

The classical Greek monographs on medicine were preserved by the Christian churches and monasteries in the Middle East. Through them, and through the Persian and Arabian physicians centered at the great library of Alexandria, medical knowledge was expanded and ultimately transmitted to Europe, influencing the establishment of the Italian medical schools in the twelfth century.

There was little advance in medical understanding or results until the seventeenth century, when William Harvey in Britain established the science of physiology. In nineteenth-century Germany, M.J. Schleiden and T. Schwann expounded theories of cellular organization and R. Virchow established pathology as the basis of disease. As organ function was clarified, methods of physical examination were refined. New inventions such as the stethoscope, introduced in 1819, facilitated understanding of disease and helped to introduce more scientific diagnostic methods. By the late nineteenth century the outline of modern practice was established, although the therapeutic tools available were limited.

The twentieth century has witnessed an exponential increase in medical knowledge. Though there has been success in treating many diseases there has also been growing difficulty in accessing the huge number of discoveries. Currently, burgeoning medical research is dramatically changing the nature of general practice.

SOCIETAL AND GOVERNMENTAL RELATIONSHIPS

The social climate in which general practice flourished in Western countries has changed. Health insurance schemes began in Germany in the late nineteenth century and in Britain in 1948, but there was no comprehensive system in North America until 1968. Until then, payment to a doctor was the responsibility either of the patient or of limited insurance schemes. The epicenter of practice was the physician's office; treatments were limited and visits to the patient's home were common. Apart from university hospitals (which were as much for teaching as for treatment) and larger community hospitals, most practice was general rather than specialized. General practitioners could reasonably apply the limited treatments available for common ailments, working in both office and hospital.

Following World War II, demand for health coverage benefits led to legislation which provided health insurance for the people of Britain, Europe, Australia, New Zealand, and Canada; in the United States, insurance was introduced in 1965 that partially covered the elderly and the poor. The intercalation of government as the paying agent eliminated economic barriers; patient visits increased sharply, with concomitant cost increases. At the same time, public perceptions of inadequate medical accountability grew. There was increased litigation against physicians, complicated by the avalanche of medical discoveries. These changes were accompanied by the spread of specialist practice to smaller community hospitals.

Recently, the public has again questioned medical accountability, and "defensive medicine" is widely practiced. General practitioners have restricted activities such as obstetric practice, or procedures have been excluded by regulation, such as denial of many surgical privileges in hospitals.

THE CHANGING ROLE OF GENERAL PRACTICE

The enormous growth of medical knowledge, the need for multidisciplinary treatment of illness, and the continuing growth and diversity of specialties are encouraging the emergence of new roles for general practitioners. In Canada and the United States, medicine is self-regulated by legislation, and specific regulatory bodies have been formed for general practice. The Canadian College of Family Practice, for example, has lengthened the period of training required; the role of "medical team coordinator" has emerged; and continuing medical education has been encouraged, although in most jurisdictions this remains a voluntary activity.

Typically, the duties of a general practitioner are now more office-centered. Where possible, patients continue to be managed completely. However, they may be referred to specialist or hospital care and it is in relation to these latter areas that general practice is experiencing the greatest change. As specialties proliferate, large areas of office medicine which were formerly the purview of general practice have been lost, in part because intrusion into highly specialized medicine invites patient litigation or professional disfavor.

In hospitals, restriction of resources and the need to demonstrate uniformly high quality have altered medical staff relationships. Medical staffs are now organized by departments based on medical specialty. Many treatments are confined to specialists of superior training and skill, thus excluding general practitioners from previously permitted activities; indeed, in many hospitals general practice is defined by what its members cannot do.

While most general practitioners operate from privately owned facilities, in some small communities offices are provided by the health authority or hospital. In North America, general practitioners have access to diagnostic facilities

and hospital beds for their patients, except in some university hospitals. In Britain, there is less availability or use of such hospital facilities as laboratory and radiology testing; general practitioners cannot usually admit their patients to hospital, but must refer them to a specialist.

Group practice with other general practitioners or specialists is now common. The recent emergence of "walk-in" clinics, providing comprehensive general medical care without appointment including management of minor emergencies, reflects the increasing separation of general practice from the hospital milieu.

Typically, the general practitioner sees office patients in succession using several examining rooms. Simple diagnostic testing may be available; "black box" testing equipment, run by office personnel, facilitates the performance of twenty or more common blood tests; and many group practices have adjacent radiology facilities.

During the day, the practitioner visits patients in the hospital, managing or assisting with treatment. An important hospital function of the general practitioner is liaison with members of the large teams that often manage complex cases such as multiple injuries, cancer, or heart surgery.

In North America, a fee for each item of service rendered is the method of remuneration, but alternative payment schemes are increasing. In Britain, a capitation fee is paid for each patient on a physician's list.

QUALITY IMPROVEMENT ISSUES

Attention has been paid by governments and by an increasingly litigious public to iatrogenic, or physician-caused, disease. In hospitals, this has provoked restriction of general practice privileges and a tightening of other quality-related regulations; however, demonstrated quality assurance in the private office remains fragmentary and inadequate.

Another major issue is the lack of support for isolated or rural practice, where normal diagnostic, therapeutic, consultative, and literature resources are often not available. In some jurisdictions, efforts are being made through computer networks to provide what is becoming known as telemedicine: medical library and database access, radiology and laboratory test interpretation, and teleconferencing with consultants.

[K.R.T.]

See also **Hospital Organization.**

GEOCHRONOMETRY

Geochronometry (< Greek *ge, geologic; chronos, time; metria, to measure*) is literally the process of *measuring geologic time*; it is used in geochronology, the science or study of time in relation to the history of the earth. The ability to measure geologic time has been sought since man began to ponder his origins, the earth on which he lived, and when it all began. Xenophanes of Colophon (ca. 570–480 B.C.) is known to have recognized changes in fossil fauna as a function of time and Herodotus (ca. 484–425 B.C.) recognized the thick accumulations of Nile sediments as indicative of the passage of geologic time. Prior to the middle of the nineteenth century, theological estimates of the rates of natural processes and the age of the earth dominated earth science. During the latter half of the nineteenth century, however, students of the earth sciences became convinced of the great antiquity of the earth and scientific approaches to the measurement of time developed rapidly. This transformation permitted the rates of geologic processes and the age of geologic events to be evaluated independently of cosmologies. Early milestones in scientific investigation of geologic time include recognition of the slow rates of change in land elevation above the sea, calculations of the earth's age based on its rate of cooling, the time required to increase ocean salinity to present levels, and documentation of the enormity of time required for accumulation of the thick sequences of sediments found on the continents.

The advance most important to the modern understanding of geologic time and *geochronometry* was the discovery of radiation by W.C. Röentgen in 1895, and of natural radioactivity by Henri Becquerel in 1896 and Marie and Pierre Curie in 1898. The Curies provided the name, *radioactivity*, for this newly recognized phenomenon and demonstrated that it was a natural property of some atoms, such as uranium (U), thorium (Th), radium (Ra), and polonium (Po). In 1899, Ernest Rutherford reported that the radiation emitted by naturally radioactive materials occurred in three different forms, which he named alpha, beta, and gamma. In 1902, Rutherford and Frederick Soddy proposed the theory of radioactive decay by which an atom of a radioactive element (the parent atom) changes spontaneously to an atom of another element (the daughter atom or product) by the emission of alpha and beta particles. In 1905, B.B. Boltwood and R.J. Strutt independently estimated the ages of U- or Th-bearing minerals by measuring the abundance in the minerals of U and Th decay products, lead (Pb) and helium (He). These advances were translated into a tool for geochronometry, *radiometric dating*, when Boltwood in 1907 and Arthur Holmes in 1913 demonstrated that the daughter/parent ratio (Pb/U) in uranium minerals increased with their geological age.

The advances necessary to measure geologic time reliably began with attempts to understand the structure of matter. In order to explain the failure of measured weights of elements to follow the whole-number relationship suggested by William Prout in 1815, William Crookes proposed in 1886 that different atoms of an element have different whole-number weights. Frederick Soddy helped resolve the question of atomic weights, naming atoms of the same element but different atomic weights *isotopes*. With the advent of the mass spectrograph or mass spectrometer (F.W. Aston, 1920), quantitative measurements of parent and daughter isotopes became possible and radiometric dating evolved to become the standard and most reliable tool for geochronometry.

PRINCIPLES OF RADIOMETRIC DATING

Spontaneous breakdown or decay of atomic nuclei is termed radioactive decay and results in the transmutation of the *radioactive parent* atom to a *radiogenic daughter* atom. Radioactive decay occurs as a reaction in the nucleus of certain isotopes as a result of a natural instability. Four different mechanisms of decay are of interest geologically: alpha decay, beta decay, orbital electron capture, and spontaneous fission. Alpha decay occurs with the expulsion of a particle equivalent to a He nucleus (two protons and two neutrons) from the nucleus of an atom. Beta decay involves emission of an electron from the nucleus of the atom as a result of the breakdown of a neutron to form a proton. Orbital electron capture occurs when the unstable nucleus incorporates one of its extranuclear or orbital electrons, neutralizing a proton and forming a neutron. Spontaneous fission, or "splitting" of an atom, occurs where the ratio of the nuclear protons to the protons plus neutrons exceeds some critical value.

The value of radioactive decay as a geochronometer derives from statistical laws of physics, which relate to *average* behavior, and only have meaning if the number of individuals in the population described is very large. The law of radioactive decay holds that for time intervals of equal length, the number of atoms disintegrating is proportional to the number of atoms present. The probability of a parent atom decaying to a daughter atom is the same for all atoms of that element regardless of temperature, pressure, or chemical conditions. Only a fixed percentage will decay in a given period of time. This probability of decay is the *decay constant*. The time required for one-half of any statistically representative number of parent atoms to decay to an equal number of daughter atoms is called the *half-life*. If the decay constant is known and one can measure the amounts of parent and daughter atoms presently in a mineral, the time since it formed or became closed to movement of those atoms may be determined.

All rocks and minerals contain at least trace amounts of long-lived radioactive elements, although their abundances may be too low for accurate measurement. These radioactive elements constitute geochronometers, or independent time clocks, that under the proper conditions allow the age of the rocks to be determined. Geochronometers are like tools; each has an appropriate use and none may be applied to every problem. The physical record of the event to be dated—commonly rock, mineral, or organic matter—must be evaluated to determine which dating methods are compatible with its mode of origin and subsequent geologic history. Only geochronometers appropriate to the types of rocks, their geologic history, and the geologic environment are selected for use. Certain fundamental principles must be met for dating to be valid.

1. The initial isotopic abundance of the parent element must be known or be determinable. Isotopes above mass forty commonly show little evidence of mass-dependent fractionation on earth, but lighter nuclides may exhibit significant fractionation related to thermal or biological phenomena. Initial abundances of cosmogenic nuclides, those produced by cosmic radiation such as ^{14}C and ^3He, vary as a function of cosmic ray flux and must be normalized.

2. For dated materials to reflect the correct age, the material dated must have been closed to loss or gain of either parent or daughter isotopes since its origin. Only under limited circumstances are corrections possible for ages modified by changes in parent or daughter abundances.

3. Any amount of the daughter isotope in the dated material at the time of origin must be correctable or the age will appear too old. Commonly, mineral phases are selected for

study which contain insignificant amounts of original daughter product.

4. Finally, sufficient concentrations of parent and daughter isotopes must be present in the sample material for reliable determination by available analytical techniques. This condition limits the useful age range of a geochronometric technique because inadequate amounts of either isotope result in imprecise age measurements. Materials with high concentrations of the parent element are dateable over a wider age range than low concentrations because measurable amounts of parent remain longer and those of the daughter accumulate more rapidly.

RADIOMETRIC GEOCHRONOMETERS

Using the principles discussed and a knowledge of the sensitivities of the dating methods to different geologic processes, appropriate geochronometers may be selected for each situation. The more commonly used methods will be described briefly with some emphasis on the geologic conditions affecting their use. Figure 1 summarizes the type of radioactive decay and half-life, as well as the parent and daughter isotopes, of the most commonly used dating methods.

URANIUM-LEAD AND THORIUM-LEAD TECHNIQUES

The earliest geochronometers, based on chemical U and Th methods, were qualitatively useful, but quantitatively invalid because neither parent nor daughter isotopes were uniquely determinable chemically. However, the discovery that three parent isotopes, ^{238}U, ^{235}U, and ^{232}Th, decay to ^{206}Pb, ^{207}Pb, and ^{208}Pb, respectively, and the development of techniques for isotopic measurement, led to highly precise dating methods. Beginning with the early work of Marie and Pierre Curie, U and Th were found to decay through specific chains or series of intermediate radioactive isotopes by both alpha and beta emission to a stable isotope of Pb. Because the half-lives of these intermediate daughters are shorter by several orders of magnitude than their parent U or Th, a *secular equilibrium* is reached after a geologically brief period such that the production rate of the stable Pb isotope equals the decay rate of the parent.

Loss or gain of U, Th, or Pb will result in incorrect apparent ages, but the uranium-lead method is one of the very few from which valuable data may be obtained after open-system behavior. Uranium-lead analysis of multiple fractions of the disturbed mineral population may reveal both the time of formation and the time of disturbance in some cases. Multiple episodes of disturbance or continuous open-system behavior (long-term diffusion), however, will commonly defeat attempts of this sort. The useful range of uranium-lead and thorium-lead methods extends from materials as young as 10–20 million years to the oldest materials known (about 4.5 billion years).

POTASSIUM-ARGON AND POTASSIUM-CALCIUM TECHNIQUES

Both these dating methods utilize the natural decay of potassium-40 (^{40}K), which has a *branched decay*, disintegrating by either beta emission to ^{40}Ca or by electron capture to ^{40}Ar. Application of the potassium-calcium technique is restricted by the large abundance of ^{40}Ca in most minerals at the time of formation, but the technique is useful in certain circumstances.

The potassium-argon dating method has been the most commonly used of all geochronometers. This method uses materials for which an assumption of zero initial ^{40}Ar is usually valid. Igneous rocks, such as granite or lava that were originally molten, are most commonly used because ^{40}Ar, an inert or noble gas, is not combined in mineral structures and is not retained in the melt. On cooling and solidification, radiogenic ^{40}Ar accumulates in the rock. Age measurement is accomplished by measuring the K content chemically and melting the rock in a vacuum to boil out and measure the amount of ^{40}Ar. Because almost 1 percent of the atmosphere is ^{40}Ar, however, a correction must be made for even the small amount of atmospheric ^{40}Ar adhering to the sample and to the extraction system itself.

Since about 1965, use of an analytical modification of the potassium-argon method has become increasingly common. Called the $^{40}Ar/^{39}Ar$ or argon-argon technique, the measurement of K is accomplished by irradiating the sample in a nuclear reactor, converting some of the ^{39}K to ^{39}Ar. By irradiating a monitor mineral of known age with the sample, the K content, the radiogenic ^{40}Ar, and the age of the unknown sample are determined by a single measurement of the $^{40}Ar/^{39}Ar$ ratio. Another advantage of the $^{40}Ar/^{39}Ar$ technique arises because both the ^{40}Ar and the ^{39}Ar are trapped in the original sites of potassium in a mineral. Consequently, the ^{40}Ar and ^{39}Ar are released in constant proportion during heating, allowing valid age measurements to be made on any increment of the total Ar.

Often more importantly, however, taking multiple increments of the Ar gas from the sample during *incremental heating* permits evaluation of the sample as an undisturbed or closed system. If an igneous rock or mineral system has been disturbed since cooling, the ages of the increments will vary. In some cases the pattern of ages obtained from a thermally disturbed sample allows valid ages to be determined by modeling the disturbance.

Problems with Argon dating methods generally relate to disturbance of Ar systems by geologic events. Ar loss is the most common problem, although rocks cooled under high pressure occasionally incorporate Ar during crystallization, a condition known as *excess Ar*. Valid ages have been measured by Ar techniques from less than 10,000 years to nearly the age of the earth.

THE RADIOCARBON OR ^{14}C TECHNIQUE

Radiocarbon dating uses the beta decay of carbon-14 (^{14}C) to nitrogen-14 (^{14}N) with a half-life of 5,730 ± 30 years. Naturally occurring ^{14}C forms in the atmosphere by cosmic ray bombardment, primarily through slow neutron reactions with nitrogen-14 (^{14}N). After formation, the ^{14}C is incorporated into atmospheric CO_2 by reaction with oxygen or by exchange with a stable carbon isotope. The $^{14}CO_2$ enters plant tissue during plant growth and remains in equilibrium with the atmospheric abundance of ^{14}C as long as the plant lives and CO_2 is exchanged. When the plant dies and exchange ceases, ^{14}C abundance decreases as the original amount decays. Because the daughter product, ^{14}N, is not retained quantitatively by the plant tissue, the age is calculated by comparing the rate of decay (^{14}C activity) in the sample to that of ^{14}C in equilibrium with the atmosphere.

Because of its short half-life the radiocarbon method is only useful in samples younger than about 50,000 years (nearly nine half-lives). Accurate dating by this method requires that the production rate of ^{14}C in the atmosphere be constant or that variations be correctable. Both the cosmic ray flux and the resulting production rate have been shown to vary substantially, related primarily to the intensity of the earth's magnetic field and solar radiation cycles. Studies of tree rings, peat bogs, and annual varve deposits in glacial lakes have established age correction curves for the last 6,000 to 8,000 years to correct for these variations. Corrections are also made for different latitudes and elevations.

LONG-LIVED, SINGLE-DECAY METHODS

Four other radiometric techniques that deserve mention may be treated together as they are closely related in both theory and practice. All use trace elements, occurring in low abundance in most rocks. These include the *rubidium-strontium* (^{87}Rb to ^{87}Sr), *samarium-neodymium* (^{147}Sm to ^{143}Nd), *lutetium-hafnium* (^{176}Lu to ^{176}Hf), and *rhenium-osmium* (^{187}Re to ^{187}Os) methods. In each case the parent isotope decays directly to a stable daughter isotope that is present in most rocks when they form. After the time of formation, the ratio of this radiogenic isotope to any other stable isotope of the daughter element in the rock system increases from its *initial ratio* as a result of radioactive decay. If this initial ratio is known, an age may be calculated directly. Alternatively, measurement of the present radiogenic to stable isotope ratio of the daughter element in multiple samples of the rock may permit both the true age and initial ratio to be calculated. The rubidium-strontium technique is the most widely used of these geochronometers, and is useful in a wide variety of igneous, metamorphic, and sedimentary rocks. The samarium-neodymium dating method is most commonly applied to geologically old, low-silica, high-iron-magnesium rocks because of the long half-life of ^{147}Sm. The lutetium-hafnium technique is very similar in application to that of samarium-neodymium, although Lu is substantially less abundant than Sm. As a technique for age dating, lutetium-hafnium is commonly restricted to the use of materials such as zircon, which are enriched in rare-earth elements. Application of the rhenium-osmium dating method is restricted by the very low abundance of Re in most silicate rocks. Its use as a chronometer is most appropriate in iron meteorites and the metallic phases of some ore deposits.

OTHER RADIOMETRIC METHODS

Disequilibrium series dating uses intermediate daughter products of uranium and thorium decay for age measurement. The most useful of these are ^{230}Th/^{232}Th (the so-called ionium-thorium method), ^{234}U/^{238}U, ^{230}Th/^{238}U, ^{230}Th/^{234}U, and ^{231}Pa/^{230}Th (the so-called ionium-protactinium method). In addition to ^{14}C, several other cosmogenic radionuclides deserve mention as useful geochronometers. Most have been employed in dating glacial ice and some are used in studies of sediments and groundwater. Beryllium-10 (^{10}Be), which decays with a half-life of 1.5×10^6 years to boron-10 (^{10}B), is created by spallation of N and O atoms in the atmosphere by cosmic-ray protons. Aluminum-26 (^{26}Al), silicon-32 (^{32}Si), chlorine-36 (^{36}Cl), and ^{39}Ar are all produced by cosmic-ray protons in the atmosphere by spallation of Ar atoms, but may be produced in rocks exposed at the surface by other reactions with cosmic rays.

OTHER GEOCHRONOMETERS

Although radiometric dating techniques as a group dominate the field of geochronometry, other physical methods may be important, especially where the materials necessary for radio-

Table 1. Most Common Radiometric Geochronometers

Parent Isotope		Daughter Isotope		Decay	Half-life (years)
Carbon-14	(^{14}C)	Nitrogen-14	(^{14}N)	β	5.73×10^3
Uranium-235	(^{235}U)	Lead-207	(^{207}Pb)	α, β	7.04×10^8
Potassium-40	(^{40}K)	Argon-40	(^{40}Ar)	ec	1.25×10^9
Potassium-40	(^{40}K)	Calcium-40	(^{40}Ca)	β	1.25×10^9
Uranium-238	(^{238}U)	Lead-206	(^{206}Pb)	α, β	4.47×10^9
Thorium-232	(^{232}Th)	Lead-208	(^{208}Pb)	α, β	1.40×10^{10}
Lutetium-176	(^{176}Lu)	Hafnium-176	(^{176}Hf)	β	3.59×10^{10}
Rhenium-187	(^{187}Re)	Osmium-187	(^{187}Os)	β	4.30×10^{10}
Rubidium-87	(^{87}Rb)	Strontium-87	(^{87}Sr)	β	4.88×10^{10}
Samarium-147	(^{147}Sm)	Neodymium-143	(^{143}Nd)	α	1.06×10^{11}

metric dating are not present. *Dendrochronology*, the study of time through the analysis of annual growth rings of trees, was practiced at least as early as 1811, when De Witt Clinton used the method to estimate the age of man-made earthworks in the state of New York. As a scientific technique, dendrochronology was proposed in 1901 by A.E. Douglass. Thermoluminescence, fission-track, alpha-recoil track, electron spin resonance, and pleochroic-halo dating are all physical geochronometric techniques based on the measurement of radiation damage to rocks or minerals. All require some calibration of the radiation flux to calculate the period of exposure and only reflect the time of exposure of the dated material to the radiation. Relative dating techniques that use rates of other physical geologic processes include hydration-rind dating, cation-ratio dating, amino-acid racemization dating, lichenometry, and pedochronology or soil-development dating.

SUMMARY

Advances in the measurement of geologic time have accelerated from the early questions through qualitative measurements to quantitative dating methods. Some techniques are now capable of precisions better than 0.5 percent. The greatest difficulties in geochronometry relate to finding materials suitable for dating that represent the event to be dated. The science of geochronology has become a mature discipline.

[R.J.F.]

See also **Archaeological Dating Methods; Fossil Record; Geologic Time Scale; Stratigraphy and Paleontology.**

FURTHER READINGS

Faure, Gunter. *Principles of Isotope Geology.* 2nd ed. New York: Wiley, 1986.

Holmes, Arthur. *The Age of the Earth.* London: Harper and Brothers, 1913.

Rankama, Kalervo. *Isotope Geology.* New York: McGraw-Hill, 1954.

Rutherford, E., and F. Soddy. "The Cause and Nature of Radioactivity" (Parts I and II). *The Collected Papers of Lord Rutherford of Nelson.* Ed. James Chadwick. 3 vols. London: George Allen and Unwin, 1962. 1:472–509.

Zeuner, Frederick E. *Dating the Past.* 4th ed. London: Methuen, 1958.

GEOLOGIC TIME SCALE

Much of geology is historical science dealing with sequences of events. This history is recorded in stratified rocks of the earth's crust. The temporal framework in which stratified rocks are arranged and studied is the geologic time scale.

About three centuries ago, Nicolaus Steno formulated a basic principle of geology called the principle of superposition. This principle states that in any sequence of undisturbed strata, the oldest layer is at the bottom and successively higher layers are successively younger. In the late eighteenth century, James Hutton, a Scottish naturalist, observed rock exposures in which steeply inclined older strata had been beveled by erosion and covered by gently inclined younger layers. The erosion surface represented an interval of time during which strata were not deposited. The surface is a chronological gap or hiatus, the duration of which can be established only by determining the age of the strata on either side. By 1800, geologists were able to understand the sequence of older to younger rocks locally, but could not relate their observations to different strata exposed at distant locations. A self-taught geologist named William Smith resolved this problem. Smith traced out strata in England and represented them on maps. He recorded the occurrence of fossils and concluded that rock units could be identified and correlated by the particular fossils they contained. He used fossils to extend correlations over greater distances to strata of different lithology or physical character, even if outcrops were not continuous. The different lithologies were inferred to be the same age because they contained the same fossils. Geologists began to subdivide rock sequences into discrete units in local areas. This produced, in rather haphazard fashion, a vast array of information that needed to be organized and managed. The relative time scale was the answer to the problem; the first attempts to construct a systematic and relative, or chronostratic, time scale began in the middle part of the nineteenth century. This time scale was based on layered rock sequences and their contained fossils and was uncalibrated as far as time is concerned.

The merging of the concept of time with the sequence of rocks deposited required a framework for describing the rocks and the time span represented by their formation. Geologists have agreed that this framework should have three types of units. *Rock* units are identifiable, genetically related units based solely on rock type. *Chronostratigraphic* or *chronostratic* units represent all the rocks formed during a specific period in the earth's history. The *system* is the primary chronostratic unit having time-constant boundaries regardless of location or rock type. *Time or chronologic* units define specific time intervals when the chronostratic units formed. The *period* is the primary unit of time and corresponds to the interval during which rocks of a system were deposited.

A more useful time scale, as discussed by W. Brian Harland et al., is the geochronologic time scale—a merger of a chronometric scale based on uniform units of time and a chronostratic scale based on rock sequences with standardized reference points. Geologists have agreed that a chronostratic scale will consist of stratigraphic divisions with agreed-on boundaries and a succession of rocks with potential for international correlation.

The calibration of a chronostratic time scale depends on some quantitative measurement of elapsed time (duration). The age of a geological event is given by the number of units of time that have elapsed between the event and a given datum, usually the present. Thus, the chronometric time scale is a numerical scale. The fundamental unit of time is the second, but since earth scientists deal with vast arrays of time, the year is used as the conventional geologic time unit.

During the nineteenth century when the relative geologic time scale was constructed, accurate calibration of this time scale proved to be impossible. Hourglass methods such as the rate of sediment accumulation and the increase in salinity of the ocean yielded inconsistent results. With the discovery of radioactivity in 1896, the way was open to develop dating methods based on long-lived, naturally occurring radioactive nuclides. These radiometric dating methods depend on the spontaneous decay of a radioactive *parent* nuclide to a stable *daughter* nuclide at a rate that can be measured experimentally. In the early part of the twentieth century a number of ages were measured based on the decay of uranium to lead. These ages were not very accurate, but they indicated that the earth may be billions of years old instead of being much younger, as some had maintained. Between 1930 and 1950, eight parent-daughter systems useful for measuring rock and mineral ages were identified. Of these, the $^{40}K/^{40}Ar$, $^{87}Rb/^{87}Sr$, $^{238}U/^{206}Pb$, and $^{235}U/^{207}Pb$ methods have the

Eon	Era	Period	Age (Ma) of base
Phanerozoic	Cenozoic	Quaternary	1.64
		Tertiary	65
	Mesozoic	Cretaceous	146
		Jurassic	208
		Triassic	245
	Paleozoic	Permian	290
		Carboniferous	363
		Devonian	409
		Silurian	439
		Ordovician	510
		Cambrian	570
Proterozoic	Sinian		800
	Riphean		1650
	Animikean		2200
	Huronian		2500
Archean	Randian		2800
	Swazian		3500
	Isuan		3800
Priscoan	Hadean		4540

Figure 1. Geologic time scale (millions of years)

greatest application to time-scale measurements. Improvements in instrumentation and measurement techniques have made it possible to measure ages with an analytical precision of better than one percent; accuracy, however, is not as good.

The chronometric time scale consists of a sequential array of individual rock or mineral ages that can be correlated with the chronostratic time scale. The ideal time-scale point is a rock on which radiometric ages can be measured, such as a lava flow, interbedded with sedimentary rocks containing fossils which are diagnostic of their chronostratic age. This circumstance, however, does not occur often in nature.

The chronostratic time scale has a hierarchy of subdivisions named eons, eras, periods, and epochs (from longest to shortest duration). This hierarchy, as reviewed by G. Brent Dalrymple, spans the entire breadth of earth history, some 4.54 billion years. However, no radiometric ages older than about 3.9 billion years have been measured on rocks from earth.

Numerous versions of the geochronologic time scale have been compiled since radiometric ages became relatively abundant. One of the latest and most comprehensive is that of Harland et al. It uses a database of several hundred radiometric ages. The time scale is summarized in Figure 1 with the age of the base of a subdivision of the chronostratic scale given in millions of years before the present (Ma).

[M.L.]

See also **Fossil Record; Geochronometry; Stratigraphy and Paleontology.**

FURTHER READINGS

Dalrymple, G. Brent. *The Age of the Earth*. Stanford: Stanford UP, 1991.

Harland, W. Brian, et al. *A Geologic Time Scale 1989*. Cambridge: Cambridge UP, 1990.

GERMAN IDEALISM

Although there is no uniform conception of time in German idealism, time still takes on a markedly different set of characteristics within that philosophical movement, especially when it is contrasted with the manners in which it is conceived within the framework of pre-Kantian metaphysics and idealism. Despite minor Spinozistic recurrences among some of German idealism's proponents and secondary Humean reassessments among some of its critics, time does not conceptually emerge within German idealism as either a metaphysically real existent

ontologically defining the being of any object whatever or a psychological facet of the human mind functionally serving as part of an empirical psychogenetic account of the origins of how a person perceives either things or his or her own mental state. Furthermore, since German idealism is best understood in terms of its pivotal yet tumultuous appropriation and revision of Kant's critical idealism and his notion of the transcendental (nonempirical) unity of apperception, it then becomes important to review briefly Kant on time in order to appreciate the reconstructions that the notion of time had undergone, primarily within German idealism's concern with apperception or self-consciousness.

In the "Transcendental Aesthetic" of the *Critique of Pure Reason*, Kant claims that time is (1) the form of inner sense and (2) the formal condition of intuiting both inner and outer empirical objects. As the form of inner sense, temporality is in the empirical self. That is to say, time is the vehicle in and through which the self is sensibly intuitive and immediately aware of its own inner mental items. Such intuited items, in contrast to externally intuited objects (that is, objects represented in space), are immediately and exclusively temporal, because they cannot be intuited separately from the happening or occurring of the mental states in which they are occasioned. The happening of a mental state (the occurring of a toothache) and a mental item (the toothache itself) are intuitively inextricable or immediately at one. Hence, the mental item is intuited as itself having temporal components and duration, because the happening of the mental state is intuitively represented as a temporally sequential process. Apart from its immediate unity with the happening of a mental state, a mental item is nothing.

As the formal prerequisite of intuiting inner *and* outer objects, time is a necessary and sufficient condition of the sensible world. What Kant affirms here is the following claim and its converse: all empirically physical and psychological objects appearing in the sensible world appear in time and all empirically physical and psychological objects appearing in time appear in the sensible world. Without going into detail, this point speaks to a notion of time which is one and ubiquitous comprising all determinate times. Accordingly, in introspectively regarding the temporally sequential happening of its own mental states, the self must conceive the happening of these states in inner sense as an objectively transpiring temporal event in the sensible world and, hence, in that single ubiquitous time. Furthermore, the self too must register its own existence or appearance as determinate in that world and, hence, in time while apprehending its own mental states. So Kant can affirm that time enables the self to interpret both the happening of its mental states in inner sense and the experience of itself as something empirically or sensibly conditioned in this world.

For J.G. Fichte, this discussion of the empirical self as itself in time neither has any bearing on the notion of the self understood in terms of Kant's unity of apperception nor any weight on how he wants to discuss temporality in the light of the apperceptive self. Bear in mind that the unity of apperception, for Kant, is the conscious awareness of the activity of thought whose existence is established automatically with such awareness and *not* with any relation to inner or outer objects or to the forms of sensibility, namely, time (and space). For Kant, this is tantamount to claiming that the apperceptive self is nontemporal and unconditioned (yet not noumenal), but also that the content of the apperceptive self's knowledge must be obtained from a source other than its own intellect. These two points enable Kant to explain the possibility of sensible intuition in terms of those forms, time, and space. This is why Kant could discuss time (and space) without recourse to the apperceptive self. However, in his *Wissenschaftslehre* (1794), Fichte wants to derive the necessity of time from the apperceptive self, since that self is to be unconditionally posited by itself. This rules out treating time as either the form of inner sense or the formal condition of all sensible existence. But it enables Fichte to interpret the apperceptive self, and not simply the empirical self, as temporal.

Since the existence of the apperceptive self is *immediately* established with that self's awareness of the activity of thought, Fichte refers to the apperceptive self as "intellectual intuition" or the self-positing subject. Here intellectual intuition does not carry the Kantian sense of a divine intelligence capable of immediate generation of and acquaintance with noumena. It does bear, however, the Kantian stamp of being a necessary component of every mental state, but it is not alone sufficient to comprise a complete mental state of consciousness. Although the details of this point cannot be argued here, it entails for Fichte that consciousness possesses a dual yet inseparable arrangement—sensible and intellectual intuition—in which consciousness is (1) aware of an empirical object via sensible intuition and (2) aware of the sensible

intuition of an object as its own via intellectual intuition. The latter reflects the identity of the self in being cognizant of itself as the one sensibly intuiting this or that; the former reveals the constraint or limitation on the self since the self relies on a relation to something other than itself in order to be a self.

Temporality emerges within the "interdetermination" between intellectual and sensible intuition, that is, within the context of the self either positing itself (awareness of representations of objects being its own) as constrained by the not-self or positing the not-self (awareness of objects) as constrained by the self. The first disjunct addresses the activity of the self as *finite* in its theoretical orientation; the latter disjunct marks the activity of the self as *infinite* in its practical orientation. Regarding the former, the self's being constrained is always the same in any imaginable case, despite the fact that each particular limitation is different. Every moment of being constrained is identical with any other moment. Each act of the self positing itself and the not-self *renders present* in the "now" a single representation, which is necessarily dependent upon and opposed to an *antecedent* representation in the past that has also been the result of the self's positing activity, and which does not have anything necessarily dependent on it. Since it is impossible for the self to have two or more representations simultaneously, the representations take on the shape of a temporal sequence or succession established by the self's positing acts yet limiting those acts ad infinitum. Past and present are generated in terms of the apperceptive self positing itself as constrained by the not-self, because of the tenable possibility of the not-self and its constraints being distinguished from the self's endeavors to establish its determining relation to the not-self in a *complete* and *spontaneous* manner. And that possibility looms constantly in the self's theoretical orientation.

Yet Fichte overrides that possibility by explicating the self in the light of its practical orientation, and it is in that practical mode that the self's relation to the *future* arises. Fichte's motive here is to reconcile the unconditioned character of the apperceptive self with its finitude and being constrained. This is done by interpreting the self as one that "*strives*," that is, as a self that strives toward determining the not-self with the aim of showing that the constraints of the not-self are wholly contingent on the endeavors of the self. The striving of the apperceptive self is equivalent to the self setting for itself the task of making limitations operative on it *self*-limitations, thereby making limitations of the not-self subject to the self's demand that they conform to its self-positing structure completely. The self's striving toward determination of the not-self delineates its orientation toward the future, because the self's goal is a charge it gives itself to fulfill incessantly and not a fact about or property of it. In this scenario, the self's goal is not directed to an isolated deed or single representation but, say, to a "form of life" in which present is not dependent on past, but both are structured by the future-oriented "strivings" or projects of the self. The matter cannot be pursued here, but Fichte's emphasis on the future is one way in which the primacy of the practical mode over the theoretical mode of "self-positing" is articulated.

Hence, in contrast to Kant, who establishes a basic gap between the apperceptive self and the temporal structure of experience, Fichte closes that rift by making it possible to understand the apperceptive self in its practical mode in terms of the temporal constitution of its existence. He thus anticipates existential and phenomenological analyses of time-consciousness.

Hegel's understanding of temporality can be seriously miscontrued if it is ensconced too comfortably in a metaphysical or theological reading of his philosophy as a whole. For such a reading engenders the absurd talk of human beings both appearing to and being an appearance of some divine substance or absolute spirit-god in the course of historical time. Of course, philosophers' misconceptions of Hegel have been his to imbue as much as theirs to imagine. But temporality will be dealt with here in the context of a *non-metaphysical* reading of Hegel which, simply and briefly put, states that Hegel's philosophy is one geared toward the self-reflexive construction, explanation, and justification of fundamental categories of thought operative not in reality, but in claims about reality.

Time arises explicitly in Hegel's *Realphilosophie*, particularly his *Philosophy of Nature*. Hegel regards it as the "truth of space" and as "intuited becoming," serving as a category of physics and mechanics enabling us to construe particular items as qualitatively and quantitatively distinct. Since space for Hegel is both the abstract plurality of points differentiable in it and the indifference to those differentiable points, time as the "truth of space" refers to the character of any point being externally alongside other points while simultaneously being simply and differentially for itself. Through being differentially for itself while being externally alongside other

points, a point is enabled to stand out from both the other points and the indifference of space. This is the enabling condition of a point which Hegel calls the "*now*." For Hegel, a now-point is distinct from this and that point. It also establishes the sequence in which it is positioned. So it is not (no longer) this point and is not (not yet) that point. But since the now-point is *intuitively* the enabling condition of any point in nature, its being differentially for itself while being externally alongside other points is leveled, so that the coming into being of persistent difference between the no longer, the now, and the not yet cannot be *conceptualized* with respect to nature where time is simply the "now." This is time as "intuited becoming," because the no longer, the now, and the not yet cannot be established *in thought* as a transitive variation, in which the no longer and the not yet steadfastly carry import. They can be construed only intuitively as "nows" whose sequential or transitively varied character is nullified. In nature, time is the now in which the intuitive registering yet ultimate leveling of the temporal distinctions between the no longer and the not yet arises.

Yet this conception of time does not offer an account of time's relation to Hegel's notion of spirit. For such an account to be given, one of two routes can be taken, namely, the Jena *Phenomenology* of 1807, or the *Philosophy of Objective Spirit*. Briefly, in the former, time is characterized as "the *concept* itself, which is there and which represents itself to consciousness as an empty intuition; because of this, spirit necessarily appears in time, and it appears in time as long as it does not *comprehend* its pure concept, i.e., as long as time is not surmounted by it. Time is the purely intuited, that which is external to the self, not comprehended by the self, i.e., the concept which is merely intuited." If spirit were incapable of self-consciousness, which means for Hegel incapable of apperceptively applying, *on nonempirical, autonomous, and atemporal conceptual grounds*, commonly held principles for explaining, evaluating, and justifying experiences, then it would be no different than any other entity of nature appearing in time. It is the Jena *Phenomenology* of 1807 showing that spirit self-consciously employs principles, and it is the *Science of Logic* that reflexively justifies the nonempirical, autonomous, and atemporal conceptual grounds of spirit's "self-determination." Time is thus subject to spirit's self-conscious conceptual reconstruction and no longer remains solely an intuitive medium in which spirit indifferently appears. It becomes a conceptualized element already shaped in accordance with spirit's autonomous grounds and constituted as something for which spirit can account *retrospectively* and acknowledge concretely as its own *qua history*.

Finally, F.W.J. von Schelling alters the Hegelian conception of time. He argues against the atemporal character of the conceptual conditions through which time is comprehended by the activities of spirit and temporal distinctions of present, past, and future are constituted. In his little-known and incomplete *Die Weltalter* (*The Ages of the World*), Schelling argues that the individual's conceptual conditions of its self-conscious activities are temporally structured. Unlike Hegel, who makes those conceptual conditions "infinite" and subjects time to the fulfillments of reason, Schelling makes them finite and subjects reason to the finitude of human temporality. Following this course leads Schelling to give existential import to the individual's self-conscious activities. Self-consciousness provides an individual with access to his or her self as they are in the present by reflecting on principles accepted decisively in the past and by reflecting on principles accepted with resolve for the future. It enables an individual to take responsibility for his or her own life history. Time is intrinsically for the human individual, because one's life as a whole makes sense retrospectively and prospectively in terms of what an individual has done and intends to do, all of which is constituted temporally.

One should bear in mind, however, that this was not Schelling's final position, since he still sought an *Urgrund*, an originary metaphysical ground on which to base this existential anthropology. Nonetheless, the existential-anthropological aspect of his philosophy clearly predelineates the moves that would later be taken by the likes of Heidegger.

[F.M.K.]

See also **Hegel, Georg Wilhelm Friedrich; Heidegger, Martin; Hume, David; Kant, Immanuel; Spinoza, Benedictus de (Baruch).**

FURTHER READINGS

Gilead, A. "Teleological Time: A Variation on a Kantian Theme." *Review of Metaphysics* 38.3 (March 1985): 529–562.

Hegel, G.W.F. *The Philosophy of Nature.* Trans. A.V. Miller. Oxford: Oxford UP, 1970. Sections 257–259.

Heinrichs, Jürgen. *Das Problem der Zeit in der praktischen Philosophie Kants.* Bonn: Bouvier, 1968.

Kant, Immanuel. *Inaugural Dissertation of 1770 (Of the Form and Principles of the Sensible and Intelligible*

World). Trans. William J. Eckoff. New York, 1894. See in particular Section 3, Paragraph 14 "Of Time.

———. "*The Critique of Pure Reason.* Trans. N.K. Smith. New York: St. Martin's P, 1968. See in particular "Transcendental Aesthetic," Section 2 ("Of Time"); and "Transcendental Analytic," Book 2, Chapter 1.

Schindler, Walter. *Die reflexive Struktur objektiver Erkenntnis: eine Untersuchung zum Zeitbegriff der Kritik der reinen Vernunft.* Munich: C. Hanser, 1979.

Sherover, Charles M. *Heidegger, Kant and Time.* Bloomington: Indiana UP, 1971.

Wieland, Wolfgang. *Schellings Lehre von der Zeit: Grundlagen und Voraussetzungen der Weltalterphilosophie.* Heidelberg: C. Winter Universitätsverlag, 1956.

GIDDENS, ANTHONY (1938–)

Giddens seeks to bring temporality to the heart of social theory. In his *Theory of Structuration* (see **Social Theory**), he connects the production of social interaction with the reproduction of social systems across time-space. Social reproduction is considered by him to be irreducibly historical and contextual, dependent on a common stock of knowledge, and guided by personal purposes, reasons, and motives.

Giddens insists that continuity and change are not opposites but mutually implicating. Stability, he argues, is always continuity over time: it is the close similarity between how things are now and how they used to be in the past. Moreover, social patterns can only be recognized if there is repetition over a period of time. Stability, order, regularity, and pattern, the traditional foci of "timeless" analyses, therefore, cannot be conceptualized without recourse to time. He suggests further that there is no choice of time scale to be made, that daily life is carried on within the boundaries of birth and death while extending into the long-term past and future. Following Bergson, Heidegger, and Braudel, he respectively calls these three levels of time, *durée, Dasein,* and *longue durée*: *durée* for the daily round of living, *Dasein* for the birth-death parameter, and *longue durée* for the historical dimension.

Giddens developed the concept of *time-space distanciation* to express the historical development towards externally stored knowledge and its association with state power. The concept alludes to a difference between traditional and large-scale contemporary societies. In the former, he argues, collective knowledge was or is tied to what individual people could remember while the latter's social knowledge is located externally and no longer dependent upon being handed down through a chain of individuals. That is to say, writing, printing, and the use of computers, for example, have vastly increased the time-space distance over which knowledge may be stretched. This involved a transfer of power from individual keepers of knowledge to the collectivity—predominantly the state and its agents—as keepers of records.

Power is associated with time in yet another important way. Power, Giddens proposes, is central to social relations that are conducted on the basis of *commodified time* (see **Social Theory**): those situations where time as an abstract quantity has become a medium for exchange. Labor time as abstract quantity and exchange value is no longer something that is merely used, passed, or filled. It has become an integral component of production, a quantity that helps to mediate exchange. The development of a standardized, context-free clock time, divisible into infinitely small units, is seen by him as a precondition for the development of social relations based on commodified time.

Writing on modernity, Giddens identifies a number of time-related characteristics associated with the globalized existence of the late twentieth century: the separation and emptying of time and space, the disembedding of social relations, and the vastly increased scope, intensity, and pace of social life. Motorized transport, electronic communication, and satellite television, for example, have changed the long-standing relationship between time and space, between distance traveled over time. The speed of contemporary systems of communication has rendered space almost irrelevant and increased the scope and the geographical distance covered by people and information. Moreover, the empty, decontextualized time may be rearranged at will, edited almost like a film, and recombined in new ways to enhance, for example, the efficiency of industrial production.

Giddens's time-sensitive social theory proposes complexity and unpredictability where previous approaches offered master narratives and certainty. It makes historical distinctions and pleads for a recontextualization of social time.

[B.A.]

See also **Bergson, Henri; Heidegger, Martin; Social Theory.**

FURTHER READINGS

Giddens, Anthony. *Central Problems in Social Theory: Action, Structure and Contradiction in Social Analysis.* Berkeley: U of California P, 1979.

———. *A Contemporary Critique of Historical Materialism: Power, Property and the State.* Berkeley: U of California P, 1981.

———. *The Consequences of Modernity.* Cambridge: Polity, 1990.

GLOBALIZATION

The time implications of globalization are manifold. They relate to the globalized present; to historical and spatial extension; to the separation and reassemblage of time and space; to time spans; to speed; and to the gap between the time of information, machines, and body movement across space.

At 12:15 A.M. local time on April 14, 1912, a distress signal was sent from a sinking ship in the North Atlantic. By early morning the news of the *Titanic*'s tragic fate had covered the globe. A disaster that would have been destined to become a secret of the sea only a few decades earlier had become a collectively knowable, global event.

With the development of the wireless telegraph, the sending and receiving of information became almost simultaneous. By the early part of this century, this technological innovation had become an essential part of a global network of communication that linked land stations and ships at sea. Equally important was the development of the telephone. It too allowed for virtually instantaneous communication across vast distances. Years, months, and days of waiting for a reply were reduced to fractions of seconds, to a gap that was almost imperceptible. Together, these innovations in communication separated the established link between time and space. They changed the relationship between movement across space and time: succession and duration were replaced by seeming simultaneity and instantaneity. The present was extended spatially to encircle the globe. This opened up an unbridgeable gap between the speeds at which information and physical bodies could travel across space. Today, this gap is incorporated into the anticipations, plans, and actions of members of industrial and industrializing societies whether these involve travel, satellite television, the movement of troops and equipment to the scene of modern warfare, or the interaction of people with their computers.

This instantaneity of communication and its attendant enmeshing of the globe with information created some further anomalies: persons making a telephone call in the morning might find that it was nighttime for their conversation partners or, odder still, they might have been communicating into the day just gone or the one to follow. A telephone conversation may have even taken place in two different months. With the standardization of time, these discrepancies were rationalized: Greenwich was established as the zero meridian; the earth was divided into twenty-four time zones one hour apart; and in 1913, the first time signal was transmitted from the Eiffel Tower and sent around the world. A global electronic network was established and with it the independence of local times began to collapse.

Jointly, these two developments—the wireless information transfer and the standardization of time—facilitated the globalization of the economy, information, transport, politics, and war. The "global embrace" meant individual and collective involvement beyond local and national boundaries: it promoted transnational practices and institutions. The World Bank, the IMF (International Monetary Fund), the OECD (Organization for Economic Cooperation and Development), OPEC (Organization of Petroleum Exporting Countries), the United Nations, and the World Commission on Environment and Development are indicative of such transnational relations and interdependencies. The existence of a global present, however, meant not merely that business meetings could take place between people in Bangkok, Bonn, and Boston without any of the participants having to leave their desks. It meant also that events in one part of the world could have effects on the other side of the globe and send ripples through the entire network. Stock markets are a case in point: excitement or problems in one financial center have inescapable and often unpredictable effects on the rest.

More recent technological innovations extended the human reach into space and thus freed the way for global surveillance in aid of the purposes of war and peace. Satellites can detect movement of people and equipment on earth. During the Gulf War, for example, military personnel of the United States stationed in Australia advised allied generals when and where to attack in Kuwait. Moreover, the global enmeshing of information, economics, and politics meant that wars were no longer affairs that could be contained within the combating countries.

A similar situation pertains to environmental problems. These too cannot be contained within their countries of origin. Acid rain, radiation, global warming, or the depletion of the ozone layer, for example, know no national boundaries: they affect perpetrator and innocents alike. They constitute an invisible reality that surrounds humanity. Nuclear material, for example, is located across the world on land, in the sea, and in the air. It is stored deep in the earth and on the bottom of the oceans. It is harnessed for both benign and hostile power and it encircles our earth in satellites. It engulfs the globe, affecting all life on earth with its potential threat: the aftermath of radiation may be immediate, or take decades, even millennia, to reveal. The concept of *half-life*—the characteristic average rate by which half of a random sample of radioactive material decays, half the remainder after that and so on—has been established not merely for radioactive decay, but has been applied equally successfully to the dissemination and fading of globally networked information.

Sociopolitical engineering and risk calculation become highly problematic social practices once the potential outcome of cultural activity is characterized by globalization and temporal uncertainty and once the time lags of cause and effect span from nanoseconds to millennia. They pose barriers to effective action because our capacity to predict and control is dependent on processes governed by sequential, linear causality. This means that instantaneity and nonlinear processes elude our conventional modes of domination: the simultaneous and potential present of global information and environmental effects render our efforts ineffective.

The global present demands that prediction, action, and control be based on different temporal principles. It necessitates response speeds outside the range of our physiological and mental capacity. It requires personal and collective responsibilities that span not just election cycles or, at best, a single generation, but hundreds of generations. It calls for a long-term perspective, since our actions today determine the present for a multitude of future generations. It links our personal and local times with global times, and connects our individual concerns with collective responsibilities for the long-term future.

[B.A.]

See also **Definition and Measurement of Time; Environment and Ecology.**

FURTHER READINGS

Featherstone, Mike, ed. *Global Culture: Nationalism, Globalization and Modernity.* London: Sage, 1990.

Giddens, Anthony. *The Consequences of Modernity.* Cambridge: Polity, 1990.

Kern, Stephen. *The Culture of Time and Space 1880–1918*. London: Weidenfeld and Nicolson, 1983.

May, John. *The Greenpeace Book of the Nuclear Age*. London: Gollancz, 1989.

World Commission on Environment and Development. *Our Common Future*. Oxford: Oxford UP, 1987.

GRAINVILLE, JEAN-BAPTISTE COUSIN DE (1746–1805)

In *Le dernier homme* (1805), translated into English in 1806 as *The Last Man, or Omegarus and Syderia, A Romance in Futurity*, Grainville inaugurated the genre of stories recounting the end of human history. His narrative combines epic, biblical, and novelistic features to portray the world's end in an undated far future that is presented as mythic rather than historical time. Grainville's doomed lovers, Omegarus and Syderia, earth's last fertile couple, must contend with a dying planet marked by exhaustion of natural resources, depopulation, and reversion of humanity's remnants to savagery amid the ruins of once-great cities. God sends Adam back to earth to persuade them not to have children so that time will end, the final judgment will take place, and eternity begin. Earth's guardian spirit tries to prevent this outcome, but fails. The book concludes with a vivid account of how Omegarus, Syderia, and a few others living through the last days experience the ensuing cataclysm and resurrection of the dead. The first parallel work in English literature is Mary Shelley's *The Last Man* (1826), in which the only survivor describes a plague that destroys the human race. This catastrophe is natural, not supernatural. Despite some gothic touches and occasional apocalyptic imagery recalling the Bible, Shelley's *Last Man* is a realistic narrative providing a futuristic version of Daniel Defoe's *Journal of the Plague Year* (1722). The realism of Shelley's *Last Man* makes it a more viable model for twentieth-century versions of apocalypse. Grainville's *Last Man* is nevertheless notable for its success in secularizing the Apocalypse by portraying its events within a mode of allegory and fantasy while also realistically depicting the tempo of human experience, especially the subjective tempo of perceived duration.

[P.K.A.]

See also **Apocalypse; Defoe, Daniel; Futuristic Fiction.**

FURTHER READINGS

Alkon, Paul K. *Origins of Futuristic Fiction*. Athens: U of Georgia P, 1987.

Wagar, W. Warren. *Terminal Visions: The Literature of Last Things*. Bloomington: Indiana UP, 1982.

GRAVITY, TIME, AND SPACE

Common sense suggests that gravity, time, and space are separate and independent aspects of nature. But in 1905, Albert Einstein (1879–1955) argued that time is not completely independent of space, but is combined with it in an entity called space-time. Later, in 1915, he explained how the various manifestations of the force of gravity could be explained in terms of a comprehensive theory of space-time. In this volume, the subject is developed under four headings: **Relativity Theory** describes Einstein's early special theory of relativity that led to the idea of space-time. **Space-Time** develops this idea in more detail; the present article outlines the general theory of relativity, which is essentially a theory of gravity; and **Big Bang** and the black holes dealt with in **X-Ray Universe** include some speculations inspired by the theory that have yet to be proved by observation.

THE FORCE OF GRAVITY

In the Middle Ages, people believed that things fall downward because they have the quality of being heavy. During the seventeenth century, Johannes Kepler (1571–1630), Galileo Galilei (1564–1642), and others maintained that this formulation explains nothing and that gravity (< Latin *gravitas* , heaviness) must be understood as a force that pulls a thing toward the center of the earth. In the 1660s, by working out a crude theory of the moon's motion, Isaac Newton (1642–1727) persuaded himself that the earth's gravity reaches the moon but is weaker there; he discovered that the force of gravity is inversely proportional to the square of the distance from the earth's center. Twenty years later, Newton returned to this subject and postulated in his great work, the *Principia* (1687), that there is a force of gravity between every two objects in the universe. It follows from Newton's laws of gravity and motion (see **Physics**) that when an object moves in a gravitational field, its orbit is independent of its size, mass, and material composition. For example, an orange in the earth's orbit would circle the sun exactly as the earth does.

THE PRINCIPLE OF EQUIVALENCE

Imagine conducting experiments in a drifting spacecraft. Two different objects, say a wrench and a pencil, are released from rest and float side by side, not changing their positions in the spacecraft. Suddenly the jets are fired. The space-craft starts to move and soon its wall hits the objects. To observers in the spacecraft it will appear that a force now exists in the spacecraft that has caused the objects to hit the wall, and that both objects have moved in exactly the same way.

Imagine now a more difficult experiment in which a very large mass is brought near the spacecraft, which is not allowed to acquire a new motion. According to Newton's principles, the wrench and the pencil will again be seen to move toward the wall in exactly the same way as before. Einstein's general theory starts with the postulate, called the principle of equivalence, that by no possible experiment could observers isolated in the spacecraft tell which of the two causes was operating. But the motions of objects in the spacecraft, which involve changes of position with time, can be completely described in terms of the coordinates x, y, z, t that situate a thing in space-time. It thus appears that the effects of gravitation can be described in geo-metrical terms.

GENERAL RELATIVITY

Einstein soon realized that in a theory of gravity, space-time must be more than a geometric mode of description; it must have physical properties and must curve just as the earth's surface does, and possess bumps and hollows as well as a general overall curvature. This curvature, how-ever, is in the four dimensions of space-time, not the two that are easily visualized. The curvature is produced by the presence of matter and ener-gy, and it also affects the motion of matter so as to produce the phenomena of gravity. It is the principle of equivalence that allows this part of physics to be expressed in geometrical terms. By 1915, the general theory of relativity was almost complete. The "curvature of space-time" can usual-ly be separated into curvature of space and "curva-ture of time." The first is almost self-explanatory; the second means simply that the rate of an idealized clock depends on where it is and that it is affected by the presence of gravitating matter.

The most delicate experimental tests of the theory so far involve planetary motion. Here, the "curvature of time" leads to equations essen-tially the same as those that follow from New-ton's laws; the spatial curvature makes small modifications that are now well verified by ob-servation. But Newton's theory and Einstein's follow different modes of explanation. In New-ton's theory, the sun exerts a force of gravity that makes planetary orbits curve around it; accord-ing to Einstein, however, there is no force, and the paths curve because the sun makes space-time curved.

It is natural to ask whether gravity is the only force of nature that can be reduced to geometry. The continuation of Einstein's program by many physicists over seventy years has led to the development of new geometries, some of which are based on more than four dimensions. It seems impossible, though, to proceed by geom-etrizing one by one the various forces of na-ture—gravitational, electromagnetic, nuclear—and so the next step seems to be the "grand unification" of all the fields into a single theory. That is for the future.

[D.A.P.]

See also **Big Bang Theory; Physics; Relativity Theory; Space-Time; X-Ray Universe.**

FURTHER READINGS

Born, Max. *Einstein's Theory of Relativity.* New York: Dover Publications, 1962.

Einstein, Albert. *Relativity.* New York: Crown Publish-ers, 1961.

Geroch, Robert. *General Relativity from A to B.* Chicago: U of Chicago P, 1978.

Will, Clifford M. *Was Einstein Right?* New York: Basic Books, 1986.

GUYAU, JEAN-MARIE (1854–1888)

Jean-Marie Guyau is mostly known as a moral and social philosopher. His importance for the study of time resides entirely in *La genèse de l'idée de temps*, published posthumously in 1890, and his only digression into psychology. This essay is one of the most fundamental and interesting texts in the psychology of time. It bears compar-ison with the work of Guyau's famous contem-poraries, Henri Bergson and William James, and antedates much of it.

Central to the argument of *La genèse* is the position that time is "simply" an acquired orga-nization of dynamic mental representations, enabling humans to store and remember past events. The cognitive functions that support this organization nearly always establish coher-ent episodes that are situated in concrete, spa-tially defined contexts. Such a position is re-markably consistent with modern cognitive views about memory and knowledge representation. Guyau illustrated his views with examples from the study of normal and pathological memory.

Why, Guyau asks, do we need a conceptual structure, an idea of time, and how do we attain such an idea? It is not present at birth, and children (as well as animals) only gradually acquire cognitive strategies allowing them to represent temporal relations. Without such strategies we are not able to organize our experiences and expectations. To acquire the idea of time is therefore an important functional adaptation. It is the result of a long process of evolution in a social context.

For the idea of time to develop, an organism must first have sensory systems that can detect differences and produce symbolic representations of distinct events. In the second place, it must be capable of perceiving the tension between its present state and its desired state or goal. In Guyau's own phrase, it must experience "the tension between the goblet and the lips." These two conditions imply that representations of events must take the form of spatial imagery. Consequently, as a representational medium space must precede time *logically* as well as *psychologically*. In Guyau's view, memory is the dynamic temporal organization of our representations of (past) events.

In support of this rather general theoretical position, Guyau specifies five mechanisms which allow us to achieve such memory organization. In contemporary terms we refer to these mechanisms as: schema formation, matching, spatial analogy, chunking, and narrative closure.

1. *Schema Formation.* The representations of events and episodes have a schematic or prototypical character. They possess more or less salient contextual features that influence the ease with which they are manipulated. Most of these contexts are culturally inspired. They are passed on from generation to generation.

2. *Matching.* The way in which schemata function will depend on the principles of similarity and uniqueness: we may understand something to the extent that it matches some fact we already know, but we learn and remember something to the extent that it differs from this fact.

3. *Spatial Analogy.* The representation of time is mediated by our representation of space and thus by the processes that operate on spatial relations. This influence is not an arbitrary one. After all, both spatial and temporal representations derive from intentional effort, from the juxtaposition of "what is and what is to be." The issue is to find out how we can get to an independent representation of time as the dimension of past-present-future.

4. *Chunking.* Reference points—temporal landmarks—help to simplify the organization of memory. As a rule they are salient experiences that are called to mind more frequently and easily than other events. More importantly, however, they enable us to "compile" our search rules: frequent use creates more compact temporal representations, so that ultimately only the first and last elements of a chain of retrieval operations are retained and all intermediate steps will be eliminated in a memory search.

5. *Narrative Closure.* Representations of events and episodes remain plastic. Memories evolve slowly but constantly. They are embellished or deformed until they finally stabilize in ways that may bear little resemblance to their initial form. This is an esthetic process that answers the cognitive need for narrative closure. Memory must remain coherent and consistent with our present "acting and undergoing" if it is to be *someone's* memory, that is, the manifestation of a *self*.

The inputs to which the cognitive procedures that shape our notion of time are responsive may vary in a number of ways. The characteristics of what we may call *temporal information* influence our perception and retention of duration. According to Guyau, these characteristics include (1) the number and stochastic properties of event ensembles; (2) the structural relations between events that specify the form or rhythm of event sequences; and (3) the cognitive, emotional, and evaluative context in which the events take place. Each of these aspects will influence our experience of duration, our awareness of time-in-passing. In addition, time estimates are based on the effort required to generate an adequate, episodically coherent representation. When in early childhood or old age, or as a result of organic or mental disorders, the regular strategies for processing this temporal information are not yet or no longer available, certain characteristic distortions or illusions of time experience will occur.

[J.A.M.]

See also **Bergson, Henri; James, William (as Psychologist; Psychology of Time.**

FURTHER READINGS

Guyau, J.-M. *La genèse de l'idée de temps.* Paris: Félix Alcan, 1890.

Michon, J. A., V. Pouthas, and J. L. Jackson, eds. *Guyau and the Idea of Time.* Amsterdam: North-Holland, 1988. This contains a reprint with English translation of Guyau's *La genèse.*

HEGEL, GEORG WILHELM FRIEDRICH (1770–1831)

The place of time in Hegel's philosophical enterprise is not prima facie prominent or obvious. One will find very few explicit remarks by Hegel on this subject. So it is incumbent on an interpreter to reconstruct those comments and draw the proper inferences in the light of Hegel's overall project.

In his Jena *Phenomenology* of 1807, specifically in the chapter entitled "Absolute Knowing," Hegel makes the following claim about time: "Time is the *Concept*, which is there and which represents itself to consciousness as an empty intuition; because of this, spirit necessarily appears in time, and it appears in time as long as it does not *comprehend* its pure Concept, i.e., as long as time is not surmounted by it. Time is the purely intuited, external to the self, not comprehended by the self, i.e., the Concept which is merely intuited." In his post-1820s *Realphilosophie*, specifically in the *Philosophy of Nature*, Hegel calls time "the negative unity of being-external-to-and-alongside-itself" and "intuited becoming." With respect to content, what do the citations from the two different texts of Hegel share and not share?

Unlike the *Philosophy of Nature*, the Jena *Phenomenology* brings time's relation to spirit into account. It is Hegel's sustained argument disclosing spirit's capability to employ self-conscious commonly held principles for explaining, evaluating, and justifying experiences. Yet Hegel also argues that the grounds which support spirit's apperceptive application of such principles are *nonempirical, autonomous, and atemporal conceptual conditions*. Hegel's *Science of Logic* is his extended reflection on the self-determined and atemporal "developmental" character of those conditions on which spirit's apperceptive account-giving hinges.

Repairing to time's relation to spirit, we get the following. Time is subject to spirit's apperceptive conceptual reconstructions. It becomes a conceptualized element already shaped in accordance with spirit's autonomous and atemporal conceptual conditions and already constituted as something for which spirit can account *retrospectively* and acknowledge concretely as its own *qua history*. Spirit here does not merely appear in time; rather time here is comprehended by spirit.

But what does it mean for spirit simply to appear in time? Answering this question re-

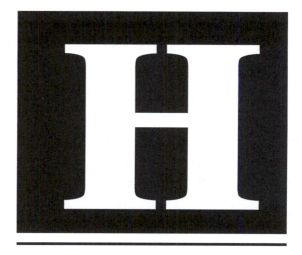

quires looking at time itself, and Hegel's *Philosophy of Nature* takes on that task. Hegel here regards time as the "truth of space" and as "intuited becoming," serving as a category of physics and mechanics and enabling us to construe particular items as qualitatively and quantitatively distinct. Since space for Hegel is both the abstract plurality of points differentiable in it and the indifference to those differentiable points, time as the "truth of space" refers to the character of any point being externally alongside other points while simultaneously being simply and differentially for itself. Through being differentially for itself while being externally alongside other points, a point is enabled to stand out from both other points and the indifference of space. This is the enabling condition of a point which Hegel calls the "*now*."

For Hegel, a now-point is distinct from this and that point. It also establishes the sequence in which it is positioned. So it is not (no longer) this point and is not (not yet) that point. But since the now-point is *intuitively* the enabling condition of any point in nature, its being differentially for itself and being externally alongside other points are leveled, so that the coming into being of persistent difference between the no longer, the now, and the not yet cannot be *conceptualized* with respect to nature in which time is simply the "now." This is time as "intuited becoming," because the no longer, the now, and the not yet cannot be established *in thought* as transitively varied and distinct, in which the no longer and the not yet steadfastly carry import. They can be construed only intuitively as "nows" whose sequential or transitively varied character is nullified. In nature, time is the now in which the intuitive registering yet ultimate leveling of temporal distinctions between the no longer and the not yet arises.

So if spirit were incapable of self-consciousness and without nonempirical conceptual conditions for evaluating experience, it would not be different from any other entity of nature appearing in time, solely in a sequence of nows without temporal distinctions. For Hegel, then, if time is to sustain temporal distinctions, it must be reflexively comprehended by spirit in accordance with the conceptual conditions necessary for comprehension.

[F.M.K.]

See also **German Idealism.**

FURTHER READINGS

Hegel, G.W.F. *Philosophy of Nature.* Trans. A.V. Miller. London: Oxford UP, 1970.

———. *The Phenomenology of Spirit.* Trans. A.V.Miller. London: Oxford UP, 1977.

HEIDEGGER, MARTIN (1889–1976)

As one of the most influential philosophers of the twentieth century, Martin Heidegger significantly reshaped the classical approach to the question of time.

Almost all philosophers have addressed the issue of time in at least a peripheral manner. What distinguishes Heidegger's approach is his belief that an examination of time holds the key to redefining the philosophical task as an attempt to re-ask the question of being (*Sein*). The uniqueness of his approach is reflected in the title of his major work, *Being and Time* (1927). For Heidegger, the philosophical tradition is characterized by its neglect of the question of being. But this neglect is directly proportional to forgetting the contribution that time makes in enabling us to understand being.

In Heidegger's view, the philosophical tradition mistakenly centered on only one aspect of being, its static character of permanent presence that is reminiscent of the Greek notion of substance (*ousia*). This too narrow view of being had a twofold root. First, there was little realization that the temporal dimension of the present is not an isolated occurrence but is really formed out of a combination of the other dimensions, of future and past. Second, time was never addressed on a plane of equal importance to being, as intrinsic to any human understanding of it; time was thereby relegated to a subservient role

and construed after the fact either as a component of entities (*Seiendes*), or as a "measure" determining their motion or change.

Heidegger, like Bergson before him, becomes the chief philosopher in the twentieth century to make the retrieval of time his overriding task. Beginning with Plato, being was defined primarily in terms of continuation, endurance, or presence, and time was determined in regard to movement and flux as a sequence of moments. Insofar as being and time were not originally grasped in their reciprocity, but rather were contrasted to each other, the subsequent philosophical tradition considered them as separate phenomena. Heidegger's entire goal lies in recovering the concealed internal relation between being and time, or the manner in which being (as permanence) is projected upon time as the precondition for its own disclosure.

Heidegger's concept of time can be described as "phenomenological"; that is, he considers the root-conception of time as experienced or lived-time. To distinguish the originality of his approach, he refers alternatively to lived-time as "primordial time" or "ecstatic temporality." According to Heidegger, the concrete experience of time is primordial when it is determined primarily out of the future as the animating power of human existence. The future arises as the extreme point and limitation demarcating all of one's possibilities, that is, the imminence of mortality or the inevitability of death, or for that matter in any projected course of deliberative activity. So conceived, temporality is a forward-looking, anticipatory movement which arises from the future, takes in the past, and forms our notion of the present. This integration of the three modes of temporality defines its "ecstatic" character. For Heidegger, temporality is a dynamic process that retrieves dormant possibilities from the past within a future context. This movement of retrieval, in which the three modes of time are integrated, defines history in the most fundamental sense. Primordial time is not itself another entity, but instead constitutes the opening of that space or historical horizon through which the advent of "world"—the collective involvement of peoples within society and the emergence of entities in nature—can unfold simultaneously. Given its "ecstatic-horizonal" constitution, temporality makes possible our understanding of being as the reciprocal interplay between the space of disclosure and the entities that subsequently appear and become present. Temporality is defined as much through its affinity with absence as with presence, which further exemplifies the internal formation of time as finite.

The same circular pattern of retrieval by which Heidegger describes our temporal experience governs his reinterpretation of the philosophical tradition. Indeed, much of the emphasis he places on the character of time as finite stems from his retrieving Kant's view of time as the organizational field for the comprehension of objects and for the formulation of moral guidelines. Thus Heidegger closely links his analysis of time with Kant's treatment of imagination as the creative capacity inherent in human beings for organizing their experience on both cognitive and moral fronts. Yet even before his concentrated exploration of Kant during the late 1920s, Heidegger had already assembled the key elements to his mature view of temporality. Foremost in this development was his examination of such prominent theological figures as Kierkegaard and Luther, as well as a familiarity with the nineteenth-century philosopher, Wilhelm Dilthey, and his hermeneutical method for interpreting history. When reinterpreted phenomenologically, the biblical tradition's view of humanity as already having been saved, of the *eschaton*, yields a vision of the past or of human "facticity" as reemerging from the future. Likewise, Dilthey's emphasis on our historical life involves more the appropriation of the past in future possibilities than a simple chronicling of previous events. In the early 1920s, Heidegger also turned to Aristotle's analysis of act-potency to identify clues for recovering the dynamic aspect of time.

Heidegger's ability to combine many different strands of the Western heritage in an original way suggests why his contribution to the study of time is of such lasting value. Even in his later writings after 1940 where he assumes a more mystical posture, Heidegger's allusion to the distinct epochs in the history of being still retains a Western sensitivity to eschatology and to the radically finite character of human experience.

[F.S.]

See also **Aristotle; Bergson, Henri; Kant, Immanuel; Kierkegaard, Sören Aabye; Plato.**

FURTHER READINGS

Heidegger, Martin. *Being and Time*. Trans. John Macquarrie and Edward Robinson. New York: Harper & Row, 1962.

————. *On Time and Being*. Trans. Joan Stambaugh. New York: Harper & Row, 1972.

————. *The Basic Problems of Phenomenology*. Trans. Albert Hofstadter. Bloomington: Indiana UP, 1982.

————. *History of the Concept of Time*. Trans. Theodore J. Kisiel. Bloomington: Indiana UP, 1985.

————. *Kant and the Problem of Metaphysics*. Enlarged Fourth Edition. Trans. Richard Taft. Bloomington: Indiana UP, 1990.

HETEROCHRONY

Heterochrony, literally "different time," is technically defined as evolution by change in timing of development. While the process is seemingly obscure, biological evolution is largely dependent on heterochrony. This is because natural selection can only produce evolutionary change if there is preexisting variation to act upon. By altering the timing with which individuals develop, heterochrony produces most of the variation in the population.

Examples of heterochronic variety surround us. Dogs are essentially juvenilized wolves. In domesticating wolves over the last 10,000 years, we selected traits such as playfulness and obedience, which are most pronounced in juvenile wolves. Humans acted as the selective agent by preferring and breeding adult dogs that tended to retain juvenile traits.

Despite its importance in evolution, most evolutionary biologists agree that heterochrony, and development in general, remains one of the most neglected aspects of evolutionary theory. It was widely studied in the nineteenth century by well-known workers such as Ernst Heinrich Haeckel and Karl Ernst von Baer. However, the twentieth century has seen little significant work in the subject, with a few conspicuous exceptions such as Gavin de Beer and Stephen Jay Gould.

KINDS OF HETEROCHRONY

There are two basic kinds of heterochrony: underdevelopment and overdevelopment. The technical names for these are paedomorphosis ("child form") and peramorphosis ("advanced form"). The dog example illustrates underdevelopment whereby adult descendants become progressively more like the juveniles of their ancestors. However, overdevelopment is also very common. In this case, the adult descendants progressively extend the development of their ancestors. For example, we humans owe most of our traits to overdevelopment of ancestral ape growth trajectories. Both our brain and body size have steadily increased over the last six million years by extending the growth pattern of these traits beyond that of our ape ancestors.

Underdevelopment and overdevelopment can occur in both anatomical and behavioral traits. Our larger body size is an example of the former, while the playfulness and obedience of dogs is an example of behavioral underdevelopment. Timing differences in development are also important in creating the anatomical and behavioral differences among individuals within a species. An adult human who shows juvenile behavioral traits, such as selfishness or lack of emotional control, is said to be immature, or has arrested development.

Underdevelopment and overdevelopment often do not affect the entire individual. Each trait in a developing individual has its own set of growth controls that can be independently altered. In humans, for example, our relative hairlessness represents a drastic underdevelopment of hair growth. This has occurred despite our aforementioned overdevelopment of brain and body size. However, there are also many examples in evolution where most if not the entire developmental process of all traits is truncated or extends beyond the ancestor. For example, many lineages show giantism while others show dwarfing.

CAUSES OF HETEROCHRONY
There are only three ways of altering developmental timing to produce all the types of overdevelopment or underdevelopment: change in onset, offset, or rate of development. All three ways have been observed in living organisms. The first method changes the onset time, or beginning of development. For example, an organ or behavior may begin development sooner than another in an individual or species. The second way to alter development is to change the offset time, or cessation of development. In this case, the organ or behavior would continue developing for a longer time in one of the individuals or species. And finally, the third method involves changing the rate of development. Here, organ or behavior development may begin and end at the same time in both individuals or species, but development occurs at a higher rate in one. Because traits can be independently altered, all three methods of altering development can affect one individual. Trait A, such as the human brain, may be overdeveloped from delayed offset (prolonged growth) relative to the ancestor. In contrast, trait B, such as the lack of human body hair, may be underdeveloped from slow development.

The three modes of altering developmental timing are ultimately caused by changes in the genes that control development. In the past, all such genes were labeled as "regulatory genes." However, recent advances in developmental biology have shown that this is a gross oversimplification in that development is controlled by a hierarchy of genes which interact in very complex ways. There are many kinds of gene mutations that affect the timing of transmission of the biochemical signals that carry out development.

[M.L.M.]

See also **Biological Revolutions; Evolution of Evolutionism; Evolutionary Progress; Saltatory Evolution.**

FURTHER READINGS
Gould, Stephen Jay. *Ontogeny and Phylogeny.* Cambridge: Harvard UP, 1977.

McKinney, Michael L., ed. *Heterochrony in Evolution: A Multidisciplinary Approach.* New York: Plenum, 1988.

McKinney, Michael L., and Kenneth J. McNamara. *Heterochrony: The Evolution of Ontogeny.* New York: Plenum, 1991.

HIERARCHICAL THEORY OF TIME

The hierarchical theory of time is a class of principles in the natural philosophy of time and a framework for interdisciplinary studies. It maintains that time is not a homogeneous single thrust in which all processes equally partake, but a hierarchically nested system of qualitatively different temporalities.

The theory elucidates certain time-related problems that have resisted more conventional approaches and raises new questions unnoticed in received teachings. This article sketches the main ideas of the theory. For a defense of those ideas and for illustrations of their applications, see *Further Readings.*

The mental present of human experience combines cognitive and affective interpretations of sense impressions with the feeling of continued identity, and with ideas about future and past. The ceaseless reclassification of events into future, past, and present is the experience of the flow of time. Humans see themselves as participating in that flow and conduct themselves accordingly. Not only humans, however, but all life forms function by a temporal ordering of their actions. They all respond to present needs to be satisfied in the future, according to patterns of behavior inherited from or learned in the past.

In stark contrast, inanimate objects do not possess needs to be satisfied nor do they have memories. This future- and pastlessness, as seen in their own terms, is reflected in the form of physical laws: they have no features to which the idea of present could correspond. Since future and past make sense only with respect to a now, the flow of time metaphor cannot be applied to the time of the physical world. Even the entropic arrow of time is only arbitrarily assigned to the thermodynamics of closed systems.

The absence of directed time from all formal statements of physical change is often cited as evidence that the foundations of the universe are timeless. This presumed timelessness, contrasted with the human certainty of passage, favors the idea of a Platonic division of the world into the eternal or unchanging and the temporal or passing. But such a division is too coarse to accommodate the nature of time as revealed through contemporary scientific knowledge and humanistic understanding.

A much richer epistemic framework is needed. It must admit and correlate the broad spectrum of qualitatively different temporal processes that are found between the chaos of radiation at one end, and the sophisticated organization of life and of cultures at the other.

The hierarchical theory of time offers such a framework. It respects the different assumptions, modes of reasoning, and tests for truth that the different fields of knowledge necessarily demand. It also reveals the dynamic structuring of what, by a single word, we call time.

The theory recognizes a nested hierarchy of five stable organizational levels in nature, along a scale of increasing complexity. Beginning with the most complex integrative level they are: the mental process and its universe of symbolic representations; the life process; the physical processes of the astronomical universe of massive matter (the world of Newton and of general relativity theory); the quantum processes of elementary objects; and the chaos of radiative energy. Each integrative level subsumes the functions and structures of the one or ones beneath it, adding to them new degrees of freedom.

When the time-related teachings of the sciences and the humanities are systematically surveyed and arranged to correspond to the hierarchy of stable organizational levels, five distinct concepts of time emerge. By a definition of reality known as the extended umwelt principle, the concepts are taken to correspond to the actuality, or reality of qualitatively distinct temporalities. Each is seen as complete for the organizational level where it is identified, even if incomplete when compared with the human experience of time.

For an appreciation of the nature of qualitatively different temporalities, intuitive notions alone are insufficient. It is difficult enough to comprehend the temporal world of an infant, let alone that of a rabbit, a flea, or a virus. And we possess no intuitions concerning the temporal worlds of galaxies, molecules, or objects that travel at the speed of light.

The description of the temporal levels that follows proceeds from the most complex yet most familiar temporality, that of the human mind, to the most primitive and therefore least familiar temporality, that of the electromagnetic world.

Nootemporality is the time of the mature human mind in its waking state. Its hallmarks are: a distinction among future, past, and present; unlimited temporal horizons; and the *mental present* with its continuously changing boundaries and cognitive content. Nootemporality may be represented by the picture of a long straight arrow: shaft, head, and tail. The mental present is not imagined as located along the shaft, but as a family of processes for which the arrow is a visual metaphor. The characteristic connectivity among events of the nootemporal world is that of symbolic causation.

Biotemporality refers to the time governing the biology of living organisms, including humans insofar as their biological functions go. Its hallmarks are: a distinction among future, past, and present, limited temporal horizons, and the *organic present* whose boundaries seem to be species-specific. Biotemporality may be represented by the picture of a very short arrow. The organic present is not envisioned as located along the shaft but as a family of processes for which the arrow is a visual metaphor. The characteristic connectivity among events of the biotemporal world is final causation.

Eotemporality is the time of "the physicist's *t*" that is, of the astronomical universe of massive matter. It is a temporality without a present and hence is one to which ideas of future, past, and the flow of time do not apply. It may be represented by the picture of the shaft of an arrow. Its characteristic connectivity is deterministic causation.

Prototemporality is the time of elementary objects dealt with in quantum theory. It is not a continuous form of time but one in which instants may only be specified statistically. The appropriate visual metaphor is the fragmented shaft of an arrow. Its characteristic connectivity is probabilistic causation.

Finally, even the picture of the fragments may vanish and we are left with a blank sheet of paper, a symbol for the *atemporal* world of electromagnetic radiation. Atemporality does not stand for nonexistence, but for a world of complete chaos: the primeval universe at the instant of the big bang, or the inside of a black hole.

These temporalities are the *canonical forms of time*. They are not different aspects of time which become noticeable as we rise to organizational levels of increasing complexity, but stable aspects of reality along the open-ended evolutionary development of nature, including that of time. Although the idea that time itself evolves appears to be a contradiction in terms, it cannot be rejected on the basis of logical reasoning alone. For just as the expanding universe does not fill preexisting space, the qualitatively different temporalities do not evolve within a preexisting expanse of time. Rather, they emerge as correlates of the different functional and structural complexities of the distinct organizational levels of nature.

[J.T.F.]

See also **Interdisciplinary Studies.**

FURTHER READINGS

Fraser, J.T. *The Genesis and Evolution of Time: a Critique of Interpretation in Physics.* Amherst: U of Massachusetts P, 1982.

———. *Time, the Familiar Stranger.* Amherst: U of Massachusetts P, 1987.

———. *Of Time, Passion, and Knowledge: Reflections on the Strategy of Existence.* 2nd ed. Princeton: Princeton UP, 1990.

———. "Human Temporality in a Nowless Universe." *Time & Society* 1.2 (May 1992): 159–173.

HIGH FREQUENCY TIMEKEEPERS

Any stable frequency is a clock. All one has to do is count the beats (vibrations, oscillations) and convert them into conventional time units (minutes, seconds, or fractions of seconds). The most accurate of mechanical clocks, the regulators that have served for astronomical observation (those developed and improved by G. Graham, S. Riefler, W.H. Shortt, and F.M. Fedchenko), were typically controlled by seconds-beating pendulums which kept a frequency of 0.5 hertz. Portable mechanical timekeepers controlled by balance wheel and spring (from pocket and wristwatches to marine chronometers) ordinarily oscillate at 2 or 2.5 hertz, although "fast-beat" watches working at twice that frequency were introduced in the 1930s as a way of improving accuracy. *Other things equal*, the "quality" (accuracy cum reliability) of a timekeeper is a function of frequency, but for swinging balance wheels, further increases in frequency of oscillation are limited by problems of inertia.

The search for better (higher-frequency) controllers moved away, then, from mechanical devices to auditory vibrators such as tuning forks. These could be made to generate frequencies in the twenty-five to the hecta- or kilocycle range. Experimental tuning-fork timekeepers were produced in the nineteenth century and by the mid-twentieth were standardized for use as regulators in scientific laboratories. These were large instruments, not intended for portable, civil use. Such application came in the 1950s with the invention by Max Hetzel of the Accutron watch, a marvel of miniaturization. Hetzel was a Swiss engineer, but his device was refused by Swiss manufacturers. It was, however, adopted and diffused by the Bulova Watch Company in the United States and later licensed to Swiss makers, who made their obligatory reference to Bulova in the smallest print possible—another marvel of miniaturization. The accutron tuning fork vibrated at a frequency of some 360 hertz, which controlled the movement of a ratchet escape wheel of exceptional fineness: 2.4 millimeters in diameter, 300 teeth, with intervals between teeth of 0.025 millimeters. Bulova guaranteed that the watch could be rated to a minute a month, or two seconds a day.

The Accutron was an electrical watch, battery driven. Other electrical timekeepers already existed, in the form of clocks driven off ordinary house current (60 hertz in the United States and Japan, 50 hertz in Europe). In all of these, accuracy was a function of the regularity of the electrical frequency as maintained by the central power station; the timepiece itself did not have an autonomous controller.

The next step in the direction of higher frequency and greater accuracy was the invention of quartz crystal controllers. These were based on piezoelectrical effects discovered and investigated toward the end of the nineteenth century: the response of a rock crystal to the passage of energy is physically to vibrate at a regular frequency determined by the shape of the crystal. These vibrations were in the hecto-cycle, kilocycle, and eventually megacycle range. They found their first application in radio transmission and reception, but the effort to ensure accurate and reliable frequencies for commercial broadcasting suggested the usefulness of such devices as clocks. The first quartz crystal clock was built in the United States by J.W. Horton and Warren A. Marrison in 1928, and this example was soon followed by many others for laboratory and astronomical use. So it was that very soon after the Shortt free-pendulum clock was introduced, it was already rendered obsolete by an entirely new technology of time measurement.

Quartz clocks necessarily vary in accuracy. They best operate in the megacycle range and are placed in thermostatic containers to minimize the effects of temperature variation. They are the temporal workhorses of laboratory work, corrected as necessary by the even more accurate atomic regulators ("disciplined oscillators"), or by radio signals based on such regulators. The most accurate of the autonomous quartz timekeepers, once settled in, will keep to 1 part in 10^{11} per day, about a second in 3,000 years; the disciplined variety should keep exact time indefinitely.

The earliest quartz clocks filled large consoles; the more recent laboratory models are about the size of a cigar box. To make them truly portable, however—that is, to produce them in the form of watches—required a major effort of miniaturization of the works itself and the power source. Here as in other instances horology benefited from work elsewhere. The miniaturization of batteries was originally undertaken for the purpose of making tiny hearing aids, while the invention of microcircuitry was a by-product of the transistor revolution and the etchable silicon chip. Even so, the first quartz watches (1969) were thick and clumsy-looking—the antithesis of centuries of the pursuit of slender elegance; their energy requirements were such as to impose a default blackout except at the demand of the wearer; and they cost a thousand dollars or more. These shortcomings were rapidly overcome: in little more than a decade, battery life was extended from one year to five; display was continuous; thickness had been reduced to a millimeter; and in a world of general inflation, price had come down to a hundredth of what it had been. Such watches at their best work to a frequency in the 10^4 range and are accurate to seconds a year, far superior to the best of the mechanicals, so that the great majority of watches now produced are quartz-controlled, whether with traditional analog or digital (numerical) display.

The continuing pursuit of greater accuracy led after World War II to the investigation of even higher frequencies. Physicists led the way here, experimenting first with molecular (ammonia gas) and atomic resonators. These were initially no more accurate than the best quartz clocks (which by 1950 were operating at a rate constant to almost ten microseconds [10^{-6}]), but they offered the great advantage of uniformity. A quartz clock, however accurate, operates at its own intrinsic frequency. A vibrating cesium atom not only has its own frequency, but this frequency is the same for all cesium atoms, anywhere in the universe.

The first ammonia clock was built by Harold Lyons of the National Bureau of Standards (USA) in the late 1940s. It was rapidly superseded by the cesium-beam resonator (L. Essen and V.L. Parry of the British National Physical Laboratory, 1955) and the hydrogen MASER (microwave amplifier by stimulated emission of radiation; developed by H.M. Goldenberg, D. Kleppner, and Norman Ramsey in 1960). The cesium resonators operate at a frequency of more than 10^9 and keep time to one part in 10^{13}; they gain or lose, in other words, less than ten nanoseconds (10^{-9}) a day. As a result of these and earlier gains in accuracy, which made possible a more precise awareness of the irregularities of the earth's rotation, previously the clock of last resort, the thirteenth General Conference of Weights and Measures redefined the second, from a fraction of an earth day to "the duration of 9,192,631,770 periods of the radiation corresponding to the transition between the two hyperfine levels of the ground state of the cesium atom 133"—in other words, from a piece of an irregular and changing interval to the sum of constant units.

The invention and development of these new instruments of high frequency time measurement has transformed both civil and scientific temporalities. Ordinary people now have ready access to far more accurate and reliable time information than ever before. Their watches and clocks need be reset only when the hour changes from standard to summer time and vice versa. Whether people have changed their habits of punctuality and use of time is another matter. Scientists, on the other hand, not only have a new time standard, but one that is so much more precise than any other measure that, whenever possible and desirable, quantities (electrical units, for example) are converted into frequencies for purposes of exact measurement and comparison. At the same time, modern industrial and communication techniques often depend on the precision of microsecond timing and better: thus the development of high frequency timekeeping has contributed much to advances in computer operations, high-density wire and wireless transmission, celestial and terrestrial navigation, missile guidance, and the like.

[D.S.L.]

See also **Definition and Measurement of Time; Standard Time: Time Zones and Daylight Saving Time; Time Measurement and Science.**

FURTHER READINGS

Bateman, D.A. "Q and Oscillator Stability." *Electronics and Wireless World* 93 (August 1987): 843–844.

Coel, Margaret. "Keeping Time by the Atom." *American Heritage of Invention and Technology* 3.3 (Winter 1988): 43–48.

Forman, Paul. "Atomichron: The Atomic Clock from Concept to Commercial Product." *Proceedings of the IEEE* 73.7 (July 1985): 1181–1204.

Good, Richard. *Britten's Watch & Clock Makers Handbook, Dictionary, and Guide.* 16th ed. (revised). London: Eyre Methuen and E. & F. N. Spon, 1978.

Jespersen, James, and Jane Fitz-Randolph. *From Sundials to Atomic Clocks: Understanding Time and Frequency.* National Bureau of Standards Monograph 155.- Washington: U.S. Government Printing Office, 1977.

Ramsey, Norman F. "History of Atomic and Molecular Standards of Frequency and Time." *IEEE Transactions on Instrumentation and Measurement* IM-21.2 (May 1972): 90–99.

HINDUISM

The name Hinduism has been used to describe a great many different religious and philosophical traditions whose common denominator is the (nominal) acceptance of the Veda as word of revelation and the caste-structure as a natural division of society. In the course of its more than 4,000 years of history, Hinduism has given rise to a great many sects and schools of thought which often hold diametrically opposed opinions on central issues, and thus also with regard

to time. Most Hindu systems distinguish between divisible and indivisible time: the first identified with empirical time and its divisions, the second an uncreated principle of the universe.

EARLY CONCEPTS OF TIME

Time was a central concern in Hinduism long before the six classical (philosophical) systems developed. The *Ṛgveda* speaks of the rotating wheel of time as having twelve spokes, and it connects the seasons with the ingredients of the all-important sacrifice. The *Maitri Upaniṣad* contains the famous passage, "Time cooks all things in the great self. He who knows in what time is cooked is the knower of the Veda" (VI,15). In the *Mahābhārata*, time appears as fate (*daiva*), or even death. Time is seen both as giver of happiness and misery; its effects are considered inescapable. In the *Purāṇas*, time (*kāla*) is often introduced as one of the uncreated principles on a par with *pradhāna* (matter) and *puruṣa* (spirit), emerging from the unmanifested being (*avyakta*). Time thus becomes a kind of demiurge. Such a conception makes it possible to leave *brahman* totally transcendent and to absolve *brahman* from the evils of the world.

The popular *Yogavāsiṣṭha Rāmāyaṇa* has a large section devoted to *kāla*: time is said to be the cause for both the creation and the destruction of the universe. By means of *niyati* (fate) it also controls the course of history. *Kāla* (time) is compared to an actor who appears on the stage, disappears, and reappears again to perform his play. The *Bhagavadgītā*, possibly the best known Hindu text, contains the famous passage where Kṛṣṇa says about himself: "Time am I, world-destroying, grown mature, engaged in subduing the world." The *Bhagavadgītā* uses this text to demonstrate that everything in this world is preordained, that all events happen by necessity, with or without human cooperation. In one of the last sections of the *Mahābhārata*, the Mausalyaparva, which is characterized by a deep sense of doom, the speaker tells us that his heroes "met with destruction, impelled by time." Time (in an embodied form) is described as wandering around the earth: "He looked like a man of terrible and fierce aspect" and was "none else but the Destroyer of all creatures." The evil deeds that the protagonists commit and which earn them their fate are ascribed to "the perverseness of the hour that had come upon them."

PHILOSOPHIES OF TIME

1. SUBSTANTIALIST NOTIONS OF TIME.

Vaiśeṣika, a thoroughly atomistic philosophical system, subscribes to a decidedly substantialist notion of time. Time is one of nine substances (*dravya*). It is described as "of three kinds, being characterised by creation, sustention and destruction" (*Saptapadārthī*).

Nyāya deals with time in the context of "valid cognition." It accepts the *Vaiśeṣika*, notion of time as a substance and attempts to work out the epistemological implications. It holds that "perception and the rest cannot be regarded as instruments of cognition on account of the impossibility of connecting them with any of the three points of time." In an attempt to rebut the Buddhist negation of a present time, the *Naiyāyikas* assert that "If there is no present time, then past and future are inconceivable, as they are relative to that. Time is not conceived in relation to space but in relation to action. It is the actually existing connection of the object and the action which present time indicates. On the basis of this we have the notion of past and future, which would not be conceivable if the present did not exist" (*Nyāyasūtra* with *Bhāṣya*).

Viśiṣṭādvaita, a school of *Vedānta*, considers the physical universe to be "the body of God" and thus invests nature with a degree of reality hardly paralleled anywhere else. Consequently, time also acquires a substantiality of its own as the manifestation of God's eternity and omnipresence. As one text says, "What is called time (*kāla*) is a particular inert substance devoid of the three *guṇas*. It is eternal and all pervasive. It is the real basis for such terms as 'simultaneous,' 'immediate,' 'long' etc. . . . All creation is dependent on time . . . likewise all dissolution. . . . Time itself is the material cause in respect to its own effect. Undivided time is eternal, its effect is non-eternal. Time is an instrument in the cosmic sport of God. In his sport-manifestation God functions as dependent on time. In the eternal-manifestation, though time exists, it has no independence."

2. RELATIVISTIC NOTIONS OF TIME.

For the Advaitin Śaṁkara (eighth century), *brahman*, which is timeless, is the only reality. One of the preliminary qualifications of a study of *Vedānta* is the capacity to discriminate between what is eternal and what is non-eternal. Manifoldness, the result of evolution in time, is produced by ignorance. Time does not possess an independent reality of its own; it is only associated with events in time. The twelfth-century Advaitin Citsukha refutes the reality of time by pointing out that it can neither be perceived by the visual nor by the tactual sense, nor apprehended by mind; it cannot be inferred, either, because there are no perceptual data from which to start. Notions such as priority and posteriority, succession and simultaneity, quickness and duration do not indicate the nature of time itself. Since the self can be regarded as the cause of the manifestation of time in events and things in accordance with their varying conditions of appearance, it is unnecessary to introduce the existence of a new category called time. Notions such as priority and posteriority do not need time as an explanation: they may be regarded as the impressions produced by a greater or lesser quantity of solar vibrations. There is, therefore, no necessity to admit time as a separate category since its apprehension can be explained on the basis of our known data of experience.

3. MOMENTARINESS VERSUS TEMPORALITY.

Patañjali defines the end and purpose of *Yoga* to be "the cessation of all modifications of consciousness" and endeavors to lead the practitioner to a transcendence of time and space. Since the ultimate condition is one of timelessness, time cannot be an aspect of reality. "Temporality" is a figment of the mind; however, the moments which cause the perception of time are real. The *Yogasūtra* says that one gains metaphysical knowledge by concentrating (*saṁyama*) on the sequence (*krama*) of moments (*kṣaṇa*). As the commentator Vyāsa explains, "Just as the atom (*paramāṇu*) is the smallest particle of matter (*dravya*), so a moment (*kṣaṇa*) is the smallest particle of time (*kāla*)." Physically a *kṣaṇa* is the amount of time which an atom in motion takes to cross a space equalling the space it occupies. The sequence of such moments cannot be combined into a "thing." Notions like "hours" or "days" are mental combinations. Time (*kāla*) is not a real thing but is based on changes in the mind. The moment, however, is a real thing in itself and constitutive of the sequence. The sequence is constituted by an uninterrupted succession of moments. Past and future can be explained on the basis of change. The world which exists in this moment undergoes instant change. *Patañjali* accepts the notions of present, past, and future. Unlike the present, however, past and future do not exist in manifest form.

When the mental condition called *dharmamegha* is reached, the sequence of changes comes to an end and the sequence can no longer sustain even a *kṣaṇa*. In *dharmameghasamadhī*, the Yogi reaches a zero-time-experience before merging his consciousness in the timeless *Kaivalya*, a condition beyond matter and *karma*.

[K.K.K.]

See also **Buddhism; Indian Traditions and Time; Jainism.**

FURTHER READINGS

Adidevananda, Swami, trans. *Yatīndramatadīpkā by Śrīnivāsadāsa.* Mylapore: Sri Ramakrishna Math, 1949.

Coward, Harold. "Time (*kāla*) in Bhartrihari's *Vākya-padīya.*" *Journal of Indian Philosophy* 10 (1982): 277–287.

Dasgupta, S.N. *History of Indian Philosophy.* 5 vols. Cambridge: Cambridge UP, 1922–1955.

Gurumurti, D., trans. *Saptapadārthi of Śiāditya.* Adyar: Theosophical Publishing House, 1932.

Jha, Ganganatha, trans. *Gautama's Nyāyasūtras with Vatsyāyana Bhāṣya.* Poona: Oriental Book Agency, 1939.

Klostermaier, Klaus K. "Time in *Patañjali's Yogasūtras.*" *Philosophy East and West* 34.2 (April 1984): 205–210.

———. "Dharmamegha samādhi." *Philosophy East and West* 36.3 (July 1986): 253–262.

Prasad, Hari Shankar. "Time and Change in Sāṁkhya-Yoga." *Journal of Indian Philosophy* 12 (1984): 35–49.

HISTAMINE AND ALLERGIC RHINITIS

Many authors have reported circadian rhythms in asthma and the nocturnal exacerbation of allergic as well as nonallergic asthma attacks is becoming well accepted. However, few physicians are aware that circadian variations can also be detected in the cutaneous reaction to histamine and in the signs of allergic rhinitis.

The circadian variation in the cutaneous response to histamine was studied in young, diurnally active volunteers. Skin reactivity to intradermal injection of ten micrograms of histamine was evaluated at six different hours of the day. Circadian variations were detected in the cutaneous erythema (skin reddening) and wheal reactions as peak and trough sensitivity occurred at 11:00 P.M. and 8:00 A.M., respectively. Similar findings were found with compound 48/80, a histamine-releasing drug.

The circadian variations in the signs and symptoms of allergic rhinitis were studied in a multicentric study on 1,052 adults suffering from allergic rhinitis. Patients used visual analog scales four times in each twenty-four-hour period to self-measure symptoms such as sneezing, runny nose, stuffy and itchy nose, coughing, and dyspnea during a seven-day span. As a group phenomenon, circadian rhythms were validated for all symptoms, with a crest time early in the morning, for example at approximately 6:00 A.M.

Circannual variations in allergic rhinitis have not been studied extensively but it is well accepted that peak allergic reactions occur in the fall.

Physicians must take into account these temporal variations in allergic diseases when prescribing medications. Indeed, studies with long-acting antihistamine drugs such as mequitazine are indicating that the evening administration of this drug is more efficient than morning or afternoon ingestion for the prevention of sneezing, stuffy, runny, and itchy nose. It is noteworthy that the ingestion of the drug at 9:00 P.M. produces less side effects than at other times of the day.

[P.G. and G.L.]

See also **Allergy and Pollen; Biological Rhythms and Medicine; Biological Rhythms in Epidemiology and Pharmacology.**

FURTHER READINGS

Reinberg, A., G. Labrecque, and M.H. Smolensky. *Chronobiologie et chronothérapeutique: Heure optimale d'administration des médicaments.* Paris: Flammarion Medecine-Science, 1991.

Reinberg, A., P. Gervais, et al. "A Multicentric Chronotherapeutic Study of Mequitazine in Allergic Rhinitis." *Annual Review of Chronopharmacology* 3 (1986): 441–444.

HISTORIOGRAPHY AND PROCESS

Time is a uniquely human phenomenon, an intuitive concept by which human beings relate to the past and present and attempt to anticipate the future. The practice of "historiography" (< Greek *historia*, "learning and knowing by inquiry"; + *graphos*, "to write") stems from the same inclination to recover and to systematize facts for posterity, as well as to inquire into causes and motives.

Seeking a dynamic purpose to history, theorists down through the ages have presupposed that temporal events comprise a systematic series of actions, are directed to a definite end, and can disclose certain immutable laws or forces which, in turn, might be used to understand why and how events occurred. In this quest for the unifying principles of history—for principles endowing experience with meaning, purpose, and direction—historiography exhibits mankind's need to understand himself, temporally, as an individual and as a species. This article surveys six millennia of such theorizing. The idea that history is a "process" governed by discernible laws reflects mankind's irrepressible need to understand his place in time.

JEWISH AND GRECO-ROMAN HISTORIOGRAPHY

In the ancient world, the historiographical impulse relied on chronology as an ordering principle. Genealogies, dynastic lists, and war inscriptions abounded in ancient Babylon and Egypt. But a coherent, "processive" historiography did not emerge until the time of the ancient Hebrews. For the Hebrews, God was the lord of history who had made a covenant with his chosen people. The notion that they occupied a special place in human history and had an obligation to live according to a divine law gave meaning, direction, and purpose to the Jewish sense of time. As a result, chastisement, deliverance, and judgment were all important aspects of Jewish historiography.

There is also evidence of the processive mode—in which history is considered to be a "process" governed by discernible laws—in Greco-Roman historiography. Historians such as Herodotus, Thucydides, and Polybius, although focusing on the great events of contemporary history (the Greco-Persian War, the Peloponnesian War, and the rise of the Roman Empire, respectively), conjectured on the deeper meanings and dynamic structures of history. The Greeks developed a cyclical theory (each civilization progressed to a point and then inevitably declined), which described the succession of civilizations. But this scheme was intrinsically limited because it precluded progress, and each civilization possessed a determined and insulated life-cycle. Influenced by the Greeks, the Romans also conceived of limited versions of processive historiography. Livy (59 B.C.–A.D. 17), for example, wrote an idealized history of the Roman Empire, which was designed to express both secular and religious Roman traditions. Livy not only suggested that Rome had been chosen for greatness

by the gods, but that it was being guided by this spiritual election, and that it embodied a unique spirit of virtue and honor.

TWELVE CENTURIES OF CHRISTIAN HISTORIOGRAPHY

Hebrew and Greco-Roman historiography share the natural inclination to systematize and pattern events. Classical conjectures about synthetic historiography also demonstrate an almost unavoidable fallacy: the tendency to interpret history selectively and restrictively and, thus, to force historical reality into conformity with philosophical ideas that were preconceived and sometimes supratemporal. Christian historiography inherited these features. Indebted for historical facts to the Old and New Testaments primarily, and borrowing key elements from Greek philosophy and from Jewish prophetic literature, the early fathers of the church developed a universal history featuring a periodical structure and an historically immanent providence. The framework of the Bible provided a way of outlining the history of mankind from Creation (Genesis) to the Last Judgment, the consummation of which is figuratively described in the Book of Revelation. Naturally, early Christian writers were concerned with chronology and with important historical markers such as the Incarnation. Writers such as Scipio Africanus (A.D. 221) conjectured about human origins, the age of the world, and the dynamics of history, accommodating as they did the Greek concept of the rise and fall of nations (which they correlated with divine favor), and the Jewish periodical scheme of four world monarchies found in the Book of Daniel. One obvious shortcoming of the processive modality, illustrated by the temporal allusions in the Epistle to Barnabas (A.D. 70–130), is the uncritical use of sources and the overriding need to make received material conform to, and support, a preconceived system. This sort of processive historiography subordinates the past and the present to the future and to the drama of the last things: an Apocalypse, a millennium of Christ's rule on earth, and the Last Judgment.

Though the infant church placed little emphasis on the past—on the lives of the saints, on proselytization, and on persecution—as it gradually became evident that the Second Coming was not imminent, Christian historiographers, notably Eusebius, revised their interpretations accordingly to consider three centuries rich in cultural history and philosophy. Since the time of Irenaeus (ca. A.D. 180), Christian historiographers consistently saw time as the medium within which God's plan for redemption was being worked out. This was, above all, an educational journey dramatized by the convergence of great events: the life of Christ (Incarnation to the Resurrection), Greek philosophy, Jewish theological history, and the establishment of the Roman Empire.

The need to accommodate theological history to great and sometimes contradictory changes has been its greatest challenge, one that St. Augustine, in the *City of God* (413–426), faced directly and undauntedly. The fall of Rome led the pagans of Augustine's time to blame Christianity for their ill fortune. Thus, in his theodicy, Augustine attempted to reevaluate the nature of mundane evil. Without compromising God's omnipotence, he reasoned that too close a causal relationship between divine authority and a temporal empire simplified reality by imposing a mundane explanation upon mysterious and inscrutable events. He explained, further, that God bestowed vicissitude on the good and the bad alike. Augustine's major innovations include differentiating profane from theological history, and repudiating historical theories, such as Cicero's cyclical view, which contradicted received dogma, and which cleared ground for heresy. Augustine commissioned Paulus Orosius to demonstrate, conclusively, that Christianity did not cause the fall of Rome, and that the world had suffered great evils before the appearance of Christianity. In the process, however, Orosius diverged from Augustine on several issues. From the viewpoint of how human history relates to eternal truths, Orosius argued for a closer correspondence between Roman history and divine providence than Augustine would have allowed. The Orosian idea of an imperial theological history would greatly influence medieval historiographers, many of whom wrongly assumed this to be Augustine's idea.

Orosius's reversion to elective historiography and his rigid providentialism shaped medieval historiography. Although genuine historical disquisitions appeared during the Middle Ages—detailed accounts of great contemporary events such as the Crusades—the biblical framework remained the governing structure. But the inexorable expansion of historical consciousness beyond Western Europe, along with other momentous events, encouraged writers to develop further the profane dimension of theological history. William of Tyre, for instance, in his history of the Crusades, reflected on commerce, on psychological motives, on military strategy, and on political policy. And even a traditional theological historian such as Bishop Otto of Friesing (*The Two Cities*, 1143–1146), although greatly indebted to Orosius, understood that the genre had to be remodeled in view of these events.

SECULAR CURRENTS IN PROCESSIVE HISTORY, FIFTEENTH TO NINETEENTH CENTURY

Processive history did not disappear with the Renaissance and the Reformation. In fifteenth-century Florence, especially, there flourished a kind of processive history that was idealistic and imperial, though no longer overtly theological. Writers such as Leonardo Bruni (ca. 1370–1444), who thought that Florence embodied the spirit of democracy, created a kind of ideological history of Florence, with the Greek city-state purportedly a cultural prefiguration. A variant on the imperial theme of Orosius, Bruni's processive historiography of Florence exemplified the weaknesses inherent to idealized history. At this juncture, the most significant theoretical development, with respect to processive historiography, was the separation of the theological from the secular. The historiography of late fifteenth-century Florence certainly idealized secular politics and culture. But with the defeat of Florentine republicanism in 1512, this idealizing penchant was displaced by a more mundane concern for accuracy through careful research.

While analytical approaches to historiography were developing in Italy—especially in the works of Macchiavelli (1469–1527) and of Guicciardini (1483–1540)—the English were preoccupied with myths of origin traced back to Noah, the ancient Britons, or the Trojans. The myth of King Arthur became especially popular with the accession of the Tudors when people were fascinated with a glorified past filled with pageantry, ideals, and a sense of historical destiny. The conflation of cultural myth and of national identity was not a new development to processive historiography, for it could trace its own intellectual origins back to the ancient Hebrews.

The most potent eighteenth-century reaction against ecclesiastical and idealized historiography generally came from Voltaire (1694–1778) and the *philosophes*. Voltaire attacked the most representative theological history, Bishop

Bossuet's *Discourse on Human History* (1681), which had been fashioned in the Augustinian and Orosian mold. Yet, ironically, in their zeal to discount the Bible as an historical source for world history, writers such as Voltaire and Condorcet (1743–1794) idealized human history, each in his own way, and like the Greeks, fashioned speculative paradigms governed by immutable principles. Among their fallacies was the tendency to view human nature as unchanging and to condemn the past as uniformly primitive and savage when contrasted to the enlightened present. Although the *philosophes* viewed history ahistorically, they contributed significantly to the development of historiography, nonetheless, by widening the cultural scope to encompass non-European cultures and disciplines other than history. They also drove a deeper wedge between theological and critical historiography.

At this historical juncture, Giambattista Vico's *Scienza Nuova* (1725), represented a significant work in the genre, one not easily categorized. Vico reacted against the radical empiricists who denied that mankind could possess any real historical knowledge; he reaffirmed the theological concept of divine providence but refined the medieval view when he said that God worked through secondary causes and human behavior. Vico's enlightened interest in the uniqueness and historical interrelatedness of cultures, and his unenlightened appreciation for ancient myth and legend, suggests that he was trying to fuse the ancient and modern perspectives and to modernize the theological format.

A largely secular form of processive historiography prevailed in the later eighteenth and early nineteenth century. Exploration, progress in science and technology, and the decline of the medieval worldview gave rise to a new form of world history, one that was more globally inclusive, optimistic, and progressive. Philosophies of history replaced theologies of history, especially in Germany where writers from Johann Gottfried Herder (1744–1803) to Georg Wilhelm Friedrich Hegel (1770–1831) devised secular theories of historical process displacing divine providence with the processes of the human mind. These speculative historiographies were operating on a different track from the "academic" historiography of the Universities of Göttingen and Berlin, where theorists such as August Ludwig von Schlözer (1735–1809) and Leopold von Ranke (1795–1886) were trying to enunciate a dogmatically unrestricted and analytical historical method.

Also idealized, preconceived, and utopian, Marx's processive historiography, like Hegel's, attempted to elucidate the underlying structures of human history. Since Marx (1818–1883) believed that nature was the source of historical patterns, he adapted to Hegel's dialectical scheme the basic notion of struggle between competing groups. The result—dialectical materialism—presumes that economic factors are the most historically significant, and that social history is dialectically processive, a history of "class struggle" in which a specific class would rule only when representing the economically productive forces of society. Hence, just as capitalism displaced feudalism dialectically, creating the new industrial order, the proletariat class (those who produced goods), on becoming the most economically productive, would replace the bourgeoisie.

Throughout the second half of the nineteenth century, academic historiography, characterized by intense and detailed research, eclipsed processive historiography. New approaches to cultural history were exemplified by H.T. Buckle's *History of Civilization in England* (1857), Jakob Burkhardt's *Civilisation of the Renaissance in Italy* (1860), and Hippolyte Taine's *Origines de la France contemporaine* (1876–1894). The question of whether or not history was a "science" was a controversial issue, as well. Wilhelm Dilthey (1833–1911) and Wilhelm Windelband (1848–1915) studied the very nature of historical knowledge. And a preoccupation with the method and grounds of historical knowledge—especially in the works of Max Weber (1864–1920), Ernst Troeltsch (1865–1923), and Friedrich Meinecke (1862–1954)—would shape the course of twentieth-century historiography.

THE TWENTIETH CENTURY: A MULTIPLICITY OF VIEWS

The study of history in the twentieth century has become an extraordinarily complex and multidisciplinary enterprise, incorporating ideas from fields as diverse as science, psychology, and linguistics. Despite the proliferation of speculative theories and of their applications, many of which have argued against the very possibility of a synthetic historiography, some twentieth-century theorists have continued to pursue a unified, processive model. The common denominator to their diversified approaches has been the intuitive conviction that "time" is meaningful, not as an abstraction, but as a dynamic and generative context for human existence, a context including the interplay of chance and of nature.

In particular, three processive historiographers of the twentieth century—Oswald Spengler (1880–1936), Arnold J. Toynbee (1889–1974), and Teilhard de Chardin, S.J. (1881–1955)—have employed a variety of approaches in the common pursuit of a unified and dynamic world history. Spengler, in *The Decline of the West* (1918), like the nineteenth-century German philosophers of history, sought a unifying perspective in his scheme of cultures. Each culture is a thriving, independent phenomenon, sharing common beliefs: each "has its own new possibilities of self-expression which arise, ripen, decay, and never return." Spengler studied two such cultures closely: what he called the "Apollonian" of ancient Greece and Rome and the "Faustian" of the medieval and modern West. His speculative analysis endowed each with a millennial life span and a four-stage growth pattern which he likened, metaphorically, to the seasons. Highly speculative, metaphoric, and evidently indebted to idealistic antecedents, especially in Germany, Spengler's sense of a Western declension is clearly processive.

Toynbee, in his massive *Study of History* (12 vols., 1934–1961), also propounds a deterministic and cyclical view of history, one featuring paradigms of descent. Unlike Spengler's approach, Toynbee's endows social history with genetic and dialectical unity. Distinguishing twenty-one known civilizations, he places them into three generations. In the twentieth century, there are eight extant civilizations, the roots of which are traced to extinct forebears. Along with the genetic and hereditary principle, Toynbee also postulated that historical societies experienced a growth cycle contingent largely upon how each reacted to environmental challenges.

A third example of modern teleological history can be found in Teilhard de Chardin's *The Phenomenon of Man* (1955; reprint, 1975). In this text, de Chardin works out a design argument in evolutionary terms. Employing the term "noosphere" to describe a wholly humanized earth, he sees God as being both transcendent to and immanent in the world. On one level, mankind is able to perfect himself by cooperating with the natural world. On a deeper level, through Christianity, mankind will be able to incorporate himself into the mystical body of Christ, a direct union with God constituting ultimate perfection. De Chardin unites Christian theology with evolutionary perfectibilism, espousing a kind of evolutionism or "cosmogenesis," whereby a steady increase in the complexity of the phenomenal world, both material and psychic, finds in man a new and higher level of possibility; the "noosphere"—creation subsumed under, and transfigured by, evolving human consciousness—would be manifested, outwardly, by a unified world-culture, and inwardly, by unity with God at the "Omega" point.

The diversity of their approaches notwithstanding, Spengler, Toynbee, and de Chardin exemplify the archetypal pursuit of a unified, processive historiography. Like the ancients, they too were motivated by the sense that time is both the matrix and the substance of inscrutable processes.

DEDUCTIONS

Intuiting time to be the medium of human experience, and guided by the relative distinctions between past, present, and future, processive historiographers have searched for dynamic forces and structures to unify history. Notwithstanding an array of modern theories (the new historicism, structuralism, deconstructionalism, and left-wing social historiography), many of which have militated against the possibility of a "world" or synthetic historiography, the pursuit of a synthetic and processive historiography remains a theoretically viable pursuit, but only so if anchored by a balanced methodology. On the one hand, such a methodology would have to be analytical, involving the critical evaluation of sources, an understanding of the complex nature of historical knowledge, and an awareness of how ideology and dogma affect history. On the other hand, it would have to be synthetic: global yet specific in scope, inclusive, and cohering around a valid, universally applicable principle.

[C.D.]

FURTHER READINGS

Breisach, Ernst. *Historiography: Ancient, Medieval and Modern.* Chicago: U of Chicago P, 1983.

Butterfield, Herbert. "Historiography." *Dictionary of the History of Ideas: Studies of Selected Pivotal Ideas.* Ed. Philip P. Wiener. 5 vols. New York: Charles Scribner's Sons, 1973. 2:464b–498b.

———. *The Origins of History.* Ed. Adam Watson. New York: Basic Books, 1981.

Collingwood, R.G. *The Idea of History.* 1946; reprint, New York: Oxford UP, 1974.

D'Arcy, S.J., M.C. *The Meaning and Matter of History: A Christian View*. 1959; reprint, New York: Noonday P, 1967.

De Chardin, S.J., Teilhard. *The Phenomenon of Man*. Introduction by Sir Julian Huxley. 1955; reprint, New York: Harper & Row, 1975.

Gay, Peter, and Gerald J. Cavanaugh, eds. *Historians at Work*. 4 vols. New York: Harper & Row, 1972.

Mohan, Robert Paul. *Philosophy of History: An Introduction. Horizons in History*. General eds. Jude Dougherty and Robert Wood. New York: Bruce Publishing Company, 1970.

Spengler, Oswald. *The Decline of the West*. Ed. Helmut Werner and Arthur Helps. Trans. Charles Francis Atkinson. New York: Knopf, 1962.

HOGARTH, WILLIAM (1697–1764)

William Hogarth is the artist who best portrayed the pervasive interest in mechanical timekeeping during the British horological revolution of 1660–1760, the latter half of which took place in his own lifetime. Why a graphic artist, rather than a poet, should have thus distinguished himself may be partially explained by Hogarth's keen awareness of time in his professional career. He began his work as an engraver of watchcases, a business which grew quickly as the watch increasingly became a part of urban daily life. Later, as a painter and engraver in his own right, he worked according to what we might now call "time management" methods. He proposed to paint a portrait in four one-quarter-hour sittings, and even arranged for some of his most famous completed paintings to be sold by timed auction.

Many of Hogarth's works are structured by the passing of time. The progresses—*A Harlot's Progress*, *A Rake's Progress*, *Marriage à la Mode*, and *Industry and Idleness*—play ironically upon the new meaning of the word *progress*, which during the seventeenth century had first come to signi-

Figure 1. A Harlot's Progress, *Plate III.*

fy a progression through time rather than through space. Works such as *Before and After* and *The Four Times of the Day* demonstrate other aspects of Hogarth's interest in portraying the passage of time.

Iconographic symbols of time also appear frequently in Hogarth's work, in which the watch, still an expensive novelty in his day, is frequently shown. The iconography of stolen watches—occurring in the climactic positions of Plate III of *A Harlot's Progress* (Figure 1), *A Rake's Progress*, and the four *Stages of Cruelty*, as well as Plates VII and IX of *Industry and Idleness*—is a favorite motif. Such scenes illustrate both the corruption of a thieving character and the corrupting value of the watch, which often represents several years of the thief's potential income in any honest capacity. It is little wonder that the small size of the watch, normally worn in the pockets of men and at the waists of women, made it a favorite target of pickpockets and cutpurses. Those who wear a watch in Hogarth's work do so because they are wealthy or have pretensions to wealth. For example, in Plate I of *A Harlot's Progress*, Mother Needham, who is procuring for Colonel Charteris, carries a watch at her waist while the as yet uncorrupted Moll carries only her needlework implements there.

In his prints, Hogarth uses the clock for both denotative and connotative purposes. Among others, the clocks in Plates I and II of *The Four Times of the Day* and in *The Battle of the Pictures* serve the denotative purpose of indicating time. In *Masquerade Ticket* (second state), the clock above denotes the lateness of the hour, but the killing of "Time" in the scene below adds connotations regarding the role of the masqueraders at the ball (Figure 2). At the ball in *Analysis of Beauty*, Plate II, the weakness of the apparently cuckolded bourgeois husband is emphasized by the manner in which he draws his wife's attention to the time. In Plate II of *Marriage à la Mode*, the tasteless and elaborate rococo clock behind young Squanderfield's head shows the lateness

Figure 2. The Masquerade Ticket.

of the hour, but is also meant to emphasize the financial and sexual excesses of the unfaithful husband. In contrast, the simple weight-driven clock of the wife's alderman father in Plate VI reflects his frugal lifestyle. But Hogarth's timepieces also carry such varying connotations as a *memento mori* message in the woodcut of Plate III of *The Four Stages of Cruelty*, a sociopolitical message in *The Times*, and a message of quiet dignity in *Miss Mary Edwards*.

Father Time appears frequently, as he does above the clock in "Morning" of Plate I of *The Four Times of the Day*. In *The Lady's Last Stake*, however, he is significantly absent. Instead, Cupid holding the scythe above the ornate clock with the message "NUNC NUNC," adds spice to the titillating dilemma of whether the lady, who has lost everything at a card game, should submit to the young officer's proposals before the sun has set. Under the clock in *The South Sea Scheme* stands a Father Time whose metamorphosis into the

devil reminds us of his almost forgotten antecedents in Saturn-Cronus (Figure 3). Father Time becomes the central figure in both *Time Smoking a Picture* and Hogarth's final work *Tailpiece, or the Bathos*, which alludes directly to Pope's *Peri Bathos*, a forerunner of *The Dunciad* (Figure 4). In Hogarth's last work—a pessimistic comment on contemporary society that hauntingly parallels Pope's final statement in *Dunciad* IV—Hogarth depicts the death of Time, whose traditional symbols including the scythe and the hourglass lie broken amidst chaos.

In the works of Hogarth's successors, James Gillray and Thomas Rowlandson, the iconography of time is conspicuously absent. Hogarth's life coincided with the peak of the fascination with mechanical timekeeping. It was perhaps only natural that an artist so concerned with the urban activities of London should show an interest in the technology which had so much impact upon the life of his city.

[S.L.M.]

Figure 3. The South Sea Scheme.

Figure 4. The Bathos, or Manner of Sinking in Sublime Paintings.

See also **Clock Metaphor; Father Time; Saturn-Cronus.**

FURTHER READINGS

Macey, Samuel L. "Hogarth and the Iconography of Time." *Studies in Eighteenth-Century Culture.* Vol. 5. Ed. Ronald C. Rosbottom. Madison: U of Wisconsin P, 1976. 41–53, and Plates 1–4.

———. *Clocks and the Cosmos: Time in Western Life and Thought.* Hamden: Archon Books, 1980.

Paulson, Ronald. *Hogarth: His Life, Art, and Times.* 2 vols. New Haven: Yale UP, 1971.

The figures are from John Trusler's Works of Hogarth *(London [1830]) in the author's possession.*

HOPEFUL MONSTERS

"Hopeful monster" is an expression coined by the evolutionist Richard Goldschmidt in 1933 for a lecture presented at the Chicago World's Fair. Having rejected the tenets of neo-Darwinism after extensive field research, Goldschmidt was interested in the mechanisms of macroevolution or saltatory evolution. The monstrosity represented a radical novelty of form or function. The hope was twofold: first for an ability of the monstrosity to breed true, either through genetic dominance, or through hermaphroditism (that is by self-fertilization, a common feature of many organisms) or, less likely, by finding a similar type of mate. The second hope was that the novelty would make the monster much better for the prevailing conditions of life than its parents, or that it would be better able to exploit an available new environment than the existing inhabitants. A tailless Manx cat was "just a monster"; an *Archaeopteryx*, the primitive reptile-bird, was a hopeful monster, and the sky was the limit to its ecological expansionism.

Under the circumstances of its introduction, the hopeful monster proposition was not taken very seriously. But Goldschmidt persisted, and revived the beast in his book, *The Material Basis of Evolution* (1941). The mechanism that produced the hopeful monster was a radical change in "position effect," that is, a change in gene expression during development due to a chromosomal mutation. This, together with the doubts he expressed about the very existence of the molecular gene, was too much for orthodoxy; by his own account, Goldschmidt had "stirred up a hornets' nest." Neo-Darwinism dictated that any monster must be hopeless because of the absence of natural selection from its conception.

However, in the light of recent advances in epigenetic research, some modern evolutionists feel that a revival of the hopeful monster is justified, at least as a catalyst for theoretical debate. The research of Barbara McClintock, the Nobel Laureate geneticist who was associated with Goldschmidt at the beginning of her career, was slow in receiving recognition. But her discovery of transposons, the "jumping genes" of the popular press, vindicated Goldschmidt's commitment to position effects and has provided an empirical basis for taking the hopeful monster seriously.

[R.G.B.R.]

See also **Evolutionary Progress; Heterochrony; Saltatory Evolution.**

FURTHER READINGS

Keller, E.F. *A Feeling for the Organism: The Life and Work of Barbara McClintock.* San Francisco: W.H. Freeman, 1983.

HOSPITAL ORGANIZATION

A hospital is a facility for the diagnosis and management of disease and the supervision of childbirth and has functions directed to the preservation of health. It usually provides inpatient and outpatient environments. In modern hospitals, the combined pressures of rising costs and increasing demand have encouraged the streamlining of procedures and practices. Ideally, the goal has been to deliver the highest possible quality of care in the least possible time.

EARLY HISTORY

In the millennium before Christ, hospitals were established in India and Sri Lanka; in Greece and Rome, healing temples were centers for the treatment of disease. Hospitals were established by the Christian church before A.D. 700 in Constantinople, Rome, Lyons, and Paris. Subsequently, monasteries and the Crusaders established many hospitals in which there was a gradual growth of the use of herbal remedies and the adoption of superior, Arabian methods of medical care. Through the Middle Ages, hospitals changed little; they were affiliated with religious organizations, cared for the indigent ill and dying, and concerned themselves more with the spiritual than the physical welfare of their patients. The Spanish and the French established the first hospitals in North America (again staffed by religious orders) in the fourteenth and fifteenth centuries, respectively. The industrial revolution in Britain and Europe hastened the building of secular hospitals, and this development was further accelerated in the nineteenth century by the growth of cities and medical advances.

INFLUENCE OF INFECTIOUS DISEASES

Prior to modern methods of treatment, hospital-acquired infection killed many patients attending hospital for other diseases or for childbirth. I.P. Semmelweis, Louis Pasteur, and Joseph Lister contributed to a new understanding of infection that changed hospital organization. Infectious cases became segregated in special wards or hospitals; this applied especially to tuberculosis because of its chronicity, frequency, and mortality. Hand-washing facilities were provided for staff in the wards of general hospitals, and special areas and equipment for disinfection were developed in operating rooms.

Better understanding of the routes of transmission of infection and the discovery of antibiotics has reversed some of these trends. Isolation of patients has decreased, the isolation ward has disappeared, and fever hospitals have been converted to other uses. However, there is growing recognition of hospital-acquired infection in patients with immune system disorders due to disease or to treatments such as chemotherapy, and this phenomenon has accompanied the development of "reverse-isolation" areas.

INFLUENCE OF MEDICAL SPECIALIZATION

The enormous accretion of new medical knowledge which has occurred in the last half-century has led to profound changes in hospitals. Prior to the twentieth century, most hospitals did not provide for the varied requirements of different types of disease; rather, each ward accommodated all diseases.

As more effective operations were devised with the help of anesthesia and antisepsis, surgical treatment areas gradually became segregated. Operating rooms became larger and more complex, and induction of and recovery from anesthesia necessitated separate facilities. Surgical bed allocation grew, and outpatient surgical areas were added. As surgical procedures became more sophisticated, postoperative recovery areas and later intensive care areas were added. The transfusion of blood, which became commonplace during World War II, accelerated these trends.

Hospital-based internal medicine lagged behind until the mid-twentieth century. The adoption of invasive diagnostic and treatment methods, the enormous growth and complexity of clinical pathology and medical imaging, and the discovery of many potent drugs provided a powerful stimulus. Endoscopy suites were constructed, and more space and resources were allocated; invasive cardiology facilities in particular experienced enormous growth and increasing complexity.

Paralleling these changes, ward nursing became specialized, and multidisciplinary treatment teams became common. This led to the development of wards aligned by medical specialty—for example, gastroenterology—or by treatment type, such as chemotherapy. Emergency departments expanded, often combining the treatment of true emergencies with treatment of less severe problems.

Hospitals also specialize in the intensity of care given. Acute general hospitals and some specialty hospitals give the most urgent care, while intermediate and long-term care hospitals cater to more chronic, often elderly patients and have less intensive staffing. Gender and age specialization occurs, but is less common.

GOVERNANCE OF HOSPITALS

In Europe, most hospitals are directly managed by the government. In Britain, regional health authorities receive money from the government, and manage regional hospitals. Recently, private clinics and hospitals have developed in response to the perceived inadequacy of resources allocated by the state.

In Canada, many hospitals are directly responsible to provincial government ministries; others are run by the boards of private societies or, less commonly, by religious organizations. Until recently, the government of Canada administered veterans' hospitals; these are now the responsibility of the provinces. In the United States, nonprofit hospitals are run by universities, societies, or cities; private and for-profit hospitals are administered by large corporations or medical groups.

The rapid growth and rising cost of hospitals has precipitated the examination of alternatives by governments, who now allocate up to one-third of their total budget to health care. Currently, the role of hospitals is being stringently examined, particularly in North America. Amalgamation of neighboring hospitals, the elimination of duplication and unnecessary competition, expansion of outpatient rather than inpatient services, and closer collaboration with other community health agencies are increasing trends. Professional administrators have replaced medical superintendents and computer-based management information systems are widely available.

FISCAL ISSUES IN HOSPITALS

Initially, hospitals were dependent on voluntary donations and a variety of fees; a few fortunate institutions were able to secure large corporate or philanthropic donations, but most were chronically underfunded. With government-sponsored health insurance, hospitals grew rapidly up to the mid-1980s. They acquired diagnostic and other equipment, and developed a much more elaborate organization. It was common during this time for hospitals to exceed their allocated budget, and to rely on automatic year-end financial adjustment by the government.

From 1960 onward, quality was improved by voluntary adherence to criteria developed first in the United States and then in Canada. In general, this process further accelerated growth in small and medium hospitals, as it tended to stress the concept that "more is better."

Growth, complexity, and expense have triggered tighter financial control in the last decade. Industrial concepts such as product-costing were adapted for hospitals using diagnostic related groups and peer-group comparisons were introduced. As a result, growth has been curbed; indeed, some hospital facilities have actually been reduced. Private hospitals have reappeared in Britain, and the desirability of two levels of health care ("two-tier medicine") is being actively discussed in Canada.

Continuous quality improvement schemes have helped to achieve more effective and efficient use of expensive hospital resources. Nonhospital treatments have been expanded for less severe illnesses, resulting in a decrease in numbers but an increase in the severity of cases admitted to hospitals. Overall, these mechanisms have slowed the previously inexorable cost escalation.

Hospitals in this century became so complex that the patient was often peripheral; while cure was achieved, care was forgotten. Recent patient advocacy and discoveries in psychobiology have rekindled the importance of care and refocused hospitals on caring for, as well as curing, the patient.

[K.R.T.]

See also **General Practice Organization.**

HOUSING AND THE AGED

There are a number of ways in which time has a bearing on the housing needs of elderly people. Needs change over the life course and between different generations, and in both cases are tempered by a recognition that factors such as cultural, economic, social, and other variations, including gender, will play a part. Such factors help to determine needs, preferences, and the ability to fulfill them, and also to determine the kinds of housing that are provided.

CHANGES OVER THE LIFE COURSE

For many centuries, few people survived to "old" age and so the question of their housing was of little relevance. Even now there is great variation in numbers surviving, and there are marked differences between developed and developing countries. However, as countries become more industrialized, large extended families may shrink and elderly people become more isolated.

For the majority of people, the first few years of life are spent within a family. Most, particularly in industrial countries, leave home to work in another area. A period of living alone may follow in lodgings or in some kind of supported environment, such as a hostel. Marriage in developed countries usually means a move to an independent home in which children are brought up. At this stage, moves may take place to accommodate a growing family though some, such as farmers, may remain where they are. When this family building stage is completed a home may be too large and a move contemplated. It is then that difficult decisions have to be made about the relative merits of moving to somewhere smaller and, perhaps, leaving an environment where everything is familiar.

Some elderly people make a move at retirement, and in some countries, movement may also take place because there is an increase in migration. For others, no change of location occurs until a specific event precipitates a move. This is usually the death of a spouse or increasing disability. Disability increases with age and problems of mobility such as being unable to climb stairs make the provision of suitable housing important. If the decision is taken to remain *in situ* it may be necessary to make adaptations. Another reason for a move on retirement may occur when older people have worked in a country which is not their homeland.

A decision to move involves a number of factors. For many elderly people the availability of kin is important, and some moves are made to be nearer relatives, usually children, so that there can be mutual help.

For others, the move may be to somewhere more suitable, perhaps smaller, in the same area. One of the biggest decisions to be taken is whether to opt for specialized or nonspecialized housing. Specialized housing includes homes that are specially designed and built with older or disabled people in mind. An example is sheltered or congregate housing where accommodation is usually grouped around communal facilities and where some care and support is available.

A further decision is whether to opt for integration or segregation with other generations; the provision of both enables elderly people to have a choice. Those in favor of integration argue that it is a more "natural" environment to be with people of all ages. Those who favor segregation argue that older people may wish to have neighbors who are of much the same age, who may share similar forms of behavior, and who would seek similar communal facilities for leisure or care. Segregated communities have been developing in many parts of the world, notably the United States and Australia, and some large retirement communities have developed. In most cases, self-contained accommodation is provided either for rent or for sale. Often, housing is of different kinds and may include residential care and nursing homes.

CHANGING NEEDS BETWEEN GENERATIONS

Rising standards of living and purchasing power, decreasing size of families, and changing perceptions of need lead to housing which varies from one generation to another. The desire for privacy and independence on the part of both elderly people and their families is leading to a decline in extended family living. Although three-generation families living together are still common in some parts of the world, such as Southeast Asia, this arrangement is generally decreasing.

Another trend is the declining participation of elderly people in the work force. This factor, together with increased survival, leads to more time spent in the home and increases its importance. Home activities, including hosting visitors, require space, and the desire for more space is a trend in developed countries. One bedroom apartments are becoming less desirable than two bedroom ones. Higher standards of central heating and other amenities are also becoming more common for elderly people as they are for other groups. However, low income groups still occupy some of the worst housing and there is need for appropriate housing for them at a cost that they can afford.

The development of technology is changing some housing for elderly people. The extension of telephone usage has been followed by the provision of alarms which enable an elderly person to contact someone in an emergency. More elaborate electronic systems can also enable an elderly person to be monitored from a distance.

VARIATIONS BETWEEN ELDERLY PEOPLE

Generalizations about elderly people are dangerous because there are as many differences between elderly individuals as there are among people of other ages. The needs of fit elderly people are very different from those of frail or sick elderly people. While social class and financial resources will often determine where elderly people live, other factors are of importance too. Cultural differences may affect the design of housing and living patterns. Even tenure in old age may be affected by cultural variations. For example, people from the Indian subcontinent arriving in Europe as immigrants may be more likely to become owner-occupiers than West Indians for example.

There are also differences based on gender. Women tend to live longer than men and more survive into old age. They are also more likely to suffer from disability. This means that most very elderly people are women who may need adaptations to their homes, as well as more help with domestic and personal tasks.

In conclusion, and for a broad spectrum of reasons indicated throughout this article, the question of time and timing is of particular significance when considering questions that relate to housing and elderly people.

[A.T.]

See also **Aging and Time; Gender Differences in Aging.**

FURTHER READINGS

Bond, John. "Living Arrangements of Elderly People." *Aging in Society*. Ed. John Bond and Peter Coleman. London: Sage, 1990. 161–180.

HUMAN FERTILITY TRENDS

Although fertility levels in modern developed societies (1.5–1.8 children per woman) are the lowest ever achieved in human history, it would be wrong to think that there is a steady diminution of fertility during the course of humankind's progression over time from preindustrial to postindustrial societies.

During the hunting and gathering era, comprising by far the greater part of the planet's occupation by human beings, fertility levels are thought to have been fairly modest (four to five children to those women surviving to the end of the childbearing period, compared to five to seven in contemporary sub-Saharan Africa). The evidence is derived from anthropological studies of groups like the Kalahari Bushmen who were still dependent on hunting and gathering livelihoods in the twentieth century. In such groups, the overall fecundity (physiological ability to conceive and bear children) was significantly lower than in contemporary societies due to delayed age at menarche (first menstruation), to adolescent infertility (delay of ovulation for some years after onset of menstruation), and to the lactational amenorrhoea (suppression of menstruation and ovulation during breastfeeding) that is widespread among mammals. Thus, sixteen years was the average age at menarche; adolescent sterility delayed the birth of the first child until nineteen; and lactational amenorrhoea kept births four years apart until the relatively early arrival of menopause at about forty. Lactational amenorrhoea is thought to be of particular importance among short, thin people like the Bushmen because the severe calorie drain of prolonged breastfeeding provides insufficient body fat for ovulation to take place. The number of Venuses and other obese female figures found in prehistoric deposits suggests that hunters and gatherers were well aware of the crucial role of body fat in fertility.

There may also have been some deliberate child-spacing among such societies. Since mothers need to be mobile, not only between camps but also in daily food gathering, they are unable to carry more than a single child on hip or back. Moreover, foods soft enough to permit the early weaning of infants are frequently unavailable to hunting and gathering peoples, so infants often have to be breast fed for three to four years. The needs for appreciable birth intervals are clear, but the methods used are not. Possibilities include post-birth sexual abstinence, coitus interruptus, and induced abortion. If all else failed, there would be resort to infanticide.

With the emergence of sedentary agriculture, many of these restraints on fertility eased. There is no longer the need to "travel light" in terms of material possessions and young children; infants can be weaned much sooner by giving them grain meal and cows' milk; and the labor needs of families increase as the collectivist and cooperative social structures of hunting and gathering societies are replaced by families working their own land. Consequently there were rises in fertility and population growth during the agricultural era.

In more recent times a distinction can be made in fertility trends between developed and less developed countries.

DEVELOPED COUNTRIES

The first significant falls in fertility in the modern era occurred in northwestern Europe between the sixteenth and eighteenth centuries (four to five children per woman, compared with six to seven thought to have been common in the world's other agricultural societies at that time). This can be attributed to a pattern of late marriage and widespread celibacy which emerged in the region in the sixteenth century. Having the means to an adequate livelihood was a prerequisite to marriage, but in many European peasant societies at the time, all available agricultural land had been taken up, so that marriages had to be delayed until the incapacity or death of the father. These inhibitive marital customs were relaxed when new employment opportunities, detached from land inheritance, became available. Thus, earlier marriages and modest fertility increases were associated with the rural cottage industries of the eighteenth century and urban industrialization of the nineteenth century. Earnings, rather than property, now became the prerequisite for family formation, and children were important members of household production teams.

The major falls in fertility in Europe, North America, and Australasia were delayed until the late nineteenth century—well after appreciable urbanization and industrialization had occurred in countries like Britain. The decisive factors encouraging a demand for smaller families at that time were: first, the transition from a famil-ial mode of production to a capitalist mode, in which the new contractual relationship between worker and employer severed the functional link within the family between reproduction and production; second, the development of universal compulsory schooling withdrew children from the internal and external labor force of the family; and third, the legitimization and moral approval by Christian teaching of the traditional family structure and its internal relationships was undermined by growing secularization, social reformist movements, and embryonic socialism, so that birth control was transformed from the unthinkable to the acceptable.

Fertility levels declined continuously until the "baby boom" era of the late 1940s to the mid-1960s, when fertility was boosted throughout the developed world by full male employment, low participation of married women in the workforce, postwar optimism, and a marked trend toward younger marriage. Fertility reduction (the "baby bust") was resumed with remarkable consistency from the late 1960s, attributable largely to the changing role of married women—in particular, their greatly increased involvement in the workforce and their pursuit of fulfillment in spheres additional to motherhood and homemaking.

LESS DEVELOPED COUNTRIES

Fertility falls, comparable to those initiated in the West in the late nineteenth century, have only become apparent in Asia, Africa, and Latin America from the 1960s. The pattern has been for little, if any, fertility reduction in sub-Saharan Africa and the Middle East, modest reduction in most countries including India and the whole of Latin America, and substantial reduction, down to two to three children per woman, in several important countries in eastern Asia.

Three factors determine this pattern. First, following the Western model, the more developed countries in terms of economic diversification, education, and urbanization have seen the greatest fertility reduction (South Korea, Taiwan, Singapore, Barbados). Second, some religions consciously bolster high fertility (Islam, Roman Catholicism, traditional African belief systems), whereas Buddhism and Confucianism have more liberal attitudes to legitimizing the notion of family limitation. Third, the strength of family planning programs varies between countries; contrast, for example, the very weak programs in sub-Saharan Africa and Latin America with the very strong programs in China, Indonesia, and Thailand.

[H.R.J.]

See also **Family Planning Policies; Population: Past, Present, Future.**

FURTHER READINGS

Caldwell, J. *Theory of Fertility Decline.* London: Academic P, 1982.

Coale, A., and S. Watkins. *The Decline of Fertility in Europe.* Princeton: Princeton UP, 1986.

Coleman, D., and R. Schofield, eds. *The State of Population Theory.* Oxford: Blackwell, 1986.

HUMAN MORTALITY TRENDS

Modern evidence from relic societies like the Kalahari Bushmen suggests that life expectancy at birth among hunting and gathering societies was about thirty to thirty-five years. For agricultural societies, the first reasonably reliable records of mortality have been provided by historical demographers from ecclesiastical registers of burials and baptisms in peasant communities in northwestern Europe in the sixteenth to eighteenth centuries. Life expectancy in these communities averaged some thirty-five to thirty-eight years, but with considerable fluctuations from year to year. Such fluctuations have often been explained by the success and failure of harvests, but scholars now place more emphasis on the unpredictable waxing and waning of epidemics and wars which are unrelated to economic conditions. Bubonic plague alone dominated mortality patterns from its European debut in the 1340s until its almost complete disappearance after 1670, when smallpox epidemics may have exerted a similar influence.

The modern period of mortality decline began in northwestern Europe in the eighteenth century. Improved nutrition has been a major factor. The widespread adoption of the new wonder crop from North America, the potato; the series of agricultural advances collectively known as the agricultural revolution; and the elimination of regional famines by the growing economic integration of national territories through road, canal, and rail development all improved the standard of nutrition and decreased the rate of mortality. During the same period, however, unsanitary and congested living conditions in major cities spawned epidemics of often calamitous proportions. In the early 1840s, life expectancy at birth was a mere twenty-five years in Manchester and Liverpool, and thirty-two years in Paris,

Lyon, and Marseille, compared with forty years for both England and France as a whole. In the cities, the reduction of mortality rates had to await public health developments in the second half of the nineteenth century, particularly the provision of sewers, refuse collections, and sand-filtered water supplies.

Until the late nineteenth century, medical developments had little impact on mortality rates. Essentially, this was because before the work of Pasteur and Koch in the 1870s and 1880s there was no appreciation of the existence of germs, their manner of reproduction and transmission, and their specificity in causing disease. Similarly, it was only after Lister's work in the 1880s that a start could be made on aseptic and antiseptic surgery through the sterilization of instruments, the use of masks, and the scrubbing of operating theaters with carbolic acid (hence the well-known statement by Florence Nightingale that the first requirement of a hospital is that it should do the sick no harm). Effective medical therapy, acting directly on the infective microorganism, was delayed until the introduction of chemotherapeutic agents, particularly sulphonamides and antibiotics from the 1930s. Probably the only medical measure to contribute significantly to mortality reduction before the twentieth century was vaccination against smallpox by the cowpox vaccine developed by Jenner in 1798.

In North America, the average life expectancy of about forty-five in 1900 grew to seventy-five years by the year 1990. This improved figure reflects the virtual elimination of deaths from infectious diseases thanks to further medical advances and higher living standards. In the mid-nineteenth century, almost half of all deaths had occurred among children because of their poorly developed immunity against infections.

Mortality reduction spread from the core area in northwestern Europe and North America to countries on the economic periphery, notably southern and eastern Europe, Australasia, and Japan. But conditions of high, fluctuating mortality persisted throughout the Third World until the 1940s. Important control measures for tropical infectious diseases were stimulated by the needs of Allied troops during World War II. So successful were the subsequent programs based on vector control, vaccination, and antibiotics, that—quite contrary to earlier Western experience—levels of mortality fell spectacularly in the 1950s, despite the continuance of largely unfavorable economic, social, and environmental conditions. The most spectacular example has been the worldwide elimination of small-pox, one of the traditional scourges of human-kind, by a World Health Organization campaign. By the 1970s, however, the rapid tempo of mortality decline in many parts of the Third World had slowed considerably, implying that the medicalized, single-disease campaign approach to health can reduce mortality levels so far, but no further.

The persistence of high infant and child mortality prevents the great majority of Third World populations from approaching the survival levels of developed countries. (Life expectancy at birth in 1990 was: Africa fifty-three years, Asia sixty-four, Latin America sixty-seven, Europe and North America seventy-five.) While deaths of children under five comprise 1–2 percent of all deaths in Europe and North America, equivalent proportions from poor countries are still as high as 25–35 percent. The major health policy response in such settings has been the promotion of primary health-care systems, which attempt to provide at least a bare minimum of accessible, affordable, and socially acceptable health services to the great mass of population which is still concentrated in rural areas.

[H.R.J.]

See also **Food Supply and Population; Population: Past, Present, Future.**

FURTHER READINGS

Halstead, S., J. Walsh, and K. Warren, eds. *Good Health at Low Cost*. New York: Rockefeller Foundation, 1985.

McKeown, T. *The Modern Rise of Population*. London: Arnold, 1976.

World Health Organization. *Primary Health Care: Report of International Conference on Primary Health Care, Alma Ata 1978*. Geneva: World Health Organization, 1978.

HUME, DAVID (1711–1776)

Hume's most sustained analysis of time appears in *A Treatise of Human Nature*. His task is to give an account of time as it appears to consciousness. In Book I, he examines the meaning time has for what he calls the understanding; in Book II, he examines its meaning for the passions. Hume begins by observing that there is no particular impression of time as there are, for instance, particular impressions of sound and color. Time is the "manner" in which impressions of all sorts appear to consciousness. Hume observes that in the experience

of five notes played on a flute, time appears, not as a sixth impression, but as the manner in which the five notes are ordered. From such experiences an abstract idea of time can be formed which is the idea of objects in succession. The parts of time are indivisible and are always filled with real existents, there being no "empty" time.

In that account of time, the self is an abstraction, the mere subject of the act of understanding; and its experience of time is simply that of before and after. But in Book II, Hume examines the self as an agent passionately involved with the world. In this more concrete conception of the self, the scope of consciousness is increased, and the abstract view of time is transformed by the passions. Time now emerges, not only as before and after, but as past, present, and future. Further, Hume observes that there is an asymmetry in the way we feel about our location in time and space. Great and small distances in space affect us differently from like distances in time. And great and small distances in past time have a different meaning for us from like distances in future time. From these different sentiments arise temporal passions such as veneration for antiquity, nostalgia, expectation, and hope.

This picture of the self as the subject of temporal passions suggests that a narrative notion of time must be one of the primary ways in which the self understands its involvement with the world. This suggestion receives some confirmation in a part of Section III of *An Enquiry Concerning Human Understanding* published in the Hendel edition, 1955. Section III is devoted to Hume's famous theory of the association of ideas. This theory is fundamental, since the disposition of the imagination to order ideas is, for us, as Hume says elsewhere, "the cement of the Universe." He argues that this disposition can best be understood by examining its productions, and the products he explores are exclusively narrative structures: biography, narrative poetry, drama, and history, suggesting that the human world is and must be a world of narratives. Hume's own attempt to understand human life through narrative is to be found in his *History of England*, which was a standard for a century, passing through at least 167 posthumous editions.

[D.W.L.]

FURTHER READINGS

Livingston, Donald W. *Hume's Philosophy of Common Life*. Chicago: U of Chicago P, 1984.

HUSSERL, EDMUND (1859–1938)

German philosopher Edmund Husserl was the central figure in the phenomenological movement in philosophy. Phenomenology is a philosophical approach that attempts through a special type of reflection to describe what is happening in first-person experience. The phenomenological investigator seeks to explicate what makes up the "stream of consciousness" and how we are able to experience everything that we experience.

Husserl's investigations concerning time focus on our experience of time, rather than on the characteristics of time itself. He attempts to discover how we are able to be aware of the temporal features both of "objects of consciousness" and of our own mental life. Physical objects and processes are extended through time and pass in time. We regularly perceive (understand, remember, and so on) the temporal extension and temporal passing of everyday things. Our own mental life (our perceiving, thinking, emoting, and so on) is also spread out in time and passes in time. This raises the question of how any given moment of our mental life is able to perceive and conceive those temporal parts of enduring things that are not simultaneous with that moment. It also raises the question of how we are able to experience the temporal extension and temporal passage of our own perceiving, thinking, and emoting.

Husserl explained our unreflective awareness of both inner and outer temporality in terms of an interlocking structure of mental life. Each phase (moment) of mental life has three features: a retention of earlier phases of mental life, an awareness of what is "now," and a "protention" of later phases of mental life. The retentional feature directly contacts the just earlier phase of mental life and "looks through" the three features of this phase to their intended objects. The retentional feature is aware of the previous phase of mental life as "just past." By looking through the previous phase's retentional feature (which itself looks through its previous phase's retentional feature, and so on), retention is aware of a series of phases of mental life with their intended objects running back into the past. This is how we are unreflectively aware of the past as a series of events trailing behind and forming a context for what is currently happening. By looking through the previous phase's now-consciousness feature, retention is also aware of the object of this now-consciousness feature as "just having been now," because this object was just experienced (through the now-consciousness feature) as present. This is how we are aware of the passing of time. By looking through the previous phase's protentional feature, retention is aware of the previous anticipation of what is now happening.

Husserl applied this analysis to hearing a melody. At any given moment we are hearing one note as now, retaining a series of earlier moments of the hearing process, and protending moments of the process to come. In retaining the just previous moment of the hearing process, we experience this whole moment to be just past. This retaining looks through the previous moment's retaining to the whole process of hearing the previous parts of the melody. The previous parts of the melody are experienced as a background which becomes less clear as it gets farther from the present note. The passing of the melody in time is experienced by retaining and looking through the previous hearing of a note as now. At any given moment we experience these earlier notes as "having been now" and so as passing away from the present.

Husserl also introduced a second level of mental life to explain our unreflective awareness of our first order mental life. He considered this second level of mental life (the "absolute flux") to be nontemporal or quasi-temporal, because it contained no content that could endure or persist. This puzzling notion of a nontemporal absolute flux led Husserl toward idealism.

[P.K.M.]

See also **Phenomenology.**

Further Readings

Husserl, Edmund. *On the Phenomenology of the Consciousness of Internal Time (1883–1913).* Trans. John Brough. Leiden: Kluwer Academic, 1991.

McInerney, Peter. *Time and Experience.* Philadelphia: Temple UP, 1991.

HUXLEY, ALDOUS (1894–1963)

Aldous Leonard Huxley was educated at Eton and at Baliol College, Oxford. The wit, intelligence, brilliant cynicism, and polished style of his novels quickly established him as a leading author. His novels used literary and bohemian characters as mouthpieces for divergent ideas rather than as vehicles for complex psychological insights. Beginning with

Crome Yellow (1921) and *Antic Hay* (1923), which are in a lighter vein, there is a growing seriousness in the later works of the 1920s—*Those Barren Leaves* (1925) and *Point Counter Point* (1928). Together with *Brave New World* (1932), these early novels are those for which he will be remembered. In later years, when he turned to Hindu philosophy and mysticism, a number of works reflect that preoccupation. The interest in mysticism cannot be entirely divorced from a late work, *The Doors of Perception* (1954), concerned with the hallucinogenic drug mescaline, which, like the *soma* of *Brave New World,* was able to remove people temporarily from the tyranny of time. Indeed, some of Huxley's very last works—*Brave New World Revisited* (1959), *Island* (1962), and *Literature and Science* (1963)— suggest that the interests of *Brave New World* were with him until the end.

As early as *Crome Yellow,* his first novel, Huxley's very reasonable Mr. Scrogan personified the dangers of the extremely rational man with cold-blooded ideas about a rationalized world. Though Scrogan has diabolical antecedents which go back in the English novel at least as far as the Gradgrind of Dickens's *Hard Times* (1854), two factors would develop by the end of the 1920s which were not yet as evident at the beginning of that decade.

First, despite increasing the sufferings of workers, the industrial revolution had provided the economic underpinning for Dickens's Bounderbys and Gradgrinds, and more indirectly for Huxley himself and the characters about whom he wrote. But even such people were not immune to the crash of 1929, and remained economically vulnerable until the production boom that derived from World War II. This provided one reason for the greater bitterness of Huxley's *Brave New World* than one finds in H.G. Wells's earlier utopias and even dystopias.

Second, the 1920s also supplied Huxley with a much more vivid model for rationalization than had been available to his predecessors. While the clock had long provided a metaphor—at first positive but later pejorative—for the reasonable and rationalized man (see **Clock Metaphor**), the time and method study of Frederick Winslow Taylor would now find its greatest exponent in Henry Ford. Far more even than the factories of the industrial revolution, the ineluctable movement of Ford's assembly lines past the attendant workers provided a stark visual image of the effects of the clock in rationalizing and mechanizing

the very people whose labor they precisely controlled. Henry Ford began the production of his Model T in 1908 and by the year 1927—when he retooled completely to produce the Model A— no less than fifteen million of the first massproduced cars had rolled off the assembly line.

It was no more than a logical and reasonable step in the furthering of rationalization for Huxley to project cynically a society in which the assembly line itself would be employed to produce workers with physical and mental levels appropriate to the labor that they would be expected to provide. Better still, most of them would possess the uniformity implied by the "bokanovskified egg," which at its best could result in "ninety-six identical twins working ninety-six identical machines." Though *Brave New World* is projected to take place in A.F. 632 (After Ford) and its citizens appropriately and mechanically make the sign of the *T* to "Our Ford," the rationalized world society is centered in England and the novel opens at the assembly line of the Central London Hatchery in Bloomsbury.

In such a society there is no undue need to stress the absolute control of clock time, though this is made abundantly clear at two critical points in the novel. Early in the novel the plot is activated when we learn that Henry Foster and the Assistant Director of Predestination pointedly turn their backs on Bernard Marx, and this occurs just after we are told that "In the four thousand rooms of the Centre the four thousand electric clocks simultaneously struck four." In a comparable manner we learn that "The hands of all the four thousand electric clocks in all the Bloomsbury Centre's four thousand rooms marked twenty-seven minutes past two" just before the novel's peripeteia or plot reversal. This occurs when Bernard is just going to be exiled to an island by the Director of the Hatchery and in a dramatic reversal Bernard himself produces the director's "wife" and the son that— horror of horrors—they had engendered viviparously without benefit of hatchery.

The curiously benevolent autocrats of the Brave New World understand all too well that even well-indoctrinated human beings cannot at all times be subjected to the clock. Conditioning begins with the Pavlovian hypnopaedic procedures at the Central London Hatchery. It is regularly reinforced through communal religious singing to "Our Ford" under the auspices of Big Henry, the Singery clock which dominates the center of London. But even when things go wrong, and particularly with the lower orders, the rulers under Mustapha Mond the World Controller and the alphas—Huxley's own class—can produce such prophylactics as "Synthetic Anti-Riot Speech Number Two (Medium Strength). Straight from the depths of a non-existent heart." For primitives there are reservations and in the worst cases misfits like the alpha plus Bernard Marx (the result of an accident on the Hatchery's assembly line), can be exiled to an island where the clock's normal restraining qualities do not apply.

But there are also occasions when "normal" citizens wish to escape from time and for this the world state supplies *soma*. For example, when physically and mentally exhausted after viewing the primitives with Bernard Marx, the beautiful and pneumatic Lenina feels an urgent need to take a "*soma* holiday." In practice, she "swallowed six half gramme tablets of *soma*, lay down on her bed, and within ten minutes had embarked for lunar eternity. It would be eighteen hours at least before she was in time again." Huxley's *soma* is too much similar to the Indo-Iranian *soma* for this to be a coincidence. *Soma* is the Sanskrit for the sacred *haoma* plant, whose fermented juice imbibed at religious ceremonies produced an intoxication that was intended to give celebrants—while still remaining confined by this earth's finite time—a foretaste of the infinite time that lay ahead of them.

The inhabitants of the Brave New World were no more likely to partake of infinite time than were the former partakers of the sacred *haoma* plant. In practice, their lives were limited precisely by the temporal confines between the Central London Hatchery and the predetermined time sixty years later, when they would enter the Park Lane Hospital for the Dying. Thereafter, each citizen—including even the alphas—would contribute his or her 3^1/2 pounds to the "four hundred tons of phosphorous every year from England alone" being collected at the Slough Crematorium. Or, as Henry Foster put it approvingly to Lenina, we can be "socially useful even after we're dead. Making plants grow."

As for ourselves, we have now arrived at a point only one tenth of the years After Ford to which Huxley projected the plot of *Brave New World*. Yet in many ways—both technologically and socially—one wonders how long the novel will be able to work as a dystopia and show by a projection into the future the further dangers into which the ideas of Ford will continue to propel us. On the technological level we are already, for the most part, well beyond Huxley's projections. And on the social and economic level, a great many of the world's peoples—deny it though they may—would be more than grateful for the benevolent aristocracy and economic stability provided by the Brave New World. Huxley might well have wondered about the irony of having unintentionally created the model for a future utopia.

[S.L.M.]

See also **Clock Metaphor; Industrial Engineering After Taylor; Taylor, Frederick Winslow; Utopias and Dystopias; Wells, H.G.**

FURTHER READINGS

Macey, Samuel L. "Clocks and Time in the Dystopias: Zamyatin's *We* and Huxley's *Brave New World*." *Explorations: Essays in Comparative Literature.* Ed. Makoto Ueda. New York: UP of America, 1986. 24–43.

Sexton, James. "Brave New World and the Rationalization of Industry." *English Studies in Canada* 12 (December 1986): 429–438.

HYPNOSIS AND PSYCHOLOGICAL TIME

Using any of several related techniques may enable a sufficiently susceptible person to experience hypnosis, a range of altered states of consciousness. Hypnotic techniques may produce both characteristic changes and suggested changes in time-related behaviors and experiences. Characteristic changes occur regardless of whether the hypnotist gives a specific suggestion; suggested changes occur only if the hypnotist gives a specific suggestion.

Some early research suggested that subjects judge duration more accurately during hypnosis; however, these studies typically lacked an appropriate nonhypnotized control condition. More recent research reveals that duration-judgment accuracy does not significantly improve during hypnosis. In fact, a major characteristic change is that subjects retrospectively underestimate the duration of a hypnotic time period. Retrospective verbal estimates of a hypnotic period are up to 40 percent shorter than those of a nonhypnotic period. Because suggestions for posthypnotic amnesia do not change the degree of this temporal constriction, and because subjects do not necessarily show decreased recall of hypnotic events, we cannot attribute the temporal constriction to failure of posthypnotic recall for hypnotic events. The finding that individuals with high susceptibility to hypnosis show greater temporal constriction than do individuals with low susceptibility suggests another explanation: A high degree of absorption in a relatively unchanging experience produces few changes in cognitive context, and subjects base retrospective duration judgments on the available number of contextual changes. The additional finding that prospective judgments of a hypnotic duration are similar to those of a nonhypnotic period does not weaken this explanation; other factors, such as attention to time, influence prospective duration judgments. This explanation for duration experience in hypnosis parsimoniously proposes that subjects use similar processes to those that subjects use in nonhypnotic duration judgment.

Researchers have also explored the possibility that time-distortion suggestions given to hypnotized subjects may influence their experiences and behaviors. For example, a hypnotist may suggest that duration is lengthened or that the rate of passing of time is decreased. Subjects usually then report that they were able to complete a task in a shorter time than ordinarily possible. Research also reveals that time-distortion suggestions influence the perceived rate at which time is passing, personal tempo, and retrospective duration judgments. Although time-distortion suggestions profoundly influence a person's experiences, there is little reliable evidence that such suggestions modify performance on perceptual, learning, memory, and other tasks.

Several researchers have altered the temporal perspective of hypnotized subjects by giving them suggestions concerning the past, present, and future. For example, a hypnotist may suggest that the present is expanded, whereas the past and the future are constricted. Many hypnotized subjects then behave more spontaneously and become more involved in sensory experiences. This is one way to study the influence of temporal orientation on experience and behavior. Interesting findings come both from nonhypnotized simulators, who reveal their beliefs about effects of the experimental manipulation, and from hypnotized subjects, who directly experience effects of the experimental manipulation.

Some psychologists argue that when hypnotized subjects report changes in experiences or show changes in behaviors, the changes are attributable to the demand characteristics of the social situation labeled "hypnosis," and assert that it is not necessary to postulate a special "hypnotic state." Because well-controlled experiments continue to find differences between hypnotized and control (simulating) subjects, this kind of explanation seems strained and unconvincing.

[R.A.B.]

See also **Cognition; Memory for Time; Prospective and Retrospective Time; Psychology of Time.**

FURTHER READINGS

Block, Richard A. "Time and Consciousness." *Aspects of Consciousness: Vol. 1. Psychological Issues.* Ed. G. Underwood and R. Stevens. London: Academic P, 1979. 179–217.

St. Jean, Richard. "Hypnosis and Time Perception." *Hypnosis: The Cognitive-Behavioral Perspective.* Ed. N.P. Spanos and J.F. Chaves. Buffalo: Prometheus, 1989. 175–186.

IMMIGRATION POLICIES

The nineteenth century saw a huge growth in international migration, largely from Europe to the New World. Since the destination countries were sparsely peopled and resources were abundant, governments placed few restrictions on immigration. Toward the end of the century, however, the surge of immigration into the United States from southern and eastern Europe began to bring charges of "cheap labor" and "unfair competition," particularly since immigrants were now concentrated visibly in inner-city enclaves such as "Greektowns" and "Little Sicilies." The first exclusions were against prostitutes, convicts, the mentally ill, and persons likely to become public charges (1875 and 1882), the Chinese (1882), the Japanese (1907), and nationals of an Asiatic Barred Zone (1917). But the ultimate expression of selective immigration control was embodied in the Quota Act of 1924, which took full effect in 1929 and continued with little modification until the mid-1960s. The Quota Act limited the annual immigration from origins outside the Western Hemisphere to 154,000, with quotas distributed among countries in the same ratio as these countries contributed to the national origin (often through several generations) of the United States population in 1920. This was flagrant ethnic discrimination, since countries like Italy and Poland that possessed only short but tumultuous migration links with the United States, were granted derisory annual quotas of 6,000 compared with 66,000 for Britain and 26,000 for Germany. Similar ethnically discriminatory immigration policies were imposed elsewhere, notably the "White Australia" policy.

From the middle of the twentieth century the great demand for migration has been for access to rich Western countries by the rapidly expanding peoples of the Third World. Western countries have responded with two major types of immigration policy.

First, the major countries of traditional settlement immigration with citizenship rights have all responded positively to Third World demands for less discriminatory immigration policies, so that formal ethnic quotas and preferences were discarded in the United States in 1965, Canada in 1967, and Australia in 1973 in favor of preferences based on family reunion, refugee and other humanitarian needs, and labor market skills. Thus, in the United States, immigrants from Asia rose from 7 percent of the total legal inflow in 1965 to 46 percent in 1985,

when the Third World contribution as a whole was 84 percent and Europe's only 11 percent. By 1990, Canada and Australia were the only countries to maintain an *expansionist* immigration policy. Traditionally, their governments have been convinced that benefits of immigration outweigh costs in their huge, resource-rich countries with some of the world's lowest population densities. A larger population has been actively sought as a means of achieving economies of scale and consolidating national sovereignty. But even in Canada and Australia the immigration issue has become controversial, largely because of growing unemployment in the 1980s and unease about the whole concept of multiculturalism.

The second type of immigration policy has been embraced by countries seeking "replacement" labor for the menial jobs being spurned by the indigenous population. The preferred policy has been to recruit foreign workers on a temporary, fixed-contract basis, with the supply being turned on and off to match the cyclical pattern of labor demand. Such policies have been the basis of migrant worker movement—generally from adjacent labor-surplus countries—into northern Europe, the oil-rich Gulf states and the gold mining areas of South Africa.

The German term for migrant workers, *Gastarbeiter*, or guest worker, suggests that migrants only move to countries for a short period at the invitation of their hosts, and that they should be grateful for the privilege. But only in authoritarian South Africa has the system worked in this way. Elsewhere, many migrant workers have managed to bring in their families, perhaps returning to their homeland only for holidays and retirement. Consequently, against a background of growing unemployment and hostility toward immigrants in the 1970s and 1980s, European governments have responded with immigration policies which embrace varying mixes of recruitment restriction, repatriation incentives, and integration programs.

[H.R.J.]

See also **Emigration.**

FURTHER READINGS

Bouvier, L., and R. Gardner. "Immigration to the United States." *Population Bulletin* 41.4 (1986).

Kritz, M., C. Keely, and S. Tomasi, eds. *Global Trends in Migration: Theory and Research on International Population Movements.* New York: Center for Migration Studies, 1981.

INDIAN TRADITIONS AND TIME

The great diversity of the Indian traditions makes it advisable to split the presentation up into three major components: Hinduism, Buddhism, and Jainism. Despite the disagreement on detail of the philosophy of time, there are several notions which are common to all and which have a bearing on the concept of time.

KARMA AND REBIRTH

From the time of the Upaniṣads onward (ca. 2000 B.C.), the universal belief in the endless round of rebirth (saṃsāra) became widely accepted in India together with the notion that it was the major task of a human being to break that cycle and attain a state of transcendent freedom. While rebirth, under the inexorable law of karma, took place in time, liberation (mokṣa, nirvāṇa, kaivalya) meant reaching a timeless state. The major differences between the competing traditions arose from differences in understanding the nature of the ultimate condition and the means necessary to achieve it.

DIVISIONS OF TIME

Regardless of the philosophical differences (which ranged from accepting time as an eternal substance to denying its existence altogether), Indians throughout the ages accepted certain divisions of empirical time which were used both in daily life and in astronomical and astrological calculations. Different though such systems were—and are—these differences are not related to different ideological conceptions of time. The major divisions of time are effected by the revolutions of moon, sun, and Jupiter (Bṛhaspati). The moonmonth is divided into a

dark half (kṛṣṇapakṣa) and a bright half (śukla pakṣa); each half is divided into fifteen tithis (each with their specific names). The solar movement divides the year into six seasons (determined by entry into certain constellations) and twelve solar months. The seasons are vasanta (spring), grīṣma (hot season), varṣa (rainy season), sārād (fall), hemānta (winter), and śiśira (cool season). The months (beginning with caitra in spring) are neither identical with the months of the Western calendar nor with the lunar months. Every now and then an intercalary month is required to realign the beginning of spring with the beginning of the month caitra (or meṣa). Different schools of astronomers issue yearly calendars or almanacs (pancaṅga) which are followed by different groups of people. Major feasts are sometimes celebrated on different days (even a month apart) because of disagreements between the calendars. For astronomical and astrological calculations the nakṣatras ("houses") are important: there are twenty-eight, each measuring 13 degrees 20 minutes of the ecliptic. Each nakṣatra is subdivided into four padas of 3 degrees 20 minutes each. Over and above the lunar and solar cycles the twelve-year and sixty-year cycles of Jupiter are important.

The twenty-four-hour solar day is subdivided into thirty muhūrtas (forty-eight minutes each). A muhūrta is subdivided into two ghati (of twenty-four minutes each). Each ghati is subdivided into thirty kāla (of 48 seconds each). Each kāla is divided into two pala (of twenty-four seconds each); each pala into six prāṇa (of four seconds each); each prāṇa into ten vipala (of 0.4 seconds each); and each vipala into sixty prativipala (0.000666 seconds each). One month in human terms is considered to be one day and night of the pitṛ (deceased forefathers); one human year is equal to one day and night of the deva (gods); 1,000 years of the deva is equal to one day of Brahmā, the "Creator." History is reckoned in manvantaras, "ages of patriarchs," of which there are fourteen, each presided over by a specific manu. The largest time frames are the kalpas (eons), equal to 4,320,000 years, and subdivided into four yugas, each successively shorter and more wicked (*Kṛta Yuga, Treta Yuga, Dvāpara Yuga, Kali Yuga*). We are at present living in a *Kali Yuga* (age of strife) which will end with a *pralaya* (total dissolution of the world) before a new age arises. As regards details of these calculations there is a certain amount of discrepancy among various authors. But the notion of a devolution of history, a gradual and irreversible worsening of the world situation, is common to all as is also the idea of a cyclic destruction and creation of the universe, regardless of whether it is attributed to the action of a deity or to an impersonal process.

APOLOGETICS AND POLEMICS REGARDING VIEWS ON TIME

Not only did the various Indian traditions develop a variety of notions of time, they also entered into vigorous debates with each other; much of their philosophical literature consists of apologetics and polemics, a critical examination and demolition of other views. A long and fierce controversy concerning the nature of time was conducted between Buddhists and Hindus. Hindu critiques of Buddhist notions of time as in Kumārila Bhaṭṭa' *Ślokavārttika* (seventh century) were countered by Buddhist critiques of Hinduism, as in Śāntarākṣita's *Tattvasaṁgraha* (eighth century), which in turn was subjected to criticism by Hindus as in Citsukha's *Tattvapradīpika* (twelfth century), and so forth. Each major Indian thinker reviewed and critiqued all other opinions on the subject before stating and defending his own position. This debate, sustained for centuries, still continues and is conducted today with references to modern scientific theories.

THE TIMELESS STATE

While Hindu, Buddhist, and Jain thinkers devoted considerable ingenuity to the investigation of time, they considered the timeless state the real objective of their theoretical and practical endeavors. Transience and mutability are the counterfoil to their visions of permanence and eternity. They all view time *sub specie aeternitatis*—time is but the rippled surface of the deep and motionless ocean of being from which we arose and into which we are bound to return.

[K.K.K.]

See also **Buddhism; Hinduism; Jainism; Numbers, History of.**

FURTHER READINGS

Balslev, Anindita Niyogi. *A Study of Time in Indian Philosophy*. Wiesbaden: Harrassowitz, 1983.

Cardona, George. "A Path Still Taken: Some Early Indian Arguments Concerning Time." *Journal of the American Oriental Society* 111.3 (July-September 1991): 445–464.

Kane, P.V. "*Kāla*." *History of Dharmaśāstra*. Pune: Bhandarkar Oriental Research Institute, 1958. Volume 1.1: Section 2.

Mandal, Kumar Kishore. *A Comparative Study of the Concepts of Space and Time in Indian Thought*. Varanasi: Chowkhambha, 1968.

INDO-IRANIAN GODS OF TIME

The gods of polytheistic religions demonstrate an overt time-related ambivalence not found in the Judeo-Christian deity, whose quality of being an only god without beginning and end makes the relationship between God and finite time particularly problematic. It is often difficult to reconcile the eternal, omniscient, and omnipotent qualities of the Judeo-Christian God with his role as the Creator of a finite and imperfect world. In the early Indo-Iranian pantheons, many of the most important deities were gods of time, who exhibited a persistent dualism which obviated the need for a reconciliation of finite time and eternity within one being. Twin gods represented respectively finite time (and usually destruction and evil) and infinite time (usually associated with creation and benevolence).

Varuna, the preeminent deity of the Aryan invaders of India during the second millennium B.C., represented finite time and possessed a foreknowledge of time. Although he was a terrifying god associated with Yama, or "death," his twin, or double, was Mitra, the benevolent god of infinite time.

In Hinduism, Varuna gave way to Rudra (later Siva), a powerful god of time who embodied the dual aspects of time represented by Varuna and Mitra. He was both the creator and the destroyer of the cosmos, at once the author of time and the transcender of time. The two personifications of Rudra-Siva's ambivalence were Maha-Kala (great time), as the god of timelessness or infinite time, and Kala-Rudra (all-devouring time), as the terrifying god of finite time. The activating energy (*sakti*) of Rudra-Siva was the goddess *Kali*, whose name is the feminine form of the Sanskrit word for time (*kāla*). Kali herself was paradoxical: she was represented both as a destroyer of life with fangs and tongue ready to consume the earth, and as a nurturer with milk-heavy breasts. She is still the most important Indian cult figure. Rudra-Sivu shared the leadership of the gods with Vishnu, a god who is comparably ambivalent as a deification of time. In his benign aspect, he was both the creator and sustainer of the universe; in his terrifying aspect, he was the destroyer, and is often depicted swallowing every form of life. The preeminence of gods of time in the Hindu pantheon reflects Hindu eschatology: time is a cyclical process in which one carries the responsibility for past actions even through repeated incarnations. In answer to a yearning to escape from this servitude to time, Buddhism promises an atemporal state, or nirvana.

Time was also a basic concept in Iranian or Persian cosmology. Zurvan, whose name means "time," was the ultimate source of good and evil. Like those of Rudra-Siva and Vishnu, Zurvan's qualities encompassed dual aspects: as Zurvan akarana, he represented infinite time, while as Zurvan dareghochvadhata, he represented finite time or "time of the long dominion," which was in later speculation set at 12,000 years. This time god was the father of the twins Ohrmazd (or Oromasdes), the bright, benevolent god of infinite time, and Ahriman (or Aremanios), the swarthy, malevolent god of finite time, who embodied Zurvan's opposing qualities of creation and destruction.

The monotheistic reforms of Zoroaster or Zarathustra (late seventh to early sixth century B.C.) attempted to eliminate all the gods of the Iranian pantheon but one. Ohrmazd became Ahura Mazda and was celebrated as the "wise lord," representing only the creative and infinite aspects of the duality of Zurvan. Ahura Mazda, like Zurvan, had twin sons: Spenta Mainyu (later called Ohrmazd as a result of the prevailing influence of Zurvanite doctrine), who aligned himself with truth and life, and Angra Mainyu (Ahriman), who aligned himself with evil and death. Early Zoroastrianism was intentionally nondualistic, but neither Zurvan-Ahriman (the devil) nor the dualism of the pre-Zoroastrian pantheon were easily forgotten. Later Zoroastrianism incorporated the dualism of finite and infinite time as a result of the merging of the identity of Ahura Mazda with that of Angra Mainyu, their coevality making Ahura Mazda necessarily finite. Although the beginnings of the two antithetical gods of infinite and finite time are left unexplained, this dualistic form of Zoroastrianism was accepted as orthodox when it became the official religion during the Sasanian period (from A.D. 224).

In Zoroastrian cosmology, Ohrmazd and Ahriman were both said to exist in infinite time but separated by a void, the one dwelling in the light, and the other in the darkness below. Ahriman made an unsuccessful attack on Ohrmazd, who realized that unless it could be settled in finite terms, their struggle would continue eternally. They made a pact limiting the time of their struggle to four successive periods of 3,000 years each. Thus finite time was born from infinite time. During the 12,000 years, the material world was created, over which Ahriman ruled, but from which he could not escape. At the end of what the Zurvanites would have called the "time of the long dominion," a final judgment would take place and finite and infinite time would merge again. In recent times, the inheritors of the Zoroastrians have modified the coeternal aspects of Ohrmazd and Ahriman. The Parsees—a group which left Iran because of persecution in the eighth to tenth centuries A.D. and settled in India—have explained Ahriman as merely an allegory of man's evil tendencies, thereby making Ohrmazd the sole omnipotent deity.

Zoroastrian dualism greatly influenced the Judeo-Christian perception of the relationship between God and Satan. The Judaic God was eternal and almighty, and therefore did not share his throne with a twin god of finite time. Before the Babylonian exile (586 B.C.), Satan was perceived as the servant of God (see, for example, Job 1:6–12 and Zachariah 3:1–2). Since the Babylonian exile, Satan acquired some of the qualities of the Iranian god of finite time, the swarthy Ahriman. For example, Satan's status becomes more nearly equal to that of God. Two versions of the same story demonstrate this change. In Samuel 24:1, written before the exile, God incites David to do evil, while in I Chronicles 21:1, written after the exile, it is Satan, in his new role as the antagonist, who provokes David. In Revelation, there is a clear dualism between the power of God and the power of Satan about who rules in this world. The cosmology expressed in Revelation is very similar to that of Zoroastrianism and in fact owes much of its imagery to the influence of Babylon.

Another development related to the rise of an independent and strong Satan was a new belief in resurrection and life after death which was encouraged by the influence of Zoroastrian eschatology. Only two passages in the Old Testament unambiguously suggest the resurrection of an individual, and both were written after the Babylonian exile (Isaiah 26:10–14 and Daniel 12:2–3). Even today the doctrine of resurrection is not a central tenet of Jewish thought. The Christians, however, quickly adopted this aspect of Zoroastrian cosmology brought to them via Mithraism, an Indo-Iranian cult whose dissemination throughout Roman Europe was almost parallel to that of Christianity. Resurrection of the dead is a prerequisite of either everlasting life or eternal damnation. Early Christian missionaries learned that offering the possibility of a future in heaven (as opposed to eternal damnation) provided an attractive reward for those who were suffering on earth. In addition, the absolute dualism between everlasting life or eternal punishment in the domains of the atemporal beings was also a powerful incentive to convert to Christianity during one's finite time on earth.

Mithraism, which at one time provided very strong competition for Christianity, spread from Persia through Asia Minor to Rome and its empire. Although Mitra, known as Mithra in Iran, gave his name to the mystery cult, he was not its main deity, despite his identification as the creator of man. To protect his creation from evil, he acted as a mediator between Zurvan Akarana or Ohrmazd (infinite time) and Ahriman (finite time). A more important Mithraic god was the lion-headed anthropomorphic god, whose iconography is very much concerned with time. It has been argued that this monstrous deity represents Mithraic Kronos or "boundless time" but it is more plausible that he represents "time that devours all" or "time of the long dominion."

Mithraism and Christianity were similar in that each worshiped a god who had assured man of eternal salvation through a single act. Both religions shared a relatively rigid moral code, both believed in the power of baptism and the sacramental meal, and both theologies stressed the importance of service under a divine commander. Also, they were missionary religions which for the most part drew their converts from those with modest means, and both religions shared comparable ideas of heaven and hell culminating in a Last Judgment. However, Christianity outlived Mithraism and flourished for a number of reasons: intellectual and popular thinkers were ready for monotheism, something which polytheistic Mithraism could not offer; "Jesus Christ was a historical rather than a mythical figure; and Christianity, unlike Mithraism, included women, thereby ensuring that religious rituals would be integrated into family life. Nevertheless, Mithraism left the Western world with a legacy from the Indo-Iranian gods of time, in the more powerful figure of Satan, and in the concepts of resurrection and of a life beyond that on this earth.

[S.L.M.]

See also **Father Time; Saturn-Cronus.**

FURTHER REFERENCES

Brandon, S.G.F. *History, Time and Deity: A Historical and Comparative Study of the Conception of Time in Religious Thought and Practice.* Manchester: Manchester UP, 1965.

Macey, Samuel L. *Patriarchs of Time: Dualism in Saturn-Cronus, Father Time, the Watchmaker God, and Father Christmas.* Athens: U of Georgia P, 1986.

Zaehner, R.C. *Zurvan: A Zoroastrian Dilemma.* Oxford: Oxford UP, 1955.

———. *The Dawn and Twilight of Zoroastrianism.* New York: Putnam's, 1961.

Zimmer, Heinrich. *Myths and Symbols in Indian Art and Civilization.* Ed. Joseph Campbell. New York: Pantheon, 1946.

INDUSTRIAL ENGINEERING [BEFORE TAYLOR]

Industrial engineering, or work study (which has gone by far too many names, and sometimes none at all) comprises two main subdivisions of time measurement and method study. Time or work measurement quantifies the period that it should take to complete a particular element of work, and the closely related practice of method study ascertains when, where, and by which person or machine such elements of work can be undertaken most advantageously. Time and method study—which has been at the forefront of the Western rationalization of manufacture—is substantially concerned with the measurement of time.

A number of factors contributing to industrialization in the second half of the seventeenth century made England an especially suitable setting for time and method study's early development. Among these factors were the benefits to British shipping of the Navigation Act of 1651; the birth of modern science, epitomized by the founding of the Royal Society in 1662; the commencement of modern mechanical technology, epitomized by the production of pendulum clocks from 1657; the introduction of British financial institutions, epitomized by the founding of the Bank of England in 1694; the trebling of London's population during the century; the rise of the "Puritan" ethic; the use of the division of labor; and the rebuilding of London after the great plague of 1665 and the great fire of 1666. Daniel Defoe says "that there never was known such a trade all over England as was in the first seven years after the plague and after the fire of London." As calamity in West Germany and Japan after World War II provided a great impetus for production, so did the plague and fire in Restoration London stimulate productivity.

Though standards of measurement were by no means entirely rationalized by this period, they were beginning to compare favorably with what had existed before. When Walter de Henley (ca. 1240) wrote a book on husbandry, he knew that, according to the nature of the land, a ploughman should be able to work a given number of acres per day with horses or oxen. But his study is clearly limited by the fact that in his time both the length of an hour and even the size of an acre could each vary by a factor of at least two according to time and place. Even when Leonardo da Vinci (1452–1519) carried out a much more detailed time study on the shoveling of earth, the "equal" hour was not universally accepted, and "the 'foot,' the piede, had a value of 17.134 inches in Milan, 14.07 inches in Padua, but 11.73 inches in Rome."

Among earlier and relatively simple activities controlled by time measurement, we know from Lucian's *Fisherman* that, under Roman rule, the length of time for which a lawyer might plead a case was customarily controlled by clepsydrae, or water clocks. In a comparable manner, simple water clocks were used in North Africa to denote the period of time during which landowners were entitled to extract water for irrigation. Also, an elementary production operation could be timed by a sandglass. This can, for example, be seen in the illustration of a medieval stamping mill from *Das Feuerwerkpuch*, a treatise on the manufacture of fireworks written in Germany about 1450.

THE DIVISION OF LABOR

The division of labor, which is related to both time and method (or motion) study, is a precondition for productivity science. In his *Republic*, much of Plato's argument for introducing specialization into the occupations and administration of men in society is based on a comparison with the trades: "More things of each kind are produced, and better and easier, when one man works at one thing." Though the division of human labor into trades was an early concomitant of urbanization, subdividing the trades themselves by using the process known as "division of labor" did not become the normal practice until at least the eighteenth century. This further rationalization followed the weakening of the guilds and their associated master craftsmen, who were responsible for making a total product.

By the middle of the eighteenth century, the division of labor is graphically illustrated and described in detail in Diderot's *Encyclopédie* that divides clockmaking into sixteen and watchmaking into twenty-one processes. The *Encyclopédie* then argues that each part of a watch or clock must therefore be perfect because it is manufactured by someone who is a specialist in producing a single element of the product.

Horology—as it did for so many of the elements that set the conditions for time and motion study—also played its part in introducing the division of labor. By the time of his death in 1713, Thomas Tompion, the father of English clockmaking, had manufactured 500 clocks and 6,000 watches. The unprecedented demand for his products seems to have led him to introduce a form of batch production. In this first step toward the division of labor, one person at one time made relatively identical individual parts. When Sir William Petty, the economist, promotes the application of the division of labor, he is almost certainly referring to the innovative procedures in Tompion's workshop: "As for Example, in the making of a *Watch*, if one man should make the *Wheels*, another the *Spring*, another shall Engrave the *Dial-Plate* and another shall make the *Cases*, then the *Watch* will be better and cheaper, than if the whole work be put upon any one Man." In *Peri Bathous* (1728), even Alexander Pope takes it as self-evident that "The vast improvement of modern manufactures ariseth from their being divided into several branches."

Half a century later, Adam Smith, in his *Wealth of Nations*, identifies watch movements as those articles whose price had been most reduced (from twenty pounds to twenty shillings), despite the inflation of the previous 100 years. By 1832, when Charles Babbage wrote his *Economy of Machinery and Manufactures*, watchmaking was divided into no less than 102 different trades. As modern work study engineers would therefore anticipate, the first detailed study of a manufacturing process dealt with pins rather than with the more complicated processes of horology.

M. Perronet's *Art de l'Epingler* (1762), offers not only a glossary of terms for pinmaking, but also describes in detail the 130 drawings on seven folio sheets through which he illustrates the trade. The study includes such detailed statistics for both the timing and cost of each operation that some seventy years later Babbage was able to compare Perronet's figures for pinmaking with his own. Perronet's work reflects the increasing interest in the division of labor during the eighteenth century. For example, comparable reports on pinmaking can be found in Ephraim Chambers's *Cyclopaedia; or an Universal Dictionary of Arts and Sciences* (1728), the *Encyclopédie*, and Adam Smith's *Wealth of Nations* (1776), which actually begins by stressing the importance of the division of labor.

Although the division of labor began to enter the industrial "climate of opinion" from the late seventeenth century, the developments discussed thus far were part of an ongoing process. Henry Hamilton notes, in *The English Brass and Copper Industries to 1800*, that pinmaking in England was a form of manufacture "probably of little importance before the middle of the sixteenth century." However, in a petition to James I barely half a century later, the pinmakers claimed that "there were no less than 20,000 people . . . employed in making pins in England." As Hamilton further points out, by 1697, the consumer demand that such a development implies had produced what he calls "a classic illustration" of the division of labor. At Dockwra's Copper Company, which specialized in the production of pins, it was claimed that "some 'top workmen' could deal with 24,000 a day."

Battery and wire drawing, which were employed in pinmaking, were the two main processes in the brass and copper industry until about 1700, but during the latter part of the period there were some new developments in metalworking. Although casting had previously been employed for bells and cannons, it was now adapted for producing small household articles, and this of itself involved a form of standardization. During the last decade of the seventeenth century, an early account describes thimbles being cast about six gross at a time in Highgate. The manufacture of a very wide range of standardized household articles was further revolutionized from about 1700, when the old process of battery was replaced by rolling mills. This was the development that heralded the introduction of Birmingham's stamped brass foundry trade.

There is a report that as early as 1686, nine frying pan plates were being battered at the same time "like a nest of Crucibles or Boxes." In a similar vein, a letter of 1705 from a grinder of convex glasses for telescopes complains about a special order because the customer is not yet aware that "the new way of making them is by working four, six, or eight together." Demand for coinage, which had been produced by battery until 1662, outstripped supply to such an extent that, despite the use of the fly press, by 1753, half the copper coinage in England was

estimated to be counterfeit. This type of demand hastened the introduction of machinery and reduced the dependence on labor. Matthew Boulton knew by 1788 that he had to set up new presses which would minimize the expense and potential errors that resulted from human handling. By 1790 he had patented a new coining press. It was to be driven by steam "in place of men's labour, as has hitherto been practised."

THE EARLY USE OF TIME STUDY

Though it would ultimately lead through mechanization into mass production, the more immediate corollary to the division of labor was time study and piecework. Conveniently for time study, the first stopwatch was Samuel Watson's "pulse watch," invented for use by physicians about 1690. Laurence Sterne's *Tristram Shandy* has some extended references to the use of stopwatches by 1761, and even by then does so in a derogatory fashion. In the same period, one of the first time recorders was installed by the time-conscious Josiah Wedgwood in his Etruria factory for clocking in workmen. And stopwatches were already clearly being employed in factories during the latter part of the eighteenth century for the purposes to which working men and women would later very much object. In a document of 1792 quoted by R.M. Currie, a man by the name of Thomas Mason promises to use his "utmost caution at all times" to ensure that no one will discover that at the Old Derby China Factory he is being "employed to use a stop watch to make observations of work done."

The achievement of Boulton and Watt in manufacturing steam engines is appropriately recognized, but far too little attention has been paid to the achievement of their respective sons. It is clear from the balance sheets that after the lapse of the patent on the steam engine in 1800, their time and work flow studies at the Soho factory both improved productivity and repaid them handsomely. When James Watt Jr. died in 1848, the man who has been referred to as "the pioneer of time and motion study and engineering costing" left a fortune of 160,000 pounds. Although Watt may have been the pioneer, there were certainly others. Sir William Fairbairn's Manchester works for steam and locomotive engines and James Nasmyth's pioneering work in the assembly-line production of machine tools at his Bridgewater Foundry offer similarly impressive examples.

Indeed, the organization of factories is far from being an attribute exclusive to the twentieth century. Ambrose Crowley III brought hand, rather than machine, workers together in an early form of factory organization at the very beginning of the period that concerns us here. From at least 1685 into the nineteenth century, his firm would employ as many as 1,000 men and make a wide range of metal products—for the most part by piecework—ranging from anchors to nails. Although Robert Owen is generally credited with being the first factory owner to have a modern social conscience, Crowley III provided a wide range of social services more than a century before Owen was involved with the Lanark mills.

THE EFFECTS ON PRICES AND LABOR

The British industrial revolution resulted in a "deflation" of the price of many products and raw materials, but it also produced a painful reduction in the living and working standards of factory hands, and especially of women and children. M.W. Flinn has noted that cotton yarn fell from 38 shillings per pound in 1786 to 2 shillings 11 pence in 1832; bar iron from about 18 pounds per ton in the middle of the century to about 8 pounds in the early 1820s; and the delivered price of coal in Manchester from 8 pence a hundredweight to 4 pence. Among Charles Babbage's many examples for manufactured goods, a better brass knob was now being turned out in Birmingham by steam engine at 1 shilling 9$\frac{1}{4}$ pence per dozen than had been previously produced by hand at 13 shilling 4 pence per dozen. The competition between factories using power machinery and those using factory hands was so unrelenting that employers could frequently no longer compete merely by increasing working hours and reducing piecework rates. This, too, meant that time and method study would be initiated by those employers who were beginning to understand it.

The early effects of the pressure on the weakest elements among the labor force are vividly portrayed, in literature, by Goldsmith's *Deserted Village* (1770), and Blake's *Songs of Experience* (1794). Robert Owen's *Observations on the Effect of the Manufacturing System* (1815) provides a later and a prosaic, but perhaps an even more telling account of what had been taking place. As Owen puts it, "Not more than thirty years since, the poorest parents thought the age of fourteen sufficiently early for their children to commence regular labour." But he notes that now, "In the manufacturing districts it is common for parents to send their children of both sexes at seven or eight years of age, in winter as well as summer, at six o'clock in the morning."

In those highly unsuitable working conditions, and with understandably reduced productivity, they remained in the factories, usually "till eight o'clock at night."

Charles Babbage—like Newton before him the Lucasian professor of mathematics at Cambridge—deals with the conflicting interests of handworker and power machine in his *Economy of Machinery and Manufactures* (1832), and he is equally aware of the paradox that at least for a time, increased production would almost inevitably entail increased suffering. As he puts the case, in what remains a fascinating book for those interested in productivity, although there had been 240,000 hand looms in England and Wales in both 1820 and 1830, the number of power looms, each doing three times as much work, had increased during that time from 14,000 to 55,000. One can well understand that such developments were resulting in "considerable suffering amongst the working classes."

CHARLES BABBAGE ON PRODUCTION METHODS

When dealing with time studies, Babbage notes that if the observer stands, watch in hand, before a person heading a pin, the workman will almost certainly increase his speed, and the estimate will be too large. A much better average will result from enquiring what quantity is considered a fair day's work. When this cannot be ascertained, the number of operations performed in a given time may often be counted while the workman is quite unaware that he is being observed. For example, the sound from a loom may enable the observer to count the number of strokes per minute, even when he is outside the building.

Babbage is concerned with the concept of "a fair day's work" long before the widespread use of the term was brought in by Frederick Winslow Taylor. For his own part, Babbage is well aware that he is himself discussing time study procedures that are already well established. He quotes from the published advice of M. Coulomb, a man with "great experience in making such observations" to suggest that work needed to be timed at various periods of the day, and that care should be taken to try and avoid workers becoming aware that their activities are under observation. This suggests that Currie's observation regarding Thomas Mason, at the Old Derby China Factory in 1792, having to give his solemn word to "prevent the knowledge transpiring" that he was "employed to use a stopwatch to make observation of work done" was by no means a unique occurrence. Although the proprietor may well have wished to avoid a change in the speed at which the worker was operating, he would also want to avoid his competitors becoming aware of such activities. Quite possibly the least of his concerns would have regard to the rights and feelings of the worker.

The chapter in Babbage's *On the Economy of Machinery and Manufactures* entitled "On the Division of Labour" deals first with the advantages of that procedure as set out by other writers. He adds perceptively that the division of labor furnishes the "first steps towards a machine." Babbage argues for the importance of the recent improvements in documenting industrial procedures. In his view, the former absence of "an extensive knowledge of machinery, and the power of making mechanical drawings" had been one of the reasons for so many failures in the early development of manufacturing. When he quotes from Perronet's studies of pinmaking, Babbage adds what he feels to be his own important addition to the value of time study, namely that it permits the manufacturer to forecast exactly the right mix of labor required for the most cost effective execution of a job. Babbage stresses that in his contribution to what we would now call method study, the savings would have been even greater had he chosen needle-making as his example. In that trade, the difference between the greatest and the least earnings were forty-fold, rather than just over four-fold as in pinmaking. As a result, the profit from choosing the right mix of labor would have been commensurately greater. But, as a true exponent of work study, Babbage has no illusions that a machine is in all situations more effective than a worker.

Babbage's next chapter is "On the Division of Mental Labour." He suffers from none of the illusions which until very recent years held back the transfer of work study methods from the factory to the office. In fact, he is convinced that procedures for mental activities, just like those for labor, should follow the practice of only employing operators who are specifically trained for the services that they provide. In the central example that he uses he describes a project in which extensive mathematical tables were created by employing three groups of people with quite different levels of training. First, a small committee of leading mathematicians produced the relevant formulae; then a section of seven or eight lesser mathematicians were employed to "convert into numbers the formulae"; and finally, a much larger group of some sixty to eighty people were engaged to carry out the "mechanical" calculations. In the subsequent editions of *Economy of Machinery and Manufactures*, Babbage—whose analytical engine was a precursor of the computer—also added to this chapter a paragraph listing ten separate managerial categories recently initiated in mining and pointed to the great improvements that had resulted from the "judicious distribution" of managerial duties "which have gradually been introduced."

THE EMERGENCE OF PROFESSIONAL MANAGEMENT

What records we do have of the organization and methods that earlier manufacturers like Crowley, Arkwright, or Wedgwood undertook are frequently with us through chance rather than through a conscious need to provide a record for scholars or historians. As working proprietors, the early manufacturers hardly felt the need to publish so that their competitors might enjoy the benefit. Although work study principles were being initiated in manufacturing by the end of the seventeenth century, and Babbage certainly had an understanding of many of its modern functions, the reticence of proprietors to publish their practices may help to explain why the early history of work study is so sparsely recorded.

It is probably not a coincidence that James Watt, Jr., the pioneer of time and motion study, also represents a transitional figure in an important and related change in the effective control of industry that would take place between his own time and the middle of our century. When the "monopoly" on steam engines came to a close in 1800 at the end of the patent, he was brought into the Soho Works in what amounted to a managerial capacity on behalf of his father and his father's partner. He reacted to what might well have proved to be disastrous competition by employing time and method study so extensively that the works did far better under his guidance than they had done under his father with the benefit of the patent. Nevertheless, he still thought of himself as an entrepreneur rather than as a professional manager or an academic. As a result he felt no need to publish his procedures.

Some of the later consultants like Charles Eugene Bedaux (1887–1944) were similarly secretive, but by the time of Bedaux, the sources and channels for the provision of venture capital had changed and management was becoming more and more divorced from the ownership of business. After 1926, Bedaux found himself employed by large corporations in the United States. He was obliged to train time and motion study engineers for them and this provided a setting in which his ideas could not continue to be kept secret.

Today's professionalism in management and the increasingly standardized methods by which managers are trained derives at least in part from the fact that managers are now employees rather than entrepreneurs. Management itself has been evolving along lines comparable to the increasing specialization associated with the division of labor. Babbage's innovative model of ten managerial functions for mining had foreshadowed this development. Frederick Winslow Taylor (1856–1915) would similarly recognize the need for specialization in management by the end of the nineteenth century. His concept of the "functional or divided foremanship" consisted of "so dividing the work of management that each man from the assistant superintendent down shall have as few functions as possible to perform." At the close of the twentieth century, Taylor's formula for the division of managerial labor has left very few of us untouched by its ever-broadening implications.

[S.L.M.]

See also **Industrial Engineering After Taylor; Taylor, Frederick Winslow.**

Further Readings

Babbage, Charles. *On the Economy of Machinery and Manufactures.* 4th ed., enlarged. 1835; reprint, New York: Augustus M. Kelley, 1963.

Currie, R.M. *Work Study.* 2nd ed. London: Pitman, 1963.

Flinn, M.W. *Men of Iron.* Edinburgh: Edinburgh UP, n.d.

———. *Origins of the Industrial Revolution.* [London]: Longmans, 1966.

Hamilton, Henry. *The English Brass and Copper Industries to 1800.* 2nd ed. London: Frank Cass, 1967.

Macey, Samuel L. "Work Study Before Taylor." *Work Study and Management Services* 18 (October 1974): 530–36.

———. *The Dynamics of Progress: Time, Method, and Measure.* Athens: U of Georgia P, 1989.

Musson, A.E., and Eric Robinson. *Science and Technology in the Industrial Revolution.* Manchester: Manchester UP, 1969.

Owen, Robert. *Observations on the Effect of the Manufacturing System.* London: Richard and Arthur Taylor, 1815.

Roll, Sir Eric. *An Early Experiment in Industrial Organization.* London: Frank Cass, 1968.

INDUSTRIAL ENGINEERING [AFTER TAYLOR]

Though some application of time measurement and organization is generally involved in industrial engineering, the problem of finding a single name for its many and changing techniques has plagued this discipline from the beginning. Elements of time measurement and organization have also been known by such names as time and method study, time and motion study, scientific management, work study, organization and methods, management services, operations management, and management consulting. In the very early days—when factory owners had no desire to advertise their techniques—the discipline generally had no name at all.

CHARLES EUGENE BEDAUX

Frederick Winslow Taylor (1856–1915)—considered the first modern practitioner of industrial engineering—was concerned mainly with time studies in industry. His work was supplemented by a number of early refinements, particularly those of Bedaux and the Gilbreths. Charles Eugene Bedaux (1887–1944), who emigrated to the United States from France when he was about twenty, made two important improvements on Taylor's work in respect of time measurement: (1) he evaluated the performance of workers by a process called "rating," and (2) he developed a method for incorporating a relaxation allowance into time study.

Unlike the procedure adopted by Taylor, time study engineers trained by Bedaux no longer needed to begin by selecting the type of person most suited for a particular job. Since they were trained by Bedaux to rate the speed at which any employee was working, such time study practitioners did not have to base their figures on the work of a previously selected ideal operative. They took into account the "soldiering" or malingering of workers by which Taylor felt himself to have been plagued. But they were also able to make allowance for the inherent differences between workers and the changing level of effort that individual workers made at different times of the working day. Bedaux used his own name as the basis of the Bedaux 60/80 rating system. In this, the normal working rate is taken to be 60 Bs per hour, or an effort comparable to walking on level ground at three miles per hour. The incentive payments were, however, based on the anticipation that a worker of average experience and skill would work at the rate of 80 Bs per hour.

Bedaux's second great innovation involved the application of relaxation allowances, and came into play at the point when incentive payments were being set up. Taylor's innovation had been to allow young women inspecting bicycle balls two ten-minute rest periods in each session, but Bedaux's relaxation allowances were based on a much more careful evaluation of working conditions. A short paper on "The Bedaux Work Unit Method," first published by H.E. Kearsey in 1934, discloses that "This relaxation allowance is not a standard allowance, but varies with conditions of work, such as atmospheric temperature, working position, periodicity of cycle, and so forth."

In 1926, Bedaux established a British company in order to train time and motion study engineers for his clients. One of his clients was Huntley and Palmers, the first company to adopt the term "work study." They did so in 1943 at the suggestion of Kearsey, who had introduced them to industrial engineering. Other clients of Bedaux included Imperial Chemical Industries and J. Lyons. Imperial Chemicals later developed one of the largest work study units in England. The professional organization that would be called the Institute of Practitioners in Work Study, Organization and Methods—now the Institute of Management Services—to which the Duke of Edinburgh devoted a five-year term as president was the brainchild of some of the work study engineers at Imperial Chemicals. The American Institute of Industrial Engineers is the American parallel to this organization.

L.H.C. Tippett introduced a new sampling technique which, after Bedaux's innovations, was perhaps the next most important development in time study between the wars, and the work of both men still influences manufacturing methods. Tippett, who worked in the English cotton mills, employed a statistical procedure then known as "snap reading method," but now called "activity sampling." This method, which is rather like that presently employed in Gallup polls, is particularly useful when a time study engineer follows in predetermined order a selected cycle of observations. The goal is to discover during what percentage of time the preselected operations are, or are not, being worked on by men or machines. By obtaining enough observations, the time study engineer can calculate the "downtime" with remarkable accuracy.

THE GILBRETHS

The Gilbreths' motion and method studies, which sought to discover "the best way" a task could be carried out, were undertaken concurrently with Taylor's time studies, which sought to measure a "fair day's work." Motion study is a component of method study and the Gilbreths were the great pioneers in both areas. Frank Bunker Gilbreth (1868–1924) had been trained as a bricklayer, and his wife, Lillian M. Gilbreth, had trained as a psychologist. They brought a remarkable combination of skills and ideas to the processes of work study, and Lillian Gilbreth continued to apply and advance their work long after her husband's death.

Frank Gilbreth had applied his ideas regarding motion economy to bricklaying while still a very young man. He later published these under the title *Bricklaying System* (1909). In the section on "Motion Study," he claims to have revolutionized a trade in which the methods had evolved over several thousand years. He is certainly entitled to his claim that "The motion study in this book is but the beginning of an era ... that will eventually affect all of our methods of teaching trades. It will cut down production costs and increase the efficiency and wages of the workman. ... To be preeminently successful. ... A mechanic ... must use the fewest possible motions to accomplish the desired result."

Essentially, there have been three major developments which have contributed to the rationalization of labor and technology through a series of increasingly subdivided divisions of labor. The first of these divisions of labor, which appears as early as Book 10 of Plato's *Republic*, was the division of labor into trades; the second was the subdivision of particular trades as occurred in clockmaking and pinmaking and was documented in the *Encyclopédie* and the work of Perronet during the eighteenth century; and the third is Gilbreth's analytical documentation of a bricklayer's motions while performing one clearly defined element in his specialized subdivision of a particular trade.

Gilbreth numbers and describes the individual motions that by long tradition had been involved in the single job of laying a brick. The four key charts that he provides are each concerned with one of the four methods of bricklaying. Each of these methods had traditionally employed eighteen motions for laying a single brick. These are listed under the heading "The Wrong Way," while Gilbreth lists his new methods under the heading "The Right Way." The new methods reduce the number of motions respectively from eighteen to $4^1/_2$, 2, $4^1/_2$ and $1^3/_4$ motions for laying a brick by each of the four methods. In *Fatigue Study* (1916), Gilbreth pointed out the important implications for time study, and notes that the elimination of unnecessary motions in bricklaying had "enabled this same bricklayer to lay three hundred and fifty bricks per hour, where he had laid one hundred and twenty bricks per hour before."

Taylor often praises Gilbreth's work in his writings. In his view, Gilbreth's achievements derived from eliminating "certain movements which bricklayers in the past believed were necessary"; teaching "his bricklayers to make simple motions with both hands at the same time"; and introducing "simple apparatus, such as his adjustable scaffold and his packets for holding bricks, by means of which, with a very small amount of cooperation from a cheap laborer, he entirely eliminates a lot of . . . time-consuming motions." The Gilbreths' studies in motion economy were very much helped by their adaptability in the application of interdisciplinary methods. For example, Gilbreth used motion picture photography, then in its infancy, for analyzing and documenting motions, and employed cyclegraphs and chronocyclegraphs to measure activity. These proved particularly useful when he analyzed all jobs into seventeen basic motions. He called them Therbligs, derived from an anagram of his name. In a comparable adaptation, the Gilbreths employed Lillian's special training. The use of both physiology and psychology in studies that adapted the design of the work setting to improve the effectiveness of workers made them among the earliest exponents of ergonomics.

HENRY FORD

Henry Ford (1863–1947) is probably the manufacturer who best illustrates the use of Taylor's scientific management. David Halberstam states the relationship clearly: "Ford, fascinated by efficiency of production, absorbed Taylor's principles and began to use them in his plant, eventually developing and applying them to an almost mythic degree." Though Ford is most celebrated for manufacturing automobiles through his introduction of the assembly line in 1913, he was also responsible for other related and innovative procedures. He standardized products, dispersed assembly plants, integrated supply industries, and organized his manufacturing by synchronizing the flow of product

components between the continuous line-to-line flow from sub-manufacturers to the central assembly line.

Ford, who had virtually no capital when he began in 1903, eventually bought out the other stockholders in his company. During the period between 1908 and 1927, the Ford Motor Company built up a surplus of nearly 700 million dollars, and produced more than 15 million Model Ts. But Ford's industrial philosophy went one step beyond the normal pace of using Western technology. Rather than wait while his rationalized production methods had time to increase the demand and subsequently reduce the price, he took what we might now call the "proactive" step of simply reducing the price unilaterally. As a result, the volume of sales was raised, thereby permitting him to improve the efficiency of production further, increase the volume further, and reduce the price further. Seemingly, this was a cycle that might continue almost indefinitely.

Ford exhibited many of the traits that myth has endowed on a number of the industrial proprietors of the eighteenth and nineteenth centuries. He was a man who could build a car with his own hands, and, though a paternalist, was genuinely interested in the well-being of his employees. But Ford also saw his workers as potential customers and when the average manufacturing wage in the United States was eleven dollars a week, he paid five dollars a day, though he certainly expected value for money. Ford, however, also had to face problems related to finance and labor that were making it increasingly difficult to continue in the old traditions of the nineteenth-century proprietor. He financed his company as far as possible out of profits, because he hated banks and Wall Street. And he actively disliked trade unions, and hoped that unionism would fade away. Yet the United Auto Workers gained from him the first union dues checkoff and union shop contract in the industry when a recognition election by the union succeeded in 1941.

The rigidity of Ford's views, which had been an important component in his success during the early days, would later cost him a great deal. His insistence that the Model T could be purchased in any color as long as it was black has become part of manufacturing mythology. But there were other examples of a continuing resistance to change. At the time when the conventional gearshift, the hydraulic brake, and the six- or eight-cylinder engine were being offered by his competitors, Ford still tried to retain the planetary transmission, the mechanical brake, and the four-cylinder engine. As a result, by the time that he retooled completely for the Model A by 1928, and produced a V-8 by 1932, it was too late to regain his dominating lead. He had manufactured half of the world's production of motor vehicles in 1920, but Ford had fallen behind General Motors by 1928, though he still remained a strong competitor.

The contrast between the methods by which General Motors and Ford were managed epitomized the difference between today's large public company with one eye on the bottom line and on Wall Street, and the old-fashioned business proprietor of the eighteenth and nineteenth centuries. The contrast was between their managements rather than their chronologies. In fact, General Motors, just like Ford's first Model T, both date back to 1908. In that year, William Crapo Durant had used profits from a successful carriage-making business to found General Motors, but he was quite unlike Ford. Much of his time was dedicated to the stock market. In 1910, he lost control of General Motors to a banking syndicate, and then took over again in 1916 by using the money that he had made from building up Chevrolet. After the financial panic of 1920, Durant was once more forced out, and by 1923, the company was firmly in the hands of Alfred P. Sloan Jr.

Although under Sloan's guidance General Motors became the largest manufacturing enterprise in the world, Henry Ford continued to epitomize heavy industry and industrial engineering throughout most of the first half of the twentieth century. In order to undercut the rationalized society that he deplored, Aldous Huxley wrote his dystopia, *Brave New World* (1931). At that time it was almost inevitable that he chose "Our Ford" as the modern equivalent of "Our Lord," and made the inhabitants of the Brave New World's mechanized society make their obeisance with the sign of the "T." Even Mustapha Mond—Huxley's World-Controller—has been equated by James Sexton with Alfred Moritz Mond (Baron Melchett). Melchett had been one of the founders of Imperial Chemical Industries, still a British leader in the use of work-study methods. But the dystopian writer who was most immediately concerned with the effects of the demands of the clock on Western society and Western technology was Yevgeny Zamyatin, a naval architect and mathematician. In his novel *We* (1920), he had made Taylor, and

"the Taylor system," the most important single target of his attack.

Ford, the greatest practical exponent of the Taylor system, had used that system to produce at the Rouge the most perfectly rationalized and integrated factory complex in the world. By the middle of the 1920s, its 1,100 acres accommodated some twenty-seven miles of conveyor belts serving 75,000 workers. One of the ironies of recent years has been the manner in which the Japanese have been credited for the time dominated JIT, or just-in-time theory, among other manufacturing procedures. By relating the supply of parts directly to the requirements on the factory floor, JIT drastically reduces the need for holding inventory. Like much else, however, this aspect of industrial rationalization had long ago been applied at the Rouge. In the course of making a toast to the head of Ford in 1982, Eiji Toyoda, of the Toyota Company, admitted quite candidly that there was "no secret to how we learned to do what we do, Mr. Caldwell. We learned it at the Rouge."

FURTHER RAMIFICATIONS OF TIME AND METHOD STUDY, INCLUDING WHITE COLLAR WORKERS AND MANAGEMENT

During the second and third quarters of the twentieth century, the building up of operations based on very small elements, which the Gilbreths had brought into motion study, was extended to several new developments. Apart from ergonomics, the new disciplines included M.T.M. (methods-time measurement) and P.M.T. (predetermined motion times) which have allowed the time required for a new job to be predicted. They do so by assembling the time elements from a battery of predetermined synthetic times that relate to a whole series of activities. More recently, these developments contributed to the British Work-Measurement Data Foundation. Beyond the confusion of titles which has already been mentioned, work study suffers from the mushrooming of the terminology and titles for various systems since World War II. Such systems have often been based on the work of the armed services. The titles of games techniques and operational research speak for themselves; CPM (critical path method) "grew out of a joint effort in 1957. . . to apply electronic computers to scheduling the design and construction of chemical plants"; PERT (program evaluation and review technique) was designed, in 1958, by the U.S. Navy's Special Projects Office "for evaluating the . . . existing schedules on the Polaris missile program"; ergonomics had earlier grown out of the necessity for aligning men and women with sophisticated machines; and cybernetics is "the study of *control systems* in man and machine."

Just as industrial engineering did not really start with Taylor, one could demonstrate that administrative and clerical work were not entirely ignored by people who were developing time and method study prior to the twentieth century. In the eighteenth century, James Watt invented not only the steam engine but also the copying machine. The copying machine was first used to duplicate his own business letters and engineering drawings. In the nineteenth century, novelist Anthony Trollope had shown that time measurement could also be applied to creative work. With remarkable candor, he documents in his *Autobiography* that it had "become my custom . . . to write with my watch before me, and to require from myself 250 words every quarter of an hour. I have found that the 250 words have been forthcoming as regularly as my watch went. . . . I wrote my allotted number of pages every day. . . . And as a page is an ambiguous term, my page has been made to contain 250 words."

Even in our own century we have not been generally convinced that creative writing can be subject to time study. The case of office work is, however, different. As recently as the last twenty or thirty years, office workers were still arguing heatedly that—despite early examples of mechanization like Babbage's calculating engine, Watt's copying machine, and the typewriter of Sholes and Remington—time and method study could only be applied to industrial operations, and indeed that this was underscored by the American term "industrial engineering." But that is a myth which—with the aid of MBAs, computers, and word processors—has been exploded only in very recent years. Currie had, however, already argued the case clearly in his *Work Study* (1963): "The old concept of method study as applying only to light repetitive work did scant justice to its potentialities. It can, in fact, be applied anywhere, since any process or procedure is open to improvement." In Currie's succinct definition, "method study involves the breakdown of an operation (or procedure) into its component elements and their subsequent systematic analysis. Thence, those elements which cannot withstand the tests of interrogation are eliminated or improved."

The growth of the various national and international institutes of work study and industrial engineering has reflected the ever increasing concern with rationalizing human activities in production and elsewhere during this century. With these developments has come a virtual deluge of publications intent upon serving a new class of managers in every aspect of productivity science.

In modern times mental labor is being divided in the same way that physical labor was once broken down. Management is being divided into a whole range of categories. There are now not only accountants, office managers, production managers, purchasing officers, sales managers, stock managers, and transport managers, but such categories are even further broken down into groups of specialized management like that for hospitals, banking, or education. And in their own turn the newly developing management-related functions are creating the need for an ever-widening range of professional and university qualifications. As a result, a large and increasing number of specialized professional journals are now being written for people in management.

Work study, or industrial engineering, represents only one area of the many discrete entities in management which have developed from the division of mental labor. However, it holds a special place insofar as it can assist all the other managers in organizing more effectively the operation of plant, tools, and workers. But beyond this it is also well placed to examine the methods of the very managers themselves, in whom incompetence or inefficiency can be far more devastating than it would be in individual workers. Since the latter part of the seventeenth century, there has been an exponential growth in material progress based on Western technology. In all its forms of temporal measurement and organizational know-how, work study has been an integral part of that progress.

[S.L.M.]

See also **Industrial Engineering Before Taylor; Measurement of Work and Applications; Predetermined Motion Time Systems; Scheduling Through Operational Research; Taylor, Frederick Winslow.**

FURTHER READINGS

Barnes, Ralph M. *Motion and Time Study: Design and Measurement of Work.* 7th ed. New York: Wiley, 1980. Includes bibliography.

Blyton, Paul, et al. *Time, Work and Organization.* New York: Routledge, Chapman, and Hall, 1989.

Gilbreth, Frank B., and Lillian M. Gilbreth. *The Writings of the Gilbreths*. Ed. William R. Spriegel and Clark E. Myers. Homewood: Irwin, 1953.

Halberstam, David. *The Reckoning*. New York: William Morrow, 1986.

Introduction to Work Study. 3rd ed. Washington: International Labor Office, 1981.

Macey, Samuel L. *The Dynamics of Progress: Time, Method, and Measure*. Athens: U of Georgia P, 1989.

Menipaz, Ehud. *Essentials of Production and Operations Management*. Englewood Cliffs: Prentice-Hall, 1984. Includes bibliographies.

Mundel, Marvin Everett. *Motion and Time Study: Improving Productivity*. 6th ed. Englewood Cliffs: Prentice-Hall, 1985.

Niebel, Benjamin W. *Motion and Time Study*. 8th ed. Homewood: Irwin, 1987.

Shell, Richard L., ed. *Work Measurement: Principles and Practice*. Norcross: Institute of Industrial Engineers, 1986.

Whitmore, Dennis A. *Work Study and Related Management Services*. 3rd ed. London: Heinemann, 1976. Includes bibliography.

INSTINCT

The subject of instinct has been surrounded by divisive scientific debate since the groundwork for the development of the concept was laid by Heraclitus (ca. 540–ca. 480 B.C.). From the beginning, it has been defined and discussed in terms of its relation to animals that possess the power of reason and, less directly, to a soul. Early philosophers from the time of the Stoics until René Descartes in the seventeenth century argued that only human beings (and the gods) had the power of reason and, because of a strong belief in an afterlife, a soul. They deduced that animals, because they lacked reason, were not free to act independently and were governed by their natural "instincts." Over time, however, various schools of thought have prevailed ranging from the classical behaviorists, who deny the existence of instinct both in humans and in animals, to those who attribute the most varied instincts to animals and humans alike (more than 6,000 specific types of actions, forms of behavior, impulses, or motives, according to L. Bernard in 1978). Between these two extremes lie the current hypotheses of scientists. Some groups have reduced the multiplicity of instincts to a few basic ones, which are interpreted as the keys to animal and human behavior, while others have assigned instincts to animal species only and deny their existence in the case of the

human species (or accept them as only vestiges of animal behavior).

Charles Darwin (1809–1882) wrote that "the very essence of an instinct is that it is followed independently of reason." A more modern definition might be "an inherited, evolutionary response by an animal to stimuli resulting in a predictable and relatively fixed behavior pattern." Inherent in these definitions of instinct are the precepts that the behavior is innate and not learned, that it is stereotyped and characteristic of the species, and that it is adaptive and thus promotes the survival of the species. Some other simple types of behavior, however, would by definition be included within this broad sweep. For instance, a *taxis* (the direct orientation of an organism in respect to environmental stimuli) is perhaps the simplest form of adaptive behavior; a *reflex* is more complicated, but is still a relatively stereotyped and fixed response to stimuli, although some variations may be seen especially in the higher vertebrates; but by far the most fascinating of the innate, unlearned behavior patterns are the *instincts*.

Our current understanding of instinctive behavior is derived from the studies of two different schools of thought converging in their investigations. One is that of the European ethologists who are zoologists and who investigate behavior under natural or close to natural conditions. Their interest has been chiefly in animals other than mammals, and they have focused mainly on parental and filial behavior, social behavior, and reproductive behavior. The second group is made up primarily of American psychologists and physiologists who are interested mainly in sexual behavior, hunger, thirst, temperature regulation, sleep, rage, fear, and so on. These investigators have worked primarily on mammals, including primates and humans. Typically, they have been interested in one limited aspect of behavior, observed under laboratory conditions, but investigated deeply for its neurophysiological mechanisms. Despite the differences in approaches of these two scientific schools, it is remarkable how similar are their findings and basic conclusions.

When all the criteria which supposedly differentiate instinctive from learned responses are critically evaluated, the only one which seems universally applicable is that instincts are unlearned. This forces us to deal with a two-class system, and such systems are particularly unmanageable when one class is defined solely in negative terms, that is, in terms of the absence of certain characteristics that define the other class. Furthermore, it is logically indefensible to categorize any behavior as unlearned unless the characteristics of learned behavior have been thoroughly explored. Thus, ontological studies of behavior in different species become extremely important, as the following examples suggest. Not all cats kill mice, for although this behavior is said to be instinctive, it turns out that kittens often must see adult cats killing mice before they do so themselves, and kittens reared with mice rarely become mouse killers. Similarly, the chaffinch, if reared in isolation from its kind, sings a much simpler song than chaffinches reared with adult birds, and the isolated bird may never be able to learn the full song of the species if it is kept isolated past one breeding season. In the ermine moth, *Yponomeuta padella*, females lay their eggs on the leaves of the hackberry plant. The eggs hatch, and the larvae eat the leaves and eventually become mature. After metamorphosis, the females of this new generation in turn select hackberry leaves on which to deposit their eggs.

Another race of the moths, however, prefers apple leaves as an oviposition site. The difference between the two races has been perpetuated, generation after generation. It would appear to be the example *par excellence* of a genetically controlled behavior trait. However, when eggs of the apple-preferring type are transferred to hackberry leaves, the larvae thrive on the new diet. Thirty percent of the females developing from these larvae show a preference for hackberry leaves when it comes time for them to deposit their eggs. The evidence is of course incomplete. It would be illuminating if the same experimental treatment could be repeated on several successive generations. Nevertheless, it appears likely that the adult moth's choice of an oviposition site is influenced by the chemical composition of the food consumed during the larval period. If this interpretation is correct, the data illustrate the fact that a complex behavior pattern may be "unlearned" (that is, genetic) and still depend upon the individual's previous history (that is, learning).

Because it is so difficult to assess the criteria of instincts, many ardent believers in the concept have been able to apply it all too freely to almost every kind of behavior in every animal, including humans. Worse than that, they use instinct as an explanatory concept, never seeking to analyze or investigate its underlying mechanisms. Thus it is said, for example, that man fights because he has a fighting instinct and that is all there is to it. However, in humans the dominant modes of adaptation are reasoning and learning; there is very little in the way of instinct or even reflex that is not greatly modified by experience; taxes in the sense of an uncomplex response to an external stimulus are essentially nonexistent.

According to Konrad Lorenz, a Nobel Laureate in ethology, an example of a human instinct is the response to a touch stimulus given by an insect crawling on the skin. Our response is to throw the insect off with a quick movement of the hand, a movement that contains both a fixed pattern and an orientation component, and is therefore a reaction of greater complexity than a mere reflex. It is usually accompanied by a subjective feeling, namely disgust. In a mammal like the rat, in contrast, reasoning is virtually nonexistent, but learning is well developed. Instincts are clearly present and important, but they may be modified by experience; some taxes are present, but only very early in ontogenetic development. The insects, relatively speaking, are poor learners, are dominated by largely unmodifiable instincts, and show taxes quite clearly. Below the level of worms, learning is not clearly recognizable and may not be a property of organisms. Instinctive patterns are relatively simple and poorly developed, and organisms are dominated by taxes and reflexes.

No bit of behavior can ever be fully understood until its ontogenesis has been described. When this task has been properly carried out for a significant number of animal species, there will be no further reason for ambiguous concepts of instinctive behavior.

[R.A.R.]

See also **Psychology of Time; Psychophysiology.**

INSTRUMENTS OF TIME MEASUREMENT TO CA. A.D. 1275

Time measurement was not a necessity to early societies. In consequence traces of it—whether archaeological, epigraphic, or literary—are scarce, and surviving examples of the instruments used are exceptionally rare. For virtually the whole of the period that concerns us here—2000 B.C. to ca. A.D. 1275—time was found, kept, and measured for specific purposes rather than because of any sense of a need to know time general to a given society. Discussion of the instruments should always relate them to the context in which they were used, as this relationship sometimes helps to explain their form. Theoretically, we may distinguish between time-finders that are used to discover what time it is in whatever system of time-reckoning is being used, time-keepers that provide a continuous reckoning of time, and time-measurers that offer a means of determining the duration of discrete periods. In practice these often become combined in a single instrument. A fixed sundial, for example, is both time-finder and timekeeper and may be used as a time-measurer, but a portable dial, which by definition is generally not permanently set up, acts only as a time-finder. In what follows instruments are described by class and their evolution from antiquity in the Near East and in Europe is described. Developments in India and the Far East, which in some cases may also find an origin in the ancient Near East and in Greece, are, however, excluded from consideration.

Hour Systems

The number of parts into which the periods of light and dark or the two together may be divided is arbitrary. For most of the period with which we are here concerned a twelve-hour division of the night and a twelve-hour division of the day was accepted, although the earliest known text concerning a sundial, an inscription on the wall of the Sarcophagus room in the Cenotaph of Seti I (1318–1304 B.C.), describes and illustrates a sundial which divides the day into only eight hours. The evidence of an older surviving dial, however, shows that a twelve-hour division of the day was already being used in Egypt—where it may have originated—by the middle of the second millennium. The twelve-hour day division which subsequently became general was, however, different from that which has prevailed in Europe since the fourteenth century. In Egypt and elsewhere, the period of daylight was divided into twelve equal parts, as was the night. Since, however, the period of day and night, thanks to the inclination of the earth's orbit around the sun, are equal to each other only at the equinoxes (the moment when the earth crosses the celestial equator), the length of the daylight and night periods varied throughout the year as, in consequence, did the length of the hours. Such hours are known as "unequal hours." By contrast, if the total period of night and day measured from sunrise to sunrise is divided into twenty-four parts, then the hours of the day and night will be the same. These "equal hours," were, however, only used in antiquity and the early Middle Ages by astronomers. They do not

Figure 1. A late antique marble sundial.

occur in civil life before the fourteenth century, and then only in Europe. All the instruments described below, therefore, show unequal hours with the exception of the astrolabe, which as an astronomical instrument sometimes included equal hour scales, and the sandglass, which by its construction can only measure equal periods. In addition, it should be noted that the point from which one begins counting the hours, be they equal or unequal, is also arbitrary. Astronomers habitually counted from midday to midday; ecclesiastical reckoning tended to be from sunrise to sunset; but counts from midnight to midnight or sunset to sunrise are also known, and may be found on instruments up to the Renaissance.

Gnomons and Shadow-Length Tables

Gnomons are specially constructed shadow-casting instruments. As such, they make up an essential part of a sundial but, in the absence of an associated hour grid, they are not in themselves sundials. They can, however, be used to find time once it has been recognized that the height and direction of the shadow cast by a vertical gnomon changes in length and direction throughout the day and throughout the year. The gnomon was thus a versatile instrument that could be used for astronomical, calendrical, and day time measurement. On the grounds that calendrical time measurements were probably more important to agricultural communities than were day time measurements, we may postulate that the use of the gnomon for calendrical purposes, and in particular for solstice or equinox observations, preceded its use for day time measurements. Certainly, to determine day time by the length of the shadow cast by a vertical gnomon, it is necessary to know how the length of the shadow varies throughout the year as a function of the change in solar declination. The shadow is longest at the winter solstice when the sun's midday altitude is at its least, and shortest at the summer solstice when the altitude is greatest. This seasonal variation of the shadow length was probably first codified in Babylon, where tables presenting it are found among the Mul Apin texts of ca. 687 B.C. At present, it is not possible to determine whether or not there was any influence of these tables on those developed in Greece during the fifth and fourth centuries B.C., from which the whole subsequent Mediterranean and European tradition of shadow-length tables derived. Such tables show unequal hours of the day in terms of the length of the shadow in feet throughout the year. The foot is a non-metrological unit, the idea being that the person needing to know the time could himself become the gnomon and that any person is approximately six times as tall as his foot is long.

Whether a gnomon shadow or a human shadow was used, the method was widespread and would have a long history. Current all around the Mediterranean basin, it was known also in pre-Islamic Iran, in India, and in China. In the fifth century A.D., simplified shadow-length tables were incorporated into Palladius's *De re rustica*, which ensured their availability in the Latin West throughout the Middle Ages. At the same time, thanks in large part to the anonymous *Libellus de mensura horologii*, often attributed to Bede but not actually by him, time-finding by shadow lengths found a place in the collection of computistical texts and even in missals used in medieval monasteries. It was thus available in both learned and popular literature, in civil and religious contexts, and was probably the commonest way of time-finding used in the medieval period.

SUNDIALS

Sundials simulate the apparent diurnal movement of the sun across the sky by means of the shadow of a gnomon falling on a specially constructed hour scale permanently associated with the gnomon. From this scale the time of day may be read in whatever system of day time measurement is being used. It is the presence of the hour scale that distinguishes sundials from the simple gnomons described earlier. In a sundial, the gnomon is but one—albeit essential—part, the shadow-caster, but it has no utility apart from its hour scale.

Sundials employ either the altitude of the sun, or its direction, to give a measure of time. Virtually all early dials are altitude dials measuring the height of the sun above the horizon by the length of the shadow cast. To be accurate, therefore, such dials have to compensate for the seasonal variation of the sun's altitude. Apart from the fact that they are divided for a twelve-hour day, the earliest dials are similar to the dial illustrated on the wall of the Cenotaph of Seti mentioned earlier. They consist of a rectangular strip fitted with a vertical block at one end which acts as the gnomon and to which a plumb is attached. Along the body of the instrument are divisions marking the hours against which time is measured when the instrument is placed on a horizontal surface with the gnomon-block directed toward the sun. Exactly when compensation for the solar declination was introduced we do not know, although it seems to have occurred during the first half of the first millennium. A small group of Egyptian dials or votive models thereof have survived from the late dynastic and Ptolemaic periods. These are of the same basic pattern as the earlier dials, but now the plane of the hour scale is inclined by an angle equivalent to that of the latitude of the place where the dial is to be used. Lines representing the different months are drawn on this plane perpendicular to the gnomon block on which the corresponding month names are usually marked, and the hours are indicated by a series of dots or lines which curve across the month lines so as to agree with the longer or shorter shadows cast at different times of the year.

At the same time as this relatively simple, probably empirically derived improvement was made in Egypt, sundials entered upon an extraordinary period of development and refinement at the hands of Greek mathematicians. Although dials may have first appeared in Greece in the sixth century, it is more likely that this is the period of the introduction of gnomon and shadow-length tables from Babylon, the true sundial not appearing until the late fifth or even fourth century. Certainly no surviving Greek dial can be dated to earlier than the third century B.C.

Whatever the date that it was introduced, the sundial in Greece found a ready reception. To mathematicians, the instrument offered a technical challenge at the same time as, in the essentially urban setting of Greek social and intellectual life, it had clear utility. Sundials supplied the time-markers by which town dwellers could fix appointments and structure their days. At the same time, sundials could be produced as massive, decorative pieces of mural or free-standing sculpture. They were thus civic adornments reflecting credit and conferring prestige upon those who erected them. The name of the donor of a Greek or Roman sundial is more likely to be inscribed on it than is that of its designer or maker.

In these circumstances dials multiplied in the Greco-Roman world. In the first century B.C., Vitruvius in a famous passage (*De architectura* IX.viii.1) could list fifteen different types of dial, eleven of them fixed, four portable, and the list is unlikely to be exhaustive. Of the types of dial that he records eight of the fixed dials can be identified among the approximately 280 ancient dials known to have survived, although it is less certain that the four known forms of portable dial can be directly identified with the four types named by Vitruvius. The typical Greco-Roman dial was spherical or conical in form, plane dials whether vertical or horizontal occurring far less frequently among known examples. As a more literal representation of the celestial vault, spherical and conical dials were perhaps more easily assimilated by the public (see Figure 1). In addition to the hour lines, most dials included lines marking the tropics and midsummer, and thus carried out some of the functions of a public calendar as well as those of a dial. Compared with plane dials, however, they were rather less accurately drawn, at least to modern eyes.

The tradition of building monumental public sundials spread throughout the Roman Empire and lasted as long, indeed somewhat longer, than the empire itself. Dials were to be found in the towns and in those urban communities in rural exile, the great villas. For travelers a number of portable dials were developed. To be effective, these needed not only to be small,

light, and preferably flat, but also to be arranged for use in more than one latitude. This may be effected either by adapting the gnomon so that it can always be set parallel to the polar axis whatever the latitude, or by drawing several scales, each for a different latitude. Portable dials drawn for only one latitude also existed for those who did not intend to travel far. Such dials seem to have developed somewhat later than their fixed public counterparts, perhaps in the second century B.C., and no surviving dial is earlier than the first century B.C. Thereafter, the eighteen known surviving dials are distributed fairly evenly from the first century B.C. to the sixth century A.D. Few though they are, it is clear that like public dials, they were an object of current manufacture throughout the period of late antiquity, and that a craft tradition of their manufacture survived the breakup of the Roman Empire to influence manufacture in Byzantium, the Latin West, and the regions of Islam.

Of Byzantine dials we know little, but there is evidence that they continued to be made before the Arab-Islamic invasions of the early

Figure 2. Receiving vessel (facsimile) of a Romano-Egyptian clepsydra.

seventh century, and traces of them reappear in the mathematical-astronomical literature of the tenth and later centuries, although the treatise on sundials by the anonymous mid-tenth-century scholar known as Hero of Byzantium has disappeared. Mathematics and astronomy did not have a high profile in Byzantine society, where the church had become the focus of intellectual life. For the needs of the church, and more especially monasteries, a dial far simpler than the mathematically sophisticated Greek constructions was sufficient. Although some conical dials have been found on monastic sites, more typical is a simple plane, semicircular vertical dial with its gnomon at right angles to the dial face and twelve hour lines radiating from the base of the gnomon.

Dials of this sort seem to have traveled with monasticism from the Near East to northwest Europe, early examples being found in northern Britain and Ireland. It was to become the typical ecclesiastical dial. Early examples retained the full complement of twelve hour lines, sometimes indicating by a cross the third, sixth, and ninth hours which had liturgical significance as being the hours prescribed for prayer. In time, however, the intermediate lines were suppressed and examples of such dials are found with four, six, eight, ten, or twelve divisions. Dials of this kind used in Anglo-Saxon England were generally treated as large two-dimensional relief sculptures. Later in the Middle Ages, by which time they were disseminated throughout northern Europe, they degenerated into small diagrams scratched on church walls as and when needed (they are for this reason usually called "scratch dials," sometimes "mass dials"), and it is not unknown for traces of several such dials to be found on the walls of a single church.

While in the Latin West sundials were thus restricted in use to virtually a single type for religious use, in the Islamic east (and west after the conquest of Spain), the recovery of Greek mathematical texts led Islamic scholars to explore the possibilities for creating new kinds of dials. Since little investigation has yet been made of surviving texts, and the remaining dials have only partially been inventoried, no general picture of Islamic dialing can be drawn, but it is clear that certain Greek forms of dial, in particular the pelecinum (so-called from its resemblance to a double-headed battle-axe), were taken over and made, at the same time as new forms were developed. One new form of portable dial—the vertical plate dial—is probably to be related

to the hour diagram found on the Egyptian inclined plane dials. One example of such a dial survives from the mid-twelfth century and it is exactly the same in principle and method of use as the pillar or cylinder dial which was to become one of the most convenient and longlasting of all dials. In both dials, a series of vertical lines represent the months and the hour lines curve across them according to the length of the shadow of the gnomon at different times of the year. The gnomon is set at right angles to either the plate or the pillar at the top of the appropriate month line and the dial directed toward the sun until the gnomon shadow lies on the chosen month line when the position of its tip among the hour lines shows the time. Self-orienting and extremely simple to use, with the solar declination compensated simply by placing the gnomon in position for the date, such dials seem to have been transmitted to Latin Europe at the same time as was knowledge of the astrolabe at the end of the tenth and eleventh centuries. Referred to as "horologium viatorium" in Latin texts and "chylindre" in Middle English ones, it was probably the most widely used portable dial of the Middle Ages and later.

WATER CLOCKS

Water clocks are probably the oldest of all time-measuring instruments. The earliest evidence that we have for them comes from an inscription in an Egyptian tomb of the sixteenth century B.C., while the earliest archaeological fragments to survive, those of the Karnak clepsydra, date from the reign of Amenhotep III (1415–1380 B.C.). This is an outflow clepsydra in which, as water flows out of the vessel by a small hole set in the wall near the base, time is indicated by the descending level of water against an hour-scale marked on the inside of the container. The Karnak instrument, however, is already a sophisticated device which compensates for the change in water pressure as the head gets smaller, and makes provision for the changing length of the unequal hour throughout the year. As the height of the water above an orifice changes so does the pressure exerted and thus the rate of discharge. If, however, the sides of the container are inclined so that the diameter of the brim is about twice that of the base, the pressure and so the rate of flow is almost equalized throughout the period required to empty the vessel. The Karnak instrument is of this truncated cone form. Marked on the inside, moreover, are not one but twelve hour scales, one for each month, with the graduations varied in a proportion of

37 — FEZ — L'Horloge de Bou-Anania, les 13 Grands Timbres - L L

Figure 3. Gongs and ball channels of a water clock, Bû'anâniyya mosque, Fez. Postcard of ca. 1920.

12:14 for the months with the longest and shortest unequal hours.

Since the earliest mention of this compensation occurs in an inscription of ca. 1580, we may assume that more primitive forms of clepsydra preceded the Karnak-type vessel in ancient Egypt. Nothing, however, is yet known of them. Nor is anything much known of the development of outflow clepsydras for 1000 years after that of Karnak. Clearly, they were not all as advanced as that of Karnak, for a clepsydra recovered from a well on the Athenian Agora datable to the fifth century B.C. is not a timekeeper, but simply measures the period of time allotted for certain speeches in the law courts. It is thus ungraduated, and similar instruments were widely used in antiquity and the Middle Ages for purposes as disparate as timing legislative assembly speeches, measuring military watches, or delimiting the period during which irrigation water would be supplied to a person's lands.

More sophisticated was the inflow clepsydra. As its name suggests, this device depends on the controlled entry of water into a receiving vessel normally cylindrical in shape (see Figure 2). Time is measured against a scale that is either drawn on the inside of the receiver or mounted above it, in which case there is a float in the receiver carrying an index that moves up the scale above as the vessel fills. The name of Ctesibios of Alexandria (ca. 300–230 B.C.) is associated with the invention of this instrument, but there is no evidence to confirm this. Ctesibios may perhaps be associated with some improvements essential to the machine. Vitruvius associates him with the introduction of the use of gold or pierced gemstones for the orifice—since these would be less liable to accretions which restrict the flow—and with that of the float and marker. Both of the latter are used in the "parastatic" clock, which Vitruvius describes as a typical clepsydra. In this clock a cylindrical recipient was filled by water from a vessel of truncated cone shape (like an outflow clepsydra) by means of an overflow tank. The overflow was placed between the reservoir and the receiving vessel. Before operation began, the overflow tank was filled with water up to the level of a small outlet set beneath the brim. When further water entered from the reservoir, the excess ran out from this overflow. The operative level of the water in the charging vessel was thus maintained constant, ensuring a constant rate of discharge into the receiving vessel. All the orifices were of gold or gemstones. A float in the receiver carried a small figure holding an index which indicated the hour on a column marked with curved hour lines crossing perpendicular month lines similar to those inscribed on the cylinder dial discussed above. Alternatively, in the absence of this scale, the rate of flow could be adjusted seasonally to give a longer or shorter hour.

Water clocks were widespread throughout the Hellenistic cultural region as were water-driven alarm clocks using either whistling siphons or the sound of a hard ball falling into a metal vessel. Such alarms may have preceded water clocks with visual indications. In the hands of a series of Alexandrian engineers between the third century B.C. and the first century A.D., the simpler, earlier machines were developed by the introduction of a range of automata marking time visually and aurally, and with astronomical and calendrical indications. This whole technology was transmitted from the late Roman world to the barbarian west, to the civilized east, and eventually to the Arab-Islamic regions as part of the same mathematical technology group as sundials and the astrolabe. Although in the west this technology virtually disappears from record, it may not have been totally lost. Some astronomical paintings which ultimately depend upon the geometrical projection that underlies the astrolabe are known, details of two eleventh-century monastic water alarms have survived, and there is good evidence for the existence of other water clocks which may have incorporated automata and displays. Certainly such displays were very quickly incorporated into public weight-driven clocks when these appeared in the late thirteenth century, which would seem to imply an existing tradition.

As in the west so in the east, but here we have far more information. In the hands of Arab scholars not only was the Greek tradition of water clocks developed, but detailed descriptions were written by the compilers of *The Book of Archimedes on the Construction of Water-Clocks* (eighth to twelfth centuries); by al-Murâdî (eleventh century); al-Khâzinî (early twelfth century); Ridwân (late twelfth to early thirteenth century); and al-Jazarî (late twelfth to early thirteenth century). However elaborate these machines became, with automata figures blowing trumpets or beating drums to sound the hour, snakes gliding toward birds singing in trees, slave girls bowing, eagles dropping balls into basins, windows lighting up regularly through

the night (one at each hour), and astronomical displays showing where the sun or moon was in the sky, most of them continued to depend on the basic techniques of the inflow and outflow mechanisms described earlier, or on the equally simple device of the sinking bowl, which consists of a basin pierced with a small hole. The basin is floated in a tank of water and sinks after a predetermined period. New techniques were, however, introduced, such as the steelyard clepsydra, in which the weight of water or sand running into a recipient was weighed before triggering off an indicator mechanism. The treatises that describe this long Islamic tradition are sufficiently detailed for reconstructions of a number of the machines to have been made in recent years. All have worked well, and it is clear that such machines were built and used in the medieval period (see Figure 3). They might be monumental public clocks set up in mosques or madrasas (colleges), or more delicate devices for domestic use. That few monumental sundials have survived from medieval Islamic lands may reflect the fact that public water clocks made them unnecessary. The remains of a fourteenth-century public water clock may still be seen today on the façade of the Qarawiyyin mosque in Fez. Such clocks were naturally an urban phenomenon. As in the Latin West they would eventually be displaced by weight-driven clocks, but in Islam this did not even begin to occur until the sixteenth and seventeenth centuries.

TIME-FINDERS BY NIGHT

The sundial by its nature is a day time-measurer. In origin, the clepsydra was probably its night-time equivalent, but in the context of temple rites where surveillance was possible. Although some of the developed Islamic monumental water clocks included night indication by means of illuminated windows, for private use something more convenient was required. This was supplied by candle clocks.

Use of the regular consumption of a combustible substance such as oil or wax to measure time, although a primitive technique, is one of which the historical origins are uncertain. In Europe, candles of known height and diameter graduated to twenty minutes are associated with Alfred the Great in England ca. 878, and similar devices are attested from later Latin sources. For example, Louis XI of France (1214–1270) employed graduated candles three feet in height to measure the amount of time that he spent in Bible reading and meditation. In Islam, the existence of a quite lengthy tradition is implied by the complex candle clocks described by al-Jazari, although he mentions only one precursor, Yunûs al-asturlâbî (mid-twelfth century). Probably to be related to the Islamic tradition, although quite different from al-Jazarî's device, is the candle clock described by Samuel el-Levi of Toledo in the Libros del Saber written in Spain in 1276.

Early time-measuring instruments, as noted above, were often specific to a particular function or social context. A clear example of this is the "nocturnal," a time-measurer developed from a combination of a sighting tube—an empty tube used by astronomers which by restricting the field of vision caused the pupil to expand, making the sighting of celestial objects clearer— with a double scale of months and the twenty-four hours which correlate the midnight position of ß ursa minoris throughout the year. By sighting the pole star through a central hole in the instrument and noting where the star stood, time could be calculated from the number of hours difference of the star from midnight as a function of date.

The nocturnal in this form was described by Ramon Llull at the end of the thirteenth century. It was intended as an instrument for seamen, and more primitive versions of the device may well go back to Gerbert (Pope Sylvester II) in the tenth century, or Pacifico of Verona in the late eighth century. But such an instrument was restricted in its use to navigators and astronomers. It played no part in civil time-reckoning.

THE ASTROLABE

Essentially the astrolabe is an astronomical instrument. A model of the heavens in two dimensions, it is primarily valuable as a calculating instrument—the first analogue computer—enabling the state of the sky at any given moment to be set up or conversions to be made between different sets of celestial coordinates without calculation (see Figure 4). For such an instrument time is an essential input, and so it is equipped for time-finding (the astrolabe has no time-measuring or timekeeping capacity). Finding time with an astrolabe is relatively simple, but astrolabes were scarce and expensive instruments in the Middle Ages. It is therefore unlikely, except perhaps in Islam where the instrument was part of the regular equipment of a muwaqit (the timekeeper of a mosque charged with announcing the times of prayer), that they were very widely used for time-finding purposes. In this sense the astrolabe is only indirectly a time instrument and should probably not be

counted as such. The same, however, is not true of most of the quadrants that were derived from the astrolabe, but as the period of greatest quadrant development falls outside the period covered by this article, they are not here further discussed.

SANDGLASSES

The origins of the sandglass are unknown. The earliest clear evidence for its existence is European and dates from A.D. 1345–46 in England, with a possible reference in a thirteenth-century Persian text. Neither of these is, however, likely to be the earliest use of the instrument, and the sandglass may well have originated in the twelfth century, or even earlier. A measurer of discrete time intervals, it was used exclusively for specific purposes in much the same way as the outflow clepsydra in antiquity. If one of its most important applications was in navigation for timing watches and, from the late thirteenth century onwards, for timing the period that a log was in the sea to measure the way made, this need not imply that the sandglass originated in a marine context. There were plenty of operations in monasteries, schools, and secular activities where the instrument was useful. But of all the early time-measuring instruments it is, with the noc-

Figure 4. Front of a late-fourteenth-century European astrolabe.

turnal, the only one not to have originated in antiquity.

[A.J.T.]

See also **Clocks and Watches: The Leap to Precision; Clocks: The First Mechanical Clocks.**

FURTHER READINGS

Field, J.V. "Some Roman and Byzantine Portable Sundials and the London Sundial-Calendar." *History of Technology* 12 (1990): 103–135.

Gibbs, Sharon L. *Greek and Roman Sundials.* New Haven: Yale UP, 1976.

King, David A. *Islamic Astronomical Instruments.* London: Variorum, 1987.

Sedillot, L.A.M. "Mémoire sur les instruments astronomiques des arabes." *Mémoires présentés par divers savants à l'Académie Royale des Inscriptions et Belles-Lettres* 1.1 (1844): 1–229.

Turner, A.J. *Water-Clocks, Sand-Glasses, Fire-Clocks* (The Time Museum, Catalogue of the Collection). Vol. I.3. Ed. Bruce Chandler. Rockford: Time Museum, 1984.

———. *Astrolabes and Astrolabe Related Instruments* (The Time Museum, Catalogue of the Collection). Vol. I.1. Ed. Bruce Chandler. Rockford: Time Museum, 1985.

INTERDISCIPLINARY STUDIES

Interdisciplinary studies of time explore the experience and idea of time through scientific understanding and humanistic insight. Working by the professional standards of the fields of learning that contribute to these studies, they lead to new approaches for many time-related problems that are of common interest to the disciplines involved.

Everyday wisdom maintains that people have no choice but to live with time. This example of practical insight loses its apparent simplicity, however, as soon as we try to answer the question: what is it that we must live with when living with time?

Traditional answers to this question have been associated with God, death, and eternity. Accordingly, for an explanation of what time is, people turned to spiritual leaders. In our age, answers are more likely to be sought in the opinions of scientists, especially physicists. The question, therefore, arises: to what field of learning does the study of time most properly belong? The sample issues that follow suggest that the study of time, as seen from the point of view of the contemporary division of intellectual labor, demands an interdisciplinary approach.

The universal human datum of time is the certainty of death. Attempts to conquer the finality of death through belief in afterlife are as old as is human identity. Such beliefs amount to theories about time, for they see life's passage as virtual, death an entry to timeless eternity. But: whom should one ask about the meaning of timeless eternity? Perhaps a psychologist who studied the nature of the mind. Or maybe a person who knows what the great spiritual leaders of mankind have said about it. Perhaps an astronomer who explores the boundaries of space and time.

Some of the early thinkers of Greek antiquity maintained that time was change, permanence was only apparent. Others would argue that ultimate reality is permanent and timeless while time and change are only appearances. This ancient debate continues in our own epoch. Are these issues questions in logic or do they pertain to the physiology and psychology of perception?

Plato separated the world into permanent, timeless ideas and changing, temporal appearances. More than two millennia later, the Platonic view of time came to be built into the foundations of experimental science in the form of (temporal) contingencies applied to (timeless) scientific laws. In Newtonian physics this separation was clear and useful. With quantum theory, however, the division between change and permanence became blurred. For the conditions of light propagation, as interpreted in special relativity theory, the distinction became meaningless. In this historical process toward increasing formalism and abstraction, life and even matter were left behind. The question of how time in the equations of physics relates to the time of human experience remains open.

Did time have a beginning and will it have an ending? Should we believe the philosophical theology of Saint Augustine, who wrote that time and the universe were coeval, or should we favor physical cosmology which asserts that time probably came about with the big bang, but its ending is uncertain?

From whatever source the answer might come, it is difficult to comprehend what is to be meant by reality before the world and time came into being or what it may mean after they vanish. But it is equally difficult to imagine time and the world not having a beginning or an ending. If this demonstrates a limitation to human thought, then we ought we consult psychology and epistemology to learn about the boundaries of human reality. Or, we may be projecting our births, lives, and deaths upon a universe in which nothing can correspond to those ideas. Or, natural languages and logical thought may be inappropriate means for exploring issues that relate to the beginning and ending of time.

Are time and history cyclic as classical Oriental thought maintained, or is time linear and history progressive, directed toward a goal, as taught by Christianity? Perhaps time is a dialectical process of the spirit as Hegel suggested, or of matter as Marx argued. Or, is history a neutral data bank to be searched by computers for recurring but otherwise meaningless temporal patterns?

In all great cultures the arts and the letters have reflected the human concern with passage. These concerns have been continuously expanding through the capacity of the mind to create representations of new worlds as, for instance, through the exact sciences. Is it necessary, however, to seek the nature of time through the odd behavior of black holes or should we, preferably, look beyond the rainbow of human imagination, laid down in the passionate self-expressions of men and women?

At the beginning of this article the question was asked, what do we live with when we live with time? The answer seems to be: with an unceasing turmoil of ideas, arising from what appears to be a simple fact of life: the experience of passage. There is an immensity of contesting ideas about the nature of time. But the mere number and vastness of the issues should not prohibit the search for an integrated view of time. For the task of the mind remains that of constructing comprehensive views of the world, and thereby to guide humans in their search for meaning and order in existence.

What is called for is an integrated understanding of time wherein creativity, common to all knowledge, is permitted to flourish and ideas about time, separately born and developed, are permitted to interact. The purpose of the interdisciplinary study of time is to make such interactions possible.

However, the enterprise so envisaged has a number of difficulties.

Each of the many fields upon which an integrated study of time must draw—be it clockmaking, folklore, or genetics—has its *language*. Each uses common words whose meanings differ from those conveyed in ordinary speech. Each field employs stock phrases whose meanings become self-justifying for insiders because of frequent use, while remaining opaque to outsiders. Additional problems arise if texts are translated because the logics and tenses of natural languages embody different judgments about the nature of time.

That which constitutes a necessary and sufficient *proof of truth* in one discipline may be judged, from the perspective of another, as neither a necessary nor a sufficient demonstration of fact. An argument may be judged by one set of standards as correct and convincing while regarded by other standards as useless verbiage.

Different fields display different *personalities*. Mathematics, neurology, literary criticism, or anthropology show different collective attitudes toward the world. The different compartments of human knowledge are emotionally loaded modes of self-expression. They represent different ways of life which those in the discipline seek because they find them satisfying. People group themselves accordingly and, thereby, create and reinforce the personalities of their professions—and their judgments as to what is significant in the nature of time.

Recognizing these problems is a necessary step toward the development of an interdisciplinary study of time. It is necessary, but not sufficient. It is equally necessary to provide a conceptual framework, such as the hierarchical theory of time. This theory respects the different languages, methods of proofs, and personalities of the established fields of knowledge. It also shows how their relevant teachings correlate and, by so doing, it assists in creating an integrated and contemporary vision of time, that moving image of a changing eternity.

[J.T.F.]

See also **Hierarchical Theory of Time.**

FURTHER READINGS

Fraser, J.T., ed. *The Voices of Time.* 2nd ed. Amherst: U of Massachusetts P, 1981.

———. *The Genesis and Evolution of Time: A Critique of Interpretation in Physics.* Amherst: U of Massachusetts P, 1982.

———. *Time, the Familiar Stranger.* Amherst: U of Massachusetts P, 1987.

———. *Of Time, Passion, and Knowledge: Reflections on the Strategy of Existence.* 2nd ed. Princeton: Princeton UP, 1990.

Fraser, J.T., et al., eds. *The Study of Time.* Volumes I-IV, New York: Springer, 1972–1981; Volume V, Amherst: U of Massachusetts P, 1986; Volumes VI-VIII, Madison: International Universities P, 1989–.

Whitrow, G.J. *The Natural Philosophy of Time.* 2nd ed. Oxford: The Clarendon P, 1990.

INTERNAL-CLOCK MODELS

The ability of people and other animals to antic-ipate the time of occurrence of a regular event and to discriminate between different durations of time suggests that they may possess internal clocks. An internal clock is a hypothetical bio-logical or psychological mechanism with some of the characteristics of a physical clock. A psy-chological model of an internal clock consists of the internal clock itself plus associated memory and decision processes.

TYPES OF CLOCKS

Various types of internal clocks have been pos-tulated as the basis for time perception and timed performance. People and animals may have a pacemaker accumulator system that serves as an interval clock, a single periodic clock, or a clock composed of multiple oscillators.

PACEMAKER-ACCUMULATOR CLOCKS

An ancient mechanism for measuring durations of time is a clepsydra, a water clock. An interval is begun when water starts dripping into an empty collecting tube and a duration of time is represented by the height of the water in the tube at the end of the interval. The dripping water serves as a pacemaker or oscillator emit-ting discrete pulses in time, and the collecting tube is an accumulator, summing the number of pulses. A pacemaker-accumulator mechanism of this sort, often called an interval clock, is an essential component of scalar timing theory, as discussed by John Gibbon, which is currently the most successful quantitative theory of tem-poral discrimination. In addition to the clock, this internal-clock model includes memory and decision processes. A pacemaker emits pulses that can be switched into an accumulator; the value in the accumulator may be stored in mem-ory; and a decision to act at a given time is based on a comparison between the value in the accu-mulator at that time and a sample (or samples) from memory. This information-processing model of duration discrimination has been trans-formed into a precise mathematical model with the specification of distribution forms, parame-ter values, and combination rules.

PERIODIC CLOCKS

Many periodic clocks consist of a pacemaker, a source of regular pulses such as a pendulum, a source of power, and an escapement to translate the back and forth movement of the oscillator to the rotary movement of a marker (the hand) around a circular face. If the hand is reset or entrained to some external stimulus, the direc-tion of the hand indicates the duration (unless the period of the clock is exceeded). Investiga-tors of circadian rhythms often refer to a "bio-logical clock" that behaves like a one-handed clock with a period of about twenty-four hours and, as discussed by Martin Moore-Ede et al., they have located the pacemaker for it in the superchiasmatic nucleus of the brain of various mammals. But a clock with a twenty-four-hour period fails to measure longer periods and is not particularly useful for discriminating between short durations, such as minutes or seconds.

MULTIPLE OSCILLATOR CLOCKS

A more useful type of periodic clock is one with several hands that move with various periods. Unlike one-handed clocks, a multiple-handed clock driven by one or more oscillators can distinguish between elapsed time and accumu-lated time—the differences, say, between one hour and one hour plus one day. As C.R. Gallis-tel suggests, such a clock is useful both for determining the phase of a short or long period and for timing the duration of a short or long interval.

BIOLOGICAL BASIS OF TIMING

As Hudson Hoagland has indicated, it is general-ly assumed that the internal clock can be iden-tified with events in the brain, and that its speed can be directly measured by both physiological and behavioral methods. The speed of the clock can be affected by drugs, stress or arousal, and diet. For example, an increase in the effective level of the neurotransmitter dopamine in-creases the speed of the internal clock and dopam-ine receptor blockers (such as the neuroleptics used to treat schizophrenia) reduce the speed of the internal clock.

EVALUATION OF INTERNAL-CLOCK MODELS

There have been various challenges to internal-clock models. Although animals and people can judge the time of occurrence of events, and they can discriminate between stimuli of different durations, it is possible that they do so without using an internal clock. For example, behavior occurs through time, and it might be used as a clock, as in timing a second by saying "one steam engine." If behavior itself were sufficient as a basis for time discrimination, the animal would not possess a clock but its behavior would be the clock. Some investigators of timing of motor performance have attempted to dispense with a pattern generator (such as a central internal oscillator) when it is possible for peripheral systems of muscles and the physics of the limb movements to produce the timing involved. Some cognitive psychologists—as indicated in Richard Block's *Cognitive Models of Psychological Time*—doubt the existence of a central internal clock primarily because there are many factors, such as events that occur during an interval, that affect the perceived duration of an interval. Like other theories, internal-clock models may be evaluated in terms of the extent to which they can provide accurate, systematic, and parsimonious explanations of a wide range of phenomena. Recent models have been quite successful in this regard, for they predict in accurate detail the data from many duration discrimination and production experiments.

[R.M.C.]

FURTHER READINGS

Block, Richard A., ed. *Cognitive Models of Psychological Time*. Hillsdale: Erlbaum, 1990.

Gallistel, Charles R. *The Organization of Learning*. Cambridge: MIT P, 1990.

Gibbon, John. "The Origins of Scalar Timing Theory." *Learning and Motivation* (Special Issue on Animal Timing). Ed. Steven F. Maier and Russell M. Church. 22.1–2 (February-May 1991): 3–38.

Hoagland, Hudson. *Pacemakers in Relation to Aspects of Behavior*. New York: Macmillan, 1935.

Moore-Ede, Martin C., Frank M. Sulzman, and Charles A. Fuller. *The Clocks that Time Us*. Cambridge: Harvard UP, 1982.

INTERNATIONAL SOCIETY FOR THE STUDY OF TIME (ISST)

ISST is a professional organization dedicated to the exploration of the idea and experience of time, and to the elucidation of its role in physical, organic, intellectual, and sociocultural processes. Since its founding in 1966, the society's meetings have provided for an exchange of ideas among its members. Selected papers from the meetings are published in *The Study of Time* (1972–) series.

A glance at a roster of contemporary professional societies will witness the radical fragmentation of human knowledge, demanded by the ever-increasing division of labor. This fragmentation persists at a time when there is an increasing need for comprehending larger segments of nature, life, and culture. The royal societies of the world, the great national academies that embraced and encouraged all forms of critical learning, date to earlier centuries.

Interdisciplinary studies by members of ISST, conducted under the critical standards of the disciplines involved, offer opportunities to counter fragmentation by working toward an integrated understanding of time. Simultaneously, the society's meetings help members gain new perspectives on time-related matters in their own specialized fields of training.

Requirements for membership include a doctoral degree earned at an accredited institution of higher learning, as well as publications in the applicant's field in the form of books and refereed papers.

[J.T.F.]

See also **Interdisciplinary Studies.**

FURTHER READINGS

Fraser, J.T., ed. *The Voices of Time*. 2nd ed. Amherst: U of Massachusetts P, 1981.

———, et al., eds. *The Study of Time*. Volumes I-IV, New York: Springer Verlag, 1972–1981; Volume V, Amherst: U of Massachusetts P, 1986; Volumes VI-VIII, Madison: International Universities P, 1989–.

Macey, S.L. *Time: A Bibliographic Guide*. New York: Garland, 1991.

ISLAM

Islam is a major global religion whose roots are in the Arabian Peninsula of the early seventh century. Its core elements were implanted in the early years and all later developments relate, in one way or another, to that core.

In pre-Islamic Arabia, some people seem to have related to time (*dahr*) as fate, an underlying force directing human and natural destiny. It was conceived as a power existing from eternity to eternity responsible for the happiness or agony of humanity. Thus the Koran (Qur'ān) refers to those who "say. . .'nothing but time can destroy us'" (45:23/24).

While time was generally seen as an impersonal force, some people sought to identify time with God or, worse still from the Islamic perspective, to use this concept to deny God's existence. The apostolic tradition (*hadith*) records Muhammad's saying that Allah commanded men not to blame *dahr*, "for I [God] am *dahr*." Later there were various groups of radical thinkers, often only vaguely defined and known primarily from polemic references, who asserted "the eternity of the course of time." Accordingly, because they denied both creation and judgment, the beginning and end of time, they were considered atheists. The term *dahrîya*, therefore, came to encompass a broad spectrum of dissenters advocating some form of atheism and/or hedonistic materialism.

Islam universally views time as created. It is God's handiwork which, like all Creation, is under God's command. God acts in and through history but, being eternal, time does not encompass Him.

According to al-Baydâwî (d. 1282) in *Anwâr at-Tanzîl wa-Asrâr at-Ta'wîl*, Time consists of *mudda*, the period of revolution of the sphere from beginning to end (that is, the totality of time); *az-Zamân*, a gross subdivision of *mudda* into long periods of time (for example, specific historical eras such as dynastic reigns); and *al-Waqt*, fine subdivisions of *zamân* into definite points of time or short intervals (for example, precise times of the five obligatory prayers).

There are some, within the Islamic tradition, who assert that time, begun at Creation, has no necessary end. Al-Ghazzâlî (d. 1111) in *Tahâfut al-Falâsifa*, speaking for the mainstream tradition, teaches that religious dogma points to a finite end to time (that is, at the day of judgment).

MEASUREMENT OF TIME

There have been many historical eras. The two most significant, in the consciousness of Muslims, are the Age of Ignorance (*al-Jâhilîya*), the dark age in Arabia before the revelation of the Qur'ân; and the Islamic age stretching from the formation of the Islamic community in A.D. 622 until the end of history at judgment. All, however, can be divided according to the calendars accepted at different times among various peoples.

There is evidence which suggests that most ancient Arabs followed a pure lunar calendar. About two centuries before the Prophet, apparently under the influence of Jewish civilization, many in Arabia adopted a lunisolar calendar. After Muhammad's transfer to Medina (the *hijra*), however, an absolute lunar calculation was mandated.

The *hijrî* year consists, in theory, of twelve months of twenty-nine days, twelve hours, forty-four minutes and three seconds. In fact, for various practical reasons, the lunar months are computed variously as having either twenty-nine or thirty days. (The *hijrî* year is about eleven days shorter than the solar year. There is no intercalation to the solar. Any particular *hijrî* date, over a period of approximately thirty-three years, will move through all four solar seasons.)

A number of Islamic societies have introduced a solar or lunisolar calendar (for example prerevolutionary Iran and Kemalist Turkey). None of these, however, has achieved any universal acceptance among the world's Muslims. It is accepted, further, that such a calendar has no support in the Qur'ân or prophetic Sunnah.

Specific points in the yearly cycle are sanctified and celebrated in various ways, and there are many local holidays and celebrations. Certain times, however, are universally acknowledged as primary Muslim holy times. The first is the month of Ramadan, during which the Muhammad's prophetic career was opened. For the entire month, Muslims abstain from food, drink, smoking, and sexual contact. The fast begins each day at the moment that there is sufficient light to distinguish white from black threads. It ends each night after the sun has completely set. Islam's "lesser feast," *'Îd al-Fitr* (feast of breaking fast), brings release from the month-long abstention.

The "greater feast" is the *'Îd al-Adhâ* (feast of sacrifice) on the tenth of *Dhû 'l-Hijjah* (the last month of the Muslim year). It celebrates the end of the holy pilgrimage and reenacts Abraham's sacrifice of a ram in place of his son (Qur'ân 37:102). The primary sacrifice is made by the pilgrims in the valley of Minâ, near Mecca. Muslims all over the world, however, also offer such a sacrifice.

In Muhammad's time the Arabs counted a seven-day week. There is evidence, however, that this is a relatively late practice imported from Babylonia (or perhaps by way of resident Jewish communities who observed the weekly sabbath). Earlier, time flow was divided according to weather and similar seasonal changes. Under Islam, the week was given significance by assigning a special status to Friday (which is not a day of rest but rather a day of communal prayer).

TIME IS A MORAL DIMENSION

> By [the token of] Time [through the Ages],
> Verily Man is in loss,
> Except such as have faith and do righteous deeds and [join together] in the mutual teaching of truth and of patience and constancy. Qur'ān 103:1–3

There are numerous Qur'ānic references to man's time and God's time. It is stated, for example, that "He rules [all] affairs from the heavens to the earth: in the end will [all affairs] go up to Him, on a Day, the space whereof will be [as] a thousand years of your reckoning" (32:5). Creation, as well, is said to have been effected in six days (32:4). Exegetes often emphasize that each of the divine days of creation, before the placement of the sun, corresponds to 1000 mortal years (and, in 70:4, to 50,000 years). Muslim scholars reiterate, however, that Allah is in no way bound by time, for He is totally transcendent.

The point, they teach, is that throughout the course of human history God maintains full control over His Creation. In His mercy he provided man with a window to His will and commanded him in the straight path. When time ends, at judgment, man will face his time compacted to God's scale. "In the immense future all affairs will go up to Him, for He will be the Judge, and His restoration of all values will be as a day or an hour or the twinkling of an eye; and yet to our idea it will be a thousand years" (Abdullâh Yûsuf Alî, *Commentary on the Holy Qur'ân*).

Time's purpose is to serve as an arena of moral action. It is the place which God has established for the exercise of will. Judgment and consequent assignment to paradise or hell-fire will mean the end of time; thus time serves solely as the setting for man's surrender (*Islâm*) to God.

[M.S.S.]

FURTHER READINGS

Houfsma, M. Th., et al., eds. *Encyclopedia of Islam*. 1st ed. Leiden: E.J. Brill, 1913–36. (See under mik̲āt, ta'rîkh, and zamân.)

Lazarus-Yafeh, Hava. *Some Religious Aspects of Islam*. Leiden: E.J. Brill, 1981.

Mernissi, Fatima. "The Muslim and Time." *The Veil and the Male Elite*. Reading: Addison-Wesley, 1991. 15–24.

Von Grunebaum, Gustave E. *Muhammadan Festivals*. 1951; reprint, London: Curzon P, 1976.

ISOLATION

Virtually all investigations of the perception of relatively long intervals of time involve a certain degree of isolation. As reported by J. Aschoff in 1985 and S.S. Campbell in 1990, the very nature of the experimental conditions under which most such studies have been conducted dictate that subjects are isolated not only from cues to time of day, but from social, environmental, and many behavioral cues as well. As such, most studies of long-term time perception in humans

are germane to the issue of isolation. Here, however, a narrower focus will be taken in order to examine a specific question regarding possible effects of the *degree* of isolation on time estimation: is "empty" time perceived differently than relatively "filled" time? Or, stated differently, does time fly when the subject being investigated is having fun?

It is generally acknowledged that an interval filled with some activity or sensory stimulation is perceived to pass more quickly than an "empty" interval of the same duration, during which one simply sits. This result has been found in virtually all studies investigating the perception of short intervals. However, the finding by Aschoff that short-term and long-term time estimations are probably mediated by different mechanisms, and therefore not necessarily subject to influence by the same factors, raises the possibility that the latter may not be influenced in the same way by the nature of the interval to be estimated. A comparison of the results of two studies conducted in the same laboratory, but under very different conditions, suggests that in the case of long-term estimation, the *degree* of isolation does not directly affect the manner in which the passage of time is perceived.

In the first study, as reported by P. Lavie and W.B. Webb, subjects lived individually in a time-free environment for two weeks, during which they were encouraged to maintain a daily schedule of activities. In the second study, as reported by Campbell in 1986, subjects lived in the same time-free environment for sixty consecutive hours, but they were confined to bed for the entire period and were prohibited from reading, writing, listening to music, and so on. Thus, subjects in the first condition may be viewed as estimating filled time, whereas those in the bed rest condition were clearly judging the passage of empty time.

In both cases, subjects were asked to estimate the time of day at irregular intervals throughout the study. Under the assumption that filled time passes more quickly than empty time, it would be expected that subjects in the extremely monotonous bed rest condition would underestimate the passage of time to a much greater extent than those studied by Lavie and Webb. This was not the case, however. The average subjective "empty" hour continued for precisely the same duration—1.12 hours—as the "filled" hour. Furthermore, J. A. Vernon and T. E. McGill have reported time estimates obtained from subjects living under even more drastic conditions of complete sensory deprivation which resulted in an average subjective hour of a similar duration (1.08 hours).

These findings clearly suggest that of itself the degree of isolation has little direct impact on the way in which people perceive the passage of relatively long intervals. However, as Campbell argued in 1986, to the extent that isolation is associated with environments and behaviors that deviate significantly from prior experience, this feature of the environment may be intimately tied to the accuracy with which the passage of time is estimated. In general, the less structured the environment, the less precise our estimation of the passage of time.

[S.S.C.]

See also **Biological Rhythms and Psychological Time; Psychology of Time; Time Perception.**

FURTHER READINGS

Aschoff, J. "On the Perception of Time During Prolonged Temporal Isolation." *Human Neurobiology* 4 (1985): 41–52.

Campbell, S.S. "Estimation of Empty Time." *Human Neurobiology* 5 (1986): 205–207.

———. "Circadian Rhythms and Human Temporal Experience." *Cognitive Models of Psychological Time.* Ed. R.A. Block. Hillsdale: Erlbaum, 1990. 101–118.

Lavie, P., and W.B. Webb. "Time Estimates in a Long-Term Time-Free Environment." *American Journal of Psychology* 88.2 (1975): 177–186.

Vernon, J.A., and T.E. McGill. "Time Estimations During Sensory Deprivation." *Journal of General Psychology* 69 (1963): 11–18.

JAINISM

Jainism, like Buddhism, originated in India in the sixth century B.C. as a movement of ascetics determined to win liberation from the endless cycles of rebirth (*saṃāra*) caused by *karma*. Their ultimate end was the return to a state of monadic bliss, *kaivalya*, a condition beyond matter and *karma*.

In order to rationalize their practices the Jains had to place them into the context of a well-developed cosmology. According to Jain teaching, the whole universe is composed of (combinations of) six *dravyas* (substances, elements) namely *jīva* (living soul), *pudgala* (matter), *dharma* (principle of motion), *adharma* (principle of rest), *ākāsa* (space or ether), and *kāla* (time). The first five are called *āstikāya*, possessing bodies—time is described as "without a body." Time is not only seen as atomic, but the time atoms can neither join to form larger units (as the other elements can do) nor combine with other elements. This understanding of time as atomic, absolute, and real is distinguished from the notion of conventional time that the Jains share with the rest of the people in India. Absolute time underlies conventional time. Absolute time is the cause for the changes (birth, growth, and decay) in all things. Absolute, atomic time, has no beginning and no end—conventional time has both beginning and end. No two instants can be found simultaneously; but each instant is indestructible. The *Dravyasaṃgraha* uses the following illustration: As heaps of diamonds consist of individual diamonds (which do not combine or fuse), so each region of the universe has a unit of time different from the others; since the regions are innumerable there is an infinite number of atoms of time, which exist independently and discretely from each other. One of the most authoritative texts, the *Sarvārthasiddhi*, says that "The function of time is to assist the substances in their continuity of being, in their modifications, in their movements and in their priority and posteriority." The commentary on his *sūtra* speaks of "two kinds of time: real time and conventional time. Real time is established by continuity of beings, and conventional time by modifications. Conventional time is threefold: past, present and future. In real time the conception of time is of primary importance, and the notion of past, present and future is secondary. In conventional time, the notion of past, present and future is of primary importance, and the idea of time is subordinate. Conventional time depends on the

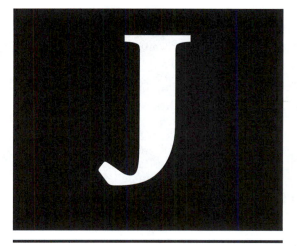

substances endowed with activity and on real time." The text also tells us that "time is a substance like space," and that the static particles of time exist throughout the entire universe-space, each time atom being located in a space-point. "Those innumerable substances, which exist one by one in every unit of the universe-space, like heaps of jewels, are the points of time." They are devoid of qualities such as shape and color and are thus immaterial. "The present consists of one instant. Still, time is said to consist of infinite instants, as the instants of the past and the future are infinite."

[K.K.K.]

See also **Buddhism; Hinduism; Indian Traditions and Time.**

FURTHER READINGS

Balslev, A.N. *A Study of Time in Indian Philosophy.* Wiesbaden: Harrassowitz, 1983.

Jain, S.A., trans. *Śrī Pujyapāda's Sarvārthasiddhi.* Calcutta: Vira Sasana Sangha, 1969.

Mandal, Kumar Kishore. *A Comparative Study of the Concepts of Space and Time in Indian Thought.* Varanasi: Chowkhambha, 1968.

Schubring, Walther. *The Doctrine of the Jainas.* Varanasi: Motilal Banarsidass, 1962.

Shanta, N. *La voie jaina.* Paris: O.E.I.L., 1985.

JAMES, WILLIAM (AS PHILOSOPHER) (1842–1910)

James is a process philosopher for whom stasis of any kind is problematic, whether of being, conceptualization, scientific facts, or moral absolutes. Therefore, his writings question how stabilities have arisen, been taken for granted, and are no longer questioned, in order to recover the indeterminacy at the core of existence and the sense of self as the ordering center of experience. Since "the fundamental fact about our experience is that it is a process of change," he raises the crucial questions of what sort of change ought to be brought about, by whom, and for what ends. As humans we are not only "incurably rooted in the temporal point of view," but also exhibit continuity over time rather than a substantial identity of self. Even the smallest pulse of consciousness includes a consciousness of passing time. The literal or specious present does not exist (although it can be conceptualized), but only the passing moment, with past and future intermixed. Even a minimal feeling has reference to the future and consists of a continuity of an earlier and a later. Thought is always off balance and in transition; its essential characteristic is this rush of thought forward through its fringes. Ideas are thus anticipations. Thinking is defined in James's *Principles of Psychology* (1890) as "a cognitive phenomenal event in time."

Temporality is a central aspect of the fringe or horizon which affects all of James's positions. In response to Darwin's demonstration that species are not natural kinds but processes of change over time and Hegel's and Comte's contentions that human consciousness developed in predictable and progressive stages, James sought to counteract the nihilistic conclusion that human events are mindlessly determined by mechanistic evolutionary forces. His radically pragmatic perspective emphasized the fragility of developmental processes and the possibilities inherent in the emergence of consciousness for guiding the further evolution of the natural and social worlds. Since temporality enters into the very constitution of the universe and of our appropriations of it, James emphasizes the finite and tentative character of all our interpretations or claims about reality, which seek to order experiences according to ends-in-view. We order experience according to selective interests because we are not passive spectators but participants already interactive with environing conditions, conscious organisms which are simultaneously the result and source of genuine novelty in the universe. Earlier moments develop into later ones, which reinterpret and correct them.

When the more narrowly cognitive dimension of such appropriations are the subject of inquiry, it is more accurate to speak of hypotheses or interpretations rather than truths or even propositions, because we are within the process and have no privileged access to ultimate reality. Interpretations are in principle always revisable because they are temporal negotiations which can only be judged by their success in satisfying the criteria we ourselves set. The satisfactions James has in mind are variously expressed as the completion of the reflex arc of incoming stimuli with outgoing response as intentionally rearranged, the successful marriage of previously funded experience with novel events or of intention with intentional object, and leadings that are worthwhile. Epistemological satisfactoriness cannot be determined apart from values or choice of good. Such undertakings are pluralistic and perspectival, since different angles of vision and interactions disclose or bring about different realities. As James stated in *A Pluralistic Universe* (1909), "What really *exists* is not things made, but things in the making."

[C.H.S.]

See also **James, William (as Psychologist); Pragmatism.**

FURTHER READINGS

Myers, Gerald. *William James: His Life and Thought.* New Haven: Yale UP, 1986.

Seigfried, Charlene Haddock. *William James's Radical Reconstruction of Philosophy.* Albany: State U of New York P, 1990.

JAMES, WILLIAM (AS PSYCHOLOGIST) (1842–1910)

William James, the pioneering American philosopher and psychologist, included a chapter on the psychology of time in his classic book, *The Principles of Psychology*. (The chapter is an almost verbatim reprint of an article published earlier in the *Journal of Speculative Philosophy*; James included a much shorter version in his subsequent book, *Psychology: Briefer Course.*) In this chapter, James reviewed research and, if there was little or no evidence on a topic, speculated. His conjectures were remarkably prescient, which partly explains why scientists continue to cite the work of someone who published essentially only one article on psychological time. Psychologists (for example, several of those represented in R.A. Block's *Cognitive Models of Psychological Time*) most frequently cite James's discussion of these issues: (1) the "sensible present," or "specious present"; (2) the transition from simultaneity to successiveness; and (3) the differences between experiences of time in passing and in retrospect.

James said that "the practically cognized present is no knife-edge, but a saddle-back, with a certain breadth of its own on which we sit perched, and from which we look in two directions into time." Its "nucleus is probably the dozen seconds or less that have just elapsed." This fits nicely with evidence that recently attended information remains in working memory for about ten to fifteen seconds.

James correctly concluded that the psychological transition from simultaneity to successiveness is in the range of several milliseconds, but that a longer time period is needed for someone to judge correctly the order of several very brief stimuli.

James distinguished between duration experiences in passing and in retrospect, and he also speculated about the effects of information content: "In general, a time filled with varied and interesting experiences seems short in passing, but long as we look back. On the other hand, a tract of time empty of experiences seems long in passing, but in retrospect short." To explain these effects, James said that tracts of time in passing seem longer when "we grow attentive to the passage of time itself," whereas the "length in retrospect depends obviously on the multitudinousness of the memories which the time affords." Recent experimental evidence tends to support these claims. Experienced duration, or prospective judgment, lengthens as attention to time increases, whereas remembered duration, or retrospective judgment, lengthens as memory contents change (although precisely what aspects of memory are involved remains unclear).

James did use some questionable terminology, such as in his titles, "The Perception of Time" in *The Principles of Psychology* and "The Sense of Time" in *Psychology: Briefer Course*. Many psychologists now think (along with J.J. Gibson) that events are perceivable but that time is neither perceived nor sensed. James also discussed some currently discredited ideas, such as the notion that there is an absolute "indifference-point," or "an interval which we judge with maximum accuracy." Some of James's speculation, such as that concerning brain processes involved in temporal experiences, is vague, incorrect, or dated. Psychologists usually overlook these aspects of James's chapter and focus instead on how he lucidly defined several issues that they are still investigating.

[R.A.B.]

See also **Memory for Time; Prospective and Retrospective Time; Psychological Present; Psychology of Time; Simultaneity, Successiveness, and Temporal-Order Judgments.**

FURTHER READINGS

Block, Richard A., ed. *Cognitive Models of Psychological Time*. Hillsdale: Erlbaum, 1990.

James, William. *The Principles of Psychology: Volume 1.* New York: Henry Holt, 1890. Chapter 15.

———. *Psychology: Briefer Course*. New York: Henry Holt, 1892. Chapter 17.

JAZZ

Jazz is music of the invented moment. It is a stylistically varied music with a history encompassing this century. From early Dixieland, to big band swing, to bebop, to the avant-garde of the 1970s, to the post-bebop of the early 1990s, the element most common to all of these styles is spontaneous improvisation in rhythmic musical phrases that are sonically derived from the expressive richness of the voice. Given the vocal orientation of jazz, its temporality is closely aligned to that of discursive speech. The significance of jazz as a musical language is not to be found in the structures of large-scale musical forms but rather in momentary and possibly surprising musical events within the context of a pulse-driven rhythm. Moreover, there is a greater tendency to value flashes of intuition and emotion than there is to value dispassionate musical thought and the comprehension of a composition through memory.

In fact, there is little in jazz that requires the use of long-term memory from the listener. (Rare exceptions are found in music composed by Duke Ellington and in that arranged by Gil Evans.) Jazz improvisation is usually supported by a repeating or continually recycling harmonic and/or melodic structure of relatively short length. (Song forms—on which much of jazz is based—generally do not exceed a length of thirty-two bars in a meter of four, or precisely 128 beats. The only indigenous harmonic and song form in jazz is the blues, which traditionally is twelve bars of a four-beat meter in length, or forty-eight beats.) In the case of the avant garde, or "free jazz" (a term originating with the music of Ornette Coleman in the late 1950s), such structures often do not exist. Avant-garde jazz improvisation may take the form of a "free association" or a "stream of consciousness" with any or none of the musicians taking a soloist role. In both cyclical and free-form structures, when each musician takes a turn at assuming a predominately solo role, he or she may perform in an individualistic manner, or at least in a fashion idiomatic to his or her instrument. This often results in remarkable contrasts as a succession of improvisations ensue. The stark individualism of each musician, plus the context of either a short cyclical or a free-form structure, alleviates the need for formal structures that extend much beyond the present moment.

Although large ensembles may rely to a significant degree on notated music, interaction between musicians in smaller ensembles is to some extent dependent upon established roles (chordal accompaniment, rhythmic accompaniment, and so on) that are mutually supportive and interactive. Even though the focus of public awareness has often been on the solo virtuosi in jazz who have a special musical identity or "voice" (such as Louis Armstrong, Benny Goodman, Art Tatum, Billie Holiday, Charlie Parker, John Coltrane, Miles Davis, to name a few), the success of those virtuosi would never have been possible without the context of a supporting and interactive ensemble. Jazz rhythm is the cohesive and underlying force in creating a unified interactive texture.

However, jazz rhythm is somewhat enigmatic. It produces an interesting tension through the practice of what is commonly called "swing." Swing can best be described as a *perpetual rhythmic motion* created by transferring the melodic or rhythmic emphasis from the stable arrival points (rest beats) in a metric structure to the motion points (motion beats). There are several ways in which this is effected:

1. Jazz musicians tend to place individual notes as anticipations and delays of rest beats. In a meter of four beats, the first and third beats are rest beats—or stable arrival points—while the second and fourth beats are motion beats, in that they are unstable points moving to or from rest beats. A four-beat meter, the one most commonly used in jazz, is somewhat complex in that it is really the composite of two two-beat meters, with the second half of the meter having less stability than the first. Therefore, beats one and three in a measure of four beats could both be considered as rest beats, but beat one provides the greater rest or arrival point. On the other hand, while both beats two and four are considered motion beats, beat four—due to its closer proximity to beat one—has the greater instability and, therefore, greater value as a motion beat.

2. When playing eighth notes (or two notes to a beat), instrumentalists will emphasize the second or the motion half of individual beats. At slow tempos, this is exaggerated by dividing a beat into triplets (three equal parts) and, although only two notes are played per beat, the second note is emphasized more by accenting it and placing it on the last third of the beat.

3. Drummers maintain the normal rest-motion structure by playing single notes on beats one and three and a "skip beat" (which precisely uses the same exaggerated device of two notes played with a triplet subdivision) on beats two and four with the "ride cymbal" (a large single cymbal). However, they emphasize simultaneously the motion aspect by playing the "high hat" (double cymbals played by the foot) on beats two and four exclusively, thereby creating an "unstable stability." This leaves them free to improvise rhythms on other drums and cymbals with the free hand and foot.

Despite an emphasis on momentary inventiveness and endless improvisational variation, there is little music in jazz that one could describe accurately as being non-goal-oriented. (The music of Ornette Coleman, Cecil Taylor, Albert Ayler, and John Coltrane provides some notable exceptions, created at a time when composers of classical music were also producing non-goal-oriented music.) Many factors—relatively clear musical phrases, often combined with goal-oriented harmonic structures, reasonably short lengths of entire musical selections, and definitive beginnings and endings—provide the listener with information about the music's past, present, and future. Nevertheless, the music's passion is in the moment. In jazz, there is no need to reinterpret the past through the present, to understand the present through the past, or to anticipate the future.

[D.M.]

See also **Music: Africa; Music: American Avant-Garde; Music: Rock; Music: Western; Rhythm and Meter in Music; Tempo.**

FURTHER READINGS
Kramer, Jonathan. *The Time of Music.* New York: Schirmer, 1988.

JEFFERSON, THOMAS (1743–1826)

More than any other colonial American, Jefferson had a lifetime preoccupation with time and its application. From his student days at the College of William and Mary to the end of his life, he habitually recorded statistics in pocket memorandum books. The entries related to various forms of measurement, whether of cash expenditures, of degrees of physical effort and the time required for them, or of unusual proportions he encountered. He recorded, for example, the time required to ferry a vessel across a river, and for a man to dig a grave. While his home at Monticello was under construction, he noted that a man could fill a two-wheel barrow in three minutes and move it a distance of thirty yards in $1^1/_2$ minutes and that it equaled four loads of a barrow having one wheel. Emerging from these notations was Jefferson's concern with the maximal use of time and motion, a concern which became a characteristic throughout his life. He may be considered as the first to devise "time and motion" studies. "No person will have occasion to complain of the want of time who never loses any," he admonished his young daughter Martha in 1787.

It is not surprising, therefore, that Jefferson had a particular preoccupation with clocks and watches, and that he acquired a large number of them both for his own use and for use as gifts. It was his practice to present each of his children and grandchildren with pocket watches when they reached a certain age.

When Jefferson required timepieces for particular purposes, he designed his own. While in France as minister plenipotentiary, he provided a sketch with measurements for a timepiece he desired for his mantelpiece which he called his "obelisk clock." Presently on display at Monticello, it was made of black marble, with the movement supported between two obelisks. It was while serving his final year as secretary of state in Philadelphia that he designed and ordered a special timepiece to be installed over the main entrance in the reception hall of Monticello. Jefferson provided written specifications for the timepiece to Philadelphia clockmaker Robert Leslie in 1793, and it was constructed by Leslie's journeyman, Peter Spruck. The clock was equipped with two dials or "faces" so that the time could be viewed inside the house as well as under the portico outside the mansion. The clock, still in operation at Monticello, strikes the hours on a copper gong installed on the roof so that it can be heard throughout the grounds as well as inside the mansion. Power for the clock is provided by cannonball-shaped iron weights attached to wires which descend along the wall into the basement. Eight weights on the left

control the striking, and those on the right control the time. The wall against which the time weights travel is marked at appropriate intervals with the names of the days of the week so that the falling top weight indicates the day and serves as a weekly calendar.

As he had need of them, Jefferson designed further timepieces for purposes other than the domestic measurement of time. In 1811, after his retirement from government, he required a precision timepiece for making astronomical observations of eclipses and other celestial phenomena. From Philadelphia clockmaker Thomas Voight he ordered a tall-case weight-driven regulator clock to be made according to his specifications. It is "intended for astronomical purposes only," he wrote, to be "divested of all apparatus for striking or for any other purpose," although it was also to indicate seconds. Jefferson marked the back wall of the clockcase with the names of the days of the week so that the descending top weight also provided him with a weekly calendar, as did the clock in the entrance hall.

While supervising the construction of the University of Virginia in his final years, Jefferson arranged for the addition of a public clock in the rotunda on campus. It was constructed according to his design by noted Massachusetts clockmaker Simon Willard. The clock remained a favorite landmark of the students from its installation in 1827 until a fire destroyed the rotunda in 1895.

[S.A.B.]

FURTHER READINGS

Bedini, Silvio A. "Thomas Jefferson and His Watches." *Hobbies Magazine* (February 1957): 36, 46–47.

———. "Thomas Jefferson, Clock Designer." *Proceedings of the American Philosophical Society* 108.3 (June 1964): 163–180.

———. *Thomas Jefferson Statesman of Science.* New York: Macmillan, 1990.

Tuttle, Kate A. "The First Bell and Clock of the University." *Alumni Bulletin* (University of Virginia) (February 1899): 111–113.

JOHNSON, SAMUEL (1709–1784)

"Time is, of all modes of existence, most obsequious to the imagination; a lapse of years is as easily conceived as a passage of hours." Upon this challenging premise Johnson builds his famous argument in the *Preface to Shakespeare* against the unity of time. To those who insisted that plays should confine their action to events of a single day (or less) and accordingly damned Shakespeare for violating this rule, Johnson replied by appealing to every reader's actual experience of time perception. He adds that "In contemplation we easily contract the time of real actions, and therefore willingly permit it to be contracted when we only see their imitation." There is thus no reason why a long interval cannot be supposed to have elapsed between a play's scenes. An epistemological disagreement underlies the dispute between Johnson and strict adherents to neoclassical dogmas about the unity of time.

Johnson's views on time perception are Lockean in the sense of being either derived from or in agreement with the remarks on duration in the *Essay Concerning Human Understanding* by John Locke. Equally important is the fact that Johnson shared Locke's empirical inclination to avoid abstract theorizing about time in favor of examining the way it is really perceived. Johnson also read treatises on chronology. These along with Locke's *Essay* furnished Johnson with a vocabulary of time words that he adapted to his purposes.

As a moralist, Johnson takes up *memento mori* themes and in other conventional ways stresses the importance of considering human relationships to time and eternity. His moral outlook on time is distinctive for the extent to which he portrays its benefits as well as its threats. Time is in Johnson's view not merely a source of pain and anxiety. Thus, in *Rasselas*, Nekayah finds it impossible to continue intensely grieving over the abduction of Pekuah. Time heals. Johnson's moral writings reflect the two ideas of time that have dominated Western thought: a tragic view of time the destroyer, our invincible antagonist; and a more reassuring view that, as Shakespeare put it in a line that Johnson quotes in his *Dictionary*, "Time is the nurse and breeder of all good." The latter view prevails in Johnson's criticism, which also takes up a remarkably wide range of relationships between reading time, writing time, time within narratives, and the clock time marking individual lives and the development of nations. Only a few examples can be given here.

In the *Preface to Shakespeare,* Johnson also insists that because all judgments except those involving morality are relative, the ultimate test of artistry is time: "length of duration and continuance of esteem." The best works will survive. For Johnson, criticism is an exercise in comparative literature that involves cross-temporal comparisons even more crucially than cross-cultural comparisons: "What mankind have long possessed they have often examined and compared; and if they persist to value the possession, it is because frequent comparisons have confirmed opinion in its favor." Implicit here as in Johnson's other criticism, and also in his discussions of moral topics, is a linear rather than cyclical view of cultural time. The test of time would be neither decisive nor really a test if the reputation of literary works merely ran in cycles.

Johnson believed in a general advance of judgment over time. "Nations, like individuals, have their infancy," he remarks in the *Preface to Shakespeare*, thus applying to literary history a familiar organic metaphor of linear progression through time from childhood to maturity. Since cultural time does not run in circles, it follows that there should be no regression to the standards that pleased during national infancy, and that some older works could even slip downward to become children's literature. This Johnson believed is the fate of medieval romances because of their reliance on magic, dragons, and the like, marvels that more advanced eras reject as impossible. In his *Miscellaneous Observations on the Tragedy of Macbeth*, Johnson suggests that only the modern reader's historical sense spares works like *Macbeth* from similar degradation: "A poet who should now make the whole action of his tragedy depend upon enchantment, and produce the chief events by the assistance of supernatural agents, would be censured as transgressing the bounds of probability, he would be banished from the theatre to the nursery, and condemned to write fairy tales instead of tragedies." This is a dismissive view of children's literature—and by implication also of most outright fantasy—as something that all readers ought to outgrow and that the best writers should avoid. But it also displays Johnson's acute awareness of literature's involvement with cultural time.

In *Rambler* 36, Johnson applies more positively to pastorals his notion that some genres have an appeal linked to the various stages of individual and cultural development from childhood onward. In opposition to those who saw pastorals as works whose action is set in a mythic past, he defines the genre by its "confinement to rural imagery." He associates pastoral with the beginnings of poetry itself in the remote past as well as with childhood reading, but says that we do not "throw it away among other childish amusements and pastimes, but willingly return to it in any hour of indolence and relaxation. . . . In childhood we turn our thoughts to the country, as to the region of pleasure, we recur to it in old age as a port of rest, and perhaps with that . . . gladness, which every man feels on reviewing those places, or recollecting those occurrences, that contributed to his youthful enjoyments and bring him back to the prime of life." Here, in addition to an almost Wordsworthian emphasis on the sustaining power of remembering country landscapes, Johnson characteristically stresses several time dimensions of reading: pastorals are for lazy hours of relaxation; their worth is measured by their continuing appeal during all stages of life, especially childhood and old age; they may induce remembrance amounting to a kind of mental time travel "back to the prime of life." Thus for older readers, Johnson proposes pastorals as a way of inaugurating an almost Proustian search for lost time.

A linear concept of distinct stages of intellectual development over time also underlies Johnson's references to reading as a means of initiation into adulthood. He mentions the *Tatler* and *Spectator*, but the most important class of initiatory literature in Johnson's view was the eighteenth century's major new genre, the realistic novel. In *Rambler* 4, Johnson remarks that novels "are written chiefly to the young, the ignorant, and the idle, to whom they serve as . . . introductions to life. . . . The purpose of these writings is . . . to initiate youth by mock encounters." He regards novels as less remarkable for the new realism introduced by Richardson and Fielding than for creating a strong appeal to young people that brings with it special moral demands on novelists to avoid attractive portraits of evil characters who might become objects of imitation. Here Johnson defines a genre primarily in terms of time relationships between works and readers. Relationships between time and writers figure most significantly in Johnson's observations about periodical literature. In *Rambler* 145, he considers essayists (like himself) who "perceive no particular summons to composition except the sound of the clock." Johnson understood that ascendancy of the printing press and the journalism it spawned profoundly changed the relationship to time of readers, writers, and literature: we live in a world dominated by writing done to the sound of the clock.

[P.K.A.]

See also **Chronology; Dramatic Unities; Locke, John; Proust, Marcel.**

FURTHER READINGS

Alkon, Paul. "Johnson and Chronology." *Greene Centennial Studies: Essays Presented to Donald Greene in the Centennial Year of the University of Southern California.* Ed. Paul J. Korshin and Robert R. Allen. Charlottesville: UP of Virginia, 1984. 143–171.

———. "Johnson and Time Criticism." *Modern Philology* 85.4 (1988): 543–557.

Gaba, Phyllis. "'A Succession of Amusements': The Moralization in *Rasselas* of Locke's Account of Time." *Eighteenth-Century Studies* 10 (1977): 451–463.

Tillotson, Geoffrey. "Time in *Rasselas*." *Augustan Studies.* London: Athlone P, 1961. Chapter 13.

Vance, John A. *Samuel Johnson and the Sense of History.* Athens: U of Georgia P, 1984.

JUDEO-CHRISTIAN TRADITIONS ON TIME

Medieval divines—Jewish, Christian, and Muslim—routinely dealt with time in the context of eternity: their theocentric conception of the universe (which they shared with the neo-Platonic thinkers) led them to assume that time was not the only form of duration of being, but that time, the specific mode of human existence, was originating from, and enveloped by, the mode of existence of God, which is to say, eternity.

This was seen as the message of the Bible, too. God created the world in time. With creation time began; but time was preceded by God's own eternity which continued to coexist with it in a mysterious manner. The eternal God was believed to have created sun and moon, by whose movements humans measured time and distinguished days and nights, weeks and fortnights, years and generations. At the end of times, God would roll up the heavens like a parchment—sun and moon would no longer be, and time would cease to exist—but God and His elect would continue to exist in an eternity beyond time. Time was seen of relevance only as religiously meaningful time, as time of salvation, as time to be used for the sake of eternity. Such time was especially the time of the divinely instituted feasts. These privileged times were seen as different from ordinary times. Ecclesiasticus, in the apocryphal text, asks, "Why is one day better than another, when each day's light throughout the year comes from the sun?" And he answers, "They have been differentiated in the mind of the Lord, who has diversified the seasons and feasts; some He has made more important and hallowed, others He has made ordinary days" (33:7ff.). The sabbath, the holy day, believed to have been instituted by God at the time of creation of the world, was kept sacred by a great many generations of Jews: during the Sabbath all ordinary work-a-day activity had to cease and the mind turn toward eternity. A special rite was introduced to part ordinary time from holy time at the beginning of each sabbath. One of the most quoted biblical texts is certainly Ecclesiastes 3:1ff.: "To all things there is a set time, and a time for every matter under the heavens—a time to be born and a time to die—a time to plant and a time to pull up what is planted, a time to kill and a time to heal. . . a time to weep and a time to laugh." The writer obviously implied that God has set the time for everything.

When the Jewish people were scattered into the Diaspora, they had to articulate their views vis-à-vis the major philosophies developed by the classical world.

Moses Maimonides (1135–1204), who wrote his *Guide for the Perplexed* in order to provide a Jewish answer to the questions of the philosophical schools, combined Jewish tradition with Aristotelian philosophical notions of time: "Time itself is among the things created; for time depends on motion, i.e. on an accident in things which move, and the things upon whose motion time depends are themselves created beings, which have passed from nonexistence to existence."

With the Enlightenment and the end of scholasticism, both the authority of Aristotle and his notion of time as an accident were generally given up—by gentile as well as Jewish thinkers. History became the paradigm of the new scholarship, and evolution and progress in time were the foci for the new sciences. Biblical religion began to be seen as a history of salvation. Thus Joshua Heschel (1907–1973) calls Judaism "a religion of history, a religion of time. The God of Israel was not found primarily in the facts of nature. He spoke through events in history." And as he puts it, "Important to the biblical understanding of history is not only the conception of a chosen people but also the concept of a chosen time; the election of a day, not only of a people." For Heschel this belief has important corollaries: "We believe that history as a whole has a meaning that transcends that of its parts. We must remember that God is involved in our doings, that meaning is given not only in the timeless, but primarily in the timely, in that task given here and now. . . . In its happenings we hear the voice as well as the silence of God."

Christian understandings of time parallel the Jewish notions, resting as they do on the Bible and the concept of *creatio ex nihilo*. On specific issues Christian thinkers adopt either Platonic or Aristotelian notions of time.

Thus Augustine, after admitting in *Confessions* 11 that "if nobody asked him, he knew what time was, but when asked, he would not know," locates the passage of time in consciousness. Our estimate of time is conditioned by expectation, attention, and memory, and time originated only after the creation of mutable beings. There is no empty time, as there is no empty space.

Thomas Aquinas, the most comprehensive thinker of the Middle Ages, undeterred by neo-Platonic criticism, fully endorses and defends Aristotle's notion of time, "the number of motion according to the before and after" (*numerus motus secundum prius et posterius*). Aquinas deals with the essence of time in the context of a treatise on God's eternity. After having ascertained that God is absolutely immutable, because of His being "pure act" without any potentiality and absolutely "whole" and indivisible, he approvingly refers to certain ancients who "as if compelled by truth itself, postulated an immobile first principle." In contrast to the deity it is the characteristic of all creatures to be mutable, always in the vicinity of nonexistence. In spite of his Aristotelian concept of time Aquinas adopts the neo-Platonic definition of eternity which Boethius had bequeathed to Christianity, namely "the complete and simultaneous possession of endless life" (*interminabilis vitae tota simul et perfecta possessio*). In contrast to Plotinus, who had maintained that an appropriate notion of the essential nature of time had to be arrived at from a true notion of eternity, Aquinas states that "as we arrive at the cognition of simple entities through composite entities, so we must come to a notion of eternity through a cognition of time." Not to leave any doubt about his intentions, he adds that "As the essence of time consists in numbering of the before and after in movement, thus in the apprehension of the uniformity of that, which is totally outside movement, consists the essence of eternity." Contrasting our perception of time with our sense of eternity, he explains that "As the apprehension of time is caused in us by our apprehension of the *flux* of the very now, thus the apprehension of eternity in us is caused insofar we apprehend the *standing* now." Eternity, he asserts, is nothing other but God himself.

Aquinas, with many other medieval theologians, accepted a mode of existence in between time and eternity, for which he chose the term *aevum*. Etymologically closely related to the Greek *aion* (and the Sanskrit *ayus*), it acquired in scholastic writings a specific meaning, designating the mode of existence of "separate intellectual substances" (called "angels" in Christianity), who relate differently both to eternity and to time. Aquinas is convinced of the necessity of postulating incorporeal creatures, given the nature of the created universe, which has to contain all possible kinds of creatures. He insists that they even exist in a "maximum number" exceeding all numbers of material entities. He attributes to them "virtual quantity" and says that "they are in a corporeal place not as contained but as somehow containing it." In consequence of the virtuality of the quantity of such beings they can move locally, but their movement is not continuous. Since they are in a locality only by way of virtual contact their movement is such a discontinuous (discrete) series of virtual contacts. Their movement, however, can be said to be in time, since there is a before and an after in it. The *aevum* can be called an "infinity of time" but it is not eternity in the sense of the divine eternity, nor is it "endless time." The "spiritual creatures" participate in three different modes of existence: "as far as their affections and insights go, where there is succession, they are in time . . . whereas regarding their natures they are measured by the *aevum* . . . what regards their vision of the divine glory they participate in eternity." Aquinas maintains that "our intellectual nature is per se beyond time." Our sensual nature, however, is subject to time. He adds that "All those acts, and only those, which look forward to gaining something in the future for the perfection of their kind are in time." Against the concept of the unity of time which Plotinus and the Platonists put forth, Aquinas makes a distinction in time: "In time there is something which is indivisible, namely the moment. And something which is continuing, namely time. But in eternity that which is indivisible and that which continues is one and the same."

Christian theologians of the modern period were less interested in the traditional issues of time and eternity dealt with by the scholastics. They focused instead on the "Heilsgeschichte" aspect, the historicity of revelation and the events reported in the Bible. The denominational strife following the split of Christendom, first into an Eastern and a Western part, then into factions within Western Christianity, turned attention of Christian scholars to details of church history in order to defend their contradictory claims. Church history, history of doctrine, development of dogma, and juridical claims based on historic documents became the major focus of interest of Christian scholars, and little attention was devoted to fresh investigations of time and eternity.

Existentialism, which topicalized the temporality of being during the first half of the twentieth century, found some resonance in Christian theological circles, while major figures like Jacques Maritain, Paul Tillich, and Karl Rahner came close to articulating a kind of Christian existentialism. In the influential encyclopedic work, *Sacramentum Mundi* (published under the editorship of Karl Rahner and some of his prominent pupils), Adolf Darlap says in an article on time that "The theological question as regards 'time' must be posed in the context of the coming (or offer) of salvation, when man is summoned to decision, to accept salvation in fact, in his freedom. Hence the theological question does not start from a notion of time derived from the natural sciences. It is concerned with man's self-understanding as a being in need of and capable of salvation—an understanding which is prior to the view of man gained from science and technology." The author then proceeds in his theological interpretation of time by fully and uncritically taking over the Aristotelian notion of time, singling out as particularly "theologically relevant" (1) the element "of succession, movement, in the duration of the temporal," and (2) "'Internal,' qualitative, time, which is seen as filled with content and measured in terms of man—time as event." Again, while first considering "cyclic time" as the "internal time of experience [which] has not yet been truly a matter of reflection," he concludes the paragraph by stating, "Hence the two properties of time, the cyclic and the linear, are theologically indispensable."

Theology of time, proper, however, is developed under the heading "The Future as the Fullness of Time." There we learn that "Man is individually and socially a being who always keeps a step ahead of himself, so to speak. He makes himself what he is by planning his future and projecting himself into the future." In addition, "[The future] is composed of single and different elements whose time runs out, and whose space is cramped." Further, "The future is the uncontrollable and incomprehensible which is not amenable to man's power." And finally, "the future is never completely detached from the past and the present. It is necessarily derivative, since it comes from the past and the present. For the present is always generating the past, and thus creating the past that will be. . . . Past and present stem from the realm of futurity. All individual and social existence is ruled by the arrival of what is to come."

According to Darlap, accepting the future means openly and optimistically accepting both its uncertainty and its "inexorable unity" with past and present. The past must be approached with the same openness, for only by accepting the past as a determinant of the future can we properly understand historical change in either the individual or society. As for the present, it can only have meaning for Christians in the light of their promised future and the gift that it involves.

Darlap concludes his essay with the words of Karl Rahner: "The purposeful active, planned construction of the intramundane future, the liberation of man as far as possible from subjection to the forces of nature, the progressive socialization of man for the sake of the greatest possible deployment of individual liberty, are regarded by Christianity as a task imposed by the God-given nature of man. Man's duty lies here, and it is here that he fulfils his real religious task, the openness of freedom, in faith and hope, for the absolute future."

[K.K.K.]

See also **Aquinas, St. Thomas; Aristotle; Augustine; Plato; Plotinus.**

Further Readings

Dales, Richard C. "Time and Eternity in the Thirteenth Century." *Journal of the History of Ideas* 49.1 (January-March 1988): 27–45.

Darlap, Adolf. "Time." *Sacramentum Mundi: An Encyclopedia of Theology.* Ed. K. Rahner. Vol. 6. London: Burns & Oates, 1973.

Delling, A. "Chronos." *Theological Dictionary of the New Testament.* Ed. G. Kittel. Vol. 9. Grand Rapids: Eerdmans, 1976.

Gloy, Karen. "Die Struktur der Augustinischen Zeittheorie im XI. Buch der Confessiones." *Philosophisches Jahrbuch der Görresgesellschaft* 95.1 (1988): 72–95.

Heschel, Joshua. *God in Search of Man: A Philosophy of Judaism.* New York: Farrar, Strauss, and Giroux, 1976.

Maimonides, Moses. *The Guide for the Perplexed.* Trans. M. Friedlander. New York: Pardes Publishing House, 1946.

Mascall, E.L. *Theology and the Future.* London: Darton, Longman & Todd, 1968.

Mayer, Anneliese. "Zeit und Bewegung," and "Die Einheit und Einzigkeit der Zeit." *Metaphysische Hintergründe der spätscholastischen Naturphilosophie.* Rome: Edizioni di Storia e Letteratura, 1955. Chapters 2 and 3.

Moltmann, J. "The Time of Creation." *God in Creation.* London: SCM, 1985. Chapter 5.

Mouroux, J. *The Mystery of Time.* New York: Sheed & Ward, 1964.

JUNG, CARL GUSTAV (1875–1961)

Jung had two conceptions of the operation of time, one associated with Western philosophical traditions and connected to the idea of causality, the second associated with Chinese esoteric and what he called "synchronicity." The first concept was chronological or historical, the usual way that people describe events, attributing causal effects to a particular occurrence in past time. However, in the Basel public schools, Jung would have been well drilled in the work of Jakob Burkhardt, a native of Basel. As the eminent historian-author of *The Civilization of the Renaissance in Italy* (1860), he was at the height of his influence during Jung's childhood. Burkhardt's view that a culture might be studied not chronologically by events occurring in history but by its essential character—its *Zeitgeist*— had led him to focus on eternally recurring motifs or mythologems. This approach to cultural studies influenced Jung, and he later drew on Burkhardt (and Plato, Augustine, and Kant) for the concept of "primordial images" or, as he would come to call them after 1919, "archetypes." It was Jung's thinking about these anhistorical and autonomously operating structures of the collective unconscious that made possible his hypothesis during the 1920s of the operation of synchronicity. This "acausal connecting principle," as he thought of it, operated through archetypal process to link events *across* and *beyond* time, rather than within the sequential framework constituted by traditional Western notions of chronological time.

This second conception of time involved circumstances in which either psychological and physical events are related or two physical events are connected to each other. The chronological conception, which looks for the causal in the past, would consider such events to be at most coincidental. But when a cause cannot be identified, the circumstances could be regarded as a "meaningful coincidence" if the events have a meaning to the individual within the context of his or her life as a whole. Jung's conception of synchronicity takes the coincidence of events in space and time as meaning something more than mere chance. Synchronistic events are not causally connected, and yet they have a meaningful relationship to one another.

Jung's understanding of synchronicity was the outcome of a long development. Two centuries before Jung, David Hume shook the philosophic world by demonstrating logically that causality is not something we actually see but rather an imputation that we read into events. According to the traditional illustration, all we perceive is one billiard ball touching another with a certain force, and then we see the second ball move away. We do not actually "see" the causality: we only infer it.

By stressing this point, Hume raised some very important issues, although he himself did not press the matter very far. All he wanted to show, he said in his *Treatise of Human Nature*, was that from the epistemological point of view, causality cannot be proven as an objective truth. Nevertheless, he conceded that for practical purposes it is necessary to believe in causality as though we knew it to be a reality. On this basis, Hume developed the idea that because of the necessities of life, causality has been accepted by everyone as the practical basis of social activity. He was still thinking in rationalistic terms, but since he was a historian as well as a philosopher, the idea suggested itself to him that causality might best be understood as a phenomenon of culture in the context of history.

It was thus in direct continuation of Hume's thought that American sociologist Thorstein Veblen, who had studied Hume and Kant very closely, added his profound analysis to show that the imputations of causality arise as "habits of thought." Veblen agreed with Hume's basic point that causality is not a truth inherent in the things themselves, but is rather an imputation that arises pragmatically through social usage. But Veblen went a step further, pointing out in *The Place of Science in Modern Civilization* that apart from the question of truth, the historical deep-rootedness of causality as a "social habit of thought" makes it the criterion that all thinking must meet to "pass muster" in modern times.

When Jung began to develop the concept of synchronicity during the 1920s, the rigidities of rationalistic causal thinking were still strongly predominant. But he was greatly stimulated and encouraged by physicists like Nils Bohr and Wolfgang Pauli, for their work seemed to suggest that no matter how objective science tried to be, the element of subjectivity, through the consciousness of the observer, was always an additional factor (see his *Synchronizität als ein Prinzip akausaler Zusammenhänge* [1952]). Jung was convinced that causality could no longer be accepted as an absolute reality in itself, and that it must be understood as a psychologically and historically conditioned point of view.

The main philosophical antecedents of synchronicity in Western culture are found in sources far beyond rationality. These antecedents are typified by Leibniz as a leading representative of those whose ideas go beyond rationalism. Leibniz's *Monadology* culminates the rich development of European alchemical thought and epitomizes the conception of man as a microcosmic expression of the macrocosm. In Jung's microcosmic/macrocosmic conception of the human psyche, to work with the materials of personality, which means to work *within* the human being, leads immediately beyond the person. This is so because at its depth, the psyche of the individual contains *reflections* of the larger universe. These reflections are images that symbolically represent aspects of the macrocosm. The images—archetypes—contained within the individual psyche are thus reflections of the universe in miniature. The movements of these within each person embody the processes of the psyche. They are the expressions in individual form of the processes and rhythms that move in the macrocosm of nature.

The conception of the archetypes helps to show how noncausal, but meaningful events, might be related. The specific archetypes that are active at the depth of an individual's existence are the means by which the general orderedness of the larger patterns of the macrocosm can come to specific expression at any moment of time. The archetypes are the vehicles by which the encompassing patterns of life are individualized in experience.

At the point where an archetypal factor becomes involved in a given situation, something more active than the conscious mind of an observer enters the picture. The archetypal element becomes an effective factor in this situation because it serves to recrystallize and reconstitute the situation as a whole. As the effective factor, it creates a new situation; it becomes the core of the new quality of orderedness that permeates and characterizes the new situation as it exists *across time*. The functioning of the archetypal element in a situation cannot be encompassed in any of the usual definitions of causality.

Many of the phenomena of synchronicity are aspects of the life history of the person. In the life of Abraham Lincoln, for example, there was a time when a man came to him asking for a dollar for a barrel of miscellaneous goods. Lincoln did not believe there was anything of value in the barrel, but he bought it anyway, reasoning that the dollar would be well spent even if he had no use for its contents. After about a year had passed, Lincoln finally opened the barrel. Inside, he discovered a nearly complete set (with only one volume missing) of William Blackstone's *Commentaries*, thus finding himself provided with the means to study law, become a lawyer, and so eventually to enter politics.

This event is an example of a meaningful coincidence. To Lincoln it was an event that occurred beyond his personal consciousness. The event did have meaning, but this meaning was brought forth by his unconsciousness, in which his archetypes played an important role.

The next step in exploring Jung's hypothesis of synchronicity is to gather instances of this type of event in the lives of a broad spectrum of creative persons.

[I.P.]

See also **Augustine; Hume, David; Kant, Immanuel; Leibniz, Gottfried Wilhelm; Plato.**

FURTHER READINGS

Jung, C.G. *Synchronizität als ein Prinzip akausaler Zusammenhänge*. C.G. Jung and W. Pauli. *Naturerklärung und Psyche*. Zurich: Rascher Verlag, 1952.

———. "On Synchronicity." *Man and Time: Papers from the Eranos Yearbooks*. Trans. R.F.C. Hull. Ed. Joseph Campbell. New York: Pantheon, 1957. 201–211.

———. *Structure and Dynamics of the Psyche*. Trans. R.F. Hull. 2nd ed. *The Collected Works*. Princeton: Princeton UP, 1968.

Progoff, Ira. *Jung, Synchronicity, and Human Destiny: C.G. Jung's Theory of Meaningful Coincidence*. New York: Crown, 1987.

Von Franz, Marie-Louise. "Time and Synchronicity in Analytic Psychology." *The Voices of Time*. Ed. J.T. Fraser. 2nd ed. Amherst: U of Massachusetts P, 1981. 218–232.

KAFKA, FRANZ (1883–1924)

The work of Franz Kafka has been characterized by a preoccupation with clocks, watches, and time, a preoccupation that penetrates into the very core and fabric of existence itself. He writes in his diary of two clocks that do not agree: the inner one rushes along in a demonic or inhuman way and the outer one continues in its own customary pace. This underlying discrepancy between inner experience and the ticking clock reveals that self and world are out of synch.

Kafka confronts his reader on the most fundamental level with situations that challenge and disturb any steady and secure hold on life that is grounded in temporal order. His prose is a stark depiction of protagonists caught in the attempt to find stability and meaning where none exists. In an instant, they may be torn from their comfortable existence and plunged into a dream-like world where the rules have all collapsed and action leads nowhere but in a circle. Here goals remain elusive and forever out of reach. Clocks move at a speed and direction all their own.

In one short parable, the narrator compares his watch to a tower clock and shocked by the discrepancy, loses his sense of direction, his confidence, the very meaning of his life. In a panic he rushes to a policeman for help in order to ask about his "way"—only to be told, "Give it up." In "The Metamorphosis," Gregor wakes to find himself transformed into a disgusting insect and unable to meet the demands of his everyday schedule. Yet he is obsessed with thoughts about time, train departures, getting to work, and resuming his accustomed routine. "Heavenly Father! he thought. It was half-past six o'clock, and the hands were quietly moving on, it was even past the half-hour, it was getting on toward a quarter to seven. Had the alarm clock not gone off?" This clock-based temporality, which defined his life before, is now no longer valid. As an insect, he *cannot* meet the constraints of a schedule. Gradually, such concerns matter less and less to him until finally he is uncertain about how much time an action takes, or how many days have passed, or how long ago events occurred. He functions more and more on an increasingly primitive level of consciousness and orders reality according to the directness of his experience. Only at his death does he again become conscious of time as the tower clock strikes 3:00 A.M., a time when the rest of the world sleeps, unaware and uncaring about his demise.

Joseph K. in *The Trial* is also torn from his everyday routine when he awakes one morning and learns that he is under arrest. The temporal order with which he was accustomed to living his life now no longer applies. His sense of time is distorted; he is either late or early for appointments and duration does not fit normal expectations. Time, as a dimension of orderly sequence of cause and effect, of sense and meaning, is torn away like a rug from underfoot, and he, like so many other protagonists, must struggle to create a different fabric that holds existence together. Unfortunately, most are doomed by the challenge and end in a paralyzed state of frustration or indecision. Their inability to break through and move forward creates the sense of temporal emptiness that is characteristic of Kafka's work.

Other twentieth-century writers also focus on the breakdown of temporal order, but Kafka's vision strikes a particularly raw nerve in modern existential experience because the plight of his protagonists awakens an uneasy and disquieting familiarity. We know this world in our dreams, in our nightmares, in the deepest recesses of our being where the façades of our living cannot sustain us. Even the process of reading Kafka's narratives is disquieting. His straightforward and direct language leaves us no time to find a comfortable stronghold before plunging us into a sequence of events that is deceptively and logically illogical. Before we know it, the sense of disruption and the struggle to find a meaningful order have become an intricate part of the reading itself. Kafka's time is representative of an age that in its frantic attempt to keep pace with its clocks has lost touch with its genuine self and does not truly comprehend that it is standing on the brink.

[M.P.S.]

FURTHER READINGS

Bloom, Harold, ed. *Franz Kafka*. New York: Chelsea House, 1986.

Corngold, Stanley. *Franz Kafka: The Necessity of Form*. Ithaca: Cornell UP, 1988.

Udoff, Alan, ed. *Kafka and the Contemporary Critical Performance: Centenary Readings*. Bloomington: Indiana UP, 1987.

KAIROS

Kairos is an ancient Greek word that means "the right moment" or "the opportune." It is traditionally associated with the sophist Gorgias (ca. 490–ca. 385 B.C.), who founded his philosophy of rhetoric upon this concept. For Gorgias, the principle guiding rhetorical invention is the occasion of discourse, the chance conjunction of circumstances confronting the one who would invent. The question "What shall I say?" can best be answered not by repeating what has already been said, but on the basis of *kairos*, the fortune of the moment, what Nietzsche called the "dice throw." Gorgias imagines the activity of invention as the fortuitous falling together of a multiplicity of factors the issue or outcome of which cannot be foreseen. Cultural practice remains innovative, he suggests, only so long as the inventor is willing to modify the existing repertoire of things to say in response to the unique opportunity offered by the situation at hand.

This insistence on circumstantial improvisation implies a view of temporal process in which the occasion of invention, far from simply continuing or prolonging what has gone before, erupts discontinuously as an *event*. In his remarkable "Theses on the Philosophy of History," Walter Benjamin (1892–1940) observes that any appeal to notions of a necessity or destiny determining cultural practice depends on the assumption of a "homogeneous, empty time," a time of predictable development in which *nothing ever happens* because the present and future are already inscribed in the past as its inevitable culmination. Benjamin would rather that cultural history be understood as an endless series of opportunities to invent. This means that the inventor must attend to "the presence of the now," a "configuration pregnant with tensions" that might make the "continuum of history explode." Indeed, the ethical force of an act of invention depends on the degree to which it is able to "wrest tradition away from a conformism that is about to overpower it." The chronological time of homogeneous unfolding in which the present is subjugated to the past can thus be contrasted with the temporality of *kairos* as rupture and discontinuity—the radically disclosive time of the now.

A similar distinction between the unvarying routine of mundane time and the disclosive temporality of *kairos* can be found in the Epicurean metaphysics of the Roman poet, Lucretius (ca. 99–ca. 55 B.C.). In *De rerum natura*, he argues that invention depends on present circumstances, whether that be the unpredictable emergence of physical structure from chaotic flux or a cultural practice that takes the occasion of thought as its point of departure. From the standpoint of Lucretian cosmology, the universe itself is a chance conjunction of circumstances, a turbulent chaos of colliding atoms in which material form and human culture arise not by necessity but purely by chance. The eternal fall of the atoms through space is periodically interrupted, he says, by a minute aleatory swerving, the *clinamen*, a microscopic chance departure from linear flow ensuing in collisions among the atoms which subsequently combine to form enduring structures. This deviation from what would otherwise amount to interminable repetition is truly an event. By swerving stochastically and unpredictably, the atoms "break the decrees of fate, that cause may not follow cause from infinity." And such is the case not only at the level of physical particles but in human affairs as well, since "what keeps the mind itself from having necessity within it in all [its] actions . . . is the minute swerving of the [atoms] at no fixed place and at no fixed time."

The Lucretian view of stochastically emergent form is cited by Ilya Prigogine and Isabelle Stengers in their *Order Out of Chaos* as a precursor to contemporary non-equilibrium thermodynamics. Nonequilibrium thermodynamics represents, for them, the recognition in the natural sciences that time is not merely homogeneous in its unfolding, but open and disclosive. What Prigogine and Stengers stress, above all, is the phenomenon of emergence. At what they call a "bifurcation point," an unstable dynamic system may choose one path of development over another in a random manner. A system destabilized by its environment—in other words, by the convergence of factors comprising an occasion of invention—may leap to a new regime stochastically. Alluding to the notion of *kairos*, they point out that a "microscopic fluctuation" occurring "at the 'right moment'" may ensue in systemic transformation. As a system becomes chaotic, suffused with random fluctuations, it becomes capable, potentially at least, of overcoming the redundant amplification of its own beginning premises. The hitherto unintelligible "noise" of its environment may provoke a system to reorganize itself, thereby giving rise to new varieties of "information." Prigogine and Stengers thus posit an opposition between the time of strict determinism and the time of stochastic emergence. And like Gorgias, Benjamin, and Lucretius, they valorize the moment of innovation. The unforeseen spontaneity of the present occasion provides the means to regenerate a system. The chronological time of predictable regularity is the time of entropic decay. Alternatively, the time of stochastic emergence, a time of risk to be sure, is also the only time when the possibility exists of reversing the slide toward dissolution. Physical systems, living systems, and cultural systems all depend upon a flow from outside for renewal. To the extent they remain closed off from their surroundings, the law of increasing entropy mandates that they can only disintegrate.

Michel Serres has drawn the lesson of Lucretian and Prigoginian physical speculation in *La naissance de la physique dans le texte de Lucrèce*. In what amounts to a materialist account, to use the traditional term, of "creativity," he maintains that thought and action should remain responsive to the unexpected novelty of heterogeneous situations. The wisdom of the garden of Epicurus, he says, is a "logic of circumstances" and "multiplicities" for which his favorite image is a vortex that varies its form in relation to the intensity of the energy flows infusing it from without, a whirlpool of metamorphic significance set amidst a flux of fertile noise. Thus drawing upon ancient and contemporary natural philosophy, Serres arrives at a position strikingly reminiscent of the claim first made by Gorgias for the inventive potential that resides in *kairos*, the radical time of the now, the always unforeseen opportunity to think and do otherwise.

[E.W.]

See also **Chaos Theory; Dynamics.**

FURTHER READINGS

Benjamin, Walter. "Theses on the Philosophy of History." *Illuminations: Essay and Reflections*. Ed. Hannah Arendt. New York: Schocken, 1969. 253–264.

Lucretius. *De rerum natura*. Trans. W.H.D. Rouse. Revised by Martin Fergusan Smith. 2nd ed. Cambridge: Harvard UP, 1982.

Prigogine, Ilya, and Isabelle Stengers. *Order Out of Chaos: Man's New Dialogue with Nature*. New York: Bantam, 1984.

Serres, Michel. *La naissance de la physique dans le texte de Lucrèce: Fleuves et turbulences*. Paris: Minuit, 1977.

White, Eric. *Kaironomia: On the Will-to-Invent*. Ithaca: Cornell UP, 1987.

KANT, IMMANUEL (1724–1804)

Immanuel Kant, the leading German philosopher of the eighteenth century, was both the heir to and the most resolute critic of the main tendencies of the German Enlightenment. His interpretation of time strongly influenced his unique approach to the more systematic questions of a fully developed critical philosophy. The main sources for his theories about time and space are the precritical *Dissertation On the Form and the Principles of the Sensible and Intelligible World* (1770), and the signature critical works, *Critique of Pure Reason,* and *Prolegomena To Any Future Metaphysics Which Will Be Able to Come Forth as a Science*.

TIME AS THE MATRIX OF SENSE PERCEPTION

The attention Kant gave to analyzing time and space grew out of his conviction about the role they played in reframing the main questions of philosophy. Time and space, he held, were pure forms of the human mode of perceiving or intuiting objects. They determined the order and structure of the appearances of objects within the experience of human subjects. As such, they are the a priori forms of all intuitions. Taken critically, time is the matrix for what is earlier and later in internal sense. Space is the structure for all side by side appearances as they arise from external sense.

The critical or transcendental philosophy of Kant is based upon an analysis of the fundamental factors he took to be typical of all human experience. A central question for him is this: How can there be true judgments about all possible objects of human experience, which are not thereby merely trivially or tautologically true? The foundations of mathematics, natural science, and metaphysics included such judgments. In Kant's phrasing, the question is: How are such synthetic judgments a priori possible? Time and space, he thought, can provide some grounds for such universal, but nevertheless factual, synthetic judgments because all of the factual, material aspects of experience have to submit to the prefiguring effects of these forms of human perception.

Kant's treatment of time and space in the transcendental aesthetic (< Greek *aisthesis*, perception or sensation) played off the conventional contrast between form and matter, and between structure and content. Other philosophers, but especially Leibniz, had held that the formal aspects of sense experience were ideas or concepts supplied by the understanding, no matter how imperfectly focused those ideas might appear in perception. Kant rejected this doctrine of the inherent rationality of all of the structuring aspects of experience. For him, there are formal factors within perception itself, namely, these pure intuitions of time and space. Time and space, his formulation has it, are empirically real but transcendentally ideal. They are real features of appearances arising in human perception. Though really given in experience, they do not arise out of appearances. Rather, they are antecedently present as enabling conditions of the human mode of experience. This antecedent, modal aspect Kant called the ideality of time and space. By their ideality, he meant to deny that space and time are objective things or relations external to and independent of experience. Rather, they are the mediating conditions of human experience, the means by which external objects can appear as objects for us.

To say that these pure forms of sensibility are distinctive marks of the human mode of perception or intuition is to say that human perception is never a direct reception of objects as they essentially are in themselves. Instead, objects undergo some change or modification as they impinge upon us. The universal forms which cut across and underlie all these modifications are time and space. In short, human perception is derivative, mediated through the time-space matrix, and never direct and immediate.

In the closing paragraphs of the transcendental aesthetic as given in the *Critique*, Kant insisted that the manner in which we perceive or intuit objects requires the presence of objects as they affect us. He did not doubt that there is a real world, a real nature, external to us. But as it appears to us, its aspects are ordered earlier and later in time, and side by side in space. These kinds of sensibility, inner and outer, or time and space, are derivative. Kant gives uneven expositions of these derivative forms of perception. In some passages, time and space are taken in a narrow sense, as unique features of the distinctive human mode of perception. But in others, he allows a broader sense, that perhaps all finite thinking beings, human or nonhuman, perceive within time and space as the pure forms of all their intuitions.

Regardless of Kant's openness on this point, it is clear that finite, human perception is derivative. He called it *intuitus derivativus*, as opposed to *intuitus originarius*. Only the latter, which would give the essence of things as they are in themselves, could be called intellectual intuition. This kind of original, intellectual intuition would be most proper for the possible primordial being, as the first cause and ground of all that is. But this primordial being would not know things under the conditions of time and space. For they are limiting conditions, and would entail the conclusion that a possible primal first being is limited if it were to know things temporally and spatially. However, dependent subjects such as humans have pure forms of sensibility which are necessary and sufficient for their special mode of being. These derivative forms of perception, taken by Kant as a given matrix appropriate to human subjectivity, are time and space.

Humans are perceiving subjects in a finite, dependent world, and time and space are a priori forms for what affects the human mind. These forms necessitate that the world as it appears to us will always be awash in the tides (times) and loci (spaces) of a commonly experienced world. All experience typical of this subjective mode of being is, on its formal side, purely, necessarily, and endlessly given as temporal and spatial. The temporal mode, reflecting our inner experience, is more universal than the spatial, and encompasses it. Accordingly, human experience is essentially and purely, inescapably and inalienably, time-bound.

[B.P.H.]

See also **Leibniz, Gottfried Wilhelm; Philosophy of Time.**

FURTHER READINGS

Al-Azm, Sadik J. *Kant's Theory of Time*. New York: Philosophical Library, 1967.

Allison, Henry E. *Kant's Transcendental Idealism*. New Haven: Yale UP, 1983.

Falkenstein, Lorne. "Kant's Argument for the Non-Spatiotemporality of Things in Themselves." *Kant-Studien* 80 (1989): 265–283.

Parsons, Charles. "The Transcendental Aesthetic." *The Cambridge Companion To Kant*. Ed. Paul Guyer. Cambridge: Cambridge UP, 1992.

Strawson, P.F. *The Bounds of Sense*. London: Methuen, 1966.

KIERKEGAARD, SÖREN AABYE (1813–1855)

Kierkegaard was a pioneer in developing our understanding of an existential awareness of temporal experience and in contributing to the so-called phenomenological view of time. For Kierkegaard, time is not merely an abstract series of moments measured by the clock, nor an objective, discrete sequence of moments determined in space. Time is rather the dynamic, non-discrete inward reality of concrete lived experience. In lived existential time, the three modalities of past, present, and future interpenetrate within the span of my present consciousness as a remembered past and an anticipated future. I become a concrete personal history in which temporal dimensions dynamically interrelate in an evolving self.

For Kierkegaard, the human individual is also a "synthesis of the temporal and the eternal." According to these terms, we are not yet an individual self, but a "process" whose task it is to become a self. To be a synthesis of temporality and eternity is to contain an insurmountable paradox or contradiction—to face an abyss between the eternal or infinite and the temporal or finite which is not subject to mediation. Yet this paradoxical existential situation gives us our task as human individuals: to become "infinitely interested in existence" in order to realize our inner reality through holding these two extremes in dynamic tension within our lives.

This is to see the task of life as the realization of "inwardness," that is, for an existing finite individual to recognize that "truth is subjectivity." Movement of the individual toward ever greater inwardness—the truth of subjectivity—means ever increasing awareness of both the eternal and the temporal. While Kierkegaard recognizes the objective time of the natural world in which things can be said to have a before and after, he is not merely emphasizing human "subjective" time as opposed to objective time. Rather, he wants to argue that the *real* existential structure of human life is the internal dynamic of temporality and its paradoxical synthesis with eternity.

Kierkegaard dramatizes life as a movement from the aesthetic to the ethical and, ultimately, to the religious stage of existence. The vast majority of people live their entire life at the aesthetic stage; they "atomize" the time of their lives into a linear series of moments, some of which are past, some of which are to come, and only one of which is real: the present. Through self-deception, people mask the anxiety and dread which characterize the temporal process of true self-realization. They avoid both experiencing the "dizziness of freedom" which gazes down into its own unlimited possibilities, and agonizing over decisions in the present about what and how one will become.

For Kierkegaard, the self-deception of the aesthetic who deals only with unrealities, never facing his or her own temporality, ultimately leads to despair. Out of this despair the ethical stage arises when the individual, through resolute decision and dread, becomes a personal history appropriating his or her past and taking responsibility for his or her future. Yet the ethical individual soon realizes that not only are there no grounds or principles on which to make these decisions, but that his or her task of realizing ever more fully the synthesis of the eternal and the temporal is beyond all possible human capacity. Thus the ethical becomes a transitional stage to the religious in which one's relationship to the eternal in time becomes the "absolute telos" of one's life. Only God, as lord over the future and its possibilities (and relied on absolutely through an ever renewed decision of faith), can make life possible for a temporally existing concrete being. And, for Kierkegaard, only Christianity, with its paradoxical claim that the eternal entered time in the person of Christ, does full justice to the contradictory existential realities of human life.

[G.M.]

See also **Existentialism; Phenomenology.**

LAWRENCE, D.H. (1885–1930)

Lawrence's presentation of time in his eleven novels and sixty stories is partly traditional and partly innovative. Unlike some other twentieth-century novelists, such as Faulkner, who scramble the sequence of events in their narratives, Lawrence uses a straightforward story line in which event follows event in normal chronological sequence. Where he becomes strikingly innovative, however, is when the sequence of normal clock time is interrupted by an experience which causes the clock—in effect—to stop. Lawrence described these happenings as exemplifying "The Eternal Moment," prompted by what he called a "transfiguration." Examples of such timelessness include his heroine's responding to a sunset in his novel *The Rainbow*, or, in the same novel, the impact on her father on seeing the interior of a cathedral: "Away from time, always outside of time." But the chief circumstance prompting the eternal moment is an overpowering sexual union as pictured in *Sons and Lovers* and *Women in Love*, or in his long story "The Man Who Died." In the latter story and in many others, the intensity of the union is enhanced by its occurring in conjunction with a keen awareness of death.

In addition to these important experiences—"points of time" as Wordsworth called them—Lawrence shows how his characters' differing attitudes toward time lead to dramatic personal conflicts. Lawrence's male characters celebrate the past, with its age-old cycles of rural living as contrasted with the corrupted present, whereas his women usually yearn for an improved, future-oriented society: "a new dawn" and a "new day," as he writes.

Critics loudly disagree whether Lawrence's writings are themselves past-oriented or future-oriented, but it would be more accurate to say simply that he lived with both senses of time. His fictional world sings (like Yeats's golden bird) "of what is past, or passing, or to come."

[G.H.F.]

See also **Novel.**

FURTHER READINGS

Ford, George H. "The Eternal Moment: D.H. Lawrence's *The Rainbow* and *Women in Love*." *The Study of Time III*. Ed. J.T. Fraser, N. Lawrence, and D. Park. New York: Springer, 1978. 512–539.

Haegert, John. "Lawrence's World Elsewhere: Elegy and History in *The Rainbow*." *Clio* 15 (Winter 1986): 115–135.

Hinz, Evelyn J. "The Paradoxical Fall: Eternal Recurrences in D.H. Lawrence's *The Rainbow*." *English Studies in Canada* 3 (Winter 1977): 460–491.

LEGAL MALPRACTICE: TIME LIMITS

A statute of limitations is the time period in which an action must be filed, at the risk of being barred entirely or being subject to a defense that will prevent the action from proceeding. For many malpractice actions, including legal malpractice actions, the time period is relatively shorter than for other kinds of actions. One or two years is not uncommon.

One reason for this is that the practice of law and similar professions require subjective judgments which might be forgotten as time passes. Statutes of limitations encourage clients to assert claims expeditiously while memories are fresh and witnesses are available. These days, however, the time period often does not begin to run until the client discovers or should have discovered the resulting injury. Earlier rules often provided that the time period began when the relationship between attorney and client ceased.

The failure to adhere to statutorily required time periods such as statutes of limitations or time periods in which pleadings in general must be filed is a frequent basis for the assertion of a malpractice claim against an attorney.

[M.H.A.]

See also **Statute of Limitations.**

FURTHER READINGS

Koffler, J.H. "Legal Malpractice Statutes of Limitations: A Critical Analysis of a Burgeoning Crisis." *Akron Law Review* 20 (Fall 1986): 209–260.

LEIBNIZ, GOTTFRIED WILHELM (1646–1716)

Leibniz held that time was ideal. By this he meant that (1) it is a relation known by abstraction from perceptual experience, and (2) its existence is dependent upon the sequences of events whose order it exhibits. Like most of his contemporaries, Leibniz coordinated his discussions of time with those of space. Thus time, he claimed, is the order of connected but incompatible existences, while space is the order of compatible existences. His definitions may be made concrete in a simple example. A perceiver's description of all the elements of a pool table in the instant just before the cue ball hits the eight ball would express a certain relational order, which would be abstracted by the perceiver as spatial. (One might here imagine what is depicted in a single movie frame.) Included in this description would be the sentence, "The cue ball does not touch the eight ball." This description could not also include the sentence, "The cue ball hits the eight ball," since this sentence would be inconsistent with the set of sentences in the first description. A second description of the pool table, however, could very well make reference to the collision. (Here the next movie frame might be imagined.) Each of the two descriptions would be consistent within itself, but inconsistent with the other, since the set of events described by each would be incompatible with one another, although obviously connected—indeed, they are causally connected. From the two incompatible but causally connected sets of events (the two successive movie frames), perceivers abstract a temporal relationship. Leibniz's belief that time is an abstract relation dependent upon events and perceivers is evident in this example.

[G.G.]

See also **Leibniz-Clarke Correspondence.**

LEIBNIZ-CLARKE CORRESPONDENCE

Leibniz and Newton were two of the finest physicists of their era. Their views on fundamental issues, however, often differed greatly. Just before Leibniz's death in 1716, the two began their final and probably most significant debate concerning the nature of space and time. It was carried out via correspondence between Leibniz and one of Newton's followers, Samuel Clarke, although we have good evidence that it was Newton himself who provided not only the spirit, but often the letter of Clarke's responses. Newton defended what is now called the theory of absolute space and time. Leibniz, by contrast, defended a theory of relational space and time. According to Newton's view, which finds its foundation in ordinary experience, both space and time exist in their own right, and are logically prior to their contents. Time thus provides a form of preexisting "container" within which the world's events and their sequences come to occur. In objecting to this view, Leibniz argued both positively, in favor of his own relationist position, and negatively, against Newton's position.

In Leibniz's theory, neither space nor time had an existence independent of objects, events, and perceivers. Time is instead merely a relational order abstracted from sets of connected events. Unless and until the event-sequences occur, and are perceived to occur, time does not exist. Leibniz's positive views are not nearly as intuitively appealing as Newton's. Leibniz's critique of Newton's theory, on the other hand, was devastating. He began from the common ground of both men's belief in a rational creator. Such a creator, Leibniz asserted, would never do anything without a sufficient reason. Yet, he continued, that is precisely what would happen if we were to assume—simply as a logical hypothesis—that the theory of absolute space and time were true. Analysis shows that the hypothesis implies that, since time was created before its contents, all moments are intrinsically empty, and thereby totally identical. This means that the creator could have no rational grounds to prefer any one empty moment over another as the moment of creation. Hence, since the original hypothesis leads to the absurd conclusion that the creator is irrational, it must be false: space and time could not be absolute. The persuasiveness of Leibniz's argument left physics with the quandary that Newton's theory of space and time was scientifically adequate but philosophically insupportable. This quandary was not resolved until Mach and his successors, including Einstein, began to grapple with it late in the nineteenth century.

[G.G.]

See also **Leibniz, Gottfried Wilhelm; Newton, Isaac.**

FURTHER READINGS

Leibniz, G., and S. Clarke. *The Leibniz-Clarke Correspondence: Together with Extracts from Newton's* Principia *and* Optics. Ed. H.G. Alexander. Manchester: Manchester UP, 1956.

LEISURE: WOMEN WITH CHILDREN IN FRANCE

When considering the leisure of women with children in any national context it is important to recognize that mothers do not constitute a homogeneous category for analysis. Although much recent sociological research—such as that by Erica Wimbush and Margaret Talbot in Britain, Nicola Le Feuvre in France, and Karla Henderson et al. in the United States—has highlighted the particular constraints that women with children face, both in access to leisure time and space and in the type of leisure activities undertaken, the nature and degree of these constraints differ considerably according to variables such as the number and age of dependent children, marital status, social class, ethnic origin, and economic resources.

In France, numerous time budget surveys carried out by the INSEE (Institut national de la statistique et des études économiques), have shown that, in quantitative terms, the amount of "constrained" time (professional activity plus domestic chores) of mothers depends, as demonstrated by Caroline Roy, to a large extent on whether or not they are economically active. Mothers who are full-time homemakers with a single child devote on average a daily total of seven hours thirty minutes to household and child care tasks, compared with a daily total of ten hours for employed mothers with one or two children. However, the constrained time of full-time homemakers increases more with the number of dependent children than in the case of employed mothers.

Roy argues further that the total leisure time of mothers also varies considerably according to the number of dependent children. This variation is again most marked for mothers who are full-time homemakers. Time budget data show that the amount of total daily leisure time of economically active mothers varies only slightly as the number of dependent children increases: from three hours with a single dependent child to two hours and fifty-five minutes with three children or more. For mothers who are not in employment, the total daily amount of leisure time decreases substantially from five hours with a single dependent child to three hours and forty-five minutes with three children or more.

Recent qualitative research has, however, questioned the reliability and validity of this type of quantitative analysis of leisure. Although many of the weaknesses of the findings are inherent in the time budget data collection process, they pose particular problems for the study of the leisure of women with children. Qualitative analysis, as Le Feuvre demonstrates, has drawn attention to the multifaceted and complex nature of the time sequences of women with children. Unlike the relatively compartmentalized temporal sequences of most economically active men, for whom work and nonwork time and space are clearly distinguished, the domestic and child care responsibilities of this category of women tend to blur the boundaries between time sequences. Insofar as time budget studies impose an a priori unitary definition on activities and measure leisure time as the residual left over after subtracting time devoted to employment, domestic activities, and personal hygiene (including sleep), they are unsuitable tools for grasping the complex nature of the leisure experiences of women with children.

The employment and family status of mothers influence not only their access to leisure time and facilities but also their subjective experiences of a range of leisure activities within and outside the home environment. Despite the fact that mothers who are full-time homemakers have, on average, more daily leisure time than employed mothers, they are more likely than the latter to devote their time to activities which take place within the home, notably television and handicrafts, and to spend their leisure time in the company of their spouses and children.

Research to date suggests that the educational qualifications of mothers play an important role in determining the relationship between paid employment, leisure, and domestic and childcare responsibilities. Mothers with the lowest school-leaving age tend to define leisure activities as those nonwork activities that take place in the company of their spouses and children and allow them to escape from the most demanding and repetitive aspects of their domestic responsibilities. Employed mothers in this category see their paid work as a barrier to more autonomous forms of leisure because they feel the need to compensate for their absence from the home during the working day by devoting themselves to their spouses and children in their leisure time. Although they may express the desire for more autonomous leisure activities, they often see the organization of these as an additional constraint which may outweigh the personal fulfillment they expect to gain from such activities.

Mothers who have undergone higher education, on the other hand, define leisure in terms of the freedom it offers from domestic and child care responsibilities. Their most valued leisure activities are those spent in the company of other adults or their spouses, but away from their children. Nonwork activities shared with children are more likely to be defined as a pleasurable aspect of their domestic responsibilities than as leisure activities. This distinction would seem to be particularly important for well-qualified mothers who are full-time homemakers and who find it difficult to identify personal space within the confines of the domestic environment where they assume primary responsibility for the synchronization of the time sequences of other family members. Rather than seeing autonomous leisure activities as being in contradiction with their primary responsibilities as wives and mothers, these women tend to stress the importance of leisure activities as "breathing spaces" which indirectly enhance their ability to assume responsibilities within the domestic sphere.

These differences illustrate some of the complex issues which need to be addressed when considering the objective and subjective leisure experiences of such a heterogeneous category as women with children in any national context.

[N.Le F.]

See also **Time for the Family; Time Structuring for Teachers.**

FURTHER READINGS

Henderson, Karla A., et al. *A Leisure of One's Own: A Feminist Perspective on Women's Leisure.* State College Oxford Circle: Venture Publishing, 1989.

Le Feuvre, Nicola J. *Etude empirique et théorique des pratiques et des représentations du loisir chez les mères de famille en France.* Unpublished Ph.D. thesis, Birmingham: Aston University, 1990.

Roy, Caroline. "L'emploi du temps des mères et pères de familles nombreuses." *Economie et statistique* 140 (1982): 59–68.

Wimbush, Erica, and Margaret Talbot, eds. *Relative Freedoms: Women and Leisure.* Milton Keynes: Open University Press, 1989.

LEVINAS, EMMANUEL (1906–)

Born in Kovno, Lithuania, French philosopher and Jewish thinker Emmanuel Levinas was educated at Strasbourg, Freiburg, and the Sorbonne, and has held academic positions at Poitiers, Paris-Nanterre, and the Sorbonne. His twenty books and close to 100 articles, spanning sixty years of philosophical creativity, articulate a unique view of the individual and of the crucial role that the interpersonal relations play in the very constitution of the individual. Levinas has consistently sought to develop this complex view through reenvisioning the nature of time. To put the matter simply, one might say that Levinas offers an inherently social understanding of temporality, thereby diverging from the interpretations of time advanced by the phenomenological and existential schools of philosophy, according to which schools temporality is an accomplishment or project of the individual subject alone.

In his early work of 1948, *Le temps et l'autre* (*Time and the Other*), Levinas argues that the individual is, at bottom, a being whose independence substantially expresses itself in the ability to break with what already exists, a power to begin or initiate based entirely on its own resources. On this basic level the subject brings the present temporal moment—"the now"—into existence by its inexhaustible and continuous capacity to commence. Yet on this basic level the subject remains confined entirely to "the now," to a succession of self-enclosed and solipsistic moments which lack orientation outside of the subject. Therefore, Levinas goes on to sketch out what must be added, from without, to this basic level of subjectivity in order to generate a temporal flow toward the future. In death, which Levinas argues (contra Heidegger) comes upon the subject from outside itself, and above all, in the concrete encounter with the other person, Levinas locates that *contact with externality* that transforms the solipsistic, continuous present of the basic level of subjectivity into a temporality flowing toward the future.

In the mature *Totalité et Infini* (*Totality and Infinity*) of 1961, Levinas derives public, objective time from the face-to-face encounter between ego and other. The other contests the ego's privilege of giving meaning to things, for the other is a self-interpreting being with his or her *own* meaning. The other thus exceeds or overflows the self-oriented horizon within which the ego pursues its wants and deals with things. Hence, Levinas will argue that the other interrupts the immediate, spontaneous self-coincidence of the ego with itself, pulling the ego "out of synch with itself," thereby generating the extra- or trans-subjective time of self-consciousness and language.

In his *Autrement qu'être ou au-delà de l'essence* (*Otherwise than Being or Beyond Essence*) of 1974, Levinas locates that contact with the other, which founds the ego's consciousness, in an "immemorially past" temporal dimension. This contact thus becomes a "pre-originary" proximity between ego and other, a proximity that has always already taken place. To speak loosely, one might say that the other reaches the ego *before* the ego has achieved its own separate, conscious identity, acting as an irritant around which the ego coagulates into identity. This proximity between ego and other transpires before, and founds, conscious time. It thus remains irrecuperably past, echoing enigmatically in our present encounters with others.

[J.M.]

See also **Existentialism; Heidegger, Martin; Phenomenology.**

FURTHER READINGS

Levinas, E. *Le temps et l'autre.* 1948; reprint, Paris: Presses Universitaires de France, 1983. (Translated by R. Cohen as *Time and the Other.* Pittsburgh: Duquesne UP, 1987.)

———. *Totalité et Infini.* 1961; 4th ed., La Haye: Martinus Nijhoff, 1980. (Translated by A. Lingis as *Totality and Infinity.* Pittsburgh: Duquesne UP, 1969.)

———. *Autrement qu'être ou au-delà de l'essence.* Dordrecht: Kluwer Academic, 1974. (Translated by A. Lingis as *Otherwise than Being or Beyond Essence.* The Hague: Martinus Nijhoff, 1981.)

LIFE-SPAN

Most living organisms deteriorate in bodily functions as they age, leading to a decline in reproduction and life expectancy and eventually to death. Organisms that reproduce solely by fission (bacteria and some invertebrates) or by vegetative means (some plants) approach immortality without showing signs of senescence. In contrast, the life-span of organisms with a separation between the soma and the germ lines (most metazoans) is finite and, although subject to modulation by environmental factors such as temperature and nutrition, is a characteristic of a species. The average length of life under natural conditions, life expectancy at birth, and the maximum longevity attained all provide estimates of the life-span of individuals of a given species. Using the last measure, some of the longest living animals are clams (more than 200 years), sturgeons (more than 150 years), turkey vultures (about 120 years), tortoises (about 150 years), and elephants (about 100 years), whereas some insects complete their life cycle from birth to death in a few weeks. The maximum verified life-span of humans is about 110 years. Among plants, the redwoods (*Sequoia* species) can attain an age of more than 3,000 years.

Since Aristotle began the biological study of aging almost two and a half millennia ago, a plethora of theories has been proposed to explain the causes of senescence and death. Theories of physiological causes of aging, traditionally the domain of gerontology, include various organismal and cellular-molecular models. Examples of the former are the "wear and tear" models (progressive deterioration due to chronic environmental abuse) and "exhaustion" models (reproductive exhaustion or depletion of some incompletely replaced resource or substance). The "rate of living" theory, an example of the latter category, was proposed by Max Rubner in 1908 and extended by Raymond Pearl in 1928. It states that, in general, the length of life is inversely proportional to the rate of living, measured as the metabolic rate per unit weight of body tissue. Each organism is thought to have a limited, predetermined amount of energy available for its metabolic functions. The model is based on three types of observations: (1) interspecific comparisons indicate that the life-span of many organisms (for example, eutherian mammals from mice to elephants) is inversely related to their metabolic rate per unit of body weight, (2) the length of life of some invertebrates varies with the temperature and the metabolic rate in a predictable manner (individuals maintained in cool conditions have a lower metabolic rate and live longer than those in warmer environments), and (3) ectothermic animals in general live longer than homeothermic animals of the same size.

Cellular-molecular theories of aging include progressively increasing pathologies in the mechanisms of cell division and cell differentiation as well as failures in metabolic functions (for example, mitochondrial malfunction, accumulation of cellular pigmented debris, metabolism-impairing "lipofuscin," and self-digestion by lysosomes). Other physiological processes associated with aging include cross-linkage of collagen molecules (the primary protein in rigid extracellular tissue that undergoes modification with age), thermal denaturation and hydrolysis of macromolecules that have a low turnover rate, and damage caused by free radicals (highly reactive molecules with unpaired electrons) that are produced both by normal enzymatic reactions and by radiation and toxic substances in the environment.

Although the physiological theories may elucidate the proximate mechanisms of aging, only two types of models address the ultimate causes of the length of life in different species: the "rate of living" model (outlined above) and the evolutionary model. The basic premise of the "rate of living" theory (that an inverse relationship exists between metabolic rate and length of life) breaks down in many interspecific comparisons between groups of organisms. For example, birds have a higher metabolic rate than mammals, and yet they live longer than mammals of the same body size. Similarly, among mammals, eutherians have a higher metabolic rate but a longer life-span than marsupials. Despite its intuitive appeal, this theory does not provide a general explanation of the length of life.

The evolutionary theory of aging was first articulated by Peter Medavar in 1946 in terms of population genetics. William D. Hamilton and Brian Charlesworth have since produced explicit mathematical analyses of the evolution of aging. The evolutionary model is based on the theoretical premise that the force of natural selection declines with increasing age of individuals in an age-structured population. In a population subjected to a constant rate of accidental death, the number of young is always greater than that of older individuals, simply due to their reduced exposure to environmental causes of death. Due to the numerical superiority of the young, any beneficial mutation early in life will have a greater effect than a similar mutation later. Conversely, any harmful mutation that occurs early in life is quickly weeded out by natural selection, whereas a similar mutation at an older age is relatively unaffected by selection. The genetic mechanisms of aging are thought to consist of (1) antagonistic pleiotropy (antagonistic effects of alleles that are beneficial early in life but deleterious later) and (2) the accumulation of mutations, neutral in young but harmful in old individuals, in the germ line over time. The force of evolution in antagonistic pleiotropy is natural selection, whereas mutation rates govern the occurrence of the second mechanism.

According to the evolutionary theory of aging, each species has a characteristic life-span, because it is subjected to a specific pattern of unavoidable, age-specific mortality that is caused by environmental factors. Ecologists have long observed that the characteristics affecting age-specific mortality and reproductive schedules (that is, life history characteristics) do not evolve in isolation but co-occur as suites of adaptive complexes. Early reproduction, a large reproductive effort per unit of time, breeding only once, a small body size, and a short life-span form one adaptive complex. The other end of the continuum consists of the reverse characteristics (late reproduction, a small reproductive effort per unit of time, repeated breeding, a large body size, and a long life-span). Therefore, the evolution of aging and the length of life should be considered in the broader context of the evolution of life histories. Many theories, such as the r-K-model and the bet-hedging model, address the environmental conditions under which particular suites of life history characteristics are likely to evolve. Tradeoffs between the energy that different organisms invest in reproduction on one hand and in growth and maintenance on the other form a prominent feature in most of these theories, but they differ in the emphasis placed on the effects of crowding and environmental fluctuations on the life history characteristics. In general, repeated reproduction and a long life-span (iteroparous life history) is thought to evolve in populations living in environments with a high ratio of juvenile to adult mortality; conversely, populations in which the risks of dying from environmental causes are greater for older individuals than for the young will evolve toward an early, massive reproductive effort and a shorter life-span (semelparous life history).

The evolutionary theory of aging provides a unifying framework within which the different aspects of aging and the length of life can be examined. Future challenges include reinterpretation of gerontological theories of aging in light of the principles of evolution and incorporation of the considerable body of life history theories more fully into the study of aging.

[K.O.]

See also **Time and Death.**

FURTHER READINGS

Behnke, J.A., C.E. Finch, and G.B. Moment. *The Biology of Aging.* New York: Plenum P, 1978.

Charlesworth, B. *Evolution in Age-Structured Populations.* Cambridge: Cambridge UP, 1980.

Ory, M.G., and H.R. Warner, eds. *Gender, Health, and Longevity.* New York: Springer, 1990.

Rose, M.R. *Evolutionary Biology of Aging.* Oxford: Oxford UP, 1991.

LOCKE, JOHN (1632–1704)

ENLIGHTENMENT "UNDERLABORER"

Known principally as the great political philosopher of the English "glorious revolution" of 1688, Locke was a scholar of broad interests which included medicine, chemistry, economics, theology, and ethics. A leading intellectual of seventeenth-century England, John Locke was an associate of Newton, Boyle, and other great scientists. He referred to himself in *An Essay Concerning Human Understanding* (1690) as a "humble underlaborer" who but clears the ground of intellectual rubbish to make way for the improvement of knowledge by the great scientific minds. His method was epistemological—he sought to trace the ideas of human understanding to their origin in sense experience and reflection and thereby eliminate the unintelligible jargon and abuse of scholastic philosophy and religious enthusiasm. The *Essay* contains three chapters on space and time (Book II, Chapters 13–15); he explains time as a concept derived from reflection on succession of other ideas in the mind. Locke elaborates a fundamentally Newtonian concept of space and time; but skeptical of the absolute certitude of any knowledge of the external world, he grounds the concepts in the certitude of self-consciousness.

THE NEW "WAY OF IDEAS": BACK TO EXPERIENCE

The spirit of Locke's project is captured well in his *Essay*: "Tis not easie for the Mind to put off those confused Notions and Prejudices it has imbibed from Custom, Inadvertency, and common Conversation: it requires pains and assiduity to examine its Ideas, till it resolves them into those clear and distinct simple ones, out of which they are compounded." Locke developed a new "way of ideas" which involves resolving complex ideas to their simple origins in "our observation" of "external sensible Objects" or "internal Operations of our own Minds, perceived and reflected on by our selves." Thus, Locke asserts that "all those sublime Thoughts, which towre above the Clouds, and reach as high as Heaven it self, take their rise and footing here." Measures of time and space, as well as the great ideas of infinity and eternity, are traced by Locke to the "simple ideas" of experience.

DURATION, TIME, AND MOTION

It is in Book II, Chapter 14 of the *Essay* that Locke analyzes time. Time is derived from a more fundamental awareness of "duration." The mind becomes aware of the *succession* of its own ideas; the perceived "distance" or "length" between the successive ideas, Locke calls "duration." Duration is not perceived by the senses; rather, it is the reflection upon the duration of the self:

"For whilst we are thinking, or whilst we receive successively several ideas in our minds, we know that we do exist; and so we call the existence, or the continuation of the existence of ourselves, or any thing else, commensurate to the succession of any ideas in our minds, the duration of ourselves, or any such other thing coexistent with our thinking." Locke broke with the Aristotelian definition of time as a measure of motion by dissociating time from external motion as such, and locating the nature of time in self-conscious awareness: "The constant and regular succession of ideas in a waking man, is, as it were, the measure and standard of all other successions." Thus, he points out that very swift and very slow motions are not perceived, there being certain bounds to the perception of quickness and slowness of succession. The part of duration perceived without succession is called an instant; many changes or motions may occur in what appears to be an instant. Locke notes that motion relative to the motion of the observer is also not perceived.

What is commonly called time is the subsequent measure of duration based upon the observation of certain things, such as heavenly bodies, which appear at "regular and seeming equidistant periods." A good measure of time must divide its whole duration into equal and regular periods. The sun and planets have been used universally, but there is no necessary connection between duration and external motion as supposed by Aristotle—any constant periodical appearance would do. Locke suggests that recurrences of illness, hunger or thirst, smell or taste, if returning at regular intervals could serve as a measure of time.

EPISTEMOLOGICAL QUANDARIES OF TIME

Locke uncovered metrical and ontological problems concerning our knowledge of time. First, there is no standard measure of time as there is a standard of extension or space, because portions of time cannot be juxtaposed one to another. Further, although "duration" is presumed to be uniform, constant, and equal, "none of the measures of it which we make use of can be *known* to do so." Thus, in fact, the motions of the earth and sun were found to be unequal when compared to a pendulum. And in its turn, the pendulum swings cannot be "infallibly known" to be equal, ad infinitum. In conclusion, Locke says that the notion of duration is clear, but our measures of it are never exact, as long as we do not know the causes of regularity in nature itself. Second, we are compelled to extend the pure idea of space and time beyond that which is sensibly present: the idea of space can be extended beyond matter and the idea of duration beyond actual motions and measures of time; thus we arrive at the notion of infinity. Duration, Locke says, is uniform and boundless; time allows us to order and position finite things in respect to one another. "Without such known settled points," Locke says, "all things would lie in an incurable confusion." In the final analysis, Locke leaves it an open question as to whether such order reflects the divine immensity or is simply the relational construct of human consciousness.

LOCKE'S LEGACY

Locke decisively turned the discussion of time away from traditional Aristotelian philosophy and theological speculation; yet he also burrowed beneath the bright certitudes of Newtonian science. On the one hand, he anticipates Hume's skepticism about our knowledge of external nature; on the other, he finds the need for a reflective idea derived from self-consciousness by which our experience is ordered and controlled; in this he anticipates Kant.

[J.P.H.]

See also **Aristotle; Hume, David; Kant, Immanuel; Newton, Isaac.**

FURTHER READINGS

Ayers, Michael. *Locke.* 2 vols. London: Routledge, 1991.

Buchdahl, Gerd. *Metaphysics and the Philosophy of Science: The Classical Origins: Descartes to Kant.* Cambridge: MIT P, 1969.

Cranston, Maurice. *John Locke: A Biography.* New York: Macmillan, 1957.

Gibson, James. *Locke's Theory of Knowledge and Its Historical Relations.* Cambridge: Cambridge UP, 1931.

Locke, John. *An Essay Concerning Human Understanding.* Ed. Peter H. Nidditch. The Clarendon Edition of the Works of John Locke. Oxford: Oxford UP, 1975.

LONELINESS AND AGING

Loneliness has been identified by some writers as the main problem associated with old age. In the literature on loneliness in the English language and in the context of time, loneliness has been perceived as a product of the twentieth century. Both loneliness and time are defined and experienced differently in the context of different languages, especially those outside the Indo-European language family and in underde-

veloped countries. In English, the semantic distinction between solitude and loneliness is clearcut, but in other languages (those of cultures where privacy and solitude are not common features of social life), there is often only one word for these two concepts. In this short article, loneliness and aging are considered only within the context of English semantics and literature in the developed world.

Loneliness is seen as having increased as a result of increased emphasis on independence, individualism, and competition. Elderly people have been assumed to be more affected by the social and cultural changes associated with urbanization, industrialization, and automation. Because of increases in the pace of change, those skills which are valued by society also change quickly. In this context, conventional wisdom suggests that elderly people are rapidly left behind, feel less useful, and are therefore likely to become lonely. There is some evidence to suggest that the prevalence of loneliness among elderly people may have increased since the middle of this century.

Any discussion of loneliness, old age, and time has to take account of different aspects of time. Since the situation in old age is influenced by the way in which the time already lived has been passed, some aspects of old age are the result of the passage of time or of aging itself. For example, retirement from paid employment places greater emphasis on the availability, use, and perception of time in the present; memory and reminiscence of time past become more salient in old age; and awareness of a limited and shrinking future changes perceptions and orientations toward the time to come. All these aspects are related to the potential for loneliness.

LONELINESS AND THE AGING PROCESS

Despite the conventional association of old age with loneliness, the literature demonstrates that the prevalence of loneliness among elderly people tends to be overestimated. In a wide range of studies in the United States and the United Kingdom, the majority of elderly people deny being lonely, on average, fewer than 15 percent describe themselves as either very lonely or often lonely. This prevalence of loneliness is no higher than for younger age groups, suggesting that it is neither the passage of time nor the aging process per se which is responsible for loneliness.

Within the elderly category (sixty-five and up), loneliness is higher in the older age groups, but not higher than in some other, younger categories. The increase of loneliness with advanced age is associated with the incremental losses of aging (widowhood, loss of friends, loss of mobility, failing health, loss of independence, and sometimes institutionalization) rather than aging itself. In other words, old people are subject to more of the experiences that are associated with loneliness at *any* age.

LONELINESS AND THE LIFE CYCLE

The network of significant others that provides help and emotional support to elderly people is the result of patterns of family fertility and marriage, migration, and to a lesser extent temperament. It has been shown that different types of support networks develop over the life cycle and that higher levels of loneliness are associated with certain types of networks. Those who have lived in the same locality since before middle age tend to belong to networks that appear to protect against loneliness in old age, while those who have moved, particularly at or after retirement, are more liable to be lonely. This difference is likely to result from the different availability of close relatives and friends in the same neighborhood.

Widowhood and living alone are more common in old age. Loneliness is more common among those who live alone and those who are widowed, but it is more likely in the early years of living alone or widowhood. The passage of time leads to a loss of companionship but also to an adaptation which mitigates that loss.

LONELINESS AND DAY-TO-DAY LIFE

Retirement removes or changes the perception of time as new structures of daily life are imposed. The pursuit of activities that give meaning to life may become necessary. More unstructured time is available and the potential for loneliness is thus greater. For those who are without a marriage partner or close friends, the search for social activities may represent a flight from loneliness.

Since loneliness is a stigmatizing phenomenon, elderly people often prefer not to talk about this experience. When they are lonely, they may feel that the ordeal is too painful or too blameworthy to discuss; when they are not lonely, they may not wish to recall the experience. They may also deny their loneliness. Loneliness has typically been measured by self-assessment, but some researchers have used aggregate measures in an attempt to overcome the tendency to deny the feeling. In one study, the aggregate

measure indicated that loneliness is more likely to be admitted if there is an acceptable reason for it, such as living alone or being recently widowed. However, loneliness is likely to be denied where such a reason is absent—if, for example, the sufferer is married or has made a decision, such as retirement migration, which has exacerbated the condition. Self-assessed loneliness may, therefore, underrate loneliness in old age.

Loneliness has been shown to be associated with a wide range of other variables. However, the main individual causes appear to include not being married, living alone, living with younger generation relatives or without any source of informal support, having poor self-assessment of one's health, and wishing for more friends.

Since the experience of loneliness may be more intense at one time than at another as a result of life events, levels of loneliness often change over time for the individual. Research indicates that increases in levels of loneliness are associated with changes in household composition that result in living alone, deterioration in mental health or physical mobility, and shifts to network types that support less independent life-styles.

LONELINESS AND REMINISCENCE

Reminiscence is one of the natural activities of old age. It has been identified as a necessary psychological developmental stage as the elderly person seeks to make sense of the life lived in anticipation of its end. The more time available for reflection, the more reminiscence is likely to be engaged in; thus, reminiscence is more common for the very old. Where there is a sense of fulfillment in the presence of supportive family, the process can be pleasant and the sharing of memories with family and friends a source of enjoyment. Where there are disappointments, a sense of failure, or an absence of anyone who knew one when one was young (particularly for those in a second homeland), a feeling of loneliness that is often associated with depression is a common experience.

LONELINESS AND DEATH

Death has been seen as a very lonely experience. But whether they anticipate it as the end of personal time or as the passage into another life, elderly people generally fear death less than the illness, pain, loss of independence, and feelings of being a burden that may precede it. It has been suggested that old people fear loneliness more than death itself but this might be interpreted as a fear of the loneliness of dying rather than a fear of being dead.

[G.C.W. and S.S.]

See also **Aging and Time; Euthanasia and Aging; Time and Death.**

FURTHER READINGS

Coleman, P.G. *Ageing and Reminiscence Processes: Social and Clinical Implications.* Chichester: Wiley, 1986.

Checkoway, B., H. Freeman, and T. Hovaguimian, eds. *Community-Based Initiatives to Reduce Social Isolation and Improve Health of the Elderly. Danish Medical Bulletin: Journal of the Health Sciences,* Gerontology Special Supplement Series 6 (1988).

Hazan, H. *The Limbo People: A Study of the Constitution of the Time Universe Among the Aged.* London: Routledge & Kegan Paul, 1980.

Wenger, G. Clare. "Loneliness: A Problem of Measurement." *Ageing in Modern Society: Contemporary Approaches.* Ed. Dorothy Jerrome. New York: St. Martin's P, 1983. 145–167.

LONGITUDE

The exact location of a place on earth can be expressed in terms of latitude, its position north or south of the equator, and longitude, its position east or west of a reference point. Latitude can be found by measuring the height of the celestial pole above the horizon. However, because the earth rotates on its axis and orbits the sun, longitude cannot be found by such straightforward observation. Finding longitude at sea remained a problem until the second half of the eighteenth century.

This article is about the problem of finding the longitude at sea from 1500, when ocean voyages began to increase, to about 1800, when the marine chronometer had been developed as a reliable and practical instrument. Several theories for determining longitude were suggested in this period. The two methods employing terrestrial measurements involved the variation of the compass and the use of sound signals. Neither was practical at the time. Several celestial methods were proposed: the three most practical and successful were the lunar distance method, Galileo's method of using the eclipses of Jupiter's moons, and the method employing a timekeeper. The latter alone will be discussed in this essay.

Longitude and time are related because the earth rotates on its axis once in a period of twenty-four hours, so there is a change of 15 degrees of longitude every hour or one degree every four minutes. Thus, longitude can be expressed in hours, minutes, and seconds of time, and time can be expressed in degrees, minutes, and seconds of longitude. Thereby, if a navigator can establish the local time of his ship and the time of a place of known longitude, then from the difference between these times the longitude of his ship can be found.

The idea of using a portable timekeeper to determine the longitude of a ship was first proposed in 1530 by the Flemish astronomer Gemma Frisius in *De principiis astronomiae et cosmographiae.* In theory, the method was simple: a clock showing the time at a place of known longitude would be taken on board the ship. When the local time of the ship was found by astronomical observation and compared to the time shown on the clock, the time difference, and hence the longitude difference, could be quickly determined. In practice, however, this straightforward method demanded that the timekeeper's performance would remain constant under the most adverse conditions. As Newton stated in 1714, "One [method] is by a Watch to keep time exactly: But, by reason of the Motion of the Ship, the Variation of Heat and Cold, Wet and Dry, and the Difference of Gravity in different Latitudes, such a watch hath not yet been made." Newton did not believe that such a watch could be made.

From the late sixteenth century onward, substantial rewards were offered by several countries as an incentive for a solution to the problem of finding the longitude at sea. In 1714, the Act of Queen Anne established the largest prizes ever offered "for such person or persons as shall discover the longitude": £10,000 for any method capable of determining the ship's longitude to within one degree; £15,000 if determined within two-thirds of a degree, and £20,000 if determined within one half degree, or in other words, thirty nautical miles. The £20,000 prize was the equivalent of millions of our dollars, a greater amount than most people could expect to earn in a lifetime. The act also provided for a permanent committee, called the Board of Longitude, who were empowered to pay one half of any reward when the majority were satisfied that the proposed method was practical and useful, capable of giving security to ships eighty miles offshore. The second half of the reward would be payable only after the method was proved not to err more than the specified amount during a voyage from England to a port in the West Indies. It is not surprising that this extraordinary incentive brought forth ideas from all realms of society. The minutes of the Board of Longitude reveal that its members endured many hours of impractical and often comical suggestions.

The first practical attempt to produce a clock to keep accurate time at sea was made by the celebrated Dutch scientist Christiaan Huygens. In 1657, Huygens developed a pendulum clock which was fitted with a device that, at least in theory, enabled the pendulum to swing, regardless of its amplitude, at a constant rate. Huygens applied this invention to his first two marine timekeepers which were tested in the early 1660s. The account of their third trial in 1664 on a voyage to the Cape Verde Islands indicates that the timekeepers enabled the longitude of the ship to be determined. On subsequent voyages, however, the timekeepers proved erratic and suitable for use at sea only under the most favorable conditions. The pendulum was affected not only by the rocking of the ship, but also by changes in temperature and variations in the force of gravity in different latitudes. Huygens also attempted to use a balance controlled by a spring in his marine timekeepers, but this method proved to be unreliable because the strength of the spring was affected by variations in temperature. Huygens published instructions concerning the use of clocks for finding the longitude in a work entitled "Kort Onderwys," printed in 1665. In 1693, his correspondence reveals that he had invented a special design of marine balance, similar to that later used by John Harrison in his first two seaclocks. Although the great mathematician was unable to solve the longitude problem, his work was of considerable influence to those who followed him.

The next serious proposal came from an Englishman, Jeremy Thacker, an ingenious maker who published an account of a marine clock in 1714. His spring-driven timekeeper was housed inside a bell jar in a vacuum, an idea that, although probably original to Thacker, had already been proposed in 1668 by an Italian maker named Antonio Tempora for his marine timekeeper. Thacker's clock embodied a form of maintaining power, a device to keep the clock running while it was being wound. Thacker was the first person to use the word "chronometer" to describe his marine timekeeper. In his account, he claims to have made the machine he describes, but no records of its use at sea or any other work he produced have survived.

In 1703, a young English watchmaker named Henry Sully, who had worked with the celebrated English horologist George Graham, became interested in producing a clock to solve the longitude problem. However, his interests were diverted by a project to establish watch factories in France. When these ventures proved unsuccessful, he settled in Paris and turned his interests to precision timekeeping, suggesting several important technical improvements for both clocks and watches. The ingenious marine timekeeper that he presented to the académie in 1724 was followed by other models, one of which was tested in 1726. Although it performed well in calm water, it did not keep time in the open sea, and Sully's untimely death two years later brought a sudden end to his promising work. His only surviving marine timekeeper is on exhibition at the Clockmakers' Museum at the Guildhall Library in London.

The failure of many of the leading scientists and horologists to produce a timekeeper capable of performing accurately and reliably at sea caused Isaac Newton to summarize the situation in 1721 as follows: "A good watch may serve to keep a recconing at Sea for some days and to know the time of a celestial Observ[at]ion: and for this end a good Jewel watch may suffice till a better sort of Watch can be found out. But when the Longitude at sea is once lost, it cannot be found again by any watch." Newton concluded this passage in his letter to Josiah Burchett by saying that the only practical method of resolving the longitude problem was through the perfection of astronomy.

Seven years later, determining the longitude at sea with a clock did not seem such a farfetched idea, because the problems of precision timekeeping on land appeared to have been resolved: an Englishman named John Harrison had produced longcase clocks that he claimed could keep time to within a second a month, would run without oil, and would need to be cleaned only once every thirty years—a remarkable achievement indeed, particularly because these clocks were made largely of wood. Harrison, a carpenter by trade, was determined to overcome the problems of making a clock to keep time at sea and about 1730, took his ideas to London in the hope of obtaining financial support for the construction of a "seaclock." George Graham was sufficiently impressed by Harrison's remarkable ingenuity to make him an interest-free loan. Harrison's first "seaclock" incorporated a special form of his "grasshopper" escapement to overcome friction, a brass and steel gridiron to compensate for changes in temperature, a device for maintaining power, and other devices that he had invented and developed for his longcase clocks. This seaclock was completed by 1735 and proved its reliability in 1736 on its return voyage from Lisbon, when it established the ship's position correctly. Harrison, however, was intent on improving the design and so began the construction of a second machine about 1737. This machine was never tested on a voyage and in 1741 Harrison embarked on the construction of a third marine timekeeper, a device that strained the limits of his ingenuity and patience for the next nineteen years. "My curious third machine," as he referred to it, was never tested at sea, for by the time it was ready, he was perfecting a timekeeper that already proved to be more reliable. This remarkable "watch," just over five inches in diameter, was completed in 1759 and tested on two voyages to the West Indies in 1761 and 1764. The man responsible for testing Harrison's machines was the Astronomer Royal, Nevil Maskelyne, who was a strong advocate of the lunar distance method of finding longitude. During the second trial, the timekeeper performed three times better than was required to win the £20,000 prize. Harrison now discovered that obtaining the reward was almost as difficult as making the watch. To obtain the first £10,000, he had to disclose the watch's mechanism and hand over his first three marine timekeepers which were damaged in transit and were not restored until early this century. Only through the intervention of King George III, who tested a fifth timekeeper that Harrison completed in 1770, did Parliament reluctantly agree to pay Harrison a further £8,750. Beaten thus at their own game, Parliament established in 1774 a new reward of £10,000. This was made so hard to win that it was never won. Harrison's marine timekeepers did not influence the subsequent design of the marine chronometer. But they proved beyond any shadow of doubt that a clock could be made to keep time at sea and thus inspired the work of other makers.

Larcum Kendall, who had been apprenticed to one of Harrison's chief workmen, was commissioned by the Board of Longitude to make a copy of the prize-winning watch. He began this work in May 1767, completing it in 1769 for £450. After a trial at Greenwich, it was taken by Captain Cook on his second voyage, in which he navigated the South Seas and crossed the Ant-

arctic Circle. So good was its performance that Cook referred to it as "our never failing guide, the Watch." The first charts of Australasia and New Zealand that Cook produced during this voyage with the aid of Kendall's watch were of remarkable accuracy. Kendall made two other similar timekeepers, one completed in 1772 for £200 and the other in 1774 for £100. The former had the distinction of being on the famous voyage of HMS *Bounty*, but neither of these watches performed as well as the first. Harrison's marine timekeepers and the copies made by Kendall are now displayed at the Old Royal Observatory, Greenwich.

Another watchmaker who examined Harrison's prize-winning watch was Thomas Mudge. Mudge, apprenticed to George Graham, the eminent master who encouraged Harrison in the construction of his first marine timekeeper, is chiefly remembered for his invention of the lever escapement, the escapement commonly used today in high-grade mechanical watches. His marine timekeepers, although inspired by Harrison's work, are remarkable in their design and construction. They did not, however, influence the development of the marine chronometer. Mudge was awarded £2,500 from Parliament for his work. His first marine timekeeper is now in the British Museum, and the other two are in the Mathematisch-Physikalischer Salon in Dresden and the Time Museum in Rockford, Illinois.

There were two important pioneers of the marine chronometer in France: Pierre Le Roy and Ferdinand Berthoud. Pierre Le Roy, the son of the celebrated French horologist, Julien Le Roy, who had worked closely with Henry Sully, revealed his ingenuity in 1748 at the age of thirty-one with his invention of a detached escapement, an escapement in which, apart from the actions of unlocking and impulse, the motion of the balance is undisturbed. In 1754, he presented to the Académie Royale des Sciences plans for a marine clock that show that he was familiar with all the problems of keeping accurate time at sea. He constructed this machine by 1756 and produced two others in 1763 and 1764. It was not until 1766, however, that he completed the marine timekeeper that would mark him as one of the most significant clockmakers of all time. This extraordinary clock, preserved in the Musée National des Techniques in Paris, embodies some of the key elements of the modern chronometer, including a detached escapement (the form he used actually employed a lever, not the spring-controlled detent that was used subsequently in marine chronometers), a temperature-compensated balance (a balance in which the device to compensate for temperature variation is contained in the balance itself and not just applied to the balance spring), and an isochronous balance spring (a spring that would cause the balance to oscillate in the same period of time regardless of the amplitude of its swing). His belief in the latter is shown by the fact that this timekeeper was not fitted with any device to equalize the force of the mainspring. Le Roy received high praise for the performance of this and another identical machine on their three trials at sea. While Harrison had proved that it was possible to make a clock keep accurate time at sea, with these machines Pierre Le Roy had laid the foundation for the development of the modern chronometer. He was, however, bitterly disappointed not to receive the financial rewards and titles that were bestowed upon his rival, Ferdinand Berthoud. Perhaps because of this, he did not complete any other marine timekeeper before his death in 1785.

Pierre Le Roy no doubt would have received more recognition for his innovative work were it not for Ferdinand Berthoud, one of the most prolific horologists of all time, both as a maker and a writer. Berthoud, who came to Paris from Switzerland in 1748 at the age of sixteen, began work on marine timekeepers in 1762, inspired perhaps by the news of the remarkable performance of Harrison's fourth marine timekeeper. On his second visit to London in 1766, he managed to obtain a description of this watch from Thomas Mudge, and indeed, his early machines show the strong influence of Harrison's work. The steady progression of his ideas can be seen through the enormous variety of marine timekeepers that he made during his lifetime. The pension that accompanied his appointment as "Horloger de la Marine" allowed him the time to devise many different types of escapements and temperature-compensated balances which were tested with varying degrees of success. While Le Roy made no further attempt to improve upon the performance of his machines, Berthoud never rested in his pursuit of ideas. A large number of his marine timekeepers can be seen in the Musée National des Techniques in Paris.

The two people who developed the manufacture of the chronometer on a large scale and brought it into widespread use were John Arnold and Thomas Earnshaw. John Arnold, the son of an English watchmaker, gained recognition for his abilities at the age of twenty-eight in 1764 by presenting King George III with a quarter-repeating watch less than a half inch in diameter mounted on a finger ring. Soon after completing this remarkable piece, for which the King awarded him the enormous sum of 500 guineas, he turned his interests to marine timekeepers, completing his first machine in 1770. Two of his timekeepers were tested with Kendall's watch on Cook's second voyage, but they performed so poorly that the Board of Longitude refused to give him further assistance until "they [had] better proof of the merits of the watches." The improvements that Arnold made over the next few years were significant: his watch No. 36, which incorporated a pivoted detent escapement, a helical balance spring, and a new form of temperature-compensated balance, performed extremely well in its thirteen-month trial at Greenwich. Shortly after this, Arnold devised a spring-detent escapement, the invention of which was hotly disputed with Earnshaw. By 1782, having developed several new forms of temperature-compensated balances and with the pattern of his chronometers basically established, Arnold concentrated on the commercial aspects of chronometer production, establishing a manufactory outside London at Chigwell in Essex. Arnold died in 1799 and was succeeded by his son, John Roger Arnold, who continued his business and in 1806 received a windfall of £1,678 from the Board of Longitude in final recognition of his father's contribution.

Thomas Earnshaw, born in 1749, became well known early in his career as a watch finisher and escapement maker. In 1780, in an attempt to improve on the pivoted-detent escapement, he devised a spring-detent escapement. He showed this under a pledge of secrecy to a watchmaker named Brockbanks, for whom he was working at the time. Brockbanks may have shown it to Arnold, for eight days later the latter took out a patent describing, in vague terms, his own version of this escapement. Earnshaw, who had a wife and four children, could not afford to patent his own idea and therefore entered into an unfortunate arrangement with a watchmaker named Wright, who patented the escapement in his own name and demanded a royalty of one guinea on each watch Earnshaw produced until the patent fee of 100 guineas was paid off. Earnshaw also introduced the design of temperature-compensated balance that became universally adopted for marine chronometers. This bimetallic balance, as Earnshaw described it, "in the full sense of the word, equal in all its parts," was cut out of a disk of steel with brass fused on to the rim. By 1791, Earnshaw had established a workshop of his own and entered his chronometers for the £10,000 longitude prize. After more than a decade of attempts, during which he came as close as anyone to winning, he requested the Board of Longitude to reward him in some manner for his efforts. Accordingly, in 1805 he was granted £3,000 minus £500 for a grant made for the construction of his timekeepers. Earnshaw, while satisfied with the monetary aspect of this arrangement, was embittered by the fact that Arnold's son was granted the same reward for his father's work.

Arnold and Earnshaw, having developed practical designs, established a division of labor for the production of individual parts and were thus able to make a far greater quantity of timekeepers for a substantially lower price. It was through this development that England became preeminent in the production of marine timekeepers. Examples of the work of both Arnold and Earnshaw can be found in many museums.

During the last two centuries, advances in technology and the development of mass-production techniques had a marked influence on the design and construction of almost every type of product, time-related and otherwise. But so refined was the marine chronometer by 1800 that its basic design remained unchanged until the whole field of portable timekeeping was revolutionized by the advent of quartz crystal controllers.

[W.J.H.A.]

FURTHER READINGS

Andrewes, William J.H. "John Harrison: A Study of his Early Work." *Horological Dialogues* (Publication of the American Section of the Antiquarian Horological Society) 1 (1979): 11–38.

Earnshaw, Thomas. *Longitude: An Appeal to the Public.* 1808; reprint, Newark: British Horological Institute, 1986.

Gould, Rupert T. *The Marine Chronometer: Its History and Development.* London: Holland P, 1923.

Landes, David S. *Revolution in Time.* Cambridge: Harvard UP, 1983.

Mercer, Vaudrey. *John Arnold & Son, Chronometer Makers 1762–1843.* London: Antiquarian Horological Society, 1972.

Quill, Humphrey. *John Harrison: The Man Who Found Longitude.* London: John Baker, 1966.

LUNAR MONTHLY AND FORTNIGHTLY RHYTHMS

The synodic lunar month is created by the moon orbiting the earth, and is defined as the 29.5-day interval between successive new moon phases. During the days around both new and full moon, the moon and the sun's tidal forces combine, producing the largest tidal exchanges on the shoreline. These are called the spring tides. Around the two times of the month when the moon and sun form right angles with the earth, their tidal forces tend to counter one another, so the magnitude of tidal exchange becomes the smallest of the month. These have been designated as neap tides. The 14.75-day interval between successive spring (or neap) tides is best called the fortnightly cycle. Many plants and animals—especially those living in the intertidal zone along the shoreline—are known to mold their behavior (especially reproductive behavior) and physiological processes into monthly and fortnightly cycles, or as they are more commonly called, rhythms.

In some cases, the organismic rhythms are simply caused by the environmental cycles, but in others, as surprising as it may seem, some plants and animals have internal, biochemical clocks that measure off and drive their fortnightly and monthly rhythms. To demonstrate the existence of these internal clocks, rhythmic organisms are simply placed in a laboratory situation devoid of nature's cycles; if the rhythm persists in the absence of environmental cues, it is then defined as being under the control of a living clock. Examples of environmentally driven and clock driven rhythms follow.

A small green flatworm called *Convoluta* lives buried in the intertidal sands in Brittany, France. During daytime intervals of low tide the worms emerge from the sand and bask in the sun. Although each worm is minute, their numbers are so great that large expanses of sand appear spinach green after they emerge. Just before the tide returns the worms reburrow and the color of the beach returns to normal. On the days of spring tides the green coloring on the sand greatly diminishes, as if many of the animals had abandoned their daily commute. But microscopic examination of the worms reveals that the cause of this seemingly reduced population is actually a self-mutilation process associated with reproduction. Just prior to the onset of the spring tides, the posterior ends of the animals become bloated with eggs. Then, when the spring tides return, the animals break off their egg laden "sterns" leaving them buried in the sand, while the anterior ends continue their daily vertical migrations. The visual result, as determined by a casual observer, is that the whole population has been suddenly halved.

Convoluta has not yet been tested to see if its egg-laying rhythm is clock controlled, but here is an example of a plant whose rhythms are clock driven. The seaweed named *Dictyota* releases its eggs and sperm at fourteen- to fifteen-day intervals in its natural setting. When specimens were collected and observed in the laboratory they continued to release their gametes on the same fortnightly schedule. Thus, in the absence of the timing cues, the seaweed maintains its fortnightly schedule by consulting its own internal clock.

The most thoroughly studied fortnightly rhythm is that of a tiny, mosquito-like midge called *Clunio*. This animal lives on the sea bottom where it practices a unique courtship. The midges reside in the deepest part of the intertidal zone where they are uncovered by the tides only twice each month during the spring tides. During these few hours of exposure to air, the males emerge from their cocoon-like pupal cases and fly to a nearby female. The male first assists the female in escaping from her pupal case, they mate, and then, because she is wingless, he picks her up and flies her to a suitable spot where she lays eggs, and the two adults die.

When these freshly laid eggs are brought into the laboratory and made to develop in the absence of tides, adults continue to emerge at roughly fortnightly intervals if one condition is met: a light simulating exposure to the full moon must be turned on for four consecutive nights. This simple one-time treatment initiates the fortnightly rhythm that will then persist for several more cycles in the laboratory. Because the four nights of "moonlight" give no information about a fourteen- to fifteen-day interval, the results indicate that the fortnightly period is innate, that is to say it is not learned from the environment. The clock controlling this rhythm is present but not functioning until started by the simulated moonlight.

Monthly rhythms are also mostly cycles of reproduction. Many of these rhythms have been studied only in the natural habitat, so whether their oscillations are controlled by a living clock is unknown. Examples follow of both field and laboratory studies.

A colorful demonstration is provided by the antics of the Samoan palolo worm. This animal lives in a honeycomb of tunnels in coral reefs. In the autumn, each worm extends its length several fold by growing a new posterior end that eventually becomes engorged with either eggs or sperm. Then, in October and November, on the day that the moon's phase reaches third quarter, just before dawn, the decerebrate posterior ends of all the worms break off simultaneously and wriggle to the ocean surface where they eventually explode, liberating their gametes into the sea so that egg and sperm unite. So punctual is this event that it appears on the islanders' calendar as "worm day." This display is actually an example of an annual and a monthly rhythm working together. The persistence of these rhythms has not yet been tested in the laboratory.

Probably the most convincing study of monthly rhythms under the control of a living clock was discovered accidentally. A planarian, a lowly worm possessing two rudimentary eyes, was being used in a study of how the animal oriented itself to beams of light. However, the day-to-day variability of the worms' orientation was so great that the investigation was about to be discontinued when the data happened to be plotted as a function of the day of the month. To the investigators' great surprise, in spite of the fact that the worms were maintained in constant conditions in the laboratory where there was no chance of seeing the moon outside, during the days centered around new moon the worms turned away from the light, but during the days around full moon they turned toward the light. Thus, the worms' internal clocks provided the accurate temporal information required to guide their monthly behavior pattern.

Monthly rhythms have been observed for humans also. Two separate statistical studies have produced the same results: the population of women between the ages of fifteen and forty have an average menstrual period length of 29.5 days—the exact interval of the synodic month. While individuals can differ widely from one another, and while menstrual cycles are not synchronized to the phases of the moon, one could postulate that the basic period could have been derived from ancestors who until rather recently lived fully exposed to the night sky.

[J.D.P.]

See also **Chronobiology; Circadian Pacemakers; Tidal Rhythms in Marine Organisms.**

FURTHER READINGS

Neumann, D. "Tidal and Lunar Rhythmic Adaptation of Reproductive Activities in Invertebrate Species." *Comparative Physiology of Environmental Adaptations.* Vol. 3. Ed. P. Pevet. Strasbourg: Karger, 1987. 152–170.

MACHIAVELLI, NICCOLÒ (1469–1527)

Certain basic themes permeate Niccolò Machiavelli's personal letters, his plays, and his famous political treatises *The Prince* and the *Discourses*. First, there is the transience and precariousness of human affairs caused by *fortuna*, that is, by chance, uncertainty, and uncontrollable forces and circumstances. Second, there is *virtu*, or the skill, ability, knowledge, and daring, which, within limits, allows individuals to overcome fortune, or at least recognize it, adapt to it, and utilize it in the pursuit of various ends. Third, what makes such action possible is, to a large extent, the constancy of the basic attributes of human nature which can be discerned from both observations in the present and the study of the past. Time, timing, temporality, and history are significant symbols in this complex of factors.

Although not identical, fortune and time are inseparable, and both have positive and negative aspects. While fortune is often personified as female, a goddess or woman, time is usually masculine. For Machiavelli, "all human things are kept in a perpetual state of movement, and can never remain stable." Time is not only the symbol of motion and change in the physical cosmos but also in the human universe. And it primarily signifies degeneration and corruption. Machiavelli turns away from the supernatural. Change, as well as order, is essentially a function of human action and human responsibility. But mortals live in the context of nature and are tied to its movement: "Time sweeps everything before him." Time, like fortune, is fickle, yet it also offers opportunity. Time, Machiavelli noted frequently, is the "father of truth," and it opens up space for action even though what is required may not be done "in time." Similarly, "times" are variable and "bring good and evil," and "never is there a time in every way fit for doing a thing." There are "times" of "adversity," but also points at which "the time" is "ripe," "right," or "fit" for doing something. It is in the course of time that things are discovered, forgotten, and remembered, and as such it sets the scene for human activity. Time is also a commodity that one "needs" and which can be "lost" or not "used" or employed properly.

History, for Machiavelli, is both the form of human time and the events that give it content. It is the longitudinal shape as well as the record of human affairs—a record that for Machiavelli largely involved politics. Although history is meaningful in that it offers potential lessons regarding the success and failure of political action, it has no intrinsic meaning or direction. It is a story of flux and change in which "states either naturally rise or decline." Yet the continuous cycles of history, marked by the rise and fall of states, was explicable and in some measure determinable through an understanding of human nature and its propensities, which in turn made possible prudential generalizations. Machiavelli's image of the human being is distinctly pessimistic. People are, in general and fundamentally, driven by self-interest which may be manifest in various forms such as the pursuit of power, wealth, and fame or the desire for liberty and security. While these drives tend to move human affairs toward disorder, they can also produce, and be manipulated so as to create and sustain, the most important of human artifacts—secular political order or political space.

Machiavelli's intention and purpose in writing *The Prince* remain essentially contested interpretative issues. Given his nationalism and his republican affiliations and sympathies in early sixteenth-century Italy, it is difficult to conclude that the short volume was offered merely as a "handbook" of detailed ruthless instruction for political entrepreneurs or "new" princes with respect to gaining and maintaining political power. At the end of this book, based on his "long experience of modern events and a constant study of the past," Machiavelli turns to the question of why Italy, once the greatest of empires, is chaotic and disunified. And he turns also to the issue of how fortune might be overcome and under what conditions a prince might come forward and achieve glory by emulating those great founders of ancient times such as

Theseus, Moses, Cyrus, and Romulus. The immediate purpose of the book was, supposedly, to secure himself a position with the Medici family who had ousted the republican regime to which Machiavelli had belonged, but, at the time, he was in the midst of writing his long discussion of republican government, the *Discourses*, and contrasting the success of Rome with the failures of Florence.

What he called his "new route" in political science was institutional artifice based on a return to the wisdom of the past—to the knowledge inherent in the actions and institutions of republican Rome. Princes are involved now as creators, since the founding of political order, as Machiavelli so strongly stresses, must be the work of one person. But it could not rest on the moral and mortal fragility of one individual. To the extent that the book is addressed to princes, it is not for those who would destroy order and seek power for themselves, but for those who would realize the greater end of creating a lasting human cosmos and gain immortality in the memory of society. But the secret to the permanence of political order was in the principles of foundation and in a periodic symbolic and practical return to those principles.

Drawing on the idea of the mixed constitution, which Polybius had elaborated in his history of the Roman republic, Machiavelli argues that order and greatness came not, as medieval Christian humanists had claimed, from social harmony, but from conflict. It was the tension between the senate and the plebs and the dynamic institutional equilibrium between the executive and the representatives of the people and nobles that created the institutional virtue of Rome. The broad popular base of government was the best foundation for both liberty and order, and, supplemented by a policy of external expansion and by a consensus grounded in a nationalistic civic religion, a regime based on this model would transcend the vagaries of history and time. As he puts it, "There is nothing more true than that all the things of this world have a limit to their existence; but those only run the entire course ordained for them by Heaven that do not allow their body to become disorganized."

[J.G.G.]

See also **Political Theory and Philosophy.**

FURTHER READINGS

Bock, Gisella, Quentin Skinner, and Maurizio Viroli, eds. *Machiavelli and Republicanism.* New York: Cambridge UP, 1990.

DeGrazia, Sebastian. *Machiavelli in Hell.* Princeton: Princeton UP, 1989.

Orr, Robert. "The Time Motif in Macchiavelli." *Macchiavelli and the Nature of Political Thought.* Ed. M. Fleisher. New York: Atheneum, 1972.

Pocock, J.G.A. *The Machiavellian Moment.* Princeton: Princeton UP, 1975.

Skinner, Quentin. *Machiavelli.* New York: Hill and Wang, 1981.

MCTAGGART, JOHN MCTAGGART ELLIS (1866–1925)

McTaggart's famed argument for the unreality of time begins with an analysis of time according to which time necessarily involves events that have both permanent positions in the "B series" running from earlier to later and changing positions in the "A series" running from the past through the present to the future. The argument, in outline, is:

1. The A series is necessary for the reality of time;

2. The A series is impossible; therefore,

3. Time is unreal.

He has a twofold explanation for section 1. First, time requires change, and the only possibility of change is a change in an event's position in the A series, for example, its shift from being future to present and from present to past. Second, time requires the B series, and the B series in turn requires the A series, since events cannot be earlier or later than one another unless they also have positions in the A series, just as notes could not have harmonic relations to each other unless each possessed an absolute pitch. The explanation for section 2 is that since these are changing positions, every event is equally past, present, and future; and when we try to rid time of this apparent contradiction by holding that an event has these positions successively, that is to say, at different moments of time, we merely transfer this apparent contradiction to a higher order B series comprising times since its moments must also form an A series. And this launches us on a vicious infinite regress.

[R.M.G.]

See also **Analytic Philosophy; Russell, Bertrand Arthur William.**

FURTHER READINGS

Gale, Richard M. *The Language of Time.* London: Routledge & Kegan Paul, 1968.

McTaggart, John McTaggart Ellis. *The Nature of Existence*. Vol. 2. London: Cambridge UP, 1927.

MALTHUS, THOMAS (1766–1834)

This English clergyman and teacher has been one of the most influential, although controversial, figures in the development of population studies and economics. In an *Essay on the Principle of Population* (1798), he argued that the power of the population to increase is greater than that of the earth to produce subsistence. He illustrated the differential by suggesting that population, when unchecked as in land-abundant North America at that time, might grow in a geometrical ratio (1, 2, 4, 8, 16), doubling perhaps every twenty-five years, whereas food production at best increases arithmetically (1, 2, 3, 4, 5). Therefore, population growth is *inevitably* checked by the positive checks of famine, disease, and war, and by the preventive checks of "moral restraint" (especially delayed marriage). Only in later editions of his essay did Malthus think that preventive checks (broadened now to include, at least implicitly, contraception) could be at all effective. His earlier views, which constitute classical Malthusian theory, have mortality-inducing positive checks as the fundamental regulators of population growth. It is ironic that Malthus should have proposed his theory at the very time when the industrial revolution was beginning to transform the productive powers of societies and thereby undermine his theory. Nevertheless, his views have been resurrected in recent decades by some writers concerned about the inexorable pressure of population growth on limited resources in many less developed countries.

[H.R.J.]

See also **Club of Rome.**

FURTHER READINGS

Dupaquier, J., A. Fauve-Chamoux, and E. Grebenik, eds. *Malthus Past and Present*. London: Academic P, 1983.

MANAGEMENT FORECASTING

As managers rise up within an organizational hierarchy, their concerns move from the present to the future. They spend less and less of their time on controlling current operations and more and more in planning for the future. The profitability of some industries, such as insurance, is based almost entirely on an ability to forecast reliably. Unfortunately, the future is always uncertain and plans for the future must be based on imprecise knowledge of this uncertainty. Forecasting is an attempt to place a degree of order and structure on an unknown future.

Generally, prediction of the future may be based on astrology, biorhythms, divination, intuition, or any one of a number of other processes. Management forecasting normally excludes most of the outlandish processes and substitutes its own series of approaches.

The subjective approach is most commonly used by managers in small companies. It is often employed through ignorance of the forecasting techniques that are available or because of a lack of specialist support. Managers using subjective approaches often pride themselves on their ability to "read the future," to drive their organizations "by the seat of the pants," and to play their hunches. They frequently seem to thrive on the risk involved. Unfortunately, they also often go out of business and are never heard of again; even the successful ones are often the lucky rather than the able.

Much management training is concerned with the avoidance or the minimizing of risk. In effect, this is the aim of management forecasting—to arrive at predictions of future situations that are within "safe" limits. The recognition of risk leads to particular policies and operational activity. The holding of buffer stocks within inventory, for example, is a recognition that demand forecasting is an imprecise activity and that there is often a risk of being unable to satisfy customer orders through a scheduled manufacturing program, even if one could adhere strictly to that program.

Such forecasting is the basis of many decisions. Some forecasts are particularly important since they have a "cascading" effect; the initial forecast affects one decision which then affects a series of related decisions. The forecasting of future product demand, for example, is the basis of a whole series of decisions related to capacity planning, inventory management, purchasing control, plant investment decisions, and so on. Many of these decisions illustrate the fact that predicting the future involves a significant degree of risk. To build a new manufacturing plant in order to fulfill an incorrectly forecasted demand for one's product is to risk losing both capital and career.

Management forecasting of the future is based on one of three fundamental approaches: qualitative analysis, causal factor identification, and time series analysis.

Qualitative analysis is essentially subjective and intuitive. However, it is more than the simple subjective assessment of risk or prediction of the future referred to earlier. It involves some form of "constructive" approach. One method in reasonably common usage is the *Delphi method* in which a number of experts in a given field are asked for their views on future developments in that field. The results are then circulated among the experts, allowing them to refine their view in the light of what their peers have suggested. The result is often a consensus view of the future. Similar approaches are used in market testing of new products where consumer panels are asked for their views. Such forms of qualitative analysis may be the only possible approaches when there is no historic data on which to base a more "scientific" analysis.

Causal factor identification, as the name suggests, involves the identification and examination of the causal influences acting on a given situation. (Remember, though, that even astrology would claim to be a "causal science.") If we are confident of the nature of the causal relationships involved, we can make some prediction of the state of one factor (the dependent variable) based on the effects of independent variables provided by any given set of causal factor values. Two common techniques are those of curve fitting and of regression analysis. Thus, from the analysis of historic data, we may be able to identify graphically a relationship between, say, the advertising budget for a product and its sales in a given period. Alternatively, we may be able to determine mathematically a relationship using regression techniques. The reliability of future forecasting is therefore dependent on our knowledge of the past—what has happened (the historic data); more importantly, why it happened (our ability to identify the causal factors); and finally, our ability to establish the nature of the causal relationship. For example, the price of raw materials may affect the price of manufactured goods (later) and influence wage demands (even later).

Naturally, in order to use this kind of analysis, we have to be confident of our ability to predict the future value of the independent variables—at least more easily than we can the dependent one. This type of analysis is often used by governments and other agencies to make predictions about national economies—data about the expected level of a large number of relatively predictable variables is fed into a computer model and predictions about a range of dependent variables emerge.

The third approach—time series analysis—is based on the fact that time is a continuum, and that the future is often a smooth transition or evolution from the past. There are few real revolutions or discontinuities. Time series analysis is the analysis of past behavior or events across a number of (generally) even time periods in order to predict behavior or events by extrapolation across the next few time periods. For example, the demand for a given product may be analyzed and plotted on a graph against time. The shape of the subsequent graph will show the relationship between demand and time, and one can make predictions about the future behavior of demand.

This is a pragmatic approach—we are not concerned as to why any relationship exists. We do, however, often need to understand something about the variable and time relationship in order to select from a range of possible approaches. If, for example, we have data from each of the last twelve months about a certain variable, we could simply make a prediction by averaging out these figures and using that average. Alternatively we could use a moving average to take account of the time-based nature of the data. Our perhaps subjective view of the nature of the data over time may dictate the nature of the moving average. For example, in some circumstances data that are twelve months old may be considered to be of little value—in another, more stable situation, twelve-month-old data may be considered to be highly reliable. In the first case we may want to use a weighted average that weights more recent data at the expense of older data. (In such cases, we must beware ignoring or weighting out effects of seasonality—see table below.)

The reliability of any resulting forecast is often a factor of the time scale of the forecast—the further ahead we attempt to forecast, the less reliable our forecast is likely to be.

Time series analysis attempts to look for:

trends:	these are consistent changes in the value of the target variable over sequential time periods;
cycles:	a cycle is a long-term relationship between time and the factor being analyzed, normally evident over a number of years; and

seasonality: a relationship with time in which the value of the factor being measured varies with the time of the year, resulting in a curve each year that has the same fundamental shape.

For example, sales of ice cream would be expected to show a seasonal pattern with increased sales when the weather is warmest. On top of this seasonal pattern, there may be a general trend toward increased consumption of ice cream due to increasing disposable income; and over a long period, it may be possible to detect a long-term cycle in which ice cream loses some of its appeal every few years, perhaps as a result of changing health and fitness awareness, only to reclaim its appeal as a particular fitness fad goes out of fashion.

A variation in the shape of the sales-time curve that cannot be attributed to one of these three factors is a random variation (as far as the analysis is concerned) and cannot be explained by simple quantitative analysis. This is where the value of experience comes in. A manager who observes apparently random variations may be able to attribute the variation to some external event, such as (in the case of our ice cream sales) a late summer heatwave.

When a particular technique or approach is selected, the first task is to carry out some form of validation—to check that the approach is valid under the particular circumstances applying. One common way is to split historical data into two periods, using the data for the first period to establish a forecast for the second period, and then comparing the results with the data derived from what is actually known to have occurred. This allows us to gain confidence in a particular approach and in the forecasts it produces.

One of the reasons that many managers prefer "scientific" techniques is this ability to validate the approach. Another is that they provide the equivalent of a financial audit trail—it is possible, in retrospect, to show clearly how a given forecast was made, and by implication, to show that it was the "right" (which is to say the most reliable) forecast at the time. Perhaps more importantly, where a forecast turns out to have been unreliable, there is a base from which to refine the forecasting methodology rather than simply having to "start again."

Quantitative techniques have proved increasingly popular over the last couple of decades. This may have something to do with the increas-

ing education of managers, but is largely a result of the widespread implementation of computers and especially software, incorporating modeling and forecasting techniques. Some data analysis used as the basis of forecasting would be impossible to carry out within the required planning horizon without such aid.

Managers should use all available approaches as appropriate and even employ different techniques at the same time. For example, we have seen that in time series analysis there exists a degree of randomness. When making predictions about the future from analyzing time-based data, the resulting forecasts should be "filtered" through or modified by other knowledge. Predicting future sales from the trends of past sales, for example, may be unreliable if a new competitor enters the market. Such knowledge about future internal or external events or policies must be used to "temper" the results of quantitative forecasting techniques. It is important to monitor the effectiveness of the various forecasting approaches used—in effect to measure their performance over time and under different circumstances.

In any situation, the choice of forecasting approach will depend on a number of factors such as: (1) the importance of the decision or decisions to be based on the forecast; (2) the availability of relevant data (some techniques need a significant number of observations if they are to be used effectively); (3) the time horizon of the forecast; (4) the cost of preparing the forecast using different approaches and techniques; (5) the time available to make the forecast; and (6) the number of times a similar forecast will be required.

Relatively unimportant decisions will almost certainly be made on the basis of some subjective forecast. As the importance increases, there is a growing tendency to make use of some quantitative analysis (assuming data exist). For very important decisions (for example, of survival or of major strategy), forecasts based on quantitative techniques can significantly aid the decision-making process. The confidence placed in forecasts obtained from such techniques may depend on past experience with the reliability of such forecasts. Additionally, techniques such as time series analysis assume that the basic underlying structure of data and of relationships between variables remains the same. This is less likely to be true for the "far future"—what constitutes the far future depends on the situation being considered.

Almost certainly for very important and for long-term decisions, subjective or qualitative forecasting will be used to "moderate" any analytical forecasts. Managers often trust their own experience and judgment as much as they do the results of management science.

[J.P.H.]

See also **Computers and Time; Time Series.**

MANIC-DEPRESSIVE ILLNESS

As the name indicates, manic-depressive illness is a condition characterized by alternating periods of extreme hyperactivity, feelings of grandiosity and impulsive behavior, alternating with periods of melancholia, inability to enjoy pleasure, psychomotor retardation, feelings of guilt and unworthiness, withdrawal into sleep, and suicidal thoughts. The modern term for this condition is "bipolar disorder." The cycle of mania and depression is not a consistent one. The patient may pass directly from a period of depression into one of mania or the two types of mental experience may be separated from each other by varying intervals of time. In many instances, the clinical picture is dominated for a long time by one or the other abnormal moods. The illness is a disorder of the middle years of life. Recent studies have demonstrated that, in a certain percentage of cases, there is a definite link to heredity. Many patients suffering from manic-depressive illness may be helped by lithium and other medications. Distortions of the sense of time are very common in this illness. Time is experienced as being short and fleeting during manic episodes and prolonged and painfully enduring during depression.

[J.A.A.]

FURTHER READINGS

Kripke, D.F., D.J. Mullaney, and S. Gabriel. "The Chronopharmacology of Antidepressant Drugs." *Annual Review of Chronopharmacology II*. Ed. A. Reinberg, M. Smolensky, and G. Labrecque. Oxford: Pergamon, 1986. 275–289.

Kripke, D.F., et al. "Circadian Rhythm Disorders in Manic-Depressives." *Biological Psychiatry* 13 (1978): 335–351.

Wehr, T.A. "Forty-Eight-Hour Sleep-Wake Cycles in Manic-Depressive Illness." *Archives of General Psychiatry* 39 (1982): 559–565.

MANN, THOMAS (1875–1955)

Thomas Mann, like other great writers of his age, probed into the problematic nature of time. The characteristic tension of opposites in his work is closely knit to the polarities of temporality and timelessness, outer and inner time, transitoriness and the myth of the eternal return. This concern with time permeates both content and form as Mann creates literary experiences that not only talk about time but also generate a sense of temporality in the reader.

The work that one most immediately associates with Mann and time is *The Magic Mountain*. Mann himself referred to it as a *Zeitroman*, a "time novel" which reflects its time, discusses time, and manipulates the experience of time through its very structure. The plot can be briefly outlined: the protagonist, Hans Castorp, goes to a tuberculosis sanatorium for three weeks to visit a cousin and ends up staying for seven years, only to return to the world as World War I breaks out. During this time he encounters a variety of people, viewpoints, and ideologies whose interaction shapes the novel more than any plot. At the beginning of his stay the events, reactions, new experiences, and impressions create a sense of temporal passage, but as he remains on the mountain, virtually cut off from the rest of the world, time begins to dissolve into a timeless stasis marked only by the taking of temperatures and meals. The changeless routine of the day makes all days the same and creates a sense of a continuous present. References to time become more and more vague: "recently" could refer to weeks, years, even a century, and the smallest unit of time is a month. Castorp's watch, once broken, is easily forgotten—it has no relevance here. Time passes without the notice of the protagonist or of the reader.

When Castorp removes himself from the time-conscious, bourgeois world below the mountain, he acquires a new freedom: freedom to pursue intellectual debate or contemplation virtually without interruption and without judgment. Here, where no time constraints apply and no theory results in action or engagement in the world, all viewpoints can be considered simultaneously; all intellectual ideas coexist in the realm of eternal potential. This is the "magic" and the freedom that Castorp experiences for seven years before he ultimately rejects it and chooses to return to the temporal and messy world below. The turning point comes when, caught in a snow storm, he has a vision that the polarities of timelessness and time, eternity and death can only be overcome with kindness and love, an ethical responsibility, and involvement in the world. Thus, the movement of the work is not based on a chronological depiction of events, but on a temporal dialectic from time to timelessness and then to a transcendence of both.

Mann is also known for his extensive use of myth and its impact on our perceptions and experiences of time. Myths are not time-bound; they operate in the present as prototypes of human existence. In the novella "Death in Venice," for example, Aschenbach wrestles with and finally succumbs to the tensions born of Apollonian and Dionysian forces: the striving for eternal and timeless ideals and the lure of passion, disease, and death. The path of the artist, who must attempt to walk between the two poles and draw on both without falling prey to one or the other, is precarious indeed and reveals the inherent danger of art.

Through myth, one can relive timeless conflicts and also recognize the roots of humanity and a temporal continuity with the past: "For it *is*, always *is*, however much we may say *It was*. Thus speaks the myth." *Joseph and his Brothers* opens with a descent into the well of mythic past, the depths of time, and of our own psyche. Time threatens to obliterate individual events and figures, but myth enables the singular to be perceived within the sphere of mystery in the timeless present: "For the mystery is timeless, but the form of timelessness is the now and the here." Through myth, one can recognize oneself in the past and find the familiar form and feel of humanity. Joseph sees himself not as an individual thrust into the irrational randomness of time, but as a single manifestation of the living myth that extends back throughout the ages. He is aware of the story in which he plays a part, unique and yet the same.

Thomas Mann is regarded as one of the most significant writers of the twentieth century and certainly one of the major so-called time-writers whose work reflects the obsession with time so characteristic of his age. With the hand of a master, he draws us to consider the problematic of time intellectually, but also to experience time as a dialectic of flux and simultaneity.

[M.P.S.]

See also **Novel.**

FURTHER READINGS

Bloom, Harold, ed. *Thomas Mann: Modern Critical Views.* New York: Chelsea House Publishers, 1986.

Mann, Thomas. *The Magic Mountain.* Trans. Herman J. Weigand. Chapel Hill: U of North Carolina P, 1964.

Stern, Joseph P. *Thomas Mann.* New York: Columbia UP, 1967.

MARX, KARL (1818–1883)

The main contribution of Karl Marx to the analysis of time comes in a large section of Volume 1 of *Capital* (1867) devoted to a discussion of the length of the working day and why this has changed over time. Developing a notion of the "commodification" of time, this analysis forms much of the basis for Marx's labor theory of value. In this theory, the key theme is that the capitalist economic order depends on the control, regulation, and exploitation of labor time. The logic of capitalist development entails the maximization of production in time, achieved either by lengthening the working day or, when this becomes impossible, intensifying the available time. It is in the logic of capitalism, Marx argues, that as much of the laborer's lifetime as possible is converted into labor time. A central Marxist argument is that as hours of work decrease management compensates by intensifying the pace of work, employing such means as stricter supervision, incentive payment schemes, and technological innovation. Reduction in working hours, Marx argues, "Gives an immense impetus to the development of productivity and the more economic use of the conditions of production. It imposes on the worker an increased expenditure of labour within a time which remains constant, a heightened tension of labour power, and a closer filling up of the pores of the working day, i.e., a condensation of labour, to a degree which can only be attained within the limits of the shortened working day." Marx adds that "This compression of a greater mass of labour into a given period now counts for what it really is, namely an increase in the quantity of labour. In addition to the measure of its 'extensive magnitude,' labour time now acquires a measure of its intensity, or degree of intensity. The denser hour of the ten-hour day contains more labour, i.e., expended labour-power, than the more porous hour of the twelve-hour working day."

For Marx, capitalism contracts the "pores" of the working day, thereby reducing all time to the influence of the cash nexus. Time, like the individual, becomes a commodity of the production process, for in the crucial equation linking acceleration and accumulation, a human value can be placed upon time. Surplus value can be accrued through extracting more time from the laborer than is required to produce goods having the value of his or her wages. The scarcity of time as a resource, and aims by management to intensify time use at work—applying the measure of time as an indicator of productivity—set the stage for a class struggle between management and labor over temporal issues at the point of production. Marx states that capitalists, left to themselves, are not capable of maintaining a standard work time schedule that all will respect. Instead this requires a body—the state—which stands above individual capitalists to institute and enforce this standard. More recently these issues of the nature of time under capitalism have been examined in studies of the labor theory of value by C. Palloix in 1976, M. Aglietta in 1979, and C. Nyland in 1990, and the making of a capitalist time consciousness has been studied by E.P. Thompson in 1967 and N. Thrift in 1990.

[J.H.]

See also **Political Theory and Philosophy.**

FURTHER READINGS

Aglietta, M. *A Theory of Capitalist Regulation.* London: New Left Books, 1979.

Marx, K. *Capital.* Trans. Eden and Cedar Paul. Vol 1. New York: Dent, 1974.

Nyland, C. "Capitalism and the History of Work-Time Thought." *The Sociology of Time.* Ed. J. Hassard. London: Macmillan, 1990. 130–151.

Palloix, C. "The Labour Process: From Fordism to Neo-Fordism." *The Labour Process and Class Strategies.* Brighton: Conference of Socialist Economists, 1976. 46–67.

Thompson, E.P. "Time, Work-Discipline and Industrial Capitalism." *Past and Present* 38 (December 1967): 61–84.

Thrift, N. "The Making of a Capitalist Time Consciousness." *The Sociology of Time.* Ed. J. Hassard. London: Macmillan, 1990. 105–129.

MATERIAL PROGRESS AND POPULATION

Two opposing perspectives have dominated thinking on the relationships between the pressures of population growth over time and the level of living standards. Following Malthus, there are those who argue that population growth presses inexorably on finite resources, leading inevitably to lower living standards *or* a restriction of population growth through some combination of positive checks (increased mortality) and preventive checks (reduced fertility). A very different perspective links other schools of thought: the pre-nineteenth-century mercantilists, who believed that national population growth promoted vigorous and beneficial commercial expansion; land economists Ester Bose-

rup and Colin Clark, who believe that population growth preceded and provoked agricultural progress; and technological optimists, like economist Julian Simon, who stand Malthusianism on its head by arguing that population growth, far from being a problem, is a golden opportunity. In Simon's "population push" view of history, technological progress overcomes Malthusian diminishing returns because population growth *causes* progress. It does this partly by demand ("challenge and response," "necessity the mother of invention") and partly by an alleged (but, to critics, incredulous) functional relationship between population size and numbers of inventions; the ultimate resource is thus regarded as people.

Much of the debate on these two opposing stances tends to be dominated by theory, preconception, and ideology, because empirical reconstruction and assessment of historical relationships between population growth and material progress are extraordinarily difficult to achieve. This is certainly the case with the first great turning point in human material advancement, the transition from Paleolithic hunting and gathering cultures to Neolithic cultivation of food and domestication of livestock. Nevertheless, an increasingly favored view is that the emergence, and especially the intensification, of agriculture occurred under conditions of growing population pressure in environments territorially confined by deserts, coasts, and mountains like the valleys of the Nile, Tigris, and Euphrates; the coastal plains of Peru; and the mountain valleys of Colombia. What is undeniable is that the food surpluses in such societies encouraged division of labor, trade, literacy, and political and economic integration over larger population groupings and territories. And all of this, in turn, encouraged population growth, a significant proportion of which became concentrated in urban centers.

The disentangling of links between population growth, technological advancement, and living standards presents equally intractable problems for that period of rapid socio-economic transformation known as the industrial revolution. The traditional view has been that linked revolutions in agriculture, industry, and transport directly stimulated both population growth and higher living standards. But there is increasing support for the causal primacy of population growth, promoting in its wake a series of economic changes. Consider, for example, the significant population growth in England well before the industrial revolution. London's population had already exceeded 0.5 million by 1700 and had almost reached 1 million by 1800. It is widely thought that the surging demand for food in London stimulated revolutionary improvements in agricultural productivity throughout the country, which in turn provided the capital necessary for incipient industrialization. This economic development permitted, indeed stimulated, further population growth, but the modern consensus among social historians is that real wages and overall living standards in Britain and western Europe did not increase significantly, if at all, until the second half of the nineteenth century.

In the case of contemporary less developed countries, it is increasingly appreciated that population growth is only one of several key influences on humanity's future survival and prosperity. The dominant neo-Malthusian paradigm in Third World development thinking in the 1960s and early 1970s had undoubtedly exaggerated the negative functional link between population growth and development. It is now widely believed that prospects for future advancement in less developed countries are not precluded by rapid population growth, although they may well be enhanced by more modest growth. Empirical analysis shows that there is no significant correlation, positive or negative, between national population growth rates and various measures of development, like per capita income growth, over recent decades among less developed countries. Variations in economic growth and development are determined much more by a range of structural and institutional factors.

But as concern about the harmful *independent* influence of population growth on humanity's future has receded, it has been replaced by growing worries about the environment's ability to sustain life in the long term. These worries are not the Malthusian ones of depletion and possibly exhaustion of non-renewable natural resources like fossil fuels and minerals. Rather, they concern the vital renewable resources of air, water, forests, topsoil, and genetic diversity, which are being threatened in such a way as to prejudice sustainable development. Thus, in analyzing any society, we are confronted with complex interactions that evolve over time between population numbers, environment, social organization, and technology. There is no obvious causal primacy in the set of interactions, but if dislocating factors affect *any* of the

basic components in the system—such as concentrated mortality reduction, technological innovation, or rapid environmental change—a chain reaction of modifications is set in motion throughout the ecological complex as a new equilibrium is sought.

[H.R.J.]

See also **Club of Rome; Malthus, Thomas; Population: Past, Present, Future.**

FURTHER READINGS

Boserup, E. *Population and Technology*. Oxford: Blackwell, 1981.

Simon, J. *Theory of Population and Economic Growth*. Oxford: Blackwell, 1986.

Wrigley, E.A. *People, Cities and Wealth: The Transformation of Traditional Society*. Oxford: Blackwell, 1987.

MATHEMATICS

This subject divides into two parts: time in mathematics, concerning the way in which mathematics represents and handles time; and mathematics in time, concerning the status of mathematics in relation to historical time.

TIME IN MATHEMATICS

Time initially entered into mathematics, in connection with astronomy, through the two ideas of sequences and motion. The earliest astronomy was concerned with such things as predicting eclipses, and for this it was necessary to find rules for determining which of the regular sequences of full moons and new moons were liable to be eclipses (of the moon and sun, respectively). These rules involved elementary arithmetic operations for constructing sequences which regularly repeated the same pattern.

More sophisticated astronomical systems were devised in antiquity to describe the continuous motion of the planets. At first time was introduced via the idea of uniform (circular) motion. This allowed theories, culminating in that of Ptolemy, to construct the nonuniform motion of the planets by combining uniform circular motions with different speeds. Subsequent mathematical developments, leading up to the work of Newton, made it possible to describe nonuniform motion directly, giving the modern concept of time in mathematics.

Newton's picture of the universe took space and time (understood in a pure mathematical sense) as absolutely fundamental, with other physical properties defined in terms of them. Building on this, he introduced into mathematics the idea of the rate of change (or, as he called it, the fluxion) of a quantity with time. Defining precisely the idea of a rate of change proved to be a difficult matter which was not fully solved until the end of the nineteenth century. Intuitively, the rate at which a quantity was changing at some given instant of time was to be calculated by dividing its change over a short period of time by the length of the period, and then repeating the calculation for successively shorter periods until, in the limit as the period became vanishingly small, one obtained the instantaneous rate of change. Newton avoided the difficulty of making this precise by appealing to change with time as a fundamental physical process that could not be analyzed further. This (with Leibniz's alternative approach that did not depend on time) was the foundation of the differential calculus.

Given the idea of rate of change, it was possible to describe much more general sorts of motion by specifying how the rate of change of a quantity depended on the value of that quantity. In particular, one could try to describe how the rate of change in the position and velocity of a planet depended on what its position and velocity was at any given instant. An equation that relates rate of change to value, for one or more quantities, is called a first order differential equation, and the motion which it describes is called a dynamical system.

While Newton made time a special feature of his mathematics, later mathematicians tended to regard time simply as another coordinate, along with the three dimensions of space. Thus, mathematically, there was no difference between the rate of change of position with time (the velocity of a point) and the rate of change of one spatial coordinate relative to another as a curve is traced (the slope of the curve). In this sense, time disappeared from the mathematics: the coordinate t was treated in the same way as any other coordinate, and time entered only into the physical interpretation which was placed on the coordinate once the mathematics had been carried out.

There are many features implicit in the idea that time can be described by a single numerical parameter t: it implies that time is one-dimensional, is continuous, and has a direction in which t increases. In addition, modern mathematics recognizes many different number systems in which t might take values: rational numbers (that is, fractions), real numbers (expressible as infinite decimals), and nonstandard numbers (which include infinitesimal and infi-

nite numbers). As a matter of convenience, rather than on physical grounds, time is regarded as described by a real number. Many writers influenced by relativity have argued that time should be represented not by points in a number system, but by points in a set having fewer properties: for instance, only the properties of order, or of one-dimensionality, without the numerical precision of numbers.

A different aspect of time appears in mathematical logic. Normally, logic is concerned with propositions that are either true or false. But, as Aristotle first explored in his celebrated passage in *De Interpretatione* on "the sea battle tomorrow," if we are talking about a future event, propositions seem to have an intermediate status, the status of possible but not yet known. This aspect of logic was given formal expression in a modification of logic (usually called modal logic) by Jan Lukasiewicz, which was in turn developed into a system of mathematical logic incorporating time (called tensed logic) by A.N. Prior.

MATHEMATICS IN TIME

It is traditional to regard mathematical truths as eternal, in the sense of having nothing to do with time. It seems absurd to suggest that the proposition $2 + 3 = 5$ might only be true on Wednesdays, because it is what philosophers call an analytic truth, contained in the definitions of "2," "3," and so on. This inclines mathematicians to be Platonists, believing that the job of mathematics is to discover truths that exist timelessly in a realm of ideas.

This view was, however, shattered: first by K. Gödel, who showed that there were some mathematical propositions for which it could not be decided, by formal mathematical proof, whether they were true or false; and then, more significantly, by P.J. Cohen, who showed that there were some propositions where one could freely choose, without fear of ever running into contradictions, whether they were true or false.

This lent weight to the idea that mathematics was not a process of discovery, but a process of creation, and so necessarily took place in time. L.E.J. Brouwer used this as the basis of his development of an alternative approach to mathematics called intuitionism. In this approach, a number like π is not to be thought of as an abstraction, living in a timeless realm. Instead, it is regarded as a process in which digit after digit can be generated, over the course of time, according to prescribed rules, but which is never completed. Mathematics, when thought of in this way, obeys a nonstandard logic called intuitionistic logic, characterized by denying the law of the excluded middle: there can be propositions for which it is not the case that they are false, but which cannot necessarily be asserted to be true. (This is closely linked with the modal logic of the previous section.)

A significant minority of mathematicians support intuitionistic logic, but probably only a minority of these adhere to Brouwer's vision of mathematics as a process in time. The remainder apply the logic of intuitionism without the ideas about time from which it arose.

[C.J.S.C.]

See also **Leibniz, Gottfried Wilhelm; Newton, Isaac.**

FURTHER READINGS

Edwards, C.H. *The Historical Development of the Calculus*. New York: Springer, 1979.

Prior, A.N. *Time and Modality*. Oxford: Oxford UP, 1957.

Heyting, A. *Intuitionism: An Introduction*. Amsterdam: North-Holland, 1956.

MATHEMATICS OF MUSICAL TIME

Music is unique among the arts in its capacity for abstract structural representation, and this has given rise since ancient times to detailed relationships between music and mathematics. Music ("numbers in motion," according to Archytas) was considered one of the four branches of mathematics in the ancient Greek quadrivium, along with number theory, geometry, and astronomy. Mathematical studies of musical proportion are found in ancient Arabic, Indian, Chinese, and Western texts, among others, referring predominantly to pitch, but also to phenomena like rhythm and duration.

Early theories of musical time often codified temporal patterns systematically. The thirteenth-century Western system of modal rhythm, for example, proposed a simple set of rhythms as a basis for all rhythmic structure. The design of these rhythmic modes exhibited a numerological bias toward the number 3, which was considered a "perfect" number. Subsequently, the idea of variable subdivision of time was developed by composer Petrus de Cruce, musician and mathematician Philippe de Vitry, and others; mensuration was born. By the late fourteenth century, complex rhythmic structures had developed in certain styles of art music (for example, the isorhythmic motet) based upon the subdivision of time units into 2, 3, 4, 5, or as many as 13 parts. Different subdivisions might be applied to different voices (parts) in a complex polyphonic texture, each of which might move at different though related rates (for example, twice or $^3/_2$ as fast). The voices were sometimes based on a central melodic pattern, which might also be retrograded. Apparently, proportioning on larger time scales was sometimes based on the golden mean ratio (1.618. . .) or the Fibonacci series, a series that is found in the works of Johannes Ockeghem and Jacob Obrecht. (The Fibonacci series begins 1, 1, 2, 3, 5, 8, 13. . .; each element is the sum of the previous two elements.)

Another early comprehensive pattern and proportion-based theory is found in the tala system of India. Using a complex system of temporal cycles and subdivisions, it provides systematic tools for overlaying multiple patterns of one length to fit within larger time cycles (for example, the *tihai*).

In Western music, the mathematical and structural orientation to music theory went into partial decline as the rise of Renaissance humanism brought rhetoric, emotion, and poetics to the foreground. The scientific founding of acoustics, beginning in the early eighteenth century, brought rigorous mathematical treatments to vibration and sound, but these developments were little mirrored in musical time theory until well into the twentieth century.

The twentieth century has in the first instance seen a continuing application of basic number theory to temporal proportion, using such sources as the golden mean, Fibonacci series, and prime numbers. For example, the Fibonacci series is used in Bela Bartok's *Sonata for 2 Pianos and Percussion*, Karlheinz Stockhausen's *Telemusik*, and works by Brian Ferneyhough and John Chowning.

Serialism, originally formulated by Arnold Schönberg in the early 1920s to organize pitch structure, was later extended to time structure. This extension was facilitated by the representation of the twelve note names per octave (C, C#, D, D#, and so on)—now called *pitch classes* (after the mathematical term *equivalence class*)—as the integers modulo 12.

The form of temporal serialism most analogous to Schönberg's pitch serialism is the *time point series* developed by Milton Babbitt in the 1960s. There, the integers 1 to 12 are taken to be, for example, the twelve sixteenth-note positions of a ³/₄ bar, allowing the familiar serial operations of inversion, retrogression, and transposition to be directly applied to time. So-called *multiserialism* also led to the serializing of other musical parameters like dynamics, timbre, and envelope attack time, and to series of lengths other than 12.

Each such formulation involves a mathematical *group*, and many mathematical properties of such groups have ready musical interpretations. For example, Jeff Pressing found that the common scale structures in Western tonal music are isomorphic to common West African time-lines in 12/8 meter.

Traditional music in all its variety contains a number of time phenomena that are readily represented mathematically. Musical meter or pulse provides a reference grid that makes it natural to treat such music as a metric space, that is, a space with a distance measuring function. Subdivision and aggregation of temporal units or note groups are readily put into mathematical representation (using arithmetic or Boolean operations). Musical repetition, scaling (stretching or compressing patterns in time), and retrogression (time reversal) can similarly be simply represented by mathematical operators, and the symbolic expression of formal structure in music has a long history.

Polyrhythm or polymeter can be represented as the quotient of integers, and this representation can indicate the degree of "temporal dissonance" between parts. Rubato (deviations from a steady tempo) may be made explicit by the use of tempo maps that show tempo as a function of score location.

With the rapid development since the 1960s in the serious application of computers for musical purposes, musical processes became increasingly susceptible to algorithmic (explicit) formulation, whether for composition, analysis, or interactive performance with humans. This made far easier the application of mathematical operations to musical entities like notes and motives. Stochastic and rule-based systems of musical time were developed. Polyrhythms and polytempo-based musical structures that were unplayable by humans now became generally realizable. (This was predated only by the pioneering *Studies for Player Piano* of Conlon Nancarrow, who realized such things as mensuration canons based upon tempi in the ratio of π.)

One of the pioneers of the application of mathematics for compositional purposes is Iannis Xenakis. He has used stochastic distribution functions to create statistical note clouds and sound masses, as in *Pithopratka* for string orchestra; set relationships to articulate musical development, as in *Herma* for solo piano; directed graph theory to indicate patterns of allowed temporal succession; and employed game theory to produce temporally interactive musical designs. The use of probability theory (distribution functions, Markov chains, transition tables, fractional noises, random walks) is now a standard resource of computer music composition.

Other applications of mathematics to musical time include acoustics (used to synthesize new sounds by solution of the physical equations of vibration), nonlinear dynamics (often used to create self-similar, or fractal, music), information theory (used to control redundancy), Latin and magic squares (used to manipulate arrays of notes or rhythms), and time series analysis (to look for correlations between musical events).

A recent and highly developed theoretical integration of musical pitch, time, and other variables is the generalized interval system of David Lewin. This provides a formalism based on abstract algebra that links sets of musical objects and their associated groups of intervals.

[J.L.P.]

See also **Computer Music; Rhythm and Meter in Music; Music: Western.**

FURTHER READINGS

Bel, B. "Time and Musical Structures." *Interface* 19 (1990): 107–135.

Kramer, Jonathan D. "Studies of Time and Music: A Bibliography." *Music Theory Spectrum* 7 (1985): 72–106.

———. *The Time of Music.* New York: Schirmer Books, 1988.

Xenakis, Iannis. *Formalized Music.* Bloomington: Indiana UP, 1971.

Yeston, Maury. *The Stratification of Musical Rhythm.* New Haven: Yale UP, 1976.

MAYA ASTRONOMY

The concept of time is expressed in various Maya languages by the word *k'in*. In addition to signifying "time," the same term also represents "day," "sun," and "feast." Moreover, the expression *ah k'in* has the meaning of "priest." Thus, the single word *k'in* reveals the intimate connection of time, calendars, astronomy, and religion in Maya thought.

Sun, moon, and Venus were principal gods in the Maya pantheon and played an important role in Maya mythology. The motions of these three bodies were of primary concern to the Maya astronomers. Time, as measured by the sun, was approximated by a year calendar of 365 days; as measured by the moon, it was recorded in a separate lunar calendar using months of 29 or 30 days; and as measured by Venus, it was approximated by a calendar of 584 days. One of the major problems of the astronomers was to commensurate the periodicity of these astronomically based calendars with the sacred round, an all-important ritual calendar of 260 days.

ECLIPSES

The Dresden Codex, a Maya hieroglyphic book dating from around the thirteenth century, contains a table that groups six and occasionally five lunar months in a sequence of seventy stations spanning forty-six sacred rounds (46 x 260 = 11,960 days). The 405 lunations of the table span, on the average, 11,959.89 days, so that the commensuration of the lunar cycle with the sacred round is in error by less than three hours. The stations in the table are those on which solar eclipses might be visible. The table also includes a subtable, with fifteen-day intervals, allowing the user to reach lunar eclipse stations. This eclipse warning table can be recycled (a variety of mechanisms, based on the structure of the table, have been suggested) so that it remains effective over long periods of time.

The Maya believed that both solar and lunar eclipses were caused by a celestial creature, identifiable as a Venus deity, that devoured the sun or moon. Eclipses aroused considerable fear since it was thought that, following an eclipse, the Venus monster would descend to the earth and devour mankind. This vision of the end of time is portrayed in the text and scene of the Dresden eclipse (see figure 1).

The first hieroglyph at A1 is an upside-down headless mannequin attached to a half-form Venus sign. It refers to the plunging monster depicted in the bottom portion of the illustration. The hieroglyphs A3 and B3 are eclipse symbols containing signs for the sun and moon, respectively, in their interiors. The pair of hieroglyphs at A4 and B4 name a Venus deity associated with the evening star. The rectangular cartouche at the base of the text is a sky band representing the sky itself. Below this are two additional eclipse symbols again containing the signs for the sun and the moon. Finally, suspended from the eclipse signs and the sky band is a monster diving earthward. Its head is a full-form Venus sign marking it as a Venus deity.

Figure 1. The final text and picture of the eclipse table, Dresden Codex, page 58 (drawing by M.P. Closs).

VENUS

The Dresden Codex also contains a table of four Venus stations, including its first appearances as morning star and as evening star, commensurated with the solar year. The commensuration formula is based on eight solar years being equal to five Venus cycles (8 x 365 = 5 x 584). This cycle is further commensurated with the sacred round to create a larger cycle of approximately 104 solar years (= 13 x 8 x 365) or 65 Venus years (= 13 x 5 x 584). The table itself can be recycled, preserving its astronomical integrity, by using calculation factors embedded in the introduction to the table.

The four Venus stations occurring in the table are coordinated with the phase of the moon when Venus first arises as morning star. This patterning leads to a Venus-eclipse cycle that is implicated in some of the base dates used in the table.

In their inscriptions, the Maya sometimes noted the stationary periods of Venus associated with maximum elongations. In addition, scribes often noted that military excursions were timed astronomically by including references to the first appearance of Venus as evening star.

OTHER ASTRONOMICAL REFERENCES

There is reasonable evidence that the Dresden Codex also includes a table commensurating the synodic cycle of Mars with the sacred round (780 = 3 x 260). There is also evidence that stationary points of Jupiter, Mars, or Saturn may have served as ritually important dates for the Maya. The existence of a Maya zodiac is strongly suggested by the existence of a sequence of thirteen constellations named in a table of the Paris Codex (another of the surviving pre-Columbian Maya books). A subset of this sequence, in the same order, is recorded on a pre-Columbian Maya structure called the Monjas, located at Chichen Itza. Here, the figures are surmounting or surmounted by a star sign.

ARCHAEOASTRONOMY

Many measurements of the orientation of buildings and the layout of sites have been obtained in the Maya area. These reliably show that the Maya architects were concerned with alignments relating to the sun, the moon, and Venus. With respect to the sun, these included an interest in the solstices and the cardinal directions.

[M.P.C.]

See also **Archaeoastronomy; Maya Calendars and Chronology.**

FURTHER READINGS

Aveni, Anthony F. "Archaeoastronomy in the Maya Region: A Review of the Past Decade." *Journal of the History of Astronomy*, Vol. 12, *Archaeoastronomy* 3 (1981): S1–S16.

Aveni, Anthony F., and H. Hartung. *Maya City Planning and the Calendar*. Philadelphia: Transactions of the American Philosophical Society (Vol. 76, Part 7), 1986.

Bricker, H.M., and V.R. Bricker. "Classic Maya Prediction of Solar Eclipses." *Current Anthropology* 24 (1983): 1–23.

Closs, M.P. "Cognitive Aspects of Ancient Maya Eclipse Theory." *World Archaeoastronomy*. Ed. Anthony F. Aveni. Cambridge: Cambridge UP, 1989. 389–415.

Justeson, John S. "Ancient Maya Ethnoastronomy: An Overview of Hieroglyphic Sources." *World Archaeoastronomy*. Ed. Anthony F. Aveni. Cambridge: Cambridge UP, 1989. 76–129.

Lounsbury, F.G. "Maya Numeration, Computation, and Calendrical Astronomy." *Dictionary of Scientific Biography*. Vol. 15, Supplement 1. New York: Scribner's, 1978. 759–818.

MAYA CALENDARS AND CHRONOLOGY

The ancient Maya inhabited a region encompassing present-day Guatemala, Belize, the western parts of Honduras and El Salvador, and the lowlands of southern Mexico (the states of Yucatan, Campeche, Quintana Roo, most of Tabasco, and the eastern part of Chiapas). The Maya have a long history, their earliest known village being dated to around 1000 B.C. while their last independent kingdom was not subdued until A.D. 1697. From A.D. 300 to 900, the Maya civilization flourished during an era known as the classic period.

One of the most exciting features in Maya civilization is their development of a system of hieroglyphic writing. The basic elements in the script are intricate logographic and phonetic signs, commonly called glyphs. These were combined in accordance with complex rules of orthography to reflect accurately the spoken word with fidelity to the grammar, syntax, and sounds of ordinary speech. Scholars have made considerable progress in deciphering this once poorly understood script and there is wide agreement on the linguistic interpretation of many glyphs.

Students of Maya writing have at their disposal a large number of pre-Columbian texts. The current inventory includes four screen-fold books, called codices, thousands of carved stone monuments, and thousands of ceramic vessels.

THE 260-DAY CALENDAR

The most basic of the Maya calendars, shared by their neighbors and predecessors in Mesoamerica, is a cycle of 260 days. It can be dated as far back as 500 B.C. In Mayanist literature, it is referred to as the "sacred round," the "sacred almanac," or the *tzolkin* ("sequence of days"). The sacred round is the product of repeating cycles of thirteen day numbers, from one to thirteen, and of twenty day names. By convention, the latter are rendered in their Yucatec names: *Imix, Ik, Akbal, Kan, Chicchan, Cimi, Manik, Lamat, Muluc, Oc, Chuen, Eb, Ben, Ix, Men, Cib, Caban, Etz'nab, Cauac,* and *Ahau.* The two cycles combine to generate 260 dates in the sacred round. The calendar days begin with *1 Imix, 2 Ik, 3 Akbal,* continuing on to the thirteenth day, *13 Ben.* The next day, the fourteenth in the calendar, is *1 Ix* (since 14 divided by 13 leaves a remainder of 1), followed by the fifteenth day, *2 Men*, and so on. After the twentieth day, *7 Ahau*, the day names begin to repeat and one arrives at the twenty-first day, *8 Imix*, the twenty-second day, *9 Ik*, and so on. This pattern continues until the 260 (13 x 20) possible combinations of day numbers and day names have been used. At this point, one again arrives at *1 Imix* and a new cycle of the calendar begins.

THE 365-DAY CALENDAR

A second calendar, often used in conjunction with the 260-day calendar, is a cycle of 365 days known as the "vague year." This is a whole day approximation of the "tropical year" of 365.2422 days and is so named because it does not preserve an alignment with the seasons over long periods of time. The vague year is also referred to as the "agricultural calendar" or simply as the "year." It consists of eighteen named "months" of twenty days each, traditionally identified by their Yucatec names *Pop, Uo, Zip, Zotz', Zec, Xul, Yaxkin, Mol, Ch'en, Yax, Zac, Ceh, Mac, Kankin, Muan, Pax, Kayab*, and *Cumku*, and a residual "month" of 5 days called *Uayeb*. The first nineteen days in the twenty-day months and the first four days in the five-day month are numbered consecutively from one to nineteen and from one to four, respectively. The last day in each of the months is sometimes indicated by prefixing a glyph signifying "end" to the month in question. When this happens, the date is transcribed with a coefficient of twenty for a twenty-day month and with a coefficient of five for the five-day month. However, the more common practice is to represent the last day of a month as the "seating" or "installation" day of the incoming month. In that case, the incoming month is transcribed with a coefficient of zero. For example, the days of the month *Yaxkin* may be enumerated as *1 Yaxkin, 2 Yaxkin, . . . 19 Yaxkin,* and *20 Yaxkin* ("end of" *Yaxkin*), but usually, the last day of the month is recorded as *0 Mol* ("seating of" *Mol*).

THE CALENDAR ROUND

The 260-day and 365-day calendars tended to be used simultaneously and a given day would be expressed by recording its date in both calendars. This double specification for a day has come to be known as a "calendar round" date. The calendar round cycle generated by the two calendars will have 18,980 (73 x 260 or 52 x 365) dates since this is the lowest common multiple of 260 and 365. Thus, the cycle is about fifty-two

years in length and dates within it are only unique within such an interval. It is theoretically possible for the two components of the calendar round to be synchronized in five different ways. However, knowing the calendar round date for any given day would be sufficient to recover the synchronization used by the Maya. For this purpose, it is convenient to use the date *4 Ahau 8 Cumku*, since this also served as the base date for Maya chronology.

MAYA CHRONOLOGY

The Maya measured time intervals between calendar dates by a composite chronological count consisting of a vigesimal count of *tuns* (periods of 360 days), and distinct counts of *winals* (twenty-day periods), and *k'ins* (days). The vigesimal multiples of the *tun* are known as the *k'atun* (20 *tuns*), the *baktun* (400 *tuns*), and the *pictun* (8,000 *tuns*). Other higher periods also occur but these are much less common. In their inscriptions, the Maya customarily recorded the calendar round dates of significant events and linked these together by indicating the chronological interval separating the dates.

If the Maya wished to anchor dates absolutely, they often expressed the chronological distance of the first date in a text from a fixed date far in the past. This base date, or zero point of Maya chronology, is a *4 Ahau 8 Cumku* that fell in the year we designate as 3114 B.C. There are around 200 carved stone inscriptions that begin their texts in this way. These records begin with a characteristic glyph, called an introducing glyph, and continue with a reference to the chronological interval separating the initial date of the text from the base date.

The Maya also recorded the dates of mythological events occurring before the *4 Ahau 8 Cumku* base by specifying the chronological distance from the mythological date to the base date. Specialized notations were introduced for this purpose.

In many cases, texts frequently anchored their dates by simply linking them to major stations in the absolute chronology, typically the ends of *k'atuns*. Since the dates of these stations repeat every 260 years, some ambiguity could enter the system if such controls were employed without a more complete reference to the absolute chronology.

THE LUNAR CALENDAR

In those instances where a date is fixed in the absolute chronology, it is normally the case to include supplementary information concerning

A   B

Figure 1. The initial sentence from the back of Stela 3 from Piedras Negras, Guatemala (drawing by M.P. Closs).

a sequence of six lunations (the lunar half-year), and the duration of the present (or preceding) lunar month as being of either twenty-nine or thirty days.

OTHER CYCLES

The Maya also employed a number of other cycles in addition to those described above. The most common of these is a nine-day cycle usually interpreted as a sequence of nine lords of the night. Each of the nine days (nights) in the sequence has a characteristic glyph.

Another cycle, of a 819-day duration and somehow involving the rain god, occurs at several sites. This cycle includes references to the four cardinal directions and their associated colors. Because the directions and their colors alternate according to a four-day pattern, the result is to generate a combined cycle of 3,276 (4 x 819) days. In addition, there is some evidence for a cycle of seven days.

AN EXAMPLE OF MAYA CALENDAR USAGE

In order to appreciate how some of these calendrical cycles and chronological periods were used in Maya writing it is necessary to look at a specific example. The illustration (Figure 1) shows the initial sentence from an inscription on Stela 3 from Piedras Negras, Guatemala. The text begins at A1 with a special introducing glyph that includes a variable element related to the month of the 365-day calendar. This is followed in sequence from B1 to B3 with a chronological count of 9 *baktuns, 17 k'atuns, 2 tuns, 0 winals,* and *16 k'ins.* The time periods are represented by the heads of zoomorphic personifications of birds at B1, A2, and B2, of a toad at A3, and an anthropomorphic monkey at B3. The numbers are indicated by "bars" having value 5 and "dots" having value 1. They occur as prefixes of the various heads representing the time periods. The crescents in the numbers at A2, B2, and B3 have no numerical value and are used for aesthetic reasons. There is a special symbol for zero prefixed to the toad head representing the period of twenty days at A3. The entire account links the current date to the base date of Maya chronology at *4 Ahau 8 Cumku* some 4,000 years earlier. The current sacred round date is *5 Cib* and is recorded at A4. The sign for the seventh station in the nine-day cycle is given at B4. The current age of the moon, twenty-seven days, is recorded at B5. (This consists of a moon glyph with a large dot in the center having a value of 20 and a superfix of 7.) A statement that this is the second moon in the lunar half-year occurs at

the position of the initial day in the lunar calendar. This is presented by a moon age count giving the age of the current moon on the day in question, the numerical position of the moon in

A6 and a note that the lunation has a duration of twenty-nine days is written at A7. The current date in the 365-day calendar, *14 Yaxkin*, appears at B7. The text continues with a description of the event occurring on this day. At A8, we find the verb "was born" and at A9–A10 the subject is named as "Lady K'atun Lord, Lady Night Lord." In summary, the initial sentence of this text names and records the birth date of a noble Maya woman, anchors it in the absolute chronology, and provides some lunar information pertaining to the birth date. In the Gregorian calendar, the date corresponds to A.D. 674, July 6.

[M.P.C.]

See also **Maya Astronomy.**

FURTHER READINGS

Closs, M.P. "The Mathematical Notation of the Ancient Maya." *Native American Mathematics*. Ed. Michael P. Closs. Austin: U of Texas P, 1986. 291–369.

Lounsbury, F.G. "Maya Numeration, Computation, and Calendrical Astronomy." *Dictionary of Scientific Biography*, Vol. 15, Supplement 1. New York: Scribner's, 1978. 759–818.

Thompson, J.E.S. *Maya Hieroglyphic Writing: An Introduction*. 3rd ed. Norman: U of Oklahoma P, 1971.

MEAD, GEORGE HERBERT (1863–1931)

George Herbert Mead was one of the key figures in the development of American pragmatism. In general, pragmatism sought to develop an alternative to both philosophical realism and idealism by emphasizing agency, dialectics, emergence, communication, and the social sources of subjectivity and cognition. Mead's version of pragmatism was particularly relevant to social theory, as was John Dewey's, because of its irreducible social ontology and epistemology. It was within that ontology that Mead, especially during the years just before his death, worked to articulate his theory of time. While his writings on temporality are somewhat scattered, the main ideas can be found in his essay "The Nature of the Past" (1929), his four Carus lectures in *The Philosophy of the Present* (1932), and in *The Philosophy of the Act* (1938).

Mead's theory of time was framed by the more general problem of order, which he expressed in terms of disruptions of ongoing societal arrangements and modes of action. He regarded such disruptions as inherent in social systems in which change and order are inseparable. Specifically, he notes that the problem of order asks, "How can things be so reconstructed that those processes which have been checked can be set going again?" The answer requires a theory of time.

The heart of Mead's theory, as argued in "The Nature of the Past," rests in the proposition that "reality is always that of a present." The present, however, implies pasts and futures. The past arises through memory and exists only insofar as there are images of the past that form the "backward limit of the present." Likewise, the future has a hypothetical existence, since it exists in anticipations. While the issue of boundaries marking off the past, present, and future was fundamental for Mead, he maintained that no matter how far we build out both ways from the present, the events that constitute the referents of the past and future always belong to the present. It is precisely in that sense that Mead's theory was a radical departure from the traditional views of the day. That departure rejected nineteenth-century positivistic assumptions that pasts, once formed, remain forever in their formed state as well as subjective idealism's assumptions that pasts are purely perceptual. As Mead expressed it in *The Philosphy of the Present*, "We speak of the past as final and irrevocable. There is nothing that is less so." Rather, "the long and short of it is that the past (or some meaningful structure of the past) is as hypothetical as the future." Therefore, it is the specious present, in which "memory and anticipation build on at both ends," that exists.

By designating the present as specious, following James, Mead regarded it as having duration. He treated the specious present, however, in terms of the social act. The act involves a span of time containing reflection and self-indication rather than merely being a sequence of isolated moments. The social and temporal nature of the present, linking the person to situations and societal contexts, leads Mead to discuss time in terms of the dialectics of continuity and discontinuity.

Continuity is produced, as Mead argues in "The Nature of the Past," through the overlapping of one specious present by another: "There is a continuity of experience, which is a continuity of presents." More than mere overlap is involved, however, as there exists a succession of events that connects phases of a continuous process. The connected events, which are related to the social organization of society, constitute the substance of continuity, or what Mead called the "passage of something." Continuity, therefore, entails both the presence of a succession of events and acting persons who recognize succession as a succession and then render it intelligible as continuity.

The process of the passing of one present into another is also a process that gives rise to discontinuity. If continuity represents the inevitable, discontinuity represents the novel. Each specious present, therefore, contains elements of discontinuity and continuity, where the discontinuous represents departures from previous presents and is created by novel and unexpected experiences. As Mead put it, "bare continuity could not be experienced"; novel events are a requirement for the experience and recognition of continuity. Mead explained in "The Nature of the Past" that "without this break within continuity, continuity would be inexperienceable. The content alone is blind and the form alone is empty, and experience in either case is impossible. The continuity is always of some quality, but as present passes into present there is always some break in the continuity—within the continuity, not of the continuity. The break reveals the continuity, while the continuity is the background for the novelty." It is because the "primal break of novelty," or what James earlier called the knife-edge present, cannot be completely recaptured that social and personal reconstructions of the past are necessary for there to be continuity.

Novelty creates problems for ongoing action, but novelty is at the same time necessary for ongoing activity. Rather than a paradox, it was for Mead a dialectic. Specious presents consist of emergent events that are products of the continuous interplay between the continuity of events and discontinuity. The uniqueness of each present renders insecure the exact shape and nature of the future, but that emergent and time-dependent nature of the present provides it with its social qualities. This is because novel and emergent events create new situations to which persons must adjust, and in those adjustment processes, previous presents are socially aligned with current presents. Accordingly, Mead's theory of time encompasses his concept of sociality—"the capacity of being several things at once," as he puts it in *The Philosophy of the Present*—insofar as adjustive processes belong to both earlier and later perspectives. Continuity and change thus are interpenetrating and inherently lodged in social acts.

Mead's analysis was very complex, and he expressed it not only in terms of philosophical debate with others such as Whitehead and Minkowski, but also in terms of theories of causation and evaluation. His position on causation is given in two conceptually complex sentences in *The Philosophy of the Present*: "Given an emergent event, its relations to antecedent processes become conditions or causes. Such a situation is a present." Unlike the purely linear theories of causation, in which cause is located in pasts, Mead located causation in the present. Causation is a process, not objects acting on other objects. The "necessity" requirement of most conceptions of causation is met through the process in which emergent events coordinate a past and a future to meet present conditions, and the "sufficiency" requirement is met through each unique present selecting out a unique past and conditioning a unique future so as to form the adjustive response to novel events. This focus on adjustment reveals Mead's embracement of Darwinian theory. He rejected the Kantian view of forms as a priori, and treated them instead as enactments that emerged from experience and action. Form and experience are dialectically related, with adjustive processes having a functional bearing of past forms on new forms, thus contributing to the emergence of new entities. Mead's theory of time, which informs his analysis of continuity and discontinuity, therefore blends together a social theory of causation and evaluation that depends neither on the assumptions of realism or idealism, but is thoroughly pragmatist.

[D.R.M.]

See also **James, William (as Philosopher); Pragmatism.**

FURTHER REFERENCES

Joas, Hans. *G.H. Mead: A Contemporary Reexamination of His Thought.* Cambridge: MIT P, 1985. Chapter 8.

Maines, David, Noreen Sugrue, and Michael Katovich. "The Sociological Import of G.H. Mead's Theory of the Past." *American Sociological Review* 48 (1983): 161–173.

Mead, George Herbert. "The Nature of the Past." *Essays in Honor of John Dewey.* Ed. John Coss. New York: Henry Holt, 1929.

——. *The Philosophy of the Present.* LaSalle: Open Court, 1932.

——. *Movement of Thought in the Nineteenth Century.* Chicago: U of Chicago P, 1936.

——. *The Philosophy of the Act.* Chicago: U of Chicago P, 1938.

Miller, David. *George Herbert Mead: Self, Language, and the World*. Austin: U of Texas P, 1973. Chapter 11.

MEANING OF TIME IN PRIMITIVE SOCIETIES

Perception, or the sensory experience of time, is filtered by systems of time-reckoning and the instruments by which time is measured and counted. In other words, time is a construction of cultures, and the meaning of time is one area of cultural diversity. In modern industrial societies, the dominant concept of time is one of duration and succession as possessing abstract and numerical quantities which are divisible into intervals of equal duration. The result is that time is apprehended as external to experience rather than embedded in it. This modern concept of time is reckoned with technologies of clock, calendar, and schedule that impose a particular sense of duration and succession on experience.

In contrast, time in "primitive" societies is fundamentally about the experience of unequal durations, the primacy of points or moments over the durative aspect of activities, and the gross discontinuities of time that lend themselves to imaginative constructions of myth, legend, and tradition. There is a perception of gaps or holes between durations which precludes their articulation into an abstracted system of chronology. Time is perceived less as flow or passage than as incommensurable qualities. It is as if the only remembrance of time were of different Christmastimes, each with its own unique qualities, but temporally unconnected to one another. Primitive time is fundamentally about the experience of different kinds of recurrent time. As E.R. Leach observed, "the notion that time is a 'discontinuity of repeated contrasts' is probably the most elementary and primitive of all ways of regarding time."

In every society there are culturally constructed experiences of time. But time as cultural experience is particularly important in societies which emphasize oral traditions and which are organized primarily by kinship. In such societies, the meaning of time is embedded in social codes and classifications, in images and icons, and in the imaginative construction of oral tradition itself.

G. Barden shows how the kinship system of contemporary aborigines of the Australian western desert performs the dual function of serving both as an organization of social life and of time.

In aboriginal society, persons are socially classified into one of four sections in a way that suppresses the experience of duration: "According to this system a man marries a woman from another section, his son becomes a member of a third section and marries a wife from a fourth section." The result is a society in which all sections are filled and no section has members who are either all dead or yet unborn. Duration is overcome by the repetition of the marriage pattern itself, a suppression of time in which there is a refusal to name dead members. The dead are exorcised by changing the names of the living who share the same name with the dead.

Barden concludes that the passage of time is not significant in the system of social classification, which is itself an image of one temporal state. The kinship system effaces any experience of historical duration beyond the lifetime of the concrete experience of an individual. Aborigines, however, do have a completely different kind of time, called the "dreamtime."

The state of actors in the dreamtime is qualitatively different from the state of contemporaries who tell their stories. There are two lived durations—sleeping and waking—both present-oriented but unconnected. The experience is not unfamiliar. Fairy tales that begin with "once upon a time" are removed from the same *kind* of time as the storyteller or listener and placed in a time of their own. No amount of traversing a distance from present to past could land the time traveler in that other time. "Then" and "now" are perceived not as two points on a continuum, but as two different kinds of experienced duration. The meanings of "then" and "now" within modern and primitive time are incompatible.

Many of the same themes appear in very complex societies that retain oral traditions and in which kinship dominates social codes of conduct. Despite a sophisticated calendar that is used to reckon multiple cycles of relatively long durations, the Balinese represent time in social codes that make intelligible their personal and collective experience.

C. Geertz, in his classic description of Balinese time and the structure of experience, shows the connection between the depersonalization of social interaction and the suppression of duration. To take only one example, a complex classification of different kinds of persons turns individuals into anonymous contemporaries despite the social reality of living in hamlets. Balinese have personal names, but these are unspoken and socially unimportant. They also have birth order names, but these are standardized and repeated after the fourth child. In short, their names merely represent a pattern that is repeated after four children. Even the classification of relatives is an iteration of form over content. Balinese have shallow genealogies and use only a few terms to refer to everyone in the same generation. The effect, according to Geertz, is the "immobilization of time" and "the celebration of an unperishing present."

The ceremonialization of public or collective conduct corresponds to a further immobilization of duration by means of the calendar. The Balinese calendar divides time into recurrent durations, but the purpose is neither to count them nor to measure durations that would result in a sense of time as flow or passage. Instead, the purpose is to create a sense of participation in many different kinds of time, each with its own qualities and duration. The Balinese calendar is a complex demarcation of recurrent durations. There are ten different cycles of day names that run concurrently. Each day can have ten different names. In this imaginative construction of time and social reality, the conjunctions of different durations have their own day names that index a special meaning for each in terms of appropriate or propitious social conduct. Such complexity and indexicality of primitive calendars is not unusual. B. Tedlock, for example, described how Maya day-keepers interpret day names of persons using a calendar that integrates time, person, and conduct.

The meaning of primitive time is discovered in the way it privileges the idea of qualitatively different *kinds* of time over quantitatively measured and calculated homogeneous time. Primitive time is concerned with socially meaningful occasions rather than linked durations. The result is that it willingly sacrifices precision in the interest of propriety. The ultimate question about the meaning of time, from the standpoint of primitive societies, is not whether time is used efficiently, but whether occasions happen according to the durations and sequence of a social code appropriate to the event.

[H.J.R.]

See also **Primitive Time-Reckoning.**

FURTHER READINGS

Barden, Garrett. "Reflections of Time." *The Human Context* 5 (1973): 331–344.

Geertz, Clifford. *Person, Time, and Conduct in Bali.* New Haven: Yale UP, 1965.

Rutz, Henry J. "The Idea of a Politics of Time." *The Politics of Time.* Washington: American Anthropological Association, 1992. 1–17.

Tedlock, Barbara. *Time and the Highland Maya.* Albuquerque: U of New Mexico P, 1983.

MEASUREMENT OF WORK AND APPLICATIONS

Time is a precious commodity. It is said that time is money, but unlike money, once lost, time cannot be regained. Hence the importance placed upon time by managements.

The measurement and monitoring of work done by people has been carried out for hundreds of years with varying degrees of precision. It is only since the late 1800s and early 1900s that any recognizable precision has been incorporated into such measurements. In truth, it is not *work* that is measured, but time taken to do the work, which means that the term "work measurement" is a misnomer. This distinction is quite important because true measurement of work (usually in ergs) is the province of *ergonomics*. However, throughout this article the term "work measurement" is used generically to describe the measurement of time to do specified work.

Since the 1960s the trend has been away from work measurement, but it will be shown that, as with most fashions, work measurement is cyclic, moving in and out of favor over the years.

There are signs of a resurgence of popularity in work measurement brought about by new technology. Rather than reducing the jobs and staff in offices, new technology has actually created work in the form of information input, and also the means by which output can be monitored electronically. Organizations are now able to monitor the actions of operators in terms of volume of information input, keystrokes, break times, and errors. Similarly, time spent talking to customers on the phone can be monitored in information centers, insurance companies, hospitals, and other such areas. Upper limits for telephone calls are set, within which all individual calls must be made. This can have the effect of pressuring people into hasty decisions, reducing sympathetic and friendly conversation, and generating an urge to get rid of people who may need the comfort of a friendly and helpful voice. In recent years there has been a drive for, and noticeable improvement in, the quality of both products and services; the "have-a-nice-day" approach. This monitoring could be incompatible with quality of service. Do we really want to sacrifice such attention in the interest of saving time?

The extent of electronic monitoring in some areas is reminiscent of the sweatshop of the late nineteenth and early twentieth centuries, thus exemplifying the cyclic nature of the history of work measurement. The urge is for more telephone calls per hour, more patients seen, more supermarket customers checked out, and more keystrokes per minute. The results of checking the rate of keystrokes are evident from the increase of RSI (repetitive stress injury) experienced in the wrist and arm muscles of keyboard data input operators achieving up to 16,000 keystrokes per hour. However, a complete return to nineteenth-century practices is unlikely in a society familiar with the teachings of Maslow, Herzberg, and others.

Thus there may be a case for restricting work measurement to jobs concerned with inanimate objects rather than extending it to all service areas, but in any case, one should be selective in how and where to apply the techniques.

Much has been made of automation, robotics, and computer numerical control of machines, but there still is a surprisingly wide range of work which needs the intervention of human beings. When there is a need to measure work that is entirely under the control of the worker—such as the examples of keyboard data capture, supermarket checkouts, and telephone calls—a completely different approach to the measurement of work is demanded. The speeds of process-controlled work can be adjusted to preset levels. In the case of the human worker who has complete control over the handwork, the output depends upon several factors. These include the ability and skill of the worker, the motivation to do the work, the perceived importance of achieving a completion time, problems encountered, and prevalent working conditions, but of course, all humans experience different perceptions of skills and conditions of work.

The goal envisaged by Frank Bunker Gilbreth in the 1920s was "a fair day's work" for everyone. This is a very subjective target open to individual interpretation. Who is the ultimate arbiter of exactly how long a particular job should take to complete? Members of a group of keyboard operators will produce different outputs over a day, but how can we tell who has done "a fair day's work"?

Clearly, there is more to consider than the time actually taken to complete a task. If everyone worked at the same rate (such as the number of keystrokes per minute), then the output should be the same. However, looking at the factors again, it is evident that people cannot achieve an identical speed. The only solution would appear to be to set a time standard which is based on the average time the majority of people take to do the particular task, and judge each individual against that standard. Unfortunately, this gets no nearer to answering the question because the practice assumes that the time standard would be for the *person,* whereas it should really be for the time to do the *job.*

A time based on how long people actually take to do a job may not be the same as how long they ought to take. The actual time taken may be considered too slow, or perhaps too fast. The missing element here is the *rate* at which people are working. Admittedly this sounds very subjective, and in fact it is, but in practice it has proved to be a much better way of arriving at an acceptable time for doing work.

Thus, the time standard for a job should be based on actual times taken modified by the respective rates at which the person was working when achieving these times. The work measurement technique of *time study,* where a person is timed by stopwatch, is one method used for obtaining a standard time for a job.

To illustrate the principles outlined above, suppose a person is doing a repetitive job, and because of differences in the pace at which he carries out the work cycles, the time varies accordingly. The table below shows the sort of recording which may be obtained by an observer experienced in taking time studies.

TABLE 1

CYCLE	RATING	TIME TAKEN
1	90 PERCENT	0.22 MINS.
2	100	0.20
3	110	0.18
4	100	0.20
5	85	0.24
6	120	0.17
7	95	0.21

In the first cycle, the observer estimated that the operator was working at 90 percent of what he thought was a good standard pace of working.

When he looked at the stopwatch, it had recorded 0.22 minutes. The next cycle was then estimated (or *rated*), and the observer assessed the rating as the standard 100, and the time from the watch was 0.20 minutes. The observer thought the next cycle was done at a higher rate than his concept of "standard rating," so he rated this one 110, and the time taken was 0.18 minutes, and so on. Notice that he rated the pace first, and only then took the watch reading when the cycle had finished. By doing so, he ensured that the rating was totally independent of the time on the watch. This is crucial to the validity of the method of time study.

When the percentages were applied to the actual times, the respective products (usually known as *basic times*) were:

Cycle:	Basic times
1	0.198
2	0.200
3	0.198
4	0.200
5	0.202
6	0.204
7	0.200

The arithmetic mean of these seven basic times is 0.2 minutes. It will be noticed that the original actual times varied from 0.17 to 0.24, the highest of the seven being 47 percent different from the lowest, whereas the basic *times* were only different by 0.06 minutes or 3 percent. Thus, the use of rating has introduced (1) higher consistency to the times, and (2) reference to a com-

Selecting the Appropriate Measurement Techniques

Generic group	technique	application ratio	precision	time unit	suitable for
PMTS level 1	Detailed Work-Factor	150 to 350	very high	0.0001 mins.	short-cycle, repetitive work.
	MTM-1	150 to 350	very high	0.00001 hr.	
level 2	Ready Work-Factor	70 to 150	high	0.001 mins.	short-cycle, repetitive work
	MTM-2	70-150	very high	0.00001 hr.	
level 3	Abbreviated Work-Factor	30-50	high	0.01 mins.	short-cycle, repetitive work
	MTM-3	30-50	very high	0.00001 hr.	
macro-PMTS	(see text)	15-40	high	various	medium cycle, repetitive work
	standard	circa 1	med./high	various	short and medium cycle, repetitive
TIMING	time study	10 to 120	medium	0.01 mins.	short and medium cycle, repetitive
	rated activity sampling	8 to 80	medium	various	medium cycle and continuous work
ESTIMATING	overall	ca. 0.001	very low	mins. or hrs.	one-off, long cycle work
	analytical	0.4 to 3	low	mins. or hrs.	one-off, long cycle work
	comparative	0.005 to 0.05	low	mins. or hrs.	one-off, long cycle work
	category	0.001 to 0.015	low	mins. or hrs.	one-off, long cycle work

Note: The application ratios are the ratios of the time it takes to set the standard time to the time it takes to carry out the work. Thus, for example, "70" means it takes 70 times longer to work our the standard time than actually to do the job, and 0.001 means that the standard time can be set in one-thousandth of the time it takes to do the job. Because of the variable nature of work, inevitably these ratios are approximate guides.

Figure 1. Measurement of Work and Applications

mon standard pace of working (albeit a subjective one).

Observers become skilled at recognizing this standard rate of working through training and subsequent experience. In practice, other factors besides pace are taken into account in the rating, such as effort exerted by the person observed, and difficulty experienced.

METHODS USED TO MEASURE WORK

The prefatory section of this article has introduced a method of work measurement known generally as time study. An essential ingredient of time study is the rating factor which is applied to extend the times actually observed to a basic time for the job. This rating factor is present in all techniques of work measurement. In some it is explicit, such as in time study, and in others it is inherent, and even introduced quite unconsciously.

There are three generic groups of techniques for measuring work: timing, estimating, and predetermined motion time systems (PMTS). Briefly, the methods available are as follows:

TIMING

This group of techniques consists of two major methods: time study (described previously) and rated activity sampling, the latter of which relies on snap observations being made at regular or random intervals of time.

ESTIMATING

The second group covers those techniques which are based on the assessment of the time a job should take, without recourse to any device for actually measuring time. The four main methods in this category are described in Example 4 later in this article.

PREDETERMINED MOTION TIME SYSTEMS

This method of time measurement relies on tables of standard times for a whole range of procedures from exceedingly small parts of jobs, to other tables containing complete jobs such as laying bricks, welding, maintenance tasks, word processing, and filing documents. A comprehensive account will be found in the article **Predetermined Motion Time Systems** and in the *Further Readings* at the end of the present article.

In the case of PMTS, rating was built into the tables of times while they were being collected during the original observations. When the techniques of estimating are used, the assessors estimate the times which would be needed to complete the tasks if the operators were working at the standard rating of 100.

The basic forms of work measurement should not just be used as an end, but also as a means to an end. Standard times created should be compiled into *standard data* (or *synthetic data*) which are a macro form of predetermined motion time systems. The difference between standard data and PMTS is just a matter of size, the element times for synthetic data being much larger than those of PMTS.

The techniques of PMTS, estimating, and standard data are "prospective," that is, they can set times for jobs *before* the work is done. This is useful for forward planning, scheduling, and cost-estimating of work before it actually exists. Timing techniques, however, can only set times for jobs *while* they are being done, and so they are referred to as "retrospective" techniques.

APPLICATIONS OF WORK MEASUREMENT

One of the most common "roadblocks" experienced by practitioners of work measurement is the objection that "You cannot measure my job; it is different from your usual kind of work." Everyone's work is different, but it can still be timed or measured in one way or another. Thus the tool kit of the work measurement practitioner must be sufficiently comprehensive to accommodate all types of work. Over the years, methods of measurement based on the three generic groupings of techniques have been designed to meet various situations encountered. But how does one decide which technique is most suitable for a particular situation? The author has developed a diagram from which one can select the appropriate technique (Figure 1):

The three most important factors which affect the choice of the most appropriate technique are: (1) the precision which one requires, (2) the extent to which the work is repetitive, and (3) the length of the work cycle. Clearly, with highly repetitive work which is going to run for many months or years, precision is quite important because any gross rounding of values will have a cumulative effect over a long period. With "one-off" (single, non-repetitive) jobs, if one job is overestimated, the chances are that another will be underestimated, resulting in a probability of compensating errors.

JOB ELEMENTS

Any job may be analyzed into smaller elements which are definable parts of the job. Elements are identified by having specific beginnings and ends. The end of one element is the start of the next adjacent element. The elements of PMTS can be measured in ten-thousandths of a minute, whereas the elements of timing techniques are usually of the order of hundredths of a minute, and those of estimating in minutes or often hours.

EXAMPLE 1: HIGHLY REPETITIVE, SHORT-CYCLE WORK

In the previous paragraph it was stated that this type of work demanded very precise standards measured to fractions of a second. The group of techniques which would satisfy this degree of precision would be PMTS. The reader is referred to **Predetermined Motion Time Systems** for a full description of the methods.

EXAMPLE 2: HIGHLY REPETITIVE, MEDIUM-CYCLE WORK

The type of work in this category would include the assembly of automobiles and electronic apparatus (radio, TV, and computers), the manufacture of components on lathes and milling machines, and clerical jobs such as word processing. Such work may be measured using time study as described earlier in this article. An example of a time study is given in Table 1. Alternatively, standard data may be used where these exist.

EXAMPLE 3: LONG-CYCLE WORK

Long-cycle work is that work which cannot easily be identified as having repetitive elements or cycles. Examples of these jobs are cleaning the inside of a boiler, hand spraying large areas of ground with insecticide, and digging a trench. Such jobs are best studied using a timing technique known as *rated activity sampling*.

This technique requires the observer to study the job continuously, taking no times, but rating the pace of the worker at intervals of time (usually fixed, though they can be random times). For example, if the time interval chosen is one minute, then the observer will make a rating, wait one minute and then look at the worker and rate him again, continuing this process every minute. One such study is illustrated in Table 1, together with an example of the calculation of basic time in the two subsequent paragraphs.

EXAMPLE 4: "ONE-OFF" AND LOW REPETITION JOBS OF LONG DURATION

This category includes repair maintenance work and jobs which may never be done in exactly the same way again. In such cases, because of the uncertainty in the probable content of the work, it is not worth using a precise, tediously lengthy method of measurement. A more appropriate generic group is *estimating*. Estimating exists in four different forms:

1. *Overall estimating* requires the estimator to judge the work and give an "off-the-top-of-the-head" assessment for the total time needed for its completion.

2. *Analytical estimating* involves analyzing a job into elements, each element being timed using standard data where these exist, or estimating for elements where data do not exist.

3. *Comparative estimating* is a more refined method, relying on estimating into target *bands of time* rather than estimating an exact amount of time. The bands are in geometric progression, and the geometric means of each band are used as the time standards. Typical jobs (or benchmarks) are provided to guide the estimator to the correct time band.

4. *Category estimating* is similar to comparative estimating but for the lack of benchmarks. Estimators use their skill and experience to select the most appropriate time band.

APPLICATIONS OF STANDARDS

This article has been concerned with the measurement of work. Once a time standard has been derived it can be used for any purpose of which the basis is *time*. The following example illustrates some of the applications of time standards derived from work-measurement techniques. These data will be used throughout the example: the standard time for assembling control board B6 is 4.8 minutes, for inspecting control board B6 is 2.1 minutes, and for packing all types of board is 1.5 minutes; the time engaged on all ancillary work is 50 minutes; the standard labor rate for a 390-minute working day is $35 per hour; and the daily rate of pay is $195 (or $30 per hour).

1. Costing.

   Total standard time for assembling, inspecting, and packing a control board of type B6 is 4.8 + 2.1 + 1.5 std. mins. (standard minutes), or 8.4 std. mins.

   Therefore, the standard labor cost per board is 8.4 / 60 x $35, or $4.90.

2. Performance or Efficiency Statistic.

   operator performance =

   $$\frac{\text{total standard time for all measured work}}{\text{total time spent on this work}} \times 100$$

In this case, if the operator assembles 60 B6 boards on one day, and does 50 minutes of other measured work, his performance or efficiency is:

[(4.8 min x 60) + 50] / 390 min. x 100 = 86.7 percent

3. Incentive payments.

The operatives are paid on an incentive payment scheme, using the formula:

today's payment = [60 + 0.5 x (performance)] x $1.2

which in this example is [60 + 0.5 x 86.7] x $1.2 = $124.02

4. Manning.

An order is received for 500 boards of type B6, which are to be made within 5 days. The total standard time required is 500 x 8.4 std. mins., which equals 70 standard hours. One man-day is 6.5 hours, so this order requires 70 / 6.5 or 10.77 man-days to complete.

5. Planning.

To plan this work to be completed within 5 days, the manpower needed is 10.77 / 5 days, or two operators, plus a small amount of overtime.

A further example of the use of time standards in planning is given in the article **Scheduling Through Operational Research.**

These are some examples of how measurements of time are essential for effective managerial control.

[D.A.W.]

See also **Industrial Engineering [After Taylor]; Predetermined Motion Time Systems; Scheduling Through Operational Research.**

FURTHER READINGS

Whitmore, Dennis A. *Management for Administrators.* London: Heinemann, 1985.

———. *Work Measurement.* 2nd ed. London: Heinemann, 1987.

MEDICINES AND AGING

As people get older the time they have left to live decreases. Does this make them keener to extend this time, and more willing to take preventative action or medicine in order to avoid life-threatening diseases or situations? Or, alternatively, do they become less willing to forego the pleasures of some risky pursuits, or to take medicines with a high level of side effects, or carry out uncomfortable exercises, all on the grounds that long-term benefits become less relevant with age? In other words, does time in itself become more precious as it becomes scarcer, or is the quality of the remaining time felt to be more important?

A study by R. Barker Bausell has supported the first of these theories. It found that people aged sixty-five or more reported greater compliance with a series of nine health-seeking behaviors than younger adults. Bausell points out that one possible explanation for this difference is that individuals who survive into older age have done so *because* they have taken better care of themselves than those who did not. Another possibility is that the disparity results from differences between generations rather than between ages. A third explanation is that older people may be in a better position than younger people to control their diet (six of the nine health-seeking behaviors showing an age difference were related to diet). A prospective study of people over time is needed to resolve this issue. In its absence, one might speculate that older people are likely to vary as much, if not more, than younger people. Habits of risk-taking or caution may persist and possibly deepen over time, although the form these take may change. Those who have heeded advice and accepted screening and preventive care in their younger days may well become the ones who, as they grow older, will seek out and accept injections to prevent influenza. Others who have ignored exhortations to give up smoking, drink abstemiously, or take exercise may continue their indulgences, although for some, ill health may moderate their habits, as indeed it is likely to do when it strikes at any age.

Illness and incapacity increase with age and with them the number of medicines that are prescribed and taken. As indicated in studies by Robert Anderson and Ann Cartwright, Ronald B. Stewart et al., and the British Department of Health, variations in patterns of illness and medicine-taking with age, and possibly the exemption of older people from prescription charges under the National Health Service (NHS), have meant that, in Britain at least, the prescription rate for older people has been rising over time, whereas among younger age groups it has fallen.

As elderly people are prescribed more medicines than younger people, the former could be considered the main beneficiaries of modern medicine. But older people are also more likely to have adverse reactions to drugs: M.R. Bliss, a consultant geriatrician, described them as "the main victims of modern drugs and the system by which they are administered." One reason for the increased sensitivity of elderly people to drugs and side effects is the increased time it takes for some drugs to be eliminated from the body as people get older and the consequent accumulation of drugs within the body. Another problem is doctors' lack of awareness of side effects and the time it takes for dangers to be recognized and action taken. This is illustrated by the millions of people around the world, many of them elderly, who, as Charles Medawar has shown, become addicted to benzodiazepine tranquillizers. But Medawar argues that the risks were always obvious and that the providers of medicine readily allowed these addictions to develop.

Confusion among older people is often cited as a reason for drug regimes being misunderstood or not adhered to, but of course, the great majority of people who are often classified as elderly on the grounds of a chronological age of sixty or sixty-five and over are not confused. Moreover, studies have shown that elderly people understand the purpose of most of the medicines they are taking. And—as Ann Cartwright and Christopher Smith, Marcel Arcand and J. Williamson, and W.J. Gilchrist et al. have shown—their doctors' records or memories are often inadequate so that doctors are unaware of a substantial proportion of the prescribed drugs their patients are taking.

These findings are from studies in Britain where almost everyone is registered with a particular general practitioner. In countries where this does not happen there may be even larger gaps in doctors' awareness of the medicines their patients are taking. The issue is particularly important for older people because they often have more than one health problem and may be taking several medicines. They are therefore more prone to drug interactions and more sensitive to them. Yet they often do not report possible side effects and interactions to their doctors and the doctors do not always monitor these adequately. Many repeat prescriptions are issued without consultation.

Given their increased needs, it is uncertain whether older people consult their doctors as frequently as expected, even when access to a doctor is free. In Britain, as Cartwright has noted, data suggest that older people consult their doctors less than younger people in relation to both their reported morbidity and their prescribed medication. Part of the reason for this may be difficulty getting to the doctor's office or

surgery and the decline in house calls by physicians.

While doctors tend to assume that patients want a prescription, many older patients are reluctant medicine-takers. Doctors may not realize this as patients are likely to feel it will seem gratuitous to say they do not want a prescription before it is offered and noncooperative to do so afterwards.

If the benefits of modern medicines are to be maximized for older people, prescribers need to take account of the attitudes and circumstances of their patients, as well as their age and frailty, and to monitor closely the effects of the often very powerful drugs they are prescribing.

[A.C.]

FURTHER READINGS

Anderson, Robert, and Ann Cartwright. "The Use of Medicines by Older People." *Self-Care and Health in Old Age.* Ed. K. Dean, T. Hickey and B.E. Holstein. London: Croom Helm, 1986.

Arcand, Marcel, and J. Williamson. "An Evaluation of Home Visiting of Patients by Physicians in Geriatric Medicine." *British Medical Journal* 283 (1981): 718–720.

Bausell, R. Barker. "Health-Seeking Behavior Among the Elderly." *The Gerontologist* 26 (1986): 556–559.

Bliss, M.R. "Prescribing for the Elderly." *British Medical Journal* 283 (1981): 203–206.

Cartwright, Ann. "Medicine Taking by People Aged 65 or More." *British Medical Bulletin* 46 (1990): 63–70.

Cartwright, Ann, and Christopher Smith. *Elderly People, Their Medicines and Their Doctors.* London: Routledge, 1988.

Department of Health (and Social Security). *Health and Personal Social Services Statistics for England.* London: HMSO, 1978, 1982, and 1991.

Gilchrist, W.J., et al. "Prospective Study of Drug Reporting by General Practitioners for an Elderly Population Referred to a Geriatric Service." *British Medical Journal* 294 (1987): 289–290.

Medawar, Charles. *Power and Dependence: Social Audit on the Safety of Medicines.* London: Social Audit, 1992.

Stewart, Ronald B., et al. "Changing Patterns of Therapeutic Agents in the Elderly: A Ten-Year Overview." *Age and Ageing* 20 (1991): 182–188.

MELATONIN

Modern urban man lives by his watch, having little regard for seasonal changes in day length: in winter he uses artificial light to overcome the limitations of dark evenings, and in summer, heavy curtains shut out the unwanted early dawn. But most species must adapt to seasonal variations in day length, temperature, and food availability if they are to survive. For many, the substance that transduces the photoperiodic message received by the eye into a chemical signal understood by the rest of the body is melatonin. This indole is produced only during the hours of darkness by the pineal, a small gland attached to the brain. Its production is suppressed by light and thus the pattern of release reflects day length—during winter melatonin is produced throughout the long nights, but in summer the period of production is short.

For sheep and goats, young must be born in spring in temperate zones to give the maximum time with plentiful food to grow sufficiently to withstand the rigors of their first winter. The long gestation period necessitates autumnal conception and the onset of sexual activity in these seasonal animals is timed by melatonin production. If melatonin is given to experimental animals late in the afternoon in summer, thus mimicking a short day or winter photoperiod, sexual activity will commence early. Conversely, in long-day breeders with short gestation periods, such as the Syrian hamster, lengthening daylight in spring induces the onset of seasonal sexual activity, while artificially extending the "night" in late summer by giving melatonin late in the afternoon results in gonadal regression.

Even the simplest of organisms need to synchronize their life cycle with circannual climatic changes. A unicellular alga, *Gonyaulax polyedra*, produces melatonin during the dark phase and reacts to photoperiodic change by forming dormant cysts. Cyst formation can be induced in certain conditions by melatonin and related compounds. Melatonin transduces photoperiodic information in organisms as phylogenetically diverse as dinoflagellates, reptiles, birds, and mammals.

In industrialized countries, any circannual rhythm in human reproduction is likely to be strongly influenced by social and cultural phenomena, for example the availability of tax concessions. In man, melatonin is probably of minor importance as a seasonal reproductive signal for varying day length. We do, however, exhibit strong circadian rhythms—society expects most people to be active during the day and to sleep at night. The sleep-wake cycle is entrained to a twenty-four-hour periodicity by time cues such as the light-dark cycle and pineal melatonin production. If, however, an individual is deprived of these zeitgebers or external cues by isolation in constant darkness, melato-

nin production will persist ("free-running")—there will still be a rhythmic pattern but the periodicity will not be twenty-four hours. As the days pass the melatonin rhythm will increasingly be out of phase with the natural day-night cycle. Long-term blindness can mean an inability to perceive the difference between light and dark; the resultant free-running melatonin rhythm is associated with desynchronization of the sleep-wake cycle causing considerable disruption to the person's life. Giving exogenous melatonin in the evening has been shown to synchronize the timing of sleep to a twenty-four-hour rhythm and to improve sleep quality in some blind people. Melatonin administration in the late evening has also been shown to advance the timing of sleep in delayed sleep phase insomnia, a rare and socially disruptive condition characterized by delayed internal rhythms probably due to defective coupling to external zeitgebers.

External and internal desynchronization of circadian rhythms occurs after transmeridian flight—the "jet-lag" syndrome. Although the periodicity of the light-dark cycle is unchanged at twenty-four hours, the phase is altered by the number of time zones crossed. Disturbed sleep, hormonal and metabolic patterns result and re-entrainment may take as long as two weeks. The rate of re-entrainment can be enhanced by giving small doses of melatonin before the journey at a time equivalent to bedtime in the new time zone, and at bedtime for a few days after the flight.

This inability of the internal clock to adapt quickly to forced phase shift also causes problems in shift work. Alertness is reduced in individuals whose rhythms are desynchronized with important implications for efficiency and safety. Preliminary work indicates that melatonin may improve daytime sleep quality during night shifts and reverse the decrease in alertness. Its effects on performance require careful evaluation.

In old age the control of circadian rhythmicity grows less robust—the elderly tend to sleep less well and for a shorter period at night and to compensate by napping during the day. Plasma melatonin levels decrease with increasing age, and in rats it has been shown that the number of brain receptors through which melatonin acts also decreases with age. We do not know whether or not these observations are linked, but perhaps in the future melatonin may be used to enhance the quality of life for our increasingly aged population.

Work on the pineal gland was first recorded in the third century B.C., when Herophilus considered that it might control the flow of thought. In the seventeenth century, the French philosopher Descartes considered that the gland was the seat of the soul and with great prescience linked it mechanistically with the eyes. The study of melatonin is much more recent—the hormone was first isolated by Aaron Lerner in 1958. Our understanding of its role in entraining the biological clock within our bodies to the time set by the astronomical clock that governs our environment is increasing but is far from complete. Its widespread occurrence across the phyla of the animal kingdom is, however, a reminder of the importance of that link. Melatonin is the hand of the biological clock. In some species it exerts primary control over circadian rhythms; in others (humans, for example), it is concerned with fine tuning of the clock itself.

[J.A. and J.E.]

See also **Biological Rhythms in Epidemiology and Pharmacology; Photoperiodism and Seasonal Rhythms: Animals.**

FURTHER READINGS

Arendt, J., D.S. Minors, and J.M. Waterhouse, eds. *Biological Rhythms in Clinical Practice.* London: Wright (Butterworth Scientific), 1989.

Borbely, A. *Secrets of Sleep.* New York: Basic Books, 1986.

Miles, A., D.R.S. Philbrick, and C. Thompson, eds. *Melatonin: Clinical Perspectives.* Oxford: Oxford UP, 1988.

Waterhouse, J.M. "Light Dawns on the Body Clock." *New Scientist.* October 26, 1991.

MEMORY FOR TIME

In everyday life memory for temporal information may often relate to specific clock times or calendar dates. Human memory for such information is not very impressive, however. For example, W.A. Wagenaar in 1986 recorded 2,400 events from his everyday life over a period of six years. The events were recorded in terms of *who, what, where,* and *when.* When memory was tested over varying lengths of time, each of these words were presented individually as retrieval cues. The order of efficacy was *who, what, where,* and *when,* with *when* proving to be virtually useless. Chronological information was usually missing from the memory of the event and could not be used as a search criterion. It therefore appears that, with the exception of a few landmark events such as important birthdays and holidays which are precisely dated, in general, events are not filed in memory by dates. Instead, they are consciously constructed from some other known autobiographical event which, in turn, depends on some socially induced reference system such as school year.

This viewpoint has been endorsed by W.K. Estes in 1985, who pointed out that in most laboratory research and also in much of everyday life, temporal memory does not take the form of explicit verbal encodings of *when* information. Instead, what appears to be stored in memory is the temporal attribute or relations between events or sequences of events. It has been argued that such temporal attributes of events are treated by the human organism as information in the same way as size, intensity, or color, and that the encoding of temporal patterns takes place in a separate representational code (as discussed, for example, by J.A. Michon in 1985). It therefore follows that temporal information should be encoded, stored, and retrieved within the human memory system in a manner similar to other information.

Memory is not one specific mechanism but is part of a complex and integrated information-processing system. It makes use of a variety of different types of mechanisms that operate on mental representations. The particular mechanism and representation that will be used at a specific time depends entirely on the type of task the individual has to carry out and the context within which the task occurs. The information-processing system has a limited processing capacity; in other words, we can only consciously attend to a certain amount of information at any given time. One distinction that is pervasive in current models of memory relates to this limited capacity issue. It distinguishes between automatic and nonautomatic or conscious access to mental contents (as discussed, for example, by L. Hasher and R.T. Zacks in 1979). Automatic memories are defined as being relatively fast retrievals that require no conscious processing, while nonautomatic memories are seen as slow retrievals that do require conscious processing.

Experimental psychologists who have explored how information is encoded, stored, and retrieved have used memory tests that examine implicit or automatic remembering as well as exertive, conscious remembering over short, intermediate, and long retention intervals. Psychologists exploring memory for temporal information have used similar measures but have done so specifically in tasks that require judgments of duration, order judgments, lag estimates, position judgments, and, as mentioned above, the dating of autobiographical memories. In general, the methodology used in temporal judgment tasks involves the following pattern: subjects are first presented with lists of letters, words, pictures, or series of events; they may be aware (intentional instructions) or unaware (incidental instructions) that temporal judgments will be required; and judgments have to be given either immediately or after short, intermediate, or relatively long retention intervals.

Judgments of duration vary according to whether estimates are made while time is elapsing, or in retrospect. The retrospective-prospective issue is not new, having been mentioned by philosophers such as Jean-Marie Guyau and psychologists such as William James. These authors were already aware that attentional rather than memory processes play an important role in the experience of time in passing since subjects who are aware of the temporal nature of the task in advance will allocate more attention to temporal aspects, and make their judgments immediately upon completion. On the other hand, it is widely recognized that memory processes play an important role in the experience of duration in retrospect. For example, in the framework proposed by R.E. Ornstein in 1969, time estimates are inferred from the amount of information stored in memory such that any interval consuming more storage space than another will appear relatively longer in duration (R.A. Block, however, in 1985 and 1989 provided an alternative explanation relating to contextual change). Such memory-related explanations have also been offered to account for age differences in the subjective passing of time. The commonly held view is explicitly summed up by Guy Penreath in his inscription on a clock in Chester cathedral (as quoted in G.J. Witrow's *The Natural Philosophy of Time*):

> For when I was a babe and wept and slept, Time crept.
> When I was a boy and laughed and talked, Time walked;
> Then when the years saw me a man, Time ran,
> But as I older grew, Time flew.

The explanations underlying this phenomenon have been described within a memory-space model. For example, Paul Fraisse in 1984 suggests that for the child, everything is new and is therefore stored in memory as nontemporal events. Estimations of durations of past intervals lengthen as the amount of information stored in long-term memory increases; for the child, intervals, therefore, appear long. For the elderly, on the other hand, there are few novel events to be stored in memory and this paucity of information decreases estimations. Developmental differences in memory storage are therefore assumed to account for the differing subjective experiences of time.

Order judgments, which are often referred to in the literature as judgments of relative recency, require recalling which of two items occurred later in a series. In the laboratory, such judgments have mainly been tested over short or moderate retention intervals. Even when subjects are unaware that order judgments will be required, memory performance consistently exceeds a chance level. Two further robust findings show that (1) performance decreases as the interval between the test and the position in the original sequence of the more recent member of the test pair increases; and (2) that memory for items which are far apart is considerably better than for items which are close together. In the studies that have explored retention over longer intervals, it appears that subjects usually overestimate the recency of events, a bias that is known as *forward telescoping*. This biasing is particularly evident with well-known events that are dated as being more recent than they really were, with the reverse holding true for less well-known events.

Absolute lag judgments require subjects to estimate the number of items presented between two different items from a series. Even at very short retention intervals, memory for this type of temporal information is poor with subjects exhibiting a central tendency, that is, tending to underestimate long lags and overestimating short ones.

Position judgment tasks have been the most successful in yielding information about the way in which memory for temporal attributes of items changes during retention intervals. Positional tasks explicitly require the recall of positional or temporal information about the appearance of an item. Within the short-term range, subjects are typically presented with a small number of items (approximately six) for a short duration interval. Immediately afterwards, they are required to recall the items in order. When rehearsal strategies are precluded by introducing a secondary task, results show that the errors which occur are of the transposition type, that is, subjects recall the letters correctly but transpose them (for example, recall D V E P J instead of D J E V P), indicating that *item* and *order* information are forgotten at different rates. Moreover, the empirical data show that while order information for the initial and final positions is accurate, judgments about items from the middle of the list are much more uncertain.

When the experimental series are divided into segments, transpositions not only appear within a segment but also between segments. In 1981, C.L. Lee and W.K. Estes provided a description of a hierarchical encoding/perturbation model which explains such data. When position judgments are explored in the laboratory over somewhat longer retention intervals using techniques that again preclude rehearsal (J.L. Jackson reviewed such studies in 1990), it is once more only the unique positions that are found to be judged accurately. As Jackson demonstrated in 1985, veridical temporal judgments are, however, possible, but these seem to require conscious processing with performance improving as a result of level of practice and use of elaborate rehearsal strategies.

It therefore appears that memory for temporal information is by and large poor, only proving to be accurate for a number of unique events. As Michon and Jackson indicated in 1984, unless we deliberately pay attention to it, "temporal information is not encoded unless noticed and not noticed unless meaningful!" In this respect, memory for temporal information is similar to that of nontemporal information and is susceptible to the same constraints within the information-processing system, namely limited processing capacity.

[J.L.J.]

See also **Guyau, Jean-Marie; James, William (as Psychologist); Prospective and Retrospective Time; Time-Order Errors; Time Perception.**

FURTHER READINGS

Estes, W.K. "Memory for Temporal Information." *Time, Mind, and Behavior.* Ed. J.A. Michon and J.L. Jackson. Berlin: Springer, 1985. 151–168.

Fraisse, Paul. "Perception and Estimation of Time." *Annual Review of Psychology* 35 (1984): 1–36.

Guyau, J.-M. *La genèse de l'idée de temps.* Paris: Félix Alcan, 1890. (Translated as *Guyau and the Idea of Time.* Ed. J.A. Michon, V. Pouthas, and J.L. Jackson. Amsterdam: North-Holland, 1988.)

Hasher, L., and R.T. Zacks. "Automatic and Effortful Processes in Memory." *Journal of Experimental Psychology: General* 108 (1979): 356–388.

Jackson, J.L. "Is the Processing of Temporal Information Automatic or Controlled?" *Time, Mind, and Behavior.* Ed. J.A. Michon and J.L. Jackson. Berlin: Springer, 1985. 179–190.

———. "A Cognitive Approach to Temporal Information Processing." *Cognitive Models of Psychological Time.* Ed. R.A. Block. Hillsdale: Erlbaum, 1990. 153–180.

James, W. *The Principles of Psychology.* Vol. 1. New York: Henry Holt, 1890.

Lee, C.L., and W.K. Estes. "Item and Order Information in Short-Term Memory: Evidence for Multi-Level Perturbation Processes." *Journal of Experimental Psychology: Human Learning and Memory* 7 (1981): 149–169.

Michon, J.A. "The Compleat Time Experiencer." *Time, Mind, and Behavior.* Ed. J.A. Michon and J.L. Jackson. Berlin: Springer, 1985. 20–52.

Michon, J.A., and J.L. Jackson. "Attentional Effort and Cognitive Strategies in the Processing of Temporal Information." *Timing and Time Perception.* Ed. J. Gibbon and L.G. Allan. *Annals of the New York Academy of Sciences* 423 (1984): 298–321.

Ornstein, Robert E. *On the Experience of Time.* Harmondsworth: Penguin, 1969.

Wagenaar, W.A. "My Memory: A Study of Autobiographical Memory Over Six Years." *Cognitive Psychology* 18 (1986): 225–252.

MENTAL DISORDERS IN AGING

Time plays a role in our comments on mental health and aging in two different ways. First, the age structure of our Western societies has changed dramatically during this century. Because of declining birth rates and increasing life expectancy, the populations of most Western industrialized countries are becoming older. Second, at the level of individual development, the passage of time, as documented through regularly noted birthdays, is virtually synonymous with aging, at least with getting older. Examining the characteristics of the individuals who represent an increasing proportion of the populations of Western countries is both fair and important. Should individuals expect to experience an ineluctable decline in the functioning of their minds and bodies? Is the popular notion of successful aging just a dream for increasing numbers of adults? If sufficient (and growing) numbers of individuals experience significant physical or mental decline, does this imply that society must devote ever more resources to caring for a decreasingly healthy population? In this article, we summarize some changes that occur with aging in one aspect of health, namely, mental health.

The major categories of mental disorders are organic brain syndromes and functional disorders. The former refer to a group of symptoms that are related to physical changes within the brain and are due to a variety of causes. The latter refer to the group of symptoms for which no physical concomitant is known. Probable causes for functional disorders include psychological and interpersonal factors. Mental disorders may occur at any point in the life-span but, like physical health problems, they appear in different proportions in groups of differing ages. One notable aging-related trend is that the incidence of first admissions to institutions tends to increase in old age for organic brain syndromes and decrease for functional disorders.

ORGANIC BRAIN SYNDROMES

Mental disorders derived from organic brain syndromes may be either chronic or acute. Chronic syndromes affect approximately 6 percent of those over sixty-five years of age, but the incidence increases dramatically in later life (the seventies and beyond). Generally, chronic organic brain syndromes are characterized by a progressive deterioration of memory and other cognitive abilities, some emotional abnormalities, and an inability to manage daily activities. Dementia is typical of organic brain syndromes. It is characterized by (1) memory impairment, (2) inability to think abstractly, (3) impaired judgment, and (4) personality changes. The most common dementia is Alzheimer's disease (AD), the cause of which remains controversial. Potential causes include genetic factors, infectious diseases, and toxic substances. AD has an insidious onset, deteriorating course, and considerable variation with respect to its duration. The rate of decline may depend in part on the age of onset. Other chronic brain syndromes include multi-infarct dementia (caused by multiple small strokes), and the less common Huntington's disease (genetically based), Parkinson's disease (a central nervous system disorder appearing in older adults), and Pick's disease (with symptoms similar to AD).

Approximately 10 to 20 percent of individuals with organic mental syndromes suffer from acute brain dysfunction, which may be due to a number of causes, including toxicity from medication use and vitamin deficiencies. Delirium is a common acute brain dysfunction that can occur at any age, but is most prevalent after the age of sixty. The causes of delirium include metabolic disorders, infections, and substance abuse. It is characterized by (1) the inability to maintain attention, (2) disorganized thinking, (3) disorientation to time, place, and person, and (4) memory impairment. Unlike chronic brain syndromes, acute syndromes are usually reversible if diagnosed and treated quickly.

FUNCTIONAL DISORDERS

Functional disorders or psychopathologies may occur at any point in the life-span. Their occurrence is moderately related to such demographic factors as health (poorer), marital status (unmarried), income (poorer), and gender (females). Common functional disorders include schizophrenia, paranoia, and depression. Anxiety disorders—disturbances typified by tension, trembling, and rapid breathing—are more common in young adults than old adults. Similarly, personality disorders—inflexible or maladaptive behavior patterns—tend to appear first in late adolescence or early adulthood.

Schizophrenia and paranoia are part of a larger category of functional disorders known as psychosis. In psychosis, normal mental activity is severely impaired and the person's perception of reality is distorted. Schizophrenia involves psychotic experiences, such as bizarre delusions, hallucinations, disturbances in thinking, and loss of contact with reality. Although clinicians once believed that schizophrenia only occurred before the age of forty-five years, new research indicates that late life onset may occur. Nevertheless, the incidence of diagnoses of schizophrenia peaks in early adulthood and declines thereafter. Approximately 1 percent of those over sixty-five years of age experience symptoms of schizophrenia. Paranoid disorders are comprised of non-bizarre delusions, such as beliefs about persecution. Intellectual functioning remains intact while mood, behavior, and thoughts are distorted. Such disorders are rare with only 1 percent of all adults experiencing delusions; however, they do tend to increase with age. The most common causes of paranoid disorders are isolation from human contact and the failure of vision or hearing.

Depression can occur at any point in time during the life-span. Theorists identify a wide range of potential causes ranging from physiological to social isolation. Symptoms of depression include sustained deep sadness, apathy, anhedonia (an inability to take pleasure in anything), inactivity and lack of interest, weight loss, difficulty in concentrating or memory loss, feelings of worthlessness, inappropriate guilt, and thoughts of death or suicide. Less than 5 percent of community-dwelling elderly adults experience major depression, the most severe type of depression, although some recent research suggests that the prevalence may increase in those over eighty-five years of age. Older adults seem to be less likely than their younger counterparts to recover fully from a depressive episode, and subsequently may be at greater risk for other problems. Depressed older adults (especially white males) are at increased risk for mortality due to suicide and other health-related causes. Despite these negative potential outcomes, depression is the most treatable functional disorder of later life.

SUMMARY

Whatever the stereotypes, aging and pathology are not synonymous. That is, increasing age does not lead inevitably to a decline in mental health. Whereas progressive deterioration is the necessary outcome of chronic organic brain syndromes, accumulating evidence suggests a more optimistic picture for older adults with reversible functional disorders. The vast majority of older adults are free of serious mental disorders, reside in the community, and lead active, relatively healthy lives. For them, successful aging is more than just a slogan.

[I.C.F. and R.A.D.]

See also **Aging and Time; Loneliness and Aging; Manic-Depressive Illness; Psychoanalysis; Social Gerontology.**

FURTHER READINGS

Cohen, Gene D. *The Brain in Human Aging*. New York: Springer, 1988.

Kaszniak, Alfred W. "Psychological Assessment of the Aging Individual." *Handbook of the Psychology of Aging*. Ed. James E. Birren and K. Warner Schaie. 3rd ed. San Diego: Academic P, 1990. 427–445.

Poon, Leonard W., ed. *Handbook for Clinical Memory Assessment of Older Adults*. Washington: American Psychological Association, 1986.

Smyer, Michael A., and Margaret Gatz, eds. *Mental Health and Aging: Programs and Evaluations*. Beverly Hills: Sage, 1983.

Teri, Linda, and P.M. Lewinsohn, eds. *Geropsychological Assessment and Treatment*. New York: Springer, 1986.

MERCIER, LOUIS-SÉBASTIEN (1740–1814)

Playwright, essayist, lexicographer, and brilliant journalist of quotidian life in his *Tableau de Paris*, Mercier published in 1771 the first utopia set in future time: *L'An deux mille quatre cent quarante: Rêve s'il en fut jamais* (The year 2440: A dream if there ever was one). The narrator dreams of sleeping 700 years to awake in a twenty-fifth century Paris where the Bastille has been demolished and despotism replaced by a benevolent government presiding over a beautiful city whose enlightened inhabitants have long been free from tyranny and superstition. The point of contrasting this utopian future with French life in 1771 was so clear that *The Year 2440* was banned in France, put on the Inquisition's list of forbidden books in 1773, and widely read throughout Europe during the rest of the eighteenth century. The Enlightenment ideals eloquently embodied in *The Year 2440* are less innovative than its future setting. Before *The Year 2440*, only four secular books (none of them utopias) had been set in future time. Mercier was the first to adopt a specific future date as the title for a work of fiction, thus paving the way for Orwell's masterful use of this device. Even more crucially for the history of literary forms, Mercier inaugurated the shift from utopia, the good place which is also no place, to uchronia: the good future time. By imagining a better future in a real place—Paris—rather than portraying, as Sir Thomas More and his immediate successors did, an ideal society on an imaginary island, Mercier connected utopia to history by offering a vision of potential change set ahead in time but explicitly proposed as a possibility for the reader's own place.

[P.K.A.]

See also **Alternate History; Futuristic Fiction; Utopias and Dystopias.**

FURTHER READINGS

Alkon, Paul K. *Origins of Futuristic Fiction*. Athens: U of Georgia P, 1987.

Baczko, Bronislaw. *Utopian Lights: The Evolution of the Idea of Social Progress*. Trans. Judith L. Greenberg. New York: Paragon House, 1989. Originally published as *Lumières de l'Utopie*. Paris: Éditions Payot, 1978.

MERLEAU-PONTY, MAURICE (1908–1961)

Transcendental philosophy from Kant forward has identified time with subjectivity: time is conceived as an immanent structure that is the condition of any possible conscious experience. Merleau-Ponty belongs to this tradition, but transforms it by grounding transcendental subjectivity in human embodiment and acknowledging that the body transcends its experience of itself—preeminently in its temporality. Time, then, cannot be simply an immanent structure, because time transcends the body that is the condition for experience. Merleau-Ponty departs from the tradition of transcendental philosophy by articulating a thesis implicit in it since its inception: the thesis of the transcendence of time.

Merleau-Ponty conceives the human body (*le corps propre*, one's own body, the lived body) as both immanent subject and transcendent object of experience. Since my body is my means of experiencing the world, the world is the correlate of my bodily experience: I touch the table only by virtue of being touched by the table. I can be touched by the table, however, only because my body, like the table, is a transcendent worldly thing. This thought transforms transcendental philosophy by displacing the dualism implicit in its characteristic reduction of the phenomenal world to an object of experience: since the world can be revealed as phenomenon only to the extent that we experience it, the phenomenal world, for a human subject, can only be the world as revealed to and structured by human subjectivity. In this manner, transcendental philosophy intrinsically asserts an ontological division between transcendence and immanence, the world that transcends experience and thereby necessarily eludes cognition must be different from the immanent world revealed to consciousness. Transcendental philosophy purports to deliver apodictic truths about the world as experienced, but only at the expense of maintaining an agnostic, ultimately skeptical, posture with regard to the transcendent world.

Merleau-Ponty transforms this tradition by showing that the body, as a condition of being the subject of cognition, must also be a thing that transcends cognition. I can experience my embodiment, my physical presence in the world I have inhabited since birth and in which I will linger until I die, but I cannot think my totality concretely (as, for example, Hegel's absolute must) simply because I cannot be present at my birth and my death. I can think of my birth and death through the abstract medium of language, and through that medium attempt to assimilate the events to which others have been and will be unproblematically present, but, for me, my concrete absence from these situations makes the fulfillment of the witnessing intention an absolute impossibility. That is part of what it means to be a finite embodied subject that is itself finally subject to the inexorable process of be-

coming: all eternal being is a fantasy that cannot exist for me. Exactly that is the meaning of eternity for me: I am finally transcended by time.

The problem of time is that it, like all world phenomena, must be both immanent and transcendent: time must be revealed, but transcend its revelation. In *The Visible and the Invisible*, Merleau-Ponty writes that "Time must *constitute itself*—be always seen from the point of view of someone who *is of it*. But this seems to be contradictory. . . . The contradiction is lifted only if the new present is itself a transcendent: one knows it is not there, that it was just there, one never coincides with it" (VI 184). The key to understanding the transcendence of time for Merleau-Ponty is in the last phrase quoted: one never coincides with the present. For Hegel, time is for-itself, self-constituting: the alienation from itself (or self-externalization) which is finally overcome in eternal self-presence or self-coincidence. For Merleau-Ponty, this self-coincidence is a reduction to immanence, a denial of temporality, a denial that one is of time. If the self-conscious subject is fully for-itself in Hegel's sense, it cannot be temporal in the manner of a living body that is destined to die from the moment of its conception.

Merleau-Ponty unself-consciously appropriates much of Husserl's teaching on the subject of time, and even reproduces Husserl's diagram in his chapter on temporality in the *Phenomenology of Perception*. But he definitively distances himself from Husserl's reduction of time to an immanent form of synthesis. The crucial term for Merleau-Ponty is *écart*: separation, dehiscence, fission. Taking up the issue of the "primal impression" which Husserl held to be the "source point" of an enduring temporal object (such as a melody), Merleau-Ponty asks an ontological question: "What is the impressional consciousness, the *Urerlebnis*?" His answer to this question constitutes a clear break from Husserl's conception of time consciousness as immanent, as internal: Merleau-Ponty says that the *Urerlebnis* is "a transcendent," "an *etwas*," and that "the 'to be conscious' of the *Urerlebnis* is not coincidence, fusion with . . . it is separation (*écart*) . . . which is the foundation of space and time" (VI 191). In order to think the temporality of the for-itself (consciousness or subjectivity) with Merleau-Ponty, one must think of a separation from itself that is not sublated, but remains always at a distance from itself, always present to a transcendent other. The transcendence, the otherness, is expressed as *écart*, as separation.

Merleau-Ponty does not deny the immanent temporality of transcendental constitution, but holds that subjective acts of temporal synthesis are separated from the autochthonous organization of transcendent time which they recapitulate. Objective time as measured by clocks is grounded in lived time, but lived time is responsive to a passage, succession, becoming that it does not constitute: it is possible to be mistaken in constituting time, and inevitable to be overtaken by it.

[M.C.D.]

FURTHER READINGS

Merleau-Ponty, Maurice. *Phenomenology of Perception.* Trans. Colin Smith. London: Routledge & Kegan Paul, 1962. (*Phénoménologie de la perception.* Paris: Éditions Gallimard, 1945.)

———. *The Visible and the Invisible.* Trans. Alphonso Lingis. Evanston: Northwestern UP, 1968. (*Le visible et l'invisible.* Paris: Éditions Gallimard, 1964.)

MESOAMERICAN ARCHAEOASTRONOMY

The sun, moon, stars, and planets were very important in the calendar system of Mesoamerica. Cultures from Mexico south to Honduras shared a unique calendar system combining a 260-day ritual almanac with a 365-day festival calendar. The emphasis in this essay is on the Aztec and Yucatec Maya; a separate encyclopedia entry treats Maya astronomy in general.

The 260-day almanac, called the *tzolkin* by the Maya and the *tonalpohualli* by the Aztecs, relates to a number of different natural cycles. According to modern Maya accounts, the 260-day period corresponds to the human gestation period of nine lunar months. The origin of this unique calendar cycle can be traced back to ca. 700–500 B.C. In pre-Columbian Mesoamerica, the calendar was used to prognosticate human destiny and to predict weather and astronomical cycles. The 260-day period coordinates approximately with the period of visibility of Venus as either the morning or evening star. Observations of Mars may also have been important in the cycle because one synodic revolution of the planet (780 days) equals three periods of 260 days.

The 260-day calendar meshed with other calendars to form larger cycles of time. Only once every fifty-two years (a calendar round) did a specific day of the 260-day calendar coincide with a given day in the 365-day calendar. The 365-day calendar, known as the *xihuitl* among the Aztecs and the *haab* among the Maya, is called the "vague" year because it only approximates the solar year of 365.25 days. Current scholarship suggests that the Maya did not adjust the *haab* for leap years. The late postclassic (A.D. 1200–1521) Aztec calendar, however, was adjusted periodically to account for leap years. Nevertheless, the 260-day calendar continued without adjustment, providing a separate chronological cycle.

The end of the Aztec calendar round of fifty-two years was celebrated with a major festival known as the new fire ceremony. Friar Bernardino de Sahagun, the sixteenth-century chronicler, notes that the ceremony was timed by the midnight zenith of the Pleiades. All fires were extinguished and the world was plunged into darkness, awaiting astronomical observations made from the "hill of the star." My own work, and the work of E.C. Krupp and Johanna Broda, suggests that the new fire ceremony corresponds to the annual solar nadir, when the sun was in the "lowest" depths of the underworld at the beginning of the dry season. Observations of the Pleiades at zenith, in opposition to the sun in Scorpius at this time, determined the exact moment the sun reached the depths of the underworld. The Aztecs feared that the sun would die and time would stand still. When the Pleiades was observed crossing the zenith, they understood that the sun continued its course unharmed, rising from the underworld to begin a new cycle of fifty-two years. At this time, the new fire was lit and carried throughout the land as a reaffirmation of the new world age.

Every eight years the 260-day calendar coordinated with five synodic Venus cycles (584 days each) and 99 lunar (synodic) months (8 x 365 = 5 x 584 = 29.53 x 99). The Aztecs celebrated this cycle in the Atamalcualiztli festival dedicated to the lunar goddess Xochiquetzal. In the Yucatec Maya area, this cycle is recorded in the Venus pages of the Dresden Codex. The Mixteca-Puebla codices also record five successive cycles of the heliacal rise of Venus.

Specific lunar and Venus events also correlated with larger cycles of time because the 104-year double calendar round is divisible by the eight-year period. This is the lowest common multiple of the 260-day sacred almanac and the 584-day synodical revolution of Venus (146 x 260 = 65 x 584 = 104 x 365). The sixty-five Venus cycles are displayed in five pages of the Dresden

Codex. The division of the table into five pages reflects different seasonal positions of Venus over the course of eight years, repeated over a cycle of 104 years. The idealized periods for Venus phases used in the Dresden Codex may also incorporate lunar intervals.

A zodiac from the Paris Codex depicts a 1,820-day period with different animal constellations biting what may be eclipse signs. Eclipse prediction tables in the Dresden Codex incorporate periods of 405 lunations equal to forty-six cycles of the 260-day calendar (405 x 29.53 = 46 x 260). According to Victoria Bricker, there may also be a seasonal calendar that correlates Venus and eclipse events in the Dresden Codex.

The classic Maya long count inscriptions, rather than focusing on a cycle of fifty-two years, trace the passage of time from a mythical starting point of about 3114 B.C. Historical dates in the long count fall within the classic Maya period, dating between A.D. 250 and 900. The work of Floyd Lounsbury and other scholars suggests that some Maya historical dates correlate with the observation of astronomical events.

Measurement of time was intimately linked to the observation of the stars. Sahagun's *Primeros Memoriales* notes that the Aztec priests observed the sky six times each night, and the Codex Mendoza illustrates a priest telling time by the stars.

Data on specific constellations in pre-Columbian Mesoamerica indicates that the Pleiades were of primary importance. According to Bishop Landa, the principal calendar stars of the Yucatec Maya were the Pleiades and Gemini (or possibly Orion), described respectively as the rattlesnake's rattle (*tzab*) and the turtle stars (*ac ek*). The Pleiades glyph and a rattlesnake that may represent the Pleiades appear in the Yucatec Maya codices (Madrid Codex, 11–18), according to my research. As noted earlier, the Pleiades were also very important among the Aztecs, who observed the Pleiades to time their most important calendric ceremony. As part of his duties as king of the Aztecs, Moctezuma was advised that he must rise at midnight to observe the *yohualitqui mamalhuatztli* (fire drill, Gemini or Orion's belt and sword), the *citlaltlachtli* (the star ball court, a northern constellation), the *tianquiztli* (the marketplace, the Pleiades), and *colotlixayac* (the scorpion, Scorpius or Ursa Major), the constellations that marked the four parts of heaven.

The Pleiades and Scorpius appear to be especially important because they were seasonal opposites in the classic and postclassic periods.

My studies indicate that the Pleiades marked the zenith sun's position entering the Milky Way at the beginning of the rainy season, whereas Scorpius marked the nadir sun's position entering the Milky Way at the beginning of the dry season. These two constellations continue to be important according to ethnographic data. The Pleiades are still observed to time the beginning of the rainy season among the Chorti and Cakchiquel Maya.

Architectural orientation also provided a way of measuring the passage of time. Structures at Xochicalco and Monte Alban were constructed with a vertical shaft that allows light to enter the interior structure on the solar zenith. The play of light and shadow on the Castillo at Chichen Itza around sunset on the equinox (March 21, September 21) creates a pattern of rattlesnake markings on the serpent-headed balustrade, an effect that was first discovered in modern times by the local Maya caretakers of the site. My research indicates that the Upper Temple of the Jaguars at Chichen Itza was oriented so that light penetrates the inner temple at sunset on the solar zenith. The Pleiades setting just before the zenith could also be observed from the temple, along with Venus on the western horizon in conjunction with the Pleiades at the onset of the rainy season.

Anthony Aveni's work indicates a number of orientations that may have been used in calendric observations. The Caracol at Chichen Itza has windows that apparently were oriented toward the Pleiades setting and Venus setting at its northern and southern extremes, events that may have been coordinated with specific seasonal cycles. Temple 22 at Copan has a window aligned to the northern extreme of Venus at the beginning of the rainy season. The Pleiades setting seems to be a major orientation for the east-west axis of Teotihuacan, and, at the time the site was constructed, this star group rose at dawn on the solar zenith in late May and marked the true zenith point—the cosmic center of the sky.

Solstice and equinox orientations were also important as calendrical markers in Mesoamerica. Anthony Aveni's work indicates that more than 90 percent of the Puuc Maya sites measured in a sample of 113 sites showed a 24–25 degree solsticial orientation. His measurements of the Aztec Templo Mayor indicate that the twin pyramid temple is positioned so that the equinox sun rises over Huitzilopochtli's temple, confirming a sixteenth-century chronicler's account that

Moctezuma wanted the temple aligned so that the sun would be in the proper position to mark the time of their annual equinox festival. This is one more indication that public ceremonies, architecture, astronomy, and calendrics were all closely linked in Mesoamerican cosmology.

[S.M.]

See also Archaeoastronomy; Aztec Calendar; Maya Astronomy; Maya Calendars and Chronology.

FURTHER READINGS

Aveni, Anthony F., ed. Archaeoastronomy in Pre-Columbian America. Austin: U of Texas P, 1977.

———. Skywatchers of Ancient Mexico. Austin: U of Texas P, 1980.

———, ed. New Directions in American Archaeoastronomy. Oxford: BAR International Series 454, 1988.

———, ed. The Sky in Mayan Literature. Oxford UP, 1992.

Thompson, John Eric S. "Maya Astronomy." Philosophical Transactions of the Royal Society of London 276 (1974): 83–98.

Williamson, Ray, ed. Archaeoastronomy in the Americas. College Park Maryland: Center for Archaeoastronomy, 1981.

METAMORPHOSIS

Metamorphosis in a literal sense is the essence of life itself, the concept that almost all organisms undergo changes in form during development. In an ontological sense, it is the goal of the seeker who wishes transformation from a less nearly perfect to a more nearly perfect being. From the biological perspective, however, which this article addresses, metamorphosis will be considered as that set of profound changes which some groups of organisms, such as insects and amphibians, undergo during development of the individual. The term, which literally means changes of form, is a misnomer since changes in biochemistry and physiology also occur, thus preparing the new form for large changes in its behavior and ecology. Since more is known about the timing and control of metamorphosis in insects, the remainder of this article will be devoted to that taxon.

It is interesting to consider how a phenomenon such as metamorphosis in insects could have evolved over time. Metamorphosis is a characteristic of all winged insects. Once wings evolved, why were they restricted to the adult stage only? Since growth and development, flight (that is, dispersal), and reproduction all have high energy demands, it would appear advantageous to separate these processes both spatially and temporally. Wings would be disadvantageous in many feeding situations and would also create problems during the discontinuous growth pattern of arthropods whose structure necessitates periodic molting of a hardened exoskeleton. Once the possession of wings was "relegated" to the adult stage, some degree of metamorphosis becomes a requirement. In the most advanced types of metamorphosis, an intermediate pupal stage is required to accommodate the profound changes associated with the breakdown of larval tissues (histolysis) and the reorganization of adult tissues and structures (histogenesis). Complete metamorphosis then allows both active life stages to exploit different food sources and habitats. It also suggests that two sets of genes are responsible for controlling development, one governing larval characters and the other adult characters. In turn, these sets of genes regulate the production of hormones which ultimately determine the type, and depth, of metamorphosis. Only three such hormones are involved in a series of profound changes from hairy caterpillar to sleek butterfly. The first (brain hormone) is produced in the brain and is common to all molts; the second (ecdysone) is produced in the prothoracic glands and initiates the moult; and the third (neotenin) from the corpora allata determines the degree of maturation. This latter hormone, sometimes referred to as the juvenile hormone, is a remarkable agent that allows development to proceed but prevents maturation. Thus the balance and timing of three hormones controls the complex series of events that culminates in a radical change of form—metamorphosis.

Another phenomenon closely allied to metamorphosis in insects is diapause, a form of suspended animation. Diapause is regarded as an important adaptation for preserving a species in regions where environmental conditions prevent continuous multiplication. In many species it results in the prevention of metamorphosis, and gives rise to some intriguing questions about biological time versus chronological time. Diapause is, in effect, a hormone deficiency syndrome that interrupts the normal sequence of growth, development, and metamorphosis. Take, for example, a family group of larvae whose diapause interrupts their moult from larval to pupal stages. Since diapause is not 100 percent effective in any one batch, a few larvae may complete development, leaving their siblings behind in the larval stage. Now suppose that these developing, nondiapause larvae are allowed (by manipulating environmental conditions) to produce further generations of off-spring. If this continues for, say, two years at the rate of one generation every three weeks, then about thirty-five generations would ensue. Now terminate diapause (again by manipulating environmental conditions) in the original group of larvae and you have the possibility of flies mating with their great, great . . . great, great (repeated thirty-three times) grand-uncles and -aunts. Intriguing possibilities if diapause could be induced in domestic animals or even in the human species!

[R.A.R.]

See also **Evolution of Evolutionism.**

MICHELSON-MORLEY EXPERIMENT

This experiment is the most famous, and perhaps the most definitive, of those which show that light does not move through space in the form of waves in an ethereal fluid as assumed in early theories of light. The experiment, first performed in 1887 by A.A. Michelson (1852–1931) and E.W. Morley (1838–1923) at Western Reserve University in Cleveland, Ohio, was designed to detect the earth's motion through this fluid. It consisted essentially in splitting a beam of light by means of a half-silvered mirror and directing the two parts along paths at right angles to each other. At the end of each path was a mirror that reflected the light back toward its source, where by observing the interference between the two beams any change in their average speeds relative to the apparatus could be detected. If one beam is directed parallel to the earth's motion it was calculated to move more slowly, on the average, than the other, transversely moving beam. The whole apparatus could be rotated so as to interchange the beams, but when this was done the expected effect of the earth's motion was not seen. Subsequently the experiment was repeated many times by many people with the same result. That such motion was unobservable in principle was a postulate of the theory of relativity that Albert Einstein (1879–1955) had published in 1905, but ironically, neither Michelson nor Morley was ever convinced by Einstein's argument and hence they did not recognize the importance of their work. To the end of their lives they believed their experiment had unaccountably failed.

[D.A.P.]

See also **Relativity Theory.**

FURTHER READINGS

Born, Max. *Einstein's Theory of Relativity.* New York: Dover Publications, 1962.

Swenson, Loyd F. *The Aethereal Ether.* Austin: U of Texas P, 1972.

MIGRATION: RURAL TO URBAN

The mobility transition model (Figure 1) suggests that as development proceeds over time, various forms of migration ebb and flow, with different types of movement succeeding one another as the dominant wave. Rural-to-urban migration characterizes those societies undergoing capitalist intrusion and transformation. In several parts of Europe, especially Britain, industrial capitalism had depended on the prior penetration of capitalist methods in agriculture. This provided a mechanism for capital accumulation, drove labor from the land through processes like enclosures, and created a food surplus to support an industrial proletariat. As capital began to find its highest returns in urban centers, it created a substantial demand for labor. That demand could not be met by the urban population itself because of the excess of deaths over births in the crowded, unsanitary nineteenth-century cities. This directly stimulated inflows of labor from the countryside.

Although the bulk of urbanward migration was from adjacent rural areas and small towns, the destabilizing role of migration has been particularly evident in the poorer, more remote upland areas of Europe. Initially, rural exodus reduced population pressure there by creating a more tolerable relationship between population numbers and resources, but because of its self-

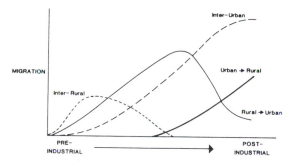

Figure 1. The major migration streams in the mobility transition model. Adapted from Zelinsky, W. "The Hypothesis of the Mobility Transition." Geographical Review 61 (1971): 219–249.

perpetuating nature, migration may proceed eventually to undermine the demographic and economic health of the community. So many young men may leave that the agricultural land cannot be worked effectively, and the population may fall below the level necessary to support vital community services. In such cases, population decline may become irreversible. The remote Scottish island of St. Kilda provides an extreme example. There demographic seepage over generations finally made the community's survival impossible, and led to the evacuation of its debilitated and demoralized population in 1930.

Less Developed Countries

United Nations estimates reveal that between 1950 and 1980 the urban population of less developed countries (excluding China) increased by almost 600 million. In 1975, for the first time in world history, a majority of the world's urban population resided in less developed countries, and by 2000 the proportion is expected to reach two-thirds. The *present rate* of urbanization in less developed countries (the increase in the urban proportion of population) is remarkably similar to that in the earlier European and North American urban transition. Thus, in the quarter-century from 1950 to 1975, the urban proportion grew from 17 percent to 28 percent in less developed countries, compared with the increase from 17 percent to 26 percent in today's developed countries between 1875 and 1900.

There are three important ways in which rural-to-urban migration in the Third World differs from its earlier counterpart in developed countries: primate (capital) city dominance, circulation, and urban underemployment. The overwhelming target of migration is the national metropolis. Resources for both investment and consumption are disproportionately allocated to the capital city because that is where the power base of the government lies. Bangkok is perhaps the most primate city of any country in the world. Containing just over half of Thailand's urban population, its population in 1960 was already twenty-six times that of the second largest city, but by 1980 this had risen to more than forty-five times. Circulation denotes a variety of movements, usually short term and repetitive, in which people leave their places of residence for varying periods but eventually return to them. The dominant movements link rural and urban areas, so that appreciable sections of the population have a dual dependence on city and village. Such bi-local lifestyles were

not uncommon in Europe during its urban transition, but the resort to circulatory movement rather than permanent migration is much greater in the contemporary Third World. In the city most circular migrants find work in the labor-intensive, low-productivity, informal sector—the so-called bazaar economy—which includes activities such as street vending, shoe shining, dishwashing, and pedicab driving. This is partly because formal sector employment demands certain levels of education and skills as well as a commitment to regular working hours. The greater absorptive capacity and flexible working arrangements of the informal sector are often much more suited to circulating workers. Third World cities have not replicated Western experience in the nineteenth century when appreciable growth of manufacturing employment was the leading edge of urbanization and labor absorption. The mushrooming numbers of "marginal" urban dwellers survive in the ever-expanding but "involuting" informal sector; this is urban growth without real development.

Counterurbanization

If urbanization or population concentration is taken to characterize the spatial redistribution of population within developing capitalist societies, then counterurbanization or population deconcentration can be regarded as the hallmark of modern, mature capitalist societies. The trend back toward a more even distribution of population over space seems to have begun in the most developed and urbanized countries like Britain, the United States, and the Benelux countries in the late 1960s but has now spread throughout the Western developed world. The term "counterurbanization" can be misleading, since there is much more to population deconcentration than the stereotype of urban dropouts fleeing to remote countrysides in a back-to-the-land idyll. Indeed, the great mass of movement is interurban (Figure 1), so that we are, in effect, experiencing a new pattern of urbanization as population shifts *down* the urban hierarchy. Thus, the "population turnaround" proceeds from a situation in which rural areas and small towns were experiencing net out-migration, to the modern experience of population losses in large cities and population gains in towns and countryside.

There are three fundamental determinants of counterurbanization: metropolitan spillover, economic restructuring, and changing residential preferences. The spillover into surrounding countrysides of largely middle-class metropolitan populations seeking superior residential and environmental conditions is a long-established feature of urban ecology, but recent developments in transport have permitted a further extension of the area in which this can take place. Economic restructuring has involved an important shift in relative attractiveness for industrial investment (and therefore for job creation and population movement) from metropolitan centers to smaller settlements. Finally, there has been a shift in residential preferences in an anti-urban, pro-rural direction as the tradeoff that people make between material enrichment and quality of life considerations shifts significantly toward the latter at high levels of economic development. Such preferences seem to underlie the population turnaround of several peripheral rural regions like the Scottish Highlands, the Massif Central, and northern New England from their traditional pattern of depopulation to one of novel growth through net in-migration.

[H.R.J.]

FURTHER READINGS

Champion, A., ed. *Counterurbanisation*. London: Arnold, 1989.

Prothero, M., and M. Chapman, eds. *Circulation in Third World Countries*. London: Routledge, 1985.

Skeldon, R. *Population Mobility in Developing Countries: A Reinterpretation*. London: Belhaven, 1990.

MILLENARIANISM

"Millenarianism" is the belief that Christ, along with the resurrected dead, will return to earth before the Last Judgment to reign over a glorious kingdom on earth. This kingdom will last for one thousand years, hence, the term "millennium" (< Latin *millenarius*, of a thousand). The designation of such an era and its cosmic significance demonstrates how time can be construed in a profoundly religious way.

The central text for the "millenarian" concept is the Book of Revelation:

And I saw an angel come down from heaven,
having the key of the bottomless pit and
a great chain in his hand.
And he laid hold on the dragon,
that old serpent, which is the Devil,
and Satan, and bound him a thousand years,
And cast him into the bottomless pit,

and shut him up, and set a seal upon him,
that he should deceive the nations no more,
till the thousand years should be fulfilled:
and after that he must be loosed a little season.
And I saw thrones, and they sat upon them,
and judgment was given unto them:
and I saw
the souls of them that were beheaded for
the witness of Jesus, and for the word of God, and which had not worshipped the beast, neither his image, neither had received his mark upon their foreheads,
or in their hands; and they lived and reigned
with Christ a thousand years.
But the rest of the dead lived not again until the thousand years were finished.
This is the first resurrection.
(Revelation 20:1–5)

It is clear from this seminal passage that the great battle between God and Satan will conclude with the fall of "Babylon," the Satanic kingdom. Satan will then be imprisoned by an angel for 1,000 years but then, surprisingly, will be permitted a resurgence culminating in a final battle at "Armageddon." After Satan is defeated, he will be thrown irrevocably into the "lake of fire." Once evil has been banished entirely from creation, the final stages of redemption will commence: a universal judgment will occur, followed by the establishment of God's kingdom on earth. In effect, time and space will be radically transformed with the coming of a "new heaven and a new earth." The millennium, interpreted both literally and symbolically, is therefore an interval of peace, a prelude to the eventual confrontation between the heavenly and the demonic forces.

Readers of the Book of Revelation since the times of the early fathers of the church have been intrigued with this apocalyptic text and with its cosmic implications for the human race. The prospect that evil will finally be overturned through divine power—through God's direct and decisive intervention into temporality—has inspired enthusiasts of every age to prophesy and to chastise the nations for straying from God's revealed law.

Both the Jews and the Christians at the time of Christ's life and thereafter expected a messianic deliverer who would not only consolidate God's people but who would also bring with him the consummation of history and a new world. Both groups at that time were oppressed minorities, tyrannized by the Roman Empire. Thus their messianic conjectures and speculations about the future were inherently revolutionary in character. They felt that the great tyrants of history would someday be thrown down by God's intervention into the world.

Many early Christians, such as St. Justin Martyr (ca. 100–165), L. Caecilius Lactantius (ca. 260–340), and Commodianus, expected Christ's imminent return. As "millenarianists," they read Revelation literally, envisaging salvation as a collective and catastrophic event. By St. Augustine's time, however, it was clear that the fulfillment of Revelation 20:1–5 was not imminent. Consequently, the concept of the millennium underwent much revision. Augustine, for example, avoided this literal interpretation when he postulated that the 1,000-year reign of Christ on earth really signified a protracted and indefinite number, and his allegorical interpretation would shape medieval responses. Yet the millenarian or "pre-millennialist" perspective of the infant church had not been entirely eclipsed. Augustine's millennial or "post-millennialist" revision, which also rejected the notion of a temporalized heavenly kingdom, was not accepted by all. Recultivated by sacred historians, such as Orosius, it reemerged among minority groups and sects.

During the Middle Ages, minority groups of all kinds reverted to the millenarian perspective to explain social injustice and to justify their sufferings. Not surprisingly, there is a revolutionary character to these reactions. The Jacquerie revolt (1358) and the Peasant revolt (1381) are overtly chiliastic, while the hope of an imminent consummation of historical time was revived by the "free spirit" movement, which exalted the holiness of poverty. Another prominent example of this kind of social chiliasm can be seen in the Anabaptist revolution in Münster (1525).

From the sixteenth to the nineteenth century, many Protestant thinkers continued to read the Book of Revelation literally and, in so doing, to expect a millenarian consummation. The "fifth monarchy men" of the English Civil War (1642–1660) were indebted to Daniel 2:44 for the notion of an everlasting and indomitable kingdom, the fifth and final one in Daniel's vision, established by God on earth: "And in the days of these kings shall the God of heaven set up a kingdom, which shall never be destroyed: and the kingdom shall not be left to other people, but it shall break in pieces and consume all these kingdoms, and it shall stand for ever."

In the seventeenth and eighteenth centuries, English-speaking Protestants also subscribed to the theory that the future could be discerned in the Book of Revelation. Their theological history and millenarian view identified the papacy with the antichrist, the battle between good and evil reputedly being a struggle between true and false Christianity. Similarly, revolutionary enthusiasts in Germany and England (notably Wordsworth, Coleridge, Southey, and Blake) considered the French Revolution to be the apocalyptic fulfillment of Revelation and the prelude to the millennium. Like the early fathers of the church, they, too, became disillusioned by events and had to revise their literal interpretations.

The millennial idea has continued to flourish, especially in Protestant circles. For the Adventists, the doctrine of the Second Coming of Christ and the establishment of the millennium is central. It has even pervaded secular theory. For example, Marxist doctrine envisions a utopian age in the future and the culmination of history in which class distinctions would disappear and a socioeconomic utopia would be realized.

The idea of the millennium demonstrates mankind's longing for a better life. Though springing from an historical context of discontent and suffering, millennial visions are generally constructive, exhibiting optimism about the future and an indomitable faith in human capability. For the millennial thinker, time is not a vacuously infinite duration. Rather, it provides a context of profound ethical struggle, involving all of creation.

[C.D.]

See also **Apocalypse; Eschatology; Indo-Iranian Gods of Time; Prophecy.**

FURTHER READINGS

Barrois, Georges Augustin. "Millennium." *The Interpreter's Dictionary of the Bible: An Illustrated Encyclopedia.* Ed. George Arthur Buttrick et al. 4 vols. New York: Abingdon P, 1962. 3:381a–382b.

Cohn, Norman. *The Pursuit of the Millennium: Revolutionary Millenarians and Mystical Anarchists of the Middle Ages.* 1961. New York: Oxford UP, 1977.

Dolan, J.P. and R. Kuehner. "Millenarianism." *New Catholic Encyclopedia.* Ed. Rev. William J. McDonald et al. 18 vols. New York: McGraw-Hill, 1967. 9:852a–854a.

Tuveson, Ernest. *Millennium and Utopia.* Berkeley: U of California P, 1949.

———. "Millenarianism." *Dictionary of the History of Ideas: Studies of Selected Pivotal Ideas.* Ed. Philip P. Wiener. 5 vols. New York: Scribner's, 1973. 3:223a–225b.

MILTON, JOHN (1608–1674)

It had been conventionally thought that Shakespeare's works revealed a world of time, and Milton's, a world of space. Like most convenient dichotomies, this one is false, but it is in relation to Milton that it errs more seriously. From early in his career to his last works, in his prose and in his grander poetry, John Milton fully engaged all of the issues raised by the Renaissance discovery of time.

Early in his career Milton was imbued with fervent new faiths, particularly as regarded the benefits of a rational plan of education and the importance of fame. Like Dante, Petrarch, Shakespeare, and many others, Milton espoused the high reward of fame as fitting the achievements of learning and literature. In his ideas on education we find the same aroused and vigorous utilization of time that was evident in other Renaissance tracts. In *Of Education*, Milton outlines the ideas that he had developed "of a better education, in extent and comprehension far more large, and yet of time far shorter, and of attainment far more certain than hath yet been in practice." Milton addresses two shortcomings; one is sloth and the other is subject matter. An earlier prolusion, "In the Morning Rise Up Early," regrets that physical laborers make better use of their time than do scholars: "We permit ourselves to be outstripped by laborers and farmers in nightly and early morning toil. . . . We guard our health against late hours and severe studies; shameful to say we leave the mind untended." This is particularly shameful, since, given diligent application and a temperate life, the scope of what humankind can accomplish is practically limitless. A Baconian prospect of the unlimited advance of knowledge unfolds before Milton's vision.

This concern for time is attended by a desire to introduce right order in the system of studies as well as more useful materials. Milton would discard the "trifles of grammarians and rhetoricians," save only what was worthy from logic, and avoid the perilous rocks of metaphysics. "With all of these things, which are of no value, despised and eliminated, it will be wonderful how many whole years we shall gain." In *Of Education,* he holds that the amount of Latin or of Greek that it had formerly taken seven or eight years to acquire, "might be learned otherwise easily and delightfully in one year." The goals of Petrarch and of Rabelais are reaffirmed by Milton "if from childhood we permit no day to pass without lessons and diligent study."

The point of recalling these earlier and fervent expressions is to indicate that when we come to the onset of Milton's most memorable poetry, from "On Time," Sonnet VII ("How soon hath time . . ."), and *Lycidas*, Milton was already engaged in the modification of these Renaissance goals from the perspective of his religious faith. In fact, one of the major themes of Milton's most serious poetry is quite simply to mount resistance to the temptations posed by those arguments of time that had so clearly emerged in the Renaissance.

In Sonnet VII, Milton's own chosen path of retirement for the purposes of study risks comparison with his more successful contemporaries. Implicit in the poem's debate is a secularized version of the parable of the talents. The evidence of the "more timely-happy" to the question of what has one to show for his talents is more apparent than that of those who have chosen a life of quiet study. In all of these works, Milton is affirming his own divine trust and religious faith as providing the ultimate support and justification of his actions: "All is: if I have grace to use it so / As ever in my great Taskmaster's eye." In the more famous Sonnet XIX, the so-called sonnet on his blindness, the responsible work (or day labor) seems to have been literally cancelled by Milton's loss of sight. Any fretfulness over an unjust calling to account implies a slight to divine wisdom: while there are those who are dispatched in God's service, constantly posting "without rest," Milton can find satisfaction in the knowledge that there are those also close to God "who only stand and wait." Although he does not uproot the notion of an active use of time, Milton still provides other alternatives to Renaissance activism.

In *Lycidas,* Milton confronts the greatest challenge to his religious faith, and that is young death and even oblivion before any work of note can be achieved. Whereas earlier Milton had attributed value to the powers of poetry and fame, here in *Lycidas,* these reliances are shown to be unstable. How is poetry to provide any stay for Milton when the very prototype of the poet,

Orpheus, whose powers Milton had earlier elevated, was helpless against the same fate of drowning that had met Edward King, whose loss at sea occasioned the poem's deep questionings. So, too, in *Lycidas*, earthly fame acquires only a mixed and subordinate value. As in Dante and Petrarch, and that line of humanists who were determined to rise above the slighter values of their day, in Milton fame is both the motive spark and the reward that inspire the heroic soul. But the very precariousness of this hope, registered by Edward King's premature drowning, exposes the fragility of fame as a primary human value. *Lycidas* continues the spiritual discoveries of Sonnet VII. As Milton had placed his labor under the supervision of a divine trust, so genuine fame finds its true reward "in the perfect witness of all-judging Jove."

These same resolutions that Milton discovered in his earlier poetry will receive fuller expression in his great series *Paradise Lost*, *Paradise Regained*, and *Samson Agonistes*. Just as Milton was obliged to overcome the strong arguments of a keen temporal accountability and responsiveness, so conversely where these arguments prevail in his large poems, whether with Adam and Eve, or more definitively with Satan, we see that chaos and destruction are the results, and that the greater glory of his highest creations, of Christ in *Paradise Regained* and of Samson, are achieved by their direct repudiation. In Book Nine of *Paradise Lost*, Eve argues for working separately from Adam by invoking the better efficiency to be gained from a division of labor. She argues that Adam, with his "casual discourse," decreases their productivity: he interrupts their "day's work, brought to little, though begun / Early," and as a result, "th' hour of supper comes unearned." Rather than trusting in God's bounty, as does Adam, Eve betrays her more personal and aggressive attitude toward time, which will become even clearer when she reaches forth to seize the forbidden fruit. Her actions summarize the Renaissance motif of *carpe florem* ("Her rash hand in evil hour / Forth reaching to the fruit, she plucked, she eat"), and behind these we hear even more fundamental motives of the Renaissance: humankind was not intended to live like a beast with its conscious powers undeveloped, but rather to shed the infantile dependence and assume the risks of good and evil. While these are the surging motives that overwhelm her, not excluding the prospect of godhead itself, Milton reminds us that her conduct is rapacious, and that she is in the grips of a blind hunger.

Satan, who had himself fallen victim to these desires, offers them as temptations to Christ in *Paradise Regained*. By pointing out Christ's obscurity, his mature years, the great promises ringing in the past about Christ's own future mission, he tries to instill distrust, temporal anxiety. Satan's need for immediate action (*carpe diem* and *carpe florem* urgings) argues and reveals a primary emphasis on secondary forces, like glory, all of which would tend to diminish any primary faith in God the father. The means he proposes are designed to destroy this larger sense of humankind's spiritual being and importance. And this seems to be the primary basis of Milton's quarrel with the newly emergent Renaissance means for combating time.

Like Dante's, Milton's own journey is complex and arduous, and in its very complexity shows its indebtedness to the heroic humanism of the Renaissance. Samson himself, like Christ, dreams of promised glory, an inspired faith in grand accomplishments and fame. These had first to be tempered by the agony of his defeats and subjected to intense spiritual scrutiny. Finally, however, the last poet of the Renaissance reasserts the early Renaissance faith. "Samson hath quit himself / Like Samson and heroically hath finished / A life heroic. . . . " His final triumph, though mortal for himself, brought to himself and his father's house eternal fame. But more importantly his own endeavor will serve as a monument for those who come after, and Samson's own heroism as a model for their conduct.

Milton was the last poet able to make large and imaginative use of the great Christian patterns of salvation history. Very early, from his *On the Morning of Christ's Nativity*, which has been called a dress rehearsal for *Paradise Lost*, Milton incorporated into his poems the cardinal points of the eschatological drama—the Creation and the Fall, the Incarnation and the Crucifixion, and Resurrection and the Last Judgment. What this means is that he was able to measure human events from another perspective, a more enduring one of larger significance. Like Dante's, Milton's understanding of human events fits into these larger controlling patterns. What Dante had anticipated, Milton experienced in full force and power: the developing new conceptions of time introduced by the culture of the Renaissance. Like Dante, Milton recoiled from some of the implications of these new discoveries, but also like his Italian compeer, he remained in his poetry and development indelibly marked by these developments. Each was responding to as well as embodying in his works an energetic and dramatic view of the world.

[R.J.Q.]

See also **Dante Alighieri; Petrarch, Francis; Shakespeare, William.**

FURTHER READINGS

Patrides, C.A. *The Grand Design of God*. London: Routledge & Kegan Paul, 1972.

Quinones, Ricardo J. "Milton." *The Renaissance Discovery of Time*. Cambridge: Harvard UP, 1972. 444–493.

Stoll, E.E. "Time and Space in Milton." *From Shakespeare to Joyce*. Garden City: Doubleday, 1944. 416–430.

MODERN AND POSTMODERN MUSIC

With the advent of film and automobiles, quantum physics and relativity theory, research on dreams and the unconscious, and an increasing interest in world cultures, the time Western composers wished to make audible in their music changed dramatically in the twentieth century. No longer was it essential to present an illusion of time, or what Suzanne Langer calls "virtual time," as continuous, unilinear, and homogeneous as in most nineteenth-century Western art music. In response to social, technological, and scientific innovations, as well as an awareness of different attitudes toward time in Eastern, African, and various indigenous cultures around the world, many Western composers began to play with and abort conventional notions of time in their music. Experimenting with discontinuity, multiplicity, heterogeneity, and non-teleological kinds of time, they initiated radical changes not only in music but also in listeners' perception of time in music.

Depending on their culture, composers reconceived musical time in various ways at the beginning of the twentieth century. Some, such as C. Debussy and I. Stravinsky, chose to slow down the rate of short-term change in their music through frequent repetition of small melodic fragments, sometimes borrowed from simple folk tunes. The effect of this turning in place—akin to W.B. Yeats's gyre and T S. Eliot's eternal present—is to shift attention away from moment-to-moment changes in the music, away from the allure of a song-like melody with its supportive accompaniment, to the movement of large sections, each relatively static, self-contained, and with what Debussy called "its own color and sense of time." To accentuate the differences between these sections, such composers eschewed conventional techniques assuring smooth transitions between ideas in favor of abruptly juxtaposing them. In this way, discontinuity became a technique capable of reorienting the listener's sense of time. This music, consisting of relatively static activity within sections and maximal change from section to section, thus made time audible on a level of form whereas previously spatial models (that is, ABA, or from A to B and back to A again) had dominated. Time in such works as Stravinsky's early ballets depends on listeners to connect the disparate parts (much as in cubist collages), that is, to experience the musical sections as somehow simultaneous, multiply present, and formally dynamic.

Other composers in the early part of this century, such as A. Schoenberg, A. Webern, and A. Berg, began to work with extreme condensation of sonic materials and to employ mirror forms. Their music requires listeners to imagine time as completely different from that of daily life and, under certain conditions, as a background to reversible symmetries. To bridge this difficulty and, after World War I, to question teleological notions of progress in general, they and neoclassical composers elsewhere turned to incorporating musical forms and styles from the past. Without necessarily replicating the sense of time these musics may otherwise carry, they used these references to revive pre-nineteenth-century values, to suggest that our sense of the future must be founded on our acknowledgement of the past, and to create opportunities to surpass past achievements.

After World War II, and as tape machines and electronically produced sound became increasingly popular, some composers turned to making works that threw into question the notion of music as a coherent sequence of sounds. In the moment forms of K. Stockhausen, for example, the music just starts and stops, without consequential beginnings and endings. It does not initiate procedures to be developed in either a continuous or discontinuous manner nor depend on the listener's accumulated memory from one part to the next. Form in these works does not involve any climax or dramatic finale and is often conceived in strictly proportional terms, with section lengths sometimes based on the Fibonacci number series.

Since the turbulent 1960s, some composers have begun to reject the increasingly difficult and often intellectual approach to music espoused by the modernists. Challenging this idea as well as the need for constant change and originality, and following the lead of such postmodernist critics as F. Jameson and J.F. Lyotard, they are returning to more accessible, easily perceptible notions of time, those that do not rely on the listener having specialized training. Some of these composers wish to renew a connection to the past, to the temporal strategies characteristic of eighteenth- and nineteenth-century compositions. Quoting previous works or incorporating sampled tape sounds and sometimes collaging a wide variety of musical materials in their music without any desire to overpower or redefine these sources, they seek not to get beyond the past but rather to extend our understanding of the present, a present in which the memory of other times is deeply embedded. Works such as L. Berio's *Sinfonia* (1968), quote from both predecessors' and contemporaries' music to construct a sense of time as embodying many times, a sense of self made of many memories.

Those espousing what H. Foster calls a postmodernism of reaction are returning explicitly to traditional forms and syntax. Sometimes, as with G. Rochberg, these serve as a foil to modernist ideas within one work; at other times, as with D. Del Tredici, they signal a wholehearted return to tonality and conventional narrative. Among those expressing, by contrast, a postmodernism of resistance, composers such as J. Adams use parody and irony when dealing with the music of the past, seeking to deconstruct the mechanisms underlying traditional musical gestures, including temporal ones. Composers such as P. Glass and S. Reich use tonal triads and continuous repetition to create non-narrative works that subvert the role of long-term memory. Many of their works place the listener in a time of pure process, pure presence, what J. Kramer calls "vertical," as opposed to horizontal, time.

In recent decades, composers are continuing to explore new kinds of musical time in widely diverse ways. At one extreme are those trying to remove the conscious, subjective role of the composer as much as possible. Some use chance procedures to generate the music, as in the work of J. Cage; others follow complex mathematical algorithms. The time sense in these works may depend on the listener to bring one to the work. On the other end of the spectrum are those

inspired by recent perceptual and cognitive studies. Such composers as F. Lerdahl hope to use the results of research on how the human mind and ear perceive time through sound to be able to control precisely the effect their music has on listeners. Other composers are returning to the time of storytelling, though in new narrative forms, or, like P. Oliveros, are working directly with the time of the human organism. Her works, which depend on the human breath for their shape and articulation, aim to affect listeners' breathing and place them in a meditative state of "deep listening." The time of such works is no longer a virtual experience, but an actual one, different for each listener.

[J.P.]

See also **Computer Music; Modernism; Music: American Avant-Garde; Postmodern Literature; Time and Narrative.**

FURTHER READINGS

Brelet, Gisèle. *Le temps musical.* 2 vols. Paris: Presses Universitaires de France, 1949.

Ermarth, Elizabeth Deeds. *Sequel to History: Postmodernism and the Crisis of Representational Time.* Princeton: Princeton UP, 1992.

Kramer, Jonathan D. "Studies of Time and Music: A Bibliography." *Music Theory Spectrum* 7 (1985): 72–106.

———. *The Time of Music.* New York: Schirmer, 1988.

MODERNISM

Modernism has long secured its position as the dominant intellectual and artistic movement of the twentieth century, and as such is worthy of being discussed in the same terms as the Renaissance or romanticism. In fact, modernism ranks with the Renaissance in the fervor, the scope, and the frequency of its addresses to time. Like that earlier period, it not only sought to alter accepted ways of regarding time, but these altered conceptions of time were in the forefront of larger changes in cultural values. "From the very beginning you began bothering about time," the accusation leveled against one of Thomas Mann's characters in his enormous *Zeitroman* (time-novel), *The Magic Mountain* (1925), could also be used to characterize Petrarch's temporal concerns in the fourteenth century. Such concerns were the vanguard to more fundamental change. But there is another, even more direct historical connection between these two periods where time figured so prominently. The nature of the time-world that began in the Renaissance and that then led the way for larger developments in the West was the very one that modernism was born to challenge and, where possible, to alter. This means, of course, that the temporal concerns presented by modernism are not to be confused with those of modernity, and that in fact, modernism lived to refashion the temporal and psychic demands of modernization.

Given these associations, it should come as no surprise that the stylistic changes of modernism have substantial philosophical roots. In the Renaissance, responses to time were at once heroic and dramatic and practical and mundane. But in the later developments of these responses, the heroic and the cosmic dimensions were lost, while the practical and the mundane reigned. This resulted in what has been called "the paradox of time," which holds—put simply—that when the practical dimensions of temporal response triumph so exclusively they produce the opposite effect, the triumph of space. Henri Bergson, Alfred North Whitehead and others provide the philosophical dimensions of modernism when they indicate that by the end of the nineteenth century, time had become spatialized. They of course refer to scientific time, wherein any specific moment is a discrete counter cut off from, but not different from, any other moment of time. If time involves a world of unrelieved sameness then not time, but space is the result. And writers, artists, and other thinkers responded to this possibility with horror.

The origins of modernism are thus metaphysical and begin in this shudder at the experience of emptiness. If we look at literary modernism, we see that in its first phase it was determined to show the collapse of those who most willfully upheld the requirements of the Western temporal dynamic. In such characters as Kurtz (Joseph Conrad's *Heart of Darkness*), Thomas Buddenbrook (Thomas Mann's *Buddenbrooks*), Gerald Crich (D.H. Lawrence's *Women in Love*), and Prufrock (in T.S. Eliot's "The Love Song of J. Alfred Prufrock"), their authors show the fatal encounter with emptiness that is the logical consequence of the system to which each of these characters adhered. In Dante's famous image concluding *Paradiso* X, the mechanical clock represents the fully harmonized workings of a spiritual universe. But in the works just mentioned, and many others, the mechanical clock is only a dull reminder of spiritual sameness. Clearly something has happened. The clock has lost its hands, and one is confronted only with blank space.

If the first phase of literary modernism presented the negative portraits of failed models—characters who themselves were representative of a system that had become dangerously single-minded—the next phase grows out of the first and offers a more positive typology. As the danger of the older method was a kind of temporal linearity, where one kind of experience would be repeated into infinity, then stylistically the aim of modernism was to disturb such predictability. This was done by introducing a style that was disjointed and jarring, with materials coming from varied and discrepant lexical levels and levels of experience. T.S. Eliot wrote that the poet must not only look into his heart but also into the "cerebral cortex, the nervous system, and the digestive tracts." A poem is an amalgamation (fragmentary, to be sure) of such discrepant experiences. If this was the case stylistically, then obviously modernism was obliged to evolve a typology suitable to register these multiform patterns of experience. Indeed, as may be seen with Tiresias (*The Waste Land*), Hans Castorp (*The Magic Mountain*), Marcel (Proust's *Remembrance of Things Past*), and Leopold Bloom (*Ulysses*), modernist "heroes" were passive, selfless, tolerant witnesses. They were characters not endowed with an enormous will, but rather characters more open to the many facets of experience.

Such a "complex central consciousness" is the receiver most suited to a complex world with multiple levels of experience. But here too, modernism shows why, as a movement, it came to characterize an entire era. It shares these same insights with other disciplines, with philosophy, psychology, and physics. This complex central consciousness, as well as other devices for reflecting multiple points of view, may be allied with the thought of Ortega, Whitehead, and Einstein. Rather than presenting a single "observer-elect," modernism inclined toward "perspectivism" (Ortega) or toward what Whitehead called a "manifold of prehensions." This means that the techniques and representations of modernism may be shown as doing for contemporary literature what Einstein's theories had done for understanding the physical universe.

The heralded fragmentariness of the modernist style does not rest there. Its aim is directed toward what has been called the "mythic method," that is, the simultaneous manipulation of episodes from modern life with scenes of mythic power from past great literature. The Ulysses story, the Parsifal story, Shakespeare's *Tempest*—these are the resonant works that modernists have used to give relief and texture to the apparently anarchic events of contemporary experience. This has rightly been called "spatial form," where meaning is not linear, or consecutive, as in narrative, but stacked up, as it were, concentric, as events are portrayed as having greater reverberations than their fragmentary natures might lead us to suppose.

Events might be fragmentary, but not for that reason random. In the course of their developments, major modernists all moved toward grasping the heart of myth itself. Modernism may thus be understood in developmental terms: its negative critiques, its complex central consciousness, its fragmentary style are actually movements toward grasping the archetypal, to restoring density and texture to experience. Indeed, like their earlier confreres of the Renaissance, they were devoted to revealing the more abiding presences of life itself.

[R.J.Q.]

See also **Bergson, Henri; Renaissance; Whitehead, Alfred North.**

Further Readings

Frank, Joseph. "Spatial Form in Modern Literature." *The Idea of Spatial Form*. New Brunswick: Rutgers UP, 1991.

Meyerhoff, Hans. *Time in Literature*. Berkeley: U of California P, 1955.

Patrides, C.A. *Aspects of Time*. Manchester: Manchester UP, 1976.

Quinones, Ricardo J. *Mapping Literary Modernism: Time and Development*. Princeton: Princeton UP, 1985.

MOLECULAR AND BIOCHEMICAL RHYTHMS

Living organisms have the ability to regulate processes in relation to time, and to use this ability for physiologically important functions. Biological rhythms that have periods of approximately one day—circadian rhythms—are taken as indicators of an underlying endogenous mechanism. Indeed, circadian rhythmicity has been documented as a prominent and pervasive feature in both animal and plant physiology, having been reported in all major eukaryotic taxa, and in prokaryotes as well. But the molecular and biochemical nature of the rhythmic mechanism remains unknown.

Under twenty-four-hour light-dark cycles, circadian systems exhibit daily rhythms in many different functions, each with a given phase relation to the imposed light-dark cycle, so that different functions may peak at different times of day. If organisms are maintained in the laboratory under conditions of constant light or dark and constant temperature, the rhythms continue essentially unabated and for indefinitely long periods. Moreover, while the periods are generally close to twenty-four hours, they are not exactly so, thus the term circadian (< Latin *circa*, about; *diem*, one day).

In higher animals, both vertebrates and invertebrates, the circadian mechanism involves the nervous system and cell-to-cell interactions. However, circadian control and expression also occur in plants, and also in single cells, without a nervous system or cellular interactions.

Molecular and biochemical changes must underlie physiological rhythms, and the molecular events are generally viewed as being closer to the biological clock mechanism itself. To be sure, certain biochemical rhythms might be part of the mechanism, but since the clock mechanism remains unknown, it continues to be difficult to distinguish actual components of the clock from those that are simply clock controlled.

At the biochemical level, knowledge of a clock-controlled component—a protein for example—can lead to knowledge concerning the clock mechanism itself. Luciferase, an enzyme involved in the circadian-controlled bioluminescence in a unicellular alga, the dinoflagellate Gonyaulax polyedra, exhibits a rhythm in its cellular concentration. It is thus an excellent biochemical correlate of the physiological rhythm. The mechanism of the daily regulation of enzyme synthesis and destruction can provide insight concerning the action of the clock at the levels of mRNA (messenger ribonucleic acid) synthesis (transcription) and its translation (protein synthesis).

An early model of the clock, the "chronon," was based on the discovery that clock function in Gonyaulax could be blocked by inhibitors of both transcription and translation. A strong prediction of this model was the existence of time-of-day specific mRNAs. Such RNAs have now been discovered in several different organisms, but whether or not they are part of the actual clock mechanism remains to be established. In the chronon model, certain key segments of the deoxyribonucleic acid (DNA) are transcribed sequentially once each day; with the synthesis of the relevant regulatory proteins, a loop is closed so as to repeat the sequence of genes transcribed, restarting at a point corresponding to about twenty-four hours earlier.

Other models have been centered on biochemical pathways associated with energy metabolism. These have not gained much support, but the discovery that creatine affects the period of the clock in *Gonyaulax* suggests that circadian timing may involve energy metabolism.

Based mostly on the effects of inhibitors of eukaryotic protein synthesis on circadian phase and period, an important involvement of proteins in the clock mechanism is now firmly established. Several different inhibitors of eukaryotic protein synthesis—for example cycloheximide, puromycin, and anisomycin—are very effective in shifting the phase of free-running circadian oscillations. Analogues of certain amino acids, which do not block protein synthesis but result in defective proteins, are also effective. Chloramphenicol, an inhibitor specific for prokaryotic protein synthesis, has no effect on phase or period.

All models involve proteins which, in one way or another, may vary in activity and cellular levels as related to time of day. As mentioned, these may be difficult to distinguish from clock-controlled proteins. Two such circadian-controlled proteins (luciferase and binding protein) are biochemical correlates of the bioluminescence rhythm in *Gonyaulax*, changing in amounts in concert with the in vivo rhythm. The binding protein is synthesized in a daily pulse of four to six hours, but the mRNA levels for this protein remain constant at different times of day, as does its in vitro translatability in a heterologous system. These facts indicate that the clock regulates the synthesis of this protein at the translational level, thus providing a clue as to how the clock exerts its effect, but not a clue concerning how it "keeps time."

We suggest a clock model involving a series of protein regulatory factors for the translation of mRNAs, each regulating the synthesis of the next regulatory protein, eventually closing a loop such that the "last" protein regulates the synthesis of the "first." These would thus constitute true "clock proteins," which might also control the synthesis of other proteins outside the loop, thus serving dual roles as clock components and transducers to overt rhythms. They would be encoded by clock genes, whose transcripts are produced constitutively and are relatively stable (a half-life of days). By contrast, the clock proteins are unstable (a half-life of hours) and synthesized in similarly short bursts, each one being regulated by a different short-lived protein.

A number of substances other than protein synthesis inhibitors have been reported to influence either the phase or period of circadian rhythms in different organisms, but sites and mechanisms of action are largely unknown. Phase-shifting effects of ion channel inhibitors and ion channels could relate to the participation of membranes in the rhythmic mechanism. Alcohols and aldehydes have significant effects, and it is possible that they influence protein synthesis. Calcium, calmodulin, and cyclic adenosine monophosphate are implicated as potential clock elements in some species; the effects observed could relate in one way or another to protein phosphorylation. Still unexplained is the effect of heavy water (D_2O), which slows the biological clock in organisms ranging from unicells to invertebrates and mammals.

Mutants exhibiting altered clock properties can be extremely valuable in the analysis of mechanism. Important results have been obtained with *Drosophila*, *Neurospora*, *Chlamydomonas*, and the hamster. In *Drosophila*, mutants of the *per* (period) gene (per^l, per^s and per^0) were isolated as long, short, and arhythmic flies, respectively. These same alleles were later shown to affect minute-long courtship rhythms similarly. Thus, rhythms having very different frequencies can be affected by a single gene, but the way in which these effects relate to the mechanism itself is unknown. The *per* gene has been cloned and characterized, and its introduction into mutant arhythmic flies has been shown to restore circadian rhythmicity. The transcript of this locus, which is expressed rhythmically in the nervous system, appears to encode a proteoglycan-like molecule, which may act by modulating gap junction conductivity. *Per* homologues have been found in a number of other species, and the *per* gene even possesses regions of homology with the functionally analogous *frq* (frequency) gene in *Neurospora*. In *Drosophila*, a *per* homologue has been shown to be crucial to normal neurogenic development.

The temporal coordination of internal physiological and cellular biochemical events is often cited as an important benefit accruing from the circadian system. This is illustrated by recent studies on oxygen-evolving photosynthesis and oxygen-labile nitrogen fixation in the unicellular cyanobacteria *Synechococcus*. In cyanobacteria with cells specialized for nitrogen fixation (heterocysts), these incompatible processes are spatially separated. In some species they occur together, but show endogenously generated daily rhythms in the two functions, with peak levels at opposite daily phases. These organisms thus make use of circadian timing as a mechanism for temporal segregation of incompatible functions.

A somewhat different example is the cycling of the luciferase molecule in the bioluminescence rhythm of *Gonyaulax*. The protein is actually degraded to the level of amino acids and resynthesized every twenty-four hours. As this organism lives in an environment limited by nitrogen but not energy, protein turnover may represent a mechanism for conserving nitrogen by degrading proteins whose function is unnecessary during a certain part of the day and then reusing their amino acids (which are retained in the cell) to synthesize new and different proteins which have functions at that time of day.

Many questions are not yet answered, but enough is known about circadian timing, in its various manifestations, to justify the conclusion that the circadian clock represents a powerful, versatile, and functional physiological mechanism.

[J.W.H.]

See also **Cellular Rhythms; Chronobiology; Circadian Pacemakers; Endosymbiosis; Internal-Clock Models; Molecular Genetics and Biological Rhythms.**

MOLECULAR GENETICS AND BIOLOGICAL RHYTHMS

Biological rhythms occur on many time scales ranging from milliseconds to years. However, the most intensely studied of these are daily, or circadian, rhythms because they are virtually ubiquitous and they encompass a myriad of behavioral, physiological, and biochemical processes. Circadian rhythms have three basic properties: They can be entrained by environmental cues (usually light), they persist under constant environmental conditions (free-run), and they run at the same rate independent of temperature (that is to say they are temperature-compensated). The second of these properties is particularly important to the molecular geneticist as it indicates the circadian clock is regulated by an endogenous, self-sustaining, genetically encoded oscillator. In fact, early pharmacological studies showed that RNA and protein synthesis (that is, gene expression) were necessary for free-running circadian rhythms. This being the case,

what are the molecular mechanisms underlying circadian clock function? To address such a global question, it has been helpful to separate the clock into three components: An entrainment pathway that transmits environmental information to the oscillator, an oscillator that can respond to the environment and accurately keep time, and output pathways that activate various overt rhythmic processes based on the phase (relative time of day) of the oscillator. Genes which function in each of these components have been found through genetic (that is to say, mutants that disrupt clock function) and molecular (that is to say, genes that have adapted their expression to the clock) means.

How is environmental information relayed to the oscillator? A recent breakthrough in this area is the discovery that light stimulates the expression of c-fos and jun–B (whose protein products combine to form transcription factor AP-1) in the suprachiasmatic nucleus (SCN; site of the mammalian pacemaker) of hamsters during the "subjective" night (when lights would be off). These observations suggest that photic inputs may be coupled to the circadian oscillator through AP1-mediated changes in transcription. Another molecule that appears to be involved in circadian entrainment is the indoleamine hormone melatonin. This hormone, which is produced in the pineal gland and (in some species) retinae, accumulates to high levels during the subjective night and binds to receptors on the SCN and elsewhere. Daily injections of this hormone in free-running mammals, birds, and lizards acts to entrain circadian rhythms. However, if the source or sources of rhythmic melatonin production is removed, there is little or no affect on circadian rhythmicity in mammals, while birds and lizards become arrhythmic. Thus, melatonin appears to function at different levels in the clocks of different species.

What do we know about the molecules and mechanisms involved in measuring time? One gene that appears to be involved in this process is the *period* (*per*) gene of the fruit fly, *Drosophila melanogaster*. Mutations in this gene can eliminate or alter the periodicity of individual or population rhythms in flies. One important aspect of *period* gene expression is the daily fluctuations of its mRNA and protein products in the head (site of the *Drosophila* oscillator) and other (but not all the other) tissues. The circadian accumulation in *period* protein lags behind that of *period* mRNA by eight hours or more, and constitutes a feedback loop where the protein appears to influence negatively the synthesis of its own mRNA. Since this feedback loop has the basic properties of a self-sustaining oscillator (that is to say, time delays and feedback regulation), it may be at least part of the circadian timekeeping mechanism in *Drosophila*. Other potential oscillator molecules include the *Neurospora* (bread mold) *frequency* (*frq*) gene product, whose mutant forms have many of the same circadian phenotypes as *period* mutants (that is, alteration or elimination of rhythmicity), and proteins within oscillator cells of certain marine gastropods (*Bulla* and *Aplysia*) and rats that cross-react to antibodies directed against the *period* protein. Further studies are needed to determine how *frequency* and *period* cross-reacting proteins are involved in oscillator function.

What molecules are involved in activating different behavioral, physiological, and biochemical rhythms at the appropriate time of day? Several specific circadian rhythmic outputs are associated with molecules that exhibit circadian fluctuations in abundance. For instance, circadian rhythms of bioluminescence in *Gonyaulax* are associated with oscillations in luciferase binding protein. Photosynthetic processes in several (and perhaps all) species of plants are associated with circadian rhythms in chlorophyll A/B binding protein mRNA. Some molecules that undergo circadian oscillations are thought to be clock outputs, but have not been associated with a specific rhythmic process. These include rod photoreceptor opsin mRNA in some amphibians and fish; DBP, a liver-enriched transcriptional activator protein involved in (at least) albumin gene regulation in rats; polyadenylated vasopressin mRNA in the rat SCN, which leads to oscillations in vasopressin neuropeptide in the cerebrospinal fluid; and rat calcitonin, a neuropeptide involved in calcium metabolism. Several putative output molecules have only been identified via oscillations in their abundance. Circadian cycling of two *Neurospora* ccg (clock-controlled gene) transcripts is dependant on the *frequency* gene as period-altered *frequency* mutants affect the periodicity of ccg transcript cycling in parallel (that is, short and long period ccg transcript cycling is seen in short and long period *frequency* mutants, respectively). The abundance of several anonymous proteins have been found to undergo circadian oscillations. One of these, a 230-kilodalton protein in *Acetabularia*, also alters its abundance in response to stimuli that shift the phase of the clock. How does the oscillator interact with input and output pathways to form a functional clock? The following model takes into account different levels of clock-regulated gene expression: Environmental stimuli induce the synthesis of AP1 or AP1-like transcription factors which act to phase-shift the oscillator by altering its expression; a *period*-like feedback loop operates as a self-sustaining circadian oscillator that modifies its cycling in response to AP1 regulation; the oscillator then affects overt rhythms by regulating the expression of output pathway molecules through the action of a *period*-like protein. As this scenario was built from observations in many different organisms, it will be interesting to see if any single organism's clock works in this way and, if not, what the differences are.

Finally, the molecules and mechanisms regulating circadian rhythms may have general significance to biological rhythms of other periodicities. This is most apparent in *Drosophila*, as the *period* gene not only affects circadian rhythms but also affects courtship song rhythms having periodicities of approximately one minute. In addition, evidence from other organisms suggests that the annual photoperiodic clock and the circadian clock have elements in common. Thus, by continuing molecular genetic studies of the circadian clock and applying what is found to other biological rhythms, we will continue to make progress in learning how organisms measure time.

[P.E.H.]

See also **Biological Rhythms in Epidemiology and Pharmacology; Chronobiology; Internal-Clock Models; Melatonin.**

FURTHER READINGS

Aschoff, J. *Handbook of Behavioral Neurobiology. Vol. 4. Biological Rhythms*. New York: Plenum, 1981.

Cassone, V.M. "Effects of Melatonin on Vertebrate Circadian Systems." *Trends in Neurosciences* 13 (1990): 457–464.

Dunlap, J.C. "Closely Watched Clocks: Molecular Analysis of Circadian Rhythms in *Neurospora* and *Drosophila*." *Topics in Inorganic and General Chemistry* 6 (1990): 159–165.

Hardin, P.E., J.C. Hall, and M. Rosbash. "Circadian Cycling in the Levels of Protein and mRNA from *Drosophila melanogaster*'s *Period* Gene." *Molecular Genetics of Biological Rhythms*. Ed. W. Young. New York: Marcel Dekker, 1992.

Rosbash, M., and J.C. Hall. "The Molecular Biology of Circadian Rhythms." *Neuron* 3 (1989): 387–398.

Takahashi, J.S. "Circadian Rhythms: From Gene Expression to Behavior." *Current Opinion in Neuroscience* 1 (1991): 556–561.

MOVEMENT AND RHYTHM

Rhythm is ubiquitous in movement. Adopting the definition of rhythm as the presence of temporal symmetry within an event, its ubiquity is most obvious in locomotion: rhythmicities can easily be identified in the wing beats of the sea gull, the strides of the sprinter, and the thrusts of the swimming leech. Internal repetitive actions are similarly rhythmic. Consider the beating of the heart or the movement of the jaw during chewing. The symmetry definition makes it reasonable to argue that even unidirectional movements about a single joint are rhythmic. The velocity profiles for such movements show a temporal symmetry in that the peak velocity occurs at approximately the midpoint of the movement's duration.

REPETITIVE MOVEMENTS OF A SINGLE LIMB

Finger tapping tasks have been used to study the control of timing in human movement. Performance may be assessed during a paced phase in which subjects attempt to synchronize their responses with a periodic signal or during an unpaced phase in which the signal is eliminated. In some experiments, the mean interresponse interval has been found to deviate consistently from the target interstimulus interval. These biases are suggestive of an internal clock process operating at a fixed frequency that provides an entrainment signal in conflict with the external stimulus.

Analysis of the variability of the interresponse intervals, however, suggests alternative internal timing mechanisms for these tasks. If the tapping rate is varied from trial to trial, one would expect subjects to be most consistent when the target of the tapping rate was a harmonic of the frequency of the internal clock. At other target rates, the mismatch between the target and intrinsic frequencies would be expected to increase the variability of the interresponse intervals. Such evidence has not been obtained. Alternative timing mechanisms that have been proposed include adjustable oscillators or delay-line processes. In the latter scheme, the temporal unit is given by the amount of time required for a process to transpire rather than by any oscillatory process. Models such as these emphasize flexibility in the control of rhythmic movements: the performer is able to produce periodic movements at any desired rate and is not constrained by intrinsic oscillatory processes. The variability data also indicate that feedback plays a minimal role during repetitive tapping.

The production of non-isochronous intervals is severely constrained to be rhythmic (temporally symmetrical). People have little difficulty producing temporal patterns when the long subintervals are integer multiples of shorter subintervals and the short subintervals add up to the longer interval (for example, a pattern composed of two 250-millisecond intervals followed by a 500-millisecond interval). Patterns which do not meet these criteria are extremely difficult to produce. A pattern composed of two 250-millisecond intervals followed by a 600-millisecond interval would violate the integer multiple constraint. A pattern composed of two 250-millisecond intervals followed by a 750-millisecond interval would violate the subinterval sum constraint. In attempting to reproduce such patterns, people will systematically distort the intervals (for example, lengthen the short intervals toward 300 milliseconds and shorten the long interval toward a multiple of the short interval).

REPETITIVE BIMANUAL MOVEMENTS

Different constraints become manifest in the course of bimanual movements. When people simultaneously reach for two objects at different locations, they make the temporal properties of the movements similar. The movements begin and end at the same time, even when this requires that the person generate very different forces in the two limbs.

In repetitive movements, this temporal coupling becomes even more apparent. Consider a task in which subjects repeatedly flex and extend their wrists. At relatively slow speeds (less than 2 hertz), only two phase relations lead to stable performance: movements made in-phase (that is, each wrist flexes and extends at the same time) or antiphase (that is, one wrist flexes while the other extends). People are generally poor at maintaining other phase relations. When the bimanual movements are made at faster rates, only the inphase pattern remains stable. If antiphase bimanual movements are gradually speeded up, a phase transition will occur to inphase movements.

These phenomena have been modeled by assuming that each limb's movement is controlled by an oscillator and that these oscillators are coupled during bimanual movements. Moreover, neural mechanisms that may produce the oscillation have been shown to interact with the physical properties of the moving object (for example, a limb). Huygens's law, originally developed to describe the period of two coupled mechanical pendulums, can also predict the rate of oscillation people adopt when swinging two pendulums of differing mass.

The coupling constraints in bimanual movements are also observed in patients who have undergone surgery in which the two cerebral hemispheres have been disconnected. It appears that these constraints are imposed below the level of the cortex.

RHYTHM AND LOCOMOTION

During locomotion the actions of the different limbs occur in a cyclic manner. This does not mean that the sequence of actions is invariant for a given species. Within a species there are a number of different gaits, each characterized by its own temporal-spatial pattern. For example, when walking, a cat only lifts one limb at a time off the ground. At faster speeds, the actions of the limbs become coupled. In pacing, a cat simultaneously extends both limbs on one side of the body, then the limbs on the other side; in galloping, the coupling occurs between homologous limbs on opposite sides of the body.

Research on locomotion has also emphasized that rhythmic behavior can be the result of relatively low-level neural mechanisms. Normal patterns of locomotion can be observed in animals with transected spinal cords. For example, cats with transected spinal cords will begin to walk when placed on a moving treadmill. Moreover, the cat's gait will pass through the appropriate phase transitions as the speed of the treadmill is increased.

This last result might suggest that rhythmic actions are regulated by sensory processes. However, sensory information is not essential for producing the basic temporal pattern. The locomotion patterns of animals deprived of sensory information remain rhythmic and are even reflected in the neural activity of in vitro segments of the spinal cord. Thus, it has been proposed that certain rhythmic actions reflect the operation of central pattern generators, neural mechanisms that intrinsically constrain the spatiotemporal pattern of fundamental actions such as locomotion, breathing, or chewing.

RHYTHM IN PERCEPTION AND ACTION

The coupling phenomena described for bimanual movements also constrain movements produced simultaneously by different individuals when these people observe each others' actions. If one person swings a leg at a given rate and phase, the leg movements of a second person will become entrained to that frequency and adopt either an in-phase or antiphase mode. It has been argued that these constraints between individuals play an important role in explaining the skill involved in rhythmic group activities such as those exhibited by the crew of a rowing team or the movements of a ballet company.

These phenomena emphasize the important relationship between the perception and production of rhythm. While mechanical analyses can predict the preferred rate of oscillation of biological systems, they fail to account for the flexibility of these systems. Similarly, central pattern generators have proven most useful in describing fundamental, fairly stereotypic rhythmic behaviors. On the other hand, people (and probably other animals) are very adept at perceiving rhythms in external events and incorporating those rhythms into their own movements. We can tap at the rate given by a metronome or match the pace of our gait to that of a running partner.

This flexibility suggests an internal timing mechanism that is relatively unconstrained in terms of establishing a basic unit of time. An additional property of such a timing process is that it is task-independent; that is, the same mechanism is invoked in both movement and perception. Neuropsychological evidence indicates that the neocerebellum may be an essential component of this internal clock. Patients with lesions in this region exhibit impairments in both movement and perception tasks that require precise timing.

[R.I.]

FURTHER READINGS

Cohen, A.H., S. Rossignol, and S. Grillner. *Neural Control of Rhythmic Movements in Vertebrates*. New York: Wiley, 1988.

Keele, S.W., and R. Ivry. "Does the Cerebellum Provide a Common Computation for Diverse Tasks? A Timing Hypothesis." *The Development and Neural Bases of Higher Cognitive Functions*. Ed. A. Diamond. New York: New York Academy of Sciences, 1991. 179–211.

Kugler, P., and M.T. Turvey. *Information, Natural Law and Self-Assembly of Rhythmic Movements: A Study in the Similitude of Natural Law*. Hillsdale: Erlbaum, 1987.

Rosenbaum, D.A. *Human Motor Control*. San Diego: Academic P, 1991.

MUSIC: AFRICA

In music-making, Africans notice and value the temporal. Early outside observers, such as Richard Wallaschek in *Primitive Music* (1893), were well aware of the attention African music gives to time. Later researchers made extended analyses, many of which rely on sound-recording devices, beginning with the cylinder phonograph in the 1890s, and continuing with computers in the 1990s.

Though much of the theoretical basis for African time-reckoning remains unknown, several principles have emerged. African musicians value concepts of motion, action, and, by extension, variation in performance. Motion is manifest in dance and, more subtly, in changes of sound patterns sung or played on instruments. Song texts allude to carefully delineated movement and action. In the text of the Kpelle woman who carved bowls with her singing voice, different words depict small adze strokes, the carving of a bowl with a large inner part, the smoothing of the wood, and the shining of the black bowl. For knowledgeable listeners, performance consists not of endless repetition (as stereotypical portrayals assert), but of intricately shifting sounds.

African musicians emphasize a qualitative approach to time-reckoning. Drummers employ mnemonic syllables to communicate not only meter and rhythm, but tonecolor and timbral dimensions. Among the Kpelle of Liberia, the distinctiveness of these patterns draws from the imitation of a bird's voice (see Figure 1). Among the Yoruba of Nigeria, this same basic pattern is expressed with a different set of mnemonic syllables (see Figure 2). The mnemonic pattern becomes a guiding principle, or (in Kwabena Nketia's term) a "timekeeper." By conceiving these sounds as a series of contrasting tone textures, musicians make no necessary assumption of linear movement.

African music revels in the juxtaposition of asymmetrical durations, joined at temporally coordinate points. Its rhythms have both individual and corporate characters, which combine in an exchange between performers, who maintain separate identities. Performers rarely follow a single organizing beat.

The royal ivory horn players of West Africa form an ensemble of six musicians. Each plays a one- or two-note motive, which precisely interlocks with the others to form a larger whole, or hocket. The motives do not merge in a main beat, but often set up asymmetrical intersections—temporal ties that in performance may shift. The Shona of Zimbabwe call one division of a mbira (plucked idiophone) performance *kushaura*, "to lead the piece," and the other *kutsihira*, "to exchange parts of the song." Two players of the Mangwilo xylophone in southeast Africa sit opposite one another and play the same instrument, the one part referred to as *opachera*, "the starting one," and the other called *wakulela*, "the responding one."

Performance in African contexts carries a contingent quality: the length of a song or event depends on relationships that develop in performance. At appropriate moments, people celebrate this quality by making token gifts of cigarettes, cane juice, palm wine, or coins. Without audience approval and feedback, performers cut their offering short. Under apt conditions, musicians emphasize the elasticity of segments, elaborating outward from a present-centered focus to create an "expandable moment."

In African music, the past informs the present moment of creation, where it dynamically affects musical sounds and textual allusions. From the past, performers call on spirits, often those of ancestors, to enter a performance; by their presence, spirits bring to the present their authority and sanction. As one Kpelle musician played his multiple bow-lute, he called out, "Gbono Kpate," naming a late, great musician and calling on him to come to the performance. Not long afterward, the lute player called out in a high pitched voice, "Ooo," to indicate that the ancestral musician had come and announced his presence in the performance, thereby adding

Figure 1. Mnemonics for drumming; Kpelle, Liberia.

Kee-kee-zi-kee zi-kee

Figure 2. Mnemonics for drumming; Yoruba, Nigeria.

kong kong ko-lo kong ko-lo

the authority of his reputation and enhancing the event.

Ethnomusicologists have made quantitative descriptions of the asymmetrical juxtaposition of sounds in African music. Rose Brandel, among others, has identified the phenomenon as hemiola, based on the play of twos and threes: horizontally over time, and vertically between parts, sounds group in a ratio of two to three. Other scholars have used terms such as "cross-rhythms" and "offbeats," which serve an explanatory purpose, even as they introduce problematic issues of translating African concepts to Western ideas of time.

Motor patterns, Erich M. von Hornbostel asserted in the early 1900s, are also an important basis of African rhythms. Though some scholars disagree, Gerhard Kubik asserts that kinetic and visual rhythms affect musicians' understanding of acoustic rhythms. Moses Serwadda and Hewitt Panteleoni point out that to teach or explain drum patterns, drummers may cite or demonstrate dance motions.

Performed throughout an area encompassing more than eleven million square miles, African music displays distinctive temporal traits: hocket, hemiola, and multiple coordinate points. Implementation of these principles shows influences within the continent and beyond. Arabic, European, African-American, Latin-American, Anglo-American, and Asian ideas of music have enriched and intermingled with local ideas of time. In areas heavily influenced by Arabic culture, music is single-voiced in intent, and less layered than elsewhere in Africa. In the twentieth century, Latin-American rhythms from reggae to rumba have infused African performances. Afro-American jazz and gospel music have been transformed in the African setting and reinfused with African dimensions of rhythm.

In Africa, drums of great variety form ensembles, where each resounds as a different "voice." Drums, as well as other instruments like lutes and horns, often highlight temporal segmentation. In east African royal courts, the *akadinda* xylophone ensembles apportion to each player simple motivic patterns of tone and time, which, with conventionally determined precision, fit together to make a complex musical whole.

[R.M.S.]

FURTHER READINGS

Berliner, Paul. *The Soul of Mbira*. Berkeley: U of California P, 1978.

Brandel, Rose. *The Music of Central Africa*. The Hague: Martinus Nijhoff, 1961.

Chernoff, John M. *African Rhythm and African Sensibility*. Chicago: U of Chicago P, 1979.

Jones, Arthur M. *Studies in African Music*. London: Oxford UP, 1959.

Nketia, J.H. Kwabena. *The Music of Africa*. New York: Norton, 1974.

Stone, Ruth M. *Dried Millet Breaking: Words, Music and Time in the Woi Epic*. Bloomington: Indiana UP, 1988.

MUSIC: AMERICAN AVANT-GARDE

The two best-known, and probably most significant, American figures of this century in the development of ideas concerning musical time are the composers John Cage (1912–1992) and Elliott Carter (1908–). Each has both contributed and inspired a wealth of theoretical and compositional work, and this has been conducive to dividing any notion of an avant-garde tendency by composers in the United States into two separate, even hostile, camps. Both recognize the inevitability of music moving, in some sense, through time, but both have challenged received notions regarding the perception of time passing in a musical composition.

Cage's espousal, in the early 1930s, of duration as the structural basis for his compositions remains as crucial as it was devastatingly simple. This brought about a radical rejection not only of tonality—and therefore of previous relationships between harmony and the perception of musical time—but of all pitch-based systems; what was favored instead were units of time assembled with reference to simple proportional schemes governed by number ratios. Cage's extensive output based on this principle went far beyond the earlier work of Igor Stravinsky, Edgard Varèse, and others, particularly in opening up composition to sounds previously regarded as unmusical, and to silence as something other than mere punctuation of a musical discourse. The perhaps misleadingly entitled *Sonatas and Interludes* for prepared piano (1946–48) offers a fine illustration; his extensive use at that time not only of the frequently percussive-sounding prepared piano, but of both conventional and unconventional percussion instruments of many kinds emphasizes these commitments.

The tendency toward the avoidance of personal expression already inherent in Cage's early work was taken much further with his move into indeterminacy from 1951, underlining the close links between the dynamics of time-structuring and attitudes to what music may be said to express. Crucial here, too, is the concern to avoid regularity or repetition of any kind: most fundamentally, from the point of view of perceiving how time passes in music—or, perhaps we may rather say, how music passes in time—is the avoidance of regular pulse or any other rhythmic iteration, elements which still played important roles in Cage's pre-chance compositions. When indeterminacy took Cage's definition of music and his compositional methods so far from the conventions of Western musical practice, listeners were challenged to deal with the passing of time in a composition with reference closer to Oriental notions of "being" rather than Occidental notions of "becoming." Christian Wolff (1934–), one of Cage's major pupils, has described the approach to time in his own early music as "*timeless*, or circular, or nonlinear. The piece is a kind of landscape: you can move about in it in different directions." *HP-SCHD* (1967–69), and *Roaratorio, an Irish Circus on Finnegan's Wake* (1979–80), are good large-scale examples of Cage's approach to time—even though, arguably, neither entirely denies the possibility of linear associations.

Carter, on the other hand, built his new notions of musical time into a more thoroughly Western approach to compositional structure, in which such matters as goal-orientation, tension and release, and the dynamics of exposition and development, climax and closure continue to play crucial roles. His refinement of previous "gearing systems" for speed changes in continuous spans of music, frequently referred to as "metric modulation," was, however, used in radical ways to effect what the composer called "perceived large-scale rhythmic tension" via a friction of "disparate rhythmic layers" that is heightened by a complex pitch foreground.

Like Cage, Carter originally attempted to invent techniques that would allow the development of music independent to a considerable degree of European classical models. His move away from thematicism, especially from the *Second String Quartet* (1959) onward, and his attempts to replace its functions in making a piece of music cohere by the invention of different "vocabularies" of musical material characterized as much by rhythm and tempo as anything else, are notable here. These bold steps—traceable in many forms throughout the twentieth century, in reducing the form-giving impact of pitch aspects and replacing them, at

least to some degree, with new developments in the domains of rhythm, meter, and tempo—established Carter's present position.

But while his work between the mid-1940s and the late 1960s is enlivened by new perspectives on rhythm and tempo derived from, or at least inspired by, the work of American composers such as Charles Ives, Henry Cowell, and Conlon Nancarrow, Carter's later output suggests a move away from the concern to establish a specifically American identity. It is tempting to make a direct link between his increasing "Europeanism" and Carter's firm, arguably also increasing, commitment to goal-direction: the essence, after all, of the European-derived sonata principle. A comparison between the "flux" of different types of musical material and speeds coexisting in his *Concerto for Orchestra* (1968–69), or even *Third String Quartet* (1971), and the greater clarity of later works such as the *Fourth Quartet* (1985–86), would point up this contrast well.

Even composers closely associated with Cage have, however, moved in the last twenty years or so closer to the "dynamic" model of musical form-building: a model more concerned with movement through time, and thus often more directly with rhythm once again, which helps to articulate this. Morton Feldman (1926–1987)—another Cage pupil—devoted the 1950s and 1960s to finding ways of overcoming our inclinations as Western listeners, whether caused by training or instinct, to connect sounds up: notably by deregulating sounds from the periodicity of a beat, as well as by minimizing any apparent connection between pitches. This substantially weakens the listener's ability to retain in the mind any sequence of sounds, or even simply the previous note or chord. As Alfred North Whitehead might have put it, memory is thus increasingly represented only by its "fringe" (that is, the present), while "anticipation" (that is, the future) is constantly qualified, often negated.

In the 1970s and 1980s, however, Feldman challenged his listeners with much longer pieces—frequently of at least ninety minutes duration, and not less than four hours in the case of his *Second String Quartet* (1983)—which, perhaps paradoxically, sometimes lock sounds into clearly audible repeating metrical patterns. Even the apparently diatonic sequences in the late music are, however, "compromised" by this very repetition and unfamiliar length, creating new ambiguities of musical time.

So-called minimalist composers, too, such as Steve Reich (1936–) and Philip Glass (1937–), have moved away from essentially nonlinear, non-Western-inspired conceptions of musical time in the 1960s, involving repeating patterns submitted to processes which, however logical and audible, and however modal, remain unhampered by goal-orientated harmony. Their new approach owes an increasing amount to Western ideas such as those concerning the evolution of counterpoint, tonal motion, and the relationships between pitch hierarchies and the dynamics of large-scale structures. Reich's *Music for 18 Musicians* and Glass's *Einstein on the Beach* (both 1974–76) fruitfully occupy the middle ground between the earlier and later approaches. While connections between *Einstein* (a music-theater collaboration with the designer-director Robert Wilson) and even the person of the scientist himself, let alone his theories, remain oblique, the concern to deal with such subject matter in a minimalist context leads to some fascinating explorations of the "relativity" of musical, and theatrical, time.

Three other American composer-theorists have had a particular impact on the theory and practice of musical time in the late twentieth century. Barney Childs (1926–) has explored a wide range of temporal ideas from a literary as well as musical perspective, arising in particular out of his own commitment to indeterminacy and its implications for the achievement of a fundamentally non-European and non-dialectic worldview. Challenging linear notions of time as a misapprehension, and the argument that the narrative curve of the sonata principle is somehow organic or natural, he argues that we "can now choose to replace . . . closed structures (and their accompanying analytic apparatus) with an extensive and complex range of art/life interweavings."

Roger Reynolds (1934–) has conducted extensive research into the perception of time in music, prompted by reflection on the differences between Oriental and Occidental notions and experience of time during a period spent in Japan in the 1960s. His many years of work in computer music have in addition facilitated the "accelerating and retarding temporal proportions logarithmically derived" that the composer himself says form the basis of his works since 1970, whether involving electronics or not.

Jonathan Kramer (1942–) has written the essential book on musical time as well as compositions that interestingly challenge such ideas as those involving the necessity for unity in a piece of music. In contrasting the railroad as "a symbol for nineteenth-century linearity" and the essentially static experience of airplane or even space shuttle travel as "an apt symbol for contemporary time experience," Kramer emphasizes the close connections that various kinds of musical time may have with everyday experience, as well as offering perceptive commentary on the differences that help music transcend the mundane realities of late twentieth-century life.

[K.P.]

See also **Computer Music; Jazz; Modern and Postmodern Music; Music: Western; Rhythm and Meter in Music; Tempo.**

FURTHER READINGS
Cage, J. *Silence*. Middletown: Wesleyan UP, 1961.

Childs, B. "Time and Music: A Composer's View." *Breaking the Sound Barrier: A Critical Anthology of the New Music*. Ed. Gregory Battcock. New York: Dutton, 1981. 102–128.

Kramer, J.D. *The Time of Music: New Meanings, New Temporalities, New Listening Strategies*. New York: Schirmer, 1988.

Reynolds, R. *Mind Models: New Forms of Musical Experience*. New York: Praeger, 1975.

Stone, Else, and Kurt Stone. *The Writings of Elliott Carter: An American Composer Looks at Modern Music*. Bloomington: Indiana UP, 1977.

MUSIC: BEGINNINGS

This article is involved with how musical works begin, rather than with the origins of music. The need to point out this potential misunderstanding is significant, partly because of the important connection between musical beginning tactics and general cultural notions of beginnings, and partly because no specialized vocabulary or classification scheme has been developed for the study of musical beginnings. It is surprising that one of music's major structural functions has been so neglected, but the same can be said of beginnings in general. Readers who attempt an electronic search for literature pertaining to beginning or beginnings will find many studies addressed to the beginning(s) of certain things, but few on the broader subject of cultural concepts of beginning or modes of beginning in the various arts.

Beginnings in literature are a welcome exception, and studies on narrative beginnings in novels, stories, plays, and poems have begun to accumulate in large number since the 1960s.

Perhaps the best known of these is Edward W. Said's *Beginnings: Intention and Method* (1975), which raises many important questions. For most critics, the standard approach to narrative beginnings has been to focus on opening lines (such as Charles Dickens's "It was the best of times, it was the worst of times . . .") and their relation to the following material, and an entire subgenre of literature has sprung up since the inauguration of the Bulwer-Lytton Fiction Contest at San Jose State University in 1983, in which contestants were asked to compose an opening sentence to the worst of all possible novels—parodying the famous opening line of Bulwer-Lytton's 1830 novel, *Paul Clifford*: "It was a dark and stormy night; . . ."

It goes without saying that many of the insights of literary theory may be profitably transferred to the study of music, once necessary changes have been made. Many musical beginnings mimic traditional figures of speech such as anacoluthon, anaphora, and antithesis. Apart from the obvious fact that music lacks the denotative properties of words, it shares with literature many of its artistic features, such as meter, referentiality, rhythm, tempo, and tone. But any successful inquiry into musical beginnings must also consider some of the unique properties of music—among them, harmony, melody, and tonality.

What can be said about beginnings in musical compositions? No doubt that a beginning is recognized as such for an obvious reason—it comes first! But there is much more to it. Composers in all historical eras and in all world regions have developed specialized beginning tactics that communicate an unmistakable sense of inception to their listeners, not only at the outset of a work but also in the many subsequent beginnings of phrases, subsections, sections, and movements. Like literature (and life), music is full of beginnings, as it is also full of endings. Some tactics may indeed be universals; others are unique to a particular place, time, style, or ethnic tradition. The following discussion concentrates on Western art music, recognizing that this is only a part of a much wider picture.

It must be acknowledged at the start that many musical works simply begin, without rhetorical emphasis or any special introductory procedures. But even in these cases there are specific objectives to be accomplished if a beginning is to do its job. These objectives include: (1) translating the listener from external time to the internal time of the composition; (2) overcoming the inertia of the surrounding zone of silence (the atemporal "frame," for which see below), often by means of considerable physical energy; (3) laying out the tonal field for the composition (often by establishing temporary high and low "edges") and suggesting tonal focus therein; (4) giving a preview of the scope of the composition and offering criteria for inclusion and exclusion; (5) initiating the listener's train of expectation, moving generally in a direction from ambiguity toward certainty; (6) establishing a feeling of motion; and (7) often serving as an announcement of the composition. Despite the tendency for beginnings to fall into conventional figures, it is astounding how many compositions can be readily recognized by their first few seconds.

There are four distinct stages in the inception process: (1) the framing silence (a buffer zone between external and internal time), (2) the attack itself, (3) time creation (in which a scale of periodicities is established for the work), and (4) formal processing (in which the first formal units are articulated). Of these four stages, the first and third are of particular interest and pertain specifically to time.

Edward T. Cone's valuable essay on "The Picture and the Frame" (see *Further Readings*) is an important contribution to the understanding of musical beginnings. He emphasizes that both silence and behavior are essential components of beginning rituals: silence, for its ear-cleansing properties and the barrier it creates between the real world and the world of art; and behavior, not only for such practical purposes as tuning and pitch-giving, but also for the traces of ritual that help to set musical events apart from ordinary daily activities. Formal musical activity (as opposed to spontaneous humming or work songs) has been traditionally set apart by multiple social frames—planning, advertising, tickets, special clothes, special halls, special times, dimming of lights, entrance, applause, acknowledgment, tuning, silence, preparation for the actual attack. What is often overlooked is that many of these framing behaviors spill over into the opening of the music—procedures for getting one's attention, for clearing one's aural palate (with relatively pure or uncomplicated sounds), for making a smoother transition from the surrounding zone of atemporality, or for announcing the substance of the work to follow. In the Western art music tradition, it is clear that listeners relish these multiple frames and depend upon them for communicating the sense of inception.

An important observation about beginnings in music is that their primary function is to entail certain consequences, as the result of the array of clues that they present in the first few seconds of a composition. Beginnings thus function not only as points of entry, but also as powerful impulses whose consequences are felt throughout a composition as it unfolds. Beginnings generally proceed by way of increase in various dimensions: increased continuity, energy, and momentum; ascent (in pitch); expansion (of range and texture); acquisition (of relationships), thus becoming increasingly implicative and referential. Beginnings generally do not decrease, dwindle, descend, disintegrate, trivialize, or become less referential.

Four particular beginning tactics have become popular in the art music of the Western world since about 1600: (1) beginning with an assertive gesture, as in Richard Strauss's *Don Juan*; (2) beginning with gradual emergence of sound (suggesting the idea of creation *ex nihilo*), as in Beethoven's Ninth Symphony; (3) beginning in a way that immediately entrains the listener into the time world of the composition, as in Brahms's *Fourth Symphony*; and (4) beginning with a long, unarticulated duration, as in Mendelssohn's Overture to *A Midsummer Night's Dream*.

Said's useful observation that "a beginning *is* its own method, because it reveals the author's intention" is equally valid in the case of music. Certain genres (most notably fugues, themes with variations, motets, and some other categories of variations) display their method unequivocally at the outset, and perhaps for that reason seldom deploy any special introductory procedures. Beginnings are generally most rhetorical in concerted pieces (symphonies and concertos) than in solo or chamber music; and they have become increasingly enlarged in music of the last three centuries, perhaps reflecting the transformation of music from private and group entertainment to public event.

Compositions do not begin *only* when an audience first encounters them. For a composer a work may begin when he first meets his teacher or first hears an influential work; it begins in quite a different sense when he conceives the first idea for a piece and continues with the rest of the composition process—incubation, sketching, revision, and final polishing. When it begins for a performer or a listener, it begins anew for its creator (if present) but in quite a different mode: as a finished product whose properties bring no surprises apart from the nuances of performance. Whether a musical work is heard for the first or twentieth time, a well-crafted beginning does its job by ushering the listener into the unique time world of the individual composition.

Musical beginnings are not products of individual genius; they are for the most part commonplaces that can be mastered by anyone competent in putting notes together. The real test of compositional skill comes later in choosing from among the musical consequences of a particular mode of beginning. Musical beginnings represent the collective accomplishment of a culture, in the form of an authorized set of opening gambits from which an infinite variety of meaningful continuations can be generated.

[L.R.]

FURTHER READINGS

Cone, Edward T. *Musical Form and Musical Performance*. New York: Norton, 1968. Chapter 1.

Kramer, Jonathan D. "Beginnings and Endings in Western Art Music." *Canadian University Music Review* 3 (1982): 1–14.

———. *The Time of Music: New Meanings, New Temporalities, New Listening Strategies*. New York: Schirmer Books, 1988. Chapter 6.

Rowell, Lewis. "The Creation of Audible Time." *The Study of Time IV*. Ed. J.T. Fraser, N. Lawrence, and D. Park. New York: Springer, 1981. 198–210.

Toch, Ernst. *The Shaping Forces in Music*. New York: Criterion, 1958. Chapter 13.

MUSIC, HISTORY OF ANCIENT

"Ancient music," from a Western point of view, is generally understood as a reference to the music of the Greco-Roman world from about the fifth century B.C. until the decay of Hellenistic culture in the early Christian centuries. Little is known about the music of earlier Western civilizations, and still less about the temporal organization of their musics—apart from the common assumption that the rhythms of music were dominated by the rhythms of a poetic text. This assumption may or may not be correct.

Some fascinating but conjectural material on music in the ancient Near East appears in *Sounds from Silence: Recent Discoveries in Ancient Near Eastern Music,* by Anne Draffkorn Kilmer, Richard L. Crocker, and Robert R. Brown (Berkeley: Bīt Enki Publications, 1976), a booklet accompanying the sound recording of the authors' transcription of a Hurrian cult song from ancient Ugarit (ca. 1400 B.C.). Scholars have long suspected that some documentary evidence also exists for rhythm in ancient Egyptian music, but the surviving material has remained in the hands of a few scholars whose caution has outweighed the urge to publish.

Most of the evidence for ancient music falls into one of two categories: (1) the visual arts (such as pottery, sculpture, and tomb paintings), and (2) surviving musical instruments. But although the iconographic evidence helps to illuminate the social context within which music was performed, and the organological material tells us a great deal about tuning and the organization of pitch, neither reveals anything about the role of time in music. Only when we turn to the music of Ancient Greece do we find hard evidence in the form of technical treatises and decipherable music notations.

The keywords for time organization in ancient Greek music are *rhythm* and *meter*, two words with a long and slippery history; they still dominate discussions of musical time today. Much of what is known about the early history of these concepts is recorded in musical treatises by Aristoxenus of Tarentum (fourth century B.C.) and Aristides Quintilianus (fourth century A.D.), as well as in treatises on poetic meters by authors such as Dionysius of Halicarnassus (first century B.C.), Hephaestion (second century A.D.), and Longinus (third century A.D.). Both concepts are grounded in the durational and accentual patterns of Greek verse (that is, in poetic "feet" such as the iambic, trochaic, dactylic, and anapestic) and both can be accurately described as temporal "scales," but their purposes were quite different.

Rhythm is a much broader concept than meter and is manifest not only in poetry but also in song, instrumental music, and dance. Meter, on the other hand, is specifically located in a poetic text. Aristides defined rhythm as "a scale of *chronoi* [time units] compounded according to some order, and the conditions of these we call arsis and thesis, noise and silence." Arsis and thesis should be understood as "lift" and "descent" (of the hand, of the leg, or—in a more abstract sense—as feelings of metric lightness and weight). Meter, according to Aristides, was "a scale of feet compounded of dissimilar syllables, symmetrical in length," and he contrasted the two terms as follows: "Rhythm is composed through similar syllables and opposing feet, but meter is never composed through having all syllables similar and seldom through opposing feet."

Despite the fact that both rhythmic and metric feet exhibit the characteristic binary opposition of arsis and thesis, as well as the same array of durational patterns, it is clear from the testimony of Aristides that the essence of rhythm was an even sequence of similar durations organized into regular groupings by our perception of the arses and theses. Meter displays a greater range of dissimilar quantities and depends lightly if at all upon the qualities of arsis and thesis. Which is simply to say that the rhythms of music are inherently more regular and dependent upon various species of accent for their structure than are the rhythms of poetry.

Rests were essential components in the structure of both rhythm and meter, despite the contentions of many classical scholars. As Quintilian observed, "There are also the following differences [between rhythm and meter], that rhythm has unlimited space over which it may range, whereas the spaces of meter are confined, and that, whereas meter has certain definite cadences, rhythm may run on as it commenced until it reaches the point of . . . transition to another type of rhythm. Further, meter is concerned with words alone, while rhythm extends also to the motion of the body. Again rhythm more readily admits of rests although they are found in meter as well."

Some of the technical terms employed by the ancient authors provide vivid glimpses of their cultural worldview, particularly with regard to concepts of time. *Meter* means nothing more than "measure," but the etymology and semantic range of *rhythm* (in Greek, *rhythmós*) are informative. For a full account of the history of this word, readers are referred to Robert Christopher Ross's 1972 dissertation, "RuqmóV: A History of Its Connotations" (U of California, Berkeley). The word apparently first appears in the writings of Archilocus in the eighth century B.C., where it signifies the "ups and downs" of human life (a possible source for the later concepts of arsis and thesis) and the characteristic temper or nature of a person. Its subsequent semantic development extends to such things as shaping a cake, focusing one's mind, the pulse beat, the motion of a battle line, the scansion of a poetic line, and the harmonic motion of the cosmos.

Rhythm, then, is the form of anything that moves in a rational or regular way, with clear internal structure and external limitations. Studies on the etymology of *rhythmós* have failed to reach any consensus on its derivation, tracing it to one of three possible root meanings: (1) to draw or pull, (2) to hold or restrain, or (3) to flow. "Flow" is what many musicians would like it to mean, but Ross contends that this meaning was a creation of the nineteenth century. No doubt several of these meanings became mingled in the historical development of the concept of rhythm.

Aristoxenus and his followers divided the subject of rhythm into five main topics: (1) the primary time unit (*chronos protos*), (2) the foot, (3) rhythmic progression, (4) rhythmic modulation (that is, to another species of rhythm), and (5) rhythmic composition. This set of topics closely resembles the set of topics by which the dimension of pitch was organized, thus suggesting that musical time and musical space were coordinate dimensions that took their characteristic shapes from the same set of universal principles—especially the principle of harmony. Aristoxenus's concept of musical time is notably atomistic, and his temporal forms (the proper proportions of rhythm) are described in much the same language used to describe geometric forms. Temporal units are called *semeia*, the same word that signifies a geometer's points, and hence his notion of rhythm resembles a child's dot-to-dot drawings. If Aristoxenus's idea of rhythm can be said to "flow," it does so within strictly defined channels and is articulated by clearly located points. No doubt this analysis conveys an inaccurate picture of the realities of ancient musical rhythm, but it also demonstrates the conceptual obstacles that impede understanding of the elusive domain of musical time—so real in the human experience of regular pulsation, durations, accents, and groupings; but so slippery in the many performance deviations that make music come alive, and in the difficulties of drawing mental comparisons between musical events widely separate in time.

Time, to the Greeks, was a scale of precise increments (at least in theory), and dealing with it was largely a matter of dividing and measuring it as precisely as possible. No wonder that the root of the Latin word *tempus* (as in *tempo*) means "to cut, divide." The best way to measure anything was to determine, in logical sequence, its basic units, patterns, proportions (the concept of *genus*), and then set forth the many ways in which phenomena could differ from one another—in magnitude, in genus, in composition (whether composite or incomposite), in proportion, in order, and in numerous other ways. Because Greek authors thought of them-

selves as binary creatures and had become accustomed to thinking in binary oppositions of exclusive categories ("on the one hand, on the other"), it seems fitting that their most powerful conceptual tool for the organization of musical time was the concept of arsis and thesis—a parallel to the concept of responion in Greek verse. No doubt the alternation of accent and non-accent is a musical universal, realized in different ways in different cultures; but it was only in the Greco-Roman world that it was elevated to such a dominant status. The overwhelmingly binary nature of our rhythm and its organization by perceptions of accentual weight and lift are the two principal legacies that music in Europe and the Americas has received from our classical predecessors.

[L.R.]

See also **Rhythm and Meter in Music; Tempo.**

FURTHER READINGS

Mathiesen, Thomas J. "Rhythm and Meter in Ancient Greek Music." *Music Theory Spectrum* 7 (1985): 159–180.

Rowell, Lewis. "Aristoxenus on Rhythm." *Journal of Music Theory* 23.1 (1979): 63–79.

———. "Time in the Musical Consciousness of Old High Civilizations—East and West." *The Study of Time III*. Ed. J.T. Fraser, N. Lawrence, and D. Park. New York: Springer, 1978. 578–611.

Sachs, Curt. *The Rise of Music in the Ancient World—East and West*. New York: Norton, 1943. Section 5, Chapter 11.

———. *The Wellsprings of Music*. Ed. Jaap Kunst. New York: McGraw-Hill, 1965. Chapter 2, X.

MUSIC: INDIA

The temporal structure of Indian music is a living demonstration of how profoundly a musical tradition can reflect the influence of cultural intuitions of time. Just as the visual arts of India have been shaped by long-standing cultural preferences for a circular disposition of space, so have music and the other performing arts responded to preferences for a cyclical disposition of time—preferences that were already clearly articulated in two hymns to time (conceived as a deity) from the Atharva Veda (ca. 900–500 B.C.).

The key word for time in Indian music is *tāla* (Sanskrit), signifying a system of hand gestures with symbolic and ritual connotations. These gestures control and integrate all aspects of a performance and serve as audible and visible signs of the temporal structures embedded in the music.

The Indian experience of music has been traditionally conceived as a confluence of two simultaneous streams of time: (1) a physical, external time whose divisions are marked by hand gestures (claps, finger counts, and silent waves), and (2) an internal stream of continuous time, devoid of any distinctions and manifest in the emission of vocal sound from deep within the human body. Reflecting this conception, the music of the Indian subcontinent has evolved into essentially a dialogue between (1) a drum accompaniment and (2) the human voice or another melodic instrument. A third component of an Indian musical performance is the continuous drone played on a tambura (a long-necked lute) or, in some modern performances, an electronic device. The drone has been interpreted as a symbol of the timeless reservoir of vital sound that fills all the space within the universe and provides a seamless continuum encompassing the self, the external world, and the divinity that abides beyond the illusory world of human perception.

Many of the words chosen or coined to represent the various temporal concepts in Indian music contain etymological clues suggesting that the time of music should be understood as a manifestation of the cosmic process of continuous creation and dissolution. *Laya*, the Sanskrit word for tempo, is etymologically linked with the third and final stage of world process in the traditional Hindu worldview, the stage in which Śiva dances in the midst of a circle of flames, trampling all created forms back into their former state as undifferentiated primal matter—as if to suggest that the world of musical experience is dissolved and reconstituted between each successive tone. (*Laya* was originally conceived as the empty interstices between musical actions, a conception that contrasts with the Western idea of tempo as the rate of speed of a particular series of perceived pulsations or beats.) *Yati*, the term for the direction of change of tempo (that is, whether accelerating, decelerating, or proceeding at an even rate of speed), is derived from the common Sanskrit root *yam* (hold, control)—as if to imply that time is a primordial power that needs to be continually restrained lest it somehow run away with us.

The *tāla* systems of Indian music may be divided into four distinct historical and geographic stages: (1) the ancient system of *mārga* (path, way) *tālas* employed in the ritual music of the Gupta theater, (2) the system of *deśī* (provincial) *tālas* that developed late in the first millennium A.D., and (3) and (4) the *tāla* systems of modern north and south India. The four systems embrace the entire range of temporal experience in music—from the shortest units (beats, rests, durations, and gestures) to the longest spans of musical structure and whole compositions—and they demonstrate a continuous evolution toward cyclical rhythm and meter. The roots of later cyclical practice are present in the system of *mārga tālas*, but the ancient ritual forms are more accurately described as modular structures with many independent parts and sharp divisions between sections. With the advent of the *deśī tālas*, a repeated rhythmic pattern became the principal means of temporal organization, and in today's *tāla* systems the rhythmic cycle (*āvarta*) has become the chief presupposition in the temporal experience of music.

Cyclical time is not, however, the only species of time in the music of India; nor is all Indian music measured by *tāla*. Most performances begin with an improvised exposition of the chosen *rāga* in a style known as *ālāp* or *ālāpana*—a nonmetrical style that is regulated not by regular pulsations and accents but by convention and the performer's breath. Its rhythm is not "free," but it lacks the constraints of uniform durations, metric structure, and the controlling *tāla* gestures. The conventional progression from (1) nonmetrical rhythm to (2) rhythm measured strictly by the patterns of *tāla* has become India's most powerful and pervasive musical archetype, and it has been explicitly linked with the first two components of world process: (1) the creation of forms from undifferentiated primal substance, under the patronage of the creator god Brahma, and (2) the sustaining of regular world process, presided over by Visnu.

Perhaps the most notable feature of the *tāla* systems is the gesture language—an assortment of audible and inaudible signals that differ slightly from one region to another and in different historical periods. The characteristic patterns of the various *tālas* are also represented by strings of vocables—nonsense syllables that convey the rhythmic properties of each *tāla* by means of typical phonetic oppositions (for example, between long and short [vowel grade], voiced and unvoiced, aspirated and unaspirated). The prominent role of silent gestures (which some have seen as a parallel to the characteristic emphasis on passive or negative concepts in Indian thought) is also a distinctive feature of the temporality of Indian music. No other world music tradition has gone as far in controlling the audible by means of the visible, or has been as explicit in associating physical gestures and recited syllables with the experience of time in music.

Another interesting feature of the temporality of Indian music is a tendency toward inflation (of patterns or components of patterns): the proportions of rhythmic patterns alter dramatically as some of their components expand by the addition of extra finger counts. The popular south Indian *tāla* Rūpaka, for example, is conceived as 2 + 3 identical durations (at whatever tempo chosen) and notated as O I_3; the circle is performed as a downward clap (on the knee) followed by a silent wave to the right, and the vertical stroke as a clap followed by two silent finger counts. But the final conceptual unit of this *tāla* may also be expanded with additional finger counts (I_4, I_5, I_7, or I_9), and consequently the *tāla* pattern would expand to a total of 6, 7, 9, or 11 durations, respectively. In this way a simple pattern is often transformed into a more complex structure, and the rhythm thereby produced can more accurately be described as "additive," rather than "divisive." This is to say that many of the most popular *tālas* were, and are, constructed from the bottom up in irregular groupings of a lowest common denominator (hence, additive), not from the top down in a nested series of even divisions of a highest common multiple (as in most of the standard meters of Western music prior to the twentieth century). From an Indian perspective, audible patterns are free to contract or expand in whole or in part, consistent with ancient teachings that time and space are infinitely contractible and expandable, forms are protean, and all matter is flexible and amenable to continuous transformation.

There is clear evidence for the impact of deep-seated cultural ideas on the temporal forms of Indian music, but such a complex and explicit system of rhythm and meter could not have developed purely from abstract ideas. More concrete temporal models were available, among them the patterns of spoken language and the regularly pulsating rhythms of the human body. The former provide a set of models for the grouping of individual durations and tones, models authorized by long habit, daily usage, and a long literary tradition; the latter provide the means for entraining these groups into an organized stream of sound. While traces of the influences of poetic meters can be detected in the music of early India, it is evident that musical rhythm had managed to free itself from the patterns of verse at a very early date, perhaps during the second half of the first millennium A.D. This is a striking contrast to the music of ancient and medieval Europe, which remained dependent upon the quantitative meters of Greek and Latin verse until the fourteenth century.

Time in Indian music can best be described as the interaction of independent rhythmic strata, controlled by symbolic gestures and implying a rich counterpoint of patterns. At least four such strata are present in most performances: (1) the metrical sequence of text syllables (in vocal music), (2) the structural gesture patterns of *tāla*, (3) the melodic rhythms of the vocal or instrumental soloists, with their profusion of ornaments, and (4) the accompanying rhythmic patterns played by the drummer(s). The crowning achievement of Indian musicians has been their evolution of the conceptual means by which these strata can be integrated into an organized, coherent stream of sound.

[L.R.]

See also **Tempo.**

FURTHER READINGS

Powers, Harold S. "India" (Sections 1 and 2). *The New Grove Dictionary of Music and Musicians*. Ed. Stanley Sadie. London: Macmillan, 1980. 9: 69–141, especially 118–125.

Rowell, Lewis. *Music and Musical Thought in Early India*. Chicago: U of Chicago P, 1992. Chapters 8–9.

———. "Thinking Time and Thinking *about* Time in Indian Music." *Communication & Cognition* 19.2 (1986): 229–240.

———. "Tāla." *Kalātattvakośa: A Lexicon of Fundamental Concepts of the Indian Arts*. Volume 2. Ed. Bettina Bäumer. New Delhi: Indira Gandhi National Centre for the Arts, 1992.

Widdess, D.R. "Rhythm and Time-Measurement in South Asian Art-Music: Some Observations on *tāla*." *Proceedings of the Royal Musical Association* 107 (1980–81): 132–138.

MUSIC: INDONESIA

For more than three and a half centuries, Indonesia has been exposed to Western music through Portuguese sailors, Dutch colonists, soldiers, and missionaries; and recently to American popular music through the mass media. Indonesian musical genres that have come under Western influence generally adhere to the time organization of the Western musical system, while those that are less affected exhibit different ways of dealing with musical time.

In indigenous Indonesian music, time exists at multiple levels, of which some are macro level, and others micro level. For example, at the macro level, in Bali, *Odalan*—a major Balinese temple festival of music, dance, and drama—is presented for the gods and mortals every 210 days; in rural Sunda, a certain music repertory is performed biannually to honor Dewi Sri, the rice goddess; in Java, birthdays may be celebrated every thirty-five days—a calendrical cycle created by the combination of the Judeo-Christian-Islamic seven-day week and the traditional Javanese five-day week.

Time proscription is concomitant with time prescription. In Bali, music may not be played during the annual twenty-four hours of total silence (*nyepi*). In the Javanese court, traditionally music is not played during the month of Ramadan (the Islamic holy month), or from Thursday noon until the following Friday noon to observe the Islamic sabbath.

A more specific time organization is found in the Javanese *wayang kulit* (shadow puppet) performance. In this theater, time is divided into three periods of unequal length. The first period is the longest (about four hours), and the last period the shortest (about two hours). These time periods parallel the three modes in each of the two Javanese tuning systems.

FORM

In the gong culture of Indonesia, musics with regular beats are usually organized by means of consistently recurring accentuation known in ethnomusicology as a colotomic pattern, an accentuation pattern created through pitch and timbre differentiation. The tendency is that the lower the pitch, the less frequently it is played. In addition to being the means of organizing time, these colotomic patterns also determine form.

The most complex colotomic rhythms are found in the Javanese court *gamelan*, an approximately twenty-five-piece ensemble composed largely of gongs and metal slab instruments. Sounding about 50 hz (hertz) *gong ageng*, or simply *gong*, is located in the lowest octave of the seven-octave *gamelan*. The *gong* is played to mark the end of a musical period. Each musical period may be composed of as many as 256 beats

or as few as four in the case of theater music. At a tempo of 15 MM (Maelzel's metronome), in a 256-beat piece, the *gong* stroke only occurs approximately every seventeen minutes. In contrast, in a composition where four beats constitute a period, at a tempo of 120 MM, the *gong* stroke occurs every two seconds. When a *gong* is required to play so frequently, a higher pitched *gong* (in the second-octave register), the *gong suwukan* or *gong siyem*, is employed.

Compositions in regular forms have consistent length of quadratic musical periods. Each period is divided into either two or four phrases of equal length by means of gongs of higher pitch called *kenong*. Depending on the length and the genre of the piece, the division may subsequently be subdivided into four or eight segments; each subdivision is marked alternately by gong-type instruments of differing pitch and timbre, *kethuk* and *kempul* or *wela* (a "colotomic rest"). Based on the tuning system used, the section in the composition, and the style of playing, each subdivision of the beat may be further subdivided into smaller segments by the *engkuk-kemong* or *kempyang*, other gong instruments with different pitches and timbres. Combined, these time markers create subtle tonal rhythms underlying musical compositions.

IRAMA

Another time scheme manifests itself in the concept of *irama*. At the first level of specificity, *irama* means tempo or, sometimes, rhythm. In the Javanese tradition, *irama* refers to the relationship between the principal beats of the piece and the number of strokes played on a given instrument as determined by the prevailing tempo.

The Javanese court music tradition recognizes four *irama*: *irama I*, or *irama lancar*; *irama II*, or *irama dados*; *irama III*, or *irama wiled*; and *irama IV*, or *irama rangkep*. The different *irama* may be distinguished by the number of strokes the various subdividing instruments idiomatically play between two principal beats. For a certain type of piece the *gambang* (a type of xylophone, which plays the fastest subdivision) may be used as a standard. The formula is roughly thus: in *irama I*, at about 50 MM, there are 4 *gambang* strokes to a beat; in *irama II*, at about 25 MM, there are 8; in *irama III*, at approximately 12.5 MM, there are 16; and in *irama IV*, at approximately 7 MM, there are 32. This means that, regardless of the *irama*, the density referent, or the frequency-per-minute, of *gambang* strokes remains the same, which is to say approximately 200 MM. Hence, what distinguishes one *irama* from another is not the tempo of the principal beat, but rather the ratio between the *gambang* or other subdividing instruments and the principal beat.

In some cultures where drummers are merely timekeepers, they usually do not occupy a particularly prestigious position in the ensemble. In the Indonesian gong culture, however, drummers usually enjoy high prestige because they are not merely timekeepers, but also dance accompanists as well as *irama* and dynamic conductors.

Traditionally, slight variants of tempo may occur owing to the context of the piece; such variants are related, for example, to whether the piece accompanies a dance, and further, the type of dance, and the regional style. Tempo may fluctuate at the transitional points of a piece. In more contemporary contexts, tempo may fluctuate because of external time constraints. In the days of recording with the 78 rpm (revolutions per minute) format, in which the maximum time was about seven minutes and twenty seconds per side, tempo tended to be faster than was normal for live performance. Another important factor in tempo variants is the temperament of the drummer himself. A good drummer and conductor is judged, among other things, on the basis of how well he controls *irama* in particular and how well he manages time in general.

Viewed broadly, in Indonesia music does not exist in a vacuum; its musical time reflects a cosmological and social ordering of events.

[H.S.]

FURTHER READINGS

Becker, Judith, and Alan Feinstein, eds. *Karawitan Source Readings in Javanese Gamelan and Vocal Music.* Ann Arbor: Center for South and Southeast Asian Studies, 1987.

Dibia, I Wayan. "Arja: A Sung Dance Drama of Bali; A Study of Change and Transformation." Ph.D. dissertation, University of California, Los Angeles, 1992.

Falk, Catherine. "The Tarawangsa—A Bowed Stringed Instrument from West Java." *Studies in Indonesian Music.* Ed. Margaret J. Kartomi. Monash: Centre of Southeast Asian Studies Monash University, 1978.

Kunst, Jaap. *Music in Java.* Ed. E.J. Heins. 3rd ed. 2 vols. The Hague: Martinus Nijhoff, 1973.

Wong, Deborah, and Rene T.A. Lysloff. "Threshold to the Sacred: The Overture in Thai and Javanese Ritual Performance." *Ethnomusicology* 35.3 (1991): 315–348.

MUSIC: PERFORMANCE

Music is with good reason widely regarded as the temporal art par excellence, and it is in the performance of music that this temporality is most richly and, as far as the performer is concerned, most testingly revealed. Since performances not only take place *in* time but also in their rhythmic properties consist *of* time (or more accurately temporal proportions), time can be regarded as both a medium for performance and as an important part of the "substance" of performance. A striking and at first sight paradoxical feature of skilled musical performance is its combination of temporal stability and flexibility: a number of authors have demonstrated that performers can reproduce the detailed temporal characteristics of their performances on different occasions, in some cases spanning many years, with very little variability, but that at least some performers also have the ability to alter radically the temporal characteristics of their performances at a moment's notice. Taken together, these two pieces of evidence have been widely understood to indicate that the temporal characteristics of a performance are generated from a relatively abstract musical conception, rather than being directly stored as properties in their own right—though this may reflect more the kind of model preferred by research in cognitive science than the representation in the musician's head. It is the stability of a performer's *conception* of the music that underlies the ability to perform the music with such precision over such long periods, and likewise the ability of a performer to change his or her *conception* of the music that results in immediate changes in the temporal properties of performance.

A number of levels of time in performance can be distinguished. At the highest level there is the global tempo of a performance; below this there is a hierarchical structure of temporal relations constituting what is conventionally termed the rhythmic structure of the music; and at the lowest level there are small scale temporal variations in the way in which the rhythmic structure is realized in performance. These three levels are thus denoted by the terms tempo, rhythm, and expressive timing. Rhythm and expressive timing are distinguished on the basis of a contrast between discrete and continuous temporal relations: in the great majority of world music (but not universally) musical rhythm consists of relations between discrete categories of duration, while expressive timing variations in performance are continuously variable. It is the operation of categorical perception that separates these two components for listeners as they hear a performance.

Two classes of mechanisms for timekeeping in performance can be envisaged. One depends primarily on some kind of central programmable internal clock which directly controls one or more levels of temporal structure in the performance (see below). An alternative approach regards timekeeping as a more distributed characteristic of the motor system, and as an emergent property of movement, rather than a parameter in its own right. Movement timing is the result of the variable elasticity of muscles and the natural periodicities of the limbs under differing conditions of muscular stress, and hence in a sense is not really "timing" at all. There seems no reason to propose these views as mutually exclusive. It seems clear on the one hand that the intimate relation between music and movement points to the latter kind of mechanism (by analogy, one would not think that the temporal characteristics of an expert tennis stroke are controlled by an internal clock; they are simply the consequence of the movements required to play the ball effectively). On the other hand, a performer's ability to control consciously the precise temporal shape of a performance indicates the operation of a central clocklike mechanism. One solution is to propose that the motor system makes use of whatever intrinsic temporal properties the motor system can generate, but that the system is driven (rather than being in some kind of free-running oscillatory state) by more abstract musical goals.

The temporal characteristics of performance seem to fulfill a number of roles. First, as noted earlier, time is the medium in which music happens, and were it not for the temporality of performance, pieces of music would collapse into timeless singularities. Even those kinds of music that aim to suspend the subjective sense of time are obliged to take place *in* time. Second, time is both a *component* of structure (rhythm) and, in its guise as expressive timing, a medium through which performers convey all manner of nontemporal structural features of the music. A well-documented example is the way in which performers indicate hierarchical phrase structure by slowing up at phrase boundaries in a manner that is proportional to their hierarchical depth. Third, expressive timing conveys to the listener a sense of movement—both the metaphorical movements of music in pitch space and

metrical space, and a more tangible sense of physical (bodily) movement. There is evidence that the time course of natural-sounding expression in music follows the laws of physical motion of bodies (particularly the human body) moving under gravity. Fourth, and somewhat controversially, it has been proposed by Manfred Clynes that the temporal microstructure of music is specific to an individual composer: for a piece by a particular composer to be played convincingly, a performer must organize the expressive timing variations (and dynamic variations) such that they reflect what Clynes has called the "composer's pulse." The empirical evidence for this proposal is equivocal, and it seems intuitively unlikely that all the music of a composer as stylistically diverse as Beethoven should be played with a single pattern of expressive timing. Lastly, along with the other expressive parameters of performance, the temporal properties of performance may perform the function of conferring a particular character or narrative structure on a piece. While a music analyst may be primarily concerned with elucidating the formal structure of music, performers are arguably more concerned with "bringing a piece of music to life"—using the expressive parameters of performance to generate what is variably referred to as a drama, narrative, or global character for the piece.

Finally, stylistic developments in twentieth-century music have had significant consequences for time in performance. Parallel with the abandonment of tonality in the early part of this century was a gradual loosening and, for some composers, ultimately a complete abandonment of metrical structure. This brings with it problems for both performers and listeners in processing expressive timing. The continuously variable fluctuations of local tempo that characterize expressive timing depend upon an underlying framework of categorical values, generated by a meter, for their effectiveness. Without this framework, the distinction between structure and expression (at least in the temporal domain) becomes impossible to maintain in the narrow sense that it has been used here, relying as it does on the contrast between the inexpressive categories of the score and the expressive modifications of the performer. Some schools of composition in this century—as, for example, the Darmstadt school—have deliberately cultivated absence of expression as a characterizing stylistic feature. Others have turned to a reinvestigation of the possibilities of meter, influenced by African and Oriental music (for example, the music of so-called minimalists). Both have investigated the possibilities of twentieth-century technological innovations—the one to counteract the deep-seated psychological tendency in human performers to organize rhythmic structures in a metrical fashion, the other to achieve perfect regularity. In electroacoustic music there has been increasing interest in the interaction of live and computer-generated elements, raising the difficult issue of whether (and how) the two might work together in a temporally flexible manner—as performers in an ensemble do. One approach is to try to develop artificial intelligence models for human rhythmic expression in the hope that computers may ultimately "perform" their music with the same degree of controlled flexibility that is encountered in human performance. That goal is still some way off, but not as remote as it once appeared. If ever achieved, it would represent the culmination of explicit attempts to understand the temporal structure of performed music.

[E.F.C.]

See also **Computer Music; Movement and Rhythm; Music: Africa; Music: India; Music: Indonesia; Music: Western; Rhythm and Meter in Music; Tempo.**

FURTHER READINGS

Clarke, Eric F. "Structure and Expression in Rhythmic Performance." *Musical Structure and Cognition*. Ed. Peter Howell, Ian Cross, and Robert West. London: Academic, 1985.

Clynes, Manfred. "Expressive Microstructure in Music Linked to Living Qualities." *Studies of Music Performance*. Ed. Johan Sundberg. Stockholm: Royal Swedish Academy of Music no. 39, 1983.

Gabrielsson, Alf. "Timing in Music Performance and its Relations to Music Experience." *Generative Processes in Music*. Ed. John Sloboda. Oxford: Clarendon P, 1988.

Shaffer, L. Henry. "Performances of Chopin, Bach and Bartok: Studies in Motor Programming." *Cognitive Psychology* 13 (1981): 326–376.

Todd, Neil P. McA. "The Dynamics of Dynamics: A Model of Musical Expression." *Journal of the Acoustical Society of America* 91 (1992): 3540–3550.

MUSIC: ROCK

Rock music was founded on and driven by the Big Beat—as defenders and detractors alike would agree. A strong beat is, of course, of central importance to any music meant to be *danced* to. In the case of rock 'n' roll it was crucial: the beat was exaggerated and amplified into an insistent rallying cry for rebellious teenagers. The beat was experienced immediately on the dance floor and in the emphasis on rhythmic instrumental styles (the basic rock lineup of guitars, bass, and drums was simply the *rhythm* section of a jazz band); moreover, the beat itself served as a metaphor for a new, postwar generation shaping a high-speed modern world in their image. The manic energy of Little Richard and Jerry Lee Lewis, the rapid-fire rhythms and rhymes of Chuck Berry, and the sheer flash and excitement of Elvis Presley defined 1950s rock 'n' roll and fueled a teenage culture full of dances, drive-ins, fast cars, fast food, and instant everything.

Rock 'n' roll compressed and divided the experience of time into a dense, exhilarating jumble of moods and moments that reflected the youth and energy of its audience. The music was custom made for two-to-three-minute 45 r.p.m. (revolutions per minute) "singles" and the ever-shortening attention span of the young rock audience. In the nonstop world of the radio and the jukebox, a new mood, tempo, or bolt of energy was always a nickel or twist of the dial away. The Big Beat charged the atmosphere around it, from the frenetic movements of the artists and audience to the frantic delivery of the radio disk jockeys and the overheated commercials forced to adopt rock's youthful velocity— just as current television commercials have adopted the look and fast-paced editing of MTV (music television).

The songs themselves were shaped by patterns of repetition that clearly articulated the songs' structure and temporal framework. A "twelve-bar blues" structure based on a specific set of chord changes was used in most up-tempo rock 'n' roll (such as Chuck Berry's "Johnny B. Goode" and Little Richard's "Long Tall Sally"). Conventional popular song models, defined by the melodies of the verses, repeated refrains, and contrasting "bridge" sections, were often used in ballads and mid-tempo songs (such as Fats Domino's version of "Blueberry Hill" and Buddy Holly's "Maybe Baby"). At the extreme end of rock's rhythm obsession, Bo Diddley's hypnotic, one-chord rhythmic juggernauts evoked a sense of nonlinear stream-of-consciousness and seemed almost arbitrarily begun, ended, and deemed a "song." The pop-oriented, melodic approach was exemplified by producer Phil Spector's "little symphonies for the kids": pop songs of grand orchestral proportions imploded into beatifically simple signature refrains ("Be My

Baby," "Baby I Love You") that froze time and etched the songs in the listener's mind.

The 1964 British Invasion of the Beatles, Rolling Stones, and a flood of other groups heralded the arrival of rock's second generation. The turbulent changes of the 1960s were mirrored in the music and in the rock culture it helped spawn and unite. Like everything else in that era, rock seemed to exist in a heightened, accelerated state, with tremendous changes occurring in a matter of weeks. Lyrics took on a much greater importance, thanks largely to the influence of Bob Dylan, who helped make rock as timely as the day's headlines. Musical styles expanded even more dramatically, delving into classical music, Indian ragas, avant-garde electronic music, and other far-flung styles for inspiration. The attempt to explore these new influences and expressive possibilities within the limitations of the three-minute single was the spark for many of the era's creative peaks, though even the hit singles grew longer and artier as rock outgrew its old constraints. (The Beatles' seven-minute "Hey Jude" shattered radio's time barrier in 1968; other lengthy songs of note include Bob Dylan's "Like a Rolling Stone," the Rolling Stones' "Going Home," Richard Harris's "MacArthur Park," Simon and Garfunkel's "The Boxer," and Don McLean's "American Pie.")

Long-playing albums were better suited to the innovations of the 1960s and soon surpassed singles as the creative vehicle of choice. In the process they grew from simple collections of disparate songs to large-scale artistic statements. The Beatles' *Sgt. Pepper's Lonely Hearts Club Band* album, released in 1967, was the culmination of rock's ascent to "art" status and the blueprint for the "concept album": an album meant to be heard as a *whole*, unified by common themes, recurring material, and musical transitions that blur the boundaries between individual songs. Other experiments with long-form conceptions included the Beatles' side-long "song cycle" on their *Abbey Road* album, the Rolling Stones' *Their Satanic Majesties Request*, the Who's "rock opera" *Tommy*, Pink Floyd's epic *Dark Side of the Moon*, several theatrical theme albums by the Kinks, and the pseudo-classical music of the Moody Blues; Emerson, Lake and Palmer; and other "art rock" bands.

The growing virtuosity of guitarists like Jimi Hendrix and Eric Clapton inspired further moves toward longer song forms that left breathing room for their solos and improvisations, while the time-blurring influence of psychedelic drugs encouraged still wilder experiments in an attempt to recreate aurally the fluid, mind-altered immediacy of that experience. The complex musical pastiche of Frank Zappa and the Mothers of Invention and the uncompromising assault of Captain Beefheart and the Magic Band, riddled with irregular rhythmic patterns, changing tempi and discordant sounds, formed the cutting edge of late sixties rock, though their music was too far removed from the crucial ingredients of rock and pop—the dance beat and clear melodies—to achieve widespread success.

By the early seventies, rock had finished its rampant expansion and set the limits that have, for the most part, defined it since. Later and disparate bands such as Led Zeppelin, King Crimson, Yes, Rush, Electric Light Orchestra, Queen, and Genesis continued experimenting with rhythmic complexities and large-scale works within the context of familiar rock textures and imagery. The disco music of the middle 1970s reaffirmed the dance beat, while punk rock rekindled rock's rebellious energy and its celebration of the all-consuming, combustible Moment.

Music videos, synthesizers, and digital technologies have been catalysts for dramatic changes in the last decade in both the recording studio and live performance. Digital sampling and editing, used most effectively in rap music (the most defiantly dense and rhythmic music to date), allows for a reshuffling of previously recorded material in new contexts and for the increased manipulation of music on all levels, including the ability to take music completely out of time in order to shape and edit it. The influence of MTV and rock videos has expanded rock's sensory landscape and added a visual dimension that, at its best, enhances the listener's experience of a song. On the negative side, videos have caused a resurgence of the claustrophobic "hit singles" format and, along with the mechanized rigidity of synthesizers and drum machines, have further squeezed the spontaneity out of live performances (which are sometimes simply lip-synched, not "live" at all).

Then again, early rock critics pointed with alarm to the use of studio "effects" such as multitracking and editing, rather than single continuous performances captured unadorned on tape, as proof of rock's musical destitution. These and other inventive uses of technology have always been hallmarks of rock's creative process and will continue to be so in the future, just as computer-assisted performance and recording are now turning time, quite literally, into a material to be shaped and manipulated.

[G.Ga.]

See also **Jazz; Modern and Postmodern Music; Music: American Avant-Garde; Music: Western; Rhythm and Meter in Music; Tempo.**

MUSIC: WESTERN

In the following account, the contention is that the main trends in the early history of Western music have been driven by two musical goals that have not been shared by other major world musical cultures—(1) harmony (the "vertical" organization of music into related, simultaneous complexes of tones, that is, "chords") and (2) literacy (the perceived need to set down the details of music in as precise and permanent a notation as possible). To achieve each of these goals, musicians have paid a price. Because of their preferences for related simultaneous sounds, early Western composers were compelled to forgo the ornate melodic structures heard in many art musics of Asia; and because of their desire to notate their compositions as accurately as possible, they found it necessary at times to introduce radical simplifications so that they did not imagine a music of greater intricacy than their scripts were able to represent. Only in the many traditions of improvisation has Western musical practice developed in relative freedom from these constraints.

The present article seeks to identify and explain the major trends in the temporality of music from the early Middle Ages until the present, focusing on the European tradition of art music and its subsequent spread to the Americas and elsewhere in the developed countries of the world. To survey this span of some 1,500 years, it is necessary to adopt a perspective that historians would describe as "distant," and thereby run the risk foreseen by the authors of the entry on "Rhythm" in *The New Grove Dictionary of Music and Musicians,* who wrote that "By the very nature of the subject, an attempt to write a history of musical rhythm would be doomed to failure." We can all be grateful that these authors chose to ignore their own advice, and since the following paragraphs parallel the chronology set forth in the *New Grove* article, readers who wish to supplement this historical account with material on a more technical level will be able to do so.

What do we mean when we refer to the time of music? Music obviously takes place in time, is situated in time. Any musical work or performance may be measured in both *elapsed* time (the time span *within which* it runs its course) and *locative* time (the time *at which* an individual work is actualized in performance). Interesting things can be said about both of these modalities of musical time, but this is not what we ordinarily mean when we refer to the time of music. We refer instead to our perception of the quantities and qualities of the stream of music itself: how quickly it appears to move, the patterns by which it is organized, its points of emphasis and de-emphasis, the sense of passage that it invokes, whether it suggests motion toward a future goal, and other such intuitions. These are the issues around which the following narrative is organized.

A.D. 500–1500: THE AGE OF MEDIEVAL MONOPHONY

The age of medieval monophony (that is, music that consists solely of a melodic line) includes many traditions of secular song and sacred chant, including, among the latter, Gregorian chant. Notation was not the problem it was later to become, because much of this heritage of song and chant was primarily an oral tradition—especially with respect to secular song. In early chant notations, rhythmic values were not as precisely notated as they would become in later centuries, because of the prevailing assumption that the rhythm of music was dictated, or at least was influenced, by the poetic structure of the text. For this diverse heritage of vocal music, the primary temporal models were the patterns of formal poetry and the rhythms of dance.

From the former, the various styles and traditions of ecclesiastical chant inherited the quantitative meters and surface patterns of Greek and Latin verse (iambic, trochaic, dactylic, and the like), which were regulated by a rough 1:2 ratio between the short and the long, and which featured highly irregular line structures that remained largely independent of any scheme of regular accents and, as a consequence, displayed no overall metrical plan. From the latter, an array of various genres and ethnic styles of secular song and instrumental dance music (most of which was never set down in notation) inherited a relatively uncomplicated rhythmic style that featured simple binary and ternary meters, with lines organized by regular stress and grouped into periodic, repetitive patterns.

In these early song and chant repertoires, we may recognize an important distinction that has persisted throughout most of the long history of melody in the West and elsewhere: a distinction between (1) a declamatory musical style modeled upon the patterns, accents, and inflections of speech, for which the musicologist Curt Sachs coined the term *logogenic* ("word-born") and (2) a more melodic, "songlike" musical style that remains independent of the constraints of speech rhythms, hence *melogenic*. The apparent domination of speech rhythms in early Western vocal music may be attributed to the fact that musicians in this part of the ancient world were uninterested in drums and drumming and were consequently motivated to seek out other models for their musical rhythm.

Among other important trends in this millennium, we note the gradual development of vernacular tongues (with their own sets of prosodic features, many of which differed sharply from those of their ancestral language) and a corresponding progression from quantitative to qualitative meters and from accents of duration (agogic accents) to accents of stress. Free from any constraints of accompaniment (although common sense suggests that accompaniments may often have been added), the vocal melodies of both monks and court musicians were often conceived and performed in a free style of recitative that reflected only faintly the underlying metrical patterns. When we hear Gregorian chant (the liturgical repertoire of the Roman branch of the medieval Catholic church) performed in the flowing, nonmetrical style that has been popular for most of the present century, it is easy to understand why it has often been described as a music, not of time, but of eternity.

A.D. 1000–1300: THE AGE OF MODAL POLYPHONY

The age of modal polyphony (music consisting of two or more simultaneous lines), and of Romanesque and early Gothic art, was an age in which church musicians began to introduce radical simplifications into the temporal structure of their music in order to cope with two new problems: (1) the need to synchronize simultaneous musical lines, and (2) the consequent reduction of melodic and rhythmic complexity so that the durational relationships within and between the various musical parts could be notated with sufficient precision.

"Modal," in the present context, refers not to the melodic structure of the chants but to the six rhythmic *modi* (trochee, iamb, dactyl, anapest, molossos, and tribrach) borrowed from classical metrics. These familiar groupings, with their stabilizing 1:2 ratio between short and long, were set within a general scheme of ternary rhythm—the "eternal triple meter of the Middle Ages," as it has often been described—and reinforced intellectually by a system of values in which the number 3 represented *perfectio* and invoked symbolic associations with the Christian doctrine of the Holy Trinity. Within this regulatory framework of periodic stress and a common repertoire of patterns, the individual parts began to develop in complex polyrhythms, which ultimately posed a severe challenge to performers. Music was written in successive layers, one part added to another, just as a cathedral was constructed in successive phases (and often with later layers in a new style, as in the contrasting spires of Chartres).

Interestingly, musicians still lacked two things we take for granted today when we describe the organization of musical time: (1) a fixed set of proportional equations among the various standard durations (a duration of two *tempora* might be notated either as a *longa* or a *brevis*, depending upon the context, and the duration of the *longa* itself was not fixed—it could last for either two or three breves, again depending upon the context), and (2) an effective means of representing the overall temporal structure. To achieve these objectives, two further things would be required—an increased set of constraints on the melodic and rhythmic complexity of the individual parts, and, most of all, a bold leap of imagination. Both came in the third decade of the fourteenth century, at the outset of the period historians have labeled as the ars nova.

A.D. 1300–1600: THE AGE OF MENSURAL POLYPHONY

The age of mensural polyphony is generally understood to include the High Gothic and Renaissance eras in music history, as heard first in the compositions of Guillaume de Machaut, Guillaume Dufay, and Josquin Des Prez, and then in works by the great masters of the sixteenth century—William Byrd, Orlando di Lasso, Giovanni Pierluigi da Palestrina, and Tomás Luis de Victoria. This era, which began with an explosion of melodic and rhythmic complexity and then continued with a progressive simplification of the musical language, was marked by two major advances in the control of musical time: (1) the system of mode, time, and prolation that was worked out by Philippe de Vitry and his French and Italian contemporaries, a system which stabilized the proportional relationships (the mensurations) between the musical durations on various hierarchical levels and thereby enabled musicians to represent the general temporal structure of the music with a single controlling "time signature," and (2) a gradual movement toward a standard pulse, which came in the form of the *tactus*—an up-and-down (or down-and-up) movement of the arm to which all the musical lines were regulated in a binary rhythm of arsis and thesis. One consequence of (2) is that the force of the stress accent diminished during this era, since the two phases of the *tactus* were conceived and felt as different in function but equal in force.

The ultimate significance of Vitry's new system is that musical rhythm was finally emancipated from the controlling meters of classical verse, triple meters no longer occupied a higher status than duple meters, and musical structure began to expand into a steep hierarchy. Musicians were at first uneasy with these new possibilities and continued to rely on isorhythmic patterns of repetition for the control of musical structure, but as their confidence grew these procedures were gradually abandoned. The significance of the *tactus* is that music for the first time came under the regulation not of individual units (whose durations were difficult to specify—just how long should a "long" be?), nor of the groupings derived from the metrical feet of Greek and Latin verse (as in the modal rhythms of the preceding age), but of a single master pulse.

These advances in the control of musical time evidently stimulated composers to increase the general level of rhythmic activity in their music, to take advantage of the deeper hierarchy now accessible to them, and to develop an intricate counterpoint of cross-rhythms in the several vocal and instrumental parts. Once again, sacred and secular music went their separate ways—not so much in style as in their preferred model of time. Sacred music, to the end of the sixteenth century, continued to exploit the complex polyrhythms made possible by the controlling presence of the *tactus*; secular music, on the other hand, became more and more attracted to the declamatory inflections of speech and the dance rhythms of instrumental music, motivated more by the emotional content of the text and the heavier stress accents of the dance.

It is debatable to what extent the rhythms of the musical lines were delineated by stress or agogic accents, but it is clear that the conceptual structure of musical rhythm could now be accurately described as *divisive*—that is to say, a set of nested divisions of a highest common multiple, for example:

$$1$$
$$1/2 \quad 1/2$$
$$1/4 \quad 1/4 \quad 1/4 \quad 1/4$$

Even at the end of the period, most music was still notated in separate part-books (instead of scores) and without bar lines, but composers had begun to write all the musical parts simultaneously and had learned to imagine their music under the control of a single master time with a conventional pulse and tempo. These achievements made possible the advances that were to come in the music of the baroque era.

A.D. 1600–1750: THE BAROQUE

The baroque era in music began with the birth of opera and continued to a grand climax in the first half of the eighteenth century with the music of J.S. Bach, George Frideric Handel, Georg Philipp Telemann, and Antonio Vivaldi. It is significant that this era, which opened with a bold attempt to reintroduce the accents, inflections, and rhythms of human speech (in a declamatory style that became known as *recitative*), drew to a close after having achieved the most highly controlled, "clocklike" concept of rhythm and meter ever reached by Western musicians. Isaac Newton's celebrated description of an "absolute, true, and mathematical time . . . [which] flows equably, of itself and from its own nature, without relation to anything external" has struck many as an appropriate description of the concept of musical time in the late baroque.

The regulating master pulse of the *tactus* was gradually replaced during this period by a set of conventionalized meters, each with its own characteristic tempo, rhythmic groupings (many derived from dance rhythms), accentual structure, and other distinctive features. The result was at once a simplification, a diversification, and an individualization of musical meter. We have noted several instances of this strategy in the preceding pages, a strategy that may be expressed with the following imperative: "Simplify the details, and thereby gain more overall control."

Notation no longer seemed a problem. Music was now set down in scores with regular measures and bar lines, and was conceived and experienced as a regular sequence of metric accents. But the greatest temporal achievement of the musical baroque was the system of tonal harmony that developed in the late seventeenth century and has prevailed until the present century—as embodied in the system of major and minor keys. In this familiar system, in which the notes are oriented vertically in "chords" (each with its own harmonic function and set of tendencies), the idea of music became transformed into a set of probabilities directed toward a future goal. The tonal aims of music included artful deviation from, progression toward, and ultimate affirmation of the chord built on the fundamental tone of the scale.

As a consequence, the temporal structure of music became increasingly linear and teleological, and this goal-directed linearity was intensified by a general increase in rhythmic activity, in dynamic level, in emotional content, and by the development of large ensembles such as the orchestra. In contrast to the previous era, the music of the mature baroque was conceived not as a set of multiple layers of time coordinated by a master pulse, but as a single integrated stream of time.

A.D. *1750–1815: The Classical Era*

The so-called classical period, from the music historian's point of view, includes a scant two generations and is defined by the music of Franz Joseph Haydn, Wolfgang Amadeus Mozart, and the young Ludwig van Beethoven. The music of this period is probably what most listeners have in mind when they speak of the "time" of music: linear, periodic, symmetrical, progressive, teleological, hierarchical, recurrent in pattern, beginning decisively and ending with a sense of finality, delineated by regular schemes of stress and tonal accents, and displaying a general binary rhythm marked by the alternation of arsis and thesis, stress and nonstress, tension and relaxation, stability and instability. The foregoing is an accurate description of the time we hear in a Mozart quartet or a Haydn symphony—a miniature universe of coordinated musical clocks. Significantly, this was the period in which the metronome was invented and came into widespread use.

Readers should not conclude from the above description that the time of music was entirely inflexible; it does not follow that a totally coordinated stream of time must also be rigid and mechanical. (And here our metaphor of a clock shop begins to break down.) In the hands of sensitive performers, music always retains the options for expressive nuances, surges of intensity, retarding and quickening, minute pauses and articulations—all those deviations that make music come alive, many of them not specifically indicated by the composer. It was perhaps among the greatest accomplishments of the classical period that such a high degree of temporal deviation could be achieved within the constraints imposed by the musical system—a system that provided a solid base for the increasing deviations of the two subsequent centuries.

A.D. *1815–1910: The Age of Romanticism*

The age of romanticism in music was the era in which the clocklike temporal world of the classical composers became gradually transformed (by composers such as Hector Berlioz, Frédéric Chopin, Franz Liszt, and Richard Wagner) into a time that took as its models the irregular rhythms of nature and the surges of human passion. The rolling waves of the sea and palpitations of the human heart seemed closer to music than the ticking of a clock. If it is reasonable to conceive of Mozart's musical world as a clock shop in which all the clocks are synchronized, as in a jeweler's window, then we may describe the clock shop of Liszt and Wagner as one in which the clocks gradually gain or lose speed, fall out of synchronization, stop unexpectedly, proceed ambiguously, or surge forward until the individual ticks fuse into a continuous stream of sound. The master beat weakened, rhythmic groupings were not as neatly confined within bar lines, and irregular beat groupings began to become popular—particularly as the art music traditions began to draw upon ethnic rhythms from the European heritage of folk song.

The temporal history of nineteenth-century music has yet to be written, because we are only now beginning to comprehend what its consequences have been for composers of the twentieth century. From the viewpoint of melody, harmony, and tonality, most listeners regard the romantic century as a stable and natural development of the tonal system brought to such a peak of perfection by the great classical composers (a perception that is not entirely accurate). But from the viewpoint of musical time, it was nothing less than a revolution.

A characteristic development in nineteenth-century music was the concept of *tempo rubato*: a fluctuating, expressive deviation from, and return to, an established tempo, as heard in the piano pieces of Chopin or the operatic arias of Giuseppe Verdi. In the course of the century, musical works became both shorter and longer.

The duration of a symphony or concerto increased from about fifteen or twenty minutes (as in the early symphonies of Haydn and Mozart) to an hour or more. Art songs and piano pieces often ran their course in a minute or less, distilling a world of emotion into a brief span of time. The temporality of music thus came to occupy a far greater range and became subject to enormous dilations and dense compressions. As we shall presently see, both of these trends continued in the twentieth century.

THE TWENTIETH CENTURY

In the music of the twentieth century, much of which still seems to perplex listeners, temporal organization has splintered into a number of controlling procedures. As a consequence, the time of music can no longer be described as a single linear, hierarchical, teleological stream—except in the music of conservative composers and, perhaps, in the frustrated expectations of those listeners for whom the above version of musical time remains a "given."

The temporal ambiguities, contradictions, dilations, and interruptions of the romantic composers, which were heard and savored as expressive deviations so long as they remained under the harmonic control of major-minor tonality, became exposed as painful dislocations as composers such as Arnold Schoenberg, Alban Berg, and Anton von Webern turned first to atonal and then to serial music. In the absence of the traditional harmonic and melodic coherence, many composers of the first half of the century became increasingly focused on the organization of musical time. Rhythmic activity increased, and many new procedures were developed—as if rhythm itself were to fill the void left by the departure or weakening of tonality. Around mid-century, composers began to experiment with imposing serial order on the elements of rhythm—durations, rests, and accents—as well as pitches; calculated order was thereby installed as a principle of temporal organization, as if to say that our clocks could be preprogrammed with variable sequences of durations. In more recent years, the advance of technology has suggested additional new possibilities for temporal organization in music.

American composer and theorist Jonathan Kramer has drawn attention to a number of new temporalities in music, among them: (1) time that remains linear but which is no longer directed toward a single future goal, (2) time that is characterized by a reordering of the apparent sequence of events, based on the perceived implications of the musical gestures, (3) time that proceeds not in an integrated stream but in a disjunct series of unrelated moments, (4) time in which all sense of dynamic motion is suspended, and, we may add, (5) multiple streams of time heard simultaneously, and (6) time in which unrelated musical events, each with its own time, are embedded in an aural collage like a collection of found objects.

The tendencies toward expansion and contraction of performance timespans have continued in the music of our century: recent minimalist operas by Philip Glass unfold in a hypnotic span of many hours, reflecting the late-century trend toward artistic marathons and suggesting the time of epic; at the other extreme of the spectrum are the chamber music miniatures of Anton von Webern, which at times consume no more than a few seconds. Approaching the end of the twentieth century, we hear a prominent trend toward an eclectic concept of musical time in which the characteristic features include the juxtaposition of seemingly unrelated musical events (often to make a political or social point, and with parody as one of the aims), and in which listeners are invited to deconstruct the relationships among these events. The history of temporality in the twentieth century would be incomplete without some mention of the cross-fertilization of the world of Western art music with first oriental music and other musics of the non-Western world, and, more recently, with the rhythms of jazz, rock-'n-'roll, rap, and other genres of popular music.

At century's end, there are few signs of any coherence emerging from this diverse mixture of genres, styles, ethnic traditions, and idiosyncratic approaches to the time of music. Perhaps the only meaningful conclusion is that, for the first time in the history of music, so much attention has been focused on the temporal dimension. For composers and analysts, the present array of temporal possibilities opens up interesting vistas for creative exploration and for a reinterpretation of our musical past. For traditional listeners, especially for those already alienated by trends in the other dimensions of music, the result has probably been to reinforce their sense of loss and dislocation, as well as to harden their preferences for musical styles in which their perceptions of temporal order and passage more closely match their own sense of what time was and ought to be.

But as cultural concepts of time continue to change—from the timeless cycles of the Middle

Ages, to the driving linear time and clockwork universe of the Enlightenment and the industrial revolution, to the scientific and technological advances of the twentieth century and beyond—we may expect to encounter music that constantly challenges our traditional values and reflects, sometimes some distance after the fact, new ways in which thoughtful and creative people are thinking about time and its role in our lives.

The preceding narrative has traced a grand curve cresting in the eighteenth century, a model of history that is not unlike some of the popular explanations that have been offered for the tonal organization of music. But there are important and inescapable differences. No one has yet succeeded in locating any bodily mechanisms on which our preferences for tones may be grounded, but our many biological clocks provide a constant standard of measure for musical time. Atonality may indeed be at least a theoretical possibility, but we cannot get our clocks out of our systems.

From the beginnings of polyphony ca. A.D. 1000 until about 1800, we have noted a progressive series of innovations designed to bring the temporal structure of music closer to what has been described as a coordinated clock shop with standardized measures and overall controls. Once achieved, this musical clock shop has endured as a base for creative and expressive deviation in subsequent years. The early history of this evolution was driven by the two most characteristic features of Western art music—harmony and literacy. It was the perceived need to assert control over the vertical dimension of harmony that motivated early musicians in their search for synchronizing devices and procedures; and it was the obsessive literacy of the medieval monastics that led to the development of relatively precise rhythmic notations. First, it was necessary to simplify music's temporal organization so that the individual parts could be aligned, coordinated, and written down; once this had been accomplished, the search turned in the direction of a standard pulse, conventional tempos, and a system of universal control. We may examine this history more closely by drawing a set of final conclusions based on five temporal ideas.

With respect to (1) *duration*, we have seen a progression from a narrow range of durations (those of the poetic meters) to a much wider range of divisions and multiples, and ultimately to irregular and irrational values; in the process,

music became more hierarchical. With respect to (2) *accent*, we have noted a gradual trend away from agogic accents and toward the combination of stress and tonal accents, a trend that is loosely parallel to the progression from quantitative to qualitative accent and from classical to vernacular verse. With respect to (3) *grouping*, the progression has been from the ternary modal rhythms of poetic feet to a steep hierarchy of nested binary divisions; as one consequence of this development, musical rhythm became independent of the controlling rhythms of poetry early in the fourteenth century.

The two remaining trends belong to the later history of time in music. With respect to (4) *passage*, the temporal stream of music became more and more linear, directional, and periodic, with an increased sense of motion, a higher energy level, and a greater range of tempos; the equilibrium and control that were achieved in the music of the eighteenth century have shown signs of progressive disintegration in the music of the two subsequent centuries. With respect to (5) *sequence*, later developments in musical form (beginning, perhaps, in the baroque era) have demanded a corresponding development of new listening skills, requiring listeners to perceive and evaluate cross-references between nonadjacent musical events; early preferences for musical form clearly favored strophic and chain structures, but gradually the preferred forms of music became more developmental and syntactical (as in the sonata-allegro form), with the interesting consequence that relationships between noncontiguous events often turn out to be more important than the actual sequence in which the musical events are heard.

[L.R.]

See also **Mathematics of Musical Time; Music: History of Ancient; Rhythm and Meter in Music; Tempo.**

FURTHER READINGS

Dürr, Walther, Walter Gerstenberg, and Jonathan Harvey. "Rhythm." *The New Grove Dictionary of Music and Musicians.* Ed. Stanley Sadie. London: Macmillan, 1980. 15:804–824.

Kramer, Jonathan D. *The Time of Music.* New York: Schirmer, 1988.

Rowell, Lewis. "The Temporal Spectrum." *Music Theory Spectrum* 7 (1985): 1–6.

Sachs, Curt. *Rhythm and Tempo.* New York: Norton, 1953.

Schuldt, Agnes Crawford. "The Voices of Time in Music." *The American Scholar* 45.4 (1976): 549–559.

NEWTON, ISAAC (1642–1727)

In the history of physics, Newton's reputation rests on two antithetical achievements. The great synthesis of terrestrial and celestial mechanics, and the exquisite experimental research on light stand in marked contrast to Newton's defense of the reality of absolute space and absolute time as independent manifolds, sets of ordered locations and moments, within which God created the material universe. While we are lost in admiration for the former, we are less than impressed by the latter. But this is too swift a judgment. To understand his position, it is quite essential to remind ourselves that Newton's physics was only a part of his project, and that he "had an eye upon such principles as might work with considering men for the belief of a Deity," as he confesses in his first letter to Bentley. Newton, Boyle, and indeed most English scientists of the day were stout defenders of the idea of "natural religion." It was hoped that God's nature and existence could be proved from a study of the nature of his creation.

Newton's views on space and time are set out in two places. They are defined explicitly in the *Principia* and accompanied by a description of two very important thought experiments by means of which he hoped to establish the existence of an absolute motion. I owe to Harvey Brown the observation that Newton himself did not offer these experiments as proofs of absolute space. Newton's considerations in favor of absolute space are to be found in the *De Gravitatione*. Nor, it seems, did Newton think that these experiments established the existence of absolute time. Given absolute space and an absolute angular velocity, ought we not immediately to arrive at absolute time? But to do so another step would have been required. It would have been necessary to find some guarantee that the measures of time used by every potential observer of the events imagined in these famous "experiments" would be the same. There is nothing in either of the experiments that could establish that. To reach a full understanding of Newton's views on space, time, and motion, however, we must also consult the Leibniz-Clarke correspondence to find their full significance and defense, and in particular their relation to the question of natural religion. It can hardly be doubted that Samuel Clarke was writing almost as Newton's amanuensis in this famous debate. Let us look first of all at the account of space and time in the *Principia*.

In the Scholium to Definition VIII, Newton writes:

I. Absolute, true, and mathematical time, of itself, and from its own nature, flows equably without relation to anything external, and by another name is called duration: relative, apparent and common time, is some sensible and external (whether accurate or unequable) measure of the duration by means of motion. . . .

II. Absolute space, in its own nature, without relation to anything external, remains always the similar and immovable. Relative space is some movable dimension or measure of the absolute spaces; which our senses determine by its position to bodies. . . .

Why should we believe in these absolute manifolds, sets of moments and of places, which allegedly exist independently of the sequences of events and structures of things that constitute the time and space of everyday life with which physics seems to deal?

In the *Principia*, Newton develops two powerful thought experiments, each of which depends on the important principle that real causes must have real effects and that real effects must be the result of real causes. As he puts it, "true motion suffers always some change from any force impressed upon the moving body." But the most important corollary of the principle is that "the effects which distinguish absolute from relative motion, are the forces of receding from the axis of circular motion." Descartes had tried to escape from the obloquy of confessing that in a Copernican universe the earth must be in motion by redefining motion to mean movement relative to whatever is next to a body. If the earth is carried round with a celestial vortex, then it is stationary with respect to the material of the vortex. Newton, to complete his case against Descartes, offered the experiment of the rotating bucket both to refute this way of defining motion and to demonstrate that the question of one kind of absolute motion could readily be established experimentally. A bucket, containing some water, is hanging by a rope, and is rotated until the rope is tightly twisted. When the bucket is released, the relative motion between the bucket and the water in it is at a maximum, but the surface of the water is still flat. As the water picks up the motion of the bucket by friction, the surface becomes more and more concave until when the water is rotating with the same velocity as the bucket, and the relative velocity between them is now zero, it has the maximum concavity. What is producing the change in the shape of the surface of the water? It cannot be the relative Cartesian motion between water and bucket, because that is now zero. It must be the rotation of the whole system. But since the effect is real—that is, the water is really concave—the motion must be real, and so absolute—that is, the bucket is rotating with respect to absolute space.

The experiment of the globes is rather similar, but it would allow one to compute the absolute velocity of rotation of the system. Two globes are connected by a string. If they are rotating there will be a tension in the string, and so the quantity and direction of the motion can be calculated. This result, Newton asserts, will be obtainable "even in an immense vacuum." Therefore, it must be a rotation with respect to absolute space, since it would be detectable, thought Newton, even in the effective absence of all other material things. The challenge to this assumption had to await the Machian criticisms of Newtonian physics, first published in *The Science of Mechanics* (1883).

Like Galileo, Newton accepted the principle of relativity for uniform motion in a straight line. If one were confined to the closed cabin of a ship on a flat sea there is no experiment with which one could discover whether one was moving forward or backward, or at what speed. Uniform velocity (inertial motion) was necessarily relative to whatever frame of reference was chosen as the inertial frame. Uniform motion and rest were alike in that in both cases no forces were acting on a body, so there was no independent way of determining whether or not it was in motion. This was quite unlike the case of rotation.

But where is God in this discussion? He makes his most dramatic appearance in the Leibniz-Clarke correspondence edited by H.G. Alexander. If there is absolute space and time, then it makes sense to ask where and when the material universe was created. Leibniz gave a number of arguments against the very asking of this question, but these need not detain us here. To explain how he conceived God to be related to space and time, Newton, through Clarke, and in his own person in Query 28 to the *Optics* (1706), draws on the analogy of the "sensorium." According to the neurophysiology of his day, perception could occur only by direct contact between a stimulus and some sensitive part of the perceiver. How then could a human being perceive a distant thing by sight? The answer was found in the idea that the thing perceived gave off a "sensible species" which was taken in by the relevant sense organ and thus into the immediate presence of the "sensitive substance." This contact was thought to occur in the "sensorium" with which each of us was equipped. Newton asks, "does it not appear that there is a Being incorporeal, living, intelligent, omnipresent, who in infinite space, as it were in his sensory [sensorium], sees the things themselves intimately, and thoroughly perceives them. . . by their immediate presence to himself." One could add, without distorting the sense of the analogy, that God was immediately present to all the events of physical time in the same way. Absolute space and absolute time were like a divine sensorium. Leibniz, who rarely missed a trick, took this analogy or image to be a serious account of the nature of absolute space and time, and berated Newton for being so naive. But at most the image of the sensorium was a mere analogy.

[R.H.]

See also **Leibniz, Gottfried Wilhelm; Leibniz-Clarke Correspondence.**

FURTHER READINGS

Leibniz, G., and S. Clarke. *The Leibniz-Clarke Correspondence: Together with Extracts from Newton's* Principia *and* Optics. Ed. H.G. Alexander. Manchester: Manchester UP, 1956.

Mach, E. *The Science of Mechanics.* Trans. T.J. McCormack. 1883; reprint, La Salle: Open Court, 1960.

Newton, Isaac. *Opticks.* 1730; reprint, New York: Dover, 1952.

———. *Sir Isaac Newton's Mathematical Principles of Natural Philosophy and His System of the World.* Trans. A. Motte. Ed. F. Cajori. Berkeley: U of California P, 1960.

NIETZSCHE, FRIEDRICH WILHELM (1844–1900)

Time-consciousness, as Nietzsche conceives it, is rooted in succession. Although he regards space (following Kant) as a subjective form of intuition, time is described as *actual*, and infinite in duration. The attention he gives to time, however, is primarily and fundamentally iconographic in nature. His published writings yield a mosaic depiction (*eine Zeitschilderung*), a vision and a riddle in which time (*die Zeit*) appears in conjunction with the moment (*der Augenblick*) as well as with eternity (*die Ewigkeit*). Time is variously represented as a river, an hourglass, a circle. The moment is a gateway, radically encountered either as midnight or as noon. Eternity is metaphorically evoked as a serpent, a woman, a golden wedding ring.

These iconographic illustrations suggest the basic characteristics Nietzsche attributes to time: its *fluidity* in ceaseless change, its *immediacy* in the living moment, its *temporality* in past, present, and future modes, its *irreversibility* in direction, its *historicity* in events "knotted" inextricably together and drawn in necessary succession, its *periodicity* in cyclical repetitions, its *circularity* in eternal recurrence, and its *transmutability* in an alchemically decisive moment emblematically designated as the "great noon" (*der große Mittag*). It is this last characteristic that reveals the moment in its most intimate relationship to time and eternity.

Time (echoing Heraclitus) is a river flowing inescapably into its own current, according to Nietzsche. It is ceaseless becoming (*Werden*), aimless, pointless, and meaningless change whose mutations frustrate any ultimate goal. So long as man illegitimately demands its metaphysical completion in timelessness, in absolute simultaneity, or in an unfaltering *nunc stans*, he experiences its circularity as futility, as the gravest burden, as a grim revelation that everything is done "in vain." Eternal recurrence expresses nihilism in its most extreme form. Time and its "it was" thwarts all human will and inspires all-too-human resentment. When man eventually succeeds in overcoming his normative aversion to time, however, his affirmation achieves its supreme formulation in the very same doctrine.

Man's encounter with the present moment (*die Gegenwart*) provides his only access either to what has already passed (*die Vergangenheit*) or to what is yet to come (*die Zukunft*). It is a gateway on whose threshold past and future collide. Only when this present moment becomes a momentous presence—when its inescapability elicits a superabundant "yes" and "amen"—is becoming disclosed as being, time, and eternity. This is the ecstatic moment which transfigures and renews history, which redeems the past and engenders the future. At this decisive midpoint in time's eternally circular course, the superman appears, willing his own innocent, independent, and omnipotent will, transvaluing all values, and so transforming necessity into freedom. Dionysos *philosophos*, the unknown god whose nature it is to appear, suddenly appears as flashing lightning. Midnight becomes noon, eternal recurrence as *circulus vitiosus deus* (the "vicious circle as god") now appears as *annulus aeternitatis* (the "ring of eternity"). It is a consummatory apotheosis. Time suddenly and unexpectedly becomes complete in the golden moment, validating its "once again."

[R.Pe.]

NOVEL

Novels slow time down to a pace corresponding to our subjective experience of temporality. Plays, motion pictures, and poetry may achieve such correspondence by extension toward novelistic magnitude or more intermittently by focusing on particular moments to represent them with an amplitude approaching that of actual experience. Epic poems most resemble novels, but are no longer a viable form. The temporal scope of works like the *Iliad*, the *Odyssey*, and the *Aeneid* is now successfully achieved (or surpassed) only in novels such as Leo Tolstoy's *War and Peace* (1865–69), Marcel Proust's *Remembrance of Things Past* (1913–27), and James Joyce's *Ulysses* (1922). The displacement of epic poems by the novel is not merely a matter of substituting prose for verse and extending the sheer length of narration as was done in those forms of prose romance that proliferated before the eighteenth-century rise of the novel. Equally crucial was replacement of epic and romance conventions by narrative methods creating a higher degree of verisimilitude that facilitates greater variety and intensity of temporal experience for novel readers along with better ability to represent human encounters with time. In novels after 1700, Western attitudes toward time have been elaborated with such richness as to preclude a reductive summary here in favor of attention to the main novelistic techniques for dealing with time, some of their consequences for readers, and a few milestones along the road to postmodernism's dubious atemporality.

MANIPULATION OF READING TIME

Among early novels, a classic example of the new techniques for representing human time and thereby involving readers temporally in ways hitherto unequalled by fiction is Samuel Richardson's *Clarissa or The History of a Young Lady*. Two volumes appeared in 1747. Five more were published in 1748. The protagonists, though wealthy, are people whom Richardson's mostly middle-class readers could identify with as they might not with more remote figures of epic or romance. So too, *Clarissa*'s temporal setting is the readers' own world of eighteenth-century England, with all action taking place over an interval of about one year. Because the story is unfolded in long letters from characters often describing the same events from different perspectives and usually going very fully into their thoughts, readers encounter something like the subjective pace as well as fullness of real life. Most brilliantly in the famous garden elopement scene, but also elsewhere, Richardson shows how an interval perceived in retrospect as a decisive moment, a chronologically specific turning point in one's life, may, while it is unfolding, dissolve into a continuous stream of sensations during which it is never clear just *when* a crucial decision has been made at some conscious or unconscious level of the mind.

Clarissa is (notoriously) not a book that can be rushed through. It imposes a slow pace even on fast readers. It does so partly by focusing on psychological response rather than outward events. It does so partly by its epistolary method since a fictive letter takes as long to read as a real one of equal length and thereby synchronizes real and fictive durations. It does so even more effectively because its ratio of pages to intervals described is high, thus creating an objective tempo that is slow in the sense of requiring many pages demanding much reading time for narration of a comparatively short period of plot time. Richardson wrote seven volumes to narrate one year rather than, as in books like Daniel Defoe's *Robinson Crusoe* (1719), one volume for narration of more than fifty years of the protagonist's life: an approximate ratio of seven to one rather than one to fifty. Richardson thereby establishes for readers a protracted subjective duration which creates the illusion of spending almost as much time with the protagonists as they spend in each other's company (or alone). To borrow from Alexander Pope a phrase that

James Boswell aptly quoted to describe the desired effect of his bulky *Life of Samuel Johnson* (1791), readers seem to "live o'er each scene" with those they are reading about.

In reaching for this effect, Boswell and other biographers writing in his widely imitated mode of very complete portrayal resort to a distinctively novelistic technique of expanding the representation of time in ways that allow for temporal identification by readers with the events described as well as for the sensation of experiencing durations that correspond to those of the narrated lifetime, even though not actually taking the same clock intervals. The result, when successful, is an illusion of having known the persons described in the way we know those about us: by having spent much time in their presence.

Of course, Richardson's readers do not require twelve months to read about the tragic final year of Clarissa's life. But going through the seven volumes (some 1,500 pages in a modern one-volume edition with large pages and small type) does occupy a considerable amount of clock time that is interwoven with the reader's daily activities just as encounters with acquaintances are distributed through other events over extended intervals. The experience of reading *Clarissa* is further protracted subjectively into what seems a long duration by the devices that Richardson uses to establish a slow tempo of narration throughout *Clarissa*. Novels of action in a comic mode, such as Henry Fielding's *Tom Jones* (1749), may establish a much more rapid subjective tempo locally while nevertheless achieving overall effects of extended duration similar in degree if not in kind to those attained by psychological novels like *Clarissa*.

For Richardson's initial readers, this sensation of spending much time with his characters and taking narrated events at the pace of real encounters was enhanced by the lengthy interval between publication of the first two volumes and appearance of the remaining five. That many imaginatively involved readers wrote to Richardson during this interval begging him to provide a happy ending is telling evidence that early episodes of *Clarissa* are experienced as present events in life are experienced: with a sense of multiple future possibilities. Though this sense of an open narrative future is to some extent a feature of all stories when they are first read, Richardson made it a distinctive attribute of *Clarissa* by what he called "writing to the moment." By this he meant telling a story in the form of letters supposed written by characters in diary-like manner immediately after each incident rather than retrospectively long after consequences are known, as in a book like *Robinson Crusoe*, where the narrator looks back as he writes in old age about the youthful follies that led to his island adventure. The temporal location of narrators, whether writing "to the moment" or retrospectively at a middle distance or great remove in time from the events they narrate, plays a major role in determining the reader's response in point of temporal (and other) involvement.

Ironically, the television soap opera with its recurrent and potentially endless episodes unfolding week after week at fixed hours may now be the novel's closest rival as fiction that mimics the tempo of life by demanding a large investment of its audience's time while resorting to methods of presentation that strongly influence perception of the story's subjective duration. Formal boundaries certainly overlap. All narrative art shares concern with time as a theme, requires time as a medium within which to unfold a story, and to some degree manipulates the subjective time sense of its audience. Nevertheless, more than any other literary form, the novel depends on protracted engagement with time for its unfolding, and shapes the reader's subjective perception of duration as well as tempo.

REPRESENTATION OF TIME

Imaginary events may be set in the past, the present, the future, or some combination of all three, as well as in alternate history, stories of history as it might have been, or in mythic realms of "once-upon-a-time" that have always served as a locus for fantasy. This statement will now seem obvious, but it was not always so. Futuristic fiction, the explicit location of narrated events in the future, was an eighteenth- and nineteenth-century development making available temporal settings unexplored by the literary imagination of previous eras. It facilitated the growth of science fiction and related forms inviting attention to things to come or to present events contemplated from a future perspective (or both). Robert Scholes is right to argue in *Structural Fabulation: An Essay on Fiction of the Future* (1975) that fiction set in the future is most appropriate for our time because it allows for retention of a moral imperative to use literature as an agent of human improvement while avoiding the epistemological problems of unsophisticated referentiality by providing constructs of

imaginary futures for contemplation as models and metaphors rather than merely attempting mimesis of what is. On this view, it follows that the most significant feature of time in the modern novel is its combination of temporal and other verisimilitudes of presentation with the liberating possibilities of future settings, thus making possible works like George Orwell's *Nineteen Eighty-Four* (1949) that speak so powerfully to our own future-oriented age.

While the turn to futuristic fiction is coincidental with the accelerating pace of change induced by industrial and political revolutions of the eighteenth and nineteenth centuries, it is no less closely associated with the rise after 1700 of the modern novel itself. Alternate historical settings are a nineteenth-century development. So are historical novels of the kind popularized by Sir Walter Scott, although his works had for predecessors Gothic fiction set in a vaguely medieval past in the manner of Horace Walpole's *Castle of Otranto* (1765). Another forerunner of the historical novel is Defoe's remarkable *Journal of the Plague Year* (1722), which imaginatively reconstructs London's devastating epidemic of bubonic plague in 1665. One key feature distinguishing the novel from earlier forms of narration is its freedom to set action in real pasts, alternate pasts, and imaginary futures as well as a sharply specified present time.

Another feature is the novel's heavy reliance on specification of temporal relationships to achieve greater realism than its predecessor forms. By explicitly or implicitly marking not only the temporal locus of action but the chronology of narrated events with respect to one another and to calendar time, novels achieve an order of verisimilitude unlike that of fiction before Defoe, Richardson, and Fielding. It must also be noted, however, that it is not only postmodern novelists who have experimented with extreme departures from the novelistic norms of temporal verisimilitude. Early eighteenth-century development of the novel was soon followed by Laurence Sterne's *The Life and Opinions of Tristram Shandy, Gentleman* (1760–67), a parody of novelistic conventions that significantly expanded the genre's repertoire of techniques for dealing with time.

Published in nine volumes over seven years, *Tristram Shandy* takes the form of a potentially endless memoir of the narrator's life and opinions. Whether it creates the sense of an ending by finishing its antecedent tale of Uncle Toby's courtship of the Widow Wadman, or just stops, is a matter for debate. Sterne might have continued it had he not died in 1768, because *Tristram Shandy*'s structure is open-ended rather than providing that definitive closure achieved by confinement to the classical Aristotelian plot of causally related events with a beginning, middle, and ending that forecloses further action. The more he writes, Sterne's narrator, Tristram, explains to his readers, the longer he lives, because writing itself takes time, and the events and opinions of that time will in their turn have to be narrated for the sake of completeness. Here, the usual convention that writing itself takes no specified time is comically though also realistically exploded by frequent self-reflexive references to Tristram's struggles with the difficulties of authorship. There is also advice for readers, including admonitions to reread and to read more carefully. *Tristram Shandy* thus offers explicit engagement with all three dimensions of literary time: writing time, written-about time, and reading time. It illustrates, too, how much is at stake in choosing between representation of story time intervals as open-ended, or as rounded off by events that define sequences primarily with reference to their manner of closure.

The paradox Tristram proposes is the inability of his narration ever to catch up with his life, with the frightening prospect of an endless book far longer than even such gigantic works as *Clarissa*: "The more your worships read the more your worships will have to read." This literary equivalent of Zeno's paradox of motion, though with the opposite implication that there can be no narrative rest, was Sterne's *reductio ad absurdum* of the novel's fundamental temporal device of expanded duration.

In other ways, too, Sterne parodied the novel's temporal verisimilitude. Instead of beginning with birth of the protagonist and moving forward to recount all or part of a life story in chronological order as most previous fiction had done whether or not written in an autobiographical mode, Tristram Shandy flouts convention by starting with an account of his conception (which was, he believes, marred by his mother's inopportune question "My dear, have you not forgot to wind up the clock?"). Moreover, *Tristram Shandy* is then largely occupied with events that took place even earlier, interspersing narration of those remote episodes with accounts of Tristram's birth and various childhood disasters. The narrative moves forward and backward in plot time. Its method, Tristram remarks, is digressive and progressive too. Episodes widely separated in calendar time are juxtaposed. Some events are partially recounted in one chapter with characters left suspended in mid-sentence or mid-motion, then picked up again many chapters later with the narration resumed almost as though nothing had intervened in the book's pages. In all this, Sterne both parodies and goes well beyond the classical precedent of starting an epic *in medias res* and only later providing an account of events leading up to the moment described in the initial episode.

Sterne thus radically decouples narrative sequence—the order in which events are narrated—from plot sequence—the chronological order of events in plot time. The extent to which narrative and plot sequence coincide or diverge is one of the most crucial variables in the novelistic representation of time. By 1767, Sterne had demonstrated the artistic value of departure from synchronization of narrative and plot sequence. Subsequent writers, especially avant-garde novelists of the twentieth century, have so much taken this lesson to heart that a full history of time in modern and postmodern fiction would be largely, though not exclusively, an account of variations on Sterne's devices for avoiding tedious coincidence of narrative and plot sequence.

In *Tristram Shandy*, Sterne rationalizes many of his games with time by referring to the concepts of duration explained in John Locke's *Essay Concerning Human Understanding* (1690). A key notion there is that the more ideas we entertain in a given interval the more our impression of its duration will be expanded. Sterne's most general application of Lockean time concepts is to justify the impression of expanded duration that *Tristram Shandy* achieves no less than more conventional novels, though partly by then unusual techniques of temporal representation involving the crowding together of digressions and associational leaps of thought from topic to topic.

Another important consequence of *Tristram Shandy*'s decoupling of narrative and plot sequence is an invitation to hold the novel's episodes in mind simultaneously rather than think of them as neatly distributed along a chronological line from first to last moment of plot time. Dates mentioned in *Tristram Shandy* make it possible to construct a master chronology of plot events that even includes the times of writing which Tristram occasionally specifies. But to do so is laborious. A reading of the novel leads instead to memories of it that match the narrative juxtaposition of matters widely separated in calendar time. In this way, Sterne drives home the point that different times usually coexist within human memory. In this way, too, Sterne achieves a simultaneous rather than sequential temporal structure of the kind identified in an influential essay by Joseph Frank as spatial form.

Critics have accepted Frank's observation that twentieth-century literature is characterized by the frequency of its resort to spatial form, that is, to various means of undercutting chronology to produce a more nearly simultaneous apprehension of elements widely distributed through plot time and narrative sequence. Critics have also acknowledged *Tristram Shandy*'s pioneering role in developing novelistic techniques for achieving spatial form. Although all the elements of such complicated works cannot, in fact, be held in conscious awareness simultaneously, there are major differences in styles of temporal representation as well as in aesthetic effects between works that demand an effort to do so and those that more easily allow themselves to be apprehended, analyzed, and remembered sequentially. The most important aesthetic consequence of spatial form is to shift the reader's focus from diachronic representation of plot-time to synchronic awareness of narrative sequence and textual relationships, thereby subordinating written-about time to reading time, which accordingly becomes the primary temporal dimension.

Of twentieth-century novels that resort to spatial form the most instructive paradigm is James Joyce's *Ulysses*. Its readers must strive to contemplate simultaneously rather than sequentially an intricate conflation of different orders of time. There is an account of Stephen Dedalus, Leopold Bloom, and Molly Bloom centered on events of June 16, 1904, in Dublin. Their actions, set in a real city at a particular moment of historical time are by various means presented as parallels to the episodes of Homer's *Odyssey* that exist for us outside history in the realm of mythic time. These Homeric references, along with other literary allusions, including stylistic parodies, also refer readers to the history of literature and thence to what might be called the quasi-historical dimension of textual time which partakes both of diachronic and synchronic relationships. Stream-of-consciousness passages like Molly's concluding interior monologue present the vagaries of subjective time.

Most fundamental to the temporal structure of *Ulysses* is enforcement of correspondences between the historical time of its Dublin action and the mythic time of Homer's epic. For readers, this means that *Ulysses* should be considered not only in its entirety but simultaneously with memories of Homer's text to appreciate, among other things, a kind of secular typology in which the Homeric figures and situations become types of all human experience. Thus, to read *Ulysses* is also to reread the *Odyssey*, and vice versa. Joyce creates a multiple temporal as well as textual experience. This is hard, but without attempting the temporal doublings invited by *Ulysses*, readers will miss a great part of Joyce's meaning as well as many ramifications of his method of investing apparently ordinary occurrences with far-reaching symbolism. Above all, they would miss Joyce's argument for continuities linking mythic, historical, and personal time in our own world.

In *The Sound and The Fury* (1929), William Faulkner explores intersections of historical and personal time while presenting too, in part one, the outlook of a retarded person, Benjy, for whom time distinctions hardly exist. It is extremely disorienting to encounter Benjy's detemporalized narrative, whose events can only be redistributed chronologically by readers who have completed the novel and return in memory or via a rereading to Benjy's section. By purging this part of the usual novelistic clues to chronology Faulkner not only invites consideration of time's role in constituting our humanity. He also forces readers to experience radical temporal dislocations and thus to some degree understand their consequences firsthand while struggling to make chronological sense of part one.

Benjy's predicament of living without understanding distinctions between past, present, and future is taken up at a more philosophical level in Jean-Paul Sartre's allegory of existential time dilemmas, *Nausea* (1938). Its protagonist despairs after finding himself unable to relate to the communal past by continuing his work as a historian while equally but more disturbingly unable to relate even to his own past and future: everything but the present moment drops out of awareness. In *Tristram Shandy*, Sterne dramatizes the comedy of hopeless entanglement in one's personal past. In *Remembrance of Things Past* Proust suggests that the past may be transcended by successful transmutation into art, with the novel proposed as the proper venue of memory and locus of human temporality. In *Ulysses* Joyce illustrates continuities that bind together mythic, historical, and personal time to constitute our common humanity. In *Nausea* Sartre dramatizes the modern world's tendency to discard such community by falling into self-entrapment in a perpetual present.

Another milestone in novelistic representation of time, although marking a dead-end road, is the fiction of Alain Robbe-Grillet and other avatars of the French "new novel." In such works as *In the Labyrinth* (1959), Robbe-Grillet presents episodes whose temporal settings and relationships are so ambiguously specified that it is never possible to work out an ordering of narrated actions with respect to one another in a coherent internal chronology, or with reference to calendar time. Unlike Faulkner's recreation of Benjy's limited time-perception, however, Robbe-Grillet's technique is designed to decouple narrative from representation. His withholding of temporal information reduces the reader's time frame to one order of time: the clock time and phenomenal time of encounter with the book. By this means the textuality of narrative is stressed as a means of rejecting the mainstream novel's reliance on all the mimetic techniques of verisimilitude epitomized by methods of accurately representing temporal relationships. This is also to reject the view that literature refers readers to realities outside their encounter with printed pages. For much postmodern fiction in the tradition exemplified by *In the Labyrinth*, the most significant dimension of literature is reading time divorced from other temporal connections. But such deliberate excursions into atemporality are unlikely to abolish widespread taste for the more instructive pleasures of connecting the durations of reading with all the sequences of human existence in time.

[P.K.A.]

See also **Alternate History; Futuristic Fiction; Modernism; Postmodern Literature; Science Fiction.**

Further Readings

Alkon, Paul K. *Defoe and Fictional Time*. Athens: U of Georgia P, 1979.

———. *Origins of Futuristic Fiction*. Athens: U of Georgia P, 1987.

Bakhtin, Mikhail Mikhailovich. "Forms of Time and of the Chronotope in the Novel." *The Dialogic Imagination: Four Essays by M. M. Bakhtin*. Ed. Michael Holquist. Trans. Caryl Emerson and Michael Holquist. Austin: U of Texas P, 1981. 84–258.

Frank, Joseph. *The Idea of Spatial Form*. New Brunswick: Rutgers UP, 1991.

Genette, Gérard. *Narrative Discourse: An Essay in Method*. Trans. Jane E. Lewin. Foreword by Jonathan Culler. Ithaca: Cornell UP, 1980.

Kermode, Frank. *The Sense of an Ending: Studies in the Theory of Fiction*. Oxford: Oxford UP, 1966.

Mendilow, A.A. *Time and the Novel*. 1952; reprint, New York: Humanities P, 1972.

Scholes, Robert. *Structural Fabulation: An Essay on Fiction of the Future*. Notre Dame: U of Notre Dame P, 1975.

Shaw, Harry E. *The Forms of Historical Fiction: Sir Walter Scott and His Successors*. Ithaca: Cornell UP, 1983.

Smitten, Jeffrey R., and Ann Daghistany, eds. *Spatial Form in Narrative*. Ithaca: Cornell UP, 1981.

Watt, Ian. *The Rise of the Novel*. Berkeley: U of California P, 1957.

NUMBERS, HISTORY OF

Though the Hindu-Arabic decimal numbering system has become the *lingua franca* of the modern world, this development was neither historically nor mathematically inevitable. Our first numbering systems lacked the generalized abstractions that we now take for granted. As early as the eighth millennium B.C., the Sumerians recorded their possessions by using small tokens of baked clay. Cone shaped tokens were used for a small measure of grain, and a sphere for ten such measures. Thus, a sphere and two cones represented twelve measures of grain, but such symbols in no sense referred to another commodity like sheep, which were represented by lenticular discs. Even in our language today there are vestiges of article-specific methods of numbering, like a pride, a gaggle, or a pack.

In Bertrand Russell's words, "It must have taken ages to discover that a brace of pheasants and a couple of days were both instances of the number two." Archaeologist Denise Schmandt-Besserat notes that it took the Sumerians some 5,000 years to produce abstract numbers, and that this occurred shortly after they began writing on tablets of clay in 3100 B.C. For these abstract numbers—employed in temples to account for large surpluses of produce—they used a small wedge for *one*, a small circle for *ten*, a large wedge for *sixty*, and a large circle for *360*. Such a numbering system—much like the later Hebrew, Minoan, or Roman systems—could hardly facilitate addition, subtraction, multiplication, or division. Georges Ifrah shows how, before the advent of the Hindu-Arabic decimal system, calculations would first be carried out in the lost but remarkably widespread art of finger writing (or rather finger calculating), and then noted down. In our millennium, the abacus, and much more recently the electronic calculator, have been similarly employed.

In the Hindu-Arabic decimal system the word Arabic refers to the traders who transferred a preexisting Indian system. And that system's need for very large numbers almost certainly derived from the Indian eternalistic eschatologies in which, for example, each *kalpa* involved a mythical period of 4,320 million years. At an early date, India already had names for the ranks leading as high as *laksa* (10^5), one hundred thousand, and *prayuta* (10^6), a million. When Buddha was courting Gopa, her father had insisted that he should first pit his abilities against those of Arjuna, the great mathematician. Arjuna had insisted that Buddha list all the numerical ranks above 100 *kotis*, the term for 10^7.

Unlike the other major numerical place value systems (which give values to numbers according to their places in a sequence), Indian numerals provided discrete notations for each number up to nine. When the zero and the decimal point were later added to this, the Hindu-Arabic decimal numbers led to the rationalization of numbering systems throughout the world. Significantly, even the binary numbers inherent in computers are being subordinated to the decimal system. Karl Menninger's illustrations (Figure 1) show the morphology of the Brahmi numbers as they moved westward through the Indian and Arabic to the sixteenth-century figures used by Dürer, which are much like our own.

There is no inherent reason why ten-base numerals should have prevailed other than the fact that—like the English language to a somewhat lesser degree—they became part of the dominant Western tradition. In fact, the number twelve, which has four divisors rather than the two divisors of the number ten, would prob-

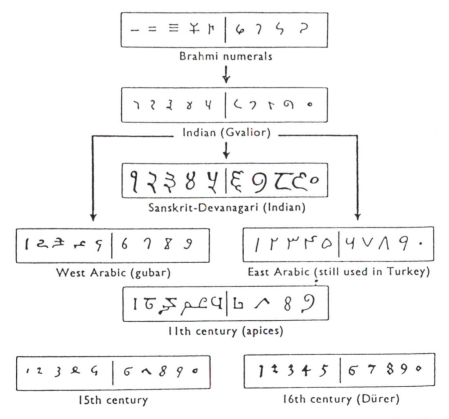

Figure 1. *The Family Tree of the Indian Numerals (Karl Menninger,* Number Words and Number Symbols, *trans. Paul Boneer. Boston, Mass.: MIT Press, 1969)*

ably have been more convenient. The generally held assumption that ten-based numbering systems derive from finger counting—much as twenty-based numbering systems derive from counting the fingers and toes—would seem to be reasonable. But what of the duodecimal and sexagesimal systems which dominated much of the numeration that has come down to us? Georges Ifrah argues persuasively that these systems derive from a long-established finger-counting method, still widely used in the Near and Far East. The duodecimal system counts to twelve by pointing with the right thumb to the twelve discrete bones on the four fingers of that hand commencing with the tip of the little finger. And this is supplemented by a sexagesimal system that indicates twelve, twenty-four, thirty-six, forty-eight and sixty by closing down each of the five fingers of the right hand starting with the little finger.

Ifrah feels that the duodecimal finger-counting method may well have been a factor in leading the ancient Egyptians to divide day and night each into twelve unequal or temporal hours. Certainly the sexagesimal numbering system was widely used by the Babylonians. They divided circles into 360 degrees—perhaps because this was close to the number of days in the year—their degrees into sixty minutes, and their minutes into sixty second minutes, which we now call seconds. The close relationship between astrology and numbers should not be overlooked. In fact, the Latin word *mathematicus* means both a mathematician and an astrologer, and our word horoscope derives from the Greek

Horoscopos thet combines *Hora* (time) and *Scopos* (observer).

Although even up to our own day they have been used in commerce and elsewhere, the duodecimal and sexagesimal number systems have remained most strongly entrenched in the measurement of the earth, and particularly of time. Yet history is clearly on the side of the decimal system of numbers. Even in time measurement, where the duodecimal and sexagesimal systems remain strongest, those measurements that were not envisaged in concrete terms before the advent of Western science and technology are now subordinated to a decimal system and terminology. Beginning with the word "century"—first used in its temporal sense in the seventeenth century—we now envisage our history, world, and universe in terms of hundreds, thousands, millions, and billions of years. Similarly, on the microscopic scale, the second is measured downwards by decimal stages through such terms as millisecond, microsecond, nanosecond, picosecond, and the chronon.

[S.L.M.]

See also **Calendar: Western; Chronology; Partitioning the Day; Historiography.**

FURTHER READINGS

Ifrah, Georges. *From One to Zero: A Universal History of Numbers.* Trans. Lowell Blair. New York: Viking Penguin, 1985.

Macey, Samuel L. *The Dynamics of Progress: Time, Method, and Measure.* Athens: U of Georgia P, 1989.

Menninger, Karl. *Number Words and Number Symbols: A Cultural History of Numbers.* Trans. Paul Boneer. Boston: MIT P, 1969.

ORIGIN AND AGE OF THE ELE-MENTS

Questions concerning the origin and age of the chemical elements must certainly date back as far as human beings have sought to understand the world about them. Only recently, however, has it become possible to begin to shed light on even such basic issues as where and when the elements were formed and whether the age of the universe is finite or infinite. In the context of the currently favored cosmological model, the Big Bang model, it now appears that the age of the universe is indeed finite. Lower limits on this age may in principle be obtained by dating the galaxies, the stars, and the chemical elements of which the universe is composed. In this regard, interesting constraints on the age of our Milky Way galaxy can be obtained by such diverse means as consideration of the ages of star clusters in the galactic halo, of the ages of the white dwarfs in the immediate vicinity of the sun, and of the age of the elements themselves. In this article, we will be concerned, specifically, with the question of the origin of the elements and its implications for the age of the elements.

Our current understanding of when and where the elements were formed reveals a complicated history but a natural chronology. The primordial fireball associated with the cosmological big bang is believed to have provided appropriate conditions of temperature and density to produce a significant concentration of ^7Li, together with hydrogen, deuterium, and the isotopes of helium, ^3He and ^4He. A hydrogen mass fraction of ~0.76 and a helium mass fraction of ~0.24 are the expected consequences of this cosmological nucleosynthesis epoch. The predicted concentrations of carbon and still heavier elements (referred to collectively as "metals" in the astrophysical literature) are, however, many orders of magnitude smaller than are observed in our galaxy today. This "primordial" abundance pattern was realized at the cosmological nucleosynthesis era, approximately three minutes into the expansion of the universe, and remained as such until galaxy formation subsequently provided the sites for stellar and supernova nucleosynthesis.

Observations of galactic sources serve to confirm the general consistency of the primordial abundance pattern with the predictions of big bang nucleosynthesis. Indeed, abundance determinations for our Milky Way galaxy and for other galaxies indicate a ^4He mass fraction of approximately 0.24, consistent with the stan-

dard model. Moreover, stars in the halo of our galaxy, which are assumed for dynamical reasons to constitute a much earlier stellar population, are found to have significantly lower metal contents—as low as ~10^{-4} to 10^{-5} that of the sun. These observations emphasize the critical roles of nuclear or "thermonuclear" mechanisms operating in stellar environments in our own galaxy, in the formation of the bulk of the heavy elements present in galactic matter. Assuming the primordial gas to have been composed of hydrogen and helium, the first generation of stars in the galaxy will then have been formed with this composition. The onset of heavy element synthesis in our Milky Way galaxy thus presumably occurred following star formation during the earliest phases of collapse of the halo. The evolution of a star is characterized both by element synthesis during various stages of nuclear burning and, ultimately, by the return of processed matter to the interstellar gas by slow mass loss of explosive ejection. There has thus followed a steady increase in the heavy element content of galactic matter to the approximately 2 percent level that characterizes the sun and solar system and the interstellar gas in our galaxy today.

The evolution of normal stars through the exhaustion of hydrogen and helium in their cores by thermonuclear "burning" processes provides appropriate environments for the synthesis of most of the carbon and nitrogen in the galaxy, as well as a substantial fraction of the elements more massive than iron and nickel. These features of stellar nucleosynthesis theory have in fact been confirmed by direct observations of stellar spectra. There exists a class of red giant stars, the "carbon stars," the atmospheres of which are seen to be highly enriched in carbon, which is believed to have been formed by helium burning in the interior and subsequently carried to the surface regions by convective mixing. Similarly, the presence of the element technetium in the atmospheres of some red giant stars confirms that nucleosynthesis is a continuing process in stellar interiors. Since there are no stable isotopes of technetium, its presence in the atmospheres of red giant stars demands that element synthesis has taken place quite recently in these stars.

The most significant nucleosynthesis sites in the galaxy are known to be supernova events, spectacular explosions of more massive stars which constitute the final stages of their evolution. Two types of supernova events are generally distinguished. Supernovas of Type II represent the final catastrophic stage of the evolution of stars of masses greater than approximately ten times the sun's mass ($10 \, M_\odot$). They are believed to have been responsible for the synthesis of most of the oxygen, neon, sodium, magnesium, aluminum, silicon, phosphorus, sulfur, chlorine, argon, potassium, and calcium nuclei present in the galaxy (and in our sun and solar system), as well as of approximately half of the nuclei in the atomic table more massive than iron and nickel. Supernovas of Type I are believed to result from the explosions of massive, dense carbon-oxygen white dwarf stars in binary stellar systems. This type of supernova synthesizes most of the titanium, vanadium, chromium, manganese, iron, cobalt, nickel, copper, and zinc nuclei present in galactic matter.

Among the heavy nuclei synthesized under the high temperature and high density conditions to which the ejecta of Type II supernovas are subjected are four unstable but extremely long-lived isotopes of thorium, uranium, and plutonium: ^{232}Th ($\tau_{1/2} = 1.40 \times 10^{10}$ years), ^{235}U ($\tau_{1/2} = 7.04 \times 10^8$ years), ^{238}U ($\tau_{1/2} = 4.46 \times 10^9$ years), and ^{244}Pu ($\tau_{1/2} = 8.3 \times 10^7$ years), where the numbers in brackets indicate the decay half-lives of these isotopes. It is particularly noteworthy that these radioactive nuclei are formed in these massive stars of very short lifetimes, which are known to have provided the first significant heavy element contamination of the gas in our galaxy during the very earliest stages of its evolution. Their presence in the gas, coupled to a knowledge of both their abundances and those of their radiative decay "daughter" products, makes possible their use in establishing a nuclear chronological age for the galaxy. Analyses of this problem indicate that the Milky Way galaxy is approximately 15 billion years old, although the various uncertainties associated with these dating techniques easily permit ages as low as 10 billion years and in excess of 20 billion years.

[J.W.T.]

See also **Age of the Oldest Stars and the Milky Way; Big Bang Theory; Cosmology; Expansion of the Universe; Solar System; Star and Galaxy Formation.**

ORIGIN OF SEX

The origin of sex comprises two separate phenomena: the origin of a life cycle that includes meiotic cell division and fusion of gametes, and the origin of maleness and femaleness. The main evolutionary advantages of sexual reproduction are in facilitating the repair of copying mistakes in the genetic material, and in promoting the formation of new gene combinations. Prokaryotes (bacteria and their relatives) are haploid and have only a rudimentary capacity for genetic recombination and sexual reproduction. Eukaryotes (all other living organisms) evolved from prokaryote ancestors approximately 1 billion years ago; their life cycles include both a haploid stage (with one chromosome set per cell) and a diploid stage (with two sets per cell). Alternation between these stages allows recombination of genes and chromosomes and maintains or increases the genetic variability that provides the raw material of evolutionary change. Most primitive forms of life are hermaphroditic, or have gametes not differentiated into sperm and egg. Separate sexes are common in some groups of organisms (such as vertebrates) and rare in other groups (such as plants). The evolution of separate sexes is typically associated with specialization of sex roles, as reflected in behaviors such as competition for mates or nurturing of the young.

[G.A.A.]

See also **Eve's Genetic Legacy; Evolution of Evolutionism.**

FURTHER READINGS

Maynard Smith, J. *The Evolution of Sex.* Cambridge: Cambridge UP, 1978.

Michod, R.E., and B.R. Levin, eds. *The Evolution of Sex: An Examination of Current Ideas.* Sunderland: Sinauer Associates, 1988.

ORTHOGENESIS

Orthogenesis, defined as "definitely-directed," implies an inherent tendency, without the influence of natural selection, that causes progressive changes as products of time. Darwin admitted the existence of a "law of growth," whereby traits lacking in any discernible utility became enhanced. A classical example of orthogenesis occurs in the lobate lines found between the shell whorls of ammonites, extinct forms of cephalopod molluscs. In the earliest strata the lines are simple curves, but with time the lines became wavy, then lobate. Some orthogenic lines of evolution seem to have resulted in a "hypermorphosis" (exaggeration of form) that brought about extinction. The shell growth of some fossil *Gryphaea* oysters became so massive that the living organism within was occluded and apparently unable to feed. The antlers of the Irish elk *Megaceros* became so large that the animals could not bear their weight.

However, all of these putative examples of orthogenesis are explained away by orthodox neo-Darwinists as no more than directional natural selection (also called "orthoselection") in action. If a particular feature has selective value in a given set of living conditions then it is likely that an augmentation of the feature, brought about by random mutation, will be selected. Hence, in a stable ecological system, the feature will continue to be emphasized until it becomes detrimental, or until the environment changes. The lobate lines of the ammonites can legitimately be correlated with improvements in the buoyancy regulation of these floating animals (similar to the modern *Nautilus*); the increases in the shell mass of *Gryphaea* helped the organism to stay out of the mud; and the antlers of *Megaceros* conferred greater sexual fitness. Extinction might very well be due to sudden or catastrophic climatic change and not to hypermorphosis at all.

These explanations and an anti-orthogenic book, *Evolution above the Species Level,* by Bernhard Rensch (1959), have removed almost all references to orthogenesis from current literature. However, molecular genetic research has detected apparent orthogenic trends at the gene level. Certain classes of genes within given species are particularly prone to duplication, sometimes with the result that thousands of copies of a particular gene may exist while a closely related species might only have the usual pair. It is thus difficult, whatever utilitarian explanation can be derived for the multiplicity, to see why the phenomenon is needed by the one species and not by the other. S. Ohno, in *Evolution by Gene Duplication* (1970), has pointed out that gene duplication allows the original type of gene to go on with its essential function, while experimental mutations can occur in the copies "out of sight of natural selection," until something useful comes along. There are numerous examples of this mechanism to be found in protein evolution. Moreover, if the duplication involves regulator genes, it is theoretically possible that radical allometric shifts might be produced; these might include major changes in the proportionate sizes of organs, such as allowed the evolution of the giraffe from its okapi-like ancestor. Thus the book is not closed on the once prominent idea of orthogenesis. However, even if it were to be recognized once more as a legitimate evolutionary process, orthogenesis would have to be seen as a minor mechanism for reshaping the existent, in contrast to the greater biological revolutions.

[R.G.B.R.]

See also **Biological Revolutions; Fossil Record; Heterochrony.**

FURTHER READINGS

Reid, R.G.B. *Evolutionary Theory: The Unfinished Synthesis.* Ithaca: Cornell UP, 1985.

ORWELL, GEORGE (1903–1950)

Though himself a left-wing writer, George Orwell (pseudonym of Eric Arthur Blair) attacked communism savagely and bitterly in his two best-known works *Animal Farm* (1945) and *Nineteen Eighty-Four* (1949). Orwell virtually always wrote from experience. A life of great poverty in London and Paris led, for example, to his early publications *Down and Out in Paris and London* (1933), and *The Road to Wigan Pier* (1937). His experiences while fighting in the Spanish Civil War are described in *Homage to Catalonia* (1938), and led to the anti-Stalinism of *Animal Farm* and *Nineteen Eighty-Four.* But on four separate occasions in the latter novel we learn that the Party of Big Brother was going to last 1,000 years; this vain boast would certainly alert readers in 1949 that communism was not the only totalitarian system being attacked.

Unlike most authors of dystopias (< Greek *dys*, ill or bad; *top[os]*, a place), Orwell projected *Nineteen Eighty-Four* only thirty-five years into the future when it was published in 1949. While this gave a much greater immediacy to a work which has acted as a powerful literary indictment of Stalinist communism, it may well be at the price of sacrificing the continuing influence of Orwell's masterpiece.

The pessimism of *Nineteen Eighty-Four* is virtually absolute. No major dystopia describes a more complete control over the human employment of time. The past and the future are annihilated while in the present, every minute of the day is regulated. The Party's slogan—repeated both early and late in the novel—maintains that "Who controls the past . . . controls the future: who controls the present controls the past." For them, "history was a palimpsest, scraped clean and reinscribed exactly as often as was necessary." The novel takes place over the last year in the life of the protagonist, Winston Smith, who at the age of thirty-nine is just old enough to have vague memories of the days before the Party. He writes in his secret diary of the present "at this moment . . . in 1984 (if it was 1984)." Though Winston "recognized himself as a dead man it became important to stay alive as long as possible" so that his work might be read at *"a time when thought is free."* And he has indeed stayed alive—his diary has become Orwell's novel. Furthermore, Winston's martyrdom was replicated physically by Orwell, whose writing and even typing of the corrected manuscript are thought to have aggravated the tuberculosis from which he died. Also, by projecting the novel no further than 1984—in order to impress his readers with the immediacy of such dangers as Ingsoc (English socialism), Big Brother, doublethink, and Newspeak—Orwell deliberately foreshortened the powerful afterlife of his own work. While the Party seeks to eliminate the chronology and history of the past as well as the hope for the future, it controls and rationalizes the present through the tyranny of clock time. When the novel opens, all the clocks are striking thirteen, and this combines a symbol of impending catastrophe with an indication that the measurement of time has been rationalized to the twenty-four-hour day. O'Brien, the leader of the Party's Thought Police, is repeatedly concerned with precise time. He not only "glanced at his wristwatch" when we first meet him, but right in the middle of the book he does so three times in the space of four pages.

One way to control people by time is to keep them busy. Winston's working week was sixty hours on normal occasions, but "he had worked more than ninety hours in five days" during Hate Week. Julia's working week was even longer than Winston's. The temporal control was just as rigid away from work. Winston informs us that "In principle a Party member had no spare time, and was never alone except in bed." The day began at "nought seven fifteen" with a high-pitched whistle from his telescreen. There were organized interludes controlled by the telescreen—like "Physical Jerks," and the "Two Minutes Hate" for which a "grinding speech, as of some monstrous machine running without oil, burst from the big telescreen"—and at twenty-three thirty the lights to his room were automatically switched off. The absolute and centralized temporal control exercised by the Party is well illustrated by the statement that "The telescreen struck fourteen. He must leave in ten minutes. He had to be back at work by fourteen-thirty."

But there are a few remaining examples of older timepieces in Mr. Charrington's junk shop, and these exercise a much less rigid and diabolical control than those of the Party. The juxtaposition of people who prefer expensive and precise diabolical clocks with those whose characters are reflected by timepieces that are old, imprecise, and benevolent has honorable antecedents among nineteenth-century novelists. In Hardy's *Far From the Madding Crowd,* one can compare the gold repeater of the Mephistophelian Sergeant Troy with the large and benevolent old watch of Gabriel Oak. And in Dickens's novels, Master Humphrey's old clock or Sam Weller's large old watch may be similarly compared with the expensive gold repeaters of Mr. Jaggers or of Scrooge.

In Mr. Charrington's junk shop we naturally associate his "long, benevolent nose, and mild eyes" with the "friendly ticking" of his "old-fashioned glass clock with a twelve-hour face . . . on the mantelpiece," and his stock of "tarnished watches that did not even pretend to be in going order." For Winston, the room above Charrington's junk shop "was sanctuary. It was as when Winston had gazed into the heart of the [antique glass] paperweight [that he bought from Charrington], with the feeling that it would be possible to get inside that glassy world, and that once inside it time could be arrested." Even when Julia and Winston visit the country, and despite the "military precision" with which the journey had to be accomplished, paradoxically and exceptionally, Winston "had no watch."

The turning point of the novel comes when Winston learns that the antique shop itself is controlled by O'Brien's Thought Police—or, on another level, that they have access to the workings of his mind. Winston's milieu now changes immediately from the apparent benevolence of Charrington's shop—where he appreciated the ability to lose his sense of time—to the so-called Ministry of Love where he is tortured because, since there are "no clocks and no daylight [,] it was hard to gauge the time." But there he loses even the sense of a present chronology. Winston estimates that he might have been there for "Days, weeks [,] months—I think it is months." In Room 101—where prisoners' individual nightmares, as uncovered by the Thought Police, are reified and turned against themselves—Winston only proves that he is worthy of loving Big Brother when he begs in desperation that Julia's body should be "thrust between himself" and the rats that terrify him. Only then and immediately after "sacrificing" Julia is he thrust back into time and we find him in the Chestnut Tree Cafe at the "lonely hour of fifteen" and at the beginning of the last chapter.

The novel, which began on a bright cold day in April, passes in seasonal sequence through the first visit to Charrington's junk shop, the purchase of the paperweight, the meetings with Julia, and their coming together in the country on "the second of May" when the "air seemed to kiss one's skin." They only succeed in making love once more during May, but meet no less than seven times during June, symbolically the month of the summer solstice. This leads up to the turning point in the plot—as also in the year—when Winston asks, "Would not the light be fading at twenty-one hours on an August evening?" And indeed, in synchrony with the passage of the seasons, the light of their love was fading during the ensuing autumn and winter when their relationship was to be tested and found wanting. In practice, the workings of the Thought Police interpenetrate the minds of men and women so completely that we can never be sure of the identity, affiliations, beliefs, and stability—let alone trustworthiness—of O'Brien,

Mr. Charrington, or even Julia, and perhaps Winston. But for those who have strayed, even in thought, from an unquestioning love for Big Brother, the only inevitability is the punishment, confession, repentance, and reintegration before death that is demanded of Winston.

When Winston and Julia meet only once again, the seasons have run through their equally inevitable pattern from the rising hope of spring and summer to the increasing death symbolism of fall and winter, but without the Christian hope for eternal bliss as Easter approaches. Winston had known from the beginning that "The past was dead, the future was unimaginable. . . . And in front of him there lay not death but annihilation." This had been confirmed by O'Brien in the last part of the novel: "You will be annihilated in the past as well as in the future." And it is further confirmed for us in the symbolism of the season when Winston and Julia last meet "on a vile biting day in March, when the earth was like iron and all the grass seemed dead." The only possibility for a glimmer of hope lay in the publication of Winston's diary in the form of Orwell's novel of warning—*Nineteen Eighty-Four*.

[S.L.M.]

See also **Utopias and Dystopias**.

FURTHER READINGS

Buitenhuis, Peter, and Ira B. Nadel, eds. *George Orwell: A Reassessment*. London: Macmillan, 1988.

Crick, Bernard. *George Orwell: A Life*. 1980; reprint, Harmondsworth: Penguin, 1982. See pp. 546 and 582–585 for Orwell "hesitating between [the titles] Nineteen Eighty-Four and The Last Man in Europe."

Macey, Samuel L. "George Orwell's *1984*: The Future That Becomes the Past." *English Studies in Canada* 11.4 (December 1985): 450–458. Reprinted in *George Orwell: A Reassessment*. Ed. Peter Buitenhuis and Ira B. Nadel. London: Macmillan, 1988. 23–31, and 189.

PARTITIONING THE DAY

Ancient Egyptians used to partition the day into a number of unequal or temporal hours. The lengths of these hours varied with the changing length of the daylight period throughout the year. At Cairo, for example, in the latitude of about thirty degrees north, there are approximately fourteen hours of daylight by the modern clock at midsummer, and ten hours at midwinter. Since the Egyptians divided the day and night into twelve unequal or temporal hours, this meant that at midsummer the hour contained seventy modern minutes during the day and fifty such minutes during the same night. But at midwinter in that town the hours contained fifty minutes by day and seventy minutes by night.

Though unequal hours may seem burdensome to us, they were not inconvenient to 95 percent of ancient Egyptians who lived and worked on the land. With almost no artificial light, most of the work had to be performed during daylight hours. Thus, shadows cast by the sun were used to mark the passage of time during daylight. In latitudes where the sun was positioned directly overhead, hours were measured by the length of the shadow, and, in more northerly latitudes, by the direction of the shadow. Originally, people kept track of time by observing the shadow cast by a tree or obelisk. The earliest extant shadow clock is a fragment from Egypt of ca. 1500 B.C. The sundial, an improvement upon the simple shadow clock, first appeared in Rome about 290 B.C., but the number of people using it had proliferated considerably by the time it was described in several forms in Vitruvius's *De architectura* in the first century A.D.

Using the entire day as a unit of time seemed natural, but choosing the number of units into which a day might be divided was more arbitrary. The twelve-hour system for day or night, on which the modern global twenty-four-hour system is based, was common but not universally accepted. Georges Ifrah feels that a widespread duodecimal finger-counting method may have been a factor in leading the ancient Egyptians to such a system. As early as 2100 B.C., the Egyptians divided the modern twenty-four-hour solar day into ten daylight hours, two twilight hours, and twelve night hours. By about 1300 B.C., this system had been simplified to twelve daylight hours and twelve night hours. The latter system was also used by the Babylonians, who, according to Herodotus, passed it on to the

Greeks. Though the Hindus came to use sixty subunits, the Chinese and the Japanese divided the solar day into twelve subunits, and Saxon sundials divided the day into four "tides," a practice still reflected in our terms *noontide* and *eventide*. Similarly, military forces divided day and night into three or four watches, a system still extant in the timekeeping of the Royal Navy. Monastic life was regulated by a daily order of work and prayer introduced by Saint Benedict in the sixth century. The eight canonical hours of matins (midnight), lauds, prime (6:00 A.M.), terce (9:00 P.M.), sext (noon), none (3:00 P.M.), vespers, and compline played an important part in regularizing life.

Though the night was also divided into unequal hours, it clearly could not be marked off by the passage of the sun. The mean solar day is now considered to begin at midnight, at the nadir of the sun's apparent motion, but in the past the beginning of the day was often marked by sunrise or sunset. We can still observe this tradition in the Jewish theological day, which begins at sunset, and in the Royal Navy's watch system, in which the first watch begins at 8:00 P.M.

Other methods of measuring time were developed which did not depend on the sun's movement. For example, short periods of time were measured by activities, and in primitive countries such methods of time measurement still exist. In Madagascar, the expression "rice cooking" means half an hour while "the frying of a locust" denotes a moment. This type of measurement, primarily of local significance, is not readily adaptable to unequal hours, yet nor were King Alfred's candles, sandglasses, the sinkingbowl type of water clock, or the water clocks known to have been used for limiting lawyers' speeches in classical times.

Sundials were relatively simple instruments that soon became the most popular devices for denoting time. Other devices created to represent the progress of time as measured by unequal hours were frequently subjected to complex adjustments. For example, the Cairo Museum possesses an early Egyptian water clock, or clepsydra, of ca. 1400 B.C. which measures time by the flow of water from a hole near the bottom. Although it would be much easier to measure equal hours with such a device, there are a series of water levels marked on the inside of this water tank which divide the average night for particular months into twelve equal parts.

The transition to equal from unequal or temporal hours began with the development of mechanical clocks in the fourteenth century, although even these machines were at first subjected to the complication of measuring unequal or temporal hours. For 300 years, the main escapement controlling mechanical clocks was the verge and foliot. Driven by weights, the escapement was not isochronous by modern standards, and so these clocks were accurate only within ten or fifteen minutes each day. Nonetheless, the verge and foliot escapement represents an invention of great importance. This device may have started out by regulating the work and prayer of monks, but it soon measured out the lives of many other humans.

The next great step in the improvement of time measurement, the pendulum escapement, derived from the demands of astronomy subsequent to the publication of the heliocentric views of Copernicus in *De revolutionibus orbium coelestium* (1543). Attempting to provide the greater precision required by Tycho Brahe and Johannes Kepler, Jost Burgi produced a crystal clock (ca. 1600) with separate rock-crystal dials for hours, minutes, and seconds; this is one of the first recorded uses of the second hand. Galileo is said to have noted the isochronous quality of a swinging lamp in the cathedral of Pisa, and to have tested this against his pulse (ca. 1581 or 1582). Astronomers were soon using pendulums maintained by hand in their observations. Christiaan Huygens united the clock and the pendulum in 1657, using the clock both to maintain the movement of the pendulum and count the number of its relatively isochronous swings. This single invention increased the accuracy of clocks more than sixty-fold. The year 1658, when the first known pendulum clock appeared

in England, marks the beginning of a British horological revolution.

Though Robert Hooke also claimed the invention, Huygens's spring-balance escapement of 1674 permitted clocks to become portable, thus making the clock available for the purposes of navigation. Since an accurate marine clock is essential in the determination of one's precise position at sea, the needs of navigators prompted the invention of chronometers. Latitude is easily determined with only a sextant and a compass, which are employed to measure the angle between the sun, the ship, and the horizon when the sun is directly to the north or the south (local noon time). Because the earth spins on its axis, it is an incomparably more difficult task to compute one's longitude. However, with an accurate clock regulated to the time at Greenwich, a seaman would be able to compare the time of the local noon with that of Greenwich noon. If local noon occurred at 3:00 P.M. Greenwich time, he could determine his longitude to be forty-five degrees ($^3/_{24}$ of 360 degrees) west of the Greenwich meridian.

The ability to determine longitude accurately was not essential when sea voyages were short and seamen could find their way by dead reckoning in known and charted waters. However, it became much more necessary to measure longitude in the late fifteenth century, when traders sought westward routes to the Far East as the era of long sea voyages from Europe began. In 1714, the British Admiralty offered a prize of £20,000 (the equivalent of more than $1 million today) for the discovery of a method to determine longitude at sea. By 1761, at the end of the horological revolution, John Harrison's fourth chronometer erred by no more than fifteen seconds after a five-month voyage to the West Indies and back.

The increased accuracy of clocks following the development of the pendulum escapement affected time measurement. It was known as early as the fifth century B.C. that the length of the solar day was not uniform throughout the year. The discrepancy between the lengths of the solar day (apparent day) and the mean solar day (clock day), known as the "equation of time," arises from two factors: the variable velocity of the earth related to its elliptical orbit around the sun, and the variable apparent velocity of the sun, which is variable because its apparent motion is in a plane inclined to the equator. Though the effect of the equation of time was to make the apparent time of the solar day fifteen minutes longer than the mean solar day in February and about seventeen minutes shorter around November, the inaccuracy of the verge and foliot escapement effectively masked this discrepancy. Although it did not obviate the need to set one's clock by a sundial until at least the latter part of the eighteenth century, the advent of pendulum clocks resulted in attempts to produce mean solar time. This was effected by adjusting sundials to allow for the equation of time, or by using the equation-of-solar-time tables printed on "watch papers" as a form of advertising from about 1700. Eventually, states imposed local mean time so that everyone in a community would use the same time. In 1780, Geneva was the first to do this, then England in 1792, Berlin in 1810, and Paris in 1816.

The industrial revolution promoted further improvements of time measurement, because it produced the post office, the railways, and the telegraph, all of which brought many local mean times into conflict. The inevitable outcome was the institution of a single time zone to cover the whole of Britain. In November of 1840, the Great Western Railway ordered that London time should be kept at all its stations and in all its timetables. Other railways quickly followed suit, and Greenwich mean time soon became the *de facto* standard for the whole country. On August 2, 1880, the Statutes (Definition of Time) Bill, which stated that any legal mention of a time would be considered as referring to Greenwich mean time, received royal assent. Britain's earlier problems with the inconsistencies of local time measurement became global problems, and so an International Meridian Conference was called in 1884. At the instigation of Sir Sandford Fleming of Canada and Charles F. Dowd of the United States, Greenwich mean time was adopted as the universal time standard. The globe was divided into twenty-four meridians that were 15 degrees apart in longitude starting from Greenwich. Each meridian was at the center of one of twenty-four time zones in which the time adopted would be uniform. This system is, by and large, the one under which the world still operates today, and it provides universal map coordinates as well as universal time measurement.

Human perception of time has changed with technological advancements. When England was still using unequal hours in the late fourteenth century, Chaucer felt compelled to explain the difference between the unequal hours used commonly and the equal hours used in astronomy in his *Treatise on the Astrolabe* (1391). In his translation *On the Properties of Things* (1398), John Trevisa listed the average number of hours in the night and day for each month. He also differentiated between the daylight day ("natural" day) and the twenty-four-hour day ("artificial" day). However, in *Utopia* (1516), Thomas More stresses that his Utopians use only equal hours. By the time of William Shakespeare (1564–1616), the use of equal hours is assumed. In Japan and some parts of the Mediterranean world, temporal hours were used well into the nineteenth century. Rejecting Western influence, Japan built its own clocks with twin verge and foliot escapements, one for day and one for night. A clockmaker would adjust the weights on each foliot about once every two weeks, to measure the average unequal or temporal hour for that two-week period. The equal hours of European time reckoning were not introduced to Japan until 1873.

Modern pressures for further improvements come not so much from marine navigators as from astronomers and physicists, the navigators of the universe, and the precision of time measurement has increased considerably. For example, Chaucer had no conception of the length of a minute, and Trevisa envisioned the quarter of an hour, a relatively long period of time by our reckoning, as a "point" in time. Shakespeare shared the modern conception of a minute, but the "second" does not appear anywhere in his canon. We are now able to measure time so precisely that leap seconds are added to clocks, and we are building clocks with an accuracy of one second in 30,000 or even 100,000 years. The measurement of the second itself is no longer related to the macromovements of the solar system; since 1967, the atomic second has been defined as the duration of $9,192,631,770 \pm 20$ particular oscillations within a cesium-133 atom.

[S.L.M.]

See also **Calendar: Western; Chronology; Numbers, History of; Standard Time: Time Zones and Daylight Saving Time.**

FURTHER READINGS

Bilfinger, Gustav. *Die mittelalterlichen Horen und die modernen Stunden*. 1892; reprint, Wiesbaden: Sändig, 1969.

Cowan, Harrison J. *Time and Its Measurement: From the Stone Age to the Nuclear Age*. Cleveland: World Publishing, 1958.

Hellyer, Brian. *Man the Timekeeper*. London: Priory P, 1974.

Hood, Peter. *How Time Is Measured*. 2nd ed. London: Oxford UP, 1969.

Macey, Samuel L. *The Dynamics of Progress: Time, Method, and Measure.* Athens: U of Georgia P, 1989.

Review of British Standard Time. London: Her Majesty's Stationery Office, 1970.

Risley, Allan S. *The National Measurement System for Time and Frequency.* Washington: U.S. Department of Commerce, National Bureau of Standards, 1976.

Springer, Max. *Mensch, Zeit, Uhr: zur Geschichte der Zeitmessung.* Berlin: Ullstein, 1927.

Standard Time in the United States: A History of Standard and Daylight Saving Time in the United States and an Analysis of the Related Laws. Washington: U.S. Department of Transportation. Office of Assistant General Counsel for Regulation, 197.

Welch, Kenneth F. *Time Measurement: An Introductory History.* Newton Abbot: David and Charles, 1972.

PASSAGE OF TIME

It is a commonplace of literature, ancient and modern, that time flows; the metaphor of a river is used again and again. One can of course make this part of one's personal definition of time and many people do, but it is not easily incorporated into a logically coherent account of the world. If I adopt such a view, do I flow with the river or not? On the one hand, I observe events passing and the world growing older around me, which suggests that I stand on the bank while the river flows past; on the other hand, I myself grow older. Perhaps I too am borne along in the river; in that case, how is it that I perceive people and things changing around me? Reflections such as these invite the question, is the passage of time a fact or is it nothing more than a somewhat faulty metaphor?

If time is really a flow, we can ask the same question that we ask of any motion: how fast is it? One might reply that time gets one second later each second, so that it flows at a rate of one second per second. Clearly this says nothing; it is as if one were to ask what a dollar is worth and be told 100 cents. The value of a dollar is determined by what goods and services it will buy; the quantity of time is measured by what happens in it. Thus we loosely define a day in terms of a revolution of the earth about its axis and the rhythm of human life which this imposes. We derive our idea of time from watching what happens to people and clocks and things that act as clocks.

There are many clocks and they do not all keep the same time. What distinguishes a good clock from a bad one? In the Middle Ages, monks painted stripes at equal spacing around a candle in order to time religious services when the sun was down. Today we have better clocks controlled by the oscillations of atoms of cesium or hydrogen, and we say that their accuracy is of the order of one second in 1 million years. What entitles us to claim that the atom is a better clock than the candle? Candles vary from one to another; the oscillating atoms in any atomic clock are all alike. Candles burn unevenly according to wind and other environmental accidents which we may not fully understand; the environments of the atoms are carefully controlled. The burning of a candle is a complicated process, but we understand very well the motions of atoms. Finally, there is a simple empirical test: several candle clocks in a room will not all burn at the same rate, whereas different atomic clocks agree to enormous accuracy.

However time is measured, it is measured by events and not by some property intrinsic to itself. It seems simplest to regard time as a scale analogous to the scale we use to measure distance. The ticks of a kitchen clock are events that help to measure time just as the markings on a yardstick help to measure distance. Ordinarily, we estimate the "passage of time" by observing the progress of events, and of all such events, the ones we know best are those that occur inside our own heads and create the orderly march of consciousness. It is events that pass, not time.

[D.A.P.]

FURTHER READINGS

Park, David. *The Image of Eternity.* U of Massachusetts P, 1980.

Williams, Donald C. "The Myth of Passage." *Journal of Philosophy* 48 (1951): 457–472.

PEIRCE, CHARLES SANDERS (1839–1914)

Charles Peirce was a scientist, logician, and philosopher whose achievements as well as ambitions invite comparison with Leibniz, if not Aristotle. His was a truly encyclopedic mind, one equipped to explore topics ranging from the pronunciation of Shakespearean English to theories of cosmic evolution; however, his energies were directed primarily toward opening new fields of inquiry (for example, semiotics or the general study of signs) and reforming traditional disciplines (philosophy, logic, and psychology). For him, the traditional discipline of philosophy was especially in need of reform; and the only way of achieving this aim was to transform philosophy into a science. In addition, he argued that the first rule of reason is: Do not block the path of inquiry. Peirce's efforts to transform philosophy into a science and his efforts to facilitate the work of virtually all scientific investigators are of a piece. On the one hand, his philosophy has, above all, a heuristic function. On the other, the discoveries of the experimental sciences, along with the disclosures of our everyday experience, provide the only materials out of which we can responsibly construct a comprehensive theory of ourselves and our world. The task of constructing such a theory is something all human beings undertake, though for the most part uncritically.

Peirce's own efforts to formulate a theory of the cosmos and of humanity's place within the cosmos culminated in a number of doctrines for which he coined rather forbidding names from Greek roots. *Tychism* was the term he devised for his doctrine of objective or absolute chance. In opposition to the determinist, the tychist maintains that the occurrence of apparently random events should not be explained away but in some cases taken as an irreducible fact about the real world. Randomness as well as regularity—chance as well as law—is a feature of nature. *Synechism* is the doctrine that the concept of continuity provides the key to understanding at least some of the most important questions of traditional metaphysics, including questions regarding the nature of time and that of being itself. In opposition to the atomist, the synechist does not suppose that any actual or even merely imaginable being can be analyzed into absolutely simple units: all things are at bottom continua of one form or another. Time itself is a continuum in which one segment flows seamlessly into another.

But, for Peirce, philosophy encompasses more than metaphysics; it also includes phenomenology and the normative sciences. The principal task of phenomenological inquiry is the elaboration of an integrated set of universal categories (concepts present in all fields of inquiry and at all levels of discourse). Peirce's own phenomenological investigations led him to the conclusion that there are three such categories—firstness (what something is in itself, apart from all else), secondness (what a thing is as a result of its oppositions to other things), and thirdness (what a thing is by virtue of connecting two or more other things—in short, by virtue of functioning as a medium). Peirce identified three normative sciences: logic, ethics, and esthetics. Logic is conceived by him in a somewhat novel manner to be the theory of self-critical and self-con-

trolled inquiry, while here ethics designates the theory of self-controlled conduct in general (inquiry being but one species of such conduct) and esthetics designates an investigation into the ideals animating and informing conduct, with special attention being paid to the ultimate aim of human action. He himself identified this aim as the continuous growth of concrete "reasonabless," a power embodied in concrete habits of action, thought, and receptivity.

Peirce's thought bears in various ways upon the topic of time. Three important respects in which it does so concern his cosmological theories (above all, his thoroughgoing evolutionism), his theory of inquiry, and his explicit, pragmatic treatment of past, present, and future. In his version of evolutionism, it is inadequate to suppose that the laws of nature are themselves fixed; rather we must suppose that these very laws have emerged in the course of cosmic evolution. The procedures, standards, and norms of investigation are also not fixed, but evolved and evolving dimensions of an irreducibly historical process (human inquiry). Finally, Peirce addressed in "Issues of Pragmaticism" (1905) the question "What is Time?" for the purpose of illustrating his pragmaticism (his distinctive form of pragmatism). According to this doctrine, the highest level of clarification is attained not by appealing to our supposed intuitions or even by producing abstract definitions, but by tracing the bearing of our words and utterances upon our experience and action. Approached thus, the *meaning* of the past is that segment of time which has attained the status of unalterable actuality and the force of an insistent presence; the present is the nascent state of the actual and the future is a more or less delimited array of possibilities.

[V.C.]

See also **Phenomenology; Pragmatism.**

FURTHER READINGS

Apel, Karl-Otto. *Charles S. Peirce: From Pragmatism to Pragmatism*. Amherst U of Massachusetts P, 1981.

Colapietro, Vincent. *Peirce's Approach to the Self: A Semiotic Perspective on Human Subjectivity*. Albany: State U of New York P, 1989.

Esposito, Joseph L. *Evolutionary Metaphysics: The Development of Peirce's Theory of Categories*. Athens: Athens UP, 1980. Chapter 5.

Hookway, Christopher. *Peirce*. London: Routledge and Kegan Paul, 1985.

Peirce, Charles S. "Issues of Pragmatism." *Charles S. Peirce: The Essential Writings*. Ed. Edward C. Moore. New York: Harper & Row, 1972. 281–299.

PERIODIZATION

"Periodization" or "periodizing" (< Greek *periodos*, circuit, period of time) is the practice of subdividing, and of interrelating, historically significant units of time. This article will consider the problems intrinsic to periodization, especially with regard to arbitrariness, complexity, scope, and flexibility; it will enumerate three approaches to periodization: the chronological, the developmental, and the individual; and it will survey the development of periodization in Western history. Periodization has proven to be an important means of comprehending history, specifically and generally.

RELATIVITY, COMPLEXITY, PERSPECTIVE

Because of its very nature, periodization can be an arbitrary and complex practice. To begin with, the measure used to subdivide history is often determined by the outlook, ability, and beliefs of the historian. Affected by many factors, such a measure must take into account all aspects of a respective culture; for example, a putatively comprehensive analysis of European history at the revolutionary juncture of the eighteenth and nineteenth century, could not possibly limit itself to political concerns and omit economic, philosophical, artistic, theological, and military factors, all of which had interacted, along with chance, circumstance, and other imponderables, to determine events and to define this particular milieu.

In addition to historical relativity and complexity, one must take perspective into account. At best, the practice of periodization is a limited endeavor, for when periodical schemes are applied to world history, inaccuracies, generalizations, and distortions are likely to increase.

Yet, despite these considerations, periodization remains a useful, if not an essential, tool in the study of history. Generalization, arbitrariness, and distortion remain ever-present dangers that can be minimized if a scheme, definition, or descriptive term, such as the "Middle Ages" or the "Renaissance," remains flexible and responsive to authentic research. Similarly, the subdivisions of geological time, and the ascription of life-forms to specific epochs, are subject to new discoveries in paleontology and geology. In a very fundamental sense, periodization provides a relative means of categorizing facts and of orientating oneself temporally. One can reasonably say that without periodization mankind would lose relative perspective and the ability to understand how ideas and institutions develop. Periodization defeats its purpose—which is to arrange natural and human phenomena on a continuum and to derive meaning from this arrangement—when it becomes self-confining, ideologically rigid, and resistant to knowledge.

APPROACHES

There are essentially three approaches to periodization that can be used independently or interdependently (Gerhard, 476b). The first, the linear or chronological, enumerates centuries, years, and key events or turning points in history. Often, the beginning of an era, such as the Judaic, Christian, or Muslim, reveals an underlying and dominant theology or philosophy. The second type of periodization is developmental: a given period is a phase in a larger evolutionary pattern. Concepts of growth and decay, of progress, and of climax are inherent in this approach. Like the chronological approach, which is arbitrary to the degree that the chronologist's beliefs determine where to begin or what to emphasize, developmental periodization presupposes a "teleology": a final cause is the goal of history and each phase or event contributes to its fulfillment. The force impelling and determining history, for example, can be either theological (providence) or secular (liberty). The third category of periodization, historical individuality, defines a period according to its essence or prevailing character, such as the "industrial" revolution, the "age of reason," and so forth. To a lesser degree in the natural sciences, where quantitative data leave less room for interpretation, these three approaches can be highly subjective; that is, the periodic historian, whether realizing it or not, will be influenced by received knowledge, by tradition, and by personal attitudes and beliefs.

WESTERN HISTORIOGRAPHY

The periodization of Western historiography incorporates the chronological, developmental, and individual approaches. Greek historiography was largely pragmatic and rational, concentrating on political analysis. Hesiod's *Theogony*, and *Works and Days,* contain evidence of periodical historiography, affirming that the human race originated in a golden age and that the human past could be divided into five contiguous eras devolving from this pristine beginning. Even though the imaginative and mythological content of Hesiod's work differentiates it from factual historiography, it indicates, nevertheless, that Hesiod did in fact think in historical terms: human history was a processive continuum, and each age possessed a distinguishing characteristic. Roman historians also had a sense of an historical beginning. Annalists such as Livy, from the second century B.C., popularized a chronological approach allegedly dating from the legendary founding of Rome (753 B.C.).

Theologians of the early church adapted the chronological concept of the creation of the world from Genesis. From the third century A.D., they constructed a chronological sequence consisting of "world periods" or *aetates* prior to Christ; each period was presumed to be a millennium, and world history consisted of six millennia altogether, a number derived from the literal interpretation of key biblical texts in both Testaments. In the seventeenth and eighteenth centuries, this dating from Creation would be replaced by B.C. A new Christian worldview developed in the Middle Ages with the formulation of the *anno domini* or A.D. designation for time posterior to the Incarnation, the central event of history. Similarly, the Second Coming and the Last Judgment were considered the terminal events of historical time. This broad eschatological framework had no other subdivisions, for the most historically (and theologically) significant time unit was the millennium.

Secular periodization complemented the eschatological schemes. For instance, the doctrine of the four world empires, derived from the Book of Daniel, was applied to the imperial historiography of Christian Rome. The Roman, therefore, was considered to be the last historical empire. From this concept came the notion of *translatio imperii*—that the empire had been transferred from the Romans to the Franks by the coronation of Charlemagne, and later of Otto the Great. Medieval historiographers would be greatly influenced by these imperial schemes, for there was still no need for the numerical subdivision of history.

The concept of *centuria*, coined by the humanists, gradually replaced the broad designation of *saeculum*, which represented a sequence of generations or even an infinite sequence of time. Terms like *siècle*, used by Voltaire in the *Siècle de Louis XIV*, periodized history more precisely. Reacting against Christian periodization, represented especially by Bossuet's *Discours sur l'histoire universelle* (1681), Voltaire spoke of "modern history" since the fall of the Roman Empire. To Voltaire, the adjective "modern" meant all of European history since the end of antiquity.

Professional historians such as Georg Hornius (1620–1670) and Christopher Cellarius (1638–1707) began to experiment with new periodical methods, emphasizing historical evolution and the uniqueness of cultures and civilizations. During the Enlightenment, the greatest strides in periodical historiography were made. From the idea of progress arose two lines of development in the philosophy of history—the positivist and the dialectical—which would influence historical periodization into the twentieth century. One major example of positivist periodization is Auguste Comte's "law of the three stages" of historical development: the theological, the metaphysical, and the positive or scientific. G.W.F. Hegel (1770–1831), Herbert Spencer (1820–1903), and Karl Marx (1818–1883) also contributed significant dialectical schemes for the understanding of history.

CONCLUSION

The purpose of this survey is to suggest that periodization is an inveterate practice employed by the greatest minds of Western history. All periodical historians, no matter what their discipline or doctrinal orientation, share the common desire to organize historical time into a discernible and meaningful pattern. Though often highly speculative, periodization has permitted historical thinkers to focus on, and to organize, history.

[C.D.]

See also **Chronology; Eschatology; Hegel, Gottfried Wilhelm Friedrich; Historiography and Process; Marx, Karl; Millenarianism.**

FURTHER READINGS

Butterfield, Herbert. "Historiography." *Dictionary of the History of Ideas: Studies of Selected Pivotal Ideas*. Ed. Philip P. Wiener. 5 vols. New York: Scribner's, 1973. 2:464a–498b.

Breisach, Ernst. *Historiography: Ancient, Medieval, and Modern*. Chicago: U of Chicago P, 1983.

Collingwood, R.G. *The Idea of History*. Oxford: Oxford UP, 1975.

Gerhard, Dietrich. "Periodization in History." *Dictionary of the History of Ideas*. 3:476a–481b.

Wellek, René. "Periodization in Literary History." *Dictionary of the History of Ideas*. 3:481b–486a.

PETRARCH, FRANCIS (1304–1374)

In the development of the Renaissance conception of time, Francis Petrarch (Francesco Petrarca) is a seminal mind and of supreme historical importance. Showing the convergence of many forces, including that of an heroic humanism with a poetic renascence, Petrarch's works, early and late, in prose as well as in poetry, regard time as a constant presence and warfare against time as one of their most persistent concerns. In his collection of sonnets and odes, the *Rime*, in his later *Trionfi*, time is a dominating presence and an object of frequent address. In his letters to friends, the collection of which has become a treasure-trove for understanding intelligent fourteenth-century opinion, he not only shows his complex awareness of the issues of this war against time, but also his own inspiration in the thought of the Roman moral philosophers. In his more systematic prose, the so-called "Coronation Oration," where temporal significance is basic to the symbolism of the laurel, his *Secretum*, *The Life of Solitude*, in the great polemics of his later life, such as *Of His Own Ignorance (and That of Many Others)*, time is a primary force against whose depredations Petrarch advocates the virtues of love and beauty, fame, and the collective powers of culture and civilization themselves. Finally, in a mode of recantation so common to the fourteenth century, time itself becomes the great force that dwarfs all human accomplishment and obliges Petrarch, in his quest for those things that endure, to look outside of time and history.

We have more precise information about the life of Petrarch than we have about the lives of any human being who lived before him (and of many who came after). This is because he himself was so careful in his letters and prose works, and in his poetry as well, to provide exact information not only as to years but to dates and even hours. Such temporal pinpointing is itself an expression of the humanist's interest in the shelter that history itself can provide. Rather than suffering all things to be dissolved in an undifferentiated flux, his aim is to redeem human discourse, and one such way is to give to events a definite connection in historical time. Petrarch's love poetry performs the same function. In his memorable sequence of poems dedicated to Laura, one of the principles of arrangement is a loose chronology. In poem after poem, Petrarch goes "counting the years," marking the anniversaries of significant points in this love affair. Such moments in time are part of the larger continuing discourse of history, one in which Petrarch rises above his time to communicate with the ancients. In fact, Petrarch may be credited with having invented the tripartite view of history that began to emerge in the fourteenth century: the great model of the classical age, an intervening middle, or dark age, and the current age of cultural rebirth, or Renaissance.

War against time was an integral part of the new heroic humanism. Petrarch gave lasting expression to this impulse when he declared, *"ingentibus animis breve nihil optabile est"* ("to the great of soul nothing brief is worthy"). The two qualities that seem to have the power to surmount time, and that thus call forth noble qualities of human nature, are love and fame. Thus it is that Petrarch can devote literally hundreds of poems to Laura, the *donna gentile*, who in the perfectness of her beauty and her ways seems to represent the best that nature can produce. His devotion to fame was among the most fervent of the Renaissance. "The immense desire for praise," serves in part to explain the inner forces that move the aspiring poet to scorn common pleasures. "The desire for glory is innate not merely in the generality of men but in greatest measure in those who are of some wisdom and some excellence." From the Roman writers (Ovid, Statius, Virgil, and others), he quotes fiery professions of the permanence of their works and of their power to confer immortality. Later Renaissance poets who would imitate Petrarch in praising the beauty of a woman, would also follow him in committing their efforts to the promises held by fame.

Petrarch gives expression to the many facets of time in the Renaissance. In an earlier letter, he is able to describe even his increased appreciation of time: "I knew that time was precious, but I did not know it was priceless." If the motivating force of this simple irreplaceability of time is heroic, the means themselves can be quite mundane. Petrarch is the first to show this dual nature of temporal response: Time as a cosmic force calls forth very mundane and diligent methods. In fact, in one of his most crucial letters on ways of compensating for life's brevity, he draws up a time schedule. He tries to get by on six hours of sleep, two hours for other necessities, and the rest for earnest study and writing. Looking ahead, we can see a more detailed version of this scheduling in Rabelais' new educational methods for his somnolent giants, Pantagruel and Gargantua. Toward his heroic end, Petrarch is prepared to utilize every moment. Like the Emperor Augustus, Petrarch, while shaving or having his hair cut, is read to, or dictates to some scribe. And in a practice he feels is unique, he does the same even when eating or riding horseback.

As there are these two cooperative responses to time—the heroic and the mundane—so there is another double aspect of Petrarch's involvement with time, but these are not so compatible. Like others of his age, Petrarch had in mind the extension of the heroic possibilities of humankind, their validity in history itself. But also like others of his age, he sensed behind him the daunting prospect of emptiness, and the vanity of human efforts. Petrarch can envision a limited manageable kind of historical time, in which human effort counts for something, but he can also imagine a time of such vastness and overwhelming power that what human beings accomplish amounts to very little. In his great *Triumph of Time*, one of his larger poetic efforts, Petrarch shows the extent of time's powers. Even to the greatest of names time is a poison. More than death, time is the great equalizer: those who have achieved great things come to the same end as those who have achieved little. Time is the great abyss into which all things slip and can only be surmounted by eternity. In the last poem of his great cycle, Petrarch, like others of his age, posits the triumph of eternity, which provides the surest way of rescuing human endeavor.

[R.J.Q.]

See also **Renaissance.**

FURTHER READINGS

Barolini, Teodolinda. "The Making of a Lyric Sequence: Time and Narrative in Petrarch's *Rerum vulgarium fragmenta*." *Modern Language Notes* 104 (1989): 1–38.

Getto, Giovanni. "*Triumphus Temporis*: Il sentimento del tempo nell'operai Francesco Petrarca." *Letterature comparate: problemie metodo.* Bologna: Patron, 1981. 1243–1272.

Quinones, Ricardo J. "Petrarch." *The Renaissance Discovery of Time.* Cambridge: Harvard UP, 1972. 106–171.

PHENOMENOLOGY

Phenomenology, in the broad meaning of the term, is a philosophical approach that investigates things as they appear, as phenomena. Phenomenology considers some subject matter as it is thought of or meant either by an individual consciousness or by a stage of culture. There are significant differences among the diverse philosophical theories and methods that have called themselves "phenomenology." Most of them share the idea that philosophical investigations must start from a description and analysis of first person experience and conception. Philosophical investigation cannot straightforwardly describe an independent reality completely as it is in itself. At least initially, it must consider things as they show themselves to or are conceived by consciousness. In describing and analyzing some subject matter as it is meant by consciousness, phenomenology tries not to impose any foreign conceptions on the subject matter, but rather to explicate the elements and features involved in it. The phenomenological explication of the elements and features involved in some subject matter also includes what is involved in the thinking of or being conscious of those elements and features.

In the broad meaning of the term, most philosophies throughout history have been in some ways phenomenological. René Descartes's (1596–1650) and other modern philosophers' concern with ideas in the mind and how the mind can know the external world was very phenomenological, although they did not use this term. The German philosopher, Immanuel Kant (1724–1804), distinguished "phenomena," that is, things as they appear within the necessary structures of the mind, from "noumena" or things as they are in themselves. Georg Hegel's *Phenomenology of Spirit* (1807) considered phenomenology to be the observation of the dialectical self-development of stages of knowledge and culture. Hegel's phenomenology observed how features of complex conceptions reveal their conflicts with each other and give rise to improved conceptions that overcome these conflicts.

In the twentieth century, the term "phenomenology" has been mainly associated with a philosophical movement whose leading figure was the German philosopher, Edmund Husserl (1859–1938). Husserl considered phenomenology to be the only method through which philosophical knowledge could be attained. The method involves a special type of reflecting on one's own first-order mental life. While suspending for itself any claims about independent reality, the reflecting consciousness observes, describes, and analyzes both what is meant in first-order consciousness and how it is meant. The reflector then seeks to discover the essential natures of what appears in first-order consciousness through actively varying individual instances in imagination. The objective is to let subject matters show themselves as they are rather than to impose classifications or theories on them. Among those who collaborated with Husserl or developed their own, revised versions of phenomenology are Max Scheler (1874–1928), Nicolai Hartmann (1882–1950), Martin Heidegger (1889–1976), Jean-Paul Sartre (1905–1980), and Maurice Merleau-Ponty (1908–1961).

Time is a central concern both for philosophers in the phenomenological movement and for phenomenological thinkers in the broad sense. Time must be considered because subject matter appears to the mind and is thought of "in time." Appearing and thinking are not timeless or instantaneous states. They themselves seem to be "spread out" through time and to occur through time. Appearing and thinking are processes that have both some type of "temporal parts," which are separated by their happening at different moments, and have some type of intrinsic unity through time, which makes the "parts" compose one process. Because appearing and thinking themselves seem to be temporal, an adequate description and analysis of the first person experience and conception of any subject matter must deal with the complexities of time.

Another reason why phenomenologists investigate time is that most things that appear have their own temporal features. The description and analysis of whatever appears has to include the temporal features of the subject matter. The phenomenological movement has been particularly concerned with the different types of temporal features that may apply to different subject matters. The temporality of physical objects may be different from the temporality of historical facts or of tools. Another important concern of phenomenologists in the narrow sense is the relationship between the temporality of first-person lived experience and the temporality of whatever appears to it. Most major phenomenologists have claimed that the temporal features of lived experience are different from the temporal features of anything that appears to lived experience. Human lived experience has different temporal features because it is free and directed toward a possible future. Human lived experience is able to change its goals, rather than automatically continuing to be what it has been. Most phenomenologists have also been idealists about time. They have concluded that the temporal features of whatever appears to human experience depend on the temporal features of human being itself.

Kant is the most well-known and influential philosopher who investigated time in a phenomenological way. Kant claimed that time is most basically a form of intuition through which everything appears to us. Time is not a real feature of things-in-themselves, but rather a structure of the knowing mind itself. Even our own thoughts appear to us to be in time, but this is the result of the form of intuition and the categories through which they appear. Kant had three main reasons for thinking that time was only a structure of the mind. One is that we can know the essential characteristics of any region of time without investigating it empirically; only if time is merely a framework of our experience could we know a priori (without sensory investigation) about its essential characteristics. Another is the supposed contradiction in the nature of time because the world must be thought both to have a beginning in time and not to have a beginning in time. The third is the supposed necessity that the mind exist outside of the causal structure of time in order that morality and freedom be possible.

Husserl's investigations focused on the experience of time. Using his phenomenological method, Husserl described the temporal features both of objects of consciousness and of the mental acts, such as perception and memory, in which we are conscious of intended objects. Both mental acts and intended objects are experienced to be spread out through time and to pass in time. This raises the question how any given moment of a mental act is able to be conscious of those moments of its intended object that are not simultaneous with it. How we are able to be aware of the temporal extension and temporal passing of our own mental acts also needs to be explained. Husserl explained the unreflective awareness of the temporal features of both mental acts and intended objects through a three-featured structure that connects the "temporal parts" of mental life. Each moment of mental life is aware of earlier moments of mental life (with their intended objects) through retention, is aware of what is "now," and is aware of later moments of mental life through protention.

Heidegger tried to elucidate what it is for things to be in terms of the temporality of things. He analyzed the different ways that different types of entities are in and through time. He was particularly concerned with the temporality of human existence, because human acting consciousness discloses and uncovers all things including itself. Human temporal existence is characterized by finding itself thrown into a historical culture, encountering and using present conditions and tools, and being directed toward a future chosen from various alternatives. Human existing in and through time is the unity of these past-, present-, and future-oriented dimensions. Human existence is a temporalizing activity that "opens up" (dis-closes) the temporally structured framework through which all things are encountered.

[P.K.M.]

See also **Descartes, René; Heidegger, Martin; Husserl, Edmund; Kant, Immanuel; Merleau-Ponty, Maurice; Sartre, Jean-Paul.**

FURTHER READINGS

Heidegger, Martin. *Being and Time.* Trans. J. Macquarrie and E. Robinson. New York: Harper & Row, 1962.

Husserl, Edmund. *On the Phenomenology of the Consciousness of Internal Time (1883–1913).* Trans. John Brough. Leiden: Kluwer Academic, 1991.

Kant, Immanuel. *Critique of Pure Reason.* Trans. Norman Kemp Smith. New York: St. Martin's P, 1965.

McInerney, Peter. *Time and Experience.* Philadelphia: Temple UP, 1991.

PHENOMENOLOGY: MUSIC AND TIME

During the latter part of the twentieth century, music scholars have become increasingly concerned with the temporally unfolding nature of musical structures. In recent years they have turned either explicitly or implicitly toward phenomenological philosophy due to its focus on the temporally unfolding nature of human experience.

The work of representative scholars exemplifies one or both of the two predominant directions of phenomenological thought—directions corresponding to the historical development of phenomenology. The first direction is defined by the work of Edmund Husserl, who in the first half of the twentieth century argued that there is no radical split between subject and objective world. Responding to the age-old philosophical problem of how subjects can adequately know a world having independent existence, Husserl argued that subject and world are essentially linked by a relation termed intentionality. Following from this essential correlation, Husserl claimed that a subject can have adequate knowledge of the objective world through a controlled investigation of how the world occurs in human experience. In other words, he argued that the attributes and principles of the objective world reflect subjective knowing.

The phenomenological turn toward experience as a basis for knowledge required a special concern for temporality since the objective world is manifested in the temporal "flow" of human consciousness. Husserl's account of temporal consciousness focused primarily on the sense of the present and its relation to the immediate past (retentional consciousness) and the remembered past. He paid scant attention to the futural dimension of time.

While the first direction of phenomenological thought is characterized by the Husserlian focus on structural features of the objective world as they occur in human experience, the second direction is represented by the philosophy of Martin Heidegger, Husserl's student. It is important to remember, however, that several later authors have further defined it (Merleau-Ponty, Sartre, Gadamer, Foucault, Derrida, and others). Building on the structural insights of a Husserlian investigation, Heidegger turned toward the subjective facets of experience, seeking to uncover the subjective conditions necessary for the experience of a world. This turning toward the existing subject and toward an interpretation of necessary conditions—the existential and hermeneutical turns—is evident in Heidegger's more radical account of temporality.

Heidegger argued that the "ordinary," or Newtonian, conception of time derives from a prior temporal experience—what he called primordial temporality. Demonstrating that the primordial experience is characterized by a spread of past-present-future, he offered a critique of and alternative to the implicit Newtonian features of Husserl's account of time. Heidegger defined five attributes of primordial temporality that are at odds with those of "ordinary" time: (1) durational quantity occurs as relational "spans"; (2) the "datability" of temporality in terms of past, present, and future is oriented by present-awareness and is not a psychological application but rather an intrinsic temporal feature; (3) by virtue of their temporal context, events have a temporal meaning or "significance" that is a defining attribute; (4) the temporality of existence is "public," recognizing and making possible human interactions in the world; and (5) experience is weighted toward the future through our cognitive attempts to anticipate the world. The attributes of the derivative, "ordinary" conception of time—those of a constant flow of objectively existing nows capable of precise quantification—presuppose primordial time. Unlike prior philosophers, Heidegger accounted for the differing conceptions of time in human experience not through a search for the one true time, but rather through an explication of the functions these differing concepts have in human experience. His approach demonstrates the extent to which his existential and hermeneutical concerns dig through the layers of human understanding.

Distinctions between the Husserlian and Heideggerian approaches to time sketched above provide a framework for understanding how representative music scholars have used these philosophical concerns to form a basis for critical and analytical studies of music's temporal structures.

Husserl's temporal model figures explicitly in David Lewin's work. Formulating a model of musical perception over time, Lewin shows how the harmonic structure of a specified present in a particular piece—the example is Schubert's tonal song "Morgengruss"—essentially includes structures of the immediate past and future, and further that as the specified present becomes another, a new harmonic structure with such past and futural features occurs that may entail a reinterpretation of the harmonic structure of a preceding present. A Husserlian interest in structural variability "over" time may be observed in some analyses in Judy Lochhead's work. The analysis of the scherzo from Webern's *Opus 28* string quartet demonstrates how strong and weak metrical beats in the movement's initial section are reinterpreted when exactly repeated due to a temporal reorientation before the repetition. In both Lewin and Lochhead's analyses, the passage of time plays an essential role in the determination of structural types.

Heidegger's concern for the diversity of temporal experience and for the existential significance of such diversity is manifest in several authors' articulation of new conceptual modes for the understanding of music's temporal structures. These modes further reflect the phenomenological stance that experience fully reveals the world; in other words, adequate knowledge of musical structures may be gained through investigation of musical experience. The new modes may be organized into five categories: (1) temporal unities, (2) succession, (3) duration, (4) "datability," and (5) simultaneity.

1. The temporal cohesion of musical unities (traditionally such things as melodies, phrases, harmonies, harmonic progressions, and so forth) is formalized in general terms, allowing the observation of a greater variety of such entities. For example, Jonathan Kramer posits a unique kind of cohesion in some recent music in which large spans of time project a single now or "moment," and Lochhead further characterizes unities by boundaries which may be clear, hazy, or absent.

2. Relations between successive musical entities (that is, order relations) are formulated according to general characteristics of a musical presentation by Kramer and Lochhead. Terms such as causal, linear, directed, and becoming characterize a "dynamic" musical succession; and nonlinear, nondirected, discontinuous, and vertical characterize a "static" succession. Formulating relations between successive temporal unities, Thomas Clifton employs categories of contrast, interruption, and temporal "intercut," the latter a special case of interruption in which the interrupted succession resumes.

3. Following Heidegger's assessment of differing ways in which durational features are manifest, Lochhead posits two durational types. In one, musical events "count out" temporal units whose simple proportional relations (1:1, 1:2, 1:3, and so forth) generate a sense of time that is quantifiable and flows continuously. In the other, events articulate temporal spans whose durational magnitude is defined in relative terms of longer and shorter.

4. Clifton, Kramer, and Lochhead formulate the "datability" of events in terms of temporal functions and their associated chronological place in a temporal process. Each author demonstrates that the functions of beginning, middle, or end may be separated from chronological place and are recognizable by features of musical events that, through convention, suggest such temporal roles. Thus, the function of beginning may occur several times during a musical presentation or in its chronological middle. Similarly, the sounds that chronologically start a piece may not project a beginning temporal function, or a piece may stop but not functionally end.

5. Clifton and Kramer articulate a category of simultaneity, showing how two kinds of autonomous strata function in musical succession. In one case, simultaneous events define distinct strands. In the other instance, successive events define distinct strands in which

the progress of one strand is momentarily suspended while the other proceeds.

Finally, the work of Lawrence Ferrara follows from the second, Heideggerian direction of phenomenological thought. His analyses offer not phenomenologically based concepts of temporal structure, but rather accounts of musical experience that illuminate more of its subjective facets. These interpretations, achieved through an "eclectic" array of analytical approaches, demonstrate a work's "ontological message" which, steeped in Heideggerian thought, is thoroughly temporal.

One may observe vestiges of phenomenological thought and a consequent turn toward temporality in some music scholarship of the 1950s, but the most significant turn away from the conception of music as an object independent of human experience and toward phenomenologically defined temporal structures occurred in the late 1960s. This new approach will likely find its most eloquent formulations in the final decade of the twentieth century.

[J.Lo.]

See also **Derrida, Jacques; Foucault, Michel; Heidegger, Martin; Husserl, Edmund; Merleau-Ponty, Maurice; Sartre, Jean-Paul.**

FURTHER READINGS

Clifton, Thomas. *Music as Heard: A Study in Applied Phenomenology.* New Haven: Yale UP, 1983.

Ferrara, Lawrence. *Philosophy and the Analysis of Music: Bridges to Musical Sound, Form, and Reference.* New York: Excelsior Music P, 1991.

Kramer, Jonathan. *The Time of Music: New Meanings, New Temporalities, New Listening Strategies.* New York: Schirmer, 1988.

Lewin, David. "Music Theory, Phenomenology, and Modes of Perception." *Music Perception* 3 (Summer 1986): 327–392.

Lochhead, Judith. "The Temporal Structure of Recent Music: A Phenomenological Investigation." Ph.D. dissertation, State University of New York at Stony Brook, 1982.

PHILOSOPHERS ON MUSIC AND TIME

Philosophers such as Augustine, Kant, and Hegel used music as an example of their ideas about time, but only in the twentieth century have philosophers developed an extended discussion of music and time. The major questions asked are: (1) How does music involve or create time? (2) Is musical time an example or symbol of other modes of time? If so, what kind of time is musical time a symbol of? Two philosophers are particularly important in this discussion: Susanne Langer and Victor Zuckerkandl.

TIME IN MUSIC

Music is the art of time in several obvious senses and some less obvious ways. First, music is an event, not an object, which is to say that it transpires and the audience perceives its beginning and end. Second, each of the basic elements in music—sounds and silences—exists for short periods of time. Third, the sounds and silences occur in succession or simultaneously. Fourth, repetition (of tones, melodies, phrases, rhythms, and so forth) is a central organizational pattern of music. Fifth, we hear movement in music. Generally, our sense of time is connected to movement—the movement of the hands on a clock, the movement of light, the rotation of the earth. Movement in music is obvious to the ear; the tones move evenly or jerkily up and down.

Rhythm and meter are the two most important temporal elements of music, and their philosophical implications have been investigated most thoroughly by Victor Zuckerkandl in *Sound and Symbol.* As tones succeed one another, the succession of long and short tones and silences is organized into patterns that have some kind of coherence and whose end is perceived as a completion. The pattern is called rhythm and can be heard in a Gregorian chant's unmetered, yet organized, flow of sounds.

Most Western music overlays rhythm with a second factor in organizing musical time: meter. Meter consists of the division of the temporal flow into a regular succession of beats, as well as the regular grouping of beats into measures. In one sense, meter acts as a clock measuring time into equal parts, but in another sense, meter is unlike a clock. Meter is not simply the division of time into beats of equal length, but is also the grouping of beats, such as, for example, the triple meter of "waltz time." Furthermore, what is important in meter is not the succession of beats in a measure, but what occurs between the beats. The first beat initiates a beginning and a moving away, the second provides momentum to continue, and the third marks the return and the demand for another journey. We hear meter when we hear each measure reach a goal and request a "once again." The succession of tones is not simple progression, but progression and recurrence. Each repetition of the wave of meter intensifies the sense of time. (Contrary to most music textbooks, Zuckerkandl shows that meter is not the result of accent.)

In Western music the rhythmic pattern of longer and shorter tones is supported by and is borne along by the metrical wave. Suppose two eighth notes are followed by a half note. In triple meter, the two short notes both occur during the first beat, while the half note is held through beats two and three. The succession of long and short notes is the rhythmic pattern that is layered over the equal (although differentiated) beats of the meter. The tension between rhythm and meter is one of the prime elements in music.

Concerning this description of meter and rhythm, Zuckerkandl asks Kant's question, "What must the world be like in order for such a phenomenon to occur?" Zuckerkandl's answer is that time itself produces meter and rhythm. He directly disputes the scientific theories that say time is a form of experience, an ordering of phenomena. He also rejects the idea that meter and rhythm are merely psychological projections added to our perception of tones.

Zuckerkandl argues that music reveals that time does not merely measure events: it produces events, such as the wave phase of meter and rhythm. He does not mean that time is something separate from the forces that produce rhythm, but that time is the activity of these forces. Time, therefore, is not merely an order or form of experience but is something that can be directly experienced in music. Zuckerkandl argues that music is a temporal art because: (1) tones are given in temporal succession; (2) music "enlists time as force"; (3) in music, time becomes perceivable; and (4) by shaping time, music creates an image of time.

TIME AND MUSIC

Zuckerkandl and Langer answer the second question—the relation between musical time and other types of time—in slightly different ways.

In *Feeling and Form*, Langer outlines the differences between both clock time and our "commonsense" version of time, and musical time. Musical time has a different logical pattern from clock time which is a contrast of various states (such as ticks) that do not themselves change. However, time in music is passage, transience. Langer claims that time in music is "virtual" in the same way that space in a painting is virtual, that is to say, an illusion. The virtual time of music acts as a symbol for our most fundamental experience of time.

Our common sense view of time is a heterogeneous composition of biological time (heartbeats, breathing), inward tensions (pressure to finish a project), outward change (a train roaring by), clock time, changes of the earth (days and seasons), psychological time, and physical sense of time (weariness or aging). For practical purposes, we allow clock time to predominate over this fragmented sense of time. However, musical time absorbs the whole of time-consciousness. Unlike our ordinary experience of time, time in music is unified and completely formed. Thus it can serve as a symbol for our life in time.

Langer agrees with many astute French musicians who recognize that Bergson's aim of finding an adequate symbol for time is fulfilled in music. Although the movement and duration we experience in music are not real, like the actual passage of time which Bergson describes so brilliantly, music is filled with tensions and their resolutions—both times share varying rhythms and pauses of tensions and releases. The similarities make music a good symbol for time. But we must not confuse the two: Unlike actual passage, which is only partly perceived, musical time is both ordered and perceptible.

Zuckerkandl agrees with Langer that music makes time perceivable and allows us to understand time. He also agrees that Bergson's analysis of time most closely resembles time as it appears in music. However, he disagrees with Langer's tendency to subjectivize Bergson's account of the passage of time and to deny the independent reality of musical time. Zuckerkandl asserts that music proves that the time Bergson described is not simply the psychological sense of time, because we find the same time in the objective phenomenon of music. As Zuckerkandl puts it, "This time cannot be 'in me,' it is not 'my time.' It is where music is; I find it where I find music—that is, in the same direction in which I find the sun, the moon, and the stars." Music proves that the physical time abstracted by scientists is not the only objective time. Hence, "he who would inquire about the nature of time would do well to consider the testimony of music, where time represents an active force, not a 'mere formality.'"

Actual, objective time appears in music, but because music is not simply time but an ordering of time, music also offers the means of beholding time. Zuckerkandl would go beyond Langer, who claims that music is a symbol of sentient life, and say that music is a symbol of time in its most fundamental sense. Zuckerkandl claims that music both is time and is a symbol of time.

[J.E.J.]

See also **Augustine; Bergson, Henri; Kant, Immanuel; Music: Western; Phenomenology: Music and Time; Rhythm and Meter in Music.**

FURTHER READINGS

Alperson, Philip. "'Musical Time' and Music as an 'Art of Time.'" *Journal of Aesthetics and Art Criticism* 38 (1980): 407–417.

Brelet, Gisèle. *Le temps musical*. Paris: Presses Universitaires de France, 1949.

Langer, Susanne K. *Feeling and Form*. New York: Scribner's, 1953.

De Selincourt, Basil. "Music and Duration." *Reflection On Art*. Ed. Susanne K. Langer. Baltimore: Johns Hopkins P, 1958. 152–160.

Zuckerkandl, Victor. *Sound and Symbol: Music and the External World*. Trans. Willard R. Trask. New York: Princeton UP, 1956.

PHILOSOPHY OF TIME

From the beginning, philosophers have been puzzled about time. In their speculations may be discerned three sorts of questions: Is time real? What is time? How is time known? Responses to these questions constitute the spectrum of philosophical theories of time.

THE REALITY OF TIME

Since unending changes in visible objects were presented in ordinary experience, and the most radical changes were manifested in the coming into being and the passing away of these objects, Heraclitus professed that all things are in flux. In the infancy of philosophy, time was linked to change; it was conceived as a measure of change, and theorizing about time, primitive as it was, instituted the separation of the variables in the flux from the mathematical fixities of measurement. The discrepancy between the static character of concepts and the flux inspired Parmenides to posit an eternal plenum of *being*—intelligible, perfect, immobile, and immutable—as the sole reality reason can attain. Change, motion, and time were cast out as not-*being*. Still the appearances of change, motion, and time demanded consideration, and in order to save these appearances, Plato offered a theory of reality with two domains: *being* (inclusive of the ideal forms) and *becoming* (embracing all the objects in flux). But Plato elevated *being* to a higher level of reality than *becoming*, and time, he suggested, is but the moving image of eternity.

The question of the reality of time did not subside after Plato. It has continued to perplex thinkers to the very present. All contemporary discussions of the question take their start from J.M.E. McTaggart's analysis. McTaggart noted that temporal change may be construed either in terms of past, present, and future or in terms of the relations of before and after. Upon this distinction he constructed two series: the A series and the B series. The passage from future through present to past is the succession of events he called the A series. The same succession of events related as before and after, earlier and later, is what he called the B series. McTaggart advanced subtle arguments to disprove the reality of time. Because every event in the A series is logically past, present, and future as regards other events, any judgment of its temporal status violates the law of noncontradiction, for it involves attributing the incompatible characteristics of past, present, and future to the same event. Hence, time in the sense of the A series is unreal. Nor does the B series rescue the reality of time. For the succession of events as before and after, earlier than and later than each other, does not capture the meaning of time unless it entails the temporal distinctions between past, present, and future. Hence, the B series is impaled on the same sort of objection that impugned the A series; it is self-contradictory. After demolishing the reality of time to his own satisfaction, McTaggart proposed a C series. In the C series, the concept of succession pertinent to the A series and the B series is abandoned, although the events are retained. In place of succession is substituted the relation of inclusion and being included in. The C series, McTaggart maintained, is real; it is logical and timeless.

Most philosophers have not followed McTaggart's denial of the reality of time. His attack on the B series rests on his assumption that it necessarily entails the use of the temporal characteristics of the A series. However, it is possible to construe the B series without resorting to past, present, and future distinctions, although to do so, McTaggart might have countered, is to eradicate temporality from the sequence. Similarly, his attack on the A series is condemned for his failure to appreciate that judgments of temporality are complex. It is consistent, and therefore not contradictory, to judge an event as past, although it was once present, and from another point in time it is viewed as future. The succession remains intact although the events in the succession undergo altered temporal status. Analytic philosophers have proposed tenseless logic, some adding that temporal terms, like "now" and "the present," are token reflexives. However damaging to McTaggart's arguments these proposals may be, they do not demolish his thesis. For they are compatible with his dismissal of the reality of time. Substituting the relations of inclusion and of being included in for relations expressive of temporal succession, McTaggart's C series offers a spatialized logical whole with affinities to Parmenidean being.

Yet for any center of experience, diminished to a mere part of this whole, the succession of objects, the ground of time in the flux, is real. While time may not exist in the same sense that other objects in the flux exist, because, in part, it is a condition for their existence, time nonetheless is. What is it?

THE NATURE OF TIME

In Book XI of his *Confessions*, St. Augustine asked what is time; he confessed that so long as this question was not raised, he knew what time is, but that, once asked, if he wished to explain what time is, he was perplexed to the point of knowing not. His admission that he knew what time is if no question were asked points toward the primary experience on which all theory rests.

The sense of time springs from the flux of immediate experience. Reflection on this primary experience indicates some generic traits which are salient in the formulation of any philosophical conception of time. First and foremost is the trait of passage, analogical to the flow of a stream or a river. Second is the trait of succession, of sequential change in terms of a before and an after. Third is the trait of directionality; the flux moves in one irreversible direction, philosophically conceptualized as from the future through the present into the past, just as a stream or a river normally flows from its source upstream to its terminus downstream. In this regard the flux is unrelenting, especially since, unlike its spatialized representation by a stream or a river, what flows temporally comes into being and passes away. Fourth are the polar traits of continuity and discreteness. The flux is experienced as continuous and unending process or change; what passes away does not abruptly exit, being in some sense present in what comes into being. At the same time the primary experience of the flux is focal; it grasps only a discrete moment in the ongoing process. From reflection on these generic traits of temporality in immediate experience philosophers have sought to construct concepts of the nature of time. Fundamental questions emerge as to whether time is subjective or objective, relational or absolute, cyclical or otherwise.

The thesis that time is subjective has been advanced on different grounds. Obviously, if arguments such as those offered by a Parmenides or a McTaggart hold, the sense of time, grounded in primary experience, is misleading when interpreted to signify reality beyond experience or consciousness, but nonetheless indicative of an important element or facet of this experience or consciousness. The stream of immediate experience, consisting of an ongoing mixture of sensation, imagination, desire, memory, and conceptualization in no strict logical sequence, does not mirror the objective order of realities. Focusing on the objective order, some philosophers have insisted that the passage of events is a myth; all events, regardless of the temporal status assigned them from the perspective of a given experiencing subject, are already fully real in an objective whole of being, just as the figures in a frieze are already fully real. Then the sense of time is merely a subjective individual's feeling, a mood of a finite consciousness as it flits through the whole of being, just as a tourist steps over the figures in a mosaic on a cathedral floor.

The philosophers who adhere to the thesis that time is subjective, however, differ in regard to other salient issues. Time as subjective has for some thinkers signified that it is psychological in a purely empirical sense. John Locke derived all ideas from experience, and further divided the sources of experience into sensation (outer sense) and reflection (inner sense). He considered the idea of time to be a complex idea of reflection. One component of the idea is duration, which he defined (perhaps unwittingly in spatial terms) as the distance between the parts of the succession of ideas or between the appearance of any two ideas in the succession in our minds. Because durations vary for different psychological subjects, the idea of time also involves the idea of constant measure. Rejecting the Aristotelian definition of time as the measure of motion, since this requires reference to space, Locke considered such motions as the diurnal rotations and annual revolutions of the earth around the sun to be the common, constant measure to complete the idea of time. They serve as the basis of clock time, with the proviso that duration is ultimately the content measured. Beginning from the discrete moments or intervals between two ideas in the succession, Locke added together these moments in an expanding series to complete the ideas of time and of eternity.

Leibniz rejected the entire Lockean program of psychological empiricism. The idea of time, like other major ideas, could not be derived merely from experience; it referred to an infinity that embraces but surpasses actualities and includes the other modalities of possibility and necessity. Further, Leibniz deemed time to be relational. It is a mode internal to each individual monad by which it represents the sequential order of things.

Kant completed Leibniz's insight while yet adhering to the subjectivity thesis. For Kant, time is a universal and necessary form of all experience. More precisely, it is an a priori form of intuition, or sensibility, and, to revert to Lockean terminology, the form of inner sense. Whatever is experienced is stamped by the form of time. While Kant acknowledged that there is an empirical conception of time based on the experience of succession, he held that the form of time is cognized by means of a pure a priori intuition. Despite affinities with Locke's notion that time is a reflective idea derived from inner sense, Kant's theory conceives time as an a priori form that shapes experience itself, and its cognition is nonempirical and pure. Thus, in special moments of consciousness, the subject may become aware of the whole of time, a linear sequential order of instants, homologous and infinite in two directions, past and future. The form of time Kant proposed is well-known to be the sort that Newtonian physics required; Kant himself sought to explain the possibility of synthetic a priori judgments in arithmetic by means of the *it*.

While Kant upheld the empirical reality of time, he yet maintained that it is transcendentally ideal. Hence time is not a structure of things in themselves; it is restricted to possible experience. Here Kant differed from Newton. What persuaded Kant that his forms (and categories) do not apply to reality were the alleged contradictions that halted reason in its attempts to apply them beyond the limits of experience. In the case of time, he articulated this argument in his first antinomy of reason. An antinomy is a pair of contradictory judgments, one of which is termed the thesis and the other the antithesis, and each of which dialectically implies the other. Simply put, the first antinomy, which treats both time and space, posits in regard to time the thesis that the world has a beginning in time and the antithesis that the world has no beginning. In somewhat tortured argument Kant sought to demonstrate that each leads logically to the other. If the world has a beginning in time, the question arises as to when it began, and if a date is determined, the further question arises as to whether there was time before that date, since the supposition of a condition prior to the world's beginning that is not itself in time is unintelligi-

ble. If the world has no beginning in time, doubt arises concerning the possibility of the occurrence of an infinite series of temporal moments terminating in the present moment, so that the occurrence of the present moment itself is rendered unintelligible. Kant thought he resolved the antinomy by restricting the form of time to possible experience; he alleged, perhaps erroneously, that the antinomy results only when reason applies the form of time outside its proper sphere. Hence, for Kant, time is subjective; but its subjectivity is a universal and necessary subjectivity. While time is denied extension transcending possible experience, it is like an envelope, a container that embraces all possible experience. Not transcendent, time is nonetheless transcendental, grounded in the very structure of the transcendental subject, whose forms, categories, and ideas constitute and regulate all possible experience.

Except for the transcendental ideality of time, Kant's doctrine incorporates Newton's absolute theory. Having declined to define time because it is "well known to all," Newton sought, however, to clarify the concept, to underscore those traits of a scientific concept of time neglected or blurred in common conceptions. He therefore specified that, on the one hand, "absolute, true and mathematical time, of itself, and from its own nature, flows equally without regard to anything external, and by another name is called duration," and, on the other hand, "relative, apparent, and common time is some sensible and external measure of duration by the means of motion." Locke's theory of the idea of time obviously has its source in Newton's treatment, but while Locke attempted to construct the idea by combining experienced durations and the idea of a measure, Newton reasoned that absolute time, expressible mathematically, is primary as a categorial envelope embracing all physical reality. Space is distinguished from time, the present moment is the same throughout the physical universe, and space and time are categories of being independent of and unaffected by the objects and events they contain. Indeed, following suggestions in Newton, some Cambridge Platonists inferred that time is part of the eternal capacity of the divine sensorium.

Newton's characterization of time as absolute does not square with common sense temporal experience. To cite an early example, Aristotle never doubted the objectivity thesis, since he deemed temporal predicates to comprise a basic, universal category of language, thought, and reality; nevertheless, he sought to elucidate this category both by means of experienced moments, "nows" and "thens," and by reference to heavenly motion. His formula for time as the measure of motion is merely one part of a sophisticated relational theory rooted in both the experience of duration and the long superseded astronomy he espoused. Although it held sway for centuries among the scientific community, it was discarded after the advent of modern astronomy and in the wake of philosophical scrutiny. The notion of relativity, alluded to even in Newton's mention of the common sense conception of time, has burst forth with new vigor since the rise of relativity theory. Accordingly, time is no longer accepted as absolute. The "absolute, true, and mathematical time" of Newton fixes every moment, so that the present moment is the same throughout the physical universe. Einstein, however, demonstrated that absolute simultaneity does not exist. If we suppose a light signal transmitted from a stationary source to be received by two bodies, one moving toward it, the other away from it, then the moment the light is received by the first body is earlier than the moment it is received by the second body, and conversely. The "now" of any event cannot be specified without reference to its spatial location and motion.

Einstein and Minkowski have theorized that all calculations concerning the temporal and spatial character of events or objects must take account of the fourth dimension of time as well as the three dimensions of space. Hermann Minkowski has projected a four-dimensional space-time matrix pervading the cosmos. This conception has invited considerable speculation, scientific, philosophic, and literary. While it is not absolute in Newton's sense, the cosmic space-time matrix, itself shaped by the matter and energy that make it up, and extending backward to the entire past and forward to the whole future, impugns real passage, upon which the reality of time rests. It makes allowances for particles allegedly moving backward and forward in time, and it is the stuff of fantasies about space travel and time machines.

As an alternative to the Einstein-Minkowski cosmic space-time matrix, with world lines traceable in all directions, stands Whitehead's doctrine of the extensive continuum. Whitehead appealed to immediate experience, just as Bergson before him had done, to find the basic components of time. These basic components, durations, are detected to be moments with a degree of spread, some overlapping or being included in and excluded from others. The mathematical point-instant is a product of abstraction—in Whitehead's phrase, extensive abstraction. Suppose a set of Chinese boxes, the largest containing the next in size recursively with the smallest box being too minute to contain any other. The last box approximates the point-instant. Since to do justice to the mathematical conception an infinite set of boxes would have to be supposed, Whitehead's thought experiment produces only an approximate notion. Later, Whitehead modified his conception of extensive abstraction with the added notion of the extensive continuum. Mathematically structured by reference to the point-instants, which are derived by means of extensive abstraction, the extensive continuum is similar to the cosmic space-time matrix. However, whereas the latter stretched backward and forward, upward and downward, in all four dimensions to encapsulate every object and event in its mathematically frigid embrace, Whitehead's extensive continuum is abstracted from the warm centers of every object and event; it embraces all that has transpired only because present events and objects, actual entities or occasions of experience in his terminology, internalize all that is past in their own being. Interaction among contemporaries is ruled out except as mediated by a common past and a future for which they share common goals. The extensive continuum is, therefore, mainly a possibility. This is particularly true in regard to the future, which is not yet come. The future is indeterminate as to its contents, which in the present are possible only. Although the structure of the extensive continuum, being a network of interrelatedness of actual entities, is determinate for the foreseeable future, it is amenable to transformation in other epochs of actual entities.

Whereas Whitehead was mathematical, Bergson had rejected the application of mathematics to time on the grounds that it spatialized duration, undermining the freedom and creativity of the present facing an indeterminate future that is not yet. Imagine a snowball rolling down a snow-covered hill. As it rolls, it gathers up additional snow and expands. Time is like the snowball; the snow it contains is the past, its circumference is the present, and the snow it will add as it rolls further is the future. This image offers a glimpse of the expansive cumulativeness of time which Bergson attempted to convey in his philosophy. As in the case of Whitehead, moreover, the future is not yet; indeterminate, it is in the making.

The primary experience of time or duration as a flux is preserved by process philosophers, such as Whitehead and Bergson. They accentuated the positive aspects of time with theories that stored up the past, and underscored the creativity and freedom in the present to constitute the future. But passage is not altogether positive. While novelties come into being, other entities pass away. Time is the harbinger of destruction, represented in folklore as an aged reaper with a scythe. Morris Lazerowitz has seized on the destructiveness of time's arrow to suggest a psychological explanation of why time is so much a topic of philosophical theorizing. Humans are anxious about passing away, about dying. Appropriate psychoanalytical therapies would eradicate this fear of death, and presumably the philosophical speculations would disappear.

Flux exists, whatever the philosophy. And the flux does not display linear progress. Rather, to some thinkers, the flux is cyclical. Perhaps the earliest notions of time, originating in ancient civilizations based on agriculture and food gathering, stressed its cyclicality, mirroring diurnal and seasonal changes. The reflection that time is cyclical has in turn spawned startling metaphysical theories, such as Nietzsche's doctrine of "the eternal return." Whatever occurs is bound to recur without end.

KNOWLEDGE OF TIME

Philosophers have offered a variety of theories as to how time is known. Some of these epistemologies have already been traversed. Empirical epistemologies have sought to locate time in the elements of immediate experience. Rational epistemologies have relied more on concepts amenable to mathematical formulation. Critical philosophy has resorted to arguments based on the structure of the subject's cognition. Speculative thinkers have resorted to a mix of theories. Hegel deemed time to be the absolute concept itself in present existence. Bergson regarded time mystically; he claimed it is attained by an intuition of duration in experience, an intuition unmarred by any conceptualization. Heidegger's theory of the human being as thrown into the world, as *dasein*, stresses the temporality of *dasein* and the temporal modalities of its consciousness.

The list of epistemologies of time is too long to be canvassed, but no account should omit William James's theory of the consciousness of time.

As a psychologist-philosopher, James approached the concept of time as he did other concepts of philosophical interest; he inquired into the psychological sense of the concept. As regards time, this led him to an analysis of the stream of consciousness with special focus on its temporal aspects. The stream of consciousness, he noted, flows from the future through the present to the past. James sought to resolve the question of the consciousness of time by reference to psychological processes such as remembering, perceiving, anticipating, and so on. He discovered that a critical point could not be easily disposed—namely, just what consciousness is conscious of when it is presently conscious. After painstaking analysis, in which the present is compared to a saddleback, which overlaps both sides, and to a razor's edge, James concluded that the present moment of consciousness is specious. It contains a part of the past and a part of the future, or as Husserl later put it in his phenomenology of the consciousness of temporality, consciousness of the present involves retention and protention.

The question remains as to how much of the past and of the future are contained in consciousness of the present. James and others have endeavored, without success, to define a fixed minimum; they have failed not only because they disagree as to the measurable duration of the fixed minimum, but also because the problem of constructing a continuum out of discrete moments surfaces, a problem whose solutions are not empirical but mathematical. Here the contributions of the mathematicians Julius Dedekind and Georg Cantor are pertinent. A.P. Ushenko has speculated that minimal durations accessible to consciousness vary for different sorts of entities and events. He has suggested that each kind of entity or event comprises a family of time, and further, that there is a hierarchy of the families of time, with the families ranked according to the extent of the moment of which they are conscious. The hierarchy stretches from the lowest, whose durations embrace very little, and the highest, who apprehend more. Except for its pluralistic twist with the added paradox that the quicker consciousness is also the more inclusive, encapsulating more in the time it takes an inferior consciousness to be aware of less, Ushenko's theory reflects the influence of Josiah Royce.

A perceptive scholar in the history of philosophy, Royce accepted James's analysis of the consciousness of time, but having studied St. Thomas Aquinas and Hegel, he added an element that James had neglected. For James never thought that the kneading together of a portion of the past and a portion of the future to constitute the present required some principle that transcended the modalities of time; he thought the empirical self, itself caught up in the flux, was adequate. Following in the footsteps of Thomas Aquinas, Kant, and Hegel, Royce thought otherwise; he posited a nonempirical self to transcend the moments in the flux. But if for the finite consciousness of time, appeal to a transcendental self was useful and necessary, then, by parity of reason, the entire stream of time, its unity and continuity, could be explained by the supposition of an absolute self who grasped in a singular vision the whole of time. The inference by a transcendental argument to an absolute self with all-inclusive eternal intuition, however, did not explain time as much as it explained time away.

[A.J.R.]

See also **Aquinas, St. Thomas; Aristotle; Arrow of Time; Augustine; Bergson, Henri; Father Time; Hegel, Georg Wilhelm Friedrich; Heidegger, Martin; Husserl, Edmund; James, William (as Philosopher); Kant, Immanuel; Leibniz, Gottfried Wilhelm; Locke, John; McTaggart, John McTaggart Ellis; Newton, Isaac; Plato; Presocratics; Relativity Theory; Royce, Josiah; Space-Time; Whitehead, Alfred North.**

FURTHER READINGS

Gale, R.M., ed. *The Philosophy of Time.* Garden City: Anchor Books, Doubleday, 1967.

Harris, Errol E. *The Reality of Time.* Albany: State U of New York P, 1988.

Lieb, Irwin C. *Past, Present, and Future: A Philosophical Essay about Time.* Urbana: U of Illinois P, 1991.

PHOTOPERIODISM AND SEASONAL RHYTHMS: ANIMALS

Most animals in temperate latitudes show marked seasonality in their behavior and physiology. Options include migration to lower latitudes or staying put to become inactive, nonbreeding, or dormant. Most nonmigratory animals restrict their breeding or activity to the favorable spring and summer months and become nonreproductive or dormant as the winter approaches. However, animals in the dry subtropics may restrict their activity to the rains, which frequently occur during the winter.

These strong seasonal rhythms are often a response to changes in day length (photoperiod-

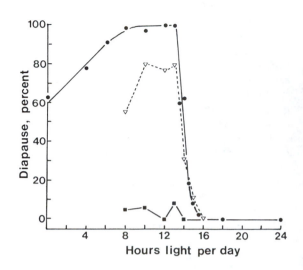

Figure 1. The photoperiodic induction of overwintering diapause in an insect (the flesh fly, Sarcophaga argyrostoma). The figure shows the proportion entering pupal diapause in different photoperiods (hours of light per day) at three temperatures, • -15 degrees C, ▽ - 20 degrees C, and ■ 25 degrees C. The "critical day length" (50 percent response) is at about fourteen hours of light per day at 15 and 20 degrees C.

ism) and imply that the animals possess an internal clock to measure the duration of the day (or night) as the seasons change.

Photoperiodic clocks are seen, for example, in the breeding patterns of birds and mammals, and in the overwintering dormancy of insects (diapause). These responses allow animals to anticipate forthcoming seasons without having to rely on the direct effects of climate. Day length is thus used as a "token stimulus" that, although not adverse or favorable in itself, is used to signal imminent and sometimes dangerous environmental change. The evolutionary advantages gained by having such a clock are often very great. For example, a bird producing a clutch of eggs too late in the year may not be able to raise her chicks, or an insect may perish if it fails to enter diapause before the first frost.

The time measurement inherent in a photoperiodic response is frequently very accurate, some insects being able to distinguish "short" from "long" days only minutes apart (Figure 1). The ability to measure abrupt changes in day length is the most important aspect of the clock because such changes separate the active condition from dormancy. In animals with a large north-south range, the critical day length becomes longer to the north. This is because winter arrives earlier in the north, often when day lengths are relatively long.

Current research into seasonal rhythmicity has focused on two main questions: (1) the relationship between photoperiodism and other biological clocks, and (2) the anatomical location of these timers and their photoreceptors that, together, enable the animal to respond to seasonal change.

In 1936, botanist Erwin Bunning suggested that photoperiodism was based on the system of daily or circadian rhythms. These rhythms have many clock-like features: persistence ("free-running") in the absence of light and temperature cues, often for weeks or months on end; a periodicity close to twenty-four hours (hence *circadian*); considerable day-to-day accuracy; and, above all, an endogenous period that is only very slightly affected by temperature. Experimental evidence for the association between circadian rhythms and photoperiodism is now available for birds, mammals, and insects, as well as plants. Many longer-lived animals such as mammals, however, also seem to rely on an internal "calendar" to regulate their annual cycles of activity and hibernation or pelt color change.

Birds and the majority of insects do not use their eyes to perceive the photoperiod and its seasonal change. Surprisingly, they use a system of "extraretinal" photoreception with the light passing directly into the brain. However, in mammals, the eyes *are* involved, although the nervous pathways are quite distinct from those used in vision, passing to a part of the brain called the suprachiasmatic nucleus (SCN), now known to house the circadian clock. The SCN is linked to the pineal organ, between the lobes of the brain, that secretes a daily cycle of melatonin ("the hormone of the night"). Melatonin then provides seasonal information to the reproductive centers of the brain through changes in the duration of its nocturnal surge. In insects, the photoperiodic clock has not been located with such accuracy, but is known to lie within the brain.

[D.S.S.]

See also **Chronobiology; Melatonin; Photoperiodism and Seasonal Rhythms: Plants.**

FURTHER READINGS

Moore-Ede, M.C., F.M. Sulzman, and C. A. Fuller. *The Clocks that Time Us*. Cambridge: Harvard UP, 1982.

Saunders, D.S. *Insect Clocks*. 2nd ed. Oxford: Pergamon P, 1982.

PHOTOPERIODISM AND SEASONAL RHYTHMS: PLANTS

The essence of photoperiodism is the measurement of time. Plants and animals measure the length (period) of light or darkness or both and respond in some way—for example, by producing flowers—when the lengths of these periods match some genetically preprogrammed length. This ensures that all plants in a population will flower at the same time, even if some started growing early or late.

Cocklebur (*Xanthium strumarium*), for example, is a so-called *short-day plant* for flowering. When nights are longer than about 8.3 hours, cocklebur leaves respond by sending a signal (a yet-to-be-identified chemical—a flowering hormone) to the buds, which then produce flowers instead of stems and leaves. That is, the plant changes from a vegetative to a reproductive state at a season appropriate for the population. In north-temperate regions between the tropic of Cancer and the arctic circle, the longer nights and shorter days cause cocklebur to flower during late summer or early autumn. Cocklebur plants raised in continuous light respond to a single long night, but flowering increases when plants receive three or more long nights, and *day* length also affects flowering of cocklebur and a few other short-day species. Although other short-day plants respond to a *single* dark period (Japanese morning glory is another example), most require several short days. Chrysanthemum, cosmos, certain strawberries, and poinsettia are examples, and short-day tobacco and soybean cultivars were important in the discovery of photoperiodism in 1920.

There are also *long-day plants* that flower when the lengthening days and shortening nights of spring and early summer reach the *critical photoperiod* for the species. Black henbane (*Hyoscyamus niger*), for example, flowers when days exceed about twelve hours. Both cocklebur and henbane flower when days are fourteen hours long, but cocklebur responds when days are *shorter* than about 15.5 hours (nights longer than 8.5 hours), and henbane responds when days are *longer* than about twelve hours. Other long-day plants include cereals (wheat, oats, rye, and barley, which usually require cold as young seedlings or moist seeds), other tobacco species and cultivars, sugar beets, and many vegetables such as lettuce and spinach, many of which are also promoted by previous cold.

Day-neutral plants flower independently of day or night length and hence may not be tied to specific seasons unless they are controlled by temperature. Examples include tomato, other strawberries, sunflower, and other tobacco species.

Many plants require some intricate combination of conditions to flower—for example, long days followed by short days—and temperatures and light levels must also be just right. White clover, by way of example, requires the short days of early spring followed by the long days of early summer; if the order is reversed, no flowering occurs. Some plants *need* a certain photoperiod to flower, while others may only be *promoted* by a suitable photoperiod, but would flower anyway.

In spite of much study, the mechanisms of photoperiodism are not completely understood. It is known that light and darkness are detected through the pigment *phytochrome*. Red light converts this pigment to a form that promotes flowering of short-day plants during the day, but inhibits flowering during the night; longer wavelengths (called far red) convert the pigment back to the red-sensitive form. As light decreases during twilight, phytochrome changes from one form to the other, and this signal initiates the processes of the dark period. Then, time is measured with a clock similar if not identical to the biological clock that controls many plant and animal *circadian rhythms* (rhythms approximately twenty-four hours long). Leaves of numerous plants, for example, move up or down according to a nearly twenty-four-hour rhythm that continues for several days in the dark at constant temperature and humidity. How the photoperiodism clock functions remains a mystery, but when the day and/or night reach the predetermined length, flowering hormone is synthesized in the leaves.

Photoperiodism in plants controls much more than flowering, although that process has been the most widely studied. Long days nearly always cause stem elongation, for example. This is not just a response to more light, because a long night interrupted with a brief period (seconds to an hour or two) of light produces the same effect as a long day; this is the definitive test for a true photoperiodism response. Other seasonal processes controlled by photoperiod include seed germination of a few species, many features of leaves (size, chlorophyll content, and so on), formation of underground storage organs (short days for potatoes, long days for onions), runner formation of strawberries, dormancy in many trees, and many other responses.

[F.B.S.]

See also **Chronobiology; Photoperiodism and Seasonal Rhythms: Animals.**

PHYSICS

Physics is the science which studies the structure and function of the material world and seeks to describe and explain them in terms of fundamental laws expressed in mathematical form. The emphasis on fundamental law is what distinguishes physics from the other sciences, and with few exceptions, all these laws involve time. "Time" is a word that has different meanings for different people, and like "atom" and other terms, it has acquired a fairly definite scientific meaning only after many centuries of use. (The word "fairly" is necessary here because the age of scientific discovery is not yet over.) This article will focus on the role of time in fundamental physics.

EARLY SPECULATIONS

The first school of natural philosophy seems to have arisen in Miletus, a prosperous seaport on the west coast of Asia Minor. There, about 560 B.C., a thinker named Anaximander tried to express the lawfulness of the world:

> The source from which existing things derive their existence is also that to which they return at their destruction, for they pay penalty and retribution to each other for their injustice according to the assessment of time.

The language is that of the lawcourt. "Injustice," in Greek law, refers to what is unlawful, but also to what is unfair or unequal. Anaximander is saying that the world tends toward a balance. The seasons alternate, drought is followed by rain, pestilences come and go, the evil deed finally catches up with its perpetrator. Law must be backed by authority, and the authority is time. The principle is general, we see it in continual operation, and, invoking time, it refers to the dynamics of the world without mentioning its structure. In all these respects it anticipates the emergence of modern versions of natural law twenty-five centuries later.

The development of logic, especially at the hands of Aristotle (384–322 B.C.), was important in the development of clear thinking, but it did little for science, since scientists arrive at most of their truths by the illogical process of trial and error. For Aristotle and those who followed him, truth *by definition* was what is arrived at by logical reasoning, and it was only gradually, as the Middle Ages gave way to the Renaissance, that the value of knowledge acquired by experiment began to be recognized.

PHYSICS IN THE SEVENTEENTH CENTURY

In Book VII of his *Physics*, Aristotle states an erroneous principle regarding motion that was accepted without question for 2,000 years: that if something is in motion it must be because it is moved by some force. Further, at least in the absence of friction or other resistance, the speed of motion is proportional to the force. At first glance this fits our experience: the harder we push something, the faster it goes, but to explain why a ball continues to move after it is thrown one had to make extravagant assumptions concerning forces exerted by the surrounding air. Further, Aristotle's principle implies that if something is dropped, its rate of fall is proportional to its weight; thus a brick would reach the ground hundreds of times more quickly than a dried pea. This conclusion is in such obvious conflict with experience that in the long run it benefited the development of science, for it encouraged thinkers to question not only other statements of Aristotle's about nature but, more important, the ways in which he arrived at them. In about 1602, Galileo Galilei (1564–1642), educated in the scholastic tradition that stemmed from Aristotle, began to show by experiment that both of Aristotle's propositions concerning motion are false and provided quantitative rules to replace them. Specifically, he found that an object in free fall drops with constant acceleration, not velocity, and also deduced that if air resistance is neglected, the acceleration is the same for all objects. Furthermore, he concluded from his experiments that if an object were set moving horizontally with no friction (say, a ball rolling on a smooth, hard, level surface) it would tend to keep on moving in a straight line at constant speed. These conclusions, however, became widely known only with the publication of his *Discourses and Mathematical Demonstrations Concerning Two New Sciences* in 1638, long after Johannes Kepler (1571–1630) had tried (1609) to explain the observed motions of the planets by constructing a mathematical theory based on Aristotle's propositions. The effort failed, of course, but it remains the first attempt to explain observational evidence on the basis of a quantitative theory of motion.

The pioneering efforts of Galileo and Kepler did not require refined conceptions of space and time; time was measured by a pendulum or a pulse or the beat of a marching tune, and distance by a yardstick. When Isaac Newton (1642–1727) set forth a coherent theory of dynamics (that is, of forces and the motions they produce) in his *Mathematical Principles of Natural Philosophy* (1687), referred to as the *Principia*, he had to analyze very carefully the words and concepts he was using, and the papers surviving from the time he was composing the work showed that this required intense thought and very specific language.

Following Galileo, Newton postulated that a body with no force acting on it will move uniformly, and that a force applied to it will produce a change in motion, an acceleration. An example would be the force of gravity that produces a constant downward acceleration in a falling body. If this constant force produces a constant acceleration, it suggests that force and acceleration are proportional, and this turns out to be true, but to state it properly is not easy. What is acceleration? It is the time rate of change of velocity, which in turn is the time rate of change of position, but velocity and position with respect to what? No use to specify them with respect to the earth, for Newton was aiming at a theory of the whole solar system, in which the earth is in motion and is no more important than any other planet. The standard that distinguishes one place from another and rest from motion must be absolute, and independent of any particular object in the universe. Newton was therefore obliged to introduce into his system something that was mysterious and unobservable:

> Absolute space, in its own nature and without reference to anything external, remains always similar and immovable. . . . Absolute motion is the translation of a body from one absolute place to another (*Principia*, Scholium to the Definitions in Book I).

Newton's principles, generally called the laws of motion, are valid in absolute space but not, for example, on a merry-go-round, for there a ball set rolling on the floor appears to move in a curve. How then do we know that we are describing motion with respect to absolute space and not some accelerated space? There must be a test, and it is provided by Newton's first law:

I. A body persists at rest or in uniform motion in a straight line [with respect to absolute space] unless acted upon by an externally applied force.

If this is true, then (the second law in words more simple than Newton's):

II. A force *F* externally applied to a body of mass *m* produces an acceleration proportional to *F*/*m* in the same direction as the force.

Finally, the third law:

III. When one body exerts a force on another, the forces of action and reaction are equal and opposite.

Thus, if the earth exerts a force of gravity on the moon, the moon exerts an equal and opposite force on the earth. This means it is not exactly true that the moon moves in an elliptical orbit with respect to the earth, for the earth moves in a small orbit too, and both orbits are described with respect to the center of gravity of earth and moon as a center.

Having carefully defined space, Newton must also say exactly what he means by time. We live in space, but time is more abstract. Still, there is an astonishing fact about it that must somehow be stated if the dynamical theory is to make sense. It is that there is only one time. Clocks tend to agree. A clock can be made by painting stripes around a candle and noting when it burns down to a certain stripe. A clock can also use falling water, or a pendulum, or the sun's apparent motion across the sky, or even one's personal impression of time. These all agree pretty well, and if they do not agree we can usually find a reason and apply a correction that makes them agree better: shield the candle from a draft; keep the water flowing without interruption; take account of the way in which changes in temperature change the pendulum's length; correct the length of the day for inequalities in the earth's rotation caused by uneven loading of the atmosphere. It seems that no matter how it is measured, provided only that it is measured carefully, what time it is is given by a single number that we perceive as advancing uniformly:

> Absolute, true, and mathematical time, of itself, and from its own nature, flows equably without reference to anything external. . . . (*Principia*, Scholium to the Definitions in Book I).

But just what these words mean is hard to say, for under examination they do not really make sense. If something flows, we may ask how fast it flows. How fast does time flow? One is tempt-

ed to answer "At a rate of one second per second," but this means nothing. As Aristotle wrote long ago,

> Time is not described as fast or slow but as many or few or as long or short. . . . Not only do we measure time by the movement but also the movement by the time, since they define each other. (*Physics*, 220)

That is, time is defined and measured not in terms of itself but in terms of what happens in it. Events are its markers, and it is events that, in a metaphorical sense, flow. We designate time by a number; it is what a clock measures. A clock, in turn, is a changing object whose law of change is known. And finally, a law of change is a physical principle that tells how the object changes in time. Considered as a string of words, these definitions move in a circle and define nothing. But the world consists of changing things, not words, and it is these changing things that define time for us. As Aristotle knew, the world is such that this circular definition is nevertheless a definition.

Today, as will be seen below, we know that we must be careful about saying that it is the same time everywhere, but we still find that one time governs all physical phenomena: we do not need different definitions of time for different purposes. This is perhaps less surprising when one considers that all matter consists of atoms, and almost all changes in matter are rearrangements of atoms, so that whatever time governs atoms, governs the world.

PHYSICS BEFORE RELATIVITY

For nearly two centuries after the publication of the *Principia*, the main work of theoretical physics was getting used to the assumptions of Newton's dynamical theory and working out its consequences. Initially, the physicists of the Continent had serious objections, and Gottfried Wilhelm von Leibniz (1646–1716) was particularly sharp in his criticisms. He accused Newton of giving space and time properties beyond those that experience requires. Leibniz preferred to define space, with Aristotle, as the totality of places that solid bodies can occupy, and time as nothing but a mental ordering of events. These objections had to be thrashed out at length before it became clear that attractive as Leibniz's definitions are, they are not strong enough to support the weight of a dynamical theory. In addition, Newton's opponents claimed that, whereas the business of physics is to explain the phenomena, Newton introduced gravity as a mysterious force represented by a mathematical recipe without making any attempt to explain how it works. To this, Newton replied that if he had known how it worked, he would surely have explained it, but since he did not, all he could do was describe it mathematically and show that the description is exact.

In the 1860s, the hegemony of the Newtonian conception of physics was broken by the development of a theory of the electromagnetic field by James Clerk Maxwell (1831–1879). Whereas early theories of electricity and magnetism had considered the fields purely in terms of forces, Maxwell showed that, in combination, they have a dynamism of their own, that they convey energy, and that, in fact, light is a rapidly changing electromagnetic field. At first, the effort was to explain the field in terms of motions in a fluid called ether that pervades all space and moves in accordance with Newton's laws, but gradually it turned out that this is impossible, and by a few years after the first paper by Albert Einstein (1879–1955) on relativity theory (1905), people understood that the field is a physical entity with a dynamics of its own, and that the time variable in this dynamics is the same as that in Newton's dynamics of matter. Relativity theory, however, revealed some unexpected subtleties.

TIME IN MODERN PHYSICS
The changes that relativity theory brought to traditional and intuitive ideas of time are described in the articles **Relativity Theory**, **Space-Time**, and **Gravity, Time, and Space**, and will only be briefly summarized here. The principal change is the disappearance of the idea of absolute simultaneity: one can no longer say without qualification that it is the same time everywhere. If two events taking place in different places are judged simultaneous by one observer, they will not be simultaneous for another observer who moves with respect to the first. Einstein assumed that Maxwell's electromagnetic theory is correct and also that its equations hold without change for observers in uniform relative motion. As a consequence, he showed that intervals of space and time are observer-dependent, and that it is necessary to modify the equations of Newtonian dynamics to take account of the fact. This does not, however, imply that there is no absolute standard of time and simultaneity, for the universe itself defines a special class of observers who are at rest with respect to the

average local movement of the matter it contains. For all such observers, anywhere in the universe, the age of the universe is given by the same number, if they can find out what it is. For other observers in motion relative to those of this special class, the number will be different. Neither relativity theory nor any other development of modern physics has anything to say concerning the individual's personal experience of time, but physics reminds us that this is a subjective experience. What we perceive are things and events; time is a mental construction based on these perceptions. As Einstein once said, "Space and time are modes by which we think, not conditions under which we live."

All the physics mentioned above is described in terms of three dimensions of space and one of time; relativity theory combines them into a four-dimensional space-time. This leads to two very important and unanswered scientific questions: why four dimensions; more specifically, why three plus one? And should we assume that *all* physical phenomena can be so described, and not just those studied so far? These questions are difficult but not necessarily unanswerable. It seems probable that if there are any processes that require more than four dimensions to define them, they would be observed at energies higher than we can produce at present or, probably, will ever be able to produce. The best hope is to find some general theory, some "theory of everything," as it is called, that explains all known properties of matter (particularly at the level of fundamental particles) and see how many dimensions it requires for its formulation. At the time these words are written, various approaches are being pursued and none has led to a definitive theory, but nevertheless, all of them, even the most extravagant, illuminate some part of our experience of the complex material world. One idea which recurs is that at the moment of creation space-time had more dimensions than it seems to have now (the numbers ten and twenty-six are required for different forms of the theory), but that subsequently all but four got rolled up. An analogy would be a sheet of paper which is rolled into something like a drinking straw. From a distance it looks like a line, but closer examination reveals its three-dimensional structure. In these theories all interactions are described in terms of the underlying geometry. Einstein showed that the gravitational interaction involves the four dimensions of our experience; the other interactions would involve the rolled-up dimensions, which are exceedingly small, but not zero. Even though some of these ideas have been worked out in great mathematical detail, they are only sketches largely unsupported by critical experiments, and the process of rolling up ("dimensional compactification") is not convincingly explained. The ideas are mentioned here because there is hope that they may some day reveal the nature of time at a deeper level of explanation.

[D.A.P.]

See also **Gravity, Time, and Space; Relativity Theory; Space-Time.**

FURTHER READINGS

Close, Frank. *The Cosmic Onion.* New York: American Institute of Physics, 1983.

Holton, Gerald. *Thematic Origins of Scientific Thought.* Harvard UP, 1973.

Pais, Abraham. *Inward Bound.* Oxford: Oxford UP, 1986.

Park, David. *The How and the Why.* Princeton: Princeton UP, 1988.

Weinberg, Steven. *The Discovery of Fundamental Particles.* New York: Scientific American Library, 1983.

PIAGET, JEAN (1896–1980)

Swiss psychologist and epistemologist Jean Piaget exerted an enormous influence on the field of developmental psychology with his theory of cognitive development and his empirical studies of the growth of knowledge in children. Within this large corpus of research and theory are many studies of the concept of time. Piaget's most important books on time are *The Construction of Reality in the Child* (1937; first published in English 1954), and *The Child's Conception of Time* (1946; first published in English 1969), (and see *The Child's Conception of Movement and Speed*, 1946; first published in English 1970). The first work includes a study of the development of infants' ability to sequence their own actions purposefully and to attend to the temporal order in which external events occur. The second work explores the stages through which preschool and school-age children pass in coming to understand time as adults do: as a uniform, continuous, all-encompassing flow, one in which the successions and durations of different actions can be uniquely integrated.

The ability to integrate logically temporal information from different actions was studied in a series of experiments. In one such study, children witnessed the movement of two me-chanical snails across a table. Although the starts and stops of the two snails were synchronous, one moved at a greater speed, thus causing it to cover a greater distance and stop farther along the table. Children were asked, among other questions, which of the two snails moved for more time. To adults it is apparent that two actions that begin and end simultaneously must be equal in duration. But Piaget discovered that children of less than seven or eight years were often misled by the distance covered or end-point of the faster snail and concluded that it moved for more time. Here, and in other experiments, he found that temporal inferences that seem elementary to adults are acquired only gradually in children. From these studies, Piaget concluded that humans' understanding of time is not intuitive, but is constructed in the course of development; it depends on the acquisition of specific mental operations that allow us to reconstruct successions, combine durations, and integrate the two kinds of information.

There have been few attempts to test Piaget's description of time in infancy, but many researchers have investigated his claims about the development of logical time in preschool and school-age children. When methods similar to Piaget's are used, studies confirm his basic findings, although children are sometimes found to reach particular stages at later ages than in the original studies. However, studies employing a variety of new measures of logical time concepts have often led to quite different conclusions about the age at which a particular ability appears, and even the order in which two abilities emerge. For example, one researcher discovered that children as young as five years can use starting and stopping times to equate the durations of two actions when the two actions do not involve spatial displacements. Other studies have shown that the order in which children seem to grasp the concepts of duration and velocity varies from one measure to another. Although these studies disconfirm some of Piaget's specific claims, his general conclusion stands: Time concepts are gradually constructed in the course of development.

[W.J.F.]

See also **Developmental Psychology.**

FURTHER READINGS

Friedman, William J., ed. *The Developmental Psychology of Time.* New York: Academic P, 1982.

Levin, Iris, and Dan Zakay, eds. *Time and Human Cognition: A Life-Span Perspective.* Amsterdam: North-Holland, 1989.

PLATO (CA. 429–347 B.C.)

Time never becomes thematic in the *Dialogues* of Plato because he considers it as twice derivative: It is a mere epiphenomenon of spatial variability, while variation itself falls out from stability.

The dialogues do, however, contain several long passages that are absolutely seminal to most later reflections on time. In interpreting these passages it is important to recall that they are incidental to often playful conversations about other subjects.

It is nevertheless possible to extract certain theses from the dialogues: (1) Being, in its self-sameness, is atemporal; only becoming is variable and temporal; (2) Time is not a substance or a substrate but a concomitant of cosmic motion and is thus secondary to space; (3) Time underlies the tenses of speech, particularly of the verb "to be." "Is," "was," and "will be" seem to correspond to the three phases of present, past, and future, but the present tense is problematic because it is actually tenseless and out of time; (4) Temporal attributions and the analysis of change give rise to several logical puzzles and paradoxes; (5) Time arises, and is known to us, as the effect of various regular, numerable cosmic cycles; (6) The course of time is imaginatively reversible, with catastrophic consequences; (7) There are immense cosmic and human epochs of time.

The three most important passages are from late dialogues: (1) The *Timaeus* (37c–47c) contains a mythico-mathematical account of the genesis of time; (2) The *Parmenides* (141, 151e–157b) contains a dialectical treatment of the logical puzzles of time and of the instant; (3) The *Statesman* (268d–274d) contains a story about the periodic reversal of time and the effect of an unwinding cosmos on human life.

THE BIRTH OF TIME

In the *Timaeus*, Plato tells in a myth how the sensible, moving cosmos was made by a divine craftsman working from an intelligible, eternal prototype, a pattern at rest but having eternal life. In order to generate a cosmos as much like the original as possible, the god places within the unmoving cosmic spatial structure of the copy a "movable image of eternity." "He made of the eternal, abiding in unity, an image going according to number, and this is what we have called 'time.'" Time is born together with the "organs of time," the revolving heavenly bodies. It comes into being with the cycles of the sun, which give us day and night as well as the year,

with the phases of the moon, which give us the month, and with the revolutions of the planets, which, when they return together to their point of origin, give us the greatest of all astronomical epochs, the "perfect year" (whose length is not given by Plato).

Thus "was" and "shall be" are astronomically generated as forms of time, while "is" belongs to the eternal being of the pattern.

In the mythical genesis, time is the name of the visible variability of the heavens insofar as they display cycles having steady, countable returns. Time is often said by Greek writers to progress, to march on, to go. The Greek word for the "eternal" is *aion*, which looks like a possible word for un-going, *a-ion*. Time, then, in the passage quoted, is an un-going, that is, not a linearly progressive, image of "un-going" eternity, which yet "goes," or progresses, numerically. It has the paradoxical nature, belonging to all images, of being the same and yet different from its original. Thus the life of the atemporal divine model is imaged in time through its association with motion. Time must image the stability of the divine model by a numerical progression which is only a regularity, not an abiding self-sameness, a cycle of returns, and not an eternal present. Time is, consequently, both eternal and ongoing, that is to say, it is everlasting, at least after its first genesis.

In this figure of time as a visible, numerically advancing image of eternity, several later notions are foreshadowed: for instance, the ideas that time is posterior to space, that it may be defined as the display of the cosmic clock, that it is connected with human counting, that it is intimately bound up with cosmic and individual life, and that its ongoing sempiternity is a counterpart of timeless eternity.

TIME PUZZLES

The *Parmenides* is a dialectical inquiry, an argument giving weight to both sides of the question, into the nature of all sorts of unity. The "one of being" is shown to be atemporal. Any sensible entity, however, any entity existing in space and time and capable of change, possesses temporal attributes. In this context, the fundamental features and expressions, as well as the perennial paradoxes and puzzles of time are, for the first time, collected:

"Is" means existence in present time, "was" existence in the past, and "will be" existence in the future; that is to say, there are three tenses in speech denoting three phases of time; in distinction from the *Timaeus*, the present is here a time. To exist is thus nothing but to partake of being with time present, a definition that incidentally prefigures a later distinction between existence and essence. Similarly, to have existed is to share in time gone by and to be about to exist is to share in time to come. Thus existence in general is understood as participation in time.

Time may be thought of as itself advancing, or, alternatively, the temporal entity may be conceived as traveling through the temporal framework.

Temporal relations are thoroughly relative. As time goes on, an entity grows older than itself and than other entities, and therefore it also grows relatively younger; yet it keeps up with itself. While it keeps the same absolute distance from a younger entity, it also comes relatively closer to it, as when two people born ten years apart seem to approach each other in age as they grow older.

Insofar as an entity becomes and is destroyed in time, it sometimes partakes of being and sometimes loses it, though not both at once. Here we have an early instantiation of the ontological law of noncontradiction.

An entity also undergoes all sorts of change, besides coming into and going out of being. Change is transition from one condition to another. When does that transition occur? Not while the entity is in the time of either condition. The transition is made in that strange, "unplaceable" thing called "the sudden," or the instant. This instant, distinguished in the dialogue from the "now" of present existence, the prototype of the "specious present," occupies no time at all. It is situated between conditions, and from it a thing passes to a new condition. The Parmenidean account of the instant bears in itself the chief problems of continuity: that the point of time is not a constituent of the continuum.

THE UNWINDING OF TIME

In the *Statesman*, after the strenuous but unsuccessful exercise of defining the true ruler, a "playful way" is introduced to show that the participants in the dialogue have made the mistake of defining an ancient divine king rather than a current human statesman. According to an old myth, at certain times the god himself helps the cosmos to go on by spinning it. When the world's rotations reach the measure of time permitted by its bodily nature, the god lets go and the heavens unwind in a catastrophic rever-

sal. (The dynamic picture is similar to that given in the *Republic*, where the planetary spheres are whorls turned on a spindle by the fates.) In the epoch when the god imparts the impulse, men are earth-born in the prime of life, and the earth nurtures them without needing cultivation. God is their shepherd and no political organization is required. In the age of unwinding, when the god releases the cosmos, men are born by human procreation as babies, and, supported by their memory of the god's age, they toil, learn the arts, and have governance. Eventually this memory fades, while the cosmos winds down and all declines into chaos. Finally, the god again takes over, and so on and on, in a prototype of the eternal return.

The age of god is called the age of Kronos. Since Kronos, the father of Zeus, was regularly identified by the Greeks with *Chronos* (time), it seems that the epoch of steady divine impulse is the era of regular time, while the age of reversal, called the age of Zeus, in which the instruments of time slow down and the human lot declines with the cosmos, is the age of temporal disorder. Not only is equable temporal progression lost, but so also is mere succession, so that "young" fails to precede "old." The tale is, however, no respecter of temporality, since it implies skepticism concerning the happiness of the "nurslings of Kronos," who do not use their even-tenored time for philosophical discourses, for inquiries into atemporal forms—as our age may.

The story foreshadows the idea of an inversion of time which is not merely a mechanical reversal but an entropic return to chaos. It posits the primacy of the time of regular divine impulses over epochs of automatic unwinding, but, countermanding the claim of the *Timaeus*, it intimates that the world is more conducive to human thought when left to its own temporally turbulent devices than as a divine cosmic order.

[E.T.H.B.]

FURTHER READINGS

Brumbaugh, Robert S. *Plato on the One*. New Haven: Yale UP, 1990.

Cornford, Francis M. *Plato's Cosmology*. London: Routledge & Kegan Paul, 1956.

———. *Plato and Parmenides*. New York: The Liberal Arts Press, 1957.

PLOTINUS (A.D. 205–270)

A central concern of Plotinus is to establish the causal connection between the ideal world and the physical world, and thereby to resolve the problem of their separation, alleged by Aristotle as grounds to reject the Platonic ideas. Plotinus reasserts against the Aristotelian critique the power of the eternal ideas to cause a derivative order in the temporal world; he goes so far in one important tractate, "On Eternity and Time" (*Enneads* III.7), to present time itself as an aspect of continuity between the changeless order of the ideal world and the ordered change of the physical world. He finds in the Platonic definition of time as "the moving image of eternity" (in *Timaeus*) the notion that the horizontal order of temporal sequence can be derived from the vertical order of ideal causation.

Plotinus's system of the universe comprises three principles. The first principle, the one, is transcendent to being and thought and therefore to both eternity and time. The second principle, being-intellect, proceeds eternally from the one as both the eternal world of ideal being and the divine intellect that eternally knows it. The third principle, soul, proceeds eternally from being-intellect as life, feeling, and movement, even before, as it were, it produces the physical world and its regular motions. The life of human souls derives from the immortal life of soul and not from the physical world. Even during their embodied life within time their immortality is manifested through rational understanding, contemplative glimpses, and fleeting moments of contact with their eternal and pre-eternal causes. A twofold vertical movement dominates this scheme: real existence descends to the embodied soul from its causes, while its real happiness occurs in a contemplative ascent toward them.

The metaphor of "emanation" compares the dependence of the lower world of physical nature upon the highest principle of the one to the light of the sun spreading about the visible world, although in a diffused and weakened form. Because the metaphor of emanation suggests that the supremely concentrated power of the one gradually dissipates, Plotinus seems at times to regret that being-intellect and soul proceeded from the one at all, that all their emergent content had not remained wrapped in timeless unity.

Thus, in "Does Happiness Increase with Time?" (*Enneads* I.5), Plotinus says that the authentic life of the human soul is scattered by its temporal life: "that is why time is called the image of eternity, since time wishes to make what is permanent in eternity disappear in its own dispersion." Elsewhere he says that the "unquiet power of the soul" mistakenly supposes that it gains content as it expands into life, whereas it actually squanders its content outside of itself instead of holding it in unity. Even divine being-intellect is said in one place to have proceeded from the one not as a free effulgence of light, but when it somehow forgot itself, grew heavy with oblivion, and so descended. In such a discouraged reading of cosmogony, the emergent qualities of the lower principles would not compensate the loss of original unity. The role of time would be entirely negative: the last, exhausted dissipation of intelligible order into mere succession. Some scholars assert that in such passages Plotinus succumbs to the Gnostic pessimism that he elsewhere utterly rejects.

The tractate "On Eternity and Time," however, gives to time a positive sense more consonant with Plotinus' usual, anti-Gnostic affirmation of the goodness of the emanated world. The Platonic definition affirms that time is the "image of eternity"; it cannot therefore be reduced to physical motions or their measure. Plotinus locates time in soul, defining it as "the life of soul in a movement of passage from one form of life to another." As an attribute of soul, one of the eternal principles, time is neither an accident nor simply a misfortune or deficiency, but an essential aspect of the unfolding of the universe.

Time precedes the physical world as the inner creative life of soul, a real but nonphysical motion. The life of soul is in turn an image of eternity, the inner life of being-intellect. This crucial stage in Plotinus' argument is an innovation in ancient Platonism. Although being-intellect is changeless and motionless, has no history, and desires nothing, its inclusive perfection has a dynamic quality as eternal life, as act and actuality gathered and poised in itself, being, possessing, and knowing itself. Time is the reflection of this compact eternal life at the lower level of the ordered evolution of soul. On this view at least, the life of soul does not scatter or squander the eternal content of being-intellect, but expands and exhibits it through time. As the inner life of soul prior to the physical world, time contains the ideal patterns of motion even before it deploys them in physical time. Time, as an attribute of soul, transmits the eternal ordering power of being-intellect to the physical world. Physical time is therefore not an empty succession that loses the present in the past, but a harmonious deployment of forms of life already contained and moving in soul. Through the inner time of soul, physical time is connected with its ideal pattern in being-intellect, whose power to cause and order the physical world is thereby confirmed.

[B.V.]

See also **Augustine; Plato.**

FURTHER READINGS

Plotinus. *Plotinus with an English Translation by A.H. Armstrong.* 7 volumes (Loeb Classical Library). Cambridge: Harvard UP, 1966–1988.

———. *The Enneads.* Trans. S. MacKenna. Ed. B.S. Page. 4th ed. London: Faber, 1969.

POE, EDGAR ALLAN (1809–1849)

Poe was an American poet, short-story writer, and critic with a Romantic predilection for the macabre. Several of his early poems had been influenced by Coleridge, Shelley, and Keats, and he in his turn was to influence Charles Baudelaire, who translated his works into French. Samuel Macey has argued that the Romantics—though not the bourgeoisie whose lives tended to proceed with clockwork regularity—turned away from the clockwork celebrated by the Newtonian watchmaker god and instead abhorred what they considered to be a clockwork devil. Like Baudelaire, Poe wrote very much in this tradition, though sometimes one cannot avoid the feeling that he is fascinated by the very clockwork that he attacks.

Like other Romantic poets, Poe's abhorrence for clockwork derives from the enslavement of men and women that he considers it to represent. In his poem "The Bells," the bells are symbols of time which, in the four stanzas that proceed from youth to death, become ever more menacing. The bells, which are continually "Keeping time, time, time, / In a sort of Runic rhyme," begin in the first stanza as "Silver bells" that belong to "a world of merriment." In the second stanza they change into "mellow wedding bells, / Golden bells." But in the final two stanzas the enslavement by time grows far more ominous. The third stanza's "alarum bells— / Brazen bells / . . . In the startled ear of night" become in the final stanza much like the terrifying warnings of Baudelaire. Poe's "Iron bells" have changed into the ghouls of clockwork diabolism and their king tolls, keeping time "To the moaning and the groaning of the bells."

In "Maelzel's Chess Player" (Johann Nepomuk Maelzel is the clockmaker honored by musicians as the inventor of the metronome), Poe questions the authenticity of the supposed clockwork automaton. But the remarkable incisiveness of Poe's arguments to demonstrate that this is a fraud demonstrates equally well the real fascination that Poe has with the very clockwork automata that he claims elsewhere to abhor. In another prose piece, "The Colloquy of Monos and Una," Poe reacts to clockwork on a different level by showing that true duration stands apart from "the irregularities of the clock upon the mantel."

It is, however, in his short stories that Poe demonstrates more than anywhere his abhorrence of the clockwork-like regularity so much celebrated by the burghers of his society. The pipe, the attention to order and method, and above all the watch are the hallmarks of such people. In "Man of the Crowd," "The upper clerks of staunch firms. . . . wore watches with short gold chains of a substantial and ancient pattern," and in "Adventure of Hans Pfaall," every burgher "to a man replaced his pipe carefully in the corner of his mouth. . . puffed, paused, waddled about, and grunted significantly." The persona of "The Business Man" tells us that "in my general habits of accuracy and punctuality, I am not to be beat by a clock," and elsewhere he praises, above all, his own "positive appetite for system and regularity." All of the above bourgeois clockwork-like qualities and more appear in Poe's "Devil in the Belfry," an amusing dystopia which is dealt with in the article on **Utopias and Dystopias.**

But Poe's questioning of clockwork-like values is by no means normally amusing. He already foreshadows the nightmarelike quality of the servitude to time that Kafka would reflect a century later. In his Kafkaesque "Pit and the Pendulum," Poe's persona—together with whom the reader also suffers—is tied down beside a rat-infested "*pit*, typical of hell" in a dark prison. Like a modern version of the sword of Damocles, there hangs over his head "the painted figure of Time as he is commonly represented, save that, in lieu of a scythe, he held what, at a casual glance, I supposed to be the picture image of a huge pendulum, such as we see on antique clocks." As the razor-sharp edge of this pendulum, tipped by a crescent of glittering steel, drops slowly and ineluctably down on the helpless man, "The whole *hissed* as it swung through the air." The snakelike hiss as the cutting edge of the diabolic clockwork pendulum itself acts as the scythe of Time foreshadows the comparably methodical engine of Kafka's "Penal Colony."

In "A Predicament," Poe gives to the very minute hand of a monster clock the consciously represented role of itself acting as the scythe of Time. Signora Psyche Zenobia, whose name would appear to mean "given life by Zeus" (a god whose own name is derived from *deus*, *dieu*, or *day*), climbs high into the massive clock of a towering steeple. In "the chamber of the belfry," she places her head through "an opening in the dial-plate," which from the street far below must have looked like "a large key-hole, such as we see in the face of the French watches." With her head resting against the hour hand, she is attracted by the figure *V* (presumably night is coming at 5:25 P.M. and with it the minute hand will effect the eclipse of day and life): "Turning my head gently to one side, I perceived, to my extreme horror, that the huge, glittering, scimitar-like minute-hand of the clock, had, in the course of its hourly revolution, *descended upon my neck*. . . . Meantime the ponderous and terrific *Scythe of Time* (for I now discovered the literal import of that classical phrase) had not stopped, nor was it likely to stop." Like ourselves, Signora Zenobia is fascinated by the very technology that is about to destroy her. As she puts it, "The ticking of the machinery amused me. *Amused me*, I say for my sensations now bordered upon perfect happiness. . . . The eternal *click-clack, click-clack, click-clack* of the clock was the most melodious music to my ears."

While it is difficult to assess how clearly Romantic poets possessed the modern sense of the dangers of technology, in "The Colloquy of Monos and Una," Poe uses the indirection of putting words into the dead Monos—"in regard to man's general condition at this epoch"—that have an uncannily modern ring to them: "You will remember that one or two of the wise among our forefathers [presumably this includes Poe]—wise in fact, although not in the world's esteem—had ventured to doubt the propriety of the term 'improvement,' as applied to the progress of our civilization." The dead Monos—and through her we the readers—can now see that if they wished to survive human beings should have submitted themselves "to the control of the guidance of the natural laws, rather than attempt their control."

[S.L.M.]

See also **Baudelaire, Charles; Clock Metaphor; Father Time; Kafka, Franz; Utopias and Dystopias.**

FURTHER READINGS

Macey, Samuel L. *Clocks and the Cosmos: Time in Western Life and Thought.* Hamden: Archon Books, 1980.

Poe, Edgar Allan. *The Complete Tales and Poems.* New York: Modern Library, 1938.

POETRY

The association between poetry and time may be viewed from several perspectives, each revealing different aspects of the relationship: how a reader responds to poetry in time, and what effect reading words arranged metrically has on the mind; the poet's awareness of treating time as a subject, of recording history, and of commenting on the enigmas of time; how different genres and metrical arrangements are used to "alter" the movement of time; and, finally, how various critical orientations bring to focus different aspects of the relationship between poetry and time.

The study of the parallels between poetry and painting—"*ut pictura poesis*"—has its roots in classical literary criticism and has focused much attention on the matter of time in poetry and painting. Beginning with the seemingly obvious distinction that a poem must be apprehended through time and a painting must be apprehended in space, critics developed this view and enumerated its implied complexities. For instance, many historical paintings are narrative. In order to be understood, they must be viewed in parts or in sequence. As John Graham has pointed out, critics such as Leo Spitzer in 1962 and Murray Krieger in 1967 have argued "that literature is an object or artifact, that poetry can ultimately be spatial or 'still,' [and] that the reader combines the sequential details into a spatial moment." Whereas cubist painting, for example, arose partly as a way of manifesting differing perspectives on a two-dimensional surface, poetry has the intrinsic advantage of being able to offer several perspectives through time. Wallace Stevens's poem, "Thirteen Ways of Looking at a Blackbird" (1923), for instance, is composed of thirteen stanzas, each describing a blackbird. The accumulation of images follows a mind's pattern of thoughts, but the impression of each stanza is generated not from a "static" picture of an image, but from the manner in which the reader moves, in time, through the poem. The impact and expectation of the final lines of several stanzas are generated from the everyday images and thoughts of the first few lines of those stanzas. The totality of a poem, therefore, cannot be experienced as a static image.

Poets have always been aware of the capacity of poetry to convey the myths and histories of their countries and of the force of poetry to outlive the poet's own time. The bards of the past were often considered visionaries with great powers of memory who could redeem the myths of a culture and preserve them in a moving narrative. Homer's *Iliad* and *Odyssey* (ninth century B.C.) record heroic events from Greece's past; and Virgil's *Aeneid* (30–19 B.C.) chronicles, in verse, the founding of Rome. The capacity to outlive its writer has been the theme of much poetry. Shakespeare's "Sonnet 18" ends with the conceit that the sonnet itself will endure to give life to the lover it addresses: "So long as men can breathe or eyes can see / So long lives this, and this gives life to thee."

A study of prosody (the theories of versification) shows how different metrical arrangements can be used to give an impression of weightiness, of moving methodically through words, or of "condensing" time to achieve the appearance of immediate experience. Iambic pentameter, one of the standard verse forms of English poetry, consists of five feet, or units, of an unstressed followed by a stressed syllable. It is generally considered to parallel closely the rhythm of standard spoken English and, because of its regularity, it contributes to a formal, even-paced reading. It has been the line frequently chosen for reflective poetry. The beginning of Wordsworth's *The Prelude* (1850), is representative: "Oh there is blessing in this gentle breeze, / A visitant that while it fans my cheek / Doth seem half-conscious of the joy it brings / From the green fields, and from yon azure sky." Many modern poets have experimented with various metrical forms, breaking up the regularity of lines to control the pace of reading, and to achieve the impression of more immediate experience by focusing different units of attention on different lines. William Carlos Williams, in "The Red Wheelbarrow" (1923), focuses on a seemingly mundane image by breaking up what is close to two iambic pentameter lines into several short lines. Each line brings attention to detail in a manner unsuited to a longer, iambic pentameter line which is more appropriate for more fully developed thoughts.

A further method of invoking temporal awareness can involve using various devices, including elision of letters from words, and changing standard syntactical patterns. Robert Creeley, for example, uses these techniques to create the illusion of experiencing a sense of imminent danger of the speaker's situation in his poem "I Know a Man" (1962).

A literary critic's orientation toward poetry may accentuate differing aspects about time. Art as imitation, originating with classical critics, promoted a realistic portrayal of the actions of life. In the *Poetics* (ca. 330 B.C.), Aristotle advances the view that art is to portray "what is possible according to the law of probability or necessity." A poem, therefore, by altering "real" time to accommodate probability rather than actuality, may achieve a more philosophical view of life than unaltered experience. Romantic critics, from the latter part of the eighteenth century onward, stressed the powers of the imagination to order reality and see relationships that were not apparent, such as those between truth and beauty. The mind has the power to liberate itself from the constraints of time, as Coleridge points out in his *Biographia Literaria* (1817). Two modern critical theories have divergent approaches to time. Deconstruction, inspired by several French philosophers, including Jacques Derrida, insists that a text has multiple meanings, and that it cannot be paraphrased. It also cannot be linked in any meaningful way to its author or to the time of its composition and is therefore ahistorical. The new historicism, a movement greatly influenced by historians and anthropologists, seeks to place a work of art in its historical context to see in which ways it seeks to promote or undermine political and historical change. In this radical and skeptical approach toward art and its relation to political power, a poem, for instance, may sustain the mythologies of a ruling elite. Norman Finkelstein, in analyzing contemporary American poetry, states that one of his critical concerns is "the critique of literary ideology, both within discrete texts and throughout the social network of poetic production."

It is conceivable that, for a further understanding of so broad a concept as time and its relation to poetry, an infinite number of perspectives is possible. This article has indicated some potential structures for thinking about time and poetry.

[R.Z.]

See also **Derrida, Jacques; Victorian Poetry.**

FURTHER READINGS

Finkelstein, Norman. *The Utopian Moment in Contemporary American Poetry*. Cranbury: Associated University Presses, 1988.

Fraser, J.T. *Of Time, Passion and Knowledge: Reflections on the Strategy of Existence.* 2nd ed. Princeton: Princeton UP, 1990.

Graham, John. "Ut Pictura Poesis." *Dictionary of the History of Ideas.* Ed. Philip Wiener. New York: Scribner's, 1973. 4:465–476.

Jackson, Richard. *The Dismantling of Time in Contemporary Poetry.* Tuscaloosa: U of Alabama P, 1988.

POLITICAL THEORY AND PHILOSOPHY

"Political philosophy" and "political theory" refer both to an academic field and to a historical subject matter. In this essay, it is part of that subject matter, the canon of classic texts, from Plato to Marx, that is discussed. Taken together, these works are often understood as a tradition of thought to which a general meaning and significance, and various attributes, such as progress and decline, have been assigned. Their unity and even the criteria of inclusion are, however, more a function of present concerns and perspectives than of inherent historical connections between the authors and books. Despite the fact that they are all part of the seamless web of Western culture, and in that sense part of an actual tradition or traditions, the designation of classical political philosophy and theory as a distinct historical genre is largely analytical and retrospective and involves abstracting the works from their particular contexts. These texts become meaningful when we distinguish various features within them that are relevant for understanding and thinking about contemporary affairs. Yet even though the constitution of this "tradition" is largely stipulative, it is possible, nevertheless, to discern or suggest certain common intrinsic characteristics of these texts, the circumstances of the authors, and the contexts of their production, and to generalize about them on this basis. Not the least of these characteristics is the relationship between political philosophy and time, between historical consciousness and the search for political order.

Although time is often construed as an objective property of the physical universe, it is ultimately a function of scientific, religious, and common sense theories and conceptions of that universe. Even if we embrace a realist metaphysic, which would posit a world independent of our theories about it, the only world we know is that sedimented in our symbolic constructions. Those constructions, and our conceptions of time, have differed historically. Although functionally we might want to say that temporality, no matter how conceived, is always a part of our vision of the universe, modern physics has tended to reduce time to space. And it is probable that ancient, as well as certain isolated modern cultures, lack any distinct language and conception of time. Time, then, is primarily a symbolic form and linguistic construction of experience that has a great deal of cultural and historical variation. The same may be said of politics. Although it is quite possible to define politics in a functional manner, such as the exercise of power or the relationship between rulers and ruled, and thereby specify it as a universal attribute of social life, politics more specifically conceived, like time, is a cultural form, a conventional dimension of human life. Both the content and the contours of what we consider political have differed historically and culturally, and, no less than time, it is a necessary mode of human existence.

Although it would be interesting to investigate empirically the relation between politics and time, that is, the manner in which time is conceived in various political societies, this essay focuses principally on the relationship between political philosophy, that is, thinking about politics, and historical consciousness. Political philosophy can be distinguished in part by its attachment to the idea that political order is the fundamental answer to the problem of the place of human beings in the world. It has characteristically borne a particular relationship to the conception of the human condition as historical. Politics, as a distinct social form, can be reasonably interpreted as having emerged in post-Homeric Greece, and political philosophy, or self-conscious systematic thought about politics, can be said to have begun with Plato and Aristotle and their confrontation with the problem of the relationship between theory and practice or knowledge and politics.

Historical consciousness arose from the transformation of the temporally and spatially compact vision of the universe characteristic of ancient mythic societies such as Egypt and Mesopotamia. Temporal consciousness and distinctions between the dimensions of past, present, and future, including the mortality of individuals and societies, are predicated upon the recognition of unique events. In the mythic *Weltanschauung*, temporality was "abolished" by the sublimation of particulars within the archetypal events of creation stories and other mythical narratives and attending rituals. Similarly, the orders of existence familiar to our experience—differentiated in terms of the spheres of god, nature, society, and individual—were compressed in an image of the world in which these distinctions were suppressed. Historical consciousness, or history as a symbolic form for ordering experience and human activity, involved both the differentiation of human beings from the other orders of existence and a conception of the particularity of human events and actions.

Historical perception entailed the realization that while the natural universe was eternal, or eternally cyclical, the human universe was not only a product of human action but tended also to move, like the life of the individual, in a linear path from birth to death. The distinctiveness of political order was in an important sense a function of the rise of historical consciousness. It was, for better or worse, the abode of human beings in the world, and its constitution, perpetuation, and relationship to the individual, nature, and deity became a problem. There were, however, radically different conceptions of both the form and content of the images of history and political order that succeeded the mythic paradigm.

For the ancient Hebrews, history was meaningful. It was the scene of the one transcendent God's providence and the story of his covenant with his chosen people. Israel was, to be sure, a political order presided over by king and priest, but, as stressed in the prophetic tradition, it was also a community of the faithful moving toward fulfillment in time. Its orientation was eschatological. The vision of history was in a sense the temporalization of the myth. Particular events, such as the exodus, gained meaning and significance as elements of an unfolding story leading to the kingship of Yahweh and the posthistorical reconciliation of humanity, nature, and god. The idea of the king as Messiah, mediating between god and society, and of Israel as a static spatial symbol was not easily reconciled with the basic elements of Hebrew theology. The tension between the kingship, which was often viewed as a manifestation or agent of covenant transgression, and the image of Israel as a dynamic historical symbol was profound. The historical memory of the Hebrews began with a flight from political order, from Egypt, and political society was always viewed in part as heretical and certainly less than the ultimate destiny of human beings. For the Greeks, the experience of history and political order was radically different.

The historical consciousness of the Greeks was also formed in the experience of an exodus—the movement, at the end of the Bronze Age, under the pressure of invasion, across the Peloponnesian peninsula to the coast of Asia Minor. The traditions that would define classical Greece emerged from this period, but in the cultural memory of the Greeks history was viewed as the scene of decline and decay, as the fall from a heroic golden age of Mycenaean kingship, recounted in Homer's epics, to a dark age of political disintegration and injustice, described in Hesiod's poems. The Greeks viewed the human condition, the life of the individual and the city, as singularly vulnerable in a universe of eternal nature and immortal gods. Human affairs were marked by a tendency toward degeneration. Change without inherent meaning was the significance of history. However, the *polis* (city-state), the community and political space, offered solace and some sense of permanence. In the creation of political order and in the deeds and words of political life a measure of immortality was achieved that transcended the destructive force of time. Human frailty was the cause of decay, but human action and its artifacts also held out the promise of overcoming, to some degree, historical entropy, of achieving justice and right order.

Aeschylus's *Oresteia* was the celebration of the impersonal law of the *polis* that lifted society out of the cycles of feudal retribution exemplified in Homer's *Iliad*, but Thucydides's story of the Peloponnesian War and the decline of Athens, and of Hellas as a whole, attested to the tenuousness of political forms. There are many ways to read Plato's *Republic*, but what distinguished his work from previous literature and can reasonably be said to have set the hallmark of political philosophy was not simply a diagnosis of social ills but the presentation of an alternative vision of political order based on access to transcendent truth. Although the *Republic* was surely an attempt to demonstrate the inadequacy of previous ideas of justice for saving the *polis*, it was less a plea for a utopian or ideal state based on the rule of philosophers than an extended exploration of the possibilities and limitations inherent in attempting to join knowledge and power. The irony in this work was the suggestion that even if the best political order did, by some miracle, come into existence, human nature, and even the nature of philosophers, was not ultimately impervious to the corruption of time. In his second most famous political work, the

Laws, Plato initiated an idea that would recur with power and frequency in Western political thought.

The image of order in the *Republic* was predicated on the existence of a certain individual or class of individuals—the philosophical ruler. If this was difficult to attain and even more difficult to sustain, the question was whether it was best at all if the purpose of political order was to provide a human cosmos that reflected in some measure the permanence of the rest of the universe. If philosophers could not be rulers, Plato suggested, might they not be founders whose psyches would be reflected in the structure of the city? Might it not be possible to create political institutions and laws in which the genius of a philosopher is manifest but which, by virtue of their construction, are self-sustaining and surpass the mortality of their creator? This was the origin of the idea of a government of laws and not persons.

Aristotle, even more explicitly than Plato, stressed the idea of the *polis* as the home of human beings in the world and as the locus of individual realization. In the creation and maintenance of the city, as a physical entity and as a space for individual human action, the inexorable movement of time, which was tied to all material things including embodied persons and their creations, was arrested. The political association was the most important, because it encompassed the whole community; political science, which aimed at the health of that association, was the master science. In an era in which the *polis* was actually being swept away in the rise of empire, a political philosophy based on this entity was in practice obsolescent, and Aristotle was considerably more tolerant of inferior types than Plato. But Aristotle's concern was still with joining theory and practice, and his moderate ideal of a mixed constitution or "polity" was a perpetuation of Plato's image of political order achieved and sustained through institutional virtue.

One of the most powerful expressions of this idea was in the work of Polybius, the Greek historian who sought to explain the success of the Roman republic. He asked why this one city-state had achieved such power and longevity and broken out of the perpetual historical cycle of rise and fall that had characterized other political regimes. Although it had happened less by design than by chance and institutional learning, Rome had evolved an ingenious mixed form of government in which the conflict between the executive and representatives of the people and nobles respectively had created an almost perpetual order based on internal equilibrium and external expansion. Machiavelli appropriated and embellished this model when confronting the political disunity of Renaissance Italy. Although *The Prince* is his most famous work, Machiavelli was a dedicated republican, and it is difficult ultimately to read his instruction to a prince for developing the necessary skill for acquiring power as other than a preface to his theory of government in the *Discourses*. For Machiavelli, the content of history was a source of knowledge, but, as a process, history signified only change and decay. He stressed that it was necessary that the founding and reformation of states be the work of one person, but, given individual mortality, the deficiencies of human nature, and the impact of *fortuna* on human affairs, institutions informed by wisdom offered the best hope for stability. The equilibrium achieved by properly designed institutional conflict was the basis for preserving both order and liberty.

Christian theology and philosophy were an important influence on political thought, but no more than prophetic Judaism was Christianity ultimately compatible with political philosophy. The life of a citizen in political space was not the end of human beings. Although Christians had endured existence in political society in the hope of future salvation, they, like the Hebrews, had conceived human history as an upward sloping line leading to the last judgment, and they finally gave religious significance to Rome, after Constantine, as the threshold of the second coming of Christ. With the fall of Rome, however, St. Augustine relegated human history and human time to its classical status of meaningless repetition. He had not dismissed the value of political order and human justice, but he had conceived it in a depreciated sense—as God's gift to sinful humanity and representative of the fallen condition that characterized the earthly city. True justice was a property of the heavenly city, the city of God, and beyond human history. Medieval Christian thought, such as that represented by St. Thomas Aquinas, attempted in various ways to reconcile reason and faith and theology and political theory, but secular political philosophy, in the classic sense, reappeared during the Renaissance and in the wake of the Protestant reformation with the separation of religion and politics.

Once again, in the seventeenth century, the idea was abroad that human beings, whatever the ultimate fate of their souls, must take on the task of creating political nature and completing the order of the universe by constructing a home for human beings in the world. The image of history was distinctly classical and Augustinian—a realm of change and without meaning. Thomas Hobbes proclaimed a science of political order that would transcend the flux of history and create coherence in human affairs by creating a *Leviathan* that would overcome and suppress the religious and secular conflicts that marked the age. Time and history for Hobbes were simply the symbols of transience and decay, of the chaos of the "natural condition" of humanity, which political science must overcome by architectonic artifice and action. Although Hobbes's image of authoritarian rule was very different from John Locke's idea of limited constitutional government and the democratic character of J.J. Rousseau's *Social Contract*, they were at one in their conception of political order as the salvation of the individual and as a bulwark against the temporal flow of unreconstructed social life. Rousseau's image of political society was a recapitulation of the structures of a hypothetical original condition where individuals had lived in harmony with one another and with nature without consciousness of history and time. James Harrington's *Oceana* pursued the republican image of constitutional balance as the source of a semi-eternal commonwealth—a theme which would find its full modern expression in the American founding and the *Federalist Papers*, but the image of history that characterized the Enlightenment fundamentally transformed political philosophy.

Heretofore, the goal had been to impose meaning and order, representing some transcendent truth, on a world of meaningless historical change. What emerged in the eighteenth century was the idea that there was meaning *in* history and that political order and human salvation were immanent in the historical process itself. Human order was now to be found in what had been characteristically understood in secular thought as the incoherent succession of time. Order was not something to be imposed on history by human action and artifice but rather history itself was the creator of order and overcame itself. The vague notion of progress in human affairs that appeared in the Enlightenment was followed by a more schematic rendering in Hegel's secularized version of the Judeo-Christian account of history as the revelation of providence. Now, however, it was the providence inherent in the march of human reason as manifest in the totality of human history and realized fully in the modern culture of the West and, particularly, the nineteenth-century political state. This image of history as the scene of human fulfillment culminated in Marx. Although Marx's conception of the end of history lay in the future and was, narrowly construed, postpolitical as well as posthistorical, it retained the persistent idea that human order required the overcoming of history.

It is difficult to characterize what, in the contemporary world, would represent the genre of political philosophy. Such a characterization would be largely academic commentary that bears little relationship to the past works that, for example, despite their ultimate lack of political efficacy, were deeply involved in the political life of their time. But the very character of the problem that informed these works has changed. We are no longer naive enough to believe that history is intrinsically meaningful. History largely appears to us once again as mere succession which we must master in order to make a home in the world, but the idea that the fundamental answer to the problem of human existence is political order is seldom expressed. And when it is expressed, the basis on which to justify either the general claim or the particular kind of political society prescribed is more difficult to define. Philosophy, in the nineteenth century, made history the repository of meaning, but the twentieth century failed to sustain that optimistic vision. Temporality once more confronts us as mere succession, but with history emptied of ultimate significance, and even human nature understood as a product of history and society, the basic idea of political philosophy might seem to be in abeyance.

[J.G.G.]

See also **Aquinas, St. Thomas; Aristotle; Augustine; Eschatology; Locke, John; Machiavelli, Niccolò; Marx, Karl; Plato; Rousseau, Jean-Jacques.**

FURTHER READINGS

Arendt, Hannah. *Between Past and Future*. New York: Viking, 1961.

Darby, W. Thomas. *The Feast: Meditations on Politics and Time*. Toronto: U of Toronto P, 1982.

Gunnell, John G. *Political Theory: Tradition and Interpretation*. Cambridge: Winthrop, 1978.

———. *Political Philosophy and Time: Plato and the Origins of Political Vision*. New Edition. Chicago: U of Chicago P, 1986.

Pocock, J.G.A. *Politics, Language and Time: Essays on Political Thought and History*. New York: Atheneum, 1971.

Rifkin, Jeremy. *Time Wars: The Primary Conflict in Human History*. New York: Holt, 1987.

Sabine, George H. *A History of Political Theory*. New York: Holt Rinehart, 1962.

Skinner, Quentin. *Foundations of Modern Political Thought*. 2 vols. Cambridge: Cambridge UP, 1978.

Strauss, Leo, and Joseph Cropsey, eds. *History of Political Philosophy*. 3rd ed. Chicago: U of Chicago P, 1987.

Voegelin, Eric. *Order and History*. Vol. 1. *Israel and Revelation*. Baton Rouge: Louisiana State UP, 1956. Vol. 2. *The World of the Polis*, 1957.

Wolin, Sheldon S. *Politics and Vision*. Boston: Little, Brown, 1960.

POLITICS AND AGING

Politics, as a reference point for aging, implies consideration of the power relationships within a given setting or society; the manner in which the governance of social affairs is conducted; and the opportunities afforded to people, including older people, to play a full role in determining arrangements for the social and economic well-being of different groups in society.

Any review of the relationship between politics and aging, with reference to time, must take as its baseline the premise that in different societies, across different historical periods, cultural variation has resulted in widely differing experiences and levels of engagement with the political process among older people. Indeed, what counts as an older person is itself contextually embedded and influenced by temporal, geographical, and cultural diversity. Nevertheless, over time globally, and over individual lifespans, it is possible to observe different trends and fluctuations in political processes and arrangements which may be located along the span from autocracy to democracy.

As an initial example, we might consider the elders of a traditional rural community in the Asian subcontinent, who may be honored and respected for their accumulated wisdom—as a result of which they might enjoy high status and political influence in the management of community affairs within a delimited location. By contrast, their peers who have pioneered an alternative life style in the West—for example, inner city Asians living in Southall, West London, may suffer invisibility. Older members of the Asian community, women in particular, may not be entered on the electoral register and may thus be prohibited from full participation in the local and national political processes; within family politics their influence may be attenuated by changes in family structure, itself the outcome of social and cultural change. Likewise, there will be variation in the roles and responsibilities held by different groups of elders within mainstream Western society—as determined by social class, gender, employment experience, health or disability, and many other factors. In other words, the relationship between aging and politics is characterized by complexity.

One of the intriguing differences that merits further examination is the dissimilar experience of aging under opposing political regimes. The social democratic convention of Western European societies affords mixed rewards to senior citizens, where a judicious balancing act is devised to accommodate a range of social and financial benefits with regard to housing, health and social care, leisure facilities, and—in exceptional cases—educational provision. This occurs alongside a pension entitlement that represents a modest fractional share of the minimum industrial wage.

In the latter stages of advanced capitalism, the role and status of elders is directly linked to their ability to control the newly colonized territory of the first-generation elderly mass consumer. Many elderly people fail to conform to this model of successful consumerism. As a result, poverty remains a constant for substantial numbers of older people who do not compete successfully as individuals pursuing the maximum private pension. Statutory support systems—provided through taxation, to which older people have contributed—remain important to many older women, ethnic elders, and those with disabilities or health care needs. Yet they are regarded as a burden to the productive members of society and receive minimal social support.

The collectivist socialist alternative offers little in material advantage for the elderly members of its varied communities. By contrast, however, social advantage may well accrue from the historical role played by this generation of elders in the early and mid-twentieth-century revolutionary struggles. As state socialism crumbles, the effects on older people should not be ignored.

One key aspect of the relationship between aging, politics, and time is the mediating effect of the different and contrasting theories of aging that have been developed to explain and interpret the combined sociobiological and/or cultural phenomenon that we refer to confidently as "growing older."

Throughout the affluent 1950s and early 1960s, in North America and Europe, the explanatory force of disengagement theory compounded popular images of a natural decline in activity levels and a gentle withdrawal from mainstream social and economic life. It thereby accorded with a politically conservative or functionalist view of the governance of human affairs. More recently, this approach has been challenged by a more radical interpretation of such a "withdrawal." Social dependency theory argues that older people are marginalized by their (weak) structural position in postcapitalist society and that their ability to achieve rewarding and independent lives is politically determined. Temporal specificity thus links the reality of the differential experience of various groups of elders with differing political explanations.

Continuing the theme of political difference and its impact on the experience of aging, there is an obvious relationship between the range of support systems that are available to promote successful aging and the way in which such systems may be used in different cultures, at different levels of intensity, with a different philosophical approach, and to quite different effect. In the more traditional form of society, and in present-day societies that favor individualism, informal care mechanisms tend to predominate. Though they may be effective where family networks are close and strong, the pressures of modern living—together with changes in family structure—have rendered the family less well able to provide direct caregiving. As formal systems have developed over time, they too have been influenced by contemporary ideas. So, for example, the biological and illness model of the early twentieth century is now challenged by a model predicated on independent living and the right to exercise choice. And the support infrastructure may be interpreted more generously as including education and leisure facilities as well as the accepted spheres of health, housing, and social care.

Finally, this consideration of politics and time must examine evidence of political activity—as one manifestation of democratic involvement over time among older people. Much interest has been generated around the issue of voting behavior. Data from different sources suggest that older voters in Western-style democracies are more conservative than younger voters. What is not clear is whether this is a cohort effect, a survival effect, a gender effect linked to the larger proportion of women, or simply a tendency to become more individualist and conservative and less collectivist and socialist with advanced age. Increasingly, this latter explanation has become suspect. What is clear, however, is that the voice of older people has had little impact on mainstream political activity and that for many, pressure-group politics has provided an alternative route to power and influence. In North America and across western Europe, the phenomenon of "grey politics" has materialized in different guises. Formal organizations of older citizens, such as the Gray Panthers or the various associations of retired persons, have intervened directly in the political process at national levels. At the same time, representational groups, such as Age Concern or Help the Aged, have extended their activities into the realms of policy and advocacy. And at a local level, there is now a burgeoning of community politics among older people which complements the more traditional forms of recreational and club activity.

In sum, the passage of the twentieth century has witnessed substantial challenge and change in terms of this complex relationship between the older person and politics, with a marked shift in awareness of what the older person as citizen can now achieve.

[D.W.]

See also **Aging and Time; Aging Populations; Ethnicity and Aging; Gender Differences in Aging; Political Theory and Philosophy; Social Gerontology.**

FURTHER READINGS

Cutler, Neal E., and John R. Schmidhauser. "Age and Political Behavior." *Aging: Scientific Perspectives and Social Issues*. Ed. Diana S. Woodruff and James E. Birren. New York: Van Nostrand, 1975. 374–403.

Cutler, Stephen J., et al. "Aging and Conservatism: Cohort Changes in Attitudes about Legalized Abortion." *Journal of Gerontology* 35.1 (1980): 115–123.

Glenn, Norval D. "Aging and Conservatism." *The Annals of the American Academy of Political and Social Sciences* 415 (1974): 176–186.

Gubrium, Jaber F. "Continuity in Social Support, Political Interest, and Voting in Old Age." *The Gerontologist* 12.4 (1972): 421–423.

Hudson, Robert B., and Robert H. Binstock. "Political Systems and Aging." *Handbook of Aging and Social Sciences*. Ed. Robert H. Binstock and Ethel Shanas. New York: Van Nostrand, 1976. 369–400.

Johnson, Gregory, and Lawrence J. Kamara. "Growing Up and Growing Old: The Politics of Age Exclusion." *International Journal of Aging and Human Development* 8.2 (1977–78): 99–110.

McIntyre, Angus, ed. *Aging and Political Leadership.* Albany: State U of New York P, 1988.

Ragan, Pauline K., and James J. Dowd. "The Emerging Political Consciousness of the Aged: A General Interpretation." *Journal of Social Issues* 30.3 (1974): 137–158.

POPULATION: PAST, PRESENT, FUTURE

The fascinating story of world population growth since the time of human beginnings tells how a few thousand wanderers a million or so years ago grew into today's billions of inhabitants in cities, towns, and countryside. *Homo sapiens* may have become distinct from its hominid predecessors about a million years ago. Between then and the beginnings of agriculture and domestication of animals about 10,000 B.C., the average rate of population growth was less than 0.0001 percent per annum, so that in this 99 percent of human history the population had increased to a mere 5 to 10 million (the number which anthropologists estimate could be supported by hunting and gathering cultures).

The concept of a population ceiling helps to explain the minimal growth or population steady state during the long Paleolithic age. Scientists have long observed that animal populations never realize, except sometimes in the short term, their often enormous biotic potential; in other words, their powers of reproduction in an optimal environment of unlimited extent free of competitors. Biotic potential is always checked, sooner or later, by environmental resistance in the form of shortages of space, food, or other sustaining resources as the carrying capacity of the environment—the population ceiling—is approached. The mechanisms that prevent the population from exceeding the carrying capacity involve some combination of increased mortality and reduced fertility. The traditional view that this was achieved in hunting and gathering societies essentially by density-dependent mortality is now being modified by an appreciation from relic societies like the Kalahari Bushmen that a combination of behavioral and nutritionally related physiological factors can also suppress fertility.

The first major population growth was associated with the emergence of agriculture in Neolithic times around 12,000 years ago, although this occurred somewhat later in the New World. There is no question that growth was stimulated by the increased carrying capacity of the habitat as humans switched from being predators and secondary and tertiary consumers in food webs to being dominantly herbivores and primary consumers. But the traditional view that population growth was accomplished largely by diminished mortality is now discredited. Concentration of population in villages and later in cities could be expected to promote transmission of diseases, and there was always vulnerability to crop failure. Population growth, therefore, is likely to have been accomplished by the increases in fertility associated with the family labor needs of peasant agriculture; in addition, grain meal and cows' milk permitted the earlier weaning of infants, thus reducing the period of ovulation suppression associated with breast-feeding.

There were some modest advances in environmental exploitation during the agricultural era, notably the development of metal tools, but the concept of a ceiling to population growth—inching up certainly at times—was still applicable. Thus, although global population grew to about 300 million by A.D. 1, and 800 million by 1750, the average growth rate was still below 0.1 percent per annum.

The modern period of population growth, when rapid technological advancement has undermined the relevance of population ceilings and carrying capacities, may be regarded as starting about 1750. Average annual growth rates climbed to about 0.5 percent between 1750 and 1900, 0.8 percent in the first half of the twentieth century, and 1.7 percent in the sec-

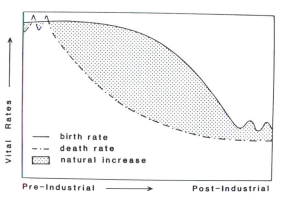

Figure 1. The standard demographic transition.

ond half. In this minute fraction of human history, the world's population has sextupled, from 0.8 billion in 1750 to 5.3 billion in 1990. In less than 0.1 percent of human history has occurred more than 80 percent of the increase in human numbers.

In developed countries, the rapid economic development and associated social modernization from the eighteenth century initially influenced mortality and then, about a century later, fertility rates were affected. If fertility and mortality declines had been concurrent, population growth in developed countries would have been fairly modest, as was uniquely the case in France, which experienced an exceptionally early fertility decline in a dominantly agrarian society. But elsewhere in the developed world, mortality decline preceded fertility decline by about a century, leading to the replacement of demographic equilibrium by the population explosion of nineteenth-century Europe and North America. In some cases there may have been a slight increase of fertility associated with new opportunities for employment and early marriage at the beginning of industrialization, further accentuating population growth in the transition. Figure 1 provides a stylized representation of the standard demographic transition, indicating how in preindustrial societies the birth rate was relatively constant, while the death rate fluctuated from year to year in response to epidemics and variable food supply. After the transition, roles are reversed: the death rate remains stable while fertility oscillates in relation to social trends and economic fluctuations.

Although the early stages of demographic transition may be observed in the Third World, there is no assurance that later stages will replicate the experience of developed countries and attain environmentally sustainable population levels. There are those who optimistically suggest that the necessary fertility regulation can be achieved. They point out that latecomers to the transition process—notably Germany, southern and eastern Europe, and Japan—all experienced a concentrated and accelerated fertility decline; that, contrary to some views, the pace of modernization in many Third World countries is actually more rapid than in nineteenth-century Europe; and that governments are now prepared and have the capability to promote policies of fertility regulation. There are others who maintain that high fertility is so institutionally interwoven with the entire cultural fabric of less developed countries that its reduction is an intractable problem. What is indisputable is that the modern period of population growth is clearly a transitory episode. If the growth rate of the 1980s were to be maintained, the population would double every forty years or so, so that in 500 years there would be standing room only on the earth's surface. Simple arithmetic, therefore, shows that a return to a growth rate much nearer zero than 2 percent per annum is inevitable, but whether this will be achieved through lower birth rates or higher death rates, or some combination of both, is the great imponderable.

[H.R.J.]

See also **Food Supply and Population; Human Fertility Trends; Human Mortality Trends; Material Progress and Population.**

FURTHER READINGS

Cohen, M. *Health and the Rise of Civilization.* New Haven: Yale UP, 1989.

Coleman, D., and R. Schofield, eds. *The State of Population Theory.* Oxford: Blackwell, 1986.

Jones, H. *Population Geography.* London: Paul Chapman, 1990.

POSTMODERN LITERATURE

Postmodernism is a radical mode of skepticism that interrogates what traditional modes of thought once took for granted about language and experience, giving these no more than a shifting and provisional status. It questions various cultural centers of authority while delighting in antiform and uncertainty. Often, theorists find it more helpful to think of postmodernism as a frame of mind rather than as a clearly defined historical period because one can cite examples of this orientation at work in many pre-contemporary cultural expressions, from the ancient European carnival tradition to Laurence Sterne's eighteenth-century antinovel, *Tristram Shandy.* At the same time, however, it is clear that this way of thinking came to dominate our culture shortly after World War II in response to a world faced with the possibility of physical and metaphysical erasure.

It is no surprise, then, to discover that postmodern literature drastically reformulates key principles of conventional literature such as authorship, audience, characterization, and narrative closure—not to mention linear presentation of time or chronology, time's technical manifestation in a poem, play, or piece of fiction. Conventional literature—particularly nineteenth-century realism, against which twentieth-century literature especially rebelled—evinces a narrative belief grounded in the passage of clock time. According to the nineteenth-century novelist Stendhal, literature's task is to hold up an impartial mirror to the world that reflects consensus reality and, hence, the communal and Newtonian time of cause and effect. Modern literature, however, rejects this view as essentially naive. Instead of emphasizing an external notion of reality, modern literature presents an internal one. If the conventional literature of an Honoré de Balzac seeks to be a photograph of the cosmos, then the modern literature of a Marcel Proust seeks to be an X-ray. Consequently, modern literature, which shares affinities with the work of Albert Einstein and Henri Bergson, focuses on relative, subjective temporality.

Postmodern literature, though, critiques *both* conventional *and* modernist portrayals of time. It does so not in order to suggest a third coherent version of temporality, but to subvert rationalist ideas of coherence and destabilize what it perceives as two fundamentally limited and limiting concepts of time. While this destabilization may occur in almost as many ways and for almost as many reasons as there are pieces of postmodern literature, the result is frequently the same: Father Time ends up on a life-support system, deformed and ridiculous, devoid of order and intelligibility. Paralleling the investigations of such poststructuralist theorists as Jacques Derrida and Jean-François Lyotard, works of postmodern literature often do not evince a tragic recognition of this destabilization, but rather a carnivalesque celebration of it. Closer to MTV (music television) than to photo or X-ray, postmodern literature embraces possibility, discontinuity, and instability.

Temporality can be destabilized on the level of content or on the level of form in a postmodern text. In terms of content, a postmodern work makes time its theme in an attempt to explore and overturn conventional and modern notions of it. Samuel Beckett, for instance, meditates upon the relentless passage of time which leads nowhere in his minimalist dramas such as *Waiting for Godot* (1952). Humbert Humbert, Vladimir Nabokov's narrator of *Lolita* (1955), tries to outdo and thereby transcend the constraints of temporality by fashioning a neoromantic love song to an unattainable young girl. Metafictionist Italo Calvino tries to imagine what the universe must have been like before the creation of time in "All at One Point," a short story in

Cosmicomics (1965), in order to privilege lyrical over scientific perceptions of temporality. In *One Hundred Years of Solitude* (1967), magical realist Gabriel García Márquez writes the saga of the Buendía family, whose lives turn out to have been nothing but the reenactment of events described in a Sanscrit parchment, while in *The Electric Kool-Aid Acid Test* (1969) new journalist Tom Wolfe creates a novel-length piece of "faction" ("fact" plus "fiction") that recounts Ken Kesey's cross-country odyssey. García Márquez and Wolfe create their novels with a deconstructive eye toward debunking time as a totalizing strategy and toward suggesting that history is a kind of literature. Science fiction, another subgenre of postmodern literature, interrogates the notion of time by generating absent futures or, more rarely, absent pasts, as in the case of Bruce Sterling and William Gibson's *The Difference Engine* (1991), which posits the invention of the computer nearly a century before the fact.

Temporality can also be destabilized on the level of form in a postmodern text by means of various structural experimentations. For example, Alain Robbe-Grillet's *nouveau romans* such as *Jealousy* (1957), involve scenic repetitions, substitutions, and permutations that lead to insurmountable contradictions in chronology. In *The Soft Machine* (1961), and other novels, beat writer William Burroughs employed "cut-ups," or verbal montages that are the linguistic equivalent of drug-induced hallucinations. Avant-pop author Thomas Pynchon generates massive temporal digressions that often go nowhere in his tome *Gravity's Rainbow* (1973). John Ashbery endlessly defers the meaning of temporality in his poem "Litany" (1979), a dialogue between two printed columns that test and subvert their own and each other's predictions about time. L=A=N=G=U=A=G=E poets such as Lyn Hejinian, Charles Bernstein, and Ron Silliman show that language can deconstruct the conventional moment and traditional assumptions about time. Writers as diverse as Beckett in *How It Is* (1961), and Kathy Acker in *Blood and Guts in High School* (1984), emphasize the contingent flow of temporality by creating the textual analog of schizophrenia.

Ultimately, then, postmodern literature's view of time is as diverse and challenging as postmodern literature itself. Its "truth" about temporality is elusive and volatile, leading readers in the end not toward a clear and conclusive product, but through an uncertain and inconclusive process; not toward a definitive answer about the nature of time, but into an infinite and interesting journey on a Möbius strip of questions.

[L.O.]

See also **Alternate History; Derrida, Jacques; Futuristic Fiction; Modernism; Science Fiction.**

FURTHER READINGS

Church, Margaret. *Time and Reality: Studies in Contemporary Fiction.* Chapel Hill: U of North Carolina P, 1963.

Hutcheon, Linda. *A Poetics of Postmodernism: History, Theory, Fiction.* New York: Routledge, 1988.

Jackson, Richard. *The Dismantling of Time in Contemporary Poetry.* Tuscaloosa: U of Alabama P, 1988.

Quinones, Ricardo J. *Mapping Literary Modernism: Time and Development.* Princeton: Princeton UP, 1985.

Tobin, Patricia Drechsel. *Time and the Novel: The Genealogical Imperative.* Princeton: Princeton UP, 1978.

PRAGMATISM

Rarely has a philosophical word been so abused, misunderstood, and sullied as has that of "pragmatism." Constantly confused with the seeking of human self-interest, with matters sheerly and exclusively practical, pragmatism as commonly used fails to connote its philosophical sophistication and epistemological importance. The classic statements of the fundamental meaning of pragmatism by Charles S. Peirce and William James, respectively, are to be found in James Mark Baldwin's *Dictionary of Philosophy and Psychology.* As Peirce puts it: "Consider what effects, that might conceivably have practical bearings, we conceive the object of our conception to have. Then, our conception of these effects is the whole of our conception of the object." Dealing with the same subject, James says the following: "The doctrine that the whole 'meaning' of a conception expresses itself in practical consequences, consequences either in the shape of conduct to be recommended, or in that of experiences to be expected, if the conception be true; which consequences would be different if it were untrue, and must be different from the consequences by which the meaning of other conceptions is in turn expressed."

Although infrequently stressed by Peirce and James, as well as by subsequent commentators, it is clear that the central thrust of this position is the ineluctable and irreducible phenomenon of time. A pragmatic theory of truth holds that propositions are precisely that, proposals, forays into the future and thereby their truth-function is time-bound. Even if one were to take a simple declaratory sentence such as "a book is on the shelf," it becomes true only if and when one reaches for it; *subsequently*, it is, in fact, there. More to the point of our present discussion, however, is the deeper meaning of "pragmatic sensibility" in our approach to making claims, offering predictions and prognostications, as well as giving advice on the basis of assumptions held at that time.

Nothing is better known, paradoxically, than the utter mystery of the meaning of time, whether it be as allegedly past, speciously present to us, or pertaining to that which inevitably is to come. Saint Augustine was incisive when he wrote in Book XI of *The Confessions*: "What then is time: If no one asks me, I know: If I wish to explain it to one that asketh, I know not."

Notwithstanding Saint Augustine's warning as to the elusiveness of the meaning of time, nor Kant's bold assertion that time is a creation of human "sensible intuition" and therefore has no ultimate reality, the "stubborn fact," to paraphrase William James, is that we experience sequence, we experience memory, and we experience both the realization and failure of our projections, hopes, fears, and contentions.

In the definitions of pragmatism given above, the key phrase in the statement by Peirce is "practical bearings." It is to be noted that he uses a present participle, thereby holding that the truth of conceptions is dependent on future outcome. For James, the key word is more direct and more helpful. He refers to "consequences" as essential to any evaluation of the truth of a conception, that is, to future experience. In his discussion of "The Construction of Judgment," John Dewey, in his *Logic: The Theory of Enquiry*, wants to "know how indispensable it is to acknowledge that judgment, like inquiry, is temporal."

If the pragmatic method for ascertaining the truth of conceptions and judgments were to be used within the framework of a traditional metaphysics, then the critics of pragmatism would be correct in holding that the meaning of nature, reality, and events would be tainted by a subjectivism. But, as with most epistemologies, the approach of pragmatism is dependent on a metaphysics. For James and Dewey, process rather than stasis, and ambiguity rather than clarity, are the major metaphors for their understanding of human activity and the affairs of nature. William James speaks of relations as experienced equivalently to our experience of objects and

Dewey insists on the transactional character of all human experience. They hold to the perpetual presence of "chance" in all that has been or is to be. For James and Dewey, reality is neither a noun, nor a thing, nor an object to be understood in any final way. Accepting the basic premise of Kant's philosophy, they believe that human knowing is more than observational or definitional. Rather, given a processive, developing, constantly changing setting, the act of human knowing is one of participating and constructing.

Consequently, and the word is used advisedly, pragmatically, it is not "time," as such, of which we can speak. Rather, we speak of our "timing" whatever is given, for it is we who segment, sequence, order, postpone, reconstitute, and project that which we come to call the world. Awake or asleep, retrospectively or prospectively, in our having experience, that is in our doing and undergoing, to use Dewey's phrasing, we are in, of, and about time, as a flow, a process, a continuum. For human beings, time is a seamless, conscious fabric which attends us in every way, every day, always.

Following James, in his "Notes for Philosophy 20c: Metaphysical Seminary (1903–1904)," finality and closure are to be avoided, for "All 'classic,' clean, cut and dried, 'noble,' fixed, 'eternal,' *Weltanschauungen* seem to me to violate the character with which life concretely comes and the expression which it bears, of being, or at least of involving, a muddle and a struggle, with an 'ever not quite' to all our formulas, and novelty and possibility forever leaking in."

Surprises, novelties, twists, and turns of meanings made and lost striate the messaging of time, its *logos*, pragmatically rendered. The beginning of the beginning is a surd and the end is not in our sight, so our passing through time passing is who we are as becoming human beings.

[J.J.M.]

See also **James, William (as Philosopher); Kant, Immanuel; Peirce, Charles Sanders.**

FURTHER READINGS

Helm, Bertrand P. *Time and Reality in American Philosophy.* Amherst: U of Massachusetts P, 1985.

PRECISION TIMEKEEPING, 1790–1900

This subject will be considered in three units, these being portable timekeepers, fixed timekeepers, and the related subject of their calibration by astronomical means.

There were considerable pressures to make timekeepers that would perform well. Initially, these pressures came from astronomers and physicists who wished to make more accurate observations, but later in the nineteenth century, pressure from railway companies, industry, and corporate bodies prompted action. A typical initiative was the establishment of the Liverpool Observatory in 1844, which was given the responsibility of providing a time standard for the town, determining the longitude of the Port of Liverpool, and testing chronometers. One of the first tasks involved the determination of the longitude of Boston by the exchange of chronometers with Liverpool. In the United States, the Naval Observatory was established in 1845 to determine the nation's time standard. In England, the railways adopted a standard time in 1852, a move that was to result in the adoption of Greenwich Mean Time for the whole of the United Kingdom in 1880. There was also a growing need to measure short time intervals accurately. Thankfully, the ingenuity of watch and clockmakers allowed them to provide solutions for this and other problems they were asked to solve. By 1850, for example, very short time intervals were being measured by clockwork-driven drum chronographs fitted with an electrically moved pen or stylus.

PORTABLE TIMEKEEPERS

During the eighteenth century in England, John Harrison, the pioneer maker of marine timekeepers, proved it was possible to produce an instrument that was adequate for navigational purposes. He was followed by Pierre Le Roy and Ferdinand Berthoud working in France. Although the instruments they made would keep time at sea, they were not articles of general commerce and it was left to others to develop more viable devices. By 1790, the English chronometer-makers John Arnold and Thomas Earnshaw had between them provided the fundamental technical basis on which all chronometers were to be built. They simplified the mechanisms so that, although still costly, they were affordable to those who needed them for their work. The principle features were (1) an escapement, which drove (2) an oscillator. The oscillator was formed of a spoked wheel (called a balance) coupled to a spiral or helical spring (balance spring) which provided the restoring force when the balance was displaced from its resting position. As well as maintaining the swings of the balance by giving it regular pushes (impulses), the escapement also counted the vibrations of the balance and was designed to interfere with these as little as possible.

The escapements fitted to chronometers were invariably of the type known as "detached escapements," and the final form was that devised by Earnshaw. Earnshaw's escapement was used because it had the advantage of not requiring lubrication on its acting surfaces, thus eliminating the effects of the long-term deterioration of oil on critical parts of the mechanism. Another requirement was a means of compensating for the elasticity change that occurred in the balance spring as ambient temperature varied. The method most widely used was that introduced by Arnold and improved by Earnshaw which employed two bimetallic rims with one end attached to the crossbar of the balance and the other fitted with weights which could move inward with a rise in temperature (and vice versa), thus compensating for the weakening of the spring by lowering the balance's moment of inertia. Earnshaw formed the bimetals as an integral part of the balance by fusing brass onto a disc of steel. Arnold introduced a technique of forming special curves ("terminal curves") on the ends of the balance spring to compensate for a lack of isochronism, and from the 1820s this method was almost universally adopted. The motive power source (mainspring and fusee) of a chronometer movement was fitted with a device for keeping the instrument running when being wound. This mechanism (maintaining power) was invented by Harrison in 1730 (see Figure 1).

An instrument built with the above features would keep time to within a few seconds a day for several months at a time. A number of residual errors remained, however, the most important of these being a deviation in timekeeping at extremes of temperature. An instrument could be adjusted to keep time at 10 degrees Centigrade and at 30 degrees, but would gain about two seconds per day at 20 degrees while at temperatures above 30 degrees and below 10 degrees it would lose time. This deviation was important in slow-moving sailing ships because it was not, therefore, possible to apply an accurate correction for the rate of the instrument. After a ten-week voyage, the error in a longitude sight could amount to more than thirty miles from this cause alone. Steamships in particular required accurate instruments because the danger of an incorrect position was likely to have

disastrous consequences, especially if steaming fast at night. This problem with compensation was discovered in the early 1800s and became known as middle temperature error. Much ingenuity and effort was expended in developing devices to overcome the problem. Early experimenters were John Poole, John Gottlieb Ulrich, Edward Massey, John Roger Arnold, Edward John Dent, and others.

In England, the two most successful early pioneers were John Sweetman Eiffe and Robert Molyneux, who almost simultaneously developed systems of small movable weights moved by levers that were attached to the balance. These became known as "auxiliary compensation devices." Other devices included small mercury thermometers perfected by Edward Thomas Loseby in 1843. These proved capable of completely reversing the error if the thermometer tubes were correctly made and fitted. Other systems were developed which restricted the movement of the bimetallic arms below certain temperatures. "Auxiliaries" were difficult to make and install and were sometimes unstable. Certain systems proved more reliable than others and were widely adopted during the second half of the nineteenth century. Exceptionally good results were obtained by the Swedish chronometer-maker Victor Kullberg, who worked in London. He used his own design for auxiliary compensation on chronometers of exceptional quality and made instruments capable of keeping time to within a few seconds a month. The problem was virtually eliminated by the use of an alloy of about 44 percent nickel and 56 percent iron (invented by the Swiss physicist Dr. Edwarde Guillaume in 1896), which was used in place of the steel in the balance.

The usual material for balance springs was hardened and tempered steel. Other materials had been used for balance springs, but all except palladium alloys, introduced in 1879 by the Swiss Charles Auguste Paillard, were abandoned. Palladium alloys had three advantages: they were nonrusting, they were not affected by magnetism, and they had a slightly reduced middle temperature error. From 1880 onward, a number of chronometer trials were won by instruments fitted with these springs, and numerous better-quality instruments were resprung using this expensive metal.

Most marine chronometers were fitted into gimbals in boxes so that they ran "dial up" with the movement horizontal, whatever list a ship might have. The effect of gravity on the balance was always in one direction except when the instrument was being wound and an important source of error (discussed when considering watches) was thus eliminated.

These improvements in the balance and spring were also applied to high-quality domestic carriage clocks which combined an attractive and pleasant case of reasonable size (thus acceptable as a piece of domestic, club, or office furniture) with a movement that could be relied on to maintain a close rate for a long period of time. Unlike marine chronometers, this form of timekeeper was sometimes fitted with a striking and/or a repeating mechanism and occasionally with a perpetual calendar (a mechanism that automatically sets the correct day of the month, adjusts for the varying number of days per month, and self-corrects for leap years).

Precision watches fitted with detached escapements were developed in parallel with the chronometer. Because of their small size they were expensive to make and had the additional disadvantage of being easily deranged by inept handling or overhaul. This was so much of a problem that instruments which had been taken aboard by navigators and other users were frequently sent thousands of miles to England for repair because of a lack of skilled local watchmakers. During the early 1800s, there was a rapidly growing demand for accurate and reliable portable timekeepers, and this coincided with the development of more robust, simpler versions of Thomas Mudge's lever escapement of 1759–60. The earliest of these were invented by the English watchmakers Edward Massey and George Savage, and were further developed to improve functioning and ease of production. English precision watches continued to hold a preeminent position worldwide during the first half of the nineteenth century, after which American and later Swiss, German, and French firms began to catch up.

The great Swiss-French watchmaker Abraham Louis Breguet had applied Arnold's idea of incurving the ends of the balance spring to the flat spiral springs used on watches. He did this by raising the outer coil of the spring and forming the curve back over the body of the spring. The widespread adoption of this technique was partly due to the practical application of the results of some theoretical work undertaken by the French engineer Edouard Philips which dealt with the correct form of the terminal curves and which were published in 1861. Additional work by the French theoretician Louis Lossier enabled watchmakers to make practical use of these

"overcoils" on watches of quite modest quality. Because of the greatly increased potential accuracy, Continental and American firms were able to dispense with the fusee (used by English makers to average out the force produced by the mainspring) and thereby make a simpler but just as accurate watch. The need for such timepieces grew during the 1800s as railways were built and their safe operation came to depend on the

Figure 1. Marine chronometer made by John Arnold and Son, London, in 1791 and fitted with a detent escapement, gold helical balance spring with terminal curves, and bimetallic compensation balance. The wooden octagonal box is original. The instrument needed to be lifted and turned over before it could be wound up by means of a separate key. By this time Thomas Earnshaw was using a system of hinged gimbals that enabled the movement to be inverted without the danger resulting from lifting and which kept the instrument horizontal while the ship was not on an even keel. (Owned by the National Museums and Galleries on Merseyside and displayed at Prescot Museum.)

locomotive drivers' knowledge of the correct time.

Portable timepieces intended to be worn in the pocket, or carried, were subject to another set of errors caused by the effect of gravity on the balance and spring as the watch changed position. Not only would the amplitude of oscillation of the balance reduce as the watch moved into the vertical position, but any offset of the center of gravity relative to the axis about which the balance moved would also affect the rate of the watch. This problem was compounded because the effect varied as the amplitude of oscillation of the balance changed. During the 1790s, a watch would be adjusted and tested in two positions, one lying on its back and the other with the pendant (position of the winding button) in the vertical position ("pendant up"), and would not, unless very expensive, have provision for temperature compensation. By the end of the 1800s, techniques were developed, principally by the German, Jules Grossman, that enabled the number of positions to be increased to six. These were dial up, dial down, pendant up, pendant down, pendant right, and pendant left. A medium-quality watch adjusted in these positions, and also for the effects of temperature and for isochronism, could be relied on to keep time to within a few seconds per day for several months at a time. This accuracy was, however, dependent on the oil not deteriorating and the watch not being mishandled, dropped, brought into the proximity of magnets, or subjected to the ingress of dirt or moisture.

Although the observatory at Greenwich was the English center for testing watches and chronometers intended for use by the government, it did not test instruments intended for civilian use. The first independent testing laboratory was the Liverpool Observatory. John Hartnup, the director, introduced chronometer-testing ovens in which the temperature could be varied at will. He analyzed the effects of middle temperature error to the extent that he was able to produce a set of formulae which could be applied to correct the rate of a chronometer, if a record of the temperatures to which it had been subjected had been kept. His testing methods were considerably in advance of those at Greenwich for a long time, and he provided a valuable service to the merchant fleets using Liverpool Docks by ensuring that their instruments were properly tested.

The civilian testing of watches in England was not undertaken until the Kew Observatory was equipped to carry out such work in 1884. In 1885, a system of marks was introduced for class A1 (excellent quality) watches with the words "Especially good" endorsed on the certificate of any watch gaining more than eighty marks. Lesser watches could be awarded a class B certificate.

The Swiss had adopted a form of *bulletin de marche* or rating certificate as early as 1828 at Neuchâtel for watches having undergone a test. However, the clock standard by which they were tested was poor, being only the passage of the sun across the meridian. The Neuchâtel makers were forced to purchase their own transit instruments until the establishment of the observatory in 1858. At Geneva, observatory trials did not start until 1873, but quickly established themselves and became very competitive, raising their minimum standards at regular intervals.

A test certificate supplied with a watch helped to inspire in the user a feeling of confidence. Testing was competitive, with much status and publicity accruing to a maker who came high in the trials. This obviously provided a great spur to produce more accurate and consistent timekeepers.

FIXED TIMEKEEPERS

During the early 1800s, the standard form of nonportable precision clock was a "regulator" based on that developed in the early 1700s by English clockmaker George Graham. The essential features were a pendulum compensated for temperature changes by means of a mercury-filled bob, a means to keep the regulator running while it was being wound, and a form of frictional rest escapement known as a "dead beat." The dead-beat escapement was so named because the second hand moved forward exactly one second at a time and—unlike the second hand on a longcase clock of the period—did not recoil. A clock such as this could be expected to keep time to within a second a day, and some were capable of a much better rate. In the medium to long term, deterioration of oil on the escapement would result in a change of arc and thus a change of rate.

In England at this time there was a dramatic increase in interest in the clock escapement and in ways of overcoming the problems inherent in the dead beat. Much interest was generated by the two "remontoire" escapements designed by Thomas Mudge. Chronometer-maker William Hardy developed a variant of his own using two locking pallets and two impulse pallets. Greenwich, together with several other British and British-controlled observatories, was supplied with Hardy's clocks, and for a brief period they outperformed Graham's. However, they were very susceptible to mishandling and were easily destroyed; as a result, a number were converted to dead-beat escapements. One remontoire escapement invented around 1813 by the Scottish clockmaker Thomas Reid, was based on the escapement developed by Mudge for his marine timekeepers. It was not widely used at that time, but during the early 1900s was adopted by a number of precision clockmakers, including Louis Leroy of Paris (see Figure 2). Another remontoire escapement, patented in Germany by Sigmund Riefler in 1889, and giving impulse via the pendulum suspension spring, enjoyed wide success.

An adequate escapement theory was developed by George Biddell Airy and published in 1827 while he was still at Cambridge University. Airy's paper laid down the criteria for an ideal escapement and provided standards against which new designs could be judged. Several new designs appeared. The most successful was that developed by Englishman Edmund Becket Denison in 1845 from a design of James Mackenzie Bloxham for the great clock at the Palace of Westminster, London, in 1862. Denison's escapement revolutionized standards of turret clock accuracy. It gave impulse to the pendulum by means of levers ("gravity arms"). The pendulum still had to unlock these by overcoming the force delivered by the wheel train, even though the torque was transmitted through long, locking levers on the escape wheel. This escapement was much improved by American Richard Bond of Boston. He designed a series of gravity and spring arm escapements, and by the mid-1860s, produced a most elegant design of a completely detached escapement. This employed a continuously rotating wheel to recock a single gravity arm. Not only was the energy expended by the pendulum during the unlocking of the gravity arm constant from cycle to cycle, but the energy delivered by the gravity arm to the pendulum to maintain its oscillations was also constant for each cycle. A series of three clocks were made with this form of escapement and were used at the Harvard Observatory, Bond's premises in Boston, and at Bidston Observatory, near Liverpool. The clock supplied to Bidston in 1868 responded so predictably to changes in barometric pressure that the observatory director was able to calculate and apply a correction factor for this error which amounted to 0.2 of a second per day for a change in atmospheric pressure of one inch of mercury. The corrected rate for the clock varied between -0.05 and +0.08 seconds per day.

The accuracy of this clock appears to have prompted Airy to design a clock for Greenwich using a variation on an escapement that he designed in 1827. This escapement was not as fully detached as Bond's because the force required to unlock the escape wheel could vary with the force transmitted by the wheel train. It was a clock version of the detent escapement as applied to marine and pocket chronometers. The clock was constructed in 1870 by the firm of Dent in London and, like the Bond clock, also varied in rate with barometric pressure. One of Airy's assistants, William Ellis, designed a barometric compensator which was attached to the clock case. It worked by moving a magnet toward or away from a steel bar attached to the pendulum. With this mechanism fitted, the clock gave satisfactory service for many years.

The effect of changes of atmospheric pressure on a clock's timekeeping had been predicted by Francis Baily in the early 1820s. In 1831, Thomas R. Robinson of Armagh Observatory in Ireland published the results of his investigations into this relationship and described the application of a mercury-in-glass barometer to the pendulum in an attempt to counteract the effect. Although Robinson stated that he had success with this method, it was not adopted, probably because it was too unstable due to the movement of the mercury in the tubes. Barometric errors were not effectively counteracted until the standard sidereal clock at Greenwich was built. Other designs of barometric compensator developed at the end of the 1800s included a weighted aneroid (a device for measuring atmospheric pressure through the use of a partial vacuum) applied to the pendulum and an aneroid mechanism mounted on the case that varied the effective length of a spring attached to the pendulum. The problem of barometric error was completely eliminated at the end of the century by enclosing pendulum and movement in an airtight case. In many instances these clocks were electrically wound to obviate winding holes and the need to seal them.

Pendulum design also developed over the same period. The Graham form, in which the mercury was contained in a glass jar, was slow to respond to temperature changes. Many different combinations of metals were tried in an

Figure 2. Precision regulator clock made by Thomas Reid, Edinburgh, in 1818 and fitted with his spring pallet escapement and zinc and steel compensation pendulum. Although not widely used in the early 1800s, the escapement was adopted in France and used on observatory clocks in the early 1900s. (Clock owned by the British Horological Institute and photographed by James Arnfield.)

attempt to produce a pendulum that was not only predictable in the amount of compensation that could be achieved but also stable in the long term. Pendulums using linkages to amplify small movements of compensation bars were originally tried in the second half of the eighteenth century but suffered instability from the effects of friction. Designers realized that free air circulation to all parts of the pendulum was essential so that all components gained or lost heat at similar rates. The types that achieved widespread acceptance were those using steel bars and zinc tubes and those using mercury in steel tubes. At the end of the century a metallurgical development, the invention of invar (a nickel and steel alloy), rendered most forms of compensation redundant. Only minimal errors remained to be corrected on clocks of the highest accuracy intended for use as time standards. With clocks of such sophistication, mechanical timekeepers had reached their zenith.

THE CALIBRATION OF TIMEKEEPERS BY ASTRONOMICAL MEANS

In 1790, the standard by which the accuracy of clocks was measured was that of the rotation of the earth. Time was determined by two methods. The first involved observing the passage of the sun over the meridian, with a correction being applied to convert solar time into mean solar time. A difference between the time indicated by a clock and that shown by a sundial had been observed following the introduction of pendulum clocks. Correction tables giving the difference over the course of a year had been produced by the English astronomer John Flamsteed, by 1670. This method was only accurate to within about ten seconds unless special methods were employed either to take and correct accurately equal altitudes of the sun before and after midday, or to observe the sun's transit over the meridian using an especially prepared aperture hole and meridian datum. Such a transit could then be observed to within about two seconds. Solar methods remained in widespread use in Britain until the adoption of the electric telegraph ensured that local post offices, telegraph offices, and railway stations received time signals.

The second and superior method for determining the time involved observing the passage of a given star for several nights past a fixed vertical reference point. Such a method was used by Harrison. However, as the day length derived by this method was sidereal and was approximately three minutes and fifty-six seconds shorter than a mean time day, a correction had to be applied. A disadvantage of this method was that the same star could not be used for long periods because the chosen star passed earlier every night and sooner or later could not be seen at all.

Originally, the problem of determining sidereal time was threefold. First, one needed a clock with a close enough rate to be able to measure the time accurately between transits of different stars. Second, it was necessary to prepare an accurate table giving the height above the horizon (declination) and the time each star would be overhead (right ascension, the celestial equivalent of longitude). Third, one required a suitable transit telescope with which to observe the star as it passed directly overhead. At this juncture, a brief description of the transit instrument is called for because it was fundamental to precision time determination.

A transit instrument was introduced by the British astronomer Edmund Halley at Greenwich in 1721, and similar instruments were used until the mid-twentieth century (see Figure 3). In its basic form, a transit instrument consisted of an astronomical telescope (inverting) fitted with a pair of trunnions rather in the fashion of an eighteenth-century cannon. The trunnions were arranged as pivots and the bearings for these were adjusted so that the telescope could be turned from the horizontal looking due south, through the vertical to the horizontal looking due north. It could, therefore, be employed to observe a slice through the sky, which if extended through the earth would pass through the center in the form of a plane surface (in practice this is not quite correct as the earth is not a perfect sphere). The telescope was fitted with vertical hairs made from spider's web (it was a specialty to select and collect the correct variety) and mounted in the tube at the joint focus of the eyepiece and objective lenses. These hairs were illuminated at night by the light of a lamp shining through one of the hollow trunnions. For a transit to be observed, the telescope tube was turned to the correct declination for the star. The star entered the field of view from the right and the observer either took the time himself by counting from a clock, or called the instant of passing to an assistant. The effect of personal error was known and it was appreciated that this varied from person to person with experiments being undertaken to ascertain differences.

In practice it was more complicated than this since an allowance had to be made for telescope errors. It was also necessary to check the instrument in order to ensure that it was correctly oriented and that the optical system was correctly set up. Unless the star was directly overhead, the angle that the telescope had to be set at to observe a transit varied from that in the star tables because the light from it was bent by the atmosphere (refraction) and this effect was greatest when the observed star was nearest the horizon. The effect also varied with barometric pressure and temperature. A separate instrument called a mural circle was originally used to measure the declination of a star, but Airy combined this with the transit instrument in 1851, when his transit circle was built.

With this equipment, and using known stars as they passed the meridian, a good operator could check the accuracy of a clock to within fractions of a second by judging the time between the beats of the clock. Observations of several stars in the course of a night would be averaged and a clock's rate could be determined to within about 0.1 seconds. By 1767, information enabling this to be done by navigators and others had been greatly refined. Tables containing this and other details, such as the predicted position of the moon, were published by the Greenwich Observatory as "The Nautical Almanac and Astronomical Ephemeris." The information in this publication was, except for one short period, refined throughout the 1800s and was used worldwide. These tables were almost universally used through the 1800s. Cartographers and chart publishers used longitude graduations based on Greenwich. Ultimately, this provided the impetus for the 1884 international agreement defining the prime meridian as the line passing due north-south through Airy's transit instrument of 1851. From this position, standard time was measured for the whole world.

In 1849, the Naval Observatory in Washington used drum chronographs to record transits, and in 1851, the Bond firm exhibited this type of equipment at the great exhibition in London. It transformed the accuracy of observations because it used a set of contacts on the clock to trigger a marking pen or stylus every second leaving a mark on the paper. (Later, with Dent's standard sidereal clock, this became every two seconds.) As the star passed the vertical hair in the transit telescope, the observer closed a contact, causing a second pen or stylus to leave a mark on the paper; the time could be determined by measurement of the relative positions of the marks. Still greater accuracy was achieved by using a number of vertical hairs with the contact being operated as the star passed each and the results being averaged.

The "American method" was quickly adopted at Greenwich during 1852 and—combined with Airy's new transit circle, which could also be used to measure declination—set standards of accuracy that were only emulated by major contemporary observatories as they in turn acquired copies of the equipment. In 1851, Airy introduced at Greenwich a "reflex zenith telescope" as an additional means of determining time. Although limited to observing a small part of the sky, it evolved to become the most accurate of all the instruments used for checking the rate of a clock.

In Britain, this greatly improved accuracy was made available to all parts of the country by means of the electric telegraph. As the century progressed with rapidly improving transport and communications, more and more towns and cities took advantage of this reliable time service and adopted Greenwich Mean Time as their standard. This process was finally legitimized in 1880 when Greenwich Mean Time was declared the standard for the United Kingdom and the whole population was able to take advantage of accurate time.

These developments in precision timekeeping came into being because there was a demand for them and because improvements in technology enabled science to progress. In turn, scientific developments were used to advance this technology. Throughout the whole period, the cooperation between the theoretician and the intelligent craftsman was close and highly productive.

[R.J.G.]

See also **Clocks: America and Mass Production, 1770–1890; Clocks and Watches: The Leap to Precision; High Frequency Timekeepers; Longitude; Standard Time: Time Zones and Daylight Saving Time; Time Measurement and Science; Timekeepers, Domestic: English Influence, 1710–1800; Watch Manufacturing in Nineteenth-Century America.**

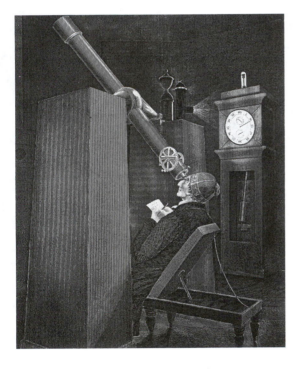

Figure 3. Transit instrument (by Thomas Jones, cost £105) and clock (by Vulliamy, cost £105) installed in the private Hartwell observatory by Vice Admiral W.H. Smyth in 1831. The "noddy" or "wobbler" at the top (by W. Hardy) showed whether the clock was securely mounted, and the quadrant device on the side of the telescope tube was for setting the instrument at the correct elevation so that the required star would pass through the field of view. (Illustration published privately in 1860 in "The Cycle of Celestial Objects continued at the Hartwell Observatory to 1859...." Photographed by David Flower, National Museums and Galleries on Merseyside.)

FURTHER READINGS

Britten, Frederick J. *Britten's Watch and Clock Maker's Handbook, Dictionary and Guide.* 16th ed., revised and edited by Richard Good. London: Eyre Methuen, 1978. The standard guide.

Bruton, Eric. *The Longcase Clock.* New York: Arco Publishing, 1964.

De Carle, Donald. *British Time.* London: Crosby Lockwood, 1947.

Eiffe's and Molyneux's Specifications for Improvements in Chronometers. 1842; reprint, Munich: Callway, 1987.

Ferriday, Peter. *Lord Grimthorpe, 1816–1905.* London: Murray, 1957.

Gould, R.T. *The Marine Chronometer.* 1923; reprint, London: Holland P, 1976.

Haswell, J.E. *Horology.* London: Chapman and Hall, 1947.

Jagger, Cedric. *The Artistry of the English Watch.* Rutland: C.E. Tuttle, 1988.

Loomes, Brian. *Complete British Clocks.* Newton Abbot: David and Charles, 1978.

———. *Grandfather Clocks and Their Cases.* Newton Abbot: David and Charles, 1985.

Randall, Anthony, and Richard Good. *Catalogue of Watches at the British Museum, VI: Pocket Chronometers, Marine Chronometers and Other Portable Precision Timekeepers.* London: British Museum Publications, 1990.

Riefler, D. *Präzisionspendeluhren.* Munich: Callway, 1981.

PREDETERMINED MOTION TIME SYSTEMS

There is an old and hackneyed expression about "reinventing the wheel." This is quite germane to the measuring of the time it should take to do a specified job, as there is a great danger that one could do just that. Many jobs bear close similarities to other jobs, so why time them over again?

The ideas put forward in the article **Measurement of Work and Applications** show how basic times for precisely defined jobs could be set by one of three fundamental methods, namely timing, estimating, and predetermined motion time systems (PMTS). The present article will describe the philosophy, use, and application of PMTS.

Whereas timing techniques rely on the actual observing of the job as it is taking place, PMTS does not. Times may be derived by visualizing the way the job should be done, analyzing this mental image into suitable elements, and allocating times to these elements.

ANALYZING JOBS INTO ELEMENTS

There is an untold number of jobs that can be done by humans, so it would not be possible to catalog even a small proportion of them. But like the twelve notes of music, work is also composed of a finite number of basic elements. PMT systems go back to basics, and back to the fundamental motions of which all manual and some mental activities are composed.

All jobs can be analyzed into smaller but distinctive parts. In turn, these parts can be analyzed into even smaller elements, until finally they are reduced to what are, in effect, the basic muscle movements. For example, a clerical job can consist of word processing, answering the phone, discussing work, using a Dictaphone, filing documents, and so on. If one considers "filing," this can be analyzed into picking up the document, going to the filing cabinet, opening the drawer, and inserting the document. Opening the drawer demands that one reach for the drawer handle, grasp it, move it toward the body, and then release the hold on it. This last analysis may seem very laborious, but it is the basic level at which systems of PMT operate.

Probably the first person to develop a viable system of PMT was A.B. Segur of Illinois in 1925. Segur called his system motion-time analysis, and based it on Frank Bunker Gilbreth's "therbligs," which describe seventeen basic human motions, analogous to the twelve notes of music.

The most widely known and used systems today are Methods-Time Measurement (MTM) and Work-Factor. Work-Factor was developed in the 1930s by J.H. Quick, J.A. Duncan, and J.A. Malcolm Jr. Roughly a decade later, the rival system of Methods-Time Measurement was published by H.B. Maynard, J.G. Stegemerten, and J.L. Schwab for use in the Westinghouse Brake and Signal Corporation. During the intervening decade several other versions of PMTS appeared, but none has enjoyed the fame achieved by these two proprietary systems. MTM has been used by many researchers as the basis for their own variations at diverse levels of data.

The systems of PMT may be separated into two generic groupings of data. One group consists of the very basic systems, usually in three levels of precision, known as *micro-PMTS,* while the second group contains systems at a much higher level of data, known as *macro-PMTS.* Micro-PMTS is composed of the basic work elements, whereas macro-PMTS is job specific. The difference is illustrated in Figure 1. Micro-PMTS can be applied to all jobs, but a particular version of Macro-PMTS can only be used in the specific area—such as clerical work or maintenance work—for which it was designed.

TYPICAL ELEMENTS OF MICRO-PMTS

All systems of PMT bear a close resemblance to each other. Many use identical names for some of their elements.

If one needed to pick up a bolt and insert it into a hole, one would follow this sequence:

1. reach out for the bolt
2. grasp the bolt with the fingers
3. move the bolt to the hole
4. reposition the bolt so that it is in line with and perpendicular to the hole
5. insert the bolt into the hole
6. push the bolt home
7. release the bolt
8. remove the hand from the area of the hole

A simple job such as this requires at least eight basic motions. From the analysis it is apparent that micro-PMTS is very time-consuming and laborious to use. This has led to a reluctance on the part of managements to employ these systems, and hence the development of other, higher levels of predetermined times.

Some of the basic motions are further qualified by the inclusion of "variables" which permit the analyst to allow for factors such as (1) distance moved by the body member, (2) the weight of the object to be moved, (3) the type of motion (such as "U" motions, or whether the hand is at rest at the beginning or at the end of the motion), (4) difficulties encountered, and (5) any care or precaution needed (such as to avoid spillage, smudging, damage, or injury). All of these factors, where they are applicable, will affect the basic time for the element.

Once the job has been analyzed into its basic motions, the elemental times may be read off the tables. An example of how this is done is shown in Figure 1.

SYSTEM LEVELS

The examples given so far have been for first-level PMTS. Responding to the problems arising from the extreme degree of precision inherent at this level, researchers have developed second-level micro-PMT systems which are far quicker to apply. In order to achieve this it has been necessary in some cases to *merge* elements, *simplify* elements, *combine* individual times into ranges of times, and generally reduce the amount of analysis required. In this connection, the Methods-Time Measurement Directorate authorized the development of a second level of their

system (MTM-2) in which the three MTM elements of reach, grasp, and release were combined into just one MTM-2 element of "get," and the two elements of move and position were merged into "put." Because around 90 percent of all manual work consists of getting objects and putting them somewhere, these two new elements were instrumental in greatly reducing analysis time. Also, the twenty-one different distances quoted for "reach" (ranging from "$3/_4$ inch or less" up to "30 inches") were reduced to just five bands of distances. Other simplifications to the rules were implemented.

Later, further amendments were made to produce an even simpler method, MTM-3.

At the macro-PMT level the systems become job specific, that is, they are particular to a trade or task group such as clerical work or maintenance jobs. Examples of proprietary products are the MTMA Office Data System, Office Modapts, Standard Clerical Data, and Basic Work Data for maintenance work.

The low-level PMT systems are used to generate the elements of macro-PMTS; in fact, most

Levels of Predetermined Motion Time Systems

first level	0.0001 mins.	*second level*	centi mins.	*macro level*
Reach to grasp bolt	70			
Grasp bolt	12	Obtain bolt	1.10	
Improve grasp	30			
Move bolt to hole	65	Move bolt to hole	0.65	Assemble bolt to hole = 3 c. mins.
Align bolt to hole	60			
Insert bolt	30	Place bolt in hole	1.10	
Push bolt home	15			
Release bolt	10			
Totals	292 = 0.0292 mins.		2.85 = 0.0285 mins.	
8 elements		3 elements		1 element

Figure 1. Predetermined Motion Systems

of them have relied upon MTM data for their development. Elements such as reach, grasp, move, release, and others are built up into large elements which include "unscrew and remove bolt," "joggle, align, and staple pages of a document," and "file a document." Clearly these elements are far quicker to apply than those of micro-PMTS levels.

PROCEDURE FOR ANALYZING BY PMTS

1. The job to be timed is described in detail.
2. The job is then analyzed into the elements of the system being used, including any factors or variables as listed above.
3. After analysis it may be considered necessary to carry out a method study to determine whether or not the job can be improved.
4. For each element, times are extracted from the PMT tables.
5. The analyses with the relevant times are entered onto a suitable PMTS analysis sheet, and the total time calculated.
6. Where appropriate, suitable allowances for personal needs, relaxation, and other causes are added to the overall time.

STANDARD DATA

A predetermined motion time analysis, or indeed any time study, should not be used as an end in itself, but as a means to an end: the end being the generation of a set of "building blocks" of elements or parts of jobs which may be used over again, whenever they occur in future jobs. This philosophy is not confined to PMTS, but should be the aim of all techniques of work measurement. The files of work element times stored for future use are known as *standard data* (or *synthetic data*).

Eventually a comprehensive library of work element times will be compiled, preferably in computer files, which may be selected and retrieved as situations arise.

There is little difference between macro-PMT systems and standard data. The main differences are that in the latter (1) the elements may be rather larger in some cases, (2) the elements are "home grown" within the user organization, and (3) the elements may be generated from techniques other than PMTS, whereas macro-PMT elements are generated from lower-level micro-PMTS.

[D.A.W.]

See also **Industrial Engineering [After Taylor]; Measurement of Work and Applications.**

FURTHER READINGS

Maynard, H.B., J.G. Stegemerten, and J.L. Schwab. *Methods-Time Measurement.* New York: McGraw-Hill, 1962.

Quick, J.L., J.H. Duncan, and J.A. Malcolm. *Work-Factor Time Standards.* New York: McGraw-Hill, 1962.

Whitmore, Dennis A. *Work Measurement.* 2nd ed. London: Heinemann, 1987. Chapter 8.

PREDICTION IN ASTRONOMY

The prediction of events and the motion of heavenly objects has been the hallmark of astronomy since the dawn of man. Early man followed the motion of the sun, moon, and planets in an attempt to understand the future behavior of the gods they represented. The megalithic monument Stonehenge, in England, is likely to have been used to predict eclipses of the moon. The Greek-Egyptian, Claudio Ptolemy, followed the motion of the planets and developed the geocentric model of the solar system not only to predict future motion of the planets, but to provide a basis for understanding of the planetary system itself. Failure of the Ptolemaic system to give accurate positions of the planets in the time of Copernicus is likely to have been one of the motivating reasons for his reexamination of the problem of planetary motion and the formulation of the Copernican heliocentric model for the solar system.

However, it was not until the development of Newtonian mechanics and its application to celestial objects that prediction in astronomy reached its fullest development. The calculus of Newton, which he called fluxions, allowed the proper understanding of the role of time in describing physical phenomena. Newton viewed time as an absolute quantity in the sense that the universe could be viewed as being filled with hypothetical clocks that all kept the same time. While the "absolute time" of Newton subsequently proved to be incorrect, it worked remarkably well in describing heavenly phenomena. The correct prediction of the return of Halley's comet was taken to be a significant verification of Newtonian mechanics and the law of gravity. Herschel's observation of the motion of stars about each other demonstrated the universality of the law of gravity. During the next several centuries Newtonian mechanics developed into a highly elegant theory through the efforts of Laplace, Lagrange, Gauss, Hamilton, Jacobi, and others. But the basis for judging the success of Newtonian mechanics and the law of gravity continued to be the extent to which they gave accurate predictions for the positions of the planets and other objects in the solar system.

It is ironic that the very tests establishing the stature of Newtonian mechanics and Newton's law of gravity should ultimately provide the basis for showing that they could not be the correct description of the physical world. By the end of the nineteenth century, the determination and prediction of the motion of the planet Mercury had shown that its elliptical orbit was itself turning in a manner inconsistent with the laws of Newton. While the presence of other planets in the solar system dictated that the orbit of Mercury should itself rotate, causing the major axis of the ellipse to precess in space, the amount of the precession missed the predicted value by forty-three seconds of arc per century. This tiny amount serves to indicate the degree of precision that had been reached by the end of the nineteenth century in both planetary observation and Newtonian theory. That this tiny amount was sufficient to overturn Newton's theory of gravity is a major testament to the integrity of scientific prediction and observation. It was a significant triumph of Einstein's theory of gravity, usually called general relativity, that it could predict the precise value of the deficit of the precession of the major axis of Mercury's orbit between observation and the Newtonian prediction.

In the three-quarters of a century since the publication of the general theory of relativity, astronomical prediction of temporal events has moved to even greater levels of precision. The discovery of the spinning magnetic neutron stars called pulsars in the 1960s and the nearly simultaneous development of atomic clocks have had results in the measurement of the temporal behavior of astronomical objects that could not have been imagined half a century earlier. Some pulsars have demonstrated a temporal accuracy that rivals the best atomic clocks. In at least two instances, pulsars orbiting close to other stars have provided tests for the general theory of relativity of unprecedented accuracy. Unlike Newtonian gravity, no disagreements between theory and observation have yet been found.

[G.W.C., II]

See also **Definition and Measurement; Gravity, Time, and Space; Relativity Theory; Solar System.**

PRESOCRATICS

Any discussion of the "presocratic philosophers" must begin by acknowledging that the line between the "first philosophers" and the mythic writers who preceded them is blurred at best. This is certainly true in regard to discussions of time. The early mythic writers in the Western tradition—such as the writer of the *Epic of Gilgamesh*, or Homer, and Hesiod—often referred to time explicitly or had an implicit account of time underlying their tales. Three brief examples are: first, in the *Epic of Gilgamesh*, Gilgamesh's deep sense of urgency to "have his name written on the walls," to accomplish renowned deeds, is brought on by the recognition of his mortality, or of what we today call "temporality." This is the experience of time in terms of our finitude, that we do not have forever to become what we will become, and the sense of urgency consequently bestowed on our actions. As the philosopher Alcmaeon poignantly but obscurely puts the point in his sole surviving fragment, "Humans die for this reason, that they cannot join together the beginning and the end." Second, in Hesiod's *Theogony*, the original mating couple of Gaia (earth) and Ouranos (sky or heaven) give birth to, among others, Kronos, who eventually overthrows his father by mutilating him, and in turn fathers Zeus and the Olympian tradition. If "Kronos" refers to "time" (the issue is one of some scholarly debate), then clearly there is a recognition here of the primordial significance of time in the world. Time, with earth and sky, "generate" the world, the coming to be and passing away of things, the seasons of the year. Third, in Hesiod's account of the "ages" of humans, from the golden, to the silver, to the bronze, to the heroes, and finally to his own age, we see an implicit account of time as historical progression, in Hesiod's view a consistent if not uninterrupted decline in the caliber of humans.

If we accept Aristotle's judgment, which has become conventional, the "first" philosophers were the Milesians—Thales, Anaximander, and Anaximenes. Of them, the one who dealt most directly with the issue of time was Anaximander. His sole surviving fragment reads, "The indefinite (*to apeiron*) is the first principle (*arche*) of things that are. It is that from which coming to be takes place, and it is that into which they return when they perish, by moral necessity, giving satisfaction to one another and making reparation for their injustice, according to the order of time." Here we have an explicit, if undeveloped, claim that the "measure" of the coming to be and passing away of things is time. With no further surviving fragments, we cannot say how, or whether, Anaximander developed this nascent theory of time. But the reference itself clearly signals his recognition of the decisive importance of time in the coursing of things, and his startling interpretation of time as implicated in a kind of cosmic justice, that the passing away of things is a "penalty" for the "injustice" of coming to be.

Of the other Milesians, Thales and Anaximander, little is known of their accounts of time. Diogenes Laertius attributes to Thales the pronouncement that of all things, time is "the wisest, for it brings everything to light," which is consistent with Anaximander's fragment, and it is instructive that Thales apparently did considerable research into the movement of the heavens, even, according to tradition, predicting an eclipse.

Pythagoras, the great mathematician, held that everything in the world had as its essence its proper number. Thus, for example, justice was 4, human being 250, "the opportune time" 7. Such emphasis on the mathematical essences of things tends to diminish the significance of time, since number is atemporal. Pythagoras could thus be said to begin that strand of Western thought that emphasizes the ahistorical, atemporal determination of the essences of things. Moreover, number is a way of ordering time, of making sense of it, and so of imposing a measure of control on the passing of things, as when I say that "this is 1992," or "I am fifty-three years old." It should further be noted that Pythagoras also held to a doctrine of reincarnation, that is, to a belief in the endurance of the soul through the generations of its instantiations. This too seems to contribute to a diminished emphasis on the significance of time in a given life.

Heraclitus, with Parmenides, one of the two giants of presocratic philosophy, gives perhaps the most distinctive emphasis to time among all the presocratics. His account of the happening of things as occurring through a tension or contradiction of opposites, and of the *Logos* as the ordered but flowing and developing source of the intelligibility of this happening, clearly implies a philosophy of time, or perhaps better, of temporality. His famous "river fragments," such as fragment 49a: "In the same river, we both step and do not step, we are and we are not," invoke the sense of the endless, if ordered, coming to be and changing of things. Most explicitly, his fragment 52 reads, "Time (*Aion*:

"time" in the sense of "lifetime") is a child playing draughts; kingship is in the hands of a child." This testifies to his evident conviction that it is time which is the source and "king" of the happening of things, a kingship, however, with the spontaneity and unpredictability of a child playing. Nevertheless, it is a rule-governed game that the child is playing; there is both order and spontaneity in the happening of time.

Parmenides, on the other hand, with his emphasis on the changelessness and eternality of being, would seem to join with Pythagoras in de-emphasizing the importance of time in an account of the *arche* of things. If being neither comes to be nor passes away but only and always "is," then clearly the happening of time, if it is not entirely illusory, is no longer decisive in an account of being.

Parmenides' follower, Zeno, does seem to invoke the importance of time, however, in some of his paradoxes, which were supposedly designed to throw the opponents of Parmenides, those who advocated change and motion, into confusion. Particularly his paradoxes of motion, such as the famous "Achilles" paradox or the "arrow" paradox, both play on the difficulties of accounting for how a thing "is" over time.

Of those presocratic philosophers after Parmenides and Heraclitus, however, the one with the most explicit invocation of time is surely Empedocles. Empedocles introduces what amounts to a cyclical view of history. According to him, the epochs of "history" circle between two poles, "love" and "strife." "Love" is a period of total, complete unity, "strife" one of equally total or complete disunity or multiplicity. The only "intelligible" periods of history are therefore the periods in-between the two poles, when the copresence of unity and multiplicity makes possible an intelligible world.

Of the remaining presocratics, neither Anaxagoras nor the atomists, Leucippus and Democritus, present a thematic account of time. The most that could be said of them is that the coming together of the "seeds" in Anaxagoras, or the coming together and breaking apart of atoms in the case of Leucippus and Democritus, must happen through time. But none of our surviving fragments of these thinkers mention this phenomenon.

Nor do the Sophists, the great espousers of the doctrine of relativism. It is plausible to surmise that if they were to make explicit their views on time, it would be some sort of relativistic account. But that, lacking explicit texts, is only speculation.

In sum, the thing to be emphasized regarding the presocratics is that the question of time was already a controversial issue. Some, such as Anaximander, Heraclitus, and Empedocles, clearly gave to time an explicit and central role. For them, time functioned in one of three basic ways: as the "measure" of the happening of things, as "temporality" (that is, the finite, temporal experience of human beings as they move toward their death), and as a nascent theory of history. Others, such as Pythagoras and Parmenides, tended to diminish the importance of time in an account of things. That debate, it is fair to say, continues throughout the Western tradition.

[D.A.H.]

See also **Historiography and Process; Periodization; Saturn-Cronus.**

FURTHER READINGS

Burnet, J. *Early Greek Philosophy.* New York: Meridian Books, 1957.

Cornford, F.M. *From Religion To Philosophy.* New York: Harper Torchbooks, 1957.

Hyland, Drew A. *The Origins of Philosophy: Its Rise in Myth and Presocratic Philosophy.* Atlantic Highlands: Humanities P, 1985.

Kirk, C.S., and J.E. Raven, *The Presocratic Philosophers.* Cambridge: Cambridge UP, 1960.

Nietzsche, Friedrich. *Philosophy in the Tragic Age of the Greeks.* Chicago: Gateway Paperbacks, 1962.

PRIMITIVE TIME-RECKONING

There are three senses in which time-reckoning systems are primitive. *Formally* primitive time-reckoning contrasts numerical and abstract systems of time-reckoning with those based on concrete phenomena and immediate experience. *Chronologically* primitive time-reckoning searches for origins of modern and ancient systems among societies organized mainly by kinship. *Instrumentally* primitive time-reckoning refers to systems of rituals, legends, and genealogies that use methods distinct from schedules, calendars, and clocks.

It is important to maintain a distinction among the three senses of primitive time-reckoning in order to understand how they are related. Formally primitive time-reckoning is found in all societies regardless of the level of complexity or development. Some chronologically older systems of reckoning time are more numerical and abstract than some recent ones.

And nearly all societies, including those considered "primitive" on the basis of social development, are of sufficient complexity to maintain a multiplicity of time modes and systems of time-reckoning. Keeping these distinctions in mind, time-reckoning primarily by concrete phenomena and oral tradition is associated with societies organized mainly by kinship.

Formally primitive time-reckoning refers to systems in which duration and succession are measured by concrete phenomena, the recurrence of which experience has taught persons to expect. The essence of primitive time-reckoning was captured best by the Danish archaeologist and historian, M.P. Nilsson. The universality of durations such as "day" and "month" rests on physical events perceived by an observer on earth—respectively, the rising and setting of the sun and the phases of the moon. The universality of the "year" is more problematic because of its relatively long duration from the standpoint of lived experience. The duration of "seasons" in conjunction with activities of livelihood is a more common denominator of the "year," on account of which greater variability is to be expected in its definition. In sum, there are universal divisions of time, but their reckoning is variable. Days have unequal periods of lightness and darkness, and years can vary significantly by the rhythms of plants, animals, and people. Two other features follow from reckoning by concrete phenomena: discontinuity of units and part-for-whole counting. The unequal durations of lived experience correspond with discontinuous time-reckoning. Days are not reckoned as parts of months, nor months as parts of years. The experience of time as a flow is premised on its infinite divisibility, which in turn depends upon its division into units of equal duration—an abstraction from experience. But primitive time is reckoned by units of unequal duration, such as the Benedictine *horarium.* Successions can be interrupted, as it were, by durations of empty or unfilled time. The long history of reconciling lunar and solar calendars rests on the problem of articulating two recurrent but unequal durations. The discontinuity of time is reflected in the *pars pro toto* method of counting. Days may be counted in "suns," months in "moons," and years by the number of "harvests." But in the absence of an abstract and articulated system of suns, moons, and harvests, counting consists of adding up isolated and incommensurable concrete phenomena that do not form part of a larger whole. There is a weak articulation of the divisions of time which, together with units of unequal duration, makes precise counting difficult. The result is a subordination of succession to duration in the system of reckoning time, together with a reduction of recurrent durations to points or moments, or what is referred to as the *pars pro toto* method of counting.

The chronologically earliest systems of time-reckoning are unknown, and we cannot say that they necessarily had the characteristics of formally primitive time-reckoning. The prehistoric record, which reduces the question of time-reckoning systems to the material residue of extinct societies, such as the stones of Stonehenge or the antler carvings found in Neanderthal burials, is silent on the question of whether abstract and numerical systems evolved from formally primitive ones. Astronomical calendars and almanacs, many of which have the mixed features of concrete and abstract systems of reckoning time, are very old.

Extant tribal societies, many of which exhibit features that extend far back into the early history of humankind to before the appearance of astronomical calendars, offer the best glimpse of formally primitive time-reckoning. These oral societies use neither clocks nor calendars to measure and count time.

The best known example is the Nuer of Sudan and Ethiopia. In E. E. Evans-Pritchard's classic account, the Nuer reckoned duration and succession of their social activities by the concrete phenomena of stars, seasons, and cattle. The Nuer, who had no generic word for time, had no encompassing abstract and numerical system of time-reckoning that articulated different series of recurrent concrete phenomena. A day was reckoned from sunrise to sunrise. Divisions of the day were based on a combination of positions of the sun and a succession of tasks related to tending cattle. The result was a Nuer day with unequal durations of many divisions around sunrise but few in midday and late afternoon. Days were unnamed and unnumbered, reflecting general disinterest of the Nuer in the succession of days within a more inclusive unit such as the "week," which was absent from their system of reckoning. Their most salient divisions of time—related to transhumant pastoralism and cattle raiding for their livelihood—were a change of seasons and age-grade rituals, respectively.

A change of seasons signaled a change in settlement pattern. The "year" consisted of a cluster of social activities associated with either dry-season camps along rivers or wet-season houses in hamlets. There was no generic word for "year," only for the wet and dry seasons that defined succession by recurrence. From succession, however, the Nuer could deduce duration only imperfectly. The reason is that durations of seasons and rounds of social activities covaried. The year was divided into twelve named "moons" of unequal duration that marked the succession from wet to dry season and back again. If the Nuer were still in their dry camps waiting for rain, then they would say it must be that named moon. But if they were still engaged in activities associated with the wet hamlets, then it must be that moon. Thus, the concrete experiences of either social or ecological phenomena were used to reckon the succession of both according to where the Nuer were and what they were doing. Working one series against the other, the Nuer would rename months, skip months altogether, or even omit years, depending on their perception and manipulation of natural or social events.

Wherever dominant modes of time are embedded in social codes and rituals of reciprocal hospitality among kinsmen, primitive time-reckoning predominates. Duration is more important than succession. Durations, however, are unequal, and the reckoning of durations tends to be reduced to a single point of recurrence, for example, the recounting of concrete events such as cattle raids. The result is a system that privileges qualities over quantities and precludes precision in favor of propriety. Primitive time-reckoning is designed to tell the "right" social time, not to measure how much time.

[H.J.R.]

See also **Meaning of Time in Primitive Societies.**

FURTHER READINGS

Evans-Pritchard, E.E. "Nuer Time-reckoning." *Africa* 12 (1939): 189–216.

Nilsson, Martin P. *Primitive Time-reckoning.* Lund: C.W.K. Gleerup, 1920.

Rutz, Henry J. "Material Affluence and Social Time in Village Fiji." *Affluence and Cultural Survival.* Ed. Richard F. Salisbury and Elisabeth Tooker. Washington: The American Ethnological Society, 1984. 105–118.

Zerubavel, Eviatar. *Hidden Rhythms.* Chicago: U of Chicago P, 1981.

PROPHECY

Prophecy (< Greek *pro*, "before" + *phetes*, "spokesman") rests on the conviction that God, in his eternal and infinite nature, creates and sustains the finite world. In his special role as God's spokesman, then, the prophet of the Judeo-Christian tradition chastises apostates, reveals God's presence in the finite and temporal world, interprets his will, exalts his transcendent power, and affirms his ability to intervene in human history.

Throughout the history of ancient Israel—from Joshua to Ezra-Nehemiah—prophets interpreted Yahweh's will, and their efforts were most intense at times of crisis. During the period of Israel's captivity, from the mid-eighth to the mid-sixth century, the prophets went to great lengths to explain precisely how and why this chosen nation had fallen into bondage. Their cultural and political responsibilities notwithstanding, prophets such as Amos, Hosea, Micah, and Isaiah of Jerusalem (eighth century), along with Jeremiah, Ezekiel, and Deutero-Isaiah (eighth century) subjected their interpretations to the unchanging principle that apostasy brings historical chastisement, and that, conversely, faithfulness brings deliverance from God, a future event envisaged as the reconstitution of the Jewish state in the promised land. Hence, their message was that fidelity to the Covenant was the only means of temporal deliverance.

Old Testament prophecies also appealed to early Christians who searched scripture for prefigurations of Christ's life. Christian exegetes developed the "typological" method of interpretation which correlated Old Testament persons, places, objects, or events with similar instances in the New Testament. Their purpose was to discern prefigurations of Christian truth in the Old Testament and to point out links between both Testaments. One example of this was the linkage between Adam and Christ. From a typological perspective, Adam is seen in his own right in Genesis, yet as a type, or prefiguring, of Christ: "death reigned from Adam to Moses, even over them that had not sinned after the similitude of Adam's transgression, who is the figure of him who was to come" (Romans 5:14). Similarly, Isaiah's allusion to the suffering servant has been construed as prefiguring Christ's passion (Isaiah 53:1–12).

The prophetic impulse was revitalized in the Middle Ages. One important example of this resurgence is Joachim of Floris, who founded his own order in Calabria, Italy, at the end of the twelfth century, and who wrote theological histories containing prophetic elements. Influenced by St. Augustine, Joachim constructed an elaborate paradigm for world history based on seven epochs and the Trinity. In works such as *The Concord of the Old and New Testaments*, Joachim interconnected three ages: (1) that of the Father (the Old Testament); (2) that of the Son (from the New Testament to the mid-thirteenth century); and (3) that of the Holy Spirit (1,000 years until the world's destruction and the Last Judgment). The third age is prospective and apocalyptic and includes the final struggle between the forces of good and evil according to the Book of Revelation. Joachist eschatology served political opportunists and religious extremists, however, until it was eventually discredited in the mid-thirteenth century. What is most important to note is that Joachist ideas were revived during catastrophes and upheavals, such as the great schism (1378–1417) and the period of the black death (1348–1350).

Though recognized primarily as an apocalyptic text, the Book of Revelation has remained the major source for visionary literature throughout the nineteenth and twentieth centuries. It has been an especially fertile source for the prospective imagination interested in interpreting current political and social upheavals in biblical terms. This kind of writing, inspired by oppression, anxiety, and faith, is radically unhistorical: writers from St. John to William Blake had considered current events as prelusive to the end of time, a concern for "the last things" overriding that for social and moral reform. Unlike apocalyptic writing, however, prophetic writing arises from historical conditions and responds to these conditions within a specific sociocultural context; hence, prophecy involves historical interpretation, and also, as we can see in the prophets Isaiah and Hosea, an informed and intuitive sense of political culture and of human behavior.

Both prophecy and apocalyptics have been popular in the twentieth century, especially in times of crisis. The prophets of the Cold War years ingeniously equated the symbolic constructs of Revelation with contemporary history and events; in such constructs, the founding of the state of Israel in 1948 was often a central and profound event, around which the forces of the East and of the West, identified dualistically as the representatives of good and evil on the earth, were gathering for an imminent confrontation. What this suggests is that prophecy has universal and perennial appeal because it speaks of the destruction of evil, of the triumph of God, and of the deliverance of the faithful. Despite this optimism, however, many prophets who have read political culture in theological terms have tended to extrapolate beyond the factual; their enunciations have tended to be historically shortsighted and spiritually farsighted, as they conceive of present circumstances as the worst that have ever been. The collapse of the communist world in the 1990s demonstrates how hazardous and speculative prospective historiography can be.

Throughout its 6,000-year history, prophecy has attempted to transcend the limitations of the human condition in the hope of endowing experience with unity, purpose, and direction.

[C.D.]

See *also* **Apocalypse; Eschatology; Millenarianism.**

FURTHER READINGS

Daniélou, S.J., Jean. *The Lord of History: Reflections on the Inner Meaning of History.* Trans. Nigel Abercrombie. London: Longmans, Green and Henry Regnery, 1964.

Gabel, John B., and Charles B. Wheeler. *The Bible as Literature: An Introduction.* New York: Oxford UP, 1986.

Greenberg, Moshe. "Prophecy in Hebrew Scripture." *Dictionary of the History of Ideas: Studies of Selected Pivotal Ideas.* Ed. Philip Wiener. 5 vols. New York: Scribner's, 1973. 3:657a–664a.

Leff, Gordon. "Prophecy in the Middle Ages." *Dictionary of the History of Ideas.* 3:664a–669b.

Trawick, Buckner B. *The Bible as Literature: The Old Testament and the Apocrypha.* 1963; reprint, New York: Barnes and Noble, 1973.

PROSPECTIVE AND RETROSPECTIVE TIME

William James eloquently discussed factors that influence prospective and retrospective time. He thought that attention "to the passage of time itself" influences psychological duration in passing, whereas memory influences psychological duration in retrospect. Modern researchers investigate these and other claims by varying the temporal paradigm. A prospective paradigm concerns duration in passing, or experienced duration; a retrospective paradigm concerns duration in retrospect, or remembered duration. The operational difference is that in the prospective paradigm, subjects know *before* a time period that they will later judge its duration, whereas in the retrospective paradigm, subjects do not have such prior knowledge.

If the two types of judgment involve different processes, there is no a priori reason to predict that one type will necessarily be longer than the other. However, many experiments have found that prospective judgments are longer than retrospective judgments, several have found no difference, and only a few have found that prospective judgments are shorter than retrospective judgments. In the latter experiments, however, all subjects first made a retrospective judgment and then made a prospective judgment. Presentation-order effects (see **Time-Order Errors**) commonly occur when subjects judge long durations, and this methodology confounds presentation order and paradigm. A meta-analysis of experiments, excluding those with this confounding, reveals that prospective judgments are reliably about 20 percent longer than retrospective ones. The meta-analysis also suggests that more than one variable influences such duration judgments.

Research reveals that several variables differentially influence prospective and retrospective judgments. For example, prospective judgments lengthen as the attentional demands of an information-processing task performed during the time period decrease. Retrospective duration judgments lengthen if a person experiences more events, more complex events, more event segmentation, more varied information-processing tasks, or more changes in external or internal context.

An attentional model provides a widely accepted account of prospective judgment. It proposes that subjects divide limited attentional resources between stimulus information processing and temporal information processing. If a stimulus-processing task demands more resources, fewer resources are available for temporal information processing, and experienced duration shortens.

An alternative view, a contextual-change model, attempts to explain both types of judgment. It proposes that prospective and retrospective paradigms differ in the amount of various types of contextual information that subjects encode. In the prospective paradigm, a person frequently attends to time, and on each occasion contextual information concerning the previous act of attending to time is automatically retrieved. Whenever this occurs, the previous time tag is retrieved, and a new time tag is encoded as part of the record of the retrieval event. Prospective duration judgment mainly involves estimating the availability of these various time tags, or temporal context changes. In the retrospective paradigm, subjects deliberately attend to time only occasionally, and so they do not encode temporal context changes as frequently. However, changes in environmental context, in emotional context, and in other external and internal contextual elements accompany the encoding of stimulus information. If there are more such changes, a person encodes a greater variety of contextual information. Someone making a retrospective duration judgment selectively retrieves memories of events and estimates the availability of these various types of contextual change. If more of them are available, the person will remember the duration as being longer.

[R.A.B.]

See also **Cognition; James, William (as Psychologist); Memory for Time; Psychology of Time; Temporal Judgment (Methods); Time-Order Errors; Time Perception.**

FURTHER READINGS

Block, Richard A., ed. *Cognitive Models of Psychological Time.* Hillsdale: Erlbaum, 1990.

Macar, Françoise, Viviane Pouthas, and William J. Friedman, eds. *Time, Action and Cognition: Towards Bridging the Gap.* Dordrecht: Kluwer, 1992.

PROUST, MARCEL (1871–1922)

French author of a celebrated novel on the theme of time, *A la recherche du temps perdu* (1913–27, translated as *Remembrance of Things Past*), Proust dedicated most of his career to this vast work. Frail in health and a chronic insomniac, Proust led a largely withdrawn adult life in a cork-lined room at 102 Boulevard Haussmann in Paris. An early novel, *Jean Santeuil* (written 1896–1900 but unpublished until 1952), represents *A la recherche* in embryonic form, but it was not until 1913 that Proust published at his own expense the first part, *Du côté de chez Swann* (translated as *Swann's Way*). Of the remaining eight parts, five appeared before his death: *A l'ombre des jeunes filles en fleurs*, 1919 (translated as *Within A Budding Grove*); *Le Côté de Guermantes I*, 1920; and II, 1921 (translated as *The Guermantes Way*); *Sodome et Gomorrhe* I, 1921; and II, 1922 (translated as *Cities of the Plain*). The remaining three appeared posthumously: *La Prisonnière*, 1923 (translated as *The Captive*); *Albertine disparue*, 1925 (renamed *La Fugitive*, translated as *The Fugitive*); and *Le Temps retrouvé*, 1927 (translated as *Time Regained*). Proust's influence on time-related fiction is particularly evident in *A Dance to the Music of Time* (1951–75)

by the English novelist, Anthony Powell. Interest in Proust remains strong: a 1981 "reworking" (mainly by Terence Kilmartin) of C. K. Scott-Moncrieff's definitive English translation of *A la recherche*; three new, independent editions of the novel (published by Grasset, Laffont, and Flammarion), as well as a new edition of *Albertine disparue* (Grasset), all following the end of copyright on the novel in October 1987; and a 1991 biography in French by Ghislain de Diesbach.

NARRATIVE CHRONOLOGY AND HISTORICAL CONTEXT

Narrated by a semi-autobiographical figure, Marcel, *A la recherche* is a detailed saga of French life in the late nineteenth and early twentieth centuries. Though vague regarding specific dates and the age of characters, the novel embraces historical events such as the Dreyfus affair and World War I, introducing in its course over 200 characters from many walks of life.

The novel's unconventional narrative chronology, as well as the narrator's linking of the intuitive inner being to the function of art, have led critics to suggest a connection with the time and memory theories of Proust's cousin, philosopher Henri Bergson. Proust denied this link, falsely believing there to be no distinction in Bergson's philosophy, unlike in his own work, between voluntary and involuntary memory.

As the novel begins, the middle-aged narrator is exploring the mental borders between sleep and waking. Various rooms from childhood come to his mind, bringing him gradually to a conscious decision to investigate the mysteries of memory. The narrative then steps back further in chronological time (as well as becoming largely third-person) in *Swann's Way*, its focus on Charles Swann setting in motion a complex chain of personal relationships around the narrator. Otherwise, the narrative continues to move from the narrator's childhood in Combray back to his middle age, when he resolves to write the book that we have by now almost finished reading.

INVOLUNTARY MEMORY AND THE RECOVERY OF LOST TIME

The novel is a sustained meditation on the effects of time and memory on the individual consciousness. The basis of Proust's search for the means to regain lost time is his distinction between voluntary and involuntary memory. The spontaneous occurrence of involuntary memory (a concept not original to Proust) through uncanny physical experiences holds the key to the narrator's eventual realization that the past may be regained through the creation of a work of art. The most celebrated of these various experiences (or "fetishes" according to one of Proust's most perceptive critics, author Samuel Beckett, in *Proust*, 1931) occurs early in *Swann's Way*, when the taste of a madeleine cake dipped in tea revives fully and joyfully for the narrator a forgotten moment of his childhood in Combray. This episode alone, says Beckett, "would justify the assertion that his entire book is a monument to involuntary memory. . . . The whole of Proust's world comes out of a teacup."

This unexpected recovery of the past persuades the narrator to investigate the reasons for his ecstasy, but its intellectual as well as its full emotional significance does not become evident to him until the final section of *Time Regained*. Shortly after the end of World War I, he is invited to a reception at the Guermantes mansion, where he meets again many of the characters, some now horribly aged, who have shaped his past. On arriving in the courtyard of the house he steps on some uneven paving-stones, whereupon the involuntary memory of a similar experience in the baptistery of St. Mark's in Venice again fills him with joy. This seemingly miraculous identification is followed, while he waits in the Guermantes library, by what Beckett calls several similar "visitations" forming a "single annunciation." These culminate in the narrator's final understanding that his inner being has witnessed the fusion of past and present, briefly rendering himself and his impressions free "from the order of time." It is, says the narrator, "to this contemplation of the essence of things I had decided therefore that in future I must attach myself." At the same time, he realizes that the only way to recapture this fleeting bliss, this "fragment of time in the pure state," is by the creation of a work of art. In his case, this will be through the precision and beauty of language. Proust thus forges what he believes to be the crucial link between the recovery of the past and the necessity of art.

[P.M.]

FURTHER READINGS

Cocking, J.M. *Proust: Collected Essays on the Writer and His Art*. New York: Cambridge UP, 1982.

Goodkin, Richard. *Around Proust*. Princeton: Princeton UP, 1991.

Kilmartin, Terence. *A Guide to Proust*. London: Chatto and Windus, 1983.

Steel, Gareth H. *Chronology and Time in "A la recherche du temps perdu."* Geneva: Droz, 1979.

Thody, Philip. *Marcel Proust*. New York: St. Martin's P, 1988.

PSYCHOACTIVE DRUGS

Many psychoactive drugs influence time-related behaviors, experiences, and judgments. These drugs include stimulants (such as amphetamines), sedative-hypnotics (such as ethanol), antipsychotics (such as chlorpromazine), anticholinergics (such as scopolamine), and hallucinogens (such as Δ^9-tetrahydrocannabinol, or THC, the active ingredient in marijuana). Psychoactive drugs are complex biochemicals that alter normal synaptic neurotransmission processes. The influence of any drug on brain and cognitive processes depends on which neurotransmitter system or systems the drug affects, whether the drug is an agonist or an antagonist, and whether the neurotransmitter is excitatory or inhibitory. Because any neurotransmitter is found in only certain parts of the brain, various types of psychoactive drugs influence psychological time in different ways. Thus, psychoactive drug effects can clarify the involvement of various brain systems in psychological time. Actions of many psychoactive drugs are not very well understood, however, so some of the following discussion is speculative.

Several drugs influence temporal behaviors and experiences by altering dopamine-based neurotransmission. For example, amphetamines are dopamine agonists: They increase stimulation of postsynaptic dopamine receptors. Phenothiazine derivatives (for example, chlorpromazine) are dopamine antagonists: They have the opposite effect. Although several brain areas contain dopaminergic neurons, apparently only one of these mediates temporal experiences. This area, located in the prefrontal cortex, is thought to be critical for maintaining an internal representation of the current information processing context. Perhaps as a result, it mediates prospective timing (experienced duration). Robert Hicks has reported converging evidence that enhanced activity in dopaminergic neurons in the prefrontal cortex increases the subjective time rate and reduced activity decreases it.

Some psychoactive drugs influence psychological time by interfering with acetylcholine-based neurotransmission in the hippocampus. This structure, along with other limbic-system structures, subserves the storage of long-term episodic memories so that subjects may explicitly retrieve them later. Anticholinergic (anti-muscarinic) drugs such as scopolamine and THC increase the subjective time rate, but also shorten the remembered duration of a time period, perhaps because they decrease the storage of new long-term episodic memories. Other psychoactive drugs affect gamma aminobutyric acid (GABA), a neurotransmitter that inhibits activity in several areas of the brain, including the hippocampus. Ethanol and THC have several different effects on the brain, but both apparently enhance the normal inhibitory effect of GABA in the hippocampus, thereby disrupting long-term memory storage. Retrospective duration judgments depend partly on explicit retrieval of long-term memories for events, which probably explains why alcohol and marijuana shorten such judgments.

The cerebellum, which relies on GABA- and glutamate-based neurotransmission, contains memory representations that subserve procedural memory. These representations, or motor programs, contain information on the timing of well-learned movements. Drugs that interfere with cerebellar neurotransmission (for example, ethanol) disrupt the coordinated functioning of motor programs.

Some psychoactive drugs also influence other temporal experiences, but researchers know little or nothing about the brain areas or neurotransmitters involved. For example, when subjected to relatively high doses of hallucinogenic drugs, people describe effects such as the loss of awareness of time; awareness only of the present; feelings of eternal, infinite, or archetypal time; or feelings that external time has slowed down so much that it has stopped. These reports suggest that duration experiences and temporal orientation are intimately connected.

[R.A.B.]

See also Cognition; Memory for Time; Psychology of Time; Psychophysiology.

Further Readings

Grilly, David M. *Drugs and Human Behavior*. Boston: Allyn and Bacon, 1989.

Hicks, Robert E. "Prospective and Retrospective Judgments of Time: A Neurobehavioral Analysis." *Time, Action and Cognition: Towards Bridging the Gap*. Ed. F. Macar, V. Pouthas, and W.J. Friedman. Dordrecht: Kluwer, 1992. 97–108.

PSYCHOANALYSIS

Psychoanalysis has a threefold significance. The term applies to a form of treatment for mental illness, a method for investigating the workings of the mind, and a branch of psychology, particularly behavioral science. The fundamental principles of psychoanalysis were formulated by Sigmund Freud. They were stimulated by his early experiences in treating patients suffering from hysteria and other neurotic disturbances. At first Freud used hypnosis and suggestion to study the nature of these disorders. Subsequently, he developed a more objective mode of investigation, namely, the psychoanalytic method. From his early observations, he concluded that the symptoms of hysteria resulted from childhood sexual experiences that had been forgotten, but which nonetheless continued to exert a dynamic influence on mental functioning. The memory of the traumatic events had been excluded from consciousness by a process of repression, but this process was only partly successful and the symptoms of hysteria constituted a disguised return of the repressed memory and its affective complement.

Freud was able to demonstrate how unconscious mental activity affected conscious mental processes and that childhood experiences have lasting effects, not only for the process of pathogenesis, but for shaping the personality in general, and that the sexual drive exerts a persistent and ubiquitous influence on mental life. He was able to demonstrate the influence of unconscious forces in mental activities that were not considered pathological, but were part of everyday experience, such as dreams, slips of the tongue, forgetting of names, unintentional acts, and character traits.

Although currently there are several different schools of thought in psychoanalysis, there are a number of principles which stand as the fundamentals of psychoanalysis as a psychology. These principles are determinism, dynamics, and topography. Determinism articulates the concept that mental events are not random but are etiologically and dynamically related to each other. This principle is best demonstrated through the use of the psychoanalytic method. Dynamics indicates that mental life is characterized by an interplay of forces in conflict, of opposing tendencies which have to be reconciled. Topography indicates that a great deal of mental activity occurs outside of the realm of consciousness. The existence of unconscious mental activity is inferred from the manifest products of the forces in conflict as they present themselves to consciousness.

In addition, psychoanalysis is characterized by the genetic approach, which applies particularly to issues of pathogenesis. It is a corollary of the aforementioned principles. The genetic approach summarizes the empirical findings of psychoanalytic investigation, to the effect that mental functioning in general and pathogenesis in particular reflect the persistent effects of the vicissitudes of childhood conflicts. Overarching all of these fundamentals of human psychology is the inherent biological tendency of the mind to seek pleasure and to avoid pain and unpleasantness. In situations of conflict among the various trends in the personality, what eventuates is some form of compromise, some mental product—a thought, an action, a fantasy, a dream, a symptom, a character trait—a mental product in which the various elements in conflict are represented in a form which minimizes pain, maximizes pleasure, and enhances adaptation.

How to conceptualize the origin of the nature of the forces in conflict in the mind has been a persistent source of controversy in psychoanalysis. Freud's final formulation visualized the functioning of the mind in terms of three principal centers of activity. The moral imperatives and the ideal aspirations collectively constitute the superego. The persistent driving tendencies, seeking gratification of sexual or aggressive wishes, constitute the id. The integrative, adaptive, reality oriented, compromise-forming functions fall under the heading of the ego, which is the agency that acts as the executant for the mind. It is the functioning of the ego that gives the final specific shape to the elements of mental life. Other analysts emphasize the self as the major organizing principle of mental functioning.

The investigative tool and the therapeutic medium of psychoanalysis is the psychoanalytic method. Its organization reflects the principles of mental functioning described above. Under standard conditions regarding schedule, length of sessions, fees, and regard for confidentiality, the patients are expected to report, as far as they are able, every presentation to consciousness that occurs to them, without censorship, omission, or distortion. This aspect of psychoanalytic investigation or treatment is referred to as free association. The analyst, accordingly, is privy to moment-to-moment variations of the interplay of forces in the patient's mind. From time to time, the analyst intervenes, demonstrating certain connections among the elements in the patient's thoughts of which the patient was not aware. Often enough, the patient had not been conscious of the connection between some thoughts and how they related to his or her difficulties. Conclusions about unconscious mental processes are inferences derived from the patient's productions. In effect, they constitute derivative representations of the patient's conscious and unconscious conflicts. The analyst draws conclusions about unconscious processes from the context and the sequence of the patient's thoughts, from the contiguity and juxtaposition of the elements in the patient's productions, from the repetitive appearance of certain themes, and from the nature of the language used, especially metaphoric images. All of these converge into a comprehensive hypothesis. The validity of an interpretation does not depend on the patient's acceptance or rejection, but is determined by its dynamic effect, that is, by the nature of the material that emerges subsequent to the intervention.

The technical goal of psychoanalytic treatment is to give patients insight into how their current problems derive from persistent unconscious conflicts, which started during childhood; how they have carried over into their current life fears, attitudes, and compromise formations from childhood; and how they have transposed them onto their current interpersonal relationships and thinking. In this regard, the analysis of the transference—that is to say, the patient's attitude and reactions to the analyst—is particularly helpful and important. It enables the analyst to demonstrate to the patient how he or she unconsciously transposes, that is, transfers unconscious fantasy wishes and conflicts from important individuals in the past onto the person of the analyst. Such transferences are always taking place outside of the treatment situation as well, but they stand out in bolder relief in therapy because the therapist does not respond to the patient's unconscious scenario. Instead, the therapist interprets it. Through this insight, the patient learns to distinguish the present from the past, reality from fantasy, and the analyst from objects of childhood conflicts.

Accordingly, psychoanalysis is a developmental psychology. Mental functioning in the adult is the product of lifelong processes of maturation and development. All experiential factors influence in one way or the other how the inevitable developmental challenges are mastered at different stages in life. The kind of compromise formations effected to master the conflicts secondary to the persistent unconscious fantasies determines the nature of character, personality, sexual orientation, choice of life vocation, and, ultimately, the issue of mental health or illness. The goal of psychoanalytic treatment is to enable the individual, through the process of insight, to adopt the best modes of dealing with his or her persistent unconscious conflicts. Psychoanalysis is suited for the treatment of neuroses and character disorders. Although it may contribute to the understanding of the psychology of psychoses and criminality, psychoanalysis is rarely effective in those conditions.

[J.A.A.]

See also **Developmental Psychology; Freud, Sigmund; Jung, Carl Gustav; Psychopathology and Time.**

Further Readings

Arlow, Jacob A. "Psychoanalysis and Time." *Journal of the American Psychoanalytic Association* 34 (1986): 507–528.

———. *Psychoanalysis: Clinical Theory and Practice.* Madison: International Universities P, 1991.

Brenner, Charles. *The Mind in Conflict.* New York: International Universities P, 1982.

Kurtz, S.A. "The Psychoanalysis of Time." *Journal of the American Psychoanalytic Association* 36.4 (1988): 985–1004.

Meerloo, Joost A.M. "The Time Sense in Psychiatry." *The Voices of Time.* Ed. J.T. Fraser. 2nd ed. Amherst: U of Massachusetts P, 1981. 235–252.

Melges, Frederick T. *Time and the Inner Future: A Temporal Approach to Psychiatric Disorders.* New York: Wiley, 1982. Bibliography 325–345.

Richter, Curt Paul. *Biological Clocks in Medicine and Psychiatry.* Springfield: Charles E. Thomas, 1965.

Sabbadini, Andrea. "Boundaries of Timelessness: Some Thoughts about the Temporal Dimension of the Psychoanalytic Space." *International Journal of Psycho-Analysis* 70.2 (1989): 305–313.

PSYCHOLOGICAL PRESENT

The psychological present is the focus of human experience. Phenomenologically, it appears as a privileged point in time, the Now. Physically, there appears to be no basis for this hic et nunc: real world events may occur simultaneously at any point t_x of a time scale, but this does not, by itself, create an experience of the present. Apparently, a privileged present requires a conscious observer capable of observing the cotemporality of these events within a single representational frame of reference. The psychological present, rather than being the durationless knife-edge between past and future, also has a certain temporal width, variously estimated to lie in a range between roughly one-tenth of a second and ten seconds. Within this *time window,* events appear to occur and to gradually recede into the past.

The psychological present allows the organism to integrate the various elements of information processing into one coherent package of information, that is, a meaningful scene, event, frame, or idea. As such, the mechanism leading to the awareness of a psychological present may be seen as a *coagulator* of reality. Incoming information and outgoing information may be continuous, but internal representations, in contrast, are syntactically and semantically discrete. Memory storage and retrieval rely on such "coagulated," interpreted inputs and outputs: we remember semantically coherent constituents of a situation, an event, or a thought, never the second half of one thought together with the first part of the next.

Considerable effort has been devoted to a specification of the functional mechanisms responsible for the psychological present. In one form or another, these mechanisms entertain the idea of a *time quantum,* a more or less fixed time interval within which information is integrated and treated as simultaneous, like the single frame of a movie picture. Much of the debate about the time quantum has focused around two models, the fixed rate "snapshot" or "movie camera" model and the "traveling window" model. No direct evidence has been found for either alternative, and the available indirect evidence appears to be inconclusive. The same uncertainty pertains to the length of the time quantum. Initially the value most often reported, as given by J.M. Stroud, was of the order of 100 ms (milliseconds); later, values around 25 ms, as given by I.J. Hirsh and A.B. Kristofferson, and even as short as 5 ms, as given by H.-G. Geissler, have been quoted. In addition, there seems to be evidence for a geometric series of time quanta at $2^n \times \delta t$ (where $\delta t \approx 5$ ms). These more recent findings are consistent with the concept of oscillator mechanisms (internal clocks). Altogether, however, at present, the evidence remains so weak and inconsistent as to leave the matter of the length of the time quantum undecided.

An additional weakness of both the fixed rate and traveling window models is that they do not take into account the structure and meaning of the situation to be coped with. Given the subtle syntactic and semantic processing that is going on all the time while a human being is interacting with his or her dynamic environment, it is likely that the psychological present—or the time quantum, if any—is intrinsically related to this cognitive activity. In other words, the psychological present and any quantization will be dictated by the syntactic and semantic structure of the environment and the actions being performed, rather than by some fixed-rate driving process or a traveling, but otherwise passive, window. Taking these structural aspects into account, a flexible and dynamic parsing model for the psychological present emerges.

The mechanism underlying the psychological present can be thought to operate as follows. In order to cope with its environment in a coherent and efficient fashion, the observer will at some point in time be induced to pay attention to a stimulus event. At that point a fresh psychological present will be initiated as a result of an elementary, automatic cognitive activity known as *tuning*. Tuning is a continuous process of parsing and interpreting the world and anticipating what will happen next, on the basis of the incoming stimulus information and aided by the cognitive strategies and expectations of the person. If, and as long as, the anticipation is confirmed by further incoming information and by the results of the parsing process, the current present will remain intact, that is, it will become longer and longer. As soon as a mismatch between anticipation and reality occurs that cannot be revised by backtracking, however, the parsing process is interrupted (and the present terminated). Its contents up to that point, if meaningful—that is, if structurally and semantically "closed"—are then transferred to permanent memory. At the same time, a new start is made, repeating the process of initializing and (dis)confirming a prediction about the events as they are expected to unfold. This process is similar to the process of parsing linguistic inputs. There, the flow of speech sounds is analyzed "on line" and then "packaged" and stored as integral constituents. Listeners do not wait for a sentence to be completed before they start interpreting it; sometimes this will lead to problems, for instance in sentences such as "The boat sailed to Rotterdam arrived at the dock."

The process of parsing, interpreting, and storing the flow of events in semantically or pragmatically meaningful chunks proceeds largely automatically. The results of this process are largely accessible to consciousness as our experience of the psychological present. This description of the "making of the present" is consistent with empirical data on the encoding, storage, and retrieval of information in human memory.

The time scale on which this process is taking place can be estimated from a variety of experimental data. Starting from the zero point of initializing a present, the onset of the parsing process may be initiated as early as 20-25 ms after stimulus onset. At 250-300 ms a present may be "aborted" if no fitting prediction can be found. This will occur if the input information is essentially random, or if stress prevents a subject from properly attending to the input. At the other end of the scale, the length of a psychological present is constrained by the capacity of working memory: to retain information in working memory continuously for more than twenty or thirty seconds, it must be refreshed (rehearsed), which will interfere with the effort to sustain the parsing and interpreting process. On average, the length of the psychological present in everyday circumstances will be found to be of the order of 2 to 5 seconds. It is no accident that many naturally and culturally determined situations and events have an internal structure with components or constituents that fall within this range.

[J.A.M.]

See also **Psychology of Time; Time Perception.**

FURTHER READINGS

Dennett, D.C. *Consciousness Explained*. Harmondsworth: Penguin, 1992.

Fraisse, P. *The Psychology of Time*. Trans. J. Leith. New York: Harper & Row, 1963.

Gale, R.M., ed. Th*e Philosophy of Time: A Collection of Essays*. Hassocks: Harvester P, 1978.

Harris, E.E. *The Reality of Time*. Albany: State U of New York P, 1988.

Jackendoff, R. *Consciousness and the Computational Mind*. Cambridge: MIT P, 1987.

James, W. *The Principles of Psychology* (Vol. 1). New York: Dover, 1950. First published in 1890.

Jones, M.R. "Time, Our Lost Dimension: Toward a New Theory of Perception, Attention, and Memory." *Psychological Review* 83 (1976): 323–355.

Michon, J.A. "The Making of the Present: A Tutorial Review." *Attention and Performance*. Ed. J. Requin. Hillsdale: Erlbaum, 1978. 7:89–111.

———. "The Compleat Time Experiencer." *Time, Mind, and Behavior*. Ed. J.A. Michon and J.L. Jackson. Berlin: Springer, 1985. 20–52.

PSYCHOLOGICAL RESPONSES TO MUSIC

Music is found in all cultures and used for a wide variety of purposes. It is ubiquitous, and this creativity of uses makes it impossible to come up with a single theory or set of outcomes that encompasses all possible responses to music. Music can be used to express or suppress emotions, create aesthetic enjoyment, entertain, convey emotions, arouse physical responses, and contribute to the continuity and integration of society.

Whatever its origins or functions, music is a human behavior that occurs within a cultural context. Learning underlies all musical behavior, whether it is emotional, affective, or otherwise. Musical meaning in a broad sense depends on being understood within a musical structure or grammar. Clearly, there is a wide range of responses to music, and this reflects differences in an individual's innate capacities, training, knowledge, and experience.

We can plausibly consider three ways in which music evokes psychological effects. The first is by means of reference to a non-musical object, event, or situation. For example, music can remind one of growing up, a love affair, or a religious experience, and thereby elicit emotions associated with those events. These responses will be different for each person and reflect idiosyncratic learned associations. Alternatively, music can incorporate natural sounds (such as bird songs, fire sirens, cannon firings), or well-known melodies to elicit emotional responses based on common experience. Music of this sort often serves a functional role, such as intensifying the formality and facilitating the drawing together in religious, military, and athletic ceremonies.

Second, music can evoke psychological effects by means of the correspondence between the dynamic form of music and the equivalent form of emotion. The ebb and flow of tension and relaxation in music created by changes in intensity, density, tempo, or rhythm mirrors the ebb and flow of tension and relaxation of emotions. Music does not represent one specific emotion, but it does represent the dynamic build up and relaxation cycle of emotion. It is this temporal cycling that brings about emotional responses.

Third, music can evoke an emotional response by means of the "collative" variables of novelty, surprise, complexity, and ambiguity related to its form and structure. The basic notion is that by means of experiences with a specific style of music, listeners build up a set of expectations about which notes and chords follow each other—which is to say, the rules of tonality—about the timing of strong and weak beats, and about the relationship between melody and rhythm. These expectations are to a large extent implicit; listeners cannot verbalize the rules. Nonetheless, these expectations guide our interpretation of music and provide a grammar to understand the relationships among the notes. L.B. Meyer argues persuasively that when expectations are violated or delayed, this creates suspense and tension. Though the tension is valueless in itself, it generates emotions if resolved in a manner that is understandable in the given context. From this perspective, music in an unfamiliar style is meaningless because the cycle of suspense and resolution cannot occur. Moreover, affective and intellectual responses to music cannot be separated because both depend on the same perceptual processes and mental organization.

There have been several approaches to understanding the emotional and affective responses to music. The first has investigated physiological responses, since it is commonplace to assume that music brings about changes in heart rate, breathing rate, or muscle tension. While our intuition is that such changes do occur, there is little evidence that these are consistent changes associated with specific pieces of music or that these changes are reflections of emotional response.

The second approach has used verbal responses to describe the emotional content of pieces of music. The listeners might be asked to "describe" what happened internally or listeners might rate musical segments employing emotional adjectives—such as happy, delicate, yearning, gloomy, or exciting—in order to characterize each segment. Following this, the next step is to correlate the specific emotional responses for each segment to its underlying musical and acoustical features.

Some listeners find this task impossible. They hear the music as music, and are unwilling to select emotional labels. Other listeners find it easy to give emotional labels to pieces of music. These labels point out in general ways that in Western culture, certain sound patterns have come to be associated with affective moods. In spite of differences in the results due to varying methodologies and musical segments, there does seem to be mood contrasts that are useful to characterize melodic music. One contrast may be termed gaiety (major scale, consonant, flowing rhythm, high pitch level) versus gloomy (minor scale, dissonant, firm rhythm, lower pitch level). A second contrast is energetic (loud, staccato articulation) versus relaxed (soft, slurred articulation), and a third contrast is serious (loud, slow, low in pitch, cultural labels) versus trivial. For melodic segments, rhythm and tempo seem to be the primary elements affecting mood responses. For rhythmic segments using only one tone, the fundamental emotional contrast is between vital and excited (high tempo, pronounced syncopation) versus dull, calm, and rigid.

Two points should be made. First, there is no apparent relationship between the mood response and the gender, age, intelligence, or musical training of the listeners. Second, mood responses depend on general cultural factors, but even with this background, emotional responses are often ambiguous. Some music can be interpreted as sad or happy equally well. Context in the form of a story (such as opera or ballet) or familiarity is needed to understand the music.

R. Francès suggests that one way of understanding the expressive language of music is by means of the relationship between the rhythmic and melodic structure of the movement and gestural schemes that accompany basic moods (such as calmness, excitement, and happiness). Each of these moods is accompanied by patterns of movements, and the translation of these patterns in terms of sound constitutes the basis for the expressive language of music. The moods evoked by the music are rooted in a context determined by individual and social experience. Thus, a sense of excitement can bring about an image of a busy city, a white-water canoe trip, or a political rally, depending on the listener's experiences.

It is important to note that music evolves in time and that expressive responses similarly evolve in time. Cycles of musical tension and relaxation mimic the cycles of emotion. Cycles of melodic and rhythmic syntactic change create ambiguities and expectations leading to expressive psychological states. Affective responses are embedded in a temporal background.

[S.H.]

See also **Rhythm and Meter in Music; Tempo.**

FURTHER READINGS

Dowling, W.J., and D.L. Harwood. *Music Cognition.* Orlando: Academic, 1986.

Francès, R. *The Perception of Music.* Trans. W.J. Dowling. Hillsdale: Erlbaum, 1988.

Meyer, L.B. *Emotion and Meaning in Music.* Chicago: Chicago UP, 1956.

Radocy, R.E., and J.D. Boyle. *Psychological Foundations of Musical Behavior.* 2nd ed. Springfield: Thomas, 1991.

PSYCHOLOGY OF TIME

INTRODUCTION: TIMING AND TIME EXPERIENCE

The starting point for the psychology of time, as Paul Fraisse put it, is that humans—and animals too—live in a world of change. First, in order to survive in such a world, it is essential that they be capable of correlating their behavior very precisely with the temporal course of events in their environment; this is known as *timing*. The precision of this timing ability is decisive for the survival potential of a species. Second, in order to cope with reality in complex situations where habitual timing mechanisms fail, individuals must generate explicit images and expectancies about the world. These cognitive representations supply the basis for *time experience* and the actual rules of conscious temporal conduct.

Generally speaking, empirical psychology is concerned with the question of which aspects of reality are dealt with "directly" or "automatically" by means of timing, and which are instead inferred indirectly by some reflexive, cognitive process. The aim of the psychology of time is to formulate an answer to this question with respect to the temporal domain.

HISTORY

1. THE FIRST FIFTY YEARS (1865–1915)

Psychology as an empirical science originated in the first half of the nineteenth century. Temporal phenomena were among the first to be studied experimentally. Two questions in particular lie at the root of the psychological study of time. First, it had been discovered toward the end of the eighteenth century that perception and thinking are not instantaneous. This insight eventually led to what we now call mental chronometry, the systematic use of reaction time as an index of mental activity. In the second place, the question was raised as to whether there is a genuine sense of time and, if so, where it is located? Although the answer was negative, the "time sense" lingers on as a convenient figure of speech.

The first truly systematic study of psychological time appeared in 1868. In his dissertation, *Die Zeitsinn nach Versuchen*, Karl Vierordt established the so-called indifference interval, an interval of roughly 0.75 seconds which is neither over- nor underestimated. Vierordt was followed by many others, including a host of students of Wilhelm Wundt, who himself showed a lively interest in the subject. Not surprisingly, E.B. Titchener, at the turn of the century, could qualify the study of time as one of the most important areas of psychological research, "a microcosm, perfect to the last detail," which, in his opinion, reflected all the major questions of psychology. In the same period several theoretical positions were proposed that would prove fundamental for the psychology of time. The most important among these were put forth by Jean-Marie Guyau, William James, and Henri Bergson. Now, a good century later, their impact is still felt.

2. LOW TIDE (1915–1957)

Interest in psychological time steeply declined after 1910, partly because of the elusive character of many temporal phenomena, and partly because of the decline of the introspective method and, at least in North America, the increasing influence of behaviorism. Only in France and some neighboring countries did a very strong tradition in the psychological study of time persist, a tradition that includes—apart from Guyau and Bergson—Pierre Janet, Gaston Bachelard, the Swiss Jean Piaget, the Belgian Albert Michotte, Henri Piéron, and, most notably, Paul Fraisse. Everywhere else, time psychology practically disappeared, with American Henry Woodrow being a notable exception.

Around 1960 the psychology of time could be qualified as a "venerable but tired topic." The field apparently lacked the inherent vitality to regain some of its former status. Hardly anyone bothered to attempt explaining timing and time experience in terms of other—more basic—psychological mechanisms. And the psychological study of time became sterile: over and over, experiments were based on the same petty paradigms, showing hardly any progress in the sophistication of the questions asked or the hypotheses put forward.

3. RENAISSANCE

From about 1960 onward, the psychology of time has undergone a quite remarkable renaissance. This revival was initiated and greatly stimulated by an epochal monograph, *Psychologie du Temps,* by Paul Fraisse, which appeared in 1957. In it, Fraisse summarized almost a century's empirical and theoretical work in the area. Since then, a steady increase in the number of substantive studies can be observed. This trend has been supported by strong methodological and conceptual undercurrents in experimental psychology. Particularly inspiring for the study of time were (*a*) the so-called experimental analysis of behavior, which emphasizes the role of internal timers, and (*b*) the cognitive "revolution" that took place around 1960, which has emphasized the symbol-processing and semantic aspects of mental activity. These two approaches to time psychology have followed somewhat oppositional lines of development, but attempts are now being made to "bridge the gap."

Recent studies tend to deal with the problem of time within the framework of more substantive problem areas. The last two decades, in particular, have brought a number of important and interesting developments related to the temporal aspects of phenomena in domains such as pattern recognition, speech perception, remembering life events, decision making, planning, and musical skills. Each of these developments extends well beyond the boundaries of classical time psychology, which primarily dealt with the perception, estimation, and reproduction of short time intervals. It should be emphasized that in the same period, tremendous progress has been made in chronobiology, the study of biological rhythms and other organic factors that influence the temporal structure of real life task performance. This too has given the psychology of time an important impetus. As a result of these developments, the psychology of time has again become part of the mainstream of experimental psychology.

THEORETICAL ISSUES

Do these achievements also lead to a more coherent theoretical explanatory framework for the psychology of time? This question will be considered briefly from three points of view—the descriptive, the functional, and the metatheoretical.

1. THE DESCRIPTIVE APPROACH

Quite a number of authors have formulated taxonomies of time experience. Many such taxonomies, like the one proposed by J.E. Orme, provide little more than a summing up of common sense experiences related to time. More relevant are taxonomies that are based on distinctions that are structural, as that of L.W. Doob, or functional, as that of P. Fraisse. But despite the heuristic value such taxonomies can have for research, they essentially beg the question, since their terms derive from the phenomena they purport to describe. In other words, they do not meet a fundamental requirement of scientific explanation, namely that the various temporal phenomena be described in terms of concepts that are extrinsic to time experience as such.

An example of an extrinsic taxonomy, one that is based on a good number of generic theoretical concepts from experimental psychology rather than on a phenomenology of time, is presented in Figure 1. This diagram relates a dichotomy of perceived versus remembered *data* to a dichotomy of automatic versus controlled (or conscious) *information processing*. The distinction between the two kinds of data involves the experience of the present as opposed to that of the past and future. The two processing modes allow a functional distinction between a number of phenomenal attributes of temporal phenomena such as, for instance, the implicit versus explicit nature of certain temporal behaviors, or

the conventional distinction between the perception and estimation of duration.

2. THE FUNCTIONAL APPROACH

A theory of time experience can conceptually rely on an extrinsic taxonomy, but when it comes to mapping the territory in a way that is consistent with present mainstream psychology, a theory of psychological time will have to be much more specific in terms of architecture (biopsychological mechanisms), process (symbolic operations), and structures (semantic representations). These so-called levels of explanation reflect recent views in the philosophy of mind as discussed by D.C. Dennett and A. Newell.

At the first level, we are dealing with the system architecture, that is, the biological mechanisms which enable the organism to cope with the temporal contingencies of its dynamic environment. Here a distinction is made between internal clocks and switches. Clocks refer, generally speaking, to periodic mechanisms; by switches we mean various kinds of "one-shot" mechanisms. The circadian rhythm and the breathing cycle are examples of the first; the eye-blink reflex belongs to the second category. A good deal of work in the psychology of time concerns

information processing mode			
		automatic	controlled	
d **a** **t** **a**	actual (presented)	perception of dynamic invariants (affordances)	perception of objects and events	"real time" conscious present
	stored (represented)	tacit knowledge procedural knowledge	episodic knowledge declarative knowledge	"simulated time" memories and anticipations
	processing characteristics	parallel distributed immediate data-driven implicit	sequential focused computed rule-driven explicit	
	conscious temporal correlates	frequency, rate recurrence	order, duration, position, "date"	

Figure 1. A taxonomy of psychological time

the nature and properties of these clocks and switches and the ways in which they may form the timing base for a particular task. However, there are so many external factors that influence temporal behaviors that it is difficult to specify a definite relation between a timing mechanism and external events or event sequences. This implies that a timing model which fails to specify in detail how processing and semantic aspects of these events affect clock rate or switching rate is deficient as a model of human time experience. Therefore, we need a second process level, at which we treat time as information. The number of events, their structure and dependencies, and the cognitive and emotional context in which the behavior is performed, all affect the experience of time. Work at this level aims at uncovering the way in which the processing of information—both temporal and nontemporal—influences estimates of duration.

These two levels of explanation have long dominated the field of time psychology. In recent years it has become clear, however, that it is impossible to give a coherent explanation of temporal experience if the "meaning," the semantic and pragmatic structure of the stimuli, is not taken into account. As a result, the attention of many researchers is now focused on the *event* as the core concept. Events have either a natural or an imposed structure and meaning. From this point of view, judgments of time are judgments about events, relative to internalized prototypical events. Thus, for instance, a (retrospective) estimate of how long it took me to get a particular book from the library yesterday morning will be determined, in part, by a behavioral scenario of "How to get a book from the library" that is an "average sediment" of my previous experiences with my favorite library, or even with libraries in general.

3. METATHEORETICAL CRITERIA

Although there is not yet a "received view" to which psychologists will spontaneously adhere when they are asked to give a general account of the psychology of time, there appears to be enough common territory to specify some of the basic assumptions underlying theory construction in the domain of psychological time.

A. A psychological theory of time experience should specify a *functional stimulus* for our "sense of time." In other words, a theory should tell us what external stimuli serve as the inputs from which the human mind can construct the apparently quite rich phenomenology of time experience.

B. The second requirement is that the *levels of explanation*, used in the theory, be specified. As argued earlier, psychological explanation requires a hierarchy of explanatory levels to account for the system's "architecture," its functional design as an information-processing system, and its reasons and intentions, respectively.

C. Even if the functionalistic (instrumentalistic) view is adopted, that time is largely a conscious product of the processes by which people organize their experience, we find that not all temporal relations in human behavior are explicit and accessible to conscious manipulation. The distinction between *implicit* and *explicit temporality* of human action, or between timing and time experience, is a fundamental one and must have its place in a theory of psychological time.

D. The explicit mental representation of time can take different forms. A basic feature of a theory of psychological time is what it has to say about various *modes of representation* and about the rules of operating upon these modes. This includes the well-known distinction between propositional and pictorial representation, but it may also involve a representational mode based on the causal or logical order of events, the so-called "temporal string representation."

E. A special issue is the role of space, or rather the role of the *spatial analogy* or metaphor, for the representation of time. Not only does the ubiquity of visual imagery suggest that space constitutes an independent medium for mental representation, space also permeates language and specifically the semantics of time.

F. It is evident that time as an organization of events relative to their being past, present, or future entertains a very close relation to our concept of memory. Time is intrinsically connected with *dynamic memory*, that is, with the memory for concrete episodic events, localized in space, that together constitute a meaningful narrative, including the personal history that we recognize as our "self" or ego.

G. Last but not least, a theory of psychological time must specify the *ontogenesis of time*, and describe how the cognitive mechanisms that produce our experience of time develop in the course of our life.

[J.A.M.]

See also **Cognition; Fraisse, Paul; Internal-Clock Models; Memory for Time; Psychology: Representations of Time; Psychophysiology; Time Perception.**

FURTHER READINGS

Block, R.A., ed. *Cognitive Models of Psychological Time.* Hillsdale: Erlbaum, 1990.

Dennett, D.C. *Brainstorms: Philosophical Essays on Mind and Psychology.* Hassocks: Harvester P, 1978.

Doob, L.W. *Patterning of Time.* New Haven: Yale UP, 1971.

Fraisse, P. *Psychologie du temps.* Paris: Presses Universitaires de France, 1957. (Trans. Jennifer Leith. *The Psychology of Time.* New York: Harper & Row, 1963.)

Gibbon, J., and L. Allan, eds. T*iming and Time Perception.* New York: New York Academy of Sciences, 1984.

Levin, I., and D. Zakay, eds. *Time and Human Cognition: A Lifespan Perspective.* Amsterdam: North-Holland, 1988.

Macar, F., V. Pouthas, and W.J. Friedman, eds. *Time, Action and Cognition: Towards Bridging the Gap.* Dordrecht: Kluwer, 1992.

Michon, J.A., and J.L. Jackson, eds. *Time, Mind, and Behavior.* Berlin: Springer, 1985.

Newell, A. *Unified Theories of Cognition.* Cambridge: Harvard UP, 1990.

Orme, J.E. *Time, Experience and Behavior.* New York: American Elsevier, 1969.

PSYCHOLOGY: REPRESENTATIONS OF TIME

A cognitive system such as the human mind is determined by its ability to represent its environment symbolically (which is what we call knowledge), and to perform operations on these representations (which is what we indicate by terms like thinking, reasoning, and learning). Some of these operations are carried out under conscious control, but many proceed automatically and, generally, are inaccessible to conscious control.

The temporal structure of events is itself a source of information—equivalent to dimensions such as the form, size, or color of objects. That is, a change in the temporal structure of a situation may, in and of itself, cause a corresponding change in behavior. Similarly, persons may learn to improve the acuteness of their "sense of time" by paying attention to the fine structure of a situation. J.J. Freyd, M.R. Jones and M. Boltz, J.A. Michon, R.N. Shepard, and others have offered considerable evidence for this position, although a few influential psychologists—most notably J.J. Gibson—and many philosophers—such as A. Grünbaum and P.C.W. Davies—claim otherwise.

Evidently, a keen sense of time, that is, a detailed repertoire of representations of time, has survival value. It allows its owner to review past experience and to anticipate future events effectively and efficiently. It expands the temporal horizon of the organism, allowing it to attune itself in intricate ways to the requirements of its dynamic environment. Given this biological significance of representing time, it is not surprising that humans possess a rich repertoire of temporal representations. These can be classified as implicit and explicit, respectively, the latter category being divided further into three subgroups—episodic, analogical, and formal—of increasing abstraction and increasingly under conscious control.

IMPLICIT REPRESENTATION: TIMING

To a considerable extent human behavior expresses time, rather than being based on explicit representations, in much the same way that the motions of the planets express rather than represent the equations of celestial mechanics. Temporal relations are expressed directly by the architecture of the human organism, a rich variety of clocks and switches (see **Time Perception**). Such mechanisms serve to organize a person's perceptual input and motoric output, including such periodic behaviors as walking, or "one-shot" behaviors like throwing a dart or catching a ball. A characteristic of these mechanisms is that their output cannot be influenced voluntarily and that they are only sensitive to a limited range of stimulus parameters. That time is not represented explicitly in this case is shown by the fact that one cannot influence these behaviors by directly manipulating the time constraints (duration) of the situation; instead, force, distance, and velocity appear to be variables affecting implicit timing performance.

The conclusion is that the temporal organization of a large proportion of everyday human behavior is expressed in behavior by means of a considerable number of temporally tuned mechanisms which do not, however, involve an explicit symbolic representation of the temporal parameters of the situation.

EXPLICIT REPRESENTATION: TIME AS A SYMBOLIC CONSTRUCT

The human environment frequently presents situations that are more complex than can be coped with by means of the repertoire of implicit timing mechanisms, whether innate or acquired. In these cases the organism is forced to switch to a controlled mode of information processing, or else it will fail to cope at all. Such switching implies the organism taking recourse to an explicit cognitive representation of the temporal relations in the problematic situation. In this case, flexibility of adaptation is gained at the cost of speed, smoothness, and ease of performance. Depending on the concreteness and familiarity of the situation to be coped with, one of the following modes of representation will be adopted.

1. *Episodic Representation.* In order to "understand" and encode the temporal structure of the situation, the subject will recall a more or less concrete *episode* (also known as scene, frame, or scenario) which is sufficiently similar in form and content to the prevailing situation to provide the required guidance for behaving appropriately under the circumstances. If the remembered situation does not quite match the actual situation, adaptive "tweaking" may be used to substitute details of the representation and obtain a better match between representation and reality.

2. *Analogical Representation.* If the impasse persists because no suitable episodic representation can be recalled, an attempt may be made to represent the temporal structure of the situation in terms of an analogy or a metaphor. This allows the mapping of certain relevant (temporal) relations by using the structural properties suggested by the analogy. "Time is money," for instance, is a clear example of such an analogical representation, allowing us to deal with time in situations where, semantically or pragmatically, it does appear as a valuable good, that is, as something to be spent, borrowed, saved, or wasted.

3. *Formal Representation.* Some analogical representations permit further abstraction; this applies, for instance, to the monetary analogy just mentioned, or the pervasive spatial analogy that seems to underlie much of our conventional conceptualization of time: time as distance, the future lying ahead of us, the remote past, and so forth. In these cases, the temporal structure of the situation may be mapped onto or into formal representations, that is, logical, numerical, or mathematical structures. In such cases we speak of models,

or even theories, of time: temporal logics and the motion equations of Newtonian or relativistic mechanics are examples. J.T. Fraser's hierarchy of temporalities, for instance, may be mapped onto a series of related psychophysical measurement scales. J.A. Michon has shown that these scales can be applied to the world as seen from several related and increasingly constrained temporal perspectives: atemporality, prototemporality, eotemporality, biotemporality, and nootemporality do correspond to nominal (unordered), ordinal, interval, ratio, and absolute measurement, respectively.

While the intricacies of these formal representations are frequently beyond the cognitive repertoire of many (if not most) humans, some appear to apply surprisingly well to the everyday experience of simple minds. This is especially true of the spatial representation of time. However, this is not a happy coincidence, but rather a direct consequence of the fact that such representations seem to fit the real-world situations to which they are applied quite closely. Nelson Goodman's dictum that "People make visions, and true visions make worlds" does indeed seem to apply to the effort which goes into creating formal representations of time that support such worlds—scientific, socioeconomic, or cultural.

[J.A.M.]

See also **Hierarchical Theory of Time; Time Perception.**

Further Readings

Freyd, J.J. "Dynamic Representations Guiding Adaptive Behavior." *Time, Action and Cognition: Towards Bridging the Gap.* Ed. F. Macar, V. Pouthas, and W.J. Friedman. Dordrecht: Kluwer, 1992. 309–323.

Jones, M.R., and M. Boltz. "Dynamic Attending and Responses to Time." *Psychological Review* 96 (1989): 459–491.

Michon, J.A. "Processing of Temporal Information and the Cognitive Theory of Time Experience." *The Study of Time I.* Ed. J.T. Fraser, F. C. Haber, and G.H. Müller. Berlin: Springer, 1972. 242–258.

———. "J.T. Fraser's 'Levels of Temporality' as Cognitive Representations." *The Study of Time V.* Ed. J.T. Fraser and N. Lawrence. Amherst: U of Massachusetts P, 1986. 114–146.

———. "Implicit and Explicit Representations of Time." *Cognitive Models of Psychological Time.* Ed. R. A. Block. Hillsdale: Erlbaum, 1990. 37–80.

Shepard, R.N. "Ecological Constraints on Internal Representation: Resonant Kinematics of Perceiving, Imagining, Thinking, and Dreaming." *Psychological Review* 91 (1984): 417–447.

PSYCHOPATHOLOGY AND TIME

To define the term psychopathology neatly and precisely is as formidable a task as providing a definition of time. Essentially, psychopathology is a discipline concerned with the systematic study of disorganized, disordered, and impaired mental functioning and behavior. The standard reference work of the American Psychiatric Association, the Diagnostic and Statistical Manual of Mental Disorders, states that "there is no satisfactory definition that specifies precise boundaries for the concept of mental disorder." Much controversy centers around the use of the concept; some regard mental disorder as a "myth"; yet there is no denying the abnormal, impaired, and maladaptive functioning that is the subject matter of psychopathology. Thus, psychopathology is primarily concerned with dysfunction, which is viewed by J.C. Wakefield as "a factual term based on evolutionary biology that refers to the failure of an internal mechanism to perform a natural function for which it was designed."

The Diagnostic and Statistical Manual presents an encyclopedic catalogue of a wide array of mental disorders and their symptomatology, including painful experiences, the impairment of perceptual and cognitive functioning, and a large diversity of disturbances in the behavioral, interpersonal, biological, and psychological spheres. Several broad categories of disorders are commonly identified and, although not completely independent of each other, seem logically well-suited for the delineation of the relationship between psychopathology and time.

Five broad categories of mental disorder are briefly described below. The first three categories are designated as psychotic. Common to the disorders classified as psychoses is the evidence of gross impairment to reality testing as demonstrated via dysfunction of the perceptual and cognitive apparatus, and general confusion and disturbed awareness of self and environment. Concomitant with these disorders are severely distorted temporal experiences. The last two categories (anxiety and personality disorders), in which temporality is relatively little affected, do not share the characterizations of the first three, especially with regard to adequacy of reality testing, which is generally not much impaired.

The first category covers organic brain disorders. These lead to temporary or permanent dysfunction of the central nervous system, which produces serious behavioral and cognitive effects, including distortions of time and temporal experience. Delirium and dementia are major characteristics of these conditions, in which reference is made to "clouded states of consciousness," confusion, broadband cognitive impairment, severe disturbances in the stream of thought, and sensory and memory defects.

The schizophrenic disorders comprise the second large category in the realm of psychopathology. Confusion, incoherent thought, "loosening of associations," and autism (absorption in self and fantasy to the exclusion of reality) are the cardinal signs of this group of disorders. Delusions and hallucinations are frequently experienced as part of the syndrome.

Affective disorders constitute the third major category. Two extremes of affective experience are represented in this so-called "bipolar" disorder. The manic phase involves "flight of ideas," distractibility, hyperactivity, and an inflated sense of self-esteem. At the other end of the affective continuum is the depressive phase (which in many aspects is a mirror image of the manic state), consisting of dysphoria, psychomotor retardation, decreased energy, and feelings of worthlessness.

In the neuroses, or the so-called anxiety disorders, there is an experience of great emotional tension, depression, worry, and psychological correlates of these states. Additionally, obsessions, compulsion, dissociation of thought, and somatic symptoms (in the absence of tissue pathology or other physical causes) are part of the dysfunctional picture of neurosis. The neurotic is engaged in a constant internal struggle in which many of the symptoms are the attempted solutions.

Finally, the personality disorders, which vary considerably in severity, constitute developmentally evolved lifestyle and trait patterns which, while maladaptive, generally show an awareness of the nature and demands of reality. Being aware of the nature of reality, however, is often unrelated to the behavior and conduct of persons with personality disorders.

The five groups of disorder, described above, are listed in order of decreasing severity—from the most severely impaired to the least—with respect to the reality awareness dimension.

The concern with specifying aspects of time perception and temporal experience in psychiatric description dates back to the very early development of the discipline more than a century ago. A part of the standard diagnostic interview of persons with mental disorder includes the testing for "orientation for time, place and person." It aims to give a rough indication of a person's awareness of self and the reality of his or her existence. In the psychotic disorders—brain syndromes, schizophrenias, and affective disorders—there is considerable disorientation and distortion in the temporal sphere. Much clinical experience and a voluminous experimental literature have been amassed in support of this observation. Due to differences in methodology of assessment and diagnostic differences in style or definition of syndromes, many contradictory findings are reported, but it is clear that in the psychotic disorders there is great difficulty in relating personal time awareness to "external" or world time. In the brain syndromes in particular, there is much impairment in perceiving, ordering, and remembering the succession of events—hence inadequate congruity with clock time. Sequence confusion is described by Eugen Bleuler in the case of autism in schizophrenia. The schizophrenic, according to Bleuler's detailed observations, "disregards" time relationships and mixes past, present, and future quite readily. Such confusion in time awareness, ordering, and discrimination corresponds to the defective and gross impairment of reality testing. In schizophrenia there is also difficulty in sequential thinking ("loosening of associations"), which affects time tracking and continuity. Often, a state of "timelessness," such as exists in dreaming states, is also present and underlies the time distortions so prevalent in this disorder.

With respect to the neuroses or the anxiety disorders, the emotional stress does not tend to affect time orientation or sequencing or time perception and estimation, as is noted in the psychotic disorders. Neither are there such difficulties in the personality disorders. Most problematic in these two groups are issues concerning time perspectives or, to use P. Fraisse's term, temporal horizons. The reference here is to the extension (in terms of world time) of self-projection into past, present, and future, and the coherence of the ordering of personalized events along these dimensions. Following the schema proposed in the work of Frederick T. Melges, and based on a review of a considerable aggregation of empirical and experimental data, the anxiety disorders tend to focus excessively on the past at the expense of the dreaded future. Future time perspective tends to be foreshortened, as is also the case in depression. Although repression may

be operative, Freudians would stress the potency of the past as a major reason for this tendency in the neuroses. On the other hand, personality disorders (especially the antisocial and sociopathic types) over-focus on the present and under-focus on the past and are especially neglectful of the future. This pattern of temporal experience is quite congruent with the impulsivity and the difficulty with postponing gratification which are major features of these personality disorders. The features seem to stem from the distrust in the subject's earliest relationships and from the resulting frustrations regarding what appears to be a not very promising future.

In conclusion, it may be stated that the different kinds of temporal experience, with the exception of the time perspectives mentioned above, remain intact in the anxiety and personality disorders. Memory, cognitive functioning, and reality testing are minimally affected in these conditions. Time perspectives are distorted in all the other classes of disorder. In the manic depressives temporal rate and rhythm are distorted, corresponding to the flight of ideas in mania and the constricted tempo in depressive ideation. In schizophrenia the distortions extend to the sequencing of time and the judgment of duration (as assessed via time estimation). Finally, in the brain disorders, orientation for time and the several other modes of temporal experience are impaired. Thus there seems to be a "hierarchy of vulnerabilities" in the relationship between temporal experience and psychopathology.

It is not at all clear whether mental disorders "cause" time distortion or the other way around. For F.T. Melges, the latter seems to be true. For the time being, however, pending further research, a relationship other than concomitance is yet to be demonstrated.

[A.I.R.]

See also **Manic-Depressive Illness; Psychoanalysis.**

Further Readings

Diagnostic and Statistical Manual of Mental Disorders. 3rd ed. Washington: The American Psychiatric Association, 1980.

Fraisse, P. *The Psychology of Time.* New York: Harper & Row, 1963.

Fraser, J.T., ed. *Time and Mind: The Study of Time VI.* Madison: International Universities P, 1989.

Melges, F.T. *Time and the Inner Future: A Temporal Approach to Psychiatric Disorders.* New York: Wiley, 1982.

Wakefield, J.C. "The Concept of Mental Disorder." *American Psychologist* 47 (1992): 373–388.

PSYCHOPHYSIOLOGY

Psychophysiology is concerned with the relations between behavioral and organic parameters. In the field of time, research has been focused on drug effects and on visceral, muscular, or brain correlates of temporal processing.

Psychomotor stimulants such as amphetamines or caffeine provoke an acceleration of subjective duration: Subjects tend to overestimate the duration of a stimulus or to produce unusually fast spontaneous tapping and unusually short response durations when required to press a button for a given time. In contrast, tranquilizers such as chlordiazepoxide or barbiturics induce underestimations. Psychotropic drugs such as mescaline or LSD (lysergic acid diethylamide) yield strange feelings as regards the experience of time, as if it stopped, passed by very slowly, or ran suddenly. These findings have prompted speculations regarding the dependency of internal time bases on biochemical factors that would regulate their frequency. Although one typical problem with pharmacological effects is their lack of specificity—many behavioral measures other than temporal judgments being affected—it has recently been suggested that these effects cannot be explained by general influences on the arousal level and are linked to the metabolism of dopamine in the neurons of the frontal cortex. The question of specificity has also been asked in regard to the fact that subjective time shortens when body temperature increases and lengthens in the case of hypothermia.

The search for body correlates of temporal processing first involved visceral mechanisms during the 1960s and 1970s. Because of their cyclic character, cardiovascular and respiratory processes were thought to generate consistent time bases in the second or minute range. The hypothesis implied that sensory-motor activities are rhythmically modulated depending on the phase of these cycles where they occur, this recurrent modulation being used as a temporal cue. Some evidence in favor of rhythmic changes was found in reflexes, reaction times, spontaneous motor activity, and temporal judgments. However, the interpretation is not straightforward. For instance, the increase in blood pressure during systole is known to have inhibitory consequences on the central nervous system through a chain of various mechanisms. The question is whether such interactions solely introduce noise in sensory-motor processes or whether they specifically function as a time base. This has proved difficult to establish.

The existence of motor or proprioceptive cues associated with time-in-passing has been postulated since the 1970s. Temporal accuracy in motor-timing tasks increases when the proprioceptive feedback derived from response execution is enhanced. This is obtained by manipulating parameters such as force and movement velocity. A "chaining" type of hypothesis held that the variations in the discharges of the slow adapting receptors located in the joints regulate the timing of fast response sequences: One movement would cause the receptors to fire, and the moment when the next movement occurs would be determined by a criterion level of the firing decrease. A "closed-loop" view proposed that the outcome of the sensory feedback deriving from response execution is compared to an internal representation of the criterion response, and that the next movement is modulated on the basis of this feedback so as to match the criterion. Nowadays, the concept of a central motor program governing response parameters is preferred to that of a peripheral control. Studies in reaction time indicate that the duration of a motor response can be programmed before execution if it constitutes a major requirement of the task. In other cases, duration may emerge from an interaction between the environmental constraints and the biomechanical properties of the motor system.

Brain mechanisms have been studied in various ways. The effects of brain lesions in humans have provided ambiguous results, since temporal deficits can seldom be disentangled from memory ones, especially when long durations are used. Lesions in frontal, temporal, and occipital areas, as well as in subcortical structures such as thalamic nuclei, induce deficits in temporal tasks. In animals, septal or hippocampal lesions provoke consistent defects even in short durations. Inhibitory and attentional mechanisms seem partly responsible for these effects.

Topographic analyses of brain activity suggest that frontal lobes are predominantly activated during the production of a motor response whose duration must be accurately estimated. Before the execution of this timed response, the supplementary motor area yields prominent activation while information concerning the particular duration to be produced is being processed. Single-unit activities recorded in the prefrontal cortex of monkeys have also been related to timing. The techniques of brain imagery, which are developing rapidly, will no doubt provide exciting advances in this field.

Electroencephalographic rhythms (such as the alpha rhythm and the hippocampal theta rhythm) have long been proposed as brain correlates of time processing, but clear-cut evidence is still lacking. More recently, certain of the "event-related" potential changes that are induced by various phases of information processing have yielded interesting data. For instance, an "emitted" potential appears around the moment when a stimulus should occur but does not, if this stimulus was delivered after a known delay in the preceding trials. One of the components of the "contingent negative variation" varies in relation to temporal accuracy. This potential change typically appears in the delay that separates two significant events when the duration of this delay is made predictable.

Unveiling the nature of the mechanisms involved in time estimation is the ultimate goal of those studies concerned with psychophysiological indices. Arguments for and against the existence of an internal timer or timers have long continued and no clear winner has yet emerged. Temporal mechanisms may differ depending on the conditions in which the time judgment is produced. Only when sufficient attention is given to temporal parameters would internal timers be efficient. Other types of temporal judgment would rest mainly on long-term memory processes. According to a classical conception, the timer function is to encode stochastic or periodic pulses during the period to be estimated: Subjective duration would be positively related to the number of pulses recorded. One possibility is that oscillatory neurons provide the time bases. Globally, frequencies of 10 to 50 hz (hertz) have been proposed as the characteristic frequency of the "temporal oscillator." Oscillatory neurons do exist, mostly in subcortical areas, but their function is still unclear. Little is also known about the possible relations between the timer function and the neural pacemakers that control certain biological rhythms. Studies on long-term isolation in natural caves indicate that both the period of circadian cycles and subjective duration within short delays lengthen in the absence of external synchronizers. However, whether biological rhythms and acquired temporal regulations share common mechanisms remains an open question.

Connectionist models involving neuronal networks have recently been proposed in the field of time. Distinct mechanisms are imagined: activity propagation times in chains of units that trigger next elements in a cascading process; cues deriving from the detection of synchronization or of complex temporal relations between patterns of spikes, and so forth. Further advances in the understanding of temporal mechanisms will certainly depend on close interactions between these various approaches.

[F.J.J.M.]

See also **Biological Rhythms and Psychological Time; Cellular Rhythms; Chronobiology; Circadian Pacemakers; Isolation; Psychoactive Drugs; Temperature and Psychological Time; Time Perception.**

FURTHER READINGS

Macar, F. *Le Temps: Perspectives psychophysiologiques.* Brussels: Mardaga, 1980.

Macar, F., V. Pouthas, and W.J. Friedman. *Time, Action and Cognition: Towards Bridging the Gap.* Dordrecht: Kluwer Academic, 1992.

PUEBLO ETHNOASTRONOMY

The Pueblo people of the Southwest United States believe in a cosmos in which nature functions with the active cooperation of humankind. The proper ceremonies must be carried out at the proper time so that the cosmic order is sustained. Traditional beliefs held that there were proper times for planting, harvesting, hunting, ceremonies, and many other activities—all embedded in a sense of sacred time. The right times for these crucial undertakings are established by astronomical observations to regulate the ritual calendar. The cycles of the sun and moon set the rhythm of Pueblo time.

The cyclical nature of the scheduling of Pueblo ceremonies must be viewed in their cosmological context. Basically, the Pueblo cosmos has a complementary, bipartite structure: an upperworld and an underworld. We live in the upperworld, but are connected to those beings in the underworld by a synchronicity of timings. When it is day here, it is night below. When it is the winter solstice here, it is the summer solstice below. A flawless planting ceremony here relates to a beneficial harvesting ceremony below—and vice versa. Hence, a fitting ceremony affects more than just the upperworld; the ritual reciprocates with the underworld's complementary ceremony.

Sacred time is ordered with different levels of periodicities. The longest appears to be the seasonal year. We have very little evidence—almost all ambiguous—that the Pueblos kept any long counts or tallies greater than a year. Until the twentieth century, with the intrusion of European concepts of time, no indigenous interest appears in tracking cycles of many years. The yearly cycle was all important; after its end, a new, equally unique one began. Within the seasonal span, ceremonies occur in a fixed sequence, in which the completion of one sets the stage for the next. The astronomical marker for the subdivision of the year is the observation of the phases of the moon. Within a night, the start and end of some ceremonies are flagged by observations of the positions of certain stars, especially the Pleiades.

The shortest unit of time reckoned by the Pueblos is the day, which begins with sunrise. The day has vague subdivisions into loose "hours," most of which are noted near sunrise and sunset by the color of the sky. For instance, at the Hopi village of Walpi on First Mesa, the sequence is white dawn, yellow dawn, sunrise (first gleam), and sunup (about twenty minutes after sunrise). About the only time of day noticed with any care is that of noon, which is typically observed by the length and directions of shadows cast by the edges of walls, buildings, trees, or sticks embedded in the ground.

A religious official has the responsibility and the authority to set the ceremonial dates within the ritual cycle. The crucial task entrusted to this official is the *forecasting* of the correct date by making *anticipatory* astronomical observations. The dates are announced ahead of time in order that the people of the pueblo can enter into proper preparations (practicing songs and dances, preparing costumes and special foods) so that the ceremony may be carried out with a "good heart" and be effective.

Typically, one official—the sun priest—performs the sun-watching for the seasonal cycle, which includes the planting schedule. He does so from a sun-watching station that is generally located within or close to the pueblo. From this fixed spot, the sun priest keeps a horizon calendar (usually at sunrise using an observation of the first gleam) against the horizon profile. He knows from experience that when the sun rises (or sets) against a certain horizon feature, so many days would elapse until, say, the winter solstice. Then he uses tally markers to count down to that day, with an announcement made to the Pueblo a few days ahead of the celebratory date. This anticipatory technique allows the sun

priests to forecast the dates of the solstices to within one day of the astronomically correct date when the sun appears to "stand still" at its sunrise point. The observations made about two weeks in advance catch the sun when the angular speed of its sunrise position is large enough to be discerned by the naked eye on a day-to-day basis. Hence, this practice neatly solves both a cultural and astronomical problem.

Moon-watching regulates timings between the seasonal and daily ones. The official responsible for tracking the phases of the moon is generally *not* the one who watches the sun. A Pueblo month begins with the observation of the first visible crescent and ends with the last. The days of invisibility are not typically counted. However, for Hopi and Zuñi, we have evidence from the nineteenth century that the moon-watcher was aided in his tally by the use of a calendar stick arrayed with notches. We do not know for certain how these sticks were used (or if they are used today), but in both cases, notches could have been used to count the days of invisibility. These calendar sticks could also have been used to forecast the date of certain phases of the moon.

The months of the year are counted starting with the first before the winter solstice ceremony. The first five (or six) are named, usually after seasonal characteristics; these same names are then repeated for the next five or six. The lunar calendar needs to be synchronized with the solar one, which is accomplished by adding an intercalary month (which can be as short as four days!) at the end of the regular count, or after the winter solstice.

Although Pueblo people feared eclipses of the sun and the moon, they had no way to forecast them. In part, this lack was related to their disinterest in keeping counts longer than a year. We also find no evidence for knowledge of the 18.6-year lunar standstill cycle, even though the moon certainly was observed rising and setting. The historic Pueblo culture did not seem to attach any importance to this astronomical cycle, so it was ignored.

[M.Z.]

See also **Anasazi Archaeoastronomy; Archaeoastronomy; Mesoamerican Archaeoastronomy.**

FURTHER READINGS

Zeilik, M. "Keeping the Sacred and Planting Calendar: Archaeoastronomy in the Pueblo Southwest." *World Archaeoastronomy*. Ed. A. F. Aveni. Cambridge: Cambridge UP, 1989. 143–166.

QUANTUM COSMOLOGY

Quantum theory is a theory that has to be applied when studying the very small; cosmology is the study of the large-scale structure of the entire universe. According to the widely accepted big bang theory of the universe, at one stage the universe itself was very small, and so we are led to quantum cosmology: the application of quantum theory to the entire universe, considered as a single physical system.

MANY FINGERED TIME

The most immediate problem to arise concerns the interpretation of the theory. Quantum theory was originally devised to describe what is seen when a microscopic system, such as an atom, is measured by a large external apparatus. The formalism of the theory gives rules for calculating the probabilities of the various possible outcomes of such measurements, at different times. If, however, we are considering the entire universe, then there is nothing "outside" that can measure the universe, and so a different interpretation of the formalism is needed. The most popular alternative interpretation is the many-worlds picture, according to which the basic object of quantum theory (called the wave function) represents the simultaneous existence of a vast number of possible universes. Each is represented by a component in the wave function, the components being added together to form the whole. There is thus a distinction between the entire universe, described by the wave function but unobservable, and the many component universes, one of which is what we observe.

At intervals measurements take place, as an event inside a component universe, not as something coming from outside: a measurement is any physical process in which the state of a part of the universe (such as an atom) is amplified and permanently recorded in another part of the universe (the apparatus). When this happens, the particular component universe in which the measurement takes place splits into many universes, each containing a different possible outcome of the measurement. If we think of time as proceeding through successive states of the universe, we then obtain a picture of the flow of time as itself branching into increasingly many streams, like a river branching into a delta, as the universe evolves. We might call this a "many fingered time"—to adapt a phrase introduced by Wheeler in a somewhat different sense.

THE FROZEN FORMALISM

Quantum theory also contains rules as to how the wave function evolves with time. In quantum cosmology (at least in many formulations of it), these rules imply that the wave function of the entire universe is unchanging, which seems to contradict our experience of an evolving universe. The paradox is resolved by distinguishing two sorts of evolution: within each component universe things evolve, but the wave function of the entire universe contains a combination of component universes of many different ages in such a way that, as the individual components evolve, the total "mix" remains unchanged. For this to be possible, we have to distinguish two different sorts of time: a global time in which the wave function as a whole evolves, and the local branches of many fingered time in the components. Global and local time do not in general keep step. The theory thus gives an intriguing combination of the unchanging universe which was favored by Einstein (or by steady state theorists such as Fred Hoyle), and the evolving universe which is now the dominant picture. At each instant of global time, the constant wave function of the universe contains snapshots of all possible universes at all possible (local) times.

COSMOLOGY WITHOUT TIME

The basic problem in quantum cosmology is to calculate the (unchanging) wave function of the universe. This is a mathematical object that associates a complex number with each possible universe; the sizes of these numbers then determines how the different universes are combined together into the total wave function. The procedure for doing this which has received most attention recently is that proposed by Stephen Hawking. He takes as a starting point the idea due to R.P. Feynman that if we know the wave function at a time t_1, then we can calculate it at a later time t_2 by the prescription called a path integral. Namely, at the later time, the number associated with a given universe can be calculated by adding together contributions from all possible histories that might have happened to the universe between t_1 and t_2, finishing with the given universe in question, each such contribution being multiplied by the value associated by the wave function at time t_1 to the initial state of that history.

This would seem to be useless for quantum cosmology, because the wave function at time t_1 is just as unknown as the wave function at time t_2 (indeed, they are identical!). Hawking gets around this problem by an ingenious way of eliminating the need for the earlier time t_1. The procedure involves two steps: first, the conversion of time into space; second, the removal of the first time-instant. For the first step, Hawking notes that a history of universes—that is, a succession of spaces at different times—constitutes a single four-dimensional space-time. In quantum theory there is a procedure for converting the dimension of time into a dimension of space for computational purposes, and then reconverting it into time after the calculation has been performed. If this is applied to the present case, then a history preceding a given universe is turned into a four-dimensional space, joining together the space at time t_1 and the space at time t_2, which form three dimensional boundaries to the four-dimensional space. For the second step, Hawking demands that the space at time t_1 simply does not exist: he uses a four-dimensional space which has a single boundary, namely the space at time t_2. (This device is possible with space, but not space-time.) The wave function of the universe is then calculable, in principle, by adding together contributions from all four-dimensional spaces having a given universe as boundary. Time is abolished in this picture and replaced by a fourth dimension of space.

STATUS OF THE THEORY
It should be stressed that much of what has been described is programmatic: a description of calculations that might be carried out, but which have not actually been done. There are strong indications that, in practice, parts of the calcu-

lations would in fact lead to inconsistencies, as is often the case in quantum theory. There is also a wide divergence of opinion about the interpretation of any theory that could result from this.

[C.J.S.C.]

See also **Quantum Mechanics; Space-Time.**

FURTHER READING
Leslie, J. *Universes*. London: Routledge, 1989.
Hawking, S.W. *A Brief History of Time*. London: Bantam, 1988.

QUANTUM MECHANICS

In order to understand the behavior of objects of molecular size it is necessary to use quantum mechanics, a theory that at first appears very different from the classical mechanics of Newton. As in classical mechanics, time is described mathematically by a real number t (see **Mathematics**). Some authors—for example, R. Penrose—have claimed, however, that the directionality of time (the distinction between past and future) may be due to the physics of quantum mechanics, both as regards physical directionality and as regards more metaphysical aspects such as the nature of becoming. Other authors, like F.J. Belinfante, reject this.

The quantum theory of any particular system, such as an atom or a particle, involves a mathematical object called the wave function, and denoted by ψ, which in the simplest case of a particle can be represented (among other ways) as a function whose value is a complex number varying with position in space and with time. If one specifies a particular sort of measurement, such as a measurement of the energy in the case of a particle, then the theory enables one to use the wave function to calculate: first, the possible values that such a measurement might yield; and then, for any one of these values, the probability, at any given time, that this value will in fact be obtained. The theory also specifies how the wave function changes with time, thereby giving the dynamics of the system.

The dispute starts with disagreement as to what this function describes physically. Those authors—following Belinfante, I shall call them objectivists—who deny that quantum theory produces time directionality claim that ψ describes what is called an ensemble of systems. This is a concept used in statistical mechanics in discussing such things as the second law of thermodynamics. It means an (idealized) collection of systems specified by some large-scale property. For example, specifying the volume and energy of a gas in a box leaves the detailed arrangement of its molecules unspecified and so defines an ensemble consisting of all possible boxes of gas having the specified properties but differing in their detailed molecular arrangements. When someone holding this view says, for example, that the probability of finding a given value for a measurement is $1/2$, he or she means that in $1/2$ of the members of the ensemble this value will be obtained. This is called the relative frequency interpretation of probability.

The remaining authors claim that ψ describes a single system. This interpretation has the merit that it refers to something, such as a particle, that in some sense might exist and be a fundamental constituent of matter; whereas an ensemble is a somewhat hypothetical entity that is certainly less fundamental than the individual systems of which it is composed. Thus they might be thought to be talking about a more basic reality, so that I shall (following Penrose) call them realists. When these authors talk about a probability, they mean the propensity that the individual system has to yield a given value. Many would argue that each individual has such a propensity, even though it can only be discovered by taking a large number of systems en masse and determining the relative frequency of the value (so building an approximation to an ideal ensemble).

Time directionality comes in, according to the realists, when a measurement is actually made on the system. At this point, the value of the energy, or whatever is being measured, becomes certainly known and is no longer probabilistic. Thus the wave function describing the system must change to reflect the change from probabilities to certainties. This is called the collapse of the wave function, and it is associated with a particular direction in time. One never finds a time-reversed collapse taking place, in which a wave function corresponding to certainty suddenly turns into one describing probabilities (that process always takes place gradually). Metaphysically, the collapse corresponds to the coming into being of a certain definite state out of a previous potentiality for many states, reflecting the passage from future potentiality to past certainty.

According to the objectivists, however, what happens when a measurement takes place is that the specification of the ensemble changes. It is as if, in the example of the gas in a box, we were told the extra information that all the molecules were in one half of the box, so that we changed our viewpoint to consider the much smaller ensemble of boxes of gas that had this additional feature. Similarly, if we discover the energy of an atom, we restrict attention to the ensemble consisting only of atoms with that energy. Thus the change in the wave function reflects the change in our information, not any actual physical change in the system. From this point of view, the time directionality is not a special quantum mechanical event, but depends on the directionality of all information-gathering processes.

The two views described do not exhaust the possibilities. It is only possible to mention here the many-worlds view (see **Quantum Cosmology**) and the relative state view (due to H. Everett III) which have their own implications for time. In addition, many authors, both realists (such as E.P. Wigner) and relative state proponents (such as M. Lockwood in *Mind, Brain and the Quantum*), have claimed that a decisive role in directionality, and hence in the nature of time, is played by human consciousness.

[C.J.S.C.]

See also **Mathematics; Quantum Cosmology.**

FURTHER READINGS

Penrose, R. *The Emperor's New Mind.* Oxford: Oxford UP, 1989.

Lockwood, M. *Mind, Brain and the Quantum.* Oxford: Blackwell, 1989.

D'Espagnat, B. *Conceptual Foundations of Quantum Theory.* Menlo Park: Benjamin, 1971.

RACING SPORTS AND THE STOPWATCH

The timing of races, and of sports achievement in general, is a modern phenomenon, one with a history less than three hundred years old. It could be argued, of course, that the technology required to time a race is itself less than three centuries of age, but such an argument ignores the motivation behind the modern interest in the timing and recording of competitive sports. Despite the Greeks' fascination with all things athletic, they and their successors showed little interest in recording the temporal achievements of their athletes. Winning was everything; how fast the winner ran was of little concern. For the ancients, and indeed for Western society until well into the Renaissance, man was the measure of all things, not the thing to be measured.

To a great extent, the rise of organized sports in the eighteenth and nineteenth centuries was characterized by the increasing importance assigned to the measurement and recording of time. A number of factors contributed to this development, not the least of which was a growing awareness of time itself, and of its ever-shrinking divisions. On the pedagogical front, German educators like J.C.F. Guts Muths were stressing the benefits of temporal records in physical education, arguing that "young people take pleasure in all endeavours if they know what they have achieved and the extent to which they have achieved more this time as compared to the last . . . there is no better incentive than the recognition of progress" (*Gymnastik für die Jugend*, 1793). Socially, an increase in leisure time led to the popularization of sport, and hence to the need for a means with which to compare athletic achievement (see **Team Sports**). And perhaps most importantly, the idea of the sports "record"—a word first used in its modern sense in the early 1880s—has a strong correlative in the doctrine of progressivism: records had to be established, because records had to be beaten, ad infinitum.

Sports timing began with the idea of racing against a set time, rather than timing a set distance. As early as 1589, an English nobleman, Sir Robert Carey, won a sizable bet by covering a set distance on foot in twelve days. In 1606, also responding to a wager, John Lepton of Kepwick rode his horse between London and York five times in one week. Gradually, the time period decreased: in 1835 New York, a $1,000 purse was offered to any man who could run a ten-mile course in less than an hour (only one of the nine

starters finished the race in time). In our own century, perhaps the most famous race against time has been the four-minute mile, finally achieved by England's Roger Bannister in 1954.

On the whole, the phenomenon of racing against a set time has given way to the practice of timing competitors over a set distance, a change that necessitated the introduction and development of the stopwatch. The origins of the stopwatch (or, as it is sometimes called, the chronograph) are somewhat obscure. Although anteceded by the "pulse watch" (ca. 1690) of Samuel Watson, most historians, such as Allen Guttmann in his *From Ritual to Record*, agree that the stopwatch originated as a device for timing races. The first stopwatch seems to have appeared ca. 1730; in 1731, there occurs the first reference (in the *Grub Street Journal*) to a stopwatch in connection with a race.

Part of the confusion surrounding the stopwatch's origins stems from a problem of definition: the earliest stopwatches were simply ordinary pocket watches that could be stopped at will. Later, designers fitted stopwatches with an independent, center, second hand that could be stopped without affecting the main train of wheels and the balance. This key difference may well explain later references to "first" stopwatches such as those of England's F.L. Fatton (1822) and Switzerland's Adolphe Nicole (1862).

Whatever its origins, the stopwatch played a fundamental role in the sporting world's ever-increasing desire for temporal exactitude. Prior to 1730, horse and foot races had been occasionally measured by means of pocket watches or clocks to within a minute, and even half a minute (ca. 1660); after 1730, and the introduction of the stopwatch, timing was done first to the second and then, in 1757, to the half-second. Up until the end of the eighteenth century, however, English race officials had this much in common with the Greeks: times, winning or otherwise, were rarely recorded. Not until the early nineteenth century did times for the turf appear regularly in racing almanacs.

As accurate as stopwatches were becoming, they remained subject to human error at the start and finish of a race. Experienced human timekeepers have a reaction time of between a tenth and a third of a second, a significant margin considering that by the 1880s English athletic clubs were using stopwatches that indicated quarters of a second. As a further complication, it became obvious that an official watching a runner approach the tape will anticipate the finish by fractions of a second. Together, inadequate reaction time and the problem of anticipation inspired the application of electronics and photography to sports timing.

Although electronic timing dates from at least the turn of the century, the idea of photographing the finish of a race and simultaneously recording the elapsed time did not surface until about 1926. Conceived by Gustavus T. Kirby, president emeritus of the United States Olympic Committee, and developed by C.H. Fetter, an engineer with Western Electric, the "Kirby Two-Eyed Camera" photographed the finish through one lens and a disk clock through another (hence the name). Registering time to a hundredth of a second, the Kirby camera was used at the 1932 Los Angles Olympics for official timing of the decathlon.

The Kirby camera antedated the "photo-finish" camera of horse racing by several years. Originally developed in France for photographing the identification numbers on passing freight cars, photo-finish cameras (also known as slit cameras) advance the film past a slit at approximately the speed of the horse; in 1938, American Harry Bellock filed a patent application for a slit camera that employed a timing device. Subsequent developments in phototiming include the Bulova Phototimer, introduced for use in track and field during the 1948 indoor season. The first phototiming device capable of timing each competitor and recording the order of finish, the Phototimer imprints time in hundredths of a second along the margin of the film; it became an official timer for the United States Olympic trials soon after its introduction.

Photography is by no means the only method of eliminating human error from sports timing. Other techniques, past and present, include the recording of the start by means of the breaking of a light beam or thread, the tripping of a gate, the contact of a starting pistol's firing pin, or the acoustic registering of the pistol's report. In some slalom events, ski-activated levers start the clock; in swimming, competitors touch pressure-sensitive pads at the ends of the pool. International athletic meets now rely on the starter's gun to initiate the timing, photography to record the finish, and, in some cases, pressure-sensitive starting blocks to detect false starts.

In the latter half of the twentieth century, exact timing has become essential to sport in general, and racing sports in particular. Major competitions and world records—whether set by man, motor, or beast—require fully automatic timing for authentication, usually accompanied by photographic documentation. Timing is done to the hundredth, the thousandth, even the ten-thousandth of a second. Sports timing has altered our very perception of the second: once an unimaginably small unit of time, it now represents the difference between victory and defeat. As Peter J. Brancazio has pointed out, a top sprinter like Carl Lewis, running at full stride, can cover thirty-six feet in just one second; in that same second, speed skaters can cover fifty feet, downhill skiers more than 100, and speed skiers more than 200. In downhill skiing, a competitor who lags the field by a full second is not even in the race: in one 1990 World Cup event, the margin between first and *tenth* place was a mere 1.04 seconds. Never has so little meant so much to so many.

The Kirby Two-Eyed Camera of the 1932 Olympics timed athletes to within a hundredth of a second, and cost some $50,000; at the 1988 Winter Olympics in Calgary, officials relied on Swiss timing technology valued at $4^{1}/_{2}$ million dollars and accurate to $^{1}/_{10,000}$ of a second. We have become fascinated with timing, recording, and comparing the achievements of our athletes, a fascination that the Greeks could never have understood. It is not that the Greeks shared our interests, but lacked our technology: they surely knew how to measure linear distance, yet we possess not a single record of the length of a javelin throw. Moreover, Greek society did time other, non-sporting events: the water clock (clepsydra) governed speeches in Athenian lawcourts, and Aristotle makes reference in the *Poetics* to tragedy competitions controlled by the same device. No, the engendering agent behind the modern thirst for sports timing was not technology, but rather a behavioral transition, some cultural divide that separates the ancients from the moderns. As Henning Eichberg puts it, "The stopwatch was . . . less a technological impetus in and of itself, but much more an objectified result of a behavioral process." The stopwatch, in other words, did not create a need to time sports; the need to time sports created the stopwatch.

Although supported by technological ability, the modern concern with sports timing—with the sports record—clearly stems from a cultural change rather than a technological advance. What this implies, of course, is that our fascination with the timing and recording of sports achievement may one day reach its apex. Technology, at least in the domain of sports timing, cannot perpetually better itself; the idea of timing human activity to three decimal places seems suspect now, and the idea of improving on this seems pointless. One day, perhaps, the cultural pendulum will swing the other way, and some future society will wonder at our mania for measurement, our tenth-of-a-second heroes.

[N.J.M.]

See also **Team Sports.**

FURTHER READINGS

Brancazio, Peter J. "Just a Second." *Discover* 12 (March 1991): 36–40.

Eichberg, Henning. "Stopwatch, Horizontal Bar, Gymnasium: The Technologizing of Sports in the Eighteenth and Early Nineteenth Centuries." *Journal of the Philosophy of Sport* 9 (1982): 43–59.

Guttmann, Allen. *From Ritual to Record: The Nature of Modern Sports.* New York: Columbia UP, 1978.

Harris, H.A. *Sport in Greece and Rome.* London: Thames & Hudson, 1972.

Schwartz, Hillel. "Games, Timepieces, and Businesspeople." *Diogenes* 99 (Fall 1977): 60–79.

Ward, F.A.B. "Chronographs." *Time Measurement.* Science Museum Reprint Series. 1936; reprint, London: Science Museum, 1970. 47–51.

RELATIVITY THEORY

The theory of relativity as developed by Albert Einstein (1879–1955) is a conceptual and mathematical framework for theories of the material world that introduces new concepts of space and time. The theory's original form, now called the special theory of relativity, was published in 1905; it originated in a study of electromagnetism, but during the next few years it was extended to cover most of the physics then known. Its treatment of gravitation was, however, unsatisfactory, and in 1915, Einstein extended it into what is called the general theory of relativity, which explained the known phenomena of gravity and predicted several new ones. This article concerns the special theory; its historical background and general conclusions are briefly summarized in the article **Physics**. For the mathematical framework see **Space-Time**; for the general theory see **Gravity, Time, and Space**.

ABSOLUTE SPACE

Most people realize that uniform motion does not produce any detectable effects. For example, such experiences as eating, drinking, and pouring liquids in an airliner in straight and level flight are no different from what they are on the ground. In fact, as long as the flight is straight and level and one does not look out of the window or use instruments that interact with the ground, there is no measurement that would tell that the aircraft is in motion or how fast it is going. This statement is a simple (and as we shall see incomplete) statement of what is called the principle of relativity: we detect only the relative motions of things inside the aircraft and not their motion with respect to anything external. One cannot draw from this any simple conclusion to the effect that "all motion is relative," for if the straight and level flight is interrupted by a moment of turbulence we know it at once. "All motion" is not relative; something about the aircraft and the things in it, including any observers, "knows" when the uniform motion is interrupted.

Isaac Newton (1642–1727), writing down the principles of his theory of mechanics in 1687, was aware of these facts without the benefit of airliners and postulated an absolute space that exists without any reference to things contained in it (see **Physics**). Things move uniformly in this space if no external force acts on them, while nonuniform motion occurs if forces are exerted. Newton explained the nature of absolute space largely in theological terms, but as time went on it came to be understood physically as well.

By the mid-1800s physicists understood that light is a wave. A wave implies a medium that is in some kind of oscillatory motion, and since light moves in interstellar space where there is no ordinary matter it was reasoned that there must be a special medium, pervading all of space, for the waves to travel in. This medium, called the ether, was generally thought to be at rest in Newton's absolute space and in fact to define it. After the 1860s the theoretical investigations of James Clerk Maxwell (1831–1879) and some brilliant experiments by Heinrich Hertz (1857–1894) showed that light is a motion of electric and magnetic fields, and a dogma developed that these motions must be explainable by a dynamical theory of the ether.

EINSTEIN'S PARADOX

Connect the ends of a piece of wire to a sensitive instrument that measures electric currents and wind the middle of it into a few turns of a coil. Push a small bar magnet through the coil. The instrument will show a momentary current. Now hold the magnet still and move the coil. Exactly the same thing happens. Only the relative motion matters, just as implied by the principle of relativity. Maxwell's electromagnetic theory, firmly anchored in the ether, explains both experiments but explains them in entirely different ways. In his paper of 1905 that announced the theory of relativity, Einstein pointed out that it obviously makes no difference which is at rest and which is moving (indeed, with the earth whirling about the sun one cannot reasonably claim that anything on it is at rest), and showed how the laws of electricity and magnetism could be rewritten so as to make this plain. But he did not merely rewrite Maxwell's theory, for he predicted several effects, strange and entirely unexpected at that time though commonplace now, that would be observed if one studied the behavior of things moving at speeds approaching that of light. Two of these effects are mentioned below.

ASSUMPTIONS AND RESULTS

Einstein's first paper was called "On the Electrodynamics of Moving Bodies" (the name relativity was introduced later), and its argument is based on two new postulates. The first (the principle of relativity) is that uniform motion through space is absolutely undetectable. It follows that the existence of an ether stationary in absolute space could have no observable consequences. The second postulate is that the velocity of a flash of light moving through a vacuum is independent of how the source of the light is moving relative to the observer. It follows from this and the relativity postulate that it is also independent of how the observer is moving relative to the source. If one tries to visualize how this can happen one arrives at confusion, for the comparatively slow motions we are fa-

miliar with do not and cannot behave this way. Nevertheless, by careful mathematical deductions Einstein resolved the paradox with which he started and drew novel conclusions. Of these the best known is the equivalence of mass and energy expressed in the famous rubric $E = mc^2$. As regards time, the most important conclusion is that by any proper experimental test, a clock observed when it is moving with respect to us will be slow as compared with the rate of an identical clock which we hold in our hand. To imagine how this happens it helps to introduce the concept of space-time, and the discussion is continued in the article **Space-Time**.

[D.A.P.]

See also **Gravity, Time, and Space; Physics; Space-Time.**

FURTHER READINGS

Einstein, Albert. *Relativity*. New York: Crown Publishers, 1961.

Rindler, Wolfgang. *Essential Relativity*. 2nd ed. New York: Springer, 1977.

Taylor, John G. *Special Relativity*. Oxford: Clarendon P, 1975.

RELIGION AND AGING

This article considers both how the aging process is regarded within some of the great world religions as well as empirical evidence on the relationship between religious expression and age. These are interrelated topics. One would expect to find increasing attendance to religious duties with age, especially within religious cultures such as Hinduism which emphasize the spiritual tasks of their elders. Unfortunately, few studies have been carried out on the subject of religiosity and age outside of Western culture.

RELIGIOUS CONCEPTIONS OF THE AGING PROCESS

Up to the present century elderly people in most times and places of the world were a small part of the population. Attention to the needs of the elderly and their position in society, however, belied their numerical unimportance. The historical roots of attitudes to old age within Western society have been the subject of much study, but the conclusions, as G. Minois indicates, are complex. The Hebrew Scriptures provide some of the most influential images of age. The range of themes in these writings is very broad: historical accounts which are realistic in their depiction of power and frailty and which above all demonstrate the importance of family life for all age groups; calls within the prophetic and psalmist writings for greater sensitivity to the needs of elderly people; and, as R.Z. Dulin notes, explicit focus on the personal dimensions of aging, especially physical deterioration, within the wisdom writers.

Although the New Testament repeats Jewish prescriptions not to neglect the elderly, Christian views of the "life course" differ from that of the Jews. As a result of the much stronger emphasis of Christianity on an ongoing life with God beyond death, old age appears to have of itself no special importance. Terms such as "life course" emerged toward the end of the Middle Ages as people began to contemplate life as a journey. Disregard of aging may also have been encouraged by the medieval characterization of Jesus's age of death as "the perfect age." Moreover, middle age was clearly depicted as the high point of life in the flourishing iconographic representations of figures ascending and descending a rising and falling staircase.

It is only recently that this image has been challenged in the West, most notably in the writings of the life-span psychologist Erik Erikson, who proposes in its place a linear, progressive model of development throughout life. A number of theologians have responded to his ideas. The "rise and fall" model has been criticized for encouraging fear of the losses of aging without recognition of its strengths and compensations, and for leading the Christian church to emphasize a "sustaining" model of pastoral work with older people rather than one which challenges them to give witness and prophecy. There is also acknowledgement of the involvement of "elders" within the early church.

However, there is no parallel in Christianity to the great respect and dignity shown to older people within Eastern traditions and religions. It is perhaps significant that the original Buddhist insights on the meaning of life were based on explicit confrontation with the painful realities of the deterioration that comes with age. Hindu thinking about age was similarly transformed. But whereas in Buddhism, old age, disease, and death came to be seen as the major enemies to be defeated by means of ascetic renunciation of the world throughout life, Hinduism located the meaning of aging within the context of a broader familial and social model of the stages of life. As S. Tilak has shown, this seems to have reflected the native "gerontophilia" of the Vedic Indians. Within Hinduism aging is recognized as a final stage of life for which a special task is appropriate. The suffering and losses are a key to the liberation experience. They waken people to reality. The resultant virtues of confrontation with finitude, the wise use of declining powers and abilities, and the creative response to limits are increasingly appreciated by Western thinkers.

CHANGES IN RELIGIOSITY WITH AGE

The evidence from the first gerontological studies in the 1950s and 1960s suggested that whereas religious activity outside the home declines in old age, religious feeling increases. However, more recent studies show high rates of religious attendance among older people at places of worship, and may reflect the fact that older people are healthier now than they were two or three decades ago. Cross-national surveys indicate that increasing church attendance is not a phenomenon of the later stages of aging but a process that continues throughout adulthood, with the most dramatic increases occurring between twenty-five and forty years of age. Detailed studies of the elderly population do confirm that the highest percentage of people reporting that religion is very important in their lives are eighty years of age and over. However, more longitudinal studies are necessary before confident assertions can be made about whether these are genuine life-cycle changes rather than cohort and period effects.

The main focus of gerontological study in this area within recent years has been on the relationship between religiosity and positive adjustment to aging and old age. As H.G. Koenig indicates, the recent evidence consistently shows that the associations of religious activities and attitudes with personal adjustment, happiness, and feelings of usefulness are generally higher among older people and tend to increase in the oldest age groups. In interpreting these findings, it is necessary to bear in mind the possibly confounding effects of health on both well-being and religious participation, and the fact that most studies have been carried out within samples of church members or within communities with a strong religious culture.

It is important to study religious practice in non-Western cultures. Worthy of mention in this context are the studies of psychological development with age carried out by David Gutmann in traditional societies around the world. He argues that greater passivity, openness to feeling, and capacity for nurturance, observed in older men in particular in these societies, allows male elders to exercise "sacred" rather than "pragmatic" power. Often this takes the form of increased involvement in religious practice and ritual. In so doing they come to represent the values that underpin their society and give moral encouragement to younger men. Gutmann's studies illustrate the importance not only of a cross-cultural approach to the study of aging but also of understanding changing religious practice with age within its developmental and social context.

[P.G.C.]

See also **Aging and Time; Aging Populations.**

Further Readings

Dulin, R.Z. *A Crown of Glory: A Biblical View of Aging.* New York: Paulist P, 1988.

Gutmann, D.L. *Reclaimed Powers: Towards a New Psychology of Men and Women in Later Life.* New York: Basic Books, 1987.

Koenig, H.G. *Successful Aging, Religion and Mental Health.* New York: Haworth P, 1992.

Minois, G. *History of Old Age: From Antiquity to the Renaissance.* Cambridge: Polity P, 1989.

Tilak, S. *Religion and Aging in the Indian Tradition.* Albany: State U of New York P, 1989.

RENAISSANCE

If the Renaissance may be credited with having invented the spatial dimensions of art, it may also be credited with having discovered time. The essential lineaments of the temporal dynamic of the Western industrialized world were revealed early in the literature and society of the Renaissance. Kipling's exhortation to "fill the unforgiving minute / With sixty seconds' worth of distance run," while making little sense to most of the world even of his day, would have been comprehensible in its essential charge to a Petrarch of the fourteenth century, or to a Rabelais of the sixteenth. New exhortations to make energetic response to the destructive powers of time began to appear in that period—the end of the thirteenth and the beginning of the fourteenth centuries—that saw the emergence of a vigorous urban life in conjunction with the growth of commerce and capitalism, the development of the mechanical clock, the growth of attitudes associated with the interests of a confident laity (such attitudes as the cultivation of family feeling, a renewed appreciation of the benefits of marriage and of children, new ways of memorializing death, and the aroused prospects of perpetuating the self after death through fame or through progeny), and finally the appearance of the first modern classics in that poetic renascence associated with Dante, Petrarch, and Boccaccio.

The new picture that begins to come clear in this period is one of a dramatic struggle between humankind and time. Erwin Panofsky has argued in his classic essay, "Father Time," that iconographically, time was invested with new and destructive implements by virtue of a mistaken association between Chronos and Kronos (Saturn). This was so, but it must also be added that writers just mentioned did not need such misperception to understand and to convey their senses of the harmful prospects of time. Very early in his great *Commedia*, Dante drew the essential lines of this great drama. In the *Paradiso*, time acquires a pair of shears, with which it shreds the glory of an aristocratic house. Only the continuous heroic activity of the house's heirs can repair this damage. "Oh our poor nobility of blood," Dante cries out,

Ben se' tu manto che tosto raccorce;
sì che, se non s'appon di dì in die,
lo tempo va dintorno con le force.

("Truly thou art a mantle that quickly shrinks, so that if we do not add to it day by day, time goes round it with the shears.")

Allied with this need to maintain the glory of a noble house is the more heroic call to fame, a call that will be heard again and again throughout the Renaissance. Showing the Roman inspiration of this new Renaissance devotion to fame, it is Virgil who spurs Dante on, urging him to recognize that ". . . by sitting of down or under blankets none comes to fame, and without it he that consumes his life leaves such trace of himself on earth as smoke in air or foam in water" (*Inferno*, 24, 46–51).

The study of time in the Renaissance shows that there was something like a Protestant work ethic long before Protestantism, and that if we wish to understand the nature of time in the Renaissance we must not lose sight of its dual nature. On the one hand, time is a cosmic force that challenges humankind to a great struggle in the balance of which lies our very hold on existence. The conflict is dramatic and the calling heroic—hence the great appeal of this new dynamic to the major writers of the Renaissance. On the other hand, while the struggle is heroic, the means employed are simple, even mundane, calling for day-to-day diligence. Attitudes of indifference, or any presumed sense of invulnerability—attitudes that could indeed be called cavalier—are most to be feared.

The figure who most fully represented these two forms of temporal response—the heroic and the practical—was Francis Petrarch (1304–1374). He could confidently declare, "ingentibus animis breve nihil optabile est"—to the great of soul nothing brief is worthy. At the same time, energy needs to be channeled and the great variety of things to be accomplished needs to be brought into some working order. Consequently, practical, down-to-earth scheduling of activities is required. "Everything consists in the ordered disposition of time," he also wrote. He was famous for his inventories, for his schedules, and for the calculated device of "doubling up"; that is, he would read while riding horseback or when eating, and he would insist on being read to when being shaved. He could not tolerate an idle moment, not simply because idleness is the devil's workshop, but because there was so much to do and so little time, and without such directed labor, the fame toward which he aspired would not be obtained. In Petrarch's response to time, two dimensions are plainly visible: one heroic and inspired, and the other practical and mundane—the abiding Don Quixote and Sancho Panza of the Renaissance soul.

Throughout Italy in the late fourteenth and fifteenth centuries, and then extending throughout northern Europe, the spirit of Petrarch was a living force, and particularly was this the case in regard to education. One of his humanistic followers urges a more intensive and scheduled use of time: "To give a fixed time each day to reading . . . is a well-tried practice which may be strongly recommended. Alexander read much even on campaign; Caesar wrote his *Commentaries*, and Augustus recited poetry while commanding armies in the field." This same writer continues, "Many leisure hours now wasted may be saved by devoting them to the recreation of lighter reading. Some wisely arrange a course of readings during dinner. . . ." Then he makes a suggestion that is memorable for bringing together the technological advances of the fourteenth century and the aroused concerns of humanism: "Of no little use would also be the placement in our libraries of clocks, well in view, which could inform us of the measured lapse of time."

The tremendous energies unleashed by this heroic calling and practical scheduling reached their culmination in the Frenchman, François Rabelais, one of the greatest writers of the sixteenth century. His young prince is a sleeping giant whose own resources are left untapped by the infelicitous teaching methods of an earlier epoch. However, his spirit catches fire as soon as it is placed in contact with the new humanistic educators. So rigorous was the scheduling of his time, so rewarding the subject matter studied, "that he lost not one hour of the day." The declaration and its motivation are simply revolutionary.

So important was this new conception of time that it became crucial in Shakespeare's presentations of those characters who succeed and those who fail in the dramas of English kings. Time is the agent of an external reality that crashes through any improvident view of the world. Richard II epitomizes the cavalier attitudes of the temporally negligent. Confronted with his defeat, Richard is brought to his final realization, "I wasted time, and now doth time waste me." The bitter reckoning that Richard suffered is spared Prince Hal. It is by Hal's own regained sense of time that Shakespeare shows him to be better representative of England and of its future than the careless and negligent Hotspur or Falstaff.

> By heaven, Poins, I feel me much to
> blame
> So idly to profane the precious time,
> When tempest of commotion like the
> south
> Borne with black vapor, doth begin to
> melt
> And drop upon our bare unarmed heads.

In this great contest, time is precious, its abuse a profanation; indeed, this "contest" is regarded as a deadly serious war, one requiring determined militancy.

This is the new attitude involved with the Renaissance discovery of time that began with Dante and that reached its culminating expression in Shakespeare's history plays. The great English dramatist has presented in Hal the prototype of the new man, the representative of the nascent energies and attitudes that would guide England into the future. In Hal, Shakespeare has given us a figure of the proto-industrial mind, whose major imperative is his need to control time.

Nevertheless, when we look back at the Renaissance from this modern perspective we can see that we run the risk of isolating certain tendencies from the fuller context. From the very beginning, alongside the dominant tendency of the need to manage time, we can find countervailing expressions of the need for temporal relaxation. Even in the *Purgatorio*, that canticle of the *Commedia* where temporal pressure is most felt, Dante encounters restrictions: he is reminded by an old friend that he could not progress an inch if he were not in the condition of spiritual readiness. In Rabelais' work, both Gargantua and Pantagruel are fired by the new possibilities of Renaissance learning, by the rich variety of new subjects as well as by the new discipline of learning, by educational scheduling. But in his utopian community, the Abbey of Theleme, there is to be no clock, and his ecclesiastical spokesman declares, "I never tie myself to hours . . . , for they are made for man, and not man for them."

In other ways, counter-tendencies are present in Renaissance thought and literature. One of the great poetic expressions of the new aggressiveness toward time is present in the theme of *carpe diem* (seize the day). In Italian, French, and English poetry of the sixteenth and seventeenth centuries this theme inspired some of the greatest utterances by major poets. One need think only of Andrew Marvell's "To His Coy Mistress." Yet this same poet wrote an even greater poem, "The Garden," where he finds in a garden retreat a repudiation of all the busyness of men. Despite the urgent exhortations to beat time, humankind's nature inclines toward reflectiveness, and the wisest of the Renaissance writers still conceived of dimensions of experience beyond time and history.

These same pressures were encountered by John Milton early in his career, as early as the ode, "On Time," and Sonnet VII ("How soon hath time"). In fact, one of the major concerns of Milton's most serious poetry is quite simply resistance to the temptations posed by the very pressures and exhortations of temporal use and management that emerged in the earlier Renaissance. The sonnet ends with an expression of divine trust and patience that will guide all of his later poetry: "All is, if I have grace to use it so, / As ever in my great Taskmaster's eye." The even more famous sonnet on his blindness will remind an energetic society on the move, a society harnessed to the engines of social change and scientific progress, that "they also serve who only stand and wait." From Milton to Wordsworth to the great modernists of the twentieth century, one major role of the poet-novelist-artist has been to serve as critic of a scientific industrialized culture, whose essential dynamic was provided by the exploitative sense of time developed in the culture of the Renaissance.

[R.J.Q.]

See also **Dante Alighieri; Milton, John; Petrarch, Francis; Shakespeare, William.**

FURTHER READINGS

Cipolla, Carlo M. *Clocks and Culture: 1300–1700.* New York: Walker, 1967.

Landes, David S. *Revolution in Time: Clocks and the Making of the Modern World.* Cambridge: Harvard UP, 1983.

Quinones, Ricardo J. *The Renaissance Discovery of Time.* Cambridge: Harvard UP, 1972. 290–443.

RESTIF (OR RÉTIF) DE LA BRETONNE, NICOLAS-EDME (1734–1806)

Autodidact, printer, and prolific writer of more than 200 volumes, Restif is best known as the author of *Le Paysan perverti* (1775), *La Paysanne pervertie* (1776), *La Vie de mon père* (1779), *La découverte australe par un homme volant, ou le Dédale français* (1781), *Les Nuits de Paris* (1788–94), and *Monsieur Nicolas* (1796–97). Despite a well-earned reputation for artistic failure and interests verging on pornographic, Restif deserves acclaim as a shrewd psychologist, an astute observer of society, and a utopian thinker whose most innovative novels point toward significant developments in prose fiction. He exploits a far-future setting with stunning originality, though without complete success, in *Les Posthumes* (1802). Here Restif portrays several million years of future history within the complicated frame-narrative of a story supposedly written by the Illuminist author of *Le Diable amoureux* (1776), Jacques Cazotte, who was guillotined in 1792. Biological evolution and vast geological changes, including the appearance of a second moon, are sketched as a backdrop for the life of Duke Multipliandre, a man born in the eighteenth century with the ability to project his mind into the bodies of other people and thus survive through succeeding eras to experience drastic social transformations along with changes in the human form. At the end of this fantasy of immortality and evolution, the story loops back to describe Multipliandre's horrifying encounters with violence during the French Revolution, a theme recalling the actual fate of *Les Posthumes*' putative author, Cazotte, and many others. The significance of *Les Posthumes* as a major step toward effective forms of futuristic fiction lies in Restif's creation of a narrative structure inviting readers to view a specific historical event of their own recent past from the estranging perspective of an imaginary future.

[P.K.A.]

See also **Futuristic Fiction.**

FURTHER READINGS

Alkon, Paul K. *Origins of Futuristic Fiction*. Athens: U of Georgia P, 1987.

Porter, Charles A. *Restif's Novels, or An Autobiography in Search of an Author*. New Haven: Yale UP, 1967.

REVOLUTION AND HISTORY

Denoting a cycle of events in time or a recurring period of time, "revolution" (< Latin "revolut[us]," to revolve) has come to signify the often violent overthrow of a government by those governed. Since the sixteenth century, theologians and philosophers have synthesized the temporal and political meanings of "revolution," endowing such political upheavals with universal significance; thus, they have expounded "teleological" (< Greek "telos," end; + "logia," science) interpretations of political revolutions, considering them to be final causes in an immanent or transcendental historical design. Focusing on the American, the French, and the Russian revolutions, this article will survey such teleological interpretations and suggest that they sometimes contradict historical reality.

From the sixteenth to the nineteenth century, there recurred throughout Western Europe the idea that a worldwide revolution was imminent. This idea was derived from apocalyptic texts in the Bible, namely the Books of Daniel and of Revelation, and involved a total revolution—a time of storm and trial, inescapably violent but absolutely necessary to the moral and institutional life of Western civilization. Not only would this paroxysm purge the world of evil, but it would also eliminate all suffering and inaugurate an era of peace, justice, and joy. In its earliest stages, and in accordance with biblical texts, this scenario was envisaged as a great battle between an inspired minority who represented the force of God and an entrenched majority responsible for institutional evil. Whether theological or secular in orientation, this global revolution would be guided by extra-historical agencies, either immanent or transcendental. And the redemption of human history is thought to be a golden age.

The idea of the radical transformation of history found especially fertile ground in Protestant countries, particularly during times of economic deprivation among a large, impoverished working class. In the fifteenth and sixteenth centuries, for example, messianic activities in northern Europe proliferated: the Taborites, Thomas Müntzer, and John of Leyden believed themselves to be God's emissaries, leading the struggle against worldly evil. In the seventeenth century, during the English civil wars, fervid messianism arose among the radical sects of the parliamentary armies, notably among the "fifth monarchy men," who derived their title from the apocalyptic chapters of the Book of Daniel. This eschatological fervor affected clergymen, politicians, and writers alike. Along with Gerrard Winstanley, who called on England to rejoice over the imminent establishment of God's reign, Oliver Cromwell and John Milton expressed eschatological interpretations of human history during the Puritan revolution. In each instance, biblical authority was used to justify political activity.

In the late eighteenth century, important thinkers viewed the American and French revolutions as apocalyptic events, inaugurating the democratic transformation of Western history. Loyalist historiography of the time, however, was strongly partisan and had propagandistic, rather than universal, motives. Many of these writers, who had emigrated to Scotland and England during the war, condemned the revolution as breaking with the tradition of English constitutionalism since 1688. Thomas Hutchinson (1711–1780), for one, argued that errors of governance had caused the revolution, but that this neither justified independence nor signified the onset of worldwide democratization. Patriotic historiographers, on the other hand, such as David Ramsay (1749–1815) and Mary Otis Warren (1728–1814), inverted the loyalist viewpoint. Whereas the loyalists degraded the revolutionaries to demagogues and rabble-rousers, the patriotic writers, many of whom were Nonconformists, elevated them to visionaries and freedom fighters and interpreted events favorable to the American cause as evidence of providential intrusion into history. Some American writers explicitly endowed the revolution with providential and global importance. Didactic histories also flourished at this time. Writers like Noah Webster (1758–1843) and Jedidiah Morse (1761–1826) portrayed the Revolutionary War as the central event shaping the American nation (a reasonable conclusion, given the fact that the country was less than five years old). When historiographers began to treat Westward expansion, they again set these events in a providential context.

To many eighteenth-century Protestant writers, philosophical affinities between the American and French revolutions suggested that extra-historical forces were indeed at work to release mankind from the bondage of oppressive government. A secular correlative to the Protestant apocalypse developed during the Enlightenment and was derived from the philosophes' notion that a great revolution in the human mind was underway, one that would eventually free the world from superstition, rivalry, and competition. Instead of the Second Coming of Christ, the philosophes envisioned the kingdom of reason organizing the world according to true, rational principles. For these thinkers, history was also in its final stage, and mankind was at the threshold of a new and progressive world.

Both religious and secular thinkers viewed the French Revolution as evidence of a worldwide democratic process, beginning in America and sweeping westward over Europe. English Nonconformist writers, such as Blake, Wordsworth, and Coleridge, reviving the millenarian tradition of Milton, interpreted the French Revolution as the biblical apocalypse portending an era of universal felicity. However, when the revolution took a violent turn in the hands of the Committee for Public Safety, which engineered the Reign of Terror, 1793–1794, many of these writers recanted their belief that France was the divine vanguard of the millennium.

The apocalyptic mythologies, attributed to the American and French revolutions, were derived from the Bible and from an extensive tradition of millenarian theological history. In each instance, historical events were proclaimed to be reflections of God's Will in history. National independence and the idea of inexorable westward expansion inspired American historiographers to reify their narratives; however, the collocation of theology and political history could not be maintained in the light of French policy from 1793 on.

The tenuousness arising from the interpenetration of idealized historiography and political revolution is nowhere more evident than in the Marxist interpretation of the Russian Revolution. Like Hegel, Marx saw world history as an interconnected process and believed that revolution was the force impelling this process from one stage to another. In the sense that he viewed his own times as the latest stage in this process, Marx was a teleological historian and a secular apocalypticist; for Marx, the final revolution, from bourgeois to communist society, was at hand. This was to be a golden age—not a city of god or of reason, but one in which an economic utopia would be established, eliminating material differences between people. This last stage in

the revolutionary process would extend over the entire world. Thus Marx invested the idea of revolution with chiliastic properties.

The "great October revolution" in Russia (1917), to Marxist thinkers, incarnated this process and represented the beginning of the end: from that beginning, sociopolitical revolution would spread throughout the entire world, with the Soviet Union as the messianic promoter and guardian of these socialist revolutions; and a communistic society was conceived to be the inevitable culmination of that struggle. Mikhail Gorbachev's official repudiation of this global mission, and the 1992 democratic revolution in the Soviet Union, evidence the disparity between theory and actuality.

The historical revolutions of modern history—in America, in France, and in Russia—have been interpreted teleologically, that is, as final causes in temporal processes, reputedly governed either by transcendental or by immanent forces. These interpretations naturally reflect the human tendency to order historical time and, in so doing, tend to subsume fact under ideology or dogma.

[C.D.]

See also **Apocalypse; Eschatology; Historiography and Process; Millenarianism.**

FURTHER READINGS

Abrams, M.H. *Natural Supernaturalism: Tradition and Revolution in Romantic Literature.* New York: Norton, 1971.

Breisach, Ernst. *Historiography: Ancient, Medieval, and Modern.* Chicago: U of Chicago P, 1983.

Brinton, Crane. *The Anatomy of Revolution.* New York: Vintage, 1965.

Bury, J.B. *The Idea of Progress: An Inquiry into its Origin and Growth.* Intro. Charles A. Beard. New York: Dover, 1987.

Cohen, Lester H. *The Revolutionary Histories: Contemporary Narratives of the American Revolution.* Ithaca: Cornell U P, 1989.

Cohn, Norman. *The Pursuit of the Millennium: Revolutionary Millenarians and Mystical Anarchists of the Middle Ages.* New York: Oxford UP, 1977.

Gilbert, Felix. "Revolution." *Dictionary of the History of Ideas: Studies of Selected Pivotal Ideas.* Ed. Philip P. Wiener. 5 vols. New York: Scribner's, 1973. 4:152a–167b.

Palmer, R.R. *The Challenge.* Vol. 1 of *The Age of Democratic Revolution: A Political History of Europe and America, 1760–1800.* 2 vols. Princeton: Princeton UP, 1962.

Stone, Laurence. "Theories of Revolution." *World Politics* 18 (1966): 159–176.

RHYTHM AND METER IN MUSIC

People move to music. We dance, march, tap our feet, bob our heads, swing our arms—in time to the beat. In other words, we entrain our bodily rhythms to those of the music we hear. We may sing tunes, but we *feel* rhythms. Thus, as performing musicians have long acknowledged, rhythm is the life blood of music. Despite its pervasiveness, however, rhythm remains imperfectly understood.

Music theorists have studied pitch organization more than temporal structure, probably because traditional Western music notation specifies tones more precisely than rhythms: there is a discrete number of available pitches but an infinite variety of durations. However, two recent developments have led to intensified efforts to comprehend rhythm and meter: (1) the availability of hardware and software to study the precise rhythmic shapes of a performance, and (2) the methods of cognitive psychology, which make it clear that the rhythmic and metric structure of a piece as printed on the page is very different from the temporal structure of a performance, which in turn differs from rhythms and meters as felt and remembered by listeners.

Although the competing treatises on rhythm and meter that have proliferated in the latter half of the twentieth century disagree on many fundamental issues, they all subscribe to one central idea: there is more to musical rhythm than simply patterns of duration. Thus, for example, two melodies that have identical note values and are performed at the same tempo may be experienced as rhythmically distinct because of their different *groupings* of tones. According to Gestalt psychology, tones that are in some way close together form groups that we perceive as rhythmic units. Factors that influence grouping include temporal proximity, pitch proximity, loudness or timbral similarity, and registral closeness, among others.

Despite its fundamental position in the vocabulary of musicians, theorists use the term "rhythm" in considerably different ways. Some take the word as an umbrella label for all temporal aspects of music, while others take it to be synonymous with grouping. However the term is defined, it is important to bear in mind several abstractions that bear on musical rhythm: (1) the distinction between time spans and time points, (2) the different types of accent, and (3) the hierarchic nature of temporal organization.

1. An important breakthrough in the development of rhythm and meter theory was the recognition of the differences between the ways time points and time spans are organized. It took theorists a surprisingly long time to clarify this distinction, which in fact not everyone accepts even today. A time point is analogous to a point in Euclidean geometry, and a time span is analogous to a line segment. A geometric point has no length and is, strictly speaking, invisible, although it can be represented visually (as, for example, the intersection of two line segments). Similarly, a time point has no duration and thus is not heard but rather intuitively sensed (as, for example, the music's beat). Music provides many cues that enable us to intuit the location of significant time points. Because musical patterns create expectations of when beats will recur, we experience certain time points as significant even when they mark no event (there is, for example, a powerfully accented silence in the first movement of Beethoven's *Eroica* Symphony).

Just as a geometric line segment has finite length, so a musical time span has a specific audible duration. Notes, phrases, sections, and entire pieces occupy time spans. Time spans structure events that exist in time, while time points structure time itself.

Time points mark off not only the beginnings and endings of time spans and events, but also the abstract temporal patterning known as meter. Meter consists of a normatively (but not invariably) repeating pattern of time points that are felt as beats of varying strength. For example, in a typical 4/4 measure, we experience the first beat as strong, the third beat as moderately strong, and the second and fourth beats as relatively weak. This pattern is quite durable in our minds. Thus, composers can invent patterns of note emphasis (called "syncopations") that contradict the meter, thereby creating interest, ambiguity, or excitement. Syncopations rarely threaten the stability of meter; we mentally project meter as ongoing even when there are temporarily no musical events to support it (for example, no notes beginning on strong beats).

2. Another important breakthrough in the development of rhythm and meter theory was the realization that there are several distinct kinds of musical accent. The type that performers generally refer to by the term "ac-

cent" is, paradoxically, the least significant to musical structure (although it is extremely important to expression and interpretation). Theorists call this kind of accent "stress" or "phenomenal." A stress accent emphasizes a note or chord by such means as a loud attack, brief preceding silence, or large melodic leap. When audiences at pop concerts clap their hands on beats 2 and 4, they are producing stress accents on weak beats. Significantly, this clapping does not turn these time points into strong beats. If listeners tap their feet to this same music, they tend to tap on the strong beats—1 and 3—despite the stress accents of clapping on beats 2 and 4. Thus "metric accents," as strong beats are sometimes called, are distinct from stress accents: stress accents ordinarily do not convert weak beats into strong beats.

A third kind of accent is sometimes called "structural," sometimes "rhythmic." A structural accent is associated with the focal point of a group. All notes in the group prior to the structurally accented event are heard to lead to it, and all subsequent notes to lead away from it. In groups with only a few notes, the structural accent usually coincides with a metric accent; in other words, the most structurally accented event of a small group begins on a metrically accented beat. In larger groups, such as the ubiquitous four-measure phrase (of approximately the duration that can be sung in one breath), the structural accent tends to come at or near the end, coinciding with the cadence, or arrival point.

Some theorists also define such accents as those of contour (high and low points in melodic lines), duration, and loudness. For other theorists, these are instead elements that contribute to stress, metric, or structural accents, depending on context. It is sometimes suggested that the time points that mark the beginnings of time spans are associated with yet another species of accent, namely the beginning accent.

3. In many musical styles—particularly in tonal music—most temporal structures are organized hierarchically. Meter is hierarchic. While listeners tend to focus on one level of metric activity (called the "primary" level, usually corresponding to the notated measure), both faster and slower metric structures exist in most music. For example, between the first and second beats of a measure, there may be several notes (such as sixteenth notes by way of example) that articulate timepoints, all of which are weaker than either beat 1 or beat 2, but all of which are nonetheless experienced metrically. Also, measures are often paired so that, for example, the first beat of the first measure may feel stronger than the first beat of the second measure.

Similarly, the respective first beats of four successive measures often act like the beats of a large, slow 4/4 measure: in the context of the four-measure unit (called a "hypermeasure"), these beats are respectively strong, weak, moderately strong, weak—despite the fact that each beat remains the strongest in its respective measure. Thus we are faced with a paradox: the cadence of a four-measure phrase is often strong (structurally accented) in one domain (that of time spans) and *simultaneously* weak (metrically weakly accented) in another domain (that of time points). From this paradox comes much of the complexity and experiential richness of even the simplest music.

On how large a level does meter exist? For some theorists, the metric hierarchy extends only to the level where the first irregularity is introduced. For example, in a context where four-measure hypermeasures are normative, the appearance of a five-measure hypermeasure is thought to destroy the sense of (hyper)meter. Other theorists feel that the accentual structure of the anomalous five-measure hypermeasure is sufficiently similar to that of the usual four-measure hypermeasures for meter still to be experienced. Still other theorists believe that meter is indefinitely hierarchic, so that a piece is not only one huge group, but also one huge hypermeasure. It is questionable whether such a large hypermeasure can actually be experienced metrically—whether, in other words, a relationship can be felt between successive beats widely separated in time. A less extreme position suggests that listeners can experience meter up to the level where two successive beats are sufficiently close in time to be present simultaneously in short-term memory. On any higher level, meter may make conceptual sense but probably cannot be experienced. If beat 1 has entered long-term memory by the time beat 2 is sensed, then meter can be conceived but not perceived.

Since meter is hierarchic, metric accents are hierarchic. This is why hypermeasures behave like large measures. And since grouping is hierarchic, so are structural accents, because the main structural accent of a large group is more strongly accented than the main structural accent of any smaller group contained within the larger one. But stress accents are not organized hierarchically, even though they may be of varying degrees of strength.

This brief sketch of rhythm and meter theory suggests the complexity behind even straightforward music. Sensitive composers, performers, and listeners have an intuitive understanding of such factors in music as accents, rhythm, meter, grouping, and hierarchies. Recently music theorists and psychologists have begun to create intellectual models for these intuitions. Even in their current preliminary stage, these models offer fascinating insights into the musical experience.

[J.D.K.]

See also **Jazz; Music: Rock; Psychological Responses to Music; Music: Western.**

FURTHER READINGS

Berry, Wallace. *Structural Functions in Music.* Englewood Cliffs: Prentice-Hall, 1976.

Brower, Candace. *Motion in Music: A Wave Model of Rhythm.* Ph.D. dissertation, University of Cincinnati, 1993.

Cooper, Grosvenor, and Leonard B. Meyer. *The Rhythmic Structure of Music.* Chicago: U of Chicago P, 1960.

Epstein, David. *The Sounding Stream: Studies of Time in Music.* New York: Schirmer, 1993.

Kramer, Jonathan D. *The Time of Music.* New York: Schirmer, 1988.

Lerdahl, Fred, and Ray Jackendoff. *A Generative Theory of Tonal Music.* Cambridge: MIT P, 1983.

Lester, Joel. *The Rhythms of Tonal Music.* Carbondale: Southern Illinois UP, 1986.

Rothstein, William. *Phrase Rhythm in Tonal Music.* New York: Schirmer, 1989.

Schachter, Carl. "Rhythm and Linear Analysis." *The Music Forum* 4 (1976): 281–334; 5 (1980): 197–232; 6 (1987): 1–59.

Yeston, Maury. *The Stratification of Musical Rhythm.* New Haven: Yale UP, 1976.

ROUSSEAU, JEAN-JACQUES (1712–1778)

Swiss philosopher, political theorist, and man of letters, Jean-Jacques Rousseau is a generally overlooked pivotal thinker in the distinctively modern philosophical reflection on the importance of time and history for the understanding of the human condition. Rousseau gave new depth to the significance of time for the accounts of human sociality, rationality, knowledge, language, aesthetics, and the general teleological problem of culture. Through his revolutionary insights into time he became a major source of most of the movements of later Continental European philosophy: German idealism, Marxism, Nietzsche, phenomenology and existentialism, Heidegger, and poststructuralism. Rousseau's thinking advanced well beyond earlier assertions of the changeability and impermanence of both human nature and culture (as in the cosmogonies of Lucretius and Descartes) by disclosing how time and history—or to use contemporary language, "historicity"—constitute the essence of human consciousness. The central failings and achievements, miseries and ecstasies of human life are grounded in or are inherently related to the experience of time.

The account of the history of the human species from quasi-human beginnings is the subject of the *Discourse on the Origin of Inequality* (1755), the second of the two *Discourses*. In this account, the passage of time is not solely something that the human species has suffered, with the result of irreparable alteration of its psychic and physical form. The acquisition of awareness of the passage of time is itself the crucial element in the change, and something that humans have instituted to their own detriment. The human experience of time is both the index of civilized life's perplexity, and the necessary object of reflection in any effort to alleviate the acquired evils. Rousseau's critical and diagnostic reflection on history is a continuation and radicalization of his earlier attack on the Enlightenment's confidence in the improvement of humanity through progress in the arts and sciences, exposed in his *Discourse on the Arts and Sciences* (1750). The terms of the *Second Discourse*'s argument are no longer, as in that earlier writing, the individualism and luxury encouraged by progress versus the cohesion and simplicity of the Spartan city-state. They are human reason itself, and society as built upon it, versus the original pre-rational and non-temporal state of nature. The loss of natural simplicity is located at the moment when human desires exceeded the individual's powers of self-satisfaction, thus forging the bonds of human dependence. But that excess is due to the activation of reason and imagination in the conception and pursuit of objects of desire extending beyond immediately necessary goods. Since such activation is inherently possible in human beings at all times (given their "perfectibility," or capacity for self-transformation, and their relative lack of instinctual determination), the periods of simplicity, peace, and freedom in human history are necessarily unstable and transient.

According to Rousseau, there is no natural potential or "entelechy" toward that activity of reason; contingent events were required to set in motion its indeterminate growth with its deleterious results. Rousseau here is only attempting to be more consistent than Hobbes and Locke in understanding the "natural state" non-teleologically. He argued that if his modern predecessors could claim that social life is not a natural perfection (as for Aristotle) but an acquired form of rationality, derived from pre-social passions, they should be willing to regard the rationality implicit in the passions themselves (fear of death, greed, envy) as acquired. More consistently than any earlier thinker, Rousseau proposed that human nature, including all the passions, is the product of an acquired rationality. He offered a "dialectical" view in which reason and passion mutually determine and expand each other, thus instituting ever greater enslavement to acquired desires and to the social life which is created to serve them. At the same time, he corrected earlier accounts of the natural state, presenting it as free of restless passion because free of the desire-expanding activity of reason. The first of the innovations of human perfectibility was the experience of time and of the world as temporally extended. Foresight, fear of death, and curiosity, which extend human awareness beyond sensation and the immediate present of the "sentiment of existence," emerged to destroy the natural state's blissful absorption in the present moment. Anxious pursuit of and flight from remote goods and evils are the normal condition of social life, where reason is active. Thus, Rousseau in a novel way identified rationality, temporality, and sociality, and he defined the central problem of human life as the discovery of strategies to correct, as much as it is humanly possible, the deformation of life brought about by the "fall" into time.

Yet the spirit of his search is pessimistic, for any effort to reconstruct and recreate the natural atemporal beginnings must employ language and thought which presuppose temporal consciousness. Language, as is argued in Part I of the *Second Discourse*, is inseparable from the use of "general ideas" that are not derivable from the mere association of sensations. Along with human judging, which compares particulars through the copula "is," as dealt with in Book IV of *Emile* (1762), language entails the rational capacity to render non-simultaneous things simultaneous. Rousseau acutely observed the inadequacy of earlier modern psychology to account for this spontaneity of thought. He admitted his own incapacity to provide an account of the genesis of language out of the original condition. At the same time these insights only reinforced the sense of an infinite gulf between reason and the pretemporal natural state. Rousseau assumed that the acquisition of reason, language, and time is irreversible, and contrary to common misreadings, his social and political reforms do not promise a utopian recovery of the natural state. The *Social Contract* (1762) is a sober (indeed somber) analysis of political life premised on the necessary temporal immanence and hence incompleteness of all social "cures" of human ills.

Yet, in the *Reveries of the Solitary Walker* (1778), Rousseau offered an account of certain experiences, granted to him as by a benevolent providence, that came very close to the recovery of the pure natural present. As he recounts it in *Reveries* V and VII, in his idyllic hours by the Lake of Bienne, engaged in botanical studies, he delighted in a self-sufficiency and contentment achieved in an obliteration of time, a state that approached the divine. The sentiment of existence alone filled him, and his activity was, to use Kant's language, an aesthetic "purposiveness without purpose." For Goethe and many others, Rousseau's redemption from time through an imaginative immersion in nature and aesthetic play with natural forms became an essential element of a metaphysics of unity found in a hidden pretemporal self or "daimon," rather than in a Platonic supratemporal world of forms and ideas. Also, an entire tradition of reflection on history as alienation—as a dialectic in which rational efforts to recover lost unity only increase the loss—arose from these Rousseauian experiences. The philosophy of history from Schelling to Heidegger and the poetry of recollected unity from Hölderlin to Proust would be unthinkable without Rousseau's striving for a transcendence of time from and within time.

[R.L.V.]

FURTHER READINGS

Poulet, George. *Studies in Human Time*. Trans. Elliott Coleman. Baltimore: Johns Hopkins, 1956.

Rousseau, Jean-Jacques. *Emile or On Education*. Trans. and ed. Allan Bloom. New York: Basic Books, 1979.

———. *The Reveries of the Solitary Walker.* Trans. and ed. Charles E. Butterworth. New York: Harper & Row, 1982.

———. *Of the Social Contract and Discourse on Political Economy.* Trans. and ed. Charles M. Sherover. New York: Harper & Row, 1984.

———. *The First and Second Discourses and Essay on the Origin of Languages.* Trans. and ed. Victor Gourevitch. New York: Harper & Row, 1986.

Temmer, Mark J. *Time in Rousseau and Kant: An Essay in French Pre-Romanticism.* Geneva: Librarie Droz, 1958.

ROYCE, JOSIAH (1855–1916)

Josiah Royce was the leading American advocate of a kind of idealism which stressed the will as the most important of the mind's powers. The view of time which grew out of such an emphasis is given in his "On Purpose In Thought" (1880), *The World and the Individual*, vol. 2 (1902), and "The Reality of the Temporal" (1909).

Especially important for Royce's philosophy was his interweaving of the themes of time and will. For him, the origin and structure of time trace back to the power and direction of the will. The will sets flowing all of the powers of mind and reason. Accordingly, time becomes for Royce an extension and objectification of the directives of the will. His concept of the will changed and became more expansive as his philosophy developed, and was finally idealized as an absolute ground. In parallel fashion, time's fortunes also changed and, with all limits finally removed, came to be seen as an aspect of the eternal. In Royce's last writings, when the more realistic, more aversive aspects of the will were given greater weight, so too does his absolute idealism and his philosophy of time become more pluralistic and more individualistic.

[B.P.H.]

FURTHER READINGS

Helm, Bertrand P. *Time and Reality in American Philosophy.* Amherst: U of Massachusetts P, 1985.

Marcel, Gabriel. *Royce's Metaphysics.* Trans. Virginia and Gordon Ringer. Westport: Greenwood P, 1975.

RUSSELL, BERTRAND ARTHUR WILLIAM (1872–1970)

Russell held that time, objectively considered, is constituted exclusively by temporal relations between events—McTaggart's B series. Time does require change, but this can be accounted for solely in terms of an object's having a property at one time that it lacks at some earlier or later time, for example, a poker being hot at one time and cold at another. While events could stand in relations of precedence and subsequence to each other in a world devoid of consciousness, they could not qualify as past, present, and future in such a world for two reasons. First, these determinations depend on the selectivity of consciousness. In the "Philosophy of Logical Atomism," Russell says that "we pick out certain facts, past and future . . .; they all radiate out from 'this,'" in which "this" denotes a sense-datum private to the speaker at the time of utterance. Second, in "On Propositions: What They Are and How They Mean," he argues that "Difference of tense . . . is not part of what is believed, but only of the way of believing it." Tensed distinctions do not qualify objective reality but merely express the psychological state of the speaker's mind in regard to whether it involves a recollective, perceptual, or anticipatory attitude toward the reported event. Herein he shows himself to be the true heir of Hume, who stripped the objective world of troublesome features by reducing them to features of our psychology that we mistakenly project onto the objective world.

[R.M.G.]

See also **Analytic Philosophy; McTaggart, John McTaggart Ellis.**

FURTHER READINGS

Russell, Bertrand. *Principles of Mathematics.* Cambridge: Cambridge UP, 1903.

———. "On the Experiencing of Time." *Monist* 25 (1915): 212–231.

———. "The Philosophy of Logical Atomism." *Monist* 28–29 (1918–19): Lecture IV.

———. "On Propositions: What They Are and How They Mean." *Logic and Knowledge.* Ed. R.C. Marsh. London: George Allen & Unwin, 1956.

RUSSIAN THINKERS ON THE HISTORICAL PRESENT AND FUTURE

A marked orientation toward the historical future, as Reinhart Koselleck and Jürgen Habermas have argued, is characteristic of "modernity," especially since 1789. But three points need to be added: (1) this future orientation has often been accompanied by a hatred and contempt for the historical *present* and a willingness—even eagerness—to sacrifice actual living persons for the sake of an imagined, merely possible, historical future; (2) there is a European tradition running from the Enlighteners through Fichte,

Feuerbach, Marx, John Stuart Mill, Nietzsche, and Heidegger for which such an orientation is obsessive; but (3) there is a less often noticed but equally robust countervailing tradition—including Kant, Kierkegaard, Hegel, and Gadamer—which has offered reasoned resistance to the dominant future orientation.

In Russia, a pronounced future orientation was characteristic of such nineteenth-century radicals as Bakunin and Pisarev as well as such Russian Marxists as Plekhanov, Lunacharsky, and Trotsky, and *all* Marxist-Leninists of the Soviet period. Most of those who *resisted* this orientation were traditionalists of one kind or another, such as Leontyev, Dostoevsky, and the unconventional (late) Tolstoy; and a Marxist turned Russian Orthodox theologian (S. Bulgakov), a Marxist turned religious existentialist (Berdyaev), and an academic liberal who perished in Stalin's *gulag* (Shpet). But one of the most eloquent critics of this orientation was the "Russian socialist," Alexander Herzen.

Future orientation has two related but distinguishable aspects: (1) a confidence that the historical future is predictable and that it holds the certain, if long-term, promise of achieved socialism or communism; and (2) the more ominous assumption that, for the sake of achieving the "radiant future" of communism, present existents—communities, cultures, and especially individual *persons*—may justifiably be treated as means for the realization of that historical end.

Dmitry Pisarev (1840–1868), who sometimes rivaled Nietzsche in rhetorical exuberance, announced in 1864 that the "realist" (read "nihilist") ideal which he championed would require "hundreds of generations" for its realization. Taking an average generation as thirty years, even 200 generations would amount to 6,000 years; 300 generations would amount to 9,000 years!

The Russian Marxist orientation toward the historical future, though less rhetorically extravagant, was no less powerful. All Russian Marxists endorsed the twin claims of the *Communist Manifesto* that the proletariat is the "class that holds the [historical] future in its hands," and that proletarian revolutionaries "have nothing to lose but their [present] chains. They have a [future] world to win." Georgi Plekhanov (1856–1918) insisted that the Marxist ideal is, in the present, the "*actuality* of the [remote historical] future." The Nietzschean Marxist Anatoly Lunacharsky (1875–1933), who asserted in 1904 that the "faith of the active human being is a faith in

future mankind," went on in 1909 to celebrate the "miracles of [socialist] culture in the year 3,000." Leon Trotsky (1879–1940)—from at least 1920, when he published *Terrorism and Communism*, until 1940, when he wrote his "Testament"—embraced an "unshaken faith in the communist future" of all mankind.

Marxist confidence in the Communist future is based—as Sergei Bulgakov (1877–1944) had made clear in 1902—not on knowledge but on an "irrational, blind faith." The "free, proud, and happy" mankind of the future is the "beyond" of the (pseudo-) religion of progress. And historical prediction is severely limited: "Perhaps the fate of mankind in the twentieth century . . . is known to us [in 1902], but we know absolutely nothing about what awaits mankind in the twenty-first, twenty-second, or twenty-third century."

In the mid-nineteenth century, Alexander Herzen (1812–1870) stood alone among his Western European contemporaries in challenging the fashionable orientation toward the historical future and the equally fashionable hatred and contempt for the historical present. He insisted that both the past and the present deserve love and respect, and he offered a sharp critique—expressed in a series of unforgettable images—of the theory and practice of sacrificing living persons on the altar of an abstract historical future. In 1850, he asked the impassioned rhetorical question: "Do you truly wish to condemn the human beings alive today to the sad role of caryatids supporting a floor for others some day to dance on?" And he asserted decisively, "The subordination of the [living] individual to [future] society. . .—to [future] humanity—is a continuation of human sacrifice."

Konstantin Leontyev (1831–1891), who admired certain of Herzen's writings, joined him in repudiating what he called "the feverish preoccupation" with the earthly welfare of remote future generations on the part of both socialists and utilitarians. Leontyev proposed to replace such future orientation by Christian *agapē*—love for the "person encountered, the person at hand—charity toward the living . . . human being whose tears we see, whose sighs and groans we hear . . . in this present hour."

Dostoevsky, who also admired Herzen and wrote a laudatory essay about him after the latter's death, has Ivan Karamazov draw from his ghastly catalogue of the abuses of small children the conclusion that no appeal to *future* happiness can possible justify such overwhelming *present* suffering. Once the suffering has occurred, it is "too late in history" for anything that may occur in the future to redeem it.

Bulgakov in 1902 added the striking, if rather gruesome, image of future generations as "vampires" sucking the blood of the present generation. He concurs with Dostoevsky that "future happiness cannot be bought with the absolute evil of [present] suffering." Tolstoy in 1908 insisted that human beings should live "not for the future but solely for the present, striving simply to fulfill *in the present* the will of God revealed . . . in [the law of] love." He brands the claim that "it is possible to know the future order of society" a "horrible superstition," one that is invoked, illegitimately, to "justify the use of every sort of violence [in the present] to support [the effort to bring about] that [future] order."

Gustav Shpet (1879–1937) remarked perceptively in 1921 that anyone who understands—as Herzen did—the true import of future-oriented worldviews which instrumentalize the present will listen with alarm to the sound of the "march" which is summoning living individuals to the "soulless city" of an impersonal future. The thunder of that march is "intended only to drown out the groans and sobs of those on whose present tears and present blood this mindless and heartless city is being erected. By his sober attitude toward such a way of thinking Herzen showed with complete clarity the subtlety of his mind and the sensitivity of his heart."

Nicolas Berdyaev (1874–1948) repeated and developed (in 1924) a number of the critical points made earlier by Herzen, Dostoevsky, and Bulgakov, but unlike them, he was able to direct his criticism at Soviet Marxist-Leninists, for whom the historical future represents "the substance of things hoped for, the evidence of things not seen." They are guilty of an "illegitimate deification of the future at the expense of the past and present." On the Marxist-Leninist

view, "every human generation, every individual . . . is but the means . . . to [an] ultimate humanity perfect in that power and happiness which is denied the present generation."

Berdyaev is as clear-eyed as Herzen, and perhaps clearer-eyed than Bulgakov, in seeing that for Marxists (and Marxist-Leninists), the relation of the historical present to the historical future is a relation of *means* to *end*. And, like both Herzen and Shpet, he has a vivid sense of the death-dealing potential of such an instrumentalizing ideology.

[G.L.K.]

See also **Berdyaev, Nicolas; Hegel, Georg Wilhelm Friedrich; Heidegger, Martin; Kant, Immanuel; Kierkegaard, Sören Aabye; Marx, Karl; Nietzsche, Friedrich Wilhelm.**

FURTHER READINGS

Berdyaev, Nicolas. *Smysl istorii: Opyt filosofii chelovecheskoi sud'by.* 1923 (Berlin); reprint, Moscow: Mysl', 1990. (Translated by George Reavey as *The Meaning of History.* 1936; reprint, Cleveland: Meridian, 1962.)

Bulgakov, Sergei. "Osnovnye problemy teorii progressa." *Ot marksizma k idealizmu.* Petersburg, 1903; reprint, Frankfurt: Posev, 1968. 113–160.

Herzen, Alexander. *S togo berega* (1850). *Sochineniia* (9 vols., 1955–1958). Moscow: Khudozhestvennaia literatura, 1956. 3:233–373. (Translated and edited by Isaiah Berlin as *From the Other Shore.* New York: Braziller, 1956.)

Kline, George L. "The Use and Abuse of Hegel by Nietzsche and Marx." *Hegel and His Critics: Philosophy in the Aftermath of Hegel.* Ed. William Desmond. Albany: State U of New York P, 1989. 1–34.

Tolstoy, Leo. *Zakon nasiliia i zakon liubvi* (1908). *Sochineniia* (100 vols., 1929–1958). Moscow: Khudozhestvennaia literatura, 1956. 37:149–213. (Abridged translation by James P. Scanlan as "The Law of Violence and the Law of Love." *Russian Philosophy.* Ed. James M. Edie et al. 3 vols. 1965; reprint, Knoxville: U of Tennessee P, 1984. 2:213–234.)

SALTATORY EVOLUTION

Saltatory evolution is a progression by leaps, rather than by a gradual accumulation of adaptations. Darwin was profoundly influenced by the geological uniformitarianism popularized by Charles Lyell, and he enthusiastically adopted the Leibniz maxim, *Natura non fecit saltum* (Nature has not made leaps). The reason for this stance was that the mechanism of natural selection, which Darwin regarded as his own invention, would be made largely redundant by saltations. It would function simply as the final arbiter rather than having shaped each gradual step.

Although the fossil record indicated the sudden appearance of new types—discontinuities consistent with saltations—Darwinists believed that in time the accumulation of more complete fossil data would support gradualism. But for many paleontologists this expectation has never been realized and the debate continues.

Biometrician Francis Galton and evolutionist St. George Jackson Mivart proposed that intermittent periods of stable equilibrium permitted some geological continuity within strata, but that there were times of disequilibrium and rapid evolution. This Victorian concept was reactivated as "punctuated equilibria" by Niles Eldredge and Stephen Gould in 1972. But even at the zenith of neo-Darwinism in the 1950s "explosive evolution" was being proposed by some eminent critics.

A saltatory mechanism was provided by Hugo De Vries's *Mutation Theory* (1901–1903), which proposed that some species were in a state of mutability and prone to large-scale mutations that could bring about speciation in a single step. But De Vries had misinterpreted his research, and soon "selection pressure" rather than "mutation pressure" was seen to be the effective mechanism in the evolution of populations.

The search for mechanisms of saltatory evolution has been characterized by biological philosopher J.H. Woodger (1929) as not so much "tried and found wanting" as "found difficult and not tried." Examples of animal "sports" (radically new types) appearing in breeding stock were cited in the early literature. Oddities such as an extra pair of wings, or legs in place of antennae, were observed in *Drosophila*. But the question remained as to what kind of accommodating mechanism could allow for radical change during development without producing a mere teratological freak. The answers lie within the

realm of investigation known as epigenetics, a study of gene expression during development, usually in an evolutionary context. This is a young science, since the necessary techniques have only recently come available with the maturation of molecular biology, so, though difficult, they are at last being tried.

[R.G.B.R.]

See also **Evolution of Evolutionism; Evolutionary Progress; Fossil Record; Heterochrony; Hopeful Monsters.**

FURTHER READINGS

Løvtrup, Søren. *Epigenetics*. New York: Wiley, 1974.

SANTAYANA, GEORGE (1863–1952)

George Santayana, an American philosopher with strong European intellectual roots, developed a philosophical system designed to accommodate the findings of physical science and to reconcile them to the values expressed in morality and religion. His inspiration was naturalistic, leading him to view the totality of existence as continuous with the human body and constituting the material world whose parts interact in space and time. With unrelenting realism, he thought of this world as the home and organ of the human mind rather than as its product.

The distinction between the hard facts of material reality and the symbolic truths of consciousness is at the heart of Santayana's philosophy. Existence embodies traits we can apprehend only in terms of the poetic language of the mind. One of its central features is temporality, which makes everything real evanescent. We have no immediate access to this *physical* time; the way it appears to the mind is not identical with it. This appearance of real physical passage in consciousness, *sentimental* time, consists of a set of centered perspectives on the future and the past.

Physical time, as best we can understand it, is a movement of material reality that raises certain qualities and relations to an "insane emphasis," endowing them with ultimately unintelligible and quickly passing existence. Although it leaves a past and rushes into the future, this burst of brute existence lives in an endless present, knowing neither its antecedents nor its products. By contrast, the mind's perception of time is laden with sentiment or feeling: it sees a present bordered by a lost past and an impending future. Consciousness broods over this certain loss and ambiguous promise, unable to escape the selfish perspectives that situate it in the apparent center of all reality in a passing now.

The experienced now, the specious present, reveals that mind inevitably arrests the flux of existence. Consciousness of passage requires that we unite the earlier and the later in a single synthetic image before the mind: only the presence of both terms of the temporal relation can convey the idea that something has changed. But if both termini of change are present, we have no real movement or alteration, only the appearance of change. The past and the future are, therefore, only painted perspectives for consciousness. They constitute a picturesque, symbolic version of the movement of material forces, a timeless picture of time.

Plato thought of time as the moving image of eternity. Santayana reverses this, declaring that eternity is the synthetic picture of time. Santayana's formulation expresses his emphasis on the primacy of time and change, but also establishes that there is an eternal record of all temporal facts. This record, made by "the wake of the ship of time," is the realm of truth. The animal in us flourishes in the material world; our mind or spirit enjoys only the contemplation of eternal essences, whose infinite number includes all truths. In this way, Santayana aligns himself with those who think that nothing but the transcendence of time leads to blessedness, though he notes that such transcendence is open only to mind and that the organ of consciousness cannot escape the ravages of time.

[J.L.]

See also **Plato.**

FURTHER READINGS

Lachs, J. *George Santayana*. Boston: Twayne, 1988.

Sprigge, T. *Santayana*. London: Routledge, 1974.

SARTRE, JEAN-PAUL (1905–1980)

Sartre's treatment of time and temporality is complex and subtle. In his early *War Diaries* he already employs the neologism "is-was" (*est-été*) to capture the ongoing and fleeting nature of temporality as well as its hard facticity. His fullest treatment of the topic occurs in Part Two, Chapter Two of *Being and Nothingness*, where the general theme is being-for-itself or consciousness. There he undertakes a "phenomenology" of the three temporal dimensions, namely, facticity, presence-to, and possibility. He insists that these are structured moments of an original synthesis. As aspects of a consciousness whose defining characteristic is to introduce negation into the world, these dimensions are described as the "no longer," the "other than," and the "not yet." Sartre distinguishes this "original temporality," which is ours before we reflect upon it, from both the inter-subjective "psychic temporality" of scientific psychology and social life, which functions inasmuch as we reflect upon it, and the objective "universal temporality" of natural processes. When Sartre moves from a philosophy of consciousness to one of praxis (roughly, human activity in its material environment) in the *Critique of Dialectical Reason*, his understanding of time becomes more dialectical and historical.

[T.R.F.]

See also **Existentialism; Phenomenology.**

FURTHER READINGS

Sartre, Jean-Paul. *Being and Nothingness: An Essay on Phenomenological Ontology*. Trans. Hazel E. Barnes. New York: Philosophical Library, 1956.

———. *The War Diaries: Notebooks from a Phoney War November 1939–March 1940*. Trans. Quintin Hoare. London: Verso, 1984.

———. *Notebooks for an Ethics*. Trans. David Pellauer. Chicago: U of Chicago P, 1992.

SATURN-CRONUS

The identification of Saturn-Cronus with time may have been in part the result of a mistaken association of Cronus with Chronos, the personification of time. Cronus (or Kronos) was the father of the gods in the Greek pantheon. He castrated his father, Uranus, with a sickle given to him by his mother, Gaia. In a vain attempt to protect himself from a similar fate, he devoured his own children, but one of his sons, Zeus, was hidden away by his mother, Rhea. Zeus eventually castrated and overthrew his father. All three "fathers of the gods" in the Greek pantheon either came to be or were originally associated with aspects of time. Uranus or Ur—who married Gaia, a marriage respectively of the air with the earth—came to have the connotation of ancient or original as in the German Ur-Faust or Ur-Hamlet; Cronus came to mean time itself; and Zeus—as in deus, dies, or day—was the god of day.

Before the arrival of the Greek pantheon, Cronus ruled heaven and the world enjoyed a golden age. He was the deliverer of all happiness to mankind because he introduced civilization, justice, and sincerity to the world. In his honor the Greeks celebrated the festival of Kronia in Attica during harvest time. In the Roman pantheon, Saturn was the agricultural god of a golden age until he was overthrown by the Cretan king Jupiter ("father of the gods"). The festival of Saturnalia, originally celebrated for only one day (December 17), bore a striking resemblance to the festival of Kronia. Both the Greeks and the Romans painted glowing pictures of the blessed times when Cronus or Saturn ruled. It was natural that Cronus and Saturn should become conflated and the figures of Zeus and Jupiter were also often coalesced.

Saturn-Cronus was inherently dualistic, representing on the one hand a violent god who had committed infanticide and parricide, and on the other hand a god who had ruled in a golden age of peaceful civilization. The blacker side of Saturn-Cronus probably stems from Cronus, because the story of the parricide who devoured his children was not originally part of Saturn's mythology. Cronus was also associated with human sacrifice, especially in Phoenician Carthage where the gods of the native Punic religion, Tanith and Baal Amon (or Hammon), required the sacrifice of children. When these gods were Hellenized in the fifth century B.C., Baal Amon became Baal-Cronus or Baal-Saturn, but retained his thirst for blood. The custom of sacrificing human beings, usually by immolation, to Saturn-Cronus reinforced the child-devouring element in his myth that was generally unacceptable not only to Christians but to pagan Greeks and Romans as well. Nevertheless, sacrifices to Cronus and Saturn were performed by Greeks and Romans themselves. An annual

sacrifice to Cronus took place on the top of Mount Cronius at the spring equinox. In Rhodes, at the autumnal festival of Cronus, a condemned criminal was put to death. The Romans publicly sacrificed victims to Saturn at the festival of Saturnalia in ca. 217 B.C. on the occasion of Hannibal's attainment of the Arno. During the reigns of Maximian (A.D. 286–305) and Diocletian (A.D. 284–305), Roman soldiers selected a mock king who would reign during the Saturnalia and then sacrifice his own life.

The planet Saturn reinforced the evil side of Saturn-Cronus. When the Greeks and Romans imported astrology from the Mesopotamians, they replaced the names of the zodiac signs and the planets with their own. Saturn replaced Ninib who, as the nightly representative of the sun, was regarded as the mightiest of the planets. The dark associations of the planet Saturn reinforced the cruel elements in the Saturn-Cronus myth. Saturn was usually a maleficent planet in the casting of horoscopes, although some ambivalence was allowed depending on his position in the zodiac. In the fourteenth century A.D., Chaucer calls Saturn a "wicked" planet in his *Treatise on the Astrolabe*. In *The Knight's Tale*, Chaucer associates Saturn with a round dozen of negative qualities: deceits, discontent, drowning, hanging, plots, poisoning, prisons, punishment, rebellion, strangling, treason, and vengeance. However, in Chaucer's tale, Saturn makes peace between Venus and Mars, and also succeeds where Jupiter failed. Chaucer's choice of Saturn as peacemaker suggests the ambivalence in the Saturn-Cronus figure.

By the time Plutarch (A.D. ca. 46–after 119) was writing, if not earlier, Saturn-Cronus was identified with Chronos, the personification of time. The pre-Socratic philosophers, Anaximander (ca. 611–547 B.C.), and Solon (ca. 639–559 B.C.), did not make a definitive identification of Cronus with Chronos, but they did suggest that time reveals evil and injustice. This conception of time was also expressed by Sophocles (ca. 496–406 B.C.) in *Electra* and in *Oedipus Tyrannus*. Later, Truth would be personified as the daughter of Time (*Veritas filia Temporis*). In the work of Pindar, who was virtually a contemporary of Sophocles, it is possible to surmise that the poet may be aligning Chronos with Cronus. Pindar calls Time the father of all things, thus ascribing to Chronos the traditional role that Cronus held as the father of the gods. The poet also identifies Truth as the daughter of Zeus (the son of Cronus) and as the daughter of Time. The personification of Time seems to merge into the person of Cronus. Cicero (106–43 B.C.) considered Cronus (or Kronos) and Chronos identical. He identifies Saturn as the ruler of the times and the seasons, Saturn meaning "sated with years" and Kronos or Chronos meaning "a lapse of time."

Originally, Saturn-Cronus did not possess temporal attributes, but eventually his traditional iconography was explained in terms of symbols of time. Macrobius (ca. A.D. 400), for whom there was no question that Cronus is Time, explains Cronus's sickle as a symbol of finite time which reaps, cuts off, and shortens all life. The child-devouring aspect of the myth of Saturn-Cronus was held to be symbolic of Time devouring the years. Nineteenth-century works on Greek and Roman mythology describe Saturn as an old man who carries a sickle, a symbol of the inevitable harvest of human lives. These works identify Saturn as both the malevolent god of time and the benevolent king of the golden age.

The importance of Saturn-Cronus began to wane with the advent of Christianity. Early Christians rejected the immortality of Saturn-Cronus and focused their arguments on his temporal attributes. They pointed out the incongruities of Saturn-Cronus's role as a god of time. In addition, they questioned whether a god of time could be the son of another god (Uranus) and also debated whether his sovereignty could be usurped by his son (Zeus). The Christian god was immortal and incorporeal, while the Greek gods were concerned with mortal and finite goals. By superimposing the Christian celebration of the birth of Christ upon the Mithraic festival of the rebirth of the sun, Christians also succeeded in upstaging the Saturnalia. Saturn retained his relationship to finite time but since he was viewed more as a mortal than a god he was no longer feted annually. Saturn nevertheless filled a gap in the monotheistic Christian worldview that did not allow for a god of finite time: Saturn-Cronus became the somber Father Time, whose sickle reminded the Christian of the transitory nature of life on earth and of his related need to prepare for eternity.

[S.L.M.]

See also **Father Time; Indo-Iranian Gods of Time.**

FURTHER READINGS

Klibansky, Raymond, Erwin Panofsky, and Fritz Saxl. *Saturn and Melancholy*. London: Nelson, 1964.

Lucian of Samosata. *Saturnalia* in *Works*. Trans. H.W. Fowler and F.G. Fowler. Oxford: Clarendon P, 1905.

Macey, Samuel L. *Patriarchs of Time: Dualism in Saturn-Cronus, Father Time, the Watchmaker God, and Father Christmas*. Athens: U of Georgia P, 1987.

Macrobius. *The Saturnalia*. Trans. Percival Vaughan Davies. New York: Columbia UP, 1969.

Roscher, W.H. "Chronos." *Ausführliches Lexikon der griechischen und römischen Mythologie*. Leipzig: Teubner, 1884–90. 1:899.

SCHEDULING OF THE LIFE CYCLE

Discussion of the life cycle encapsulates many of the difficulties of temporal analysis. Conceptual problems affect the very terminology to be used, even when the discussion is limited, as this is, to Western industrialized countries. Since "cycle" implies repetition and human beings do not repeat their lives as such, it can be argued that for the purposes of empirical analysis the term "life course" is preferable. This immediately raises the question of the interaction between different temporal levels. Anthony Giddens distinguishes three different levels: daily routine, the life course, and the *longue durée*, but as Barbara Adam has observed, assumptions about stable, integrative levels can make it difficult to capture inherent social dynamics. This article explores some of the issues involved. Its essence is that we should be aware of the constantly changing shape and character of the life cycle; yet the fact of change is not enough to invalidate its usefulness as a concept. As with many, perhaps all, temporal concepts, there is a permanent tension between continuity and change.

When we think about the scheduling of the life cycle from a chronosociological perspective, there are three principal and interrelated dimensions to be borne in mind: duration, sequence, and temporal rigidity. Duration refers to the length of the life cycle and the different units which comprise it. Significant shifts are occurring here, as people on average live longer than preceding generations and the amount of time spent in the various stages of the life cycle changes. Life expectancy at birth in OECD (Organization for Economic Cooperation and Development) countries has risen by between seven and ten years over the last three decades. The increase in the number of years has not been evenly distributed across the life cycle, being principally concentrated in the period after employment is finished, in what is coming to be called the third age. Similarly, but not symmetrically, the first age—the period of initial dependence—has also been extended with the prolongation of initial education. The number of such periods can of course be multiplied—medieval models of the life cycle run up to twelve or more—but the important point is that in a simple linear sense the shape of the life cycle is changing.

Second, the sequencing of stages in the life cycle is changing. Some models suggest a steady progression from one discrete stage to the next, with heavily normative connotations attaching to the notion of "progression." But two characteristics of modern society can be used to illustrate the growing complexity of the process. Education is no longer seen as an initial phase in life, but as something which recurs—or should recur—throughout one's life; and family formation is far from a simple linear process, with divorce and remarriage generating family structures of increasingly Byzantine complexity. There are, of course, still dominant patterns, but the probability of individuals following a predictable sequence is changing. Women in particular seem to establish new patterns, many now completing their "initial" education *after* having had children.

Third, the extent to which the shape of the life cycle is attached to chronological age is changing. Here there are conflicting trends. It has been argued, notably by Martin Kohli, that there is increasing "chronologization," with people becoming more firmly tied to age norms. On the other hand, there are aspects which are apparently becoming uncoupled from age: Michael Young and Tom Schuller have, for example, reported on the increasing diversity in the age at which people finish paid employment.

This very simple framework generates many lines of inquiry. Any model of the life cycle should reflect social variables such as class and gender, as well as cultural variations across and within societies. Yet this is commonly ignored at both conceptual and policy levels. Take gender: the increased duration referred to above has led to growing concern about the aging of societies and the position of older people, but women have for decades, even centuries, experienced old age as a significant component of their life cycle. Female life cycles have always exhibited more complex sequencing. And women are on the one hand more tied to certain chronological staging posts related to childbearing, but on the other hand depart from assumed norms about age-related activities. The conventional notion of a career as a continuous and predictable occupational pathway is difficult to sustain when matched against women's efforts to sustain an identity combining occupational and family roles.

It is already obvious how a temporal approach to the analysis of the life cycle exposes the norms and assumptions involved in its scheduling. As usual, however, temporal analysis must be turned on itself, for the observations offered above are themselves crucially dependent on the temporal framework employed. In its simplest sense, this is to say that our ideas of what is changing in the patterns outlined above depend absolutely on the period of time to which we choose to refer either implicitly or explicitly. Thus, the "break-up of the family" may be a politically salient issue in contemporary terms, but only by reference to the recent past (and even then, arguably, to a mythologized one); not so many decades ago, death rather than divorce dissolved many marriages at an early stage, so that expectations of long and settled coupledom were low then. In a more compressed time frame, the fluctuations of the labor market have meant rapid oscillations in the state-transmitted messages about when old age should begin, with older workers being first encouraged to stay in the labor market, then eased out or ejected, and so on in cycles of a decade or less.

Beyond this the concepts themselves demand reflection. Sequencing implies linearity, if not necessarily progression, and Karen Davies has argued powerfully that this accords more closely with male than female structures and patterns; women's time is more recursive and multi-stranded. Even duration, with its apparent objectivity, requires multiple interpretation, as the passage of time appears differently to different agents in different contexts (which is why pace is added as a discrete dimension in some frameworks). While clock time is comfortably applicable without real difficulty to the life cycle, there are areas in which perceptions of duration become as important to our understanding of the scheduling process as the actual hours or years involved.

The life cycle is shaped by the interaction of biological, cultural, and individual factors, all of which change over time at varying rates. Scheduling implies precision and predictability, but only up to a point; where that point is will always remain to be defined.

[T.S.]

See also **Feminist Perspectives; Giddens, Anthony; Social Theory; Time and Death.**

FURTHER READINGS

Adam, Barbara. *Time and Social Theory*. Cambridge: Polity P, 1990.

Davies, Karen. *Women and Time: Weaving the Strands of Everyday Life*. Lund: University of Lund, 1989.

Giddens, Anthony. *The Constitution of Society: Outline of the Theory of Structuration*. Cambridge: Polity P, 1984.

Kohli, Martin. "Social Organization and Subjective Construction of the Life Course." *Human Development and the Life Course*. Ed. A. Sorenson, F. Weinert, and L. Sherred. Hillsdale: Erlbaum, 1986. 271–292.

Young, Michael, and Tom Schuller. *Life After Work: The Arrival of the Ageless Society*. London: HarperCollins, 1991.

SCHEDULING THROUGH OPERATIONAL RESEARCH

Managements are charged with the responsibility of achieving the aims and objectives of the organization for which they work. To do this they must have *control* of the resources of those organizations.

There is no control without feedback of information and data which can be compared with the standards and targets to be achieved. Many of the standards are stated in terms of time: the time to complete a job, the time to fulfill a contract, and times which can be used for scheduling work.

The techniques for scheduling are grouped under a discipline known as operational (or operations) research (OR). This essay discusses in brief the most important techniques of OR.

When goods and services are distributed through a chain of delivery routes they must be scheduled in order to use the most efficient and cost-effective network. Several techniques have been developed to achieve these goals.

Scheduling is the process of achieving efficiency by arranging tasks into chronological sequence or by priority. Methods grouped under the generic title of critical path analysis (CPA) or network analysis are used to plan and schedule the tasks which comprise major projects. These include shipbuilding, civil engineering, and equipment construction. The times needed for CP analysis are starting dates, completion times, and completion dates. Completion times for tasks are obtained through the use of techniques such as those described in **Measurement of Work and Applications** and **Predetermined Motion Time Systems**.

Waiting lines or queues are found everywhere, from supermarket checkouts and ticket offices to aircraft stacking over an airport and waiting to land. Documents waiting for attention in an "in-tray" and components in a buffer stock of an assembly line are other examples of waiting lines. Queuing theory is used to solve problems and rationalize queues.

Replacement theory is concerned with optimizing the time to replace components of a system consistent with effectiveness and cost.

Product mix is an OR technique which seeks to determine the optimum mix of component materials or situations to maximize profit, minimize costs, or optimize other factors. It is applicable to such disparate situations as minimizing costs of compound animal feeds and optimizing hours worked by a group of operatives.

OR relies heavily on probability theory and statistical analysis for its solutions. Methods such as simulation using random sampling numbers, and the probability curves of the Poisson, exponential, beta, gamma, and normal (Gaussian) distributions are of particular value.

It will be seen that not all of the techniques of OR are time-based. Only those which have connections with time will be described here.

QUEUING

Problems involving queues include calculations of the number of service points needed in certain situations, determination of the optimal queue lengths, and calculations of waiting times in queues.

When queues are investigated, three of the most important factors to consider are (1) the arrival pattern, (2) the service routine, and (3) the discipline of the queue. Research has identified at least two probability distributions which are associated with these patterns.

The pattern of arrivals examines whether people or objects (the queue elements) join the queue systematically or randomly, as well as the rate at which they arrive (number within a certain time period). The appropriate probability distribution curve is known as the *Poisson* distribution, and from the resulting values the mean arrival rate and dispersion in terms of standard deviation can be calculated.

Service times are described by the *exponential* probability density function. From this, the probabilities of any service time being between any two selected limits of time can be calculated, using the standard exponential function.

Some queues are self-regulating; for example, items awaiting sale become obsolete, or degenerate, thus leaving the queue. Customers faced with long waiting lines will leave, or be discouraged from joining the queue in the first place. Arrivals can be systematic, which means that the queue elements arrive at fixed intervals of time (such as every two minutes, or every quarter of an hour), or random (that is, at any unpredictable and variable rate). Similarly, service times can be systematic or random.

A typical problem which could face the OR specialist is to determine the number of service points of sale required to ensure that queues do not exceed a certain length, so as not to discourage or displease customers. If the mean service times and arrival rates are known there are two main ways of effecting a solution. One is by *simulation*. This involves using fixed or random service times and rates of arrival, depending on the patterns which prevail in actual practice. Systematic times are easy to use but random times and rates must be found from random number tables which are reproduced in most good statistics textbooks (or using computer-generated random numbers). For example, if one checkout in a supermarket is considered, random numbers between 1 and 9 read off the table may be 2, 6, 7, 4, 8, 3, 1, 1, and 2 which can represent the service times of two minutes for customer 1, six minutes for customer 2, seven for customer 3, four for customer 4, and so on. Rates of arrivals can use a different set of random

numbers extracted from the tables, such as 4, 2, 3, 1, 6, 5, and so on. If the periods considered are five minutes, these random numbers can indicate that four customers arrive in the first five minutes, two in the second five minutes, three in the third, and so on. Using these sets of data in conjunction with each other the progress of customers through the checkout and fluctuations in queue length can be simulated. Computer programs are available to carry out such simulations.

Alternatively, formulas have been developed which will estimate the lengths of queues, waiting times to be served, actual service times, and other characteristics of queues.

REPLACEMENT

Even the most reliably produced components tend to age, deteriorate, and fail at some stage. Some may be in awkward places, or be so prolific (as in street lights) that they are continuously needing replacement. Furthermore, because they are frequently used, they almost inevitably fail *during* use.

Two main policies are available to deal with such circumstances. One is to replace faulty components as they fail, and the other is systematically to change *all* components in one scheduled operation. The first method means that only those components which have failed will be changed, whereas the second demands that even those which are still operational will also be changed. However, the second method al-

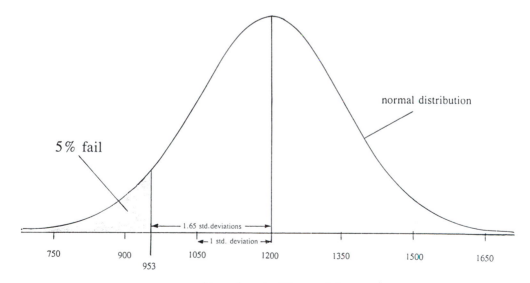

Figure 1. Normal distribution

lows the replacements to be carried out at times when the equipment is not being used, such as during vacations, overnight, or at other convenient periods. Also, travel time can be reduced if all components in the group are replaced during the same visit.

Of these two options neither can be said to be the "best," or most efficient, as the preferred option depends on the circumstances.

The replacement of street lamps provides an example. Clearly, these will fail randomly; one way to deal with the situation is to send out trucks with gantries to enable engineers to climb up and replace the failed lamps. This can be costly in traveling time. On the other hand, the engineers could work down each street changing all lamps as they go. Provided the parameters of the lamp-life are known, the optimum time for changing the lamps can be calculated. Figure 1 shows this graphically. The failure pattern for lamps roughly equates to the normal distribu-

tion. Normal distributions are always the same shape and the standard deviations are always at fixed positions on the normal distributions. Suppose the mean life for lamps is 1,200 hours. They will not all fail exactly at 1,200 hours of use: some will fail before and some after this time. The dispersion of the times can be measured by the *standard deviation* of time. Suppose also that the standard deviation is 150 hours, then this, and the mean, can be superimposed upon the standard normal distribution as shown. If the policy tolerates no more than a 5 percent lamp failure rate, then normal distribution tables (found in statistics textbooks) will say how many standard deviations from the mean represent 5 percent of the total area. In this case it is 1.66 standard deviations. This produces 150 x 1.66 standard deviations, or approximately 250 hours. Thus, all lamps must be changed about 250 hours before the 1,200 hours is up, or in other words, every 950 hours.

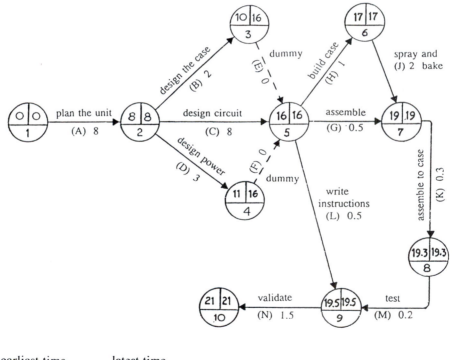

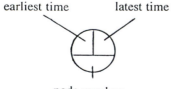

Figure 2. Critical path analysis (CPA) Arrow Diagram

As before, a cost analysis will show which policy is the better to pursue. The methods are widely applicable where replacement of large quantities of components or planned maintenance schemes are in operation.

CRITICAL PATH ANALYSIS

Large-scale projects are usually composed of many distinctly identifiable subunits. In construction, for example, subunits include clearing the site, marking out, laying the supplies, laying foundations, building the frame and floors, and so on. Assessing the total completion time is not just a matter of summing all these subunit times because many tasks can be carried out concurrently, making the overall calendar time much shorter than the sum of all the individual parts.

To arrive at an overall time it is necessary to schedule the subunits graphically, for which purpose computer programs are readily available. The technique used is called critical path analysis (CPA) or network analysis. Several versions of the basic method exist, under names such as PERT (project evaluation and review technique) and CPM (critical path method). Probably the original one was PERT, used to plan and schedule the production of the Polaris nuclear program.

All graphical methods use "nodes" linked together by arrows. The tasks or subunits are identified either by the arrows in one group of systems, or by the nodes in the other group. It is tasks by arrows which will be discussed here.

The project is first analyzed into its subunits or tasks, and constructed into a network showing the precedence or order of their execution. Each task is represented by an arrow emanating from a tail node and ending at a head node. Each head node for one task is also the tail node for the following task or tasks. Figure 2 illustrates the production of a customized control unit built from standard components and designed on a standard basic design and will be used here as the vehicle for describing CPA.

When the arrow diagram has been drawn, the times which are put to each job are derived using the techniques described in the article **Measurement of Work and Applications**. A basic rule of CPA is that no task can commence until all other tasks preceding it have been completed. Thus, tasks G, H, and L cannot start until B, C, and D have finished, and it will be seen from the figure that this will be after the

longest (that is to say task C) is completed in eight days, or sixteen days after the start of the project. It will also be seen that if task C takes eight days, the other two concurrent tasks, B and D, will have some idle time (known as "float") because they are of shorter duration than task C. The figure shows that although there are thirteen tasks in the project, taking a total of twenty-seven days, the overall calendar time for the project between nodes 1 and 10 is only twenty-one days, via nodes 1, 2, 5, 6, 7, 8, 9, and 10. This route is known as the *critical path* because all tasks which lie on it must be completed on time in order not to jeopardize the completion date. Tasks such as B, D, G, and L are not critical, as they have some idle time.

Critical path analysis has been used in many large-scale ventures and has proved its worth as a means of scheduling complex projects.

[D.A.W.]

See also **Industrial Engineering [After Taylor]; Measurement of Work and Applications; Predetermined Motion Time Systems.**

FURTHER READINGS

Lockyer, K.G. *Critical Path Analysis and Other Project Network Techniques*. 5th ed. London: Pitman, 1991.

SCIENCE FICTION

It is almost certainly wise to restrict any short discussion of science fiction—often referred to as "sf," an acronym that also includes "speculative fiction"—to what may fairly be described as the dominant form of this area of fantastic literature. That dominant form is the genre science fiction which—taking much of its initial subject matter from the fantastic-voyage tales that began with Lucian or earlier, from the future invasion tales whose first mature example was Colonel Chesney's *The Battle of Dorking* (1871), from the United Kingdom scientific romance as created by H.G. Wells, from the dime novel tale of fantastic inventions, and from the long tradition of the utopia and dystopia—came into being around 1926, with the founding of the first United States pulp magazine to be devoted exclusively to the genre.

It is this genre science fiction that inspired, and that sometimes crippled, the ambitions of the most famous American science fiction writers of the twentieth century from Robert A. Heinlein and Isaac Asimov down through Philip K. Dick, Ursula K. Le Guin, and Gene Wolfe. And it is this genre science fiction whose main venue would seem—deceptively—to suggest a consuming interest in what might be called the matter of time in science fiction writers. That main venue, from 1926 on to the present day, is the future itself. Genre science fiction can indeed be distinguished from all its predecessors by an inherent presumption, implied though not necessarily articulated in almost every story which belongs within its boundaries, that the future may be *taken for granted* as a venue. To set a story in A.D. 2200 is not, in most genre science fiction, to set up a dynamic of discourse between that year and the present. That dynamic may be an inherent element in any utopian or dystopian discourse written in the form of fiction, but most genre science fiction simply uses a future setting as a form of enabling *license*, a device that frees the writer to engage in certain kinds of plots (often garish, though frequently intriguing in their unshackled scope), and to make certain a priori cultural and scientific assumptions about the nature of existence some time hence.

The consequence of this liberty is fairly evident once realized, though perhaps not obvious before it is articulated. It is this. Setting a tale in the future has absolutely nothing to do, in imaginative or cognitive terms, with the matter of time. In purpose and in its consequences, it is entirely different from carrying a protagonist forward through time into a new setting; or from speculating upon the mysteries of time-to-be. Indeed, such speculations, because they transform the literary device of future setting into a problematic, are actively avoided by most writers of genre science fiction. As a whole, then, science fiction is not about time.

There are, however, two kinds of genre science fiction that escape this self-censorship. Tales involving **Time Travel: Future** and **Time Travel: Past** do exist in genre science fiction and in their two highly contrastive ways both subgenres have generated incisive patterns of speculation, and both have made imaginative use of the profound mystery of time. One further kind of genre science fiction may be mentioned at this point. The science fiction tale of cosmogony is generally written by authors (they include Asimov and Wolfe, as well as Poul Anderson, James Blish, Larry Niven, and Dan Simmons) who are scientifically numerate, and whose fictions of origin and destiny necessarily incorporate a sophisticated sense of the twentieth-century paradigm in physics which argues that space and time are no more than (put vulgarly)

different expressions on the face of ultimate reality. Such fictions from genre writers, however numerate, tend, however, to slur over or to make hyperbolic use of hard physics; and it is perhaps more useful to think of matters of cosmogony in their own right.

[J.C.]

See also **Cosmology; Futuristic Fiction; Physics; Time Travel: Future; Time Travel: Past; Utopias and Dystopias.**

FURTHER READINGS

Aldiss, Brian W. *Trillion Year Spree: The History of Science Fiction.* New York: Atheneum, 1986.

Eizykman, B. "Temporality in Science-Fiction Narrative." Ed. R.M. Philmus. Trans. R. Rosenthall and B. Eizykman. *Science-Fiction Studies* 12 (March 1985): 66–87.

Huntington, John. *The Logic of Fantasy: H.G. Wells and Science Fiction.* New York: Columbia UP, 1982.

McConnell, Frank. *The Science Fiction of H.G. Wells.* Oxford: Oxford UP, 1981.

Philmus, Robert M. *Into the Unknown: The Evolution of Science Fiction from Francis Godwin to H.G. Wells.* Berkeley: U of California P, 1970.

Russell, M.S. "Time in Folklore and Science Fiction." *Foundation: The Review of Science Fiction* 43 (Summer 1988): 5–24.

SHACKLE, G.L.S. (1903–1992)

George Shackle, a radical subjectivist *par excellence*, devoted a lifetime to reflecting on the complex nature of time. In order to understand the essence of individual decision, Shackle insists, we must adopt an "inside" view of time, in contrast to the "outside" view of time of the detached observer, as exemplified by the historian's panorama or by the mathematician's treatment of time as a spacial dimension. He refers to the time *in* which the individual recollects, perceives, feels, reflects, imagines, and decides as the "solitary present" or as the "moment-in-being." From the perspective of human consciousness, the moment-in-being is the only actuality, the past and future existing only in present recollections and in present imaginings. The moment-in-being—reminiscent of Bergson's "real concrete live present"—is to be conceived of not as an instant nor as a point in time but as a brief span whose contents the mind somehow grasps as a whole. Dynamic movement in time may be regarded, from the inside, as the inexorable evolution of one moment-in-being into another or, from the outside, as the movement of the moment-in-being through calendric time.

If an individual must perforce live in the solitary present, his thoughts will range over calendric time and, indeed, much of his present enjoyment will derive from imaginative contemplation of the future. Shackle suggests that an individual, in choosing among those alternative courses of action which he perceives to be open to him, will create mental images of their possible consequences, these imagined sequels constituting his vista of expectations. The individual will decide on, and commit himself to, that course of action whose imagined possibilities afford him, in the moment of being, the most desirable anticipated future experiences.

If an individual possessed perfect foresight, choice would merely involve the mechanical selection of that course of action with the most desirable consequence. Perfect foresight would render individual decision empty. Yet, in a universe without order, there would be no discernible link between action and consequence and no distinction between expectation and fantasy. Complete ignorance would render individual decision pointless. Shackle insists that, in everyday discourse, we use the word "decision" to mean decision which is neither empty nor pointless, but which is *creative*. True decision must, therefore, involve neither perfect foresight nor complete ignorance, but choice in the face of *bounded uncertainty*. Thus, the individual is constrained in his imaginings to what he believes to be in some degree possible, that is, the images which he creates must be congruous with his beliefs about human nature and about the physical world. In particular, where an image relates to a specific date in the future, any implied change in his situation between "now" and "then" must seem to him to be possible. It is fundamental to Shackle's vision that there is both order in the universe and scope for individual inspiration: what seems possible is bounded but not prescribed.

On this basis, Shackle has relentlessly challenged the conception of the history of the universe as the inexorable unrolling of some complete and determinate design. He insists that there is no objective future waiting to be discovered; rather, the future is created afresh from moment to moment. The source of the spontaneous emergence of essential novelty is the individual's freedom to create images of the future, images which may involve an *ex nihilo* element not deducible from what has gone before. Decision, in the true sense of the term, constitutes a "cut" between the past and the future, and thereby introduces an essentially novel element into the course of history.

Shackle emphasizes that much economic behavior involves merely habitual and passive responses to circumstances rather than true decisions. However, just as the precise nature of a scientific discovery cannot be predicted before its time, an outside observer cannot predict the precise nature of a creative decision before its time, nor even when an individual will next forsake habitual response and make a creative decision. Consequently, for Shackle, there can be no legitimate predictive dynamics of the individual. However, to the extent that there may be lags in the impacts of individual creative decisions on the economy as a whole, Shackle does concede that short-term predictive aggregate dynamics may be legitimate.

While Shackle's works have been a source of inspiration to many economists, his ideas have not found much favor among mainstream economists. This is hardly surprising. Mainstream economic theory is squarely based on the infinitely divisible, uniformly flowing and purely quantitative time of classical mechanics. Much of orthodox economic theory involves examining choice by an individual endowed with perfect foresight. Where uncertainty is admitted, it is typically supposed that an individual's expectations of the future can be deduced, more or less mechanically, from his past experiences and from the information available to him. Furthermore, for many economists, prediction is the *raison d'être* of the discipline. Rather than confront Shackle's arguments, mainstream economists have tended to dismiss him as a nihilist, a label which he has insistently rejected.

Shackle was born in Cambridge, England, in 1903. He received his Ph.D. in 1937 from the University of London. After lecturing at the London School of Economics, he was professor of economics at the University of Liverpool from 1951 until his retirement in 1969. He continued into his eighties to write about the complex nature of time with a command of the English language which is unparalleled among economists.

[M.C.]

FURTHER READINGS

Frowen, Stephen F., ed. *Unknowledge and Choice in Economics: Proceedings of a Conference in Honour of G.L.S. Shackle*. London: Macmillan, 1990.

Shackle, G.L.S. *Time in Economics*. Amsterdam: North-Holland, 1958.

———. *Decision, Order, and Time in Human Affairs*. Cambridge: Cambridge UP, 1961.

———. *Epistemics and Economics. A Critique of Economic Doctrines*. Cambridge: Cambridge UP, 1972.

———. *Time, Expectations and Uncertainty in Economics: Selected Essays of G.L.S. Shackle*. Ed. J.L. Ford. Aldershot: Edward Elgar, 1990.

SHAKESPEARE, WILLIAM (1564–1616)

From his sonnets through his final romances, William Shakespeare has provided the fullest, most memorable address to time of any writer of the Renaissance. He caps and transcends many of the speculations in an age when speculation was abundant. We know that time was an important part of the exciting new dramaturgy of the stage, and that it entered crucially into Shakespeare's presentation of a new scheme of values. But even more importantly, on almost every page, Shakespeare expresses his fervent war against time, testing once again the human resources of fame, children, and love as means of offsetting time's depredations. In Shakespeare's works time itself becomes an enormous antagonist in a worldview that is itself dramatic.

Time became an even more threatening enemy because, as the Renaissance developed and humanism promoted a greater faith in human resources, fame, children, and love became even more precious and precarious embodiments of this faith. Shakespeare's sonnets record this ongoing warfare, and their declarations of war have resonated in memory since. The first seventeen sonnets urge a young man to forego his presumed invulnerability, and make some defense against time by means of marriage and procreation. "When I do count the clock that tells the hour, / And see the brave day sunk in hideous night. . . ." Sonnet 12 proceeds to detail the later defeats that follow upon youth's promise, arriving at the conclusion,

And nothing 'gainst Time's scythe can
    make defense
Save breed to brave him when he takes
    thee hence.

However applicable these sonnets might be to the development of Prince Hal (who himself seems determined to deny his historical identity), they seem mundane in comparison with the more stirring affirmations about the power of poetry and love. Sonnet 60 ("Like as the waves make toward the pebbled shore. . ."), Sonnet 61 ("Against my love shall be as I am now / With Time's injurious hand crush'd and o'erworn. . ."), sonnets 64 and 65 ("When I have seen by Time's fell hand defaced" and "Since brass, nor stone, nor earth, nor boundless sea, / But sad mortality o'ersways their power. . .")—in these and many other sonnets Shakespeare asserts the power of his verse to preserve that which time destroys so relentlessly and remorselessly. And even more memorably, in Sonnet 116, he can bravely affirm that "Love's not Time's fool, though rosy lips and cheeks / Within his bending sickle's compass comes. . . ." All of these faiths and affirmations will live to be tried, affirmed, defeated, and reaffirmed in the course of Shakespeare's remarkable development.

Shakespeare's history plays, particularly the second tetralogy commencing with *Richard II* and culminating in *Henry V*, are not only historical in subject, they are historical in value. Crucial in the formation of this new political ethic is Shakespeare's conception of the reality and power of time. In episode after episode, Richard II is brought to realize that he has wasted time. "Call back yesterday, bid time return, and thou shalt have twelve thousand fightmen," is the bitter and belated recognition that is the cost of his dilatoriness. But more than an argument for punctuality, the addresses to time in the history plays are part of a new scheme of values, dashing Richard's own presumed impunity. If time is a principle of reality, then Richard's journey of discovery is a journey toward a proper understanding of his nature in time:

How sour sweet music is
When time is broke, and no proportion
    kept!
So is it in the music of men's lives.
And here have I the daintiness of ear
To check time broke in a disordered
    string;
But for the concord of my state and time
Had not an ear to hear my true time
    broke.
I wasted time and now doth time waste
    me;
For now hath time made me his
    numb'ring clock.

Richard becomes Bolingbroke's Jack-of-the-clock, the passive tool and instrument of his own accession as Henry IV.

But the great danger to Bolingbroke's yet tenuous hold on legitimacy is the attitude of his own wayward son, fostering the fear that the

Prince Hal might yet prove to be a Richard II. In both Hal and Richard we might see some of the attitudes that Shakespeare sought to correct in his addresses to the young man of the sonnets. In each, the sense of the destructive reality of time as well as the possibility of proper response come together to form a dramatic basis for struggle. Where Richard falters, Hal recovers in time, and in each instance, time itself is an important factor in his conversion. Time then is more than an agent of depredation; it is a major force in the new Renaissance argument, one involving the possibility of humankind to secure some kind of stability and order in a world of dangerous and rapid historical change. In his attention to time, Hal is more than a Renaissance prince, he is the prototype for a new world that is being formed, one where control of time is an essential ingredient to success.

If the history plays reveal the possibility of triumph in the war against time, the tragedies show the defeat of all the affirmations that were unfurled in the sonnets. Not children, not family, not fame, not love, none is finally triumphant or effective. Hamlet avers that there will be no more marriages, and Kent can wonder whence comes the hardness of heart in Lear's daughters; women are frail, and men are demonized with jealousy. In the histories, the garden can be well kept if the gardener is vigilant, but in the tragedies, the fertility of the garden is clotted at the source. The world of moderate possibility that the history plays opened is closed in the tragedies; we cannot really know the world and darkness reigns supreme.

The pessimistic vision of the tragedies is itself altered in Shakespeare's last plays, and here once again time is not only a major subject of address, but itself a major speaker in the regeneration. The last plays all cover large stretches of time: twelve, fourteen, sixteen and twenty years have elapsed since the tragic events, and in this larger encounter time is now a healing force. If the tragedies present the eye of the storm, the last plays take place long after the storm has passed. Here the human family is given the chance to reconstitute itself, but in much reduced terms. The large and confident addresses of the sonnets are no longer heard; instead humankind is gathered in to itself, as an infinite universe is envisioned by Prospero:

> . . .the gorgeous palaces,
> The solemn temples, the great globe itself,
> Yea, all which it inherit, shall dissolve,
> And like this insubstantial pageant faded

> Leave not a rack behind. We are such stuff
> As dreams are made on, and our little life
> Is rounded with a sleep.

After such a vision it would be hard to ever again give full credence to the kind of affirmations heard in Shakespeare's sonnets and sustained in his history plays. If formerly human achievements were dwarfed in relation to eternity, now they are dwarfed in relation to infinity. It would appear that Shakespeare's dramatic vision of humankind's drama, like that of the Renaissance itself, exists on a brief "shoal of Time," after the lapse of the controlling aspect of eternity and before the daunting vision of infinity.

[R.J.Q.]

See also **Renaissance.**

FURTHER READINGS

de Romilly, Jacqueline. *Time in Greek Tragedy*. Ithaca: Cornell UP, 1968.

Poulet, Georges. *Studies in Human Time*. Baltimore: Johns Hopkins P, 1956.

Quinones, Ricardo J. *The Renaissance Discovery of Time*. Cambridge: Harvard UP, 1972.

Sypher, Wylie. *The Ethic of Time: Structures of Experience in Shakespeare*. New York: The Seabury P, 1976.

SHIFT WORK

When employees take turns laboring in the same enterprise over an extended number of hours of the day, each turn is called a shift. The word is also used to describe a job schedule outside the customary span of daylight.

Economic motives for shift work include its quick response to increased demand; its ability to multiply production without further investment in the physical plant; and the fact that, because there are no additional interest payments in using equipment that would otherwise remain idle, unit costs decrease and profits rise. Working to meet deadlines and relying on speed in economic competition also foster overnight activity. The workers and other persons outside their homes after dark create an additional demand for services, including protecting, transporting, feeding, retailing, and providing recreation for them. This attracts more commercial enterprises, and enlarges the size of the work force in those hours. Another spur to shift work is the increase in worldwide interactions through transportation and communication, which call for staffing the participating enterprises in any given time zone over more hours.

Shift work organizations assign relays of workers to tasks, and those on one shift are expected to stay until their replacements appear. However, the higher the rank of the job, the less likely its incumbents will work evenings and nights. Typically, there is an intermittent presence of upper echelon personnel and a substituted presence of those at lower echelons. This staffing arrangement brings on fluctuations in the authority structure and command process. After dark, certain kinds of decisions are postponed, there is greater decentralization of authority, and more reliance is placed on contingency rules to cover situations for which decisions cannot be postponed. When there is a great emergency or circumstances calling for a major decision, the reluctance to waken a powerful sleeper to deliver bad news often results in a serial awakening of executives, traveling up the hierarchy one rank at a time, so that the chief is often the last person to be informed.

Lower echelon personnel are viewed as interchangeable. Inasmuch as the work situation may not remain the same from shift to shift (as in hospitals where the conditions of some patients are unstable), there is increased dependence on information updating through logbooks or meetings at changeover times. There is also diffusion of responsibility when job incumbents are repeatedly substituted. If tasks are left for the next persons to complete, resentment is kindled between shifts, often reducing the amount of communication given during the changeovers.

The main factors influencing the decision of individuals to work at night include economic need, vigor, a willingness to assume more risk after dark, and the seizing of opportunities where competition is lower. Economic need also prompts parents who are both employed to take turns providing child care in the household, usually resulting in one of them working after dark. More males, more younger persons, and more members of minority groups work on shifts than their proportions in the total population. The availability of shift work permits economically disadvantaged persons to hold both a day and a night job, and these "moonlighters" are estimated at 5 percent of the work force in industrialized nations.

The organization's schedule to achieve staffing has potent consequences for the workers and their families. The task of allocating personnel to ensure coverage requires fitting together assignments for individuals who customarily work a fixed number of hours and days a week (for example, in the United States five eight-hour spans). The allocation is complicated by the imperfect divisibility of the week into those sets, because 168 hours does not subdivide evenly into forty-hour shares, and seven days does not subdivide evenly into shares of two days off per person. As a result of this and other staffing constraints, the scheduling puzzle is hard to solve. Consequently, shift workers' schedules are often erratic, with juggled combinations of work and days off, and subject to last-minute changes. Moreover, since relatively few employees want to work steadily after dark, schemes are introduced for many of them to take turns rotating among the shifts. Even those who are on regular evening and night shifts rotate themselves to a daytime schedule on days off, in order to be with their family and friends.

One effect of switching the times of work, recreation, and rest is the disruption of an employee's physiological rhythms, which results in the person suffering from inferior sleep, fatigue, and a lack of alertness. This sluggishness and malaise (similar to what is popularly known as jet-lag syndrome) results in performance deficits. Also, because seniority or job promotion is customarily the basis of moving experienced workers to daytime assignments, a less well-versed group is on duty after dark. For both reasons, night workers commit more mistakes and are more frequently subject to serious accidents.

The schedules also block easy participation in an outside social life. Workers become frustrated through trying to cope with erratic assignments that undermine personal commitments and prevent them from planning even for the near future. They encounter obstacles to easy association with friends who work standard daytime schedules. Members of households are drawn away from their families during the evening or night, thereby diminishing regular chances for interaction. The worker is not available or ready to join in at usual mealtimes, and complaints and arguments can be provoked when that person's sleep is disturbed by lively children playing and by others making noise in the household. Indeed, when the spouse tries to match the shift worker's schedule so that the two may have time together, the biological and social dislocations can frequently affect the spouse as well.

Shift assignments offer job opportunities that may not be available otherwise. They also offer the serenity of commuting against the main direction of traffic during rush hours, a more relaxed and egalitarian work setting after dark because of the absence of higher executives, and more flexibility in shopping or making appointments during the daytime workweek. At the same time, those workers and their families also bear the indirect costs of strain and friction.

[M.M.]

See also **Frontiers in Time and Space.**

FURTHER READING

Hertz, Rosanna, and Joy Charlton. "Making Family Under a Shiftwork Schedule." *Social Problems* 36 (December 1989): 491–507.

Hinrichs, Karl, William Roche, and Carmen Sirianni, eds. *Working Time in Transition: The Political Economy of Working Hours in Industrial Nations*. Philadelphia: Temple UP, 1991.

Melbin, Murray. *Night As Frontier: Colonizing the World after Dark*. New York: Free Press, 1987.

United States Congress, Office of Technology Assessment. *Biological Rhythms: Implications for the Worker*. Washington: (OTA-BA-463), September 1991.

Winston, Gordon. *The Timing of Economic Activities*. New York: Cambridge UP, 1982.

SIMULTANEITY, SUCCESSIVENESS, AND TEMPORAL-ORDER JUDGMENTS

> Time is not measured by a watch, but by moments.
> — Chinese fortune cookie

Most work on simultaneity, successiveness, and temporal-order judgments involves stimuli presented for durations measured in milliseconds. Stimuli are initially processed by low-level sensory mechanisms that have evolved for analyzing dimensions such as spatial location and motion. As such, stimulus-driven (bottom-up) processing of low-level attributes may subserve the discrimination of temporal characteristics of brief events. Temporal information concerning events that occur with longer durations or interstimulus intervals may also involve concept-driven (top-down) memory and cognitive processes.

If a very short interval (that is, an interstimulus interval of less than several milliseconds) separates two or more brief stimuli, under many conditions the stimuli will seem simultaneous. As the interval increases slightly, a person may experience successiveness but be unable to judge correctly which stimulus occurred first. As the interval increases further, a person may be able

to judge correctly the temporal order of the events. The relevant variables and processes underlying these observations are now becoming understood.

SIMULTANEITY AND SUCCESSIVENESS

Different sensory systems transduce different kinds of energy in different ways. The auditory system transduces pressure waves of air molecules by means of mechanical effects on sensory neurons, whereas the visual system transduces electromagnetic energy by means of photochemical reactions in sensory neurons. The latency and variability of the resulting neural signals differ between sensory systems, and as a result thresholds for detecting simultaneity versus successiveness also differ. Two brief auditory stimuli will sound successive if the interstimulus interval is greater than three to four milliseconds, but two brief visual stimuli will appear successive only if the interstimulus interval is greater than five to twenty milliseconds.

These values are thresholds for the transition from simultaneity to successiveness under ideal conditions; many variables may increase the successiveness threshold. If several stimuli occur within a short interval, they may be experienced as simultaneous under some conditions, but the upper limit for the experience of simultaneity is never more than about 100–150 milliseconds. Early theorists attempted to explain evidence concerning this upper limit by proposing that processing occurs in temporally discrete "psychological moments" of about 100 milliseconds, but many authors now explain that evidence in terms of persistence, or enduring neural activity in sensory systems following the offset of stimulation. Whether two stimuli appear simultaneous or successive also depends on attention. If a person attends to a particular spatial location, a visual stimulus occurring there will seem to occur up to fifty milliseconds earlier than a visual stimulus occurring in an unattended location. Another important factor is distance from the observer. The speed of light is faster than that of sound, yet the transduction into neural signals is slower for vision than for audition. As a result, the distance from a source to an observer at which visual and auditory stimuli seem simultaneous (the "horizon of simultaneity") is about ten meters.

If several identical stimuli occur in rapid succession in the same spatial location, observers may experience them as a single, prolonged stimulus that is "flickering" (if the stimuli are visual) or "crackling" or "wavering" (if they are auditory). Under these conditions, well-known persistence effects prolong each sensation so that it partially overlaps with the sensation of the next stimulus.

Temporal Order

Although a person may experience successiveness of two or more stimuli, he or she may be unable to judge correctly which occurred first if the interval separating them is short. Thus, successiveness discrimination is necessary, but not sufficient, for order discrimination. Theorists agree that sensory systems vary considerably in the threshold of successiveness; however, they disagree concerning the threshold for temporal-order discrimination. Some argue that the threshold does not depend on stimulus modality and that subjects can discriminate temporal order only if the interstimulus interval is at least twenty milliseconds. Others suggest that there is no fixed threshold and that subjects can sometimes correctly discriminate temporal order at much shorter interstimulus intervals (for example, several milliseconds).

If two visual stimuli occur in rapid succession at different spatial locations, an observer may experience apparent motion of a single object, a phenomenon studied for centuries under many different conditions. Stimulus parameters such as spatial or temporal separation influence the phenomenon. Depending on these parameters, it may be seen only at intervals of a few milliseconds, or it may be seen at intervals ranging from several milliseconds to several hundred milliseconds. If two visual stimuli occur such that an observer perceives apparent motion, the direction of the apparent motion may serve as a cue for temporal order. However, apparent motion is not necessary for temporal-order discrimination of closely adjacent stimuli, which may be possible at intervals as short as a few milliseconds.

If two differently colored lights appear in rapid succession at different locations, it may appear that a single stimulus has moved from the first location to the second and has changed color abruptly in mid-trajectory. This phenomenon, the color phi effect, seems paradoxical if one assumes that the neural representation of the color of the apparently moving stimulus must change in an appropriate way before the second stimulus has occurred. The apparent paradox vanishes if one assumes that stimulus processing is distributed temporally as well as spatially. Various brain systems analyze attributes such as location, color, and motion at different

rates, and the analyses are blended into a representation of a single perceptual event. (Recently, some researchers have suggested that global synchronous brain oscillations, or neural firing patterns, that occur at 40–60 hz (hertz) intervals, or about once every twenty milliseconds, may be the neural basis of this blending process.) Thus, the color information may have been analyzed only after the motion information, and no paradox occurred. In short, color phi and other phenomena show that when stimulus durations are brief, low-level sensory mechanisms may underlie temporal-order discrimination.

Although modality-specific areas of the brain subserve temporal-order discrimination of brief events, memory for temporal order of longer events seems to require the normal functioning of a dorsolateral area of the prefrontal cortex. Experiments on recency judgment present a series of items and then test subjects by presenting two items and asking them to decide which event occurred more recently in the series. Patients with prefrontal-cortex damage show impaired memory on this temporal-order judgment task, but the deficit is not a global memory deficit, because usually the patients can correctly recognize the events. Damage to the left hemisphere prefrontal cortex impairs temporal-order memory for verbal items (such as words), but not for visual or other nonlinguistic items (such as pictures), whereas damage to the right hemisphere prefrontal cortex impairs temporal-order memory for both kinds of items. Thus, information about the temporal order of external events apparently involves the right prefrontal cortex more critically than the left. However, other evidence reveals that subject-initiated ordering of events more heavily involves the left prefrontal cortex.

General Conclusions

No fixed interval, common to all sensory modalities, signifies the transition threshold from simultaneity to successiveness. Experiences of brief events depend on stimulus parameters such as sensory modality, spatial separation, and intensity, along with more cognitive factors such as attention. There may be no fixed interval common to all sensory modalities that signifies the transition threshold from successiveness to order. Some temporal phenomena reflect a pervasive process by which different low-level sensory analyses are blended to form a single perceptual event. Sensory processing areas of the brain subserve temporal experiences and judgments concerning brief events and intervals, and a specialized area in the prefrontal cortex subserves memory for temporal order.

[R.A.B. and R.P.]

See also **Cognition; Film; Memory for Time; Psychology of Time; Time Perception.**

FURTHER READINGS

Dennett, Daniel, and Marcel Kinsbourne. "Time and the Observer: The Where and When of Consciousness in the Brain." *Behavioral and Brain Sciences* 15 (1992): 183–247.

Milner, B., M.P. McAndrews, and G. Leonard. "Frontal Lobes and Memory for the Temporal Order of Recent Events." *Cold Spring Harbor Symposia on Quantitative Biology* 55 (1990): 987–994.

Patterson, Robert E. "Perceptual Moment Models Revisited." *Cognitive Models of Psychological Time*. Ed. Richard A. Block. Hillsdale: Erlbaum, 1990. 85–100.

Pöppel, Ernst. *Mindworks: Time and Conscious Experience*. Trans. T. Artin. Boston: Harcourt Brace, 1988.

SLEEP-AWAKE CYCLES

Alternating periods of sleep and wakefulness occur every twenty-four hours in adult humans living under normal light-dark conditions, the sleep-awake ratio being approximately 1:2. Both the periodicity and the manner in which these cycles are synchronized with geophysical cycles undergo ontogenetic and phylogenetic changes. Human newborns follow sleep-awake cycles of approximately 3.5 to 4.5 hours which entail a sleep-awake ratio of approximately 1:1; the twenty-four-hour cycle emerges during the first year of life. The consolidation process comprises the diminution in number and the shortening of length of sleep episodes during the day, and their increased number and prolongation during the night. The waking episodes show opposite trends. Sleep-awake cycles, or the more primitive rest-activity cycles found in less advanced animals, can be found throughout the animal kingdom, but the durations of bouts of sleep and wakefulness, their periodicity, and the degree and type of synchronization with the light-dark cycle, vary from species to species. The sleep-awake ratio is generally dependent upon the size of the animal, that is, large animals have a lower ratio than small ones.

Until the mid-twentieth century it was believed that the sleep-awake cycle is a behavior that simply arises in response to the environment. In recent years, however, much research has shown that the cycle is generated within the organism. It is called a circadian cycle (< Latin *circa*, about + *dies*, day, that is, cycles of about one day). Humans isolated from all cues from the environment show persistent sleep-awake cycles for many months. However, in these circumstances the circadian rhythm "free runs" with a periodicity longer than twenty-four hours, usually within the range of twenty-five to twenty-nine hours. This results in systematic delays in bedtimes and awakening times in relation to the geophysical time. Humans isolated in such "time-free" environments are reported to show dramatic alterations in time perception. When estimating the length of time in isolation, they almost invariably err by considerably underestimating the duration in question. This is because they are unaware of the change in the length of their sleep-awake cycle, and continue to rely on their normal sleep behavior for time estimation. Thus, they estimate every bedtime as "about midnight" and every awakening as "about seven o'clock," which produces a large accumulated misjudgment.

Other species isolated from time cues follow cycles which deviate from twenty-four hours. Light-dark cycles are shown to be the most important agent for synchronizing the sleep-awake cycle to the environment. Light is perceived by the retina, which sends neural signals by a special neural tract (different from the optic tract) to the brain. Although there is no clear information concerning the site of the neural mechanism that generates the endogenous sleep-awake cycle, it is considered to be in the vicinity of the suprachiasmatic nucleus of the hypothalamus. Animal studies have revealed that lesions in this area of the brain completely abolish the circadian rest-activity cycle.

[P.L.]

See also **Chronobiology.**

SOCIAL GERONTOLOGY

Social gerontology is the study of social behavior and social issues in old age. Social gerontologists work in psychology, sociology, biology, anthropology, history, and economics, among other fields. They may consider the quantity, quality, and importance of social activity in old age, and often focus on these in relation to the well-being and health of older adults.

Time is a theme throughout social gerontology, and is nowhere more apparent than in the methods of study. When we compare people of different ages, we must determine whether observed differences are due to intra-individual developmental changes with age, or to the people having been reared in different times with different standards of conduct or opportunities for learning. Research designs that measure the same people on multiple occasions across their lives are called longitudinal designs. Age differences that appear in longitudinal studies might be due to aging or development, but might also be due to differences in the social or educational climate at the times of measurement. Research designs that compare people of different chronological ages are called cross-sectional designs. Age differences that appear in cross-sectional studies can be due to aging or development, or to different social or educational conditions during the upbringing of the individuals. So, neither of these designs can conclusively separate developmental change from the effect of an era, but more complicated designs are available to do so. In addition to studying age differences and change processes, social gerontologists consider the similarities among age groups and generations, and the stability of needs and dispositions over time.

TIME IS BASIC TO SOCIAL GERONTOLOGY

Aging, the interaction of time and biology, results in pervasive, recognizable differences between younger and older organisms. Age is measured not just chronologically, but biologically, socially, psychologically, and subjectively. These alternative indices of age concern the amount of change a person has undergone, rather than simply the amount of time since their birth. Such indices are often better predictors of the way a person will function than is chronological age.

The physical differences between young and old constitute some of the core issues of interest to social gerontologists. For instance, the surface features of oldness (grey hair, wrinkled skin) suggest to perceivers a homogeneity in the aged population that is not really present. In fact, older adults are the most heterogeneous of age groups. The misperception of homogeneity results in stereotyping, and potentially in the unfair treatment of older adults—phenomena known as "*ageism*." Attitudes and stereotypes concerning older adults range from negative to positive, with people often believing the aged to be kind and wise (a positive stereotype) but cognitively incompetent (a negative stereotype).

Experience comes with the passage of time, and hence with age. In some instances, older adults' past experience can be a cause for greater respect and better treatment, as when it is la-

beled wisdom. In other instances, elders are perceived as obsolete, because their experiences are with forms and contexts that are no longer viable.

Another aspect of time relevant to aging, leading to differences in the social behavior of old and young, is the *passage of time*. This can be invoked to explain age differences that are not due to aging or experience. For example, if an older adult spends more time talking about the past than does a younger adult, we should not hastily attribute this to poor memory for recent events, or to the possibility that older adults are "stuck in the past." The passage of time, greater in the old person's case, might be responsible. Because the older adult's past is as much as three times as long as the younger adult's, a randomly selected story from the older adult's life is more likely to be drawn from the distant past than is one from the younger adult's life.

Rates of behavior decrease with age in all spheres of physical and mental activity, including speech. Because speech is central to human communication, its slowing has implications for the social lives of older adults. When older adults speak slowly, they may be perceived by others as suffering from pervasive age-related cognitive deficiencies. Word-finding difficulty that would go unnoticed in a younger person becomes cause for concern in an older one. This slowing of speech production can activate ageist stereotypes, eliciting "accommodative" strategies from conversational partners. That is, people speaking to older adults may slow and simplify their speech, or speak loudly and use babying intonations. This adjusted communicative style is called over-accommodation, because it goes beyond what is necessary, compensating for imagined rather than actual cognitive shortcomings. The basis of over-accommodation is the incorrect belief that all mind and body systems decline at the same rate, another instance of time's relevance to social gerontology.

SOCIAL TIES IN OLD AGE

Older adults socialize less and report fewer confidants than do younger people. Reductions in rates of social activity were once explained by disengagement theory advanced by Elaine Cumming and William E. Henry in *Growing Old: The Process of Disengagement* (1961). Until then, sociologists attributed older adults' lower rates of social activity to society's unkind rejection of the old. Cumming and Henry's interviews with older adults suggested an alternative view, namely that older adults willingly participated in the separation of themselves and society, and that the effects of the separation were mutually beneficial. They believed that nearness to the time of their death encouraged older adults to weaken their ties to others, so that the transition from life to death would be gradual and easy rather than sudden and painful.

Disengagement theory has not remained popular, however. Too many studies have found that among older adults, high rates of social activity are correlated with high rates of well-being. Activity theory, based on these findings, claims that social relations remain vital to well-being across the life span and into old age. Contrary to stereotypes of them as indolent television-watchers, many older adults are active, involved community members. After retiring from the paid workforce and its built-in opportunities for social contact, older adults may continue their participation in the local or global community by socializing, volunteering, going back to school, or traveling.

AGING AND THE FAMILY
Although old age has been called the "roleless role," older adults have meaningful roles to play in families and society. One of the most celebrated is grandparenthood. Grandparents are largely positive about their role, and may serve various functions such as family historian, playmate, or substitute parent.

Women tend to outlive men and, correspondingly, outnumber men in old age. For married women, the average length of widowhood is twelve to fifteen years. This constitutes a period nearly as long as childhood, or child-rearing, yet it is one for which few cultures or individuals prepare. Men's shorter life expectancy only partially determines this phenomenon; the tendency for women to marry men older than themselves exaggerates it. Widowhood is difficult for men and women alike, and the typical response is a year or more of mourning for the lost spouse. Widowers are more likely than widows to eventually remarry, partly because of the greater availability of female partners, but also because fewer widows wish to remarry.

Family members, usually female, provide most of the care and assistance received by older adults. The study of family members who care for ailing older adults has uncovered both joys and stresses associated with the caregiving role. The time and difficulty of caring for an ailing family member can lead to distress for the caregivers and the care recipients alike, and social

scientists have been seeking solutions to caregiving difficulties in recent years.

Within Western society and across the world, social gerontologists are trying to understand the social strengths and social problems of older adults in various cultures and life circumstances. In this pursuit, they assist in the exchange of knowledge and care between young people and the elderly.

[C.L.C.]

See also **Aging Populations; Gender Differences in Aging; Loneliness and Aging.**

FURTHER READINGS
Binstock, R.H., and L.K. George. *Handbook of Aging and the Social Sciences.* San Diego: Academic P, 1990.

Perlmutter, M., and E. Hall. *Adult Development and Aging.* New York: Wiley, 1992.

Giles, H., N. Coupland, and J.M. Weimann. *Communication, Health, and the Elderly.* Manchester: Manchester UP, 1990.

SOCIAL PSYCHOLOGY

Social psychology is a discipline that deals with phenomena at each of several system levels—from relatively micro features of individuals as social creatures, through phenomena at interpersonal and small group levels, to phenomena at larger system levels such as organizations, communities, and so on. There are temporal issues involved in the phenomena at all of these levels. Furthermore, these levels differ not only in size and scope of the social unit being studied (for example, individual, group, organization), but also in the scope of the activities and processes being considered (from specific steps or activities, to major tasks, to large and complex projects), and in the temporal scope involved (social psychological phenomena may involve time periods as short as seconds, as long as years or even generations). At all of these levels, temporal issues enter into social psychological phenomena in both of two functional capacities: On the one hand, temporal features of the embedding context within which behavior takes place can affect various social psychological processes. On the other hand, various social psychological factors can affect the temporal patterning of behavior. Both of these are of concern for a social psychological perspective that takes account of temporal issues.

There follows a list of ten temporal topics that are important for a social psychology that intends to incorporate a temporal perspective. Each of these topics embeds a number of crucial research questions. Together, these topics span the different system levels that social psychology encompasses and deal with both the context and the temporal patterning of behavior. But the topics cannot be neatly classified into those system levels and functional capacities, and some of the topics are covered from other perspectives under other headings. Some of those temporal topics have received considerable systematic research; others have not as yet been given the attention their importance warrants. Systematic study of all of them would provide a substantial basis for the study of time as a subdiscipline of social psychology.

After discussion of these ten topics, there are some concluding comments about the role of temporal issues in the conceptual and methodological underpinnings of social psychology as a discipline.

1. TIME AND THE SELF

One major topic for a time-centered social psychology is the construction and development of the self-concept. Most prior work on the self assumes a continuing and well-developed self schema, persistent over time and circumstances, and independent of the research process. Recent work done from a temporal perspective questions these assumptions. That work proposes that a self-conception elicited from a given respondent at a given time is affected by at least three temporal factors. First, it is constructed from remembrances (past) and anticipations (future) from cognitive stores. Second, the elicited picture of self is influenced by the time orientation (past, present, future) that is salient for the respondent at the time of elicitation. Third, the self-conception depends on the respondent's temporal location with regard to life stages (such as a twenty-first birthday) and event cycles (such as graduation or a new job) operating at the time the self-conception is given.

On a related topic, there has been considerable study of temporal orientations that characterize individual cognitive, affective, and behavioral patterns. That work has given particular attention to future orientation, which is regarded as a central feature of certain motivational forces (such as high need achievement) and certain personality patterns (such as the Type A syndrome). Moreover, there is evidence that optimism about the future—even unrealistic optimism—may be beneficial to individual mental health. Such temporal orientations are strongly influenced by cultural and subcultural values. It is not yet clear, however, whether such tempo-

ral orientations reflect continuing, transitutional, individual predispositions (that is, "traits"), rather than situation-contingent states, and to what extent such orientations are influenced by the person's location in life cycles and event cycles.

2. THE TEMPORAL SIDE OF JUDGMENT PROCESSES

Another important temporal topic has to do with temporal effects on a range of judgment processes. Some of these have received considerable research attention. For example, people tend to attribute the causes for one's own actions more to situational factors, and to attribute the causes of others' actions more to traits or dispositional factors. This tendency diminishes as the time between the event and the judgment of that event increases.

There is a growing body of work regarding effects of passage of time on decisions. Most of it shows that payoffs are discounted (that is, their subjective value is diminished) and instrumentalities are attenuated (that is, people are less confident about the effectiveness of proposed actions) as the time between judgments and the events being judged increases. These effects are monotonic but nonlinear over time. There is also research suggesting a "risky drift"—that is, that decisions become riskier as cognitive processing time increases.

There is a very large body of work on effects of a number of stimulus parameters and judgment conditions on judgments of the passage of time. One major finding in this domain is that judgments made retrospectively (that is, when the respondent does not know in advance that a time judgment is to be elicited) differ, often dramatically, from judgments made prospectively (that is, when the respondent is aware, in advance, that estimates of time interval are to be elicited). Retrospective judgments, for example, tend to be overestimates of clock time to the extent that the interval was densely filled with complex cognitive material; whereas prospective judgments tend to be underestimates of clock time under those same conditions. Recent studies by a number of researchers provide elegant theoretical models for interpretation of such time judgment data from a rich variety of studies.

3. THE TEMPORAL SIDE OF MOOD, EMOTION, AND MOTIVATION

Study of temporal effects on mood and emotion is just beginning. There is some evidence that variations in mood influence the experience of time, and also influence the temporal patterning of interaction. There is growing evidence of a strong relation between dysfunction of temporal orientation and depression. Both achievement motivation and Type A personality have important temporal components. The Type A personality syndrome involves impulsivity, impatience, and a high pace of activities. Achievement motivation involves a future orientation and temporal persistence.

4. PLANNING AND SCHEDULING AS TEMPORAL ALLOCATION

There has been limited but very interesting work on macro-level planning. Some studies have suggested that future orientation is a prerequisite for planning, and that the pattern of development of a future orientation is a function of gender, social class, education level, and socialization.

Regarding actual time allocations, there is a considerable body of research using time diaries, dealing with actual (self-reported) time allocations, often over extensive periods of time. In addition to the sampling problems that are always embedded in such evidence, time diary evidence has two major limitations. First, diary entries are usually coded into categories representing concrete activities—often categories predetermined by the investigator. These may only reflect epiphenomena, rather than deeper and psychologically more meaningful (though more abstract) categories of behavior. Second, time diary studies seldom include direct observational evidence that could serve as a check on the accuracy of self-reported time use. Nevertheless, the extensive time diary work is a major contribution to our knowledge about how people distribute time in day-to-day activities, and how those time distributions may differ across cultures, generations, and social standings.

One major feature of all planning efforts is the requirement that specific sets of activities by specific people be scheduled into specific periods of time. Such planning must take account of some rather complicated features of the "match" or "fit" between times and activities. The uniformity of our Newtonian-based clock and calendar times notwithstanding, time is experienced in social behavior as epochal rather than homogeneous; that is, all time periods are not experienced as equivalent and interchangeable for all activities. For one thing, task activities tend to confront us in "natural" bundles. No set of task activities is totally "modular"; it cannot be aggregated or disaggregated without limit. On the one hand, there is a limit on the extent to which a given bundle of activities can be broken down into smaller units to be carried out in small and distributed time units (for example, ordinarily people do not launder one garment at a time). On the other hand, there is a limit on the extent to which a given kind of activity can be "saved up" and done all in one concentrated block of time (for example, a worker cannot save up a whole week's commuting to do all in one long agonizing afternoon).

Furthermore, some time periods are more versatile than others—they can accommodate a wider range of types of activities. For example, for many people, early morning hours are not very versatile; and in some communities, the range of activities that one can do on Sunday mornings is greatly limited. Moreover, some bundles of activities are inflexible with respect to when they can be done. (For example, in many communities, one cannot buy groceries in the middle of the night.) At the same time, some bundles of activities are elastic with respect to the length of time it takes to do them. (It has been said that work expands, and contracts, to fit the time available for it.) Thus, time-activity matches must be made on a particularistic basis, and some of those particularities vary among individuals and among social contexts. This domain has seen only very limited social psychological research.

5. TIME-SHARING: DOING MORE THAN ONE THING AT A TIME

Although there is a cultural prescription that "you can't do more than one thing at a time (and do it well)," people try to violate that prescription all the time. They deliberately fill relatively "empty" intervals—waiting for a bus, riding a bus, waiting for an appointment time—by carrying out a second task (for example, reading a book, making lists). At the level of individual task performance, there has been extensive human engineering research on time sharing for multiple tasks, and there has been some cognitive science work on parallel processing. At a more macro level, and with regard to more social psychological processes, however, there has been only limited systematic research to date.

How well humans can do more than one activity in the same block of time—for example, a business golf match, a business lunch, reading on a trip—depends on the relation of the activities to one another and to the environmental conditions under which they are being carried out. Doing multiple activities simultaneously can work well if: (a) the activities do not use the same input and output modalities; (b) the activities have interspersible temporal patterns (that is, at least one of them does not require continuous action or monitoring); and (c) each task is helped (or at least not hindered) by the same ambient conditions.

6. SYNCHRONIZATION AND COORDINATED ACTION (ENTRAINMENT)

Research on the cyclical aspects of human physiological processes (for example, on circadian rhythms) has led to considerable work on the temporal aspects of individual behavioral processes as well. This in turn has led in recent years to some research attention to the many rhythmic or cyclical patterns in social psychological processes.

Many aspects of individual social behavior are temporally patterned—that is, rhythmic or cyclical. Often, those cycles are consistent or regular for any one individual over time, but show substantial and stable individual differences (in cycle length, phase, and magnitude). Under some conditions, such cyclical patterns become mutually entrained (that is, synchronized with regard to phase and periodicity of the cycle) for interacting partners. There is evidence that interactions are more pleasant when there is smooth entrainment (that is, synchronized cycles) between partners. But there is also evidence that high predictability of behavior of the other—both as to time and as to content—can be associated with dissolution of relationships (as in marital disruptions). This suggests that a combination of synchrony in timing but differentiation in content is the most pleasant and effective pattern. It also suggests that relationships may work best when there is loose coupling between interacting partners (that is, when the synchronization between interacting partners is neither too predictable nor too chaotic).

7. DEADLINES AND OTHER TIMEMARKS (EXTERNAL ENTRAINMENT)

There is a large and relatively unexplored set of questions involving how people use deadlines and other "timemarks" (analogous to landmarks) to regulate work and to help structure their behavioral fields. One issue is whether deadlines function in the same way as does the setting of specific quantitative goals. Another is whether self-imposed deadlines function in the same way, sociopsychologically, as do externally imposed deadlines.

A closely related set of issues has to do with how deadlines alter the flow of work in groups and under what conditions the presence of time deadlines can entrain the timing of interaction and task performance of groups. Empirical research suggests that project deadlines pace group work in nonlinear patterns. The time remaining before the deadline, rather than the amount of work already done, defines successive "phases" of group work activity on a given task. Deadlines on early periods of work on a given type of task can entrain both the task performance rate and the pattern of interaction for later work periods on the same task. Those entrainment patterns depend on the nature of the task, and on other activities or conditions affecting the group during that same period of time. Some evidence suggests that such entrainment patterns may persist for extended periods of time (several days); but other findings suggest that a major change in task type or working conditions can "disentrain" those patterns.

8. TEMPORAL EFFECTS OF COMPLEX TECHNOLOGY

An intriguing new area of study involving temporal issues at the sociopsychological level has to do with the effects of complex technology on work groups. Research in this domain, mostly dealing with computers and related electronic technology, raises a number of interesting sociopsychological questions, including a number of temporal issues. There is a growing body of research evidence on these questions.

Electronic media have pervasive temporal effects. Computer systems can be space and time bridging systems; they make it possible for members of work groups to "meet," or at least to communicate, even if the group's members are not all in the same place, and even if they are not all available at precisely the same time intervals. At the same time, these media alter the timing of components of the communication process (for example, composition, editing, transmission, and reception times); they modify transmission and feedback lags; and they make the flow of information in interaction more turbulent.

Furthermore, communication that is mediated via electronic systems is greatly constrained as to its modalities (compared to face-to-face communication). Ordinarily, such systems transmit information only in text and graphics forms; nonverbal and paraverbal cues carried in ordinary face-to-face communication are lost. Thus, much of the social and contextual information by which people interpret communication is lost, as are many of the cues by which groups regulate the flow of their communications. Use of computers therefore alters the richness of the information that can flow, and thereby makes achieving a consensus harder and slower for work groups. They generally increase the time needed by a group to complete tasks requiring consensus.

Hence, the temporal flow of interaction for computer mediated groups is likely to be far more chaotic than is usually the case in face-to-face meetings. The extent of such disruption, and its consequences for the group and its task productivity, depend on a number of features of the group (for example, its own history, and its experience with the medium and with the task), and of the task and working conditions.

In addition to research on temporal consequences of computers, there is some work on temporal patterning consequences of the introduction of other kinds of very complex high-tech systems, such as those in medicine, nuclear physics, and systems engineering. This area of study needs much more attention than it has received.

9. STAGES OF GROUP DEVELOPMENT

One time-related issue that has long been of interest to social psychologists is the idea that there might be a more-or-less fixed sequence of stages in the development of a group. Most attention in the past has been given to a four- or five-stage developmental pattern assumed to characterize the developmental sequence of a wide range of groups. The four stages in the early formulations of that theory were paraphrased as: "forming, storming, norming, and performing"; a fifth stage, "adjourning," has been added more recently. A number of researchers have questioned the generality of such a fixed sequence of stages, arguing that no one pattern of group development fits all or even most groups, but rather that such regularities are contingent on such factors as member attributes, aspects of group composition and structure, and features of the goals, tasks, technology, and context. Empirical evidence has been mustered in support of both views, but the latter (contingency) position seems to have the stronger support. Some of the factors on which patterns of group development depend include changes in membership, differences in socialization practices by which individuals become group members, dif-

ferences in task type and difficulty, differences arising in the group's own history, and differences in the degree to which the group's environment is variable and uncertain versus stable and predictable. Many questions remain unanswered here.

The end points of the group development life cycle—the issues of birth and death, so to speak—represent distinct but related topics of study. There has been relatively little systematic inquiry into the conditions underlying group formation and dissolution. Here too, many interesting questions remain unaddressed.

10. PHASES OF GROUP TASK PERFORMANCE

Closely related to the issue of stages of group development discussed above is the question of whether there are regularities in the patterns of behavior by which groups carry out their tasks—regularities that transcend specific groups, tasks, and situations. The central question here is: what regularities are there (that is, modes or phases) in the paths by which groups perform tasks (solve problems, make decisions), and to what degree are those regularities contingent on the group's composition, its task(s), and its context?

The classic work on this problem postulated regularities in the form of a fixed sequence of problem-solving phases. Those phases involve a shift in the relative attention given—in successive periods of group work—to orientation and information exchange, to evaluation of choices related to that information, and to decisions or final action on the group's task. In that view, the task (or instrumental) activities are punctuated intermittently with personal and interpersonal (that is, socioemotional or expressive) activities that are necessary for continued group effectiveness but that are irrelevant to the specific task at hand.

Empirical evidence on this issue is highly mixed. More recent theorists have postulated a contingency view; that is, that groups generate different alternative paths regarding phases or modes of both task activities and group relations, and that those phases are a function of features of group composition and the group's own history, its task, and the conditions under which the group is operating. Some researchers also have postulated (and found evidence for) the idea that groups exhibit much unorganized (chaotic) behavior that fits no phase sequence at all. As with the related question of stages of group development, many questions about patterns of group task performance over time remain unanswered.

CONCLUDING COMMENTS: TEMPORAL ISSUES IN THE INTELLECTUAL UNDERPINNINGS OF THE FIELD

In addition to the many interesting temporal features of the substantive phenomena of social psychology that have been discussed, temporal issues are also important in the conceptual and methodological underpinnings of this field. There are many temporal assumptions and temporal issues deeply embedded within the dominant conceptual paradigm of the culture within which social psychology takes place, and especially within its dominant "theory of method" (logical positivism). The idea of equilibrium is broadly and deeply entrenched in the concepts of social psychology (as it is in the concepts of many related behavioral and social science fields). This leads to a strong preference on the part of theorists and researchers for dealing with social units as if they were stable rather than continually changing and dynamic systems. In the currently dominant methodological paradigm, there are crucial temporal assumptions regarding the relation of temporal order and causal order, the cause-effect interval as a specification of causal process time, choices among alternative research strategies (for example, field studies, laboratory experiments, sample surveys), and choices among study designs to carry out those strategies (for example, interrupted time series versus static comparisons versus longitudinal and cohort designs). Furthermore, there are a number of strong temporal assumptions built into the "measurement theories" underlying the construction of measurement operations as used in social psychology.

Many of these temporal issues often go unnoticed. Nevertheless, all of them influence how effectively researchers can deal with potential threats to the validity of the empirical evidence obtained in their studies. Other conceptual paradigms (for example, constructionist, contextualist, deconstructionist, and feminist perspectives), which have been proposed as alternatives to the currently dominant logical positivism paradigm, raise somewhat different but equally crucial temporal issues. Thus, the conceptual and methodological underpinnings of social psychology, as well as many of its substantive phenomena, need extensive attention to temporal matters.

[J.E.M.]

See also **Cognition; Memory for Time; Prospective and Retrospective Time; Psychology of Time; Temporal Judgment (Methods); Time Perception; Time Perspective and Its Measurement.**

FURTHER READINGS

Friedman, W.J. *About Time: Inventing the Fourth Dimension.* Cambridge: MIT P, 1990.

Gergen, K., and M. Gergen, eds. *Historical Social Psychology.* Hillsdale: Erlbaum, 1984.

Jaffe, J., and S. Feldstein. *Rhythms of Dialogue.* New York: Academic P, 1970.

Kelly, J.R., and J.E. McGrath. *On Time and Method.* Newbury Park: Sage, 1988.

McGrath, J.E., ed. *The Social Psychology of Time: New Perspectives.* Newbury Park: Sage, 1988.

McGrath, J.E., and J.R. Kelly. *Time and Human Interaction: Toward a Social Psychology of Time.* New York: Guilford Press, 1986.

Melbin, M. *Night as Frontier: Colonizing the World After Dark.* New York: Free P, 1987.

Michon, J.A., V. Pouthas, and J.L. Jackson, eds. *Guyau and the Idea of Time.* Amsterdam: North-Holland, 1988.

Nuttin, J.R. *Future Time Perspective and Motivation: Theory and Research Method.* Hillsdale: Erlbaum, 1985.

Rappaport, H. *Marking Time: How Our Personalities, Our Problems, and Their Treatment Are Shaped by Our Anxiety About Time.* New York: Simon and Schuster, 1990.

Robinson, J.P. *How Americans Use Time: A Social-Psychological Analysis of Everyday Behavior.* New York: Praeger, 1977.

Voce, F.A., ed. *Making Time: Ethnographies of High-Technology Organizations.* Philadelphia: Temple UP, 1988.

Young, M., and T. Schuller, eds. *The Rhythms of Society.* London: Routledge, 1988.

Zerubavel, E. *Hidden Rhythms: Schedules and Calendars in Social Life.* Berkeley: U of California P, 1981.

SOCIAL THEORY

The social sciences are intimately tied to modernity and post-Enlightenment culture and thought: to the development of *objective science*, the *control over nature*, and to the *rational organization* of every sphere of life. Not surprisingly, analyses of social time emphasize the organization of Western life to the objective, metronomic beat of the clock, the control over time, and the standardization of time across the globe. Time theories, in other words, parallel the social sciences' concern with objectivity, rationality, and the scientific study of Western, industrial societies. Even where the focus is on qualitative experience, the objective time of the clock permeates analyses: in anthropological studies "non-Western" time is defined against the back drop of clock time and contrasts are established between linear and cyclical time as characteristics of Western and non-Western societies, respectively. Historians have taken a similar approach, identifying earlier periods as, for example, oriented toward tasks rather than organized by the clock or as living in sacred rather than profane time.

The dominance of clock time overshadows alternative visions. Time-generating practices (see **Feminist Perspectives**) as well as contemporary processes of simultaneous global action and instantaneous communication, for example, tend to be subsumed under the classical approaches to social time: Karl Marx's theory of the commodification of time and its necessary link with control and power or Emile Durkheim's establishment of the social nature of time and its association with social order. Irrespective of context, therefore, we find time to be theorized as a social resource that is used either as an abstract exchange value or a device that helps us to order, synchronize, and regulate social life. In both these approaches time is assumed to be a parameter within which social life is conducted; a quantity to be measured, allocated, sold, and controlled; a finite, nonrenewable resource to be consumed; and a standardized measure to be imposed on the processes of the natural environment and cultural life. The clock is the dominant metaphor in such social theories of time. More recently, the discrepancy between the time of the clock and some contemporary aspects of time has been elaborated. This has been achieved through a shift in emphasis from the mere use and discussion of time to an explicit focus on its multiple expressions. The implications of these findings, however, have not yet affected the social sciences at the level of theory where assumptions based on clock time still hold sway. The problem can be made explicit by an elucidation of clock time.

The clock presents time visually as distance traveled in space, as a spatial measure of the length of time. Clock time is constituted on the basis of homogeneous, invariable, context-independent, infinitely divisible but finite units which ensure that the hour between 3:00 and 4:00 is the same regardless of whether it refers to the afternoon or the night, in Greenland or Greece, during summer or winter, in a nursery

school or the board room of a multinational company. It is tied to an expression by number. The meaning of time, in contrast, is dependent on its relation to real environmental changes: night and day, summer and winter, waxing and waning moons. Moreover, the invariant measure is an abstraction that bears no relation to the repetitive processes with variation on which it is based; nor does it encompass the living time of regeneration where birth and growth triumph over the finite resource and death. In its artifactual form time is intimately linked to industrial time. As a quantity of "empty time" and as measured duration, time can be freely exchangeable with all other times. It allows for standardization, global synchronization, and transformation into money. As abstract exchange value, it can be bought and sold as a commodity on the labor market. While the characteristics of abstraction, invariability, divisibility, sequence, and duration are central to theories of industrial societies, there are other aspects of time that cannot be reduced to those of the clock.

Feminists have shown that the preoccupation with clock time and its consumption neglects time giving and the generation of time. Contemporary social theorists such as Elias and Giddens have introduced further aspects of time. Elias stresses the synthesizing role of clock time on one hand and the importance of reflexivity as a nonlinear, nonsequential, and noncausal process on the other. Giddens emphasizes the importance of the severance of time and space through innovations in transport, print, and information technology. His *Theory of Structuration* unites what has been separate in traditional social theories—structure and change, repetition and transformation, large-scale historical changes and daily routines—and it demonstrates that all are fundamentally dependent on time. These are essential contemporary advances in social theory but they do not yet go far enough. They are not yet sufficient to conceptualize the temporal changes heralded by innovations in technology, transnational economics and politics, and contemporary environmental problems.

Developments in information technology and satellite television, for example, have brought the temporalities of simultaneity and instantaneity to center stage. Time as motion and as distance traveled in space has been reduced to nothingness, the very meaning of instantaneity. Moreover, feedback loops and amplification make the original condition irrelevant and future ones unpredictable. This means that networks and cybernetic relations have to be superimposed on the time principles of the clock. To take these changes in temporal principles seriously is important since they provide a theoretical bridge to ecological thinking and to the pressing environmental problems that cannot be tackled with the conceptual tools of a previous century. Equally important are the changes in time spans associated with nuclear power and computers respectively. Not only have socially relevant time-spans increased and decreased by a factor of $10^{\pm 6}$, but they have to be dealt with, and thus conceptualized, simultaneously. Nuclear wastes that outlast us by millennia are part of the same reality as computers with their operating speeds of nanoseconds. Time spans outside the capacity of human imagination and control on one hand and reaction and computation on the other coexist, creating an ever vaster future in the present. Millennia and nanoseconds, however, have not replaced seconds, minutes, and hours enduring and passing just as instantaneity, simultaneity, and unpredictability have not superseded sequence, duration, and predictability. All are mutually implicating.

Social scientists are beginning to recognize that clock-time conceptualizations are no longer sufficient either for their theories or for the social lives they must explain. Gradually, the artifactual time is understood and appreciated alongside the complexity of times embedded in cosmic, living, and cultural processes. This emergent shift in social science emphasis forms part of a more general move away from master narratives and the construction of opposites toward recognition and acceptance of a multitude of voices speaking simultaneously and with equal authority.

[B.A.]

See also **Durkheim, Emile; Elias, Norbert; Environment and Ecology; Feminist Perspectives; Giddens, Anthony; Marx, Karl.**

FURTHER READING

Adam, Barbara. *Time and Social Theory.* Cambridge: Polity; Philadelphia: Temple UP, 1990.

Durkheim, Emile. *The Elementary Forms of Religious Life: A Study in Religious Sociology.* Trans. J.W. Swain. London: Allen & Unwin, 1915.

Elias, Norbert. *Über die Zeit.* Trans. H. Fliessbach, and M. Schröter. Frankfurt: Suhrkamp, 1984.

Giddens, Anthony. *A Contemporary Critique of Historical Materialism: Power, Property and the State.* London: Macmillan, 1981.

Marx, Karl. *Grundrisse.* Harmondsworth: Penguin, 1973.

SOCIAL TIME

Two broad sets of arrangements and activities involving time are affected by or expressed in human activity. One is time reckoning and the other is the temporal order of society.

In time reckoning, although the rotation of the earth and astronomical cues are the basis of standard time measurement (days, months, years), humans have introduced partitions that have no basis in nature. These culturally created units include the hour, minute, and second. Developments in time reckoning are historically associated with the social organization of production. As society's endeavors enlarged from hunting and gathering to agriculture and to industrialism, people's awareness of time changed progressively toward finer discriminations, more categories, and more standardization. (In Europe in the Middle Ages the hour was divided into forty parts, called minutes, but by the Renaissance it had been split into sixty parts, still called minutes.)

Of the culturally created temporal units, the week is most influential. It appears to have emerged when humans had a stable and more abundant food base, and was introduced as a market interlude during which people traded their surpluses. Its cycle occurs in lengths of three to ten days throughout the world even in the latter half of the twentieth century. Institutionalized religion, and astronomical attentions linked to it, resulted in standardizing the interval at seven days, and the days of the week were named after planets and other heavenly bodies or gods. This calendar marker became so entrenched for economic and religious reasons that when French and Soviet political revolutionaries (more than a century apart) tried to alter it from seven to ten days for the French and to five (later six) days for the Russians, their efforts failed. The week seems to have become institutionalized as the community's main period for such recurrent events as religious observance, receiving wages, shopping, and recreation.

Nature also delivers cues that directly affect the temporal order of life in society. These include working mainly during daylight, attending to the time of sunset for observances of the sabbath, and seasonal guides to school terms, vacations, and festivals at harvest time. Biological age is used to establish social rankings (age grades) and roles. Among the most notable are norms for mandatory attendance in school, laws of permission (for marriage, voting, license to drive a car), and regulations for when retirement from work will occur.

However, each culture also creates temporal norms and tempos that are independent of nature. Morally appropriate durations have been established for mourning in bereavement, for the intervals before widowed persons may remarry with propriety, for the number of years after a crime that a person may still be charged with committing it, and for prison terms that calibrate punishment temporally for specific convictions. Standard time spans are used in economic practices for the payment of rent or repayment of installment loans, for wages by the hour or week, and for salaries by the month or year. A financial tactic, fees based on the time when a service is used, is introduced to spread demand over more hours of the day as public utilities become overloaded; its familiar forms include lower rates for long distance telephone calls and for electricity in the evenings, and a lower charge for public transportation during the middle of the day. Political institutions have legal norms for periodic elections and length of terms of office. The rationales vary across all these instances, but all of them reflect an integration of social life with the basic dimension of time.

There is also variation among cultures as to the valuation of time and the tempo of endeavors. Ideas of national character are partly based on the pace of life observed, and the emphasis on temporal precision (as in making the trains run on time). Societies have pace norms, such as how fast to move in courtship, the speed of learning (via slow and fast "tracks" in school), degree of promptness, and appropriate timing in reciprocating a gift or an invitation (not too early, not too late). People in different cities and nations walk at different speeds and have different degrees of exactness in their sense of time.

Synchronization of effort becomes pivotal for individuals in different specialties where there is great division of labor, and where there is worldwide (across time zone) interaction. Scheduled obligations and punctuality become imperative. In these endeavors being late or early makes people tense and managers distraught. Time is intolerably wasted if one has to wait; work is jumbled if some actions are undertaken before they are expected. In advanced industrial societies speed has become an ideal.

Daily activity is so tightly coordinated and meeting deadlines emphasized so consistently that people have begun to suffer and complain of the stressful pace and tempo of their lives.

Social inequality, a characteristic of almost every known society, is also revealed in how people are distributed in time. Deference, for example, is conveyed by coming earlier and waiting for an honored individual; not keeping that person waiting is a sign of respect. Higher status individuals arrive later at ceremonial or social affairs, and the more elevated one's rank, the more time others allow that individual to be late without penalty. In a traditional society, members of a household will assemble to dine around the communal food platter and wait until the ranking elder begins eating before they do so themselves. In the same vein, the annoyance felt by having to wait at home all day for a repairman is aggravated by the norm that a lower-status person should not keep a more powerful one waiting.

Moreover, the social order is formally embodied in time queues and phase distributions. Primogeniture is a rule of inheritance by which the firstborn inherits an estate or title. In labor union contracts, seniority is often the basis for privilege or promotion. The patent office is an institution for channeling rewards to the first person to register the design for an invention that several may achieve. As for phase distributions, the curfew is a formal tactic of social control, keeping some elements of the population away from certain places at certain times while permitting freedom of movement to more powerful persons. In a related scheme, licensing and zoning laws have stipulated closing times, a way that the dominant interest groups restrain other members of the community from potential intrusions or disturbances in their preferred way of life.

[M.M.]

See also **Cultural Differences; Social Theory.**

FURTHER READING

Levine, Robert, and Ellen Wolff. "Social Time: The Heartbeat of a Culture." *Psychology Today* 19.3 (1985): 29–35.

Melbin, Murray. *Night as Frontier: Colonizing the World after Dark*. New York: Free Press, 1987.

Young, Michael D. *The Metronomic Society: Natural Rhythms and Human Timetables*. Cambridge: Harvard UP, 1988.

Zerubavel, Eviatar. *Hidden Rhythms: Schedules and Calendars in Social Life*. Chicago: Chicago UP, 1981.

———. *The Seven Day Circle: The History and Meaning of the Week*. New York: Free Press, 1985.

SOCIOBIOLOGY

Sociobiology is the study of conflict and cooperation among individuals in animal societies based on the theory of evolution. Although the term had been used previously, Edward O. Wilson was the first to apply it to a unified discipline in 1975 with the publication of *Sociobiology: The New Synthesis*, in which he integrated ethology, population biology, and genetics into the study of social behavior. The central tenet of sociobiology is that the same biological principles that govern morphological evolution also apply to animal social behavior, and that both have been shaped by natural selection through time. Behavioral patterns, therefore, are subject to adaptation, and those that enhance the reproductive success of their bearers under specified conditions will increase in frequency over time.

Sociobiology has drawn attention to the conflicts of interest that exist between an individual and the social unit to which it belongs. An extreme example is the development and maintenance of sterile castes that, among some social insects, forego reproduction and work for the benefit of the colony. William D. Hamilton's concept of inclusive fitness (individual reproductive success plus additional reproductive success of relatives due to the individual's cooperation) has shown how apparently altruistic behavior can arise and persist in animal societies. Other analytical and conceptual advances in sociobiology include the models from game theory, first advocated by Hans Kalmus and later promoted by John Maynard-Smith, and Maynard-Smith's own notion of evolutionary stable strategies in analyzing conflicts between individuals over the use of space and resources and in the allocation of energy. The examination of the costs and benefits of social behaviors in terms of the reproductive success of individuals has provided insights into the evolution and maintenance of these behaviors in animal societies over time.

In *Sociobiology: The New Synthesis*, Wilson extended the evolutionary approach into the study of human societies, thus bringing sociology, traditionally the study of proximate causes of human behavior, into the realm of biology. The extent to which sociobiology can explain human behavior is controversial and subject to much debate. Sociobiology has recently become an integral part of the broader discipline of behavioral ecology (the evolutionary study of how animal behavior, including social behavior, contributes to individual reproductive success under different environmental conditions), and the word "sociobiology" is gradually falling into disuse.

[K.O.]

See also **Social Theory.**

FURTHER READINGS

Kitcher, P. *Vaulting Ambition: Sociobiology and the Quest for Human Nature*. Cambridge: MIT P, 1985.

Wilson, E.O. *Sociobiology: The New Synthesis*. Cambridge: Harvard UP, 1975.

SOLAR SYSTEM

In 1905, Einstein published his special theory of relativity, which concluded (in addition to the relationship between mass and energy, $E = mc^2$) that an observer sees time pass more slowly on objects moving by at high speed. Soon after, Einstein turned his attention to the phenomenon of gravitation, and by 1911 he demonstrated that time should also be slowed by proximity to mass. In fact, he could reproduce all of the results of Newton's law of gravitation without introducing a force of gravity at all, simply by assuming that objects in free fall take the shortest path through time. A baseball thrown up in the air which lands back on earth a short time later will experience a shorter time for the trip by rising and then falling. This allows the baseball to spend time farther from the earth, where time travels faster, and hence it can get to its destination on the ground faster than if it did not rise and fall. However, since this version of gravitation gave the same answers as Newton's laws for the trajectories of objects moving in a gravitational field, observing such trajectories could not discriminate between the two theories.

Einstein proposed, however, a comparison of clock rates on the sun and on earth. Consider light leaving the sun. The electromagnetic waves of a spectral line vibrate at a characteristic frequency, the number of waves emitted per second. Spectral lines from atoms on the sun must have the requisite number of waves in a lengthened second, since time there is slowed by proximity to the sun's mass. On earth, with much weaker gravity from both the sun and earth, seconds are shorter. In a shorter second, there is less time to count crests of the electromagnetic waves from the sun, and fewer waves means a lower frequency, corresponding to longer wavelength and redder color. This is termed a gravitational redshift. Although small, it has been measured for the sun and found to be consistent with Einstein's prediction to an accuracy of 2 percent. Every five and a half days, a clock on the sun would show one less elapsed second than a clock on earth.

A similar test, involving a much larger red shift, was performed by measuring spectral lines from gases in the much stronger gravitational field of the white dwarf companion of Sirius, the brightest star in the night sky. Accurate clocks have also measured the different clock rates at various heights above the earth's surface (and around other planets as well), and the gravitational red shift has been seen for spectral lines rising from the earth's surface. The slowing of time by mass is well tested.

By 1915, Einstein realized that this explanation of gravity was incomplete; if mass slowed time in its vicinity, it would also distort the space around it. This is now generally stated by saying that mass distorts (or curves) the space-time around it. At low speed, travel through space is negligible compared to travel through time (where travel time is multiplied by the speed of light, c, to convert the trip into spacelike units). However, when an object travels at high speed through a gravitational field, the shortest distance through space-time is different than the shortest distance through just time, and thus its trajectory would be different if it followed Einstein's theory rather than Newton's law of gravitation. To test the 1915 version, Einstein proposed two additional tests that could be performed in the solar system. These were the motion of the perihelion of Mercury and the deflection of starlight passing near the sun as observed during a total solar eclipse. Mercury, the planet closest to the sun, is hence the fastest traveling of all planets in the solar system. In Einstein's view, the sun's mass distorted the space-time around the sun, and as Mercury orbited at high speed its orbit would differ very slightly from predictions based on Newton's laws. The fact that Mercury was observed to move in accordance with Einstein's concept was strong support for the new general theory of relativity.

There are two reasons why a ray of starlight deflected by the sun would take longer to reach the earth if it traveled in what a distant observer would envision as a straight line, rather than what appears to be a slightly curved path that does not get as close to the sun. By not approaching as close to the sun, the light ray avoids the slight delay caused by time passing more slowly the nearer one is to the sun. Also, the increased warpage of space the nearer one gets to the sun means that there is more actual distance to travel closer to the sun. Light takes what is actually the shortest path through space-time to reach us, even though the path looks curved to an external observer. Such a path is called a geodesic. In the total eclipse of 1919, the deflection of starlight was measured and found to be consistent with Einstein's laws, instantly making Einstein and the theory of relativity household words.

The effects are small; the difference in the deflection of starlight between Newton's and Einstein's 1915 theory is less than one second of arc. Hence, gravitational fields in the solar system are called weak fields, and solar system tests of general relativity are therefore tests of weak fields. Strong field tests must be performed around neutron stars or, the ultimate in strong gravitational fields, black holes, but such measurements are much more difficult than tests within the solar system.

In the years since 1915, other theorists have proposed variations of general relativity, and the solar system has remained the prime testing ground of whether any of the new theories were as accurate as Einstein's. This requires considerably greater precision than the measurement of starlight in 1919 and usually involves radio or radar telescopes. Each October, when the sun appears to pass between two quasars in the sky, the sun's gravitational field appears to bend radio waves from the quasars in opposite directions. With radio telescopes connected as interferometers, the deflection can be measured with much smaller errors than was possible with optical telescopes during an eclipse. Results confirm Einstein's prediction to an accuracy of about 1 percent.

Whereas this test measured the direction of radio waves, another test measured the delay in radar signals caused by the slower time and extra space introduced near the sun by its mass. When Mars is on the far side of the sun as seen from earth, a radar signal from earth to Mars and back again must pass close to the sun twice. Since the orbits of Mars and earth are known to great precision, the expected time for the trip if the sun were not present can be well calculated. The observed time delay to radar transponders on the Viking landers, however, was about 0.0002 seconds longer. The results confirm predictions from Einstein's relativity to an accuracy of 0.1 percent.

Since time is indeed slowed by proximity to mass, then one must reexamine definitions of time. If clocks tick at slightly different rates in different parts of the solar system, which one should we use as our standard? In calculating motions of bodies orbiting the sun, the convenient definition is to use the calculated rate of a clock located at the barycenter (or "center of mass") of the solar system as a whole. Time at this location is called TDB for the French translation of barycentric dynamical time. To compute the position of a body as seen from earth, it is convenient to use time as kept by clocks on earth; this is terrestrial dynamical time (or TDT). TDB and TDT are defined to run at the same average rate over the course of a year, but during the course of a year they can differ by up to .00166 seconds. About half of the difference between the two times results from the fact that, as the earth moves first closer, then farther, from the sun in the course of its elliptical orbit about the sun, the slowing of time on earth due to the sun's gravitational field must also change. The remaining difference results from changing clock rates on earth due to variations in orbital speed of the earth around the sun. It is a tribute to the extreme stability of modern atomic clocks that such slight effects on clock rates caused by the weak gravitational fields in the solar system must be considered when establishing standards of time.

[G.H.N.]

See also **Definition and Measurement of Time; Physics; Relativity Theory; Space-Time.**

FURTHER READINGS

The Astronomical Almanac for the Year 1992. Washington: United States Government Printing Office, 1991. B5, M2, M10.

Calder, Nigel. *Einstein's Universe.* New York: Penguin Books, 1980.

Will, Clifford M. *Was Einstein Right? Putting General Relativity to the Test.* New York: Basic Books, 1986.

SPACE-TIME

The terms time and space, as used by physicists, are discussed in the article **Physics.** Their union into space-time, as required by Einstein's **Relativity Theory,** is explained here.

Already in the eighteenth century, people were saying that the new science of mechanics, which describes how things move under the influence of forces, is geometry in four dimensions, the dimension of time having been added to those of space, but this is not what is expressed by the idea of space-time; the situation is much more subtle, since the idea belongs to the theory of relativity. This article will first present some formulas of special relativity and then point out a feature of them that suggests an interpretation in terms of a geometry uniting space and time; finally it will mention some applications of this geometry that go beyond the terms of special relativity.

THE LORENTZ TRANSFORMATIONS

Albert Einstein (1879–1955) published his special theory in 1905. The results which generated the most public discussion, though not the ones most used by physicists today, are those that describe anomalies in the measurement of space and time. In 1904, they were first given, in rather clumsy form, by Dutch physicist Hendrik Antoon Lorentz (1853–1928), but it was Einstein who understood their meaning and generality and gave them a neater form in his theory. In three spatial dimensions they are complicated, so only one dimension will be used here.

Let an observer O, equipped with apparatus to measure times and distances, study the motion of an object M that moves in a direction called x. We will compare observer O's measurements with those found by another observer O¢ who is in motion with respect to O but travels along the same axis, and observes the same object. Let Dx and Dt be respectively a spatial displacement and an interval of time relating to M as measured by O, and Dx' and Dt' be the same quantities as measured by O'. The formulas connecting them, called the Lorentz transformations, are

$$Dx' = \gamma(Dx - vDt) \, , \; Dt' = \gamma(Dt - vDx/c^2) \qquad (1a,b)$$

where v tells how fast O' is moving with respect to O and c is a universal constant whose value is equal to the value of the speed of light, about 3 x 10^8 meters per second. (The meaning of this constant will be further explained below.) The quantity γ is an abbreviation for

$$1/\sqrt{1-v^2/c^2}$$

It is always greater than 1, but for the speeds we are familiar with it is very close to 1. If v becomes greater than c, then γ becomes imaginary and these formulas no longer apply.

The equations just given can be solved for Dx and Dt: the result is

$$Dx = \gamma(Dx' + vDt') \, , \; Dt = \gamma(Dt' + vDx'/c^2) \qquad (2a,b)$$

so that the relations as seen by O are the same as those seen by O′ except for the sign of v; that is, if O thinks O′ is moving with speed v, then O′ thinks O is moving with the same speed in the opposite direction.

With a little practice these formulas are easy to read. Suppose the object M is a watch held by O′. In the interval Dt' between two ticks the watch does not move according to O′ and therefore, in (2b), $Dx' = 0$. Thus, $Dt = \gamma Dt'$, and O's careful measurement of the interval between two ticks of the watch will give not Dt', but something larger. To O, the watch O′ has is slow, and the same argument with O and O′ interchanged shows that to O′, O's watch is slow. This is not contradictory however, since the two results refer to different watches measured according to different procedures. By similar arguments using (1) it is seen that if O′ holds a yardstick pointing in the direction x, O will judge its length to be shorter than a yard by a factor γ.

The representation of these results in terms of space-time begins with the simple calculation which shows that regardless of the value of v,

$$c^2 Dt'^2 - Dx'^2 = c^2 Dt^2 - Dx^2 \qquad (3)$$

This expression is thus *invariant* under a Lorentz transformation. It has the same value for every observer and must, therefore, have a special significance. Imagine that we are O, watching a moving O′ who holds a watch. For O′, as before, $Dx' = 0$, and Dt' is O″'s own time, called the *proper time* and usually written Ds. The invariant quantity Ds^2 is given by

$$c^2 Ds^2 = c^2 Dt^2 - Dx^2 \qquad (4)$$

SPACE-TIME

In about 1908, mathematician Hermann Minkowski (1864–1909) noticed the existence of the invariant Ds^2 and realized its geometrical significance. An analogous situation occurs if we draw a stick of length l on a sheet of graph paper with one end at the origin of coordinates and the other at a point with coordinates x and y. However the paper is oriented with respect to the yardstick, such that

$$x^2 + y^2 = l^2 \qquad (5)$$

the quantity l^2, which has physical significance as the square of the stick's length, is invariant under rotations of the coordinate system, just as Ds^2 is invariant under Lorentz transformations. The fact that the stick, as viewed from various directions in the plane, seems to change in length is an effect of perspective. In Minkowski's geometry, the changes in apparent spatial and temporal dimensions given by the Lorentz trans-

formations are similarly an effect of perspective. Note that this is perspective in four dimensions, since for simplicity two of the spatial dimensions have been omitted in writing (3) and (4).

We see now the role of the constant c. In (5), the quantities x and y must obviously be expressed in the same units, but for historical reasons we measure the distances and times of (4) in different units; c is merely a constant that makes the units the same. Finally, there is the negative sign in (4). This announces a new kind of geometry. Equation (5), for constant l, defines a circle, but (4), for constant Ds, defines a pair of hyperbolas. The negative sign in (4) expresses the distinction, in our experience of the world and physical theories that describe it, between intervals of space and intervals of time. From any standpoint an observer makes the distinction with perfect clarity; this is, in fact, the reason why it took so long for the underlying space-time symmetry to be noticed.

Space-time is the stage on which the drama of our physical and intellectual lives is enacted, and in the formulation of physical theories it and its generalizations have become increasingly important. It is not necessary to formulate special relativity in terms of space-time, but general relativity is a theory of space-time which tells how it is distorted by the presence of matter to produce the effects of gravity, and cosmologists represent the entire universe as a structure in curved space-time.

[D.A.P.]

See also **Gravity, Time, and Space; Physics; Relativity Theory.**

FURTHER READING

Born, Max. *Einstein's Theory of Relativity*. Revised ed. New York: Dover, 1962.

Minkowski, Hermann. "Space and Time," in H.A. Lorentz, A. Einstein, H. Minkowski, and H. Weyl, *The Theory of Relativity*. London: Methuen, 1923.

Taylor, Edwin F., and John A. Wheeler. *Space-time Physics*. San Francisco: Freeman, 1966.

SPACE-TIME AND THE CONTEMPORARY WORLD

To specify an event in the universe requires knowledge of its location in time as well as space. In a real sense, the concept of time is as essential in describing the physical world as is that of space. This is the basis of the notion of space-time. Language has automatically incorporated this concept, for if we say "there is a book lying on the table" we implicitly mean "now." That "now" has the same meaning to all people able to discourse with one another is the happy result of the speed of light being so much greater than the speed of sound. Information about an object's existence can propagate through the universe no faster than the speed of light. Thus, if "now" is to mean the same thing to two different observers, they should be separated by a distance that is short so that the light travel time between them is small compared to the scale of their temporal perception. This has been traditionally true for the inhabitants of earth, but is beginning to change. Global communication through satellites has resulted in the appearance of phenomena associated with the finite speed of light. Should you place a transoceanic phone call, it is likely that your call will be carried by one or more communications satellites. These satellites lie in geostationary orbit about 26,000 miles above the earth so that their orbital revolution about the earth will equal the earth's axial rotation. The result is that the satellite remains above nearly the same point on the earth's equator, making it easy to find and use. The typical transoceanic phone call will start out over land lines traveling a few hundred miles before reaching a satellite link. It then travels 26,000 miles to the satellite and a similar distance back to the earth where it again travels over land lines to the party being called. When the party replies, the call retraces the same path traveling a round-trip distance of more than 100,000 miles. The speed of light is 186,000 miles per second, so the time required for the response is greater than half a second. That is a very long time in social discourse and can lead to the impression that the party who is responding is rather slow. Similar problems have been encountered in television where a foreign correspondent may seem slow and inattentive compared to the local anchor man, again due to the finite speed of light.

These apparently trivial concerns become far more important when communicating with spacecraft moving through the solar system. Here the round-trip light travel time can approach a good fraction of a day. This makes interactive work with such a craft virtually impossible. Responses based on information sent from the spacecraft may take many hours to return to the spacecraft from the earth. Speeds of probes to other planets often reach tens of thousands of miles per hour when they pass near a planet and a several-hour delay may mean that opportunities are missed or that the spacecraft is endangered.

Astronomers must deal with this time delay in their everyday observation of the universe. If "now" is to have clear meaning with respect to the object, then the distance to the object should be similarly short. If not, then the best that the observers on earth can do is agree that they are seeing an image of the object as it was in the past. It has been said that astronomers' telescopes are time machines for they provide a view of the universe as it was. Alternatively, our observers could agree that they will define the "present" to be that which they can sense about the universe at any instant of local time. In this case, the presently perceived universe will contain objects whose "age" depends on their distance. This is not a small effect, for the light from the nearest star takes about four years to arrive at the earth. For the nearest galaxy similar to our own, the travel time is nearly two million years. Thus, the more deeply we probe the night sky, the further we look back in time and see objects as they were when the universe was younger.

One of the great triumphs of the twentieth century has been the discovery that the constituents of the universe (isolated galaxies and clusters of galaxies) are steadily receding from one another with a speed proportional to the distance that separates them. It is as if at some point in the past they all violently separated from each other and those which were traveling faster simply have traveled farther. This view of the universe has been dubbed the "expanding universe," the beginning of which is called the "big bang." Although it is not without some problems, it has proven to be the most successful cosmology of the twentieth century. One of the consequences of this view is that when we look deeply into space we see the universe when things were closer together. If one follows this logic to its ultimate conclusion, one can imagine looking deeply enough into space to observe matter in the universe when it was tightly bunched in roughly the same place at the same time. With everything crammed into a small volume of space-time, one might be somewhat amazed that we can observe it in whatever direction we look. Yet this is the case. The material matter of the universe would then be confined to a small volume and presumably be in a state much different from matter relatively nearby us. One can calculate the state of matter when the density became such that light can escape from it. That is, we can ascertain what the state of matter would be when it becomes relatively transparent. The matter would mimic that found on the surface of the typical star. However, the extreme rate at which we appear to be receding from it causes the light from this early material to be doppler shifted to the far red and to appear much cooler than the typical star. In the early 1960s, Arno A. Penzias and Robert W. Wilson found just such radiation while they were testing a very sensitive radio amplifier at the Bell laboratories in New Jersey. They received the Nobel Prize for their discovery and that radiation is today being subjected to exhaustive tests for what it can tell us about the state of the early universe. Its most significant hallmark is that it is seen in whatever direction we look in the sky.

THE GLOBAL GEOMETRY OF SPACE-TIME
The idea of seeing a "point" or at least a very small volume of space spread out over the entire sky immediately suggests that the large-scale geometry of space-time is not the flat Euclidian geometry of common experience. There is nothing new in the local nature of geometry being a poor guide to large-scale geometry. Early man thought the world was flat for that appeared to be the case. The concept worked well for the cosmology of the common man until well into the fifteenth century. Although the spherical nature of the earth had been known to the Greeks and was known to the educated at the time of Columbus, it would have confused the typical European serf. There would have been questions like "What holds people on the other side of the globe to the earth?" There is similar confusion today when people are exposed to phrases like the "edge of the universe." It is perfectly reasonable to ask, "If the universe has an edge, what lies beyond it?" At least the medieval serf could perceive in three dimensions so he could picture the world as a globe. Unfortunately, we are unable to perceive the four dimensions of space-time with our senses so visualizing the true nature of the universe is difficult. However, with practice one can imagine spaces of higher dimension than three and specifically the four-dimensional world of space-time.

We can draw analogy to the Flatland of the Reverend Edwin Abbott where creatures can only perceive in two dimensions. Flatlanders cannot perceive up or down. Therefore it never rains in Flatland. Houses are simply polygons with a gap in the perimeter for the door. It is fair to question if a Flatlander could determine if he really lived on a Euclidean plane or on the surface of a very large sphere. The answer is yes, for he could determine whether the postulates and theorems of Euclidian plane geometry applied to his physical world or whether the postu-

lates and theorems of spherical geometry were correct.

Our Flatlander could even determine if his universe was expanding much in the same way we do by observing the doppler shifts of distant objects in the universe. Consider what the Flatlander would see should he indeed live on the surface of a very large expanding sphere. The local environment would look convincingly flat in a Euclidian sense. However, images of distant galaxies would appear closer to each other than they did locally since they exist on the surface of a much earlier and smaller sphere. If our Flatlander could look deeply enough into space, he could view an epoch of his universe when matter was packed tightly together, and the view would not depend on the direction in which he looked. In principle, if the observer could look through the tightly packed matter he would perceive the Flatland version of the big bang itself, that instant of time when everything was packed into the same place. If the Flatland observer was wedded to the concept of Euclidian flat space, he would call that location the edge of the universe. However, to ask what is beyond the edge of the universe is equivalent to asking what came before the big bang. The answer to that question is beyond the realm of science.

The analogy between the Flatlander's expanding universe and our own is not a bad one. The distribution of the primeval fireball across the night sky is a result of the large-scale geometry of space-time with different epochs existing at different distances, all tied together by the finite speed of light. The ill-conceived concept of the edge of the universe is the same in both worlds. The term "edge of the universe" is as misleading in our world as it is in Flatland for it presupposes Euclidian flat space as the appropriate geometry of space-time. A far less prejudicial term is *particle horizon*, for it is within this volume of space that all information carried by particles, including light, can reach the observer. Therefore, it is not possible to have any information about the state of the universe beyond the particle horizon, and hence that state lies beyond the scope of scientific enquiry.

[G.W.C., II.]

See also **Space-Time; Big Bang Theory.**

FURTHER READINGS
Abbott, Edwin A. "Flatland." *The World of Mathematics.* Ed. J.R. Newman. New York: Simon and Schuster, 1956. 2385–2396.

Collins, George W., II. "Dragons at the Edge of the Universe." *The Astronomy Quarterly* 21 (1988): 5–25.

SPECIATION

Speciation in the classical sense is defined as the formation of two or more new species from a single ancestral stock. It involves the development of both morphological and reproductive differences between the diverging lineages. Most often an ancestral stock becomes subdivided by an external geographical barrier such as a mountain range, body of water, or other region of unfavorable habitat. Alternatively, though more rarely, an internal barrier (such as a change in courtship behavior in a bird population, or host preference in a parasite or plant-feeding insect) can arise within a species. The establishment of barriers to reproduction between diverging populations is accompanied or followed by the development of morphological differences, effected by natural selection or random genetic drift. Speciation is most commonly a gradual process, in which differences between diverging lineages accumulate over many thousands of generations. The actual time required for divergence varies greatly; American and Eurasian sycamores remain incompletely divergent after more than 20 million years, whereas desert pupfish of California have speciated within 30,000 years. Apparent instances of abrupt speciation, occurring over one or a few generations, also exist. In such instances, a mutation or chromosomal rearrangement occurring in a few individuals may, in a single step, alter both their morphology and their interfertility with other members of their species.

[G.A.A.]

See also **Extinction; Evolution of Evolutionism.**

FURTHER READINGS

Otte, D., and J.A. Endler, eds. *Speciation and Its Consequences.* Sunderland: Sinauer Associates, 1989.

SPINOZA, BENEDICTUS DE (BARUCH) (1632–1677)

The most significant fact about a theory of time in Spinoza's *Ethics* lies in its conspicuous absence. When Spinoza wishes to discuss what one would look for under the rubric of temporality, the closest he comes to this remarkably absent subject is to be found in the sparse remarks on duration. Thus, according to Spinoza, time is relegated, and restricted, exclusively to the domain of "duration."

In Part II, Definition 5, of *Ethics*, Spinoza defines duration as the indefinite continuance of existing. In the explication of this definition, he states, "I say 'indefinite' because it can in no wise be determined through the nature of the existing thing, nor again by the thing's efficient cause, which necessarily posits, but does not annul, the existence of the thing." A definite duration neither belongs to the nature of the thing nor is it posited by the thing's efficient cause, which is responsible for its existence as such, but not for its length of duration.

Probably the closest Spinoza came to a conception of time lies in his discussion of definite duration—which cannot belong, he insists, to a thing's essence. He is writing an ethics, albeit an ethics *sui generis*; the scholastic word "thing" (*res*) Spinoza uses to refer primarily to "human being." Thus, a human being is not born with an essence to live, say, for twenty-three or thirty-two or eighty-four years. This would somehow seem demonic, perhaps even cruel. Nor can the extent of some one person's duration be determined by his efficient cause, which solely affirms its effect to the extent of its ability.

The key phrase here is "to the extent of its ability," not only with regard to the efficient cause, but also and more importantly with regard to the nature of the thing itself. In Part III, Propositions 6 and 8, Spinoza maintains that "Each thing, insofar as it is in itself, endeavors to persevere in its being." It is the very essence of a thing to persevere in its being as far as it can. This endeavor, *conatus*, does not involve a finite time, but indefinite time. What, then, limits the thing's endeavor to persevere? The power of external causes. In Part II, Proposition 31, and its corollary, after stating that we have only a very inadequate knowledge of the duration of both our own body and of particular things external to us, Spinoza goes on to say that "all particular things are contingent and perishable. For we can have no adequate knowledge of their duration, and that is what is to be understood by contingency and perishability. For apart from this is no other kind of contingency."

The same lack of interest and difficulty that Spinoza had in explaining finitude surfaces with regard to the question of time. In Part II, Proposition 45, he conceived duration as "existence, insofar as it is considered in the abstract as a kind of quantity." Existence in the abstract true sense refers to things insofar as they are in God. Things, insofar as they are in God, are eternal, not temporal. It is the human mind in its "intellectual love of God" that can truly attain blessedness and freedom. As Spinoza argues in Part V,

Proposition 36, "The mind's intellectual love toward God is the love of God wherewith God loves himself not insofar as he is infinite, but insofar as he can be explicated through the essence of the human mind considered under an aspect of eternity. That is, the mind's intellectual love towards God is part of the infinite love wherewith God loves himself."

As Spinoza saw it, our essence, if we are able to realize it, is eternal, not temporal. He makes the point at the very end of *Ethics* that "The ignorant man, besides being driven hither and thither by external causes, never possessing true contentment of spirit, lives as if he were unconscious of himself, God and things, and as soon as he ceases to be passive, he at once ceases to be at all. On the other hand, the wise man, insofar as he is considered as such, suffers scarcely any disturbance of spirit, but being conscious, by virtue of a certain eternal necessity, of himself, of God, and of things, never ceases to be, but always possesses true spiritual contentment."

[J.S.]

FURTHER READINGS

Alexander, Samuel. *Spinoza and Time*. London: Allen & Unwin, 1921.

Hallett, Harold Foster. *Aeternitas: A Spinozistic Study*. Oxford: Clarendon P, 1930.

Spinoza, Benedictus de. *Ethics*. Trans. Andrew Boyle and revised by G.H.R. Parkinson. London: Dent, 1989.

STANDARD TIME: TIME ZONES AND DAYLIGHT SAVING TIME

Standard time is the civil time of day in any of the world's twenty-four time zones, usually the mean solar time of the zone's central meridian. One time zone usually covers 15 degrees longitude from pole to pole and differs by one hour from its neighboring zones.

This global system of zoned time is based on the equivalence of time and longitude (one hour = 15 degrees longitude and twenty-four hours = 360 degrees). As the earth rotates once in approximately twenty-four hours, the sun appears to traverse 15 degrees longitude per hour. Almost all of the countries of the world cooperate to observe this system, but in some places the zone boundaries deviate from the convention to accommodate local time preferences.

The starting line for calculating longitude is the prime meridian (0 degrees longitude) running through Greenwich, England. The zones west of Greenwich are calculated successively in one-hour increments and expressed with reference to Greenwich time ($+1^h$, $+2^h$, $+3^h$, up to $+12^h$). The zones to the east of Greenwich are similarly calculated and expressed in one-hour subtractions (-1^h, -2^h, up to -12^h). A few countries use increments in fractions of an hour. Each zone can also be expressed as a letter of the alphabet. The calendar date changes at the International Date Line, an imaginary line that roughly follows the meridian at 180 degrees. To the east of the date line, the calendar date is one day earlier than to the west.

HISTORY

The division of the globe into twenty-four zones one hour apart occurred in 1884 at the International Meridian Conference in Washington, attended by delegates from twenty-five countries in the Americas and Europe. The conferees not only divided the globe, but also recommended that the nations of the world establish a prime meridian at Greenwich; count longitude east and west from the prime meridian up to 180 degrees in each direction; and adopt a universal day beginning at Greenwich at midnight. Although the International Meridian Conference had no authority to enforce its suggestions, the meeting resulted in the gradual worldwide adoption of the time-zone system based on Greenwich as prime meridian in use today.

Organized international support for fixing a common prime meridian had emerged at the International Geographical Congress held at Antwerp in 1870. Scientists interested in establishing a coordinated time system for their worldwide observations met throughout the decade to discuss the desirability of a standard time for the world. Sandford Fleming, engineer-in-chief of the Canadian Pacific Railway, was the first to publish a systematic scheme for a global system of time zones in *Uniform Non-Local Time (Terrestrial Time)* in 1876.

By the time of the International Meridian Conference in 1884, Sweden (1879) and Great Britain (1880) had each adopted a national standard time, and the railroads of North America had already begun their own experiment with zoned time. Within a single European country, the time of the capital city could serve as a national standard because longitudinal differences were small. But in North America, by the 1880s, it had become impractical to operate on a single time because of the enormous differences in longitude from east to west.

On November 18, 1883, Standard Railway Time went into effect in North America. That day, most United States and Canadian railroads replaced a profusion of nearly fifty local times with five zones—Intercolonial, Eastern, Central, Mountain, and Pacific—each of which had a uniform time within its boundaries. The zones were calculated on meridians, 15 degrees apart, based on Greenwich as the prime meridian (0 degrees longitude), following North American shipping practice. Fearing government intervention, the railroads voluntarily introduced the new system to help organize the ever-increasing traffic of passengers and freight. The railroads' transition from multiple times to zoned time was orchestrated by William F. Allen, publisher of *Travelers' Official Guide* and secretary of the railroads' two organizations for coordinating timetables, the General Time Convention and the Southern Railway Time Convention.

Although pockets of local resistance to railroad standard time persisted into the twentieth century, most large cities in North America immediately adopted the railroads' artificial time. The Standard Time Act of 1918 made the system federal law in the United States, and Canada adopted similar legislation that same year. In the United States, the Interstate Commerce Commission was responsible for drawing and changing the zone boundaries, which have been adjusted many times since then. Today the U.S. Department of Transportation has responsibility.

STANDARD TIME AND DAYLIGHT SAVING TIME

Daylight saving time provides more hours of daylight in the evening by adjusting the clock one or two hours ahead of standard time. Although Benjamin Franklin facetiously suggested a plan for saving daylight in a 1784 essay, the modern system is credited to English builder William Willett, who proposed it in his 1907 pamphlet "The Waste of Daylight." Germany, the first nation to adopt daylight saving time, advanced its clocks in 1915 during World War I as a measure to save fuel. Great Britain followed in 1916.

The first legislation establishing both standard time and daylight saving time for the United States also came during World War I. On March 19, 1918, in an effort to promote industrial efficiency, Congress approved the division of the country into five zones—-Eastern, Central, Mountain, Pacific, and Alaska—measured from the Greenwich meridian, and prescribed that the time in each zone was to advance one hour for the seven months beginning the last Sunday in March and ending the last Sunday in October. Canada approved daylight saving time in the same year.

But with the end of World War I, a deluge of protests—many of which came from farmers whose work days were based on sun time rather than clock time—caused the United States Congress in 1919 to repeal the daylight saving provision of the original act. President Wilson vetoed the repeal twice, but was overridden. The Canadian law was in effect only for the summer of 1918.

At the outbreak of World War II, the United States and Canada once again adopted extended daylight saving time. In the United States, this "War Time" began February 9, 1942, and continued year-round until September 30, 1945. Canada began on the same date and ended two weeks earlier.

Although many states and localities observed daylight saving time between the wars and after World War II, no national time legislation took effect again in the United States until the Uniform Time Act of 1966, which placed time-zone matters under the Department of Transportation. The act also provided for eight time zones and required all states choosing to observe daylight saving time to do so uniformly—from the last Sunday in April to the last Sunday in October. The mnemonic—"spring forward, fall back"—came into common usage as a reminder for altering the nation's clocks.

In response to the energy shortage of 1973, the United States Congress extended daylight saving time. The measure, controversial and short-lived, was observed from January 6 through October 27, 1974 and from February 23 through October 26, 1975. In 1986, Congress once again extended daylight saving time to begin, starting with the 1987 season, on the first Sunday in April rather than the last.

The worldwide observation of daylight saving time, or summer time, varies considerably. Many countries do not advance their clocks in the summer months, and those which do advance them do so on widely different dates.

[C.E.S.]

See also **Longitude; Partitioning the Day.**

FURTHER READINGS

Bartky, Ian. "The Adoption of Standard Time." *Technology and Culture* 30 (January 1989): 25–56.

Howse, Derek. *Greenwich Time and the Discovery of the Longitude*. Oxford: Oxford UP, 1980.

O'Malley, Michael. *Keeping Watch: A History of American Time*. New York: Viking, 1990.

Thomson, Malcolm. *The Beginning of the Long Dash: A History of Timekeeping in Canada*. Toronto: U of Toronto P, 1978.

STAR AND GALAXY FORMATION

The formation of galaxies and stars represents the formation of the largest highly structured forms in the universe and their primary constituents. Little is known about the former while a reasonably compelling scenario exists for the origin of the latter. One of the primary problems in developing unambiguous theories for the formation of both these classes of objects rests in the relatively small fraction of their lifetime required for their formation. Thus, any random collection of these objects will provide a small sample of representatives that are in the formation stage. In addition, stars and galaxies represent heterogenous collections of objects having very different lifetimes.

THE FORMATION OF STARS

In our galaxy of stars at least as much material lies between the stars of the galactic disk as is in the stars themselves. It is from this material that stars form. The basic picture of the processes that take place consists of the gravitational contraction of a clump of interstellar matter with a density significantly greater than the surrounding material. The detailed nature of these density fluctuations and the very early conditions of star formation is still an area of some controversy. However, once the initial collapse of the proto-star cloud begins, the situation becomes increasingly clear.

The central regions of the collapsing cloud coalesce rapidly, forming a stellar core. Eventually the core becomes dense enough so that the energy released by the in-falling matter cannot easily escape. Being trapped within, it then heats the core. In stars with masses less than a few times the mass of the sun, material will continue to rain down on the stellar core increasing the mass of the configuration by a significant fraction of the final total. The resulting proto-star will continue to contract producing more energy from the gravitational squeezing of the stellar gas. In the early phases of this process half of this energy is carried to the surface by convection where it is radiated away into space as light. The remaining half carries on heating the interior of the star. The result is that the star continues to shrink in size, maintaining about the same surface temperature while the central temperature continues to increase. Eventually, the internal structure changes so that energy is transported more slowly than by convection and the shrinking star experiences a marked increase in its surface temperature. After a further time, the central temperature of the contracting star reaches a point where nuclear reactions begin to take place in its most central regions. The energy produced by these reactions is sufficient to stop further contraction and the star has reached the point in its evolution where it will spend about 90 percent of its total life. The formation process is complete.

The time required for the formation process to take place is known as the *Kelvin-Helmholtz contraction time* and was initially developed in the nineteenth century in an attempt to reconcile the age of the sun with the geologically determined age of the earth and the time required by Darwinian theory for the development of the higher species. Nuclear processes were unknown and no chemical process could even begin to provide the luminous energy liberated by the sun for more than a short time. The gravitational energy liberated by the in-fall of the material making the sun its present size will permit it to shine at its present rate for a specific amount of time; this Kelvin-Helmholtz contraction time for the sun amounts to about 14 million years. Prior to the discovery of nuclear reactions, this time was thought to provide the best estimate for the maximum age of the sun. While it is significantly greater than the age allowed by chemical reactions, it fell far short of the time required by the theory of evolution to yield complex species on the earth. It was on this basis that Lord Kelvin wrongly rejected Darwin's theory of evolution. Nuclear processes provide a present age for the sun of about five billion years. This age is consistent with the estimated age of the earth, moon, and meteorites.

THE FORMATION OF GALAXIES

Not only does the short formation time of galaxies inhibit our understanding of the details of that process, but it appears that galaxies formed very early in the history of the universe. Since the light from distant objects takes considerable time to arrive at the earth, we must expect that young galaxies will only be found at great distances from the earth. This makes their detailed study difficult. If these two problems were not enough to confuse our knowledge of the early phases of a galaxy's life, there is still an additional confounding difficulty. Galaxies, like stars, preferentially form in groups or clusters. However, unlike stars, the typical separation of members in a cluster of galaxies is not much greater than the size of the typical galaxy. Thus, as the galaxies move around within the cluster under the influence of their mutual gravity, they are far more liable to collide with each other than do stars in their clusters. The result is that the structure of many galaxies may be dominated by collisions that occur after their formation. These collisions will introduce morphological changes which conceal the nature of their initial state. Such difficulties result in a theory of galactic formation that is more speculation than fact.

With these reservations in mind, the present view of galactic formation suggests that the earliest stages are governed by gravitational contraction from preexisting density fluctuations in the intergalactic medium. The source and nature of these fluctuations constitutes one of the central problems of contemporary cosmology. The rapid gravitational collapse of the intergalactic cloud will then give rise to star formation and in the later stages may perhaps yield galaxies called "starburst galaxies" containing large numbers of bright blue stars. The continued collapse of the proto-galaxy leads to the observed form of the galaxy with a great concentration of stars and gas near the center. It has even been speculated that the gravitational collapse yields such a large concentration of mass in the central regions that one or more massive black holes may form, giving rise to that most energetic phenomenon called a quasar.

[G.W.C., II]

See also **Age of the Oldest Stars and the Milky Way; Cosmology.**

FURTHER READINGS

Collins, George W., II. *The Fundamentals of Stellar Astrophysics.* New York: W.H. Freeman, 1989. Chapter 5.

STATUTE OF LIMITATIONS

A statute of limitations refers to a specified period of time in which a legal action must be filed in a court of law. If it is not filed within the time period, either it may not be filed later, or if it is filed, the running of the time period can be used as a defense in the action. The time period and effect of the statute varies according to the kind of case, and may in certain instances be extended, for example when a person whose action would be barred is a minor. Some kinds of actions, such as prosecution of murder, have no statute of limitations.

Statutes of limitations may apply in both civil cases (an action by one person or organization against another) or in criminal cases (prosecution by the state for violations of the criminal code). In criminal cases, the statute is generally held to constitute a bar to prosecution, that is, to prevent the state from bringing an action altogether. In civil cases the statute may not bar the filing of the action, but it can be asserted as a defense and may prevent the plaintiff from proceeding further with the action.

In criminal cases, more serious crimes generally have longer time periods in which the crime can be prosecuted. For example, a statutory scheme might state that felony prosecutions (excluding murder) must commence within six years, misdemeanors within two years, and minor misdemeanors within six months. These time periods might have certain exceptions; for example, that an action for a crime involving fraud may be brought within a year of being discovered by the injured party or that the time period for prosecuting an action against a public official's misconduct may extend past the time the person ceases to be a public official.

In civil actions the time periods of statutes of limitations vary widely, depending on the kind of case. One statutory scheme, for example, provides for a twenty-one-year period for actions to recover real estate; a fifteen-year period for actions based upon written contracts; a six-year period for actions not in writing; a four-year period for torts such as trespass, recovery of personal property, fraud, and medical malpractice; a two-year period for actions for wrongful death or bodily injury; and a one-year period for libel, slander, and certain malpractice actions.

In civil cases, in which a statute of limitations has the effect of denying recovery to a particular party, there are frequently exceptions which permit actions to be filed after (sometimes even long after) the statute of limitations would have barred the action. The most common example is that of a minor, who is often permitted to bring an action after reaching adulthood. In the case of a minor injured as an infant this could have the effect of extending a short statute of limitations for as long as twenty-one years. The statute may also be extended for persons under disability. In other situations a statute may be extended if war occurs or if the defendant leaves the state, hides, or otherwise defeats the court's jurisdiction during the period of limitation.

Statutes of limitations in civil cases are often extended by rulings concerning the time when the statutory period begins. There is a substantial body of case law concerning when the periods begin to "run," much of it depending upon when the injured party or other plaintiff knew or should have known that there was cause to sue the opposing party. Where the driver's negligence in an automobile accident is the cause of injury, for example, the injured party is usually on notice of the cause of injury. In a medical malpractice or product liability case, though, it may be years before the injury or its cause become known.

In the area of criminal law, it is also sometimes necessary to extend the statute of limitations to cover situations in which a party may not know about, or is somehow unable to file a complaint about, the criminal conduct. In cases of incest, for example, the criminal conduct may be repressed until long after the child has become an adult. Some states have adopted statutes specifically permitting the crime to be prosecuted at that time.

The legal rationales for statutes of limitations in civil cases are similar to those urged in criminal cases. Statutes of limitations are necessary because of the difficulty of preserving evidence, the frailty of memory, and the fact that witnesses may die or otherwise become unavailable. These statutes are intended to encourage timely and efficient assertion of claims by plaintiffs or the state, and to provide a period of time after which defendants may rest assured that a claim will not be asserted against them.

As a practical matter, statutes of limitations are often based on an interplay between two factors—the difficulty of proving the case after a period of time has passed, which may burden both the court system and the parties, and the seriousness of the harm or crime. Thus, when criminal offenses such as murder or incest are involved, the law may permit the bringing of the action long after the misconduct occurred, despite the difficulties of proof. Similarly in civil offenses, the period allowed for bringing an action concerning a written contract will generally be longer than the period allowed for an oral contract, because proof in the former situation is less dependent on the fallibilities of memory.

When social values suggest a need for flexibility, the law often provides special mechanisms to lessen the harshness of statutes of limitations. For example, when a company manufactures a dangerous product but conceals the evidence of the danger, the law may provide that the statute does not begin to run until the defect is or reasonably could be discovered. A balance is thus struck between the social interest in having time limits to litigation and the social interest in maintaining the litigation system as a deterrent to corporate misconduct. A somewhat similar balancing rationale underlies the related legal concept of *laches*.

[M.H.A.]

See also **Time Periods and the Law.**

FURTHER READINGS

Bintliff, B. "Statutes of Limitations for Court Actions in Colorado." *The Colorado Lawyer* 12 (June 1983): 895–902.

Dworkin, T.M. "Product Liability of the 1980s: 'Repose Is Not the Destiny' of Manufacturers." *North Carolina Law Review* 61 (October 1982): 33–66.

Josling, J.F. *Periods of Limitation: With Practical Notes.* 5th ed. London: Oyez, 1981.

McGovern, F.E. "Status of Statutes of Limitations and Statutes of Repose in Product Liability Actions: Present and Future." *Forum* 16 (Winter 1981): 416–450.

Williams, Jeremy S. *Limitations of Actions in Canada.* 2nd ed. Toronto: Butterworths, 1980.

STRATIGRAPHY AND PALEONTOLOGY

Stratigraphy (the study of stratified, or layered, rocks) is arguably one of the broadest of geological disciplines and can be investigated from a variety of viewpoints. These include the details and processes that cause sediments to form, as well as their subsequent deformation, alteration, and—in many cases—removal from the rock record. Because of the temporal aspect that accrues to the origin of sedimentary rocks, and the power of this to aid in our understanding of the geological history of the earth, the treatment here links stratigraphy with paleontology (the study of remains of past life). The study of paleontology is, among other things, the primary means by which the progress and process of the organic evolution of life through time is documented. The successional aspect of evolution permits paleontologists to identify and recognize the chapters of elapsed time during which life on our planet has evolved. The following discussion focuses on the complementary ways in which stratigraphy and paleontology aid our evaluation of the past history of the earth and, especially, its biosphere (living organisms). Advances in geochronology, based on the decay of radioactive isotopes, and upon the reversals of the earth's magnetic field, are also incorporated here.

BASIC PRINCIPLES IN STRATIGRAPHY

It is not surprising that stratigraphy and paleontology have been inextricably linked for at least 150 years. Yet the power of stratigraphy to reveal events that could be tied to the history of our planet's development was illustrated as early as ca. 1669 when the Danish scholar, Nicholas Steno, articulated three principles that are still fundamental to the study of Earth's history. These principles can be conveniently illustrated as follows:

1. *The Principle of Superposition.* According to this principle, the layer encountered at the bottom of a succession of sedimentary rocks was deposited first, and is the oldest. Successively higher layers are thus successively younger. This automatically gives a relative age framework with which to interpret the timing of geological events as reflected by information found in the sedimentary succession or sequence.

2. *The Principle of Original Horizontality.* In Steno's time, philosophers thought that all rocks of the earth had been precipitated in a primeval ocean. Recognizing that a volume of material settling or forming in an aqueous medium eventually acquired an even and horizontal upper surface, Steno proposed that the boundaries between sedimentary units would be effectively horizontal. The obvious ramification of this principle is that sedimentary rocks which are now tilted with respect to the horizontal have acquired that attitude subsequent to their original formation. Even though geologists now recognize that certain alluvial fan deposits can form at relatively high initial angles of repose (up to about 20 degrees), Steno's principle still holds in virtually all cases.

3. *The Principle of Original Continuity of Strata.* Since they were precipitated in a primeval ocean, all sedimentary layers would be expected to be of global (or at least basin-wide) distribution such that there would be no interruption to the layer's distribution except as provided by islands of topography "poking through" or by the layer eventually feathering out to a thin edge at a shoreline. The Grand Canyon now cuts through more than one mile of virtually horizontally bedded sedimentary rocks that can be projected to have been previously continuous from one wall of the canyon to the other. By Steno's third principle, the cutting of the Grand Canyon can be seen to have taken place after the deposition of the sediments it now exposes to our view.

USING STENO'S PRINCIPLES

Within 100 years of the publication of Steno's principles, mining geologists (by profession or avocation) were proposing scenarios designed to account for the sequential evolution of the strata of the earth. Abraham Gottlob Werner (1750–1817) is likely the most prominent of these students, and his theories epitomize the strengths as well as the failings of the methodology of his day. Basically, these workers built on the principles of Steno to develop an understanding of the history of the sedimentary succession of that part of the world with which they were cognizant. The fundamental principle was that all rocks had precipitated from an original ocean, and thus the proponents of this scenario became known as *Neptunists*. In various nomenclatures, these successions usually identified a "primitive" unit (the basal, or oldest, represented by rocks now metamorphosed by geological processes into units having only a few remnant features of their originally sedimentary nature, that is, unfossiliferous gneisses, schists, and slates now found as cores of many mountains). The "primitive" rocks were followed in age by a sequence of "transition" rocks (mostly marble) containing ancient forms of life, and showing evidence of having been formed, in part, by running water. Thus the ancient oceans were starting to recede. Next formed were the "stratified" rocks, with abundant fossils preserved in sandstone, coal, slate, and limestone. Finally, after the seas retreated wholly, the last series of sediments was formed by stream deposition and was identified as consisting of "alluvial" rocks (gravels, loosely consolidated sands, and the like).

A basic tenet in these reconstructions is that one could identify the age of a rock on the basis of what kind of a rock it was. Nowadays, one recognizes that this principle is likely to be severely wrong, although still useful in limited situations. Thus, a wide variety of rocks may form at a given point in time and, under the proper conditions, similar rocks can form at a wide variety of times.

FAUNAL SUCCESSION

The British surveyor and engineer of canals, William Smith, was a keen observer of sedimentary rocks in southwestern England. He needed to be. Various strata had singular properties important to building canals across them. Over time, Smith observed that not only were there distinct sequences of rock in the regions where he worked, but also that there were distinct sequences of fossil invertebrates contained within them. He further observed that whereas in more distant locations the details of rock composition might change, the succession of fossils remained the same. Thus, fossil assemblage "A" always occurred stratigraphically below fossil assemblage "B" regardless of details of the lithology. Not only was the sequence of fossils repeated from place to place, but each assemblage had a unique position in the sequence, and thus appeared to represent a distinct interval of time that could be recognized thereupon. Thus, Smith found that he could recognize the age relationships of the various strata on the basis of the fossils they contained. We owe to William Smith the *principle of faunal succession* which underscores all of the faunal zonation schemes that we use today. One of the most important points to remember about Smith's proposal is that he observed and used the changes in the invertebrate faunas as a basis for temporal correlation but he did not understand the reasons behind those changes, as we do now. Thus, Smith's operation was purely empirical.

UNIFORMITARIANISM, HUTTON, AND THE GEOLOGICAL PERSPECTIVE

James Hutton, a gentleman farmer and avid naturalist, published his *Theory of the Earth* in 1795. Publicized by John Playfair in 1802 as "Illustrations of the Huttonian Theory of the Earth," Hutton's work presented evidence that modern-day processes and the natural laws of physics and chemistry that govern them could account for features seen in ancient sedimentary rocks. The concept, known as *uniformitarianism*, is commonly paraphrased as "the present is the key to the past." Whereas we now recognize that a literal reading of the statement is inappropriate to geological processes that require a very long time over which to operate, uniformitarianism placed the study of the earth on a naturalist basis and focused attention on the amount of time required to form geological features. An important ramification of this, also supported later by the proposals of Darwin and Wallace, is that—contrary to what at the time was espoused in the scriptures and widely held to be true—the earth is very old.

DARWIN AND EVOLUTION

A naturalistic view of the world was further supported in 1858, when Charles Darwin and Alfred Wallace jointly presented their bases for believing that the multiplicity of organisms in the modern world stemmed from a process of gradual modification over time that can be summarized as "evolution by natural selection." This meant that new species arose, and others became extinct, by their ability (or inability) to adapt to inevitable changes in the natural environment over the course of geologic history. The concepts of Darwin and Wallace formed a partial underpinning for Smith's ideas as to the rationality of faunal change and its temporal significance. We now appreciate that each organism, once evolved, has a unique temporal span; after becoming extinct, it is extremely unlikely that anything exactly like it ever will evolve again.

THE MODERN SYNTHESIS

Thus, by the mid-nineteenth century, the disciplines of stratigraphy and paleontology had been placed on a modern footing, in that their study could be undertaken by scientific inquiry based on natural laws and processes. In 1866, Gregor Mendel established the science of genetics, which we now appreciate as governing the bases for the evolutionary changes observed by Darwin and Wallace. It is important for biologists to understand the genetical bases for the variations in morphology shown within and among species, and paleontologists usually attempt to reconstruct "populations" of fossil species, keeping in mind the ranges of variation found within, and the limits between, modern forms. At the same time, a stratigraphic paleontologist, who attempts to use fossils to describe, identify, and recognize intervals of time in the stratigraphic record, is more concerned with the results of evolution than with its processes. William Smith, of course, knew nothing of evolution or genetics.

STRATIGRAPHY, FIDELITY, AND PALEONTOLOGY: PRECISE CORRELATION

Stratigraphy provides the framework that contains the fossils used to construct temporal zonations of the rock record. The principle of superposition underscores and precedes that of faunal succession. Once having been stabilized by stratigraphy, however, faunal succession is paramount in developing stratigraphic units that represent the passage of time and that are recognizable over wide geographic (even global) distances.

GOALS

A major goal of chronostratigraphy (time as based on stratigraphy) and geochronology (determining the age of events in the evolution of the earth) is to devise a scheme of temporal intervals that neither overlaps nor contains gaps in information; all of geologic time is thus completely and unambiguously represented. Having accomplished this, the further goal is to demonstrate correlations of distant sites relative to the original sequence that are as closely time-correlative as possible.

The operation begins with the usual practice that the base of each unit defines the top of the unit just below, and that each base is defined on a temporally significant novelty which, in paleontology, means the advent of a new species. Of course, to be useful in this operation of correlation, the basis for recognizing the beginning of the new unit should be discernable as widely and unambiguously as possible. The new species should be widespread and its spread considered to have been "instantaneous" geologically. It is also imperative that the new species is defined. What does this mean?

OPERATIONS IN CORRELATION

In this context, one must clearly recognize that the term "definition" takes on a formal meaning, as does the term "characterization." The lower boundary of each chronostratigraphic unit must be defined in order to be unambiguous. The unit itself can be recognized on the basis of a number of taxa that are characteristic of it.

The definition of a chronostratigraphic boundary occurs at two operational levels. The first is that the boundary should be defined on the first stratigraphic occurrence of a single taxon. Unless extrinsically forced, it is unlikely that two or more taxa will have exactly the same temporal duration. A group of taxa that nearly or absolutely occurs solely within the limits of the unit under discussion can be used to characterize it. Thus, if one or more of the characterizing taxa are recognized in a peripheral site, those rocks can be correlated as being coeval with some part of the original unit. Only if the defining taxon is present in the peripheral site can those rocks be considered as correlating nearly or precisely with the base of the original unit. If the new (defining) taxon is believed to result from a regional dispersal (immigration) event, then recognizing the base of the unit should be straightforward, being stratigraphicaly unambiguous. The new species will be seen to occur abruptly in a stratigraphic succession.

The situation is at once more complex, but also more secure, in a case where the new taxon is thought to arise from an *in situ* evolutionary first occurrence. This is the second aspect of definition: defining the morphological basis on which the presence of the species is to be recognized. Here, it is especially important that the criteria for recognizing the presence of the taxon be clearly set out, so that its presence or absence also can be defined. One drawback of the "paleo-populational" concept of fossil species is a common presumption that a certain threshold of abundance of a particular morphology needs to be surpassed before a new species can be interpreted to have arisen. This adds a statistical complexity to the operation of species definition. The dilemma can be resolved if one recognizes that each species consists of a number of temporally and geographically overlapping morphologies. Thus, each species can be characterized on the combined presence of a number of the morphologies by which it is represented but its chronological beginning can be *defined* on the first stratigraphic occurrence *of a single specimen* having the morphology determined to *define* that species. All of the above presumes, of course, that any species being proposed for a boundary definition be thoroughly studied in advance as to its morphology, and geologic and geographic range.

Both of the operations discussed above regarding definition and characterization can evoke queries, and from the same direction. Basically, what does one do if the defining taxon or its morphology cannot be found? The dilemma is typical of the present state of affairs, and is not unique to the ideas summarized here. In the case where defining taxa or morphologies cannot be recognized, one still can correlate to "within" the zone or interval, or "within" the span of a species, but just cannot address the question of identifying the stratigraphic position of a boundary. That problem impacts all of stratigraphic paleontology and is not unique to the present discussion.

FIDELITY OF THE RECORD

A tacit assumption of many textbooks on stratigraphy is that in most cases, the record is complete enough for the purposes of reconstructing geological history. Certainly, one would not propose to define chronostratigraphic boundaries at breaks, hiatuses, or other points in a stratigraphic sequence showing evidence of the activities of extrinsic processes. At the same time, unconformities (breaks in the stratigraphic record where strata—and information—have been lost due to erosion or non-deposition) are also well known. An important realization most fully appreciated in the past few decades, however, is that even seemingly "complete" sequences are probably not entirely so, and that even in those sequences important information as to succession and duration of phenomena is missing. Although this has been stated, at least in principle, for more than 100 years, modern research is arriving at a growing recognition that the fidelity of the stratigraphic record systematically becomes worse in progressively older parts of the geologic time scale due to the cumulative effects of erosion and other destructive geological processes. On the one hand, this realization promotes the development of statistical proposals to address the probability that the physical record of a taxon's sojourn in time accurately reflects its geological lifespan. A decision on this point thus has implications for evaluating the validity of perceived "first" or "last" occurrences of taxa, both singularly and collectively (that is, individual or mass originations or extinctions). On the other hand, we, as chronostratigraphers, continually need to strive to be aware of where important breaks are or are not in the stratigraphic record.

ISOTOPIC AND MAGNETIC POLARITY INFORMATION

Fundamentally all subdivisions of the geologic time scale used today were developed over the past 150 or more years by combining the stratigraphic and paleontological records. Progressively in the past fifty or so years, however, radioisotopic and magnetic polarity methods have materially aided our ability to correlate rocks of the earth's crust. During this time, scientists have recognized that various "parent" isotopes of radioactive elements decay into "daughter" products at rates that are virtually unaffected by most geologic processes. Among those known, the radioactive decay series from isotopes of uranium to lead, strontium to rubidium, potassium to argon, and argon to argon are among the most popular as pertaining to meaningful geological situations. In all cases, remains of the parent mineral and the new daughter isotope must be retained in the crystal lattice involved in the analysis. The radiocarbon dating method can be used to evaluate the age of rocks as old as about 50,000 years, but for older samples the margin of analytical error is too large to allow a precise determination of the age to be made.

In order to be useful, any isotopically determined age must be analytically precise, and in most systems the precision usually is within ± 2 percent of the stated age or less. All of the isotopic calibration systems provide a numerical "date," but in progressively older parts of the geologic time scale the margin of error can become quite large in terms of the actual span of years it embraces. This factor must be kept in mind when assigning ages to various events of the ancient past.

Studies of the magnetic properties of rocks over the past few decades have revealed that the magnetic field of the earth spontaneously reverses, and that intervals of either normal (present-day) or reversed polarity have an average duration of about 300,000 years. Although the underlying mechanism for this process is not well understood, it appears that the polarity change transpires over an interval of about 10,000 years. In geological terms, this is virtually instantaneous, and is global in extent. If a polarity change can be uniquely identified in geological contexts it provides an extremely powerful tool for correlation, and a global magnetic polarity time scale has been built up for the past 200 million years based on spreading rates calculated from the magnetic reversal pattern displayed in the basalts of the ocean floor.

We now know that the sea floor is formed anew at oceanic ridges, and is carried laterally to disappear eventually down oceanic trenches. As each new increment of sea floor basalt is generated at the ridge, it receives the magnetic polarity domain then in effect, and over time, a pattern of normal and reversed polarity signatures is preserved in the now cooled oceanic crust. Ages of reversal boundaries within the overall pattern can be calculated by assuming effectively linear spreading rates relative to the distance between the boundary and the oceanic ridge which produced that part of the sea floor. Thus, a global magnetic polarity time scale can be established, at least for the present ocean's basins. Because oceanic crust is ultimately consumed in oceanic trenches, there is a finite limit to the age of oceanic crust now preserved in the world's ocean floors. The oldest crust is about late Jurassic in age, or about 150 million years old. An effective, continuously developed, and preserved magnetic polarity reversal history thus extends from the present to about the late Jurassic. Whereas magnetic polarity changes can be preserved in older rocks, it is more difficult to compile a linear pattern of change comparable to that for the late Jurassic to Recent.

Nevertheless, magnetic polarity patterns also can be preserved in volcanic and sedimentary sequences developed on land and in the sea, and ages applied to them from other sources (paleontological, radioisotopic, and so on). By these means, composite magnetic polarity reversal histories can be developed for pre-Jurassic rocks. Using the same principles, magnetic reversal patterns preserved in continental rocks of post-Jurassic age can be supplied with ages derived from the global time scale.

Magnetic polarity and radioisotopic information is also useful in assessing the relative completeness of sedimentary sequences. Some continental successions contain both well-displayed magnetic polarity stratigraphies and a useful number of interbedded volcanic units amenable of isotopic dating. In at least one instance, the accumulation rate for the sedimentary sequence appears to be slower when the ages assigned to it are derived solely from a correlation to the global magnetic polarity time scale instead of being calculated on the bases of the isotopic ages of the interbedded volcanic rocks. This does not mean that spreading-rate ages assigned to the magnetic polarity time scale are in error, but rather that some of the global magnetic polarity record is missing in the sedimentary sequence under discussion. This indicates that some of the polarity boundaries in the continental section occur at hiatuses, and thus that the record is incomplete.

To summarize, the joint disciplines of paleontology and stratigraphy are still important and viable in identifying events important to chronostratigraphy and ordering them in a relative framework; other methods help develop local and regional chronologies and correlations; and refinements in paleontology still potentially give chronostratigraphic increments with a precision and accuracy at least equal to those of other systems. All systems, however, should be used synergistically to their collective improvement and to continue to refine the accuracy of our reconstructions of the events that shaped the lithosphere, biosphere, and atmosphere through time.

[M.O.W.]

See also **Archaeological Dating Methods; Catastrophism; Evolutionary Progress; Evolution of Evolutionism; Extinction; Fossil Record; Geochronometry; Geologic Time Scale; Saltatory Evolution; Time Available for Evolution.**

FURTHER READINGS

Barrell, J. "Rhythms and the Measurement of Geologic Time." *Geological Society of America Bulletin* 28 (1917): 745–904.

Berry, W.B.N. *Growth of a Prehistoric Time Scale, Based on Organic Evolution.* London: Blackwell Scientific Publications, 1987.

MacFadden, B.J. "An Overview of 'Chronostratigraphy of Cenozoic Terrestrial Sediments and Faunas.'" *Journal of Geology* 98 (1990): 429–432.

Murphy, M.A. "On Chronostratigraphic Units." *Journal of Paleontology* 51 (1977): 123–219.

Sadler, P.M., and D.M. Strauss. "Classical Confidence Intervals and Bayesian Posterior Probabilities for the Ends of Local Taxon Ranges." *Mathematical Geology* 21 (1989): 411–427.

Woodburne, M.O., ed. Preface and Introduction. *Cenozoic Mammals of North America: Geochronology and Biostratigraphy.* Berkeley: U of California P, 1987. ix-xii, and 1–8.

———. "Principles, Classification, and Recommendations." *Cenozoic Mammals of North America, Geochronology and Biostratigraphy.* Ed. M.O. Woodburne. Berkeley: U of California P, 1987. 9–17.

STREAM OF CONSCIOUSNESS

Stream of consciousness is a modern technique employed in fiction and concerned with the attempt to delve (as with the *monologue intérieur*) into the interior life of a character. Much of the material in stream-of-consciousness fiction is recaptured through the mind of the protagonist from past experiences, the recalling of which is triggered by an experience in the present. As a result, the present time line of the action tends to be relatively short. Since the present time line can easily be as limited in length as one day, the resulting time structure may be compared with the classical dramatic unities of time, action, and place. Techniques comparable to stream of consciousness also became widely adapted to the new medium of film, for which one uses the term "flashback."

Stream of consciousness cannot be entirely realistic because consciousness is presumably not an exclusively verbal or grammatical medium. However, in undertaking to reproduce consciousness in the raw, stream of consciousness does differ from and go beyond the earlier long passages of introspection as found in Henry James and Dostoevski. Moreover, there is clearly a new Freudian influence in this important development. Under "Virginia Woolf," the *Dictionary of National Biography*, edited by her father, stresses not only the early influence on her of Henry James, Henri Bergson, and Freud, but adds, "As for Sigmund Freud, she was partly responsible for the publication in English of some of his works and for the vogue of psychoanalysis in England especially in 1918–22."

Some of the earliest of the major works concerned with stream of consciousness appeared in the period 1922–27, immediately following the introduction of Freud into English and the related vogue of psychoanalysis. Among these are James Joyce's *Ulysses* (1922), Virginia Woolf's *Mrs. Dalloway* (1925), and François Mauriac's *Thérèse Desqueyroux* (1927). In *Ulysses*, for example, the novel ends with Molly Bloom's interior monologue of some forty-two pages; in *Mrs. Dalloway* the present time line of the novel is restricted to a day in the life of the protagonist; and in *Thérèse Desqueyroux*, the present time line of the first third of the novel is restricted to a train ride by the protagonist. Though not a major work, it is noteworthy that in Freud's home town of Vienna, Arthur Schnitzler had used a comparable technique in his *Leutnant Gustl* as early as 1900. Stream-of-consciousness techniques became as quickly employed in the short story as they were in the novel. Early examples include Katherine Mansfield's "Daughters of the Late Colonel" (*The Garden Party* [1922]) and Virginia Woolf's "The New Dress," which first appeared in *Forum* (1927).

Though the technique is not as well suited to novels of action, stream of consciousness can readily be used for psychological novels that are concerned with insights over a considerable length of time and, if necessary, such insights can also be presented in chronological order. For example, Margaret Laurence's *Stone Angel* (1964), restricts its present time line to the last few weeks of Hagar's ninety years of life. But the author is able to reveal the inner workings of that life through chronological incidents in the present that take Hagar back to corresponding but also chronologically ordered incidents throughout her entire past existence.

[S.L.M.]

See also **Bergson, Henri; Dramatic Unities; Film; Freud, Sigmund; Novel; Psychoanalysis.**

FURTHER READINGS

Cohn, Dorritt. *Transparent Minds: Narrative Modes for Presenting Consciousness in Fiction*. Princeton: Princeton UP, 1978.

Friedman, Melvin. *Stream of Consciousness: A Study in Literary Method*. New Haven: Yale UP, 1955.

Humphrey, Robert. *Stream of Consciousness in the Modern Novel*. Berkeley: U of California P, 1954.

Kumar, Shiv K. *Bergson and the Stream of Consciousness Novel*. London: Blackie, 1962.

Steinberg, Erwin R. *The Stream of Consciousness and Beyond in* Ulysses. Pittsburgh: U of Pittsburgh P, 1973.

SYMBIOSIS

The derivation of the term *symbiosis* means "life together," and so in the loosest sense, symbiosis implies any kind of association between organisms of different types, such as plant/animal, fungal/algal, animal/bacterial, and so on, from which both parties derive some benefit. The numerous technical terms for the various degrees of intimacy between the symbiotic associates are reduced here to the most essential. "Symbiosis" will be taken as the generic term, although "mutualism" is also popular.

Endosymbiosis is the most intimate association, involving the intracellular presence of the symbionts in the host cells. Such a symbiosis is "holobiotic"; that is, the symbionts are found in the reproductive cells, and so are vertically or directly transferred from generation to generation.

Commensalism is the least intimate of the symbiotic associations. Meaning, by derivation, "eating at the same table," it includes such examples as anemones that live anchored to the shell apertures of hermit crabs, sharing the food of the latter and providing some protection from predators. Also included are cleaner-fish that remove growths and parasites from their hosts while sharing their food.

Some of the more intimate symbioses have had a major impact on the evolution of the biosphere. Endosymbiosis produced the eukaryotic cells that accelerated the oxygenation of the atmosphere and gave rise to the lines of multicellular plants and animals. A symbiosis between dinoflagellate algae and primitive polyps produced the coral reefs in barren tropical oceans, along with their highly diverse ecosystems. The invasion of the land by plants was made possible by an association of algae and fungi that combined their advantages to free mineral salts from the soil and protect the associates from dehydration. Most existing plants continue to depend on "mycorrhizal" (fungal-root) symbioses with fungi for their survival. When insect ancestors invaded the land they found that the greatest potential resource was plant cellulose, which they could not digest. Consequently, some of them formed symbioses with cellulose-digesting bacteria and protozoans. In turn, the insects provided an important link in the terrestrial food chain, as food for the tetrapods and their reptile, bird, and mammal descendants. Grass-eating mammals have also had to depend on cellulolytic bacteria in their stomachs to be able to digest their food.

Symbioses represent wholes that are greater than the sum of their parts. Features that in the independently living organisms would have been detrimental or toxic, requiring excretion and the expenditure of energy, are often mutually useful in symbiosis, so the negative becomes the positive. Thus, symbioses have contributed not only to the establishment of major ecosystems, but have also been responsible for some of the greatest biological revolutions. Furthermore, the establishment of a new symbiosis is a legitimate example of saltatory evolution, since the integration is a single-step complexification rather than a cumulative adaptation.

[R.G.B.R.]

See also **Biological Revolutions; Coevolution; Endosymbiosis; Gaia Theory; Saltatory Evolution.**

FURTHER READINGS

Baucher, D.H., ed. *The Biology of Mutualism*. Oxford: Oxford UP, 1988.

TAYLOR, FREDERICK WINSLOW (1856–1915)

Frederick Winslow Taylor (1856–1915) has generally been considered the pioneer of industrial engineering, and it has been customary to credit him, as R.M. Currie does, with "having first evolved the principle of breaking a job down into detailed elements to determine a time to be allowed for the job." Taylor's work was essentially, though not entirely, concerned with time studies, but we now know that time and organization studies in industry really begin in the Restoration and eighteenth century (see **Industrial Engineering [Before Taylor]**).

Unlike his predecessors, Taylor, born in Germantown, Pennsylvania, was neither a scholar like Charles Babbage nor the son of a factory owner like James Watt Jr. Rather, he had been apprenticed as a machinist and patternmaker, and was engaged as an employee. At the Midvale Steel Company, where he was engaged as a gang boss, Taylor had recognized the need for measuring a "fair day's work" as early as 1880 or 1881. This led him to undertake a series of time studies and related investigations in association with men like his assistant at Midvale, Henry L. Gantt, and F.A. Halsey, who specialized in studies concerned with work incentives. Taylor—who objected to the term, "Taylor system"—insisted on referring to his work as Scientific Management.

At Bethlehem Steel, during the Spanish-American War, Taylor was able to show how 80,000 tons of pig iron, for which there had been no market before the war, could be loaded by using his systems in little more than one-quarter of the man-hours that had been needed in the past. By employing work measurement, he was able to estimate that instead of the previous maximum of 12$^{1}/_{2}$ tons per day selected men would now be able to handle forty-seven tons per day. As a result of work that he had completed previously with Carl G. Barth, Taylor was aware of the relationship—in this case, a forty-two-pound pig of iron could only be carried for 43 percent of the working day—between the weight that a man carried and the time that he could be under load. In order to translate this knowledge into practical results, Taylor offered a carefully selected workman $1.85 per day instead of the customary $1.15 per day. But he did so with the explicit agreement that the workman accepted "having a man . . . who understood Barth's law, stand over him and direct this

work day after day, until he acquired the habit of resting at proper intervals."

Typically, what Taylor paid to the workman was only a small part of the money that he expected to save because of his time management system. When thus applying the Towne-Halsey system of limited incentives, Taylor defends himself by claiming that "This system . . . diminishes soldiering, and . . . since the workman only receives say one-third of the increase in pay that he would get under corresponding conditions on piece work, there is not the same temptation for the employer to cut prices." Taylor has some very clear opinions about "soldiering," or shirking work, and notes that when he arrived at the Midvale Steel Company in 1878, he soon realized that the workmen "had set a pace for each machine throughout the shop, which was limited to about a third of a good day's work." He protests that such activities would ultimately benefit neither the men, their employers, nor the consuming public. And he notes that English employees "more than in any other civilized country, are deliberately restricting their output because they are possessed by the fallacy that it is against their best interest for each man to work as hard as he can."

In a remarkably early foreshadowing of what would take place first in England and later in North America, Taylor argues the necessity for restraining both labor and management from self-serving activities at the expense of "the third party (the whole people)." It was also his view that to give workers much more than a 60 percent increase in wages, whatever the increase in efficiency, would encourage "many of them [to] work irregularly and tend to become more or less shiftless, extravagant and dissipated." But he also felt strongly that the public "will no longer tolerate the type of employer who . . . merely cracks his whip over the heads of his workmen and attempts to drive them into harder work for low pay." Nevertheless, Taylor felt, too, that the public, for its part, would "No more . . . tolerate tyranny on the part of labor which demands one increase after another in pay and shorter hours while at the same time it becomes less instead of more efficient." The Western world has still been largely unable to resolve the problems related to what Taylor has to say regarding labor.

By a series of carefully controlled studies related to shoveling, Taylor was able to show that "whatever the class of material they were to handle," men did more work per day with a shovel-load averaging twenty-one pounds than they could achieve with any other size. As a result of his experiments related to this work, Taylor reduced a work force from between 400–600 to 140 men; increased the load moved from sixteen tons per man-day for $1.15 to fifty-nine tons per man-day for $1.85; and decreased the cost of shoveling one ton from seventy-two cents to thirty-three cents. And he did this notwithstanding the fact that his methods involved a considerable increase in managerial and clerical work. In attempting to counter the widespread fear that workers might lose their jobs through the effectiveness of scientific management, Taylor cited the fear that English hand weavers had experienced when they expected power looms would have a comparable effect: "In Manchester, England, in 1840, there were 5,000 operatives, and in Manchester today there are 250,000 operatives . . . there now comes out of Manchester, England, 400–500 yards of cotton cloth for every single yard that came out in 1840."

The improved level of productivity achieved by Taylor derived in great measure from dividing each operation into a series of simple elements and setting down the results of timing those elements: "thousands of stop-watch observations were made to study just how quickly a laborer . . . can push his shovel into a load of materials and then draw it out properly loaded." But Taylor's method first required that he select and time the work of someone whose ability to perform the job in hand was considerably above average. This meant that whereas for his studies in loading pig iron he had sought men "of the type of the ox," when it came to his studies on the inspection of bicycle balls he needed to seek out girls "born with unusually quick powers of perception accompanied by quick responsive action."

Taylor writes that "when the bicycle craze was at its height some years ago . . . the writer was given the task of systematizing the largest bicycle ball factory in this country." Starting with the process that modern industrial engineers call "creaming the business," Taylor had begun his study with the 120 girls employed in inspection: "In most cases . . . there exist certain imperfections in working conditions which can at once be improved with benefit to all concerned. . . . A most casual study made it evident that a very considerable part of the ten and one half hours during which the girls were supposed to work was really spent in idleness because the working period was too long."

As occurs with management elsewhere in Taylor's studies, when the girls in the bicycle factory were asked to vote on whether they would accept a reduction in working hours for the same pay, they "wanted no innovation of any kind." However, Taylor nonetheless shortened the working day from $10\frac{1}{2}$ to $8\frac{1}{2}$ hours by using successive thirty minute reductions. Furthermore, in order that they should not work for more than $1\frac{1}{4}$ hours at a time he also instituted two recess periods of ten minutes each in both the morning and afternoon. Some remarkable savings were achieved even though the over-inspecting of millions of small metal balls for defects and considerable additional managerial and clerical costs were added to the price of quality control. As Taylor reports, "thirty-five girls did the work formerly done by one hundred and twenty. And . . . the accuracy. . .at the higher speed was two-thirds greater than at the former slow speed." In addition to reducing the working day from $10\frac{1}{2}$ to $8\frac{1}{2}$ hours, the employees not only benefited from a Saturday half holiday, but their wages also increased by, on average, "from 80–100 percent."

The work on bicycle balls derived from America's remarkable boom in the bicycle trade at the close of the nineteenth century. However, between 1899 and 1904, this boom in production dropped off from 2 million to .25 million units per year. Happily for both Taylor and for American manufacturing, the decline in bicycle production occurred only shortly before the introduction of mass-produced automobiles. In fact, 15 million of Henry Ford's Model Ts had been sold by the late 1920s, using production methods much influenced by Taylor.

Taylor's work on time measurement was by no means confined to the operations of labor.

His longest, most difficult, and probably most satisfying undertaking was concerned with ascertaining and documenting the optimum feeds and speeds for machine tools. In addition, his work with J. Mansell-White resulted, in 1898, in what is now called the Taylor-White process of treating tool steel. This employed quite a different method for improving the effectiveness of machine tools. In one of many examples, steel made with the Taylor-White process could cut at the rate of sixty feet per minute against twelve feet per minute with a tool made from the best carbon tool steel. In addition, Taylor's work with lathes resulted in improved criteria for standardizing, organizing, and paying for machine production. Furthermore, as already indicated, his job measurements entailed wages being calculated on the basis of "a proper day's work."

For the most part, the work of Taylor and his associates—who were mainly Americans—occurred during the thirty or so years leading up to World War I. Their contribution to industrial productivity has been widely criticized, particularly for its supposed "mechanization" of human beings. When they began, England was still the most highly industrialized country in the world, but Taylor and his associates did much to change the effectiveness of the American workforce. The increased effectiveness of the American workforce must at least, in part, be credited for the radical change in the relative economic positions of Britain and the United States which took place between, during, and after the two world wars.

[S.L.M.]

See also **Industrial Engineering [Before Taylor]; Industrial Engineering [After Taylor].**

FURTHER READINGS

Macey, Samuel L. "Work Study before Taylor: An Examination of Certain Preconditions for Time and Motion Study that Began in the Seventeenth Century." *Work Study and Management Services* 18 (October 1974): 530–536.

———. *The Dynamics of Progress: Time, Method, and Measure.* Athens: U of Georgia P, 1989.

Taylor, Frederick Winslow. *Scientific Management.* Comprising *Shop Management, The Principles of Scientific Management,* and *Testimony Before the Special House Committee.* New York: Harper and Brothers, 1947.

TEAM SPORTS

Each of the leading team sports of the Western world—cricket, hockey, football, baseball, and basketball—began its rise to prominence in the latter half of the nineteenth century. Most of these sports had, of course, been played in variable forms for years, even centuries before, but with the growth of mass leisure was born the modern sports fan, perhaps the single greatest influence on the history of sport. No longer could the rules of a game vary from week to week, field to field; spectators demanded standards, the only means by which they could compare the merits of rival teams or players. Of equal importance, no longer could sporting events last for indefinite, unregulated periods of time, as they had in their infancy.

Although the late nineteenth-century sports fan possessed newfound leisure time, that time was nevertheless limited by the clock, the controller of work time and—consequently—of playtime. (Though John Whitehurst of Derby invented the first factory time clock in 1750, such machines did not achieve their modern prominence until around 1880, and the "timecard" followed shortly thereafter.) With the clock on the factory or shop wall counting every moment of their free time, spectators sought games of known temporal limits. Thus, the needs of the spectator led not only to the standardization of the *rules* of sport, but also to the delimiting of the *duration* of sport.

With one notable exception, every prevailing team sport of the twentieth century is subject to the confinement of the clock. Basketball, the youngest of these sports, has had time limits since its invention by James B. Naismith on December 21, 1891. Naismith divided his game into fifteen-minute halves; they have since been extended to twenty minutes in college basketball, while games of the National Basketball Association consist of four twelve-minute quarters. In 1871, England's Rugby Football Union fixed the length of its games at ninety minutes; American football officials reduced their game to sixty minutes (fifteen-minute quarters) in 1906, while association football (soccer) has retained the full ninety minutes, with forty-five-minute halves. After 1875, Canadian hockey adopted the forty-five-minute halves of rugby football; in 1909, the National Hockey Association introduced the present system of three twenty-minute periods. Even cricket, arguably the least time-bound of these sports, has not entirely escaped the domination of the clock: since 1939, the year of the last so-called timeless test, matches between member nations of the International Cricket Conference—tests—have been limited to thirty hours over five days.

Moreover, in recent years the Marylebone Cricket Club—cricket's voice of authority—has shown considerable concern with "time-wasting" during the game (see, for example, Law 31 of the 1980 Code).

The introduction of the clock into team sports events did more than limit a game's duration; it also provided spectators with a third competitor—the clock itself. In the 1930s, Herbert Chapman, then manager of the Arsenal Football Club of London, proposed the use of a large white time clock to make the game more enjoyable for spectators. League officials rejected his plan, but their early conservatism was not to last. Unlike their British counterparts, however, Canadian hockey officials responded quickly to the growing desire of the spectators for temporal information. In 1931, visitors to the Montreal Forum or Maple Leaf Gardens could, for the first time, measure the action on the ice against a giant time clock. Designed by Fenton A. Roth, the clock was four-sided, with four-foot-square canvas clocks facing each wall of the arena, and—in the words of a Toronto *Globe* reporter—allowed fans to "watch every minute of the game tick off." The clocks soon spread to every indoor rink in Canada.

Basketball, football, hockey, and cricket—each of these sports takes place within the time of the clock, and, from the fans' perspective at least, enjoys the added dimension of competition against time itself. But there remains one team sport that neither accepts the clock's domination nor suffers from its absence—baseball.

On the baseball field, time is measured in outs, not moments. Unlike other athletes, a ballplayer cannot "beat" or "kill" the clock—there is no clock to beat or kill. As Baltimore Oriole manager Earl Weaver once said, "You've got to throw the ball over the goddamn plate and give the other man his chance. That's why baseball is the greatest game of them all." Because of the clock's absence, baseball time can only be reckoned by the passage of events; in fact, time in baseball has no meaning *apart* from events. In other team sports, commentators and spectators refer to the time elapsed or remaining; in baseball, however, the game's progress can only be measured by innings, outs, or strikes—by events.

Baseball is a game without clocks, a game that possesses the unique ability to escape temporality itself. Thus, more than any other sport, the game admits of infinity. As Roger Angell says in *The Summer Game*, "Since baseball time is measured only in outs, all you have to do is succeed utterly; keep hitting, keep the rally alive, and you have defeated time." In a tie—a perfect balance of forces—a baseball game can last forever. In his 1986 novel, *The Iowa Baseball Confederacy*, W.P. Kinsella plays with this eternal aspect of baseball, featuring as the core of the novel a game that lasts for 2,648 innings—forty days, a figure that, through its Biblical associations, invites a non-literal interpretation.

In *How Life Imitates the World Series*, Thomas Boswell calls baseball "an antidote to modern life, a free pass back to the tempo of an earlier time." The game achieves this preindustrial, almost pastoral tempo through its reliance on event time, rather than on the clock time that has dominated team sports since the turn of the century. Baseball, in short, is a revolt against the clock, and against a clock-dominated world. In Bernard Malamud's *The Natural* (1952), Roy Hobbs reifies this revolt: "in the second game at Ebbets Field, [Roy] took hold of himself, gripped Wonderboy, and bashed the first pitch into the clock on the right field wall. The clock spattered minutes all over the place, and after that the Dodgers never knew what time it was."

Team sports came of age in the modern era; it is therefore hardly surprising that they should, with the exception of baseball, be dominated by the symbol of that era—the ineluctable clock. Baseball, too, may yet succumb to the conquest of the clock: the rigidly time-bound world of television has never been comfortable with the game's protracted, unpredictable, and possibly infinite duration. In North America, baseball has long since lost its position as television's premier sports event to football, partly because of the latter's willingness to adapt its rules to the temporal needs of television—such as the creation of time-outs to accommodate commercials. (In Japan, the networks terminate baseball broadcasts at a set time, regardless of whether or not the game has ended.) And, since television largely determines the games we watch, the conflict between baseball's event time and television's clock time may one day spell the game's demise. In the interim, however, we as spectators can participate vicariously in baseball's temporal rebellion, and allow the game—as Roger Angell puts it—to "hold us in its own continuum and mercifully release us from our own."

[N.J.M.]

See also **Racing Sports and the Stopwatch.**

FURTHER READINGS

Angell, Roger. *The Summer Game*. 1962; reprint, New York: Popular Library, 1972.

Boswell, Thomas. *How Life Imitates the World Series.* New York: Penguin, 1983.

Guttmann, Allen. "Why Baseball Was Our National Game." *From Ritual to Record: The Nature of Modern Sports.* New York: Columbia UP, 1978. 92–116.

Morrow, Don, et al. *A Concise History of Sport in Canada.* Toronto: Oxford UP, 1989.

TELECOMMUNICATIONS

Telecommunications, or communications over long distances, are concerned with the high-speed transmission of information from one point to another by automated, dynamic electric and electronic means, and are at the heart of the "global information age" and our sense that time is "speeding up." Major inventions since the end of World War II—in particular, the transistor, the laser, and fiber optics—have taught us that time is not absolute. In our short history on earth, our sense of time has evolved from rituals and language to calendars to clocks to computers and is about to make a further leap into photonics. As telecommunication technologies improve, they become smaller and take up less space, generate less heat, use less energy, and become more economical to produce and market. Conversely, these minute information carriers are designed to bridge ever larger distances with picture, sound, and data, not only on earth, but also throughout our solar system.

The hardware of telecommunication technologies tends to be integrated and systemic—computer, television, cable, satellite, laser, fiber optic, and microchip technologies combining to form a vast interactive information and communications network that can potentially give each person on earth access to every other person, and make every byte and datum available to anyone. Following World War II, burgeoning telephone and television traffic requirements on overland routes were met through the use of microwave repeater systems, whose towers are a familiar sight in the developed nations. Microwaves travel in straight lines and repeaters must be stationed at intervals of twenty to thirty miles. Placing a repeater in a satellite, therefore, became an economic asset as well as an enormous technical advantage. The horizon, as "seen" from a communications satellite located several thousand miles above earth, spans whole continents and oceans. The communications satellite era began in 1958 with Project Score Satellite and developed rapidly in the 1960s into synchronous communications systems—a series of stationary satellites which remain at a designated altitude of 22,300 miles while completing one revolution around earth in twenty-four hours. With only three satellites it is possible to provide global coverage of television news and entertainment.

Because of the inventions of the last fifty years, millions of people live, work, travel, communicate, and perceive time differently. In the developed nations of this postindustrial era, whole populations are experiencing fundamental changes in lifestyle as information technologies—such as new telephone systems, faxes, and electronically linked industrial and personal computers—expand into giant industries and spawn new consumer products, all designed to "save time." But by speeding up the flow of activity, we may actually be decreasing the amount of time available to deal with the volume of information and the resulting workload. Further, the electronic production, use, storage, and dissemination of massive amounts of information is affecting global demographics, economies, employment, politics, education, social systems, and the human ability to make and sustain unique cultures within individual nations and groups. The speed of telecommunications also appears to be accelerating human impatience because as our brains master diverse computer functions and the buttons of electronic gadgets, we increasingly feel that such devices are "too slow."

The *concept* of telecommunications originated early in the nineteenth century with crude models of an electric telegraph system later improved by Samuel Morse. Together with telegraphy, the telephone was the chief catalyst for the development of telecommunications and continues in that role today. But the quantum leap into the electronic age occurred in 1947 when three Americans, Walter Brattain, William Shockley, and John Bardeen, invented the transistor that made possible the computer and a host of products—such as calculators, electronic watches, pacemakers and hearing aids, battery operated radios and TVs, and more—that are now common to daily life. In addition, transistors are the cornerstone of space flight and modern aeronautics and are the driving force behind satellite communications.

With lasers and fiber optics, or light wave communication that is the optical equivalent of the transistor, we are evolving now from the electronic age into the photonic age. The photonic computer will be at least 1,000 times faster than today's best stand-alone, mainframe computer, making possible *networked computing* as fiber optics gain prominence in postal, telephone, cable television, radio, videotext, and other systems. Fiber optic and satellite telecommunications technologies now link (but do not unify) the world's nations. As a result, the same TV and radio programs can be seen and heard simultaneously by billions. Increasingly in the developed nations, people find themselves living and working inside "fibered" office and apartment buildings, campuses, hospitals, and homes, environments that tend to separate people from each other as electronic communications devices make it unnecessary to conduct business, shop, or even attend school *in person*. As E.M. Forster suggested in his short story "The Machine Stops," our descendants may live in single rooms, rarely leaving their controlled environments, but still able to make instant TV contact with any person anywhere on earth.

Today, in an effort to improve and prolong life and to save time, major urban centers are beginning to transform themselves into "intelligence islands." By the end of the century—using broad-band fiber optic cables carrying data at two billion bits a second—these urban centers will be able to deliver a wide range of health care, education, entertainment, and public services to every home, school, and business. Some cities, such as Berlin and Tokyo, are using fiber optics connected to a teleport, a giant earth station, to link themselves to virtually every other city in the world. Japan, Germany, and Hong Kong are building telecommunication systems to transmit voice, video, and text at any speed or volume from one point to another or to millions of locations simultaneously. In the United States, more than two-thirds of the work force is involved in the electronic information industry. As in other developed nations, United States corporations are moving their headquarters out of major cities now that corporate decisions, affecting millions of people, can be made on airplanes, by faxes, and on computers and instantly communicated to branch offices anywhere in the world ("global localization").

At the most local level, our individual homes, such commonplace devices as video cassette recorders and telephone answering machines continuously recall and eliminate the past by recording and replaying information we prefer not to miss while we are elsewhere. We then erase and repeat the process, as we "catch up" by

attempting to see and reconstruct the past, accelerate or slow down the present, and anticipate the future. Of course, all that we ever experience is the past, but the effort to understand and control time will continue to give rise to new technologies aimed at expanding, perhaps one day even replacing, the functions and intellect of the human brain and its consuming concern with forestalling death.

[J.O.]

See also **Film; Television.**

FURTHER READINGS

Clarke, Arthur C. *Profiles of the Future.* New York: Holt, Rinehart and Winston, 1984.

Davidson, George E. *Beehives of Invention: Edison and His Laboratories.* Washington: Office of Publications, National Park Service, 1973.

Diebold, John. *The Innovators.* New York: Truman Talley Books, 1990.

Dutton, William H., Jay G. Blumler, and Kenneth L. Kraemer, eds. *Wired Cities: Shaping the Future of Communications.* Boston: Hall, 1987.

O'Neill, E.F., ed. *A History of Engineering and Science in the Bell Laboratories: Transmission Technology (1925–1975).* Short Hills: AT&T Bell Laboratories, 1983.

TELEVISION

Television (TV), the offspring of film, is the simultaneous electronic transmission and reception of transient moving images and sound, originally by electromagnetic radio waves, but increasingly by fiber optic cables. Since 1919 and the invention of the first tiny TV picture tube, since 1927 when the first simultaneous telecast of image and sound was transmitted over any distance, and since 1931 and the first transatlantic telecast, the TV picture tube has become capable of receiving more than 100 channels with the potential for hundreds more through the use of fiber optic cables. Through mass marketing techniques and technological advances developed since 1950, TV has effected the fastest transformation of life in modern times, especially in industrialized nations, where many people spend an average of fifty hours per week viewing TV programs, organizing daily activities around program schedules, and growing used to moving visually from one time and place to another in a fraction of a second, through the flick of a button, without ever leaving the room. TV viewers watch images of the past, but because they remain in one place engaged in the same activity, it is as though they exist in a continuous present. Many homes have several

TV sets to accommodate the viewing preferences of different family members, and this often results in the isolation of people in separate rooms, each viewing the past in a personal present.

Like film, TV systems use the phenomenon of *persistence of vision*, the eye's ability to break a scene into tiny separate segments and reassemble it in one seemingly continuous flow of action apparently occurring at one time. The pictures we see on TV screens in our homes usually originate on videotape in TV studios in cities that may be thousands of miles away, though increasingly they are broadcast live by microwave link to a transmitting station floating above earth. Unlike film, which is laboriously constructed for viewing much later, TV pictures, we are told, can be viewed "live" as we watch them, no matter where we may be, because images and sounds are transmitted at the speed of light. But what we are really seeing is an electrical wave *description* of the image and sound, which stay in their original place and perish as soon as they happen.

A "pickup tube" inside a studio or field camera converts an optical image into a corresponding image composed of varying electrical charges. Unlike the strip of film that is projected onto a screen in a movie theater, the TV image is scanned by an electron gun, with 525 scanning lines comprising a single image. In over-the-air broadcasting, the TV camera's electrical and sound signals (more than 7 million per second) are synchronized and superimposed on a carrier frequency, or channel; then the channel and signal is fed to a broadcast antenna, or transmitter, which emits the carrier and signal as powerful electromagnetic radiations to a receiving antenna; in turn, the antenna feeds the radiations to the tuner in our TV sets. The tuner selects the desired frequencies (channel) and the signal is removed from the carrier, amplified and fed into the picture tube, where the image is reconstructed—just as it is in the human eye or in a film camera—by reversing the original pickup operation. Whenever we "change channels," we cause the above process to occur, and the speed and ease of the operation increases still further our sense that events are occurring in present time.

Technological advances in satellites, the introduction of cable TV, constant surplus program production, increasing democratization and privatization of broadcast facilities around the globe, and the ever-expanding home video market enable production companies to capitalize on TV's almost infinite recyclability—programs can be repackaged and rerun in perpetuity. Switching channels can immediately show a program made in 1950, a movie made in 1925, a "live" newscast happening at that moment, or a prediction of an election outcome made before the polls have closed. We can also create our own channel by playing home movies made with our own video cameras and shown through videocassette recorders on our TV sets. Just as the original still cameras enabled us to freeze ourselves in time by creating photographic images of our living selves, so does TV permit us to immortalize ourselves in an even more lifelike way—moving and talking on videotape that can be replayed frequently.

Television both globalizes and regionalizes human life. These parallel tendencies are made possible by orbiting satellites that permit simultaneous telecast of the same information to all parts of the globe at the same moment, reaching billions of viewers and potentially creating a single cultural consciousness. Because the bulk of TV production is still concentrated in a few centers in less than a dozen developed nations, information flows from developed to developing nations. A New Guinea hunter can now view the same newscast as an American computer analyst, though they live in different time zones and cultures. And though all living creatures are temporally related to their environments, TV's electronic time zones are competing increasingly with—some would say replacing—our internal biological clocks to determine our sense of time.

As language, with its time-conscious verb tenses, is tailored to the short-range goal of TV—conveying the simplest message to the largest number of people for maximum, instantaneous effect—words become "sound bites" instead of extended thoughts that allow for pause and reflection. Acquiring knowledge, as opposed to mere information, requires a sense of open-ended time that permits blunders, stops, and starts as individuals progress beyond basic literacy to a deeper, richer understanding of their world and their place in it. Educators and policy makers are increasingly concerned that the predominantly visual environment fostered by TV may be contributing to functional illiteracy as people absorb pictures rather than words, yet are required to learn more at faster speeds to keep pace with the volume of transmitted information. The so-called "slow learner" may actually be an ordinary learner who is trying to pause and think between "sound bites." As we advance toward the next century and encounter the wall-size holographic screens of acute sensory refinement that may be installed in millions of homes and replace books and movies altogether, TV will continue to present major educational, cultural, psychological and political challenges for future generations.

[J.O.]

See also **Film; Telecommunications.**

FURTHER READINGS

Avery, Robert K. *Public Service Broadcasting in a Multichannel Environment.* New York: Longman, 1992.

Barnouw, Erik. *The Image Empire: A History of Broadcasting in the United States, Volume III—from 1953.* New York: Oxford UP, 1970.

TEMPERATURE AND PSYCHOLOGICAL TIME

Several early experiments suggested that brain temperature changes may influence time-related behaviors, experiences, and judgments. Hudson Hoagland found a correlation between body temperature and the experience of time in passing, or prospective temporal judgment. When his wife experienced a fever, he asked her to tap at the rate of once per second. During a fever the hypothalamus, which is the part of the brain that is the master regulator of body temperature, does not activate compensatory mechanisms, and therefore brain temperature increases. Hoagland's wife tapped more rapidly as her body temperature increased, and Hoagland reported that the data followed the well-known equation for temperature-sensitive chemical processes.

Some recent studies, which used diathermy to raise a person's body temperature artificially, have yielded similar results. Other observations also suggest that when body temperature is artificially lowered, experienced duration shortens. The French geologist, Michel Siffre, spent two months living alone in a cold cave, perhaps in a state of near-hypothermia. On leaving the cave, he estimated that less than a month had elapsed. Another study found a relationship between body temperature and the rate of counting in scuba divers measured before and after a period of cold-water immersion. An alternative hypothesis may provide a better explanation for these findings, however: Psychological variables like isolation or arousal level may have caused the changes in temporal estimation instead of or in addition to brain temperature.

These positive findings are somewhat surprising, because if an external factor influences body temperature, the hypothalamus activates compensatory mechanisms and behaviors, such as perspiring or shivering. Thus, one would expect little or no change in any internal clock that may subserve temporal judgment. Several recent studies found that artificially raising or lowering body temperature has no effect on duration judgment, whether measured by verbal estimates or productions. (Using the method of production, the experimenter verbally states a to-be-estimated duration, and the subject attempts to delimit a time period of that length.) Another anomalous finding is that marijuana decreases body temperature but increases the subjective time rate (that is, shortens temporal productions).

Experiments investigating the correlation between normal circadian variations in body temperature and temporal judgments are also equivocal. One study found a close correlation between circadian fluctuations in temperature, productions of fifteen- to sixty-second durations, and verbal estimates of ten- to thirty-second durations. However, another study found little correlation between circadian variations in body temperature and productions of 10-second durations. Chronobiologists usually assume that changes in environmental temperature do not influence the period of reliable endogenous pacemakers. Circadian pacemakers apparently do compensate for temperature, because circadian rhythms change only slightly as a function of temperature. For these reasons, it is somewhat ironic that many theorists consider temperature effects to support internal-clock models of psychological time.

One could interpret the positive evidence as consistent with the view that brain temperature influences any internal clock which may underlie timing behavior and temporal judgment. The prefrontal cortex, for example, plays a critical role in prospective timing, and perhaps changes in brain temperature influence its functioning. However, in much the same way that brain temperature may influence hypothetical neural systems which serve as internal clocks, it may also affect other areas of the brain. This includes those that subserve cognitive processes, such as attention and memory, which influence psychological time in well-known ways.

[R.A.B.]

See also **Biological Rhythms and Psychological Time; Cognition; Internal-Clock Models; Time Perception.**

FURTHER READINGS

Block, Richard A., ed. *Cognitive Models of Psychological Time*. Hillsdale: Erlbaum, 1990.

Doob, Leonard W. *Patterning of Time*. New Haven: Yale UP, 1971.

Hoagland, Hudson. *Pacemakers in Relation to Aspects of Behavior*. New York: Macmillan, 1935.

TEMPO

The Italian word *tempo*, now firmly entrenched in English usage, means "pace, rate of speed." Although the present article focuses on music, questions of tempo are in no way restricted to the production and perception of musical sounds. Anthropologists and linguists have identified distinctive norms for moving and speaking in various world cultures, while other researchers have investigated the phenomenon of personal tempo, its causes, and its variations. The results of tempo determine athletic contests, military engagements, and success in business, as well as piano competitions; and the psychological interpretation of time as passage is a major factor in the meanings we assign to the entire range of human temporal experience—from the most mundane activities to our evaluation of the pace of life itself. The following discussion will address three principal issues: how tempo is measured, tempo evaluations, and—of great importance for musicians—how to determine the proper tempo.

If our main concern with tempo is to measure it properly, to come up with a number or numbers, the matter is a simple one; accurate devices are available. Part of the problem, for musicians at least, lies in the frequent confusion of two important aspects of tempo: (1) tempo as speed, and (2) tempo as character or mood (as in the Italian words *allegro*—in which the progression of meanings develops from the original "gay" to "lively" and hence "fast"—and *grave*, "weighty" and hence "slow"). In the latter two cases, we are trying to get at an appropriate tempo by roundabout means, by finding a tempo associated with feelings of liveliness or heaviness. It often works, but equally often it is misunderstood.

A second question concerns the standards for measuring and evaluating tempo. Are they absolute or relative? Are they biological, psycho-logical, cultural, or a mixture of all three? And which phenomena do we single out in the music (or other activity) and say that the rate of *this* specific series of units or events is what we wish to measure? Music usually presents many such rates, including (1) the fastest rate of activity that can be detected in the music, often referred to as the musical "surface," (2) the rate of the conductor's gestures, (3) the pulsations that organize the music into beats, measures, and measure groupings, and (4) the rate at which phrases and themes succeed one another—the tempo of "events."

Whichever one of these we select, it must then be measured against some known or felt standard—the precise clicks of a metronome set to a predetermined number of units per minute, the pulse rate, the rate of respiration, a moderate walking tempo, the syllabic pace of one's own language, or even, as one seventeenth-century author suggested, the pace of chopping vegetables! Tempo is, then, a ratio between (1) an arbitrarily selected but audibly verifiable series of phenomena, and (2) some extramusical standard of measure, whether it be biological, cultural, or mechanical. There is evidence that the range between sixty and eighty pulsations per minute is the band within which we often assign priority to a particular series of phenomena.

Although tempo is generally regarded as a constant and linear measure within which durations remain proportionate as the rate of speed increases or decreases, research has shown that such is not the case. Because limits exist for the performance and perception of very short durations, longs tend to become shorter and shorts tend to become longer as the tempo increases (for example, in a series of iambs or trochees, the ratios alter irrationally as the speed becomes faster). Hence, any concept of tempo as a precise and proportionate measure of constant durational values is unrealistic, given the inevitable limitations of human performance and cognition.

Civilizations have conceived of tempo in different ways. Ancient Indian musicians located tempo (*laya* in Sanskrit) in the empty silences between events, not in the events themselves. Tempo in Javanese music (*irama*) is understood as a ratio between two selected levels of pulsation in the music, as marked by strokes on gongs of different sizes; but while this ratio remains constant, the actual speed of the music may increase or decrease. In Western art music, tempo is usually expressed as the ratio between what is perceived as the primary rate of pulsation (identified as "the beat") and some absolute standard.

The etymology of the word *tempo* sheds some light on how our Indo-European ancestors conceived of time in general. The relevant Latin words are *tempus* (time divided into seasons or periods, finite time) and *templum* (a space set apart, cut off from the surrounding profane space). Related words in Greek are the verb *témno* (cut) and the noun *témenos* (that which has been cut, a section or division of space or time). Evidence thus points to a hypothetical Indo-European root TEM (cut), which may itself be a development of an earlier Indo-European root TEMP (pull, draw, extend). The implicit message in this line of semantic development is that European time, like European space, has been conceived as something to be divided and delineated by regular rhythms and periods. Western musicians have not ignored this injunction.

For musicians, finding the right tempo borders on obsession. Every musician has had the frequent experience of recognizing that a particular performance captures to perfection the rhythmic structure and energies of the music, and of recognizing at other times how badly the performer has missed the mark. The musical concept of *tempo giusto* (the *right* tempo) has been a staple topic in rhythmic theory and performance practice for the last 400 years, but the literature on this subject is, for the most part, a quaintly dismal record of failures to define these ideal tempos and to suggest objective procedures for finding them. There has been a general consensus that no absolute standards can ever exist for different pieces, different composers, different eras, and different styles, and that rigid, mechanically accurate tempos are the death of music. Most authorities agree that the choice of tempo must take into account such variables as the acoustics of the hall, the nature of the instruments being played, the temperament of the performer(s), the physical demands of the composition, and perhaps even such things as the time of day and the type of audience.

Johann Mattheson wrote, in his *Der vollkommene Capellmeister* (1739), "Many a one would like to know how the true *mouvement* of a musical work can be known. Such knowledge, alas, is beyond words. It is the ultimate perfection of music, accessible only through great experience and talent." And, recently, David Epstein endorsed this conclusion: "The search for 'right' tempo involves a mixture of musical intuition

and 'received' information, communicated in a score by verbal description or metronome indications. Uncertainty seems to remain the product of it all: intuitions vary and the vocabulary of tempo lacks a universal standard."

A powerful argument advanced by Epstein and others is based on the contention that we are biologically predisposed to prefer *proportional* tempos. The artistic consequence of this predisposition is a single "master pulse" that governs, or ought to govern, all tempo relations within a given composition, and within which all major tempo relations are nested in simple whole-number ratios (generally 1:1, 2:1, and 3:2). This is in fact the same argument put forward by Aristoxenus of Tarentum more than 2,000 years ago, in which the same ratios were thought to integrate and regulate not only the artistic rhythms of music, dance, and verse, but also the physiological systems of the human body, the deliberations of political assemblies, and the structure of the cosmos. It is safe to say, however, that most musicians do not see their temporal experience in such a tidy way, and the contention has so far not been supported by reliable evidence.

What conclusions can be drawn from this discussion? Perhaps these: It is undeniable that cultural norms do exist for such things as language and walking. For instance, a linguistic tour of Europe from south to north will demonstrate a general progression toward slower tempos of speech and increasing precision in articulation. Cultural norms of this type are no doubt reflected in music in one way or another—not only in choice of tempo but perhaps also in accentual weight and other related features. But the music of the world is simply too diverse to justify any sweeping claims on behalf of a universal theory of tempo. If there are any biological predispositions toward particular tempos or tempo ranges, and there *may* be, they can obviously be overridden by contextual factors.

[L.R.]

FURTHER READINGS

Epstein, David. "Tempo Relations: A Cross-Cultural Study." *Music Theory Spectrum* 7 (1985): 34–71.

Hall, Edward T. *The Dance of Life.* Garden City: Anchor P, 1983.

Kolinski, Mieczslaw. "The Evaluation of Tempo." *Ethnomusicology* 3.2 (1959): 45–57.

Reale, Paola, ed. *Tempo e identità.* Milan: Franco Angeli, 1988.

Sachs, Curt. *Rhythm and Tempo.* New York: Norton, 1953.

TEMPORAL JUDGMENT (METHODS)

Time is an essential dimension for humans' adaptation to their environment. Yet no sense or sense organ by which time can be perceived directly is known, nor is it clear what information humans use to make time judgments. Recent research indicates that there is no single, natural temporal code in human memory. Moreover, time judgments are highly dependent on context. There are four temporal dimensions that might be subjected to temporal judgment: (1) simultaneity versus succession (were two different events occurring at the same time?), (2) temporal order (which came first?), (3) recentness (how long ago did an event happen?), and (4) duration (how long did an event last?). Time judgment, however, is a process associated mainly with the last dimension—duration, whereas the first three temporal dimensions are measured by directly asking subjects to determine if one event occurred simultaneously with another, the order in which two events occurred, and how long ago a specific event took place.

Time judgment methods are defined in terms of three elements: the paradigm, the procedure, and the mode of response. In a retrospective paradigm, a subject is requested to judge the duration of a target interval only after it was terminated, whereas in a prospective paradigm, subjects know before an interval starts that its duration is to be judged. Both of these paradigms are mediated by different cognitive processes. In a retrospective paradigm, awareness of time during a target interval is low and time judgments are constructed on the basis of information retrieved from memory. In a prospective paradigm, awareness of time is high during the interval and duration judgments are based on the processing of temporal cues such as rhythmic, repetitive events occurring during the target interval. In the absence of such cues, subjects tend to produce them by tapping or counting.

Time judgment procedures can be classified into two major categories. One is duration scaling, where subjects are asked to judge the perceived durations of a set of temporal intervals which can be easily differentiated. When subjects are asked to distinguish among a set of highly similar intervals, the task is called duration discrimination. Duration scaling can be carried out via procedures of "temporal production" (subjects are asked to produce a given time interval by marking its beginning and ending), reproduction (subjects produce an interval of the same duration as that of a target interval after the latter was terminated), and synchronization (subjects are presented with a series of brief events and are requested to reproduce a sequence of responses at the same rate). In comparison procedures, two duration values are presented sequentially on each trial, where the number of trials can be varied from one to many. Usually, one value is constant within a block of trials and is referred to as the standard, while the other value varies from trial to trial and is referred to as the comparison. Psychophysical procedures for the measurement of psychophysical properties of judged time are mostly comparison procedures.

A major distinction between duration scaling and discrimination is the high dependency of the latter on memory. Temporal judgments produced via comparison procedures are relative judgments, whereas those produced via scaling procedures are absolute ones. Thus, when, for example, a retrospective paradigm and a comparison procedure are used jointly, the role of memory is more influential than when a prospective paradigm and a scaling procedure are used together.

A third category of time judgment is duration anticipation. In this case, a subject is asked to judge the time it will take for a specific event to reach a specific ending.

The temporal response can be either verbal or motorical. In a verbal time-estimation method, subjects are requested to give a verbal response in temporal units. Verbal responses require internal transformation of temporal experience to verbal categories. Since the ability to verbalize temporal units can depend upon culture or language, verbal methods may not be reliable for all subjects. Time judgment methods which use verbal reference to conventional time units (for example, seconds or minutes) are reported to yield data showing greater intersubject variability than other methods. Another possible verbal response is a numeric one—not in terms of temporal units but rather as a representation of the magnitude of a perceived duration relative to a specified standard duration, as occurs in the method of magnitude estimation. Another type of response which is not verbal but still dependent on linguistic terms is category rating, where subjects are asked to locate the perceived duration of a target interval in one of several predefined, ordered categories.

Motorical responses can take many forms. For example, subjects might be asked to activate or deactivate some device for a predefined clock time (production), or for a duration that reflects the perceived duration of a target interval (reproduction). Another form of motorical response involves asking subjects to draw a line of a length representing the perceived duration of a target interval (scaling) or its relative duration, where a standard line represents the duration of a standard interval (comparison). Motorical responses—which are reported to be more reliable than verbal responses—are useful when a translation to verbal temporal units is undesirable, as in the case of young children. However, motorical responses might be influenced by factors such as drugs or fatigue which affect the response itself, thus invalidating the time judgment obtained.

The number of combinations of the three elements of temporal judgment is large and undefined. Each combination generates a different context within which time judgment is made. Context, however, affects temporal judgments. The major contextual factors which should be considered are level of awareness of time during a target interval, clock-time duration, the structure and presentation of the order of events occurring during a target interval, and the amount of nontemporal information the subject must process during the procedure. It should be kept in mind that contextual factors interact with each other.

A review of the relevant literature indicates that no single method can claim superiority over others in terms of accuracy and internal consistency. Nevertheless, it is unclear whether time judgments obtained by one method can be generalized to others. It is usually assumed, however, that in all temporal judgment methods the transformation of stimulus time to perceived time is a simple linear one. Thus, in order to validate that duration is indeed the measured dimension, it is important to measure more than one clock time duration in any time judgment experiment.

Because of the methodological complexity characterizing the measurement of perceived duration, time judgment is meaningful only when there is a theory to account for the processes underlying the specific time judgment method.

[D.Z.]

See also **Cognition; Memory for Time; Prospective and Retrospective Time; Simultaneity, Successiveness, and Time-Order Judgments; Time-Order Errors; Time Perception.**

FURTHER READINGS

Allan, L.G. "The Perception of Time." *Perception & Psychophysics* 26 (1979): 340–354.

Bindra, D., and H. Waksberg. "Methods and Terminology in the Studies of Time Estimation." *Psychological Bulletin* 53 (1956): 155–159.

Block, R.A. "Experiencing and Remembering Time: Affordances, Context and Cognition." *Time and Human Cognition: A Life Span Perspective.* Ed. I. Levin and D. Zakay. Amsterdam: North Holland, 1989. 333–363.

Zakay, D. "The Evasive Art of Subjective Time Measurement: Some Methodological Dilemmas." *Cognitive Models of Psychological Time.* Ed. R.A. Block. Hillsdale: Erlbaum, 1990. 59–84.

THANATOCHEMISTRY

The word *thanatochemistry* (< Greek *thanatos* = death + chemistry) was first used in a formal sense in 1985. To understand its meaning, a brief historical look at both chemistry and the practice of embalming is necessary.

It is generally believed that the modern term "chemistry" is a derivative of the ancient term "alchemy." Over the years a number of approaches have developed to this study of the nature of matter and the changes that matter undergoes. The major divisions of chemistry became identified as inorganic chemistry, organic chemistry, and biochemistry. These terms evolved, however, in a somewhat unusual fashion because until 1828, there were only inorganic chemistry and organic chemistry. Organic chemistry studied substances produced by living matter and inorganic chemistry studied nonliving substances. In 1828, when Friedrich Wohler, a German chemist, synthesized urea, a waste product of animal metabolism, from ammonium cyanate, an inorganic compound, the so-called vitalistic theory of organic chemistry came to an end. A new division called biochemistry replaced what had been formerly called organic chemistry, and organic chemistry was redefined as the study of certain carbon compounds.

Since the days of the early Egyptians, there has been interest in the chemical processes that can be used to preserve a human body. The effectiveness of the Egyptian procedure is evident: 3,000- and 4,000-year-old mummies remain preserved today in museums throughout the world. Some Egyptian embalming was performed into the sixth century. Although other early cultures such as the Hebrews, Greeks, Romans, and early Christians had funeral rituals, none of them made use of chemicals as did the Egyptians for the preservation of their dead. After the Egyptians, embalming was not performed again until late in the fifteenth century in Europe and then only for scientific and research purposes. Preservation of remains as specimens became increasingly important as physicians became interested in anatomy.

Embalming in the United States gained widespread interest with the advent of the Civil War. The bodies of military casualties had to be shipped considerable distances for final disposition, thus necessitating some method of temporary preservation. About the same time, a number of embalming schools emerged to teach the new techniques of preservation and disinfection. Chemistry became part of the curriculum of these schools, which took selected aspects of inorganic chemistry, organic chemistry, and biochemistry and applied them to the process of embalming. The branch of chemistry called embalming chemistry, then, developed as a specific response to a specialized need.

In 1985, the term "thanatochemistry" was coined to provide the antithesis to biochemistry, that is, just as biochemistry is the chemistry of life, thanatochemistry is the chemistry of death. The term first appeared in the title of the textbook, *Thanatochemistry: A Survey of General, Organic, and Biochemistry for Funeral Service Professionals*, which has gained widespread recognition among funeral service practitioners. Through time, then, the term thanatochemistry has replaced the earlier term of embalming chemistry. While embalming chemistry is essentially concerned with those aspects of inorganic chemistry, organic chemistry, and biochemistry that pertain to the disinfection and preservation of human remains, thanatochemistry is more inclusive, and thoroughly studies the very process and decomposition that embalming attempts to retard.

[B.M.H.]

See also **Biological Corruption.**

FURTHER READINGS

Dorn, J.M., and B.M. Hopkins. *Thanatochemistry.* Englewood Cliffs: Prentice-Hall, 1985.

THEOPHYLLINE

Theophylline is a medication widely used in the treatment of asthma. Chemically, theophylline is classified as a methylxanthine. Although it has been employed in the treatment of asthma for several decades, scientists still do not know the exact mechanisms by which the drug exerts its beneficial effect. The medication may function as a bronchodilator, by relaxing the muscles of the airways and thereby making breathing easier; it may modulate the inflammation of the airways; or it may have other effects which are still to be fully understood.

Theophylline may be dosed by a variety of routes—orally as tablets or elixirs, intravenously as parenteral solutions, or rectally as suppositories. Today, it is most commonly ingested in so-called sustained-release oral dosage forms, either twice daily in equal doses and equal intervals (that is, in the morning upon arising from sleep and in the evening twelve hours later) or once every evening for patients who suffer from nocturnal asthma symptoms.

The rate and extent of theophylline absorption from the gastrointestinal tract can differ greatly according to the time when the tablet medication is ingested with reference to the staging of critical circadian (twenty-four-hour) rhythms. Among others, these rhythms include those of gastric acid secretion and gastric emptying. Oral dosing of some sustained-release tablet theophylline products results in a more rapid absorption and higher blood concentration of the drug following morning than evening administration. This seems to be the case especially for asthmatic children. Patients who suffer from nighttime asthma symptoms which interrupt sleep may not obtain complete relief from a twelve-hour, equal-interval, equal-dose treatment regimen of sustained-release theophylline tablets. This is because day-night and dosing-time differences in the amount and rate of drug absorption from the gastrointestinal tract may result in subtherapeutic concentrations of the drug overnight and because patients who are prone to nighttime asthma require a higher level of theophylline in the lungs during the night in comparison to the day to avert asthma symptoms.

A chronotherapeutic approach to dosing theophylline tablets results in an optimization of drug effect for asthma. Chronotherapeutics is the timing of special dosage forms of medications in relation to the body's requirements and takes into account known day-night patterns of diseases and their symptoms as well as the effects of circadian bodily rhythms which influence the absorption, distribution, and elimination of specific medications. Once-a-day, sustained-release theophylline tablet formulations dosed in the evening constitute a chronotherapy of theophylline, especially for those patients who suffer from nighttime symptoms. With these new, specially formulated tablet theophylline medications, elevated drug blood levels are achieved at the very time when the biological need for asthma medication is greatest in order to avert symptom breakthrough. It is of interest that the effect of theophylline on the airways is stronger when the drug is dosed in the evening rather than in the daytime. This means that the airway response to theophylline is greater overnight than during the day. The chronotherapy which involves a once-daily administration of theophylline tablets in the evening constitutes a chrono-optimization of the drug by potentiating its effectiveness and safety in the treatment of asthma patients, especially those who suffer from nocturnal symptoms of the disease.

[M.H.S.]

See also **Asthma; Beta-Agonist Medications.**

THERMODYNAMICS

Thermodynamics is that branch of science which extends the theory of energy to those situations in which thermal energy (heat) is involved, as well as other forms of energy. This extension was not achieved until the nineteenth century, although there are indications that Newton was aware of the need for it. The great relevance of thermodynamics to the study of time is that it provides a criterion of time's direction which is independent of the human consciousness of "time passing." It is thus applicable to the order of events occurring in the universe before there was any life.

THE FIRST LAW
A precise statement of the First "Law" is rather technical, but it is related to the familiar principle of the conservation of energy. This states that in any physicochemical system which is completely isolated from its environment, the total energy in all its forms (such as thermal, mechanical, chemical, and so forth) remains constant. This is naturally of great importance to science and engineering, but it need not be elaborated here as it has little bearing on time studies.

THE SECOND LAW
The Second Law arose from the work of Carnot, Clausius, and Kelvin, and was based on the fact that natural processes are always irreversible when considered in their entirety. A familiar instance is the mixing of tea with milk in a cup, for we never observe "unmixing" to occur. Other examples are the combustion of fuels, the equalization of temperatures, and so on. Of course, many natural processes can be *partially* reversed. For instance, following the mixing of two liquids, they can often be separated again by distillation. But that would not amount to a complete reversal of the original mixing because the distillation requires a supply of heat from an external source. That source thereby falls somewhat in temperature, and can only be brought back to its original temperature by having heat supplied to it by a second external source, and so *ad infinitum*. It follows that the liquids can only be "unmixed" at the expense of something else which will be left in a changed condition. Similar considerations always apply. Arthur S. Eddington, who had a genius for apt analogies, remarked that the impossibility of putting Humpty-Dumpty together again nicely expresses the essential idea behind the Second Law.

In spite of what has just been said, reversibility can be approached as a *limiting case*, and this normally requires the carrying out of the process in question exceedingly slowly, through a sequence of states which are very close to being equilibrium states. For such a sequence the change in what is called the *entropy* is measurable. For purposes of simplicity its definition will here be restricted to processes occurring at some constant absolute temperature T. We suppose that we are concerned with a physicochemical system which is made to pass from a state 1 (as specified by its volume, chemical composition, and so forth) to a state 2. Let Q be any heat transfer to or from the system (taken as positive for an intake) required to hold the temperature at the constant value T. Then if S_1 and S_2 are the system's entropies in states 1 and 2 respectively, their difference is taken *by definition* as being:

$$S_2 - S_1 = Q/T,$$

so long as the process is made to occur close to the reversible limit.

With entropy difference so defined, it can be shown that the entropy of any system which is insulated against any inflow or outflow of heat can *never* decrease; it increases during any irreversible process occurring in such a system and remains constant in the limiting case of a reversible process.

These statements are the Second Law of thermodynamics. Clausius put the First and Second Laws together in a famous claim: "The energy of the universe is constant; the entropy of the universe tends to a maximum." But it is controversial whether it makes scientific good sense to speak of the energy and entropy of the whole universe. What is entirely clear is that, concerning any thermally insulated system, if its entropy is not already at a maximum some process of entropy maximization will occur. (But thermodynamics gives no guidance whatsoever concerning how fast or how slow that will be.)

THE MEANING OF ENTROPY

The foregoing definition of entropy difference expresses the Second Law in sufficient terms for many important scientific and engineering applications. However, with the development of atomic and quantum theory it has been found possible to define a "statistical entropy" which is closely similar to the thermodynamic entropy and has the advantages: (1) of being calculable, in sufficiently simple instances, as an absolute value, and (2) of providing a more intuitable notion of the essential meaning of entropy.

Consider a quantity of gas, liquid, or solid, enclosed in a rigid container whose walls transmit no heat or other forms of energy. Even though the enclosed material will be supposed to have reached a state of equilibrium, its component molecules will yet be in constant motion, bumping into each other and changing their individual energies at each encounter. As a consequence the material has a truly immense number of distinct "states" when these are reckoned on the quantum scale. Any one of them may be momentarily occupied. Let their number be W. Then a satisfactory definition of the statistical entropy is

$$S_{BP} = k \log W,$$

where the subscripts stand for Ludwig Boltzmann and Max Planck who developed the theory (k is a universal constant having the value 1.380×10^{-23} in SI units). It follows that entropy can be interpreted as a measure of the amount of randomness in the enclosed material since any one of its W quantum states can be momentarily occupied.

Several other interpretations of entropy have been put forward—notably as "mixed-up-ness," as "disorder," as "disorganization," and as "lack of information." Although some of these may seem superficially convincing, counter-examples exist against all of them. Since even a single counter-example renders a proposition useless, it follows that the current journalistic use of the term "entropy," as a sort of vogue word imply-

ing deterioration or degradation, is to be discouraged. The notion of entropy should only be used where it belongs—in physical science.

ENTROPY AND TIME

The notion of time's "arrow" or "direction" can be looked at in two alternative ways: (1) Time "goes forward" in that direction which we are aware of as "time passing"; it goes toward those events which are later than "the present"; and (2) time's direction may be defined as the direction in which entropy increases in those thermally isolated and macroscopic systems which are in the process of change.

Whereas (1) above is dependent on consciousness, (2) has the advantage of showing "time's arrow" to be a fully objective feature of the natural world.

[K.G.D.]

See also **Physics**

FURTHER READINGS

Denbigh, Kenneth. *Three Concepts of Time*. New York: Springer, 1971.

Denbigh, Kenneth, and Jonathan Denbigh. *Entropy in Relation to Incomplete Knowledge*. Cambridge: Cambridge UP, 1985.

Grünbaum, Adolph. *Philosophical Problems of Space and Time*. Dordrecht: Reidel, 1973.

Reichenbach, Hans. *The Direction of Time*. Berkeley: U of California P, 1956.

TIDAL RHYTHMS IN MARINE ORGANISMS

The tides on the shorelines of most oceans rise and fall twice each lunar day. A lunar day is the interval between consecutive moonrises, and has an average period length of twenty-four hours and fifty minutes. The interval between the peaks of successive high tides is thus half that, twelve hours and twenty-five minutes. Because of the fifty minute difference between the length of the lunar day and the solar day (the twenty-four-hour interval between successive sunrises), we humans, using clocks based on the interval of the solar day, see the tides return, on average, fifty minutes later each day.

The shoreline washed by the ebb and flow of the tides is called, quite naturally, the intertidal zone. In spite of the rigors of having to live in an ambience alternately changing from water to air, the intertidal zone is an area rich in animal and plant life. All such inhabitants must and do adjust to this profound periodicity. Among the many examples are clams and oysters that open their shells during flood tide, and hold them tightly closed after the tide recedes; some crabs that live hidden under rocks during low tides (thus avoiding predatory birds), but emerge to forage during each high tide; and some fish that migrate between inshore feeding grounds and offshore deeper water with each tidal cycle. Clearly the ebb and flow of the seas strongly mold intertidal inhabitants' behavior and physiology into a tidal waveform pattern.

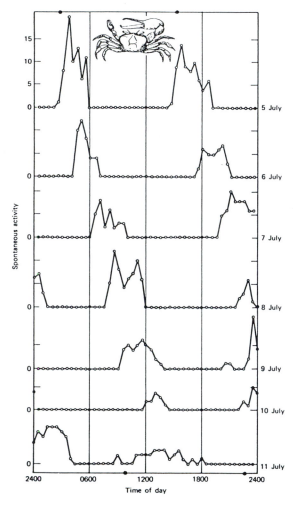

Figure 1. *The spontaneous locomotor activity of a fiddler crab (*Uca pugnax*) exposed to continuous dim light and unvarying temperature in the laboratory. On the first day in isolation the two peaks of activity occur at the times of low tide in nature. After that the period of the rhythm increases so that each peak is expressed about 100 minutes later each day. From J. Palmer,* An Introduction to Biological Rhythms. *New York: Academic Press, 1976.*

Scientists have now studied a great many of these organisms in the laboratory in the absence of the most obvious environmental periodicities: temperature and light intensity are held constant, and, of course, the tides are precluded. Still, in that environment devoid of obvious periodicities, the experimental subjects continue to act as if they were back on their home shorelines: they alternate their activity and rest, and feeding/nonfeeding behavior, in a pattern that seems almost to mimic the tides outside. This behavior is repeated with such beat-like monotony that it is described as a tidal rhythm. A fine example comes from the fiddler crab. It lives in self-dug burrows during high tides, but emerges to scurry over exposed mudflats to feed, fight, fossick, or mate during low tides. As seen in Figure 1, when the animal's activity is monitored in the constancy of the laboratory, a rather precise pattern of activity and rest is still displayed. With the individual shown, the rhythm persisted for six days, but the duration is variable, depending on the species under study, and the tenacity of each individual; under laboratory conditions, the rhythms of some individuals have continued for more than nine months.

While the rhythms do endure in the laboratory, they change slightly. By following the daily progression of the original morning activity peak in Figure 1, one sees that it moves across successive days at a rate greater than the expected fifty minutes per day. In fact, the average period length was about twenty-five hours and forty minutes for the six-day study. This lengthening (shortening is also found in some individuals) is a basic property of such rhythms, and is thought sufficiently significant to warrant the prefix *circa* (about) to rhythm names. Thus these organismic cycles are designated circatidal or circalunidian rhythms. The actual length of a circa period is specific to each individual and to the set of conditions to which the animal is exposed in the laboratory. Period lengths become circa only in constant laboratory conditions.

The fact that these rhythms persist away from the tides is interpreted as indicating that within the bodies of organisms is a living clock that takes over their timing needs in the absence of the tides. In fact there are many clocks present, one or more in every cell. This can be said with certainty because when parts of an organism are surgically removed and transformed to a culture medium that sustains life, the rhythmic processes continue unchanged in the fragments.

But even though individual organisms contain many clocks, one or two of them function as master, enslaving all the rest to the directions of their clockworks. And by raising animals from egg to adult in the laboratory, totally isolated from environmental change, it has been shown that when a living clock develops to a point where it begins to function, its interval has been genetically predetermined, which is to say that the interval is innate rather than learned by exposure to the tides.

What is the basic period of the living clock governing tidal rhythms? The traditional view is that it matches the basic interval of time elapsed between each tide: about twelve hours and twenty-five minutes. However, beginning in 1986, new properties of these organismic rhythms were discovered that cannot be adequately explained by such a clock. For instance, under laboratory conditions the two peaks that are expressed each day may act quite independently of one another. To give just two examples, the periods of the peaks may differ, meaning that one will scan the solar day faster than the other; or one peak may disappear spontaneously and reappear days later, without having any effect on the other peak. Findings like these have resulted in the formulation of a new view called the circalunidian clock hypothesis. It speculates that tidal rhythms are controlled by two clocks, each of which runs at a fundamental period of about twenty-four hours and fifty minutes, and each of which controls one of the two tide-associated peaks displayed each lunar day. Most of the time the two clocks are coupled together 180 degrees out of phase, so that the standard single peak every twelve hours and twenty-five minutes is displayed. But when the coupling breaks down, as it sometimes does in the unnaturalness of constant laboratory conditions, then, and only then, the separate peaks are free to act independently of one another, and they do.

However, scientists still need to locate where in an organism's body the master clock or clocks reside, and just how these clockworks function. Because living horologues are present in almost all plants and animals, the accomplishment of such tasks is of the greatest importance.

[J.D.P]

See also **Lunar Monthly and Fortnightly Rhythms.**

FURTHER READINGS

Morgan, Elfed. "An Appraisal of Tidal Activity Rhythms." *Chronobiology International* 8 (1991): 283–306.

Naylor, E. "Rhythmic Behaviour of Decapod Crustaceans." *Symposium of the Zoological Society of London* 59 (1989): 177–199.

Palmer, John D. *Biological Clocks in Marine Organisms: The Control of Physiological and Behavioral Tidal Rhythms.* New York: Wiley, 1974.

———. "The Rhythmic Lives of Crabs." *BioScience* 40 (1990): 352–358.

———. "Contributions Made to Chronobiology by Studies of Fiddler Crab Rhythms." *Chronobiology International* 8 (1991): 110–130.

TIME AND DEATH

> Death be not proud, though some have called thee
> Mighty and dreadful, for thou art not so,
> For those whom thou think'st thou dost overthrow,
> Die not, poor death, nor yet can'st thou kill me. . . .
> One short sleep past, we wake eternally,
> And death shall be no more, Death thou shalt die.

John Donne, not only a poet but also one of the greatest preachers any dean of St. Paul's has ever been, was able to summon some of the majesty of Death to his aid in order to confront death. He was writing in the seventeenth century not long after the King James Bible was published in English. He was writing at a time when it was possible not to feign to believe but actually to believe that after Death has summoned us, "we wake eternally."

Some such belief has been at the heart not just of Christianity but of many other religions as well. The fear of not having a future, the fear of one's life having an end, a final, undeniable, ineluctable end, has always been difficult for almost anyone to accept. Even older people have been rare who could say to themselves, as David Hume, the Scottish philosopher, said—"a man of sixty five, by dying, cuts off only a few years of Infirmities." So, in face of the fact that death has so far been 100 percent and that the dead monarch is just as dead as the dead beggar, people have generally chosen to call death a mystery and, since they cannot be plainly contradicted by anyone who comes back with a firsthand account of that bourn from which no traveler returns, they have given themselves the benefit of the doubt and constructed a future in order to avoid having none. If one time has a stop, another time will then be wound up again promptly enough in a different domain, and the different domain is not subject to the same dread scarcities which tell out our lives as they tell out our seconds.

The basic model of reassurance is readily to hand for everyone. It comes from life at its most elemental, the particular common feature of all living creatures and plants being that they reproduce themselves and preserve their species (or strive to) even while the individual members of the species die, and, indeed, preserve their species *because* as individuals they die. Birth and death are each other's very necessary partners. The seeds are blown by the wind, some of them are new kinds of seed and the tree is born again; and so it is with people.

Contemplating this process of punctuated continuity gives rise, readily enough, to the notion, the myth, the belief that after death there will be a resurrection or a reincarnation. It does not take any great genius to imagine people being reborn in some other world as they are reborn (with some strange differences, it is true) in their own children; it does take genius to invent and elaborate the myths and symbolic forms that do solemn justice to the fears and guilts, the hopes and the doubts, which lie at the back of the minds of the only creatures whose sense of time allows them the luxury of worry about a future which they are not going to share.

I started with John Donne for two reasons: the first in order to point out that some such belief as his (although expressed in so many different ways) is still very much sound currency in the minds of the greater part of the population of the world; the second in order to register how much change there has been in societies like the dean of St. Paul's own since industrialization has enfolded them. The majority of people even in the most industrialized countries still affirm a belief in some kind of afterlife. But a large and influential minority has adopted some variety of the secular humanism which has found no place for an afterlife and which has also had a profound influence even upon those who do not accept its tenets. Religion has been constrained to take account of, if not come to terms with, science, and the outlook which makes science and technology possible. The span of human control, and the span of individual lives, has been extended and the accent has been very much on the achievements which have accompanied the enlargement of control rather than on the event which sets those achievements at naught for those who can no longer benefit from them.

But very few of the secular humanists who share in the characteristic value system of modern society would argue that death poses no problem. They can make a great deal of the continuities which bind single lives into the ongoing stream of life. They can seek support in science and take some comfort from the general conservation of energy and matter. They can take from genetics the example of the immortal (or semi-immortal) gene which is preserved so marvellously from one carrier to another. They can recognize the force of tradition which is handed on, like knowledge, from one generation to another as part of a great collective enterprise which continues over many millennia, and recognize too the part that individuals play in conserving, and in small, even tiny, ways adding to that body of tradition and knowledge. The fear of death is in a sense the greatest egocentricity there is since it rests on the assumption that the end of any individual is *the* end.

Perhaps more important still is the recognition that the scarcity of time which is a continuous series of endings on the way to the final ending is humankind's greatest gift, which is no less a gift because its value is hidden. Without death—if that can be imagined—there would be no scarcity, or at least it would be an extraordinarily different kind of scarcity. All beauty, all love, all achievement is made poignant by the passage of time; and without that poignancy there would be no beauty, no love, no achievement of the kind we recognize. There are fates worse than death.

The humanist creed is not without appeal. Bertrand Russell was a famous atheist who stated it in his *Autobiography*:

> Three passions, simple but overwhelmingly strong, have governed my life: the longing for love, the search for knowledge, and unbearable pity for the suffering of mankind. . . . I have lived in the pursuit of a vision, both personal and social. Personal: to care for what is noble, for what is beautiful, for what is gentle: to allow moments of insights to give wisdom at more mundane times. Social: to see in imagination the society that is to be created, where individuals grow freely, and where hate and greed and envy die because there is nothing to nourish them. These things I believe, and the world, for all its horrors, has left me unshaken.

To that has now to be added the necessity for harmonization of human beings with the cycles of nature, and for death to be accorded its honored place in the great pageant.

For a secular philosophy still leaves a void. Death is certainly a humdrum, everyday, every minute occurrence. But we cannot avoid dreading it and indeed, if we did not, humankind would not have survived at all. Death therefore deserves to be treated as of the utmost importance, and not just to the dying and the bereaved. Death cries out to be treated not as humdrum but with reverence, as "mighty and dreadful." How that is to be done remains a problem for our collective future. Meanwhile, if there is a void it will continue to be filled in one way, by thought and, particularly, by the thought that what was most majestic about the death of Christ, or Socrates, and many others was their acceptance of death.

[M.Y.]

See also **Life-Span.**

TIME AND NARRATIVE

Traditionally, various disciplines have viewed the human experience of time from diverse, often incompatible, perspectives. Over the last two decades, however, there has occurred what might be called a multidisciplinary convergence of interest in time and its representation in narrative form. This new line of inquiry stems, first of all, from the inherently temporal character of narrative; even the simplest stories contain beginnings, middles, and ends. Without this temporal configuration, a story does not make sense. In fact, philosopher Paul Ricoeur argues that time and narrative are so closely linked that it is difficult to speak of either concept in the absence of the other. As he put it in 1980, "I take temporality to be that structure of existence that reaches language in narrativity and narrativity to be the language structure that has temporality as its ultimate referent." In addition to this internal characteristic of narrative, there is a growing recognition of the important and ubiquitous role that stories play in the social construction of reality; they are central to the construction and maintenance of groups, they figure prominently in the socialization of children, we tell stories to explain why things happened in a particular way, and so forth. These activities, like all human endeavors, involve a temporal component. The fact that they are so often represented in the form of narratives has

led scholars like David Carr to hypothesize that there may be a uniquely narrative quality to the way people think about and experience time.

Because the ability to tell and understand stories is so deeply ingrained in consciousness and so much a part of everyday communication, it is difficult at first glance to appreciate any but the most superficial of linkages between time and its representation in narrative. In order to understand this relationship more fully, it is necessary to define briefly what constitutes a narrative. At a bare minimum, constructing a narrative, as discussed by D.R. Maines, comprises three elements: selecting events, which are simply actions or occurrences that can be referred to; utilizing these events in the construction of plot, character, and setting; and arranging the selected events in a temporal sequence.

Although these elements are intertwined, plot is arguably the most important. When a sequence of events is emplotted, there occurs a transformation of what would otherwise be, at most, a chronicle. The plot grasps together the heterogeneous elements of a story and configures them into a temporal whole. It does this by combining two temporal dimensions: the chronological and the nonchronological. As D.E. Polkinghorne puts it, "The chronological dimension characterizes the story and shows that it is made of events along the line of time. The nonchronological dimension lifts events into a configuration so that . . . they form a significant whole." Through the act of emplotment, events are placed in significant relationships to one another and lifted above the level of mere succession. This dialectical character of the plot, its ability to preserve linear time while simultaneously transcending it, creates a temporal gestalt that confers meaning on events. In and of itself, as Ricoeur argues, a singular occurrence is not particularly meaningful; events take on meaning to the extent that they contribute to the development of the plot.

While many scholars would agree that humans constantly create temporal wholes out of scattered experiences and events through the use of narratives, their role in the actual experience of time is a matter of considerable debate. At one extreme, there is the argument, expressed most forcefully by Hayden White, that narratives are retrospectively imposed on actions and events in an attempt to create a sense of order from the flux of experience. In this view, the world does not present itself in the form of well-made stories. Instead, it presents itself more in the form of annals or chronicles, "as mere sequence without beginning or end or as sequences that only terminate and never conclude." Our tendency to narrativize, to treat events as if they tell their own stories, reflects a desire for coherence that is lacking in our experience of the world. Although we may use narratives to reconstruct the past and plan for the future, their capacity to represent reality is a fiction that we maintain and not something dictated by the human experience of temporality.

Paul Ricoeur pursues a modified version of this argument. Like White, he maintains that narrative imposes structure on inchoate experience. However, as Polkinghorne has observed, he differs from White in that he does not draw such a sharp distinction between narrative and reality. The two are not congruent, but there is significant overlap. Our experience in the world, according to Ricoeur's argument in *Time and Narrative*, is characterized by a "prenarrative structure." Episodes of life contain elements that lend themselves to narration. These episodes are potential "(as yet) untold stories." In explicating this idea, Ricoeur points to the example of psychoanalysis. In a therapeutic situation, the patient "presents bits and pieces of lived stories" with the aim of constructing a unified narrative that makes one's life more manageable and intelligible. While this narrative does serve to order fragmented experience, it does so against a background of lived, but previously untold stories. In Ricoeur's scheme, narrating is not simply a literary act of construction divorced from the reality it purports to explain; narrative is the proper form in which to describe the experience of time because, in the realm of human action, narrative elements are already present. Stories are simply waiting to be told.

A third approach to narrative and the experience of time goes well beyond Ricoeur's notion of prenarrative structures. In this line of thinking the temporal structure of experience and action is identical to the structure of narrative. David Carr, for instance, draws on Husserl's analysis of time experience to argue that time, conceived of as moments along a line, while theoretically possible, cannot be experienced in that manner. According to Carr, consciousness spans past and future to encompass an experience or action as a whole. Any particular moment within this complex is experienced as a part of the whole. This conception of time expe-

rience preserves the notion of sequence, but it sees sequences as configured, as displaying a structure analogous to the beginning, middle, and end structure of narrative. Furthermore, this configurational quality of time experience is not imposed after the fact. Rather, it is prereflective and inherent in lived reality. In short, we use the narrative form to describe temporal experience because this is the form in which time reaches consciousness. Thus, our experiencing and acting in the world can be thought of as a constant process of narration to ourselves and others. As Carr puts it, this is simply "our way of living in time." Even at the level of the group, whose existence can span great lengths of time, actions and events are experienced narratively. In fact, groups owe their temporal existence to the stories that are told about them; new actions and experiences are undertaken and make sense in light of the group's ongoing story.

Thus far, much of the research that has been conducted around the topic of time and narrative remains at a rather abstract, speculative level. Perhaps the most that can be said with any certainty is that narrative discourse plays an important role in making sense of the past and planning for the future; the prospect of a more precise description of its place in the lived experience of time remains problematic. In the end, the question is circular: is the narrative representation of time a mere convention derived from the realm of literature, or is something more fundamental involved? Like other questions where the nature and direction of causality defies specification, the answer to this one remains elusive.

[J.C.B.]

See also **Husserl, Edmund.**

FURTHER READINGS

Carr, David. *Time, Narrative, and History*. Indianapolis: Indiana UP, 1986.

Maines, D.R. "Narrative's Moment and Sociology's Phenomena: Toward a Narrative Sociology." *The Sociological Quarterly* 34.1 (1993): 17–38.

Polkinghorne, D.E. *Narrative Knowing and the Human Sciences*. Albany: State U of New York P, 1988.

Ricoeur, Paul. "Narrative Time." *Critical Inquiry* 7 (1980): 169–190.

———. *Time and Narrative*. Vol. 1. Chicago: U of Chicago P, 1984.

White, Hayden. "The Value of Narrativity in the Representation of Reality." *Critical Inquiry* 7 (1980): 5–27.

TIME AVAILABLE FOR EVOLUTION

The age of the earth, as inferred from decay rates of radioactive elements in meteorites and moon rocks, is approximately 4.6 billion years. The oldest known fossils are of blue-green bacteria, and are about 3.5 billion years old. For more than 2 billion years life on earth was unicellular and structurally simple. Over this time, however, cells evolved the ability to carry out complex biochemical processes, including fermentation, photosynthesis, and aerobic respiration. Eukaryotic cells (cells that contain a nucleus and other internal membrane structures) appeared in the fossil record about 1.6 billion years ago. The evolution of complex multicellular body forms is much more recent; the oldest such fossils are from the soft-bodied Ediacaran fauna first found in Australia, and are about 600 million years old. The subsequent fossil history of earth has been rich and complex. It is divided into three eras. In the Paleozoic ("old life," 570 to 245 million years ago), many marine invertebrates, the first land plants, and the first fishes and reptiles evolved. In the Mesozoic ("middle life," 245 to 65 million years ago), dinosaurs, the first birds, and the first flowering plants appeared. In the Cenozoic ("recent life," 65 million years ago to the present), modern life forms (including humans) have appeared and reached their present abundance.

[G.A.A.]

See also **Chemical Evolution and the Origin of Life; Coevolution; Evolution of Evolutionism.**

FURTHER READINGS

Cowen, R. *History of Life*. Boston: Blackwell Scientific, 1990.

Stanley, S. M. *Earth and Life Through Time*. New York: W.H. Freeman, 1985.

TIME FOR THE FAMILY

In the early postwar period, writers analyzing social time in Western societies were identifying the family, as does Maurice Halbwachs in 1950, as a social unit with its own peculiar time structures, symbolic representation of time, and calendar of events. Family time could thus be distinguished from that of its individual members and of other social groups.

The seminal proposition of P.A. Sorokin and R.K. Merton in 1937 that social time is "qualitative and not purely quantitative" is now almost universally accepted. Accordingly, the family, as constituted in advanced industrial societies, offers a useful microcosm for observing the qualitative dimensions of time and acts as a chrysalis for examining the multiplicity of time reckoning systems, the multifaceted and localized nature of time, and the means whereby activities are coordinated and synchronized.

The family has been defined in a number of ways. Even formal or official definitions vary from one country to another. For the purposes of this article, the family is conceptualized broadly as the unit constituted by two or more related or cohabiting individuals, whether or not they are married, with or without children. It may be composed of a couple whose children have left home, a single parent (including the divorced and widowed) with a child, or a group of more than two generations. The term "household," which can include a person living alone or any group of individuals living under the same roof and sharing resources, does not have the same moral and emotional overtones as the term "family." Most of the illustrations presented here refer to families with children, and in many countries the presence of children is the criterion for a household to be considered as a family. Even when a loose definition is being used, the family should not be considered as an immutable unit within society. Although it has demonstrated a remarkable ability to survive over time as a social institution, its structure is perpetually changing. The place of any individual over his or her life cycle within a family is also undergoing continual change, implying that the immensely complex time structures which have to be managed are forever being renegotiated and adapted to fit changes in family constitution, roles, and circumstances, and also plans for the future.

Time has long been identified as a problem for any society at the macro-social level. Today, issues such as the congestion and stress created by the excessive concentration of vehicles on the roads during rush hours and peak holiday periods or the problems of unemployed adolescents who do not know how to occupy their time attract the interest of the media and of policy makers. Governments can thereby legitimize their intervention and the introduction of social policy measures designed to influence time structures. Attempts to restructure working hours, which are the most common example of state intervention, are not solely a response to the demands of economic agents but also to pressures exerted by individuals and groups seeking a better quality of life through the reappropriation of time, a more equitable distribution of free time, and what has been promoted in France, in particular, as a more creative use of time (*Echange et projets,* 1980).

The impact of government intervention is felt at the micro-social level within the family which is a social organization acting as a meeting place or melting pot for the time frames of its members. This interactional process is itself rarely unproblematic. The family must serve as a buffer or shock absorber for the externally imposed rules governing both clock time and event time at the workplace, school, in public services, or the commercial sector, while also being subjected to the individual and often incompatible temporal demands of its members, whether they be socially, biologically, physically, or psychologically determined. The family is one of the major sites where the pressures, conflicts, and constraints associated with combining the different patterns and schedules of individuals are most acutely experienced and where the repercussions of the control over time by external agents are most strongly felt.

An additional complication in studying time for the family within societies and across nations is that conceptions of time which are considered natural and accepted by the majority of the members of one social group or culture and used as criteria for regulating their activities may not be applicable in another social context. As Rudolf Reszoházy has shown, each society and each social stratum can be said to develop its own patterns of behavior which are shaped by its concept of time, and these patterns are learned during the process of socialization. As a primary socialization agent the family, therefore, plays a major part in transmitting the characteristic time patterns of a society from one generation to the next and in reproducing social constructions of time.

Because it is a microcosm of society and a mirror for social processes, the family unit affords an ideal context in which to study the intersection between different social times, the multiplicity of meanings of time, the diversity of time patterns, the process of change, and the emergence of new social value systems. The family also offers examples of the way in which precedence may be given to the schedules of individual members and of the solutions adopted to avoid potential conflicts over the control of time. Ultimately it serves to illustrate the possible consequences of any failure to find compromise.

THE TIMING OF FAMILY EVENTS

A review of the timing of family events is crucial to any understanding of the time patterning of family life. The family calendar spans a vast array of events, their sequencing, and their rhythms. It includes the way the family is constituted, the timing of marriages and births, length of dependency of children, life expectancy, and the incidence of divorce or other forms of separation, as well as the temporal organization of working and nonworking life. Seasonal events such as holidays or feast days also serve as important bench marks or *Zeitgeber*, structuring the organization of family life.

Since World War II, and particularly since the mid-1960s, all postindustrial societies have experienced a reduction in family size; the age at marriage and the timing of childbirth have been delayed, and life expectancy has increased. Although young people remain dependent on their parents for a longer period due to the extension of schooling and training, the net effect of these changes is that parenting and production today occupy a much smaller proportion of the total life-span. Even if several generations no longer cohabit, contact with the wider family network has not ceased. On the contrary, it continues to play an important part in people's lives and to be demanding in terms of time, as for example in the case of daughters caring for aging parents or retired grandparents looking after their grandchildren. As Linda Hantrais has argued, while a much shorter part of the life-span is today spent raising children, the peak time for motherhood is likely to coincide with the period during which patterns of employment outside the home are being established, resulting in the need for strategies to reconcile the demands of professional and family life.

A visible effect of the difficulty in adapting to changing circumstances and of the pressures created within the family is the rapid increase in the divorce rate in older as well as younger generations. Individual differences within the family in time patterning and in the degree of adaptability to change may be important contributing factors in the breakdown of marriage, which can theoretically now last much longer than in the past.

Although most of these demographic changes are common to all advanced societies, many cultural differences can be identified. For example, although the birthrate has declined markedly throughout the developed world over the postwar period, among the twelve member states of the European community, Ireland, the United Kingdom, and France have maintained much higher levels of fertility. Marriage and divorce rates, age at marriage, and age at the birth of the first child also vary from one country to another. The very marked discrepancy in life expectancy between the sexes in France (8.2 years at birth) means that couples there can anticipate spending a smaller number of years together after their children leave home than in many other European societies. Although female activity rates and continuity of employment have increased over the past decade, very different patterns can be identified from one country to another: in Denmark almost 80 percent of women aged fifteen to sixty-four are economically active, compared with less than 40 percent in Greece and Spain. In Belgium, Ireland, Luxemburg, and Portugal, activity rates amongst married women decline from the age of twenty-five during a period when motherhood is likely to be occupying a substantial amount of time, whereas in Denmark, Germany, Greece, and Italy, rates increase rapidly in the twenty-five to thirty-four age group. Part-time work is a common strategy used in some countries to combine employment with raising a family. The proportion of women in part-time work is particularly high in the Netherlands, with almost 60 percent, whereas it falls to 10 percent in Greece, Italy, and Portugal.

These variations show how family time is structured in quite different ways in societies which would appear to be similar in many other respects and how the family calendar of events is to some extent culturally determined. Sociological analysis suggests, moreover, that differences within societies between socio-occupational groups may be as great as those between nations.

THE IMPACT OF EXTERNAL TIME FRAMES ON THE TIME STRUCTURING OF FAMILY LIFE

All families are interacting continuously with agents outside the home, whether it be through school, work, domestic labor, and related activities, such as access to public and commercial services, or through leisure. The temporal demands made on family members by external agents, the relationship between the time frames of individuals and their social and professional trajectories both inside and outside the family result in a complex and multifaceted patterning of time.

Hantrais et al. have shown that the impact of work time as a bench marker for the organization of family life and other nonwork time is at the source of much of the early sociological literature on the development of leisure and flexible working hours. The time structuring of paid employment remains a powerful force affecting the control of time within the family. Working hours in different sectors are usually controlled either by central government legislation or by employers' contractual arrangements, often as a result of collective bargaining involving trade unions. France is an example of a country where central government exercises a strong control over working hours. In Britain, by contrast, negotiation is more often at plant or company level, and individual employers therefore exercise much greater control. Comparison of the two countries suggests that central government intervention in France has resulted in a much tighter control over working hours and imposed a more rigid nationwide system than in Britain. In societies where governments have made visible and explicit efforts to control working hours paid employment is more likely to be a dominant influence structuring family time.

The impact of external time is not the same for all family members. As Caroline Roy has demonstrated, quantitative comparisons of the time structure of daily life in different countries, across socio-occupational and age groups and according to gender, show the cumulative effects of time pressures and the inequalities in the distribution of time within families. Gender differences cut across other social variables to affect the meanings attributed to time. Whereas men would seem to lead a more compartmentalized existence, the interactive process is perhaps most salient for women, for whom the different areas of family and professional life are interdependent and tightly enmeshed in one another. Rather than following the linear pattern which is characteristic of the male career, women's time is more likely to be organized around simultaneity and the addition of activities such as paid employment, housework, and child care. It is, as Karen Davies and others have shown, more subject to the fluctuations of the labor market than for their male counterparts. Rather than bringing about any far-reaching changes in the distribution of tasks within the household, in most advanced Western societies, women's increased participation in the labor force has resulted in overload and greater time pressure.

Research suggests that the relative importance to individuals, both quantitatively and qualitatively, of time spent within the family, in comparison with work, school, or individual leisure pursuits, is not to be underestimated. Despite the changes in its structure and functions, recent surveys of public opinion in Western Europe confirm the centrality of the family as a source of well-being and satisfaction. A growing body of evidence is showing how the demands of the family affect work time: for example, the availability of women for work at particular times of the day or week, the time people are prepared to spend traveling to and from work, and their geographical mobility. Family demands and expectations have also been shown to have an important bearing on other areas of life: even though for most people work still gives a meaning to life and a sense of social identity, any increase in the amount of free time available is generally sought primarily in order to be with other family members.

CONTROL OVER TIME WITHIN THE FAMILY

One of the consequences of the rapid changes which have occurred in recent years in the timing and sequencing of family events and in female activity patterns is that the temporal demands on family members are constantly changing, probably at a faster rate than in the past. Individuals may, however, be able to exercise a greater degree of personal control and choice over events, for example, through the increased freedom to choose whether to marry or cohabit, or the opportunity to decide about the spacing and timing of childbirth. Family events may be less inexorable, but they do require a higher degree of flexibility, adaptability, and personal organization than in the past.

The increased element of individual choice may not necessarily be welcome, since for most people the need to structure their own life is not easily assumed. At some stages in life, time may be associated with boredom and emptiness, particularly as changes occur in the life course, for example when children leave home, when a marriage is dissolved, or a partner dies. Although external bench marks may exercise a form of oppression, they also provide a structure, without which many people feel lost and unable to organize themselves, as exemplified by the unemployed, retired, and divorced, or by the situation of women who have stayed at home to look after their children and then find themselves isolated and deprived of a socially determined time frame and a sense of purpose and direction.

Who exercises control over time within the family and how decisions are reached are less studied phenomena than the reciprocal influence of work or school time on the family. Feminist literature generally presents the family as the context in which women are irrevocably subordinated to men, and where women's time in all its manifestations is at the disposal of family members. Women can and do, however, influence the temporal organization of family life in a number of ways: it is generally the woman, particularly if she is employed, who decides on the timing of childbirth; the woman most often petitions for divorce and she chooses whether or not to work, although the degree of choice is often very relative. In some countries women are more often deciding to take upon themselves the sole responsibility for raising children, with clear consequences for the way in which they organize their lives.

SYNCHRONIZING TIME FOR THE FAMILY

The problems of ensuring that the different life paths of individual family members can be synchronized have become increasingly complex in contemporary societies. The particular problems for women of reconciling employment and childrearing provide a good example of the complex interweaving of time schedules. In their dual roles as wage earners and homemakers, women need to organize and plan not only in terms of their own future but also with reference to that of their spouses and their children; they have to be able to cope with and take account of present constraints while also juggling with the timetables of other family members. Where women with young children are employed full-time outside the home, their schedules may be very tightly packed and a large part of their daily and weekly time is subjected to or determined by external constraints. The period when family members can be engaged in activities relating to family togetherness is limited and compact and calls for efficient time management.

Even when children are at school, major problems still have to be resolved in synchronizing work and school hours. The problem is made more difficult in countries where the school day, week, or year is largely out of step with standard working hours. In France, for example, where there is no schooling on Wednesdays before secondary level, provision has to be made for young children on that day. Since French schools operate on Saturdays when most parents are free, the weekend does not have the same impact and meaning for all family members. This arrangement can also have negative consequences for family cohesion by restricting opportunities for togetherness. In Germany, the practice of morning-only schooling is an important constraint for women wanting to work full-time, and in Britain, to take another example of the problem of incompatibility, the relatively short school day and the absence of provision for children after school hours make it impossible for many women with young children to undertake a full working day.

School holidays are a major source of scheduling problems for economically active women with children. The French are often cited as an example of a nation where the preference is to pursue leisure activities during blocks of time (extended weekends, three- to four-week blocks of holiday from the five weeks of statutory paid annual leave), and the organization of the school year is at odds with the interests of most families with children of school age.

The nature of the problems and solutions adopted to synchronize the activities of family members also differs from one country to another: in France, it is the weekly and annual organization of school time which requires most attention, whereas in Britain or Germany, it is the scheduling of the school day. The solution, or most common strategy in Britain and Germany is for women to limit family size, to interrupt their career, opt for part-time work, and not work during school holidays, with the consequent loss of status and promotional opportunities. In France and Denmark, parents have access to a much more extensive support network, provided largely by the state, in the form of childminding facilities, care outside school hours, and local authority holiday centers.

In complex advanced societies the ability to manage time, in the absence of realistic sharing of tasks, is determined to a great extent by the availability of other forms of support, not least those provided by local authorities. The possibility of having time off with pay to look after sick children, statutory provision for parental leave (in some cases with pay), or the practice of keeping open positions for women who take more than the standard maternity leave or want to switch from full-time to part-time and back again are all arrangements which help families to find a solution to the problem of coordinating various time schedules. Increasingly, the importance of being able to bring together social agents so that they can synchronize their various activities and time sequences is recognized as a crucial factor in the smooth functioning of any society, and particularly its economic insti-

tutions, to the extent that, where the state has been reluctant to intervene, employers often take the initiative by setting up schemes which take account of women's temporal demands, organizing shift systems, career breaks, and other forms of flexible work time designed to make family life more compatible with paid employment outside the home.

THE COMPLEXITY OF FAMILY TIME

Clearly the relationship between different social times within the context of the family is far from being simple or linear. The family group is constantly evolving and requires perpetual adaptation to new temporal demands. It is a source and a meeting point of temporal constraints, dysfunctioning, and conflicts over time, since it is the place where changes in time structures elsewhere are most likely to have an impact. The family is the environment in which not only the scarcity but also the abundance of time are most strongly felt and the context in which temporal aspirations can be realized. In several countries, women who are successful in organizing their work and home lives are, for example, also found to be those who are most satisfied with their leisure activities and feel they are living their lives to the full.

Comparative analysis of the way in which time is conceptualized, structured, used, and controlled within the family context in more than one society points to a number of interesting variations. Although temporal patterning displays several universal features, culturally determined differences are easily identified: individuals in some societies are found to lead a more stressful existence or have greater expectations of governments and other external agents in searching for reconciliation strategies.

If in organizational sociology a major problem, as Peter Clark has put it, is how to "incorporate a notion of the plurality of time-reckoning systems which are embedded in the social constructs of organization members and in their individual biographies," the same can be said of the problem of studying time as a social phenomenon within the context of the family. Although a relatively small number of members make up a family unit, the diversity of their activities and their contacts with external agents is such that any analysis of time for the family involves a multiplicity of time-reckoning systems and of conceptions of time. By the same token, the family affords a fascinating environment in which to examine the many dimensions of time as a social phenomenon: time within the family is not simply synonymous with obligations, rights, and rituals; the family is also a unit which assumes its own temporal momentum and where group projects are planned and executed.

[L.H.]

See also **Cultural Differences; Feminist Perspectives; Human Fertility Trends; Human Mortality Trends; Leisure: Women with Children in France; Population: Past, Present, Future; Time Structuring for Teachers.**

FURTHER READINGS

Clark, Peter A. "A Review of the Theories of Time and Structure for Organizational Sociology." *Research in the Sociology of Organizations* 4 (1985): 35–79.

Davies, Karen. *Time and the Weaving of the Strands of Everyday Life.* Aldershot: Avebury, 1990.

Echange et Projets. *La révolution du temps choisi.* Paris: Albin Michel, 1980.

Gurvitch, Georges. "La multiplicité des temps sociaux." *La vocation actuelle de la sociologie.* Paris: PUF, 1957.

Halbwachs, Maurice. *La mémoire collective.* Paris: PUF, 1950.

Hantrais, Linda. *Managing Professional and Family Life: A Comparative Study of British and French Women.* Aldershot: Dartmouth, 1990.

Hantrais, Linda, Peter A. Clark, and Nicole Samuel. "Time-space Dimensions of Work, Family and Leisure in France and Great Britain." *Leisure Studies* 3 (1984): 301–317.

Rezsohàzy, Rudolf. "The Concept of Social Time: Its Role in Development." *International Social Science Journal* 24 (1972): 26–36.

Roy, Caroline. "Les emplois du temps dans quelques pays occidentaux." *Données sociales.* Paris: INSEE (1990): 223–225.

Sorokin, Pitrim A., and Robert K. Merton. "Social Time: A Methodological and Functional Analysis." *The American Journal of Sociology* 42.5 (1937): 615–629.

TIME IN CHINESE PHILOSOPHY

Time (*shih*) is a fundamental experience, category, and problem in Chinese philosophy: not only is time deeply rooted in the metaphysical consciousness of Chinese philosophers and thus forms the onto-cosmological cornerstone of almost all if not all philosophical concepts, but it is also incorporated into the practical and cultural life of both individuals and communities as the motivating force for conscientious, self-aware moral action and cultural practice. One may say that a pervasive concern with time is

both a metaphysical principle of reality and existence and a principle of moral action and cultural transformation in Chinese philosophy. Chinese philosophy may therefore be characterized as the philosophy of time (on the metaphysical level) and the philosophy of timeliness (on the ethical level).

The primary and primordial paradigms of the Chinese understanding of time come from the philosophy of the I Ching or Zhouyi (a system of symbols developed much earlier than 1200 B.C., with original texts composed around 1200 B.C., and ten commentaries written from the fifth to the fourth centuries B.C.). As the *I Ching* (*Book of Changes*) was one of the best preserved Chinese classics from antiquity, and has continued throughout every stage of Chinese history since the Han dynasty (206 B.C.-A.D. 220) to be the book most commented on and annotated by scholars of all persuasions, it is generally considered to have been the fountainhead of Chinese metaphysics and of the Chinese mode of philosophical thinking. The *I Ching* offers a comprehensive truth of comprehensive being based on a comprehensive observation (called *quan* in the *I Ching*) of things over a comprehensive range (namely, heaven, earth, and man) and in a comprehensive period of time.

Because this method of "comprehensive observation" operates without any religious or philosophical presuppositions (an approach apparently unique among world philosophies—see **Philosophy of Time** and its cross references), the philosophy of the *I Ching* readily adapts itself to a comprehensive theory of reality, an awareness that things naturally undergo changes from integration and coordination to differentiation and opposition (as well as the comparable processes in reverse); that changes occur on different levels and across different dimensions of a system or situation; and that there are patterns of change which can be described as a balance of opposites and a harmonization of differences. This means that the philosophy of the *I Ching* is in fact a philosophy of change (*i*) which presents change in all directions, in all manners, and with all possible combinations, yet preserves the fundamental unity and simplicity of change (*i*) as directly experienced, whether consciously or unconsciously, and is capable of identifying and presenting the source and direction of all these changes. How this is possible depends on our understanding the non-methodology of presuppositionless "comprehensive observation" (*quan*): it is the achievement of this non-methodology, devoid of any a priori suppositions, to have discovered the fundamental mode of change in all changes in time and all things in change in the macrocosms of both nature and society over a long period of time.

Thus, one may even suggest that *quan* consists of observing how time presents itself not on one single level of linear change but on many levels of nested, nonlinear change. As a methodology, *quan* is therefore able to present a "configurational theory of change" and consequently a "configurational theory of time." Since reality is thus seen as change-in-time and time-in-change, there is nothing more real than changes and time, and the methodology of *quan* is coextensive with a metaphysics of changes and time. (Though it is outside the main concern of this article, it is important to note that the *I Ching* has been known popularly as a practical book of divination. This is because a knowledge of the manner in which man and his surroundings configurate may be expected to enable man to initiate and participate in changes rather than merely to receive or suffer from them.)

THE TAO AND THE T'AI-CHI

Based on the comprehensive observation of change and a consequent comprehensive reflection on the nature of changes, the *I Ching* brings out a hidden understanding of the source of time and change through the notions of the *tao* (the way) and *t'ai-chi* (the great ultimate). What then is the *tao*? What is the *t'ai-chi*? In order to understand these, we have to once again focus on the notion of change (*i*) and then explain the *tao* and the *t'ai-chi* as two sides of the *i* in terms of the following six observations:

1. Change (*i*) is a process which on the one hand can be regarded as the comprehensive activity of production, reproduction, and sustenance of things by an underlying force, and the continuous manifestation of all things thus produced, reproduced, and sustained on the other. In this sense, change is creative (it brings out things from where things were not) and life-creative (it brings out things which are full of intrinsic life, namely, things that are capable of bringing out more life by virtue of their being rooted in the source of change). Thus the Hsi Tzu I-5 in the *I Ching* says that "To be productive of production is called *i*." This is strictly a remark based on the comprehensive observation of change as phenomenon. When the *i* is thus phenom-

enonally observed one may also see that change, being creative, neither obeys any external order nor concentrates on any direction or forms any substance which is not itself subject to change. The Hsi Tzu II-8 has a good description of this *i*-creativity: "When the *i* is considered in the book, it has examples close at hand. When it is considered as the way, it is always changing. It moves and stays nowhere. It circulates among six vacuities [referring to the six lines of the hexagram symbolizing six positions of the movement of the *i*]. It moves upward and downward without constancy. It interchanges the soft with the firm and vice versa. Nothing is to be taken as a fixed norm. The change changes where it fits."

2. The underlying power of change, the activity of the power of change, and the resulting manifestations of change are not to be separated so that there is no absolute bifurcation between phenomena and reality as in Greek philosophy. In fact, the underlying power of change can be said to find its reality only in the things it produces just as things find their destinies only in being the productions of the underlying power of change. What matters is the *process* of production and transformation. However, this is not to deny the importance of the individuation of things, but to accentuate instead the fact that all things are interrelated in a process of production and transformation, and in this sense each individual thing can be said to be self-productive and self-transformative. The underlying power of change—which is invisible by itself and which is constantly creative in bringing about things—is called the *tao*, whereas things produced and transformed are called the *hsiang*. T'ai-chi is then the *tao* when conceived as the source and origin for all things or all *hsiang*. In other words, *t'ai-chi* is when we focus on the *tao* as the source and origin or equivalently when we conceive the *tao* under the form of source and origin. Conversely, we can refer to the *tao* as the *t'ai-chi* when we conceive or focus on the *t'ai-chi* as a process of production and transformation. *T'ai-chi* and *tao* are two sides of the same coin and are thus internally linked as a unity. This unity is the unity of process and source of the change (*i*), for it is in the nature of change that change is a process from an origin and an origin of change always gives rise to a process.

3. *Tao* as the process of change, even though full of infinite potentiality and obeying no external order, has an intrinsic order of its own and this intrinsic order is expressed in terms of the differentiation, opposition, interaction, interchange, complementation, integration, innovation, and creation of two forces called *yin* and *yang* or alternately named *ch'ien* and *kun*. All are in fact terms descriptive of two aspects of the *tao* and signify the dialectical changes of differentiation, complementation, and integration. They also represent the results of such changes which in turn perform such changes. This is how the formation of the cosmological world and the things in it are to be explained. Thus in its infinite creative activities the *tao* makes a world cosmology possible. In this cosmology of the *tao* everything has its place and everything is intrinsically linked in the cosmological process of *yin-yang* or *ch'ien-kun* interchange. Thus, everything can be said to form a microcosm of its own whereby all associations and complexes can be understood in terms of a cosmos-making or cosmos-forming interaction or relation of the *yin-yang*. The Hsi Tzu I-5 says of this cosmos-forming, this interchange of the *yin-yang, that* "One *yin* and one *yang* in alternation is called the *tao*. To follow this is good (*shan*), to accomplish this is nature (*hsing*)." Not only things are formed in this fashion: so too are the individuality and the value of things which consist in their cosmogenetic rooting in the *tao* and in their well-placedness and positioning in the process of the *tao*.

4. Phenomenologically speaking, *yin* is a feature of darkness, softness, and rest which one may notice in things and states of affairs. This feature is, however, only symptomatic, because as a state and as a function of the *tao*, *yin* is actually the power and ability to contain, hold, and sustain. In this sense *yin* is called the principle or virtue of *kun* (the power of conforming). On a par with the *yin*, there is the feature of brightness, firmness, and movement which we call the *yang*. As a state and as a function *yang* is actually the power and ability to create, innovate, and lead. In this sense *yang* is called the principle or virtue of *ch'ien*. As with the *yin*, there is no limitation to the way in which the *ch'ien* may function and act. Overall, *yin* and *yang* represent two functions and consequently two features and two states as well as two prin-

ciples for the performance of the process of change called the *tao*. It is important to see that *yin* and *yang* are determined relative to each other and thus constitute two aspects of the same reality. There is no atomistic reduction of things to *yin* and *yang*; rather things themselves bring about a complex of relativities of *yin* and *yang* as is natural with the ways of change.

The Hsi-Tzu I-11 says, "Thus the *i* has the *t'ai-chi*, which generates the two norms [*yin* and *yang*], two norms generate the four forms and four forms generate eight *kua* [triagrams]." The symbolic system of the *i* thus produces a well-formed cosmological sequence of configurations of things in the form of triagrams and hexagrams. On the basis of the same principles of differentiation and integration, sixty-four hexagrams are formed which represent a new level of reality in distinction from but in connection with the level of eight triagrams. As far as the symbolic meanings of the eight triagrams and the sixty-four hexagrams are concerned, the level of eight triagrams represents the natural world, whereas the level of sixty-four hexagrams represents the human world. These two worlds are connected in such a way that the human world cannot be fully understood without understanding the natural world and the natural world cannot be fully appreciated without reference to culture and humanity.

5. This connection between the natural and the cultural should lead to considerations on the place of man in the onto-cosmology of change. It is clear that man is a part of the universe, and in view of the onto-cosmology of change participates in the creative change of the *tao* and forms a *t'ai-chi* of his own. Occupying a higher level of reality than things and animals, man is endowed with a nature which can pursue goals, accomplish tasks, and achieve happiness, with a heart/mind (*hsin*) which can form judgment and achieve understanding. It is because of the nature of man and because of his *hsin* that he is able to act freely and creatively and to think, feel, and experience reality in its ultimate form. His nature and *hsin* make his moral freedom possible, but they are what they are because they are the embodiment of the *tao* and the agency for the *t'ai-chi*. This makes man a supreme vehicle for change and transformation not only of things external to him through the employment of his intellectual

mind, but also of himself through the activation of his nature. The Hsi Tzu I-10 speaks of the way of the sage (*sheng-jen*) in this way. A sage cultivates his nature and opens his mind and heart to the things in the world. A sage is capable of doing this because he lets out his nature and *hsin* without selfishness and obstruction and thus puts himself in the middle of the change of things. In this sense a sage is like the *i* itself which "does not do anything; but being still without movement is responsive to subtle changes and thus comprehends reasons and causes of these changes." It is with this ontological sensibility that the sage is able to transform people and the world in terms of his resolution of doubt and consolidation of feelings, which are needed for achieving great deeds.

6. The onto-cosmology of change in the *I Ching* is marked by the creativity of the *tao* as *t'ai-chi* or *t'ai-chi* as *tao* which leads to the creation of the self-creative human being. The high mark of man is not only that he is able to act freely but that he is able to act efficaciously and thus to bring well-being and harmony into the world. In order to do so, however, he has to understand change (*tung-p'ien*; to comprehend change). To understand change in the sense of *tung-p'ien* is to penetrate change and master change so that one can correctly adjust oneself or transform oneself toward a better or more facilitated realization of goodness as change. The latter effort and achievement is called *p'ien-tung* (to change for going through) in the Hsi Tzu. The Hsi Tzu I-11 has the following explanation of the *p'ien* and *tung*: "Thus to close gate is called *kun*, to open gate is called *ch'ien*. One closing and one opening is called change (*p'ien*); to go and come without limit is called *tung*."

We may draw the conclusion that the Chinese theory of time as exemplified and as founded in the *I Ching* is radically different from Western theories of time in not only identifying time with change, but also in identifying time with timelessness. In this manner one can speak of time of change as well as change of time, the timelessness of time as well as the time of timelessness. In light of this well-worked out philosophy of time, the character "*i*" (transformation) acquires the meanings of change (*p'ien-yi*), non-change (*pu-yi*), and simplicity (*ch'ien-yi*) all at the same time. This is not to deny that time, change, and timelessness cannot be separated in

meaning, but only to underscore the fact that a theory of time needs to be as extensive, comprehensive, and profound as any theory of cosmos, man, and reality and their interrelatedness.

The *I Ching* paradigms of time become embodied and developed in later schools, primarily in Taoism, Confucianism, neo-Taoism, and neo-Confucianism, but also in other philosophies and religions, such as Chinese Buddhism, which are beyond the scope of this article.

TAOISM

Even though the *Tao Te Ching* may have been written later than the time of Confucius, the thoughts of the *Tao* as articulated by Lao Tzu (ca. sixth century B.C.) can be seen to have an earlier origin based on the *I Ching*. First, although the idea of the *tao* is not explicitly mentioned as a central concept in the *I Ching* divination text (the original text of the *Zhouyi*), the unfolding and the deployment of the *kua* in a timely sequence which encloses all cosmological and human-related developments exhibit the timely working of an underlying force and principle which cannot be defined or characterized in any form or image it has produced. Hence the first statement of the *Tao Te Ching* that "The *tao* that can be spoken is not the constant *tao*" betrays the understanding that underlying all changes there is the timelessness which is time as a whole and as a creative power which motivates everything or enables all things to be moved by themselves. The unspoken and unspeakable nature of the *tao* is very important for understanding the *i*, for it signifies the understanding of the unity of change and non-change or the unity of time and timelessness. Following this basic idea, all the Taoist ideas of Lao Tzu such as "All things hold the *yin* and embrace the *yang*" and "Do nothing and everything will be done" naturally fall into place and present an implicit theory of time as the *tao* and the implicit theory of the *tao* as the process and substance of time.

The essential point of Taoism is that we are able to imitate and embody the *tao* if we void ourselves of desires and prejudiced, partial knowledge of the world, things, or ourselves. This means that time has an aspect of voidness (*wu*) which we call no-time or timelessness and which makes time resistant to being characterized or identified in any reifying manner, just as the *tao* itself resists permanent definition.

After Lao Tzu, Chuang Tzu (369–286 B.C.) showed that the *tao* can and should be seen as the self-identity and self-transformation of individual things, that there exist relativities of perspectives and existential values among all things, and consequently that there exist ontological equality and cosmological interrelatedness among all things. Chuang Tzu speaks of the beginning of the not-yet-beginning of the beginning of time (yu-wei-shih-yu-fu-shih-che-yeh), which means that there is no absolute beginning of time as every moment of time is a beginning of time for life and death, and hence for being and nonbeing. He says in Ch'i Wu Lun that "There is now life, there is now death; there is now death, there is now life," and also that the best way of understanding time and being is to "reach to the center or axis of the circle which is the tao and respond to infinity in infinity [te-chi-huan-chung-yi-yin-wu-chiung]." One important implication here for time is that although we think of time and reality in a linear fashion, in actuality, reality is nonlinear (that is, it resists linear characterization), and our thinking on reality or time actually comes to itself in a circle; thus, we would fare better if we reach for and reside in the center of this circle of thinking so that we can be freed from limitations in our exercise of creativity.

CONFUCIANISM
Confucius (ca. 551–479 B.C.) does not say much specifically about time. In the Analects, however, he describes a creek as quickly flowing away, a comment that is essentially a remark on the fleeting nature of time. As with the tao, time creates and as it creates it also flies away. This means that human beings should cultivate themselves and create as many values as possible so they can realize and lead worthwhile and significant lives. Confucius says of himself that he studies hard and sometimes even forgets to eat, knowing not that old age will arrive. It is true that if a person works hard and concentrates on a significant project, time ceases to exist for him. This means that he transcends time and reaches a state of timelessness in terms of his activity and achievements which exist in time in a different sense. It is in light of this unity of time and timelessness that we can speak of the timeliness of one's action and one's work, with timeliness (shih-chung) understood as penetrating into the core of things in a situation and bringing out their potentiality toward a fruitful achievement of good, including achievement of desirable transformation, harmonization, and upliftment.

In this light, we can see Confucius's efforts to teach his disciples to attain virtues and bring peace and harmony to the people as efforts to teach self-realization and the realization of others, which are two forms of time- and timeless-ness-realization in a timely manner. These two forms of time- and timelessness-realization are the core of personal and social morality, as morality is no more than reaching self-realization and helping others toward realization in time, and toward timelessness. In order to do this, Confucius speaks of realizing jen. Simply put, jen is consideration and respect toward others: it is the effort to preserve a harmonious and humane society or community so that civilization may flourish. Jen is therefore the effort to extend humanity from oneself to others and to create an environment in which all may obtain a good life. But in acting out jen, one has to do things in time, to respond to people when they require a response. To care for and to understand people is to understand people in terms of time-relations and time-consequences. Thus to worry about one's parents being old, to respect one's elder brother, and so forth can all be said to be a matter of considering time-values in human relationships. Hence acting according to time is a moral imperative for Confucianism. To put this in an abstract manner, we may see jen as giving one's time-potentiality for benefiting others, and as such transcending oneself and therefore one's lifetime in an effort to reach the values of timelessness.

Classical Confucianism cannot be completely understood without discussing Mencius (372–289 B.C.). The importance of Mencius's contributions to classical Confucianism lies in his disclosing the self-motivating nature of the human being for moral action. Morality in both duty-performance and virtue-comprehension is in line with and also derives from human existence. Mencius clearly states the need for both a teleology of goodness and virtues and a deontology of justice and duties. Again morality is considered as doing the right thing at the right time in the right place. His example of saving one's sister-in-law by giving her a helping hand illustrates the principle of exigency in time. In fact, one has to take into consideration the specific circumstances of time when fulfilling duty and demonstrating benevolence. In this sense one may even see Mencius's distinction between "nature" (hsing) and "destiny" (ming) as full of time-significance.

Ontologically, "nature" comes from the activity of heaven (a principle of creativity of time; called t'ien-tao or ch'ien-tao), whereas "destiny" results from the passivity of earthly life (a principle of receptivity of time; called ti-tao or kun-

tao). Human life and human existence are made of both "nature" and "destiny." But a human being can always use his creative nature to overcome his limiting destiny, precisely in the sense of developing his nature in time so as to transcend time and achieve the values of timelessness, even while still being bound by time on the physical level. Mencius argues that man's nature is naturally creative of goodness and this should be regarded as a manifestation of the natural and spontaneous creativity of time, on the basis of which man can use time to achieve timeless values and to apply these values to the creativity of time in a timely manner. To be timely is a matter of profound wisdom which comes from seeing the intricate relationships of things and events in a situation being interwoven and produced in time, from time, and from the ultimate reality (the *tao*) behind them. Mencius has called Confucius "a sage of time or timeliness" and this no doubt betrays Mencius's own profound understanding of time in the spirit of the *I Ching* tradition.

Late in his life, Confucius reached a full metaphysics of man and heaven in his reflections on the original texts of the *I Ching*. What has been quoted and explained with reference to the Hsi Tzu commentary of the *I Ching* belongs to the results of these reflections which are elaborated and articulated by his disciples. Thus the *I Ching* philosophy of time as based on the Hsi Tzu and the rest of the commentaries in the Ten Wings can be said to be both a disclosure of the pristine wisdom of the *I Ching* authors and a testimony of Confucius's own experience, and in this sense provides the primary and foundational understanding of time in the Chinese indigenous tradition and the native Chinese mind.

Another relevant document in this connection is the Chung Yung (the Doctrine of the Mean) from the *Li Chi* (the *Book of Rites*). Like the Hsi Tzu, the Chung Yung sees reality in terms of creative transformation and self-fulfillment in time, of time, and by time. Man in particular is given the time-potentiality for realizing his own nature, the nature of others, and the nature of all things. If a man can fulfill his time-potentiality in an authentic way (*ch'eng*, having a genuine desire and making the utmost effort to do this), he is able to form a trinity with heaven and earth, and hence is able to participate in the creative, transformative process of heaven and earth. In other words, he is to be one with the *tao* and achieve full freedom and unlimited creativ-

ity in the unity of time and timelessness in the origin-time. In fact, this ideal of developing a person is also confirmed and embraced in the Tuan commentary of the *I Ching*.

NEO-TAOISM

Neo-Taoism developed during the second to fourth century A.D. as an intellectual and philosophical response to the needs and times of the Wei-Ch'ing society. The neo-Taoist philosophers and poets deepened their studies of Chou Yi, Lao Tzu, and Chuang Tzu for the purpose of freeing themselves from worldly worries. They called their studies "learning of metaphysical profundities" (*hsuan-hsueh*). It is clear that they explicitly dealt with the metaphysical problems of *wu* (nonbeing, void, voidness) and *yu* (being, things, existents) from the very start. For our purpose here we shall restrict ourselves to two contrasting positions of neo-Taoism and assess their philosophical implications for time. Wang Pi (226–249), the foremost neo-Taoist philosopher, argued for *wu* as the foundation and source of all things in the world. With this fundamental thought he made his epoch-making commentary on the Chou Yi and went on to reinterpret Lao Tzu and the *Analects*. He argues that all things must come from oneness and return to oneness and this oneness must be conceived in terms of *wu*, since it is only from *wu*'s lack of characteristic that the diversity of things can be said to have originated. The innovation of Wang Pi is that he points out why *wu* by its very nature of not being any *yu* must be the origin of all *yu*. Thus, Wang Pi may be said to have attained an insight into the natural creativity of the *wu*. For this reason he sees *wu* as an essential characteristic of the *tao*, *tao* being the name given to focus on the all-penetrating character (*wu-pu-tung*) of the *wu*.

On the basis of the *wu*, Wang Pi stresses also the original quietude of the *tao*. By spontaneous creativity rest gives rise to motion and yet because of the original quietude of the *tao* all things will return to rest which of course is oneness. He further speaks of the substance (*ti*)/function (*yung*) relation between *wu* and *yu*, *tao* and things, and emphasizes their inseparability, which means that *yu* always has *wu* as its sustaining source. Thus time can be considered as having two sides which may be said to function like *yin* and *yang* in the unity of the *t'ai-chi*. Wang Pi's philosophy of *wu* has brought out very vividly the creativity of time and its ontological nature of self-emptiness and self-emptying.

Kuo Hsiang (?–312), a later neo-Taoist, attempted to contradict Wang Pi by insisting on the logical understanding of *wu*. Unlike Wang Pi, he refuses to see *wu* as dynamically and spontaneously creative. In order to explain the diversity of things, Kuo Hsiang appeals instead to *yu* in the sense of *ch'i*. Although Wang Pi also refers to *ch'i* (vital breath, vital force, and energy of all forms) in his annotation on Lao Tzu, he did not elaborate on its unifying and transformative nature. Kuo Hsiang seizes upon the notion of *ch'i* from Lao Tzu (and even more from Chuang Tzu) and makes it a principle of creativity and transformation for the diversity of things.

Like Chuang Tzu, Kuo Hsiang considers life and death, and the formation and destruction of things, as results of the gathering and dissipation of *ch'i*. But in terms of the significance of Kuo Hsiang's philosophy of *ch'i* for time, it is clear that even though *ch'i* can be used to identify time as change, one must specify the timeless in terms of the self-transcendence of *ch'i*, but not simply in terms of its permanent presence in all things, for the timeless is a notion in which time has voided its own existence in any concrete form. This problem then leads to the development of the position called neo-Confucianism.

NEO-CONFUCIANISM

Neo-Confucianism contains far more rich resources for thinking on being and time than philosophers in previous periods in Chinese philosophy. It is also remarkable that the neo-Confucianists, almost without exception, conscientiously sought inspiration from and were inspired by the philosophy of the *I Ching*. In fact, many of them—apart from having their own philosophical systems inspired by the *I Ching*—have contributed directly to the enriched interpretation and development of the *I Ching*'s philosophy.

Chou Tun-i (1017–1073), the founder of the Sung neo-Confucian philosophy, developed the diagrammatic system of the *t'ai-chi* as an illustration of the cosmogenesis and the homogenesis. His "Discourse on the Diagram of the *T'ai-chi*" cannot, however, be regarded simply as a cosmological theory of time-transformation; it must also be seen as an ontological reflection on the nature of the reality of time-change. He affirms the subtle creativity of the *wu* (called *wu-chi* or the ultimateless now) toward *t'ai-chi* (the great ultimate or the primary *yu*) and incorporates the theory of five powers (*wu-hsing*) into the philosophy of *yin-yang* for an onto-cosmo-

logical explanation of the creation of all things and man. But he also speaks of the return of the *t'ai-chi* to the *wu-chi*, and of *tung* (motion) to the *ching* (rest). In this sense he sees the ontological reciprocity, duality, and unity of *wu* and *yu*, being and nonbeing, motion and rest, just like Wang Pi. But he also sees everything as a *t'ai-chi* and therefore all things can be said to change and transform by themselves. In this he shares the same insight on individual creativity as Kuo Hsiang. In combining these two aspects of neo-Taoism, Chou Tun-i shows how a human being can achieve creative transformation of himself and thus reach the unity of man with heaven or the *tao*. One may see in Chou the reciprocity, duality, and unity of man and heaven in terms of the two realms of time, which are metaphysically bound together and which function in a complementary fashion.

Chang Tsai (1020–1077) has continued the thinking about change/time and *t'ai-chi/tao* in regard to their reciprocity, duality, and unity. An important development of Chang Tsai is his combining of the positions of Wang Pi and Kuo Hsiang in terms of the unity of the notion of "great void" (*t'ai-hsu*) and the notion of "great harmony" (*t'ai-ho*). His contemporary Shao Yung (1011–1077), by concentrating on the formation of structures and rational patterns of change and time-transformation in the philosophy of the *I Ching*, has tremendously enriched the form-number (*hsiang-shu*) interpretation of its process of onto-cosmological change and transformation.

Neo-Confucianism advanced to a new stage of development with Ch'eng I (1033–1107) and Chu Hsi (1130–1200), both of whom have written commentaries on the *I Ching* and whose philosophies thrive on the interplay of *li* (order) and *ch'i* as two primitive onto-cosmological categories and principles of reality. As the *li/ch'i* theory pervades human existence in terms of the composition of human nature (*hsing*) and heart/mind (*hsin*), one may also see why and how man should and can reach for unity with heaven in the sense of reaching for a higher realization of time, namely the level of realization of time-creativity and timeless-unity in the human person and through the human person.

The discussion on the *li/ch'i* relationship and their relationship to *hsing/hsin* has continued from the time of Chu Hsi and Lu Hsiang-shan to the time of Wang Yang-ming and Wang Fu-chih. It has even continued into contemporary neo-neo-Confucianist efforts on rethinking and reconstructing Confucian philosophy for the modern and postmodern world. Though the views of Hsiung Shih-li, Liang Shu-ming, and Hsiung's speculative disciples such as Mou Tsung-shan and Tang Chun-yi and their significances for the Chinese philosophy of time need separate treatment, their views have taken inspiration, like so many of their predecessors, from the primary paradigms of time in the philosophy of the *I Ching* and thus have inherited a distinctive wisdom related to the classical Chinese understanding of time.

[C.C.-Y.]

See also **Cosmology (Philosophy); Philosophy of Time.**

FURTHER READINGS

Chang Tsai. "Correcting Youthful Ignorance [*Cheng Meng*]." *A Source Book in Chinese Philosophy*. Trans. and ed. Wing-tsit Chan. Princeton: Princeton UP, 1963. 500–514.

Cheng Chung-ying. "Greek and Chinese Views on Time and the Timeless." *Philosophy East and West* 24 (1974): 155–160.

Chou Tun-i. "An Explanation of the Diagram of the Great Ultimate [*T'ai-chi-t'u shuo*]." *A Source Book in Chinese Philosophy*. Trans. and ed. Wing-tsit Chan. Princeton: Princeton UP, 1963. 463–465.

Chu Hsi. *The Philosophy of Human Nature*. Trans. J. Percy Bruce. London: Probsthain, 1922.

———. *Learning To Be a Sage: Selections from the Conversations of Master Chu*. Trans. Daniel K. Gardner. Berkeley: U of California P, 1990.

Chuang Tzu. *Chuang-Tzu: A New Selected Translation with an Exposition of the Philosophy of Kuo Hsiang*. Trans. Yu-lan Fung. 2nd ed. New York: Paragon, 1964.

———. *Chuang-Tzu: The Seven Inner Chapters and Other Writings from the Book Chuang-Tzu*. Trans. A.C. Graham. Boston: Allen & Unwin, 1981.

Confucius. *The Analects of Confucius*. Trans. Arthur Waley. New York: Vintage, 1938.

Graham, A.C. *Two Chinese Philosophers: Ch'eng Ming-tao [Ch'eng Hao] and Ch'eng Yi-ch'uan [Ch'eng I]*. London: Lund Humphries, 1958.

I Ching: The Book of Changes. Trans. John Blofeld. London: Allen & Unwin, 1984.

Lao Tzu. *The Tao Te Ching [Classic of the Way and the Virtue]: A New Translation with Commentary*. Trans. Ellen M. Chen. New York: Paragon, 1989.

Mencius. *Mencius*. Trans. W.A.C.H. Dobson. Toronto: U of Toronto P, 1963.

Wang Pi. *Commentary on the Lao Tzu*. Trans. Ariane Rump and Wing-tsit Chan. Honolulu: UP of Hawaii, 1979.

Wilhelm, Hellmut. "The Concept of Time in the Book of Changes [the *I Ching*]." *Man and Time: Papers from the Eranos Year Books*. Trans. Ralph Manheim.

Ed. Joseph Campbell. New York: Pantheon, 1957. 212–232.

TIME IN THE PLASTIC ARTS

Gotthold Ephraim Lessing's *Laocoön: An Essay on the Limits of Painting and Poetry* (1766) provides the *locus classicus* for the argument concerning the temporal nature of poetry and the spatial nature of the plastic arts. Lessing's work questions the assumptions of his contemporary, critic Johann Joachim Winckelmann, and also those implied by Horace's "ut pictora poesis" (poetry resembles painting). He argues rather that there is a difference between the temporal limitations on poetry and those on the plastic arts. He also makes it clear at the end of his preface (as given in the translation of Edward A. McCormick) that he is dealing with both poetry and painting in the widest possible terms: "by 'painting' I mean the visual arts in general . . . [whereas] under the name of poetry, I shall . . . devote some consideration also to those other arts in which the method of presentation is progressive in time."

The essence of Lessing's argument is that the poet in describing a scene—for example the flight of Philoctetes's arrow—is not restricted in his use of time. But the plastic artist who must catch a single moment of time needs to be particularly careful in choosing that moment. The main point, as given in Chapter 3, is that "the artist can never make use of more than a single moment in ever-changing nature." And therefore "the more we add in our imaginations, the more we must think we see. In the full course of an emotion no point is less suitable for this than its climax."

The reason why the artist is best served by choosing the moment just prior to the climax is demonstrated by the group statuary of Laocoön, which provides the title for Lessing's work. According to legend, Laocoön was a Trojan priest of Apollo who was punished for dissuading the Trojans from admitting the wooden horse into Troy. While offering a sacrifice to Poseidon, he rushed to the defense of his two sons when he saw two serpents leaving the sea to attack them. The serpents—as illustrated in the much celebrated statuary which had been disinterred at Rome in the sixteenth century—encircled all three of them and crushed the father and his sons. What Lessing demonstrates is that the artistic effect of the piece is far more poignant because the sculptor has chosen the moment just before the climax of death. In this way each of us as onlookers can carry the scene forward to the climax by using the imagination in our mind's eye.

This effect is by no means restricted to moments of tragic climax. As Lessing notes in Chapter 18, regarding the folds of a woman's dress in a Raphael painting, "since that part of the drapery which lies on the foot immediately follows it in its forward motion," the artist has shown the leg to have moved forward under the gown whereas the drapery is illustrated at the moment just before it will follow the limb that it covers. The effective use by the artist of that brief moment to which painting is limited allows for a comparable though much more pleasing play of the imagination than that which occurs in *Laocoön*.

Though Lessing's theory regarding the temporal limitations imposed on the plastic arts has by no means gone unquestioned since his own times, the new technologies of the twentieth century have clearly changed the ground rules. Film, television, telecommunications, and the even more recent multimedia of computers have provided new forms of visual art that are very much concerned with the "fourth dimension" of time.

But since the advent of film the plastic arts themselves seem sometimes to have been influenced by the persistence of human vision that has permitted separate frames of film to be seemingly fused into a realistic and temporally seamless visual scene. Marcel Duchamp's *Nude Descending a Staircase* (1912), and M.C. Escher's *Kringloop Cycle* (1938), depicting a man similarly occupied and similarly shown as a series of men in the process of descent make one wonder whether comparable work could have been done before our century and an awareness of the temporal factors involved in projecting a sequence of film frames. Certainly William Hogarth's progresses are a beginning but they deal with a progress over time (whether ironically or otherwise) in a rather different manner.

Though the increasing use of time in the plastic arts can be credibly related to the advent of film at the turn of the century, there are parallel developments such as Henri Bergson's concept of *durée* in his *Creative Evolution* (1907), and the related influence on Cézanne argued by George Hamilton. One can also assume a strong influence on cubism from scientific developments including Hermann Minkowski's 1908 paper of which Samuel Alexander writes in *Space, Time, and Deity* as early as 1920, "a world in Space and Time which was formulated by mathematical methods by the late H. Minkowski . . . had been used or implied in the memoirs of Messrs. Lorentz and Einstein, which along with Minkowski's memoir laid the basis of the so-called theory of relativity . . . every point has four co-ordinates, the time co-ordinate being the fourth." Various aspects of the incorporation of time into the plastic arts along the lines suggested above are dealt with in articles by William Rubin, Paul Laporte, and Linda Henderson. Jeoraldean McClain has argued further that art critics should follow the lead of Joseph Frank's "Spatial Form in Modern Literature" (*Sewanee Review*, 1945), which shows that literature in our century often describes "a dynamic tension between narrative progression and spatial form in works such as Joyce's *Ulysses*" (see **Stream of Consciousness**). In McClain's view, since literature has gone beyond the spatial limitations imposed on poetry by Lessing, the time has come for art critics to recognize the extent to which twentieth-century artists have also gone beyond the temporal limitations that Lessing imposed on the plastic arts. Like a good professor, Lessing's remarkably prescient views in *Laocoön* are now providing even his recalcitrant modern students with contemporary insights into their sister arts.

[S.L.M.]

See also **Bergson, Henri; Film; Hogarth, William; Stream of Consciousness; Telecommunications; Television.**

FURTHER READINGS

Baudson, Michel, ed. *Zeit, die vierte Dimension in der Kunst.* Weinheim: Acta Humaniora der VCH, 1985.

Gombrich, E.H. "Moment and Movement in Art." *Journal of Warburg and Courtauld Institutes* 27 (1964): 292–306.

Hamilton, George. "Cézanne, Bergson and the Image of Time." *College Art J* 16 (1956): 2–12.

Henderson, Linda. "A New Facet of Cubism: The Fourth Dimension and Non-Euclidian Geometry Reinterpreted." *Art Quarterly* 34 (1971): 411–433.

Laporte, Paul. "Cubism and Science." *Journal of Aesthetics and Art Criticism* 7 (1949): 243–256.

Lessing, Gotthold Ephraim. *Laocoön: An Essay on the Limits of Painting and Poetry* (1766). Trans. Edward A. McCormick. Baltimore: Johns Hopkins UP, 1984.

McClain, J. "Time in the Visual Arts: Lessing and Modern Criticism." *Journal of Aesthetics and Art Criticism* 44.1 (Fall 1985): 41–58.

Rubin, William. "Cézannism and the Beginnings of Cubism." *Cézanne: The Late Work.* Ed. William Rubin. New York: Museum of Modern Art, 1977. 159–169, 189.

Souriau, Etienne. "Time in the Plastic Arts." Trans. Marjorie Kupersmith. *Journal of Aesthetics and Art Criticism* 7.4 (June 1949): 294–307.

TIMEKEEPERS, DOMESTIC: ENGLISH INFLUENCE 1710–1800

This article deals with watches and clocks and does not cover sundials even though most people in eighteenth-century England still relied on sundials to set their timepieces.

The 1700s were a period of greatly increasing ownership of domestic timekeepers. The cost of these remained steady in a period of increasing wealth and thus a wider section of the population could afford to buy them. "Secondhand" or "previously owned" clocks became available as families "traded up" by disposing of the old and unfashionable and purchasing the new. Watches were being handed down generation to generation and new cases and dials were supplied for old movements when the latter were of high enough quality to merit restoration. A number of technical developments in England during this period greatly influenced domestic horology worldwide.

Ever since their invention, watches have always been valued not only for their utility but also as pieces of jewelry. With the adoption of the balance spring at the end of the seventeenth century the utility of watches increased enormously, since timekeeping was now possible to within one or two minutes a day. Although the use of a balance spring to regulate the motion of the watch balance (the mechanism that controls or governs a watch escapement) had been proposed in the 1660s, it was not until the 1680s that its use became universal. Early experiments with balance springs prompted a redesign of the basic watch movement. The running time, or period of "going," was increased from about eighteen hours to some thirty hours. This meant that the watch needed winding only once a day. The method of changing the rate of a pre-balance spring watch was to vary the force delivered by the mainspring. The famous watchmaker, Thomas Tompion, introduced an alternative method by varying the effective length of the balance spring. This method remained standard until the end of the 1700s, when a simple lever was adopted. There was a problem of showing hours and minutes in such a manner that a customer, accustomed to the single-hour hand on a longcase clock, could understand the dis-

play. One method adopted was to have a moving twenty-four-hour dial (sun and moon) set behind an aperture in the main dial and a separate minute hand. However, the method involving concentric hour and minute hands, still in use today, quickly became established and was in widespread use by 1730. By this date, the

Figure 1. Eight-day musical striking clock by Joseph Finney, Liverpool, about 1770. There is a different tune for each day of the week and the moving shutters at the top of the dial enable sunrise and sunset to be shown by means of a moving sun. This was a very expensive clock when new and was constructed using the finest materials and imported timbers. (Owned by the National Museums and Galleries on Merseyside and displayed at Liverpool Museum.)

design of basic watches had become so standardized that watches similar in style were being made for the next 150 years.

An ordinary English watch consisted of a movement and dial housed within a double case. The outer of the two cases served as a dust cover and was removed every day to wind the watch, the key being inserted through a hole in the back of the inner case. The outer cover was decorated or not, depending on the purchaser. The inner case protected the movement and had a hinged bezel holding a watch glass through which could be seen the dial and hands. To set the hands, the owner opened this bezel and placed the winding key on the square boss at the center of the minute hand. The hands could then be turned to set the time. When the watch required regulation, the movement was unlatched and swung out of the case on the same joint as the bezel. The winding key was again used, this time to turn a disk with a circle of numbers located on the back of the movement known as a "Tompion" regulator. The numbers gave an indication of how far the disk had been turned and an indication of the likely adjustment made. The movement was engraved on the visible backplate and the balance cock (which supported the balance in position) was also pierced and engraved. The maker's name and town were frequently engraved on metal dials, but later in the century, when enamel on copper dials were the norm, one could only find the maker's name on the back of the movement.

The movement was of a form known as "full plate" and consisted of two parallel brass plates drilled with bearing holes for the train of wheels. The balance was mounted outside the back plate beneath a balance cock and the lower bearing for the balance arbor (the shaft or staff on which the balance turns) was held by a bracket riveted (later screwed) to the back plate. The dial was pinned to a plate (brass edge), which was in turn pinned to the bottom plate (pillar plate) of the movement. In early watches, pins were the primary means for securing the components together, but later in the century increased use was made of screws.

Such an "ordinary" English-made watch was an expensive item, costing about five pounds at the beginning of the 1700s for one with a silver case. This was at a time when an educated, skilled man might earn one pound a week and a laborer five shillings for a six-day week. English watches did, however, have a good and deserved reputation for quality. In 1746, Johann Heinrich Zedler's *Universal Lexicon* stated that "The English watches are considered best of all, especially the so-called repeating watches. After the English watch come the French, Augsburg, Nürnberg and Ulm watches. The Geneva watches are thought little of, because they are to be had so cheaply; they are made in such quantities that one buys them in lots." Production centers in Switzerland were forced to imitate the styles set by English makers in order to compete. English watches at this time were well made with good quality, well-finished components and well-cut gear teeth on the wheels and pinions. Those from the best makers were superb. But by the end of the century they seemed heavy and expensive when compared with those manufactured overseas. Ownership of this type of watch involved routine activities that must have become almost ritualistic because of the care needed.

From the mid-1600s, it had been usual for the watchmaker to purchase finished or partly finished watches from the specialist movement producers and finishers around Liverpool in Lancashire. The Lancashire horological trade workers, unrestricted by guild influence, were capable of producing some of the finest work ever seen and the widespread use of specialists who could undertake the manufacture of individual parts ensured that the cost was not unduly high for the standard of workmanship. Their products were supplied to vendors who had to satisfy discerning middle- and upper-class customers who were not too interested in the mechanism, but who expected reliability over many years.

The above system of manufacture depended on access to a number of specialized tools developed in the Lancashire area during the early 1600s, tools that gave the Lancashire makers the great technical lead that they held until the end of the 1700s. This toolmaking expertise became renowned throughout the watchmaking world. During the mid-1700s, makers such as George Sanderson introduced improvements in manufacturing methods, but these appear not to have been widely adopted. This indicated a lack of versatility among those making watches, a problem that was to become gravely serious in the nineteenth century. Notwithstanding the reluctance to change fundamental manufacturing methods, English-based makers were prolific in developing escapements and other refinements that improved timekeeping capabilities.

In 1704, the Swiss, Facio de Duillier, along with Peter and Jacob Dubaufre, invented a method of producing drilled jewels that could be used as bearings in watches. Such bearings reduced friction and, because of the inert material from which they were made, enabled oil to remain fresh for longer periods than was possible with brass bearings. The fact that they were unable to obtain a British patent for their invention led to its widespread use on the best watches by the middle of the century. This technical lead was enjoyed by English watchmakers until well into the 1800s.

By 1725, George Graham had developed the escapement proposed by William Houghton, Edward Barlow, and Thomas Tompion in 1695. The cylinder or "horizontal" escapement, as it was then known (to distinguish it from the verge or vertical escapement), became widely used among the best makers, for whom it gave very good results. After Graham, John Ellicot Senior and Junior, Thomas Mudge, Benjamin Gray, and Justin Vulliamy were among the first watchmakers to use this escapement widely. The performance was improved by employing ruby cylinders. Graham also used center seconds hands and this feature was taken up quickly by Mudge and then by others.

Although the eminent watchmaker Thomas Mudge is well known for his work on marine timekeepers, it was the lever escapement which he applied to a watch in 1769–70 that stands as his greatest horological achievement. This escapement was "detached," that is to say the balance only came into contact with the lever for a small part of its oscillation. It also gave impulse to the oscillating balance assembly in both directions, which was beneficial in watches subject to movement. Though not greatly used in Mudge's lifetime, the lever escapement was developed by others into the "universal" escapement employed in most portable mechanical timekeepers until the present day.

Josiah Emery, a Swiss maker long resident in London, was the first maker to use the lever escapement after Thomas Mudge, and made his first watch so fitted in 1782. Thereafter he produced about thirty lever watches up to 1795. John Leroux also used the lever escapement and was probably the first to introduce the feature known as "draw" in 1795. Draw enabled the lever to be held clear of the balance staff when not actually giving impulse to the balance. Better timekeeping resulted and draw became universally used on watches with lever escapements and remains a feature of such escapements even today.

Thomas Tyrer patented the "duplex" escapement in 1782. The duplex became one of the few escapements to approach the detached chro-

Figure 2. Thirty-hour clock by Henry Deane, Honiton, Devon about 1770. This typifies the less costly clocks made during the second half of the eighteenth century. The case is of oak and simply constructed. (Owned by the National Museums and Galleries on Merseyside.)

nometer escapement for long-term consistency. It required highly skilled escapement makers for it to work effectively in handmade watches and was difficult to keep in order when components became worn. Its greatest success came when used in very cheap, mass-produced watches made in the United States.

Peter Litherland patented the rack lever in 1792. Although this was similar to that invented by Abbé Hautefeuille in 1722, there is no reason to believe that Litherland had any knowledge of the earlier invention. This robust and reliable escapement gave effective results because it allowed the balance to have a relatively high arc of vibration. The fact that it became popular meant that it was made on a large scale which in turn resulted in an abundance of skilled craftsmen who were available to Edward Massey when he moved to Lancashire in 1820 to manufacture his new designs of lever escapement. These were intended as ordinary watches for domestic use and they gave a greatly improved accuracy of timekeeping over that possible with the verge and cylinder escapements.

The eighteenth-century English contribution to domestic watches was considerable, not only because of the quality of the product, but also for the development of the lever escapement that became so widely used. English makers were to keep their lead in the production of quality watches until the middle of the nineteenth century. Omitted from this article is the development of the chronometer, temperature compensation, and better methods of springing, all of which greatly influenced the domestic watch by the end of the century.

CLOCKS

Domestic clocks underwent enormous and rapid development after the adoption of the pendulum as the timekeeping part of a clock and the invention of the recoil escapement which enabled a small pendulum arc or swing to be used. These seventeenth-century developments resulted in a uniquely English style of clock case in which to house the movement. The weight-driven longcase clock became, for many British households, the most expensive and prestigious piece of furniture owned. Case styles on the more expensive clocks were influenced by the current taste for classical architecture. The design of movements was increasingly refined and this, combined with the use of good metals and excellent craftsmanship, resulted in reliable clocks having very long working lives.

The market for clocks increased greatly during the 1700s as the country's economy was strengthened by the huge increase in general manufacturing capacity that took place. Families needed an increased knowledge of time to improve the organization of their lives. In towns, the workforce was increasingly subject to the rigors of a more widespread factory system and

relied more and more on clocks to ensure punctuality. The application of mechanisms to show the phases of the moon was of great benefit to those planning night journeys at a time when there was no street lighting. In maritime areas many clocks were fitted with tide indicators, and for the amusement of those who could afford it, clocks were fitted with musical trains that could play a different tune every day at set times.

There is a great diversity in the style and quality of surviving eighteenth-century English longcase clocks and this reflects the diverse production of these items. In general, the level of dexterity and range of equipment needed to make a clock was not as great as that required for a watch. The supply of clocks was not on the same basis as the supply of watches. Makers of clocks did not rely on the supply of unfinished movements to anything like the same extent as did "watchmakers." Clockmakers could purchase ready-made components from specialist suppliers in Lancashire who made sets of wheels, pinions, steelwork, and castings. At one extreme a maker might produce the whole clock movement himself and have the case made by a furniture or cabinetmaker. Some makers even had their own brass foundry. At the other extreme, a complete clock might be purchased from a specialist supplier.

This diversity meant that clockmakers could match their products to the pockets of their customers. In wealthy areas, clocks purchased from the trade or those made locally to the highest standards could be sold. In poorer areas, materials, design, and quality reflected the incomes of local customers (see Figures 1 and 2). Two areas where this is vividly illustrated are Liverpool and central Wales. In Liverpool, the very finest mahogany was converted into superb cases while movements were made from the best materials and were frequently of complicated design and function. Such clocks cost upwards of twenty pounds and were purchased by the wealthy Liverpool merchants and ship owners. This can be contrasted with central Wales where cases were made from local timbers by nonspecialist joiners and movements were basic in the extreme. Here, complete clocks could be purchased for as little as three pounds and were bought by tenant farmers and small holders. At their best, eighteenth-century English longcase clocks led the world with a unique combination of well-proportioned, well-made cases with technically superior movements capable of a performance adequate even by today's requirements for domestic use. They were exported to all continents and copied by makers in many countries.

Other forms of clocks became popular, especially in more fashionable society. The spring or bracket clock used the power of a coiled spring to drive the mechanism and was far less obtrusive as a piece of furniture. It had the added advantage that it could be carried from room to room. This need for portability ensured that the verge escapement survived for much longer in spring clocks than it did in the longcase clock as it was the escapement least likely to become deranged when the clock was moved. Many were fitted with repeating work to enable the time to be told at night, on demand, by pulling a cord, thus making it unnecessary for the owner to light a candle. The cases of early spring clocks were made with styling features similar to those found on longcase clocks but quickly became more ornate. Later in the century the recoil escapement became the norm. Clocks so fitted were not intended to be moved regularly and this resulted in a wide range of case styles unencumbered by the need to have a substantial carrying handle on the case top.

English spring clocks used a mainspring in conjunction with a "fusee" to even out the force delivered by the mainspring, and this feature continued throughout the 1700s. The fusee required a special and relatively expensive tool for its manufacture. Because spring clocks were more difficult to make than weight-driven clocks, they were only occasionally made outside the major horological manufacturing centers and were more expensive than longcase clocks. Provincial "makers" usually purchased their spring clocks from these centers as their customers required them. Continental makers were influenced by spring clocks and many copies similar in style were made. Later in the century, however, the innate stylistic conservatism of English makers was not followed by Continental makers. They very quickly stopped using the fusee and relied on a long, thin mainspring that gave a longer going time, of which only a small part was used. Smaller movements were developed that could be used in a wide variety of cases and because of the flexibility of styling that this made possible, Continental-made clocks gradually displaced English-made clocks, even though English clocks were capable of better timekeeping.

Other styles of clock were also made in England during this period. Wall hanging or mounted clocks ranged in size from large "tavern" clocks to small (eight inches in diameter) "dial" clocks intended for domestic quarters. These were sometimes fitted with striking movements, and although some are found with ornate and decorated cases, most are fairly plain.

During the whole of the period under discussion, the method of manufacturing these items remained essentially that of hand craftsmanship. Techniques in use were considerably more primitive than those used by watchmakers. In particular, the method of hand filing the addenda of wheel teeth and the hand filing of the teeth of pinions did not change. These methods were time-consuming but required little capital in the way of specialized engines. It was usual for each clock movement to be marked out separately and the components made to fit the plates and each other. These English production methods, relying to such a large extent on hand manufacture, could only produce items affordable by the more affluent members of society. A clockmaker was capable of making some twenty to twenty-four clocks a year and only a limited demand could therefore be met. This low production meant that at the end of the eighteenth century the English clock industry was wide open to attack by more efficient producers capable of satisfying a mass market of prospective purchasers who were aware of the advantages of possessing domestic timekeepers and had only limited funds for purchasing such an item. The boom of imported American clocks in the nineteenth century was set to succeed.

[R.J.G.]

See also **Clocks: America and Mass Production, 1770–1890; Clocks and Watches: The Leap to Precision; Clocks: The First Mechanical Clocks; Instruments of Time-Measurement to ca. A.D. 1275; Longitude; Precision Timekeeping, 1790–1900; Watch Manufacturing in Nineteenth-Century America.**

FURTHER READINGS

Beeson, C.F.C. *English Church Clocks, 1280–1850*. London: Antiquarian Horological Society, 1971.

Bird, Anthony. *English House Clocks 1600–1850*. New York: Arco Publishing, 1973.

Britten, Frederick J. *Britten's Watch and Clock Maker's Handbook, Dictionary and Guide*. 16th ed., revised and edited by Richard Good. London: Eyre Methuen, 1978. The standard guide.

Bruton, Eric. *The Longcase Clock*. New York: Arco Publishing, 1964.

Jagger, Cedric. *The Artistry of the English Watch*. Rutland: C.E. Tuttle, 1988.

Loomes, Brian. *Complete British Clocks*. Newton Abbot: David and Charles, 1978.

———. *Grandfather Clocks and Their Cases*. Newton Abbot: David and Charles, 1985.

Smith, Alan, ed. *A Catalogue of Tools for Watch and Clock Makers by John Wyke of Liverpool*. Charlottesville: U of Virginia P, 1978.

———. *The Guinness Book of Clocks*. Enfield: Guinness Superlatives, 1984.

Weiss, Leonard. *Watchmaking in England 1760–1820*. London: Robert Hale, 1982.

TIME MANAGEMENT

The resources under the control of the manager are manpower, materials, machines and plant, money, space, and time. These resources are all replaceable if lost—except for *time*. Thus time is a precious resource and must be used effectively and exploited fully. In many respects, the effective use of time applies to everyone in many respects, and not just to managers.

The management of time has two aspects: the management of one's own time, and the management of that of others. Before the time of people can be controlled it must be measured and planned. This is dealt with in the article **Measurement of Work and Applications**.

THE NEED FOR TIME MANAGEMENT

Time management not only has the advantage of saving time which can be used for other purposes, it also contributes to the avoidance of psychological problems.

Everyone needs a stimulus to work well, and this can be provided by stretching people, both physically and psychologically. Obviously, too high a workload creates problems, but so also does too light a load. A person who does not manage time properly will often appear to be overworked, and this can lead to stress. There is no absolute measure of the workload which can cause stress in people. Everyone has a different threshold, but even this varies according to circumstances. Some people are only happy when they are heavily loaded with work, while others succumb under the same burden.

Even if stress does not manifest itself, backlogs of work can build up causing failure to meet deadlines. Because there is insufficient time, work tends to be left half finished, or is ignored altogether. Whatever the outcome, the result is inefficiency, for which overloading is blamed, rather than the real cause—bad planning. People who feel that they are overworked can become irritable, doing irrational things that are out of character, and taking actions that later are regretted.

SOME ASPECTS OF TIME-WASTING

Poor Communication. The cause of much time-wasting as well as of frustration and anger can frequently be ascribed to poor communication. More people should borrow from total quality management the policy of doing things "right the first time." Much time can be lost when orders and requests are misinterpreted, and hence wrongly carried out. The good communicator will (1) check that instructions are clear and free from ambiguity and (2) check with the delegatee that he or she understands what is required before the task is begun.

Another aspect of communication which contributes to time-wasting is "The Meeting." For some people, working life becomes an endless round of meetings; meetings are occasionally even cancelled so that one can attend other meetings.

The first useful thing one can do is to question the necessity of the meeting. Many "Weekly Progress" meetings are merely information-disseminating gatherings, which give out information that could be read from short reports. On the other hand, it may be the most effective and user-friendly way of making important announcements to a body of people. Meetings in which individuals report on progress that is of no use or interest to others in attendance waste everyone's time. Reports like this can be dealt with privately outside the meeting.

Meetings which *are* necessary may still be time-wasters. There are no bad meetings in this category, just bad chairpersons. Members of a meeting are prone to wandering off the subject, quoting anecdotal matter, riding hobbyhorses, or discussing points dear to their hearts rather than those on the agendas. According to Pareto's rule, about 80 percent of the meeting is hogged by about 20 percent of its members. The skilled chairperson will keep the meeting on course and avoid diversions. A dilemma facing the chair is whether to bring the quiet members into the discussions or save time by ignoring them; the dilemma involves a balancing of human relations against effectiveness. Participants themselves can help by ensuring that they avoid the various pitfalls, thereby assisting the chair in keeping within the temporal limitations of the meeting.

A meeting should be a forum for the *meaningful* discussion of important matters, which

DAILY SCHEDULE

6 October

Things to do		Time Schedule	Accomplished
1. Do DPE report	07.00		
	07.15		
	07.30		
	07.45		
	08.00		
2. See Jim Brown	08.15		
	08.30		Dealt with
	08.45	View E-mail	E-mail
	09.00		W-P letter to Kahn
3. Phone Harry	09.15	W-P letter to Kahn	W-P letter to Jackson
	09.30	Buffer time	Made 2 phone calls
	09.45	Interview Wilson	Wilson late - did expenses
	10.00		Interviewed
	10.15	Do expenses for week	Wilson
	10.30	Dictate letters to Jackson /Allen	Dictated letter to Allen
	10.45	Prepare for meeting	Did prep.
	11.00	Attend Planning meeting	Attended meeting
	11.15		
	11.30		
	11.45		
	12.00		
	12.15		
	12.30	LUNCH	Meeting over-ran
	12.45		LUNCH
	13.00		
	13.15		
	13.30	Prepare for interview	Did prep
	13.45	Interview Candidate 1	Interviewed
	14.00		
	14.15	Discuss	
	14.30	Interview Cand. 2	
	14.45		
	15.00	Discuss and make	
	15.15	a decision	
	15.30	Buffer time	Interview over-ran
	15.45	Make any accumulated	Dealt with outstanding
	16.00	phone calls	problems
	16.15	Read and sign mail	Read and signed mail
	16.30	Deal with any outstanding	Made two phone calls
	16.45	problems	Made third call
	17.00		Finished expenses
	17.15		Left for home
	17.30		
	17.45		

Figure 1. Daily Schedule

avoids the provision of a platform for exhibitionists. Again, this is where the skillful chairperson will have carefully thought through the meeting's agenda. The chair should ensure that all necessary topics are included, while such matters as requests for statistics or personal questions to the chairperson which could readily be dealt with by memorandum or telephone are weeded out. This avoids the opportunity for that other time-consumer, "Other Business," to be used for railroading through motions that would have stood little enough chance on the main agenda.

Minutes, if they are absolutely necessary, should be as brief as possible consistent with their need to form a useful and accurate record of the important points raised and decisions made.

Telecommunication. This is another potential time-waster. Fortunately, fax machines are unidirectional and cannot immediately support a discussion. They also have the capability of saving time that would have been lost in waiting for documents to arrive through the mail. On the other hand, the telephone can embody both timesaving and time-wasting, depending on its use. It can save time by substituting for a face-to-face meeting, and waste time through idle or verbose chatter. When making calls, one should first write down the points to be made, make them as succinctly as possible, and end the call. But there are situations in which this might be neither diplomatic nor profitable. The time "wasted" in listening to the anecdotes of clients may be good for business relationships, while curtness may even lose an account. The "caring services" are in a comparable position: the doctor who cuts short the telephone call from a patient might well be censured as uncaring rather than lauded as time-conscious.

Much time is wasted on calling and re-calling a person who intentionally or otherwise is difficult to contact. When the subject *does* return the call, the original caller may not be there to receive it. All in all, the telephone respondent must be assertive, restricting the call to the matter in hand, and breaking off politely at the earliest opportunity: it is not *what* one says, but rather the *way* one says it that matters.

Delegation. Delegation is often cited as a practice that allows a person to save time. The saving for the person is real enough, but the *overall* time taken on the delegated task may in fact be greater, particularly if the delegatee is not equally experienced. Passing the task to another also passes the time necessary to do the work. Because time is saved only when one delegates to an expert or to someone more experienced in the task being delegated, it is essential to be careful about what one is delegating.

A PLAN OF ATTACK

The main problem with most programs of time management is that they demand a firm, persistent commitment to the program in question. The textbooks and courses tell us what to do and enthuse over how we can create more leisure time, but this is more easily said than done. One must have the willpower to put aside the time required to plan the day. Some people are lucky enough to be gifted with a logical mind and will plan naturally, while others will need to discipline themselves consciously. What often happens in practice is that one arrives at work full of good intentions only to be faced with a crisis which must be tackled straight away. Busy people need to get on with their jobs and frequently claim that they do not have time to sit and plan the day, but can they really afford to ignore this process? Sadly but understandably, one can all too quickly lose the habit of preplanning.

The age-old investigatory questioning techniques of work study and organization and methods (O & M) are still as applicable today as they were sixty years ago. Jobs are analyzed into the five functions of: operation (doing things), transport (moving things), inspection (checking things), storage (of things), and delay (causing things to wait for attention). The only one of these functions that contributes anything useful is *operation*; the others (except for the neutral function of "storage") are all time-wasters. Ironically, it is not the time-wasters that are attacked by O & M but rather the function of "operations." One should ask first of all, "Is the job necessary?" And one does so because if the job is not necessary, all the associated inspections, storages, delays, and transports will have also been automatically eliminated. At first, it may be thought that if work is performed it *must* be necessary, but surprisingly a great deal of work is done just because it has always been done, or perhaps because no one ever told people to stop doing it.

These principles are not confined to the province of the O & M practitioner, but can be used by everyone. There is a lesson to be learned from this: "Ask if such procedures as the job, or meeting, or paperwork, or call are really necessary." If they are not, then avoid them.

The first task when implementing time management is to find out about oneself. However difficult it may be, this should take the form of an honest self-analysis of personal strengths and weaknesses. From such an assessment, one can begin to appreciate the aspects of time-wasting to which reference has been made above. For example, on the debit side of the balance sheet one might list such qualities as "puts off disagreeable jobs," "indecisive," or "bad at coming to the point on the phone." Having identified the weaknesses, the task is to overcome them, perhaps by tackling the disagreeable jobs first and getting rid of them.

On a day-to-day level, the effective and efficient use of time demands good planning to ascertain *what* needs to be done, and scheduling to determine *when* these things should be done. This requires a plan in itself, and one such plan is given below.

1. *Work for the Day.*

   This will be (*a*) work about which the subject has prior knowledge, it being either booked in the diary previously, or a regular event such as weekly meetings, routine paperwork, and "walkabouts," or (*b*) ad hoc work such as problems, accidents, or unexpected visitors which occurs at random times.

   The plan will be based on type (*a*) work which can be scheduled, and type (*b*) work which will have to be fitted into the plan as and when it occurs. In order to schedule type (*b*) work, some sort of priority rating is needed.

2. *Prioritizing.*

   Even the best planner occasionally will not have enough time to cope with all the demands that arise. Accepting this, the astute person will assess the importance or value of the tasks ahead, and order them by priority. Sometimes the less important problems do, in practice, go away.

   Human beings often have a habit of wanting something trivial done right away and therefore insist that it is urgent, but urgency is not synonymous with importance. Short jobs such as signing things, be they urgent or trivial, *can* often be dealt with right away in order to delete them from the list of things to do. The temptation to put off disagreeable or worrying tasks and do the easy or enjoyable ones first often leads to procrastination, which results in little or nothing getting done. Thus it is advisable to tackle disagreeable or worrying tasks first (provided, of course, that these

are important or do not take very long), thereby leaving one relieved and with the motivation to proceed with the other tasks.

The plan for the day will already have previous entries for obligations such as meetings and interviews. Around these can be placed periods set aside for correspondence, phone calls to be made, and reading to be done. Like all flexible plans this should be capable of being updated, and the planner must be prepared for last-minute adjustments. An example is given in Figure 1. Any blanks in the schedule will serve as buffers, and no doubt will be filled with unavoidable crises and other unforeseen occurrences.

The next task is to put such priorities against the items in the plan such as (*a*) important, (*b*) urgent, (*c*) less important or urgent, or (*d*) do if and when time permits. The items marked (*a*) can be dealt with at the first opportunity between the appointments, and if they are very important it may even be necessary to change appointments.

Long-term projects can be listed separately, but can also be prioritized. These can either be planned by placing aside a set period each week, or inserted into time saved by the effective planning which has (or should have) been achieved (see Figure 1).

Another useful technique is the "bring-forward system." This can be based on an "elephant file" marked with the days of the month. Each note or document is studied and then allocated to the file. Some will be for immediate attention, but others can be put into the pockets dated some days ahead. Documents for meetings can be filed under the date of the meeting. Each day the relevant pocket is emptied and the contents dealt with, sometimes by relegating unimportant items to a later date in the file.

Effective time management in one's business and personal life is a very important and useful subject to which many aspire but which few entirely achieve. The reader is referred to further literature on the matter.

[D.A.W.]

FURTHER READINGS

Atkinson, P.E. *Achieving Results through Time Management.* London: Pitman, 1988.

Godefroy, Christian H., and John Clark. *The Complete Time Management System.* London: Piatkus, 1990.

Pedler, M., and T. Boydell. *Managing Yourself.* London: Fontana, 1985.

TIME MEASUREMENT AND SCIENCE

Science, in the sense of the study of the natural world, has always had a special interest in time and its measurement. For one thing, time is one way to mark and situate events—for the record and for comparison; for another, time is a key dimension of process and change and makes it possible to answer such questions as, how long? or, how fast?

This scientific interest goes back to the first attempts to study, track, and eventually predict the movements of celestial bodies, originally for purposes of astrology. It is no accident that in the ancient world, astronomer-astrologers were the first to divide the twenty-four-hour day into equal hours (as against the usual fractions of light and dark, varying necessarily with the season and between day and night), by way of facilitating comparisons of temporal data.

This link between astronomy and timekeeping continued through the Middle Ages, so much so that Derek de Solla Price, a student of the history of scientific instruments, argued that it was the effort to reproduce the movements of celestial bodies that led mechanics like Richard of Wallingford and Giovanni de' Dondi, builders of planetaria in the mid-fourteenth century, to invent the mechanical clock to serve as driver-controller of their complicated machines. This thesis has not withstood scrutiny, but there is a softer version by John North that, while conceding that the ordinary, time-telling mechanical clock well predates these complex devices, argues nevertheless that it was probably an astronomer who invented the mechanical clock. This is possible, but we have no way of knowing.

In the centuries that followed, however, it was primarily scientists who took the lead in promoting better timekeeping. Where the master clockmakers competed to produce the most complicated and ingenious mechanisms, combining calendrical and celestial indications with life-imitating automata for the wonder and amusement of wealthy patrons, a handful of technicians worked with scientists to improve the accuracy and precision of time measurement. The motive, as before, was to permit the recording and comparison of astronomical observations, the more so as it was now customary (beginning with Christoph Rothmann, in Cassel, at the end of the sixteenth century) to use time as one of two coordinates to define location on the celestial sphere. (The other coordinate was elevation above the imaginary celestial equator.)

But there were now further reasons for scientific interest: the attempt to determine longitude at sea by the use of an accurate, reliable clock that could keep the time of a place of known longitude and compare it with time at the ship's location; and a growing effort to understand and specify the laws of motion. Clockmakers such as the Swiss, Jost Burgi (1552–1632)—Burgi was also a good mathematician—played an important role in this pursuit of accuracy; but increasingly their hands were guided by savants whom we would call scientists. The most important of these were Galileo Galilei (1564–1642), Florentine astronomer and physicist, discoverer of the (quasi-) isochronism of a swinging pendulum; and Christiaan Huygens (1629–1695), Dutch mathematician and physicist, inventor of the pendulum clock in 1657 (Galileo had designed one but never built it), and the balance spring controller in 1675.

The invention of the anchor ("recoil") escapement (by William Clement in 1671), which made possible a smaller arc of swing and hence a far more accurate pendulum clock, gave scientists for the first time a machine that would keep time to a few seconds per day and respond with comparable sensitivity to changes in the physical environment. It was now possible to accumulate much truer astronomical observations and derive better predictions of the path and timing of celestial bodies; to detect differences in gravity that reflected not only variations in altitude but irregularities in the shape of the earth; and to relate heat to the expansion of metals. In return, science contributed to horological technique, most notably in the mathematics of gearing, which made possible the construction of more precise tools.

The one disappointment of these decades of the pendulum revolution was the inability of these clocks to serve on shipboard for the calculation of the longitude, to the point where even so brilliant and imaginative a scientist as Newton gave up the hope of a horological solution. The best chance, he said, lay with astronomy, which was working toward comparing the time of a given celestial event as seen at a given place and the time of the same event as seen from a place of known longitude: the difference in time could be converted into a distance in space. In fact, the astronomical solution, using lunar angular distances, was achieved at about the same time as a horological one (John Harrison's marine chronometer, completed in 1759, tested successfully in 1761). The scientists preferred the astronomical way, difficult and complicated as it was, and did their best to impose it; it was their kind of thing, and they mistrusted mysterious black boxes; but it was the horological solution that triumphed in practice.

After the adoption of the anchor escapement, the longcase, normally seconds-beating pendulum clock was further improved, by ca. 1730, by the invention of the dead-beat escapement by George Graham and, at about the same time, of devices for compensation of temperature variation. These reduced variance to a tenth of a second per day and yielded a clock that remained the standard for 150–200 years. Advances in the nineteenth and twentieth centuries—electric circuits and breakers, airtight or vacuum containers, free pendulums—further reduced error and yielded clocks (S. Riefler, ca. 1900; W. H. Shortt, 1921) that would keep time to .01 seconds, eventually .002 seconds a day (two parts in 10^8) and confirmed for the first time what some scientists had long suspected, namely, that the rotating earth, the clock of last resort, kept in fact an irregular rate.

As scientific research called for ever greater temporal fineness and accuracy, this irregularity was bound to pose the question whether such a rate could serve as a general time standard. One temporary solution was to define the second as a fraction of a given solar year—the tropical year 1900. But such an unreferrable, unverifiable standard could not meet scientific requirements. A better answer was found by the invention of superior timekeepers using high-frequency controllers: quartz, molecular, and finally atomic clocks. These last made it possible to work to nano- (10^{-9}) and picoseconds (10^{-12}) and led physicists to call for a redefinition of the second in terms of vibrations of the cesium atom rather than as a fraction of some past astronomical interval.

These horological advances gave scientists an extraordinarily powerful tool of both measurement and control. Any regular frequency can serve as a clock, and a good clock will serve to generate and control a regular, countable frequency. The new nanosecond frequencies made possible comparably fine specification of a given phenomenon, and scientists proceeded to convert nontemporal as well as temporal measures into the new standard. Increasingly, moreover, high technology depended on the squeezing of signals into very small intervals—crucial to the operation of computers, missile and satellite guidance, high-density telecommunication, and a wide array of procedures requiring close synchronization.

All of this was on the instrumental level of experiment, research, and performance. But time is also of interest to science on a metaphysical level: What is it? Is it continuous or a series of infinitesimal basic temporal particles? Does it have a direction (time's arrow)? Is it absolute or relative? Does it have a beginning or end? All of these, with the possible exception of the absolute-relative dichotomy, are questions that do not lend themselves to experimental testing and unambiguous answers. Much depends on definition. In the Newtonian universe, time was absolute, always passing in ever-equal units; in an Einsteinian universe, time is relative and is influenced by motion and mass. The behavior of high-precision clocks moving at different speeds is consistent with the Einsteinian paradigm. Can time go backwards? In science fiction, surely. In the real world? That would imply the possibility of multiple presents and would seem intrinsically illogical and physically impossible, if only because two objects cannot occupy the same space at the same time. Was there a time before time? Modern cosmology thinks of time as coeval with the universe, starting with the big bang, to the point where the words "time" and "universe" are used as synonyms—a notion reminiscent of the Bible: "In the beginning. . . ." But if one defines time as a factitious dimension, a linear system of measure like the series of positive and negative integers, then it has neither beginning nor end but rather extends to infinity in both directions.

[D.S.L.]

See also **Clocks and Watches: The Leap to Precision; Clocks: The First Mechanical Clocks; High Frequency Timekeepers; Longitude; Precision Timekeeping, 1790–1900.**

FURTHER READINGS

Decaux, B. *La mesure précise du temps en fonction des exigences nouvelles de la science.* Paris: Masson, 1959.

Defossez, L. *Les savants du XVIIe siècle et la mesure du temps.* Lausanne: Journal suisse d'horlogerie et de bijouterie, 1946.

Jesperson, James, and Jane Fitz-Randolph. *From Sundials to Atomic Clocks: Understanding Time and Frequency.* National Bureau of Standards Monograph No. 155. Washington: Government Printing Office, 1977.

Landes, David S. *Revolution in Time: Clocks and the Making of the Modern World.* Cambridge: Harvard UP, 1983. (French edition, revised and enlarged: *L'heure qu'il est: les horloges, la mesure du temps et la formation du monde moderne.* Paris: Gallimard, 1987.)

Morris, Richard. *Time's Arrows: Scientific Attitudes Toward Time.* New York: Simon & Schuster, 1984.

TIME-ORDER ERRORS

Researchers have found presentation-order effects ever since Gustav Fechner discovered the phenomenon of *Zeitfehler* (time errors) in 1860. Time-order errors are systematic distortions in comparative judgment of stimuli. In judging the duration of two or more events (stimuli) or sequences (series of stimuli) that are equivalent in all respects except for presentation order, a *positive time-order error* occurs if an observer judges the first or earlier duration to be longer than the second or later duration; a *negative time-order error* occurs if the observer judges the second to be longer than the first. Research on comparative duration judgment shows both positive and negative time-order errors. The methodological conditions likely to produce one type of error or the other remain unclear, and theorists do not agree on how to explain time-order errors.

If the duration of each of two brief stimuli is less than a few seconds, and if an observer judges several such stimulus pairs, judgments usually show a positive time-order error for shorter durations and a negative time-order error for longer durations. The duration for which there is no time-order error is commonly called the *indifference point* or *indifference interval*. Early theorists attributed special significance to this value, which tended to be about .5 to .7 seconds. Later research revealed that the indifference point varies widely, even within a single observer, and that the range of stimulus durations affects it.

In experiments using durations less than about ten seconds, negative time-order errors are more common than positive ones. A fading-memory hypothesis, which can explain such negative time-order errors, assumes that the judgment involves comparing the faded memory trace of the first stimulus with the direct perceptual experience of the second stimulus. Other explanations also propose that the effect is perceptual or memorial, but that adaptation processes or differential weighting of sensation magnitude causes time-order errors. Still other explanations attribute time-order errors to other kinds of response biases, decision processes, or general judgmental processes. The available evidence does not unequivocally support any one of these explanations. Several processes may contribute to time-order errors involving brief-duration stimuli, and whether any process is relatively more influential may depend on methodological details.

If the duration of each of two event sequences is many seconds or minutes, observers' judgments usually show a positive time-order error. This kind of judgment requires long-term memory, but presumably observers do not simply base their duration judgments on the relative strength of the memory traces; a fading-memory hypothesis would predict a negative time-order error. Evidence suggests that the remembered duration of a relatively long time period depends on the remembered amount of change in cognitive context during the period. Subjects may judge the first of two sequences to be longer than the second because cognitive context changes more rapidly at the start of a new kind of experience.

Time-order errors in comparative duration judgment represent more than just methodological nuisances or curiosities. They are genuine effects that may ultimately reveal the nature of duration-judgment processes. At present, the various causes of time-order effects are not very well understood.

[R.A.B.]

See also **Cognition; Memory for Time; Psychology of Time; Temporal Judgment (Methods); Time Perception.**

FURTHER READINGS

Allan, Lorraine G. "The Time-Order Error in Judgments of Duration." *Canadian Journal of Psychology* 31 (1977): 24–31.

Block, Richard A. "Contextual Coding in Memory: Studies of Remembered Duration." *Time, Mind, and Behavior.* Eds. John A. Michon and Janet L. Jackson. Heidelberg: Springer, 1985. 169–178.

Hellström, Åke. "The Time-Order Error and Its Relatives: Mirrors of Cognitive Processes in Comparing." *Psychological Bulletin* 97 (1985): 35–61.

TIME PERCEPTION

INTRODUCTION

The term *time perception* is metaphorical, and like space perception it is a relational term. As psychologist James J. Gibson put it in 1975, "Events are perceivable but time is not." Equally metaphorical is the term *time sense*. The physicist, Ernst Mach, writing in 1865, may have been the last person to have seriously searched for a genuine *Zeitsinn*, which he expected to find somewhere in the ear.

Not being able to perceive time directly does not imply that behavior is temporally incoherent. We know quite well how to dance to the music of time, but most of our activities are timed implicitly. That is, much of the temporal organization of our behavior is established indirectly by our ability to control such variables as velocity and force.

Duration is defined and measured in a relative fashion by comparison with other durations (see **Time Measurement and Science**). Humans as well as many animals can "perceive" the duration of an event by comparing it with some internal reference event generated by an internal clock or timer, or by comparing it with a "mental image" or representation of the event itself (see **Psychology: Representations of Time**).

Altogether, what is conventionally called time perception is a fairly complex cognitive activity rather than an immediate sensory process. Despite the fact that humans and animals lack a proper organ for the perception of time, their ability to detect differences in duration of otherwise indistinguishable events justifies the widely used terms *time perception* and *time sense*.

METHODS OF MEASUREMENT

Time perception, thus understood, is conventionally studied within the methodological framework of *psychophysics*. Subjects are presented with one or more stimuli in succession, and are requested to detect the presence or absence of a stimulus, or a difference between stimuli. The nature of temporal stimuli requires some adaptations of standard psychophysical practice. First, since no "pure" temporal stimuli exist they must always be embedded in a more complex stimulus situation: listening to a tone with a certain frequency and loudness, watching for a pot to boil, or attending a performance of Shakespeare's *Hamlet*. The nature of these embedding stimuli may, and frequently does, influence the perception of the temporal aspect; this is known as the *kappa-effect*. Second, if two or more durations are to be compared it is impossible to present them simultaneously in the way two colored stimuli can be shown side by side. The forced sequential presentation of temporal stimuli may, and frequently does, influence the perception of the temporal aspect; specifically, the most recent of two successive time intervals tends to be perceived as longer than the first. This phenomenon, known as the time-order error, is also observed, for instance, when two equally loud tones are presented in succession. In that case the most recent tone will be judged as the louder (see **Time-Order Errors**). Third, the relative character of the way in which we perceive time has proved to be a source of considerable confusion. The statement that subjects are "underestimating" a time interval, for example, must be qualified by indicating whether the target interval is underestimated relative to the internal reference or the other way around, or by specifying whether the target interval is underestimated relative to another external reference interval.

Four psychophysical methods have been favored by chronopsychologists to determine the characteristics of the time sense:

1. *production*: a numerical value (usually in seconds) is given for the duration of an interval and the subject produces an interval of the required length, for instance by pressing a button;

2. *verbal estimation*: a stimulus interval is presented and the subject is required to estimate the duration of this interval by quoting a numerical value (for example, in seconds or arbitrary numbers);

3. *comparison*: two or more stimulus intervals are presented in succession and the subject is required to judge which of these stimuli was longest (or shortest); and

4. *reproduction*: a stimulus interval is presented and the subject is required to reproduce the duration of this interval, for instance by keeping a button pressed down.

These four methods differ in two respects. Production and estimation involve abstract, numerical representations of duration, whereas comparison and reproduction are based on actual time intervals. On the other hand, estimation and comparison elicit verbal judgments, whereas production and reproduction have the subject generate a real time interval of the required duration.

Apparently, the four methods lead to quite different outcomes: the correlations between results obtained with these methods tend to be very low. This does not argue against their use, but it underscores the indirect character of what we call time perception. It also points out the need for a careful task analysis in the context of an explicit theoretical framework before embarking on an experimental study of time perception.

SENSITIVITY

The *time sense* is not a particularly keen organ; judgments of duration usually vary approximately up to 10 percent around the mean. Studies involving professional musicians and dancers have shown, however, that its sensitivity can be improved at least five- or even tenfold by extended practice.

The precision with which individuals can perceive duration is indeed highly dependent on the characteristics of the embedding stimulus conditions. This dependency has been studied extensively for a broad range of stimulus parameters and under a wide variety of conditions (for example, time pressure and solitary confinement), personal variables, and experimental methods. Together, these studies constitute the bulk of the empirical work in time psychology during the past 125 years. Unfortunately, the lack of theoretical concern of many authors has made it nearly impossible to integrate the literally hundreds of papers demonstrating that this or that factor does or does not lead to over- or underestimation of particular time intervals (see **Psychology of Time**). In the past twenty-five years, however, there have been numerous attempts to understand the human "time sense" by means of explicit, quantitative models, such as those provided by various authors in recent volumes edited by R.A. Block in 1990; J. Gibbon and L. Allan in 1984; F. Macar, V. Pouthas, and W.J. Friedman in 1992; and J.A. Michon and J.L. Jackson in 1985.

SIMULTANEITY, SUCCESSION, AND ORDER

Consider two simultaneous stimuli—brief tone pulses for instance, or weak light flashes. That they coincide perceptually does not necessarily mean that they are physically cotemporal. Conversely, events that are physically non-simultaneous may well be perceptually simultaneous. There is a rich literature dealing with the distinction between simultaneity and succession, involving such phenomena as apparent (stroboscopic) movement, streaming (that is, the separation of interleaved tonal sequences into independent melodic lines), forward and backward masking, and the "cutaneous rabbit" (regarding which see, for example, various chapters in the 1986 handbook of K.R. Boff, L. Kaufman, and J.P. Thomas).

Stimuli that are separated by a very brief time interval do not normally give rise to an impression of duration. A brief sound pulse falling on the left ear, followed by an identical pulse on the other ear some 0.1 milliseconds later, will be perceived as a single sound pulse to the left of the median plane of the observer. Stimuli with separations of the order of ten milliseconds are not perceived as two distinct stimulus events either. Instead subjects will usually report some discontinuity in what is otherwise perceived as a single stimulus.

Only if two successive stimuli are at least twenty to twenty-five milliseconds apart can they be discriminated reliably as separate events. This does not mean, however, that their order can be judged correctly as well. Order perception is largely determined by the meaning of the stimuli. R.M. Warren and C.J. Obusek, for instance, have demonstrated that the order of four natural but unrelated speech sounds presented in quick succession can be identified correctly if presented at twenty-five-millisecond intervals. If, on the other hand, the four sounds are arbitrary beeps, plonks, or hisses, their order can be determined correctly only if they follow each other at 150–200 milliseconds, or even more if the subject is inexperienced.

The perception of simultaneity has fundamental significance for the integration of sense impressions. Attempts have been made to identify the properties and underlying mechanisms of the subjective present (see **Psychological Present**). Recently, philosopher Daniel Dennett has proposed a model that is supposed to incorporate a considerable number of seemingly inconsistent findings all related to the conscious experience of being present in a coherent, integrated world. Dennett's *Multiple Draft Model* assumes that this experience rests on the parallel activity of a large number of comparatively simple mechanisms, or modules, each capable of handling only a small part of the information stream. This model stands in strong contrast with the conventional view of consciousness as a central executive function. Rather than collecting all relevant information before integrating it into a stable impression, perception takes place in a partially ordered, more or less data-driven way, gradually solidifying into a final representation. Even so, however, the time constants of the separate modules that contribute to this dynamic evolvement should be within the 100–150 millisecond range.

DURATION

Paul Fraisse has more than once emphasized the transition from perception of succession or rhythm to the perception of duration: only beyond the range of 100–150 milliseconds will subjects be able to discriminate time intervals as being of different duration. Many studies have been carried out over the past century to determine the relation between perceived duration of an interval and its physical (clock) duration. In 1976, H. Eisler reported well over a hundred such studies and the number must have increased since then. Most studies indicate that average adult subjects under average conditions will judge duration veridically; that is, an interval that is twice as long will also be judged twice as long. Moreover, one subjective second—occasionally called a *chron* or a *temp*—is roughly equal to one clock second. In other words, perceived duration (t_p) equals clock duration (t_c), that is, $t_p = t_c$. For average adult subjects this relation holds upwards from about half a second.

Rather than proving that time perception is veridical, however, this simple linear relation may be the result of a long process of learning to use the many temporal cues that the environment provides. As Michon indicated in 1975, the relation breaks down under a number of characteristic conditions, suggesting that the more naive relation (variously called natural, immediate, or impressionistic) may follow a power law: $t_p = \alpha t_c^\beta$. In young children up to about five years of age the exponent ß is of the order of 0.5, which means that perceived duration is proportional (by a factor of a) to the square root of clock time. Later the exponent gradually increases to reach the value ß equal to 1.0, specifying the linear relation, at approximately age fourteen. Many animal species perceive duration along similarly impressionistic lines. As H. Eisler has shown, the exponent ß varies, according to species, between 0.5 and 0.8. Furthermore, Michon has found, in a very detailed experiment, that in normal adults ß equals 0.5 for short intervals between 100 and 400 milliseconds. For intervals longer than this ß equals 1.0, at least for intervals up to approximately twenty to thirty seconds. Beyond that limit, which represents the upper retention boundary of working memory (without rehearsal), the judgment of duration may either be veridical (ß = 1.0) or impressionistic (ß = 0.5). The latter case will arise when the subject does not pay explicit attention to what is happening during the interval, or if the subject is suffering from a brain condition leading to the loss of short-term memory.

THE FLOW OF TIME

By far the most dramatic aspect of what we call perception of time is the variability in the rate at which time seems to pass. The subjective flow of time covers a broad spectrum, ranging from a practical standstill in certain states of trance or depression, to the feeling that "time flies like an arrow" or that one's "whole life flashed past" in the instant between falling off the cliff and landing, two seconds later, in the haystack twenty meters below.

There have been many attempts to understand this phenomenon in terms of explicit, quantitative models. Broadly, these can be classified as timer models, information processing models, and case-based models.

The timer models consist in principle of a pulse generator producing a train of (not necessarily isochronic) pulses which from the onset of the interval to be judged is fed into a counting mechanism which sums the pulses until the offset of the stimulus interval. Several authors in the volumes edited by Gibbon and Allan in 1984, and by Macar, Pouthas, and Friedman in 1992, have dealt with the way in which this counter is then "read off" and the result stored in memory for later comparison, production, verbal estimation, or reproduction. Variability in the flow of time is thought to reflect the rate of the pulse generator. This rate may be affected by physiological factors, such as body temperature (fever) or drugs, or by task-related, cognitive, and environmental factors.

Information processing models describe the various stages of task performance in terms of working memory, attention, task complexity, and so forth. Variations in the rate of temporal flow are attributed to variations in the demands that a particular task is imposing on these information processing mechanisms. A particularly elegant, generic model to account for the variations in perceived temporal flow was proposed by E.A.C. Thomas and W.B. Weaver in 1975. The model makes a distinction between temporal information (t) and nontemporal (substantive and background) information (I). Also, it distinguishes between immediate (f) and remembered (g*) information. The model is summarized by the following equation:

$$t_p = \alpha f(t) + (1 - \alpha)g^*(I,t)$$

The equation essentially states that perceived duration (t_p) is a weighted function of immediately attended temporal information (t) and retrieved information. The latter is itself a mixture of the substantive cum background information (I), and the temporal information contained in the interval. This model can accommodate a variety of phenomena related to the subjective flow of time, including the persistent finding that time which seems long in passing will seem short in retrospect, and vice versa.

Case-based models, finally, would seem to be recent additions to the explanatory repertoire of time psychology inspired by modern cognitive psychology. Michon, Pouthas, and Jackson have argued, however, that this kind of model was already proposed a century ago by Jean-Marie Guyau. In essence, these models assume that subjects, when perceiving events, compare these experiences with representations of similar events they have encountered earlier in their lives. Temporal information about order, date, and duration will usually be stored as part of these representations, or it may, on occasion, be reconstructed from them. Unlike timer models and information processing models, case-based models are amenable to syntactic and semantic analysis. Consequently, they can contribute to the discussions about cognition, complexity, consciousness, representation, and other fundamental topics in mainstream cognitive science.

[J.A.M.]

See also **Cognition; Guyau, Jean-Marie; Memory for Time; Psychological Present; Psychology of Time; Psychology: Representations of Time; Time Measurement and Science; Time-Order Errors.**

FURTHER READINGS

Block, R.A., ed. *Cognitive Models of Psychological Time.* Hillsdale: Erlbaum, 1990.

Boff, K.R., L. Kaufman, and J.P. Thomas, eds. *Handbook of Perception and Human Performance.* New York: Wiley, 1986.

Dennett, D.C. *Consciousness Explained.* Harmondsworth: Penguin, 1992.

Eisler, H. "Experiments on Subjective Duration 1868–1975: A Collection of Power Function Experiments." *Psychological Bulletin* 83 (1976): 1154–1171.

Fraisse, P. "Perception and Estimation of Time." *Annual Review of Psychology* 35 (1984): 1–36.

Gibbon, J., and L. Allan, eds. *Timing and Time Perception.* New York: New York Academy of Sciences, 1984.

Gibson, J.J. "Events Are Perceivable But Time Is Not." *The Study of Time II.* Ed. J.T. Fraser and N. Lawrence. New York: Springer, 1975. 295–301.

Macar, F., V. Pouthas, and W.J. Friedman, eds. *Time, Action and Cognition: Towards Bridging the Gap.* Dordrecht: Kluwer Academic, 1992.

Mach, E. "Untersuchungen ueber den Zeitsinn des Ohres." *Sitzungsberichte der Kaiserlichen Akademie der Wissenschaften (Mathematisch-Naturwissenschaftliche Klasse) Wien* 51–II (1865): 133–150.

Michon, J.A. "Time Experience and the Memory Process." *The Study of Time II.* Ed. J.T. Fraser and N. Lawrence. New York: Springer, 1975. 302–312.

———. "Timing Your Mind and Minding Your Time." *Time and Mind: The Study of Time VI.* Ed. J.T. Fraser. Madison: International Universities P, 1989. 17–39.

Michon, J.A., and J.L. Jackson, eds. *Time, Mind, and Behavior.* Berlin: Springer, 1985.

Michon, J.A., V. Pouthas, and J.L. Jackson, eds. *Guyau and the Idea of Time.* Amsterdam: North-Holland, 1988.

Thomas, E.A.C., and W.B. Weaver. "Cognitive Processing and Time Perception." *Perception and Psychophysics* 17 (1975): 363–367.

Warren, R.M., and C.J. Obusek. "Identification of Temporal Order Within Auditory Sequences." *Perception and Psychophysics* 12 (1972): 86–90.

TIME PERIODS AND THE LAW

Time limits and time periods provide structure to the legal system in ways that often pass unnoticed because they are so common. Courts frequently have "terms," or periods when they are in session, as do legislative and administrative bodies; and courts also have "calendars," or schedules for pending cases. Procedural rules define time periods in which certain pleadings must be filed, or certain actions must be taken—if they are not performed within a certain period, the court or an opposing party may take action. There are statutes of limitations which define time periods in which different kinds of cases must be filed in court. If they are not filed in time the case may be either barred absolutely or defended by asserting the statute of limitations.

Some of these time periods in effect create substantive rights; for example, a statute of limitations can prevent the prosecution of a criminal case. Other time limits merely give direction to parties or the court and can be waived; for example, the court can grant an extension of time in which to file a motion. In law, time limits must be understood in terms of what or whom they limit, and in terms of potential consequences arising from failure to adhere to them. For example, if a rule provides that an answer must be filed in a court within thirty days or the court may, but need not, grant default, the time limit puts the answering party at risk but does not limit the court.

The trial of a criminal case incorporates important time limits at almost every stage of the process. "Speedy trial" provisions require that many criminal cases come to trial within a certain time. This in turn requires that parties adhere to time schedules. For example, a time limit may be provided for discovering evidence needed for trial. Preparation for trial must be coordinated with the court's calendar. In criminal cases involving incarceration, the court's power is defined in terms of time limits beyond which a party may not be put in jail. While these time limits may not always be important in cases in which the court is unlikely to impose a maximum sentence, they are important initially because they define the extent of the defendant's exposure to a penalty upon being charged—it makes a significant difference that someone is charged with a crime carrying a maximum penalty of ten days rather than twenty years.

Time limits are also important in the area of non-criminal law (in the American system this is called "civil" law), although they will usually not be as important in determining the ultimate result (which will normally involve the payment of an amount of money rather than a term in jail). Statutes of limitations limit the time period in which most civil actions can be filed. Rules of procedure also define time periods in which pleadings must be filed and evidence discovered. There are also time limits for appealing cases.

Most of these kinds of time limits are designed to secure orderly court administration. Statutes of limitations (and the related doctrine of *laches*) serve this and other functions. Statutes of limitations are designed to encourage diligent assertion of claims before memories, witnesses, and evidence disappear or deteriorate. They are intended to promote fairer and more accurate cases, and to provide repose to potential defendants after some period of time.

In actual practice there is an interplay among the seriousness of the misconduct sought to be deterred by the bringing of the legal action, the difficulty of proof after time passes, and the length of the statute of limitations. The statute of limitations for written contracts will often be longer than a statute of limitations for oral contracts. Frequently, however, there is no statute of limitations for murder even though evidence has deteriorated. In some situations courts will rule that statutes of limitations do not begin to "run" until the injured party learns, or at least should have learned, of the injury.

Much of this same interplay underlies the doctrine of *laches*, an "equitable" defense (asserted in certain kinds of cases or courts referred to as cases or courts in "equity") that generally means that it is now unfair, because of the passage of time, to permit the plaintiff to have a particular remedy. If a person were, for example, to seek an injunction to prohibit someone from building a structure that interferes with his or her view, but waits until the building has been completed instead of when it could have been stopped with less cost, *laches* might be asserted as a defense.

In this situation it is not a predefined period of time, as in the statute of limitations, which acts as a defense; instead, the defense relies on the relationship between the passing of time and the particular circumstances of the case. At some point, the law recognizes, the mere passing of time changes things. The doctrine of adverse possession also illustrates this principle. If a property owner permits a party to use property adversely to the owner (for example, by permitting part of it to be used as a driveway, or by permitting the adverse party's building to remain on the property) for a substantial period of time (usually twenty-one years), then the adverse party may gain title to the property, or the ongoing right to that particular use of the property.

The rationale for this is, again, that at some point claims which would normally be asserted should be asserted, and if they are not, other people have a right to assume that there is no longer any interest in doing so. As property comes to be used in a certain way over time, expectations are established that the use may continue and will eventually be recognized even though they conflict with the recognized legal title rights. The realities of time, use, and expectation, in other words, may eventually override the abstractions of the law, even in the courts of law.

[M.H.A.]

See also **Statute of Limitations.**

FURTHER READINGS

Buswell, Henry Foster. *The Statute of Limitations and Adverse Possession: With an Appendix Containing the English Acts of Limitation.* Boston: Little, Brown, 1889.

Côté, L. "The Operation in Time of the Statute of Frauds and of the Statute of Limitations." *Revue de Droit, Université de Sherbrooke* 16 (1985): 315–349.

Lindgren, Kevin E. *Time in the Performance of Contracts: Especially for the Sale of Land.* 2nd ed. Sydney, Australia: Butterworths, 1982.

Pineus, Kaj. *Time-Barred Actions.* London: Lloyds of London P, 1984.

Wood, Horace Day. *A Treatise on the Limitations of Actions at Law and in Equity.* 4th ed. Revised by Dewitt C. Moore. 2 vols. Albany: M. Bender, 1916.

TIME PERSPECTIVE AND ITS MEASUREMENT

Time perspective refers to the subjective ordering and evaluation of the past, present, and future. It is both prospective and retrospective, and is based on reference points that are located at different distances in one's temporal space. For example, an individual lives not only in the present, but in a present that makes reference to the past and future. Time perspective also refers to the more or less conscious and continuous elaboration of the views of the past, present, and future which are subject to the individual's needs and value orientation.

Time perspective is also thought to underlie some facets of human behavior. For example, a person's anticipation of the future or recollection of past events may influence present as well as future behavior. Time perspective encompasses the idea that behavior is "time-bound" in that it occurs in reference to some goal or motivation which is anchored in some point in time. K. Lewin defined time perspective in 1951 as "the totality of the individual's view of his psychological future and his psychological past existing at a given time."

Time perspective has been the primary focus of much of the psychological research on time. Although research in this area had its beginning with the early work of N. Israeli in the early 1930s, L.K. Frank and K. Lewin subsequently developed the conceptual framework for the study of time perspective. Frank viewed time perspective as influencing behavior since an individual's perception of the future determines current action. Thus, for Frank, it is the anticipated consequences that regulate behavior, with the avoidance of negative consequences and the acquisition of desirable results serving as the motivating influences.

Lewin conceived of time perspective as a part of the individual's psychological "field." The development of one's psychological field is reflected in the degree to which it is differentiated in terms of time and space. As the person matures, the psychological field contains a broader time perspective which is not limited by the immediate future. Thus, the process of physical and psychological maturity is expected to be accompanied by an increase in the complexity of one's life style, long-range planning, and a view of the future that is long term. As a person matures, expected events may contain differential complexity, remoteness, clearness, and reality along with a differentiated life space.

As a theoretical construct, time perspective has been found to be multidimensional. Following the early work of Frank and Lewin, M. Wallace proposed that time perspective also contains the properties of extension and coherence. Extension is defined as "the length of the future time span which is conceptualized" by the individual—that is, how far into the future a person projects himself.

Coherence, on the other hand, refers to the manner in which anticipated future events are logically ordered and organized. Two other qualities of time perspective, density and directionality, were added later to the model of time perspective by R. Kastenbaum. According to Kastenbaum, density refers to the degree to which the individual's general conception of the future contains specific future-based events. The greater the number of expected events, the more "dense" the time perspective. But while density is concerned with quantity, directionality focuses on the quality of the individual's time perspective. Thus, directionality is defined as the "relative preference for a directional, active conception of time, as contrasted with a preference for a static conception of time." Directionality in this sense is concerned with the "flow" of time and is measured by the use of metaphors.

The last dimension of time perspective is attitude. The attitude dimension of time perspective is concerned with the individual's attitudes toward time and time constructs. Since attitudes influence thoughts and behavior, it has been posited that an individual's attitude toward time exerts an important influence in several areas. For example, being optimistic or pessimistic about time, as studied by J.M. Goldrich; being fatalistic, as studied by L.K. Heimburg; or being anxious, submissive, possessive, and flexible or inflexible relative to temporal matters, as studied by R. Calabresi and J. Cohen, are all dimensions that are affected by a person's individual attitudes toward time and which may influence his or her assessment of events.

Numerous methods for assessing time perspective have been used by researchers. These can be categorized into five basic approaches: (1) the telling of stories; (2) the listing of life events; (3) the assignment of ages to life events; (4) using graphic representations of time perspective; and (5) Likert-type scale ratings—which involve giving graded values to responses—of time perspective. These methods parallel the development of the construct of time perspective and have been aimed at its different conceptual levels. Research in the area of time perspective has continued the development of this concept.

[A.G.]

See also **Psychology of Time.**

FURTHER READINGS

Calabresi, R., and J. Cohen. "Personality and Time Attitude." *Journal of Abnormal Psychology* 73 (1968): 431–439.

Frank, L.K. "Time Perspectives." *Journal of Social Philosophy* 4 (1939): 293–312.

Goldrich, J.M. "A Study in Time Orientation: The Relation between Memory for Past Experience and Orientation to the Future." *Journal of Personality and Social Psychology* 6 (1967): 216–221.

Heimburg, L.K. "The Measurement of Future Time Perspective." *Dissertation Abstracts International* 24 (1963): 1686–1687.

Israeli, N. "Some Aspects of the Social Psychology of Futurism." *Journal of Abnormal and Social Psychology* 27 (1930): 209–213.

———. "Measurement of Attitudes and Reactions to the Future." *Journal of Abnormal and Social Psychology* 28 (1933): 181–193.

Kastenbaum, R. "The Dimensions of Future Perspective: An Experimental Analysis." *Journal of General Psychology* 65 (1961): 203–218.

Lewin, K. "Time Perspective and Morals." *Civilian Morals*. Ed. G. Weston. Boston: Houghton Mifflin, 1942.

———. "Defining the 'Field at a Given Time.'" *Psychological Review* 50 (1943): 292–310.

———. *Field Theory in Social Sciences*. New York: Harper & Row, 1951.

Wallace, M. "Future Time Perspective in Schizophrenia." *Journal of Abnormal and Social Psychology* 52 (1956): 240–245.

TIME SERIES

A *time series* is a collection of measurements taken sequentially through time. Examples arise in most branches of science, as well as in industrial, commercial, and everyday applications. Because the analysis of *time series* involves a knowledge of statistics that many readers will not possess, this article will concentrate on indicating, through examples, the pervasive nature of *time series*, on considering how they can be used, and on discussing their relationship with forecasting.

EXAMPLES

Example 1. Many companies record the total number of sales in successive calendar months (or perhaps in successive weeks or some other period). The sequence of sales values forms a time series. These data enable the company to spot any trends in sales and help to forecast future sales.

Example 2. Many *economic* time series are regularly recorded by government agencies, economic organizations, and others. For example,

the Dow-Jones average is recorded every day in New York and provides a guide (or index) to movements in the stock exchange. Similarly, the *Financial Times* share index is recorded every day in London, England. Numerous other examples arise in most countries such as the number of unemployed recorded every month, exchange rates recorded every day, export totals in successive months, and company profits in successive years. The title "econometrics" is given to the measurement and analysis of economic data, and as the latter often appear as time series, a knowledge of time series analysis is indispensable. Econometrics is vital in increasing our understanding of how to plan and control the economy.

Example 3. Much data are collected regularly in *meteorology*, including the temperature at noon on successive days at a recording station, monthly rainfalls, and weekly hours of sunshine. Many time series also occur in other branches of the physical sciences, such as marine science and geophysics.

Example 4. Much *medical* data are recorded. For example, a continuous trace measuring brain activity, called an EEG, is a time series. Measurements of the heartbeat, called an ECG, also form a time series. Other medical examples include the weight of a particular person measured daily, and the weight of a newborn baby measured at successive checkups.

Example 5. Many time series arise in areas other than commerce or science. Examples include the number of American tourists visiting the United Kingdom in successive years, and the number of deaths from road accidents in a particular state in successive months.

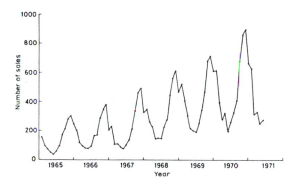

Figure 1. An example of a time plot showing the sales of a particular engineering company in successive months.

LOOKING AT TIME SERIES

The analysis of time series constitutes an important branch of statistics. As in other branches of statistics, the choice of methods for analyzing data ranges from the simple and straightforward to the very complicated. We only introduce some simple ones here. The key aspect of time series data is that the *order* in which the data were collected is crucial and must not be disregarded.

The first step in looking at a time series is to plot it on a graph called a *time plot*. This is simply a plot of the observations against time, of which an example is shown in Figure 1. Time is always put on the horizontal axis.

Plotting a time series is a vital part of a time series analysis as it will generally show up features, such as trend and seasonal variation, described below. Plotting a "good" graph is not as easy as it may seem. The choice of scales, and the way the points are plotted—for example, as separate dots or as a continuous line—may substantially affect the way the graph looks. Therefore, the analyst must exercise care and judgment and perhaps try several different ways of producing the graph. Since computer software can sometimes produce very poor graphs, the need for sound judgment has not been eliminated by the arrival of the computer age. In particular, it is still important to ensure that a plot has a clear, self-explanatory title, and that the scales are clearly labeled. In the time plot illustrated, the horizontal time axis is marked in years, although observations are taken monthly, and the vertical axis shows the total number of sales by the company in each month.

Graphs which are not clearly labeled should be used with caution because some people dishonestly exaggerate or minimize changes through an improper choice of scales.

PROPERTIES OF TIME SERIES

There are several features to look for in a time plot. If the measurements are steadily increasing, or steadily decreasing, then there is a *trend* in the data. For example, prices have shown a steady upward trend for many years albeit with occasional smaller downward movements. Trend may loosely be defined as "long-term change in the average level."

A second feature to look for is the presence of *seasonality*, which arises when measurements are typically higher, or typically lower, at a particular time of the year. For example, temperature measurements are typically higher in summer than winter. Related to the idea of seasonality is the possible presence of other cyclic variation. For example, many animals show a twenty-four-hour cycle in their behavior (the so-called "circadian rhythm"), and this can be measured in various ways, including brain activity.

A third feature to look for is the presence of unusual observations which do not appear to be consistent with the rest of the series. Statisticians call such observations *outliers*. For example, a company may have a strike and hence sell a very low or even zero number of items in the period during or just after the strike, while rainfall figures will show a sudden large increase when a tropical storm passes. An outlier may arise because of an error in taking the measurement or because of a genuine extreme observation, and these two situations call for quite different action. Where possible, an error should be corrected, while genuine extreme observations need to be looked at separately.

Finally, a series may occasionally show what statisticians call a *step change*; this occurs when there is a sudden change in the general level or gradient of values in the time series. For example, the price of oil has demonstrated some sudden changes reacting to special events in the Middle East, such as the Six-Day War in 1967.

Over and above any systematic effects, such as trend, there will usually be some *irregular fluctuations* which may be much more difficult to describe and understand. For example, the time plot in the illustration shows the presence of a fairly steady upward trend (sales are generally much higher in 1971 than in 1965), and there is also a clear seasonal effect (sales are higher in November and December than in June and July). There are, however, also some small irregular fluctuations which are more difficult to explain and which will probably be impossible to predict.

It is worth noting that time series may be classified as *discrete* or *continuous*. Measurements are usually taken at regular intervals, such as every month, to give what is called a *discrete* time series. However, measurements are sometimes recorded continuously by a mechanical recorder as a continuous trace. This provides what is called a *continuous* time series. For example, all the economic series referred to earlier are discrete. However, temperature could be recorded as a discrete or continuous series. If it is measured just once a day or once an hour, then we get a discrete time series, but if temperature is recorded by a machine as a continuous trace, then we get a continuous series. The two types of data are quite different.

OBJECTIVES

When time series data are recorded, there may be a variety of reasons for wanting to look at the data. The simplest objective in analyzing the data is to *describe* the properties of the series. This can sometimes be effected by just plotting the series ("a picture is worth a thousand words"). In addition it can be useful to calculate some simple average from the data. For example, with monthly sales, it may be helpful to calculate the average sales per month over the last year, and perhaps compare it with the average in the previous year. This will help to assess the size of the trend, if one exists. In order to assess seasonality, it may also be helpful to calculate the average sales in each month of the year, perhaps over the last five years. A quantity, like an average, which is calculated from the data, is called a "statistic," and statistics books can be referred to for information about more sophisticated quantities for measuring trend, seasonality, and other sources of variability.

A second objective is to try to *explain* the variation in one series from the variation in a second series. In particular, an economic variable is known as a "leading indicator" if a change in that variable will eventually lead to a change in some other variable. For example, an increase in the interest rate will generally lead to an eventual increase in unemployment.

A third objective is to *forecast* future values of a time series. This is an important task in sales forecasting, in inventory control, in economic planning, and in industrial control problems. The need for sales forecasting in order to plan production and marketing is clear. Likewise, inventory control requires an estimate of likely demand. Finally, much of manufacturing industry is concerned with controlling a manufacturing process, and if one can predict that a process is going to move off target, then appropriate corrective action can be taken. Thus forecasting and control are inextricably linked.

A fourth objective is to *monitor* changes. For example, in medicine, seriously ill patients may be connected to a machine to measure heart or brain activity, and any sudden change in the measured activity would lead to intervention by the medical staff.

METHODS AND DANGERS OF FORECASTING

Forecasting is the term used to describe procedures for foretelling the future. An alternative term is "prediction," and most writers use the terms interchangeably. Unfortunately, some writers do not. One or other term is sometimes used to denote a systematic (usually statistical) method of looking into the future, whereas the other term is sometimes used to mean any kind of looking into the future (including subjective guessing). Since writers do not always agree as to which term is used for what, this article uses the two terms interchangeably. Forecasting is often carried out in a *subjective* way using judgment, intuition, background knowledge, and any other relevant information. Methods range from "bold freehand extrapolation" (the BFE method), to the so-called Delphi technique, which involves a group of people using an iterative procedure to produce a consensus forecast, with controlled feedback of preliminary predictions from other people in the group. In other words the Delphi technique is a pretentious name for trying to induce a group of people to agree on a forecast.

Statisticians generally prefer to produce a more *objective* forecast by fitting a *model* to the data. There are many types of models, including many mathematical models, and they are too complicated to describe here. However, one of the most common models for describing economic data, namely the *random walk* model, should be mentioned briefly. This model holds that the "measurement in a particular time period" is equal to the "measurement in the previous time period" plus "a random error term" which cannot be forecasted in any way. Many economic time series, especially share indices such as the Dow-Jones average, can be approximated by a random walk model. The implication of this is that the best forecast of tomorrow's price turns out to be equal to today's price.

Since a time series is a collection of measurements taken sequentially through past time as seen from the present, it is not surprising that such information should be used in many disciplines as a basis for forecasting the future. But the very act of forecasting is fraught with danger. It is a form of extrapolation which is always a dangerous activity, although there are situations in which it has to be done. When making a prediction, the forecaster often implicitly assumes that the future will be like the past in some sense. This is not always the case and many forecasts have been quite wrong. When unforeseen events occur, forecasts—whether made using subjective judgment or a statistical model—may prove to be seriously incorrect. This possibility should always be borne in mind. Thus forecasting has been described as "driving a car blindfolded with the help of an assistant who is looking out of the rear window." For example, current forecasts suggest that there will be so many cars by the year 2050 that drivers will not be able to move at all. Presumably something will happen to prevent this, perhaps a savage increase in the cost of gas or the development of an alternative form of transport. Introductory statistics books often give only one method of forecasting, namely, they show how to fit a straight line to a set of data and project it into the future. This is rarely a sensible thing to do as the trend is unlikely to be exactly on a straight line and a method is required which adapts to local changes in slope. Perhaps the best advice for the experienced forecaster is to remember the old adage that "Forecasting is the art of saying what will happen and then explaining why it didn't."

[C.C.]

See also **Management Forecasting.**

FURTHER READINGS

Chatfield, C. *The Analysis of Time Series*. 4th ed. London: Chapman & Hall, 1989. Suitable for readers who have studied statistics for at least a year or two.

Kendall, Sir Maurice, and J.K. Ord. *Time Series*. 3rd ed. Sevenoaks: Edward Arnold, 1990. Suitable for readers who have studied statistics for at least a year or two.

Moroney, M. *Facts from Figures*. 3rd ed. Harmondsworth, Middlesex: Penguin Books, 1956. Suitable as an introductory statistics text for the complete novice. It also contains a short chapter on "Time Series and Fortune Telling."

TIME STRUCTURING FOR TEACHERS

Georges Gurvitch has shown that the concept of time has a plurality of meanings. Teaching is a profession where the distinction which is generally made between work time and non-work time would seem to be an oversimplification, given the multiplicity of activities involved. In this sociological and cross-cultural comparison similarities and differences in the time structuring of secondary school teachers are reviewed in two advanced societies, using qualitative analysis. The essay examines effects of the employment context (working conditions, recruitment, promotional, and hierarchical structures) on the time organization of women teachers. Individual factors influencing their time structuring and perceptions of time are considered with reference to social and national characteristics and their position within the profession.

As shown by Linda Hantrais, national differences between Britain and France in daily, weekly, and annual time organization are particularly apparent at the secondary level of schooling. In Britain, schools are open continuously from Monday to Friday and from about 8:45 A.M. to 3:30 or 4:00 P.M., with fifty to sixty minutes or less for lunch. In France, the week is generally divided into two parts, with no classes on Wednesdays and a half-day on Saturdays (afternoon); teaching hours are generally from 8:00 A.M. to noon and 2:00 P.M. to 4:00 or 5:00 P.M. Despite these differences in daily patterns, pupils spend approximately the same number of hours in class per week in the two countries.

The situation is different for teachers. In France, they are expected to be on school premises only when they are teaching, whereas in Britain they have to be at school throughout the working day. In addition to their own teaching hours they are required to cover for absent colleagues, provide "pastoral care" and carry out administrative duties. They spend 1,265 hours a year on professional activities, including about thirty to thirty-five teaching periods a week. In France, teaching hours vary according to status and qualifications from 15 to 18 hours a week and from 450 to 540 hours over the year, excluding time spent on preparation and marking. The length of a teaching period is also different: in England a period lasts for thirty-five minutes, and some lessons are spread over two consecutive periods; in France a period (*cours*) lasts for fifty-five minutes. In addition, British teachers spend more time on work-related activities at school than their French counterparts: in France, marking and preparation are more often done at home and in Britain more often at school, particularly for women teachers with children.

School timetables have an impact on other aspects of time organization. Whereas the strategies used by British women teachers to coordinate their time schedules with those of their family can be compared with the arrangements made by other women working full time, in France, full-time teaching hours more closely resemble part-time working hours. French women teachers can choose and adapt their timetables so that they can look after their children. The teaching profession is therefore more readily compatible with family life for women in France than in Britain.

The status of the profession also differs between the two countries, and this affects attitudes toward time organization. In Britain, teachers are appointed and employed by the schools and paid by local authorities. Since the Education Reform Act of 1988, promotion is based on experience and performance. Recruitment and promotion are competed for on the open market. In France, teachers are civil servants (*fonctionnaires*), employed and paid by the state at the national level. Access to the profession is via competitive examinations (CAPES [*certificat d'aptitude au professorat de l'enseignement secondaire*] or *agrégation*) taken after a degree, and not at the end of a formal training course like the British PGCE (postgraduate certificate of education). Qualified teachers are guaranteed a post and promoted by the state on the basis of qualifications and length of service. Since opportunities for promotion are very limited, teachers do not feel they have to strive continuously to reach a higher level or to improve their performance in the classroom, as do their counterparts in Britain.

The relationship between the time commitment required of them and promotional structures means that British teachers are more concerned with extracurricular responsibilities than their opposite numbers in France. Some French teachers argue that their priority is to cover the syllabus and that they cannot afford to waste time on other activities. The status of teachers in Britain and the way in which the educational system is structured seem to encourage them to spend more time on professional duties. Since the 1988 Education Reform Act, British teachers claim they feel under greater time pressure. This type of pressure is less apparent in France, most probably because of the difference in status (job security and a well-defined promotional path).

The situation within each country is not, however, uniform across the teaching profession. As Caroline Roy has indicated, time budget surveys in Britain and France show how time spent on different activities fluctuates according to the gender variable. In addition to gender roles in society and in the household, marital status and the family situation have an impact on the time structures of individuals. These variables are found to produce differences in time organization in the teaching profession within the two countries concerned. French women teachers seem to be more involved in activities not directly concerned with teaching than men. In both countries, women teachers find they need to prioritize their tasks to a greater extent if they have family responsibilities. Women with young children often complain they cannot work in the evening until after their children's bedtime. Teachers who are single or couples who do not have children devote more time to their leisure, their social

and professional life, and extracurricular activities. The age and number of children, the spouse's occupation, the time of year, and the subject taught are other factors which have an impact on time organization.

These differences show how subjective a topic time is and how perceptions of an occupation can influence attitudes toward time. One feature of the teaching profession which is common to Britain and France, however, is the view that teaching is "a job which is never finished."

[M.F.]

See also **Leisure: Women with Children in France; Time for the Family.**

FURTHER READINGS

Ferrero, Magali. *Le temps de travail et la vie hors travail des enseignantes de collège: étude exploratoire auprès de deux collèges d'Aix-en-Provence.* Mémoire de DEA d'Economie et de Sociologie du Travail. LEST, Université d'Aix-Marseille II, 1990.

Gurvitch, Georges. *La multiplicité des temps sociaux.* Paris: Centre de Documentation Universitaire, 1958.

Hantrais, Linda. *Managing Professional and Family Life: A Study of British and French Women.* Aldershot: Dartmouth, 1990.

Roy, Caroline. "Les emplois du temps dans quelques pays occidentaux." *Données sociales.* Paris: INSEE (1990): 223–225.

TIME TRAVEL: FUTURE

There are two kinds of time travel in the literature of science fiction. The more problematical of these is dealt with in the article **Time Travel: Past.** The less difficult kind of time travel, in which the direction traversed is simply that of time's arrow, is not only easier to comprehend (as it can be imagined as simply a radical *speeding up* of narrative time), but easier to contemplate in what must be called a moral sense. Time travel to the past is a literary device conceived in disillusion and executed with a kind of contempt for the given world. Time travel to the future, too, can represent a form of escape from an intolerable present; but more normally it works as a narrative springboard that allows the protagonist of a tale to *surf* forward (as it were) along time's great wave to a place where his or her (in the nineteenth century almost invariably his) present world has been more completely fulfilled.

It will be convenient to treat as functionally almost identical various literary devices that, during the nineteenth century, accomplished the goal achieved by time travel as a device. The notion of an actual time machine, as immortalized in H.G. Wells's *The Time Machine* (1895), came surprisingly late; for much of the century it was far more normal to impose some form of suspended animation upon the protagonist, and to awaken him decades or centuries later, when the new world can be properly contemplated. The device of suspended animation features in another Wells novel, *When the Sleeper Wakes* (1899; revised as *The Sleeper Awakes* 1910), and the category of science fiction that uses the device has come to be known as the sleeper-awakes tale. It is most frequently found in straightforward utopias, like Edward Bellamy's *Looking Backward* (1888), where novelistic instincts tend to be subordinated to the didactic, and where the simplest form of conveyance futurewards tends, therefore, to be selected. Extremely close in literary function to the sleeper-awakes convention was the use of dreams in which the protagonist only "seems" to awaken after long slumber in a newfound land; novels based on dreams generally closed with the "true" awakening, back in the present. Some novels—usually the more didactic—dispensed with the suspended animation or the dream, and had simple recourse to a waking "vision"; but the failure of this category of tale to provide any suspension of disbelief restricted its use. And other tales simply had recourse to some unexplained catastrophe which casts the protagonist forward in time. But all of these devices—however simply or elaborately they may be described in any one text—are formally very similar: they are all time machines.

As the nineteenth century progressed, and as the blank spaces on the map progressively shrank, authors of utopias found it more and more convenient to utilize one or another of these devices; but the value of time travel (or of the awakening sleeper) extends rather further than mere geographical convenience in a crowded world. For authors like Bellamy or Wells, the movement from the present to the future sets up a dialectic between the two poles, providing an ideal structure for arguments of comparison and contrast to be made within the body of the tale. Time travel to the future, therefore, is like a *verb*. In the neatest possible manner, it argues the complex sentence (or case) of utopia. Time travel to the future—because it depends upon a *confirmation* of the proper movement of time or progress—tends almost always to suggest lessons.

Until recently, the authors who used the device did so generally in the belief that the lessons they were imparting were lessons of hope, though of course Wells—as almost always—is exceptional. *The Time Machine* itself, by casting its protagonist hundreds of thousands of years hence in the first instance (and to the very end of time in the second), overleaps the mid-distance perspective of most utopias, and expresses through its vast compass of time traversed a *fin-de-siècle* pessimism about the prospects of humanity. This pessimism, which embodies a recessional tone typical of the late days of most empires, represents a typical British response to the challenge of Darwinism and to the dubious sidebar philosophy of social Darwinism. The Eloi and the Morlocks of *The Time Machine* are evolutionary outcomes, a lesson for the late nineteenth century that homo sapiens, given a sufficient temporal perspective, must be seen as part of the process of evolution, not its outcome. The imaginative force of that lesson was great in 1895, and remains convincing as literature a century later. Beyond Wells's very considerable skills as a writer of fiction, the reason for this continued impact lies almost certainly in his use of time travel within the tale as the element which, once established beyond all (fictional) doubt, renders all else entirely believable. Time travel, as a device, can be seen as an *earth* which grounds disbelief. Once it is accepted by the protagonist (and the reader) of the tale, anything can be believed, and brought home.

Despite its reputation as a voice proclaiming an optimistic agenda for humanity, generic science fiction in the latter twentieth century has not, however, been much interested in the uses of time travel to the future as an exploratory or didactic device. There are two main reasons for this.

The first of these lies in the nature of generic science fiction, which may almost be defined in practical terms as a literature set in the future, and which can be distinguished from most of its predecessor genres by that simple fact. In generic science fiction, as a consequence, there is relatively little need for the device of time travel to the future; and most science fiction stories that feature time travel to the future do so in a very particular manner, by bringing characters and/or artifacts forward from our own past to our present or (more often) to some point in our own future, which may be profoundly affected by the revelations entailed. (This category of time travel generally carries with it some version of a myth of origin, very often transporting to our time evidence from the deep past that the human race was seeded on this planet from afar, or some such dislocation; and in this sense can be seen as an analogue of the myth of destiny inherent in most tales embodying time travel to the far future.)

The second reason for the absence of imaginative interest in traveling to the future in science fiction lies in the nature of the future as a prospect. In generic science fiction, that prospect can be thought of as being divided into three parts: the near future, the middle future, and the far future.

The middle future, where most science fiction adventure novels and many other categories of science fiction are set, can be imagined as a kind of *tabula rasa* on which tales may be inscribed: far enough forward so that our current history can be thought of as having been "solved," but not so far forward that images of ultimate destiny dominate. Very few stories involve time travel to this middle distance, which is treated in the literature as a given rather than a goal or an example.

Time travel to the near future might, therefore, be thought to be far more common, and indeed in all logic *should* be more common. But generic science fiction, for most of its history, has been an entertainment genre, a genre of consolation (even though these consolations are sometimes grippingly cognitive), and it is increasingly difficult to think of the near future as a locus for consolation. Inhabitants of the late twentieth century do not, as a whole, anticipate much pleasure from the immediately ensuing decades. For readers of fiction, there seems little point to imagine themselves transferred in their minds' eye from the frying pan of the present into the frying pan of the Near Future. It is in any case a psychological truism that all change is painful and it is clear that any novel which embodies a transition from now to a point within its reader's anticipated later life will necessarily evoke images of pain, loss, alienation, and death. A novel like Sheri S. Tepper's *Beauty* (1992)—to name one of a singularly small number of relevant titles—carries its protagonist to the beginning of the next century and into the heart of darkness, into a devastating wasteland where she ages with astonishing rapidity, and which represents in symbol and actuality the end of humanity as a species. To travel to the near future, in generic science fiction, is to travel into death.

Only the far future remains, and once again, a morbidness infuses any tale in which characters jump from the present toward the end of time. That—taken far enough beyond the immediate coils of our mortality—this morbidness can convey a melancholy pleasure may explain the rather larger number of generic science fiction stories which, in one way or another, engage a present consciousness with the pleasures and languors of a dying earth, a term taken from *The Dying Earth* (1950) by Jack Vance, which established the far future as a complexly landscaped twilight zone where technology and magic interfuse, and where—as in the similar *The Book of the New Sun* (1980–83), by Gene Wolfe—geology devotes itself to the analysis of millennia of human remains. The latter volume features a great deal of time travel, backward and forward, but almost exclusively as a device further to illuminate the complex sieve of the present-time of the novel. This interweaving expansion and complexification of the sense of the present is characteristic of the far future novel, and makes any analysis of time travel within the context of the far future punishingly difficult—for the far future, in the minds of those who inhabit it in their imaginations, can almost be defined as a period when time itself has relaxed its stays.

A new kind of device of travel—it is also used in some near future novels—comes into play in most tales of the far future. Instead of obeying the artificial notion of time travel itself, most writers of the far future strongly tend to create protagonists who are themselves simulacra of long-ago beings, generally created through computer reconstructions of time past, and who are topologically difficult to distinguish from "actual" travelers from long ago. As in Robert Silverberg's *Sailing to Byzantium* (1985)—a text which sums up many previous versions of the same strategy—the created or re-created consciousness serves a function analogous to the visitor to any nineteenth-century utopia. Such visitors examine, puzzle over, have explained to them, and finally judge the new territory. There is one profound difference, however. The judgments of the visitors to utopia were almost universally ethical or political in nature, and their very presence in the utopian land or construct was very frequently—in those texts constructed to read as fictions—sufficient to expose the utopia as in fact dystopian. But the experiences of the simulacrum in the dying earth differ in that—so far as they are not simply expressions of the trauma of change—they tend to be essentially aesthetic. Within the generic framework of a destiny defined in terms of universal entropy locally countered by the languid savoir-faire of the dying earthers, the time traveler or simulacrum sees the Far Future as a labyrinth of consolations, a perceptual puzzle to be unlocked, in twilight, for the quiet joy of the thing done.

It may be guessed that, as the twenty-first century dawns upon a troubled world, time travel into the twilight where time itself has maternally softened will seem, more and more, a solace to long for. The end of time on earth is a return to the womb.

[J.C.]

See also **Futuristic Fiction; Science Fiction; Time Travel: Past; Utopias and Dystopias.**

TIME TRAVEL: PAST

As the entry on **Science Fiction** makes clear, it must be emphasized that the term "science fiction" is itself a misnomer, and that the flaws and accomplishments of this form of literature, which is generally known by its students and readers simple as "sf," have been systematically misunderstood. Nor can it be argued that this wide misapprehension of the true nature of the genre is restricted to those readers and critics whose perception of science fiction is crippled by the assumption that it is in essence a pulp-based ghetto literature mainly occupied in the generation of adolescent fantasies on vulgarized issues of science; many readers and critics within the field, too, have shaped their responses to science fiction to accord with the premise—proclaimed by its name when written out in full—that science fiction is a handmaid of the march of progress. In the end, it is best perhaps to use the acronym alone, because sf does not only stand for science fiction. It can also stand for speculative fiction.

Within the remarkably wide remit of science fiction narrative types and strategies, nowhere does the misunderstanding of the genre—as being shaped by the forward thrust of science through the years—do more harm than when one attempts to understand science fiction's uses of the concept of time travel. There are, of course, two radically different categories of travel through time. In the entry on **Time Travel: Future**, the more traditional category is discussed, and it is made clear in that entry that time travel to the future is in essence a literary device to carry protagonists forward into a world—often utopian or dystopian—to which the author wishes to gain imaginative access, and to describe. But time travel to the past is by no means as simple a device, either to describe,

or to understand, or (in the end) to feel comfortable with on ethical grounds.

Time travel to the future has existed as an imaginative device ever since the civilizations of Western Europe began to embrace the concept of change. Time travel to the past, though it had been adumbrated in some essays and sketches, was not created as an imaginative device until nearly the end of the nineteenth century. Mark Twain may not normally be thought of as an author of science fiction—especially by critics who find it difficult to accept the argument that science fiction encompasses far more than the "genre science fiction" which dominated the American magazine scene for much of the twentieth century—but a great deal of his short work is clearly science fiction, and in *A Connecticut Yankee in King Arthur's Court* (1889), he wrote the first full-fledged work of fiction to feature time travel to the past. The device by which the Connecticut Yankee travels backwards to the sixth century—it is nothing more than the blow on the head which more usually causes a protagonist to slip into suspended animation, and to travel forward in time as a result—is of course rudimentary; but it must be emphasized that time travel is a literary device, and that when even the most rigorously numerate science fiction writers of today make use of the device, they are writing fantasy. They know that; and most of their readers know that as well.

They also know that the primary purpose of that device in the twentieth century—just as Twain's was in the nineteenth—has been to haunt the reader with a kind of profound transgression of normal reality. It cannot be overemphasized that time travel to the future is nothing more than a form of rapid transit, while time travel to the past is a violation of time's arrow, and an assault upon the sense many readers have that it is peculiarly blasphemous to attempt to reenter (and thus to change) that which ineluctably is. There is a strong argument to suggest that—in ethical discourse and in fiction alike—to alter that which is subverts the grounds of moral choice, and creates a world of the imagination in which anything goes, but where nothing ultimately counts. Time travel to the past violates, in the mind's eye, the sense that we, as human beings, have legitimately staked our all on time's irreversibility. And if we are creatures of time, and if our brief *floruit* is tied ineluctably to what we earn in time, then that violation must be profound.

When Twain's Yankee travels back to King Arthur's court, and becomes the Boss, we enter a world of transgression and denial. Twain clearly had some inkling of this, and it seems fairly certain that he used the device as one of his many tricks of concealment, ways of disguising from his wife, his readers, his society, and (at times) himself the iconoclasm, despair of God and man, and bitter disillusion that increasingly governed his thoughts (and necessitated the circumlocutions of so much of his later work); it is also perfectly clear that Twain had only a marginal sense of the nature of the imaginative frontier he had opened out. The Boss's rewriting of Arthurian history has, for instance, little or no consequence in the current world; the godhood of the Boss is a local affair, without temporal outcome. The undoing of history, in *Connecticut Yankee*, as the Boss brings Yankee ingenuity to bear on the Dark Ages, is merely hinted at; there is no malefic unraveling of the constitution of the world in Twain's bitter but uncontaminating tale. The forward movement of time converges over the Boss's works, in a vast melancholy wave.

It is a sign of the psychic danger of time travel to the past that most science fiction writers in the century since Twain have concentrated on two kinds of story (if time paradox tales, in which protagonists marry their own grandmothers, and so forth, are left to one side as the gimmicks that they are). The first kind of story is the tale—it usually constitutes part of a series—in which some form of "time patrol" attempts to maintain a *cordon sanitaire* around the lesions of transformation. Science fiction novels structured around attempts to maintain reality include Sam Merwin's *House of Many Worlds* (1951) and *Three Faces of Time* (1955); Isaac Asimov's *The End of Eternity* (1955); H. Beam Piper's Paratime series, from "Time Crime" (1955); Poul Anderson's extremely influential "Time Patrol" from the series comprising *Guardians of Time* (collection 1960) and *Time Patrolman* (collection of linked novellas 1983), *The Year of the Ransom* (1988), *The Shield of Time* (collection of linked stories 1990) and *The Time Patrol* (omnibus 1991); John Brunner's *Times without Number* (1962); Avram Davidson's *Masters of the Maze* (1965); Gregory Benford's *Timescape* (1980), Jack L. Chalker's *Downtiming the Night Side* (1985); Frederik Pohl's *The Coming of the Quantum Cats* (1986); and John Crowley's *Great Work of Time* (1991). The list could be extended to hundreds of titles. All share—centrally or *en passant*—a melancholia about human life and history; and most treat the manipulation of already-lived lives as a moral and physical hemorrhage.

The second kind of story, seemingly different, can be seen on analysis to convey a very similar sense of defeat. This second variety is the pastoral, and consists of stories whose protagonists return to an earlier time, not to change that time so as to "perfect" the present, but as to a golden age. Much of the fiction of science fiction writers like Ray Bradbury, Jack Finney, and Theodore Sturgeon either makes explicit use of time travel to express an almost intolerable nostalgia for a simpler period, or expresses that nostalgia in tales whose melancholia derives from the inaccessibility of the past. Either way, the protagonists of these stories—and arguably their authors—have a death-bound air to them. The return to the past is a return to a world which never existed (Bradbury's and Finney's visions of nineteenth-century America, in particular, are suffocatingly simplistic and rose-colored), to a womb which has closed; and the failure to return to the past constitutes a failure to live in the real world. The only author of science fiction pastorals of time travel to maintain a seemly balance may well be Clifford D. Simak, a Wisconsin author whose pastoralism—it is grounded in a specific area in southwestern Wisconsin—is constrained, consistent, and unflaggingly honest. From *Time and Again* (1951) to the stories assembled in his eighties as *The Marathon Photograph* (collection 1986), he made it clear that the modern urban world made intolerable charges on its human victims, and that (in stories at least) he would argue for pockets of rural sanity. Viewed strictly, his escapism was as deleterious as Bradbury's; but in the end much could be forgiven an author whose longings were so translucent and so chaste.

Simak tended not to change the past but to welcome its message of solace, and was in that sense chaste. But time travel to the past, for the century of its life as an imaginative device, has seemed anything but that. For much of this century, the device has been used to express terror, anger, vengefulness, and (perhaps most pervadingly) the sense that in a technological society, reality has an arranged-for air. Time travel to the past is perhaps the central twentieth-century device to express our sense that the texture of reality is thinning.

[J.C.]

See also **Futuristic Fiction; Science Fiction; Time Travel: Future; Utopias and Dystopias.**

USE OF TIME

One of the characteristic features of modern affluent societies is an obsession with the use of time. Time is regarded as an individual's most valuable resource, one which may be spent, sold, bought, saved, wasted, or even killed.

Economists have typically modeled an individual's decision about the use of time as an allocation between market work and leisure, both measured in time units, where leisure comprises all uses of time other than market work. An individual's decision as to how many hours he or she would wish to work per week will depend on the hourly wage rate. The individual's supply curve for labor services shows for each wage rate the corresponding number of hours the individual would wish to work per week. This supply curve may well be "backward-bending," that is, starting at some relatively low wage rate, increases in the wage rate may initially result in the individual wishing to work longer hours per week but, beyond a certain point, further increases in the wage rate may induce the individual to wish to work shorter hours per week. The explanation for this is that an increase in the wage rate involves two effects, referred to by economists as an "income effect" and a "substitution effect." On the one hand, an increase in the wage rate means that the individual is now more affluent. Since an individual normally wishes to have more leisure as he or she becomes more affluent, the "income effect" of an increase in the wage rate induces the individual to wish to work *shorter* hours per week. On the other hand, an increase in the wage rate means that the "price" of leisure has now risen, that is, taking an extra hour's leisure means giving up more in earnings. This induces the individual to wish to work *longer* hours—that is, to "substitute" labor services for leisure—since leisure is now more expensive relative to the commodities on which the consumer spends his or her earnings. Thus the overall effect of an increase in the wage rate depends on the relative strengths of these two opposing forces. This may well result in a backward-bending supply curve: at low wage rates, the substitution effect outweighs the income effect so that an increase in the wage rate results in an increase in the individual's supply of labor services, but at higher wage rates, the income effect predominates so that a rise in the wage rate leads to a reduction in the individual's supply of labor services.

Following the industrial revolution, the specialization and segmentation of roles and activ-

ities associated with the division of labor and the rise of the factory system produced a need for temporal coordination. In particular, many occupations involve standard working times—in recent decades, the proverbial "nine-to-five"—so that many workers, in fact, have limited control over the lengths of their working days. However, empirical studies do suggest that, at least in the United States, the supply curve of labor to the market by males is backward-bending. This has been invoked as a major explanation of the significant secular decline in the average working week as a result of economic development: in the United States, the average hours worked by males fell from around sixty hours per week in 1900 to about forty hours per week in 1945. In contrast, empirical studies suggest that the wage rates of American females are still sufficiently low that they respond to increases in wage rates by working longer hours.

Even forty hours a week devoted to market work leaves a considerable amount of time to be allocated among other uses: to categorize as "leisure" all these other uses of time is not simply crude but also very misleading. Females, in particular, frequently devote a considerable amount of time to household work. In 1965, Gary Becker produced the seminal theoretical contribution on the allocation of time. Seeking to develop a general theory of time allocation, Becker insists that the household be regarded as a production unit as well as a consumption unit. A household's utility, or satisfaction, is assumed to depend on its consumption of certain "more basic commodities" which are, in turn, "produced" by the household using inputs of time and of market goods. For example, the production of breakfast would involve inputs of time for preparation and inputs of market goods, such as groceries, electricity, and the use of a microwave oven. The "full cost" of a unit of a basic commodity comprises the cost of the time used in its production as well as the cost of the market goods. The household's optimal allocation of time and its demands for market goods will depend on its tastes, the prices of market goods, earnings opportunities, and the technology relating the outputs of the basic commodities to the inputs of time and of market goods.

A fundamental insight from this approach, substantiated by subsequent empirical studies, is that a rise in earnings may well induce a substitution of market goods for time in household production activities. For example, a mother may respond to enhanced earnings opportunities by entering the labor force and by using nurseries for child-care, purchasing precooked foods, and so forth. Changes in household technology, such as the development of microwave ovens, can in turn lead to a greater responsiveness of female labor supplies to wage rates. More speculatively, Becker suggests that the tendency in affluent societies for individuals to be seemingly profligate with material goods yet obsessively economical with time—despite the significant increase in "free" time—may not be paradoxical but simply attributable to an increase in the productivity of time in market work *relative* to the productivity of time in household activities.

The household production approach has proved to be very powerful in analyzing the impact of economic incentives on the use of time. A recent study even indicates that the lengths of time individuals choose to sleep are inversely related to wage rates. The original Becker model has since been modified to accommodate, for example, the possibility that an individual may derive intrinsic satisfaction from the time devoted to particular activities, such as childcare. A significant theoretical development of the household production approach is Gordon Winston's 1982 "time-specific" analysis. He argues that Becker's model is concerned not with the allocation of the household's time but with the allocation of its endowment of labor; the fact that labor services are measurable in time units does not make them into time. The key feature of Winston's own time-specific analysis is that it encompasses not simply the duration of activities but also the *timing* of activities, that is, precisely *when* activities are to be performed during the day.

[M.C.]

FURTHER READINGS

Becker, Gary S. "A Theory of the Allocation of Time." *Economic Journal* 75 (September 1965): 493–517.

Biddle, Jeff E., and Daniel S. Hamermesh. "Sleep and the Allocation of Time." *Journal of Political Economy* 98 (October 1990): 922–943.

Bryant, W. Keith. *The Economic Organization of the Household.* Cambridge: Cambridge UP, 1990. Chapter 5.

Juster, F. Thomas, and Frank P. Stafford. "The Allocation of Time: Empirical Findings, Behavioral Models, and Problems of Measurement." *Journal of Economic Literature* 29 (June 1991): 471–522.

Winston, Gordon C. *The Timing of Economic Activities.* Cambridge: Cambridge UP, 1982. Chapters 8 and 9.

UTOPIAS AND DYSTOPIAS

The term *utopia* meaning nowhere (< Greek *ou*, not; *top[os]*, a place) was first used for the title of Thomas More's *Utopia* in 1516. It has come to refer to a work in which the author describes an ideal society removed by place or time from the society of the reader. Though an irony is clearly inherent in the meaning of the title (and probably was so in More's work itself), the term *dystopia* (< Greek *dys*, ill or bad) is now used for novels intended to have the reverse effect on the reader. Samuel Butler's *Erewhon* (1872) already conveys this reversal of meaning through his title.

Since they are almost entirely concerned with the ways in which human society should or should not be organized it is hardly surprising that utopias and dystopias, particularly during the past 300 years, should have been increasingly concerned with clocks and time. In the earlier period utopias placed less emphasis on time other than the present for another somewhat different reason related to clocks. Until the advent of the marine chronometer in the hands of such seamen as Cook, Bligh, and Vancouver (the discovery of Tahiti produced its own brand of sensual and exotic utopias) there were great tracts of land and sea unknown to European human beings and certainly uncharted by them. Indeed, as late as 1700, more than half of the world had not been charted by European navigators. Thus Plato's *Republic* and its many imitators—including such Renaissance reincarnations as More's *Utopia* (1516), Campanella's *City of the Sun* (first written in 1602), Andreae's *Christianopolis* (1619), and Bacon's *New Atlantis* (1626)—though they could not yet employ the clock as their paramount image of the careful regulation for the urban machine, did have the advantage of being able to situate quite enormous islands in hitherto unexplored territories.

In Plato's *Timaeus,* the large, beautiful, and prosperous island of Atlantis placed outside the entrance to the Mediterranean is eventually swallowed up by the sea because of the lack of piety among its inhabitants. Two thousand years later, Bacon could still situate his *New Atlantis,* an island no less than "five thousand six hundred miles in circuit," quite realistically somewhere between Peru, China, and Japan. Even as late as 1726, Swift can do better still by placing his Brobdingnag (some three to five thousand miles wide and six thousand miles long) in the general area of the west coast of North America, precisely where this article is now being typed. Within less than half a century, Cook and the marine chronometer had begun to ensure that such creative geography would no longer be acceptable or realistic. As late as 1872, Butler could still place a much smaller Erewhon in the unexplored uplands of the South Island of New Zealand, but there are now few if any sites in the world where utopias or dystopias can be located. The Shangri-La in the Tibetan mountains of James Hilton's *Lost Horizon* (1933) provides a very late exception, but even his *Valley of the Blue Moon* would not escape early discovery and mapping in today's world of spy satellites.

After the great voyages of discovery and mapping, writers of utopias and dystopias were increasingly obliged to situate their imaginary sites beyond this world—Marjorie Hope Nicolson's collection of eighteenth-century *Voyages to the Moon* (1948) suggests the alternative—or to go outside the present period. The heightened sense of chronology, which can itself be related to the invention of the pendulum clock in the third quarter of the seventeenth century, made it more difficult to change the past with any credibility. As a result, beginning with Louis-Sébastien Mercier's *L'An 2440* (1768–71), utopias and dystopias alike began to be transported more and more into the future. Sometimes the time machine as in H.G. Wells, or the awakened dreamer as in Mercier, does not even have to move to another city. Christopher Collins has noted that Wells's utopias were "usually set in remote time or space, were generally preceded either by disastrous world wars (in one case, an atomic war) or by a period of decay, an Age of Confusion." In our own century, Wells's terrifying *The Time Machine* (1895), *The Sleeper Wakes* (1899), and even the more optimistic *Modern Utopia* (1905) controlled by a puritanical elite have been followed by Yevgeny Zamyatin's *We*

(written in 1920) and Aldous Huxley's *Brave New World* (1932). These later works employ a comparable projection into the future, and like their predecessors, do so in order to reflect upon the present human condition. Much the same might be said of the projection into the future of shorter works like E.M. Forster's *The Machine Stops* (1929), or Ray Bradbury's *Farenheit 451* (1953). Only George Orwell among the modern dystopian writers who have made a powerful impression on the reading public has had the courage to project his work for so short a period as that between 1948 and 1984. Samuel Macey has suggested that he may yet have to pay the inevitable price.

The possibility that the clock would eventually take over the role of epitomizing urban society has been implicit in the genre from the beginning. In his *Republic,* where he applies Spartan values to urban organization—Lewis Mumford has demonstrated that the idea of utopia derives from the early city-state—Plato cannot yet use the mechanical clock as an image to demonstrate a mechanized form of society. Instead, he employs throughout the work the first stage of the division of labor—the division of work into particular trades—as an analogy to illustrate the advantage of people being trained for a specialized role in society. In his view leaders or soldiers, just as people like blacksmiths, would benefit from being trained to a particular role.

It took more than 2,000 years for the next major step in production methods—the subdivision of labor—to be instituted as it was during the latter part of his life by Thomas Tompion (ca. 1639–1713). Tompion, the father of English clockmaking, worked in the vanguard of the efflorescence that grew out of the seminal inventions of the pendulum and balance-spring escapements for clocks and watches. These led in their turn to the marine chronometer and the British industrial revolution which placed England in the vanguard of all other nations. By the time that Swift wrote his dystopia, *Gulliver's Travels* (1726), the Lilliputians, who lack advanced technology, can say of the bourgeois Gulliver that his great silver watch is "the God that he worships," whereas the Brobdingnagians, who are themselves expert in clockwork, think that Gulliver is himself "a piece of Clockwork." At first most people were proud of the technological progress that clockwork epitomized, but by about 1760 when Laurence Sterne's *Tristram Shandy* satirized the clockworklike nature of Walter Shandy, a division was beginning to take place. The bourgeoisie continued to be proud of their clockwork regularity, but artists leading up to the Romantic movement and indeed to our own time successfully began to equate automaton-like clockwork qualities in both individuals and the state with a new form of diabolism.

If we compare Etienne Cabet's utopia, *Voyage en Icarie* (1840), with Edgar Allan Poe's dystopian tale, "Devil in the Belfry," of the same period, the contrast of authorial attitudes is clear. Cabet praises the clockwork-like labor habits frequently lauded by writers of utopian literature. His persona, Lord William Carisdall, approves of the state in which the people "form a single and vast machine of which each wheel regularly performs its function" and in which the inhabitants follow a routine closely regulated by the clock. Cabet's Icarie is circular and symmetrical; Poe's Vondervotteimittiss takes the image even further in a town in which clocks and cabbage control the lives of the bourgeois inhabitants and in which the town itself clearly emulates the face of a clock: "Round the skirts of the valley . . . extends a continuous row of sixty little houses. These . . . look . . . to the centre of the plain, which is just sixty yards from the front door of each dwelling." Needless to say, their clock-dominated activities are heavily ridiculed by the dystopian author.

Helped by the rise of the anti-mechanical mode in literature throughout the nineteenth century, dystopias have continued strongly into the modern period. Ian Tod and Michael Wheeler argue that our own period "has been a century of anti-utopia," with the main utopian thrust sidetracked into great projects like the New Deal, the Soviet five-year plans, the long-term strategies of large international corporations, and the dreams of world government epitomized by the United Nations. An examination of the monumental *Utopian Thought in the Western World* by Frank E. Manuel and Fritzie P. Manuel quickly makes evident how dramatically the output of utopian literature has fallen off in our own century.

If we read as representative dystopias of our own century Zamyatin's *We*, Huxley's *Brave New World*, and Orwell's *1984*, we cannot but recognize that they are permeated with the anti-mechanical and anti-clockwork-like mode that we have been discussing. Zamyatin wrote *We* at the time when he was translating the works of H.G. Wells into Russian. As a naval architect and mathematician, he was understandably the dys-

topian writer most aware of the influence and tyranny of the clock. Moreover, in 1920, this anti-clockwork attitude combined readily with a conscious antagonism toward the extensive time studies of Frederick Winslow Taylor that were transforming American production methods. As the most important single target of his attack, Taylor and "the Taylor system" are named directly some seven times in Zamyatin's novel. The image of the clock dominates throughout the work, as it does when "At the end of the avenue . . . the Accumulator Tower hummed sternly. . . . The huge clock atop the Tower was a face; leaning from the clouds, spitting down seconds, it waited indifferently."

Though the oppressive temporal controls on society are equally in evidence in his *Brave New World* Huxley could benefit from the fact that Henry Ford—the leading exponent of the Taylor system—had by then produced his assembly line, an even more potent symbol of clock-dominated organization. Appropriately, Huxley's new world order dates itself from 632 A.F. (After Ford), and its "religion" involves making the sign of the *T*.

Orwell's *1984* (first published in 1949) differs from most other dystopias because of its limited projection into the future. Since the novel is projected only some thirty-five or thirty-six years after the time it was written, Winston in his fortieth and last year frequently deals with memory rather than history. Yet, living in the clock-dominated world of Big Brother he knows that history, memory, chronology, and even dreams can be manipulated. The Party's slogan—which appears in both the first and the last part of the novel—maintains that "Who controls the past . . . controls the future: who controls the present controls the past." But the elimination of the past and the future means that "Nothing exists except an endless present."

And yet there must be some slight possibility that Winston, like the inhabitants of Dante's *Inferno*, can pass on his story. Seemingly, the writer of dystopias needs to feel that however hopeless the domination of technology in the present a slim hope for the future, precarious though it may be, must be tolerated if only in a place beyond the pale. Such are the green land outside the Green Wall in Zamyatin's *We*, the island in Huxley's *Brave New World*, the Homeless of Forster's *The Machine Stops*, and the book people in Bradbury's *Farenheit 451*. But like the satirist, the dystopian writer can only touch briefly on the positive alternatives. To do otherwise would be to blunt the message regarding the present and translate the stark dystopian nightmare into a mere utopian dream.

[S.L.M.]

See also **Chronology; Clock Metaphor; Clocks and Watches: The Leap to Precision; Futuristic Fiction; Huxley, Aldous; Industrial Engineering [After Taylor]; Longitude; Orwell, George; Science Fiction; Taylor, Frederick Winslow; Time Travel: Future; Wells, H.G.**

FURTHER READINGS

Cabet, Etienne. *Voyage en Icarie*. 1840; reprint, Paris: Editions Anthropos, 1970.

Collins, Christopher. *Evgenij Zamjatin: An Interpretive Study*. The Hague: Mouton, 1973.

Macey, Samuel L. "The Role of Clocks and Time in Dystopias: Zamyatin's *We* and Huxley's *Brave New World*." *Explorations: Essays in Comparative Literature*. Ed. Makoto Ueda. Lanham: University P of America, 1986. 24–43.

———. "George Orwell's *Nineteen Eighty-Four*: The Future that Becomes the Past." *George Orwell: A Reassessment*. Ed. Peter Buitenhuis and Ira B. Nadel. London: Macmillan, 1988. 23–31.

Manuel, Frank E., and Fritzie P. Manuel. *Utopian Thought in the Western World*. Cambridge: Belknap P of Harvard UP, 1979.

Mumford, Lewis. "Utopia, the City and the Machine." *Utopias and Utopian Thought*. Ed. Frank E. Manuel. Boston: Houghton Mifflin, 1966. 3–24.

Tod, Ian, and Michael Wheeler. "Utopia or Oblivion?" *Utopia*. London: Orbis, 1978. 149–155.

Zamyatin, Yevgeny. *We*. Trans. Mirra Ginsburg. New York: Viking, 1972.

VICTORIAN CRITICISM

A major characteristic of English literary criticism from the 1830s through the end of the nineteenth century is a self-awareness of living in a time of great change. In "The Spirit of the Age" (1831), John Stuart Mill observed that "The first of the leading peculiarities of the present age is, that it is an age of transition. Mankind have outgrown old institutions and old doctrines, and have not yet acquired new ones." The anxiety provoked by this self-awareness led critics to a series of questions about the function of literature that serves to give perspective to the major intellectual currents of the Victorian age. Critics asked whether, in an age of great advances, literature could compete with science as a basis of knowledge. Might literature supply a source of spiritual and moral authority made necessary by the erosion of traditional religious belief? Finally, is literature to be utilitarian—must it serve a practical end—or might it be enjoyed for its own sake, as the "aesthetes" during the latter part of the century were to imply?

In "Southey's Colloquies on Society" (1830), Thomas Babington Macaulay champions the positive points of progress, seeing the approximation of a perfect society as time advances. Whatever obstacles have been the by-product of progress, Macaulay implies, have been more than outweighed by the positive breakthroughs in science and the management of society. "History," according to Macaulay, "is full of the signs of this natural progress of society." Not seeing the potential of literature, viewing it as entertainment and a source of knowledge, Macaulay questioned whether progress in science might one day render poetry impotent and eventually obsolete. Many critics reacted against this complacent confidence about the progress of their own time by attacking the "philistinism" of their audience, pointing out the dangers of worshipping materialistic progress. In "Signs of the Times" (1829), Thomas Carlyle lamented that "Only the material, the immediately practical, not the divine and spiritual, is important to us." This debate, about the function of literature, was articulated throughout the century by three of the major critics of the time: Thomas Carlyle, Matthew Arnold, and Walter Pater.

Many of Thomas Carlyle's works are the record of a struggle to declare the importance of literature in a materialistic society. In 1831, Carlyle foretold the burden that many thought

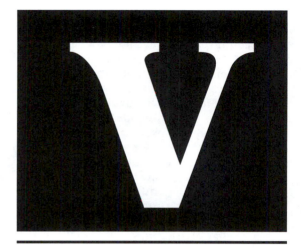

literature had to bear when he proclaimed, "Literature is but a branch of Religion, and always participates in its character: However, in our time, it is the only branch that still shows any greenness; and, as some think, must one day become the main stem" ("Characteristics"). Searching for constancy amid flux, in *Heroes and Hero-Worship* (1840), Carlyle distinguishes the universal from the particular, identifying the genius of the individual as a guiding force in history. The genius may be called a prophet or a poet or by other names, depending on the age he lives in, but he may exist in any time. In *Past and Present* (1843), Carlyle ponders the state of affairs of his own era—a time of high unemployment and of economic turmoil—and turns to the past for a paradigm. He finds one in the faith and work ethic of a twelfth-century monk who directs his energies to organizing his monastery. In the dialectic which emerges from this "dialogue" between present and past, time is redeemed in order to serve as guide for the future.

Matthew Arnold's critical concerns, in his major essays, emphasize the importance of the humanities, and enumerate those classical texts of value to his own time. For Arnold, "seeing" things correctly meant being distant from the immediate preoccupations of one's own time. In "The Function of Criticism at the Present Time" (1864), Arnold urges the critic to be "disinterested." This is to be achieved "By keeping aloof from what is called 'the practical view of things.'" Arnold's classicism, in effect, seeks to remove the critic from his own time. In viewing literature from a broad perspective, the critic is better able to judge its merits. In "The Study of Poetry" (1880), Arnold uses the touchstone method whereby lines of "great" poetical works are juxtaposed against each other in order to discern the relative value of the works from which they have been taken. Arnold's aim is to arrive at a "real" estimate of a work of literature, based on its literary merits. His aesthetic value is grounded on a work's "timelessness." A great work of art is not only of its time. Distinguishing the "real" estimate from two misguided estimates—the "historical" and the "personal"—Arnold points to problems that may arise when a critic is not distanced from his own time and preoccupations; one may exaggerate the value of a work of literature because of its influence on other works or because it treats a subject of close personal interest. Most of Arnold's critical works advocate a similar classicism, a restraint from the excesses of one's own time, and seek a middle ground whereby "sober" interpretation may regulate literary judgment. Between a didactic or useful literature and a literature to be appreciated for its own sake only is the regulating force of the timeless classics.

The interest and controversy created by Walter Pater's *Studies in the History of the Renaissance* (1873) attest to the Victorian fascination with the past and to its complex response to its own time. Widening the traditional definition of renaissance, Pater's subjects include artists from the twelfth century to the eighteenth century, emphasizing a common sensibility as a uniting force for his study. The Victorian audience was also intrigued (and some were troubled) by the implied aesthetic of Pater's work. For Pater the experience of art was important; any work of art, from any time, could give its audience pleasure. As Pater writes in the conclusion to *The Renaissance*: "For art comes to you proposing frankly to give nothing but the highest quality to your moments as they pass, and simply for those moments' sake."

Victorian critics, self-conscious of the time they were living in and of the unprecedented changes around them, reacted by trying to preserve the importance of literature in an era that challenged its existence. In so doing they developed a dialogue with the past and introduced the world to modern approaches to time. Jerome Hamilton Buckley, in *The Triumph of Time*, has pointed out that, to the Victorians, "The notion of public time, or history, as the medium of organic growth and fundamental change, rather than simply additive succession, was essentially new."

[R.Z.]

See also **Victorian Poetry.**

FURTHER READINGS

Buckler, William E., ed. *Prose of the Victorian Period.* Boston: Houghton Mifflin, 1958.

Buckley, Jerome Hamilton. *The Victorian Temper.* New York: Random House, 1964.

———. *The Triumph of Time.* Cambridge: Harvard UP, 1966.

Houghton, Walter E., and G. Robert Stange, eds. *Victorian Poetry and Poetics.* Boston: Houghton Mifflin, 1968.

Levine, George, ed. *The Emergence of Victorian Consciousness.* New York: Free Press, 1967.

Pater, Walter. *The Renaissance.* Ed. Donald Hill. Berkeley: U of California P, 1980.

VICTORIAN POETRY

The Victorian age was a time of great social and spiritual upheaval. As England became more industrialized and urbanized, many experienced a new and disorienting way of life. Advances in science, including geological discoveries and the work of Darwin and other scientists, raised questions about traditional religious beliefs. Victorian poets were neither orthodox nor heterogeneous in their reactions to these advances. A nostalgia for a romanticized past of certitude, along with a sense of mission for confronting the present, were predominant concerns of the major Victorian poets, Alfred Tennyson, Robert Browning, and Matthew Arnold.

Many of Tennyson's poems are framed in past or mythologized settings. Often they are dramatic monologues allowing for the commentary of contemporary life through a distance of time and place, thereby "insulating" the poet from the speaker. "Mariana" (1830)—a character from Shakespeare's *Measure for Measure*—waits for a lover who never comes. As the landscape signals the passing time, and as the days, the nights, and the seasons pass, her unrequited love weighs more heavily, and she wishes to escape her anxiety in death—the annihilation of time. In "The Lotus-Eaters" (1832), Ulysses's crew, returning home from the Trojan War, becomes shipwrecked on an island of lotus-eaters, "in which it seemed always afternoon." When the crew is offered the fruit, they are "distanced" from time. Although they have memories of families and lives left behind, they know that "all hath suffered change" and that their deeds will be "half-forgotten." They contemplate remaining in the land of the lotus-eaters and not confronting the objects of memory. Thus the poem confronts a Victorian preoccupation: Is the past knowable and certain? Is it retrievable? "In Memoriam" (1850), a long and ambitious poem, is a eulogy to the poet's friend, Arthur Henry Hallam. Ending in a Christian affirmation of God's divine plan, the poem follows the mind's vicissitudes as it tries to come to terms with death. "In Memoriam" is, in part, an affirmation of the healing nature of time. "Idylls of the King" (1885), a series of poems about the King Arthur legends, uses its highly stylized setting to delineate moral virtues. The ambiguities of Tennyson's own time were therefore implicitly contrasted to the "nonexistent" mythological England of King Arthur's knights.

Many of Robert Browning's poems scrutinize the past and its relation to the present. Often written as dramatic monologues, they probe the possibilities and limitations inherent to an individual ego. Bound in their own time, the speakers of Browning's poems reveal both the vices of their own time and the elements of humanity assumed to be universal. In "The Bishop Orders His Tomb at St. Praxed's Church" (1845), for instance, there is much of the materialism of the Renaissance, but also of the vices of the body. John Ruskin, a critic of Italian art, marveled at how the poem captured the "spirit" of the Renaissance. In two of his well-known works, "Andrea Del Sarto" (1855) and "Fra Lippo Lippi" (1855), Browning contrasts two views of art. Fra Lippo Lippi reveals himself to be an inspired artist; Andrea Del Sarto, an excellent craftsman. In choosing two historical personae from the same era, Browning allows his readers to make moral judgments from a "safe" distance in time. This objectivity affords a glance at another time but also a mirror to one's own time. "The Ring and the Book" (1868–69), Browning's most ambitious poem, recounts a 1698 murder trial in Florence. Browning is able to probe the motivations of the people involved as they unfold dramatically. A reliable picture of the happenings finally emerges from the "partial" stories told. In choosing a fantastic and sordid incident from the remote past, set in another culture, Browning is able to hold the interest of his Victorian audience, which remains "distanced" from the events and is therefore dispassionate.

Although Matthew Arnold's poetry was not as popular or as prolific as Tennyson's or Browning's, it is, in many ways, closer to the spirit of our own time. The tone of Arnold's poetry is often detached and stoic, displaying little emotional involvement with his characters and no optimistic affirmation of life as is apparent in Tennyson or Browning. In "Stanzas From the Grande Chartreuse" (1855), the speaker finds no spiritual "resting place":

> Wandering between two worlds, one
>   dead,
> The other powerless to be born,
> With nowhere yet to rest my head,
> Like these, on earth I wait forlorn.

In "Dover Beach" (1867), perhaps Arnold's best known poem, the comfort that lovers may find with each other is contrasted to the world in which "The Sea of Faith / Was once, too, at the full, and round earth's shore. . . ." The final image of the poem finds the two lovers isolated in a "nightmare" image:

> And we are here as on a darkling plain
> Swept with confused alarms of struggle
>   and flight,
> Where ignorant armies clash by night.

Arnold produced a large body of prose explicating his theoretical pronouncements about his age and his poetry, much of which signals a dissatisfaction with the "philistinism" and materialism of his own age. Whether Arnold's poems were set in the past or not, he sought classical models to give perspective to his own time. Championing the ancients as models in "Preface to Poems" (1853), Arnold believed they would help young writers to "escape the danger of producing poetical works conceived in the spirit of the passing time, and which partake of its transitoriness."

Manifestations of Victorian poets' interest in the past is evident throughout the era. The "pre-Raphaelite" poets, including Dante Gabriel Rossetti, developed a cult around medieval culture. Far from being an aberration, their poetry illustrates a mixture of escapism and an attempt to treat topics of profound importance to their audience. The major Victorian poets, Tennyson, Browning, and Arnold, also had a deep-rooted consciousness about the changing times they were living in. The choice of settings from the past is one of the most intriguing critical issues about their achievements; studying these issues reveals how the present may be given perspective by the past.

[R.Z.]

See also **Poetry; Victorian Criticism.**

FURTHER READINGS

Bradbury, Malcolm, and David Palmer, eds. *Victorian Poetry*. Vol. 15 of *Stratford-Upon-Avon Studies*. London: Edward Arnold, 1972.

Buckler, William E., ed. *The Major Victorian Poets: Tennyson, Browning, Arnold*. Boston: Houghton Mifflin, 1973.

Chell, Samuel L. *The Dynamic Self: Browning's Poetry of Duration*. Victoria: U of Victoria, 1984.

Johnson, E.D.H. *The Alien Vision of Victorian Poetry*. Hamden: Archon Books, 1963.

Zweig, Robert. "'Death-in-Love': Rossetti and the Victorian Journey Back to Dante." *Sex and Death in Victorian Literature*. Ed. Regina Barreca. London: Macmillan, 1990. 178–193.

WATCH AND CLOCK TRADE

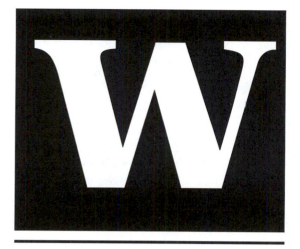

From its beginnings in the late thirteenth and early fourteenth centuries, clockmaking had its international aspect: the mobilization of skills and talent for the construction of tower clocks often entailed the import of nonlocal, even foreign, technicians and craftsmen. These machines were large objects, not easily transportable, and it was the workers who moved rather than the product. With the manufacture of movable and portable domestic clocks (small format), however, it was the merchandise that moved.

In theory, this contravened guild regulations, which aimed at protection against foreign competition and restriction of sale to products of one's own fabrication. Yet such constraints could not be maintained in the face of consumer preference. Some centers of manufacture (*fabriques*) did better work than others and found customers far and wide. Similarly, some makers did better work than others and found that demand exceeded capacity, while others could not afford to open their own shop or found it hard to compete with the more fashionable makers; so the latter worked in their room and sold their labor to the former.

In this way, the best makers were soon able to sell their clocks and, more often, watches and watchcases far beyond local markets. They did this directly by traveling about with stock; but makers could ill afford to give up time from work to sell their product, so that increasingly sales came to be handled by merchant intermediaries who could collect a varied selection from a number of makers and satisfy diverse market preferences.

The first major centers of clock and watch manufacture were linked to court patronage: the makers gathered around the buyers. Thus grew centers at Blois in France, amid the *châteaux de la Loire*, and Augsburg in Bavaria, then the seat of the ruler of the Holy Roman Empire. Geneva, a dour Calvinist republic that discouraged sumptuary display, was the exception. It owed its development (sixteenth to eighteenth centuries) not to local custom but to export, and it grew by sacrificing guild constraints to the requirements of large-scale manufacture (division of labor, regional specialization, incorporation of women and children into the work force, batch production). All of these centers inevitably developed characteristic specialties reflecting the taste of the market. One looked to Blois for colorful, artistic enamel watch cases and dials; to Augsburg and other cities in southern Germany for elaborate table clocks and automata; and to Geneva for Islamic watches with moon phases and Turkish numerals, for downscale enamels, for sacred and profane motifs for clerics and macaronies (respectively, one hopes), and for plain, utilitarian watches for gentlefolk and merchants.

The critical technical advances that turned the clock and watch from luxury accessories to necessary instruments (though without eliminating their aesthetic interest) were the invention of the pendulum (ca. 1660) for the former, and of the balance spring (ca. 1675) for the latter. These innovations substantially enhanced their reliability and accuracy, so that domestic and personal time came very close to true; your time was my time and my time yours. This meant that social action (coming and going, meeting and parting, the ordering of work and transport) could be and was increasingly organized on the assumption of common access and obedience to temporal information. Along with this increase in demand went a steady improvement in manufacturing technique, hence lower prices for timekeepers; and a slow, irregular, but significant growth in personal income and in urbanization.

The first centers to take advantage of these new opportunities were Geneva (as above) from the seventeenth century on; England (especially London) from the late seventeenth and early eighteenth; and the upland Jura districts north and northwest of Geneva from the mid-eighteenth century on. In contrast, such older centers as Paris-Blois, south Germany, and Italy had become complacent in their earlier success, were unable to adjust to new tastes and methods, and subsequently withered. Some of this was concealed by the readiness of the dominant *fabriques* to sell their work unsigned, for appropriation by makers elsewhere; thus, most watches signed as of Paris in the second half of the eighteenth century were actually from Geneva or the Jura.

In the eighteenth century, English clock- and watchmaking led the market, sustained on the supply side by innovations in product (*inter alia*, the seconds-beating pendulum, the compensated pendulum, and the anchor and dead-beat escapements for clocks; repeater mechanisms, jeweling, and the cylinder escapement for watches); and on the demand side, by the wealthiest (per head), most urbanized (even the rural areas), most time-conscious society in Europe. But these improvements were copied and adapted—and where commercially advisable, debased—by competitors in the Swiss *fabriques* (Geneva, Neuchâtel, Erguel, and the bishopric of Basel); so that beginning in the early nineteenth century, English production leveled off and Switzerland rose to a position of dominance such as had never been seen. By the middle of the nineteenth century, well over half of world output was coming from the villages and hamlets of the Jura, with a small, higher-quality increment from the *cabinotiers* of Geneva. (See Table 1.)

Table 1. Estimated output of watches by number and value in selected countries, 1870:

	Number	Value
	(thousands)	(thousand dollars)
Switzerland	1,600	17,600
France	300	3,300
Great Britain	200	3,200
United States	100	1,500

Source: Edward Young, *Labor in Europe and America*. Washington: U.S. Bureau of Statistics, 1875, p. 608.

This did not mean that the losers were standing still. In Britain, the Liverpool area rose to become a major center alongside London by building on a long experience in the manufacture of parts and rough movements (*blancs* or *ébauches*). In revolutionary France, the government determined to develop a watch *fabrique* in Besançon as a counterweight to Geneva and Neuchâtel, where political and labor troubles were dissolving the loyalties of the skilled *cabinotiers*. But neither of these new centers grew enough to challenge Swiss hegemony. Competi-

tion came instead from an unexpected quarter, the United States, first in clockmaking, then in watches. The American challenge was based on a process innovation: mass production based on interchangeable parts—what later became known as the American system of manufacture. This new technology appeared first in clocks (first decade of the nineteenth century) because tolerances were greater in large-format pieces and because duplication of parts was facilitated by the extensive use of wood, a more "forgiving" material than metal. It took another fifty years to work out similar techniques in watch manufacture, and then, in the matter of a decade (1860s and '70s), Swiss watches found themselves losing American customers and faced with serious competition in third markets.

Technology based on interchangeable parts was, of course, not unknown to European makers. It was implicit in the earlier shift to batch production and the separation of fabrication of movements in the rough on the one hand from finishing and adjustment on the other. The extensive mechanization of *ébauche* manufacture by Frédéric Japy (Montbéliard and Franche-Comte) in the 1780s and 1790s signaled and affirmed the new possibilities. Uniformity by mechanization was in the air. During the revolution (1790s), the French government thought to move in this direction as part of a general rationalization of manufacture, but it found it easier to imagine than to execute, especially in time of war. After the return of peace, Swiss watch manufacture took intermittent and tentative steps along these lines, but these often aborted, and in any event did not constitute full conversion to mechanized manufacture. That did not come until American competition compelled it, and then only gradually and progressively, as new plants embodied interchangeable parts technology and older cottage shops and home benches were abandoned.

By World War I, the Swiss industry had largely completed the transition to the new technology, while the American manufacture had begun to level off. Now, the focus of innovation shifted from process to product, and here the Swiss had an important advantage: the range and diversity of their manufacture and the rapidity of their response to taste and fashion. The Swiss were particularly quick to appreciate and act on the potential demand for women's watches, for specialty and novelty pieces, for watches designed to appeal to particular cultural and national markets, and above all, for wristwatches as against pocket watches.

The wristwatch, originally appearing (from the early nineteenth century) as a bracelet watch for ladies of means and style, was popularized and masculinized by its usefulness in war (the first examples were often pocket watches converted for wrist wear by the addition of soldered strap loops) and represented the future of the trade. The Swiss, with their long experience in making ultra-small calibers for women's wear, took to this new market far more easily than the American companies, with their conservative styling ("if you'll take 'em the way we make 'em, you'll get 'em cheaper") and their single-purpose machines. As a result, the Swiss found themselves before and after World War II once again the undisputed masters of the trade, accounting for more than half of world output. The only barriers to complete monopoly were national industries, usually protected by tariffs or subsidies, in individual countries such as France, Germany, the Soviet Union, and Japan.

At this point two things changed the picture. The first was the introduction of the American Timex, a mass-produced, lower-end watch made with truly interchangeable parts using tools and materials developed in World War II, advertised as indestructible, and sold in general retail outlets such as variety stores, drugstores, and airport shops. This aggressive marketing made the Timex an instant success and threw the lower reaches of the Swiss industry into confusion. The next blow, more serious, came with the quartz revolution, beginning around 1970. This marked a major change in the character of the product. The watch was no longer driven by a spring and regulated by a mechanical controller in the form of an oscillating balance. It was now powered electrically and kept time to the frequency of vibrating quartz crystals. By using integrated circuits, the wheel train could be eliminated entirely (digital display) or reduced to driving the hands of an analog dial. At one stroke, the advantage of 200 years of accumulated Swiss skill and experience was substantially devalued.

This was a change that the Swiss were quite capable of mastering, for they had the scientists and technicians and were among the pioneers in electronic research for horological use. But that was in the labs; the *fabricants*, comfortable with the prestige of their houses and product, were reluctant to adopt the new technology, which they initially dismissed as a fad. This was a mistake, because in the time it took them to wake up to the threat, their conservatism allowed their competitors in the United States

and, even more, in Asia, to win a substantial share of the international market. The result was a purge of the Swiss industry, which lost two-thirds of its jobs (89,400 in 1970, 29,800 in 1987), and most of its share (in number of units produced) of the world watch trade. Where Switzerland accounted in 1960 for about half the units produced and an even higher percentage of those shipped abroad, by 1991 they were down to 16 percent, and the leading makers were Japan and Hong Kong. Japan, moreover, was contracting for production "offshore" in mainland Asia, and the tendency has been increasingly for the primary makers to concentrate on design and "software," while leaving the "hardware" to cheap but skilled workers abroad. Some firms, for example, the Japanese maker Seiko, divide the tasks: higher-quality watches are made at home by capital-intensive, robotized techniques that minimize human intervention, while lower-end pieces are made abroad, in Hong Kong, Korea, or Malaysia; and as wages rise abroad in response to this demand for labor and direct investment, production is shifted to new lower-wage centers.

In the meantime, after a bad start, the Swiss industry has not let itself be wiped out by the new technology and the new competition. It has reorganized and rationalized production; adopted where possible the latest process innovations; and accepted the quartz controller while sticking to traditional analog dials, where Swiss experience with wheel trains gives them a comparative advantage. Digitals are for Asians and other low-cost producers and the Swiss, like the Japanese, have learned to subcontract to offshore producers, to the point where it is no longer clear what is meant by "Swiss Made." One of the greatest success stories has been the Swatch (Swiss watch), which combines new, simpler design, robotic manufacture, fashion-conscious and style-setting appearance, and all-points marketing to tempt and generate an extraordinary consumer appetite. The Swatch has been, in effect, the Timex of the 1980s; in 1989, it accounted for half the Swiss output of complete watches.

Most important, the Swiss have largely abandoned the lower end of the market (*le bas de gamme*) for more costly and decorative pieces: the watch as jewel, as symbol of taste and prestige, as signifier of wealth and status. There is still a demand for mechanical watches for those who delight in the wonder and beauty of these masterpieces of miniaturization, so different from the cold, immobile, unlovable efficiency of an integrated circuit. At their best and most complicated, these machines command prices in six figures. Issued sometimes in limited, specially numbered series, they command a rarity premium from the start. Even the modestly priced Swatch has been able to play this game by commissioning artistic, signed dials—to the point where some of these pieces, sold originally for less than 100 Swiss francs, have subsequently been bought at auction for tens and hundreds of thousands.

As a result, Swiss watches, though representing only about 10–15 percent of units produced worldwide (the share varies with the estimates and definitions), account for about half of total value. (See Table 2.) Average factory price of a finished Swiss watch in 1989 ran 170 Swiss francs, as against twenty Swiss francs for a Japanese watch, and nine Swiss francs for one made in Hong Kong (*Neue Zürcher Zeitung*, April 18, 1990). Whether Swiss makers can continue to maintain this supremacy in top-of-the-scale watches is hard to say, but at the moment they clearly dominate in smartness, aesthetics, and distinctiveness. Japanese makers have been sending their most gifted artists to Switzerland to learn design, but as of now their work is essentially derivative and, to this observer, unexciting.

Table 2. World output of watches and movements by number and value, 1991:

	Number (millions)	Value (million Swiss francs)
Japan	386	3,586
Hong Kong	170	1,200
Switzerland	132	7,400
Other	140	1,820
Total	828	14,006

Source: Estimates of the Fédération de l'Industrie Horlogère, Switzerland, cited in Jacqueline Henry Bédat, *Une région*, pp. 202–203.

[D.S.L.]

See also **Clocks: America and Mass Production, 1770–1890; Clocks and Watches: The Leap to Precision; French Clocks and Watches, 1660–1830; High Frequency Timekeepers; Watch Manufacturing in Nineteenth-Century America.**

FURTHER READINGS

Chapiro, Adolphe. *La montre française du XVIe siècle jusqu'à 1900*. Paris: Les Editions de l'Amateur, 1991.

Henry Bédat, Jacqueline. *Une région, une passion: L'horlogerie. Une entreprise: Longines*. N.p.: Cie des Montres Longines Francillon SA, 1992.

Landes, David S. *Revolution in Time: Clocks and the Making of the Modern World*. Cambridge: Harvard UP, 1983. (French edition, revised and enlarged: *L'heure qu'il est: les horloges, la mesure du temps, et la formation du monde moderne*. Paris: Gallimard, 1987.) [2522]

WATCHMAKER GOD AND ARGUMENT FROM DESIGN

In the Newtonian clockwork universe, the most appropriate metaphor for God was that of the watchmaker. The emerging worldview during the British horological revolution of 1660 to 1760 was increasingly mechanistic. The clock, in particular, appealed to the optimism of the eighteenth century and the sense of order in its heliocentric universe. The status of the clock as the epitome of mechanical engineering and technology provided a metaphor for many things from the lowest animal to the universe itself. In such a universe, God was seen as the watchmaker who created the cosmic clockwork.

In the work of Newton and Leibniz, the Watchmaker God was an implicit figure, but the nature of God varied according to their separate views of creation. Leibniz, the champion of eighteenth-century optimism, saw the universe as a perfectly functioning perpetual motion machine that only needed to be set in motion by the Watchmaker God. Newton, on the other hand, perceived the clockwork as less than perfect; he believed it continually ran down and required adjustments and rewinding by the Watchmaker God. Although Clarke, arguing for Newton, disputed with Leibniz about the two perceptions of the Watchmaker God within the clockwork universe, he never questioned the mechanistic and mathematical nature of the model. In this dispute, Liebniz made the following claim: "I maintain it [the universe] to be a watch that goes without wanting to be mended by him [God]: otherwise we must say, that God bethinks himself again. No; God has forseen every thing before hand; there is in his works a harmony, a beauty, already pre-established." Clarke disagrees and explains that God gains rather than loses stature by "his continual government and inspection of his clockwork."

The argument from design, which did not assume the implicit presence of a Watchmaker God, used the analogy of the universe as a watch to prove the existence of God. This argument gained popularity during the British horological revolution and continued to be expounded by theologians well into the nineteenth century. Echoes of the argument are still heard today, although they no longer employ the metaphor of a watch. The argument from design argues that just as the existence of a watch both necessitates and demonstrates the existence of a watchmaker, the existence of the universe necessitates and demonstrates the existence of a creator. To the extent that one believes that the universe is not only like a watch but actually operates like clockwork along mechanical lines, the argument from design can become very persuasive despite its implicit syllogism.

The argument from design appeared in England in Philip Mornay's 1587 translation of *A Worke concerning the Trewnesse of the Christian Religion*, at about the same time as watches were beginning to be made in that country. However, there are more examples appearing during the horological revolution. These include the watch analogies in John Smith's *Select Discourses* (1660), Lord Herbert of Cherbury's *De Religione Gentilium* (1663), John Spencer's *A Discourse concerning Prodigies* (1663), and N. Fairfax's *A Treatise of the Bulk and Selvedge of the World* (1774). Matthew Hale, in *The Primitive Origination of Mankind* (1677), introduces the subject by discussing a broken timepiece found in a field, much as does Simon Patrick in *A Brief Account of the New Sect of Latitude-Men* (1662). Hale speaks of "the Artist that made this Engin [a watch]." Boyle does not expound the argument from design but alludes to it: "And shall we readily allow so much foresight & contrivance to a Mechanicall artificer, and shall we scruple to allow much better mechanisms to (the Author even of Artificers) the Omniscient God himself, in the Production of his Great *Automaton*, the World?"

One finds comparable references in Cudworth's *Treatise concerning Eternal and Immutable Morality* (published after his death), Blackmore's *Creation* (1712), and Voltaire's pithy epigram:

Le monde m'embarasse, et je ne puis pas
   songer
Que cette horloge existe et n'a pas
   d'Horloger.

In general, the earlier references to God as a watchmaker tended to be short. But John Ray's *The Wisdom of God Manifested in the Works of the Creation*, which had reached its ninth edition by 1727, both extends the theme and couples the argument from design with "Rule, Order, and Constancy" in the heavens. He also attempts to relate the mechanical image to an intriguing but disputed passage in Cicero's *De Natura Deorum* 2.34.

William Derham, the rector of Upminster and fellow of the Royal Society who wrote the first creditable manual of horology in English, *The Artificial Clock-Maker* (1696, much enlarged in 1700), later wrote the influential *Astro-Theology; or, A Demonstration of the Being and Attributes of God from a Survey of the Heavens* (1715), which drew on his knowledge of clocks and watches to propound the argument from design. In it, he offers his version of the argument: "If we consider that those Motions are wisely ordered and appointed, being as various, and as regular and every way nicely accomplished, as the World and its Inhabitants have occasion for. This is a manifest sign of a wise and kind, as well as omnipotent CREATOR and ORDERER of the World's affairs, as that of a Clock or other Machine is of Man." Derham emphasizes the qualities of order, regularity, and constancy in this universe. His work was to be influential for more than a century.

Later in the eighteenth century, Tucker, in *The Light of Nature Pursued* (1768), discusses at some length the "divine artist" who directs the clockwork universe. In doing so, he refers to the views of both Newton and Leibniz, although he does not directly allude to them. Although Tucker has been considered an immediate influence on Paley's *Natural Theology*, Paley writes some passages that are remarkably close to Chamberlain's much earlier translation of Nieuwentyt's *Religious Philosopher* of 1718.

The most influential work on the argument from design was undoubtedly William Paley's *Natural Theology; or Evidence for the Existence and Attributes of the Deity Collected from the Appearances of Nature* (1802), which enjoyed such popularity that no less than twenty editions were printed in eighteen years. More than eighty years after its initial publication it was revised by F. Le Gros Clark "to harmonize with modern science," and continued its influence in modified form. Six hundred pages, of which the first two chapters describe "Paley's Watch," are devoted to the argument from design. Paley concludes that "after all the schemes and struggles of a reluctant philosophy the necessary resort is to Deity. The marks of design are too strong to be got over. Design must have a designer. That designer must have been a person. That person is God."

By the end of the horological revolution in 1760, poets, scientists, and philosophers were beginning to question the clockwork model of the universe and, in the case of poets, even to regard it with horror. However, both the Watchmaker God and the clockwork universe lived on through much of the nineteenth century because theologians and the bourgeoisie continued to propound the argument from design. During the Romantic reaction against clockwork diabolism, the Watchmaker God shed some of the negative accretions from his association with the clockwork metaphor by devolving them upon a dualistic counterpart, the clockwork devil. In another guise, the Watchmaker God largely remains the god of Western society because the bourgeoisie still worship the concept that "time is money." Even in the churches, the existence of the Judeo-Christian God is often "proven" through the beauty of his creation. Though the Watchmaker God and his clockwork universe are no longer with us, the argument from design, albeit in a much modified form, continues to be persuasive.

[S.L.M.]

See also **Clockwork Metaphor.**

FURTHER READINGS

Alexander, H. G., ed. *The Leibniz–Clarke Correspondence.* Manchester: Manchester UP, 1956.

Derham, W. *Astro-Theology: Or a Demonstration of the Being and Attributes of God, from a Survey of the Heavens.* London: W. Innys, 1715.

Macey, Samuel L. *Clocks and the Cosmos: Time in Western Life and Thought.* Hamden: Archon Books, 1980.

————. *The Patriarchs of Time: Dualism in Saturn-Cronus, Father Time, the Watchmaker God, and Father Christmas.* Athens: U of Georgia P, 1987.

Paley, William. *Natural Theology: Or, Evidences of the Existence and Attributes of the Deity, Collected from the Appearances of Nature.* 4th ed. London: R. Faulder, 1803.

WATCH MANUFACTURING IN NINETEENTH-CENTURY AMERICA

The history of American watch manufacturing and particularly manufacturing at the Waltham Watch Company is a history of continuous technological change throughout the nineteenth century, both in watch movement design and in production machinery development. Watch manufacturing was the most complex manufacturing process in the last century, at one time requiring some 3,746 different operations on the 150 parts of each Waltham watch.

The Waltham Watch Company and the Elgin National Watch Company dominated the American watch industry, pioneering most of the technical innovations and setting the economic and technological terms on which all jeweled watch manufacturers were forced to compete.

Efforts to produce watches in America date back to the War of 1812 and Luther Goddard of Shrewsbury, Massachusetts, and include an abortive 1830s effort by Henry and James Flagg Pitkin in Hartford, Connecticut, who actually produced some 400 to 800 watches. However, real progress was not made until 1849 when Aaron L. Dennison, the father of American watch manufacturing, joined with clockmaker Edward Howard and others to begin the effort that culminated in the firm known as the Waltham Watch Company.

Between 1849 and 1857, the Waltham Watch Company grew gradually under various corporate identities. Its primary technician was Aaron Dennison, who invented much of the first generation of watch manufacturing machinery. Other mechanics joined Waltham in its early years, most notably Charles S. Moseley, who is credited with having invented the split collet and the three-bearing or sliding-spindle lathe. Waltham mechanics developed precision grinding techniques to produce large quantities of precision collets and spindles.

The company fell prey to the panic of 1857 and was sold at auction to Royal Robbins, who pumped new capital into the venture and hired new mechanics. That same year (it is unclear exactly when and under what circumstances), Ambrose Webster came to work at Waltham. Webster understood the critical importance of the factory's machine shop as a center for developing and making machine tools as well as setting and maintaining standards. He possessed organizational skills learned during his employment at the Springfield Armory, where the American government was mass-producing guns.

This *American System of Manufactures*, as the process came to be known, consisted of first producing a *model* clock or gun, then producing a set of master go/nogo gauges to fit the model, and finally making a set of inspector's or working gauges for use on the shop floor based on the model and the master gauges. As each clock or gun part was finished, it was accepted or rejected by testing it against its respective go/nogo gauge.

It was this process of gauging and the specialized production machinery that Aaron L. Dennison saw on his tour of the Springfield Armory that inspired him to mass produce watches.

Using the Springfield Armory paradigm, the Waltham mechanics adapted the concept to watch manufacturing. The most important transfer of technology from the armories to the watch factories was the imposition of a rigid system of organization and the elevation of the machine shop to a position of supremacy. Ambrose Webster took charge of the Waltham machine shop in 1859 and through this position made his greatest contribution to the Waltham Watch Company.

Waltham's mechanics quickly learned that the go/nogo gauging system, while adequate for clocks and guns, was hopelessly inadequate for the fine tolerances and large number of parts in a watch. They abandoned the go/nogo gauge, which had no specific mathematical measurement and was literally a specially shaped piece of steel. In its place they developed a new gauging system, based on the European *douzième* gauge, that produced a mathematical measurement. They designed precise measurements for each watch part. Each watch part was made to its specific measurement, within given tolerances. In the 1850s, this was a revolutionary method of measuring and gauging, and an entirely new manufacturing method. Today, it is common practice throughout the world (see Figure 1).

In 1868, Waltham mechanics abandoned the English measuring system of a thirtieth of an inch and adopted the centimeter as the standard unit of measure throughout the factory. The Waltham Watch Company was the first American manufacturer to adopt the metric system.

During the first decade of its existence, Waltham produced many of its own parts, but continued to rely heavily on English suppliers for such items as hands, mainsprings, and hair springs. The company eventually manufactured virtually all its own parts.

The American Civil War was a fortuitous event for the Waltham Watch Company. Although it lost many operatives to military service—the company guaranteed all soldiers their jobs upon return—the company prospered from an insatiable demand for its watches, the disruption of imported English watches, wartime inflation, and the fact that it was the only American firm producing low-priced watches. Waltham succeeded technically in the late 1850s and economically in the early 1860s.

In the late 1860s, the company took advantage of its strong economic position and began to invest heavily in additions to its factory and in new automatic machinery. A host of brilliant mechanics worked at Waltham in the late nineteenth century, including Edward A. Marsh, Charles Vander Woerd, and finally Duane Church. They systematically revolutionized the production of watch parts, from hand production to fully automatic machine tools.

Typical of this factory-wide change was the evolution of screw making machinery. Since the number of screws in a nineteenth-century pocket watch was roughly one-fourth the total number of parts, there is little doubt why Waltham mechanics turned their attention to automatic screw machinery at an early date.

In the early years, Waltham operatives apparently used the traditional screw plate to cut each screw by hand. Waltham's first screw cutting machinery was in use by 1858. It consisted of two machines: a specialized lathe to cut the screw threads, and a milling machine or saw to slot the screws.

In 1871, Charles Vander Woerd developed the first automatic screw machine. Its design remained in use at Waltham through the 1950s. Vander Woerd's machine employed the conventional three-bearing, sliding-spindle lathe and double slide rest (as had the first machine), but it was activated by a series of cams running parallel to the lathe spindle. This machine was especially suited to large case and plate screws (see Figure 2).

Edward A. Marsh patented an automatic screw machine in 1885 that supplemented Vander Woerd's machine. In design, Marsh's machine departed radically from that of Vander Woerd in which a single workpiece was acted on successively by different cutting tools brought to a single place. Marsh's screw machine employed the same tools working simultaneously on numerous workpieces, carried in a large drum. It was noted for its production of smaller screws, such as balance and timing screws. Duane Church subsequently produced an improved version of the Vander Woerd screw machine.

Duane Church was also responsible for a major change in manufacturing theory. Church did nothing less than do away with jigs and fixtures, as he believed that a part "should not be released [from its machine] until fully completed." Church pioneered the use of compressed air in cylinders with cam-operated piston valves on many machines to prevent shock during the various processes. As Waltham's chief toolmaker, Church built this theory into the manufacture of most watch parts.

The evolution of screw making technology over a thirty-five-year period is typical of the continual evolution of machinery at Waltham. Between 1849 and the death of Duane Church in 1905, there was never a period of technological stagnation at Waltham.

Edward A. Marsh, Waltham's master mechanic and historian, wrote about productivity improvements in watch manufacturing that in "1857, [the Waltham Watch Company] employed about ninety people and produced five watches per day,—one watch for each eighteen workmen. At that rate of production there would be required 56,394 people to produce the 3,133 movements per day, which were made in 1907 by 4,300 people, being one movement for each 1.37 people."

Although Waltham mechanics mechanized the production of watch parts, they did not mechanize assembly and adjustment. The upper floors of the factory were filled with highly skilled watchmakers assembling and adjusting watches. Depending on the grade, adjusting could take as long as five months. Escapement manufacture best illustrates the challenges faced in these processes. The escapement consisted of some fifty-six parts, including the hairspring and the balance wheel.

"Matching the escapement" involved cementing the pallet jewels into the pallet fork using heated shellac. Despite the production of wheels and forks and jewels to precise standards, each had to be matched independently during

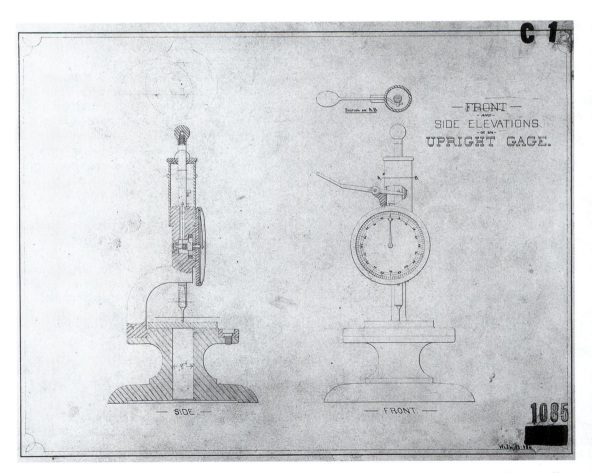

Figure 1. This "Upright Gage" [sic], drawn at the Waltham Watch Company on March 11, 186?, may well coincide with Waltham's change from the English system of measurement to the metric system in 1868. Its adjustable dial is graduated in hundredths. The gauge is designed for quick and easy use, with a lever at the left which raises and lowers the spindle in the center of the table. The needle sweeps around the dial indicating the distance the spindle is raised. Waltham Watch Company Drawings, Smithsonian Institution Specimen. Courtesy Smithsonian Institution, National Museum of American History, negative no. 83–12683.

the process of assembly. The pallet fork and its jewels were designed to be adjusted as an integral part of the assembly process, as were other parts of the watch.

Waltham mechanics evolved statistical techniques to match hairsprings and balance wheels based on the weight of the balance and the gauged strength of the hairspring. Even after such careful matching, an operative necessarily vibrated and adjusted each assembly prior to its incorporation into its movement. John Logan and Thomas Gill were noted for their innovations in this area of production, gauging, and assembly.

The Waltham Watch Company made innovations in other areas besides production and assembly. As early as 1864, it pioneered the full product line, offering the consumer a full variety of grades and prices. By 1867, Waltham offered twenty-four different grades of watch movements. This was relatively easy in watch manufacturing, as many parts (for example, plates, wheels, and screws) were interchangeable within a particular model, and jeweling, balance type, and regulator type usually determined the grade. The higher grades had more jewels, a temperature-compensated balance, and a micrometer regulator. Later in the century Waltham expanded its line and offered more than 200 different styles of dials (including special order dials) and numerous styles of hands. Mass production in the watch industry did not force product uniformity on the public. Indeed, quite the opposite was the case. Mass production offered the buying public a greater diversity of watch styles, grades, and prices.

Figure 2. Automatic Screw Machine patented by Charles Vander Woerd in 1871. This example, designed for larger screws such as plate and case screws, seems to date from about 1875 and its nickel plating suggests it may have been shown at the American Centennial at Philadelphia in 1876. Courtesy Smithsonian Institution, National Museum of American History, catalogue no. 316,564, negative no. p65727.

With Waltham's economic success in the 1860s came competition, notably from Elgin. Between the late 1860s and early 1890s, a host of other firms entered and left the market. The late-nineteenth-century watch industry was highly competitive, but Waltham and Elgin had the upper hand with rapidly advancing technology and deep market penetration. By 1910, only seven jeweled watch manufacturers remained in America: Waltham, Elgin, Hamilton, Illinois, Hampden, Rockford, and South Bend.

Waltham and Elgin did not satisfy every market, and in the late 1870s and 1880s, new firms created new products to meet the demand. These manufacturers, most notably the Waterbury Watch Company and its successors, produced inexpensive watches that came to be called "dollar" watches because of their price. These low grade, usually unjeweled watches were notable for their innovative use of materials never before employed to make watches. Some "dollar" watches featured such cost-saving parts as stamped plates, lantern pinions, paper dials, celluloid crystals, and stamped, plated cases. They usually had duplex or pin pallet escapements. Tens of millions were made and at least one maker is still in production.

Much remains to be researched and written about American watch manufacturing. No one has written a history of America's largest watch manufacturer, the Elgin National Watch Company. The Elgin company produced some 55 million watches, while its rival, Waltham, produced 34 million watches. There are intriguing bits of Elgin history. In the 1870s, for example, Elgin conducted a time and motion study of undetermined nature and concluded that it could make watches much faster and cheaper if it vastly increased its output. Elgin subsequently did so and soon cut the prices of its watches by 50 percent. Within a decade, Waltham and Elgin had joined to share patents for the newly designed pendant-setting watches then coming into fashion. They drove several small firms (Aurora and Columbus) out of business. Here is an exciting story, not only of technological innovation, but also of entrepreneurs who understood and used the power born of their technological advantage in dealing with competitors. As history suggests, Waltham and Elgin were not shy about using their mechanical muscle and the economic leverage it provided.

American manufacturers enjoyed great success in the late nineteenth and early twentieth centuries. Their products savored a worldwide reputation and their production methods were adopted by their Swiss and (belatedly) English competitors. Much of the technology they developed, notably new gauging techniques and methods of automated production, were adopted throughout industry, and many are still used today.

[D.R.H.]

See also Clocks: America and Mass Production, 1770–1890; Precision Timekeeping, 1790–1900.

FURTHER READINGS

Hoke, Donald R. *Ingenious Yankees: The Rise of the American System of Manufactures in the Private Sector.* New York: Columbia UP, 1990.

———. *The Time Museum Historical Catalogue of American Pocket Watches.* Rockford: Time Museum, 1991.

WELLS, H.G. (1866–1946)

Herbert George Wells, despite an early life bedeviled with poverty, and the need to work from the age of fourteen, won a scholarship four years later to study biology at the Normal School of Science, South Kensington, London, where one of his teachers was Thomas Henry Huxley, the defender of Darwinism and grandfather of Aldous Huxley. By 1888, Wells had graduated from London University, and by 1900, his combination of journalism with a great fecundity of astronomical and biological fantasy had set him well on the path to literary success. The standard was set by his wonderfully imaginative first novel, *The Time Machine: An Invention* (1895), and was followed in short order by such comparable scientific romances as *The Wonderful Visit* (1895), *The Island of Dr. Moreau* (1896), *The Invisible Man* (1897), *The War of the Worlds* (1898), *When the Sleeper Wakes* (1899), and *The First Man in the Moon* (1901). In addition, there were at least three books of collected short stories during the same period, including *Tales of Space and Time* (1899).

Among Wells's works were a series of utopian (< Greek *ou*, not; *top[os]*, a place) and dystopian (< Greek *dys*, ill or bad) novels that influenced the great dystopias of Yevgeny Zamyatin, Aldous Huxley, and George Orwell in successive decades of our own century (see Utopias and Dystopias). The inventor-scientist in *The Time Machine* is projected by his machine into a series of future ages that become increasingly terrifying; and in *When the Sleeper Wakes*, mass enslavement results from future developments in technology. But in the period immediately following, Wells became for a while more optimistic, and the idea of biological evolution led him to believe in a parallel sociological evolution that might lead toward utopia. Such are the ideas that appear in *Anticipations* (1901), *Mankind in the Making* (1903), and *A Modern Utopia* (1905).

The much increased knowledge of cartography and geography by Wells's time meant that unlike Jonathan Swift's dystopian *Gulliver's Travels* (1726), or Thomas More's original *Utopia* (1516) Wells's utopias and dystopias had to be set in future time. But his *Time Machine* involves interesting speculation on time as the fourth dimension which seems to predate relativity theory, Hermann Minkowski's paper of 1908, and possibly even the influence of such ideas on cubism. As the Time Traveller puts it to his friends in 1895, almost at the beginning of the work, "There are really four dimensions, three of which we call three planes of Space, and a fourth, Time. . . . *There is no difference between Time and any of the three dimensions of Space except that our consciousness moves along it.* . . . Time is only a kind of Space." The Psychologist disagrees, "You can move about in all directions of Space, but you cannot move about in Time." The Time Traveller responds, "you are wrong to say that we cannot move about in Time. For instance, if I am recalling an incident very vividly I go back [through my consciousness] to the instant of its occurrence." Here again is the germ of a temporal idea being currently studied by Freud that would later lead to a new literary mode (see **Stream of Consciousness**).

Most of *The Time Machine* is concerned with the far future in particular with the year 802,701, when the Time Traveller, together with a girl of the future named Weena whom he saves from drowning, meet both the weak rulers called Eloi and the more sinister subterranean people called Morlocks, who he feels are responsible for the disappearance of his time machine. Toward the end of the work, the time machine takes him on a voyage into the very distant future. Life as we know it has almost disappeared from the world and "The green slime on the rocks alone testified that life was not extinct." With the sun setting, and the snow beginning to fall in the bitterly cold surroundings, the horrified Time Traveller sets the levers on his time machine for a return to his laboratory and his friends in the present of the nineteenth century. Though the friends learn about his journey in the twelfth and last chapter of the book, he does not stay with them. In the brief epilogue, we learn from the narrator that the Time Traveller has seemingly been lost in time and space for some three years now. Since his machine can also travel backwards in time, he might be in "the Age of Unpolished Stone . . . the Cretaceous Sea . . . Jurassic times . . . or the lonely saline lakes of the Triassic Age." Alternatively, might he have gone "forward, into one of the nearer ages . . . with the riddles of our own time answered and its wearisome problems solved?"

But Wells is not quite ready for the utopias that the epilogue to *The Time Machine* might foreshadow. Instead, *When the Sleeper Wakes* is a dystopia in which Wells uses the contrivance employed by Louis-Sébastien Mercier in *L'An 2440* (1768–71) when the plots of utopias and dystopias alike began to be set more and more into the future. Harper and Brothers provided the following blurb to advertise Wells's book: "The sleeper is a typical liberal-minded man of means of the nineteenth century, and he awakens from a cataleptic trance in the year 2100. . . . his struggle for power—inspired by an enthusiastic girl—with the great political organiser Ostrog, gives the great structural lines of the story." Or, as the *Bookman* reviewed it more succinctly, "He fell to sleep a fanatical democrat—a socialist: he woke a tyrant; he died fighting with the people against the tyranny he had unconsciously fashioned while he slept." As the *Daily News* put it in language that must have been music to a young author's ears, "Mr. Wells beats Jules Verne on his own ground." By way of contrast in the utopian novels that immediately followed, *Modern Utopia* is controlled by a puritanical elite which oversees a satisfyingly structured technological society. These were the years when Wells became an active socialist and for a short time in 1903 even joined the Fabian Society.

Wells's *Tales of Space and Time*, though not dystopias, clearly play with the four dimensions of space and time as used in scientific fantasies. The five tales are "The Crystal Egg," "The Star," "A Story of the Stone Age," "A Story of the Days to Come," and "The Man Who Could Work Miracles." The first two stories are concerned with space: through the crystal egg we can see Mars and they can presumably see us; the star is a rogue celestial body which almost crashes into the earth and the story concludes by comparing the reaction of human beings and Martian astronomers to this momentous event. (In *The War of the Worlds,* the unconquerable Martians had landed in London and in a frightening foreshadowing of what might happen to us in an atomic holocaust—deriving from none other than the relativity and four dimensions with which Wells was concerned—the Martians are finally overcome by our bacteria.)

The final three of the *Tales of Space and Time* deal, as one might expect, with time by removing us from the normal present. The first moves back to the Stone Age, the second moves forward several generations from the Victorian Mr. Morris to his descendant, Mwres, and the last example moves out from the natural present to the supernatural present of miracles ("something contrariwise to the course of nature done by power of Will.")

Wells became increasingly pessimistic as a result of the two world wars and he never achieved the more polished prose to which academic writers aspired. Yet he wielded a very great measure of influence over at least two generations of readers. Apart from the comic novels of his middle period, he will surely be best remembered for the scientific fantasies that so often escaped either from the space of this world or along the time line of the fourth dimension.

[S.L.M.]

See also **Futuristic Fiction; Huxley, Aldous; Orwell, George; Relativity Theory; Science Fiction; Time in the Plastic Arts; Time Travel: Future; Time Travel: Past; Utopias and Dystopias.**

FURTHER READINGS

Hollinger, V. "Deconstructing the Time Machine." *Science-Fiction Studies* 14 (July 1987): 201–221. Includes bibliography.

Huntington, John. *The Logic of Fantasy: H.G. Wells and Science Fiction.* New York: Columbia UP, 1982.

Jacobs, Robert G. "H.G. Wells, Joseph Conrad, and the Relative Universe." *Conradiana* 1 (1968): 51–55.

Lake, D.J. "Wells's Time Traveller: An Unreliable Narrator?" *Extrapolation* 22 (Summer 1981): 117–126.

McConnell, Frank. *The Science Fiction of H.G. Wells.* Oxford: Oxford UP, 1981.

WHITEHEAD, ALFRED NORTH (1861–1947)

Alfred North Whitehead taught mathematics and logic at Cambridge University and at the University of London. In 1924, at the age of sixty-three, he came to the United States to serve as professor of philosophy at Harvard University. He remained in the United States until his death in 1947.

Discussions of time and temporality occupy a central place in Whitehead's scientific and metaphysical writings. Accordingly, he is often associated with philosophers like Henri Bergson and Samuel Alexander, who (in Alexander's phrase) "take time seriously"—either by placing primary emphasis on the subjective experience of flux and becoming, or by defending the notion of "pure becoming" and temporal passage as real rather than illusory.

These traditional associations are somewhat misleading. Whitehead is first and foremost philosopher of space rather than of time. He devotes a significant portion of his most important work, *Process and Reality* (1929), to a complex discussion of the geometrical relations comprising what he termed the "extensive continuum."

Specifically, Whitehead does *not* (as did Bergson and Alexander) portray time itself as something primordial, existing prior to and independent of discrete entities themselves. Neither, however, does Whitehead's focus on space and geometrical relations lead him to follow the example of those like Albert Einstein and Hans Reichenbach, who deny the reality of the apparent asymmetry in the present-past and present-future relationships, and who accordingly attempt to reduce temporality and the experience of temporal passage and becoming merely to a set of space-like relations.

The "Epochal Theory" of Time. In *Process and Reality*, Whitehead frequently uses a phrase borrowed from John Locke to describe time as "[a] perpetual perishing." Uniquely in Whitehead's thought, temporality, passage, and what Arthur Eddington described as the "arrow of time" arise as a consequence of a more fundamental fact of nature: the becoming and the "perishing" of episodic events or occasions of discrete experience. The genesis of, and the transition between, these "quanta" of experience define Whitehead's "epochal theory" of time.

The quantized episodes or events, which Whitehead (following Descartes) terms *res verae* or "actual entities," are "actual" in two possible senses. Each event is "actual" in a primary sense of being *active* and actively self-relating, coming-to-be by constituting itself as a subject out of elements (or "objective data") drawn from its past. Whitehead describes this primary activity as the *"concrescence* of an actual occasion." Once fully constituted and determinate, an event "perishes": that is, it *ceases* to be active or to experience its own subjective immediacy. In contrast to the views of some of his interpreters, however, Whitehead did not hold that this fully constituted event then disappears or evaporates into oblivion. Rather, each no longer active "actual entity" remains "actual" in a secondary, but equally important sense: that is, as *efficacious*. Each determinate entity now, in its turn, serves as an objective datum or element for inclusion within the self-constitution of *subsequent* (present) active occasions of experience.

This process of the becoming of actual entities, and of their subsequent "perishing" (that is, their transition from a state of active, subjective immediacy to one of fixed, passive, unchanging objective determinateness) defines a "flux of becoming" and gives rise to the experience of temporal passage. Concrescence defines the present, the event as subject. The perishing of subjectivity, the no longer active event serving as object, defines the past. Each actual entity, at different phases in its career, functions as both subject and object: constituting itself out of its own past, and, in turn, serving as an objective datum in the past subsequent (present) active occasions. This transition from present subjectivity to past objectivity thus defines the "arrow" or asymmetrical vector-quality of temporal passage.

Finally, since past objectified events literally serve as the "material cause" (in Aristotle's sense) of present activity, "actual entities" can thus be related, in analogy with J.M.E. McTaggart's "B series," as "earlier" and "later": earlier entities are those which serve as objectified data in the constitution of the later. This causal relationship of past to present is further asymmetrical, in that the relations of present (or "later") entities to their past (or "earlier") antecedents are always *internal* (or constitutive); while the relations of past entities to subsequent (present) entities are always *external* to (that is, non-constitutive and unaffected by) their inclusion in the self-constitution of some later event.

This ontology of present (subjective) and past (objective) events gives rise, however, to a dramatic departure from McTaggart. In Whitehead's case there can be no such thing as a determinate "future" event.

In contrast to "the present" as locus of activity, and "the past" as locus of determinate potentiality, "the future," on Whitehead's account, is merely the locus of unrealized possibilities which may or may not come to be actualized in any of a variety of ways. A present moment is (to use an awkward phrase) "as far forward into time" as one can go, since there is nothing "further on or beyond" the present activity of the self-constitution or concrescence of actual occasions. In contrast to McTaggart, the Whiteheadian "B-series," the asymmetrical causal relation of earlier to later events, thus does *not* entail that there are "future events" of some

determinate sort, moving steadily ever closer to, and finally "sliding into the shining present," and then moving out the "other end" of the present and receding ever farther into the past.

There is nothing in Whitehead's account, then, analogous to McTaggart's "A series" of events, unrolling like fixed images on a spool of motion-picture film and giving rise to the illusion of future present past time as a "moving image of eternity." If one were to press this image in Whitehead's case, instead of "unrolling" an already produced picture film, the passage of time would be like the actual ongoing manufacturing of each successive frame of the not-yet-completed film. Each successive present moment would consist of composing yet another new "frame" (episode or quantum of experience) as a unique synthesis of elements found in the preceding frames, and adding this new one on to the front of the ever-lengthening film strip.

No matter how incomplete the metaphors one employs, however, the important point to be borne in mind is that Whitehead's event ontology succeeds in providing an account of time that squares with common experience without rendering that experience illusory or reducing it to something utterly unlike it, as Einstein and the positivist philosophers have done. Whitehead also avoids the troublesome proposals from Bergson and Alexander to elevate time itself to the status of some mysterious metaphysical abstraction "within which" our temporal experiences somehow occur.

[G.R.L.]

See also **Alexander, Samuel; Arrow of Time; Bergson, Henri; Descartes, René; Locke, John; McTaggart, John McTaggart Ellis.**

FURTHER READINGS

Kline, George L. "Form, Concrescence, and Concretum." *Explorations in Whitehead's Philosophy.* Ed. Lewis S. Ford and George L. Kline. New York: Fordham UP, 1983. 104–146.

———. "'Present,' 'Past,' and 'Future' as Categoreal Terms, and the 'Fallacy of the Actual Future.'" *Review of Metaphysics* 40.2 (December 1986): 215–235.

Whitehead, Alfred North. *An Inquiry Concerning the Principles of Natural Knowledge.* Cambridge: Cambridge UP, 1919.

———. *The Concept of Nature.* Cambridge: Cambridge UP, 1920.

———. *Science and the Modern World.* New York: Macmillan, 1925.

———. *Process and Reality.* New York: Macmillan, 1929.

———. *Adventures of Ideas.* New York: Macmillan, 1933.

WITTGENSTEIN, LUDWIG (1889–1951)

Wittgenstein's philosophical concerns stand quite apart from many other modern philosophers in that time figures very little in either his early or his later work. According to the realistic ontology of his early *Tractatus Logico-Philosophicus* (1921), "Space, time and color (being colored) are forms of objects" (2.0251). Here objects are timeless, logical simples which make possible the "logical pictures" that are the core of the ability of language to represent the world truly or falsely. As a form of object, time serves in the configuration of these logical simples and aids in producing the material properties of the world we describe (2.0231).

Wittgenstein's later philosophy, which culminates in the *Philosophical Investigations* (1953), drops this realist metaphysics and criticizes all metaphysics. Although logical possibilities continue as the presupposition of all description, these are now identified as grammatical possibilities located in the "depth grammar" of our ordinary languages. Hence, what we mean by reality—which includes time—cannot be separated from language and its grammatical possibilities, and the idea of metaphysical investigations going beyond grammatical investigations is nonsensical. Time is not a problem, since it is a conventional way of talking inseparable from our ordinary everyday activities. And time may not be a problem in Wittgenstein's philosophy for yet another reason. Some scholars have compared Wittgenstein's work to Zen Buddhism as pointing to an unsayable aspect of life for which time is irrelevant. This may be in part the sense of the remark in his 1935 lectures at Cambridge that "we might say it is the whole of philosophy to realize that there is no more difficulty about time than there is about this chair."

[G.M.]

FURTHER READINGS

Wittgenstein, Ludwig. *Philosophical Investigations.* Trans. G.E.M. Anscombe. 2nd ed. Oxford: Blackwell, 1958.

———. *Tractatus Logico-Philosophicus.* Trans D.F. Pears and B.F. McGuinness. Rev. ed. London: Routledge and Kegan Paul, 1975.

WOLFE, GENE (1931–)

No writer of genre "science fiction" can be exempt from considerations of time, but most remain content to base their inventions on what might be called the platform of the future, without much examining the grounds upon which that platform represents an argument about time itself. It cannot be said of Gene Rodman Wolfe, who is perhaps the most significant American writer now alive whose literary roots are in genre science fiction, that he has in any consistent manner constructed his fictions as an analysis of the nature of time; but it is certainly the case that several of his most important works have been deeply immured in what might be called the coils of time, and that they can only be understood when one attempts to understand the workings of time within their narrative structures.

His third novel, *Peace* (1975), may serve as an example. It was published as a non-genre book, and was reviewed (quite favorably) as a nostalgic reminiscence in fictional form of an idyllic Midwestern childhood; once decoded, however, the tale turned out to be nothing so benign as *Winesburg, Ohio,* revisited. *Peace* is, in fact, an afterlife fantasy. The narrator—whose voice dominates the entire proceedings—has been dead for many years before the tale begins, though he gives no evidence of understanding that he is in effect a ghost; and his autobiographical musings—as is typical in afterlife fantasies—constitute a sorting out and coming to terms with the life he had led. But this sorting and reconciliation are told within a temporal context which is not only unadmitted, but is also unfixable to any chronology. All we know—after decoding the text—is that Dennis Weer is long dead. The true time of the telling of the tale—always central to a reader's apprehension of its significance—cannot safely be determined. That—coupled with the fact that we gradually grow to suspect not only that everybody else in the novel is also long dead but that Weer has himself killed several of them—generates a sense of near nausea in the reader. Without the capacity to coordinate his "recollections," we find ourselves facing nightmarish abysses within abysses, as Weer continues telling tales that never end on the page, but could never find a secure aesthetic haven even if an ostensible final word were penned. Without time to govern our apprehension of the text, we as readers find ourselves in a profound limbo; we begin to learn that there is nothing so terrifying as the absence of time.

Other Wolfe novels—*Free Live Free* (1984), which retells the film version of *The Wizard of Oz* (1939) within a time-paradox frame; and *Castleview* (1990), which encapsulates the Arthurian legends within a temporally compressed contemporary frame—make use of typical science-fiction narrative conventions, through which time can be seen as a device rather than a subject matter in itself. More significant than these, however, both as literature and as an effective demonstration that science fiction "devices of time" can generate legitimate contemplation of temporal mysteries, are the four separately published volumes that have come to be known by their overall title: *The Book of the New Sun*. The four installments—*The Shadow of the Torturer* (1980), *The Claw of the Conciliator* (1981), *The Sword of the Lictor* (1982), and *The Citadel of the Autarch* (1983)—cannot in fact be read as in any sense autonomous, and go together to make one tale. This story, which is written down by its protagonist as a first-person narrative an unknown number of years forward in time, recounts the life of Severian in a far-future earth, here called Urth. He is parentless; he is brought up from infancy in the heart of the Autarch's citadel to become a torturer; he sins against his calling, is exiled, makes a huge circuit of the domain of the Autarch, and returns to the citadel to become Autarch himself. At this level, the story is much like a great deal of romantic science fiction, or any other popular literature, and any related plays with time are correspondingly routine.

But Severian is not only a typical orphan who becomes king. He is an avatar, and in his growing and difficult saintliness fully embodies in the flesh an ancient redeemer known as the conciliator. And the conciliator, as Wolfe makes amply clear, is Christ. As Christ (and as Apollo), Severian is a patent representation of the Parousia, or Second Coming. But the Second Coming is *represented* in the text through a most complex play of religious imagery and science-fictional time-travel tropes, which intermingle inextricably. Events double and redouble themselves, progressively unveiling their true meaning as they do so. Severian himself is twice-told: he is himself, and he is the prior (or parallel) "Severian" who was, or is, the conciliator. He is told by time. He is both a traveler through the "corridors of time" and a representation of the mystery of return. Time transubstantiates him.

Time, in *The Book of the New Sun*, is a handmaiden of holy mysteries, and therefore far removed from the set of literary devices familiar to most readers of science fiction or, for that matter, non-generic fiction as well. Time here is an articulation of the holy play of revelation, a

servant of God. Time is the *means* of Holy Writ in *The Book*. Science fiction—which is inherently an unreverential genre—is unlikely ever to see a deeper contemplation of time as God's word.

[J.C.]

See also **Science Fiction; Time Travel: Future.**

WORK AND TIME

In the course of history, it was primarily the development of work forms, along with technological progress, which necessitated a differentiation of time concepts. At the same time, such a progression would have been unthinkable without the steadily expanding temporal consciousness of man himself. The more extensive work processes become, and the more they are based on the division of labor, the more they require coordination in the medium of time. Consider, for example, the elaborate time concepts and methods of measurement used in the construction of the pyramids, or in the planning and undertaking of great maritime expeditions and military campaigns of antiquity. Throughout history, technical and economic progress broadened the horizons of planning; as a result, time increasingly took on the character of a progressive continuum on a linear axis.

WORK AND LIFE RHYTHMS

Through industrialization, man's rhythm of life and work has become increasingly independent of natural temporal determiners (*Zeitgeber*). The standard division between working and non-working (not job-related) time is based predominantly on the need for an efficient organization of the production of goods and services in a society. The prevailing time structures and standards of modern societies (work times, opening times, time schedules, and so on) are chiefly the result of industrial conflict and other negotiatory processes that are geared both to fulfill production requirements and to effect a compromise between life and work. In this respect the prevailing time structure of the society is a convention. Only the circadian rhythm of the human body has remained a predominantly natural constant to the present day. Man cannot accustom himself to working constantly at night without suffering damage to his health. On the other hand, the weekly transition from work to leisure time is based on societal or religious tradition. The seven-day rhythm of the week and its associated concept of a regular rest period stems from the Judaic tradition and, via Christianity and the expansion of the so-called Western life style, has now spread throughout the world, although the designated periods in the various cultures (for example, Friday, the sabbath, Sunday, or the weekend) are not identical.

Time and Economy

One of the achievements of modern capitalism is the discovery of time not only as a medium for coordinating activity, but as an economic resource in and of itself. Toward the end of the eighteenth century, advocates of classical economics such as David Ricardo explained economic value primarily through amounts of labor used in the production of goods. In order to reduce time expenditure and resultant costs, the division of labor was propagated by Adam Smith. Karl Marx summed up the classical teachings on the value of work by saying that all economics is, in the end, economics of time. In the twentieth century, proponents of neoclassical economics also stress—although against a different theoretical background—the special significance of the time factor in workforce deployment. Accordingly, the market competition rewards the most cost-favorable supplier; this is achieved by employing the maximum time saving factors for the specific end product that is required.

Work Duration and Work Intensity

One of the great historical achievements of capitalism is the establishment of time discipline as a generally accepted behavioral pattern. Industrialization also marked the initial breakthrough on a broad basis for regular work times and normal working hours. As a result, among other things, the general use of the time factor for measuring work productivity took hold. The early capitalists thought that optimum profits and productivity could be attained by maximizing work time. The labor unions, however, fought for a reduction in working hours, their goal being humane working conditions as well as a just distribution of the wealth accrued within society. Work time as a measuring basis for work productivity also calls for a temporal standardization of the inner structure of the work process. Work organization using scientific methods was introduced at the beginning of the century by F.W. Taylor, who laid the foundation for the current systems of work studies. The aim of the widespread Taylorist school of thought is to identify ways in which work could be performed more rapidly. The opinion which has taken hold recently is that the pace of work can no longer be accelerated with traditional Taylorist methods. Group work appears to be taking its place. This allows the now traditional temporal dismemberment of the work process to be largely eliminated, because the productivity of labor is established in another way.

Work Time Flexibility and Self-Determined Work Time

The interest in having an increasing say about one's own time has led the more self-assured individuals in modern societies to demand that work time based on daily, weekly, yearly, and lifelong cycles should take a greater account of the diversity of life-styles. At the same time, however, business and industry have recognized the value of time more clearly than ever before. In many industries the demand exists for an extension of the weekly machine running-time to as much as 168 hours. This affects the production of goods as well as the service sector. In the past two decades, a large variety of new, flexible time models have emerged worldwide in theory and practice. Flex-time serves firms primarily by increasing their profitability. But employees hope that flex-time will result in an improved balance between family and occupation through self-determined work times. Even within the unions, the views on whether flex-time will bring the employees more temporal self-determination in the end, or merely new job dependencies, are widely divergent. From the management perspective, flexible work times have generally received a positive assessment.

[J.P.R.]

See also **Frontiers in Time and Space; Industrial Engineering [After Taylor]; Industrial Engineering [Before Taylor]; Social Theory; Taylor, Frederick Winslow.**

Further Readings

Colquhoun, W.P., and J. Rutenfranz. *Studies of Shiftwork*. London: Taylor and Francis, 1980.

Elias, Norbert. *Über die Zeit*. Frankfurt: Suhrkamp, 1984.

Rinderspacher, Jürgen. *Gesellschaft ohne Zeit: Individuelle Zeitverwendung und soziale Organisation der Arbeit*. Frankfurt: Campus, 1985.

Zerubavel, Eviatar. *The Seven Day Circle: The History and Meaning of the Week*. New York: Free Press, 1985.

X-RAY UNIVERSE

From stars, galaxies, and other more exotic forms of matter, radiation in the form of visible light is streaming through space in all directions. But these cosmic beacons also emit radiation *not* visible to the human eye. Just as ultrasound is a vibration whose wavelength is too short for people to hear, X-rays are a form of light whose wavelength is too short for people to see. Although by now the study of the universe in X-rays is an important subfield of astronomy, the natural emission of X-rays by celestial objects was unknown until only recently. This is because X-rays are completely absorbed by the earth's atmosphere and so cannot be observed with telescopes on the ground. How then was it ever ascertained that the sky outside our precious atmosphere is aglow with X-rays? In 1949, Herbert Friedman first discovered X-rays from the sun by using a sensitive detector similar to a geiger counter bolted on to a German V-2 rocket. Then, in 1961, during another rocket flight, X-rays from another star were detected. Since this was the strongest X-ray source in the direction of the constellation Scorpius, the stellar X-ray source was named Sco X-1. Almost simultaneously, astronomers discovered that the entire sky glows dimly in X-rays. Thus, an era of X-ray astronomy began that by now has seen several much more sensitive X-ray telescopes launched into space. These in their turn have revealed a wealth of new information about the universe.

X-rays carry more energy than visible light, more even than ultraviolet light. Since they are so energetic, X-rays are emitted only by those relatively rare cosmic activities that are themselves intensely energetic—due either to great heat, explosions, or to intense gravitational or magnetic fields. X-rays are emitted by the remnants of the violent stellar explosions called supernovae and also by the rarefied gas that pervades clusters of galaxies, in which temperatures of 100 million degrees may be created. Similar temperatures may be found in binary star systems where the collapsed corpses of stars—white dwarfs, neutron stars, or black holes—are slowly digesting the gaseous atmospheres of their companion stars. Gases heated to such high temperatures are called plasmas. In a plasma, the atoms are ionized—very high temperatures have stripped the atoms of some or all of their electrons. Plasmas are thus a mixture of charged particles: the negative electrons, and the positively charged ions to which they were once bound. Interactions between these rapidly

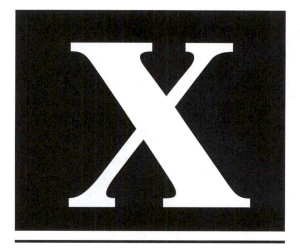

moving particles cause large changes in their energy that are given off as X-rays.

X-rays emitted by plasmas are not only found in the exotic and violent arenas mentioned above. More modest plasma temperatures of "only" several million degrees can be found in our own solar system. Even though stars in general are not the strongest X-ray emitters, the sun, being the star closest to us, appears bright in X-rays. The sun emits X-rays only from its thin, tenuous outer corona, where temperatures are the highest. X-ray images of the sun have revealed a strong association between areas of the sun that are X-ray bright, and areas that have strong magnetic fields. The twisting and buckling of magnetic lines of force in the sun is thought to heat the solar corona, thus causing X-ray emission. Occasionally, highly magnetized regions create bursts of energetic particles and radiation called solar flares that follow the eleven-year sunspot cycle. Bursts of X-ray emission accompany these flares. On other stars, much more powerful flares occur almost continuously. Though near and dear to us, the sun is just one X-ray emitting star of which there are likely to be billions of examples throughout our galaxy.

Less common but far more powerful sources of X-ray radiation are supernovae and their remnants. When a massive star has burned up most of the fuel in its dense core, the outward force of radiation no longer supports the star's outer layers under the tug of the star's own enormous gravity. By the time this happens, however, the core of the star has become as dense as the nucleus of an atom, and is composed mostly of neutrons. The dense core is like a solid wall against which the collapsing outer layers rebound in a tremendous explosion, blowing the outer layers into space and leaving behind only the hot, dense neutron star. The explosion, or supernova, emits a blast of radiation often more intense than the combined light of all the stars in the galaxy. But even after the blast has subsided, the aftermath of the supernova continues to be observable in X-rays. Shock waves created by the expanding debris sweep up and heat the interstellar gas until vast bubbles and filaments of hot plasma surrounding the neutron star begin to emit X-rays.

Much of the rotational and magnetic energy of the original star is preserved in the neutron star. The resulting combination of fast rotation (up to a thousand times a second) and powerful magnetic fields creates strong electric fields and hot plasma near the surface of the neutron star. Energetic electrons stream around the magnetic field lines at velocities approaching the speed of light, and radiation sweeps outward from the poles of the star as from a lighthouse. If the magnetic poles happen to beam toward earth, regular pulses of radiation can be detected by our X-ray and radio telescopes. In the center of the Crab Nebula, for instance, the pulsing neutron star, or pulsar, is barely visible, but is easily detected with today's X-ray telescopes.

A collapsed stellar remnant may also produce X-ray emission if it has a companion star. In these X-ray binaries, as they are known, the compact stellar remnant may be a fairly common white dwarf star, a neutron star, or even a black hole. Black holes are massive objects so dense that even light cannot escape their gravity. Since black holes are by definition invisible, they can only be inferred from their influence on other matter. Sometimes the gravity of the black hole or other compact secondary star is strong enough to pull off gas from its primary companion star. Gas from the primary spirals down onto the compact secondary, where the release of gravitational energy heats the gas so much that it emits X-ray radiation. X-ray binaries are responsible for most of the X-ray emission from normal galaxies like our own.

Some very distant, extremely luminous galaxies have compact cores so bright that they appear to be mere points of light and are often mistaken for stars. These quasi-stellar objects, better known as quasars, radiate such enormous amounts of energy that they can be seen at far greater distances than any other objects in the cosmos. Quasars allow astronomers to probe distances of billions of light-years, reaching back toward the earliest epochs of the universe, when galaxies were still forming from the diffuse gas and dust of space. Many quasars are strong X-ray sources, and most of their X-rays originate in the compact active galactic nucleus, or AGN. Rapid changes in the luminosity of the AGN prove that they must be very small by galactic standards. But the luminosity of the AGN is so great that it cannot be accounted for by any accumulation of stars in such a small region. It is now thought that a supermassive black hole sits at the center of the nucleus. The gas, dust, and stellar debris that funnel too close to this black hole form the fuel for an enormous gravity-powered engine that radiates powerfully across a wide frequency range, often from radio waves to light to X-rays. Over the span of billions of years, the black hole may swallow all the matter within reach, exhausting its available fuel, so that the active galaxy begins to appear more normal. There is some evidence that normal galaxies like our own Milky Way may harbor exhausted supermassive black holes in their centers that long ago could have been luminous, X-ray emitting quasars themselves.

Though X-ray observations of quasars imply the presence of unimaginably dense black holes, X-rays may also be emitted from regions where the density of matter is extremely low. Clusters of galaxies are a dominant feature of the X-ray sky, and most of their emission is from very hot and diffuse gas that pervades the space between galaxies in the cluster. However, even where there is no cluster, galaxy, star, or other known counterpart, X-ray radiation is still observed. This X-ray background, discovered very early in the history of X-ray astronomy, is smooth and appears to come from all directions. The source of the X-ray background is not entirely resolved. Is it from a very hot gas like that in the clusters, but one that fills the entire universe? Such a solution seems to create more problems than it solves, in part because there is no known source of energy that could heat so much gas. Is the X-ray background instead the summed contributions of a huge number of individual quasars and galaxies, many of which are too dim to detect in any other part of the electromagnetic spectrum? Astronomers are still studying and debating these questions even as new X-ray data are gathered from orbiting satellites. X-rays have enabled us to see the universe, literally, in a new light.

[P.J.G.]

See also **Big Bang Theory; Cosmology; Expansion of the Universe.**

FURTHER READINGS

Culhane, J. Leonard, and Peter W. Sanford. *X-Ray Astronomy*. New York: Scribner's, 1981.

Margon, Bruce. "Exploring the High-Energy Universe." *Sky and Telescope* 82 (1991): 607.

Tucker, Wallace, and Riccardo Giacconi. *The X-Ray Universe*. Cambridge: Harvard UP, 1985.

INDEX

Page numbers in **bold print** refer to subjects that form all or part of an article in the text.